Lecture Notes in Computer Science 3733

Pınar Yolum Tunga Güngör
Fikret Gürgen Can Özturan (Eds.)

Computer and Information Sciences – ISCIS 2005

20th International Symposium
Istanbul, Turkey, October 26-28, 2005
Proceedings

Springer

Volume Editors

Pınar Yolum
Tunga Güngör
Fikret Gürgen
Can Özturan
Boğaziçi University
Department of Computer Engineering
34342 Bebek, Istanbul, Turkey
E-mail: {pinar.yolum, Gungort, gurgen, ozturaca}@boun.edu.tr

Library of Congress Control Number: 2005933721

CR Subject Classification (1998): H, C, B, D, F, I

ISSN 0302-9743
ISBN-10 3-540-29414-7 Springer Berlin Heidelberg New York
ISBN-13 978-3-540-29414-6 Springer Berlin Heidelberg New York

Springer is a part of Springer Science+Business Media

springeronline.com

Printed in Germany

Typesetting: Camera-ready by author, data conversion by Scientific Publishing Services, Chennai, India
Printed on acid-free paper SPIN: 11569596 06/3142 5 4 3 2 1 0

Preface

This volume collects a subset of the high-quality papers that were accepted for presentation at the 20th International Symposium on Computer and Information Sciences (ISCIS). ISCIS 2005 was organized by the Department of Computer Engineering of Boğaziçi University and was held in Istanbul, Turkey during 26–28 October, 2005.

Following on the success of previous ISCIS symposia, ISCIS 2005 attracted a total of 491 papers. The submitted papers went through a rigorous submission period with the help of the Program Committee and external reviewers. Keeping up with the tradition of previous editions of ISCIS, the selected papers cover a wide spectrum of topics in computer and information sciences. The main topics of ISCIS 2005 can be listed as: computer networks, sensor and satellite networks, security and cryptography, performance evaluation, database systems, algorithms, multiagent systems, e-commerce, machine learning, natural language processing and information retrieval, image and speech processing, and theory of computing.

In addition to the paper presentations, the symposium enjoyed four invited talks. The honorary chair of ISCIS 2005, Erol Gelenbe from Imperial College, London, gave a talk on a probability model of natural or artificial infection. The second talk was by Onn Shehory of IBM Haifa Research Labs, on online auctions. Jacques Stern from Ecole Normale Supérieure, France, focused his talk on alternatives to RSA. The last invited speaker, Yanghee Choi from Seoul National University, Korea, delivered a talk on location and address issues in ubiquitous computing.

Many individuals and organizations contributed to the making of the 20th edition of ISCIS. Authors from 30 countries submitted their papers. The Program Committee members reviewed the submissions diligently in a short time span. A substantial number of external referees helped with the reviewing. The staff at the Computer Engineering Department of Boğaziçi University not only offered their help in setting up and in maintaining crucial facilities, but also advised us in setting up high standards for ISCIS 2005. The Scientific and Technical Research Council of Turkey (TÜBİTAK), the Turkey Section of the Institute of Electrical and Electronics Engineers (IEEE), and the Boğaziçi University Research Fund supported our activities financially. We are deeply indebted to them all.

October 2005

Pınar Yolum
Tunga Gungör
Fikret Gürgen
Can Özturan

Symposium Organization

Symposium Organizers

Fatih Alagöz	Boğaziçi University, Turkey
Tunga Güngör	Boğaziçi University, Turkey
Fikret Gürgen	Boğaziçi University, Turkey
Can Özturan	Boğaziçi University, Turkey
Tuna Tuğcu	Boğaziçi University, Turkey
Pınar Yolum	Boğaziçi University, Turkey

Local Organizing Committee

İlker Demirkol	Boğaziçi University, Turkey
Hatice Köse (Bağcı)	Boğaziçi University, Turkey
Arzucan Özgür	Boğaziçi University, Turkey
Fatma Canan Pembe	Boğaziçi University, Turkey
Albert Ali Salah	Boğaziçi University, Turkey
Burak Turhan	Boğaziçi University, Turkey

Program Committee

Bülent Abalı	IBM T.J. Watson Research Center
Mohammed Abdel-Hafez	UAE University
Sibel Adalı	Rensselaer Polytechnic Institute
Özgür B. Akan	Middle East Technical University
Lale Akarun	Boğaziçi University
Levent Akın	Boğaziçi University
Sahin Albayrak	TU Berlin
Reda Alhajj	University of Calgary
Ethem Alpaydın	Boğaziçi University
Emin Anarım	Boğaziçi University
I. Budak Arpinar	University of Georgia
Cevdet Aykanat	Bilkent University
Fevzi Belli	Universität Paderborn
Ufuk Cağlayan	Boğaziçi University
Mariacarla Calzarossa	Università di Pavia
K. Selçuk Candan	Arizona State University
Uğur Çetintemel	Brown University
Gabriel Ciobanu	Romanian Academy
Vedat Coskun	Turkish Naval Academy

Andrea D'Ambrogio	Università di Roma "Tor Vergata"
Tuğrul Dayar	Bilkent University
Oğuz Dikenelli	Ege University
Iain S. Duff	Rutherford Appleton Laboratory
Eylem Ekici	Ohio State University
Marc Emmelman	TU Berlin
Cem Ersoy	Boğaziçi University
Jean-Michel Fourneau	Université de Versailles
Laura Galluccio	University of Catania
Attila Gürsoy	Koç University
Michael Hadjitheodosiou	University of Maryland
Jane Hillston	University of Edinburgh
Giuseppe Iazeolla	Università di Roma "Tor Vergata"
Carlos Juiz	Universitat de les Illes Balears
Manolya Kavaklı	Macquarie University
İbrahim Körpeoğlu	Bilkent University
Sastri Kota	Harris
Ulaş Kozat	DoCoMo Labs
Albert Levi	Sabancı University
Giacomo Morabito	University of Catania
Kemal Oflazer	Sabancı University
Sema Oktuğ	Istanbul Technical University
Bülent Örencik	Istanbul Technical University
Mehmet Orgun	Macquarie University
Füsun Özguner	Ohio State University
Gültekin Özsoyoglu	Case Western Reserve University
Tamer Özsu	University of Waterloo
Yusuf Pisan	University of Technology, Sydney
Faruk Polat	Middle East Technical University
Ramon Puigjaner	Universitat de les Illes Balears
Mohammad Salamah	East Mediterranean University
Cem Say	Boğaziçi University
Martijn Schut	Vrije Universiteit Amsterdam
Nahid Shahmehri	Linköpings Universitet
Boleslaw Szymansky	Rensselaer Polytechnic Institute
Abdullah Uz Tansel	Bilkent University
Petia Todorova	Fraunhofer Institute Fokus
Borahan Tümer	Marmara University
Alper Üngör	University of Florida
Alessandro Vanelli-Coralli	University of Bologna
Branimir R. Vojcic	George Washington University
Kainam Tom Wong	University of Waterloo
Robert Wrembel	Poznan Universtity of Technology
Adnan Yazıcı	Middle East Technical University
Bülent Yener	Rensselaer Polytechnic Institute

Additional Reviewers

Johan Aberg
Osman Abul
Adnan Acan
Tarig M. Ahmed
JinHo Ahn
Yusuf Sinan Akgul
Mahmut F. Aksit
Aylin Aksu
Mustafa Aktan
Songul Albayrak
D. Turgay Altilar
Ergin Altintas
Oguz Altun
Witold Andrzejewski
Oya Aran
Sabri Arik
Juan Antonio Rodriguez Artamendi
Burak Galip Aslan
Kubilay Atasu
Tolga Ayav
Isik Aybay
Umut Ayhan
Ulas Bagci
Hayretdin Bahsi
Serif Bahtiyar
Mehmet Balman
Necla Bandirmali
Mario Barbera
Antonio Barili
Erhan Basri
SungUoon Bauk
Burak Bayoglu
Serkan Bayraktar
Zeki Bayram
Ilker Bekmezci
Carlo Bellettini
Ayse Basar Bener
Bilge Bilgen
Haluk Bingol
Zafer Bingul
S. Ilker Birbil
Aysenur Akyuz Birturk
Mehmet Bodur
Ilkay Boduroglu
Tibor Bosse
Omer Ozgur Bozkurt
Rimantas Butleris
Feza Buzluca
Gul Calikli
Prasad Calyam
B. Barla Cambazoglu
Seyit Ahmet Camtepe
Idil Candan
Alejandro Carrasco
Cagatay Catal
Zehra Cataltepe
F.V. Celebi
Buluc Celik
Coskùn Celik
Ebru Celikel
Heung Seok Chae
Nizamuddin Channa
Alexander G. Chefranov
Jessica Chen
Xiao Chen
Yan Chen
Haengrae Cho
Dae-Young Choi
Jin-Hee Choi
Lynn Choi
WoongChul Choi
Selim Ciraci
Diogo Costa
Mate J. Csorba
Haydar Cukurtepe
Tomas Danikauskas
Hakan Delic
Engin Demir
Engin Deveci
B. Taner Dincer
Banu Diri
Erdogan Dogdu
Ugur Dogrusoz
Inshil Doh
Mehmet Yunus Donmez
Claudiu Duma
Gunhan Dundar
Nurcan Durak
Taner Dursun
Tobias Eggendorfer
Atilla Elci
Nahit Emanet
Kayhan Erciyes
Zeki Erdem
Nadia Erdogan
Riza Cenk Erdur
Murat Ergun
Gurdal Ertek
Y. Murat Erten
Sarp Erturk
Mustafa Taner Eskil
Yu Fei
Dan Feng
Fernando Zacarias Flores
Mario Marques Freire
Peng Fu
Alexander Gelbukh
George Ghinea
Katja Gilly
Sertan Girgin
Berk Gokberk
Erek Gokturk
Janaki Gopalan
Robert Griffioen
Ugur Gudukbay
Cigdem Gunduz
Gurkan Gur
Burak Gurdag
H. Altay Guvenir
JungHyun Han
Su-Young Han
Sofía Galicia Haro
Jed Hassell
Eui Kyeong Hong
David C. Hooge
Mark Hoogendoorn
Jia Hou
Zhang Hu

Adriana Iamnitchi
Sinan Isik
Ali Iskurt
Jie Jiang
KyoHong Jin
Hu Jun
Kyungkoo Jun
Eui-Hyun Jung
Jinhee Jung
Fatih Kahraman
Ozan Kahramanogullari
Utku Kalay
Oya Kalipsiz
JungMin Kang
NamO Kang
Seokhoon Kang
Aylin Kantarci
Ahmet Kara
Dervis Karaboga
Dilek Karabudak
Cem Keskin
Hurevren Kilic
Cheol Hong Kim
Dong Seong Kim
Jangha Kim
Seong-Woon Kim
Young-Pil Kim
Fatih Koksal
Ahmet Koltuksuz
Can Komar
Hyunjang Kong
Jung-Shik Kong
Rabun Kosar
Alexander Kostin
Gurhan Kucuk
Ugur Kucuk
Ayse Kucukyilmaz
Tayfun Kucukyilmaz
Erhun Kundakcioglu
Sukru Kuran
Marek Kurzynski
Mustafa Kuscu
Jong Wook Kwak
Bo-Hee Lee
Chang-Gun Lee
Chang-Hwan Lee
Junsoo Lee
Kangsun Lee
ShinHyoung Lee
SungYoung Lee
Yong-Jin Lee
Ricardo Lent
Bin Li
Huaqing Li
Jinyan Li
Minglu Li
Weimin Li
Jinqian Liang
Hyotaek Lim
Hyung-Jin Lim
Ming-Hua Lin
Fuyu Liu
Jian-Wei Liu
Alok Madhukar
Margarida Mamede
Alessandro Marchetto
Robert L.R. Mattson
Carlos Alexandre Barros de Mello
Boanerges Aleman Meza
Alok Mishra
Sangman Moh
Higinio Mora Mora
Omer K. Morgul
Syed Shariyar Murtaza
Lauro Nakayama
Kim Anh Pham Ngoc
Hu Ning
Kazuhiro Ogata
Hasan Ogul
Hayoung Oh
Onur Onder
Tolga Onel
Ertan Onur
Zeynep Orhan
Cemil Oz
Selma Ayse Ozalp
Ender Ozcan
Mahmut Ozcan
Ibrahim Ozcelik
Ali Haydar Ozer
Atay Ozgovde
Bulent Ozguc
Eray Ozkural
Ahmet Ozmen
Ercan Oztemel
Tansel Ozyer
Lale Ozyilmaz
Hasan Palaz
Jaesung Park
Jihun Park
Jun-Cheol Park
Jungkeun Park
SungHoon Park
Saeed Parsa
Ferhan Pekergin
Zhang Peng
Rui G. Pereira
Viara Popova
Jae-Young Pyun
Franck Quessette
Behnam Rahnama
Omar Ramadan
Ren Ren
Ana Regina C. da Rocha
Joel J.P.C. Rodrigues
Minsoo Ryu
Ali Vahit Sahiner
Pinar Sanac
Kristian Sandahl
Hasan Sarper
Erkay Savas
Yucel Saygin
Onur Tolga Sehitoglu
Canan Senol
Jungtaek Seo
Gabriela Serban
Ahmet Sertbas
Erdogan Sevilgen
Huagang Shao
Alexei Sharpanskykh
Dongyu Shi
Xuanhua Shi
Nikolay V. Shilov
SungHoon Shim

Table of Contents

Invited Speakers

Computer Networks

Sensor and Satellite Networks

Security and Cryptography

Performance Evaluation

E-Commerce and Web Services

Multiagent Systems

Machine Learning

Information Retrieval and Natural Language Processing

Image and Speech Processing

Algorithms and Database Systems

Theory of Computing

Epilogue

Keeping Viruses Under Control*

Erol Gelenbe

Dennis Gabor Chair,
Department of Electrical and Electronic Engineering,
Imperial College London SW7 2BT
e.gelenbe@imperial.ac.uk

We introduce a probability model for populations of conflicting agents such as computer software (cells) and computer viruses that interact in the presence of an anti-viral agent. Cells can be infected by viruses, and their longevity and ability to avoid infection is modified if they survive successive attacks by viruses. Viruses that survive the effect of the anti-viral agent may find that their ability to survive a future encounter with molecules of the anti-viral agent is modified, as is their ability to infect a uninfected cell. Additionally, we assume that the anti-viral agent can be a cocktail with different proportions of agents that target different strains of the virus. In this paper, we give the state equations for the model and prove its analytical solution in steady state. The solution then provides insight into the approriate mix or "cocktail" of anti-viral agents that are designed to deal with the virus' ability to mutate. In particular, the analysis shows that the concentration of anti-viral agent by itself does not suffice to ultimately control the infection, and that it is important to dose a mix of anti-viral agents so as to target each strain of virus in a specific manner, taking into account the ability of each virus strain to survive in the presence of the anti-viral agent.

* Research supported by US Army ARO under Contract No. DAAD19-03-1-0135. Full text of the paper is available in the *Performance Evaluation* Section.

P. Yolum et al.(Eds.): ISCIS 2005, LNCS 3733, p. 1, 2005.

Online Auctions: Notes on Theory, Practice, and the Role of Agents

Onn Shehory

IBM Research Lab in Haifa—The Tel Aviv Site,
Haifa University, Mount Carmel,
Haifa 31905, Israel
onn@il.ibm.com

On-line auctions constitute a multi-billion market, which is still growing in size and reach. Classical theory of auctions offers on-line auctioneers opportunities for maximizing gains, as long as they carefully select appropriate mechanisms for the market of interest. Studies in recent years have provided auctioneers with additional, improved mechanisms and strategies for maximizing profits. In this respect, on-line auctioneers utilize the state of the art in auction theory, in practicality. In contrast, bidders in electronic auctions hardly use optimal strategies known in classical auction theory, let alone more recent results on optimal bidding. Researchers have suggested that agents could simplify the implementation of optimized bidder strategies. Such solutions, although well studied, analyzed and demonstrated, are rarely found in commercial applications. In this lecture we will present examples of current commercial online auctions and the gains they provide the auctioneer side with. We will further present some recent research results on automated and optimized bidding and the use of agents for such bidding. Following these, we will discuss the major enables and inhibitors of commercial bidder side agents. We will conclude with an open discussion on the future of bidder-side agents.

P. Yolum et al.(Eds.): ISCIS 2005, LNCS 3733, p. 2, 2005.

A Unified Approach to Survivability of Connection-Oriented Networks

Krzysztof Walkowiak

Chair of Systems and Computer Networks, Faculty of Electronics,
Wroclaw University of Technology, Wybrzeze Wyspianskiego 27,
50-370 Wroclaw, Poland
Krzysztof.Walkowiak@pwr.wroc.pl

Abstract. This paper deals with problems of computer networks survivability. We present and discuss survivability aspects of Content Delivery Networks (CDNs) and other services based on the anycast paradigm. After that, we propose a new unified approach to network survivability. This approach assumes using jointly survivability mechanisms for both kinds of traffic: anycast (one-to-one-of-many access to content servers) and unicast (one-to-one exchanging of data between individual users). We formulate a new optimization model for this scenario that can be used for development of algorithms. The optimization problem is NP-complete. The objective function is function of lost flow due to a failure of any single link. To our knowledge this problem have not received much attention in the literature. We provide also a numerical example to illustrate the proposed approach.

Keywords: Survivability, MPLS, anycast, CDN.

1 Introduction

Nowadays we watch an increasing role of computer networks, caused mainly by the growth of the Internet as well as introducing many new services. Telecommunication companies and operators focus on new ideas and concepts to enable radical transformation of networks and service infrastructures. One of the most vital attributes of current networks is provision of QoS guarantees with some survivability aspects. Service disruptions in networks are significant, since loss of services and traffic in high-speed fiber systems could cause a lot of damages including economic loses, political conflicts. Therefore, new self-healing restoration methods to provide network survivability are being deployed.

In general, current networks offer two kinds of services: access to content servers (anycast traffic) and exchanging of data between individual users (unicast traffic). Most of previous work in the field of network survivability focus on restoration and protection methods developed for unicast communication, for techniques like MPLS (Multiprotocol Label Switching).

Connection-oriented techniques use similar approach to enable network survivability. The main idea of this approach is as follows. Each connection, i.e. label switched path in MPLS, has a primary route and a backup route. The primary route is used for

P. Yolum et al.(Eds.): ISCIS 2005, LNCS 3733, pp. 3 – 12, 2005.

transmitting of data in normal, non-failure state of the network. After a failure of the primary route, the failed path is switched to the backup route [1], [8].

Less papers address survivability issues of anycast traffic and CDNs (Content Delivery Networks). There has not been any study, we are aware of, that gives specifics on how to apply jointly restoration methods of connection-oriented (c-o) networks and CDNs. Therefore, we propose a unified approach that improves survivability of networks carrying two types of traffic: unicast and anycast. We formulate a detailed optimization model that can be used for static assignment of network flows using a unified survivability approach. The optimization model can be applied for development of heuristic and exact algorithms. In order to illustrate theoretical analysis we provide a numerical example that shows robustness of the proposed approach. Results of this work can be easily modified in order to deploy a framework for dynamic optimization of network flows using the unified approach to survivability.

2 Survivability of Content Delivery Networks

Content Delivery Network (CDN) is defined as mechanism to deliver various content to end users on behalf of origin Web servers. The original information is offloaded from origin sites to other content servers located in different locations in the network. For each request, the CDN tries to find the closest server offering the requested Web page. CDN delivers the content from the origin server to the replicas that are much closer to end users. CDN techniques are based on caching of Web pages. Traffic of CDN is modeled as anycast flow. For more information on caching, replication, anycast communication refer to [2-6], [11].

Since modeling and optimization of CDN is a very complicated issue, in this work we consider a simplified model of CDN. We assume that CDN offers the same content replicated in a number of different locations called content servers or replicas. We can treat the origin server itself as simply one of the replicas. Obviously, we are not considering the case where there is a content server on every network node. A user is assigned to a number of these servers using the redirection mechanism. A variety of approaches exist for requests redirection [7]: client multiplexing, IP multiplexing, DNS indirection, HTTTP redirection and anycast.

One of CDN's advantages is the survivability it offers. Since data is replicated in different locations in the network, CDN can cope with failures of the network or Web servers. Even if one of the content servers becomes unreachable, other servers can provide necessary data to. Additionally, CDN reduces network flow what also improves survivability of the network. If there are more resources of spare capacity in the network, the restoration process can be performed more effectively.

In c-o networks an anycast demand consists of two connections: one from the client to the server (upstream) and the second one in the opposite direction (downstream). Upstream connection is used to send user's requests. Downstream connection carries requested data.

To improve the survivability of an existing CDN we suggest two approaches [9]. The first one uses a backup content server. Each client is assigned to two content servers: the primary one, used in non-failure state of the network, and the backup one, that is applied when the primary server is unavailable due to network failure. In c-o networks it is arranged in the following way. Each client has four routes assigned: two primary (downstream and upstream) between client and primary content server and two backup (downstream and upstream) between client and backup server. Both backup routes are activated after a failure of one of primary connections, because the client can be assigned to another content server and two routes (downstream and upstream) must be provisioned to the new server. This scenario can protect the network against network element (e.g. link, node) failure or replica failure.

In the secondary approach, a client is assigned to the same replica. All four routes: primary downstream, primary upstream, backup downstream and backup upstream connect the same pair of nodes. If any of two primary routes is broken, it is switched to the backup route. There is no need to change the route of the second primary route if it is not failed. This scheme protects only against a failure of network element.

3 Unified Approach to Network Survivability

It has become increasingly evident that existing computer networks offer users two main kinds of services:

- Access to popular content providing various types of information and data. Content servers can be organized in a Content Delivery Network, i.e. the same information is replicated in many locations. Users can be connected to any of available servers. Flow of these kinds of services is referred to as anycast flow.
- One-to-one communication between individual users in the network modeled as unicast flow.

Examples of the former type of services are: popular WWW sites, archives of electronic entertainment (MP3 files, movies), FTP, peer-to-peer applications, electronic libraries, software distribution. The latter kind of services is: Voice over IP, teleconferences, exchanging of files, VPN, less popular WWW servers.

The central idea of this work is to provide survivability to the consider network using jointly restoration mechanisms developed for c-o networks (ATM, MPLS) and special capabilities offered by CDNs. We propose to combine using the backup routes for protection or restoration of unicast traffic and backup content servers for protection or restoration of anycast traffic. In many existing network there is no need to protect all services. Some clients don't require any network survivability, while others are willingly to pay extra for guarantees of data delivery in spite of failures. Therefore, we introduce four classes of traffic:

- Protected unicast (PU) – flow associated with communication between two individual users protected by a backup route.
- Unprotected unicast (UU) – flow associated with communication between two individual users not protected by a backup route.
- Protected anycast (PA) – flow associated with communication between an individual user and a content server protected by a connection to a backup server.
- Unprotected anycast (UA) – flow associated with communication between an individual user and a content server without any protection.

4 Optimization Model of Survivable Unified Network

According to our knowledge, the combinatorial optimization problems presented below have not received much attention in the literature. A unicast demand is defined by a following triple: origin node, destination node and bandwidth requirement. An anycast demand is defined by a following triple: client node, upstream bandwidth requirement and downstream bandwidth requirement. An anycast demand must select one of many content servers. Therefore, the destination node hosting a replica is not defined and must be found.

We assume that estimated bandwidth requirements for all classes of demands are given. In order to solve the problem three kinds of variables must be determined: selection of content servers, primary routes and backup routes. Primary routes are selected to satisfy all demands. Sets containing proposals of primary and backup routes that conform selected rerouting strategy are given.

We consider an existing facility network, i.e. location of content servers; link capacity and network topology are given. We assume that each anycast demand is divided into two connections: upstream and downstream. Both connections associated with one anycast demand must be considered jointly, i.e. the destination node of downstream connection must be the same as the origin node of associated upstream connection and vice versa. Furthermore, both associated connections either must be restored using the same backup replica, or both connections are lost.

To mathematically represent the problem, we introduce the following notations:

V Set of $|V|$ vertices representing the network nodes.

A set of $|A|$ arcs representing network directed links.

R set of $|R|$ CDN's servers (replicas). Each server must be located in a network node.

P set of $|P|$ connections in the network. A connection can be of three types: unicast, downstream anycast and upstream anycast.

P_{CL} set of $|P_{CL}|$ connections included in a particular class, CL={PU,UU,PA,UA}.

Π_i set of routes proposals for connection i; $\Pi_i = \{\pi_i^k : k = 1,...,l(i)\}$. For unicast connection set includes routes between origin and destination nodes of considered demand. Anycast connection set consists of routes between the client's node and nodes that host a content server.

X_r set of primary route selection variables x_i^k, which are equal to one. X_r determines the unique set of currently selected primary routes

Π_{im}^k set of backup routes of connection i using primary route π_i^k after failure of arc m; $\Pi_{im}^k = \{\pi_{im}^{kh} : h = 0,1,...,l(i,k,m)\}$. Route π_{im}^{k0} is an "null" route. If π_{im}^{k0} is selected it means that connection i using the primary route π_i^k is not restored after failure of arc m.

Y_r set of backup route selection variables y_{im}^{kh}, which are equal to one. Y_r determines the unique set of currently used backup routes.

c_j capacity of arc j.

Q_i bandwidth requirement of connection i.
$\delta(i)$ index of the connection associated with anycast connection i. If i is a downstream connection $\delta(i)$ must be an upstream connection and vice versa.
a_{ij}^k binary variable, which is 1 if arc j belongs the route π_i^k and is 0 otherwise.
b_{imj}^{kh} binary variable, which is 1 if arc j belongs the route π_{im}^{kh} and is 0 otherwise.
$o(\pi)$ origin node of route π.
$d(\pi)$ destination node of route π.

A function that represents the flow lost due to failure of link m is a follows

$$LF_m(X_r,Y_r) = \sum_{i\in P_{PU}} \sum_{\pi_i^k\in\Pi_i} a_{im}^k x_i^k y_{im}^{k0} Q_i + \sum_{i\in P_{PA}} \sum_{\pi_i^k\in\Pi_i} a_{im}^k x_i^k y_{im}^{k0}(Q_i + Q_{\delta(i)}) \quad (1)$$

Function $LF_m(X_r,Y_r)$ is a sum over all connections using arc m ($a_{im}^k = 1$) and are not restored after a failure of this arc ($y_{im}^{k0} = 1$). If anycast connection $i\in P_{PA}$ is not restored we must also add bandwidth requirement of connection $\delta(i)$ associated with i, because if one of two anycast connections is broken and not restored, the second one is also removed from the network and lost.

The objective function $LF(X_r,Y_r)$ is formulated as follows

$$LF(X_r,Y_r) = \sum_{m\in A} LF_m(X_r,Y_r) \quad (2)$$

We consider a single failure of any arc $m\in A$. Therefore, the function $LF(X_r,Y_r)$ is a sum of functions $LF_m(X_r,Y_r)$ over all arcs. However, the objective function can include also other failure scenarios, e.g. multiple links failures.

The optimization problem is formulated as follows

$$\min_{X_r,Y_r} \quad LF(X_r,Y_r) \quad (3)$$

subject to

$$f_{jr} = \sum_{i\in P} \sum_{\pi_i^k\in\Pi_i} a_{ij}^k x_i^k Q_i \quad \forall j\in A \quad (4)$$

$$\hat{f}_{jr}^m = \sum_{i\in P_{PU}} \sum_{\pi_i^k\in\Pi_i} a_{im}^k x_i^k a_{ij}^k Q_i + \sum_{i\in P_{PA}} \sum_{\pi_i^k\in\Pi_i} a_{im}^k x_i^k \left(a_{ij}^k Q_i + \sum_{\pi_d^k\in\Pi_{\delta(i)}} x_d^k a_{dj}^k Q_d \right) \quad (5)$$

$$f_{jr}^m = f_{jr} - \hat{f}_{jr}^m + \sum_{i\in P} \sum_{\pi_i^k\in\Pi_i} \sum_{\pi_i^{kh}\in\Pi_{im}^k} x_i^k y_{im}^{kh} b_{imj}^{kh} Q_i \quad (6)$$

$$\sum_{\pi_i^k\in\Pi_i} x_i^k = 1 \quad \forall i\in P \quad (7)$$

$$\sum_{\pi_{im}^{kh}\in\Pi_{im}^k} y_{im}^{kh} = x_i^k \quad \forall m\in A; i\in(P_{PU}\cup P_{PA}) \quad (8)$$

$$y_{im}^{k0} = y_{\delta(i)m}^{k0} \qquad \forall m \in A; i \in P_{\mathrm{PA}} \tag{9}$$

$$f_{jr} \le c_j \qquad \forall j \in A \tag{10}$$

$$f_{jr}^{m} \le c_j \qquad \forall j, m \in A; j \ne m \tag{11}$$

$$\sum_{\pi_i^k \in \Pi_i} x_i^k d(\pi_i^k) = \sum_{\pi_j^k \in \Pi_{\delta(i)}} x_j^k o(\pi_j^k) \qquad \forall i \in (P_{\mathrm{PA}} \cup P_{\mathrm{NA}}) \tag{12}$$

$$\sum_{\pi_i^k \in \Pi_i} \sum_{\pi_{im}^{kh} \in \Pi_{im}^k} x_i^k y_{im}^{kh} o(\pi_{mi}^{kh}) = \sum_{\pi_j^k \in \Pi_{\delta(i)}} \sum_{\pi_{jm}^{kh} \in \Pi_{\delta(i)m}^k} x_j^k y_{jm}^{kh} d(\pi_{jm}^{kh}) \qquad \forall m \in A; i \in P_{\mathrm{PA}} \tag{13}$$

$$x_i^k \in \{0,1\} \qquad \forall i \in P; \pi \in \Pi_i \tag{14}$$

$$y_{im}^{kh} \in \{0,1\} \qquad \forall m \in A; i \in (P_{\mathrm{PU}} \cup P_{\mathrm{PA}}); \pi_i^k \in \Pi_i; \pi_{im}^{kh} \in \Pi_{im}^k \tag{15}$$

Variable r denotes the index of sets X_r and Y_r that include information on current primary routes (variables x) and backup routes (variables y). (4) is a definition of arc flow. Formula (5) defines flow of arc j released from the network after failure of m. This approach is called stub release [1]. We sum bandwidth requirements over connections, which primary routes include: the failed arc ($x_i^k a_{im}^k = 1$) and the considered arc j ($a_{ij}^k = 1$). Additionally, for each anycast connection i which is broken due to failure of m, we also remove from the network flow of connection $\delta(i)$ if primary route of $\delta(i)$ includes j. (6) shows the flow of arc j after a failure of m and network restoration. The last term denotes the new flow on j allocated on backup routes. Condition (7) states that each connection can use only one primary route. Consequently, (8) denotes that for selected primary route of connection i we either can decide not to restore this connection or select only one backup route. Equation (9) guarantees that both connections associated with anycast demand are altogether either restored or lost. Condition (10) is a capacity constraint in non-failure network and (11) is a capacity constraint after failure of link m and network restoration. Constraint (12) guarantees that two primary routes associated with the same anycast demand connect the same pair of nodes. Analogously, (13) ensures that backup routes associated with the same anycast demand connect the same pair of nodes. Constraints (14-15) guarantees that decision variables are binary ones.

Optimization model (3-15) can be applied to both restoration methods discussed in previous sections. The only difference is in sets of routes proposals for anycast connection. If we use backup server method, sets of primary and backup routes should include paths to (upstream) and from (downstream) various nodes hosting replica servers. In the second restoration method, all backup routes of the same anycast demand should be between the same pair of nodes as the primary route.

The presented optimization model could be modified to embrace some other constraints. For instance we can optimize also location of replica servers by introducing for each network node a binary variable indicating whether or not the considered node hosts a server. In another possible extension we propose to assign to each demand a priority as discussed in Section 4. Priorities could be included in the objective function of lost flow as a multiplication factor of bandwidth requirement to impose better restoration of high-valued demands.

5 Simulation Study

We now describe our simulation setup and scenarios. We run the experiments for 2, 3 and 4 replica servers located in various nodes in the network. In total, 18 different servers' locations are tested. For each anycast demand we select content server closest (in terms of the hop number) to the client's node. If two or more servers are located in the same distance, we select a server with the highest capacity node calculated as a sum of capacity all arcs leaving the node in which the server is located. For assignment of primary routes (two routes for each anycast demand and one route for each unicast demand) we use an algorithm for non-bifurcated flows proposed in [10].

Next we simulate network failures. We assume a single failure of each arc, according to [1] it is the most probable failure scenario. Upon each arc cut, all of the affected connections are identified. Next, all broken connections are sequentially processed using a greedy method in the following way. For each connection it is checked if a feasible backup route can be found. If such a route exists, the available capacity is updated and the next connection in the sequence gets its chance, and so on until all affected connections have had a chance to find a backup route. If there is not a feasible route, flow of the considered connection is lost. For unicast connections we simply sum all un-restored connections' bandwidth requirements to obtain the lost flow. If one route of anycast connection is affected by the failure and the backup route cannot be established we add to the lost flow bandwidth requirements of both: downstream and upstream connections associated with the same anycast demand.

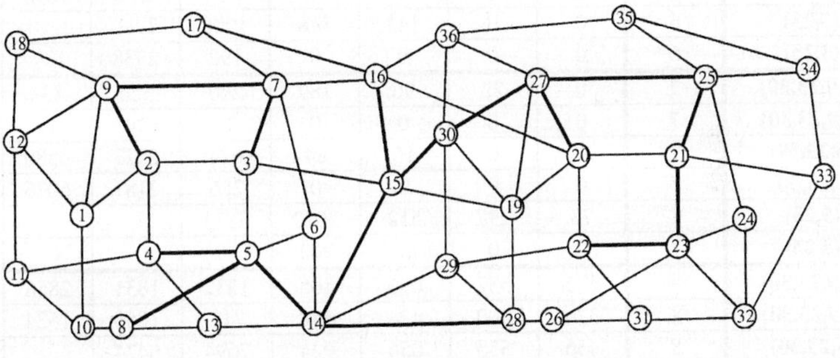

Fig. 1. Topology of sample network

The goal of the simulation study is to compare the performance of various survivability approaches for an example network topology and to study the impact of the unified approach on network restoration process in terms of the lost flow function. The network consists of 36 nodes and 144 directed links (Fig. 1). The bold lines represent links of size 96 units while other lines are links of size 48 units. The link capacities were chosen to model capacity ratio of OC-48 circuits. During simulations, the link capacities were scaled by a factor 10 to enable establishing of many connections. In the experiment it is assumed that there is a full mesh of unicast demands. Thus, the total number of unicast demands is $|V|(|V|-1)=1260$ between each node pair. In one particular experiment the unicast bandwidth requirement (U_BR) for each demand is the same. We run simulation for the following values of U_BR={6, 7, 8, 9, 10}. Additionally, there are 5 anycast demands for each node in the network. Therefore, the total number of anycast demands is $5|V|=180$. As above, anycast demands tested in one experiment have the same bandwidth requirement. Since, more data is received by clients then is sent to replicas, we make an assumption, that traffic between clients and replicas is asymmetric. Consequently, volume of downstream anycast connection is usually much higher than volume of upstream anycast connection. Therefore, we assume that upstream bandwidth is always set to 1. The following values of downstream anycast bandwidth requirement (A_BR) are tested A_BR={5,10,15,20,25,30,35,40}. We assume that all demands in the network are protected and have the same priority. Overall, for each tested location of replicas we simulate 5x8=40 various demands patterns.

In the simulation we use two restoration approaches. In the approach A all demands of type PU and PA are protected using the backup route method. Therefore,

Table 1. The lost flow function for various scenarios, demand patterns and servers' location

Server location	**U_BR**	**A_BR (Anycast Bandwidth Requirement)** 5	10	15	20	25	30	35	40
A(5,9,23,30)	6	0	0	0	0	0	0	72	492
B(5,9,23,30)	6	0	0	0	0	0	0	0	0
A(5,23,30)	6	0	0	0	0	104	1395	2760	7603
B(5,23,30)	6	0	0	0	0	0	279	1896	6250
A(5,23)	6	0	0	144	378	1908	7980		
B(5,23)	6	0	0	0	0	192	2338		
A(5,9,23,30)	7	0	22	96	189	260	324	438	1252
B(5,9,23,30)	7	0	0	0	0	0	14	42	63
A(5,23,30)	7	0	0	16	84	624	2522	6580	
B(5,23,30)	7	0	0	0	0	286	2181	6076	
A(5,23)	7	78	297	512	2079	5873			
B(5,23)	7	0	0	0	903	2493			
A(5,9,23,30)	8	472	587	696	805	1232	1831	2856	4347
B(5,9,23,30)	8	376	400	424	448	712	1056	1524	2010
A(5,23,30)	8	456	556	656	924	2694	6474		
B(5,23,30)	8	336	336	336	483	2174	5699		
A(5,23)	8	816	1800	3688	6867				
B(5,23)	8	336	744	1880	4410				
A(5,9,23,30)	9	2544	3227	3865	4575	5395	6868		
B(5,9,23,30)	9	2412	2952	3465	4050	4693	5814		
A(5,23,30)	9	2322	2927	3574	5481	9698			
B(5,23,30)	9	2178	2652	3174	4956	8944			
A(5,23)	9	3894	5880						
B(5,23)	9	3330	4736						

Table 2. The network flow various demand patterns and servers' location

Server location	U_BR	A_BR (Anycast Bandwidth Requirement) 5	10	15	20	25	30	35	40
(5,9,23,30)	6	27042	28191	29346	30033	31170	32319	33462	34581
(5,23,30)	6	27390	28840	29900	31362	32830	34364	35989	37974
(5,23)	6	27402	29244	31074	32916	34958	37428		
(5,9,23,30)	7	31058	32204	33322	34419	35558	36704	37878	39010
(5,23,30)	7	31427	32870	34327	35826	37290	38719	40442	
(5,23)	7	31861	33640	35538	37464	39619			
(5,9,23,30)	8	35470	36619	37720	38853	40026	41143	42356	43529
(5,23,30)	8	35828	37302	38728	40194	41652	43218		
(5,23)	8	36248	38088	40008	42072				
(5,9,23,30)	9	39996	41121	42156	43326	44517	45765		
(5,23,30)	9	40296	41746	43169	44619	46096			
(5,23)	9	40797	42660						

anycast flow is restored using the same replica server that is used for primary route. In the second approach, referred to as B, we apply the backup server method.

In Table 1 we report the value of lost flow function for three servers locations: (5,9,23,30), (5,23,30) and (5,23). Both restoration approaches A and B are considered. Empty cells of the table indicate that for the particular demand pattern and servers' location the algorithm cannot find a feasible solution. The experiment confirms that the unified approach proposed in the paper is more efficient then the traditional approach. The lost flow obtained for approach B is lower than for approach A. In some cases the difference is substantial. Analysis of results suggests that increasing the number of replica servers improves the lost flow function drastically. Moreover, if the number of servers grows, more demands with higher bandwidth requirements can be satisfied. The above analysis shows that applying the unified approach is reasonable and provides considerable reduction of lost flow. Another important observation is that when the proportion of the anycast flow in the overall network flow increases, adding new replicas improves the network survivability more robustly. It is in harmony with our understanding of the unified approach. Using the backup content server approach can improve the network survivability proportionally to the ratio of the anycast traffic to the whole traffic in the network.

Applying caching influences the network survivability also indirectly. When users can access the data in caches located nearby, the overall network flow decreases. Hence, more spare capacity is left for restoration of failed connections. In Table 2 we present the network flow allocated by the algorithm for the same cases as in Table 1. It is obvious that locating new replicas reduces the network flow. However, the reduction is not substantial. Comparing Table 1 against Table 2 we see that relatively small decrease in network flow can yield significant reduction of the lost flow for both tested approaches. This follows from the backup content server method. The second observation is that, as above, when the proportion of the anycast flow in the overall network flow increases, adding new replicas reduces the network flow more significantly than for other cases.

6 Conclusion

In this paper, we have studied the performance improvements as the survivability mechanisms of c-o networks and restoration capabilities of CDNs are used in cooperation in one network. We have presented and discussed basic restoration methods used for unicast flow (ATM, MPLS) and anycast flow (CDNs). We have formulated a new optimization problem of providing survivability in a unified method. This problem is NP-complete. The objective condition is the function of lost flow due to a failure of a single link. Using this optimization model new algorithms can be developed. Although our goal in this paper is biased towards the c-o techniques, we believe that the results should be generally applicable to different network techniques and restoration methods. We have provided a numerical example to illustrate the proposed approach. Simulations have provided positive results to show that using the unified survivability approach is indeed useful. In future work we plan to develop new heuristics and also an exact algorithm solving the presented optimization problem. Next, we want to make extensive test in order to evaluate presented approach.

Acknowledgements. This work was supported by a research project of the Polish State Committee for Scientific Research carried out in years 2005-2007.

References

1. Grover, W.: Mesh-based Survivable Networks: Options and Strategies for Optical, MPLS, SONET and ATM Networking. Prentice Hall PTR, Upper Saddle River, New Jersey (2004)
2. Hao, F., Zegura, E., Ammar, M.: QoS routing for anycast communications: motivation and an architecture for DiffServ networks. IEEE Comm. Magazine, 6 (2002), 48-56
3. Krishnamurthy, B., Wills, C., Zhang, Y.: On the Use and Performance of Content Delivery Networks. in Proc. of ACM SigComm Internet Measurement Workshop, 2001
4. Markowski, M., Kasprzak, A.: An approximate algorithm for replica allocation problem in wide area networks. In Proc. of MMB & PGTS 2004, VDE Verlag: Berlin, 161-166
5. Markowski, M., Kasprzak, A.: The web replica allocation and topology assignment problem in wide area networks: algorithms and computational results. Lectures Notes in Computer Science, LNCS 3483 (2005), 772-781
6. Peng, G.: CDN: Content Distribution Networks. Technical Report, sunysb.edu/tr/rpe13.ps.gz, (2003)
7. Rabinovich, M.: Issues in Web Content Replication. Data Engineering Bulletin 4 (1998)
8. Sharma, V., Hellstrand, F. (ed.): Framework for MPLS-based Recovery. RFC 3469 (2003)
9. Walkowiak, K.: Designing of survivable web caching. in Proc. of 8th Polish Teletraffic Symposium (2001), 171-181
10. Walkowiak, K.: A New Method of Primary Routes Selection for Local Restoration. Lectures Notes in Computer Science, LNCS 3042 (2004), 1024-1035
11. Weber, S., Cheng, L.: A Survey of Anycast in IPV6 Networks. IEEE Comm. Magazine, 1 (2004), 127-132

SCTP Based Framework for Mobile Web Agent

Yong-Jin Lee[1], Ho-Sang Ham[2], and M. Atiquzzaman[3]

[1] Department of Technology Education,
Korea National University of Education, 363-791, Korea
yjlee1026@daum.net

[2] Electronics and Telecommunication Research Institute,
161 Kajong-Dong, Yusong-Ku, Taejon 305-700, Korea
hsham@etri.re.kr

[3] School of Computer Science, University of Oklahoma,
200 Felgar Street, Norman, OK 73019, USA
atiq@ou.edu

Abstract. The stream control transmission protocol (SCTP) is a new transport protocol, which provides multi-streaming and multi-homing features. Especially, recent SCTP extensions with dynamic address reconfiguration supports transport layer mobility. We address web agent framework supporting seamless transport layer mobility in the wired and wireless environment. Our proposed framework for mobile web agent deploys SCTP with dynamic address reconfiguration. Mean response time is an important performance measure of web agents. Our simulation results show that our SCTP based framework reduces the mean response time of a typical transmission control protocol (TCP) based framework remarkably.

1 Introduction

Hyper text transfer protocol (HTTP) is an application protocol used by the web agent to retrieve objects in the Internet. Since HTTP is a connection-oriented protocol, it currently uses transmission control protocol (TCP) as the transport protocol. HTTP/1.0 does not provide the means to request multiple objects, thus, we must establish a new TCP connection for retrieving each object from the server. This protocol is particularly inefficient because it requires two extra round trip times (RTT) in setting up a new TCP connection between the client and the server. HTTP/1.1 can reduce the extra setup time with persistent connections. Furthermore, it allows the client to send all requests simultaneously by using pipelining. However, even though we use any other enhanced HTTP versions including HTTP/1.1, there is a mismatch between the requirements of HTTP and the functionality provided by TCP. When multiple embedded objects are being transferred using HTTP, it is desired that each object should be reliably transferred in the aspect of TCP. However, ordered delivery of these objects is not a requirement in HTTP. Instead, it is more important to reduce the perceived latency of user. In fact, most users are only concerned about the quick response time.

The Stream Control Transmission Protocol (SCTP) [1] has been proposed by IETF to overcome deficiencies of TCP such as performance degradation, head-of-line (HOL) blocking, and unsupported mobility. The performance degradation problem is alleviated in SCTP by incorporating the enhanced features of TCP congestion control

P. Yolum et al.(Eds.): ISCIS 2005, LNCS 3733, pp. 13 – 22, 2005.

schemes. For example, fast retransmit algorithm, based on selective acknowledgement (SACK), is deployed. This scheme speeds up loss detection and increases the bandwidth utilization [2]. The use of SACK is mandatory in SCTP as compared with TCP. To overcome the HOL blocking problem of TCP, we can make use of SCTP's multi-streaming feature to speed up the transfer of web objects. If one object is lost during the transfer, the others can be delivered to the web agent at the upper layer while the lost object is being retransmitted from the web server. This results in a better response time to users with only one SCTP association for a particular HTML page. Finally, to deal with the unsupported mobility problem of TCP, we utilize the extended SCTP multi-homing feature. SCTP multi-homing allows a single SCTP endpoint to support multiple IP addresses. In its current form, multi-homing support of SCTP is only for redundancy. The extended SCTP multi-homing feature (called dynamic IP address reconfiguration [3]) is capable of supporting transport layer mobility. This feature provides a mechanism that allows an SCTP endpoint to dynamically add and delete IP addresses during the lifetime of an SCTP association. Mobile SCTP [4] and transport layer seamless handover (SIGMA) [5,6] are schemes to utilize the dynamic IP address reconfiguration. These schemes do not require any modification to the IP structure.

While SCTP can solve several deficiencies of TCP, it does not provide the location management function that Mobile IP supports intrinsically. Hence, location management in SCTP is performed with the help of the domain name server (DNS) in the application layer [5] or the mobile IP in the network layer [4]. However, the scheme to use DNS can cause scalability problem; on the other hand, the scheme used in mobile IP can result in complexity and inefficiency in the network. In this paper, we consider a web agent that always initiates the connection setup to web server. Thus, we do not consider the location management problem.

We propose a web agent framework using SCTP with the dynamic IP address reconfiguration. The most important performance measure in web environment is the mean response time between HTTP requests and replies. To compare the performance of the proposed framework and a typical TCP based framework, we have carried out the simulation on our experimental testbed. Results show that our framework's mean response time is less than the TCP based framework by more than ten percents.

The main contribution of this paper are: (i) proposing an architecture for the mobile web agent framework, (ii) description of functions of the managers in the web agent framework, and (iii) demonstration of performance enhancement of the suggested SCTP based framework over the typical TCP based framework.

The rest of the paper is organized as follows. We begin by describing the suggested framework for web agent in Section 2. Section 3 compares mean response time of TCP based framework with that of SCTP based framework. Section 4 discusses the performance evaluation, and Section 5 concludes the paper.

2 Mobile Web Agent Framework Based on SCTP

We present the framework for the mobile web agent in Fig. 1. The framework is mainly composed of the mobility support manager and the data manager. Components of the mobility support manager are movement detector and handover manager. Data

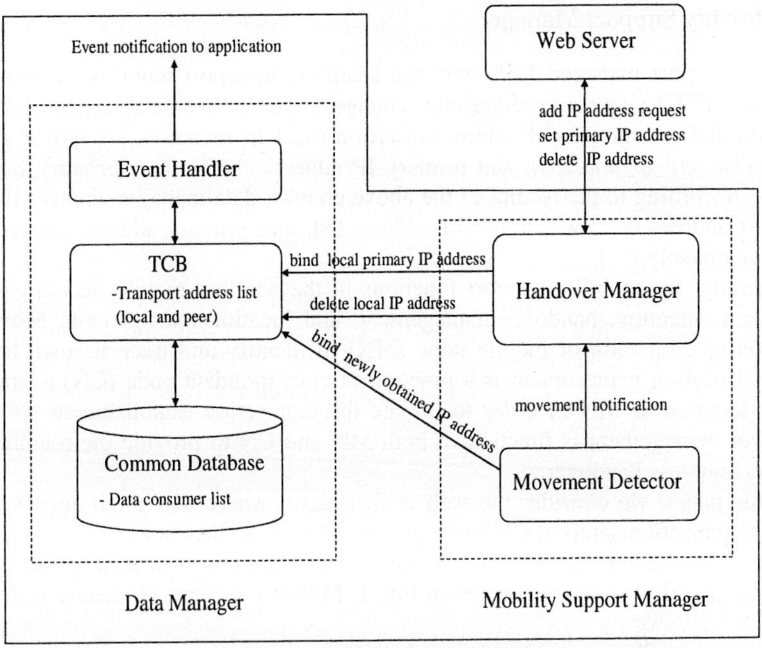

Fig. 1. Mobile web agent framework

manager includes event handler, transmission control block (TCB), and common database. Event handler passes events occurred in mobility support manager to application via TCB. Common database and TCB maintain information related with the current association and mobility support.

2.1 Data Manager

Data manager defines necessary parameters for the protocol implementation. Common database is necessary for SCTP instance as follows: (i) Data consumer list related with the currently connected association. Data consumer means process identification information, such as file descriptor, pipe pointer, and table pointer. (ii) Secret key for the security of end-user. (iii) Address list indicating end points. (iv) Port number indicating the bound port number of end point.

Some important parameters are stored in TCB per association as follows: (i) Peer verification tag indicating the authentication value of the corresponding node (ii) My verification tag indicating the authentication value of local node (iii) State indicating the current status of SCTP such as the connection complete, shutdown, and stop (iv) Peer transport address list indicating the transport address list of the corresponding node (v) Local transport address list indicating the local IP address list (vi) Primary path indicating the primary destination address of the corresponding node.

2.2 Mobility Support Manager

Mobility support manager deals with the seamless transport mobility of web agent using the SCTP address configuration change (*ASCONF*) extension [6]. ASCONF extension defines the new IP address insertion (*add_ip_address*), the old IP address deletion (*delete_ip_address*), and primary IP address change (*set_primary_address*) chunks. According to the receipt of the above chunks, data manager changes the peer transport address list, local transport address list, and primary address stored in the TCB dynamically.

Generally, the mobility support functions in the wireless mobile network include movement detection, handover management, and location management. Movement detection is a function of mobile node (MN) to identify and trace its own location change. Location management is a function of correspondent node (CN) to trace the current location of MN in order to initiate the connection establishment with MN. Handover management is function of both MN and CN to provide the roaming MN with the seamless handover.

In this paper, we consider the web environment, where MN (web agent) always initiates connection setup to CN (web server). Thus, CN does not need location management. Nevertheless, if the location management function is necessary, we can add it into the mobility support manager in Fig. 1. Mobility support procedure is depicted in Fig. 2.

(1) Movement detector
Initially, mobile web agent hears router advertisement (RA) from old access router (AR), and finds the network prefix included in RA (1, Fig. 2). Web agent acquires its own IP address by using stateless auto-configuration of IPv6 based on the network prefix (when using IPv6) or inquiring to dynamic host configuration protocol (DHCPv4/v6) server (when using IPv4/IPv6). Web agent and web server establish the association by exchanging IP address. At this time, each end point specifies the primary IP address on which data is sent (2, Fig. 2). Information related with the association is recorded in each TCB of web agent and web server, followed by exchange of data.

The web agent, while communicating with the web server, moves from the coverage of old AR to the overlapped region which is covered by both old AR and new AR. Web agent hears new router prefix from new AR (3, Fig. 2), and detects its movement into new network by comparing its current network prefix (1, Fig. 2) with new network prefix (3, Fig. 2). If web agent uses IPv6, it can itself configure new IP address using stateless auto-configuration based on the network prefix. Otherwise, it can acquire a new IP address from the DHCPv4/v6 server (4, Fig. 2), which increases the required signaling time. Anyway, newly obtained IP address is bound on the local transport address list in the TCB of web agent (5, Fig. 2). These events are delivered to the application via event handler.

(2) Handover manager
After binding the new IP address on TCB, web agent informs the web server that it will use the new IP address by sending *ASCONF add_ip_address* (6, Fig. 2). Web server modifies its own TCB by adding the received new IP address of web agent and replies to the web agent by an *ASCONF add_ip_ack* (7, Fig. 2). At this time, web

agent becomes multi-homed, and is thus reachable by two different networks. It can receive data on both old and new IP addresses. Consequently, if there is a physical problem with the path related to the primary address, the new IP address can be used as an alternate address.

As web agent leaves the overlapped region and enters the coverage of new AR, it experiences more packet loss on the primary path. If the amount of received packets on new IP address is greater than on the primary IP address, web agent sends out the *ASCONF set_primary* chuck to web server. This makes the web server to use the new IP address as primary address for data communications (8, Fig. 2). Web server replies to the *ASCONF set_primary_ack* chunk to web agent (9, Fig. 2).

As the web agent continues to move into the core coverage of new AR, the previous primary IP address becomes obsolete. Web agent sends out the *ASCONF delete_IP* chuck to web server, which eliminates the previous primary IP address (10, Fig. 2). The reason to delete the obsolete IP address is as the follows: We assume that the newly set primary path is broken in the coverage of new AR. If we did not delete the previous primary IP address in the binding list, it might become an alternate path. Thus, the data from web server may be redirected to the alternate path. However, the previous primary IP address cannot receive any data in the coverage of new AR. As a result, there exists the unnecessary traffic in the network. Handover is completed by the web server when responding by *ASCONF delete_ip_ack* to web agent (11, Fig. 2).

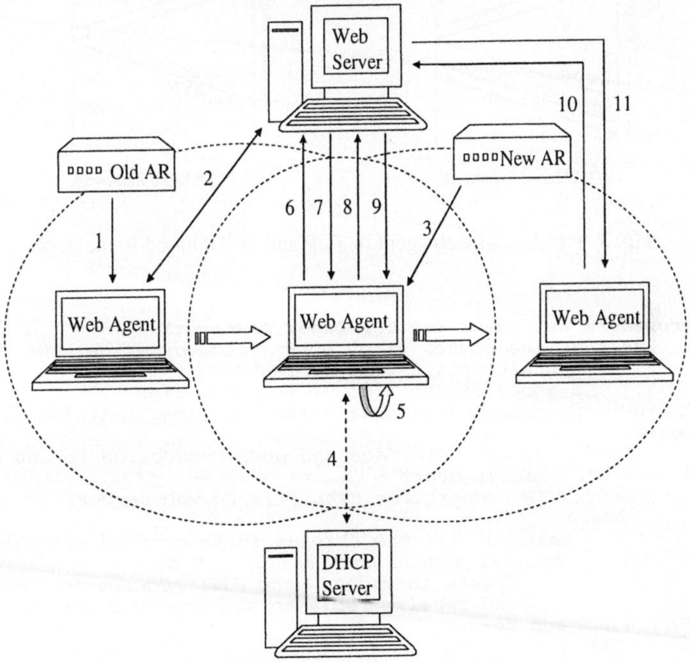

Fig. 2. Mobility support procedure of web agent

3 Mean Response Time for TCP and SCTP Based Framework

In this section, we describe TCP based framework and the SCTP based framework. We use HTTP 1.1 on both frameworks (HTTP hereafter refers to HTTP 1.1).

3.1 Mean Response Time for TCP Based Framework

In the TCP based framework, timeline of web agent using pipelining is depicted in Fig. 3 (a). Response time is defined as the time taken between the initial request from the client to the server, and the completion of the response from the server to the

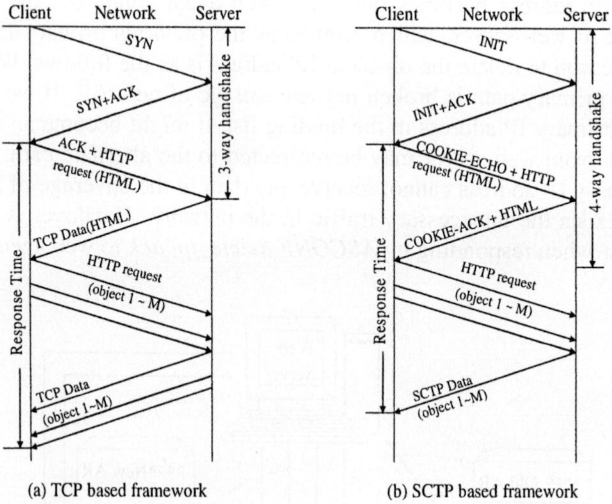

Fig. 3. Timeline of web agent in TCP and SCTP based frameworks

```
Procedure web agent for TCP based framework
Variable M: the number of objects imbedded in the HTML file
         t_start: start time of response time
         t_stop: finish time of response time
         response_time: total response time
Begin
     Create socket interface and open connection to web server;
     Start timer(t_start
     Send HTTP request for HTML file to web server;
      begin
          Wait for all the threads to be created are terminated;
           for all k such that k=1,2,..,M do
               Create thread to send HTTP request for object
               and receive reply to and from web server
           end for
      end
     Stop timer(t_stop);
     Set response_ time = t_stop - t_start;
End
```

Fig. 4. Web agent for TCP based framework

client. After 3-way-handshake, client receives the HTML file with *M* embedded objects. Then, the client that supports persistent connections and pipelines sends its requests. That is, the client sends *M* requests simultaneously using pipelining. A server sends its responses to those requests in the same order that the requests were received.

In order to compare TCP based framework with SCTP based framework fairly, we have to use the same test environment such as operating systems, hardware, and programming language. Thus, we use the same approach for TCP based framework and SCTP based framework. Web agent for TCP based framework is represented in Fig. 4: we simulate the pipelining using *M* threads that send its own request simultaneously. Meanwhile, client receives HTTP reply sequentially from the server.

3.2 Mean Response Time for SCTP Based Framework

In the SCTP based framework, the initialization of a SCTP association is completed after the exchange of four messages. The passive side of the association does not allocate resources for the association until the third of these messages has arrived and been validated. Last two messages of the four-way handshake can already carry user data. With this piggybacking, SCTP has the same connection-establishment delay as TCP, namely one round trip time. Since SCTP has multi-streaming feature, it avoids the head-of-line blocking. Furthermore, SCTP does not limit maximum number of objects for pipelining. We depicted the timeline of web agent for SCTP based framework in the Fig. 3 (b).

```
Procedure web agent for SCTP based framework
Variable  M: the number of objects imbedded in the HTML file
          t_start: start time of response
          t_stop: finish time of response time
          response_time: total response time
Begin
    Create socket interface and open connection to web server;
    Start timer(t_start);
    Send HTTP request for HTML file to web server;
    Fork the current process;
    If the process is parent for sending
        begin
          Wait for all the threads to be created are terminated;
          for all k such that k=1,2,..,M do
               Create thread to send HTTP request for object
               to web server
          end for
        end
     else if the process is client for receiving
        begin
           Wait for all the threads to be created are terminated;
           for all k such that k=1,2,..,M do
                Create thread to receive HTTP reply for object
                from web server;
           end for
        end
    end
    Stop timer(t_stop);
    Set response_ time = t_stop - t_start;
End
```

Fig. 5. Web agent for SCTP based framework

Web agent for SCTP based framework is shown in Fig. 5: we first fork two processes- parent and child. In the parent process, *M* threads simulate the pipelining for sending *M* HTTP requests for objects to web server. In the child process, *M* threads simulate the multi-streaming for receiving *M* HTTP replies from web server. To summarize, main difference between TCP based framework and SCTP based framework is that SCTP can receive multiple objects in parallel by using its own multi-streaming feature.

4 Performance Evaluation

4.1 Experimental Setup

In this section, we compare the performance of web agents for TCP based framework with SCTP based framework in terms of mean response time. For this experiment, we wrote two Linux C server programs which simulate HTTP over TCP and SCTP server, respectively. We also wrote two Linux C client programs according to procedures which are presented in Figs. 4 and 5 to simulate pipelining and multi-streaming, respectively. The main reason for the simulated HTTP server and client using our own program is due to the lack of adequate support of SCTP by current HTTP client/server. To simulate TCP based framework, each web agent sends requests for *M* objects. In response, the TCP server sends the requested *M* objects to the web agent sequentially using one TCP connection. On the other hand, SCTP server sends *M* objects in different streams on a single SCTP association. Table 1 shows the host and network configurations of the testbed. We used the CISCO-7102 router to control the bandwidth between web agent and web server. We measured the response time using *t_start*() and *t_stop*() system calls defined in *timval* structure of Unix system.

Table 1. Host and network configuration of testbed

Node	hardware	software	Operating system	network
Web Server	CPU: Intel Pentium-4/1.7 GHz, RAM: 512 MB NIC: 3 Com PCI 3cDSOHIO 100-TX	TCP /SCTP server program	Fedora Core 2 Linux Kernel 2.6.5-1	210.93.87.0
Web Agent	CPU: Intel Pentium-4/1.7 GHz, RAM: 512 MB NIC: 3 Com PCI 3cDSOHIO 100-TX	TCP /SCTP client program	Fedora Core 2 Linux Kernel 2.6.5-1	210.93.83.0
Router	Cisco-7102		IOS	

Table 2 represents test parameters used for our experiment. For example, to investigate the multi-streaming effect of SCTP over TCP according to the object size (*O*), we used 8 KB, 10 KB, and 13.5 KB. In this case, the number of objects (*M*) and bandwidth (*bw*) are 10 and 2 Mbps, respectively.

Table 2. Test parameters for the experiment

test parameters	object size (KB)	number of objects	bandwidth (Mbps)	round trip time (ms)
object size (*O*)	8, 10, 13.5	10	2	-
number of objects (*M*)	13.5	3, 5, 10	2	-
Bandwidth (*bw*)	13.5	10	0.064, 2, 8	-
round trip time (*RTT*)	13.5	10	2	55, 80, 256

4.2 Experiment Result

Fig. 6 ~ Fig. 9 shows mean response times corresponding to test parameters in Table 2. Mean response times are computed for 50 trials at each test parameter for TCP based framework and SCTP based framework, respectively. Fig. 6 shows that the mean response time is directly proportional to the object size. This is due that the transfer time is increased in proportional to the file size. In Fig. 7, the difference of mean response time between TCP based web agent and SCTP based web agent is increased as the number of objects becomes larger. This means that large number of objects in SCTP based framework can reduce the mean response time of TCP based framework. Fig. 8 shows that the mean response time is inversely proportional to the bandwidth. It is natural that larger bandwidth decreases total transfer time, which reduces the mean response time. In Fig. 9, we found that the increase rate of the mean response time in TCP based framework is about 100 % between 55 ms and 256 ms, meanwhile, which in SCTP based framework is only 30 %. Since TCP can not utilize the multi-streaming feature, all objects experience large *RTT*. On the other hand, multiple objects in SCTP based framework experience only one *RTT*. Thus, as the number of objects and *RTT* are increased, the performance benefit of SCTP over TCP will be increased.

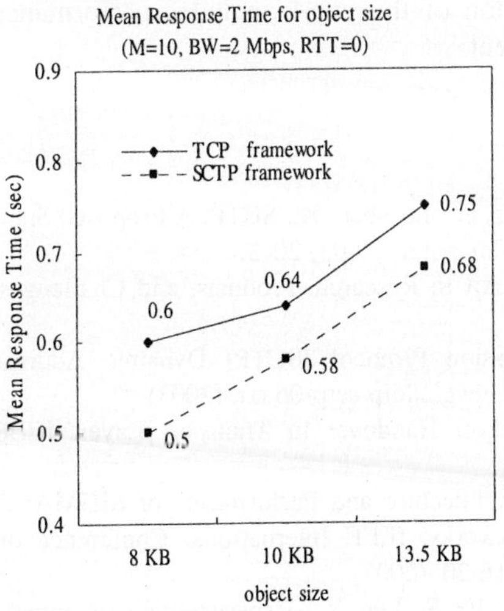

Fig. 6. Mean response time for object size

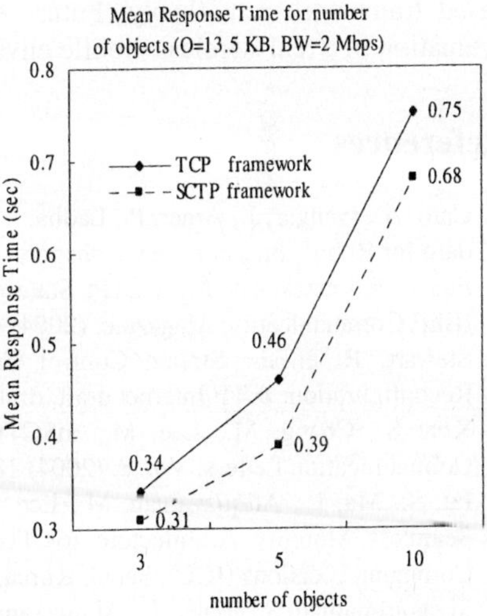

Fig. 7. Mean response time for number of objects

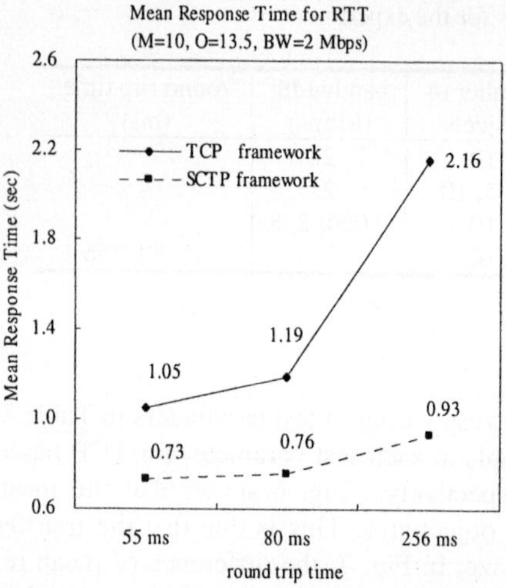

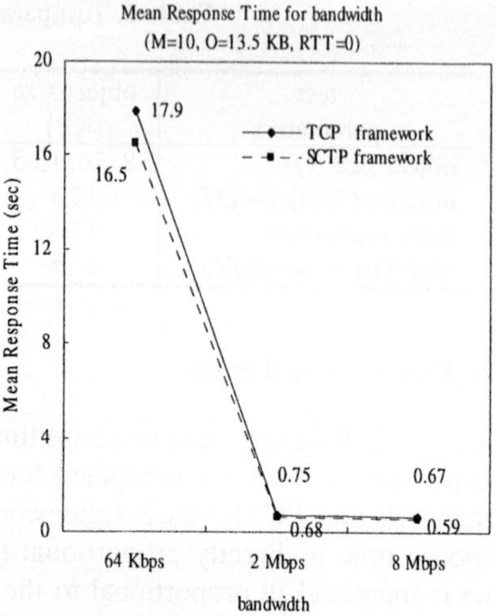

Fig. 8. Mean response time for bandwidth

Fig. 9. Mean response time for round trip time

5 Conclusions

In this paper, we have proposed and evaluated a stream control transport protocol based web agent framework. We have also investigated and described important characteristics and functions necessary to implement the web agent to support seamless mobility. To compare the performance of our SCTP based framework with typical TCP based framework, we have carried out experiment in testbed. Results show that our web agent framework can reduce the mean response time over a typical TCP based framework remarkably. Future extension of this work includes performance evaluation in a real wireless mobile environment.

References

1. Caro, A., Iyengar, J., Amer, P., Ladha, S., Heinz, G. and Shah, K.: SCTP: A Proposed Standard for Robust Internet Data Transport. IEEE Computer. (2003) 20-27.
2. Fu, S., Atiquzzaman, M.: SCTP: State of the Art in Research, Products, and Challenges. IEEE Communication Magazine. (2004) 64-76.
3. Stewart, R. et al.: Stream Control Transmission Protocol (SCTP) Dynamic Address Reconfiguration. IETF Internet draft, draft-ietf-tsvwg-addip-sctp-06.txt. (2003).
4. Koh, S., Chang, M., Lee, M.: mSCTP for Soft Handover in Transport Layer. IEEE Communication Letters, Vol. 8. (2004) 189-191.
5. Fu, S., Ma, L., Atiquzzaman, M., Lee, Y.: Architecture and Performance of SIGMA: A Seamless Mobility Architecture for Data Networks, IEEE International Conference on Communi- cations (ICC), Seoul, Korea, May 16-20. (2005).
6. Sivagurunathan, S., Jones, J., Atiquzzaman, M., Fu, S., Lee, Y.,: Experimental Comparison of Handoff Performance of SIGMA and Mobile IP, IEEE Workshop on High Performance Switching and Routing, Hong Kong, May 12-14. (2005).

An Agent-Based Scheme for Efficient Multicast Application in Mobile Networks*

Qian Wu[1], Jian-ping Wu[2], Ming-wei Xu[1], Yong Cui[1], and Hui Deng[3]

[1] Department of Computer Science and Technology, Tsinghua University, Beijing 100084, China
{wuqian, xmw, cy}@csnet1.cs.tsinghua.edu.cn
http://netlab.cs.tsinghua.edu.cn

[2] Department of Computer Science and Technology, Tsinghua University, Beijing 100084, China
jianping@cernet.edu.cn

[3] Hitachi (China) Investment, Ltd., Beijing 100004, China
hdeng@hitachi.cn

Abstract. Mobile communication is playing an increasing role in our lives. Mobile users expect similar kinds of applications to static ones. Multicast not only brings attractive applications, but also has the benefit of saving scarce bandwidth in wireless environment. In order to achieve efficient multicast in mobile networks, we propose an agent-based scheme called Mobile Multicast with Fast Handoff and Hierarchical Architecture (FHMM). This scheme introduces two kinds of agents: *Multicast Agent* (MA) and *Domain Multicast Agent* (DMA). Through the cooperation between MAs in adjacent networks, FHMM accomplishes fast multicast handoff. And through the use of DMA, FHMM achieves a hierarchical mobile multicast architecture which can isolate the local movement from outside and improve the stability of the main multicast delivery tree. The simulation results show that FHMM is effective with low packet loss rate, high multicast packet delivery efficiency and little multicast maintenance overhead.

1 Introduction

"Anywhere and anytime access to the Internet" fuels the requirement of more applications supporting mobile environment. In the mean time, mobile network often comes with the wireless infrastructure, so the scarce bandwidth becomes the main drawback and baffles the use of many applications. Since multicast can efficiently deal with multi-destinations delivery, it can not only bring attractive applications, but also give the benefit of network bandwidth saving and releasing the burden of replications from the source. It will be fruitful to bring these two together, especially in the next generation IP networks.

* This research is supported by the National Natural Science Foundation of China (No. 60373010), the National 973 Project Fund of China (No 2003CB314801), and Cooperative research project on Mobile IPv6 Multicast between Hitachi (China) and Tsinghua University.

P. Yolum et al.(Eds.): ISCIS 2005, LNCS 3733, pp. 23–32, 2005.

Providing multicast support for mobile nodes [1,2,3,4,5] is challenging because the protocol must deal not only with dynamic group membership but also with dynamic member location. It causes many new problems [6,7], such as routing inefficiency, multicast group state and delivery tree maintenance overhead, handoff latency and packets loss. The current multicast protocols of the Internet are developed implicitly for static members and do not consider the extra requirements to support mobile nodes. Every time a member changes its location, the reconstruction of the multicast delivery tree will involve extreme overhead, while leaving the multicast delivery tree unchanged will result in inefficient sometimes incorrect delivery path. Mobile IP [8] and Mobile IPv6 [9], proposed standards by the IETF, provide two approaches to support mobile multicast, i.e., bi-directional tunneling (MIP-BT) and remote subscription (MIP-RS). But both of them have severe drawbacks, such as routing inefficiency, tremendous protocol overhead, etc, and can not solve the mobile multicast problems well.

In this paper, we propose a new agent-based scheme called FHMM (Mobile Multicast with Fast Handoff and Hierarchical Architecture). It based on the MIP-RS and solved its main drawbacks. There are two kinds of agents in this scheme: *Multicast Agent* (MA) and *Domain Multicast Agent* (DMA). Through the uses of these two kinds of agents, FHMM achieves a hierarchical mobile multicast architecture which can shield the local movement from outside and efficiently reduce the change of the main multicast delivery tree and decrease the multicast protocol overhead related to handoff. In addition, FHMM introduces a fast multicast handoff technology through which the MA of expected foreign networks can be notified to join the multicast group in advance, and then both the handoff latency and the packet loss rate can be reduced. We have verified our argument through the simulation and the results show that our scheme has an improved performance over other existing protocols. What's more, the fast multicast handoff technology is used in both intra-domain and inter-domain handoff procedure that makes FHMM being a global solution for mobile multicast.

The rest of the paper is organized as follows. In section 2 we introduce the background of fast handoff for Mobile IPv6 and the existing mobile multicast protocols. Section 3 describes FHMM scheme in detail. Section 4 presents our experiments using OMNet++ [10] and result analysis. Finally, we conclude this paper and introduce future works.

2 Background and Previous Works

2.1 Fast Handoffs for Mobile IPv6

Mobile IPv6 handoff procedure includes movement detection, IP address configuration, and location update, which is often sufficient to affect realtime applications. Fast Handovers for Mobile IPv6 (FMIP6) [11] proposes a way to reduce the handoff latency. It enables a mobile node (MN) to quickly detect its movement to a new network and configure a new CoA (NCoA) when the MN is still connected to its current network. Hence, the latency due to movement detection,

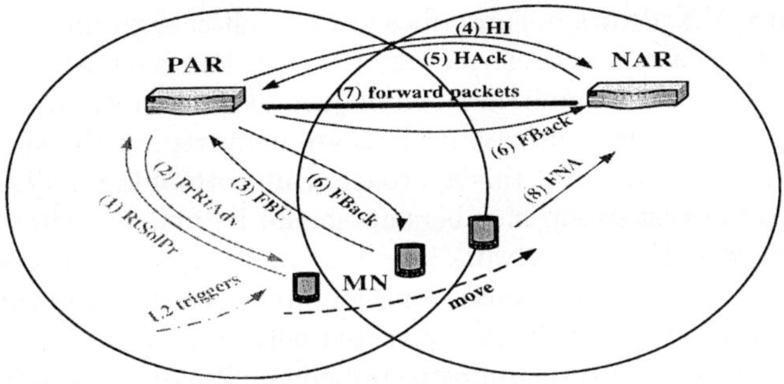

Fig. 1. The operation of FMIP6

new prefix discovery and new address configuration is reduced. And a tunnel mechanism is used to reduce packet loss.

The operation of FMIP6 is shown in Fig 1. FMIP6 begins when MN discovers the connection to a new Access Router (NAR) by the reception of a link-layer specific event. Then MN sends a Router Solicitation for Proxy Advertisement (RtSolPr) message to its current AR, also called previous AR (PAR), to acquire the network layer information of NAR. PAR responds with a Proxy Router Advertisement (PrRtAdv) message. Then MN constructs a prospective NCoA and sends a Fast Binding Update (FBU) message to PAR. PAR relays NCoA information in a Handover Initiate (HI) message and sends it to NAR. NAR replies with a Handover Acknowledge (HAck) message to notify the usefulness of NCoA or to provide another address for MN when the NCoA is not acceptable. PAR relays the operation results to MN using a message called Fast Binding Acknowledgment (FBack). At this time, a tunnel between PAR and NAR is established and PAR begins to tunnel packets to MN's NCoA.

As soon as the MN is handoff to NAR, it sends a Fast Neighbor Advertisement (FNA) message to announce its attachment, which enables MN to immediately receive packets from NAR while MN is still in binding procedure.

2.2 Mobile Multicast Protocols

MIP-BT and MIP-RS proposed by Mobile IPv6 provide basic multicast support for mobile nodes. But they can't well address the new problems arising from extending multicast to mobile nodes. In MIP-BT, MN subscribes to multicast group through its home agent (HA), and uses the bi-directional tunnel between them to receive multicast packets. In this manner, there is no need to update multicast group state and multicast delivery tree after MN's handoff, so there is no multicast maintenance overhead. But MN's multicast delivery path of is far from optimal, and routing inefficiency and bandwidth wasting become the main drawbacks. In addition, the HA should replicate and deliver packets to all its MNs through those tunnels, and this kind of burden will increase with the number of MNs that it services. Sometimes the HA may become an *error point.* To some extent, the multicast is degraded to unicast.

In MIP-RS, MN always re-subscribes to the multicast group when it changes the attachment to a new access network. MN does this re-subscription using its NCoA through the local multicast router just like the static one in the local network. Obviously, the multicast packets are delivered on the shortest paths. This is the main advantage of this approach. But both of the multicast delivery tree and the multicast group membership should be updated after the handoff occurs, which would cause network overhead and computation overhead. The re-subscription behavior also causes long join and graft latency when there are no other group members in the newly visited network.

MobiCast [1] is a protocol aiming to provide multicast to mobile nodes in an internetwork environment with small wireless cells. It uses a hierarchical mobility management approach. Each domain has a Domain Foreign Agent (DFA), and it subscribes to the multicast group on behalf of the MNs in its domain. For every multicast group, DFA provides a unique translated multicast address in the domain. Multicast packets are at first delivered to DFA, and then DFA changes the group address to the translated multicast address. The Base Station (BS) in the domain subscribes to the translated multicast group, and forwards packets of the group to the MN after re-translating them into original multicast group. In order to achieve fast handoff within the domain, as soon as the MN has subscribed to the multicast group, its affiliated BS will inform the physically adjacent BSs to join the corresponding translated multicast group and buffer multicast packets. These BSs form a virtual domain called Dynamic Virtual Macro-cells (DVM). By the use of DFA, MobiCast hides the MN's movement from outside, and avoids the update of main multicast delivery tree. The other advantages are the reduced handoff latency and packets loss. But because a mass of unnecessary multicast packets are forwarded to adjacent BSs while there is no group members, the main drawback of MobiCast would be bandwidth waste, which is critical for mobile environment. What's more, every time the mobile handoff occurs, it will cause several BSs to join the multicast group while others to leave and this will result in significant multicast protocol cost. Finally, MobiCast does not give the inter-domain handoff mechanism.

Most of the other solutions attempt to solve some drawbacks of MIP-BT or MIP-RS, or combine the advantages of them in order to provide better performance, such as MoM [2], RBMoM [5], MMA [3], and MMROP [4]. But none of them provides a global architecture and must be investigated further [6, 7].

3 Proposed Scheme

3.1 Overview

FHMM bases on MIP-RS approach because it maintains most of the merits of multicast. There are two main drawbacks of MIP-RS, one is the multicast maintain overhead and tree stability problem caused by handoff, and the other is long handoff latency and high packet loss rate. FHMM solves these two problems well through the use of hierarchical mobile management architecture and fast multicast handoff technology respectively, and achieves visible performance.

The basic FMIP6 protocol only focuses on the unicast data delivery, and can't facilitate multicast performance during handoff. If the newly visited network has no other group members, protocols based on MIP-RS are facing with additional handoff latency - waiting for the newly visited network to join the multicast group. FHMM extends the capability of AR in FMIP6 and achieves fast multicast handoff. We call this kind of extended AR as Multicast Agent (MA). MA is responsible for providing multicast service to mobile nodes in the access network. The improved multicast handoff performance can be seen in simulation result of section 4.

FHMM achieves hierarchical mobile management through the use of Domain Multicast Agent (DMA). There is no restriction on DMA excepting being a multicast router. Administrators can divide and manage sub networks conveniently. FHMM uses a translated multicast group technology which is similar to MobiCast in the domain, but the former has some advantages over the latter:

First, in order to achieve fast handoff, MobiCast requires all the BSs within the DVM of the MN's affiliated BS to join the multicast group and buffer multicast packets. As we can see in section 4, this requirement would result in poor multicast packet delivery efficiency and high multicast maintain overhead. FHMM decreases this kind of additional cost yet still achieves satisfied handoff performance by using fast multicast handoff technology.

Second, when MN moves between domains, MobiCast just directly uses either MIP-BT or MIP-RS approach. The drawbacks within these two approaches will still exist. In FHMM, the fast multicast handoff technology is also used in inter-domain with which is superior to MobiCast. We believe this method can well fit the situation, because the inter-domain handoff will not occur frequently.

3.2 Hierarchical Structure

In our hierarchical mobile structure, DMA manages multicast within its domain. Multicast group subscription and multicast packets delivering related to MN should both be done through the DMA. This requires DMA to be the root of the multicast delivery tree in the domain, and we satisfy it by using the translated multicast group technology. DMA subscribes to multicast groups which MN interests in, for example (*,G)[1] , and creates a unique translated multicast group in the domain, such as (DMA,G'). MAs and other multicast routers in the domain should join group (DMA,G'), not group (*,G), and thus the translated multicast delivery tree with the root of DMA is built. The pair of multicast group addresses, (*,G)<->(DMA,G'), forms the *Domain Translate Multicast Group* (DTMG) table.

In FHMM, DMA uses a message named as DMAUdp to multicast new DTMG entry to all the MAs within its domain. DMA also uses DMAUdp message to advertise its presence periodically.

---

[1] Multicast group address can be either (*,G) or (S,G), we uniformly use (*,G) for convenient.

When MN moves within the domain, only the translated multicast delivery tree need to be updated, so there is no influence on the main multicast delivery tree, and the multicast protocol overhead can be reduced too.

3.3 Multicast Group Joining Procedure

The multicast group joining procedure of MN is shown in Fig 2(a). Normally, MN sends a MLD [12] message to its current MA to subscribe to a multicast group, e.g. (*,G). The MA searches its DTMG table at first. If there is an entry for (*,G), then the only thing needs to be done is to join the corresponding translated multicast group, and the joining procedure ends. Otherwise, the MA relays the subscription to DMA through a message named as DMAReq. Upon receiving DMAReq message, DMA subscribes to the requested multicast group (*,G), creates a translated multicast group (DMA,G'), and multicasts this new DTMG entry within the domain. In response, all the MAs in the domain update their DTMG table and those interested in this multicast group will subscribe to the translated multicast group. Then the whole joining procedure finishes, and MN can begin to receive multicast packets.

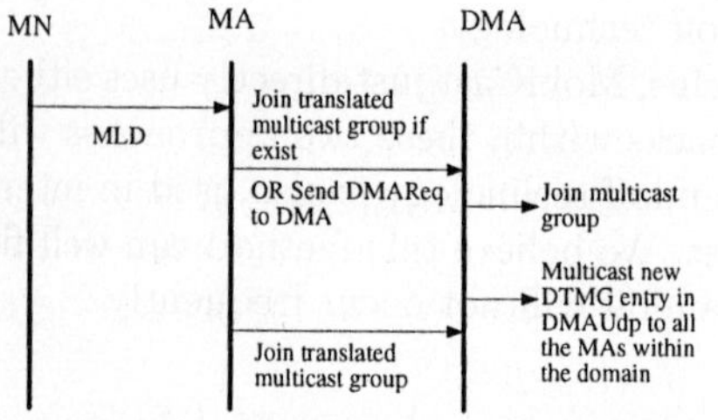

(a) Joining multicast group procedure

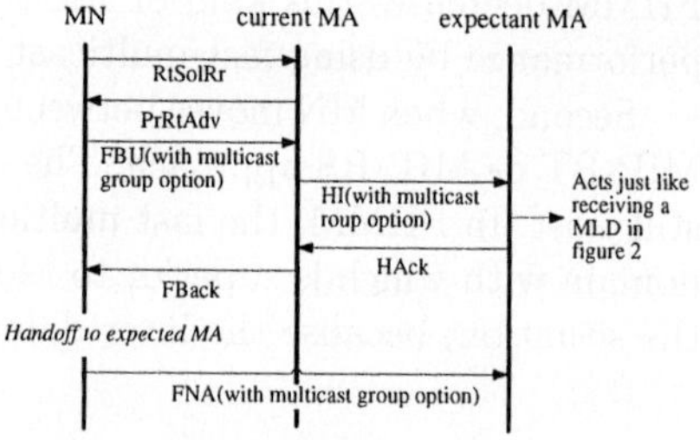

(b) Fast multicast handoff procedure

Fig. 2. Operation details of FHMM

3.4 Multicast Packets Transmitting

The process of transmitting multicast packets is as follows: The packets of group (*,G) sent by the source travel along the main multicast tree and reach DMA firstly. Then DMA translates them into group (DMA,G') and multicasts them in the domain using translated multicast tree. When these translated packets reach the MA which MN attaches to, they will be re-translated back to (*,G), and forwarded to MN in the end. So the multicast group joining procedure and multicast packets receiving manner of MN remain no change. This is one of the advantages of FHMM.

3.5 Handoff Procedure

Multicast handoff in FHMM is fast and efficient. FHMM introduces a new option, *multicast group option*, to the basic FMIP6. Through the exchange of this option, expectant MA of new access network can join the dedicated multicast group in advance which helps MN to receive multicast packets more quickly after handoff.

MN starts fast multicast handoff procedure as soon as it discovers the availability of a new access network by some link-specific methods when it is still connected to its current network. AS shown in Fig 2(b), the procedure begins with the exchange of RtSolPr and PrRtAdv messages. The operation of this phase remains the same as FMIP6. In the next phase, FHMM modifies FMIP6 by adding the multicast group option to the FBU message. This option includes the information of multicast group that MN has subscribed to. Then MN's current MA extracts the option and adds it to the HI message destined to expectant MA. The extended HI message notifies expectant MA to join the multicast group in advance. The expectant MA treats every multicast group option as a joining request and acts just like receiving a MLD message as shown in Fig 2(a). When the MN is disconnected from the previous network and moves to the new access network, it uses FNA message to quickly announce its attachment to the expectant MA. For robustness, FNA message also includes the multicast group option. Hence, for case that MN moves so fast and has no time to send FBU message during handoff, the expectant MA can still be quickly notified to join the multicast group.

The fast multicast handoff mechanism is used in both intra-domain handoff and inter-domain handoff. For the intra-domain handoff, the expectant MA can find the requested multicast group in its DTMG table, and then join the corresponding translated multicast group. The fast multicast handoff procedure ends. If the expectant MA can't find the requested entry, it can be concluded that the handoff occurs between domains and then the DMAReq message is sent to DMA. The remaining procedure is the same to Fig 2(a).

Comparing with MobiCast protocol which requires all adjacent BSs to join multicast group, FHMM only asks MAs with high probability to join. This results in significant performance improvement and reduced multicast cost. Moreover, FHMM achieves fast multicast handoff through the manner of piggyback which further reduces multicast protocol overhead.

4 Performance Evaluation

4.1 Network Model and Methodology

FHMM is compared with MobiCast, MIP-RS, and MIP-BT in terms of packet losses, multicast packet delivery efficiency and multicast tree maintenance overhead by changing the parameters of multicast group size (from 5 to 80) and mobile node's maximal speed (from 5 to 30 m/s).

The topology in our simulation is a 10*10 mesh network in which each node acts as a multicast router of local network and also a MA for MN. The distance between two nearby MAs is 100 meters, and the power range is 71 meters. There are another 4 DMA routers in the topology, and each DMA is responsible for 25 (5*5) MAs.

For simplicity, there is one multicast group with one data source. Besides, we assume that the packet transmission is reliable and the losses are only due to handoff. The source generates multicast packet with the length of 300 bytes at intervals of 20 ms to simulate the multicast conference application. Originally, mobile nodes are randomly located at the mesh. The move model is the Random Waypoint Mobility Model (RWP) [13], and MN selects its speed randomly between 0 and maximal speed. We run each simulation for 500 seconds.

4.2 Simulation Results

The first experiment is to study the packet loss rate. As shown in Fig 3(a) and 3(b), FHMM achieves the lowest packet loss rate due to the fast handoff mechanism it uses not only in the domain but also between domains. MobiCast has good performance too, but the use of MIP-RS as its inter-domain mechanism causes a loss rate that is little higher than FHMM. MIP-BT has the highest packet loss rate because MN must wait until its new address has been configured and registered with HA. For the no need of waiting for registration, the handoff latency of protocols based on MIP-RS is better than those of MIP-BT, especially when the new access network has already joined the multicast group.

Fig 4(a) and 4(b) compares the multicast packet delivery efficiency. MIP-BT is the most inefficient one because the delivery path of multicast packets is far from optimal. Multicast packets detour to HA at first and then to MN, and this results in high network transmitting overhead and device processing overhead. MIP-RS has the best efficiency. The result of FHMM is better than MobiCast because it does not need to ask all the BSs in DVM to receive and buffer multicast packets. FHMM is worse than MIP-RS because it needs to ask one or more expectant MAs to join the multicast group and receive data, and this kind of behavior would introduce redundant data.

Fig 5(a) and 5(b) shows the multicast maintenance overhead of these four mechanisms. The overhead contains all the packets sent for maintaining multi-

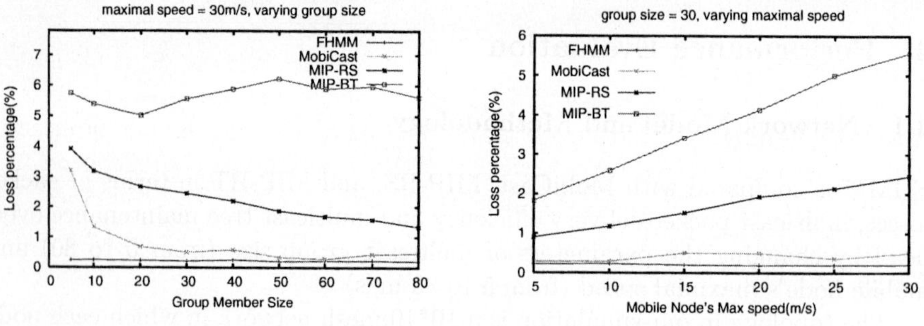

(a) Varying group size (b) Varying mobile node's maximal speed

Fig. 3. Comparison of packet loss percentage

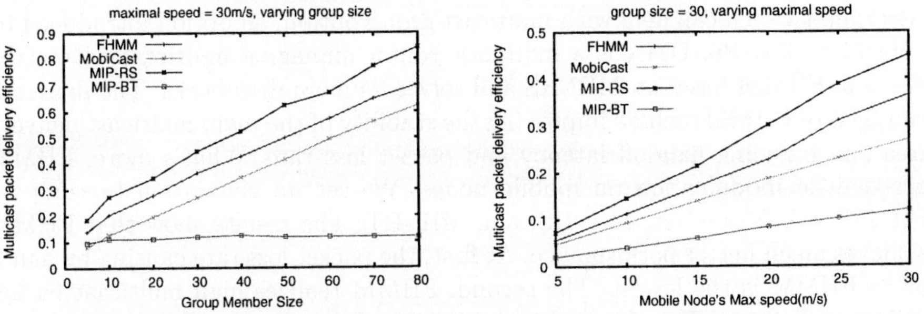

(a) Varying group size (b) Varying mobile node's maximal speed

Fig. 4. Comparison of multicast packet delivery efficiency

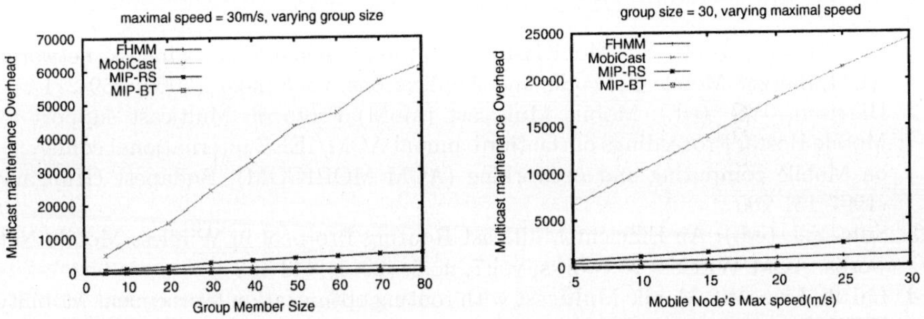

(a) Varying group size (b) Varying mobile node's maximal speed

Fig. 5. Comparison of multicast maintenance overhead

cast delivery path, such as MLD packets and those packets used to update the multicast delivery tree. We do not count the multicast data piggyback on other packets, such as FMIP6 packets with multicast group options or the usual mobile IPv6 packets. As shown in Fig 5, MIP-BT achieves the best performance this time because only HA needs to trace the situation of MN and this can be entirely fulfilled by usual mobile IPv6 packets. FHMM's performance is between MIP-BT and MIP-RS. MobiCast has tremendous overhead than the others because of the complex messages it introduces, i.e. the messages exchanged between BSs within the DVM.

5 Conclusion and Future Work

In this paper, we propose a multicast scheme called FHMM to mobile nodes in the Internet. It introduces two agents, MA and DMA, to achieve fast multicast handoff and hierarchical mobile multicast management. MA is the extended access router which can deal with multicast group option, an option introduced by FHMM to FMIP6. DMA is a multicast router managing multicast within the domain. FHMM bases on MIP-RS and solves its main drawbacks. The main advantages of FHMM include improving the stability of the main multicast delivery tree and reducing handoff latency and packet loss rate. What's more, FHMM needs little modification on mobile nodes. We set up simulation to compare FHMM with MobiCast, MIP-RS, and MIP-BT. The results show that FHMM achieves much better performance. At first, the packet loss rate causing by handoff in FHMM is the lowest. The second, FHMM realizes high multicast packet delivery efficiency. The third, the multicast maintenance overhead is low especially when comparing with MobiCast scheme.

In the future more efforts should be down for FHMM to give good performance to mobile senders too.

References

1. Lin.Tan, C., Pink, S.: MobiCast: a multicast scheme for wireless networks. ACM/Baltzer Mobile Networks and Applications, vol.5, no.4. (2000) 259-271
2. Harrison, T.G. (ed.): Mobile Multicast (MoM) Protocol: Multicast support for Mobile Hosts. Proceedings of the third annual ACM/IEEE international conference on Mobile computing and networking (ACM MOBICOM), Budapest (Hungary) (1997)151-160
3. Suh, Y.J. (ed.): An Efficient Multicast Routing Protocol in Wireless Mobile Networks. ACM Wireless Networks, vol.7, no.5. (2001) 443-453
4. Lai, J., Liao, W.: Mobile Multicast with routing optimization for recipient Mobility. IEEE Transactions on Consumer Electronics, vol.47, no.1. (2001) 199-206
5. Chunhung, R.L., Wang, K.M..: Mobile Multicast Support in IP Networks. IEEE INFOCOM 2000, Tel Aviv (Israel) (2000)1664-1672
6. Romdhani, I., Kellilm, M., Lach, H-Y., Bouabdallah, A., Bettahar, H.: IP Mobile Multicast: Challenges and Solutions. IEEE Communications Surveys & Tutorials, vol.6, no.1. (2004) 18-41
7. Gossain, H., de Morais Cordeiro, C., Agrawal, D. P.: Multicast: Wired to Wireless. IEEE Communications Magazine, vol.40, no.6. (2002) 116-123
8. Perkins, C. (ed.): IP Mobility Support for IPv4. RFC 3344, August (2002)
9. Johnson, D., Perkins, C., Arkko, J.: Mobility Support in IPv6. RFC 3775, June (2004)
10. Omnet++ Community Site. http://www.omnetpp.org
11. Koodli, R.: Fast Handovers for Mobile IPv6. Internet Draft, draft-ietf-mipshop-fast-mipv6-03.txt, October (2004)
12. Vida, R. (ed.): Multicast Listener Discovery Version 2 (MLDv2) for IPv6. RFC 3810, June (2004)
13. Bettstetter, C., Hartenstein, H., Perez-Costa, X.: Mobility, modeling, and management: Stochastic properties of the random waypoint mobility model. MSWiM'02 (2002)

An Enhanced One Way Function Tree Rekey Protocol Based on Chinese Remainder Theorem

B. Parvatha Varthini[1] and S. Valli[2]

[1] Department of Computer Applications, St. Joseph's College of Engg.,
parvathavarthini@mailcity.com
[2] Department of Computer Science, College of Engineering Guindy,
Anna University, Chennai - 25, India
valli@annauniv.edu

Abstract. Group communication is the basis for many recent multimedia and web applications. The group key management is one of the most critical problems in a large dynamic group. All group rekeying protocols add communication as well as computational overhead at the Group Key Controller (GKC) and group members. The trade off between these overheads depends on different levels of security required for different types of multicast applications [10,12,16]. This proposed work introduces a new key management algorithm based on Chinese reminder theorem (CRT). This algorithm uses CRT tuple of smaller remainders instead of keys of larger bits. So, any computation on these keys is carried out in parallel using remainders. Thus this approach reduces overall computational overhead. This algorithm reduces communication over head during the join event highly without compromising security.

Keywords: GKC, Group key, Logical key Graph, OFT, CRT, Rekeying.

1 Introduction

Multicasting is an efficient communication mechanism for applications like stock market, data distribution, video conferencing, interactive group games, IP-TV, virtual classes and distance learning. Security is essential for these distributed applications because they run on dynamic network architectures and communicate through the Internet. Data integrity, data confidentiality, group/source authentication are the minimal multicast security requirements [13]. These requirements are achieved by encrypting messages with the cryptographic traffic encryption key (TEK) which is also known as the group key.

Group communication architecture is classified as centralized and decentralized architecture. In centralized architecture [2], the GKC manages the entire group. This architecture lacks scalability. In a distributed architecture like Iolous [7] the group members are organized into subgroups. Each subgroup is managed by a Subgroup Key Controller(SGKC) with independent TEK. This architecture solves scalability issues and the *1 affects n* issue. But it also introduces a new challenge of translation latency between subgroups.

P. Yolum et al.(Eds.): ISCIS 2005, LNCS 3733, pp. 33–43, 2005.

Group key management plays an important role in group communication. Group key must be changed from time to time to safeguard its secrecy. The group key must be changed for every membership change also [11, 12, 18, 19]. Group Key management should include Backward Secrecy, Forward Secrecy and Collusion Freedom. In order to meet the above requirements a rekey process should be triggered after every join/leave operations. Rekeying in a group before the join/leave is trivial, but after the join/leave is more complicated. This proposed key management algorithm meets the requirements of maintaining backward secrecy, forward secrecy, collusion freedom, scalability and flexibility.

This paper is organized into 7 sections. Section 2 classifies and discusses about the existing group key management protocols and rationale for this work. Section 3 presents the mathematical support of this work. Section 4 addresses the overview of the proposed architecture and the analytical model of the proposed work. Section 5 summarizes and compares the performance of this approach with the other group key management algorithms in a quantitative way. Section 6 deals with security enhancement in this approach. Section 7 concludes this work.

2 Existing Work

There are different literatures [1-6,8-11,15,17] focusing on key management solutions. These existing solutions are classified as Simple Approach, Hierarchical key Graph, Periodic Rekeying and Flat table.

2.1 Simple Approach

2.1.1 n Nodes – One Controller

In this group keying scheme [2] all members are connected to one GKC. GKC generates the group key and encrypts the group key separately for each of the members of the group. When a member joins/leaves the group, GKC creates a new key. GKC encrypts and sends the new key to every member separately. Its computational and communication complexity is linear in-group size.

2.1.2 Group Key Management Protocol (GKMP)

In GKMP [5,6] initially GKC selects a member and initiates the creation of a group key packet (GKP). The packet contains the current group traffic encryption key (GTEK), and a key (GKEK) to deliver the future GTEK. To handle future rekeys, GKC then creates a digitally signed group rekey packet (GRP), which consists of the earlier created GKP encrypted with the GKEK. When a member joins, GKC selects a member and creates a new GKP containing a new GTEK.

2.2 Hierarchical Key Graph

2.2.1 Logical Key Hierarchy Graph (LKH)

LKH [1,2,3] is an efficient rekeying method for large groups. GKC creates a rooted balanced tree. Each leaf node of the key tree is associated with a member of the group. GKC shares a separate unique secret key with every member through unicast. GKC creates internal node keys and sends only a subset of them to every member. Each member receives the keys of all the nodes in its path to the root. The number of keys each member holds is equal to $log\ n$. When a member joins the group, GKC does $2log\ n$ encryptions and transmissions. When a member leaves the group, GKC does $2log\ n$ encryptions and transmissions.

2.2.2 One Way Functional Tree (OFT) OFT [3,17,20] is also a logical key tree used for rekeying with better leave rekeying compared to LKH. GKC uses a one-way function 'g' to compute a blinded key corresponding to each key in the tree. Each member receives the blinded keys of the sibling of the nodes in the path from its associated leaf node to the root of the tree. Each internal node key is computed by applying a mixing function f-XOR to the blinded keys of its child node key. When a member joins, the GKC needs to encrypt and send $2log\ n+1$ blinded keys. When a member leaves, GKC sends $2log\ n+1$ keys.

2.2.3 Efficient Large-Group Key (ELK)

ELK [4] protocol uses a hierarchical tree and is very similar to the OFT in the sense that a parent node key is generated from its child keys. ELK uses pseudo-random functions (PRFs) to build and manipulate the keys in the hierarchical tree. A PRF uses a key K on input M of length m to generate output of length n. ELK does not require any multicast messages during a join operation. When the members are deleted, new keys have to be generated for those nodes in the path from the removed node to the root.

2.3 Batch and Periodic Rekeying

In large and highly dynamic groups, to reduce rekeying overhead, a GKC may choose to rekey a group periodically [8,15,22], or process group membership changes in batches. Commercial applications of the Internet or satellite TV distribution may use batch or periodic rekeying. Trade-offs in batch rekeying are departing members continue to get access to group data for a brief period after they leave against forward secrecy and joining members are put on hold until the next rekeying instance. In Marks [8] Group members may join the group at any time, but the departure time must be known at the time of join. During registration GKC sends seeds that are necessary for a member of the group to compute group keys for its entire life duration in the group.

2.4 Centralized Flat Table

It changes the hierarchical tree to a flat table [3] with the effect of decreasing the number of keys held by GKC. The table has one entry for the TEK and $2w$ more entries for keys, where w is the number of bits in the member *id*. A member knows only the key associated with the state of its bit. In total, each member holds $w+1$ keys. This scheme is susceptible to collusion attacks.

So a group key management protocol that has a balanced trade off between scalability, security, efficiency and flexibility is needed. The proposed EOFT concentrates on these fields and provides an improved key management solution.

3 The Chinese Remainder Theorem

One of the most useful elements of number theory is the Chinese remainder theorem (CRT). In essence, the CRT says it is possible to reconstruct integers in a certain range from their residues modulo using a set of pair wise relatively prime moduli. Let $M = m_1 * m_2 * m_3 * \ldots m_k = [m]$ where the m_i are such that $gcd(m_i, m_j) = 1$ for $1 \le i, j \le k$, and $i \ne j$. We can represent any integer A as $A \leftrightarrow [a_1, a_2, a_3, \ldots a_k]$ where $a_i \in Zm_i$ and $A = a_i \ mod \ m_i$ for $1 \le i \le k$. For every integer A such that $0 \le A \le M$ there is a unique k-tuple $(a_1, a_2, a_3, \ldots a_k)$ with $0 \le a_i \le m_i$ that represents it, and for every such k-tuple $(a_1, a_2, a_3, \ldots a_k)$ there is a unique A in Z_M. Operations performed on the elements of Z_M can be equivalently performed on the corresponding k-tuples by performing the operation independently in each coordinate position in the appropriate system. Consider
$A \leftrightarrow (a_1, a_2, a_3, \ldots a_k); B \leftrightarrow (b_1, b_2, b_3, \ldots b_k)$ then
$(A + B) \ mod \ M \leftrightarrow ((a_1 + b_1) \ mod \ m_1, \ldots, (a_k + b_k) \ mod \ m_k)$
$(A - B) \ mod \ M \leftrightarrow ((a_1 - b_1) \ mod \ m_1, \ldots, (a_k - b_k) \ mod \ m_k)$
$(A * B) \ mod \ M \leftrightarrow ((a_1 * b_1) \ mod \ m_1, \ldots, (a_k * b_k) \ mod \ m_k)$

One of the useful features of the CRT is that it provides a way to manipulate potentially very large numbers in terms of tuples of smaller numbers.

4 Enhanced OFT Protocol – EOFT

In EOFT, GKC constructs a rooted balanced tree. Every group member is associated with a unique leaf node. The root of the tree is associated with the group key. Each internal node represents a logical subgroup. Each member shares a secret key with GKC through the registration protocol. These keys are received in a secured way through unicast. Each member needs keys of the internal nodes in its path to the root for computing the group key. But GKC does not send all these internal node keys to the member directly. Instead it sends pseudo key tuples of the siblings of the internal nodes that are needed to compute their ancestors' keys.

A pseudo function P is used to generate pseudo keys corresponding to each key. 'P' is a one way hash function or simple transformation function of bits depending on the required security level. GKC generates a random number M which is equal to $m_1 * m_2 * m_3 * \ldots m_p$ where $gcd(m_i, m_j) = 1$ for $1 \le i, j \le p$, and $i \ne j$. M is used to find reminder tuple corresponding to each key. To compute keys of logical internal nodes, every member applies an arithmetic function R on pseudo key tuples of the internal node's siblings. The function R can be +/-/*/ a repeated combination of odd number of these three operations. But existing works use only hash for P and XOR for R.

4.1 Initialization of EOFT

Consider a balanced tree with members A, B, C, D, E, F, G, H as leaf nodes. GKC shares a unique secret key $K_a, K_b, K_c, K_d, K_e, K_f, K_g, K_h$ with each mem-

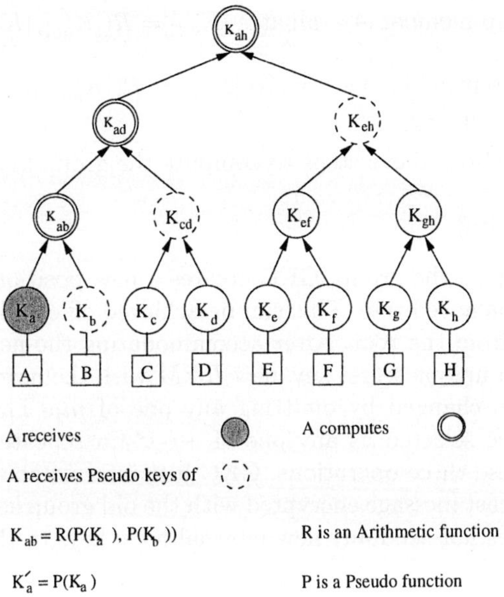

Fig. 1. EOFT Initial Tree Structure

ber respectively through unicast at registration time. GKC generates a random number $M = [m] = m_1 * m_2 * m_3 * \ldots m_p$ where $gcd(m_i, m_j) = 1$ for $1 \leq i, j \leq p$, and $i \neq j$. GKC sends the tuple $[m_1, m_2, m_3, \ldots m_p]$, the pseudo function P and the arithmetic function R to every group member. The point to be noted is that p is independent of size of the group.

Each member computes its own pseudo key using P and the corresponding tuples using M. The Pseudo keys of leaf nodes are K'_a, K'_b, K'_c, K'_d, K'_e, K'_f, K'_g, K'_h and their corresponding tuples are $[K'_a], [K'_b], \ldots, [K'_h]$. GKC sends not all the pseudo key remainder tuples of internal nodes but only that of the internal nodes in the path of associated leaf node to the root to every member in the group. Group members compute the keys associated with each logical internal node hence computes the group key. This process is illustrated in Fig. 1. An algorithm given below describes the steps involved in this process.

Algorithm for computing the group key (in view of a group member A)

Step 1: The group member A receives its secret key K_a through unicast registration protocol from the GKC.

Step 2: GKC sends Pseudo function P, Arithmetic function R, a random number M to every member. Also it sends the pseudo key remainder tuples of the siblings of the internal nodes along the path from the member A to the root. They are $[K'_b], [K'_{cd}], [K'_{eh}]$.

Step 3: The group member A evaluates its pseudo key using P and then $[K'_a]$.

Step 4: The group member A evaluates $[K_{ab}] = R([K'_a], [K'_b])$ and $[K'_{ab}] = P(K_{ab})$.

Step 5 : The group member A evaluates $[K_{ad}] = R([K'_{ab}], [K'_{cd}])$ and $K'_{ad} = P(K_{ad})$.
Step 6 : The group member A evaluates $[K_{ah}] = R([K'_{ad}], [K'_{eh}])$ and then K_{ah}, which is the group key.

Each member evaluates above steps to compute the group key.

4.2 Join Rekeying

When a member joins the group, GKC creates a new position in the tree such that the tree is a balanced tree. This can be achieved efficiently by splitting the nearest leaf node from the root. After accommodating the new member in the tree, GKC shares a unique secret key, new $R\&M$ with the new member through unicast. M can be changed by omitting any one of m_i. The new arithmetic operation R can be selected as any one of +/-/*/ a repeated combination of odd number of these three operations. GKC just informs about new R and M through one multicast message encrypted with the old group key. Unlike in *OFT* & *LKH*, GKC does not send any new internal node keys to the other members in the join event.

4.3 Leave Rekeying

When a member leaves the group, GKC reconstructs the tree as a balanced tree. If the departing members sibling is a leaf node, it gets associated with its parent node or that assumes its parent's position in the tree. GKC needs to rekey to maintain forward secrecy. Unlike in LKH, GKC does not change all the

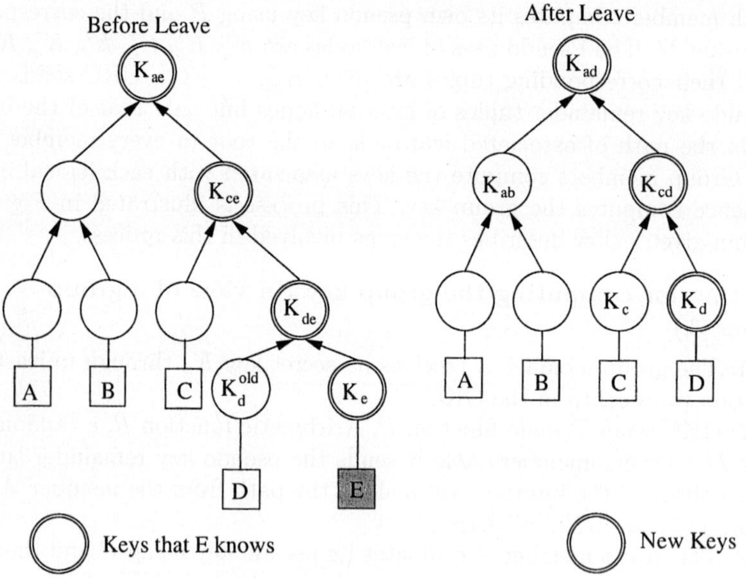

Fig. 2. EOFT Leave Rekeying

keys that the departing member knows. Since GKC does not use any pseudo keys to encrypt any message, it does not change all the pseudo keys supplied to the departing member. GKC rekeys as follows: For the sibling leaf node of the departing member, GKC sends a new key encrypted with its old key. It rekeys all the keys from rekeyed node's position to the root. It is illustrated in Fig. 2.

A new key K_d encrypted by the old key K_d^{old} is sent to the member D. A new pseudo key K'_d encrypted by K_c is sent to the member C as well as K'_{cd} encrypted by K_{ab} is sent to members A and B by GKC.

5 Performance Analysis

This section shows the efficiency of the proposed work by comparing it with the other group key management schemes. The performance of the proposed scheme on both communication and computational complexities are evaluated in a quantitative way. Table 1 & 2 compares the proposed scheme with the other group key management schemes on computational complexity. Computational complexity is measured by storage and process requirements at the group members & GKC and with the operations for deriving / generating / forwarding the key. Table 3 compares the proposed scheme with the other group key management schemes on communication complexity. The major measure of communication complexity is the number of messages and size of the messages used for transmitting key update.

Notations used in Table

n - Size of the group (excluding the leaving member and including the joining member)
T - The count of time intervals during when the group exists
t - The count of time intervals during when the member persists
d - Height of the tree = *log n* if tree is balanced
E - Encryption operation

Table 1. Computational Cost Comparison with respect to processing needed at join & leave

Group Key Management Algorithm	GKC		MEMBER (maximum)		
	JOIN	LEAVE	JOIN		LEAVE
			Other	New	
n nodes ↔ GKC	nE	nE	D	D	D
GKMP	2E	nE	2D	2D	D
LKH	(2d+1)E+ (d+1)G	2dE+dG	dD	(d+1)D	dD
OFT	2G+(d+2)g+ (2d+1)E+df	df+G+dg+ (d+1)E	D+g+ dD+df	D+g+df	D+g+df
EOFT	dR+2E	G+dP+dR+ (d+1)E	D+dR	D+P+dR	D+P+dR

Table 2. Computational Cost Comparison w.r.to Storage Requirement

Group Key Management Management	GKC (Keys)	MEMBER (Keys)
SIMPLE REKEYING		
n nodes ↔ GKC	n	1
GKMP	2	2
HIERARCHICAL KEY GRAPH		
LKH	2n-1	d+1
OFT	2n-1	d+1
ELK	2n-1	d+1
EOFT	2n-1	d+1
PERIODIC REKEYING		
MRRKS	TK	tk
CENTRALISED TABLE		
FT	(2I+1) keys	I+1 keys

Table 3. Communication Cost w.r.to Messages Passed

Group Key Management Algorithm	Join Messages From GKC to		Leave Messages From GKC to Members
	Other group members	New members	
n nodes ↔ GKC	(n-1)	1	N
GKMP	2	2	New group setting
LKH	d	d+1	2d
OFT	d+1	d+1	d+1
ELK	0	d+1	d+1
EOFT	1	d+1	d+1
MRRKS	-	t	$2log(t/2)$
FT	2I	I+1	2I

D - Decryption operation
I - Number of bits in the member id
G - Key Generating Function
g - infeasible function
f - mixing function
P - Pseudo function
R - +/-/*/ a repeated combination of odd number these three operations

Table 4 compares the proposed scheme with the other group key management schemes on provision of security in terms of Backward secrecy, Forward Secrecy and Collusion Freedom.

LKH+2 [19] method reduces the communication overhead of the LKH method by half in a leave, but in a join it has the same communication cost as the LKH. Another protocol [9], using Boolean function minimization (BFM) for key management, allows some collusion attacks for decreasing the communication cost. This proposed algorithm works in bottom-up approach [20] rather than top-

Table 4. Comparison of Backward Secrecy, Forward Secrecy, Collusion Freedom, Flexibility

Group Key Management Algorithm	SECURITY			Flexibility
	Backward	Forward	Collusion free	
n nodes ↔ GKC	√	√	√	√
GKMP	√	×	√	√
LKH	√	√	√	×
OFT	√	√	√	×
ELK	√	√	√	×
EOFT	√	√	√	√
MRRKS	√	√	√	×
FT	√	√	√	×

down. This work reduces the joint event's communication cost to one message without compromising security.

6 Security Analysis

The security of the proposed group communication scheme depends on the secrecy of the group key. The components used in this algorithm to generate the group key are a random number M, a pseudo function P and an arithmetic function R. The tackling of maintenance Backward and Forward secrecy by this group key algorithm in terms of these components is discussed below.

- Random number: The relatively pairwise prime number m_i of random number M are sent by GKC to every group member securely through unicast protocol. When a member leaves the group, the random number M is changed. When a new member joins the group, a new random number is derived by removing m_i form M. In both the cases the only possible attack on M is Brute Force and it needs $\Omega(2^n)$ effort where n is the number of bits in M.
- Arithmetic Function: The arithmetic function R used in the group key construction is not same throughout the session. It changes whenever the group membership changes. Its domain is a wide random set $\{+, *, -, +++, +**, \ldots\}$ whose cardinality is $3(9^n - 1)/8$ if R is containing $2n - 1$ operations.
- The Pseudo function used to compute Pseudo Keys belongs to Hash family of functions if the required level of security is high. Basically these functions are highly vulnerable to attack against weak collision resistance and hence have resistance to Brute Force attack. Even for a Birthday attack, these function needs $\Omega(2^{n/2})$ effort for a hash of length n bits
- Secret keys: The keys used to encrypt the key update messages and the keys included in that messages are not sufficient to derive the Group key because they are not used directly in the group key constructions. So active and passive adversaries are not benefited from cryptanalysing these messages.

From the above arguments it is clear that

- A new member who joins the group cannot compute the old group keys since he cannot derive the random number and the arithmetic function R.
- A member who leaves the group cannot compute the new group keys since he knows nothing about the new random number and is not easy for him to derive the arithmetic function R.

7 Conclusion

This proposed approach uses short rekey messages and tuples of smaller size reminders. Thus it reduces overall computational overhead. It reduces join rekeying complexity compared to OFT. It provides flexibility in selection of group key generating functions. It maintains provides forward secrecy, backward secrecy and collusion freedom.

References

1. Wong, C.K., Gouda, M.G., Lam, S.: Secure group communications using key graphs, IEEE/ACM Trans. Networks., (2000), 16–30.
2. Wallner, D., Harder, E., Agee, R.: Key Management for Multicast: Issues and Architectures, **RFC 2627**, (1999).
3. Waldvogel, M., Caronni, G., Sun, D., Weiler, N., Plattner, B.: The VersaKey framework: Versatile group key management, IEEE Journal Selected Areas in Communications (Special Issue on Middleware), (1999), 1614–1631.
4. Perrig, A., Song, D., Tygar, J.D, Elk.: A new protocol for efficient large-group key distribution, In Proceedings of the IEEE Symposium on Security and Privacy, Oakland, Calif., (2001), IEEE Computer Society Press, Los Alamitos, Calif.
5. Harney, H., Muckenhirn, C.: Group Key Management Protocol (GKMP) Specification, **RFC 2093**, (1997).
6. Harney, H., Muckenhirn, C.: Group Key Management Protocol (GKMP) Architecture, **RFC 2094**, (1997).
7. Mittra, S.: Iolus : A framework for scalable secure multicasting, In Proceedings of the ACM SIGCOMM, **27**, 4, New York, (1997), 277–288.
8. Briscoe, B. Marks.: Multicast key management using arbitrarily revealed key sequences, In Proceedings of the 1st International Workshop on Networked Group communications, Pisa, Italy, (1999).
9. Chang, I., Engel, R., Kandlur, D., Pendarakis, D., Saha, D.: Key management for secure internet multicast using Boolean function minimization technique, In IEEE INFOCOM, **2**, New York, (1999), 689–698.
10. Judge P., Ammar, M.: Security Issues and Solutions in Multicast Content Distribution : A Survey, IEEE Network, (2003), 30–36.
11. Rafaeli S., Hutchison, D.: A Survey of Key Management for Secure Group Communication, ACM Computing Surveys, (2003), 309–329.
12. Challal Y., Bettahar H., Bouabdallah A.: SAKM : A Scalable and Adaptive Key Management Approach for Multicast Communications, ACM SIGCOMM Computer Communications Review, **34**, (2004), 55–70.

13. Canetti R., Gacay J., Itkis G., Micciancio D., Nao M., Pinkas B.: Multicast Security: A Taxonomy and Some Efficient Constructions, Proceedings of IEEE INFOCOM, New York, (1999), 708–716.
14. Lee F.Y., Shieh S.: Scalable and Lightweight key distribution for secure group communications, International Journal of Network Management, Int. J. Network Mgmt, **14**, (2004), 167–176.
15. Xs L., Yr Y., Mg G., Ss L.: Batch rekeying for secure group communications, In Proceedings of 10th International Conference World Wide Web, (2001), 525–534.
16. Horng, G.: Cryptanalysis of a Key Management Scheme for secure Multicast Communications, IEICE Trans Commun., **E85-B**, 5, (2002), 1050–1051.
17. Ku W.C., Chen S.M.: An Improved Key Management Scheme for Large Dynamic Groups Using One-Way Function Trees, Proc. ICPPW'03, (2003), 391–396.
18. Canetti, R., Garey, J., Itkis, G., Micciancio, D., Naor, M., Pinkas, B.: Multicast security : A taxonomy and efficient constructions, Proc. IEEE Infocomm'99, **2**, (1999), 708–716.
19. Rafaeli, S., Mathy, L., Hutchinson, D.: LKH+2 : An improvement on the LKH+ algorithm for removal operations, Internet Draft, draft-rafaeli-lkh2-oo.txt, (2002).
20. Sherman A.T., McGrew D.A.: Key Establishment in Large Dynamic Groups Using One-Way Function Trees, IEEE transaction on software engineering, **29**, 5, (2003).
21. Setia, S., Koussih, S., Jajodia, S.: Kronos: A Scalable group re-keying approach for secure multicast, In Proceedings of the IEEE Symposium on Security and Privacy, Oakland Calif., (2000), IEEE Computer Society Press, Los Almitos, Calif.

Admission Control for Multicast Routing with Quality of Service in Ad Hoc Networks*

Kaan Bür and Cem Ersoy

NETLAB, Department of Computer Engineering,
Boğaziçi University, Bebek 34342, İstanbul, Turkey
{burk, ersoy}@boun.edu.tr

Abstract. Ad hoc networks, being able to organize themselves without user intervention, can easily provide their users with mobility, multimedia support and group communication. However, they have to combine quality of service (QoS) and multicast routing strategies. This article defines the resource management and admission control components of the ad hoc QoS multicast (AQM) routing protocol, which achieves multicast efficiency along the network. When nodes wish to join a session, a request-reply-reserve process ensures that an appropriate QoS route is selected. Nodes are prevented from applying for membership if there is no QoS path for the session. To cope with the continuous nature of multimedia, AQM nodes check the availability of bandwidth in a virtual tunnel of nodes. Objection queries are issued prior to admission in order to avoid excessive resource usage by the nodes which cannot detect each other. New performance metrics are introduced to evaluate AQM's member and session satisfaction rates. Simulation results show that AQM improves multicast efficiency both for members and sessions.

1 Introduction

The evolution of wireless communication technologies has reached a point where it is easy to integrate them to handheld computing devices. Today, a new generation of portable computers is available, offering users more computational power than ever, in addition to mobility, multimedia support and group communication. However, these devices confront consumers with the heavy task of configuration. It becomes increasingly important that, once a mobile device is operational, it is able to configure itself with networking capabilities, asking its users only for their personal preferences and making the administrative work transparent. This requirement popularizes ad hoc networks, which are self-organizing communication groups formed by wireless mobile hosts. They make their administrative decisions in a distributed manner without any centralized control. They are free from the boundaries of any existing infrastructure. They are considered for many applications, including group-oriented computing such as disaster relief, community events and game playing.

---

* This work is supported in part by the State Planning Organization, Turkey, under grant numbers DPT98K120890 – DPT03K120250 and the university research program of OPNET Technologies.

P. Yolum et al.(Eds.): ISCIS 2005, LNCS 3733, pp. 44 – 53, 2005.

In order to meet the mobile users' quality of service (QoS) expectations for such applications, ad hoc networks need to manage their scarce resources efficiently, which makes admission control a fundamental requirement. Multicast routing can improve wireless link efficiency by exploiting the inherent broadcast property of the wireless medium. The advantage of multicast routing is that packets are only multiplexed when it is necessary to reach two or more receivers on disjoint paths. Combining the features of ad hoc networks with the usefulness of multicast routing, a number of group-oriented applications can be realized.

The ad hoc QoS multicast (AQM) routing protocol is presented as a composite solution to the problem [1], which tracks QoS availability for each node based on current resource reservations. In this article, the join process of AQM is enhanced with: (a) virtual tunnels of bandwidth to avoid excessive resource allocation; (b) objection queries to control admission. Simulations show that AQM significantly improves multicast efficiency for members and sessions through QoS management.

The rest of this article is organized as follows. Previous research related to QoS systems and multicast protocols in ad hoc networks is reviewed in Section 2. After a short summary of AQM, the virtual tunnel approach to bandwidth availability and the objection query mechanism for admission control are introduced in Section 3. The performance of the proposed system is evaluated in Section 4. Final remarks and future work are presented in Section 5.

2 Quality of Service Systems and Multicast in Ad Hoc Networks

A QoS system consists of several components, including service differentiation, admission control, and resource allocation [2, 3]. Service differentiation schemes use QoS techniques such as priority assignment and fair scheduling. Priority-based mechanisms change the waiting times of the frames and assign smaller values to high-priority traffic. Fair scheduling algorithms partition resources among flows in proportion to a given weight and regulate the waiting times for fairness among traffic classes [2]. Measurement-based admission control schemes observe the network status, whereas calculation-based mechanisms evaluate it using defined performance metrics. Without admission control, the provision of QoS only by differentiating flows and coordinating channel access order is not effective for high traffic loads [3]. A contention-aware admission control protocol (CACP) introduces the concept of an extended contention area covering the carrier sensing range of a node [4]. Admission decisions are based on the available bandwidth information collected from the neighbours in the contention area.

Another important feature of a QoS system is congestion control. Congestion occurs when the data sent exceeds the network capacity and causes excessive delay and loss. It is avoided by predicting it and reducing the transmission rate accordingly. If congestion is local, it can be handled locally by routing around the congested node without reducing the data rate [5]. A multicast congestion control scheme for multi-layer data traffic is applied at the bottlenecks of the multicast tree using the queue states [6]. Some flow information is maintained at each node, and data layers are blocked and released to solve congestion and adjust the bandwidth rate.

Various protocols are proposed to maintain a multicast graph and perform routing in ad hoc networks. However, they do not address the QoS aspect of the subject, which becomes important as the demand for mobile multimedia increases.

Independent-tree ad hoc multicast routing (ITAMAR) provides heuristics to find a set of independent multicast trees, such that a tree is used until it fails and then replaced by one of its alternatives [7]. Maximally independent trees are computed by minimizing the number of common edges and nodes. Some overlapping is allowed since totally independent trees might be less efficient and contain more links. Thus, the correlation between the failure times of the trees is minimal, which leads to improved mean times between route discoveries.

Lantern-tree-based QoS multicast (LTM) is a bandwidth routing protocol which facilitates multipath routing [8]. A lantern is defined as one or more subpaths with a total bandwidth between a pair of two-hop neighbouring nodes, whereas a lantern path is a path with one or more lanterns between a source and a destination. A lantern tree serves as the multicast tree with its path replaced by the lantern-path. The scheme provides a single path if bandwidth is sufficient or a lantern-path if it is not.

Probabilistic predictive multicast algorithm (PPMA) tracks relative node movements and statistically estimates future relative positions to maximize the multicast tree lifetime by exploiting more stable links [9]. Thus, it tries to keep track of the network state evolution. It defines a probabilistic link cost as a function of energy, distance and node lifetime. The scheme tries to keep all the nodes alive as long as possible. It models the residual energy available for communication for each node, which is proportional to the probability of being chosen to a multicast tree.

3 Admission Control in the Ad Hoc QoS Multicasting Protocol

Since the main structure of the AQM protocol has been previously defined [1], the design details are not repeated below. Instead, following a short summary of AQM session management, special emphasis is laid on admission control and the means of dealing with mobility. The virtual tunnel approach to checking bandwidth availability and the objection query mechanism are introduced as enhancements to the protocol.

3.1 Session Management

When a node broadcasts a join request (JOIN_REQ) for a session, its predecessors (MCN_PRED) propagate the packet upstream as long as QoS can be satisfied. They maintain a request table to keep track of the requests and replies they have forwarded and prevent false or duplicate packet processing. Tables of active sessions, known members and neighbours are also maintained at each node. A forwarded request eventually reaches members of that session which issue replies (JOIN_REP) back to the requester if QoS can be satisfied. Prior to replying, however, they send a one-hop objection query (JOIN_OBJ) to their neighbours to check if a possible new resource allocation violates the bandwidth limitations of these. The objection query mechanism is explained in Section 3.3. Downstream nodes that have forwarded join requests forward the replies towards the requester. During this process, they also exploit the objection query mechanism since it is possible that they qualify as forwarders. The originator of the join request selects the one with the best QoS conditions among the replies it receives. It changes its status from predecessor to receiver (MCN_RCV) and sends a reserve message (JOIN_RES) to the selected node. The reserve packet propagates along the selected path and finally reaches the originator of the reply. Intermediate nodes on the path become forwarders (MCN_FWD). If this is the first receiver, the session initiator (MCN_INIT) becomes an active server (MCN_SRV).

3.2 The Virtual Tunnel of Bandwidth

The continuous nature of multimedia applications requires a new method of checking bandwidth availability to see if the QoS requirements of a new join request can be met. Being within the transmission range of each other, a session server about to allocate resources for its first member and the forwarding node immediately following it share the bandwidth of the same neighbourhood. Therefore, a server has to ensure that its successor also has enough bandwidth available to forward multicast data packets that it receives. In other words, twice as much bandwidth has to be available in the neighbourhood than the amount required by the QoS class of the session.

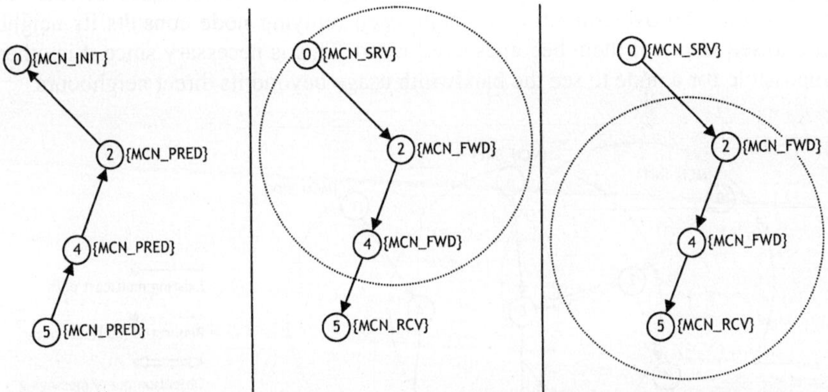

(a) Join request of node n_5 | (b) View of replying node n_2 | (c) View of replying node n_4

Fig. 1. The virtual tunnel approach to checking bandwidth availability: (a) JOIN_REQ of n_5 propagates towards n_0. Prior to sending a JOIN_REP, n_0 checks for two times QoS bandwidth since it has to ensure that n_2 can also forward packets. (b) n_2 checks for three times QoS bandwidth since, in addition to its predecessor n_0 and itself, it has to ensure that n_4 can also forward the data. (c) Finally, n_4 checks for two times QoS bandwidth since n_5 is only a receiver.

Following the path downstream towards the new member, a forwarder has to deal with its predecessor as well as its successor. Once the multicast session starts, it receives packets from its predecessor, rebroadcasts them, and allows its successor to forward the packets further downstream. Therefore, an intermediate node about to take part in the packet forwarding process has to check for availability of three times as much bandwidth than the amount needed by the session, since it shares the available bandwidth of the same neighbourhood as its immediate predecessor as well as successor. A similar judgement can be made for the rest of the intermediate nodes. Fig. 1 shows the virtual tunnel approach to checking the bandwidth availability.

Thus, nodes have to check for availability of the necessary bandwidth according to their position within the multicast tree before accepting a new request. When it is time to reserve resources, however, each node is responsible only for itself, i.e., nodes allocate only the amount of bandwidth that is necessary for the session of a particular QoS class. For a member already forwarding packets of that session, this requirement is met automatically since the node has already been through this allocation process.

3.3 The Objection Query Mechanism

A node decides whether or not to take part in a session as a forwarder based on its current resource availability. While this approach prevents the node from overloading itself, it is not enough to help other nodes balance their loads. Although a node does not allocate more bandwidth than available in its neighbourhood, the overload problem arises as a result of the admissions made by its neighbours which cannot directly detect each other. In other words, a node can be surrounded by several neighbours, some of which are not within the transmission range of each other. The node experiences overload due to excessive resource usage in its neighbourhood, which cannot be foreseen since the surrounding nodes are not aware of each other's reservations. To overcome this problem, each replying node consults its neighbours first to see if any of them becomes overloaded. This is necessary since it is otherwise impossible for a node to see the bandwidth usage beyond its direct neighbours.

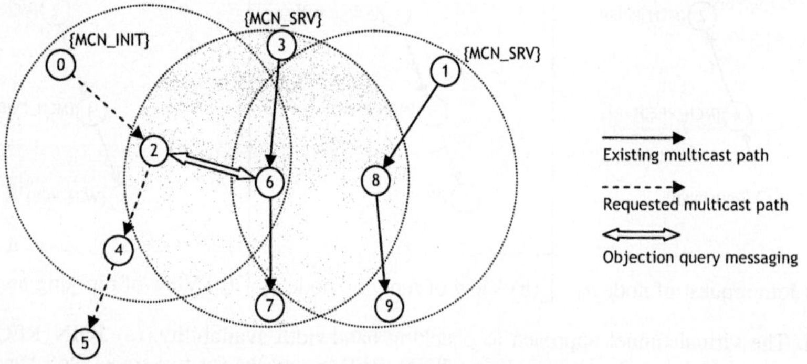

Fig. 2. The objection query mechanism: During the reply phase of a join process, the nodes n_0, n_2 and n_4 issue one-hop objection queries before sending their replies. At the time n_2 sends its query, n_6 is already sharing the bandwidth in its neighbourhood with n_3, n_7 and n_8. However, n_2 is not aware of this since it cannot directly detect the others. Thus, n_6 objects to n_2 offering their common resources to n_4 if the total allocation exceeds the capacity of n_6's neighbourhood.

A node having received a reply issues an objection query prior to forwarding the reply. This one-hop message containing information on the requested bandwidth allows the neighbours to object to a possible data flow along this path, if they start suffering from overload as a result of the allocation. If the new reservation causes the limit to be exceeded, the neighbour sends the objection to the node which has queried it. Otherwise the query is discarded. If the node having sent the query receives any objection, it discards the reply. Otherwise the query times out, indicating that the new node can be safely admitted. Only those neighbours who are serving one or more sessions may object to new allocations. It is not important that a silent node becomes overloaded. Fig. 2 shows a situation where the objection query mechanism is utilized.

A session initiator, which is about to get its first member, or an intermediate node about to forward a reply towards a requester have to issue an objection query first. An active member forwarding packets of a session does not need to query objections for each new join request since it has previously consulted its neighbours.

3.4 Dealing with Mobility

One of the major concerns for ad hoc communications is the ability of the routing infrastructure to cope with the dynamics of node mobility. In order to maintain connectivity and support QoS with maximum possible accuracy under mobility conditions within their neighbourhood, nodes perform periodic update and cleanup operations on their session, membership and neighbourhood tables.

The session information is refreshed periodically via session update packets (SES_UPDATE) sent by the session initiator. They are propagated once as long as the QoS requirements of the session can be fulfilled, even if they belong to a previously known session and come from a known predecessor to ensure that all new nodes in a neighbourhood are informed on the existence of the ongoing sessions they can join.

Lost neighbours are removed from the neighbourhood, session, membership and request tables. Additional action can be necessary depending on the status of the lost neighbour as well as that of the node itself. When an active session member, e.g., a forwarder or a receiver, loses its preceding forwarder or server, this means that it loses its connection to the session. It changes its own status to a predecessor, i.e., a regular node which is aware but not an active member of the session. It also informs its successors with a lost session message (SES_LOST) if it is a forwarding member of the session. Downstream nodes receiving the lost session messages interpret them similarly to update their status regarding the lost session and forward the message if necessary. This mechanism, combined with the periodic updates, keeps nodes up-to-date regarding the QoS status of the sessions and ready for future membership admission activities. It also prevents them from making infeasible join attempts.

4 Computational Performance Experiments

The simulations are conducted using OPNET Modeler 10.5 Educational Version with the Wireless Module [10]. They are repeated 20 times for each data point and results are aggregated with a 95% confidence interval for a multicast scenario with four QoS classes representing a sample set of applications. Nodes initiate or join sessions according to a certain probability. Generated sessions are assigned randomly to one of the four QoS classes defined in Table 1. Thus, the ad hoc network supports four types of multicast applications simultaneously and manages the QoS requirements of each application depending on its class definition. To comply with the sample bandwidth and delay bounds given as part of these QoS class definitions, nodes are restricted to certain minimum bandwidth and maximum hop count regulations. In other words, a node may join a session only if it can find a path to the server with more bandwidth available than the minimum and less hops away than the maximum allowed.

A node can take part at only one application at a time as a server or receiver, whereas it can participate in any number of sessions as a forwarder as long as QoS conditions allow. Apart from that, there is no limit to the size of the multicast groups. The effect of mobility on the performance of AQM is observed under the random waypoint mobility model. In contrast to previous performance evaluations, which limit their simulations to a few minutes and a single session, four hours of network lifetime have been simulated to get a realistic impression of the behaviour of multiple multicast sessions being maintained simultaneously in a distributed manner. The parameters of the mobility model and other simulation settings are given in Table 2.

Table 1. QoS classes and requirements

QoS Class	Bandwidth Requirement	Average Duration	Delay Tolerance	Relative Frequency	Application Type
0	128 Kbps	1,200 s	Low	0.4	High-quality voice
1	256 Kbps	2,400 s	High	0.2	CD-quality audio
2	2 Mbps	1,200 s	Low	0.3	Video conference
3	3 Mbps	4,800 s	High	0.1	High-quality video

Table 2. Simulation parameters

Parameter Description	Value
Area size	1,000 m x 1,000 m
Greeting message interval	10 s
Maximum available link bandwidth	10 Mbps
Mobility model	Random waypoint
Node speed	1-4 m/s (uniform)
Node pause time	100-400 s (uniform)
Node idle time between sessions	300 s (exponential)
Session generation / joining ratio	1 / 9
Session update message interval	60 s
Wireless transmission range	250 m

The evaluation of QoS multicast routing performance in ad hoc networks requires novel criteria that are both qualitative and measurable. The main concern of this article is to test the efficiency of AQM in providing multicast users with QoS and satisfying the service requirements of multimedia applications. Therefore, it is necessary to focus on member satisfaction. The member overload avoidance ratio O_{Member} is introduced as a new performance metric in terms of QoS requirements, which is the number of overloaded nodes o divided by a weighted sum of the number of servers s and forwarders f, subtracted from the maximum possible unit ratio of 1:

$$O_{Member} = 1 - \frac{o}{s + \alpha f} . \tag{1}$$

The coefficient α points out that the impact of overloaded nodes on forwarders is greater than that on servers, due to the fact that the former are intermediate nodes affected by both their predecessors as well as their successors.

The efficiency of ad hoc multicast routing protocols is typically measured by the session success rate, or the member acceptance ratio A_{Member}, which is defined as the number of accepted receivers r divided by the number of session join requests q:

$$A_{Member} = \frac{r}{q} \,. \tag{2}$$

It should be noted that O_{Member} and A_{Member} present a trade-off with regard to member satisfaction. While improving the former with QoS restrictions, an efficient QoS multicast routing protocol should be able to keep the latter at an acceptable level.

Fig. 3(a) compares the member overload avoidance ratio of AQM to the non-QoS scheme, where $\alpha = 0.5$. In AQM, where QoS support is active, nodes do not make allocations exceeding the maximum bandwidth available in their neighbourhood. The number of overloaded members is kept to a minimum with the introduction of the objection query mechanism. In the non-QoS scheme, nodes accept join requests if they can find a path towards the session server. Since they do not care about available resources, they soon become overloaded. As the number of network nodes grows, more sessions are initiated, and more requests are accepted without considering the available bandwidth, which causes a drastic decrease in the ratio of members not overloaded for the non-QoS network. The results show that AQM outperforms the non-QoS scheme with its ability to prevent members from being overloaded.

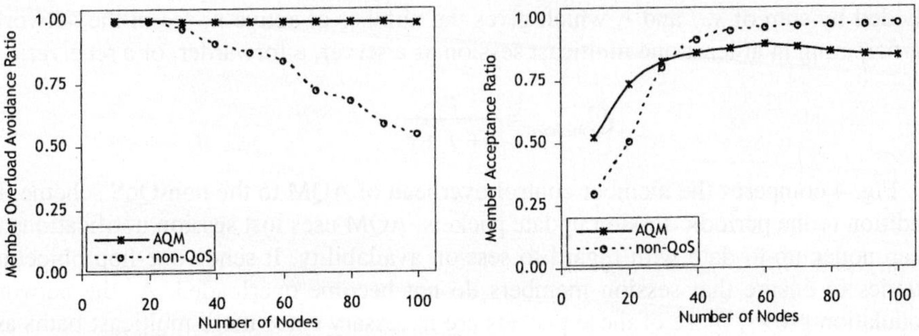

(a) Overload avoidance (b) Member acceptance

Fig. 3. AQM vs. the non-QoS scheme with regard to member satisfaction

Fig. 3(b) compares the member acceptance ratio of AQM to the non-QoS scheme. A decrease in the member acceptance of AQM is expected as a result of the tight resource management and admission control precautions taken by the protocol. However, in networks with a small number of nodes and low connectivity, AQM performs even better than the non-QoS scheme since it informs its nodes periodically on the availability of ongoing sessions and prevents them from making requests for sessions that are not reachable any more. As the network density grows and more requests are made, the performance of AQM remains close to the non-QoS scheme. In AQM, where QoS restrictions apply, nodes do not accept new requests if they cannot afford the required free bandwidth. Thus, not all requests are granted an acceptance

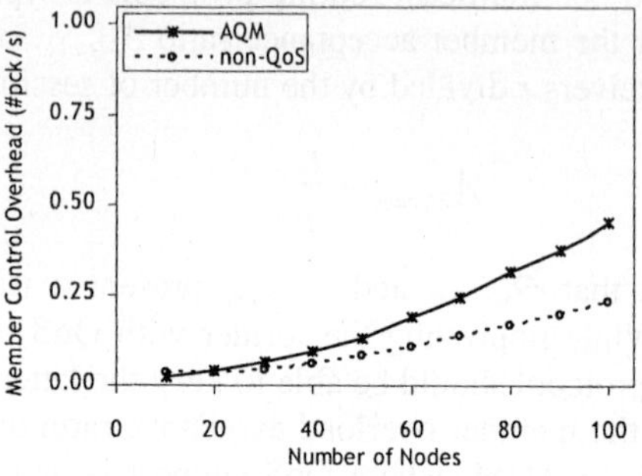

Fig. 4. AQM vs. the non-QoS scheme with regard to member control overhead

and the member acceptance ratio is lower than the non-QoS scheme. However, AQM is still able to achieve an acceptance ratio close to the non-QoS scheme due to its ability to eliminate infeasible join requests before they are issued by keeping its nodes up-to-date regarding the QoS conditions in the network and the status of the sessions.

It is inevitable that the computational overhead of a routing protocol increases with its complexity. However, it is possible to keep it at an acceptable level while adding QoS functionality to the protocol. The member control overhead of a multicast session member C_{Member} is formulated as the number of control packets processed p divided by sum of s, f and r, which gives the number of active nodes in the network, participating in at least one multicast session as a server, a forwarder, or a receiver:

$$C_{Member} = \frac{p}{s+f+r} . \quad (3)$$

Fig. 4 compares the member control overhead of AQM to the non-QoS scheme. In addition to the periodic session update packets, AQM uses lost session notifications to keep nodes up-to-date with regard to session availability. It sends one-hop objection queries to ensure that session members do not become overloaded. As the network population grows, more of these packets are necessary since more multicast paths are possible in a more crowded network. It can be concluded from the figure that AQM provides QoS with an acceptable overhead. In fact, by rejecting some of the join requests, AQM cuts further communication with those nodes, whereas the non-QoS scheme communicates with all requesters until their routing information is delivered.

5 Conclusion

The increasing amount of multimedia content shared over wireless communication media makes QoS-related, resource-efficient routing strategies very important for ad hoc networks. AQM provides ad hoc networks with these features. It keeps the network up-to-date on the availability of sessions with regard to QoS considerations. It controls the availability of resources throughout the network and ensures that users do not suffer from QoS degradation. AQM takes the continuity property of multimedia data into consideration and checks bandwidth availability along a virtual tunnel of nodes. It also facilitates an objection query mechanism to inform nodes on possible overload on others. AQM also sets limits to path length in terms of hop count and checks them in order to satisfy the delay requirements. Thus, it utilizes efficient admission control mechanisms, sustains QoS along the ad hoc network and eliminates infeasible membership requests proactively at their sources.

Service satisfaction is the primary evaluation criterion for a QoS-related scheme. Simulations give a good insight to the quality of AQM. By applying QoS restrictions, AQM achieves lower overload on members and improves the multicast efficiency for members and sessions. Without a QoS scheme, users experience difficulties in getting the service they demand as the network population grows and bandwidth requirements increase.

A future research direction for this work is the assessment of the recent multicast routing protocols to have an alternate view to their performance in terms of QoS as experienced by the user. A second topic is the efficient rerouting of multicast sessions when changes occur in the network topology as a result of mobility or varying QoS conditions. It is also a good idea to evaluate ad hoc network protocols with multiple mobility models. Ad hoc applications with team collaboration and real-time multimedia support necessitate group mobility, which improves performance if protocols take advantage of its features such as multicast routing.

References

1. Bür, K., Ersoy, C.: Ad Hoc Quality of Service Multicast Routing. Elsevier Science Computer Communications, to appear, (2005)
2. Pattara-Atikom, W., Krishnamurthy, P.: Distributed Mechanisms for Quality of Service in Wireless LANs. IEEE Wireless Communications **10**(3) (2003) 26-33
3. Zhu, H., Li, M., Chlamtac, I., Prabhakaran, B.: A Survey of Quality of Service in IEEE 802.11 Networks. IEEE Wireless Communications **11**(4) (2004) 6-14
4. Yang, Y., Kravets, R.: Contention-Aware Admission Control for Ad Hoc Networks. IEEE Transactions on Mobile Computing **4**(4) (2005) 363-377
5. Barry, M., Hogan, B.J., McGrath, S.: Congestion Avoidance in Source Routed Ad Hoc Networks. In: Proceedings of the IST Mobile Summit, Lyon, France, (2004) 682-686
6. Peng, J., Sikdar, B.: A Multicast Congestion Control Scheme for Mobile Ad-Hoc Networks. In: Proceedings of IEEE Globecom, San Francisco, USA, (2003) 2860-2864
7. Sajama, S., Haas, Z.J.: Independent-Tree Ad Hoc Multicast Routing (ITAMAR). ACM Mobile Networks and Applications **8**(5) (2003) 551-566
8. Chen, Y.S., Ko, Y.W.: A Lantern-Tree-Based QoS On-Demand Multicast Protocol for a Wireless Mobile Ad Hoc Network. IEICE Transactions on Communications **E87-B**(3) (2004) 717-726
9. Pompili, D., Vittucci, M.: A Probabilistic Predictive Multicast Algorithm in Ad Hoc Networks (PPMA). In: Proceedings of MED-HOC-NET, Mugla, Turkey, (2004)
10. OPNET Technologies Inc, Bethesda, MD, USA. available at http://www.opnet.com

An Efficient On-line Job Admission Control Scheme to Guarantee Deadlines for QoS-Demanding Applications*

Jungkeun Park[1], Minsoo Ryu[2], and Seongsoo Hong[3]

[1] Computing Lab., Samsung Advanced Institute of Technology, Korea
jung-keun.park@samsung.com

[2] College of Information and Communications,
Hanyang University, Korea
msryu@hanyang.ac.kr

[3] School of Electrical Engineering and Computer Science,
Seoul National University, Korea
sshong@redwood.snu.ac.kr

Abstract. In this paper we present a novel admission control scheme for a mixed set of periodic and aperiodic tasks with hard deadlines under EDF, which can achieve near optimal performance with practical utility. The proposed admission control scheme is based on a novel schedulability measure for a deadline-constrained task, called *utilization demand*, which can be viewed as a combination of the processor time demand and the utilization factor. We first show that this new schedulability measure provides a necessary and sufficient schedulability condition for aperiodic tasks. We then present an efficient schedulability test for a mixed set of periodic and aperiodic tasks under EDF. The resulting schedulability test can be implemented as an on-line admission control algorithm of $O(n)$ complexity, which in practice incurs sufficiently low overhead. Our experimental results show that the proposed admission control scheme outperforms existing approaches with respect to achievable processor utilization.

1 Introduction

Guaranteeing deadlines is essential in providing high levels of QoS (Quality of Service) in many networked applications. In general, QoS and real-time applications share the common constraint that services are required to meet timing requirements such as deadline and rate. Examples include interactive distance learning and online trading, which require timely processing and delivery of requested data. However, despite recent developments in real-time computing,

* The work reported in this paper was supported in part by the Korea Research Foundation Grant KRF-2003-003-D00340, in part by IT Leading R&D Support Project funded by Ministry of Information and Communication, and in part by the research fund of Hanyang University HY-2003.

P. Yolum et al.(Eds.): ISCIS 2005, LNCS 3733, pp. 54–63, 2005.

current real-time scheduling theory cannot be directly applied to those applications since most real-time research has focused on the periodic task model [6,2], in which task arrivals and related timing attributes are deterministic and known in advance. On the other hand, recent networked applications have the distinguishing characteristic that processor usage patterns include both periodic and aperiodic tasks. For example, a query for continuous multimedia involves periodic tasks for delivery and processing of continuous data, and a query for static data types involves aperiodic tasks.

There have been many attempts to deal with a mix of periodic and aperiodic tasks in the context of real-time scheduling. The authors of [9,5] proposed static-priority algorithms for joint scheduling of periodic and aperiodic tasks. They address the problem of minimizing the response times of soft aperiodic tasks while guaranteeing the deadlines of hard periodic tasks. Specifically, aperiodic tasks are handled in the background at a lower priority level, or at some fixed priority level by a special periodic task which serves aperiodic requests with a limited capacity. Considerable research has also focused on dynamic-priority scheduling algorithms, exemplified by the EDF (earliest deadline first) algorithm [6], and the static-priority approaches of [11,9] have been extended to dynamic-priority versions [9,10]. Chetto and Chetto [4] and Ripoll et al. [8] proposed optimal dynamic-priority algorithms with regard to specific criteria, for example, response time or processor utilization.

However, in the above mentioned cases, it is assumed that aperiodic tasks do not have hard deadlines, and periodic tasks are given preferential treatment. Although the scheduling and analysis algorithms proposed in [4,8,5] can be extended to handle hard aperiodic tasks, their computational complexity makes them inadequate for on-line usage in networked applications. Specifically, they require construction of a table that contains slack times present in the processor schedule for the hard periodic tasks over a specific time interval, hyperperiod (least common multiple of the task periods) [4,5] or Initial Critical Interval [8], and use the table of slack times to determine the schedulability of incoming hard aperiodic tasks. The significant computational cost of these approaches limit their applicability for on-line applications with dynamic periodic and aperiodic request arrivals.

In this paper, we attempt to provide deadline guarantees via admission control for both periodic and aperiodic tasks under EDF. Our approach differs from the approaches mentioned above in that aperiodic tasks have hard deadlines and are scheduled by the same scheduling policy as the periodic tasks, and that it can be used for on-line admission control as it incurs sufficiently low run-time overhead. Our major contribution is two-fold. First, we propose the combined use of the processor time demand [2] and the utilization factor [6] as a schedulability measure for deadline-constrained tasks. The new schedulability measure, called *utilization demand*, is defined for each task as the ratio of the processor time required for meeting its deadline to the time remaining until its deadline expires. We show that this new schedulability measure provides a necessary and sufficient schedulability condition for aperiodic tasks. Second, we extend the utilization demand analysis to handle periodic tasks as well, and develop an efficient schedulability test for a mix of periodic and aperiodic tasks under EDF. The resulting schedulability analysis can be implemented as an on-line admission control algorithm of $O(n)$ complexity, which can achieve near optimal performance with practical utility.

2 Models and Assumptions

Consider a set of independent aperiodic tasks $Q = \{\tau_1, \tau_2, \ldots, \tau_i, \ldots\}$. Every aperiodic task $\tau_i \in Q$ has an arrival time A_i, a worst-case execution time e_i, and a relative deadline d_i that is defined from its arrival time. The absolute deadline D_i of τ_i is given by $D_i = A_i + d_i$. At any given time t, we can define $Q(t) \subset Q$ as the set of current tasks that have been admitted by t and whose deadlines have not expired by t. Thus, the current aperiodic set $Q(t)$ can be described by $\{\tau_i | \tau_i \in Q, A_i \leq t, D_i > t\}$.

We use similar notation for periodic tasks $P = \{\tilde{\tau}_1, \ldots \tilde{\tau}_i, \ldots, \tilde{\tau}_N\}$. Periodic task $\tilde{\tau}_i$ with period $\tilde{T}_i$ can be considered as an infinite sequence of aperiodic tasks. Such aperiodic tasks are referred to as *periodic task instances* which are denoted by $\tilde{\tau}_{i,j}$. Each periodic task instance $\tilde{\tau}_{i,j}$ has a common relative deadline $\tilde{d}_i$ and a common worst-case execution time $\tilde{e}_i$. We use $\tilde{A}_i$ to denote the arrival time of $\tilde{\tau}_i$, and thus the absolute deadline $\tilde{D}_{i,j}$ of $\tilde{\tau}_{i,j}$ is computed by $\tilde{D}_{i,j} = \tilde{A}_i + (j-1)\tilde{T}_i + \tilde{d}_i$.

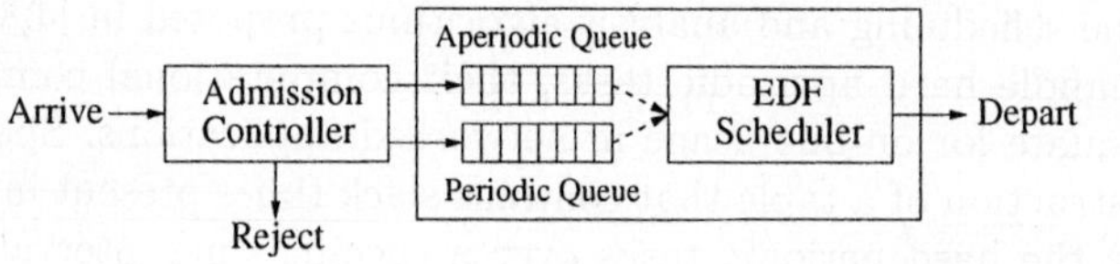

Fig. 1. System architecture composed of an admission controller, admit queues, and a task scheduler

In our discussions, we assume a generic system architecture that consists of an admission controller, admit queues, and a task scheduler, as in Figure 1. The admission controller, through admit or reject, is responsible for ensuring that the system can provide the promised deadline guarantees for all tasks accepted. Every admitted task is then put into an appropriate admit queue depending on its type. There are two separate queues, one for aperiodic tasks and the other for periodic tasks. The task scheduler then uses EDF (earliest deadline first) algorithm to select the task with the highest priority from the admit queues, and allocates the processor to it.

3 Utilization Demands as Schedulability Measures

In this section we first define a point-wise version of utilization demand and then extend it to an interval-wise version, which will be used for admission tests for a mix of periodic and aperiodic tasks.

3.1 Point-Wise Utilization Demands

Consider a set of independent aperiodic tasks $Q(t) = \{\tau_1, \ldots, \tau_i, \ldots, \tau_n\}$. We associate each task $\tau_i \in Q(t)$ with two dynamic variables, residual execution time $e_{i,t}$ and lead time $d_{i,t}$. At time t, the residual execution time $e_{i,t}$ represents the maximum remaining processor time required to complete τ_i, and the lead time $d_{i,t}$ represents the difference between its absolute deadline D_i and the current time t, i.e., $D_i - t$.

We define utilization demands using residual execution times and lead times. Formally, utilization demand $U_{Q(t)}(\tau_i)$ is defined for $\tau_i \in Q(t)$ as the processor time required to meet its deadline divided by its lead time. Let $Q(t, hp(\tau_i)) \subset Q(t)$ be the set of tasks whose priorities are equal to or higher than τ_i's priority. The utilization demand of τ_i is defined by

$$U_{Q(t)}(\tau_i) \stackrel{\text{def}}{=} \frac{\sum_{\tau_j \in Q(t,hp(\tau_i))} e_{j,t}}{D_i - t}. \tag{1}$$

The following theorem shows that the use of utilization demands provides a necessary and sufficient schedulability condition for aperiodic task set $Q(t)$. The proof is rather straightforward, and we do not provide proofs here due to space limitation.

Theorem 1. *Aperiodic task $\tau_i \in Q(t)$ is schedulable with respect to $Q(t)$ by a work-conserving priority-based scheduler if and only if*

$$U_{Q(t)}(\tau_i) \leq 1. \tag{2}$$

Note that the schedulability of $\tau_i \in Q(t)$ does not imply the schedulability of $\tau_i \in Q$, since Q may contain some high-priority tasks that will arrive later in the interval $[t, D_i]$ and they would preempt τ_i. Therefore, the schedulability test in Ineq.(2) is valid only until the next arrival time of a task. This necessitates the testing of the schedulability at every task arrival. In general, to check if $\tau_i \in Q$ is schedulable, it suffices to show $U_{Q(t)}(\tau_i) \leq 1$ at every arrival time until the deadline of τ_i expires. The following theorem formally states this.

Theorem 2. *Aperiodic task $\tau_i \in Q$ is schedulable with respect to Q by a work-conserving priority-based scheduler if and only if*

$$U_{Q(A_j)}(\tau_i) \leq 1 \tag{3}$$

at every arrival time A_j of $\tau_j \in Q$ such that $A_i \leq A_j \leq D_i$.

3.2 Interval-Wise Utilization Demands

We describe an extended concept of utilization demand called *interval-wise utilization demand*, that is defined over a given time interval. Let $Q(t, t') \subset Q$ be the set of tasks whose arrival times are no later than t' and absolute deadlines are later than t, i.e., $Q(t,t') = \{\tau_i | \tau_i \in Q, A_i \leq t', D_i > t\}$. In other words, $Q(t,t')$ includes the tasks that are admitted in the interval $[t,t']$ as well as the tasks of $Q(t)$. We define the interval-wise utilization demand for $\tau_i \in Q(t,t')$ by

$$U_{Q(t,t')}(\tau_i) \stackrel{\text{def}}{=} \frac{\sum_{\tau_j \in Q((t,t'),hp(\tau_i))} e_{j,t}}{D_i - t} \tag{4}$$

where $Q((t,t'),hp(\tau_i)) \subset Q(t,t')$ represents the set of tasks that have priorities equal to or higher than τ_i. By using Theorem 1 and Theorem 2, the above definition immediately leads to the following schedulability conditions.

Theorem 3. *Aperiodic task $\tau_i \in Q(t,t')$ is schedulable with respect to $Q(t,t')$ by a work-conserving EDF scheduler if and only if*

$$U_{Q(t,t')}(\tau_i) \leq 1. \tag{5}$$

Theorem 4. *Aperiodic task $\tau_i \in Q$ is schedulable with respect to Q by a work-conserving EDF scheduler if and only if*

$$U_{Q(A_i,D_i)}(\tau_i) \leq 1. \tag{6}$$

The notion of interval-wise utilization demands allows us to handle periodic tasks as well as aperiodic tasks. Consider a periodic task set $P = \{\tilde{\tau}_1, \tilde{\tau}_2, \ldots, \tilde{\tau}_N\}$. Essentially, all instances of periodic tasks can be considered as aperiodic tasks. That is, an instance $\tilde{\tau}_{i,j}$ of periodic task $\tilde{\tau}_i$ can be thought of as an aperiodic task τ_k that has arrival time $A_k = \tilde{A}_i + (j-1)\tilde{T}_i$ and deadline $d_k = \tilde{T}_i$. Without loss of generality, we can say that any periodic set P has an equivalent aperiodic set Q_P which consists of all task instances generated by P. We refer to this aperiodic task set Q_P as the *pseudo-aperiodic set* of P. It is obvious that P is schedulable if and only if all the tasks in Q_P are schedulable. Thus, we can use Q_P to treat periodic tasks and aperiodic tasks in a similar manner.

4 Utilization Demand Analysis for a Mixed Set

Consider a mixed set S of aperiodic set Q and pseudo-aperiodic set Q_P. Based on Theorem 4, whenever a new aperiodic task τ_x arrives, we can guarantee the schedulability of $S = Q \cup Q_P \cup \{\tau_x\}$ by ensuring that the utilization demand $U_{S(A_i,D_i)}(\tau_i)$ does not exceed 1 for any $\tau_i \in S$. However, this straightforward approach is inappropriate for on-line admission control because we have to perform schedulability checks for an unbounded number of periodic task instances in Q_P. In this section, we introduce a notion of *uniform boundedness* of utilization demands, and then use this notion to develop an $O(n)$ schedulablity test for a mixed set under EDF.

4.1 Uniform Boundedness of Utilization Demands

We first show an important property of periodic task sets. The following theorem states that if P is schedulable, then the utilization demand $U_{Q_P(t,t')}(\tau_i)$ of any task $\tau_i \in Q_P$ can never exceed the aggregate processor utilization of P.

Theorem 5. *Let* $U_P = \sum_{i=1}^{N} \frac{\tilde{e}_i}{\tilde{T}_i}$ *be the utilization of periodic task set* $P = \{\tilde{\tau}_1, \tilde{\tau}_2, \ldots, \tilde{\tau}_N\}$ *where* $\tilde{d}_i = \tilde{T}_i$. *If* P *is schedulable by EDF, then*

$$U_{Q_P(t,t')}(\tau_i) \le U_P \tag{7}$$

for all $\tau_i \in Q_P(t,t')$ *and for all* $t < D_i$ *and* $t' \ge A_i$.

Theorem 5 demonstrates the notion of *uniform boundedness* of utilization demands. Let Ω_Q be a schedule obtained by scheduling Q with an EDF algorithm. We say that the utilization demands of Ω_Q are *uniformly bounded* if there exists a positive constant $M \le 1$ such that $U_{Q(t,t')}(\tau_i) \le M$ for all $\tau_i \in Q(t,t')$ and for all $t < D_i$ and $t' \ge A_i$. Thus, by Theorem 5, any pseudo-aperiodic task set Q_P has a uniform bound U_P if P is schedulable, i.e., $U_P \le 1$.

The following theorem shows another important property. It shows that scheduling a mixed task set generates a uniformly bounded schedule if each of the individual task set has a uniform bound and if the sum of the individual bounds is no greater than 1.

Theorem 6. *For two given task sets* Q_1 *and* Q_2, *suppose that* Ω_{Q_1} *and* Ω_{Q_2} *have uniform bounds* M_1 *and* M_2, *respectively, on their utilization demands. If* $M_1 + M_2 \le 1$, *the utilization demands of the mixed schedule* $\Omega_{Q_1 \cup Q_2}$ *are uniformly bounded by* $M_1 + M_2$.

4.2 Utilization Demand Analysis Based on Fluid-Flow Model

Theorem 5 and 6 suggest that if the processor utilization U_P of Ω_{Q_P} is no greater than 1 and the aperiodic schedule Ω_Q has a uniform utilization bound no greater than $1 - U_P$, we can guarantee all the deadlines of $Q \cup Q_P$. To do so, we need to isolate the aperiodic schedule Ω_Q from the mixed schedule $\Omega_{Q \cup Q_P}$ and bound the utilization demands of Ω_Q. This approach can be viewed as exploiting the "separation" mechanism of the fluid-flow scheduling discipline of GPS (generalized processor sharing) [7], which divides the processor bandwidth into separate flows and tasks are scheduled independently within the separate flows. Recall that we adopted EDF, not the fluid-flow GPS algorithm, for task scheduling. EDF interleaves tasks and has no separation mechanism. However, because EDF is an optimal algorithm, fluid-flow based analysis allows for safe admission tests. That is, if tasks are schedulable by the fluid-flow GPS algorithm they are also schedulable by EDF.

Suppose that a new aperiodic task τ_x arrives at time $t = A_x$. Let $Q' = Q \cup \{\tau_x\}$ and $S' = Q' \cup Q_P$. We define $U_{ad}(\tau_i)$ for any $\tau_i \in Q'$ as the pure aperiodic utilization demand that is obtained from the isolated schedule $\Omega_{Q'}$. Here, we want to admit τ_x only if the pure aperiodic utilization demand $U_{ad}(\tau_i)$ remains uniformly bounded by $1 - U_P$. It is important to note that for the mixed schedule $\Omega_{S'}$, the sum of the residual execution times of aperiodic tasks does not give the pure aperiodic demand $U_{ad}(\tau_i)$ because of the interference caused by periodic task instances. In fact, it would give a larger value than the actual $U_{ad}(\tau_i)$ since aperiodic tasks can be delayed by periodic tasks.

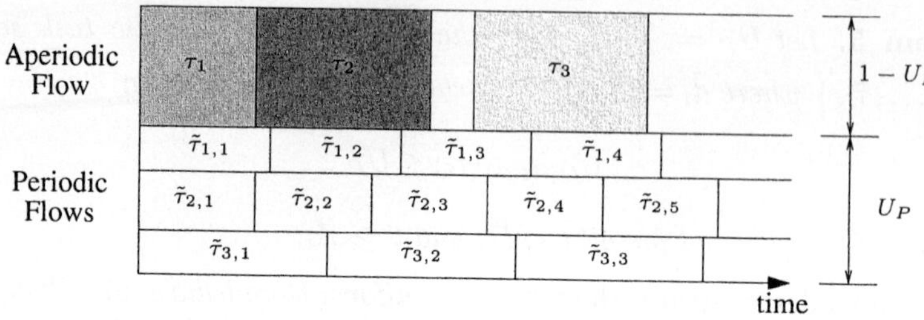

Fig. 2. Schedule of a mixed set with fluid-flow GPS discipline

To compute an exact value of $U_{ad}(\tau_i)$, we first need to assume that all the aperiodic tasks are mapped to a single flow with processor bandwidth $1-U_P$, while each periodic task $\tilde{\tau}_i$ is mapped to a separate flow with processor bandwidth $\tilde{e}_i/\tilde{T}_i$. Figure 2 illustrates our fluid-flow analysis model, where three aperiodic tasks are mapped to a single flow with bandwidth $1-U_P$ and periodic tasks are mapped to separate flows collectively contributing a constant utilization demand U_P. Based on this, the exact value of $U_{ad}(\tau_i)$ can be obtained by simulating the fluid-flow GPS scheduling as proposed in [7]. But this would requires a complex algorithm like Virtual Clock algorithm [12]. Instead, in this paper we present a simpler method that can be implemented as an algorithm of $O(n)$ complexity with a very small data structure.

If we consider the isolated schedule $\Omega_{Q'}$, it is easy to see that the pure aperiodic demand $U_{ad}(\tau_i)$ is affected by two types of interference from other aperiodic tasks in Q'; (1) preemption by higher-priority aperiodic tasks that are admitted during the interval $[A_i, D_i]$, and (2) backlogged execution time requirements caused by previous higher-priority aperiodic tasks that were admitted before A_i but whose deadlines have not expired by A_i. If we use P_i and B_i to denote the preemption time and the backlog time, respectively, the pure aperiodic utilization demand $U_{ad}(\tau_i)$ is given by

$$U_{ad}(\tau_i) = \frac{B_i + P_i + e_i}{D_i - A_i}. \tag{8}$$

In Eq.(8), the preemption time can be easily obtained at run-time. The preemption time P_i for τ_i is initially 0 at its arrival time A_i, and is incremented at every admission of a high-priority task in the interval between its arrival time A_i and deadline D_i. Formally, the preemption time P_i is defined by

$$P_i = \sum_{\tau_j \in PREEMPT(\tau_i)} e_j. \tag{9}$$

where $PREEMPT(\tau_i) = \{\tau_j | A_j \geq A_i \text{ and } D_j \leq D_i \text{ for } \tau_j \in Q'\}$.

We now describe how to compute backlog execution time B_i. In Figure 3, the shaded area B_i represents the backlog execution time caused by previous high-priority tasks including $\tau_{k+1}, \ldots, \tau_{j-1}, \tau_j$. Let $\hat{f}_j$ be the completion time of τ_j in the isolated schedule $\Omega_{Q'}$. Note that $\hat{f}_j$ differs from the actual completion time

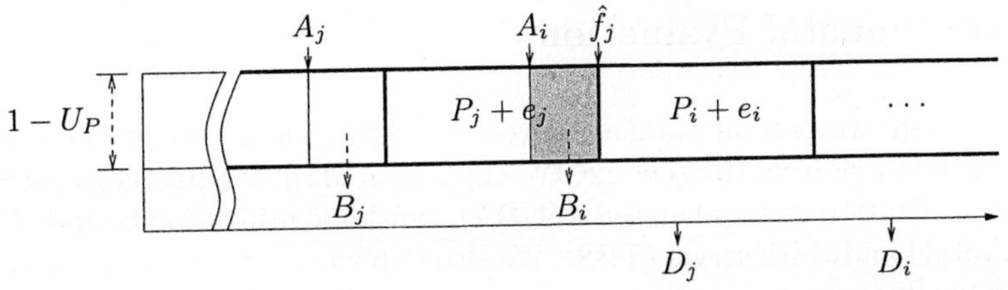

Fig. 3. Computation of backlog execution time in the isolated schedule $\Omega_{Q'}$

of τ_j in the mixed schedule $\Omega_{Q_P \cup Q'}$. We refer to $\hat{f}_j$ as the virtual completion time of τ_j. It is easy to see from Figure 3 that if $B_i \geq 0$,

$$B_i = (1 - U_P)(\hat{f}_j - A_i). \tag{10}$$

Also from Figure 3, the virtual completion time $\hat{f}_j$ of τ_j is given by

$$\hat{f}_j = A_j + \frac{B_j + P_j + e_j}{1 - U_P} = A_j + \frac{(D_j - A_j) \cdot U_{ad}(\tau_j)}{1 - U_P}. \tag{11}$$

Thus, it immediately follows that

$$B_i = U_{ad}(\tau_j) \cdot (D_j - A_j) - (1 - U_P)(A_i - A_j) \tag{12}$$

where the task τ_j is defined as the task that has the lowest priority task among the tasks in $Q((A_i), hp(\tau_i)) - \{\tau_i\}$. Since B_i is no less than 0

$$B_i = \max\{U_{ad}(\tau_j) \cdot (D_j - A_j) - (1 - U_P)(A_i - A_j), 0\}. \tag{13}$$

Eq.(8), Eq.(9), and Eq.(13) allow us to compute $U_{ad}(\tau_i)$ in an iterative manner. This means that the fluid-flow GPS simulation is not necessary in practice. Now, the following theorem summarizes our results showing that it suffices to consider only aperiodic tasks to guarantee the schedulability of a mixed set $S = Q \cup Q_P$.

Theorem 7. *A mixed set $S = Q \cup Q_P$ is schedulable by an EDF scheduler, if $U_{ad}(\tau_i) \leq 1 - U_P$ for each aperiodic task $\tau_i \in Q$.*

Using Theorem 7, one can easily determine the schedulability for a mixed task set by merely considering the utilization demands of aperiodic tasks. Note that our fluid-flow based admission test loses optimality in the sense that aperiodic tasks which may be admitted if exact EDF admission tests were done may well be rejected. However, our admission control scheme significantly reduces the complexity of exact admission test without seriously compromising the optimality. From an implementation point of view, the system has only to maintain a very small data structure for current aperiodic set $Q(t)$. On the arrival of an aperiodic task τ_x, the system only needs to compute $U_{ad}(\tau_i)$ for each $\tau_i \in Q(t) \cup \{\tau_x\}$. Thus, the admission control algorithm has a run time of $O(n)$, where n is the number of current aperiodic tasks in $Q(t)$.

5 Experimental Evaluation

In this section, we present simulation results to provide a performance evaluation of our admission control scheme. We implemented three admission controllers based on utilization demand analysis (UDA), synthetic utilization bounds (SYN) [1], and total bandwidth server (TBS). We also implemented a workload generator that can produce periodic and aperiodic requests with various task parameters.

Processor utilization was used as a performance metric in our simulations. For each simulation, we measured actual processor utilization and compared it to the generated input workload that ranged up to 150% of total processor utilization. We also used the *density* defined as $\frac{e_i}{d_i}$ to capture the tightness of deadline for task τ_i.

Figure 4 shows the measured processor utilization for mixed task sets and compares the UDA-based scheme and the SYN-based scheme. Each of mixed task set consists of 10000 aperiodic tasks and 5 periodic tasks with processor utilization $U_P = 0.1, 0.2, 0.3, 0.4$. All the task sets have the average density value of 0.1. It can be seen that the UDA-based scheme gives a faster convergence to 100% utilization compared to the SYN-based scheme throughout the experiment, and the maximum improvement was around 13% when the average density was 0.4 and the input workload was 100%.

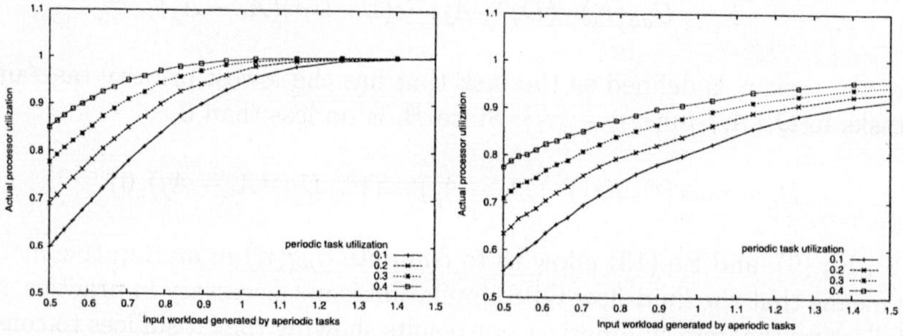

(A) (B)

Fig. 4. Measured processor utilization: (A) UDA scheme and (B) SYN scheme

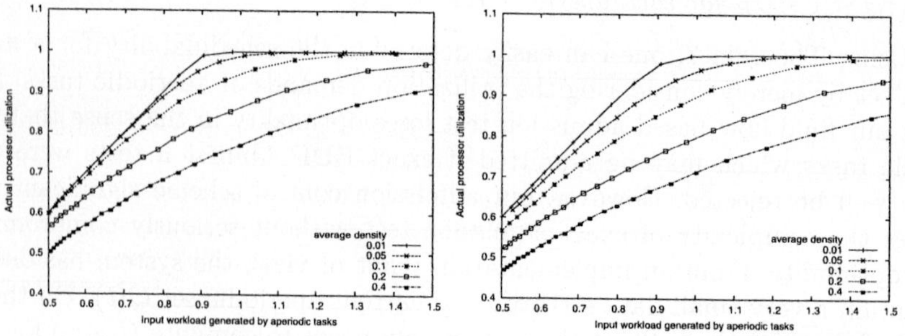

(A) (B)

Fig. 5. Measured processor utilization: (A) UDA scheme and (B) TBS scheme

Figure 5 compares the UDA-based scheme and the TBS-based scheme for mixed task sets. For this comparison, we used a common periodic utilization 0.1 for periodic tasks and varied the average density from 0.01 to 0.4. It can be seen that the UDA-based scheme achieved better processor utilization as the density value increased. The maximum improvement was around 6% when the density was 0.4 and the input workload was 100%.

6 Conclusion

In this paper, we investigated the problem of guaranteeing hard deadlines for a mixed set of periodic and aperiodic tasks. Our major contribution is two-fold. First, we introduced the notion of utilization demand, which provides a necessary and sufficient schedulability condition for pure aperiodic task sets. Second, by combining the utilization demand analysis with the fluid-flow scheduling model, we developed an effective admission control scheme for a mixed set of periodic and aperiodic tasks.

References

1. Abdelzaher, T., Sharma, V., Lu, C.: A utilization bound for aperiodic tasks and priority driven scheduling. IEEE Transactions on Computers **53** (2004) 334–350
2. Audsley, N., Burns, A., Richardson, M., Wellings, A.: Hard real-time scheduling: The deadline-monotonic approach. Proceedings of IEEE Workshop on Real-Time Operating Systems and Software (1991) 133–137
3. Buttazzo, G., Sensini, F.: Optimal deadline assignment for scheduling soft aperiodic tasks in hard real-time environments. IEEE Transactions on Computers **48** (1999) 1035–1052
4. Chetto, H., Chetto, M.: Some results of the earliest deadline first scheduling algorithm. IEEE Transactions on Software Engineering **15** (1989) 1261–1268
5. Lehoczky, J., Ramos-Thuel, S.: An optimal algorithm for scheduling soft-aperiodic tasks in fixed-priority preemptive systems. Proceedings of IEEE Real-Time Systems Symposium (1992) 110–123
6. Liu, C., Layland, J.: Scheduling algorithm for multiprogramming in a hard real-time environment. Journal of the ACM **20** (1973) 46–61
7. Parekh, A., Gallagher, R.: A generalized processor sharing approach to flow control in integrated services networks: the single-node case. IEEE/ACM Transactions on Networking **1** (1993) 344–357
8. Ripoll, I., Crespo, A., Garcia-Fornes, A.: An optimal algorithm for scheduling soft aperiodic tasks in dynamic-priority preemptive systems. IEEE Transactions on Software Engineering **23** (1996) 388–400
9. Sprunt, B., Sha, L., Lehoczky, J.: Aperiodic task scheduling for hard-real-time systems. The Journal of Real-Time Systems **1** (1989) 27–60
10. Spuri, M., Buttazzo, G.: Scheduling aperiodic tasks in dynamic priority systems. Journal of Real-Time Systems **10** (1996) 1979–2012
11. Strosnider, J., Lehoczky, J., Sha, L.: The deferrable server algorithm for enhanced aperiodic responsiveness in hard real-time environments. IEEE Transactions on Computers **44** (1995) 73–91
12. Zhang, L.: VirtualClock: A new traffic control algorithm for packet switching networks. Proceedings of SIGCOMM (1990)

A Methodology of Resilient MPLS/VPN Path Management Under Multiple Link Failures

J.T. Park, M.H. Kwon, and W.H. Lee

School of Electrical Engineering and Computer Science,
Kyungpook National University, Daegu 702-701, Korea
jtpark@ee.knu.ac.kr

Abstract. Recent advent of IP-based broadband networks makes the availability of information and communication service to network and system failures to become a critical issue. In this paper, we propose a dynamic MPLS VPN path management methodology which can rapidly find an optimal backup service path, while satisfying the TE resilience requirements from customers under multiple link failures. Specifically, we have derived the conditions for testing the availability of feasible backup paths satisfying the resilience constraints in a special MPLS VPN network in which the VPN path has monotonic property. We present fast VPN backup path construction algorithms which can dynamically make the MPLS VPN service to be available with minimal disruption, satisfying the resilience requirement from the customers. The simulation has been done to evaluate the performance of the approach.

1 Introduction

Recent advent of IP-based broad bandwidth networks makes the availability of information and communication service to system failures to become a critical issue. The resilience implies the capability of recovery from these failures. In multi-protocol label switching (MPLS) VPN network [1], it is necessary to provide a contracted reliable service to the customers with minimal or no disruption of service in case of unexpected multiple failure occurrences. Currently, active research work including those of international standard bodies [2, 3] is going on for modeling and realizing the resilience in an MPLS network.

Traditionally, VPNs have been mostly provided by the leased lines, but the development of new technology such as (MPLS) enables the service providers to look for the better cost-effective solutions in terms of scalability, security and quality of service. The provisioning of VPN over MPLS among different Autonomous Systems has been being standardized by IETF [4], and several vendors are already providing proprietary solutions such as Cisco's BGP/MPLS VPN, Nortel's MPLS-based Virtual Router, and Lucent's Virtual Router. MPLS could provide Internet service with QoS guarantee to the customers over MPLS backbone.

In IP/MPLS VPN, the IP traffic of a VPN customer site is transmitted through a provider's connection-oriented data paths, i.e., the label-switched paths (LSPs) of an MPLS backbone. In order to provide better manageability, availability, and performance, the IP/MPLS VPN is often configured in a full mesh structure for multi-point

P. Yolum et al.(Eds.): ISCIS 2005, LNCS 3733, pp. 64 – 73, 2005.

connectivity [4]. In this paper, we present a MPLS VPN path management methodology for sustaining high service availability under multiple simultaneous link failure occurrences. We present a dynamic path management strategy in a mesh-type MPLS VPN network. We have designed the testing and recovery mechanisms for an MPLS VPN network which can rapidly find an optimal backup service path which satisfies the TE resilience constraints from customers under multiple link failures. The survivability of MPLS paths is represented in traffic engineering (TE) resilience attributes for LSP of MPLS [5,6].

Lee and Griffith [7] presented a hierarchical scheme to resolve multiple failures at the MPLS networks. Their scheme assigns the failed primary path with high-priority to the pre-reserved path and the other failed path to the shared backup path. However, they did not consider segment restorations. Clouquer and Grover [8] analyzed the availability of the span-restorable mesh networks under dual-failure scenarios. However, their approach is limited to dual failures. We recently presented a resilience model and the mechanism for VPN service path management in a MPLS VPN network with a full-mesh configuration [9]. In the current paper, we have presented VPN service path management in a special mesh-type MPLS network where the primary path of MPLS network has the monotonic property, i.e., either increasing or decreasing sequence of degrees. A fast dynamic MPLS VPN path management algorithm has been proposed and simulation results are presented to evaluate the performance of the proposed approach.

In Section 2, we present the recovery model of IP/MPLS backbone with resilient constraints. In Section 3, we derive the existence conditions for fast backup path construction for a MPLS VPN with monotonic path configuration. In Section 4, we present a fast recovery mechanism which can dynamically maintain backup paths in case of multiple failure occurrences, and shows the simulation results for the evaluation of the performance. Finally, we conclude in Section 5.

2 Resilience Model for VPN Path Management in MPLS Network

In MPLS, a *primary path* is the working path along which the VPN data traffic follows. A *backup path* is the path along which the VPN data traffic follows when the primary path is unavailable due either to the failure of links or nodes. An explicit route for VPN LSPs is determined by a path selection process which usually utilizes a constraint-based routing technique. After the path selection process is performed, the VPN LSPs may be instantiated by signaling protocols. In an MPLS restoration mechanism, backup paths can be pre-provisioned without resources being allocated. After failures occur, the resources for the backup path can be allocated, and then a failed primary path can be switched to the backup path. This approach may greatly reduce the setup time in comparison with restoration mechanisms in which no backup paths are pre-provisioned.

In MPLS, a set of attributes is defined to control LSPs, and among these, the resilience attribute is used to determine the behavior of LSPs when failures occur [10]. In [9], the path resilience is defined to be a normalized ratio of the fraction of the protection region of a path. A primary path is said to have k-protection if any segment of the path, consisting of (k-1) adjacent nodes and k links connecting these nodes is

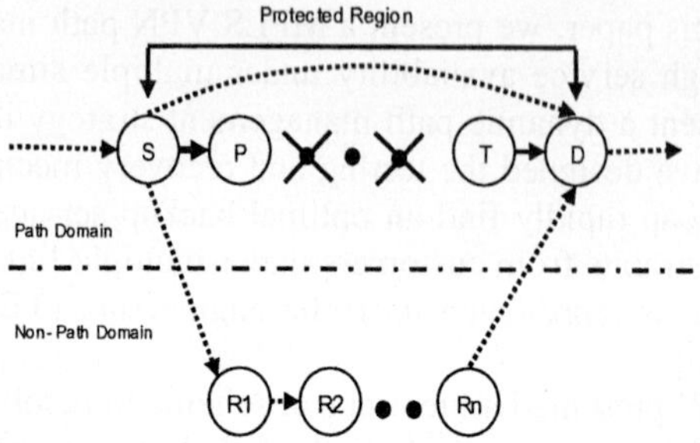

Fig. 1. Backup path candidates for VPN path recovery

protected by the backup paths [9]. In this case, the primary path is said to have a protection region of length k. We assume that the resilience constraint determines the length of the protection region, i.e., the k-protection. Path domain denotes the set of nodes in the primary path, and non-path domain implies the set of nodes not in the primary path which can be used for the construction of backup paths.

For the segment recovery mechanism, we use the backup path design rule in [9]. It says that the backup paths, for a given primary path, should follow the same sequence of nodes and links of the primary path in the sub-paths shared in both the primary and backup paths. Furthermore, no component in the protection region of a primary path should be used for the construction of backup paths, except for the beginning and ending nodes of the protection region. Applying the rule to segment recovery, we have two types of backup segment candidates: Type-1 and type-2 candidates. Type-1 consists of two nodes, the beginning node and ending node of the protection region, and the direct link connecting them. For example, the sub-path consisting of only nodes S and D in Fig. 1, which is indicated by a dotted line, is such a candidate backup segment. The type-2 candidate is the sub-path <S, R1, R2, … , Rn, D> in Fig. 1, where S and D are the beginning and ending nodes of the protection region, respectively. R1,…,Rn are the nodes in the non-path domain. There aren't any other types for the construction of the k-protection backup segments. The beginning nodes of the primary paths in MPLSVPN network have knowledge of the whole network. This is possible because MPLS employs IP-based routing protocols such as OSPF to which the whole network topology and all link status are available.

3 Conditions for Testing Backup Path Availability

We derive the condition which guarantees the existence of backup path under multiple failure occurrences satisfying the resilience constraint in a special mesh-type MPLS network. Let **P** and **R** denote path domain and non-path domain, respectively. Let $<P_1, P_2, \ldots, P_n>$ be a primary path in an MPLS network with N nodes. Let $U(P_i)$ be a unit step function such that it becomes one if there exists a direct link from a node P_i to a node P_{i+k}, otherwise zero, where $P_i, P_{i+k} \in \mathbf{P}$ for $i \in \{1,2,\ldots,(n-k)\}$. Let f be a function $f : \mathbf{P} \rightarrow \mathbf{R}$ such that for a given path, f is the number of direct links from a node P in path domain to nodes in non-path domain.

Theorem 1: For a general mesh-type MPLS network, let us assume that there exists a sub-path <P_1, P_{k+1}, P_{2k+1}, …, $P_{k(2m-1)+1}$, P_{2km+1}> of the primary path such that the degree of the nodes of the sub-path for the links from path domain **P** to non-path domain **R** is monotonic decreasing, i.e., $f(P_{ik+1}) \geq f(P_{(i+1)k+1})$ if i = 0,1,2, …, 2m-1, and the sub-graph consisting of only nodes in **R** is connected. Suppose that there are no direct links between any non-adjacent nodes of the primary path, and n = 2km+1 for some positive integers k and m. Then, the sub-path <P_1, P_{k+1}, P_{2k+1}, …, $P_{k(2m-1)+1}$, P_{2km+1}> of the primary path has *k-protection* even though (ζ - 1) number of links from {P_1, P_{k+1}, P_{2k+1}, …, $P_{k(2m-1)+1}$, P_{2km+1}} to **R** fails, where $\zeta = \sum_{j=1}^{m} f(P_{(2j-1)k+1})$.

Proof: We prove it by induction. Let **P'** be {P_1, P_{k+1}, P_{2k+1}, …, $P_{k(2m-1)+1}$, P_{2km+1}}. Let ζ be the minimum number of link failures from the subset **P'** to the non-path domain **R** which would not permit the construction of any primary path with k-protection. Let us consider for the case m = 1. In this case, **P'** is equal to {P_1, P_{k+1}, P_{2k+1}}. Thus, if all the links, i.e., $f(P_{k+1})$ from the node P_{k+1} to the nodes in **R** fail, there is no way to construct any k-protection backup paths. Since $f(P_{ik+1}) \geq f(P_{(i+1)k+1})$ if i = 0,1,2, …, 2m-1, the number $f(P_{ik+1})$ is a minimum number of link failures from **P'** to the non-path domain **R** which would not allow the construction of k-protection backup path. Therefore, ζ is equal to $\zeta = \sum_{j=1}^{m} f(P_{(2j-1)k+1})$ for m = 1.

Now, let us assume that the minimum number of link failures from **P'** to the non-path domain **R** is equal to $\sum_{j=1}^{n} f(P_{(2j-1)k+1})$ for m = n. For m = n + 1, if $f(P_{(2n-1)k+1+2k})$ links from the node $P_{(2n-1)k+1+2k}$ to the nodes in **R** fail, there is no way to construct any k-protection backup path for the sub-path <$P_{(2n-1)k+1+k}$, $P_{(2n-1)k+1+3k}$>, i.e., <P_{2nk+1}, $P_{2(n+1)k+1}$>. Since $f(P_{(2n-1)k+1}) \geq f(P_{(2n-1)k+1+2k})$, we know that the minimum number of link failures becomes $\sum_{j=1}^{n} f(P_{(2j-1)k+1}) + f(P_{(2n-1)k+1+2k})$. Since $f(P_{(2n-1)k+1+2k})$ is equal to $f(P_{(2(n+1)-1)k+1})$, this leads to the fact that ζ is equal to $\sum_{j=1}^{n+1} f(P_{(2j-1)k+1})$ for m = n +1. Since any one link from the ζ number of link failures, if it does not fail, could be used to construct a k-protection backup path, (ζ - 1) is the maximum number of allowable link failures which guarantees the existence of a k-protection backup path. This completes the proof. ■

Now, let us consider the more general case in which all the nodes in the primary path have a monotonic decreasing sequence of degree.

Theorem 2 (Optimality Theorem): For a general mesh-type MPLS network, let us assume that the degree of the nodes in the primary path <P_1, P_2, …, P_n> for the links from the path domain **P** to the non-path domain **R** is monotonic decreasing, i.e., either $f(P_i) \geq f(P_j)$ if i ≤ j for i, j = 1,2, …, n, and the sub-graph consisting of the only nodes in **R** is connected. Suppose that there are no direct links between any non-adjacent nodes of the primary path. Then, the primary path with n nodes has *k-protection* even though (ζ - 1) number of links from **P** to **R** fails, where $\zeta = \sum_{i=1}^{k}\sum_{j=1}^{m} f\left(P_{(2j-1)k+i}\right)$ and n < N, n = 2km +1+ ℓ for ℓ = 0, 1, …, k.

Proof: Without loss of generality, let us assume that the primary path has the configuration shown in Fig. 2, in which the primary path is partitioned into the groups of 2k links and the remaining ℓ -1 links. Let us partition the nodes of the primary path into a collection of subsets of nodes such that $\mathbf{P} = \mathbf{P}_1 \cup \mathbf{P}_2, \ldots, \cup \mathbf{P}_k$, where $\mathbf{P}_1 = \{P_1, P_{k+1}, P_{2k+1}, \ldots, P_{k(2m-1)+1}, P_{k(2m-1)+1}\}$, $\mathbf{P}_2 = \{P_2, P_{k+2}, P_{2k+2}, \ldots, P_{k(2m-1)+2}, P_{k(2m-1)+2}\}, \ldots, \mathbf{P}_k = \{P_k, P_{2k}, P_{3k}, \ldots, P_{k(2m-1)+k}\}$. Then, according to Theorem 1, we know that the minimum number of link failures which would not allow to build a k-protection backup path for the subset $\mathbf{P}_i$ for i = 1, 2, …, k, is $\sum_{j=1}^{m} f(P_{(2j-1)k+1})$. Since there are k subsets which are built from the partition, the total number of link failures from **P** to **R,** which would not permit constructing the k-protection backup path, becomes the sum of link failures associated with subsets $\mathbf{P}_i$ for i = 1, 2, …, k, i.e., $\sum_{i=1}^{k}\sum_{j=1}^{m} f\left(P_{(2j-1)k+i}\right)$. ■

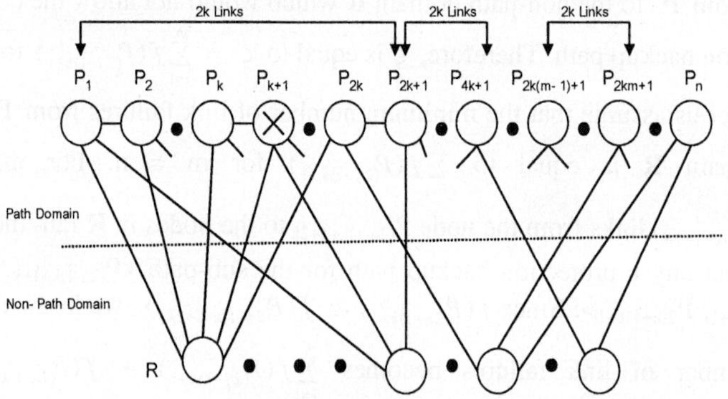

Fig. 2. A general k-protection primary path with monotonic decreasing degrees of nodes

(ζ - 1) is the maximum number of allowable link failures which guarantees the construction of a k-protection backup path under any *multiple* failure occurrences in a MPLS VPN network. It should be noted that we can prove the monotonic increasing case similarly if we count the indices of the nodes in the primary path from the ending node to the beginning node. The beginning nodes of the primary paths in the MPLS VPN network have knowledge of the whole network. This is possible because MPLS employs IP-based routing protocols such as OSPF-TE whereby the whole network topology and all link status are available. When failures occur, the MPLS signaling protocol such as RSVP-TE can be used to detect the failures and to send the failure notification message to the beginning nodes.

For segment **S** of the primary path P, let ζ(**S**) be defined as the minimum number of link failures which would not allow the construction of the k-protection backup path in S. Let $U(X_i)$ be a unit step function, such that it becomes one if there exists a direct link from node X_i to node X_{i+k}, otherwise zero, where $X_i, X_{i+k} \in S$ for $i = 1,2, \ldots, (n-k)$, and $\mathbf{S} = \{X_1, X_2, \ldots, X_n\}$.

First, we derive the upper bound of the number of failed links which guarantees the existence of the Type-1 backup segments which satisfy the resilience constraint, i.e., resilience-guaranteed backup segments.

Lemma 1. For a general mesh-type MPLS network, let us assume that the degree of the nodes in the segment $\langle X_1, X_2, \ldots, X_n \rangle$ for the links from the segment S to the non-path domain **R** is zero, i.e., $f(X_i) = 0$ for $i = 1,2, \ldots, n$. Then, the segment with n nodes has *k-protection* even though ($\zeta(\mathbf{S})$ - 1) number of links of the nodes in S fails, where $\zeta(\mathbf{S}) = \sum_{i=1}^{n-k} U(X_i)$ and $n \geq k$.

Proof: Type-1 candidate can only be constructed by using the links which directly connect two nodes in the segment **S**. Since there are n nodes with $n \geq k$ in the segment **S**, we can construct a backup segment with length k from X_i to $X_{(i+k)}$ if a direct link exists between X_i to $X_{(i+k)}$ for $i = 1, 2, \ldots, (n-k)$. Thus, $\zeta(\mathbf{S})$ is equal to $\sum_{i=1}^{n-k} U(X_i)$. If any one link is non-faulty from these direct links, we can construct a k-protection backup segment. ■

Now, let us consider the segment recovery in an MPLS network, in which the nodes $\langle X_1, X_2, \ldots, X_n \rangle$ of the segment **S** have the monotonic property. Let the total number of link failures, which are not in **P** and are incident to the nodes in **S**, be denoted as $\varepsilon(\mathbf{S})$.

Theorem 3. For a general mesh-type MPLS network, suppose that there exists a segment **S** of the primary path **P**. Suppose that the nodes in **S** have a monotonic property. Then, **S** has *k-protection* as long as there exists n nodes in **S** with $n \geq k$ and $\varepsilon(\mathbf{S}) \leq (\zeta(\mathbf{S}) - 1)$ where

$$\zeta(\mathbf{S}) = \begin{cases} \sum_{i=1}^{k}\sum_{j=1}^{m} f(X(2j-1)k+i) + \sum_{i=1}^{n-k} U(Xi) & \text{for } \ell \leq k \\ \sum_{i=1}^{k}\sum_{j=1}^{m} f(X(2j-1)k+i) + \sum_{j=1}^{\ell-k} f(X(2m+1)k+j) + \sum_{i=1}^{n-k} U(Xi) & \text{for } \ell > k \end{cases} \quad (1)$$

and $n = 2km + \ell$ for $\ell = 0, 1, \ldots, (2k-1)$, and m is a non-negative integer.

Proof. We should consider two types of backup candidates: Type-1 and Type-2. First, for Type-1, according to Lemma 1, we know that $\zeta(\mathbf{S})$ is equal to $\sum_{i=1}^{n-k} U(X_i)$. Next, let us consider Type-2 candidate. Since $n \geq k$, the k-protection backup path can be constructed within **S**. Furthermore, since the nodes in **S** have a monotonic decreasing sequence of degrees, we know according to Theorem 2 that if $\varepsilon(\mathbf{S}) \leq (\zeta(\mathbf{S}) - 1)$ with

$\zeta(\mathbf{S}) = \sum_{i=1}^{k}\sum_{j=1}^{m} f\left(X_{(2j-1)k+i}\right)$, it is possible to construct a k-protection backup segment in **S** for n = 2km +1+ ℓ, ℓ = 0, 1, …, k. This is because a segment itself can be treated as a primary path with the length n.

In the case of $\ell > k$, it should be noted that the links from the nodes $X_{(2m-1)k+1+2k}$ can be used for the construction of the k-protection backup segments. Therefore, since $X_{(2m-1)k+1+2k}$ is equal to $X_{(2m+1)k+1}$, all links from the node $X_{(2m+1)k+1}$ to the nodes in **R** should be accounted for when calculating the minimum number of link failures. Similarly, the links from the set of nodes $\{X_{(2m+1)k+2}, \ldots, X_{(2m+1)k+(l-k)}\}$ to the nodes in **R** should be accounted for when calculating the minimum number of link failures. Thus,

$\zeta(\mathbf{S}) = \sum_{i=1}^{k}\sum_{j=1}^{m} f\left(X_{(2j-1)k+i}\right) + \sum_{j=1}^{\ell-k} f\left(X_{(2m+1)k+j}\right)$ for $\ell > k$. Finally, by summing up both the results from Type-1 and Type-2, the proof is completed. ∎

When multiple failures are notified from segments in the primary path of MPLS network, we can quickly determine whether a k-protection backup segment can be constructed by counting the number of failure notifications associated with the segment **S**. The testing condition of Theorem 3 enables fast decision-making to be possible. If the number of failure notification exceeds the upper bound, the existence of backup segment with k-protection is not guaranteed. In the worst case, there will be no resilience-guaranteed backup segments so that the search time might be extremely large.

4 Dynamic Path Management Strategy and Simulation Results

We present the MPLS path management methodology which is described in Procedure Dynamic_Path_ Management. It should be noted that the computational complexity of the Procedure Dynamic_Path_Management is mainly dependent on Procedure Fast_Backup_Path_ Construct in Step 3-3. It is found that the computational complexity of Procedure Fast_ Backup_Path_Construct is found to be O (N^2) in [9]. Ler MaxNumber is defined as the value of ζ for the primary path **P**.

Algorithm. Dynamic_Path_Management (Total Number of Link Failures, Resilience Constraint);/* Test the availability of the k-protection backup path. If available, construct the backup path with minimal cost. */

```
Begin
  Step1: Construct backup paths in advance according to   the
  user QoS requirement on resilience, and distribute the input
  traffic load to both primary and backup paths according to
  the load sharing policy;
  Step2: If multiple failures occur, test whether the backup
  path is available, and switch the input traffic to the
  available backup path;
  Step3: Otherwise, construct another backup path satisfying
  the resilience constraint by testing the existence condi-
  tions of Theorem 3 as follows:
```

```
Step3-1: If Upon receiving the multiple failure notifica-
tions, update the MPLS configuration database;
Step3-2: Calculate MaxNumber for the construction of the k-
protection backup path availability;
Step3-3: If the Total Number of Multiple Link Failures <
MaxNumber
Then {Find all the feasible backup paths running the algo-
rithm Fast_Backup_ Path_ Construct in [9];}
Step3-4: Select the backup path with minimal cost from the
set of feasible backup paths for the k-protection primary
path;
End
```

In Fig. 3, we show the test configuration of the MPLS backbone for simulation, consisting of 9 nodes, and the links between them representing logical connections. In Fig. 3(a), the primary path is <N1, N3, N5, N7, N9> and there are two backup paths: Backup Paths 1 and 2. Backup Path 1 is <N1, N2, N6, N9> and Backup Path 2 is <N1, N4, N8, N9>. Here, N1 and N9 are target MPLS end nodes, i.e., the source and destination nodes, respectively. Here, the resilience value of the primary path in this case could be 1 if only one backup path is reserved, and 2 if both backup paths are reserved.

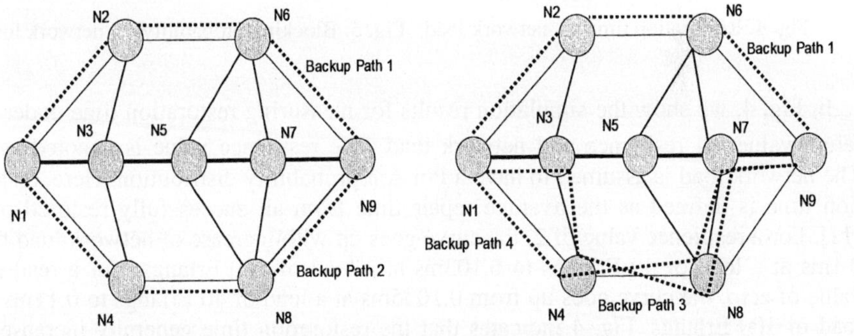

(a) Test for resilience values: 1 and 2 (b) Backup paths for resilience values: 0.4 and 0.7

Fig. 3. Test configuration of MPLS VPN backbone for simulation

Applying the restoration time testing condition, the MaxNumber from the path domain {N1, N3, N5, N7, N9} to the non-path domain {N4, N8} for 4-protection is 1, and it is also 1 to the non-path domain {N2, N6}. Thus, the minimum number of link failures which would not allow the construction of a 4-protection backup path is 2 since the MaxNumber is 2, taking into account both independent non-path domains {N2, N6} and {N4, N8}. Fig. 3(b) shows the backup paths, Backup Path 3 and Backup Path 4, for building the primary paths with 2-protection and 3-protection, respectively. In the simulation environment shown in Fig. 3, the input data traffic enters into the node P1, and is transmitted to node P9. Here, P1 and P9 serve as the source node and destination node, respectively. We simulate about 10,000 calls for each simulation. When simulating the recovery procedure, it is assumed that the node adjacent to the failure location can detect and localize the failures. A failure notification message is then sent directly to the source node using the MPLS signaling protocol. The source node usually waits for a very short time interval to check whether there are other failure notification messages, and then tests the condition for backup availability if a backup path is not reserved or damaged. If the testing condition is satisfied, it can rapidly reconstruct the backup path using the backup path design algorithm. The source node can then immediately switches the input data traffic to the backup path, resulting in high service availability with minimal service disruption. Before transmitting the input data, the source node also checks whether the input buffer at the MPLS node is available. If available, it delivers the data to the buffer. If not available, it either discards the data or switches the data to the available backup path according to the load sharing policy.

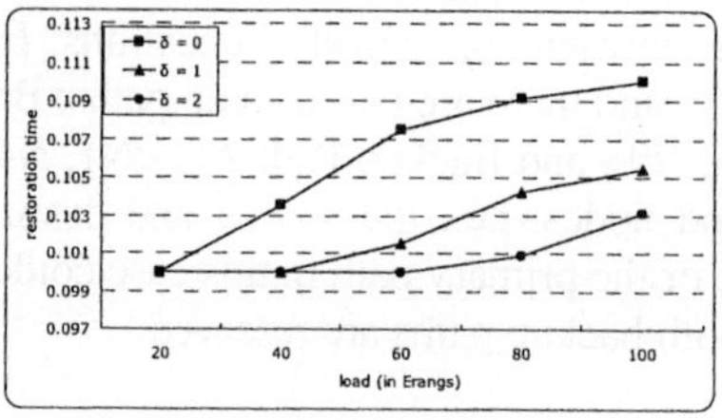

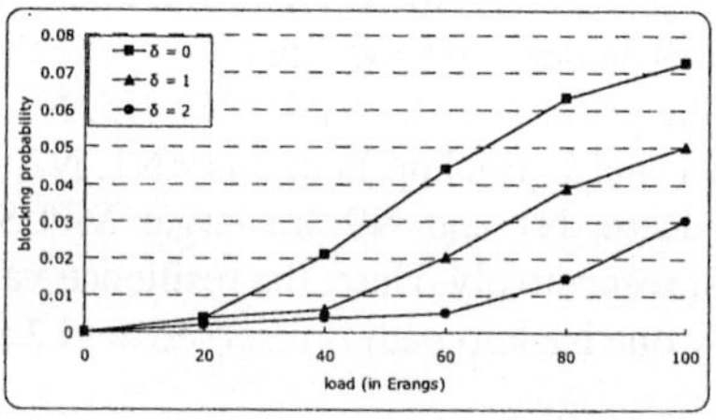

Fig. 4. Restoration time vs. network load **Fig. 5.** Blocking probability vs. network load

In Fig. 4, we show the simulation results for measuring restoration time under different values of resilience and network load. The resilience value is denoted as δ. The network load is assumed to have a Poisson probability distribution. Here, restoration time is defined as the average repair time from all successfully restored paths [11]. For a resilience value of 2, the curve goes up with increase of network load from 0.1ms at a load of 40 Erlangs to 0.103ms at a load of 100 Erlangs. For a resilience value of zero, the curve goes up from 0.1035ms at a load of 40 Erlangs to 0.11ms at a load of 100 Erlangs. Fig. 4 indicates that the restoration time generally increases as the network load increases. This is due to the fact that the larger resilience value encompasses with the greater load sharing.

In Fig. 5, we show the characteristics of blocking probability for resilience values: 0, 1, and 2. The blocking probability is defined as the ratio of the number of unsuccessful connection requests to the total number of connection requests in a network [11]. For a resilience value of 2, the curve goes up with increase of network load from 0.002 at a load of 20 Erlangs to 0.03 at a load of 100 Erlangs. For resilience value of zero, the curve has value of 0.004 at a load of 20 Erlangs to 0.075 at a load of 100 Erlangs. Fig. 5 indicates that the blocking probability also increases as the network load increases. However, the blocking probability decreases as the resilience values become larger. This is because with the increasing value of resilience, the signaling data can be delivered more reliably.

5 Conclusion

IP/MPLS VPN is a promising solution to service providers, which supports IP-based connectivity to customers over shared MPLS infrastructure. In this paper, we have presented an efficient resilient path-management strategy and detailed algorithm for resilient MPLS VPN service management. More specifically, we have derived the conditions to test the availability of backup paths which satisfy the resilience constraint for a special mesh-type MPLS VPN network in which the primary path has monotonic property. By testing these conditions for backup path availability, the VPN path recovery mechanism can find rapidly the optimal backup path which satisfies the resilience constraints under multiple link failures. Along with these existence conditions, an efficient dynamic backup path management strategy has been developed. Simulation results show that the proposed dynamic mechanism provides faster service recovery than the conventional rerouting mechanism of IETF standards.

References

1. Rosenbaum G., Lau W., Jha S.: Recent Directions in Virtual Private Network Solutions. Proceedings of IEEE ICON 2003 conference (2003)
2. Nagarajan A.: Generic Requirements for Provider Provisioned Virtual Private Networks (PPVPN). IETF Standard, RFC 3809 (2004)
3. Rosen E. C., Rekhter Y.: BGP/MPLS IP VPNs. IETF Internet Draft (2004)
4. Lasserre M., et al: Virtual Private LAN Services over MPLS. IETF Internet Draft (2003)
5. Mannie E. et al.: Generalized MPLS Architecture. IETF Internet Draft (2003)
6. Awduche D. et. al.: Requirements for Traffic Engineering Over MPLS. IETF RFC 2702 (1999)
7. Lee S.K., Griffith D.: Hierarchical Restoration Scheme for Multiple Failures in MPLS Networks. Proceedings of the 2002 ICPP Workshops (2002) 177-182
8. Clouqueur M., Grover W. D.: Availability Analysis of Span-Restorable Mesh Networks. Journal on Selected Areas in Communications, Vol. 20, No. 4. IEEE (2002) 810-821
9. Park J.T.: Resilience in MPLS Path Management: model and mechanism. Communications Magazine, Vol.42, No.7. IEEE (2004) 128-135
10. Sharma, V., Hellstrand F.: Framework for Multi-Protocol Label Switching (MPLS)-based Recovery. (2003)
11. Wang J., Sahasrabuddlhe L., Mukherjee B.: Path vs. Subpath vs. Link Restoration for Fault Management in IP-over-WDM Network: Performance Comparisons Using MPLS Control Signaling. Communications Magazine. IEEE (2002)

Comparison of Hyper-DAG Based Task Mapping and Scheduling Heuristics for Wireless Sensor Networks

Yuan Tian, Füsun Özgüner, and Eylem Ekici

Department of Electrical and Computer Engineering,
The Ohio State University
{tiany, ozguner, ekici}@ece.osu.edu

Abstract. In-network processing emerges as an approach to reduce energy consumption in Wireless Sensor Networks (WSN) by decreasing the overall transferred data volume. Parallel processing among sensors is a promising approach to provide the computation capacity required by in-network processing methods. In this paper, Hyper-DAG based Mapping and Scheduling (HDMS) algorithms for energy constrained WSNs are introduced. The design objective of these algorithms is to minimize schedule lengths subject to energy consumption constraints. Simulation results show that the CNPT-based HDMS algorithm outperforms other heuristic algorithms with respect to schedule lengths and heuristic execution times subject to energy consumption constraints.

1 Introduction

In-network processing is shown to be an effective approach to reduce energy consumption in Wireless Sensor Networks (WSN) by decreasing the overall transferred data volume [1]. In-network processing methods demand considerable computation capacity subject to timeliness requirements and energy consumption constraints. Sensors' computation power can be a bottleneck to process data given timeliness requirements. [1], [2], [3] propose collaborative data processing architectures by executing low level tasks on sensing sensors and offloading all other high level processing tasks to cluster heads. However, processing high level tasks can still exceed the capacity of cluster heads' computation power.

Parallel processing among sensors is a promising solution to provide the computation capacity required by in-network processing. Task mapping and scheduling has been extensively studied in the area of high performance computing [4] [5], but remains largely unexplored in WSNs. Task scheduling problem in WSNs has been considered in the literature recently. In [6], an online task scheduling mechanism (CoRAl) is presented to allocate the network resources between the tasks of periodic applications in WSNs. However, CoRAl does not address task mapping problem. Task mapping mechanisms in wireless networks have been presented in [7], [8]. Both [7] and [8] assume an existing underlying network communication mechanism without explicitly discussing communication scheduling

P. Yolum et al.(Eds.): ISCIS 2005, LNCS 3733, pp. 74–83, 2005.

between tasks. Task mapping and task scheduling have been considered jointly for mobile computing in [9]. However, the communication model adopted in [9] is not well suited for WSNs.

In this paper, three Hyper-DAG based Mapping and Scheduling (HDMS) algorithms for WSNs are introduced. The design objective of the algorithms is to minimize schedule lengths subject to energy consumption constraints. The performance of these algorithms is evaluated through simulations. Simulation results show that the CNPT [10] based HDMS algorithm outperforms the other heuristic algorithms with respect to schedule lengths and heuristic execution time subject to energy consumption constraints.

2 Network Assumptions and Task Mapping and Scheduling Problem

Our proposed HDMS algorithms are designed for applications executed within a cluster of homogeneous wireless sensor networks. The following assumptions are made for the sensor network: 1. Sensors are grouped into single-hop clusters with a clustering algorithm. Cluster heads create and coordinate schedules for communication and computation within clusters. 2. Sensors within a cluster are time synchronized. 3. Computation and communication can occur simultaneously on sensor nodes. 4. The communication within a cluster is isolated from other clusters through channel-hopping mechanisms.

An application executed in a cluster is modeled by a Directed Acyclic Graph (DAG) $T = (V,E)$, where the vertex set V denotes the tasks to be executed and the edge set E denotes the communication and dependency between the tasks. The computation cost of a task is represented by the number of CPU clock cycles to execute the task. The communication cost is denoted by the data volume to be transferred between tasks. Let $v_i \in V$ denote a task of the application and $e_{ij} \in E$ denote the connection between tasks v_i and v_j. v_i is the immediate predecessor of v_j and v_j is the immediate successor of v_i. A task without predecessors is called an *entry-task* and a task without successors is called an *exit-task.* A DAG may have multiple entry-tasks and one exit-task.

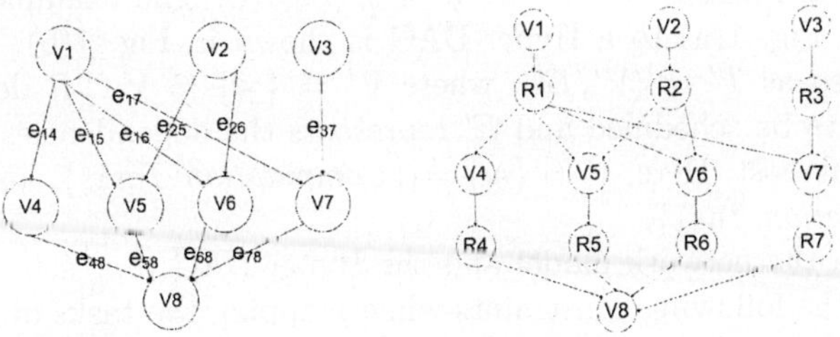

(a) A DAG Example (b) Hyper-DAG Extension

Fig. 1. DAG and Hyper-DAG Example

Fig. 1(a) shows a DAG example, where V1 is an entry-task, V8 is an exit-task, and V5 is the immediate successor and predecessor of V1 and V8, respectively.

Let $H^x = \{h_1^x, h_2^x, ..., h_n^x\}$ denote a set of mapping and scheduling decisions of an application T on a network G. Each element $h_i^x \in H^x$ is a tuple of the form $(v_i, m_k, s_{ik}, f_{ik}, c_{ik})$, where m_k represents the sensor to which task v_i is assigned, s_{ik} and f_{ik} represent the start time and finish time of v_i, and c_{ik} represents the energy consumption of v_i on node m_k, respectively. For convenience, let $pred(v_i)$ and $succ(v_i)$ denote the immediate predecessors and successors of task v_i respectively, $m(v_i)$ denote the sensor on which v_i is assigned, and $T(m_k)$ denote the tasks assigned on sensor m_k. The target problem P^o is to find an $H^o \in \{H^x\}$ that has the minimum schedule length under the energy consumption constraint. P^o is an NP-complete problem in general [5]. Therefore heuristic algorithms to solve P^o are needed.

3 Hyper-DAG Based Mapping and Scheduling Basics

The proposed HDMS algorithms are based on the observation that the communication channel is shared by all members of a cluster. In a single-hop cluster, there can be only one transmission on the wireless channel at a given time. Therefore, the wireless channel can be modeled as a virtual node *CH* that executes one communication task at any time instance [6]. Hence, a single-hop cluster can be modeled as a star-network where all sensors only have connections with the virtual node *CH*. The communication latency between sensor nodes and *CH* is considered zero since all wireless communications are accounted for by the tasks executed on *CH*. Assuming that a cluster has p sensors that are denoted as $M = \{m_k\}$ $(0 \leq k < p)$, a cluster can be represented by a connected, undirected graph $G = (M',N)$, where the set $M' = M \cup \{CH\}$, and the set N denotes the links between the nodes of M'.

To implement the wireless channel model above, communication should be explicitly represented in task graphs. Thus, the DAG representation of applications is extended as follows: For a task v_i in a DAG, we replace the edges between v_i and its immediate successors with a *net* R_i. R_i represents delivery of $v_i's$ result to all of its immediate successors in the DAG. This extended DAG is a hypergraph and is referred to as *Hyper-DAG*. The example of converting the DAG in Fig. 1(a) to a Hyper-DAG is shown in Fig. 1(b). A Hyper-DAG is represented as $T' = (V', E')$, where $V' = \{\gamma_i\} = V \cup R$ denotes the new set of tasks to be scheduled and E' represents the dependencies between tasks with zero link cost. Here, $V = \{v_i\} = \{\textit{Computation Tasks}\}$, and $R = \{R_i\} = \{\textit{Communication Task}\}$.

Based on the network model and the Hyper-DAG representation of DAGs, HDMS has the following constraints when mapping the tasks of a Hyper-DAG: 1. Computation tasks can be assigned only on sensor nodes; 2. Communication tasks can have multiple copied assigned on sensor nodes and *CH*; 3. Communication tasks assigned on a sensor node have zero execution length and energy cost; 4. To meet *Dependency Constraint*, a non-entry computation task v_i assigned on a sensor m_k must have all of its immediate predecessors $pred(v_i)$, which are communication tasks, assigned on m_k.

With the constraints presented above, HDMS-based task mapping algorithms need to obey the following rules. If a computation task v_i does not have all of its predecessors on the target sensor m_k, the absent predecessor $v_n \in pred(v_i) - T(m_k)$ has to be duplicated to m_k: if $v_n \in T(CH)$, a copy of v_n is duplicated to m_k starting from $f_{n,CH}$; otherwise, a copy of v_n is first duplicated to CH from the source starting at the earliest available time of CH for v_n, then from CH to m_k. To schedule a copy of task v_i from sensor m_s to CH and from CH to sensor m_r are equivalent to scheduling data broadcast and data reception in the physical world, respectively. The sender m_s and receiver m_r of task v_i need to be updated with the corresponding energy consumption. This communication task duplication procedure is referred to as "Communication Scheduling".

4 Heuristics

In this section, E^2-CNPT, H-MinMin, and H-BottomsUp algorithms are introduced. These are implementations of CNPT [10], Min-Min, and Bottoms Up [9] algorithms using Hyper-DAGs following the constraints and the rules presented in Section 3.

E^2-CNPT: The E^2-CNPT algorithm is based on the Critical Nodes Parent Trees (CNPT) algorithm [10]. E^2-CNPT has two stages: *Listing Stage* and *Sensor Assignment Stage.* After the Listing Stage, all tasks in V' are enqueued into *mappable task queue* L in the order that the most critical path comes the first and a task is always enqueued after its predecessors. The listing procedure of E^2-CNPT is similar to that of CNPT except for the definitions of Earliest Start Time EST and Latest Start Time LST,

$$EST(v_i) = \max_{v_m \in pred(v_i)} \{EST(v_m) + w_m\}, \tag{1}$$

$$LST(v_i) = \min_{v_m \in succ(v_i)} \{LST(v_m)\} - w_i, \tag{2}$$

where w_i equals to the execution length on sensor nodes if $v_i \in V$ or to the execution length on CH if $v_i \in R$.

In the Sensor Assignment Stage, it is assumed that an increased number of sensors involved in computation decreases the schedule length. The sensor assignment algorithm iteratively searches the task mapping and scheduling solution with the maximum number of computing sensors under energy consumption constraints. Here, a computing sensor is a sensor that executes non-entry-tasks. The E^2-CNPT with q computing sensors is described as follows:

1. Dequeue a task v_i from the *mappable task queue* L created in *Listing Phase.*
2. Find the sensor m^o that gives the minimum Earliest Execution Start Time (EEST). A non-entry computation task $v_i \in V$ can only be assigned on one of the q computing sensors. If a task depends on its immediate predecessor assigned on another sensor, the "Communication Scheduling" procedure in Section 3 is executed to meet *Dependency Constraint.*

3. Assign v_i to m^o.
4. Repeat step 1 to 3 until L is empty.

Among the schedules with different number of computing sensors, the one with the minimum schedule length subject to the energy consumption constraint is chosen as the solution. If no schedule meets the energy consumption constraint, the solution with the minimum energy consumption is chosen.

H-MinMin: The Min-Min Algorithm in [9] is extended with a fitness function for task mapping and scheduling in WSNs. Let EB be the energy consumption constraint, $PE(v_i, m_k)$ be the partial energy consumption of the cluster after assigning task v_i to sensor m_k, f_{v_i,m_k} be the scheduled finish time of task v_i on sensor m_k, $MFT(v_i, m_k)$ be the maximum finish time of the tasks assigned prior to task v_i, $NPE(v_i, m_k) = PE(v_i, m_k)/EB$ be the normalized partial energy consumption of assigning v_i on m_k, and $NPT(v_i, m_k) = f_{v_i,m_k}/MFT(v_i, m_k)$ be the normalized partial execution time of assigning v_i on m_k. Using α as the weight parameter, the fitness function of assigning a task v_i on sensor m_k is defined as:

$$fitness(v_i, m_k) = \alpha \cdot NPE(v_i, m_k) + (1 - \alpha) \cdot NPT(v_i, m_k). \tag{3}$$

The H-MinMin algorithm is summarized as follows.

1. Initialize a mappable task list L with entry-tasks.
2. For each task $v_i \in L$, find the sensor m_i^o that gives the minimum fitness value $fitness(v_i, m_i^o)$. The "Communication Scheduling" procedure is executed to meet *Dependency Constraint* if necessary and the corresponding energy consumption is counted into the $fitness(v_i, m_k)$ calculation.
3. From the task/sensor pairs found in step 2, find the pair (v^o, m^o) with the minimum fitness value.
4. Remove task v^o from L and assign v^o to sensor m^o.
5. Update L with any new mappable tasks after step 4.
6. Repeat steps 2 to 5 until all tasks are scheduled.

In the algorithm above, a "mappable task" is either an entry-task or a task that has all *immediate predecessors* already assigned. Among the schedules with different values of α ($\alpha = 0.1 \cdot i, i = 0, 1, ...10$), the schedule with the minimum schedule length subject to the energy consumption constraint is chosen as the solution. If no schedule meets the energy consumption constraint, the one with the minimum energy consumption is chosen.

H-BottomsUp: The fitness function of the modified Bottoms Up [9] is the same as that of the H-MinMin algorithm. Different from H-MinMin, a mappable task in Bottoms Up is either an exit-task or a task that has all *immediate successors* already mapped. The H-BottomsUp algorithm can be outlined as following:

1. Assign levels to the tasks: entry-tasks have level zero; a non-entry-task is one level higher than the maximum of its immediate predecessors' levels.
2. From the highest level to the lowest level, consider all mappable tasks within each individual level.

3. For each mappable task v_i in the current level, find the sensor m_k that gives the minimum $fitness(v_i, m_k)$. Execute the "Communication Scheduling" procedure to meet *Dependency Constraint* if necessary.
4. From the task/sensor pairs found in step 3, find the pair (v^o, m^o) with the minimum fitness value, assign v^o to m^o.
5. Repeat step 3 to 4 until all tasks in the present level are assigned.
6. Repeat step 2 to 5 until all tasks are mapped.
7. Schedule the tasks in the reverse order that they were assigned.

In the algorithm above, the "Communication Scheduling" procedure is similar to that presented in Section 3 except that the absent *immediate successors* of a computation task are duplicated instead of the absent immediate predecessors. In [9], a weight factor $\alpha = 0.52$ is reported to provide best performance under all scenarios. In this paper, the H-BottomsUp algorithm with $\alpha = 0.52$ is evaluated (referred to as F-BottomsUp). To further study the performance of the H-BottomsUp algorithm in WSNs, the H-BottomsUp algorithm is also executed with α ranging from 0 to 1 in steps of 0.1 (referred to as E-BottomsUp).

5 Performance Evaluation

The performance of E^2-CNPT, Min-Min, F-BottomsUp, and E-BottomsUp algorithms are evaluated through simulations. The performance of the distributed computation architecture (referred to as DCA) [1] [2] is also evaluated as a benchmark. DCA is extended such that several sensors perform entry-tasks and send intermediate results to cluster heads for further processing. We have run simulations to investigate the following aspects: 1. Effect of energy consumption constraints; 2. Effect of number of tasks in applications; 3. Effect of communication load between tasks; 4. Comparison of Heuristic Execution Times.

In these simulations, we observe energy consumption and schedule lengths. The energy consumption includes computation and communication energy expenditure of all sensors. The schedule length is defined as the finish time of the exit-task of an application. In the last set of experiments, the execution times of E^2-CNPT, H-MinMin, F-BottomsUp, and E-BottomsUp are normalized by the execution time of DCA, which serves as a relative metric of the algorithm complexity. The simulation results presented in this section correspond to the average of two hundred independent runs.

Simulation Parameters and Energy Consumption Model: In our simulation study, the bandwidth of the channel is set to 1Mb/s and the transmission range to 10 meters. The sensors have the clock frequency of 100 MHz. The energy consumptions of transmitting and receiving l-bit data over distance d are defined as $E_{tx}(l,d) = E_{elec} \cdot l + \varepsilon_{amp} \cdot l \cdot d^2$ and $E_{rx}(l) = E_{elec} \cdot l$, where $E_{elec} = 50$ nJ/b and $\varepsilon_{amp} = 10$ pJ/b/m^2 [11]. The energy consumption of executing N clock cycles (CC) with CPU frequency f is given as: $E_{comp}(V_{dd}, f) = NCV_{dd}^2 + V_{dd}(I_o e^{\frac{V_{dd}}{nV_T}})(\frac{N}{f})$ and $f \simeq K(V_{dd} - c)$, where V_T is the thermal voltage and C, I_o, n, K and c are processor dependent parameters [2]. In our simulation,

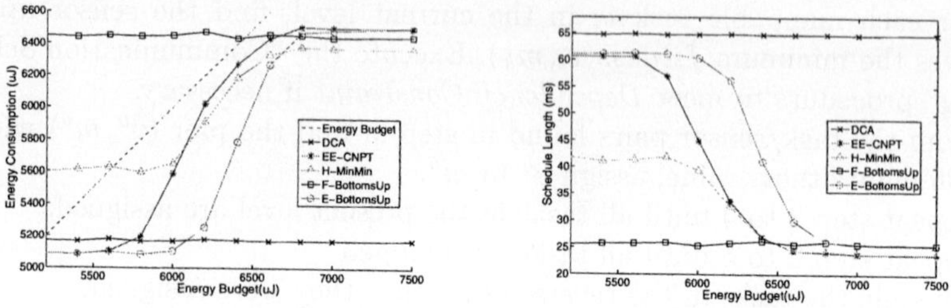

(a) Energy Consumption (b) Schedule Length

Fig. 2. Effect of Energy Budget

we consider the StrongARM SA-1100 microprocessor, where $V_T = 26$ mV, $C = 0.67$ nF, $I_o = 1.196$ mA, $n = 21.26$, $K = 239.28$ MHz/V and $c = 0.5$ V [1], [2].

Simulations are run on randomly generated DAGs, which are created based on three parameters, namely, the number of tasks *numTask*, the number of entry-tasks *numEntry*, and the maximum number of immediate predecessors *maxPred*. The number of each non-entry task's immediate predecessors, the computation load, and the resulting data volume of a task are uniformly distributed over [1, *maxPred*], [300 KCC ±10%], and [800 bits ±10%], respectively.

Effect of Energy Consumption Constraints: We investigate the effect of energy consumption constraints with randomly generated DAGs. The parameters of DAGs considered for this set of simulations are $numTask = 25$, $numEntry = 6$, and $maxPred = 3$. The energy consumption and schedule length are observed for different available energy levels (referred to as Energy Budget). According to Fig. 2, when the energy budget is small, H-MinMin and F-BottomsUp fail to meet energy constraints while E^2-CNPT and E-BottomsUp succeed. When the energy budget increases, the schedule lengths of E^2-CNPT, H-MinMin, and E-BottomsUp decrease while DCA and F-BottomsUp hardly improve their schedule lengths. With sufficient energy supply, E^2-CNPT and H-MinMin improve schedule lengths up to 63% while F-BottomsUp and E-BottomsUp obtain 60% improvement in comparison to DCA. From the simulation results, we can see that E^2-CNPT comprehensively outperforms H-MinMin, F-BottomsUp and E-BottomsUp with respect to meeting energy constraints and shortening schedule lengths.

Effect of Number of Tasks in Applications: To investigate the effect of number of tasks in applications, three sets of simulations are run on randomly generated DAGs with 20, 25 and 30 tasks ($numEntry = 6$, $maxPred = 3$). According to the simulation results in Fig. 3, energy consumption and schedule length are dominated by the number of tasks. When the number of tasks increases, the energy consumption of DCA and F-BottomsUp increases proportionally. E^2-CNPT, H-MinMin, and E-BottomsUp on the other hand adapt themselves to the increasing energy budget. For small energy budgets, the schedule lengths of all five algorithms increase when the number of tasks increases. However, for

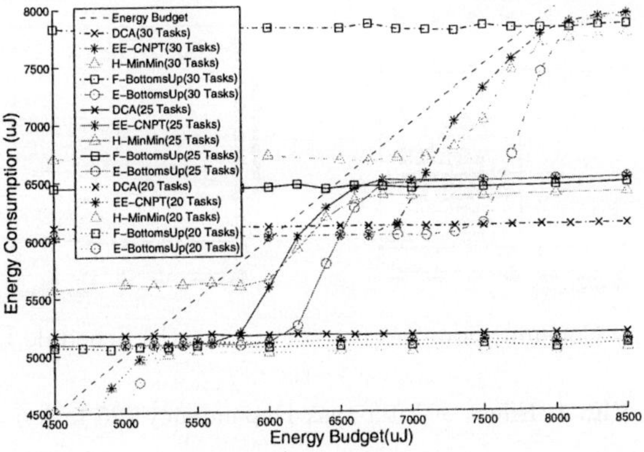

(a) Energy Consumption

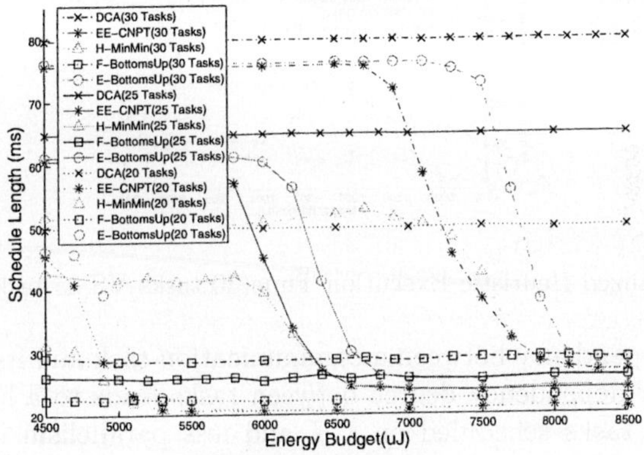

(b) Schedule Length

Fig. 3. Effect of Number of Tasks (30 tasks VS 25 tasks VS 20 tasks)

E^2-CNPT, H-MinMin, and E-BottomsUp, the schedule lengths reduce when the energy budget increases. However, the schedule lengths of DCA and F-BottomsUp increase proportionally when the number of tasks increases.

Effect of Inter-task Dependency: Inter-task dependency is determined by the in/out degree of application DAGs. Two sets of simulations with $maxPred =$ 3 and $maxPred = 6$ ($numTask = 25$, $numEntry = 6$) are executed. According to Fig. 4, inter-task dependency has almost no effect over the performance of DCA. Both of the energy consumption and schedule length increase when inter-task dependency increases in E^2-CNPT, H-MinMin, F-BottomsUp, and E-BottomsUp. The robustness of DCS against inter-task dependency change is because DCA has most tasks executed on cluster heads with the least need for communication. Regarding E^2-CNPT, H-MinMin, F-BottomsUp, and E-BottomsUp, increasing the in/out degree of DAGs does not introduce new communication tasks but

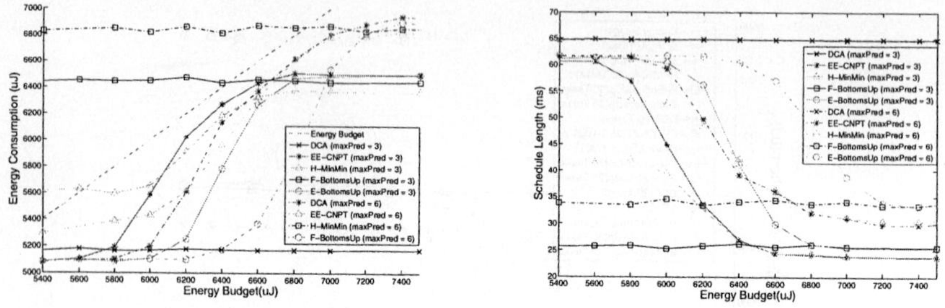

(a) Energy Consumption (b) Schedule Length

Fig. 4. Effect of Inter-task Dependency (25 tasks)

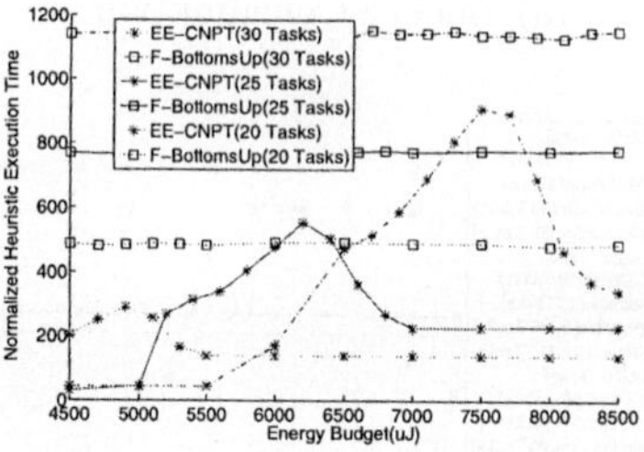

Fig. 5. Normalized Heuristic Execution Time(30 tasks VS 25 tasks VS 20 tasks)

increases the dependency between a communication task and its immediate successors. Greater dependency degree between tasks leads to a higher number of communication tasks scheduled on *CH* and less parallelism between sensors, which causes more energy consumption and longer schedules.

Comparison of Heuristic Execution Times: The heuristic execution times are investigated with three sets of simulations run on randomly DAGs with 20, 25 and 30 tasks ($numEntry = 6$, $maxPred = 3$). For fair comparison, the execution times of E^2-CNPT, H-MinMin, F-BottomsUp, and E-BottomsUp are normalized by the average execution time of DCA with 20 tasks. According to the simulation, the normalized execution times of H-MinMin and E-BottomsUp are over 5000 and significantly higher than E^2-CNPT and F-BottomsUp. Thus, only the normalized execution times of E^2-CNPT and F-BottomsUp are shown in Fig. 5. The execution time of F-BottomsUp almost keeps constant with different energy budget. When the energy budget increases, the execution time of E^2-CNPT first increases, then decreases after reaching a peak value. E^2-CNPT iteratively searches computing sensor space for optimal solutions. The searching algorithm converges faster in the scenarios with limited or sufficiently large energy budget and converges slower with intermediate scenarios. When the number of tasks increases, the execution time of F-BottomsUp proportionally increases while E^2-CNPT adapts according to energy budgets. In all scenarios, the execution time of E^2-CNPT is shorter than that of F-BottomsUp with the same number of tasks. Thus, E^2-CNPT has better scalability compared with H-Min-Min, F-BottomsUp, and E-BottomsUp.

6 Conclusion

In this paper, a wireless network model, the Hyper-DAG application representation, and communication scheduling rules are introduced for task mapping and scheduling in wireless sensor networks. Three HDMS algorithms are presented, which aim to minimize schedule lengths of applications under energy consumption constraints. Simulations with randomly generated DAGs show that E^2-CNPT provides superior performance in comparison with DCA, H-MinMin, F-BottomsUp, and E-BottomsUp algorithms.

References

1. Shih, E., Cho, S., Ickes, N., Min, R., Sinha, A., Wang, A., Chandrakasan, A.: Physical layer driven protocol and algorithm design for energy-efficient wireless sensor networks. In: Proc. of ACM MobiCom'01. (2001) 272–286
2. Wang, A., Chandrakasan, A.: Energy-efficient DSPs for wireless sensor networks. IEEE Signal Processing Magazine (2002) 68–78
3. Kumar, R., Tsiatsis, V., Srivastava, M.B.: Computation hierarchy for in-network processing. In: Proc. of the 2nd ACM international conference on Wireless Sensor Networks and Applications (WSNA'03). (2003) 68–77
4. Dogan, A., Özgüner, F.: Matching and scheduling algorithms for minimizing execution time and failure probability of applications in heterogenous computing. IEEE Transaction on Parallel and Distributed Systems **13** (2002) 308–323
5. Garey, M., Johnson, D.: Computers and Intractability: A Guide to the Theory of NP-Completeness. W. H. Freeman and Co. (1979)
6. Giannecchini, S., Caccamo, M., Shih, C.S.: Collaborative resource allocation in wireless sensor networks. In: Proc. of Euromicro Conference on Real-Time Systems (ECRTS'04). (2004) 35–44
7. Basu, P., Ke, W., Little, T.D.C.: Dynamic task-based anycasting in mobile ad hoc networks. Mobile Networks and Applications **8** (2003) 593–612
8. Kumar, R., Wolenetz, M., Agarwalla, B., Shin, J., Hutto, P., Paul, A., Ramachandran, U.: DFuse: A framework for distributed data fusion. In: Proc. of The ACM Conference on Embedded Networked Sensor Systems (SenSys'03). (2003) 114–125
9. Shivle, S., Castain, R., Siegel, H.J., Maciejewski, A.A., Banka, T., Chindam, K., Dussinger, S., Pichumani, P., Satyasekaan, P., Saylor, W., D.Sendek, Sousa, J., Sridharan, J., Sugavanam, P., Velazco, J.: Static mapping of subtasks in a heterogeneous ad hoc grid environment. In: Proc. of Parallel and Distributed Processing Symposium. (2004)
10. Hagras, T., Janecek, J.: A high performance, low complexity algorithm for compile-time job scheduling in homogeneous computing environments. In: Proc. of International Conference on Parallel Processing Workshops (ICPPW'03). (2003) 149–155
11. Heinzelman, W.B., Chandrakasan, A., Balakrishnan, H.: An application-specific protocol architecture for wireless microsensor networks. IEEE Transactions on Wireless Communications **1** (2002) 660–670

A Markov-Based Model to Analyze the Temporal Evolution and Lifetime of a Sensor Network

Mario Barbera, Salvatore Incardona, Alfio Lombardo, and Giovanni Schembra

DIIT - University of Catania, Viale A.Doria 6 - 95125 Catania – Italy

Abstract. Wireless sensor networks are made up of low-cost sensor nodes that can communicate with each other in a wireless manner, have limited computing capability and memory, and operate with limited battery power. Nodes go out of service when their batteries run out of energy, and the whole network moves to a global out-of-service state. The target of this paper is to define an analytical framework to evaluate the transient behavior of a sensor network in which sensors implement the energy-saving technique of idle/active states. The model captures the behavior of the battery lifetime of each sensor, and is therefore able to evaluate the distribution of the lifetime of all the sensors in the network. Some important metrics are defined to evaluate network connectivity over time.

1 Introduction

In recent years there has been a peak of interest in sensor networks. Applications of this kind of network are manifold, ranging from military applications to civilian applications, such as for example environmental or building monitoring. To enable communication between sensors not within each other's communication range, the sensors form a kind of multi-hop ad-hoc network. A characteristic of sensor networks is that sensors have limited resources, such as limited computing capability, memory and energy supplies, and they must balance these restricted resources in order to increase the lifetime of the network. Nodes go out of service when the battery runs out of energy. Of course, when the number of out-of-service nodes increases, network connectivity rapidly decreases, and therefore the whole network moves to a global out-of-service state. Therefore, a key challenge in the design of a wireless sensor network is maximizing its lifetime.

A large amount of work has been devoted to optimizing the lifetime of the energy available to the network, designing low-power signal processing architectures, low-power sensing interfaces, energy efficient wireless media access control and routing protocols [1,2], low-power security protocols and key management architectures [3]. However, most of the work aimed at defining architectures and algorithms, was often based on the empirical observation of phenomena, or assessment via simulation. To the best of our knowledge, however, very little effort has been devoted to defining analytical paradigms to evaluate and optimize the performance of sensor networks.

Early analytical models of sensor networks addressed analysis of the capacity of large stationary ad hoc networks [4]. Two Markov models were defined in [5,6] to capture the widely employed energy-saving technique of placing nodes in a low-power operational mode, the so-called *sleep* mode, during idle periods [7]. The model

P. Yolum et al.(Eds.): ISCIS 2005, LNCS 3733, pp. 84–93, 2005.

in [5] predicts the sensor energy consumption, although only the single node is represented by a Markov chain, while the network energy status is derived via simulation. The model proposed in [6] is the first analytical model that specifically represents the sensor dynamics in the sleep/active mode, while taking into account channel contention and routing issues. The model is used to investigate system performance in terms of energy consumption, network capacity, and data delivery delay. In [8] the so-called "spatial, fluid-based approach" is proposed to model wireless sensor networks considering the number of nodes as a continuous variable, and approximating the sensor node distribution over the network area by introducing the concept of *sensor density*. However, as mentioned previously, one of the main characteristics of sensor networks is time variability due to energy consumption. To model this peculiarity, two aspects of the network have to be considered in addition to what has already been captured by previous models: 1) battery evolution; 2) network topology variation due to the progressive death of active sensors.

The target of this paper is to define an analytical framework to evaluate the transient behavior of a sensor network in which sensors implement the energy-saving technique of idle/active states. The proposed model starts from that defined in [6], where only steady-state behavior was considered and batteries were assumed as fully charged, i.e. the network topology as constant in time. This paper, on the other hand, captures the behavior of the battery lifetime for each sensor, and is therefore able to evaluate the distribution of the lifetime of all the sensors in the network. In addition some metrics are defined to evaluate transient network evolution and the lifetime of the whole network, and to evaluate the connectivity level of the network over time.

The paper is organized as follows. Section 2 describes the network scenario and discusses the assumptions made. Section 3 presents the model in detail. Section 4 gives the numerical results obtained. Finally, Section 5 concludes the paper.

2 Description of the System

We consider a network topology of N identical stationary sensor nodes collecting information about events in their neighborhood and sending data to a gathering center called a *sink*. Sensors have an omni-directional antenna with a maximum transmission range r, so each one can only communicate with a few sensors called *next-hop* nodes. We assume that sensors can choose an arbitrary transmission power level for each data transmission, provided that their transmission range does not exceed r. Communication with the sink is possible via a succession of next-hop nodes (*multi-hop* communication). A transmission from a generic sensor i to a generic sensor j will be successful if their distance, $d_{i,j}$, satisfies the following conditions: C1) $d_{i,j} \leq r$; C2) $d_{i,k} > r$, $\forall k$: k is a sensor simultaneously receiving; C3) $d_{k,j} > r$, $\forall k$: k is a sensor simultaneously transmitting.

We assume that sensors employ the CSMA/CA mechanism; collisions may therefore only occur with RTS/CTS messages, while the transmission of data units is always collision-free. Data units are of a fixed size, K. We consider time as being divided into time slots with a duration equal to the time needed to receive or transmit a data unit. Sensors cannot, of course, receive and transmit data units in the same time slot. The wireless channel is error-free and propagation effects are neglected. The resources of sensor nodes include a FIFO buffer containing at most B_S data units, and a battery with a total energy of E_S Joule.

A generic sensor can perform four fundamental functions: *sensing* the environment, *transmitting* and *receiving* data units, and *listening* to the channel. A different amount of energy consumption is associated with each of these functions. The energy consumed in sensing the environment can be neglected in most applications, so we will not consider it. In the *listen* mode, also called the *idle* mode, although a sensor does not transmit and receive data units, it must keep its radio equipments active, because it does not know when it will be the receiver of a message from one of its neighbors. For this reason, when the sensor is in the *idle* mode, we assume a constant energy consumption value $E^{(radio)}$ (expressed in Joule/slot). When a sensor receives a data unit, it also has to activate the transceiver electronics and processing functions (such as demodulation and decoding). The energy consumption in the *receive* mode, $E^{(RX)}$, therefore has an additional contribution, $E^{(elec)}$ (expressed in Joule/slot), which is proportional to the size of a data unit, K. The most consuming operating mode in terms of energy is surely the *transmit* mode, in which the energy consumption of the RF amplifier, $E^{(amp)}$ (expressed in Joule/slot), has to be added to the aforementioned contributions. We assume that $E^{(amp)}$ is proportional to both data-unit size and the squared distance between the transmitter and the receiver. Therefore, the total energy consumption in the *transmit* mode, $E^{(TX)}$, is:

$$E_{i,j}^{(TX)} = E^{(radio)} + E^{(elec)} + E_{i,j}^{(amp)} \tag{1}$$

Likewise the approach used in [6], we propose an analytical model of the sensor network, consisting of three building blocks: a sensor model, a network model and an interference model.

3 System Model

In this section, following the same approach as [6], we propose an analytical model of the sensor network, consisting of two building blocks: a sensor model (Section 3.1), and a network model (Section 3.2). In Section 3.3 we will illustrate the iterative procedure, called *Fixed Point Approximation (FPA)*, based on the exchange of parameters between the building blocks in order to obtain a global model. Finally, in Section 3.4 we define some metrics to evaluate network performance.

3.1 Sensor Model

The model of the behavior of a generic sensor is obtained by a discrete-time Markov chain (DTMC), in which the duration of a time slot is assumed to be equal to the time interval needed to transmit a data unit. In order to derive the DTMC we need to introduce some input parameters for the sensor model. Let us indicate:

- p and q, the probabilities that the sensor moves from *active* to *sleep*, and vice versa;
- g, the probability of generating a data unit for sensing activity;
- α, the probability of receiving a data unit from neighbor nodes;
- β, the probability of transmitting a data unit to the next-hop nodes.

Note that $\alpha + \beta \leq 1$ must hold because a transmission and a reception cannot occur simultaneously. The parameters p, q and g are the input of the global model (composition of the three building blocks) and are assumed as identical for all sensor nodes; α and β, on the other hand, are different for each sensor and are estimated by the iterative procedure in Section 3.3. We define the state process of the sensor at the slot n as $S^{(\Sigma)}(n) = \left(S^{(M)}(n), S^{(Q)}(n), S^{(H)}(n), S^{(E)}(n)\right)$, where:

- $S^{(M)}(n) \in \{S, A, R\}$ is the state variable that accounts the sensor operating mode. We consider three operational states: S (the sensor is disconnected from the network: *sleep mode*), A (it can perform all the functions of the *active* mode) and R (it can only relay data units still in the buffer at the end of active period).
- $S^{(Q)}(n) \in \{0,1,\ldots, B_S\}$ is the number of data units in the sensor buffer at the slot n.
- $S^{(H)}(n) \in \{W, F\}$ takes into account the state of the next-hop nodes. If $S^{(H)}(n) = W$ it means that all the next-hop nodes are in the S or R state, and therefore they are not able to receive data units; when $S^{(H)}(n) = F$, on the other hand, at least one next hop is in the A state.
- $S^{(E)}(n) \in \{0,1,\ldots, e\}$ models the energy level in the sensor node battery. When $S^{(E)}(n) = v$, the residual energy of the sensor is in the interval $]\,(v-1)\Delta J, v\Delta J\,]$. Of course, $S^{(E)}(n) = 0$ denotes the death of the sensor. Clearly $e = E_S/\Delta J$.

In order to simplify the model derivation, we initially neglect the state of the next-hop nodes and the state of energy level. Therefore the sensor state is $S^{(M,Q)}(n) = \left(S^{(M)}(n), S^{(Q)}(n)\right)$. Let $s_1^{(M,Q)} \equiv \left(s_1^{(M)}, s_1^{(Q)}\right)$ and $s_2^{(M,Q)} \equiv \left(s_2^{(M)}, s_2^{(Q)}\right)$ be two generic states of $S^{(M,Q)}(n)$. We derive the transition probabilities as follows:

$$P_{n,n+1}\left(s_1^{(M,Q)}, s_2^{(M,Q)}\right) \equiv \text{Prob}\left\{S^{(M,Q)}(n+1) = s_2^{(M,Q)} \,\middle|\, S^{(M,Q)}(n) = s_1^{(M,Q)}\right\} =$$
$$= \begin{cases}
1-q & \left(s_1^{(M,Q)}, s_2^{(M,Q)}\right) = ((S,0),(S,0)) \\
q & \left(s_1^{(M,Q)}, s_2^{(M,Q)}\right) = ((S,0),(A,0)) \\
(1-g)(1-\alpha)p & \left(s_1^{(M,Q)}, s_2^{(M,Q)}\right) = ((A,0),(S,0)) \\
(1-g)(1-\alpha)(1-p) & \left(s_1^{(M,Q)}, s_2^{(M,Q)}\right) = ((A,0),(A,0)) \\
\beta & \left(s_1^{(M,Q)}, s_2^{(M,Q)}\right) = ((R,1),(S,0)) \\
(1-g)\beta p & \left(s_1^{(M,Q)}, s_2^{(M,Q)}\right) = ((A,1),(S,0)) \\
[g(1-\alpha-\beta)+\alpha(1-g)]p & \left(s_1^{(M,Q)}, s_2^{(M,Q)}\right) = ((A,i),(R,i+1)) \quad 0 \leq i < B_S \\
[g(1-\alpha-\beta)+\alpha(1-g)](1-p) & \left(s_1^{(M,Q)}, s_2^{(M,Q)}\right) = ((A,i),(A,i+1)) \quad 0 \leq i < B_S \\
g\alpha p & \left(s_1^{(M,Q)}, s_2^{(M,Q)}\right) = ((A,i),(R,i+2)) \quad 0 \leq i < B_S - 1 \\
g\alpha(1-p) & \left(s_1^{(M,Q)}, s_2^{(M,Q)}\right) = ((A,i),(A,i+2)) \quad 0 \leq i < B_S - 1 \\
\beta & \left(s_1^{(M,Q)}, s_2^{(M,Q)}\right) = ((R,i),(R,i-1)) \quad 1 < i \leq B_S \\
1-\beta & \left(s_1^{(M,Q)}, s_2^{(M,Q)}\right) = ((R,i),(R,i)) \quad 0 < i \leq B_S \\
(1-g)\beta p & \left(s_1^{(M,Q)}, s_2^{(M,Q)}\right) = ((A,i),(R,i-1)) \quad 1 < i \leq B_S \\
(1-g)\beta(1-p) & \left(s_1^{(M,Q)}, s_2^{(M,Q)}\right) = ((A,i),(A,i-1)) \quad 0 < i \leq B_S \\
[\beta g+(1-\alpha-\beta)(1-g)]p & \left(s_1^{(M,Q)}, s_2^{(M,Q)}\right) = ((A,i),(R,i)) \quad 0 < i \leq B_S \\
[\beta g+(1-\alpha-\beta)(1-g)](1-p) & \left(s_1^{(M,Q)}, s_2^{(M,Q)}\right) = ((A,i),(A,i)) \quad 0 < i \leq B_S
\end{cases} \tag{2}$$

Now we introduce the state variable $S^{(H)}(n)$ to take into consideration the state of next-hop nodes. To this end we need to consider two new parameters, w and f, defined as the transition probabilities from F to W, and vice versa. Again, w and f are different for each sensor and are calculated by using the iterative procedure shown in Section 3.3. Let $s_1^{(M,Q,H)} \equiv (s_1^{(M,Q)}, s_1^{(H)})$ and $s_2^{(M,Q,H)} \equiv (s_2^{(M,Q)}, s_2^{(H)})$ be two generic states of the state process $S^{(M,Q,H)}(n) = \left(S^{(M,Q)}(n), S^{(H)}(n)\right)$.

The transition probabilities related to $S^{(M,Q,H)}(n)$ can be obtained as follows:

$$P_{n,n+1}\left(s_1^{(M,Q,H)}, s_2^{(M,Q,H)}\right) \equiv \text{Prob}\left\{S^{(M,Q,H)}(n+1) = s_2^{(M,Q,H)} \middle| S^{(M,Q,H)}(n) = s_1^{(M,Q,H)}\right\} = $$
$$= P_{n,n+1}\left(s_1^{(M,Q)}, s_2^{(M,Q)}\right) \cdot \begin{cases} 1-f & \text{if } s_1^{(H)} = W \text{ and } s_2^{(H)} = W \\ f & \text{if } s_1^{(H)} = W \text{ and } s_2^{(H)} = F \\ 1-w & \text{if } s_1^{(H)} = F \text{ and } s_2^{(H)} = F \\ w & \text{if } s_1^{(H)} = F \text{ and } s_2^{(H)} = W \end{cases} \tag{3}$$

In order to correctly evaluate the transition probabilities in (3), when $S_1^{(H)}(n) = W$ we have to substitute $\beta = 0$ in (2). Finally, we complete the derivation of the DTMC related to the whole space state $S^{(\Sigma)}(n)$, by introducing the state variable $S^{(E)}(n)$ which models the energy level in the sensor node battery. Let $s_1^{(\Sigma)} = (s_1^{(P,Q,H)}, s_1^{(E)})$ and $s_2^{(\Sigma)} = (s_2^{(P,Q,H)}, s_2^{(E)})$ be two generic states of the process $S^{\Sigma}(n)$. The transition probabilities related to the complete Markov chain can be obtained as follows:

$$\begin{aligned} P_{n,n+1}\left(s_1^{(\Sigma)}, s_2^{(\Sigma)}\right) &\equiv \text{Prob}\left\{S^{(\Sigma)}(n+1) = s_2^{(\Sigma)} \middle| S^{(\Sigma)}(n) = s_1^{(\Sigma)}\right\} = \\ &= P_{n,n+1}\left(s_1^{(M,Q,H)}, s_2^{(M,Q,H)}\right) \cdot M_{[s_1^E, s_2^E]}\left(s_1^{(M,Q,H)}, s_2^{(M,Q,H)}\right) \end{aligned} \tag{4}$$

where $M_{[h,k]}\left(s_1^{(M,Q,H)}, s_2^{(M,Q,H)}\right)$ denotes the probability that the battery energy moves from level h to level k when $S^{(M,Q,H)}(n)$ transits from $s_1^{(M,Q,H)}$ to $s_2^{(M,Q,H)}$. In order to evaluate $M_{[h,k]}$ we need to consider the energy cost $C\left(s_1^{(M,Q,H)}, s_2^{(M,Q,H)}\right)$ associated with each transition from $s_1^{(M,Q,H)}$ to $s_2^{(M,Q,H)}$. This cost is independent of the next-hop state $S^H(n)$, and can be calculated on the basis of the considerations in Section 2:

$$C\left(s_1^{(M,Q,H)}, s_2^{(M,Q,H)}\right) = C\left(s_1^{(M,Q)}, s_2^{(M,Q)}\right) =$$
$$= \begin{cases} E^{(sleep)} & \left(s_1^{(M,Q)}, s_2^{(M,Q)}\right) \in \{((S,0),(S,0))\} \\ E_T + E^{(sleep)} & \left(s_1^{(M,Q)}, s_2^{(M,Q)}\right) \in \{((S,0),(A,0))\} \\ E^{(radio)} & \left(s_1^{(M,Q)}, s_2^{(M,Q)}\right) \in \left\{\begin{matrix} ((A,0),(S,0)); \quad ((A,i),(A,i)) \quad 0 \le i \le B_S; \\ ((R,i),(R,i)) \quad 1 \le i \le B_S; \\ ((A,i),(R,i)) \quad 1 \le i \le B_S \end{matrix}\right\} \\ \left(E^{(elec)} + E^{(radio)}\right)\alpha(1-g) & \left(s_1^{(M,Q)}, s_2^{(M,Q)}\right) \in \left\{\begin{matrix} ((A,i),(A,i+1)) \quad 0 \le i < B_S; \\ ((A,i),(R,i+1)) \quad 0 \le i < B_S \end{matrix}\right\} \\ E^{(elec)} + E^{(radio)} & \left(s_1^{(M,Q)}, s_2^{(M,Q)}\right) \in \left\{\begin{matrix} ((A,i),(A,i+2)) \quad 0 \le i < B_S - 1; \\ ((A,i),(R,i+2)) \quad 0 \le i < B_S - 1 \end{matrix}\right\} \\ E^{(elec)} + E^{(radio)} + \overline{E}^{(amp)} & \left(s_1^{(M,Q)}, s_2^{(M,Q)}\right) \in \left\{\begin{matrix} ((A,1),(S,0)); \quad ((A,i),(A,i-1)) \quad 1 \le i \le B_S; \\ ((A,i),(R,i-1)) \quad 2 \le i \le B_S; \\ ((R,1),(S,0)); \quad ((R,i),(R,i-1)) \quad 2 \le i \le B_S \end{matrix}\right\} \end{cases} \tag{5}$$

Let us note that in the last row of (5) we consider the average energy spent in the sensor amplifier on transmission to a generic next-hop node. This is not a severe approximation because the distance distribution between a sensor and its next-hop nodes generally has a low variance, and therefore can be considered as constant.

Let $E_h = \Delta J \cdot (h-1)$, where $1 \leq h \leq e$, be the energy values representing the thresholds dividing the total energy into different states. The elements of the matrix $M_{[h,k]}$ for each transition from $s_1^{(M,Q,H)}$ to $s_2^{(M,Q,H)}$ are:

$$M_{h,k}\left(s_1^{(M,Q,H)}, s_2^{(M,Q,H)}\right) = \begin{cases} \dfrac{E_{h+1} - C\left(s_1^{(M,Q)}, s_2^{(M,Q)}\right) - E_k}{\Delta J} & E_h \leq E_k + C\left(s_1^{(M,Q)}, s_2^{(M,Q)}\right) \leq E_{h+1} \quad h \neq 0, k \neq 0 \\ \dfrac{E_{k+1} + C\left(s_1^{(M,Q)}, s_2^{(M,Q)}\right) - E_h}{\Delta J} & E_h \leq E_{k+1} + C\left(s_1^{(M,Q)}, s_2^{(M,Q)}\right) \leq E_{h+1} \quad h \neq 0, k \neq 0 \\ 1 - \sum_{\forall k \neq 0} M_{h,k} C\left(s_1^{(M,Q)}, s_2^{(M,Q)}\right) & h \neq 0, k = 0 \\ 1 & h = 0, k = 0 \\ 0 & \text{otherwise} \end{cases} \quad (6)$$

Equation (6) completes the derivation of the transition probability matrix of the DTMC associated with the state process $S^{(\Sigma)}(n)$. If we indicate the state probabilities as π^{Σ} (we omit the dependence of time slot n in order to simplify the notation), we can easily obtain some useful parameters that we need for further derivations. More specifically we will consider:

- the probability that the sensor is in the S, R, A or D (*dead*) state in a time-slot:

$$\pi_S = \sum_{j=1}^{e} \left(\pi^{S,0,W,j} + \pi^{S,0,F,j}\right) \qquad \pi_R = \sum_{i=1}^{B_S} \sum_{j=1}^{e} \left(\pi^{R,i,W,j} + \pi^{R,i,F,j}\right)$$
$$\pi_A = \sum_{i=0}^{B_S} \sum_{j=1}^{e} \left(\pi^{A,i,W,j} + \pi^{A,i,F,j}\right) \quad (7)$$

$$\pi_D = \sum_{i=0}^{B_S} \left(\pi^{S,i,W,0} + \pi^{S,i,F,0} + \pi^{R,i,W,0} + \pi^{R,i,F,0} + \pi^{A,i,W,0} + \pi^{A,i,F,0}\right) \quad (8)$$

- the average number of data units generated in a time slot (*generation rate*):

$$\Lambda_G = g \cdot \pi_A \quad (9)$$

- the average number of data units transmitted in a time slot (*throughput*):

$$T = \sum_{i=1}^{B_S} \sum_{j=1}^{e} \left(\pi^{A,i,F,j} \cdot (1-\alpha) + \pi^{R,i,F,j}\right)\beta \quad (10)$$

- the average number of data units in the buffer in a time slot:

$$B = \sum_{i=1}^{B_S} i \sum_{j=1}^{e} \left(\pi^{R,i,W,j} + \pi^{R,i,F,j} + \pi^{A,i,W,j} + \pi^{A,i,F,j}\right) \quad (11)$$

- the average number of data units lost in a time slot:

$$\Lambda_L = \sum_{j=1}^{e} \left[g\alpha\left(\pi^{A,B_S-1,W,j} + \pi^{A,B_S-1,F,j}\right) + (g\alpha + b)\left(\pi^{A,B_S,W,j} + \pi^{A,B_S,F,j}\right)\right] \tag{12}$$

In following we will add a superscript to distinguish between the output parameters relating to each sensor in the network. The superscript 0 will refer to the sink.

3.2 Network Model

In this section, given the output parameters of the sensor model for each node, we compute the throughput for all the sensors from the point of view of the entire network, seen as an open queueing network. The network throughput may be estimated as follows:

$$\underline{T} = \underline{T} \cdot \mathbf{Z} + \underline{\Lambda}_G - \underline{\Lambda}_L \tag{13}$$

where $\underline{T}$ is a row vector containing the network throughput for each sensor, while $\underline{\Lambda}_G$ and $\underline{\Lambda}_L$ are row vectors containing the corresponding output parameters of the sensor model for each node. Finally, the matrix **Z** contains the percentages of traffic that a sensor sends to its next-hop nodes. We have:

$$z_{i,j} = K\pi_A^j \prod_{m \in H(i,j)} \left(\pi_S^m + \pi_R^m + \pi_D^m\right) \qquad 1 \le i \le N; \quad 0 \le j \le N \tag{14}$$

where K is a normalization constant such that the sum of each row in **Z** is equal to 1, and $H(i, j)$ is the set of next-hop nodes for sensor i with a greater priority than the next-hop j.

The output parameters of the network model are the transmission rates $\lambda_{i,j}$, i.e. the traffic from node i destined to node j. They can be calculated as follows:

$$\lambda_{i,j} = T_i \cdot z_{i,j} \qquad 1 \le i \le N; \quad 0 \le j \le N \tag{15}$$

3.3 Iterative Algorithm

In order to analyze the evolution of a sensor network from a given initial condition until the energy resources of all the sensor nodes run out, we have to estimate the state distribution of each sensor at each time slot. From the Markov theory we have:

$$\underline{\Pi}^{(i)}(n+1) = \underline{\Pi}^{(i)}(n) \cdot P_{n,n+1}^{(i)} \qquad \forall n > 0 \quad 1 \le i \le N \tag{16}$$

where $\underline{\Pi}^{(i)}(n)$ is the vector containing all the state probabilities of sensor i in slot n and $P_{n,n+1}^{(i)}$ is the unknown transition probability matrix of the sensor i between the slots n and $n+1$.

Given the initial distribution $\underline{\Pi}^{(i)}(0)$, where $1 \le i \le N$, we have to estimate the unknown parameters α, β, w and f of the transition matrix for each sensor.

If we assume the state distribution at slot n to be known, the matrix $P^{(i)}_{n,n+1}$, where $1 \le i \le N$, is estimated by an iterative procedure consisting of the following steps:

1. Set the following initial values for the unknown parameters for all the nodes: $w(n)=0$, $f(n)=1$, $\alpha(n)=0$ and $\beta(n)=1$;
2. Solve the network model, obtaining the transmission rates: $\lambda_{i,j}(n)$;
3. Solve the interference model, obtaining the parameters $\beta^{(i)}(n)$, $1 \le i \le N$, as in [6];
4. Estimate the transition probabilities of the next-hop state as follows:

$$\pi^i_W(n) = \prod_{k\in H(i)} \left(\pi^k_S(n) + \pi^k_R(n) + \pi^k_D(n)\right) \qquad 1 \le i \le N$$

$$f^{(i)}(n) = 1 - \prod_{k\in H(i)} \left(1 - p\frac{\pi^k_A(n)}{\pi^k_S(n) + \pi^k_R(n) + \pi^k_D(n)}\right) \qquad 1 \le i \le N$$

$$w^{(i)}(n) = f^{(i)}(n)\frac{\pi^i_W(n)}{1-\pi^i_W(n)} \qquad 1 \le i \le N$$

5. Solve the sensor model for each node by using the updated values of the parameters. Note that to this end evaluation of the parameters $\alpha^{(i)}(n)$ is needed. They are calculated by an internal loop in the sensor model in which the parameter α is set so that the throughput computed from the sensor model and those estimated from the network model are equal.
6. If the infinite norm of the difference between two successive estimates of the network throughput is over a given threshold T, we go back to step 2, otherwise we exit the procedure.

3.4 Transient Network Analysis

To analyze the temporal evolution of the network we use the following metrics:

- Network capacity, i.e. the number of data units received by the sink in a time slot:

$$C(n) = \sum_{i=1}^{N} \left(\Lambda^i_E(n) - \Lambda^i_L(n)\right) = T^0(n) \tag{17}$$

- Average delivery delay, i.e. the average number of time slots required to deliver a data unit to the sink:

$$D(n) = \frac{1}{C(n)} \sum_{i=1}^{N} B^i(n) \tag{18}$$

- Network energy consumption per time slot, i.e. the energy spent by the entire network in a time slot:

$$E(n) = \sum_{i=1}^{N} \left[\pi^i_S(n)\left(E^{(sleep)} + qE_T\right) + \left(\pi^i_R + \pi^i_A\right)E^{(radio)} + T^i(n) \sum_{j\in H(i)} E(i,j) z_{i,j}(n) \right] \tag{19}$$

where $E(i,j) = 2E^{(elec)} + E^{(amp)}_{i,j}$

- Probability that the lifetime of the sensor is n slots (to simplify the notation we have not indicated the sensor index):

$$
\begin{aligned}
l(n) &= \Pr\left\{S^{(E)}(n) \neq 0, S^{(E)}(n+1)=0\right\}= \\
&= \sum_{\forall s_1^{(M,Q,H)}} \sum_{\forall s_2^{(M,Q,H)}} \sum_{\forall s_1^{E}\neq 0} \Pr\left\{S^{(\Sigma)}(n+1)=\left(s_2^{(M,Q,H)},0\right) \middle| S^{(\Sigma)}(n)=\left(s_1^{(M,Q,H)}, s_1^{(E)}\right)\right\}\cdot \Pr\left\{S^{(\Sigma)}(n)=\right. \\
&= \sum_{\forall s_1^{(M,Q,H)}} \sum_{\forall s_2^{(M,Q,H)}} \sum_{\forall s_1^{E}\neq 0} P^{\Sigma}_{n,n+1}\left(s_1^{(\Sigma)}, (s_2^{(M,Q,H)},0)\right)\cdot \pi^{s_1^M, s_1^Q, s_1^H, s_1^E}(n)
\end{aligned}
\tag{20}
$$

4 Numerical Results

In this section we apply the proposed model to analyze the transient evolution of a sensor network in a case study. We consider a network topology in which the sensor distribution is defined as follows: 100 sensors are located on 5 concentric rings with the sink at the center. Each ring contains the same number of sensors, equally spaced out and symmetrically located in such a way that all the sensors on the same ring have the same statistical behavior. The input parameters we used are: $r = 25\text{m}$, $M = 5$, $p = 0.1$, $q = 0.1$, $B_S = 2$, $E^{(radio)} = 0.25$ mJ/slot, $E^{(sleep)} = 500$ nJ/slot, $E_T = 0.5$ mJ, $e^{(elec)} = 50$ nJ/(bit·slot), $e^{(amp)} = 100$ pJ/(bit·m^2·slot), $K = 4000$ bit, $E_S = 1$ J, $\Delta J = 20$ mJ.

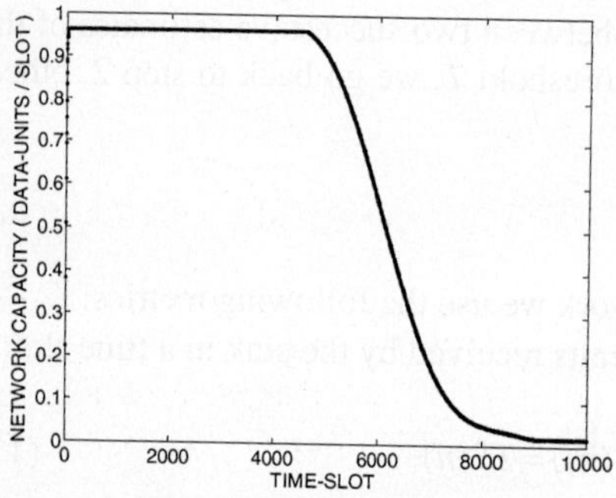

Fig. 1. Network capacity

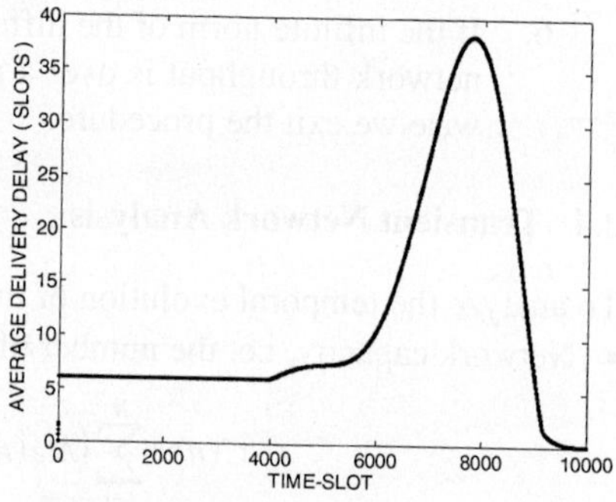

Fig. 2. Average network delivery delay

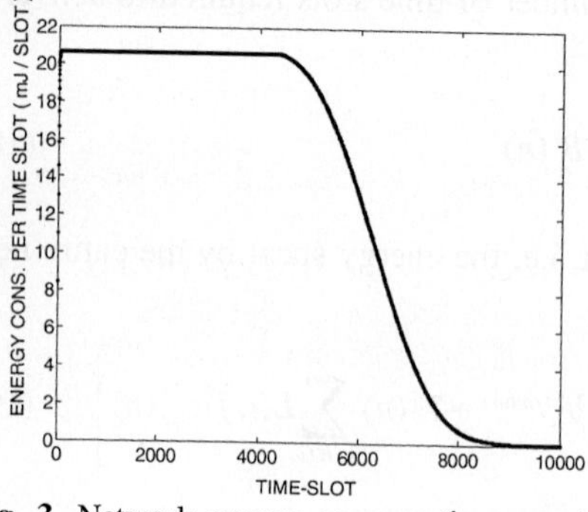

Fig. 3. Network energy consumption per time slot

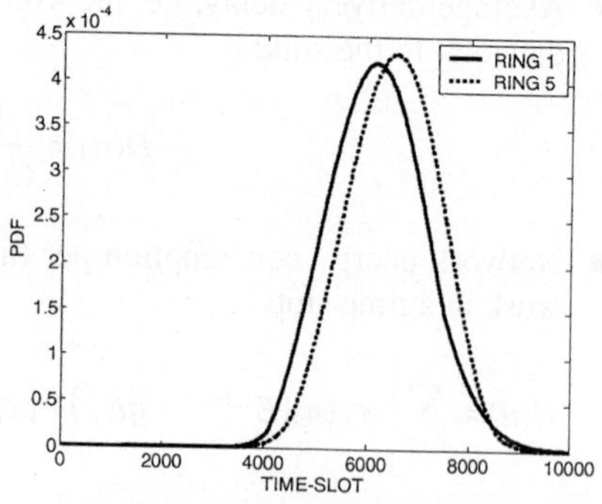

Fig. 4. Sensor lifetime pdf

In Figs. 1 – 4 we show the temporal trend of network capacity, average network delivery delay and network energy consumption per time slot, respectively. These metrics allow us to establish the time interval in which network performance is acceptable, i.e. when it meets some given constraints. We observe that, for a given period of time, in this case equal to 4600 slots, the network presents steady behavior. The bell-shaped trend in Fig. 2 is the result of two opposite phenomena: the inverse dependence between capacity and delay, and the direct dependence between buffer occupancy and capacity. In Fig. 4 the probability distribution of sensor life is presented, comparing that of the sensors in the ring closest to the sink (ring 1), with that of the sensors belonging to the farthest ring (ring 5). Note that sensors closer to the sink spend more energy to relay packets from other nodes, so their lifetime is shorter.

5 Conclusions

The paper proposes an analytical framework to evaluate the transient behavior of a sensor network in which sensors implement the energy-saving technique of idle/active states. With respect to previous literature, the proposed model is, to the best of our knowledge, the first analytical model which allows us to evaluate the battery lifetime of each sensor, and specifically the distribution of the lifetime of all the sensors in the network. Moreover network capacity, average delivery delay, network energy consumption, and distribution of the number of live sensors at a given instant, are defined and analytically derived in a case study.

References

1. Das, B., Bharghavan, V.: Routing in Ad-Hoc Networks Using Minimum Connected Dominating Sets. In Proc. of ICC, 1997.
2. Heinzelman, W. R., Chandrakasan, A., Balakrishnan, H.: Energy-Efficient Communication Protocol for Wireless Microsensor Networks. In Proc. of IEEE HICSS, January 2000.
3. Perrig, A., Szewczyk, R.. Wen, V., Tygar, J. D.: SPINS: Security protocols for Sensor Networks. In Proc of 7th Annual International Conf. on Mobile computing and Networking, 2001.
4. Gupta, P., Kumar, P. R.: The Capacity of Wireless Networks. IEEE Trans. on Information Theory, vol. 46, Mar. 2000.
5. Mini, A. F. et al.: A Probabilistic Approach to Predict the Energy Consumption in Wireless Sensor Networks. In Proc of 4th Workshop de Comunicao sem Fio, So Paulo, Brazil, Oct. 2002.
6. Chiasserini, C.F., Garetto, M.: Modeling the Performance of Wireless Sensor Networks. In Proc. IEEE INFOCOM 2004, Hong Kong, March 7-11, 2004.
7. Sinha, A., Chandrakasan, A. P.: Dynamic Power Management in Wireless Sensor Networks. IEEE Design and Test of Computers Magazine, Vol. 18, No. 2, Mar.-Apr. 2001.
8. Gribaudo, M. et al.: A Spatial Fluid-based Framework to Analyze Large-scale Wireless Sensor Networks. In Proc of DNS 2005, Yokoama, Japan, June 2005.

Power-Efficient Seamless Publishing and Subscribing in Wireless Sensor Networks

Junseok Park[1], Yeonghwan Tscha[2], and Kyoon-Ha Lee[3]

[1] Smart Interface Research Team, Post-PC Research Group, ETRI,
Daejeon 305-350, Korea
parkjs@etri.re.kr

[2] Department of Computer Engineering, Sangji University,
Wonju, Kangwon 220-702, Korea
yhtscha@sangji.ac.kr

[3] Department of Computer Engineering, Inha University,
Incheon 402-751, Korea
khlee@inha.ac.kr

Abstract. Query slipping may happen when a query propagating along a subscribe trajectory moves through a publish trajectory without obtaining desired information, even though two trajectories intersect geometrically. It can result in considerable time delay and in the worst, looping in the trajectory or query flooding the network causing inefficient power consumption and bandwidth utilization because it follows by resubmission of the query or initiation of another subscribe trajectory. In this paper, we consider the trajectory construction for power-efficient *seamless publishing/subscribing* in a multihop wireless sensor network. We address the problem by dividing each radio cell into smaller virtual grids. For the seamless trajectory development, we propose a grid-based next-hop selection algorithm. Our algorithm not only attempts to make the trajectory straight but also considers the nodal density of recipient nodes and the seamless grid-by-grid multicast. Simulation results turns out that our algorithm dissipates significantly less power, compared to the non grid-based method, as greedy forwarding.

1 Introduction

Portable computers and wireless technologies make feasible the implementation of small-sized intelligent sensor nodes [1]. We now witness a rush toward wireless sensor networks of several hundreds or thousands of nodes [5,9,10]. The networks are usually characterized by high nodal density, functionally/physically duplicated nodes, and infrastructure-less architecture. Power saving is essential in such networks to prolong the lifetime of the network, as they will be deployed using battery-powered nodes. An efficient message dissemination is one of fundamental issues on wireless sensor networks [9,12]. *Trajectory* paradigm [2,13,14,15] is worthy of giving attention for efficient data acquisition and dissemination in wireless sensor networks.

In contrast to the strict quorum system [7], the paradigm does *not* require the explicit membership management and *decouples* the trajectory itself from the address-centric nature of the conventional path. This is very important because nodes in

P. Yolum et al.(Eds.): ISCIS 2005, LNCS 3733, pp. 94 – 102, 2005.

wireless sensor networks may go into doze-mode, fail or move occasionally. In *trajectory* paradigms, the trajectory usually progresses in some *direction* without any particular destination in mind. A source or server *publishes* or *updates*, perhaps periodically, information contents or available service list along a path called *publish* trajectory, while a sink or destination attempts to access it by propagating a *query* about its interests through a *subscribe* trajectory. *Matchmaking* usually takes place at the nodes where two trajectories intersect in common. Unfortunately *query slipping* can occur when a query propagating along a subscribe trajectory moves through a publish trajectory without obtaining desired information, even though two trajectories intersect geometrically[1]. Query slipping results in considerable time delay and in the worst, looping within the trajectory or query flooding over the network causing inefficient power consumption and bandwidth utilization because it follows by resubmission of the query or initiation of another subscribe trajectory.

In this paper, we address the problem and suggest a solution for seamless storing/propagation of update and query messages along the trajectory. The remainder of this is organized as follows. In Section 2, we define the trajectory slipping problem. Section 3 defines the network model that we adopt, and grid index is introduced to embed various-sized grids within a cell. Section 4 concentrates on a grid-based next-hop selection algorithm that exploits a geographic grid-by-grid multicast. In Section 5, the power-saving ratios are given for the performance evaluation. Finally, we conclude our work and describe future work in Section 6.

2 Trajectory Slipping Problem

Even though two trajectories intersect geometrically, there exists a *non-zero* possibility that they do not possess commonly interesting nodes in the overlapped space.

Definition 1: Given a trajectory T, nodes associated with it are as follows: 1) a node v explicitly chosen by some next-hop selection, i.e. packet forwarding algorithm, is said to be *repository node*; 2) a node u which is not repository but adjacent to a repository node v is said to be *quasi-repository* if it possesses publish/subscribe information, for instance, by overhearing advertising/subscribing packets to and from the repository nodes or other messaging with the repository nodes; 3) repository node v and quasi-repository node u are *quorums*; 4) any non-quorum node w that resides in a cell defined by a repository node v is *quorum hole*.

Similar to *pseudo-quorum* [2], in this paper, the term "quorum" means any network node that has some advertising or subscribing message required for the trajectory-based matchmaking.

There are three cases, as in Fig. 1, when T_P and T_S intersect. Matchmaking succeeds in both cases of a) and b), while it does not for case c). *Query slipping* occurs if some query along a subscribe trajectory T_S moves through quorum holes made by a

---

[1] Given two straight line segments respectively connecting each pair of two nodes given by their positions, i.e., (x,y)-coordinate values, we can easily verify whether such segments geometrically intersect or not in Euclidian plane using some well-known algorithm in computational geometry area, see [12], for instance.

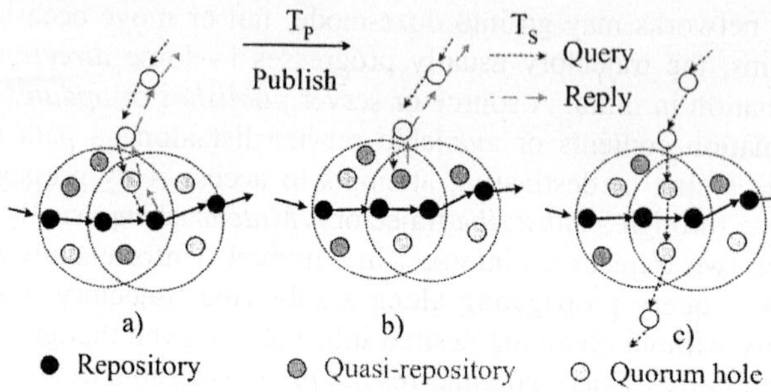

Fig. 1. Matchmaking and query along the route

publish trajectory T_P without obtaining its desired information, provided that T_P and T_S intersect geometrically. In case c), it usually follows by resubmission of the query message or initiation of another subscribe trajectory. Thus, query slipping may result in unnecessary time delay and in the worst, looping within the trajectory or query flooding over the network causing inefficient power consumption and bandwidth utilization.

We address the problem by dividing each radio cell into smaller virtual grids. For the seamless trajectory development, we propose a grid-based next-hop selection algorithm that initially considers the grids horizontally intersecting the line in the direction. Additionally, it regards the adjacent ones depending on the nodal density and the criteria needed to store the publishing/subscribing message seamlessly.

3 Virtual Grid Model and Grid Index

As shown in Fig. 2 a), we logically partition each radio cell of radius R(m) into $(2k_0+1)\times(2k_0+1)$ virtual grids according to (1) where, each grid is a square of $r\times r$(m) and $k_0\geq 0$.

$$(k_0 r+r/2)^2 + (k_0 r+r/2)^2 \leq R^2 \,. \tag{1}$$

Definition 2: Denote by $g(p,q)$ a grid whose (x,y)-coordinate value is (p,q) in Euclidian plane represented by virtual grids as Fig. 2 b). Given $g(s,t)$ and $g(e,f)$, let $d = max\{|s-e|_a,|t-f|_a\}$ where, $s,e,t,f\geq 0$, $|A|_a$ denotes the absolute value of integer A, and $max\{U,V\}$ means U if $U\geq V$ and V otherwise. Then, we say that $g(s,t)$ and $g(e,f)$ are *d-distanced* each other.

Fig. 2 a) shows embedding of various-sized grids within a cell where, k_0=1,2,3. We call k_0 grid index, as it determines the size of the grid and finally, the number of grids per cell. Note that the grid index is a tunable parameter. For instance, it may be used to create many small grids for the dense networks or a few large grids for the sparse networks. It also closely relates to the length of a nominal radius R of a cell.

We assume that every node in the network is aware of its own geographic position, and using some link-level protocol, a node exchanges its grid id with its 1-hop neighbors, i.e. up to k_0-distanced nodes. For instance, grids $g(2,2)$ and $g(5,1)$ are 3-distanced and are neighbors for k_0=3, but not neighbors for k_0=2.

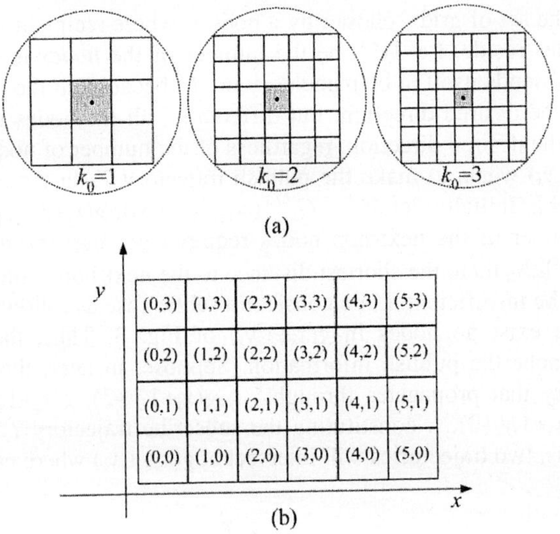

Fig. 2. Virtual Grid Model

In this paper, we consider the cross-shaped trajectory [2,13,14,15] for its simplicity and favorable success rate in matchmaking. We assume that the trajectory always makes it possible to progress toward four directions: East, West, North, and South.

This implies that there exists at least one node in $k_0 \times (2k_0+1)$(=rows×columns) grids laid in the direction of the trajectory progress. Even though the grid index k_0 is tunable at the network level, it solely can not accommodate the dynamic situation such as node failure or congestion in the sensor networks. Depending on the nodal-density, the recipient nodes may also distribute over several grids. Thereby, we deploy multicasting for the development of the trajectory.

4 Grid-Based Next-Hop Selection Using Multicast

Considering the density of the sensor networks, we ignore the position of the originating node and try to keep the trajectory close to the straight line in the desired direction, as in [2,15]. However, the nodal density-awareness and grid-based multicasting are exploited for the sensor networks to be free from the query slipping. Careful consideration is also made to guarantee the seamless storing/propagating of the publishing/subscribing messages.

Definition 3: Suppose that a node s in a grid $g(x_s,y_s)$ develops its trajectory in some direction d. Then, a set of k_0 grids which intersect the line segment to d from s is said to be *default repository set* G_s^d such that $G_s^{East} = \{g(x_s+1,y_s), g(x_s+2,y_s), \ldots, g(x_s+k_0,y_s)\}$, $G_s^{West} = \{g(x_s-1,y_s), g(x_s-2,y_s), \ldots, g(x_s-k_0,y_s)\}$, $G_s^{North} = \{g(x_s,y_s+1\}$, $g(x_s,y_s+2), \ldots, g(x_s,y_s+k_0)\}$, $G_s^{South} = \{g(x_s,y_s-1), g(x_s,y_s-2), \ldots, g(x_s,y_s-k_0)\}$ for each direction respectively, where k_0 is the grid index.

Let M_s^g denote the set of grids, chosen by a node s, where recipient nodes, i.e. the set of next-hop nodes reside. Let $|M_s^g|$ be the number of the *nodes* in M_s^g. The default repository set G_s^d lends itself to be mandatory in M_s^g because all the grids in G_s^d intersect the line in the desired direction. Put differently, all the nodes in G_s^d lay on the shortest path to the desired direction, regardless of the number of nodes in it. Suppose a node s in $g(x_s,y_s)$ wants to make the publish trajectory T_P in the east, as shown in Fig. 3 where, k_0=2. Initially, let $M_s^g = G_s^{East}(=\{g(x_s+1,y_s), g(x_s+2,y_s)\})$. Denote by N_0 the minimal number of the next-hop nodes required per hop in order to develop a trajectory. If $|M_s^g|\geq N_0$ then, the shortest distance to the next-hop could be made. However, this would be insufficient. Let's consider a subtle case as follows.

Assume there exist no nodes in $g(x_s+1,y_s)$ of Fig. 3. Thus, the nodes only in $g(x_s+2,y_s)$ will cache the publish information. Suppose, in later, there follows some subscribing query that propagates through …, $g(x_s+1,y_s-2)$, $g(x_s+1,y_s-1)$, $g(x_s+1,y_s)$, $g(x_s+1,y_s+1)$, $g(x_s+1,y_s+2)$,… constituting the subscribe trajectory T_S in the direction of the north. Thus, two trajectories will intersect at $g(x_s+1,y_s)$ where no nodes reside.

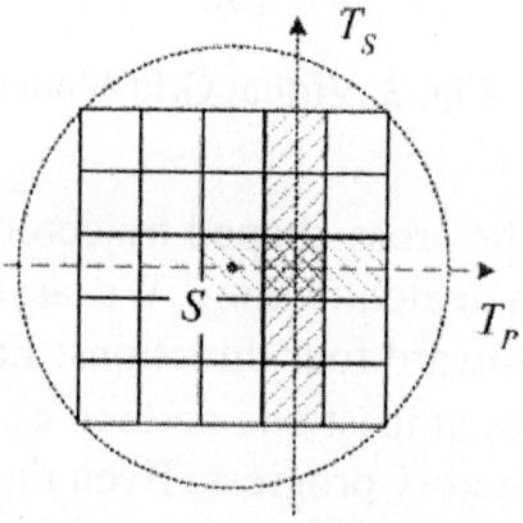

Fig. 3. Intersecting grid where no nodes reside

The query slipping will occur unless other node in the grids along T_S keeps the publish message. To exclude this uncertainty, we are required to add $g(x_s+1,y_s+1)$ to M_s^g, since $g(x_s+1,y_s)$ is empty, i.e. $|g(x_s+1,y_s)|=0$. Next turn may be $g(x_s+1,y_s-1)$ if $g(x_s+1,y_s+1)$ is empty. The similar argument will go on (x_s+1,y_s-2), $g(x_s+1,y_s+2)$, …, and so on. There exist two questions: one is about the maximum number of iterations needed for applying such procedure and the other is the naming of the set of recipient grids M_s^g. Answer to the former comes from $k_0\times(2k_0+1)$ grids given by the assumption on the trajectory development in the previous section. Our naming scheme always identifies the minimal rectangle or square comprising the desired grids including their neighbors, if necessary. To cope with these requirements, we introduce the definition of *i*-distance left/right set, as follows.

Definition 4: Given G_s^d, its i-distance left/right set $G_s^d(i,l)/G_s^d(i,r)$ is given as follows for each direction: $G_s^{East}(i,l)/G_s^{East}(i,r) = \{g(x_s+1,y_s+/-i), g(x_s+2,y_s+/-i), …, g(x_s+k_0,y_s+/-i)\}$, $G_s^{West}(i,l)/G_s^{West}(i,r) = \{g(x_s-1,y_s-/+i), g(x_s-2,y_s-/+i), …, g(x_s-k_0,y_s-/+i)\}$, $G_s^{Noth}(i,l)/G_s^{North}(i,r) = \{g(x_s-/+i,y_s+1), g(x_s-/+i,y_s+2), …, g(x_s-/+i,y_s+k_0)\}$, $G_s^{South}(i,l)/G_s^{South}(i,r) = \{g(x_s+/-i,y_s-1), g(x_s+/-i,y_s-2), …, g(x_s+/-i,y_s-k_0)\}$ where, $i\in\{1, 2, .., k_0\}$.

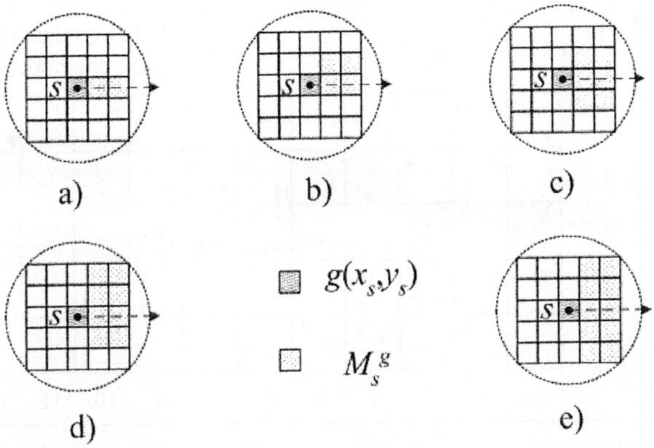

Fig. 4. Grid-based next-hop selection using *i*-distance left/right set

Given Fig. 4 a), if either $g(x_s+1,y_s)$ or $g(x_s+2,y_s)$ in the default repository set, G_s^{East}, is empty then, its 1-distance left node set, $G_s^{East}(i,l)$ (=$\{g(x_s+1,y_s+1), g(x_s+2,y_s+1)\}$), is firstly added to M_s^g as in b). Now, if $|M_s^g|\geq N_0$ and each row in M_s^g has at least one node then, all nodes in M_s^g become the next-hop nodes. If not, we add the 1-distance right set, $G_s^{East}(i,r)$ (=$\{g(x_s+1,y_s-1),g(x_s+2,y_s-1)\}$), as shown in c). If the updated M_s^g still does not satisfy the termination conditions below, additional steps will follow until $i=k_0$(=2 in this example), as in d) and e).

At last, nodes in the final M_s^g will be the next-hop of the trajectory *s*. And one of them, farther away from the current node, *s*, and is closest to the line in the direction is assigned to the *backbone* node n_s. The node is responsible for finding the succeeding next-hop nodes and multicasting the publishing and subscribing message. *Termination condition set of the next-hop selection* is as follows: 1) if $|M_s^g|\geq N_0$ and 2) either $i=k_0$ for $G_s^d(i,r)$ or every row in M_s^g contains at least one node.

Fig. 5 shows an example of the trajectory setup by the algorithm depicted in Fig. 4. Given N_0=2, at least, two nodes per hop are required to find M_s^g, and the 2-distanced grids are reachable at most by each n_s.

Initiating node X is in $g(2,2)$ and the trajectory goes for the eastward thus, we have $G_X^{East}=\{g(3,2),g(4,2)\}$. Because all grids in G_X^{East} have nodes and $|G_X^{East}|(=4) > N_0(=2)$, the first hop is finished. Note that all the nodes in the default repository grid set become the next-hop nodes regardless of how many are in it. Let's assume n_X=D, the farthest from X, even there are B, C, D in $g(4,2)$. As D is in $g(4,2)$, it follows $M_D^g = G_D^{East} = \{g(5,2),g(6,2)\}$. Since $|g(5,2)|=0$, the 1-distance left set, $G_D^{East}(1,l)(=\{g(5,3), g(6,3)\})$, is added to M_D^g. Now, M_D^g becomes $\{g(5,2),g(6,2),g(5,3),g(6,3)\}$ and $|M_D^g|=N_0(=2)$ such that each row in the direction of the trajectory of M_D^g has node E and F, respectively. The second hop halts and C_D^g, the name of M_D^g, is given by <(5,2),(6,3)>. Similar argument is also applicable to the rest hops. For *M*, initially, $M_M^g = G_M^{East}$ (=$\{g(9,2),g(10,2)\}$), and $|M_M^g|=N_0(=2)$ but, $g(10,2)$ is empty. Hence, $G_M^{East}(1,l)$ (=$\{g(9,3),g(10,3)\}$) is added to M_M^g. In case of node P, $|G_P^{East}|$ = $|\{g(11,3),g(12,3)\}|$ = 0 thus, $G_P^{East}(1,l)$ = $\{g(11,4),g(12,4)\}$, and $G_P^{East}(1,r)$ = $\{g(11,2),g(12,2)\}$ is added. Making M_P^g = $\{g(11,2), g(12,2), g(11,3), g(12,3), g(11,4), g(12,4)\}$ and $|M_P^g|=2(=N_0)$, it follows n_P= R, the destination.

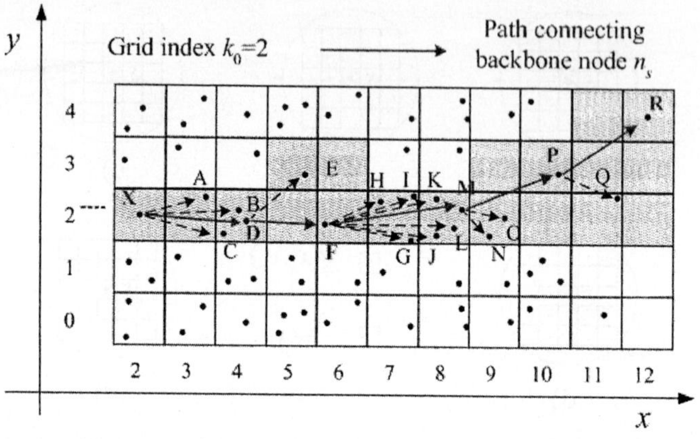

Fig. 5. Trajectory setup example

5 Experimental Performance Results

Consider the nodes which are residing in the grids under the radio umbrella defined by each backbone node n_s, but not chosen as the next-hop in the trajectory. And let them go periodically to 'sleeping' state for power-saving. We don't want to repeat the state-transition diagram or procedure for such a typical power-saving mode. Readers may refer to [16] for more detail.

Assuming the uniform distribution of nodes, a server or client that deploys our next-hop selection algorithm given in this paper for the establishment of the *cross-shaped* trajectory occupies $4k_0+1$ grids in the best case and $(2k_0+1)\times(2k_0+1)$ grids in the worst. Non grid-based protocols, such as greedy forwarding[12] or MFR[9], always cover the area of πR^2, i.e. slightly wider than the area of $(2k_0+1)\times(2k_0+1)$, where $R=[(2k_0+1)r/\sqrt{2}]$ by Eqn. (1). Let A be the area corresponding to the set of grids per cell used by the proposed algorithm. Denote by B, πR^2, the area covered by the non-grid based forwarding method. The ratio by equation $1 - (A/B)$ is said to be *power-saving neighbor (node) ratio for a server(or client)* because once the trajectory has been set up the only node that reside in the selected grids are concerned with subsequent publishing and subscribing. Unlike a server or client that initiates its trajectory into four directions, a 'transit' backbone node which simply relays a publishing or subscribing message from one neighbor to another neighbors certainly dissipates less power of neighbors, as its trajectory is set up in the direction of a column(or row)-wise. In this paper, however, we have not covered this subject.

To validate and measure the saving ratios of the proposed algorithm, we wrote a simulation program that calculates various power-saving ratios under different combinations of grid index (k_0), nodal density per grid (ρ), and number of next-hop nodes (N_0).

We first vary k_0 from 1 to 4, while using ρ=0.5. Fig. 6 shows the power-saving ratios when N_0 is given as 2, 8, 10, respectively. It is seen that the simulation results converge to about 80%, as k_0 and N_0 increase and fall between the theoretical bounds. The saving ratios hardly depend upon N_0. This is because the number of grids chosen

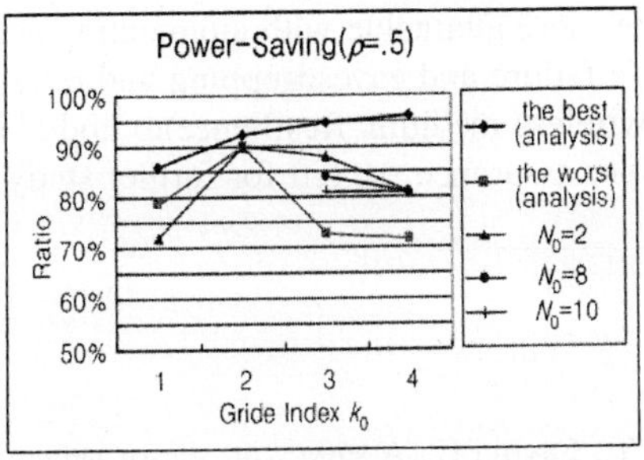

Fig. 6. Power-saving vs. grid index

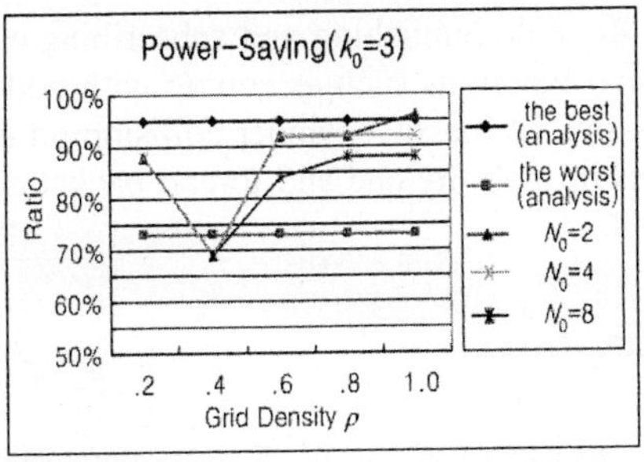

Fig. 7. Power-saving vs. grid density

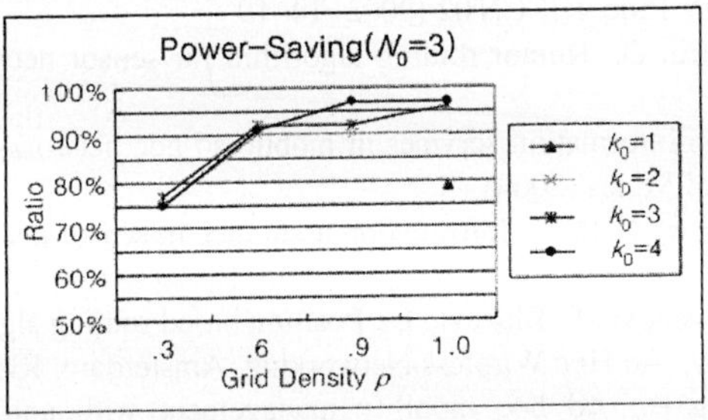

Fig. 8. Power-saving vs. grid density

by the proposed algorithm is given as a multiple of k_0 and can tolerate relatively large N_0, say 4 or 7 for k_0=3 or 4. This property is particularly useful for the multicast-based next-hop forwarding. Fig. 7 plots power-savings as functions of ρ and N_0 while fixing k_0=3. As ρ increase, the savings approach to 85% and more. Increasing N_0 slightly degrades the power-saving ratios. Fig. 8 shows the power-saving ratios when ρ varies in the range [0.3, 0.6, 0.9, 1.0], as functions of k_0, while fixing N_0=3. As expected, the savings become more apparent as ρ increases. It is shown that for $\rho \geq 0.6$, more than 90% saving is achievable.

6 Conclusions

In the trajectory-based publishing and subscribing approach, matchmaking may fail without obtaining desired information, even if two trajectories intersect geometrically. In this paper, we studied the *power-efficient seamless publishing and subscribing* for the trajectory-based matchmaking paradigm in wireless sensor networks. We addressed the issue by logically dividing the space of the whole network into smaller grids and proposed a new next-hop selection algorithm by taking advantage of the seamlessly grid-by-grid multicasting. Our analysis and simulation show that our algorithm significantly saves the power of 1-hop neighbors, compared to the non-grid-based protocol. Tuning grid index k_0 appropriately so that the grid density is about 1, 85% or more of power-savings are achievable. This is quite different form the previous fixed-grid approach as [8] that is required to have more than two nodes per grid for the power-saving.

Reliable publishing and subscribing can be more attainable with augmenting additional functions such as coping with node n_s's failure and eavesdropping and retransmission of messages under collision on the wireless medium. Resilience to node failures or mobility and end-to-end packet-delivery assurance are left for further study as well.

References

1. Akyildiz I. F., Su W., Sankarasubramaniam Y., Cayirci E.: A survey on sensor networks. IEEE Communications Magazine, Vol. 40, No. 8 (2002) 102–114
2. Aydin I., Shen C.-C.: Facilitating match-making service in ad hoc and sensor networks using pseudo quorum. Proc. ICCCN'02 (2002) 14–19
3. Braginsky D., Estrin D.: Rumor routing algorithm for sensor networks. Proc. WSNA'02 (2002) 22–31
4. Camp T.: Location information services in mobile ad hoc networks. TR MCS-03-15, The Colorado School of Mines (2003)
5. Deb B., Bhatnagar S., Nath B.: Information assurance in sensor networks. Proc. WSNA'03 (2003) 160–168
6. Giordano S., Stojmenovic I., Blazevic L.: Position based routing algorithms for ad hoc networks: a taxonomy. Ad Hoc Wireless Networking, Amsterdam: Kluwer (2003)
7. Hass Z. J., Liang B.: Ad hoc mobility management with uniform quorum systems. IEEE/ACM Transactions on Networking, Vol. 7, No. 2 (1999) 228–240
8. Hou T.-C., Li V.: Transmission range control in multihop packet radio networks. IEEE Transactions on Communications, Vol. 34, No. 1 (1986) 38–44
9. Intanagonwiwat C., Govindran R., Estrin D.: Directed diffusion: a scalable and robust communication paradigm for sensor networks. Proc. MobiCom'00 (2000) 56–67
10. Kahn J. M., Katz R. H., Pister K. S. J.: Mobile networking for smart dust. Proc. MobiCom'99 (1999) 271–278
11. Karp B., Kung H. T.: Greedy perimeter stateless forwarding for wireless networks. Proc. MobiCom'00 (2000) 243–254
12. Krishanamachari B., Estrin D., Wicker S.: Modelling data-centric routing in wireless sensor networks. USC Computer Engineering Technical Report CENG 02-14 (2002)
13. Niculescu D., Nath B.: Trajectory based forwarding and its applications. Proc. MobiCom'03 (2003) 260–272
14. Stojmenovic I.: A scalable quorum based location update scheme for routing in ad hoc wireless networks. SITE TR-99-09, University of Ottawa (1999)
15. Tchakarov J. B., Vaidya N. H.: Efficient content location in wireless ad hoc networks. Proc. MDM'04 (2004)
16. Xu Y., Heidemann J., Estrin D.: Geography-informed energy conservation for ad-hoc routing. Proc. MobiCom'01 (2001) 70–84

Group-Oriented Channel Protection for Mobile Devices in Digital Multimedia Broadcasting*

Woo-Hun Kim[1] and Kee-Young Yoo[2,**]

[1] Department of Information Security, Kyungpook National University, Daegu 702-701, Republic of Korea
whkim@infosec.knu.ac.kr

[2] Department of Computer Engineering, Kyungpook National University, Daegu 702-701, Republic of Korea
yook@knu.ac.kr

Abstract. In 2004, Huang et al. proposed a new key distribution scheme for media delivery in Pay-TV Systems based on a four-level key hierarchy. A three-key distribution scheme is proposed in Huang et al.'s paper. They use an exclusive-OR operation and a one-way hash function for key distribution in order to reduce the computational cost. One of the key distribution schemes for subscription channel protection, the group oriented key distribution scheme, however, is inefficient for the digital multimedia broadcasting (DMB) service in resource-limited mobile phones. In this paper, we show that Huang et al.'s scheme is inefficient regarding subscription channel protection. As a result, we propose an improved scheme to reduce this inefficiency by applying a two-level key hierarchy method for a resource limited device, such as the DMB service in mobile phones.

Keywords: Digital multimedia broadcasting, Conditional access system, Key distribution, Channel grouping.

1 Introduction

In January 2005, the Republic of Korea started to experiment with the broadcasting of three video channels and six audio channels through a digital multimedia broadcasting (DMB) service, via a satellite system for mobile phone service. Until now, Korea has deployed satellite DMB for commercial service with mobile phones. With the DMB service for mobile phone market growth, more and more media service providers will be able to deliver various channels to suit their own interests.

* This research was supported by the MIC(Ministry of Information and Communication), Korea, under the ITRC(Information Technology Research Center) support program supervised by the IITA(Institute of Information Technology Assessment.

** Corresponding author is Kee-Young Yoo. (Tel.: +82-53-950-5553; Fax:+82-53-957-4846.)

P. Yolum et al.(Eds.): ISCIS 2005, LNCS 3733, pp. 103–112, 2005.

Traditionally, a conditional access system (CAS) is employed by the Pay-TV systems in order to charge subscribers who watch their selected television programs [1-3]. Charges for pay channels should be paid by viewers to media service providers based on the key distribution performed in the set-top box on the TV. Traditional key distribution schemes for a CAS, however, required that the high performance device covers complication computation costs [4-6]. In order to provide appropriate CAS service for resource limited mobile devices such as mobile phones, an efficient and secure key distribution scheme is required.

In 1998, Tu et al. [7] discussed various levels of key hierarchy and proposed a four-level hierarchy key distribution scheme for a CAS and the Digital Broadcasting System (DBS). Due to the need for frequent CW encryption operations, they concluded that the two-level key hierarchy system is not suitable for the broadcasting system.

In 2004, Huang et al. [4] proposed a new key distribution scheme for media delivery in Pay-TV systems. A three-key distribution scheme was proposed in Huang et al.'s paper: two for subscription channels, and one for pay-per-view channel protection. They used simple exclusive-OR operations and a one-way hash function for key distribution in order to reduce the computational costs. Huang et al. asserted that the authorization key (AK), distribution key (DK), and secret key (SK) are never disclosed by a smart card. Unfortunately, after issuing the smart card, frequently updated information such as the AK (e.g. daily) is vulnerable when protecting short term information [8][9]. However, one of the key distribution schemes for subscription channel protection, the group-oriented key distribution scheme, GKD scheme, however, is inefficient for a DMB service in mobile phones. The GKD scheme should maintain a four-level key hierarchy.

In this paper, we state that the GKD scheme is inefficient for the a DMB service. Then, we propose a two-level key hierarchy scheme for DMB service with a limited-resource device such as mobile phones.

2 Review of the GKD Scheme

In this section, we review the group-oriented key distribution scheme proposed by Huang et al. [4]. The notations used throughout this paper are defined in Table 1.

Their scheme is divided into two phases: (1) initial phase, and (2) update phase. The key generation performed in the initial phase for the service provider (SP) is described as follows:

(1) SP randomly generates $\langle DK_{SP} \rangle$, where $\langle DK_{SP} \rangle = [dk_1, dk_2, ..., dk_m]$.
(2) SP derives new $\langle AK_{SP} \rangle$ by performing the following procedures:
  (i) $ak_1 = D \oplus dk_1$, where D is a random number.
  (ii) $ak_j = ak_{j-1} \oplus dk_j$, $2 \le j \le m$.

The key generation performed in the initial phase for each subscriber (S_i) is described as follows:

Table 1. The notations used in Huang et al.'s group-oriented key distribution scheme

Notation	Description
G_j	Channel group of identity j, where $j = 1, 2, ..., m$
S_j	Subscriber j, where $j = 1, 2, ..., n$
SG_i	Channel groups ordered by subscriber S_i.
$h()$	One-way hash function.
dk_j	The DK for channel group j, held by SP.
ak_j	The AK for channel group j, held by SP.
dk_j^i	The DK for channel group j, held by subscriber S_i.
ak_j^i	The AK for channel group j, held by subscriber S_i.
$\langle DK_{SP} \rangle$	A vector of DKs and is held by SP.
$\langle AK_{SP} \rangle$	A vector of AKs of all channel groups and is held by SP.
$\langle DK_i \rangle$	A vector of DKs and is held by subscriber S_i.
$\langle AK_i \rangle$	A vector of AKs held by subscriber S_i

(1) SP generates the vector $\langle DK_i \rangle$ for each subscriber S_i, where
  (i) dk_j^i is randomly generated, for $G_j \notin SG_i$.
  (ii) $dk_j^i = (dk_1 \oplus \cdots \oplus dk_j) \oplus (dk_1^i \oplus \cdots \oplus dk_{j-1}^i)$, for $G_j \in SG_i$.
(2) After generating $\langle DK_i \rangle$, the SP encrypts $\langle DK_i \rangle$ using the secret key SK_i of S_i.
(3) SP transmits $\{\langle DK_i \rangle, D\}_{SK_i}$ to S_i, where D is the random number used to generate $\langle AK_{SP} \rangle$.
(4) Subscriber S_i derives new $\langle AK_i \rangle$ by performing the following procedures:
  (i) $ak_1^i = D \oplus dk_1^i$.
  (ii) $ak_j^i = ak_{j-1}^i \oplus dk_j^i$, $2 \leq j \leq m$.

The distribution keys in $\langle DK_i \rangle$ are generated one by one in an ascending group order. In the initial phase, if group j is subscribed, dk_j^i is generated to satisfy the formula $dk_j^i = (dk_1^i \oplus \cdots \oplus dk_{j-1}^i) \oplus (dk_1 \oplus \cdots \oplus dk_j) = dk_j$, which is held by the SP. Otherwise, if group j is not subscribed to, the corresponding dk_j^i will be randomly generated and will not equal the dk_j, held by SP.

The update phase for the service provider (SP) is described as follows:

(1) SP generates a random number R.
(2) SP derives new $\langle AK_{SP} \rangle$ by performing:
  (i) $ak_1 = R \oplus dk_1$.
  (ii) $ak_j = ak_{j-1} \oplus dk_j$, $2 \leq j \leq m$.
(3) SP transmits $(R, h(R))$ to all subscribers.

The update phase for each subscriber (S_i) is described as follows:

(1) After receiving $(R, h(R))$, S_i checks $h(R)$ for the integrity of R.
(2) S_i derives new $\langle AK_i \rangle$ by performing:
  (i) $ak_1^i = R \oplus dk_1^i$.
  (ii) $ak_j^i = ak_{j-1}^i \oplus dk_j^i$, $2 \leq j \leq m$.

The new AKs in the vector $\langle AK_{SP} \rangle$ and the vector $\langle AK_i \rangle$ are generated one-by-one in the ascending group identity order. In order to verify the integrity of the received R, the SP broadcasts R together with its digest, $(R, h(R))$, where $h()$ is a one-way hash function known to the SP and the subscriber's smart cards. In the update phase, if channel group j is subscribed to, the dk_j^i, held by subscriber S_i, is equal to the dk_j, held by the SP. Thus, subscriber S_i is able to derive an ak_j^i, that is equal to ak_j held by the SP.

For example, subscription channels are divided into three groups, G_1, G_2 and G_3. In the initial phase, the service provider (SP) randomly generates three distribution keys, dk_1, dk_2 and dk_3. The SP then derives the three authorization keys, ak_1, ak_2 and ak_3 by performing the equations described above. In this example, the legitimate subscriber S_1 subscribes to the subscription channel groups, G_1, G_2, and G_3. Fig. 1 shows an example of the initial phase of S_1.

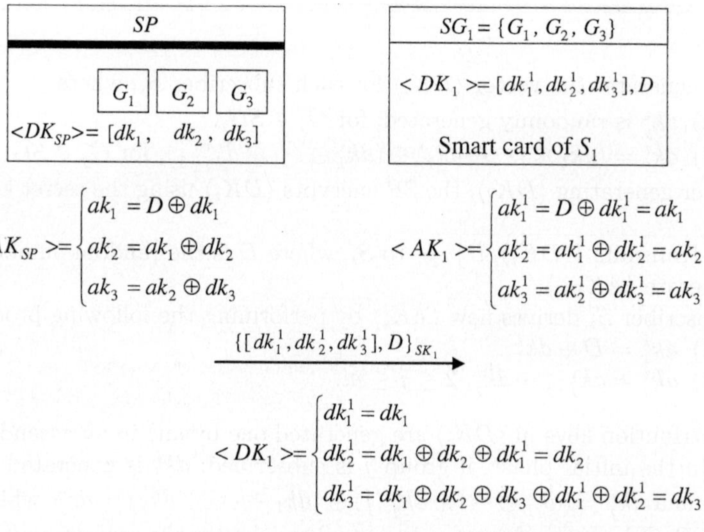

Fig. 1. Example of the initial phase of S_1

The distribution keys held by subscriber S_1 are derived as follows:

(1) dk_1^1 is the same as the distribution key (dk_1) held by SP.
(2) $dk_2^1 = dk_1 \oplus dk_2 \oplus dk_1^1 = dk_2$.
(3) $dk_3^1 = dk_1 \oplus dk_2 \oplus dk_3 \oplus dk_1^1 \oplus dk_2^1 = dk_3$.

After deriving the distribution keys, the subscriber S_1 continuously derives the authorization keys for the subscribed channel groups G_1, G_2, and G_3, as follows:

(1) $ak_1^1 = D \oplus dk_1^1 = ak_1$, where D is the random number used to generate the authorization keys for S_1.
(2) $ak_2^1 = ak_1^1 \oplus dk_2^1 = ak_2$.
(3) $ak_3^1 = ak_2^1 \oplus dk_3^1 = ak_3$.

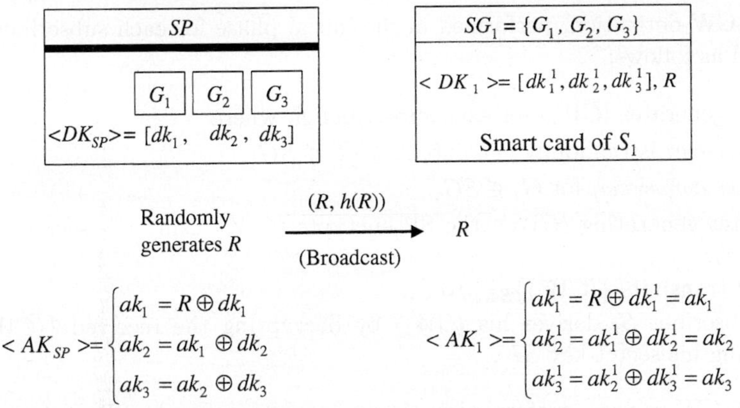

Fig. 2. Example of the update phase of S_1

Upon updating the authorization keys, the SP broadcasts a random number R to all subscribers. The SP derives a new $\langle AK_{SP} \rangle$, as described above. Then, all subscribers update their authorization keys. Fig. 2 shows an example of the update phase of S_1. The key generation process, performed in the update phase for the legitimate subscriber S_1, is described as follows:

(1) After receiving $(R, h(R))$, S_1 checks $h(R)$ for the integrity of R.
(2) S_1 derives new $\langle AK_1 \rangle$ by performing:
  (i) $ak_1^1 = R \oplus dk_1^1 = ak_1$.
  (ii) $ak_2^1 = ak_1^1 \oplus dk_2^1 = ak_2$.
  (iii) $ak_3^1 = ak_2^1 \oplus dk_3^1 = ak_3$.

3 The Proposed Group-Oriented Key Distribution Scheme for the DMB Service

In the group-oriented key distribution scheme, customers subscribe to channels by group. The proposed scheme is based on a two-level key hierarchy: Control Word (CW), and Secret Key (SK) for computational efficiency.

The CW is used encrypt/decrypt programs on the channels. Each channel has a unique CW at a specific time. The SK is used to encrypt/decrypt the CW. The SK is distributed to the subscriber's mobile device upon registration and can be stored securely. Only the encrypted random-value R by the SK is broadcasted frequently (e.g. 5-20 sec) for higher security.

The distribution of the CW consists of two phases: Initial phase and update phase. In the initial phase, a service provider generates the vector $\langle CW_{SP} \rangle$. Upon subscribing to the channel groups, the service provider uses $\langle CW_{SP} \rangle$ to encrypt programs on the subscribed channels. By assuming that there are n subscribers and m groups of channels in the proposed scheme, the generated CW, performed in the initial phase for the SP, is described as follows:

(1) SP randomly generates $\langle CW_{SP} \rangle$ where $\langle CW_{SP} \rangle = [cw_1, cw_2, ..., cw_m]$.

The CW derivation, performed in the initial phase for each subscriber, is described as follows:

(1) SP generates $\langle CW_i \rangle$ for each subscriber S_i where
  (i) cw_j^i is randomly generated for $G_j \notin SG_i$.
  (ii) $cw_j^i = cw_j$ for $G_j \in SG_i$.
(2) After generating $\langle CW_i \rangle$, the SP encrypts $\langle CW_i \rangle$ using the secret key SK_i of S_i.
(3) SP transmits $\{\langle CW_i \rangle\}_{SK_i}$ to S_i.
(4) Subscriber S_i derives his $\langle CW_i \rangle$ by decrypting the received $\{\langle CW_i \rangle\}_{SK_i}$ using his secret key SK_i.

The CW update, performed in the update phase for the SP, is described as follows:

(1) SP generates a random number R.
(2) SP derives new $\langle CW_{SP} \rangle$ by performing:
  (i) $cw_j = R \oplus cw_j$, $1 \le j \le m$.
(3) SP transmits $(R, h(R))$ to all subscribers.

The CW update, performed in the update phase for each subscriber, is described as follows:

(1) After receiving $(R, h(R))$, S_i checks $h(R)$ for the integrity of R.
(2) S_i derives new $\langle CW_i \rangle$ by performing:
  (i) $cw_j = R \oplus cw_j^i$, $1 \le j \le m$.

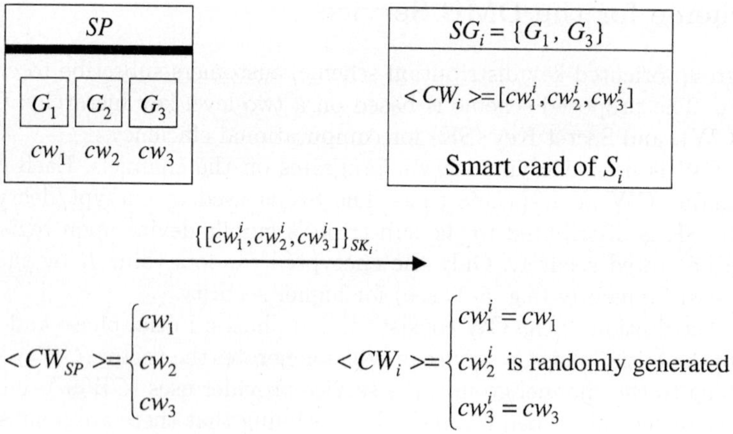

Fig. 3. Example of the initial phase of the proposed scheme

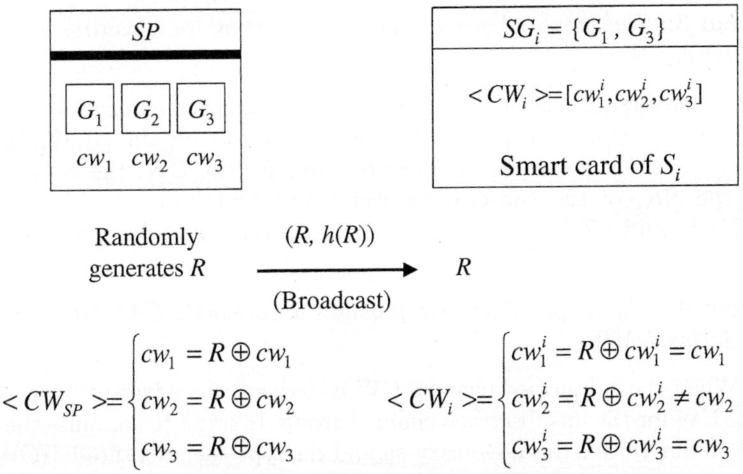

Fig. 4. Example of the update phase of the proposed scheme

The new CWs in vector $\langle CW_{sp} \rangle$ and vector $\langle CW_i \rangle$ are generated in the ascending group identity order as the GKD scheme. Fig. 3 shows an example of the initial phase of the group-oriented key distribution scheme. In this example, the subscription channels are divided into three groups, G_1, G_2, and G_3. The subscriber S_i subscribes to the subscription channel groups, G_1 and G_3.

Upon updating the CWs, the SP sends an encrypted random number R to each subscriber. Then, the SP and all subscribers update their CWs, as shown in Fig. 4.

4 Security Analysis

In this section, we analyze the requirements of our proposed scheme.

Theorem 1. *The proposed scheme is not susceptible to the subscriber's secret key compromise.*

Proof: An adversary tries to reveal the subscriber's secret key (SK) from the public values. With the assistance of a smart card, it is still difficult to derive the SK after issuing the smart card from the smart card producing center. Then, the subscriber's secret key can not be revealed to the adversary.

Theorem 2. *The proposed scheme is not susceptible to a subscriber impersonation.*

Proof: An adversary tries to impersonate a legal subscriber by forging the mobile device. It is impossible, however, to derive the CW without the legal subscriber's secret key (SK), which is stored in each subscriber's smart card. Thus, the adversary can not impersonate a legal subscriber.

Theorem 3. *The proposed scheme is not susceptible to a control word (CW) compromise.*

Proof: An adversary wishes to derive the CW from the transmitted messages of the initial and update phase. The adversary can obtain $\{\langle CW_i \rangle\}_{SK_i}$ and $(R, h(R))$ from the network. In order to compute the CW, the adversary can obtain the SK_i of the subscriber's secret key. Obtaining the SK_i from the $\{\langle CW_i \rangle\}_{SK_i}$ and $(R, h(R))$ is difficult because the smart card has to be broken.

Theorem 4. *The proposed scheme provides an adequate CAS for channel protection in the DMB.*

Proof: When the subscribed channel CW is derived, the adversary tries to compute the CW for the unsubscribed channel group. In order to compute the unsubscribed channel CW, the adversary should decrypt the encrypted $\{\langle CW_i \rangle\}_{SK_i}$ with S_i's secret key SK_i, which is legally subscribed to the channel group SG_i. It is impossible to decrypt the $\{\langle CW_i \rangle\}_{SK_i}$ without the legal subscriber S_i's secret key, SK_i. This is because the subscriber's secret keys are securely distributed with the assistance of a smart card.

Theorem 5. *The proposed scheme provides selective channel group watching for each subscriber in the DMB system.*

Proof: After completing the update phase, the subscriber can derive independent CWs for channel group watching. It means that each subscriber can subscribe to the channel group of his/her own choice. Also, the service provider can control the subscriptions to all channel groups for their own interest.

5 Comparison

In this section, we compare the proposed scheme and the previously proposed schemes with regard to several features. Table 2 summarizes the main features of the previously proposed schemes and our proposed scheme.

In Tu et al.'s scheme, the number of encrypted messages and transmitted messages are the same as those of the subscriber groups with a four-level key hierarchy. If the groups are divided into many groups, this scheme is not suitable for resource-limited mobile devices.

In the GKD scheme, one random number is broadcast to all subscribers for the updated AKs. They use a simple exclusive-OR function to derive the AKs with a four-level key hierarchy. Regardless of the efficient operation (e.g. one-way hash function and XOR operation) for the AK update, they apply a four-level key hierarchy.

In our scheme, the subscriber can only generate the CWs for the subscribed channel group. This is efficient and cost effective when the resource-limited mobile device is used for the DMB service.

Table 3 summarizes the key refresh interval of the previously proposed schemes and our proposed scheme. Usually, the keys for each level are used to encrypt

Table 2. Comparison of proposed scheme and previously proposed schemes

Scheme	Tu	GKD	Proposed
Key hierarchy level	4	4	2
Message transmitted for update AK/CW	(AK) m	(AK) 1	(CW) 1
Computational cost for update AK/CW	m enc	1 hash	1 hash

† m : number of the subscriber groups, enc : encryption operation.

Table 3. Comparison of key refresh interval

Scheme	Tu	GKD	Proposed
Key refresh	SK : permanent DK : monthly AK : daily CW : 5-20 sec	SK : permanent DK : monthly AK : daily CW : 5-20 sec	SK : permanent CW : 5-20 sec

and decrypt the keys for the previous level. All keys, except the SK are updated periodically in order to maintain a high level of security. Previously proposed schemes make use of the four-level key hierarchy in order to reduce the update computation costs. It is interesting to note, that the GKD scheme uses a four-level key hierarchy even though their scheme's update operation is a simple XOR operation. It is not necessary to use a four-level key hierarchy if the key update operation requires low computational costs (e.g. XOR operation).

6 Conclusions

In this paper, we have demonstrated that the GKD scheme is inefficient for the DMB service. In the environment of resource-limited mobile devices, the four-level key hierarchy operation should be a burden to the operation. To overcome this inefficiency, we have proposed a new group-oriented channel protection scheme for the DMB service with mobile devices. Our scheme makes use of the two-level key hierarchy and a simple operation that only requires low computational costs in mobile device. Furthermore, our scheme makes use of the two-level key hierarchy for the CW update without additional encryption operations. The proposed scheme does not only apply to the CAS for Pay-TV but it is also applicable to resource-limited devices for the DMB service.

References

1. Kamperman F., Rijnsoever B. V.: Conditional access system Interoperability through software downloading, *IEEE Transactions on Consumer Electronics*, vol. 47, no. 1, (2001), 47-53.
2. Song R., Korba L.: Pay-TV System with Strong Privacy and Non-Repudiation Protection, *IEEE Transactions on Consumer Electronics*, vol. 49, no. 2, (2003), 408-413.

3. Liu B., Zhang W., Jiang T.: A Scalable Key Distribution Scheme for Conditional Access System in Digital Pay-TV System, *IEEE Transactions on Consumer Electronics*, vol. 50, no. 2, (2004), 632-637.
4. Huang Y.L., Shieh S., Ho F. S., Wang J. C.: Efficient Key Distribution Schemes for Secure Media Delivery in Pay-TV Systems, *IEEE Transactions on Multimedia*, vol. 6, no. 5, (2004), 760-769.
5. Macq B. M., Quisquater J. J.: Cryptology for digital TV broadcasting, *Proceedings of the IEEE*, vol. 83, no. 6, (1995), 944-957.
6. Coutrot F., Michon V., "A single conditional access system for satellite-cable and terrestrial TV", *IEEE Transactions on Consumer Electronics*, vol. 35, no. 3, (1989), 464-468.
7. Tu F. K., Laih C. S., Toung S. H.: On key distribution management for conditional access system on Pay-TV system, *in 1998 IEEE Int. Symp. Consumer Electronics (ISCE'98)*, vol. 45, Taipei, Taiwan, R.O.C., (1998), 151-159.
8. Monnin G.: Smart Cards Exclusive Advantages in Pay-TV, *IEE Broadcasting Convention IBC. International Conf.*, vol. 3-7, (1992), 418-421.
9. Anderson R., Kuhn M.: Tamper Resistance - a Cautionary Note, *Proc. Second USENIX Workshop Electronic Commerce*, (1996), 1-11.

IP Traffic Load Distribution in NGEO Broadband Satellite Networks – (Invited Paper)

Tarik Taleb[1], Abbas Jamalipour[1,2], Nei Kato[1], and Yoshiaki Nemoto[1]

[1] Graduate School of Information Sciences, Tohoku University, Sendai 980-77, Japan
{taleb, kato, nemoto}@nemoto.ecei.tohoku.ac.jp

[2] School of Electrical and Information Engineering, University of Sydney, Sydney, NSW 2006, Australia
a.jamalipour@ieee.org

Abstract. Given the fact that more than half of the world lacks a wired network infrastructure, satellite networks are seen as an important alternative to achieve global coverage. Since most of the world population lives around the equator or in middle-latitude regions, satellite constellations have to deal with different communication requirements from different regions. The traffic requirements become further unbalanced as the population density varies among urban and rural areas. This results in the congestion of some satellites while others remain underused. The issue of traffic engineering over satellite networks can be resolved by distributing the traffic in a balanced way over underutilized links. This paper proposes an Explicit Load Balancing (ELB) routing protocol which is based on information of traffic load at the next hop on the remainder of the path to the destination. A satellite with high traffic load sends signals to its neighboring satellites requesting them to decrease their sending rates before it gets congested and packets are ultimately dropped. Neighboring satellites should accordingly respond and search for other alternate paths that do not include the satellite in question. The performance of the proposed scheme is evaluated through simulations. From the simulation results, the proposed scheme achieves a more balanced distribution of traffic load, and reduces the number of packet drops and queuing delays. The resulting satellite constellation is a better-utilized and traffic-balanced network.

1 Introduction

Along with the rapid globalization of the telecommunications industry, the demand for Internet services is growing in terms of both the number of users and types of services to be supported. Along with this steady growth, provision of a plethora of wide-band Internet applications to metropolitan areas with a potentially large number of users, regardless of time and space limitations, is a challenging task for current terrestrial and wireless networks. Because of their extensive geographic reach and inherent multicast capabilities, satellite communication systems are seen as an attractive infrastructure to accommodate these high bit-rate services with diverse Quality of Service (QoS) requirements [1].

P. Yolum et al.(Eds.): ISCIS 2005, LNCS 3733, pp. 113–123, 2005.

Communications over satellites began successfully with the use of individual satellites in geostationary orbits. However, due to high signal delays caused by the high altitude of geostationary satellites, focus has been directed towards the development of new Non-Geostationary (NGEO) satellite communication systems called Low Earth Orbit (LEO) and Medium Earth Orbit (MEO) satellite systems. NGEO systems promise to offer services with much lower latency and terminal power requirements than those offered by geostationary satellites. The design and development of these satellite networks have been thus the subject of extensive research in recent literature (e.g. Teledesic [2], Skybridge [3]).

NGEO satellite networks exhibit different characteristics from the traditional satellite or wired networks. The success of NGEO satellite networks in delivering high-speed access hinges on the ability of the underlying Internet protocols (IP) to function correctly and efficiently in NGEO satellite systems, systems characterized by rapidly time-varying network topologies [4]. The effect of such a communication environment on the working of IP protocols has been the focus of a large body of prior works [5]. Another important factor that the performance of IP protocols depend on in NGEO systems is related to routing. Indeed, whilst use of Inter-Satellite Links (ISLs) in multi-hops NGEO constellations provides more flexibility, it leads to complex dynamic routing [6]. The routing complexity becomes more substantial as NGEO satellites change their coverage areas on the Earth surface due to their continuous motion, and accordingly have to transmit different amounts of traffic load. This ultimately results in an unbalanced distribution of the total traffic over the entire constellation [7]. Support for IP routing within the satellite constellations is highly important for the implementation of Integrated or Differentiated Services (DiffServ) architectures to support QoS over satellite systems.

To route traffic over dynamic satellite constellations, several strategies have been proposed. Dynamic Virtual Topology Routing (DVTR) [8] and Virtual Node (VN) [9] protocols are the best known concepts. Based on these two schemes, important research efforts have been elaborated in the recent years with respect to IP proprietary routing over satellite constellations [10]. While most of these pioneering routing protocols search for the shortest path with the minimum cost, they do not take into account the total traffic distribution over the entire constellation. Indeed, while searching for only short paths for communication, some satellites may get congested while others are underutilized. This phenomenon leads to unfair distribution of the network traffic, and ultimately to higher queuing delays and significant packet drops at some satellites in the constellation.

As a remedy to the above issue, this paper proposes an explicit routing protocol which is based on prior information of traffic load at the next hop. A satellite with high traffic load sends signals to its neighboring satellites requesting them to decrease their sending rates before it gets congested and packets are ultimately dropped. Neighboring satellites should accordingly respond and search for other alternate paths that do not include the satellite in question. This operation can be accomplished without changing the routing protocol in use. It can be easily implemented over any routing protocol, such as DVTR or VN routing schemes. The proposed concept targets only the packets of delay-insensitive applications. Delay sensitive applications are not subject to the proposed scheme and can be dealt with according to any traditional routing protocol. The proposed scheme is dubbed *Explicit Load Balancing (ELB)*.

The remainder of this paper is structured as follows. Section 2 surveys the ongoing research efforts tailored to IP routing over NGEO satellite communication systems. Section 3 presents the key design philosophy behind the proposed scheme ELB. Section 4 portrays the simulation environment used to evaluate the performance of the proposed scheme and discusses the simulation results. The paper concludes in Section 5 with a summary recapping the significance of the research work elaborated in this paper.

2 Related Work

Current terrestrial Internet routing protocols, such as Open Shortest Path First (OSPF) [11] and Routing Information Protocol (RIP) [12], rely on exchanging topology information upon a change or set-up of a connection; that is in a connection-oriented manner. Applying such schemes to the rapidly and regularly-changing NGEO satellite network topologies incurs substantial overhead [13]. Several connectionless algorithms have been thus proposed to route data traffic over satellite constellations. They can be classified into two categories, namely constellation periodicity-based routing and onboard routing schemes.

Although satellite constellations experience frequent topological variations, these variations are highly periodic and predictable because of the strict orbital movements of the satellites. The basic idea behind protocols of the first category is to make use of this periodic and predictable nature of the constellation topology. Various schemes fall into this category. DVTR [8] and VN [9] protocols are the most worth-mentioning concepts.

In DVTR, the system period is divided into a set of time intervals. Over each interval, the topology remains constant. Link activation and deactivation are performed only at the beginning of intervals. Over each time interval, optimal shortest paths and alternate paths can be established using well-known methods such as the Dijkstra shortest-path algorithm. These routing tables can be then stored onboard and retrieved upon a change in the topology. One major credit of this operation consists in the removal of online computational complexity. However, this computation simplicity comes at the expense of large storage requirements, weak fault tolerance, and quasi-null adaptive capabilities.

In the VN scheme, virtual nodes (VNs) are assumed to be set in fixed positions relative to the surface of the Earth. A VN is embodied at any given time by a certain physical satellite, and a virtual network topology is set up with these VNs. The virtual topology is always embodied by the satellite constellation. When a satellite disappears over the horizon, its corresponding VN becomes represented by the next satellite passing overhead. The virtual topology remains accordingly unchanged. Each VN keeps state information, such as routing table entries or channel allocation information, pertaining to the users within its coverage area. Upon a satellite handoff, the state information is transferred from the first satellite to the second. Routing is performed in the instantaneous virtual topology using a common routing protocol. In such a manner, topology changes are hidden from routing protocols running on the constellation.

In the onboard routing mechanisms, as the name infers, routing tables are calculated onboard the satellites based on real-time information related to the network state. A potential number of onboard routings has been proposed in the recent literature. To mention a few examples, Henderson *et. al.* propose an onboard distributed routing protocol that selects the next hop based on minimization of the remaining geographic distance to the destination [14]. [15] proposes an onboard routing protocol specifically designed for multi-layered satellite constellations composed of LEO, MEO, and GEO satellites. In the proposed scheme, satellites in low layers (e.g. LEO) are grouped according to the footprint area of their corresponding satellites in the higher layers (e.g. MEO). This grouping is performed in each snapshot period. Higher satellites receive delay measurement reports from their group members in lower layers. Based on these reports, the higher-layer satellites compute the minimum-delay paths for their corresponding lower-layers members. While most of onboard routing schemes exhibit important adaptive capabilities, they impose significant challenges for the space devices in terms of the required computational and processing load. They ultimately question the scalability of their routing tables. Moreover, since these routing schemes focus on only finding paths with the shortest delays, they may turn unfavorable for the support of certain QoS requirements. They may be appropriate for only best-effort light-load traffic.

Given the important correlation between efficient routing strategies and the support of QoS, tremendous research efforts have been elaborated in recent years with respect to QoS over satellite constellations [16]. Most of these pioneering research works are based on the above-mentioned schemes. [10] provides a thorough discussion on the main merits and downfalls of these previous research works and indicates areas of possible improvements.

In the sphere of QoS over constellations with ISLs, the focus of earlier research work was on the integration of dynamic satellite networks with the Asynchronous Transfer Mode (ATM) [17][18]. Because of its provision of different levels of QoS guarantees and its concept of virtual path, ATM has been seen indeed as a promising solution for the provision of QoS over mobile satellites. However, the rapid growth of Internet-based applications motivates satellite operators to consider IP traffic as well. For IP-based satellite constellations, a number of interesting solutions has been proposed to provide QoS over satellites. In [19], Donner *et. al.* developed a Multi-Protocol Label Switching (MPLS) networking protocol for NGEO satellite constellations. The protocol is still in its infancy, and some important practical problems related to rerouting and maintenance overhead are still unsolved and deserve further study. On the other hand, [20] proposes a Traffic Class Dependent (TCD) routing algorithm. Different traffic classes are considered. The protocol differentiates between packets belonging to each traffic class and provides accordingly different levels of services. The

TCD protocol whilst attempts to guarantee QoS for different traffic classes, it may assign a single route for a specific class with huge traffic data and may ultimately result in heavily overloading the chosen path. This would intuitively affect the balancing of traffic load over the entire satellite constellation.

Another issue that is common among most conventional routing algorithms consists in the fact that route decision is based primarily on propagation delay. Given the fact that queuing delays may also contribute largely to the total delay that a packet may experience mainly in case of heavy loads, a more appropriate routing cost metric has to be selected. In this context, [21] proposes a Minimum Flow Maximum Residual (MFMR) routing protocol where the minimum-hop path with the minimum number of flows is selected. One of the main drawbacks of the protocol consists in the fact that it implies knowledge of the flows over the constellation and does not consider the case where the flows count increases along the selected path. Given the fast movements of satellites, such scenario may occur frequently. This would lead to the congestion of the chosen MFMR paths and ultimately unfavorable performance. In [22], a Probabilistic Routing Protocol (PRP) is proposed. The PRP scheme uses a cost metric as a function of time and traffic load. The traffic load is assumed to be location homogeneous. The major drawback of the protocol consists in this assumption as it is far away from being realistic. Indeed, newly coming traffic can easily congest the chosen PRP path and leave other resources underutilized. In [23], Jianjun *et. al.* propose a Compact Explicit Multi-path Routing (CEMR) algorithm based on a cost metric that involves both propagation and queuing delays. At a given satellite, the queuing delay is predicted by monitoring the number of packets in the outgoing queue of the satellite over a time interval. It is assumed that the network state over each time interval is updated before routing calculation is carried out. While the used cost metric gives a good insight about the queuing delay that may be experienced by a packet at a given satellite, it does not reflect the congestion state of the next hop, nor does it estimate the queuing delay a packet may experience there. It does not reflect the likeliness of packets to be dropped by the downstream hop either. To avoid packet drops and to more efficiently distribute traffic burden over multiple satellites, further study is needed to optimize the performance of the existing routing schemes. This challenging task underpins the research work outlined in the remainder of this paper.

3 Explicit Load Balancing Scheme

This section gives a detailed description of the proposed scheme, *Explicit Load Balancing (ELB)* scheme. First is an outline of the key components of multi-hop NGEO satellite constellations.

A multi-hop satellite constellation forms a mesh network topology. It is composed of N orbits and S satellites uniformly distributed over each orbit. The first and N^{th} orbits are neighbors in both sides due to the spherical shape of the Earth. Depending on the constellation type, each satellite is able to set up M ISLs with its neighboring satellites. Satellites along the counter-rotating seam

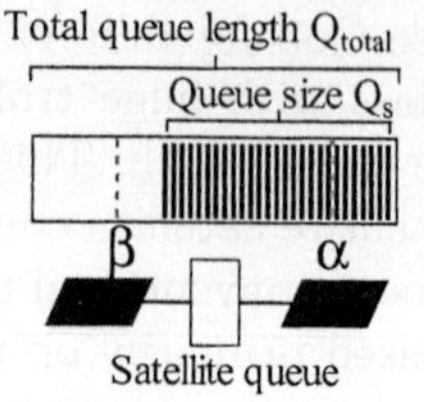

Queue ratio Q_r	Satellite State
$Q_r < \alpha$	Free
$\alpha \leq Q_r < \beta$	Fairly Busy
$\beta \leq Q_r$	Busy

Fig. 1. The three network states of satellites

have less neighboring satellites. There are two types of ISLs. Links between adjacent satellites in the same orbit are called Intra-plane ISLs, and links between neighboring satellites in adjoining orbits are called Inter-plane ISLs. Intra-plane ISLs are maintained permanently, but some Inter-plane ISLs may get temporarily deactivated when the viewing angle between two satellites is above a given threshold. In the remainder of this paper, we assume that each satellite is aware of the ISLs established with its neighboring satellites.

As previously discussed, while most traditional routing algorithms use different routing cost metrics to search for the most appropriate route, they do not take into account the congestion state of next hops on the remainder of the path to the destination. If the chosen next satellite is congested or about to be congested, the forwarded packets may either get discarded or experience a long queuing delay. To tackle this issue, neighboring satellites should mutually and dynamically exchange information on the states of their queues. In deed, at each satellite three representative states are defined based on the queue ratio[1] as shown in Fig. 1. The considered states are as follows:

- Free state: When the queue ratio (Q_r) is inferior to a predetermined threshold α ($Q_r < \alpha$), the satellite is considered to be in a free state.
- Fairly-busy state: Having the queue ratio between the threshold α and another predetermined threshold β ($\alpha \leq Q_r < \beta$), the satellite is considered to be in a fairly-busy state.
- Busy state: The satellite changes its state to busy when its queue ratio exceeds the threshold β ($\beta \leq Q_r$).

The choice of the thresholds α and β as queue ratios to indicate the congestion state of satellites is similar in spirit to the idea of major intelligent packet-discard policies such as Random Early Marking (REM) [24] and Random Early Discard (RED) [25].

Upon a change in the queue state of a given satellite, the latter broadcasts a *Self-State Advertisement (SSA)* packet to its M neighboring satellites informing them of the change occurrence. The SSA signaling packet carries information on the satellite ID and its state. It should be emphasized that SSA packets are broadcast to only the neighboring satellites and not over the entire connection path. Given their small size, overhead in terms of the bandwidth consumed by these signaling packets should not be an issue. When a satellite receives a

[1] The ratio of the queue size Q_s to the total queue length Q_{total} ($Q_r = \frac{Q_s \cdot 100}{Q_{total}}$).

SSA packet, it uses the enclosed information to update its *Neighbors Status List (NSL)*. Each NSL contains information on the current queue state of each neighboring satellite. When a satellite A experiences a state transition from free to fairly-busy state, it sends a warning message (via a SSA packet) to its neighboring satellites informing them that it is about to get congested. The neighboring satellites are then requested to update their routing tables and start searching for alternate paths that do not include satellite A. When the queue state of satellite A changes to busy, all neighboring satellites are then requested to forward (χ%) of traffic that has been transmitted via satellite A to other alternate paths. If the traffic includes different applications with different requirements, delay insensitive applications are to be first forwarded via the alternate paths. Packets of delay sensitive applications can be transmitted via satellite A if that would guarantee the delay requirements of the applications. It should be noted that the working of the proposed scheme can be accomplished without changing the routing protocol in use.

4 Performance Evaluation

Having described the details of the proposed scheme, focus is now directed on its performance evaluation. This section verifies how the proposed system is efficient in avoiding packet drops and enhancing the system throughput. The performance evaluation relies on computer simulation, using Network Simulator (NS) [26].

To better explain the mechanism of the proposed scheme, we consider the network topology example depicted in Fig. 2(a). The figure shows the case of the Iridium constellation where each satellite maintains ISLs with four other satellites ($M = 4$). All up-links, down-links, and ISL links are given a capacity equal to 25Mbps. Their delays are set to 20ms. In order to remove limitations due to small buffer sizes on the network congestion, buffers equal to the bandwidth-delay product of the bottleneck link are used [27]. Due mostly to its simplicity,

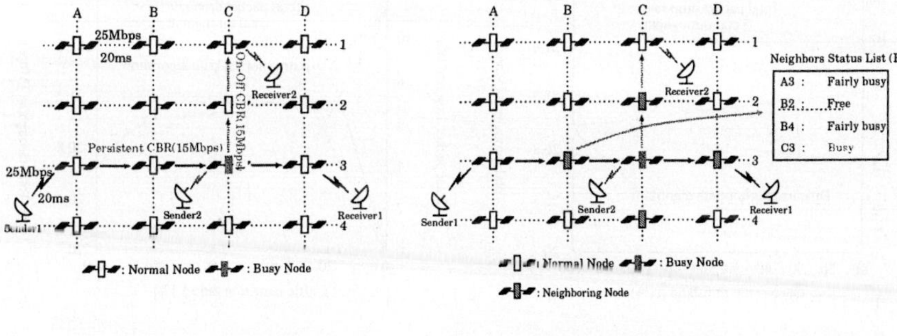

(a) Traffic concentration at satellite C3

(b) Exchange of network state information among satellites

Fig. 2. An example showing the main operations of the ELB scheme all satellites use Drop-Tail as their packet-discarding policy. The abstract configuration considers the case of two Constant Bit Rate (CBR) connections over two different routes, namely A3-D3 and C3-C1 (Fig. 2(a)). The sending rate of the two connections is set to 15Mbps. While the connection on the (A3-D3) route is simulated as a long-lived CBR flow, the traffic over the (C3-C1) route is modeled as a non-persistent On-Off connection. The On/Off periods of the connection are derived from a Pareto distributions with a shape equal to 1.2. The mean On period and the mean Off period are set to $200ms$. The packet size is fixed to 1 kB. Simulations were all run for $20s$, a duration long enough to ensure that the system has reached a consistent behavior. It should be noted that the above-mentioned parameters are chosen with no specific purpose in mind and do not change any of the fundamental observations about the simulation results. While the proposed scheme can be implemented over any routing protocol, in the performance evaluation, we consider the scenario of the proposed scheme over the Dijkstra's Shortest Path algorithm. The latter is used therefore as a comparison term.

Having all the traffic concentrated at satellite C3, this latter issues a SSA packet to its neighboring satellites (B3, C2, C4, and D3) indicating that its state has become "Busy". In response to the SSA packet, neighboring satellites set the state of C3 to Busy and update their NSL list accordingly. As satellite B2 is free, satellite B3 starts transmitting a portion of the (A3-D3) traffic via satellites B2, C2, D2, and finally the edge satellite D3 (Fig. 2(b)). This operation is continued until satellite C3 transits to a free state. By so doing, the overall network traffic becomes better distributed.

To investigate the effect of the threshold β on the system performance, we plot the total throughput and total packet drop rate experienced by the two connections for different values of β. α is set to half the value of β and the traffic reduction ratio χ is set to 70%. Fig. 3(a) shows the simulation results. The figure indicates that setting β to larger values leads to lower throughput and higher packet drops. Note that the case of ($\beta = 100\%$) refers to the use of

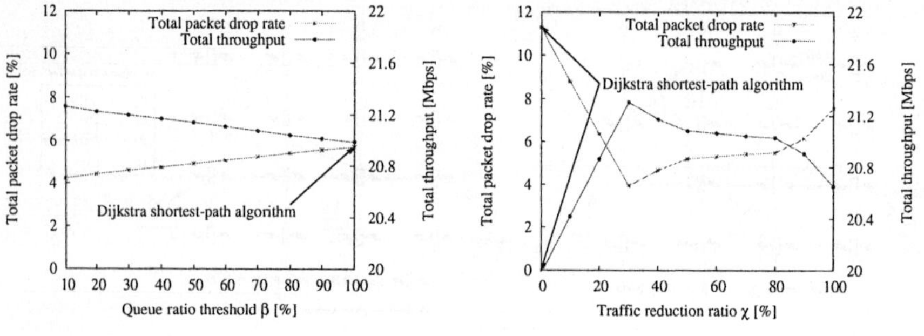

(a) Effects of β on the packet drops ($\chi = 70\%$)

(b) Effects of χ on the packet drops ($\beta = 80\%$)

Fig. 3. Performance evaluation in terms of packet drops

only Dijkstra algorithm. The achieved performance is intuitively due to the fact that by setting β to high values, the proposed scheme would not have enough time to accommodate the traffic bursts and the queue ends up by discarding a high number of packets. This is ultimately translated into degraded throughput. In order to investigate the effect of the traffic reduction ratio χ on the system, we plot the total throughput and total packet drop rate experienced by the two connections for different values of χ in Fig. 3(b). We vary the value of χ from zero to 100%. While the case of ($\chi = 100\%$) refers to the extreme case when all packets are forwarded via other links, the case of ($\chi = 0\%$) refers to the case when the proposed scheme is not implemented and only the Dijkstra algorithm is in use. The queue ratio threshold β is set to 80%. From the figure, it can be deduced that the system exhibits its optimum performance when the value of χ is set to 30%. This result is attributable to the fact that smaller values of χ put most of the traffic burden on satellite C3, whereas higher values of χ congest satellite C2. Both scenarios lead to higher packet drop rates and degraded throughput. Setting χ to optimum values helps also to avoid the re-distribution cascading issue that may occur to the already-distirubted portion of traffic. While this result is promising, it should be observed that it comes at the price of higher delays. In deed, packets have to traverse more hops than in case of traditional routing algorithms. For delay insensitive applications, this should not be an issue. For delay sensitive applications, a tradeoff between the number of packet drops and the parameters β and χ should be established. This forms the basis of our future research work.

5 Conclusion

In this paper, we proposed an Explicit Load Balancing routing protocol to efficiently distribute traffic over multi-hop NGEO satellite constellations. The key idea behind the proposed scheme is to reduce the sending rate of data traffic to nodes that are about to be congested and use instead nodes that are in free states. For this purpose, the proposed scheme uses information of traffic load at the next hop on the remainder of the path to the destination. This information is exchanged among neighboring satellites via signaling packets. The efficiency of the proposed scheme in distributing traffic data and accordingly avoiding packet drops is investigated through simulation using a simple satellite topology. While the setting of the scheme parameters (β & χ) deserve further study and investigation, the simulation results obtained so far are encouraging. In the performance evaluation, the authors considered the case of a small part of the Iridium constellation, as future research works, they are currently working on the performance evaluation of the scheme over the entire satellite constellation.

References

1. Taleb, T., Kato, N., Nemoto, Y.: On-demand media streaming to hybrid wired/wireless networks over quasi-geostationary satellite systems. Elsevier J. on Computer Networks, Vol. 47, No. 2, Feb. 2005, pp. 287-306.

2. Kohn, D.M.: Providing global broadband Internet access using low-earth-orbit satellites. Computer Networks and ISDN Systems, Vol. 29, No. 15, Nov. 1997, pp. 1785-1768.
3. Fraise, P., Coulomb, B., Monteuuis, B., Soula, J.L.: SkyBridge LEO satellites optimized for broadband communications in the 21st century. in Proc. of 2000 IEEE Aerospace Conf., Big Sky, Montana, USA, Mar. 2000.
4. Taleb, T., Kato, N., Nemoto, Y.: Recent trends in IP/NGEO satellite communication systems: Transport, routing, and mobility management. to appear in IEEE Commun. Mag..
5. Taleb, T., Kato, N., Nemoto, Y.: An explicit and fair window adjustment method to enhance TCP efficiency and fairness over multi-hops satellite networks. IEEE J. on Selected Areas in Commun., Vol. 22, No. 2, Feb. 2004, pp. 371-387.
6. Wood, L., Clerget, A., Andrikopoulos, I., Pavlou, G., Dabbous, W.: IP routing issues in satellite constellation networks. Int. J. Sat. Commun., Vol. 19, 2001, pp. 69-92.
7. Jamalipour, A., Katayama, M., Ogawa, A.: Traffic characteristics of LEO-based global personal communications networks. IEEE Commun. Mag., Vol. 35, No. 2, Feb. 1997, pp. 118-122.
8. Werner, M.: A dynamic routing concept for ATM based satellite personal communication networks. IEEE J. Select. Areas in Commun., Vol. 15, No. 8, Oct. 1997, pp. 1636-1648.
9. Mauger, R., Rosenberg, C.: QoS guarantees for multimedia services on a TDMA-based satellite network. IEEE Commun. Mag., Vol. 35, No. 7, Jul. 1997, pp. 56-65.
10. Nguyen, H. N.: Routing and quality-of-service in broadband LEO satellite networks. Kluwer Academic Publishers, Nov. 2002.
11. Coltun, R., Fuller, V.: The OSPF NSSA option. Network Working Group, RFC 1587, Mar. 1994.
12. Meyer, G., Sherry, S.: Triggered extensions to RIP to support demand circuits. Network Working Group, RFC 2091, Jan. 1997.
13. Uzunalioğlu, H., Akyildiz, I.F., Yesha, Y., Yen, W.: Footprint handover rerouting protocol for LEO satellite networks. ACM-Baltzer J. Wireless Networks, Vol. 5, No. 5, Nov. 1999, pp. 327-337.
14. Henderson, T.R., Katz, R.H.: On distributed, geographic-based packet routing for LEO satellite networks. In Proc. Globecom 2000, San Francisco, CA, USA, Dec. 2000.
15. Akyildiz, I.F., Ekici, E., Bender, M.D.: MLSR: A novel routing algorithm for multilayered satellite IP networks. IEEE/ACM Trans. on Networking, Vol. 10, No. 3, Jun. 2002. pp. 411-420.
16. Molinaro, A.,De Rango, F., Marano, S., Tropea, M.: A scalable framework for end-to-end QoS assurance in IP-oriented terrestrial-GEO satellite networks. IEEE Commun. Mag., Vol. 43, No. 4, Apr. 2005, pp. 130-137.
17. Chen, J., Jamalipour A.: An adaptive path routing scheme for satellite IP networks. Int. J. Commun. Sys., Vol. 16, No. 1, Feb. 2003, pp. 5-21.
18. Werner, M., Dellucchi, C., Vogel, H.J., Maral, G., Ridder, J.: ATM-based routing in LEO/MEO satellite networks with intersatellite links. IEEE J. Select. Areas in Commun., Vol. 15, Jan. 1997, pp. 69-82.
19. Donner, A., Berioli, M., Werner, M.: MPLS-based satellite constellation networks. IEEE J. Select. Areas in Commun., Vol. 22, No. 3, Apr. 2004, pp. 438-448.
20. Svigelj, A., Mohorcic, M., Kandus, G., Kos, A., Pustišek, M., Bešter, J.: Routing in ISL networks considering empirical IP traffic. IEEE J. Select. Areas in Commun., Vol. 22, No. 2, Feb. 2004, pp. 261-272.

21. Kucukates, R., Ersoy, C.: High performance routing in a LEO satellite network. in Proc. 8th IEEE Int. Sym. on Comp. Commun. (ISCC 2003), Washington, DC, USA, Jun. 2003.
22. Uzunalioglu, H.: Probabilistic routing protocol for low earth orbit satellite networks. in Proc. of IEEE Int. Conf. Commun. 1998. Atlanta, GA, USA, Jun, 1998.
23. Jianjun, B., Xicheng, Lu., Zexin, L., Wei, P.: Compact explicit multi-path routing for LEO satellite networks. in Proc. of 2005 IEEE Workshop on High Performance Switching and Routing, Hong Kong, P.R. China, May. 2005.
24. Athuraliya, S., Li, V.H., Low, S.H., Yin, Q.: REM: Active queue management. IEEE Network, Vol. 15, No. 3, Jan. 2001. pp 48-53.
25. Floyd, S., Jacobson, V.: Random early detection gateways for congestion avoidance. IEEE/ACM Trans. on Networking, Vol. 1, No. 4, Aug. 1993.
26. UCB/LBNL/VINT: Network Simulator - ns (version 2). http://www.isi.edu/nsnam/ns/
27. Goyal, R, Jain, R.: Buffer management and rate guarantees for TCP over satellite-ATM networks. Int. J. Satell. Comm., Vol. 19, No. 1, Jan.-Feb. 2001, pp 111-139.

Cross-Layer Management of Radio Resources in an Interactive DVB-RCS-Based Satellite Network—(Invited Paper)

Paolo Chini[1], Giovanni Giambene[1], Danilo Bartolini[2], Michele Luglio[2], and Cesare Roseti[2]

[1] CNIT - Dipartimento di Ingegneria dell'Informazione - Università degli Studi di Siena, Via Roma, 56 - 53100 Siena, Italy
giambene@unisi.it
[2] Università degli Studi di Roma "Tor Vergata", Via del Politecnico, 1 - 00133 Roma, Italy
{luglio, cesare.roseti}@uniroma2.it

Abstract. Recently, the request for multimedia broadband services via satellite has been rapidly increasing. We envisage a group of terminals that have to transmit (uplink) to a *Network Control Center* (NCC) via a geostationary bent-pipe satellite; the NCC is interconnected to the Internet through a router. Terminals employ the DVB-RCS standard to communicate with the NCC. Due to both the intrinsic propagation delay and the presence of a lossy radio channel, the *Transport Control Protocol* (TCP) is particularly inefficient in the satellite scenario. Therefore, we propose a novel cross-layer mechanism where resources are allocated by the *Medium Access Control* (MAC) layer at the NCC depending on the TCP behavior at remote terminals. Moreover, the MAC layer can also intervene on the TPC data injection rate to avoid system congestion. Simulation results show that: (*i*) our scheme prevents the occurrence of TCP timeouts (due to the satellite network congestion), thus improving the utilization of radio resources; (*ii*) it reduces the mean file transfer time for ftp applications with respect to a classical allocation scheme. This paper has been carried out within A&TCP research group of the "SatNEx" NoE project (URL: www.satnex.org; contract No. 507052) belonging to the 6-th framework of the European Commission.

Index Terms: *Satellite Networks, DVB-RCS, TCP.*

1 Introduction

Satellite communications have an important role since they can be the sole communication medium in unaccessible regions on the earth or in the Oceans. Moreover, satellite networks are the best candidate to allow a fast provision of broadband communications in different areas.

Towards the full protocol integration between terrestrial and satellite communication systems, it is important to study techniques to support TCP traffic

P. Yolum et al.(Eds.): ISCIS 2005, LNCS 3733, pp. 124–135, 2005.

with adequate efficiency and throughput also in satellite systems [1]. Typical characteristics of TCP are the gentle probe of system resources by progressively increasing the injection rate of data in the network by using sliding windows with dynamically adapted width; in such mechanism, a fundamental role is played by the *congestion window* (*cwnd*) [2]. This approach is needed since the network is a 'black box' and the TCP sender has no mean to know the network congestion status before sending data. Congestion is revealed by the loss of TCP segments with the consequent possibility of TCP timeouts that lead to the *cwnd* to be reset to its initial value (typically 1 or 2 TCP segments) with a sudden and significant TCP throughput reduction.

The TCP congestion control scheme leads to well-know inefficiencies in the satellite scenario due to both the high *Round-Trip Time* (RTT) and the frequent errors (with related losses of data) on the radio channel. TCP does not distinguish between segment losses due to network congestion and those caused by the radio link. Whereas, in the presence of a radio channel, many errors will be produced with consequent frequent *Retransmission TimeOut* (RTO) expirations that drastically reduce the throughput. However, these losses are not due to network congestion and the *cwnd* reduction is not appropriate.

Referring to TCP-based applications, we have that the traffic injected in the network is time-varying owing to the *cwnd* mechanism: *cwnd* can increase on an RTT basis (slow start or congestion avoidance case) or suddenly decrease in the presence of segment losses. On the basis of the above, a fixed bandwidth allocation to a given TCP flow is particulary inefficient. Also a classical dynamic channel allocation (considering the current state of radio resource allocation and the behavior of the physical layer) can be quite inefficient, being unable to track the TCP dynamics. Satellites are typically bandwidth and power limited. Hence, to achieve a better utilization of radio resources in the presence of TCP flows, we propose here a novel type of *Dynamic Bandwidth Allocation* (DBA), centrally controlled by a *Network Control Center* (NCC), that operates as follows [3],[4]:

- As far as resources (layer 2) are available, the NCC tries to allocate transmission uplink resources to a terminal so as to follow the behavior of its *cwnd* (layer 4).
- When all resources are allocated, the NCC (layer 2) stops a further increase in *cwnd* (layer 4) of the terminal.
- Resources are assigned according to a suitable prioritization scheme that privileges flows having less allocated resources.
- Resources are allocated so that connections of the same type and in similar conditions are fairly served (this entails resource rearrangements to avoid that more recent connections are starved by older ones).

According to the above, at the remote terminals we have envisaged a cross-layer dialogue so at to make resource requests to the NCC that are TCP-aware (interaction from layer 4 to layer 2). The NCC allocates resources to terminals on the basis of these requests; in case of congestion the NCC is also able to stop temporarily a further increase in the *cwnd* value of remote terminals (interaction from layer 2 to layer 4). Hence, there is a twofold cross-layer exchange of control information in our scheme [5],[6]. We have obtained that our resource allocation technique permits to reduce the occurrence of TPC timeouts due to congestion, since congestion is signaled in advance in the satellite network. Moreover, the available resources are better utilized, thus reducing the mean delay to transfer files with the ftp application (*elephant connections*).

2 System Architecture

In this paper we focus on an *Interactive Satellite Network* (ISN), based on the DVB-RCS standard [3],[4]. In particular, we consider a *GEOstationary* (GEO) bent-pipe satellite, *Return Channel Satellite Terminals* (RCSTs) and a *Network Control Center* (NCC) that is connected to a router to access the Internet (see Fig. 1). RCSTs are fixed and use the *Return Channel via Satellite* (RCS) that allows transmitting data or signaling. The NCC is the heart of the network: it provides control and monitoring functions and manages network resources allocation according to a DBA approach.

Typically, the RCST is connected to a local network where different terminals are present. For the sake of simplicity, in the following analysis we refer to a single terminal (user) connected per RCST; the extension of such study to the case of multiple terminals per RCST generating concurrent TCP flows is feasible[1], but beyond the scope of this paper where we are interested to prove the importance of the cross-layer interaction between layers 2 and 4 in order to achieve both a higher TPC throughout (layer 4) and an efficient utilization of resources (layer 2). In such a scenario, it is also possible to employ a *Performance Enhancing Proxy* (PEP) and to have a split of the TCP connection at the NCC [7]. While it is widely acknowledged that the deployment of split-based solutions may lead to a considerable performance improvement, we lose the typical end-to-end semantics of TCP causing congestion at the intermediate buffers and the risk of undelivered packets [8]. Finally, the IPsec protocol for secure transmissions requires that TCP operates end-to-end. Hence, we focus here on an end-to-end solution, leaving the comparison with the PEP approach to a further work.

3 DVB-S and DVB-RCS Air Interface Resources

DVB-S is used for the *forward link* (from NCC to RCSTs) and DVB-RCS is employed for the *return link* (from RCSTs to NCC); in both cases, a QPSK modulation is used. DVB-S can achieve a (layer 2) maximum data rate of 38 Mbit/s, whereas DVB-RCS has a maximum data rate of 2 Mbit/s. DVB-S has been conceived for primary and secondary distribution (*Fixed Satellite Service*, FSS) and

[1] In such a case, we may expect that the RCST aggregates the traffic needs coming from the current *cwnd* values of its different TCP flows; when congestion occurs, the RCST receives from the NCC a notification to stop the increase in the injection of traffic, so that the RCST can block the increase of the *cwnd* values according to a local criterion.

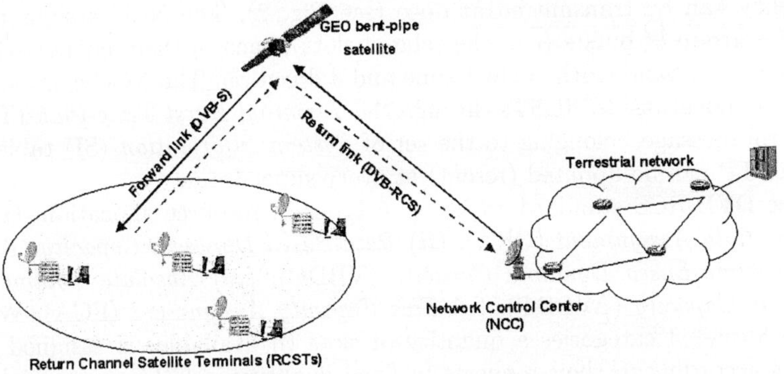

Fig. 1. System architecture

Broadcast Satellite Service (BSS), both operated in the Ku (11/12 GHz) band [9]. Such system is used to provide a direct reception from the satellite (*Direct-To-Home*, DTH) for both a single user with an integrated receiver-decoder and a collective access.

Below the transport layer and the IP layer we have the *Multi Protocol Encapsulation* (MPE) that provides segmentation & reassembly functions for the production of MPEG2-TS (*Transport Stream*) packets of fixed length (188 bytes) that are transmitted according to time division multiplexing. To the block of data coming from the application layer, a TCP header of 20 bytes, an IP header of 20 bytes and an MPE header+CRC trailer of 12+4 bytes are added; the resulting blocks are fragmented in payloads of MPEG2-TS packets. Then, transmission is performed according to several steps, such as: channel coding (external Reed-Solomon coding, convolutional interleaver, internal convolutional coding, puncturing), baseband shaping of impulses, and QPSK modulation.

The DVB-RCS air interface is of the *Multi Frequency - Time Division Multiple Access* (MF-TDMA) type: resources are time slots on distinct available carrier frequencies with different possible available bandwidths. DVB-RCS resources are divided in super-frames that are characterized by suitable portions of time and frequency bands. The DVB-RCS standard considers that the maximum super-frame length is 93.2 s. Each super-frame is divided in frames that are composed of time slots; the frames can have different duration, bandwidth and composition of time slots. An RCST can have assigned slots belonging to the same frequency or to different frequencies with the constraint that only one

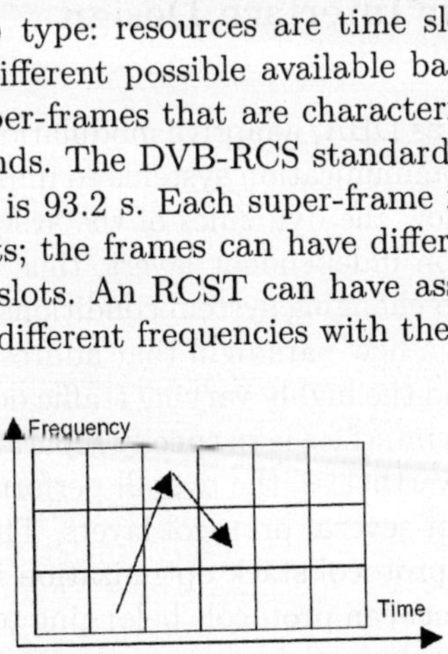

Fig. 2. Use of MF-TDMA slot resources on different carrier frequencies

frequency can be transmitted at once (see Fig. 2). The NCC assigns to each RCST a group of bursts (i.e., the related slots), each of them characterized by a frequency, a bandwidth, a start time and a duration. The NCC communicates resource allocations to RCSTs through the *Terminal Burst Time Plan* (TBTP), a control message belonging to the set of *System Information* (SI) table. Note that TBTP can be updated (resent) at every super-frame.

The DVB-RCS standard envisages 5 types of resource allocation: (*i*) *Continuous Rate Assignment* (CRA); (*ii*) *Rate-Based Dynamic Capacity* (RBDC); (*iii*) *Volume-Based Dynamic Capacity* (VBDC); (*iv*) *Absolute Volume-Based Dynamic Capacity* (AVBDC); (*v*) *Free Capacity Assignment* (FCA). Whereas in the former 4 categories a quantity of slots (if available) is assigned to the RCSTs according to their requests (a fixed quantity in CRA or a variable one in the other 3 cases), the FCA assignment strategy allocates the resources not used in a given super-frame (after the satisfaction of the other types of assignment requests), without explicit requests made by the RCSTs (a sort of *bonus* to reduce possible delays). Since in this paper we need to employ a DBA scheme, the two major candidates are VBDC and AVBDC due to the fact that in both cases time-varying resource requests are made by the RCSTs. In the VBDC assignment, an RCST dynamically requests the total number of slots needed to idle its queue; requests are cumulative. Such category is typically used for Web-browsing traffic. Whereas, in the AVBDC case, an RCST dynamically requests the number of slots, but requests are absolute (not cumulative). Even if VBDC is the default mode in the DVB-RCS standard, it seems that an AVBDC-like scheme should be used in our scenario, since, according to the envisaged cross-layer approach, requests are not exactly related to the status of the buffer and are not cumulative, but rather they refer to the prospected next value of the congestion window *cwnd* for each TCP flow (mapped here to a single RCST).

4 Cross-Layer Air Interface Design

Several techniques (such as DBA, adaptive modulation and coding, etc.) need to be adopted in satellite communication systems to improve their efficiency. These techniques permit to follow the dynamics of the system. The conventional OSI protocol stack is based on independent layers, thus precluding the adaptation of each layer according to changing system conditions. The cross-layer approach proposed in this paper is a new paradigm that addresses adaptation considering both system dynamics and the highly varying traffic demand of applications. The classical way to design an interface is to specify separately physical, link, network and transport layers. Nevertheless, the overall performance can be improved by means of a joint design of several protocol layers. This is the aim of the cross-layer approach, where a protocol stack optimization is achieved by introducing novel interactions even between protocols belonging to non-adjacent layers. Due to the specificity of the optimization process, the cross-layer design needs to be suitably tailored for our DVB-RCS scenario.

In the light of the above, this paper proposes the definition of a layer 2 MAC protocol that on the RCST side exploits information coming from TCP [5],[6] and interacts with the layer 2 on the NCC side for resource allocation decisions. Different methods can be used to implement the cross-layer exchange of information, as described in [10]; among them, particularly interesting solutions are the use of packet headers or the adoption of *Internet Control Message Protocol* (ICMP) signaling to create holes in the layers of the protocol stack so that messages can be propagated across layers.

4.1 Dynamic Resource Allocation for TCP Flows with Interactions Between Layer 2 and Layer 4

Referring to the network architecture shown in Fig. 1, our resource management scheme (centrally coordinated by the NCC) is described below considering the protocol stacks detailed in Fig. 3. In what follows, we refer to the TCP NewReno version where some packet losses can be recovered without a timeout expiration by means of the duplicated ACK mechanism [11],[12].

In the return channel, RCSTs send their resource requests to the NCC on the basis of the expected behavior of their *cwnd* values in the next RTT; this is obtained through a special message from layer 4 to layer 2 of the RCST and, then, to layer 2 of the NCC. Then, the NCC looks at the available uplink resources of the MF-TDMA air interface and sends a broadcast response every super-frame to update the resource allocation to the RCSTs (forward channel) by means of the TBTP message. Hence, resource allocation to RCSTs is dynamic on the basis of the behaviors of their congestion windows. Moreover, resources are fairly shared among competing flows of the same type. When a further increase in the

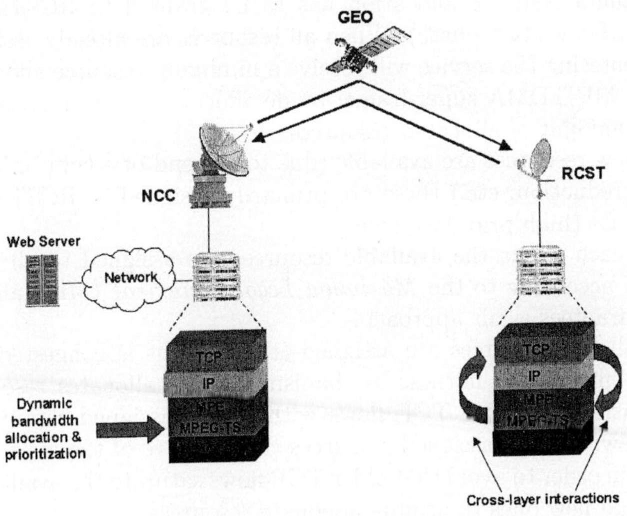

Fig. 3. Protocol stack and cross-layer interactions (view of both the RCST side and the NCC side)

need of allocated resources to an RCST cannot be fulfilled by the NCC (all the MF-TDMA time slots are assigned and no reassignments are possible), layer 2 of the NCC sends a special message to layer 4 of this RCST to stop temporarily further increases in *cwnd*.

The MAC header in the resource request message sent by the RCST to the NCC contains the two following data that are essential for our resource allocation scheme: (*i*) the TCP phase flag; (*ii*) the estimate of the congestion window value ($cwnd_{next}$) for the next RTT. The NCC filters any incoming packet in order to compare the $cwnd_{next}$ value with the amount of resources already assigned (a_{res}) to the corresponding RCST (in terms of packets). Two cases are possible:

- If $cwnd_{next} < a_{res}$, the NCC considers that a packet loss has occurred so that the *cwnd* has been reduced; then, for the next RTT $cwnd_{next}$ resources will be allocated to the RCST and $a_{res} - cwnd_{next}$ resources will be made available and equally shared among the connections of other RCSTs (this is the typical case of a channel loss).
- If $cwnd_{next} > a_{res}$, the NCC considers that the RCST (i.e., TCP sender) needs a capacity increase in the next RTT. Such resource request is managed as outlined below.

The request is inserted in either a high-priority queue or a low-priority one, respectively depending on the slow start phase or the congestion avoidance one, as specified by the TCP phase flag in the MAC header. Requests in the queues are served as follows:

- The NCC allocates further resources (in the next RTT through the broadcast TBTP message) first to requests in the high priority queue; then, requests in the low-priority queue are considered if there is still available capacity.
- A minimum resource allocation has to be granted to RCSTs starting to transmit (slow start phase). When all resources are already assigned, a new RCST entering the service will receive a minimum resource allocation of one slot per MF-TDMA super-frame, by de-allocating it from RCSTs with the highest amount of allocated resources.
- When new resources are available (due to the end of a connection or due to a *cwnd* reduction, etc.) these are primarily assigned to RCSTs in the slow start phase (high priority queue).
- Within each queue the available resources are assigned to all the pending requests according to the *Maximum Legal Increment* (MLI) algorithm [13] that guarantees a fair approach.
- When all the resources are assigned (the systems is congested), the DBA scheme envisages a fairness mechanism that de-allocates resources on an RTT basis from those TCP flows with higher assigned resources in favor of those with lower assigned resources (irrespective of the related TCP flow phases) in order to avoid that older TCP flows saturate the available capacity and forbid new ones to acquire adequate resources.

If the resource request of a given RCST cannot be fully satisfied in the current super-frame, the NCC creates a “waiting list” to assign resources in the next super-frames. If also the amount of the needed resources exceeds the available resources in an RTT, the NCC defines a *cwnd** value lower than the current $cwnd_{next}$ value determined by the RCST; the *cwnd** value, conveyed in a field for TCP options in the segment overhead, is sent back to the RCST up to layer 4 to modify the current *cwnd* value used by the RCST as: $cwnd \leftarrow cwnd^*$. Such procedure is repeated until the congestion persists; hence, during congestion periods, an RCST has a flat *cwnd* behavior forced by layer 2 of the NCC. Such approach is quite important: since the NCC has a complete control over the resources of the ISN, it can stop (in the presence of congestion) further increases of *cwnd* that would only cause packet losses and throughput reduction at the TCP level.

Note that in typical (non-cross-layer) DBA implementations, the buffer at the MAC level of an RCST has a value equal to the *Bandwidth-Delay Product* (BDP) of the ISN. Hence, MAC requests a certain number of resources according to the contents of the buffer with DBA. Whereas, in our DBA case with cross-layer approach, the MAC layer requests resources according to the *cwnd* value estimated for the next RTT; therefore, the MAC buffer contains only those packets waiting for transmission (i.e., the packets to which resources are assigned and that wait for the corresponding slots).

5 Simulation Results

We have implemented a simulator in the ns-2 environment to test the potentialities of our proposed cross-layer approach [14]. We have modified the C++ code and created two new specific classes: "Cross-layer" and "DBA-algorithm". The former (inside the RCST) performs the functions for the exchange of information between TCP and MAC and the functions for the estimation of the requested resources for the next RTT (i.e., $cwnd_{next}$). The latter (inside the NCC) implements the algorithm to allocate/deallocate resources to RCSTs with the evaluation of *cwnd**. The simulator is realized through one node for the NCC, one node for the GEO-satellite and one node for each active RCST.

Our simulation scenario is numerically characterized as follows: RTT (GEO satellite) = 540 ms; a single frequency carrier; super-frame length = 54 ms (10 super-frames = 1 RTT); TCP segment size = 1444 bytes plus headers of TCP (20 bytes), IP (20 bytes), and MPE (16 bytes for header and trailer), so that the resulting packet length is of 1500 bytes; layer 2 (MPE) buffer length = 50 packets; bit-rate on a carrier = 2 Mbit/s; transport protocol = TCP NewReno; Ku band channel model of the AWGN type for clear sky conditions with *Packet Error Rate* (PER) $\in (5 \times 10^{-4}, 5 \times 10^{-2})$; ftp transfer with file size = 5 Mbytes or 7.5 Mbytes (elephant connections); ftp traffic model = ACK clocked; the receiver window has been assumed infinite not to limit the transmission window. We have adopted a resource granularity of 1 slot (minimum resource allocation) corresponding to 4 packets (1500 bytes), i.e., a train of MPEG2-TS packets, transmitted in a burst (slot).

Fig. 4 shows the operation of the resource allocation algorithm that permits to assign resources to a single RCST according to the behavior of its *cwnd*. This graph has been obtained for a single RCST having to transfer a file of 7.5 Mbytes (i.e., 5000 packets) with a PER $= 3 \times 10^{-4}$. The initial *ssthresh* value is 50 packets. The cross-layer technique permits to request to the DBA controller an amount of resources corresponding to the estimated *cwnd* value for the next RTT; such request is fulfilled only if there are available transmission resources.

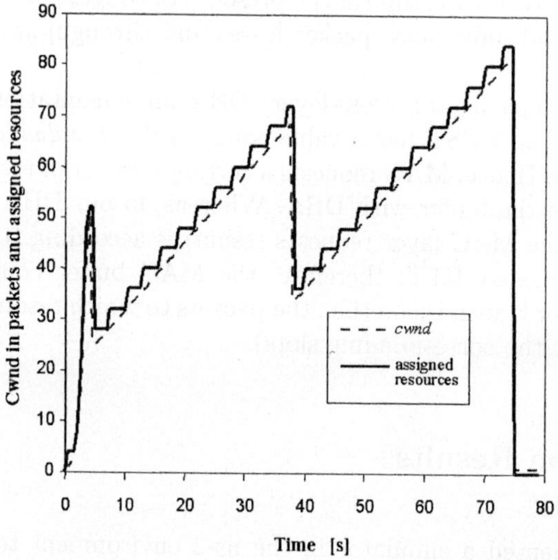

Fig. 4. Behavior of the TCP congestion window as compared to the assigned resources per RTT

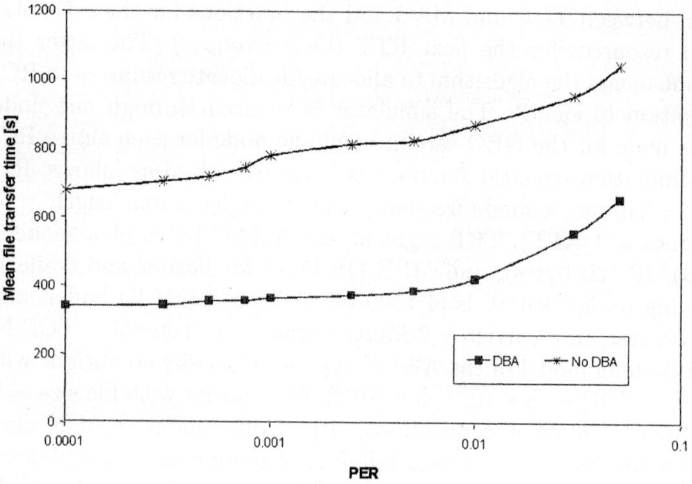

Fig. 5. Mean file transfer time as a function of PER for both our scheme (DBA) and the classical fixed channel allocation ('no DBA')

cwnd reductions are due to packet losses caused by the radio channel. In such cases, the *cwnd* value is halved, according to the NewReno scheme, and the DBA technique is able to change adaptively the resource allocated on an RTT basis. It is important to note that no TCP timeouts occur with our algorithm.

The behavior of the mean file transfer time (for files of 5 Mbytes) as a function of PER is shown in Fig. 5 for 30 RCSTs connections (starting at regularly spaced intervals of 10 s). This graph shows that the mean file transfer time in the fixed allocation case ('no DBA', i.e., fixed share of the available capacity among the

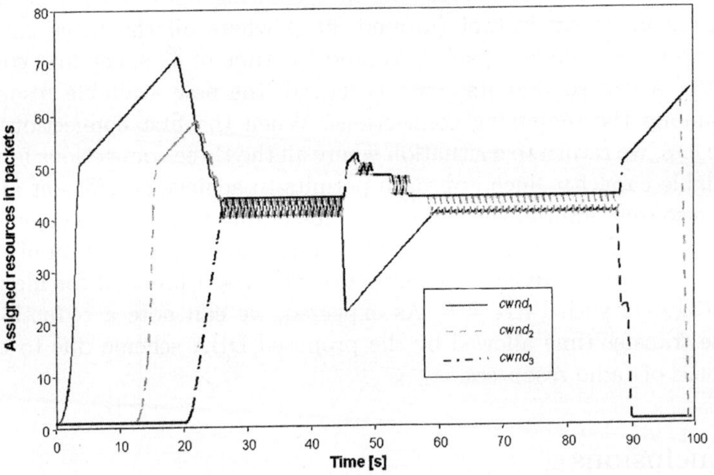

Fig. 6. Behavior of assigned resources in the time in the presence of three concurrent TCP connections

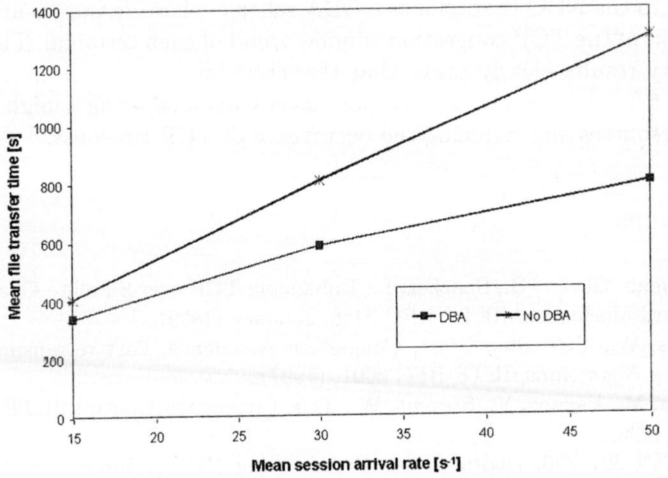

Fig. 7. Mean file transfer time for both DBA and fixed channel allocation ('no DBA') as a function of the mean arrival rate of ftp connections (PER = 0)

RCSTs) is much higher than that in the proposed DBA scheme. We note that the mean file transfer time increases with PER since the TCP goodput is affected by errors; of course, the proposed DBA scheme takes advantage of both the efficient use of resources and the reassignments in case of packet losses so that the mean file transfer time is significantly reduced with respect to the classical 'no DBA' scheme.

Fig. 6 refers to a case with 3 RCSTs starting ftp connections at different instants with PER $= 1.5 \times 10^{-4}$ and files to be transferred of 7.5 Mbytes. These TCP-based connections start at different times; hence, even if the first connection saturates the available resources, the new entering ones entail a deallocation of resources up to an instant (around 30 s) where all the three connections fairly share the available capacity. Around the time of 45 s, the first connection experiences a loss so that its *cwnd* is halved; the new available resources are shared among the remaining connections. When the first connection recovers from the loss, we return to a situation where all the three connections fairly share the available capacity. Such approach permits to achieve an efficient utilization of radio resources even in the presence of losses due to the radio channel.

Finally, Fig. 7 presents the mean file transfer time as a function of the mean rate for the arrival of RCST ftp connections (Poisson process) for file transfers of 7.5 Mbytes/s with PER = 0. As expected, we can note a reduction in the mean file transfer time allowed by the proposed DBA scheme due to the more efficient use of radio resources.

6 Conclusions

DVB-RCS is an open standard for interactive broadband satellite services. We have considered a group of terminals that, using TCP as transport protocol, send data to the NCC that adopts a DBA scheme where resources are allocated on the basis of the TCP congestion window trend of each terminal. The obtained preliminary results clearly prove that this cross-layer approach permits to improve the performance at the transport level while achieving a high utilization of radio resources and reducing the occurrence of TCP timeouts.

References

1. M. Allman, Glover, D., Sanchez, L.: Enhancing TCP over Satellite Channels using Standard Mechanism, IETF RFC 2488, January (1999).
2. Stevens, W.: TCP Slow Start, Congestion Avoidance, Fast retransmit and Fast recovery Algorithms, IETF RFC 2001, (1997).
   Allman, M., Paxons, V., Stevens, W.: TCP Congestion Control, IETF RFC 2581, April (1999).
3. ETSI EN 301 790. Digital Video Broadcasting (DVB); Interaction Channel for Satellite Distribution Systems. V1.3.1, (2003).
4. ETSI TR 101 790. Digital Video Broadcasting (DVB); Interaction Channel for Satellite Distribution Systems; Guidelines for the use of EN 301 790. V1.2.1, (2003).

5. Shakkottai S., Rappaport, T. S., Karlsson, P. C.: Cross-Layer Design for Wireless Networks. IEEE Commun. Mag., October (2003), 74-80.
6. Guainella, E., Pietrabissa, A.: TCP-Friendly Bandwidth-on-Demand Scheme for Satellite Networks", ASMS conference (2003).
7. Border, J., Kojo, M., Griner, J., Montenegro, G., Shelby, Z.: Performance Enhancing Proxies Intended to Mitigate Link-related Degradations, IETF RFC 3135, June (2001).
8. Floyd S., Fall, K.: Promoting the use of end-to-end congestion control in the Internet, IEEE/ACM Trans. on Netw., vol. 7, pp. 458472, Aug. 1999.
9. ETSI EN 300 421. Digital Video Broadcasting (DVB); Framing structure, channel coding and modulation for 11/12 GHz satellite services. V1.1.2, (1997).
10. Wu G., Bai Y., Lai J., Ogielski A.: Interactions between TCP and RLP in wireless Internet, Proc. IEEE GLOBECOM'99, December (1999).
11. Allman, M., Paxons, V., Stevens, W.: TCP Congestion Control, IETF RFC 2581, April (1999).
12. Floyd, S., Henderson, T.: The NewReno Modification to the TCP's Fast Recovery Algorithm, IETF RFC 2582, April (1999).
13. Acar, G., Rosenberg, C.: Algorithms to compute for Bandwidth on Demand Requests in a Satellite Access Unit, Proc. of the 5th Ka-band Utilization Conference, (1999), 353-360.
14. NS-2 Network Simulator (Vers. 2.27), URL: http://www.isi.edu/nsnam/ns/ns-build.html

Aggressive Back off Strategy in Congestion Management Algorithm for DBS-RCS — (Invited Paper)

Tuna Tuğcu and Fatih Alagöz

Department of Computer Engineering, Bogazici University,
34342 Bebek, Istanbul, Turkey
{tugcu, alagoz}@boun.edu.tr

Abstract. This paper investigates an aggressive back off strategy as part of the congestion management algorithms developed for Direct Broadcast Satellites with Return Channel Systems (DBS-RCS). The satellite architecture considered in this work is based on an asymmetric architecture with the high capacity forward link provided by the DBS and low speed return channel is provided by a constellation of Low Earth Orbiting (LEO) satellites. The network carries both Moving Pictures Expert Group (MPEG) coded video traffic and other data traffic having available bit rates (ABR) which is based on Reliable DBS Multicast Protocol (RDMP). Due to overwhelming complexity of real DBS-RCS systems, unless unduly simplifications are made, an exact analysis of this system becomes impossible. Therefore, we rely on the testbed results for investigation of the proposed aggressive back off strategy. In this paper, we first present a brief background on adaptive resource allocation and management (ARAM) system developed in our earlier work [1]. Then, we provide the proof of concept experiments for the newly introduced aggressive back off strategy. We show that the distributed control provided by the watermarks provides performance comparable to the baseline ARAM model. We also show that an aggressive back off strategy should be used for increased QoS.

1 Introduction

The future broadcast satellite system is under investigation for an asymmetric architecture with high capacity forward link provided by the Direct Broadcast Satellites (DBS) and lower speed return link provided by either a terrestrial link or a constellation of Low Earth Orbiting (LEO) satellites [1]. The challenge is to manage the dynamic bandwidth needs of Moving Pictures Expert Group (MPEG) video traffic while maintaining their Quality of Service (QoS). The purpose of this paper is to present an adaptive control approach for multiplexing heterogeneous traffic types over a Direct Broadcast Satellite (DBS) to end-users located in different regions experiencing varying channel conditions. When the MPEG coded video bit rates are at peak values, then network congestion will typically occur unless the network is designed to accommodate such peaks. Such congestion will degrade performance as evidenced by in-creased packet delays and packet losses for both the variable bit rate traffic as well as other traffic in the network. However, if the network is designed for peak rates, then it will be over designed for nominal rates resulting in excess capacity.

P. Yolum et al.(Eds.): ISCIS 2005, LNCS 3733, pp. 136 – 144, 2005.

Due to stringent service requirements of integrated satellite networks, the admission control and resource management scheme may become more challenging than traditional wired/wireless networks. [2] presents the performance of a movable boundary accessing technique, detailing the admission control and resource allocation procedure, in a multiservice satellite environment. [3] provides performance results for both conventional and dual movable boundary schemes. [4] presents the simulation results for an end-to-end connectivity planning and admission control for a multibeam satellite network with on-board cross-connectivity. [5,6] propose an adaptive call management system real-time (low-interactive) VBR traffic over GEO satellite links. [7] presents simulation results for the performance of the combined/fixed reservation assignment scheme for aggregated traffic. [8] presents the simulation results for the medium access control of the broadband satellite networks. [9] presents the performance of end-to-end resource management in ATM GEO satellite networks. [10] presents an integrated connection admission control scheme for multiple wireless systems, ranging from terrestrial cellular networks to satellite networks.

The admission control approach described in this paper is based on the Adaptive Resource Allocation and Management (ARAM) algorithms described in [1]. ARAM is intended to ameliorate these problems in three ways:

- Design the network to leverage the statistical multiplexing effects, i.e., not all peaks occur at the same time,
- Adjust the rates of Available Bit Rate (ABR) traffic with less stringent latency requirements,
- Scale the MPEG video to operate within the bandwidth if all else fails.

In this way a balance is maintained between meeting user needs without an over designed network. The rest of this paper is given as follows. Section II presents a brief description of the system architecture envisioned for deployment of the above techniques. Section III presents the aggressive back off strategy in adaptive control algorithm of the forward link satellite channel. Section V describes the testbed and protocol work. Section V presents proof of concept experimental results. Section VI concludes this study.

2 Background

Figure 1 portrays the system concept that is based on an asymmetric architecture such that existing technology may be most effectively employed. The system delivers high volumes of information (data, imagery, video) from Source Systems located in safe havens to Application Platforms, i.e., user systems experiencing different channel problems. The system uses a high capacity forward link provided by a DBS to multicast data, imagery, and video packets from Source System hosts to DBS Field Terminals (DFTs) located at the satellite down link facility. Upon receipt of these packets, the DFT routes them to the user Application Platform (AP). The DFT is a combination of DBS antenna, RF system, and DVB decoder with an IP router. The interface

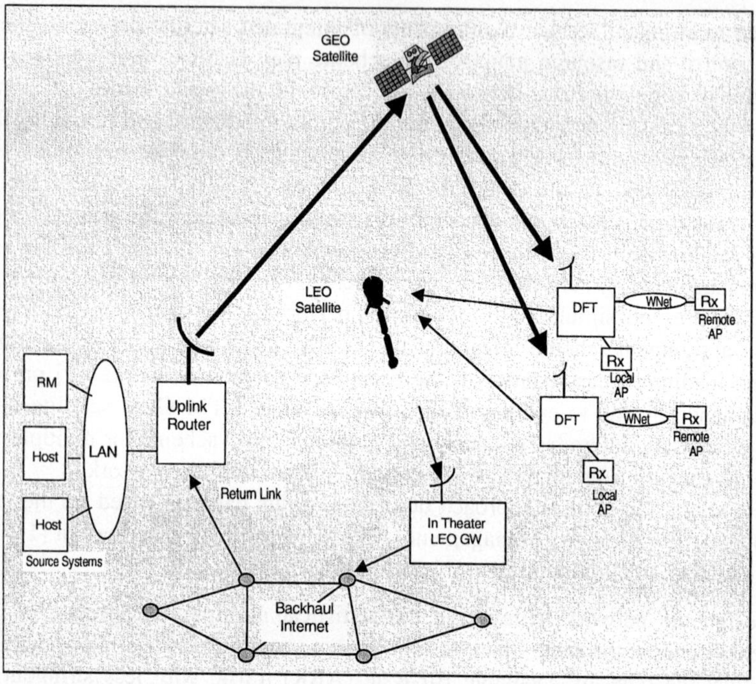

Fig. 1. System Architecture

between the DFT and Application Platforms may be either: local area network, or remote connection by a terrestrial wireless network.

The low speed return link is provided by a constellation of Low Earth Orbit-ing (LEO) satellites. Since the area of coverage of the LEO satellite may not in-clude the Source Systems, the LEO will downlink return packets to an in-theater gateway. The LEO gateway will then transmit the packets to the Source System via a terrestrial backhaul network. To deliver large volumes of information, this system utilizes the IP multicast protocol as the integrating technology.

The system provides the following two types services:

- Available Bit Rate (ABR) service for the reliable multicast of data and imagery,
- Variable Bit Rate (VBR) service for the MPEG video.

The ABR provides the error free delivery of data (files, images, or objects) to each receiving entity resident in the AP. In the case of transmission errors, it notifies both the sending application and network management for a retransmission. This service which is implemented by the Reliable DBS Multicast Protocol (RDMP), guarantees the reliable delivery of messages to receivers or identifies an error condition [3]. The RDMP concept in terms of its ARQ (Automatic Repeat reQuest), flow control, synchronization, and recovery capabilities are described in [3]. Based on network congestion, it transmits its packets at a rate ranging from (T_{min}, T_{max}).

The VBR provides the delivery of variable rate MPEG video via IP multicast from one source to many receivers. Since this service operates in a real-time mode, it does not utilize any acknowledgment techniques but relies on the quality of the underlying network to ensure an acceptable error rate. Analogous to ABR, the VBR service adjusts its offered data rate based on network conditions. While it requires the fixed delivery of 2 GOPs per second, the length of the frames may be adjusted over a range (L_{min}, L_{max}) to control the MPEG coding rate [7].

3 Aggressive Backoff Strategy in Adaptive Control Algorithm

The Adaptive Control concept for multiplexing the ABR and VBR traffic allows for an arbitrary mix of ABR and VBR traffic. A Resource Manager allocates available capacity to the ABR and VBR services based on priority, time window when service is needed, and cumulative queuing time of a request. Since the VBR services operate with a variable data rate, this allocation assumes some statistical multiplexing of VBR services will occur. As described in [1], the number of services allocated is based on the assessment that the capacity allocated to the VBR services will only exceed the assigned capacity a fixed percentage of the time.

The control algorithm is based on the concept of watermarks, as measured in the uplink router queue [12]. The traffic will be multiplexed from several hosts over a LAN to a router that is directly connected to a satellite uplink facility. Since the LAN will have a higher data rate than the satellite uplink, the uplink will be a bottleneck. Therefore, congestion will be detected at the uplink router where packets are passed to the satellite ground station for transmission. In this concept, the watermark is measured as the uplink queue utilization in the router. The router will periodically multicast its "uplink queue watermark" over a network management socket to all of the Source System Hosts. When hosts serving ABR traffic receive a watermark message on the net management socket, they will adjust their transmission rate according to its watermark action table which will specify the fraction, f_k, for adjusting the transmission rate for level k. When the watermark indicates the queue utilization is low, then the ABR transmission rate will be increased to T_{max}. Analogously, when the queue is heavily utilized, the transmission will be backed off to T_{min}. When the watermark message is received indicating the current utilization is between Level k-1 and k, the host will determine the closest match in the action table, e.g., Level k. Then if the watermark has changed from the previous report, then the new transmission rate will be set with the rate factor, f_k, at:

$$T_{new} = T_{min} + f_k * (T_{max} - T_{min})$$

The adjustment of the VBR traffic is done analogously except the frame length is adjusted based on the watermark, but the transmission rate stays the same. For example, the new frame length would be determined as:

$$L_{new} = f_k * L_{nom}$$

where L_{nom} is the frame length at the nominal compression rate and fk is the scaling factor. With watermarks, source systems are alerted of congestion by watermark messages and take action by reducing the source rates. The watermark table may be static or dynamic. For example, as the number of active users changes over time, it is desirable to modify the granularity of the adjustments being made. For example, when congestion occurs with a small number of users, large adjustments per user will be required to alleviate congestion while if there are a large number of users, smaller adjustments may suffice. Therefore, as the number of users changes the Resource Manager may update the watermark action tables.

Since digital signals over satellites have a very abrupt threshold, the video quality may completely degrade when the signal falls below the threshold. When the error rate threshold has been less than the acceptable threshold for N (typically 5) periods, then the FEC rate is increased to the next level. Because of the curves are very steep, decreasing the FEC rate by one level from levels of 7/8, 5/6, or even 3/4 may provide no improvement in performance. Therefore, the ARAM Resource Manager will reduce the FEC rate to either 1/2 or 2/3.

4 Testbed and Protocols

Figure 2 depicts the logical layout of the testbed. Source Hosts (MPEG, emulated MPEG, and RDMP), Resource Manager implements the algorithms, Uplink Router implements the queue management algorithms, Satellite Emulator introduces the

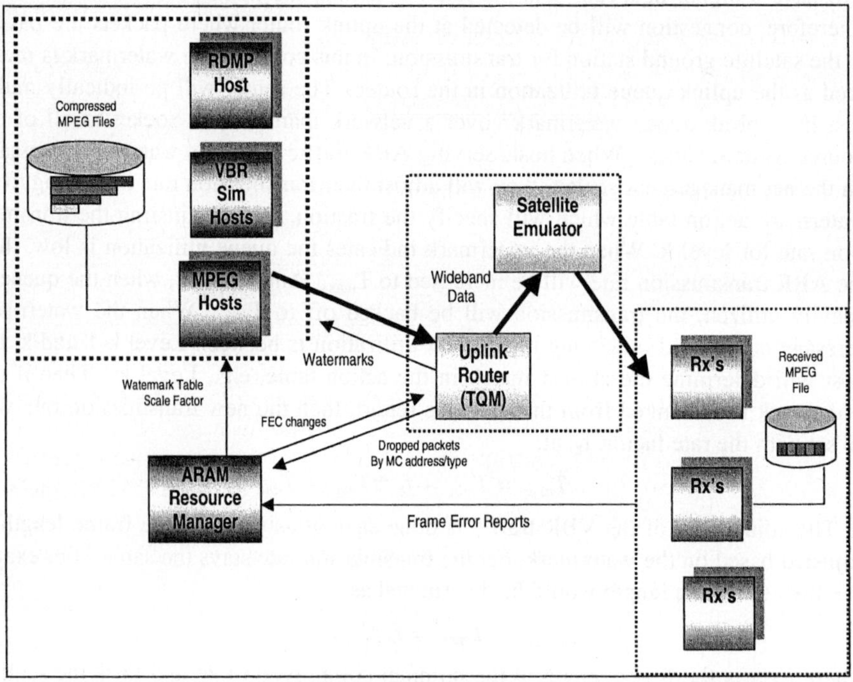

Fig. 2. Testbed Concept

delays and error rates representative of DBS satellites, and set of VBR and ABR receivers. The testbed elements are implemented using PCs or workstations. Although theUplink Router and Satellite Emulator represent separate physical elements, they are implemented in the same PC to minimize testbed resources.

The representation of ARAM in the testbed is a simplified version of simulations because the testbed has the capability to model only a small number of MPEG flows (compared to the 30-40 flows in the simulation). As depicted in the figure, the Resource Manager is driven by the Frame Error Rate report from the Receivers and the Dropped Packet Reports from the Uplink Router. Based on these inputs, the Resource Manager resets the FEC rate and informs the Source Systems of the FEC change via the Scale Factor message. The Scale Factor reflects the change in information capacity due to the change in FEC rate. It is defined as the ratio of current FEC rate to the starting FEC rate. For example, if the starting FEC rate is 3/4 and the current rate is 1/2, then Scale Factor = (1/2)/ (3/4) = 2/3.

Introduction of the real MPEG stream into the testbed was difficult because of the heavy processing load required for MPEG encoding. Therefore, MPEG compression was performed off-line MPEG data was stored on disk with four compression rates (shown by the four color coded files in the figure). When the ARAM algorithm indicated a change in the compression rate was required, the source selected the corresponding MPEG file for transmission over the network. The decoder then received a video stream with the compression rate changing over time (shown by the file having four shades).

The emulated traffic was introduced using a superposition of two first-order autoregressive, AR(1), processes; one captures the short, and the other captures the long term dependencies of MPEG coded video traffic [12].

RDMP was developed to provide a reliable multicast service over a DBS satellite with a low speed return link. It operates over UDP because it has been developed as a UNIX application. For an operational system, RDMP would be modified to run directly over IP and reside in the UNIX kernel. Details on RDMP and the details of RTP-MPEG header encapsulations are described in [13].

5 Proof of Concept Experiments

This section describes the physical layout and the data display developed to show the experimental results as tests are being conducted. First, Figure 3 depicts the hardware layout, organized in Source and Receiver Systems. It also shows the functional residency of each device in terms of RDMP sender/receiver, Emulated VBR sender/receiver, and MPEG sender/receiver. For ease of implementation, one of the RDMP receivers (DBS3) collects the watermark, scale factor, and RDMP throughput data and sends it to the MPEG Display host (APOLLO) such that an integrated d isplay can be produced. However, this is for display purposes only and would be implemented in an operational system.

The watermark strategy employed in the experiments was to first backoff the RDMP transmission rate and then backoff on the MPEG rates. The RDMP watermark tables were set to begin backing off when the watermark hit a 50% level. At the 50% level, the RDMP transmission rate was adjusted to 90% of the maximum rate while when the watermark hit 100%, the transmission rate was reduced to 50% of the maximum value.

For the MPEG traffic, the backoff began when the watermark hit 80%. The following adjustments were used:

80% - transmit at 95% of nominal rate,
90% - transmit at 90% of nominal rate,
100% - transmit at 90% of nominal rate.

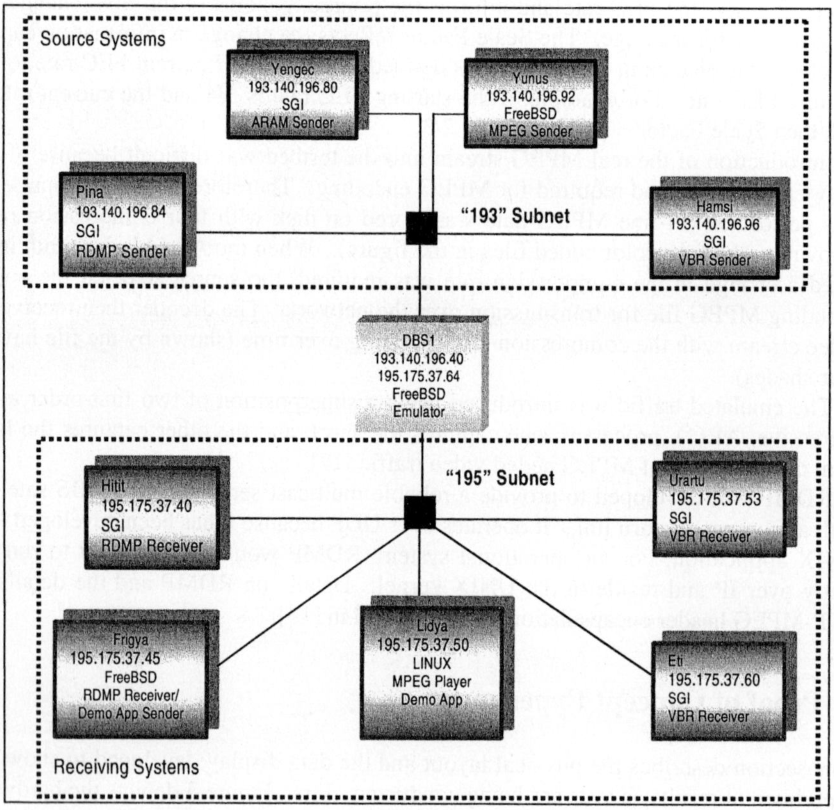

Fig. 3. Hardware Layout

These rates are very aggressive because there are only two MPEG streams. In order to display results as the experiments are being performed, the real-time display is developed. The proof of concept experiment was successfully conducted for both a good channel scenario and a Gilbert channel alternating between good and bad channel conditions. It was demonstrated that the source rates for both the emulated and actual MPEG streams and the RDMP stream could be successfully changed in response to the watermark message. It was also demonstrated that the FEC rate could be

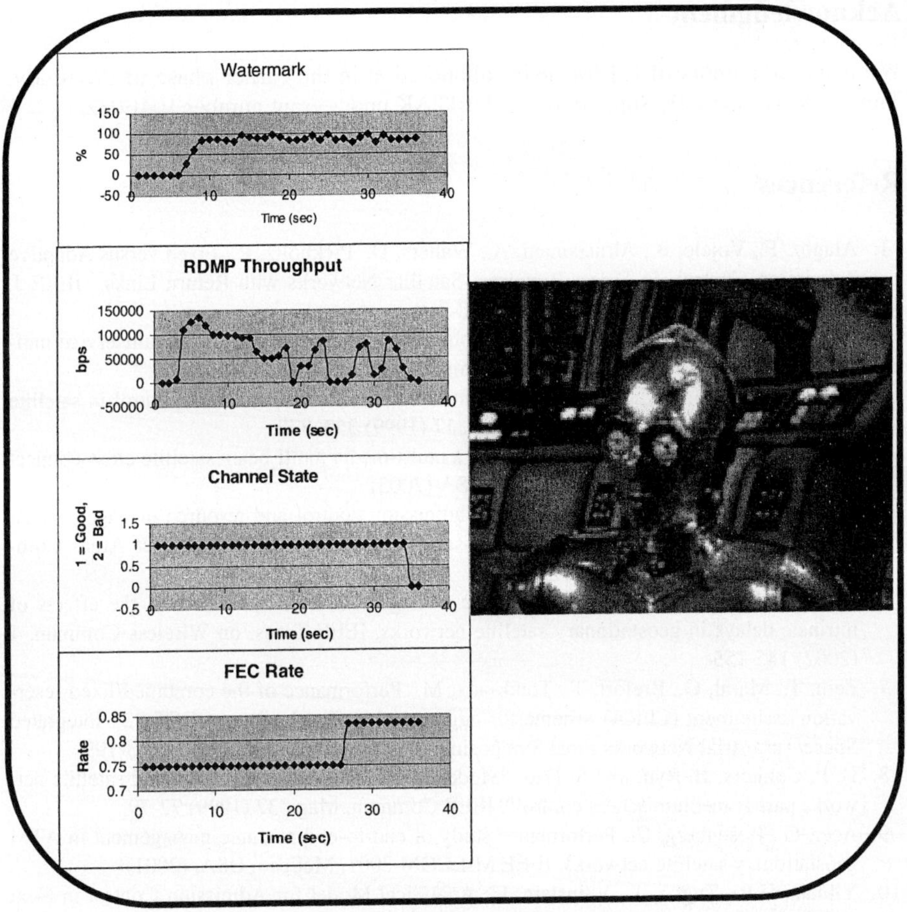

Fig. 4. Representative Screen Display

adjusted by the ARAM algorithm. Figure 4 depicts the representative screen display showing data captured during the experiments.

6 Conclusions

In this paper we presented the testbed performance results of an aggressive back off strategy for congestion control in integrated satellite networks. We demonstrated a proof concept for implementation of the adaptive resource allocation and management (ARAM) algorithms based on the use of watermarks, to detect congestion in the system. It has been shown by simulation that the distributed control provided by the watermarks provides performance comparable to the baseline ARAM. Also, the testbed results show that utilizing an aggressive back off strategy, i.e., back off later rather than sooner, provides a higher quality of service even though more frames are dropped because performance will not be unnecessarily reduced.

Acknowledgment

We thank co-authors of [1] for their collaboration in the earlier phase of this study. This work was partially supported by TUBITAK under grant number 104E032.

References

1. Alagöz, F., Vojcic, B., Alrustamani, A., Walters, D., Pickholtz, R.: Fixed versus Adaptive Admission Control in Direct Broadcast Satellite Networks with Return Links. IEEE J. Selected Areas in Commun. 22 (2004) 238-250.
2. Bohm, S., et al: Analysis of a movable boundary access technique for a multiservice multibeam satellite system. Int. J. Satellite Commun. 12 (1994) 299–312.
3. Koraitim, H.,Tohme,S.: Resource allocation and connection admission control in satellite networks. IEEE J. Select. Areas Commun. 17 (1999) 360–372
4. Hu, R.Q., et al.: Call admission control in a multi-media multi-beam satellite cross-connect network. IEEE ICC 2003, Anchorage, USA (2003)
5. Iera, A., Molinaro, A., Marano,S.: Call admission control and resource management issues for real-time VBR traffic in ATM-satellite networks. IEEE J. Select Areas Commun.18 (2000) 2393-2403
6. Iera, A. Molinaro, A., Marano.S: Traffic management techniques to face the effects of intrinsic delays in geostationary satellite networks. IEEE Trans. on Wireless Commun. 1 (2002) 145-155
7. Zein, T., Maral, G., Brefort, T., Tondriaux, M.: Performance of the combined/fixed reservation assignment (CFRA) scheme for aggregated traffic. In Proc. COST 226 Integrated Space/Terrestrial Networks Final Symposium, Budapest, Hungary, (1995) 183-199
8. D. P. Connors, B. Ryu, and S. Dao, "Modeling and simulation of broadband satellite networks part 1: medium access control", IEEE Commun. Mag., 37 (1999) 72-79
9. Açar, G., Rosenberg. C.: Performance study of end-to-end resource management in ATM geostationary satellite networks. IEEE MILCOM 2001, McLean, USA, (2001)
10. Yilmaz, H.B., Tugcu, T., Vainstein, F.: Analytical Model for Admission Control in Next Generation Wireless Systems. In Proc. CONWIN Workshop on Convergence of Heterogeneous Wireless Networks, Budapest, Hungary, (2005)
11. Sudame, P., Badrinath B.R.: On Providing Support for Protocol Adaptation in Mobile Wireless Networks. Mobile Networks and Applications, 6 (2001) 43-55
12. Alagöz, F.: Approximations on the Aggregated MPEG Traffic and Their Impact on Admission Control. Turk. J. of Electrical Eng. and Computer Sci.10 (2002) 73-84
13. Walters, D.: Reliable Multicast for the Digital Battlefield. 3393 SPIE Aerosense, Orlando, USA (1998)

TCP-Peach++: Enhancement of TCP-Peach+ for Satellite IP Networks with Asymmetrical Bandwidth and Persistent Fades—(Invited Paper)

Jian Fang[1] and Özgür B. Akan[2]

[1] Broadband & Wireless Networking Laboratory,
School of Electrical & Computer Engineering,
Georgia Institute of Technology, Atlanta, GA 30332
jfang@ece.gatech.edu

[2] Department of Electrical and Electronics Engineering,
Middle East Technical University, Ankara, Turkey 06531
akan@eee.metu.edu.tr

Abstract. In this paper, an improvement to TCP-Peach+, called TCP-Peach++, is proposed to improve the throughput performance for satellite IP networks with asymmetrical bandwidth and persistent fades. The delayed SACK scheme is adopted to address the problems due to bandwidth asymmetrical satellite links. A new protocol procedure, Hold State, is developed to address the link outages due to persistent fades. The simulation results show that TCP-Peach++ improves the throughput performance during rain fades and addresses the bandwidth asymmetry problems in Satellite IP Networks.

1 Introduction

Satellite networks will play a crucial role in the global infrastructure of the Internet. They do not only provide global coverage, but also are capable of sustaining high bandwidth levels and supporting flexible and scalable network configurations. Satellite networks can also be used as a backup for existing networks, e.g., in case of congestions or link failures, traffic can be rerouted through satellites. Satellite networks have high *bit error rate* (BER) and *long propagation delays*[1]. Traditional TCP schemes usually perform poor in these situations [6] and thus, TCP-Peach and its enhancement, TCP-Peach+, [1] have been proposed to address these problems. However, satellite IP networks are also characterized by the following problems, which are not directly addressed by the TCP-Peach and TCP-Peach+ [1]:

– *Low Bandwidth Feedback Link:* The feedback link is usually not faster than several hundred Kb/s for small satellite terminals and a few Mb/s for larger satellite terminals [3]. This causes bandwidth asymmetry between the capacities of forward, i.e., from satellite to terminals, and feedback links, i.e.,

P. Yolum et al.(Eds.): ISCIS 2005, LNCS 3733, pp. 145–151, 2005.

from terminals to satellites. This leads to congestion in the feedback link resulting in severely degraded network performance. A terrestrial feedback link to the sender has been proposed in [4]. However, this is not practical in some cases, especially for mobile receivers, which need to use low-bandwidth uplink channel as the feedback link.

- *Persistent Fades:* Satellite link channels may also experience persistent link fades, i.e., intermittent link blockages and signal losses, due to handoff or signal fading by environmental obstructions such as tunnels, bridges, mountains, and varying weather patterns such as rainstorms [2,5]. The congestion control algorithms must address the persistent fades to reduce performance degradation and unnecessary transmissions when the links are unavailable.

In this paper, in order to address above challenges, we propose an improvement to TCP-Peach+, called TCP-Peach++, to improve the throughput performance in satellite IP networks with asymmetrical bandwidth and persistent fades. The delayed SACK scheme is adopted to address the bandwidth asymmetry problems and a *Hold State* is incorporated into the congestion control in TCP-Peach+ to address the persistent fades. Performance evaluation shows that TCP-Peach++ effectively addresses these challenges and hence improve the throughput performance in satellite IP Networks.

2 TCP-Peach++

In this section, the details of the developed protocol algorithms are presented.

2.1 The Delayed SACK

TCP-Peach+ [1] uses the selective acknowledgment (SACK) options to assure reliable data segment transmission. TCP-Peach+ sink continuously sends a SACK back to the source for each data packet it receives. If the data packet size is 1KB and SACK size is 40 Bytes, then the ratio of the traffic in the forward and feedback channels is 25 : 1, i.e., no congestion will occur in the feedback channel only if the bandwidth asymmetry does not exceed 25 : 1. However, satellite IP networks have low bandwidth feedback links usually not faster than several hundred Kb/s for small satellite terminals and a few Mb/s for larger satellite terminals [3], i.e., the bandwidth asymmetry may exceed 25 : 1. Thus, sending one SACK for each data packet may cause congestion in the feedback channel resulting in overall performance degradation.

In order to reduce the number of SACKs in the feedback channel, we adopted the *delayed SACK scheme* into the TCP-Peach++ protocol algorithms. The TCP-Peach++ sink maintains a delayed-SACK factor, d, and sends one SACK for every d data packets received if the sequence numbers of the received packets are increased accumulatively. Otherwise, it sends a SACK back to the satellite immediately. As a result, the amount of traffic in the feedback channel is controlled by adjusting the delayed-SACK factor d. Note that if d is sufficiently large, no congestion will occur in the feedback channel.

2.2 The Hold State

TCP-Peach++ congestion control contains two new algorithms: *Jump Start* and *Quick Recovery* [1] as well as the two traditional TCP algorithms, *Congestion Avoidance* and *Fast Retransmit.* In order to address the persistent fades due to varying weather patterns, such as rain fades, the *Hold State* is incorporated into the congestion control in TCP-Peach++. The flow chart of TCP-Peach++ congestion control algorithm is illustrated in Figure 1.

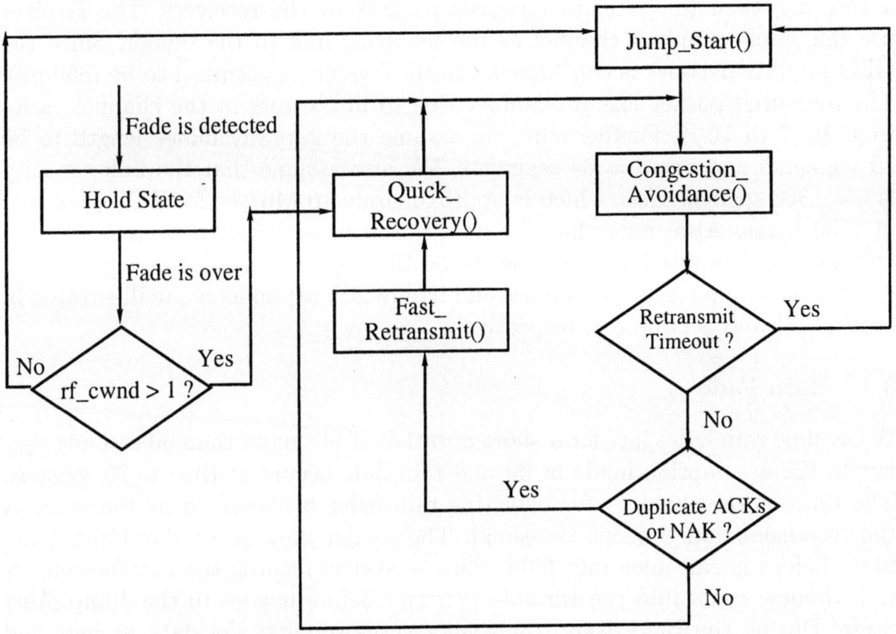

Fig. 1. TCP-Peach++: Flow Chart

The sender receives SACKs for reliability control purposes. If the sender does not receive any SACK from the receiver for a certain period of time T_f, it infers this condition as a result of persistent fade and goes to the Hold State. In the Hold State, the sender first records the current congestion window *cwnd* in the variable rf_cwnd. The sender then freezes all retransmission timers and starts to send NIL segments to the receiver periodically in order to probe the link availability. Upon receiving a probing NIL segment, the receiver sends a SACK immediately to the sender to report its current buffer status.

If the sender receives the SACKs for the probing NIL segments, it infers that the persistent fade is over and resumes sending data packets. If rf_cwnd=1, it goes to the Jump Start State, otherwise, let $cwnd$=rf_cwnd. In the latter case, the sender first transmits $rwnd - cwnd$ NIL segments [1] to probe the available bandwidth, where *rwnd* is the receiver window size, and then enters the Quick Recovery State to recover the missing packets. Hence, with the help of Hold

State and NIL segments, TCP-Peach++ source can quickly recover its original congestion window size after the persistent fade is over.

3 Performance Evaluation

For the performance evaluation purposes, we developed our own simulation model using a *c++* development environment. In the simulation topology, there are 10 senders and 10 receivers. The senders send packets to the satellite through a gateway, then the satellite forwards packets to the receivers. The receiver use the satellite uplink channel as the feedback link to the sender. Since the GEO satellite network is considered, the RTT values is assumed to be ($550ms$). The measured packet loss probability due to link errors in the channel varies from 10^{-6} to 10^{-2}. Furthermore, we assume the gateway buffer length to be 50 segments and $rwnd$ = 64 segments. We also assume that the link capacity is $c = 1300$ segments/sec which is approximately 10 Mb/sec for TCP segments of 1000 bytes. Also, note that the application is assumed to be reliable data transport and simulation time is set to be 100 secs.

The performances for rain fades and bandwidth asymmetry are illustrated in Section 3.1 and Section 3.2, respectively.

3.1 Rain Fade

We assume rain fades last for a short duration of not more than 60 seconds similar to the assumption made in [5] and rain fade occurs at time t=20 seconds. The timeout threshold T_f for detecting rain fades is chosen to be the same as the retransmission timeout threshold. The sender may go to the Jump Start State before it can infer rain fade, thus, it always records the current congestion window $cwnd$ into the variable rf_cwnd before it goes to the Jump Start State. During the Hold State, the sender stops sending any data packets and freezes all retransmission timers to avoid unnecessary transmission. However, it periodically sends NIL segments [1] as probing packets to detect when rain fade is over. To investigate the performance improvement by the Hold State, we also consider TCP-Peach++ without the Hold State, i.e, TCP-Peach+, where the sender keeps going into the Jump Start State when the transmission timer expires. The throughput performance for TCP-Peach++ with and without the Hold State is shown in Figure 2.

As shown in Figure 2, the throughput with the Hold State is always higher than that without the Hold State. Note also that the relative throughput improvement achieved is approximately constant for different rain fade periods. For the rain fade period of 60 seconds, TCP-Peach++ with Hold State achieves throughput improvements of 67% over TCP-Peach+ as shown in Figure 2. The reasons that TCP-Peach++ with the Hold State achieves higher throughput can be outlined as follows:

- In the TCP-Peach++ with Hold State, the sender uses NIL segments [1] as probing segments to obtain the exact information about link loss situation.

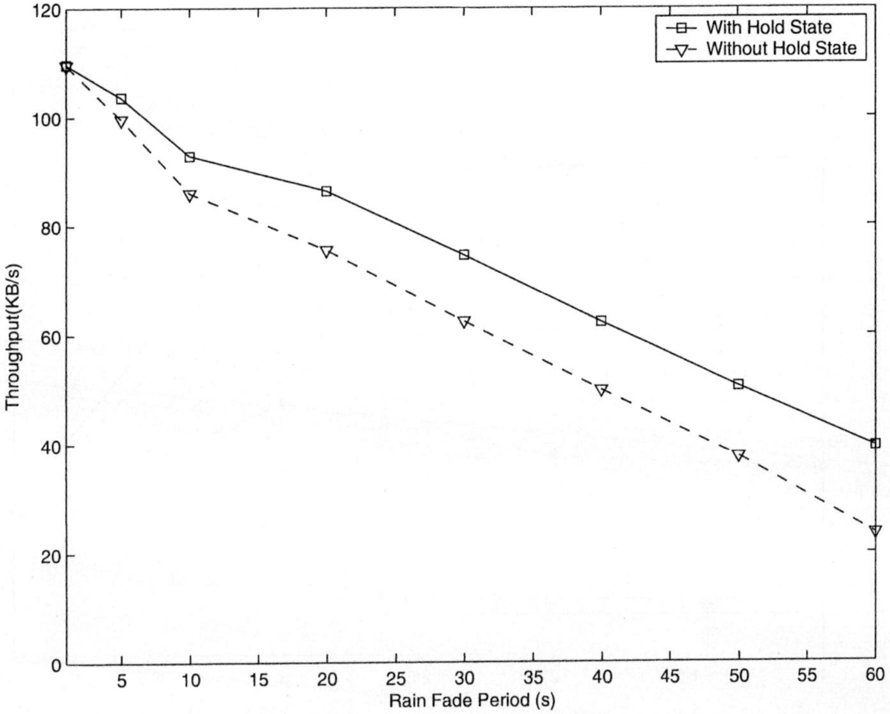

Fig. 2. Throughput vs. rain fade period

On the other hand, without the Hold State, the sender has to wait for the retransmission timer to expire and then goes to the Jump Start State to send packets to the receiver.

– With Hold State, the TCP-Peach++ sender records its current congestion window when the persistent fade occurs and keeps this congestion window after fade is over. However, without the Hold State, the sender always goes to the Jump Start State and the congestion window is set to 1.

Therefore, TCP-Peach++ improves the throughput in persistent fade conditions by incorporating the new Hold State procedure.

3.2 Bandwidth Asymmetry

Since the feedback link capacity is usually very low for satellite networks, the delayed SACK scheme explained in Section 2.1 is adopted to address the bandwidth asymmetry problem, i.e., the receiver sends one SACK for a certain number of received data packets. This number is called the delay factor, d. We investigate 3 cases of the bandwidth asymmetry problems, i.e., the feedback link bandwidth is 1 Mb/s, 100 Kb/s and 64 Kb/s, respectively. Also, assume the link capacity from the sender to the receiver is 10 Mb/s. The throughput performance with respect to different delay factors is shown in Figure 3.

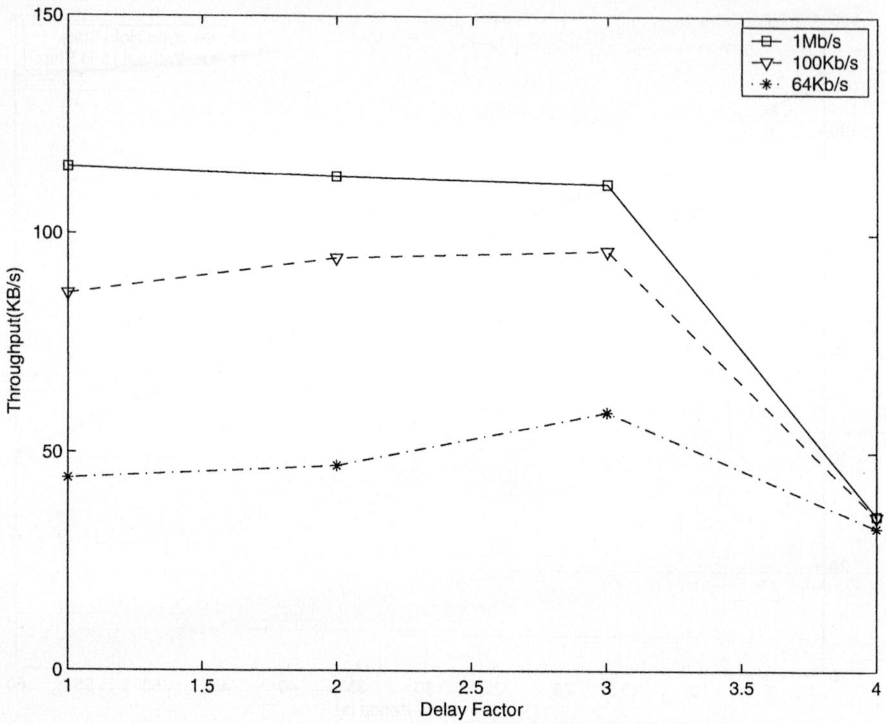

Fig. 3. Throughput vs. delay factor

When the feedback link bandwidth is 1 Mb/s, the throughput performance is not degraded for this bandwidth asymmetry ratio. The reason is that the ACK size is usually about 40 Bytes, which is much smaller than the data packet size 1 KB, thus, the feedback link is not congested. However, the throughput performance decreases with increasing bandwidth asymmetry ratio. For example, the throughput drops to 86.223 from 115.425 KB/s when the feedback link bandwidth is 100 Kb/s and the delayed SACK scheme is not used, i.e., $d = 1$. For the cases where the feedback link bandwidth is 100 Kb/s and 64 Kb/s, the throughput increases with increasing delay factor d by 11.5% and 34.5%, respectively, and reaches the highest value when delay factor is 3, which is close to the throughput for 1 Mb/s. However, since TCP operation relies on the ACK clock to transmit packets, the delay factor cannot be too large, which degrades the throughput performance for very high bandwidth asymmetry ratios. This is also observed in Figure 3 as the throughput decreases approximately 20% when the feedback link bandwidth is 64 Kb/s and the delay factor is $d = 4$.

4 Conclusions

In this paper, we introduced TCP-Peach++ to improve the throughput performance of TCP-Peach+ for satellite IP networks with asymmetrical bandwidth and persistent fades. The delayed SACK scheme is adopted to address the bandwidth asymmetry problems and a Hold State is developed to address persistent fades. Simulation results show that TCP-Peach++ improves the throughput performance during persistent fades and addresses the bandwidth asymmetry problems.

References

1. Akyildiz, I. F., Zhang, X., Fang, J.: TCP-Peach+: Enhancement of TCP-Peach for satellite IP Networks, *IEEE Commun. Letters,* vol. 6, no. 7, (2002) 303-305
2. Akyildiz, I. F., Fang, J.: TCP Peachtree: A Multicast Transport Protocol for Satellite IP Networks, *to appear in IEEE Journal of Selected Areas in Communications (JSAC),* February (2004)
3. Henderson, T. R., Katz, R. H.: Transport Protocols for Internet-Compatible Satellite Networks, *IEEE Journal on Selected Areas in Communications,* vol. 17, no. 2, February (1999) 326-344
4. Jung, M., Nonnenmacher, J., Biersack, E. W.: Reliable Multicast via Satellite: Unidirectional vs. Bi-directional Communication, in *Proc. KiVS 1999,* Darmstadt, Germany, March (1999)
5. Koyabe, M. W., Fairhurst, G.: Performance of Reliable Multicast Protocols via Satellite at EHF with Persistent Fades, *the 7th Ka-Band Utilization Conference,* Santa Margherita Ligure, Genoa,Italy, September (2001)
6. Marchese, M.: Performance Analysis of the TCP Behavior in a GEO Satellite Environment, *Computer Communications Journal,* Vol. 24, (2001) 877-888

Automatic Translation of Serial to Distributed Code Using CORBA Event Channels

Saeed Parsa and Omid Bushehrian

Iran University of Science and Technology
{parsa, bushehrian}@iust.ac.ir

Abstract. Automatic Distribution of computationally intensive object oriented programs is one of the active research areas. To distribute a serial code over network, automatically, the class dependency graph extracted from the program code can be clustered using a genetic clustering algorithm. The clusters are then distributed across the network. To balance the distribution gain achieved by each cluster, a new algorithm is presented in this paper. Automatic conversion of ordinary method calls into asynchronous inter-cluster calls has been achieved by developing a new simple data dependency analysis algorithm. The layered architecture of our suggested environment has provided a general pattern to create distributed code which can be easily implemented within different infrastructures.

1 Introduction

One of the primary challenges to create a distributed application is the need to partition and place pieces of the application. Although successive generations of middleware (such as RPC [1],CORBA [2]) have brought the advantages of service-location transparency, dynamic object instantiation, and object-oriented programming to distributed applications, the process of distributed application decomposition has changed little: programmers manually divide applications into subprograms and manually assign those sub-programs to machines [3],[4],[12]. Often the techniques used to choose a distribution are platform dependent.

We argue that system software should partition and distribute applications, instead of the programmer. To partition a given object oriented program, first a class dependency graph is extracted from the serial program code. Then, the graph is partitioned such that the most similar classes are placed in the same cluster. The main problem is to determine the amount of similarity amongst the classes such that the resultant clustering yields distributed software with a better performance in comparison with the serial one. In order to achieve this, a similarity metric based on a distribution gain is presented in Section 3. To support platform independency a general layered architecture using a Connector component to access the distribution middleware is presented in Section 2. To automatically convert method calls to asynchronous inter-cluster calls, data and control flow analysis algorithms may be employed to locate the very first positions where the results of the asynchronous call are required. However, due to complexity of these algorithms a simple algorithm to perform inter-cluster data dependency analysis is presented in Section 5. Some conversion rules to convert sequential code to the distributed code using the middleware components are presented in Section 5 as well.

P. Yolum et al.(Eds.): ISCIS 2005, LNCS 3733, pp. 152–161, 2005.

2 A Layered Architecture

To simplify the task of transforming serial code into functionally equivalent distributed code, it is beneficial to design an environment which handles the communication aspects and allows the programmer to concentrate on the functional aspects of the serial system [5],[9]. Figure 1 shows a layered architecture within which the various aspects of communication and synchronization are transparent to the application program.

In the highest level, the serial program code is analyzed and re-modularized into a number of modules using our clustering environment called DAGC [6],[7]. Within this environment, parsing the source code of the program to be distributed, the program class dependency graph is extracted and clustered based on a similarity criterion described in Section 3. To distribute the resultant clustering over the network, the serial code should be analyzed to find inter cluster invocations. Then each inter cluster invocation is transformed into an asynchronous invocation via the *Port* component. This component is implemented as a Java class which can be generated automatically as will be described in Section 4.1. The middleware components functionality can be summarized as follows:

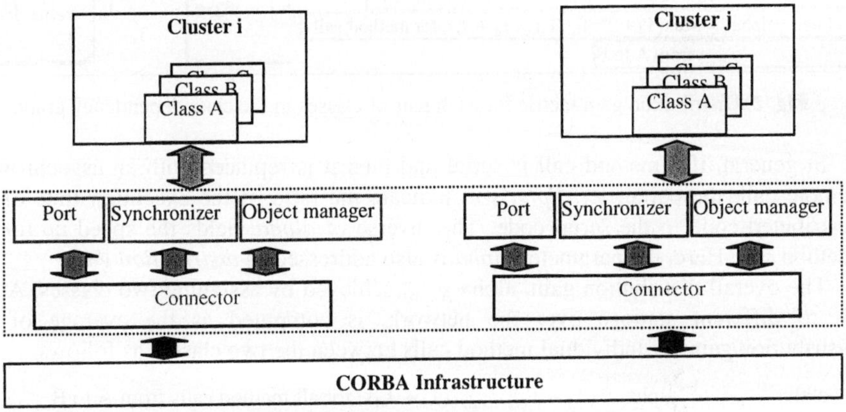

Fig. 1. The main components of the proposed environment of classes

- **Port:** This component acts as an interface for each cluster. Remote invocations are performed through the Port component. The Port component is further described in Section 4.1.
- **Synchronizer:** Asynchronous remote calls are controlled via a Synchronizer component. This component provides the synchronization capabilities to the distributed application. The Synchronizer is fully described in Section 4.2.
- **Object Manager:** This component manages creation of distributed objects. Object Manager creates an object and assign it a GUID (global unique identifier) when an object creation request arrives from a remote cluster. The object manager is described in Section 4.3.
- **Connector:** The Connector component is responsible for sending and receiving events between clusters. This component is further described in Section 4.4.

3 Optimal Partitioning

To distribute a given program over the network, the program code should be partitioned. The partitioning criteria are described in Section 3.1 Each partition is then assigned to a separate station. Here, the optimal number of stations is computed within the DAGC clustering environment [6], [7].

3.1 Distribution Criteria

A main reason for the distribution of a program code is to speed up its execution. As shown in Figure 2, the amount of speedup is affected by the communication and synchronization overheads between the distributed components. To measure the amount of speedup, a parameter *alpha* is calculated in Figure 2.

Let N = number of invocations
T_d = execution time of the called method
T_c = remote invocation elapsed time
T_s = elapsed time between the call statement and the first use of the call results within the caller
Then $alpha_i = Max(T_d + 2 * T_c, T_s) / (T_d + T_s)$ for method call i from A to B

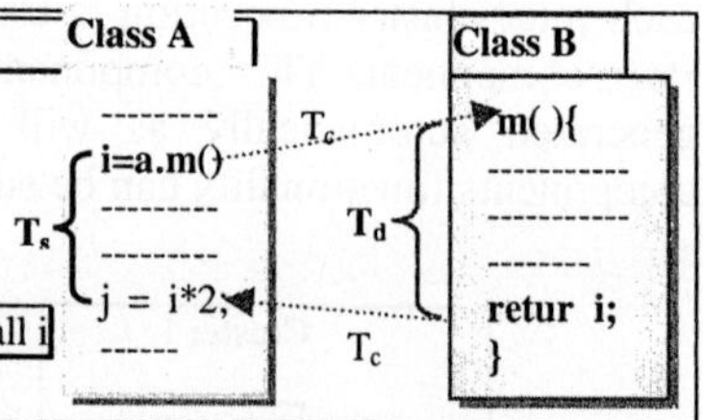

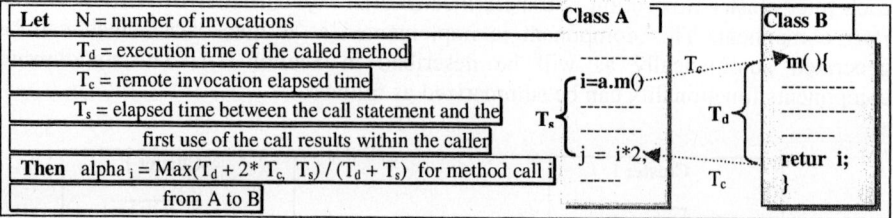

Fig. 2. Distribution gain metric for each pair of classes in the class dependency graph

In general, if a method call is serial and then it is replaced with an asynchronous remote call, the parameter *alpha* will indicate the ratio of the execution time of the distributed code to the serial code. The inverse of *alpha* yields the speed up for the method call. Here, the parameter *alpha* is also addressed as *distribution gain.*

The overall distribution gain, $alpha_{A,B}$, achieved by assigning two classes, A and B, to different stations over the network, is computed as the average of the distribution gains of individual method calls between the two classes as follows:

$$alpha_{A,B} = \sum alpha_i * (T_s + T_d)_i \;/\; \sum (T_s + T_d)_i, \text{ for all method calls from A to B}$$

In the above relation, the nominator is the total time elapsed when the method call is remote and the denominator is the total time elapsed when the method call is serial. If the calculated alpha, is less than or equal to one, the distribution will increase the performance (i.e. execution time) otherwise the distribution is not beneficial. The maximum speed up is achieved when T_s equals '$T_d + 2T_c$'. In this case, if T_c equals zero then the speedup will be equal to 2, which is the maximum speedup.

3.2 Clustering Objective

Before partitioning the class dependency graph, the edges of the graph are labeled with the amount of speedup gained by distributing the nodes of the graph. The main objective is to partition the class dependency graph into modules which are weakly coupled while the classes residing in a module are highly coherent.

Obviously there are certain criteria, rather than cohesion and coupling that may be considered for software decomposition. Here, for automatic distribution of serial code, the following three constraints are applied:

1. To support modular understandability criterion, certain nodes can be defined to share a same cluster
2. To support load balancing in a distributed environment the nodes appearing in clusters should be balanced.
3. To limit the number of clusters produced on a given graph G with N nodes, the maximum and minimum number of clusters can be defined by the user, such that:

$$\text{min.no.clusters} \leq \text{no.clusters} \leq \text{max.no.clusters}$$

4 Distributing Components

After a program code is partitioned, to distribute the partitions over the network, as shown in Figure 1, four major components Port, object manager, synchronizer and Connector are augmented to each partition of the program code. In this Section each of these components and their interfaces are described. The process of using the components to convert an ordinary method call into a remote asynchronous invocation is shown in Figure 3, below.

> ***Step1.*** *For each cluster A, create a port class Port_A.*
> ***Step2.*** *Find an inter cluster invocation o.m(prarlist) between cluster A and cluster B.*
> ***Step3.*** *Suppose object o is of type class1.*
> ***Step4.*** *Add an inner class, class1, to Port_A and Port_B*
> ***Step5.*** *Add a method m(Handle guid, parlist) to class1*
> ***Step6.*** *Convert the method call o.m(parlist) to Port_A.class1.m(o , parlist)*
> ***Step7.*** *Add a Synchronizer.wait(varName) statement in the first place in which the values affected by the call statement are required.*

Fig. 3. Converting a serial code into distributed code

For instance, consider the Java code fragment, presented in Figure 5. There is an ordinary call, obj1.m (obj2), in line 3 of this code fragment from within class A to class B. The reference parameter, obj2, and the return value, k, are affected by the call statement. The first position where the return value, k, is required is line 10.

```
void caller_method
{  Integer k;
 1 class1 obj1=new class1();  // remote class
 2 class2 obj2=new class2();  //local class
    ...
 3 k=obj1.callee(obj2); //inter cluster invocation with a reference parameter
    ...
 //first use of k variable
 10 if k.intvalue() > expres ... ;          ...  }
```

Fig. 4. Serial source code

To support the distribution of the above code fragment, the three components ObjectManager, Port and Synchronizer are used. Below, in Figure 5 the use of these four components to transform the above serial code into a corresponding distributed code is shown.

```
void caller_method{ Integer k;
 1- ObjectManager objman1=...//get the reference of the remote ObjectManager
 2- Handle  obj1=objman1.CreateObject("class1"); //remote class
 3- ObjectManager objman2=...//get the reference of the local ObjectManager
 4- Handle2 obj2=objman.CreateObject("class2")  //local class
    ...
 5- Port_A.class1.calee(obj1,obj2);
    ...
 //first use of k variable
 6- k=(Integer)Synchronizer.wait(obj1)
    if k.intvalue() > expres  ... ;  ...  }
```

Fig. 5. Distributed code

4.1 Port

A *Port* component is created for each cluster to communicate with the other clusters. *The Port* component performs outgoing inter-cluster invocations and delegates incoming invocations to the appropriate classes in the cluster. To generate a *Port* component, *Port_A*, for a cluster A to communicate with the other clusters, all the remote invocations between A and the other clusters and the destination class names of the remote invocations are determined. For each remote invocation such as a.m(parlist), from cluster A to B, first the callee class, class 1, is determined then this class is inserted as an inner class into the *Port_A* and *Port_B* classes. The called method, *m(parlist)*, is added to *class1* with an additional parameter of type *Handle* to access the remote object.

```
Static class Port_A {  //port for cluster A
 Static class class1 {Void m (Handle h, parlist  )
   { //call the connector layer
    Connector.SendEvent( "class1",h,
                          "m1" ,parlist);  }
   ...   } //class1
   ... }//Port_A
```

```
Static class Port_B {  //port for cluster B
 Static class class1 { Void m (Handle h,  parlist  ){
      class1  c=(class1)ObjectManager.GetObject(h)
      r=c.m(parlist);//delegate the incoming cal
      connector.ReplyEvent(h, r, "class1");  }
      ...  }//class1
   ...  }/ /Port_B
```

Fig. 6. Port classes

As shown in the above example, to access the method *m(Handle h,parlist)* from within the cluster *A*, an object of type *class1* is created by calling the method *createObject* of the object manager component, described in Section 4.2 below. The object manager creates the object and returns a global unique identifier of type *Handle* to access the object, remotely. Using the *Port* as an interface for inter-cluster communications, each ordinary inter-cluster method call such as *O.m(par1,...)* in cluster A is replaced with *Port_A.class1.m(handle, par1,...)*. As shown in Figure 6, remote method calls are performed via the sendEvent( ) method of the connector component as follows:

Connector.SendEvent("class1", h,"m1",parlist);

The SendEvent method is used as a carrier to deliver a remote method invocation to the destination object, via the network. In *Port_B* another call to the connector layer is made after the invocation:

Connector.ReplyEvent(h, r, "class1");

4.2 Object Manager

The Object Manager component provides two methods CreateObject and GetObject to construct and access remote objects, respectively. The component exposes the following standard interface:

Interface ObjectManager {Handle CreateObject(String classname);
Object GetObject(Handle guid) ; }

In the above interface definition, the method CreateObject is invoked, remotely, to construct a new object of type *classname* and assign a global unique identifier, *guid* of the type Handle. The *GetObject* method, returns the object corresponding to the requested *guid.* In fact this method uses the unique identifier *guid* as an index to locate the corresponding object within a list of objects, constructed remotely. The pseudo code for CreateObject method is as follows:

Handle CreateObject(String classname){ String guid; guid=getNextguid();
object o=class.forname(classname).newInstance();ObjectTable.add(guid,o);}

4.3 Synchronizer

The Synchronizer component manages synchronizations between the caller and callee methods in asynchronous invocations. The component interface definition is:

Interface Synchronizer { void register(Handle h); object wait(Handle h);
void callback(Handle h,Object r); }

The *register(Handle h)* method registers the object addressed by the handle h in a waiting list, *WaitTable*. The *wait(Handle h)* waits for the completion of a remote method execution addressed by the handle h. The *wait* method also receives the return value and the values of any reference parameters passed to the remote method. Every time that a Connector component receives a return value *r* from a remote cluster, it calls the *callback* method of the Synchronizer. This method updates the *WaitTable*.

Reference parameters in Java can only be instances of class data types. A handle for each reference parameter is created within the caller and passed to the method instead of the reference parameter. The remote method can then access the methods of the reference parameter through its handle.

4.4 Connector

The Connector component is the platform aware part of our suggested architecture, shown in Figure 1. The component uses a CORBA event channel to handle remote method calls. Below is an interface description of the component:

Interface connector{SendEvent(String classname, Handle h, String methodname, ParamList parlist)
void ReplyEvent (Handle h , Any returnValue); }

The SendEvent method of the Connector is called by the Port class of the caller component and the ReplyEvent is called by the Port component of the callee. The SendEvent method packs the remote call details in an event structure. These details include a unique identifier of the remote object, the name of the class to which the object belongs and finally the method name and its list of actual parameters. The event is then pushed into the event channel, by calling the *Push* method of the *eventChannel* object. To use a CORBA event channel for passing parameters, the following structure should be added to the CORBA IDL file.

```
typedef sequence <Any> ParamList;
Valuetype Event{ String classname; Any guid; /* expected object uid*/
          String methodname; /* expected method name*/ Any returnvalue; // the returned value
          int reply; /* determines if this event is request or reply */ Paramlist par; };
```

Bellow is an implementation of the SendEvent method in CORBA:

```
SendEvent(String classname,Long guid,String methodname,ParamList parlist)
 { EventChanel *Myeventchannel=geteventchannel(classname); Event r;
  //fill the r fields
  r.classname=classname; r.methodname=methodname; r.parlist=parlist; r.guid=h;
  any a; a<<= r; Myeventchannel->push(a); }
```

Passing the *classname* parameter to the method *geteventchannel()*, the event channel of the target cluster is obtained. The return value is transferred to the caller via the *ReplyEvent* method of the connector component:

```
void ReplyEvent(Handle h , Any returnValue, String classname)
  { EventChanel *Myeventchannel=geteventchannel(classname); Any a; Event r;
   r.guid=h; r.reply=1; a<<=r; Myeventchannel->push(a); }
```

This above method acknowledges termination of the remote method. The Connector component always listens to the event channel to accept incoming events including SendEvents or ReplyEvents. When the connector receives a SendEvent, it runs the requested method by invoking the proper method of its local *Port* :

```
Any a; MyEventchannel.pull(a); Event r; a>>r; switch(r.classname)
  { case "A": If (r.methodname="m1" ){ par1=r.par[1]; par2=r.par[2]; ...// others parame
              Port.A.m1(r.guid,par1,par2,...); } Case "B" : ..... }
```

The connector updates entries in the *WaitTable* corresponding to a *guid* when the return value for that guid is received via the *callback* method of the Synchronizer.

5 Data Dependency Analysis

Dependency analysis approaches are performed on sequential code to identify the inherent parallelism within the code [10]. In a data analysis approach, a def-use chain [10] can be constructed to find the first locations within a program code where the values affected by a remote method call are required. In this section, a simple algorithm to analyze dependencies is proposed in Figure 7. The algorithm uses a list of objects called DependencyList to keep track of all the values affected by the remote method. This list includes an array of tuples *(variable, handle)* where, the parameter *handle* addresses the remote object and the parameter *variable* is the name of the object affected by the remote method call. Each variable reference in the subsequent statements is searched in the DepenedencyList to find its corresponding handle. If a handle is found, the execution should be suspended until termination of the callee. Statements of the serial source code are analyzed using a Java analyzer library *Compost*[11].

```
//Let DependencyList be a list to hold the name of the variables, affected by an asynchronous call
Set statement=Compost.NextStatement();
Switch (statement.Type) of
  //If the statement Type is a new class instant creation
  Case New Class :
      //Ask the object manager to create a new instance of classname and return its unique handle
      Code.Insert( "handle=ObjecManager.CreateObject(classname);" )
  // If statement.Type is a call to a method in another cluster
  Case intra-cluster invocation :
     // Add each reference parameter and the return value, x, in the DependencyList
     Let h be the invocation object handle
  For each variable x in{x I x is Passed By Reference or x is a return value}DependencyList.add(x, h);
     // Ask the synchronizer to register the handle of the invocation
     Code.Insert("Synchronizer.Register(" + h  + ");")
     If (LoopDepth > 0) then Add the invocation handle to the List of inLoops
     //Convert an ordinary call obj.m(params) into a remote call, Port.className.m(handle, params),
       Set m=statement.MethodName(); Set ParList=statement.ParList;
       Set ClassName= statement.RefName.Type;
       Code.Insert( "Port." + ClassName + "." + m + "(handle," + ParList +")"
     //Insert a wait statement before any use of any variable affected by a remote call
      Case VariableReference
        if(statement.name is in DependencyList) handle=get_handle(DependencyList, statement.name);
        Code.insert("Synchronizer.wait(" +  handle + ")" );
     //Increase a nested loop number, LoopDepth, when entering a block in the body of a loop
      Case StartOfLoopBlock
           LoopDepth ++ ; // This variable indicates whether there is a loop block
     // At the end of each Loop block insert a wait statement for all the invocation within the loop block.
      Case (End of Loop Block)
           For each (invocation handle h in the inLoop list) do
            Code.Insert("Synchronizer.LoopWait(" + h + ");" ); LoopDepth--  //exiting a loop block
```

Fig. 7. Data dependency analysis and transformation rules

6 A Case Study: TreeMaker

In this section, a simple example representing advantages of distributing a computationally intensive application code is presented. This case study contains 15 Java classes implementing three graph manipulating algorithms called Kruskal, Prime and ShortPathExtractor. Each of these algorithms is developed as a class. Before building a spanning tree for a given graph, a class called ComponentExtractor is accessed to extract the connected components of the graph.

The result of clustering of this case study is shown in Figure 9. Considering this clustering, The STP class may call Kruskal and Prime classes in parallel. This distributed architecture contains two components. Each component is assigned to a node in the network to execute.

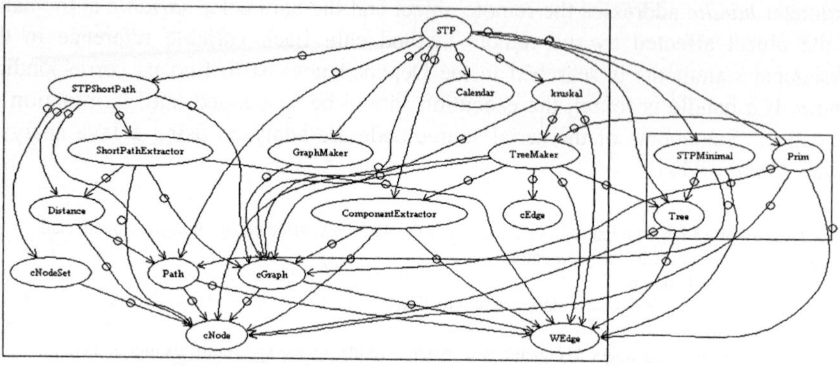

Fig. 8. TreeMaker Clustering

Considering the clustering criteria described in Section 3, the resultant distribution outperforms the sequential one (Figure 9). A distribution of a sequential program may perform worse than the original sequential version if, the distribution criterion is not well defined. To demonstrate the efficiency of our clustering approach, we moved the class ComponentExtractor to the same cluster as Prime. It is shown, below in Figure 9, that after the movement the performance decreases.

nodes	edges	sequential time(ms)	Distributed time (ms)
220	450	1639.038	785
200	410	1432.658	676
180	380	1189.569	568
160	330	875.589	445
140	280	436	250
120	250	158	123
100	200	99.36	98

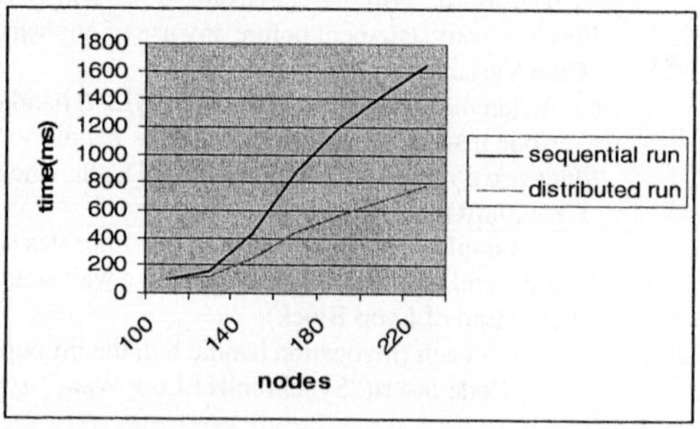

Fig. 9. A comparison of the sequential and distributed code execution times

7 Conclusions

Object oriented programs can be automatically transformed into distributed code. Optimal distribution of the program code can be achieved by applying a genetic clustering algorithm to the program class dependency graph where each edge of the graph is labelled with the amount of speedup achieved by distributing the two connecting nodes. To apply certain constraints imposed by the network architecture, user policy, and environmental conditions, interactive clustering algorithms are preferred.

Parallelizing compiler techniques can be applied to detect the inherent concurrency in object-oriented programs. To accelerate the detection process, concurrency could be identified by simply performing data dependency analysis on inter-cluster invocations. CORBA event channels could be used as a means for inter-cluster communications. Each cluster should be supplied with a connector object to transfer / receive remote method calls and their results through the event channel.

References

[1] OMG. The Common Object Request Broker: Architecture and Specification, Technical Report formal/01-02-01, Object Management Group, 2001.

[2] Bolton F.: Pure CORBA: A code-intensive premium reference, SAMS publishing, 2002.

[3] de Wachter B., Massart T., Meuter V.: dSL: An environment with automatic code distribution for industrial control systems", 7th International Conference on Principles of DistributedSystems, La Martinique, France, December 2003

[4] Haase J., Eschmann F., Klauer B., Waldschmidt K.: The SDVM: A Self Distributing Virtual Machine for Computer Clusters, 17th International Conference on Architecture of Computing Systems, Germany, 2004.

[5] Parsa S, Bushehria O., Rajabi M: Auto-Distributor: An Environment for Automatic Distribution of Programs, CSIC2005, Tehran, IRAN (in Persian).

[6] Parsa S, Bushehria O.: A Framework to Investigate and Evaluate Genetic Clustering Algorithms for Software modularization, LECTURE NOTES IN COMPUTER SCIENCE, Vol. 3037 (June 2004), SPRINGER-VERLAG.

[7] Parsa S, Bushehria O.: The Design and Implementation of a tool for Automatic software modularization, journal of Supercomputing, Volume 32, Issue 1, April 2005.

[8] Keahey K., Gannon D.: PARDIS: CORBA-based Architecture for application-level parallel distributed Computation, Proceedings of the IEEE/ACM SC97 Conference November , 1997, San Jose, California.

[9] Hunt G. C., Scott M. L.: The Coign Automatic Distributed Partitioning System, Proceedings of the 3th Symposium on Operating Systems Design and Implementation, 1999

[10] Zima H.: Super-compilers for Parallel and Vector Computers, ACM Press, 1990.

[11] http://i44s11.info.uni-karlsruhe.de/ ~ compost, Software Composition System.

[12] de Wachter B., Genon A., Massart T.: From static code distribution to more shrinkage for the multiterminal cut, White Paper, University of Brusels, 2004.

[13] Doug K., Roth T.: A Tool for Partitioning Distributed Object Applications Based on Communication Dynamics and Visual Feedback, Proc of the Advanced Technology Workshop, Third USENIX Conference on Object-Oriented Technologies and Systems. Portland, OR, June 1997.

Fault Tolerant and Robust Mutual Exclusion Protocol for Synchronous Distributed Systems

Alexander Kostin and Erhan Basri

Department of Computer Engineering, Eastern Mediterranean University,
Magusa, via Mersin 10, Turkey
{alexander.kostin, erhan.basri}@emu.edu.tr

Abstract. A novel symmetrical, fully distributed, robust and fault-tolerant protocol for mutual exclusion with low message traffic is proposed. The protocol is based on reliable multicast communication in a network of processes. A brief description of the protocol is given. Guidelines for choice of time-outs and delays are presented, and complexity issues of the protocol are outlined along with a sensitivity analysis for robustness. The protocol was implemented as a detailed simulation model in terms of a class of the extended Petri nets. The results of the simulation study of a distributed system with the proposed protocol of mutual exclusion, for different numbers of processes in the group and different loads, are discussed.

1 Introduction

Mutual exclusion is intended for serializing the accesses of a number of concurrently running processes to a common *shared resource* (SR), with the exclusive use of SR by not more than one process at a time. Those parts of process programs which deal with the access of the processes to SR are usually called *critical sections.* If processes run at different nodes of a network system, we have a distributed mutual exclusion task.

A number of publications have been done on the subject during the past 20 years. Excellent surveys of the related works can be found in [1 – 4]. Actually, all known distributed mutual algorithms and protocols can be divided into two basic classes, which are *token-based* [6 – 9] and *permission-based* [10 – 15] protocols. A detailed classification scheme, which includes an additional, hybrid class and subclasses for each class, is given in [4]. Unfortunately, known algorithms and protocols of distributed mutual exclusion, with their static configuration assumption, do not scale well to group size and runtime dynamics, and become impractical.

In this paper, a new scheme of distributed mutual exclusion is proposed which logically belongs to the permission-based class, uses a reliable multicast mode of interprocess communication, but does not require transmitting explicit permission messages to a requesting process from all other processes. Instead of sending an explicit permission message as a response to each request for accessing SR, each process, which received a multicast request, agrees "silently" to satisfy the request if possible or explicitly objects if it uses the SR at the time of receiving of the remote request. In case of objection, the process responds by transmitting a corresponding

P. Yolum et al.(Eds.): ISCIS 2005, LNCS 3733, pp. 162 – 172, 2005.

message which will be received by the requesting process to inform it that the SR is being used at this time. More than that, in the normal mode of operation of the protocol, each process in the group will be aware of whether SR is being used by some other process and will not send its request if SR is being used. Only when SR becomes free for the exclusive use, one or more processes may send a request for accessing the SR, which can result in conflicts between requesting processes. These conflicts are resolved in a way similar to the known collision resolution technique in a LAN of Ethernet type [5].

The rest of the paper is organized as follows. Section 2 presents a system model and assumptions used in the proposed protocol. In Section 3, a general description of the protocol is given. Section 4 contains guidelines for the choice of time-out values for the protocol. In Section 5, communication complexity of the protocol is discussed. Finally, Section 6 describes the results of a simulation-based performance study of the protocol.

2 The System Model and Assumptions

We consider a *synchronous* distributed system consisting of N identical processes which use some shared resource (SR) in a mutually exclusive way. Logically, this system can be viewed as a finite-population queuing system with N client processes and one *non-preempted* SR server. In agreement with the general framework for distributed mutual exclusion [10], there are alternating intervals of main work and accessing a shared resource by each client process in the system. We assume that probability distributions for durations of a step of main work and of using SR are exponential, with given mean values depending on the desired server's load. With these assumptions, the *idealized* model of the distributed system under study is an $M/M/1/N$ finite-population queuing system [16].

For communication, the processes send only multicast messages. This means, in particular, that communication between processes is anonymous, so that each process needs to know only the group address. There are different forms used to deliver multicast messages [17]. For the proposed protocol, it is sufficient that multicast messages are delivered to participating processes in the single-source FIFO order. Since multicast and group membership management are strongly interrelated [19], it is assumed that the group membership management is part of the underlying multicast scheme.

Further, multicasting is assumed to be reliable [18]. Protocols for reliable multicasting over wide area networks are still evolving, but for LANs a few efficient solutions exist [27].

One more assumption is that the distributed system in which the protocol runs is *synchronous*. In a synchronous system, there is a *known upper bound* on message delay which includes not only the time required to transmit the message by the underlying transmission media, but also the delays associated with buffering, sending and receiving of the message [19].

In addition to a group address, each process is assumed to know the *approximate* size of the group to which it belongs. This information is used by processes to calculate the probability of issuing a request for SR.

Finally, the proposed protocol takes into account possible crashes of processes. The processes crash by halting failures in any of the process's states, with subsequent recovering. This corresponds to a crash-recovery model [28].

3 Description of the Protocol

The proposed protocol uses three types of messages: a request for SR (message of type R), SR is free (message of type F), and SR is being used (message of type E). Each process is either performing a step of main work, or accessing SR, or waiting for SR to become free.

Consider the behavior of some process *P* informally. After finishing a step of main work, process *P* checks the current state of SR by the use of its local state variable RSTA. This variable represents the process's knowledge of the state of SR and can take the following values: 0 - SR is free, 1 - SR is being used by this process, 2 - SR is being negotiated by some other processes or used by some other process. If, from the point of view of process *P*, SR is not free or is being already negotiated for the access by some other processes, process *P* will enter its waiting state until SR becomes free.

If SR is free then the process multicasts, *with some probability*, a message R to inform all other processes in the group about its *desire* to access SR and starts its time-out T_1. Message R includes the estimated duration of the intended use of SR. If, according to the calculated probability, the process makes decision not to request SR, then it delays for some time (*slot* time) and, after elapsing this time, can make a new attempt if SR is free.

If, after transmission of the request message, process *P* did not receive any *conflicting* message R from any other process during time-out T_1, it deduces that no other process intends to access SR and starts using SR. In this case, due to reliable multicast, all other processes in the group receive the message R from *P*, learn from the message the estimated duration of the use of SR by *P*, and set the corresponding state of SR in their local variable RSTA. The duration of the intended use of SR will be used to calculate the upper limit of a crash-recovery time out T_2. Process *P*, after finishing the use of SR, multicasts a message of type F which forces all other processes in the group to set the free state of SR.

On the other hand, if process *P* receives at least one message R from some other process during time-out T_1, it understands that there is a conflict with another process, and starts a random back-off delay T_3. The same action will be done by each conflicting process. After elapsing of T_3, the behavior of process *P* and of all other processes involved in the conflict, is determined by the state of SR as seen by each conflicting process.

Fig. 1 illustrates the work of the protocol, for a group of three processes, in a conflict scenario. To simplify the timing diagram, the moments of delivery of a multicast message are shown the same for all destinations. It is assumed that all processes have initially RSTA = 0. This means that, from the point of view of processes, SR is initially free. This happens when processes start running and also after any process completes its use of SR and multicasts message F.

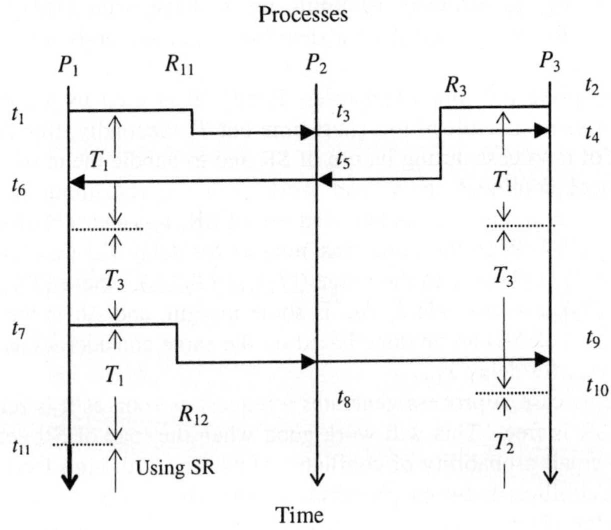

Fig. 1. A scenario for three processes, with a conflict (two processes request SR concurrently)

4 Time-Outs and Delays Used by the Protocol

The proposed protocol uses the following time-outs and random delays: T_1 – conflict-detection time-out; T_2 – deadlock-resolution and crash-handling time-out; T_3 – back-off delay; T_4 – p-persistence delay (or slot time).

When two or more processes request a SR at about the same time, a conflict arises. Conflicts are not errors, they are normal events in the work of the protocol. They initiate a mechanism for arbitration of processes in their attempts to access SR. This mechanism consists of two parts: *detection* of a conflict, and *back-off stepping* to resolve the conflict.

The detection of a conflict is carried out with the use of time-out T_1 that has a fixed maximal period. The back-off step is governed by random delay T_3.

Let τ_d be an upper bound on delay in delivering of a multicast message in the underlying network from a source process to all processes in the group. The value of time-out T_1 must satisfy the inequality

$$T_1 > 2\tau_d, \tag{4.1}$$

where $2\tau_d$ is a *conflict window* which is the amount of time for the message to propagate from a source process to the most remote process in the group and back.

A random back-off delay T_3 is used for the resolution of conflicts between processes. It starts in processes after elapsing of time-out T_1 if a conflict has been detected by the involved processes. The purpose of this delay is to *spread out* the moments of awakening of all conflicting processes as far as possible to decrease the probability of a repeated conflict. There exist different back-off strategies [20]. We choose a uniform probability distribution for delay T_3. The rationale behind such a choice and the way to estimate the limits for T_3 have been explained in [21] in connection with the development of a distributed contention-based load balancing protocol.

Time-out T_2 plays two important roles. Firstly, it is used to resolve a deadlock which could arise as a result of too short time-out T_1. Secondly, this delay serves to detect a crash of a process during its use of SR and to handle the crash in such a way that the protocol continues its normal work with the remaining processes. Each process knows the duration of its intended use of SR, τ_{SR}, and includes this duration in its request for SR. With the same reasoning as for delay T_3, a uniform probability distribution for T_2 is chosen, in the range $((T_2)_{min}, (T_2)_{max})$, where $(T_2)_{min} = \tau_{SR} + \Delta t_m$ and $(T_2)_{max} = (T_2)_{min} + \Delta t_r$. Here Δt_m is some margin, and Δt_r is the length of the range. The choice of Δt_r can be done based on the same considerations as the choice of $(T_3)_{max} - (T_3)_{min}$ for delay T_3.

In the extreme case, a process generates a request as soon as it is ready to use SR and sees that SR is free. This will work good when the load of SR server is low so that there is a small probability of conflicts. However, with high load of SR server, probability of conflicts between processes wanting to access SR will considerably increase, with the number of processes involved in a conflict depending on the group size. This would severely affect the scalability of the protocol with respect to the number of processes in the group.

To solve this problem, the protocol uses a probabilistic persistence, or *p-persistence* scheme similar to one proposed once for p-persistent carrier sense multiple access with collision detection (CSMA/CD) in local area networks [22]. According to this scheme, a process that is ready to access SR generates a multicast request for SR with some probability. If a decision was made to generate a request, the process sends the request and then activates time-out T_1. On the other hand, if the process made a decision not to generate its request for SR at this moment, it makes a delay T_4 called *p-persistence* delay. After elapsing this delay, if RSTA = 0, the process may do a new probabilistic attempt to generate a request. If, after elapsing T_4, RSTA $\neq 0$, then the process routinely activates deadlock-resolution time-out T_2 as was described above.

Like in p-persistent CSMA/CD, p-persistence delay in the proposed protocol should be of order of the collision window (4.1). It is also desirable to make the p-persistence delay random, so that different processes would finish this delay at different moments of time. Taking into account these considerations, a uniform probability distribution in range $(T_1/2, T_1)$ was chosen for p-persistence delay T_4 in the protocol.

5 Communication Complexity of the Protocol

In this section, communication complexity of the proposed protocol is discussed. The *communication complexity* is defined as the expected number of messages sent by a process, per use of SR. As was explained in Sect. 3, the protocol uses multicast messages of types R, F, and E. Messages of type E are sent by a process only occasionally and therefore will not be taken into account in the evaluation of the protocol's complexity.

Message of type F is sent exactly once per each access to SR, at the end of using SR by each process. On the other hand, a process can multicast a random number of messages of type R before it wins the competition for SR among other contending processes.

Below, two limiting cases are considered. The first case corresponds to a low load of SR server, and the second one corresponds to its high load. It is assumed initially that a process generates a request for SR with probability one.

The load of the SR server, ρ, can be expressed in terms of a finite population queuing system, with parameters λ and μ, as defined in [16]. When load ρ of SR server approaches zero, there is no competition for SR and, thus, there are no conflicts between processes, so that each process accesses SR actually at will. Obviously, in this case each process wanting to access SR will send only one request message of type R so that, taking into account a message of type F, the *minimal* communication complexity will be 2 multicast messages per use of SR by a process.

The case of high load is more complex for analysis, since in this case conflicts between processes wanting to access SR at about the same time are frequent and considerably complicate the picture. For the assumed 1-persistence scheme, up to $N-1$ processes can send their request message R at about the same time, detect a conflict each and, after elapsing of time-out T_1, start their back-off delay T_3. Assuming for simplicity that only one repeated conflict can happen and using the reasoning described in [21], it can be shown that, for this simplified pattern of process contention, the expected number of messages of type R sent by each process competing for SR is not less than

$$3-(1-p_r)^{N-2}, \tag{5.1}$$

where p_r is probability of the repeated conflict. Since, for high load, this probability is not small, expression (5.1) yields, even for moderate number of processes N, the expected number of messages of type R close to 3. Together with one message of type F, the expected total number of messages per use of SR is *not less* than 4 for high load.

In the p-persistence scheme, if SR is free, each process that is ready to use SR issues a request message with some persistence probability p. Correspondingly, with probability $1-p$ the process defers, enters a *p-persistence delay*, after which it will make a new attempt to issue a request message if SR is still free. Recall that in Section 4 p-persistence delay was denoted by T_4.

By delaying, the process temporarily refrains from competition for SR which results in the decreased message traffic. As explained in Section 4, p-persistence delay should be of order of collision window $2\tau_d$. It can be shown that the total expected delay associated with p-persistence is

$$\frac{1-p}{p}E(T_4), \tag{5.2}$$

where p is persistence probability and $E(T_4)$ is mean value of p-persistence delay.

Unfortunately, it is difficult to mathematically derive the exact expression for persistence probability. Instead, we propose a simple heuristic functional form

$$p(N,\lambda,\mu)=1-e^{-k\frac{\mu}{\lambda N}}, \tag{5.3}$$

where λ and μ were specified at the beginning of this section, N is the number of processes in the group, and k is a nonnegative coefficient.

The intuition behind the proposed form (5.3) is as follows. When the number of processes N is large and/or the rate of steps of main work λ is high (with fixed μ, this corresponds to high load of SR server), persistence probability should be small to keep at low level the number of processes who will issue a request message. On the other hand, small values of N and/or λ correspond to decreased load of SR server, and in this case persistence probability should be increased. The functional form (5.3) for persistence probability satisfies both of these requirements. Coefficient k can be used as a configuration parameter to control the behavior of persistence probability when N and λ change.

To use expression (5.3), each process needs to know the number of all processes in the group, N, rates λ and μ, and coefficient k. Coefficient k is a system-wide parameter. Since processes are assumed to be members of some group, each process can get values of variables N, λ, and μ as part of group membership information. If the values of these variables provided by the membership management system are different from their actual values, the protocol will continue its proper operation, probably with decreased performance. This is in contrast with many known algorithms of distributed mutual exclusion where each process usually needs to know the exact number of processes in the group.

6 Performance Study

To investigate the proposed protocol of distributed mutual exclusion in more depth, its detailed formalized model was developed and an extensive simulation study was carried out. As a modeling formalism, a class of extended Petri nets, which are colored timed Petri nets with attributed tokens, was used [23]. The simulation was carried out in the simulation system Winsim based on these Petri nets and implemented in Windows XP operating system [24], [26]. The simulation model, in terms of extended Petri nets, was organized as a set of segments, with each segment representing activity of one process. All these segments were linked to a model of a network of Ethernet type. The number of segments representing processes could be varied to simulate the protocol with different number of processes in the group.

The model of each process has a number of constants and variables, with values assigned at start-up time of simulation. For a simulation run, constants are duration of time-out T_1, number of processes in the group, N, coefficient k in expression (5.3), limits $(T_3)_{min}$ and $(T_3)_{max}$ of uniformly distributed random delay T_3, values $(T_4)_{min}$ and $(T_4)_{max}$ for random slot interval T_4, mean time of a step of main work $1/\lambda$ and mean time of using SR $1/\mu$ fixed at 500 ms in all our simulation experiments.

As a performance measure of the protocol, the average number of messages sent by a process per use of SR was used. The term "average" denotes here the sample mean. The *average number of messages* reflects communication complexity of the protocol. As explained in Section 5, this measure is the average sum of messages of types R and F per use of SR by a process.

Almost all simulation experiments have been carried out for three loads of SR server: low (0.1), medium (0.5), and high (0.9). For each load, the number of processes in the model was varied as 3, 6, 9, …, 21. For each of the three loads of SR server, and given number of processes, the following values of coefficient k in expression (5.3) were tried: 10, 1, 0.5, 0.25, 0.1, and 0.05. The value $k = 10$ in expression (5.3) was chosen so as to make persistence probability $p(N, \lambda, \mu) \approx 1$. Thus, the value $k = 10$ actually corresponds to 1-persistence scheme. The values 1, 0.5, 0.25, 0.1 and 0.05 of coefficient k correspond to a p-persistence scheme, with the decreasing persistence probability.

In the model of the communication network, *delivery time* of multicast messages was assumed to be random, with uniform probability distribution in the range (2, 4) ms. This is in agreement with actual delivery time of frames with the size of about 500 bytes in a LAN of Ethernet type [25].

Based on the above specified delivery time of messages in the model of the underlying network and taking into account considerations of Section 4, the following values of time-outs and random delays were fixed in simulation experiments: $T_1 = 20$ ms, $(T_3)_{min} = T_1/2$, $(T_3)_{max} = 100$ ms, $(T_4)_{min} = T_1/2$, $(T_4)_{max} = T_1$. Values of Δt_m and Δt_r in the limits of time-out T_2 were fixed at $2T_1$ and 100 ms, respectively.

Since, from a simulation point of view, the protocol can be considered as a *non-terminating* system, its steady-state performance measure is of interest. To decrease the effect of the transient state, each simulation run was done long enough to ensure that each process accesses SR about 5000 times.

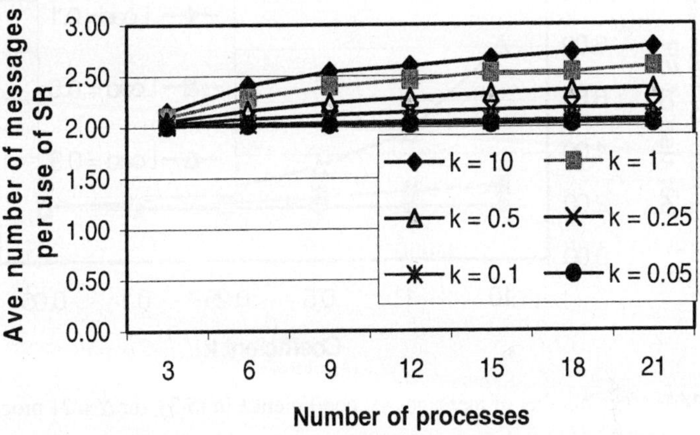

Fig. 2. Average number of messages vs. number of processes, for medium load of SR

Figs. 2 and 3 show graphs of the average number of messages per use of SR versus the number of processes in the group, for medium and high loads of SR server and different values of coefficient k in expression (5.3). Fig. 4 reflects the behavior of the performance measure versus coefficient k, with $N = 21$ processes in the group, for three loads.

From the results of simulation, we can make the following observations:

1. When load of SR server is low, average number of messages per use of SR by a process is very close to 2, independent of what persistence scheme is used – 1-persistence scheme or p-persistence one. This is in full agreement with the complexity analysis in Section 5.

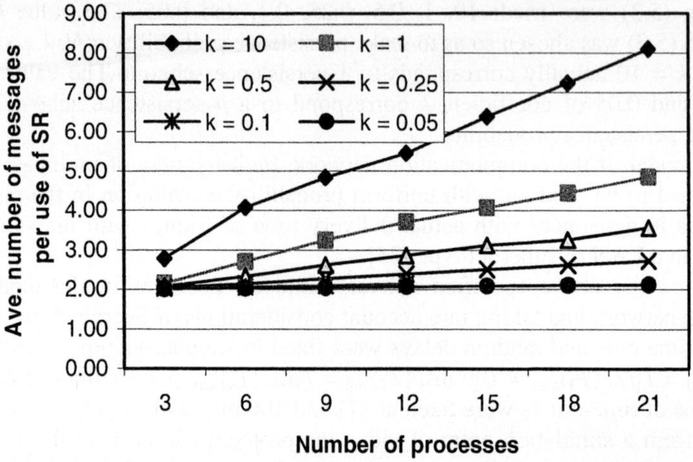

Fig. 3. Average number of messages vs. number of processes, for high load of SR

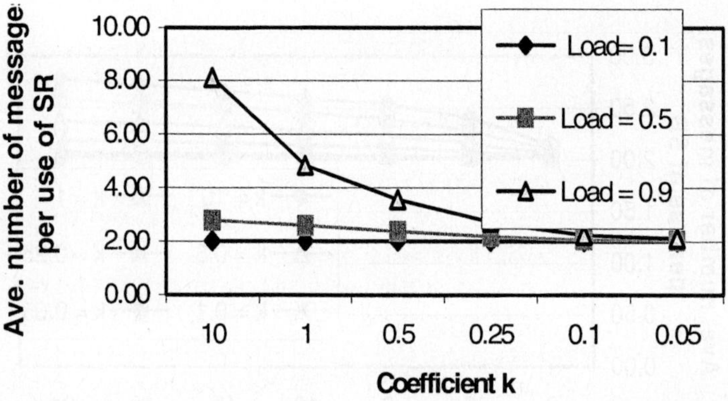

Fig. 4. Average number of messages vs. coefficient k in (5.3), for $N = 21$ processes

2. As Figs. 2 and 3 show, when load of SR server increases, average number of messages per use of SR demonstrates a definite dependence on coefficient k in expression (5.3). In particular, for the 1-persistence scheme the performance measure grows almost linearly and rather steep with the number of processes in the group. On the other side, the p-persistence scheme yields much better results. For example, with coefficient $k = 0.05$ in (5.3), the performance measure is almost independent of the number of processes, with average number of use of SR by a process close to 2. The favorable effect of the p-persistence scheme, for 21 processes, is clearly demonstrated by Fig. 4. Thus, the p-persistence scheme, with a reasonably small value of coefficient k, essentially eliminates the dependence of the protocol's behavior on the number of processes in the group, which makes the protocol scalable with respect to the number of processes.

3. As can be seen from Table 1, the protocol did not demonstrate a significant change in the average number of messages per use of SR, when value of time-out T_1 changes in the range from 10 to 50 ms. Since other delays depend on time-out T_1, one can conclude that the protocol is robust with respect to values of all used time-outs and delays.

Table 1. Average number of messages per use of SR with respect to time-out T_l, for $N = 21$ processes and coefficient $k = 0.05$ in expression (5.3)

Load of SR server	Value of time-out T_l, ms				
	10	20	30	40	50
0.1	2.006	2.005	2.005	2.005	2.005
0.9	2.155	2.124	2.117	2.115	2.117

7 Conclusion

A fully distributed and fault-tolerant protocol of distributed mutual exclusion is described and investigated by extensive simulation. The protocol is based on reliable multicast and assumes a bounded delivery time of messages. To decrease the negative effect of competition of processes for shared resource (SR), a probabilistically persistent scheme is used by each process in its decision to issue a request for SR. As results of simulation show, this scheme dramatically decreases average number of messages per use of SR by a process.

References

1. Srimani, P.K., Das, S.R. (Eds.): Distributed Mutual Exclusion Algorithms. IEEE Press (1992)
2. Raynal, M.: A Simple Taxonomy for Distributed Mutual Exclusion. ACM Operating Systems Review, vol. 25, no. 2 (1991) 47 –51
3. Singhal, M.: A Taxonomy of Distributed Mutual Exclusion. Journal of Parallel and Distributed Computing, vol. 18, no. 1 (1993) 94 – 101
4. Chang, Y.-I.: A Simulation Study on Distributed Mutual Exclusion. Journal of Parallel and Distributed Computing, vol. 33, no. 2 (1996) 107 – 121
5. Loshin, P., Kastenholz, F.: Essential Ethernet Standards: RFC's and Protocols Made Practical. John Wiley & Sons (1999)
6. Raymond, K.: A Tree-based Algorithm for Distributed Mutual Exclusion. ACM Transactions on Computer Systems, vol. 7, no. 1 (1989) 61 – 77
7. Nishio, S., Li, K.F., Manning E.G.: A Resilient Mutual Exclusion Algorithm for Computer Network. IEEE Trans. on Parallel and Distributed Systems, vol. 1, no. 3 (1990) 344 – 355
8. Mueller, F.: Prioritized Token-based Mutual Exclusion for Distributed Systems. Proc. of the Parallel Processing Symposium IPPS/SPDP (1998) 791 – 795

9. Banerjee, S., Chrysantis, P.K.: A New Token Passing Distributed Mutual Exclusion Algorithm. Proc. of the 16th International Conference on Distributed Computing Systems (ICDCS'96) (1996) 717 – 724
10. Sanders, B.A.: The Information Structure of Distributed Mutual Exclusion Algorithms. ACM Transactions on Computer System, vol. 5, no. 3 (1987) 284 – 299
11. Ricart, G., Agrawala, A.K.: An Optimal Algorithm for Mutual Exclusion in Computer Networks. Communications of the ACM, vol. 24, no. 1 (1981) 9 – 17
12. Maekawa, M.A.: $\sqrt{N}$ Algorithm for Mutual Exclusion in Decentralized Systems. ACM Transactions on Computer Systems, vol. 3, no. 2 (1985) 145 – 159
13. Singhal, M.: A Dynamic Information Structure Mutual Exclusion Algorithm for Distributed Systems. IEEE Trans. on Parallel and Distributed Systems, vol. 3, no. 1 (1992) 121 – 125
14. Jayaprakash, S., Muthukrishnan, C.R.: Permission-based Fault-tolerant Distributed Mutual Exclusion Algorithm. International Journal of Computer Systems Science and Engineering, vol. 14, no. 1 (1999) 51 – 60
15. Lodha, S., Kshemkalyani, A.: A Fair Distributed Mutual Exclusion Algorithm. IEEE Trans. on Parallel and Distributed Systems, vol. 11, no. 6 (2000) 537 – 549
16. Banks, J., Carson, J.S., Nelson, B.L., Nicol, D.M.: Discrete-Event System Simulation, 3rd ed., Prentice-Hall (2001)
17. Floyd, S., Jacobson, V.,Liu, C., McCanne, S., Zhang, L.: A reliable Multicast Framework for Light-weight Sessions and Application Level Framing. IEEE/ACM Transactions on Networking, vol. 5, no. 6 (1997) 784 – 803
18. Hadzilacos, V., Tueg, S.: A Modular Approach to Fault-Tolerant Broadcasts and Related Problems. Technical Report TR94-1425, Dept. of Computer Science, Cornell Univ. (1994)
19. Coulouris,, G., Dollimore, J., Kindberg, T.: Distributed Systems: Concepts and Design, 3rd ed., Pearson Education (2001)
20. Hastad, J., Leghton, T., Rogoff, B.:Analysis of Backoff Protocols for Multiple Access Channels. SIAM Journal on Computing, vol. 25, no. 10 (1995)
21. Kostin, A., Aybay, I., Oz, G.: A Randomized Contention-Based Load-Balancing Protocol for a Distributed Multiserver Queuing System. IEEE Transactions on Parallel and Distributed Systems, vol. 11, no. 12 (2000) 1252 – 1273
22. Tobagi, F. A., Hunt, V.B.: Performance Analysis of Carrier Sense Multiple Access with Collision Detection. Computer Networks, vol. 4, no. 5 (1980) 245 – 259
23. Kostin, A.E.: Models and Algorithms for Organization of Distributed Data Processing in Information Systems. Diss. D.Sc., Moscow Institute of Electronic Technology (Technical University) (1989) (in Russian).
24. Simulation System Winsim Based on Extended Petri Nets: User Manual, http: //www.daimi.au.dk/PetriNets/tools/db/winsim.html
25. Held, G.: Local Area Network Performance: Issues and Answers. John Wiley & Sons (1994)
26. Kostin, A., Ilushechkina, L.: Winsim: A tool for Performance Evaluation of Parallel and Distributed Systems. Lecture Notes in Computer Science, vol. 3261, Springer-Verlag (2004) 312-321
27. Maxemchuk, N.F.: Reliable Multicast with Delay Guarantees. IEEE Communications Magazine, vol. 40, no. 9 (2002) 96 – 102
28. Rodrigues, L., Raynal, M.: Atomic Broadcast in Asynchronous Crash-Recovery Distributed Systems. Proc. Of the 20th International Conference on Distributed Computing Systems ICDCS '00 (2000) 288 - 297

Exact Best-Case End-to-End Response Time Analysis for Hard Real-Time Distributed Systems

Lei Wang[1,2], Mingde Zhao[1], Zengwei Zheng[1,3], and Zhaohui Wu[1]

[1] College of Computing Science, Zhejiang University,
310027 Hangzhou, R.P. China
{alwaysbeing, zmdd48, zhengzw, wzh}@cs.zju.edu.cn
[2] UFSOFT School of Software, Jiangxi University of Finance & Economics,
330013 Nanchang, R.P. China
alwaysbeing@sohu.com
[3] City College, Zhejiang University, 310015 Hangzhou, R.P. China
zhengzw@zucc.edu.cn

Abstract. The prediction of best-case response time is quite necessary to guarantee control accuracy and stability of distributed hard real-time systems. Published time analysis techniques can precisely dealt with the precedence relations between tasks on different processors, but usually ignored or inaccurately estimated the effects from the precedence relations between tasks on the same processor. This leads to a pessimistic analysis. This paper presents an algorithm to analyze the best-case end-to-end response time for hard real-time distributed systems. This algorithm extends the traditional analysis technique by exploiting the precedence relations between tasks on both different processors and the same processor and achieves a more accurate analysis. Simulation results have shown that this algorithm can achieve more accurate results than existing methods.

1 Introduction

Distributed control systems are is superior to the traditional centralized control systems in performance, capability and robustness. Therefore, they are increasingly deployed in current industry and products. There are strict deadlines placed on the response times of control processes. Failure to meet the deadline may result in catastrophic consequences. However, adoption of the distributed architecture increases the complexity to predict the temporal behavior of control systems. In order to verify that a given distributed control system is capable of providing the required control quality, a means to predict response times is required. Preferably, this information should be available at an early design stage.

The technologies to predict whether the tasks can be completed before their deadlines, also known as schedulability analysis, have been well studied for single processor systems [1, 2] and also been extended to multi-processors systems and distributed systems [3, 4]. In order to provide guarantees for tasks meeting their deadlines, traditional analysis has focused on the analysis of worst-case behaviors. However, there are situations where it is also necessary to predict best-case performance. One such situation is in the calculation of response jitter, the maximum

P. Yolum et al.(Eds.): ISCIS 2005, LNCS 3733, pp. 173 – 182, 2005.

variation in the response time of a task or a sequence of tasks, which is an important parameter in real-time control systems. Since the executions of control algorithms precisely depend on the periodic samplings and actuations, large variations in these periods can result in inaccurate measurement and unstable output. In order to guarantee the control accuracy and stability it is important to find tight bounds of such variations. An exact best-case analysis is necessary for this purpose.

Palencia et al. have developed Tindell's method [4] with an approximation estimate of best-case response times [5]. They found a lower bound on the response time of a task by optimistically assuming that all higher priority tasks finish at the instant when the analyzed lower priority task is released (after having experienced their best-case response times). This results in a correct lower bound for the best-case response times of tasks, but it is not exact. Henderson et al. tried to find the exact best-case response times [6]. However, their solution leads to a numerically intractable search through all possible orderings of higher priority task executions, prior to the release of the analyzed low priority task. After that, Redell et al. presented a simple and exact method to solve this problem [7]. Although the accuracy to predict the best-case temporal behaviors has been improved, existing methods consider a model of independent tasks and precedence relations between tasks are only considered in the calculation of jitters, which are somewhat pessimistic since the precedence relations among tasks are not sufficiently exploited.

Based on the best-case phasing given by Redell et al. [7] and the canonical form transformation proposed by Harbour et al. [8], this paper proposes a more exact best-case end-to-end response analysis, where the precedence relations between tasks in the same processing nodes are directly considered.

The remainder of the paper is organized as follows: the next section describes the assumptions and computational model used in this paper. Section 3 presents the methods to compute end-to-end response times and release jitters. Then the best-case response time analyses for precedence relations are presented in Section 4. Simulation results are given in Section 5. Finally, we conclude the paper in Section 6.

2 Assumptions and Computational Model

In this paper we consider the event-driven software system. In this system a set of external event sequences activate tasks. These tasks may generate internal events (signals as well as data) that activate other tasks, and so on. We assume that a task immediately activates its successors at the end of its execution. All tasks, which are in precedence relation by their activation, are grouped into entities that we called transactions. The assignment of the tasks to the processors is given and all the tasks of the same transaction are not necessary assigned to the same processor. Each transaction has a period and deadline. We assume the deadline is less than or equal to their period. Tasks within the same transaction have the same period and deadline with the transaction. We exclude the possibility that the execution of multiple instances of a task can be underway, i.e., a task must complete before its next arrival. In the computational model referenced in this paper, each task has one direct predecessor at most, which may run on the same or different processor. A task may have one or more successors on the same or different processors.

On each processor, tasks are statically assigned unique priority and scheduled under a fixed priority preemptive strategy. The assignment of priority is not the focus in this paper, but we assume that predecessors are always assigned higher priority than their successors on the same processor. This is reasonable since successors in a transaction are always released after their predecessors complete. To reduce the complexity of response time analysis, the communication costs between processors is neglected in this study. Actually, the response time of messages can be analyzed with the similar method by modeling each network as if it were a processor, and each message as if it were a task [10].

Let P be the set of processors. There is a set $\Gamma = \{t_1,\ldots, t_n\}$ of n periodic tasks in the system. Each task t_i is characterized by $(T_i, C^B_i, D_i, \pi_i, p_i)$ where T_i is the period of task t_i, C^B_i is its best-case execution time (BCET), D_i is its deadline, π_i is its priority and $p_i \in P$ is the processor to which it is allocated. Γ_p denotes the task set allocated to the processor $p \in P$.

Let k be the total number of transactions in the system. There is a set $X = \{x_1,\ldots, x_k\}$ of k transactions in the system. Each transaction x_i is characterized by (T_i, TS_i, D_i) where T_i is the period of transaction x_i, TS_i is the set of all the tasks in this transaction and $TS_i \subseteq \Gamma$. D_i is the deadline of the transaction and $D_i \leq T_i$. Each task in TS_i has the same period T_i and deadline D_i.

If tasks do communicate with each other, they are said to be precedence constrained since a task is blocked until its direct predecessors activate it. Each transaction has one beginning task and one or more terminative tasks. We denote *end(x)* the set of terminative tasks of transaction $x \in X$.

3 End-to-End Response Time and Release Jitter

The end-to-end response time of a transaction is measured from the activation time of the first task to the finishing time of the last task in the transaction. To obtain the end-to-end response time of a transaction, we can calculate its individual task response times and sum them up [3]. We define *local* response time r_i for a task t_i which is measured from the local arrival time of t_i and define *global* response time R_i of t_i in a transaction which is measured from the beginning of the complete transaction. The global best-case response times of t_i, R^B_i can be expressed as:

$$R_i^B = R_{i-1}^B + r_i^B \tag{1}$$

where r^B_i is the best-case local response time of t_i, R^B_{i-1} is the best-case global response time of its direct predecessor task and $R^B_0 = 0$. Obviously, the end-to-end response time of a transaction is its terminative tasks' global response time. Thus, the best-case end-to end response time R^B_x of transaction x can be expressed as:

$$R_x^B = \max_{j \in end(x)} (R_j^B) \tag{2}$$

In periodic distributed systems, transactions composed of precedence-constrained tasks will begin periodically. However, tasks except the first in a transaction will suffer variation in release time since they will inherit variants in response time (jitter) from predecessor tasks. The presence of jitter can affect the response times of lower priority tasks [9]. Therefore, we need to compute the release jitter for each task.

The release jitter of a task is defined as the maximum variation of its release time. Traditional analysis of distributed response time assumes that the release jitter of a task is the worst-case response time of the task which directly precedes it and the best-case response time of the predecessor task is assumed to be small and is ignored. However, this will lead to a pessimistic calculation of response times, since jitter may increase rapidly with each additional precedence step in a transaction. Given the global worst-case and best-case response times of its direct predecessor, the release jitter J_i of task t_i can be more accurately computed through the following equation:

$$J_i = R_{i-1}^W - R_{i-1}^B \tag{3}$$

where R^W_{i-1} is the global worst-case response times of its direct predecessor of t_i. The calculation of worst-case response time is not the focus in this paper.

4 Task Best-Case Response Time Analysis

From a scheduling point of view, an execution sequence is defined by the release times and executions of all instances of all tasks. Such execution sequence represents exactly one possible execution of a real-time application. The best-case response time computation for a transaction needs to find an execution sequence, called best-base phasing, for which the transaction has experienced its smallest global response time. Redell et al. have proposed a best-case phasing for a model of independent task with jitter. They have proved that for a set of independent tasks with jitter [7]:

*The best-case phasing of a task occurs whenever **it finishes simultaneously** with the release of all its higher priority tasks and these have experienced their maximum release jitter.*

Based on the best-case phasing, Redell et al. also proposed a method to calculate the best-case response time r_i^B. Given a schedulable set of independent fixed priority scheduled tasks with deadline equal to or smaller than their periods, r_i^B can be computed through the following iterative equation:

$$r_i^{B*} = C_i^B + \sum_{j \in hp(i)} \left\lceil \frac{r_i^B - J_j - T_j}{T_j} \right\rceil_0 \cdot C_j^B \tag{4}$$

where $\lceil x \rceil_0 = \max(0, \lceil x \rceil)$. r_i^B can be found by iteration over this equation starting with a value $r_i^{B*} = r_i^W$ or $r_i^{B*} = T_i$. When the iteration has converged, the corresponding r_i^{B*} is equal to the best-case response time of task i.

The method above can accurately calculate the best-case response time of independent tasks. However, when the precedence relations of tasks are considered, this method does not provide correct results. This can be illustrated by the following example. Consider the task set on a processor p shown in Table 1. If we neglect the precedence relations in the task set, the best-case response time of t_2 and t_4 are 2 and

Table 1. The task set on processor $p3$

Task	Transaction	Period	Direct predecessor	BCET	Priority
t_1	x_3	8	None	2	4
t_2	x_1	30	None	2	3
t_3	x_3	8	t_1	3	2
t_4	x_1	30	t_2	5	1

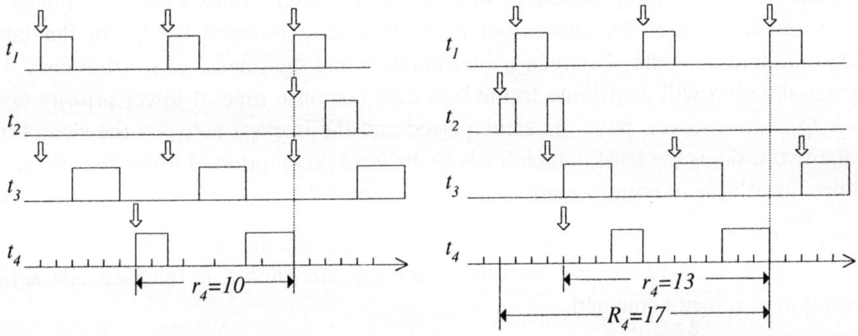

Fig. 1. The best-case phasing of t_4: (a) Tasks are independent; (b) Dependences are considered

10 respectively based on the method above. The best-case phasing of t_4 is shown in Fig.1(a). The interval between the release of t_2 and the termination of t_4 is 2+10=12. However, when the precedence relations are considered, the result is different. As shown in Fig.1(b), t_4 is released at the end of t_3 and t_3 is released at the end of t_1. The best-case response time of t_4 is 13 and the best-case interval between the release of t_2 and the termination of t_4 is 17.

From this example we can see that the precedence relation between two tasks does not affect the execution of the predecessor, this is because the predecessor always has a higher priority than its successors on the same processor. The precedence relations between tasks on different processors have been considered in the calculation of global response time (Equation 1). In order to extend the response time analysis for precedence relations between tasks on the same processor, we consider the following two cases on a processor p. t_i is a task running on p.

Case 1: The calculated task t_i has no direct predecessor on p.
Case 2: The calculated task t_i has a direct predecessor on p.

Case 1: t_i has no direct predecessor on p. Let's consider the task scheduling on p. When calculating t_i's response time, we do not consider the effects from its indirect predecessors on p, since they do not preempt the execution of t_i. Although these indirect predecessors may affect the release time of t_i, these effects are indirect and are transferred to t_i's direct predecessor, which is on another processor. The dependence on its direct predecessor has been taken into account in the calculation of global response time of t_i (see Equation 1). As a result, t_i's execution is only affected by the tasks on p with higher priority and belonging to other transactions. We denote the set of these tasks as S, so S can be expressed as $S = \{t_i \mid t_i \in hp(i) \wedge t_i \notin V(i)\}$, where $hp(i)$ is the set of tasks on p which have higher priority than t_i and $V(i)$ is the set of tasks in the transaction of t_i. If the tasks in S have no precedence relations among them (no two tasks belong to a common transaction), the precedence relations between tasks on p will not affect the execution of t_i. The best-case phasing for t_i is the instant when it finishes simultaneously with the release of all the tasks in S.

Consider the case that two tasks in S have a precedence relation. Let the two tasks be t_j and t_k, and t_j is the predecessor of t_k. t_k may be released just when t_j terminate its execution or released by successors of t_j (indirectly released by t_j). In the latter situation there is a delay between t_j's termination and the release of t_k. Obviously, the former situation will contribute to the best-case response time of lower priority tasks (task t_i), since t_j and t_k have the same period and the interval between the executions of the two tasks is the least, which leads to the least preemption of lower priority tasks before the release of them. Lemma 4.1 and Lemma 4.2 can prove this.

Lemma 4.1: In the task set of a processor p, task t_j is the direct predecessor of task t_k. If t_k's release time is brought forward to the instant when t_j is released, the actual execution of t_k is not changed.

Proof: According to the assumptions, t_j and t_k has a common period and t_j has a higher priority than t_k. t_k is released when t_j terminates. Consider the phase illustrated in Fig.2 with $\pi_i > \pi_j > \pi_k$. The white arrow denotes the release instant of tasks when the precedence relations are considered. a2 is the instant when t_j is terminated and t_k is released. $a1$ is the instant when t_j is released and is denoted by the first black arrow. It can be seen that if t_k is released at $a1$, it will have no change to execute before the termination of t_j in the same instance of their transaction. This is because that t_j and t_k are released simultaneously at $a1$ and t_j has a higher priority than t_k. That is to say the execution of t_k will not be different whether it is released at $a1$ or $a2$. Since t_j and t_k have the same period, this is true for all the following instances of t_k. ∎

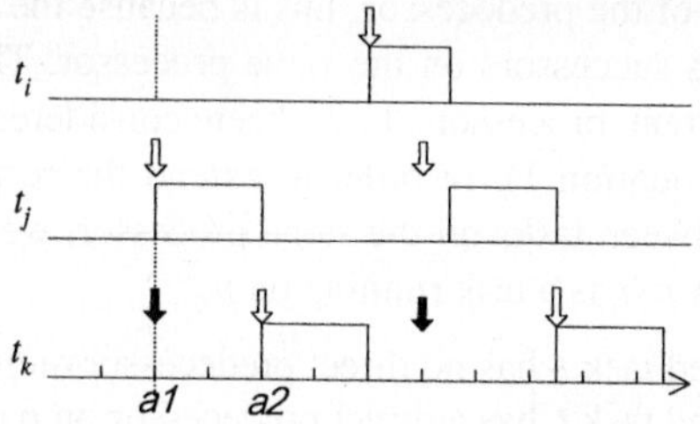

Fig. 2. Bringing forward t_k's release time to $a1$ dose not change t_k's actual execution

Theorem 4.2: In the task set of a processor p, task t_j and t_k belong to the same transaction x and task t_j is a predecessor of task t_k . For another task t_i, which has lower priority than t_j and t_k and does not belong to x, the case t_j is the direct predecessor of t_k will contribute to the best-case phasing of t_i, which occurs when t_i finishes simultaneously with the release of t_j.

Proof: When the precedence relation between t_j and t_k is not considered, the best-case phasing of t_i occurs when it finishes simultaneously with the release of the instances of t_j, t_k and all other tasks with higher priority than t_i [7]. Consider the precedence relation between t_j and t_k. If t_j is the direct predecessor of t_k, according to Lemma 4.1, t_i remains in its best-case phasing, just like the case that instances of t_j and t_k are released in the same time just after t_i has terminate its best-case execution. ■

According to Lemma 4.1 and Theorem 4.2, the calculation of t_i's best-case response time can be performed as if t_i finishes simultaneously with release of all the tasks in S. Therefore, the precedence relations between tasks in S will not affect the best-case phasing of t_i.

As a result, no matter whether there are precedence relations between tasks in S, according to the theory of Redell et al., t_i's best-case local response time, r_i^B, can be computed through the following iterative equation:

$$r_i^{B*} = C_i^B + \sum_{j \in \Gamma_p \cap hp(i) \wedge j \notin V(i)} \left\lceil \frac{r_i^B - J_j - T_j}{T_j} \right\rceil_0 \cdot C_j^B \tag{5}$$

An initial response time, $r_i^{B*} = r_i^W$ or $r_i^{B*} = T_i$, may be assumed. The newly computed response time, r_i^{B*}, replaces r_i^B on each iteration. When the iteration has converged, the corresponding r_i^{B*} is equal to the best-case local response time of task t_i. The convergence of the equation has been proved in [7].

Case 2: The calculated task t_i has a direct predecessor on p. An example for this case is the task t_6 on Fig.3, which has a direct predecessor t_5 on the same processor. To calculate the best-case local response time of t_i, we need to consider the effects from its predecessors. We introduce the *consecutive sub-transaction* to compute the response time of t_i.

Definition 4.1: The *consecutive sub-transaction* of a task t_i is the sub-transaction in which all the consecutive tasks are on the same processor and t_i is the last task in this sub-transaction.

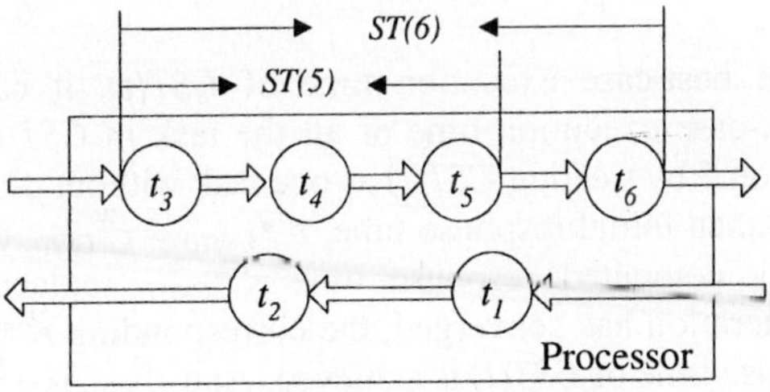

Fig. 3. Consecutive sub-transaction

In Fig.3, the consecutive sub-transaction of t_5 and t_6 are shown. We denote the consecutive sub-transaction of t_i as $ST(i)$. Obviously, t_i and $ST(i)$ have the same global response time. The best-case global response time of t_i can be expressed as:

$$R_i^B = R_{fst(i)-1}^B + r_{ST(i)}^B \tag{6}$$

where $fst(i)$ is the first task in $ST(i)$, $r^B{}_{ST(i)}$ is the best-case local response time of $ST(i)$ which is measured from the release time of the first task to the termination of the last task t_i in $ST(i)$.

To calculate $r^B{}_{ST(i)}$, we introduce the concept *canonical form* proposed by Harbour et al. [8]. A transaction or sub-transaction is said to be in canonical form if it consists of consecutive tasks that do not decrease in priority. Harbour et al. have proved that converting a precedence chain into a canonical form does not change its completion time. Therefore, we can calculate $r_{ST(i)}$ by transforming $ST(i)$ to a canonical form. We denote the canonical form of $ST(i)$ as $CST(i)$. The canonical transformation can be performed by applying the following algorithm:

Algorithm 1. Canonical transformation
t_i is the last task in $ST(i)$;
while t_i is not the first task of $ST(i)$
  If $\pi_{i-1} > \pi_i$ **then** $\pi_{i-1} = \pi_i$;
    $i = i-1$;
end

Since the consecutive tasks in a consecutive sub-transaction have descending priorities, after the canonical transformation, all the tasks in $CST(i)$ have the same priority π_i. Due to the tasks in $CST(i)$ also have the same period and each task is immediately released when its direct predecessor terminates its execution, when calculate its response time, $CST(i)$ can be treated as a single task with priority π_i and period T_i. According to the definition of $ST(i)$, this assumed task has no direct predecessor on p. This is just the case indicated by Case 1. Therefore, the best-case local response time $r_{CST(i)}$ (equal to $r_{ST(i)}$) can be expressed in the following iterative form:

$$r_{CST(i)}^{B*} = C_{CST(i)}^B + \sum_{j \in \Gamma_p \cap hp(i) \wedge j \notin V(i)} \left\lceil \frac{r_{CST(i)}^B - J_j - T_j}{T_j} \right\rceil_0 \cdot C_j^B \tag{7}$$

where $C^B{}_{CST(i)}$ is the best-case execution time of $CST(i)$, it can be achieved by summing up the best-case execution time of all the task in $CST(i)$. This equation is deduced from Equation 5 by treating $CST(i)$ as one task without direct predecessor.

To calculate $r^B{}_{CST(i)}$, an initial response time, $r^{B*}{}_{CST(i)} = r^W{}_{CST(i)}$ or $r_i^{B*} = T_i$, may be assumed. The newly computed response time $r^{B*}{}_{CST(i)}$ replaces $r^B{}_{CST(i)}$ on each iteration. When the iteration has converged, the corresponding $r^{B*}{}_{CST(i)}$ is equal to the best-case local response time of $CST(i)$ is achieved. And $r^B{}_{ST(i)}$ is equal to $r^B{}_{CST(i)}$.

Based on Equation 1, 2, 3, 5, 6 and 7, the best-case end-to-end response times of transactions in distributed systems can be calculated.

5 Assessment of Effectiveness

In order to evaluate the performance of the proposed method, simulations were conducted with different task sets whose execution times, periods and priorities were generated randomly. These results are compared with those using the method proposed by Redell et al. [7].

Fig.4 compares the transaction best-case response times obtained using Redell's technique for independent tasks, R_{indep} with the response time obtained using the algorithm presented in this paper, R_{dep}. The Y-axis presents the average ratio R_{dep}/R_{indep}. The X-axis represents processor utilization. The results are presented for three different ratios of the maximum transaction period over the minimum transaction period, T_{max}/T_{min}. The figure shows the results for a set of 5 transactions with 8 tasks per transaction, in four processors. It can be seen that the ratio will increase with the ratio of T_{max} over T_{min}. For normal utilization levels of around 70% and T_{max}/T_{min} =100, the average best-case response time in the analysis with our algorithm are roughly 15% larger than analysis with independent tasks.

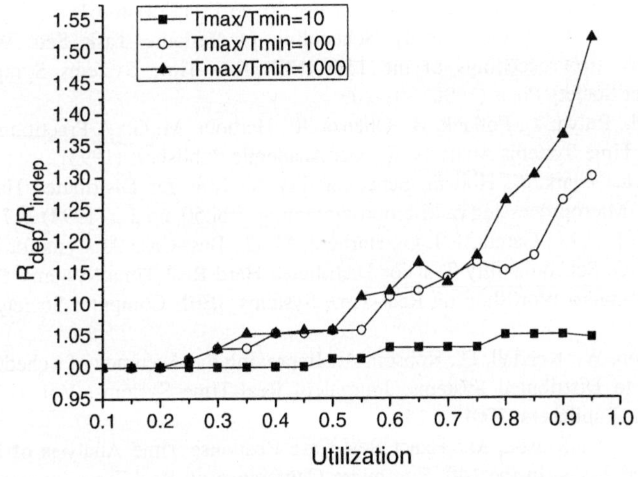

Fig. 4. R_{dep}/R_{indep}, 4 processors, 5 transactions, 8 tasks per transaction

6 Conclusion

In this paper we have addressed the problem of best-case end-to-end response analysis in distributed hard real-time systems, which is necessary to guarantee the control accuracy and stability. To achieve an accurate analysis, we extend the current best-case response time analysis techniques to exploiting the precedence relations between tasks on both different processors and the same processor. The analysis technique is based on the best-case phasing given by Redell et al. [7] and the canonical form transformation proposed by Harbour et al. [8]. We have found that the effects of precedence relations can be easily added in the end-to-end analysis if it is guaranteed that predecessors are always assigned higher priority than their successors in the same processors. Simulation results have shown that this algorithm can achieve more accurate results than existing methods.

Our further work includes the optimization of scheduling for distributed systems based on both worst-case and best-case end-to-end response time analysis. This will help system designers to improve the performance and reliability of a complex distributed system at an early design stage.

Acknowledgments

This work is supported in part by the National Hi-Tech Research and Development 863 Program of China under Grant No. 2003AA1Z2140 and 2004AA1Z2180.

References

1. Liu, C. L., Layland, J. W.: Scheduling Algorithms for Multiprogramming in a Hard Real-Time Environment. Journal of the ACM, Vol.20, no.1 (1973) 46-61
2. Lehoczky, J. P.: Fixed Priority Scheduling of Periodic Task Sets With Arbitrary Deadlines. In Proceedings of the 11th IEEE Real-Time Systems Symposium. IEEE Computer Society Press (1990) 201-209
3. Klein, M., Ralya, T., Pollack, B., Obenza, R., Harbour, M. G.: A Practitioners Handbook for Real-Time Systems Analysis. Kluwer Academic Publishers (1993)
4. Tindell, K., Clark, J.: Holistic Schedulability Analysis for Distributed Hard Real-Time Systems. Microprocessing & Microprogramming, Vol.50, no.2-3 (1994) 117-134
5. Palencia, J. C. G., García, J. J. G., Harbour, M. G.: Best-Case Analysis for Improving the Worst-Case Schedulability Test for Distributed Hard Real-Time Systems. Proceedings of 10th Euromicro Workshop on Real-Time Systems, IEEE Computer Society Press (1998) 35-44
6. Henderson, W., Kendall, D., Robson, A.: Improving the Accuracy of Scheduling Analysis Applied to Distributed Systems. Journal of Real-Time Systems, Vol.20, no.1. Kluwer Academic Publishers (2001) 5-25
7. Redell, O., Sanfridson, M.: Exact Best-Case Response Time Analysis of Fixed Priority Scheduled Tasks. In the 14th Euromicro Conference on Real-Time Systems (2002) 165-172
8. Harbour, M. G., Klein, M. H., Lehoczky, J. P.: Fixed Priority Scheduling of Periodic Tasks with Varying Execution Priority. In Proceedings of Real-Time Systems Symposium. IEEE Computer Society Press (1991) 116-128
9. Audsley, N. C., Burns, A., Tindell, K., Richardson, M., Wellings, A.: Applying New Scheduling Theory To Static Priority Pre-emptive Scheduling. Software Engineering Journal, Vol.8, no.5 (1993) 284-292
10. Tindell, K., Burns, A., Wellings, A. J.: Analysis of hard real-time communications. Journal of Real-Time Systems, Vol.9. Kluwer Academic Publishers (1995) 147–171

A Formal Policy Specification Language for an 802.11 WLAN with Enhanced Security Network

Handan Gül Çalıklı and Ufuk Çağlayan

Department of Computer Engineering, Boğaziçi University,
Bebek, İstanbul 34342, Turkey
{gul.calikli, caglayan}@boun.edu.tr

Abstract. In Wide Area Networks (WANs)inconsistencies among the security policies of Administrative Domains (ADs) may cause severe security flaws. Recently, security policies are written in natural language and as they get more complicated, even for an expert it might be impossible to detect such inconsistencies. However, when a formal language is used, it might be possible to make verification of security policies by automated theorem proving tools. Due to the existence of mobile devices such as laptops, PDAs and mobile agents, we need a formal language that is capable of defining the concept of mobility. In this paper, we extend Mob_{adtl} [1] according its refinement methodology to obtain a formal policy specification language for an 802.11 WLAN with enhanced security network.

Keywords: Administrative Domain, 802.11 Wireless Local Area Network (WLAN), Mob_{adtl}, Security Policy.

1 Introduction

In this paper we extend Mob_{adtl} [1] according to its refinement methodology to form a formal policy specification language for an 802.11 WLAN with enhanced security network. Refinements are made by adding axioms for system information, architectural operations and file access operations to existing axioms of Mob_{adtl}.

In the literature, there are network-aware formal models. Ambient Calculi are aimed to be used in the design process of programming languages for mobile environments. Among the Ambient Calculi we examined, there were Mobile Ambients [6] and its variants Mobile Safe Ambients [7], Socure Safe Ambients [8] and Boxed Ambients [9]. However, the semantics and syntax of Ambient Calculi are complicated. The model proposed by Cuppens and Saurel in [10] use deontic logic for modelling the concepts of permission, obligation and prohibition with a modal logic of action. In [11], Ryutov and Neuman propose a model that is capable of representing existing access control mechanisms such as *Access Control List* (ACL) and *Condition*.

P. Yolum et al.(Eds.): ISCIS 2005, LNCS 3733, pp. 183–192, 2005.

Finally, Mob_{adtl} is an ensemble of a model, a logic to formalize the model and a methodology required to structure, refine and compose specifications to obtain other specifications [1]. Compared to Ambient Calculi, functional units of Mob_{adtl} remain relatively simple while enabling the specification of rich co-ordination policies in an incremental manner. In addition, unlike most models such as Boxed Ambients and Mobile Ambients, Mob_{adtl} does not base its model on a basic security mechanism. Thus each authority can define and modify its own security policy.

In order to form axioms for architectural operations and system information, necessary information is extracted from IEEE 802.11 [12] and IEEE 802.11i [13] standards, respectively.

The rest of this paper is structured as follows. Overview of security aspects of IEEE 802.11 and IEEE 802.11i standards is given in Section II followed by an overview of network-aware formal models in the literature and Mob_{adtl}. Examples for enforcement of proposed formal policy language are given in Section III. Finally, Section IV summarizes the work done and mentions future work.

2 Background

The formal policy specification language, we formed refinening Mob_{adtl}, contains axioms for architectural operations and system information.Information required to form axioms for architectural operations and system information was extracted from IEEE 802.11 and IEEE 802.11i Standards, respectively. This section also includes an overview of Mob_{adtl} and other related network-aware formal models.

2.1 Overview of IEEE 802.11 and 802.11i Aspects

The most basic component of the 802.11 wireless network is station (STA)which is any device containing conformant medium access control (MAC) and physical layer (PHY) interface to the Wireless Medium (WM). The building block of an IEEE 802.11 WLAN is basic service set (BSS) and it consists of a group of any number of STAs. 802.11 wireless networks can exhibit two different basic architectures which are infrastructure basic service set and independent basic service set (IBSS). In an IBSS a STA communicates directly with one or more other STAs and a minimum IEEE 802.11 WLAN may consist of only two STAs. Mobile STAs must be within the range of each other to communicate. This type of operation is often referred to as an ad hoc network. An infrastructure basic service set is a BSS with a component called access point (AP). An AP is any entity that has STA functionality and provides access to the distribution services, via WM for associated STAs [12]. In an infrastructure BSS, STAs communicate via AP, but not directly with each other. Distribution System (DS) interconnects a set of BSSs and integrated local area networks (LANs) to create an extended service set (ESS) [12]. IEEE 802.11i [13] standard inherits basic security aspects from IEEE 802.1X standard which is the standard for port based network access control. The operation of port based access control has the effect of creating two distinct points of access to the authenticator system's point of attachment to the LAN. One of these two distinct points of attachment is the uncontrolled port which allows port data unit (PDU) exchange regardless of the authorization state; whereas the other is the controlled port which requires port to be authorized for allowing PDU exchanges. The authenticator Port Access Entity (PAE) uses the uncontrolled port for the purposes of exchanging protocol information with the supplicant. If MAC is physically or administratively inoperable, then no protocol exchanges of any kind can occur on either the controlled port or uncontrolled port. A STA can be part of an ESS, only if it is associated to an AP. If 802.1X EAP authentication is used, for association it should be followed by four way handshake. 802.1X EAP authentication process in an ESS can be initiated either by the supplicant or authenticator. If the EAP authentication succeeds, IEEE 802.1X controlled port is blocked so that general data traffic is not allowed. Authenticator associated with AP exchanges authentication messages only with supplicant which made a request for authentication (or to which the authenticator has sent authentication request message). When 802.1X EAP authentication is used in an IBSS, each STA will need to include 802.1X authenticator and authentication server. During IEEE 802.1X EAP authentication, each STA's supplicant will send an EAPOL-Start message to every other STA to which it wants to authenticate and each STA's authenticator will respond the identity of the credential it wants to use. For a STA to be a member of an IBSS, it should authenticate to each STA in that IBSS. In addition, four way handshakes should be performed in a mutual manner.

2.2 Overview of Network-Aware Formal Models and Mob$_{adtl}$

In [10] Cuppens and Saurel model the concepts of permission, obligation and prohibition using deontic logic with a modal logic of action. Temporal representation is introduced to the model via boolean attributes *Before*, *After* and *During*. Ryutov and Neuman present in [11] a model based on set and function formalism. *Mobile Ambients* (MA) [6] describe the movement of processes and devices through and within ADs. In MAs, interaction is *one-sided* and one of the two partners simply undergoes the action of moving or opening an ambient. In Mobile Safe Ambients (SA) [7], which is a variant of MA, a *mutual agreement* between the two partners undergoing an action is required. Secure Safe Ambients (SSA) [8] is a typed variant of SA. This type system provides for static detection of security attacks such as Trojan Horses and other combinations of malicious agents. Boxed Ambients (BA) [9] is a variant of MA and it provides finer grained abstractions for resource protection and access control in systems of distributed and mobile agents. Finally Mob$_{adtl}$ [1] is an ensemble of a model, a logic to formalize the model and a methodology required to structure, compose and refine specifications to obtain other specifications. $\triangle$DSTL(x) [2] is an asynchronous, distributed, temporal first order logic used to formalize the model of Mob$_{adtl}$. It adds a temporal structure and the concept of event on the top of DSL(x), which is a first order logic for reasoning on properties of distributed systems. The syntax of DSL(x) formulae defined in [3] is as $F :: A \mid \perp \mid \neg F \mid F \Lambda F' \mid \forall F \mid \exists F \mid m_i F$.

In the syntax of DSL(x), formula A is an atomic first order formula, $\perp$ is the constant *false*, m_i is a modality for locality built using the name of component m_i. $\overline{m}_i$ is used to denote the dual of m_i satisfying the following equation $\overline{m}_i = \neg m_i \neg F$.

$\triangle$DSTL(x) owns operators which relate conditions in different states of a computation. These operators and their functionalities are listed below:

- *STABLE* is used to state that a condition will keep staying *true* once it is established,
- *INIT* defines conditions holding in the initial state of a computation,
- *LEADS_ TO* expresses a *liveness* condition and defines the *sufficient* causes for a condition to hold,
- *BECAUSE* expresses a *safety* condition and defines the *necessary* causes for a condition to hold.

The concept of *event* (i.e. becoming *true* of a condition) is defined using the formula of the form $\triangle$F which is a part of $\triangle$DSTL(x) syntax.

In the model of Mob_{adtl} [1] *neighborhood* is a bounded environment where both stationary and mobile components live. *Components* have unique names determined by their initial neighborhood. Each neighborhood is associated with a stationary component called the *guardian.* The components are location aware due to the knowledge of their guardians. Communications are based on asynchronous message passing and they occur between components via guardians. A guardian intercepts messages and decides which of them can enter or leave the neighborhood it controls. Similarly, the guardians intercept components and decide which of them can enter or leave their neighborhood. Inter-operability of Mob_{adtl} provides enforcement and implementation of the security policies by different security mechanisms. Most models for secure mobile systems base their models on a specific security mechanism. For instance *Mobile Ambients*(MA) [6] specifies and enforces access control policies of mobile agents via capability based type system. In *Boxed Ambients* (BA), the resource access control framework defined is an instance of the standard *Mandatory Access Control* policies in multi-level security environments. Mob_{adtl} provides each guardian(authority) with the ability to define its own security policy. It also allows each authority to modify its own security policy by adding new restrictions. Since Mob_{adtl} separates functionality from coordination, it can specify both component functionalities and the security requirements independently at the abstract level. Mobility in Mob_{adtl} is subjective, in other words mobile units can control their location. In Seal Calculus, seals are moved by their parents, thus mobility is objective and cannot be controlled. Ambient Calculus is a hybrid; ambients can decide to move, but they carry their sub-ambients with themselves so that sub-ambients are moved in an objective way. The fact that MA supports both subjective and objective mobility can be seen as a source of interferences and wrong behaviors. *Safe Ambients* (SA) [7] introduces a form of control centralization with the notion of single thread and constrains subjective and objective moves via co-actions and synchronization, and thus it has similarities with Mob_{adtl}.In SA, only one process in each ambient can have the capability of making a move. Such notion of authority is similar to that of guardians in Mob_{adtl}. Secondly, co-action mechanism is similar to the interaction protocol between an agent and its guardian. Finally, reasoning on policies in Mob_{adtl} is automatized giving us the opportunity to make verifications in order to detect the security flaws in the overall system using MaRK [1].

3 Mob_{adtl} Specialized for 802.11 WLANs with Enhanced Security Network

In our work, refinements and additions are made to the theory for mobile devices which was given as an example for usage of Mob_{adtl} in [1]. *Neighborhood* is used to model ADs. An AD may consist of a hybrid of IBSS and ESS topologies. Sometimes an AD can consist of two or more mobile devices, as in ad-hoc networks. Moreover, when a mobile device has no connection with a mobile device or an AP, then its neighborhood it itself. The *guardian* concept of Mob_{adtl} model is used to model the central authority of a neighborhood which decides to forward or veto mobility, message and file access requests according to that neighborhood's security policy. In addition, a *guardian* is able to detect approaching and leaving STAs as well as reachability of a STA [1]. A *component* can be both a mobile and stationary device.

The axiom set for architectural operations consists of axioms for ESS/BSS and IBSS topologies. These axioms are encodings of the necessary extracts from IEEE 802.11 standard and are given in Table 1. Axioms for system information include EAP 802.1X authentication, and four way handshake procedures extracted from IEEE 802.11i standard as shown in Table 2. Axioms in Table 3, concern the basic file access operations which are *read, write* and *execute* respectively and data flow.

Table 1. Axioms for Architectural Operations

EL1: *S(associatedTo(AP)) Λ AP(guardedby(G)) LEADS_ TO G(guarding(S))*
EL2: $\overline{S}$*(associatedTo(AP)Λ associated to(AP′) → AP ≠ AP′)*
EIBL3: *G(reachable(S)Λ satisfies(S,P)) LEADS_ TO G(guarding(S))*
EL4: *G(△exit(S,P))LEADS_ TO G(moving(S))*
ES1: $\overline{AP}$*(guardedby(G))*
EIBS2: *S(guardedby(G)) BECAUSE S(associatedTo(AP)) V (S(ibssAuthTo (S′))Λ S′(ibssAuthTo(S)))*
ES3: *S(associatedTo(AP)) BECAUSE S(mutualAuthTo(AP))*
IBL1: *S(ibssAuthTo(S′)) LEADS_ TO S′(ibssAuthTo(S))*
IBL2: *S(ibssAuthTo(S′))LEADS_ TO G(guarding(S)Λ guarding(S′))*
IBS1: *S(ibssAuthTo(S′))BECAUSE S(mutualAuthTo(S′))Λ S′(mutualAuthTo (S))*

Table 2. System Information Axioms

SIL1: *S(△EAPAuthenticateTo(A)) LEADS_TO A(△protocol_msg(EAPOL–Start, S, A)*

SIL2: *A(△EAPAuthenticate(S)) LEADS_TO S(△protocol_msg (EAPRequest, A, S))*

SIL3: *A(△protocol_msg(EAPOLStart,S,A)) LEADS_TO S(△EAPAuthenticatingTo(A) V toBeVetoed(protocol△msg(EAPOLStart, S, A), D))*

SIL4: *A(△protocol_msg(EAPOLStart, S′, A) Λ EAPAuthenticating(S)Λ S≠S′) LEADS_TO S′(△toBeVetoed(protocol_msg(EAPOLStart,S′,A),D))*

SIL5: *S(△EAPAuthTo(A)) LEADS_TO A(△portAuthorized) Λ △block(ControlledPort, S)*

SIL6: *S(△mutualAuthTo(A)) LEADS_TO A(¬block(controlledPort, S))*

SIS1: *G(△DataIn(D, G′)V G(△DataOut(D, G′)) BECAUSE A(¬block(controlledPort, S) Λguardedby(G)) Λ S(guardedby(G))*

SIS2: *S(mutualAuthTo(A)) BECAUSE S(EAPAuthTo(A))*

SIS3: *G(exit(S,P)) BECAUSE (S(¬mutualAuthTo(AP)) Λ AP(guardedby(G))) V (S(¬ibssAuthTo(S′))Λ S′(guardedby(G)))*

SIS4: *A(¬macEnabled) BECAUSE A(Disconnect)*

SIS5: A(Disconnect) BECAUSE A(EAPAuth(S) *Λ* (¬KeyAvailable V TimeOut))

Table 3. Axioms for File Access Operations, Mobility, Communication and Data Flow

FL1: *S(△Read(F, O) Λ guardedby(G)) LEADS_TO G(△read(F, S, O))*

FL2: *G(△read(F,S,O) Λ guarding(S)) LEADS_TO S(△toBeVetoed(ftp–Connection, D))V G′(△read(F, S, O) Λ guarding(O))*

FL3: *G(△read(F, S, O) Λ guarding(O)) LEADS_TO S(△toBeVetoed (read(F, S, O),D)) V S(△readIn(F, O))*

FL4: *S(△Write(F,S,O) V △Execute(F,S,O)) Λ S(guardedby(G)) LEADS_TO G(△write(F,S,O))*

FL5: *G(write(F, S, O) V execute(F, S, O)) LEADS_TO G(read(F,S,O))*

FS1: *P(△ReadIn(F,S)) BECAUSE G1(guarding(S) Λ allow(P, Connect, ftp-Port)) Λ G1(allow(P, Read, F) V allow(P, Write, F) V allow(P, Execute, F))*

FS2: *S(Read(F,O) Λ △ failure_msg) BECAUSE S(guardedby(G))Λ G(¬reachable(O))*

MS5: *G2(△moving(S)) BECAUSE G1(guarding(S) Λ allow(S,moveTo,G2))*

CS1: *P(△in(M,S)) BECAUSE G1(guarding(S) Λ allow(S, Send, (M,P)))*

DF1: *∀ G1, G2, G3,F . G2(△DataIn(F,G1))Λ G3(△DataIn(F,G2)) → G3(△DataIn(F,G1))*

3.1 Examples of Enforcement of Formal Policy Specification Language for 802.11 WLANs with Enhanced Security Network

In this section, examples for the enforcement of the axioms we formed as an extension of Mob_{adtl} to make verifications for 802.11 WLANs with enhanced security network are given.

For instance, a component of an AD may want to read a file F owned by entity O. If O or (and) S does (do) has no connection with a STA, then response of the query requesting read access to file F will be a failure message. This is stated in axiom FS2 of file operations axiom set in Table 3. If a STA is not part of an BSS/ESS, then it is not mutually authenticated to an AP. On the other hand, if a station is not part of an IBSS/ESS, then there is not a station S′ so that S and S′ are mutually authenticated to each other. These facts are stated in axiom SIS3 in Table 2. If S and S′ are not part of the same IBSS, then this means that either (or both) of them did not mutually authenticate to each other as stated in axiom IBS1 in Table 1. Thus, if S is not mutually authenticated to a station, the reason for this might be,

- S might have performed 802.1X EAP authentication successfully. However, a problem may have occurred during four way handshake. This might be due to the fact that either Pairwise Master Key (PMK for ESS/BSS architecture, and it is PSK for IBSS architecture) is not received by authenticator (i.e. $A(\neg KeyAvailable)$) or after supplicant receives the message with Anonce (Anonce is a random number generated by authenticator during four way handshake in order to be used in derivation of PTK) from the authenticator, it sends no response to the authenticator (i.e. $A(\triangle TimeOut)$), or
- Neither authenticator nor supplicant wanted to perform 802.1X EAP authentication, (i.e. $S(\neg EAPAuthenticateTo(A))\ \Lambda\ A(\neg EAPAuthenticate(S)))$ which is supposed to be followed by four way handshake for the mutual authentication, or
- The supplicant wanted to initiate 802.1X EAP authentication and it received a veto message, (i.e. $S(\triangle veto(protocol\_msg(EAPOL\_Start,S,A))))$ or
- The authenticator wanted to initiate 802.1X EAP authentication and it received a veto message, (i.e. $A(\triangle veto(protocol\_msg(EAPRequest,A,S)))$) or
- Supplicant has not yet finished 802.1X EAP authentication and it is authenticating to the authenticator, (i.e. $S(EAPAuthenticatingTo(A))$), or
- Supplicant has successfully performed 802.1X EAP authentication and has just started four way handshake. Thus, controlled port of the authenticator is blocked for data exchange, (i.e. $A(\triangle block(controlledPort,S))$) and only messages related to four way handshake are allowed.

The possible reasons for why S is not mutually authenticated to a station can be written in Mob_{adtl} as follows:

$$S(\neg mutualAuthTo(A))\ BECAUSE\ A(\neg KeyAvailable)\ V\ A(\triangle TimeOut))\ V$$
$$(S(\neg EAPAuthenticateTo(A)\ \Lambda\ A(\neg EAPAuthenticate(S))\ V$$
$$S(\triangle veto(protocol\_msg(EAPOLStart,S,A)))\ V$$
$$A(\triangle veto(protocol\_msg(EAPRequest,A,S)))\ V$$
$$S(EAPAuthenticatingTo(A))\ V\ A(\triangle block(ControlledPort,\ S))$$

As mentioned before, serious security flaws arise as a result of the inconsistencies among the policy elements of different ADs. Detection of such inconsistencies is possible by using a verifiable formal language.

Figure 1 shows a system consisting of three ADs together with their security policies. In the security policy representation of Figure 1, we used the model

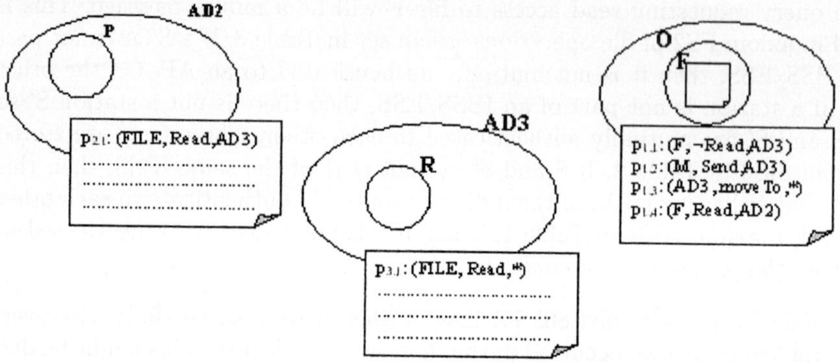

Fig. 1. A system consisting of three administrative domains

based on *Set and Function Formalism* proposed in [11] by Ryutov and Neuman. Thus, security policy of each AD consists of *Elementary Policy Statements.* As it is stated in [11], an *Elementary Policy Statement* consists of an object component, a positive or negative access component and zero or more conditions. In our representation an object component can be a *file* (F), a *message* (M), an AD, a *port*, etc. On the other hand, positive access right component can be *Read, Write, Execute,* (for a file F), *Connect* (for a port), *MoveTo* (for an AD), *Send* (for a message M), etc. Negative access right components indicate that an entity is not to allowed for an action related to an access right (i.e. *¬Read, ¬Write,¬Execute, ¬Connect, ¬MoveTo, ¬Send*). Finally, the condition is the AD in which the entity, that wants to access the object, resides for the case when access right is Read/Write/Execute (a file F) or target AD to which an entity wants to send a message or wants to move . The sign " * " is used denote any AD.

In Figure 1, security policy of AD1 contains elementary policy statement $p_{1,1}$ which restricts the components of AD3 to read file F. However, the same security policy contains the elementary policy statements $p_{1,2}$ and $p_{1,3}$ which allow every component of AD1 to send message to the components of AD3 and to move to AD3, respectively. Since a component of AD1 can attach file F to the message it sends to a component in AD3, there is an inconsistency between $p_{1,1}$ and $p_{1,2}$. Moreover, since $p_{1,3}$ allows every component of AD1 to move to AD3 and thus S which owns file F can move to AD3 and become a member of AD3, there is also inconsistency between $p_{1,1}$ and $p_{1,3}$. These are the examples of inconsistencies among the elementary policy statements of a security policy of a single AD and the basic operations that can be performed for the information contained in file F to be transmitted from one AD to another (i.e. *G2(DataIn(F,G1))*) are as follows:

- A component in an AD downloads file F owned by a component of another AD (i.e. *P(△ReadIn(F,S) Λ guardedby(G2)) Λ S(guardedby(G1))*) to perform one of the file operations which are read, write and execute, respectively

- A component in an AD sends a message M, with file F attached to it, to a component in another domain (i.e. *P(△in(M,S) Λ guardedby(G2)) Λ S(guardedby(G1) Λ attached(F,M))*).
- A component in an AD, which owns file F (i.e. *S(owns(F))*), moves to another AD (i.e. *G2(moving(S)*) and becomes the component of that AD.

All these above statements can be written as one specification in Mob_{adtl} as follows:

G2(△DataIn(F,G1)) BECAUSE (P(△ReadIn(F,S) Λ guardedby(G2)) Λ S(guardedby(G1))) V (P(△in(M,S) Λ guardedby(G2)) Λ S(guardedby(G1) Λ attached(F,M))) V (G2(moving(S) Λ S(owns(F)))

We use *ReadIn(F,S)* because we assume that if a component has the right to execute a file (i.e. *G1(allow(P, Execute, F))*) then it also has the right to write to it (i.e. *G1(allow(P, Write, F)))* and any component which has the right to write to a file has the right to read it (i.e. *G1(allow(P, Read, F)))*. In addition, for a component to read (or write or execute) a file owned by another component, it should be allowed to access the ftp port by the security policy of AD where file owner resides (i.e. *G1(guarding(S) Λ allow(P,Connect, ftpPort)))*. This is stated in axiom FS1 in Table 3. Similarly, if a component P receives the message M sent by another component S (i.e. *P(△in(M,S)))*, it is required that the security policy of AD of which S is a component, allows S to send message M to P (i.e. *G1(guarding(S) Λ allow(S, Send, (M,P))))*. Axiom CS1 in Table 3 states this fact. Finally for a component S to move from one AD to another (i.e. *G2(△moving(S))*), it is required that security policy of AD, to which S belongs, allows S to leave (i.e. *G1(guarding(S) Λ allow(S, MoveTo, G2)))* as explained in axiom MS5 in Table 3.

In Figure 1, there is also an example of an inconsistency among two elementary policy statements which belong to security policies of different ADs. One can see that in the system shown in Figure 1 components in AD2 are allowed to read file F due the existence of elementary policy statement $p_{1,4}$. Once P reads file F owned by O, it owns a copy of file F and since elementary policy statement $p_{2,1}$ of security policy of AD2 allows the components of AD3 to read any file owned by the components of AD2, $p_{1,1}$ is violated by allowing the flow of information contained in file F from AD1 to AD3. In order to prevent such violation, axiom DF1 in Table 3 is added to the set of axioms.

4 Conclusion

In this paper, we formed a formal policy specification language for an 802.11 WLAN with enhanced security network adding axioms and making refinements to Mob_{adtl}[1] axioms. In the long run, a verification system that will employ the policy specification language formed in this work can be constructed. The verification system can be used to design security policies, which are for ADs inside the boundaries of the same domain (i.e. domain of a university, hospital, firm, etc.), free of security flaws.

Acknowledgements

This work has been partially supported by Boğaziçi University Research Fund.

References

1. Semprini, S.:Specification and Verification of Mobile Systems, PhD Thesis, Department of Informatics, University of Pisa,(2004)
2. Montangero, C., Semini, L.: Distributed States Temporal Logic, http://arxiv.org/abs/cs.LO/0304046s, (2003)
3. Montangero, C., Semini, L.: Distributed States Logic, Proceedings of Nineth International Symposium on Temporal Representation and Reasoning (2002), Manchester
4. Semprini, S.: Mark: Mob_{adtl} Reasoning Kit, http://www.sra.itc.it/people/semprini
5. Ferrari, G., Montangero, C., Semini, L., Semprini, S.: Multiple Security Policies in Mob_{adtl}, Proc. Workshop on Issues in the Theory of Security (2000)
6. Cardelli, L.: Mobility and Security, Lecture Notes for Marktoberdorf Summer School, (1999)
7. Levi, F., Sangiorgi,D.: Controlling Interference in Ambients, Proceedings of POPL (2000), 352–364
8. Bugliesi, M., Castagna,G.: Secure Safe Ambients, Proceedings of the 28th ACM SIGPLAN-SIGACT Symposium on Principles of Programming Languages (2001), London
9. Bugliesi, M., Crafa, S., Castagna,G.:Boxed Ambients,Proceedings of Fourth International Symposium on Theoretical Aspects of Computer Software (2001), Sendai, Japan
10. Cuppens, F., Saurel, C.: Specifying a Security Policy: A Case Study, 9th IEEE Computer Security Foundations Workshop (1996), 123–134, Kenmare, Ireland
11. Ryutov, T., Neuman, C.: The Set and Function Approach to Modeling Authorization in Distributed Systems, Workshop on Mathematical Methods, Models and Architecture for Comp. Networks Security (2001), Russia
12. ANSI/IEEE 802.11 Standard, (1999)
13. IEEE P802.11i/D9.0 Standard, (2004)

A Generic Policy-Conflict Handling Model

Taner Dursun

Tübitak Uekae
tdursun@uekae.tubitak.gov.tr

Abstract. This paper presents a policy-conflict handling model, which is independent of both technical details of policy enforcement architecture and syntax of policy-specification language. The model primarily focuses on handling the application-specific (semantic) conflicts [1]. This model has been applied to the POLICE Policy-Based Network Management (PBNM) framework in [2-4]. The POLICE framework does not suffer from the modality conflicts [1] since it does not support negative policies whereas application-specific (semantic) conflicts are handled according to the model described in this paper. We are able to rely on a common schema in our model since almost all policy specification languages include subject, target and action concepts and the fact that all languages can be modeled in an approximately similar way allows our model to be designed independently of other details of the language.

1 Introduction

Policy-Based Network Management (PBNM) concept simplifies the management of systems by using business-level policies. A *policy* is defined as combination of one or more sets of rules that dictate actions according to conditions to help automate network, system, and service management. In other words, policies dictate the conditions that must be met before the specified actions can be taken. Research activities in PBNM community have generally focused on languages for specifying policies and architectures for managing and deploying these policies. However, achieving a complete consistency between the policies used within a PBNM framework is a difficult problem waiting to be solved. When the number of policies increase, the ability to handle conflicting policies becomes crucial. However, in the conflict detection and resolution field, a perfect solution or a standard meeting all the requirements has not appeared yet.

There has been considerable amount of research about handling modality conflicts [1], which can be detected automatically by analyzing the policies. However, proposals for handling semantic conflicts stayed limited due to the fact that researchers showed more interest in modality conflicts than in semantic conflicts, except a few groups [1], [5].

A formal model proposed in [5] aims detecting and solving modality conflicts along with some semantic conflicts by using policy constraints. A well-known study employs meta-policy concept [1] for semantic conflicts. However, both of these studies do not consider runtime conditions in conflict handling since they rely on static policy specifications. This paper introduces a unique solution to fulfill the requirements for handling semantic conflicts. The primary design goal of our model is

P. Yolum et al.(Eds.): ISCIS 2005, LNCS 3733, pp. 193 – 204, 2005.

to make conflict handling independent of the implementation details of both PBNM system and policy language syntax.

Remainder of this paper is organized as follows. Sections 2 and 3 introduce some background for the reader. The conflict detection and resolution issues within our model are discussed in Section 4. Section 5 includes evaluation of the related work and the last section presents our conclusions.

2 PBNM Background

In order to facilitate policy management activities it is necessary to use an easy-to-understand policy language and an integrated toolkit for the deployment and enforcement of the policies within the system. Recent works like Ponder [6], [7], [8] have introduced object-oriented languages to specify general-purpose management policies. Almost all objects in these languages represent elements of managed systems and the methods of these objects function as management interfaces of these elements. The elements in a managed system may be substituted for subjects and targets. According to the well-known definition, the term *Subjects* refers to users or automated manager components, which have management responsibility, and the term *Targets* refers to objects affected by the activities of subjects. Method invocations on targets allow subjects to access targets. Policies can be defined as the set of rules managing these invocations by means of *Actions* that specify what must be performed or what is permitted according to conditions of the system.

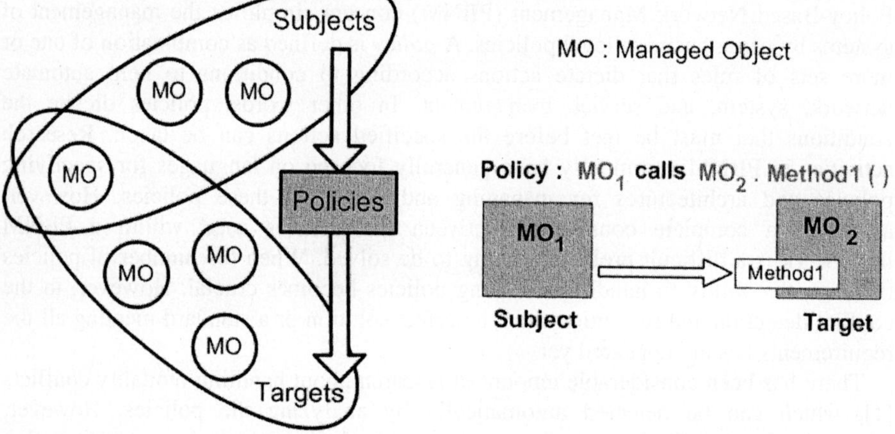

Fig. 1. Visualization of policy concept

Our conflict handling model assumes that all policies relate to objects which have interfaces defined in terms of methods as shown in Fig. 1.

Policies are basically classified into two main categories in the literature: Authorizations provide subjects with legitimate power to perform actions, Obligations give subjects the imperative to carry out actions.

In a generic PBNM system, three types of elements, Policy Decision Point (PDP), Repository and Policy Enforcement Point (PEP), are involved in the execution process. PDP acts as policy manager, which stores policy in a policy repository and distributes them to PEPs. Once policies are received from PDP, PEPs analyze them and extend their behavior. In the PEP architecture, all access requests originated from subjects to targets are intercepted and checked whether they are granted required permissions according to authorization policies. In the case of obligation policies, if their constraints are fulfilled, the subjects are ordered to perform access operations.

Policy repository is a specific data store that holds policy rules, their conditions and actions, and related policy data. In our model, the policy related data includes the information model of the managed system, so-called *System's Information Model (SIM)*. SIM models managed objects as the instances of *Model Classes.* A model class includes methods which serve as a model of the management interface of the corresponding real managed object. In addition to managed objects, the application specific (semantic) relationships (R_i) between managed objects are also modeled in SIM. Incidentally, our conflict handling model relies on these relationships. Fig. 2 shows an example of SIM.

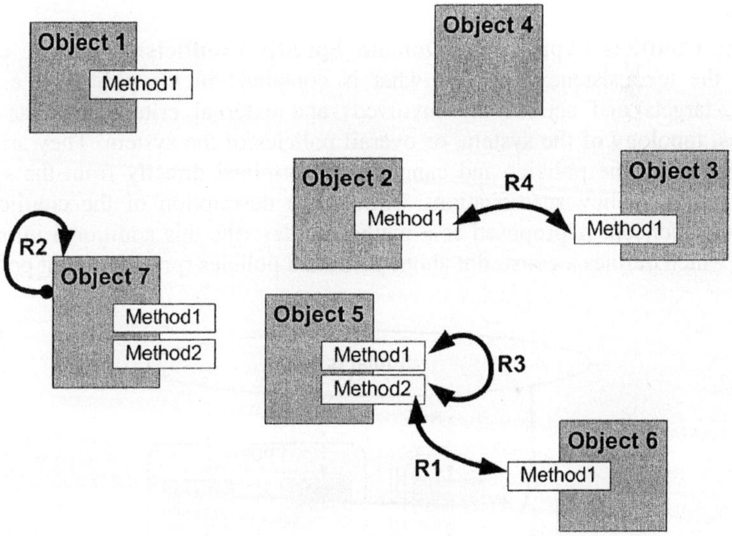

Fig. 2. Sample scenario including semantic relationships between managed objects

The content of SIM is kept up-to-date with a node discovery mechanism running on PEPs, and with administrator intervention for the nodes that are not supporting auto discovery. The vendor/deployer of a system prepares a node profile including objects for the managed elements and special relationships between them. When this node joins PBM system SIM is extended with the addition of the node profile. Thus, the managed system itself provides semantic relationships and the program pieces to be run to ensure that policies are enforced considering these relationships. Some relationships and the profiles of nodes that are not supporting node discovery are entered into the system manually.

3 Policy Conflicts

A conflict may occur if one policy prevents the activities of another policy from being performed or if the policies interfere in some way that may cause the managed objects to be put into unwanted states [9]. A policy conflict occurs when the conditions of two or more policy rules that apply to the same set of managed objects are simultaneously satisfied, but the actions of two or more of these policy rules conflict with each other. Basically, the conflicts are classified into two groups: Modality and Semantic conflicts. (A detailed conflict classification can be found in [9])

Conflict of Modalities: Modality conflicts [9] are inconsistencies in the policy specifications, which may arise from existence of both a positive and a negative authorization or obligation policies that apply to the same set of managed objects. Conflicts of modalities are independent of the exact identities of the managed objects and objectives of the policies. Without any knowledge about the managed system or activities, syntactic analysis of the policies can detect conflicts of modalities prior to deployment of the policies. Existing studies in detecting conflicts mostly focuses on modality conflicts.

Semantic Conflicts (Application-Domain Specific Conflicts): Semantic conflicts refer to the inconsistency between what is contained in the policies (i.e., which subjects, targets and actions are involved) and external criteria such as limited resources, topology of the system, or overall policies of the system. They arise from the semantics of the policies and cannot be determined directly from the syntactic analysis of the policy specifications without the description of the conflicts. The *Meta-policy* concept is proposed as a method to describe this additional information in [1,9], which defines a constraint about permitted policies (policies about policies).

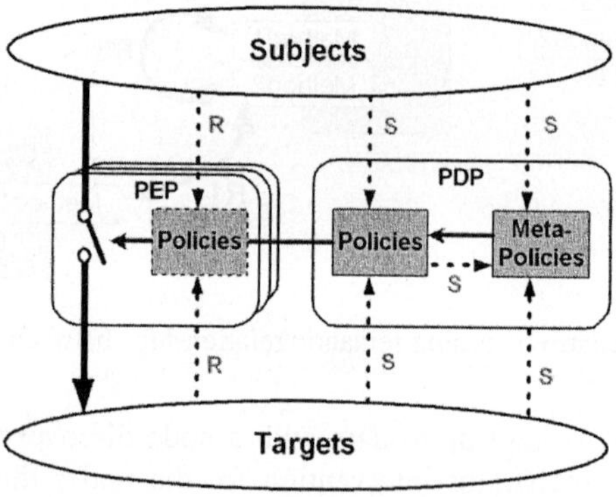

Fig. 3. Meta-policy based conflict handling

Fig.3 illustrates meta-policy based conflict handling. As shown in the figure, meta-policies are located and evaluated at PDP. The meta-policy evaluation process uses only *static data* including policy definitions and identities of subjects/targets of policies. According to the result of this evaluation, some of the ordinary policies are eliminated due to possible semantic conflicts. Remaining policies (subset) are deployed to PEPs, evaluated and enforced there to manage the interactions between subjects and targets. The dashed lines represent inputs of related blocks, and the dark lines show the control flows. The letter R means runtime data which is related to the status of managed objects and available only at policy enforcement time, whereas the S represents static data which is related to the policy definitions and available at any time (before and after policy deployment).

4 Proposed Conflict Handling Model

The relationships between subjects or targets show implicitly the relationships of policies applied to them. In [9-12], it is claimed that a conflict may occur between two or more policies if there is an overlap between the subjects or the targets. Thus, they assert that if there are no common subjects and targets between two policies (disjoint policies), there is no possibility of conflict. However, these assumptions are true for only modality conflicts, and they may be false for semantic conflicts since there may be system-specific associations between the subjects or the targets of the policies even these policies are disjoint (implicit conflicts). In such cases, the enforcement of these policies may result in semantic conflicts. As specified in the previous section, semantic conflict detection process needs to have additional knowledge of the managed system.

Although the meta-policies are created to handle semantic conflicts, they cannot always fulfill the requirements to solve the problem. Therefore, the administrator must specify meta-policies for all possible, runtime situations, which may result in conflicts. It is almost impossible for the administrators to take into account all implicit relationships that may cause conflicts in the managed system. Moreover, in many cases, the fact that there are policies related explicitly or implicitly to each other does not mean a conflict will certainly occur at runtime because the runtime conditions required for conflicts may not be fulfilled exactly. Meta-policies are based on static data instead of runtime data. Thus, the conflicts detected via meta-policies prior to policy enforcement, may not appear at runtime.

The current design of our model does not address modality conflicts. In case of semantic conflicts, however, as an alternative to meta-policy based approach, we have developed a policy conflict handling mechanism based on the relationships between the objects of the system being managed. In order to make our model run, all associations between managed objects (subjects/targets) must be modeled in the Repository (SIM) prior to policy enforcement. By evaluating these associations, *direct or indirect relationships* between the policies to be enforced on these managed objects can also be determined. Our model wraps these evaluation processes in special scripts, so called as *Evaluation Code* (E-Code). There are two possible ways to add E-Codes into conflict investigation process. These scripts can be obtained from the managed system itself during node discovery process performed by PEPs. In this case, the E-codes which have been placed into the managed device or system by vendor or administrator are passed on to related PEP in addition to the information model of the managed system or device. In the other case, administrators can write E-Codes via management console of PDP. The PEPs investigate the likelihood of conflicts at runtime by executing E-Codes. In order to do this, the PEPs must first look for any relationship involving the subjects or targets of the policies for which these PEPs are responsible. If there is a relationship, PEP has to get the E-Code related to this relationship from the repository and run. E-Codes may include any command that can run on the system to determine the real conflict. If needed, the PEPs can communicate with other PEPs or PDPs. PEPs enforce their subjects according to the results of the executions of E-Codes. E-Codes make it possible to figure out the runtime picture of the conflicts accurately.

As shown in Fig. 4, E-Codes running on PEPs use both static and runtime data to perform conflict analysis. The meanings of the lines and letters in Fig. 4 are the same as those in Fig. 3. E-Codes do not only use static data such as policy definitions (represented with letter S) but also run time data (represented with letter R) related to the managed system such as attributes of managed objects (subjects, targets), subjects and targets of policies, system time, and so on.

Unlike Ponder, performing central and static conflict analysis on policies at PDP, postponing the decision on whether there is any conflict (conflict decisions) until the enforcement time makes our model more consistent and accurate on determining the real conflicts. In addition, using E-Code concept instead of meta-policies provides more flexibility because our model does not involve any restrictions for policy specification language. In contrast to meta-policies, the syntax of the E-Codes is independent of policy specification language and an E-Code can include more complex statements of any interpreted computer language such as Java, TCL. We prefer BeanShell [13] which is a script language based on Java. In contrast to the flexiblity provided with E-Codes, meta-policies can contain only limited number of pre-defined statements, in order to stay analyzable by an automated software. E-codes need not to be analyzed due to the fact that they are independent of the policy language.

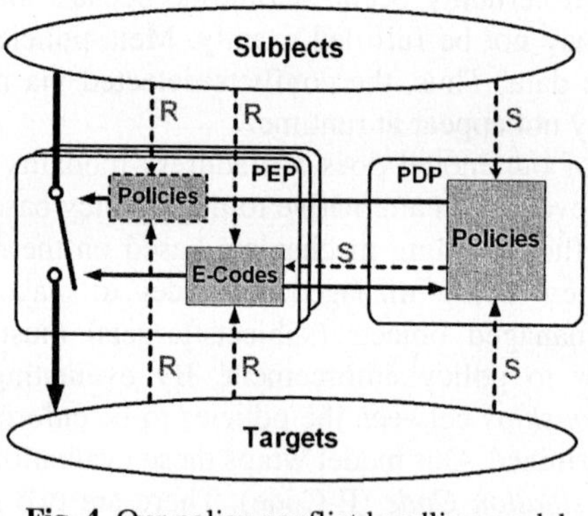

Fig. 4. Our policy conflict handling model

Our model has been first applied to POLICE policy based management framework which has been developed in TÜBİTAK [2]. In order to provide a standard format in E-Codes' statements, we have also developed an E-Code Application Programming Interface (API) including the interfaces in order to access to PEP, PDP, Repository and other modules of PBNM framework. In order to Provide an abstraction layer between E-Codes and PBNM systems, this API includes various abstract classes such as PEP, PDP, ManagedObject, Method, Relationship, Policy, PolicyList, Filter, and so on. Any PBNM framework conforming to this API can run the E-Codes prepared for conflict handling. The main points highlighting advantages of our model over meta-policy model are listed below:

- The administrators specifying policies do not have to worry about possible conflicts (faster and easier specification). The policy conflict analysis logic is embedded into the managed system itself and performed by PEPs.
- Our policy conflict tests are executed independently of any change in the policy data stored in the Repository, but the evaluation of meta-policies is repeated in each modification (adding, deleting policies or managed objects) of the policy data stored in a central Repository.
- Our conflict tests (E-Codes) are executed if there is an application-specific relationship related to the subjects or the targets of the policies being enforced. Only The e-code related to this relationship is run.
- Our conflict test covers only a small subset of the entire policy set stored in the Repository whereas meta-policies are evaluated at PDP and on entire policy set.
- If the policies are edited (add | remove | update) frequently, meta-policy model, which has a central conflict analysis repeated after each edit operation, becomes unscalable, whereas our model remains scalable because policy edits may affect only the policy list which will be involved in the next run of any E-Code. However, if the policy set is not changed frequently, the conflict test overhead of the meta-policy based model is zero. Nonetheless, Meta-policies always require specifications and these specifications are difficult to define.
- In our conflict tests performed during enforcement operations, better suited data to detect actual conflicts (data at enforcement time) is used.
- The meta-policies can include logic for only conflict detection, whereas E-Codes can also include conflict resolution logic.

The sample problem explained below indicates how both meta-policy based model and our model handle semantic conflicts:

Conflict of duty which is a well-known application specific conflict type in literature can be expressed as "*There should be no policy pair authorizing a subject to perform two separate operations that must be performed by different subjects*" [1].

Meta-policies are used to define application specific constraints in Ponder model to limit the permitted policies in the system, or prohibit the simultaneous execution of conflicting policies. The Ponder meta-policy for detecting the conflicts similar to the one mentioned above is shown below:

```
inst meta budgetDutyConflict raises conflictInBudget(z) {
 [z] = self.policies → select (pa, pb |
 pa.subject → intersection  (pb.subject)→notEmpty and
 pa.action → exists (act | act.name = "submit") and
 pb.action → exists (act | act.name = "approve") and
 pb.target → intersection (pa.target)→oclIsKindOf (budget))
 z → notEmpty ;
}
```

This meta-policy prevents a conflict of duty in which the same person both approves and submits a budget. It searches for policies with the same subject acting on a target *budget* in which there are actions *submit* and *approve*. If it is found, `conflictInBudget event` is raised which may trigger an obligation policy.

Unlike the usage of meta-policies in Ponder model, we embed the conflict detection logic into PEPs. Instead of catching conflicts by defining and analyzing meta-polices at PDP, we prefer a flexible and distributed mechanism in which policy analysis is performed by PEPs. In case of "*separation of duty*" type conflicts, the E-Code which will be executed by the PEPs is as follow:

```
boolean EC_DutySeperation ( Method submit, Method approve) {
    p1 = PDP.getAllPolicies();

    f1 = new Filter(ACTION, EQUAL, submit);
    f2 = new Filter(ACTION, EQUAL, approve);
    p2 = p1.search(f1); // find policies whose action is submit
    p3 = p1.search(f2); // find policies whose action is approve

    conflictedList= new PolicyPairList();
    //find policies from p2 and p3 not having same subject
    for (policy:p2.iterator()){
     PolicyList tmp = p3.search(new
            Filter(SUBJECT, NOT_EQUAL, policy.getSubject() ));
      //match policy with tmp policies
     conflictedList.addPair(policy,tmp);
   }// for
    return (conflictedList.size()==0);
 }
```

4.1 Handling of Well-Known Semantic Conflicts

A detailed scenario including five policies is given in Fig. 5 to explain how our model is capable of handling semantic conflicts specified in [1].

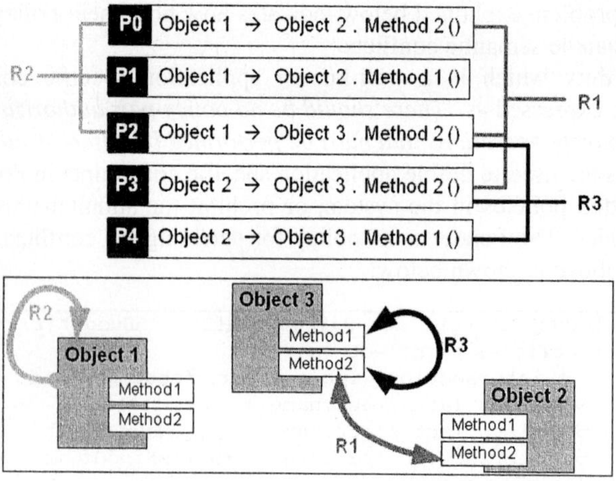

Fig. 5. Sample scenario

- **Conflict (separation) of duties:** This type of conflict occurs, if some tasks must be performed by different subjects but assigned to the same one. Let $Object_2.Method_2$ be check-signing operation and $Object_3.Method_2$ be the authorizing payment of check. In order to avoid a conflict, the system must guarantee that only different subjects can call these two methods. Therefore, a relationship specifying this exclusion is represented by $\mathbf{R_1}$ in Fig. 5. Then, the policy sets $\{\mathbf{P_0}, \mathbf{P_3}\}$ or $\{\mathbf{P_2}, \mathbf{P_3}\}$ ordering different subjects to carry out these two methods may cause a conflict. The E-Code for this conflict is already presented in the previous section.
- **Multiple Managers:** Accessing a common target, multiple subjects may cause a conflict when the management operations to be performed on this target object are not independent. Let $Object_3.Method_1$ and $Object_3.Method_2$ be dependent on each other (for example, both may modify the common variable). Then, different subjects accessing these two methods may affect the operation of each other. This case is represented with $\mathbf{R_3}$. So, the policies set $\{\mathbf{P_2}, \mathbf{P_4}\}$ and $\{\mathbf{P_3}, \mathbf{P_4}\}$ must be enforced carefully.

```
boolean EC_MultipleMng ( Method method1, Method method2) {

 p1 = PDP.getAllPolicies();
 f1 =new Filter(ACTION, EQUAL, method1);
 f2 =new Filter(ACTION, EQUAL, method2);

 p2 = p1.search(f1); //find policies whose actions is method1
 p3 = p1.search(f2); //find policies whose actions is method2

 conflictedList = new PolicyPairList();
 for (policy:p2.iterator()){
  PolicyList tmp = p3.search( new  Filter(SUBJECT,
                                         NOT_EQUAL,
                                         policy.getSubject()));
  conflictedList.addPair(policy, tmp);
 }
 return (conflictedList.size()==0);
}
```

- **Conflict of Resources/Priorities:** This type of conflict occurs when the amount of resources (target objects) available is limited. Object accesses are performed in the control of the Resource Controllers at PEP's. The Resource Controllers can already eliminate this kind of conflicts. Thus, the limit on the critical resources must be determined by an E-Code similar to the one shown below so that Resource Controller can keep the usage of the critical resources under control. In order to achieve this, the resources are marked by associating them with relationships and each relationship are associated with an instance of the E-Code shown below.

```
boolean EC_ResourceLimit ( ManagedObject mo1, int amount) {
    return PEP.setAccessLimit(mo1,amount); //resolution of conflict!
}
```

- **Conflict of interests:** This describes a situation where a single subject has tasks relating to two different targets, and carrying out both tasks together conscientiously may be impossible. Let be a requirement that $Object_1$ can manipulate only either of the $\{Object_2, Object_3\}$. In this case, $\mathbf{R_2}$ is described to specify that $Object_1$ can call only the methods of either $Object_2$ or $Object_3$. So, the policy sets $\{\mathbf{P_0}, \mathbf{P_2}\}$ or $\{\mathbf{P_1}, \mathbf{P_2}\}$ ordering $Object_1$ to access different targets may cause a conflict and they must be enforced carefully.

```
boolean EC_Interest ( ManagedObject mo){
  //find policy pairs whose subjects is mo but targets are
  //different

  p1 = PDP.getAllPolicies();
  f1 = new Filter(SUBJECT, EQUAL, mo);
  p2 = p1.search(f1); //find policies whose subject is mo

  conflictedList= new PolicyPairList();
  //find policy pairs whose targets are different
  for (policy:p2.iterator()){
   tmp=p2.search(new Filter(TARGET,NOT_EQUAL, policy.getTarget()));

   //match policy with tmp policies
   conflictedList.addPair(policy, tmp);
  }
  return (conflictedList.size()==0);
}
```

5 Related Work

Although majority of working groups from PBNM community have realized policy conflicts can occur, neither have they distinguished between modality and semantic conflicts nor do any of them say how conflicts will be detected. However, some groups tried conflict handling by means of various methods.

The Ponder framework includes a conflict analysis tool performing static analysis of policies [1], [11]. The tool also allows various forms of precedence to be specified to resolve policy conflicts. By using this tool, static analysis is repeated for each new policy to see if it conflicts with existing ones. Such an operation results in long delays when the amount of policies grows. For semantic conflicts, Ponder model benefits from meta-policy concept.

The technology independent model proposed in [5] aims detecting and solving modality conflicts and some semantic conflicts by means of policy constraints. However, it is not flexible because it is only based on policy constraints for the semantic conflicts.

On the other hand, there has been considerable effort in logic-based approaches to specify policies, as described in [12], [15], [16], [17]. The policies are in a logical representation, existing formal calculus methods, and running tools in this area provide a means to check the consistency of policies [12], [18]. However, they do not easily map onto implementation mechanisms.

Representing policies by using IETF format [19] may allow using logic based tools, an expert system or theorem-proving approach. However, using formal methods in the analysis of policies may result in unreasonable completion time in the multi-purpose and complex systems. Moreover, static analysis of policies during specification phase may not be right approach to detect all conflicts since some kinds of conflicts may or may not arise at runtime depending on the conditions.

Another study [20] examines the conflicts that may occur in multi-agent systems. In a multi-agent system, agents share and carry out tasks collaboratively. Because of the possible dependencies between the tasks, the task distribution should be done appropriately. While the agents perform their tasks, possible conflicts can be solved by defining policies for the agents. Conflict resolution typically entails a conversation in which agents negotiate over the interaction, generally making an agreement to either avoid the interaction through a change in the planned activities or by temporally sequencing their activities. We conclude that the model used to solve the conflicted tasks in [20] can also be employed in PBNM systems to detect and solve the conflicted policies. Moreover, our SIM concept may provide an infrastructure for the multi-agent systems because they define associations between the tasks as we do while establishing our relationships between managed objects.

6 Conclusions and Future Work

There are two main approaches about policy specification and implementation issue; implementing policies as a piece of code and interpreting them as objects [21]. *Policy as code* is more flexible using a standard programming language. However, Verma stated that in case of policy as code, it is quite difficult to determine if the policies are mutually consistent [12]. Policies specified in *policy as object fashion* are easier to analyze than policies specified as computer programs [11].

Although some authors [1], [12] suggest keeping the policy specifications simple, the majority of the working groups think that such systems, not supporting policies defined as computer programs, have several limitations and it will be inevitable to take into account more complex policies, even though their analysis is so hard.

In the conflict detection and resolution field, an excellent solution or a standard meeting all the requirements of both *policy as code* and *policy as object* fashions has not appeared yet. Our proposition, however, is able to overcome this shortage since it provides a conflict detection mechanism which is independent of the complexity of the policies. Thereby, it offers a novel conflict detection model fulfilling most of the requirements for comprehensive policy-based management. However, our model can be extended further, especially in the following areas:

- Using intelligent and/or mobile [22] enforcement agents to handle conflicts,
- Improving E-Code API especially in the issue of PEP inter-communication,
- Testing how the proposed model meets the requirements of various management domains and works in practical applications,
- Further exploration of the relationships between policies, in relation to conflicts between them,
- Running/Integrating our model within a framework such as Ponder which has already a modality conflict handling mechanism,
- Then, adding support for modality conflicts,
- Scalability analysis of E-Codes.

References

1. Lupu, E., Sloman, M.: Conflicts in Policy-based Distributed Systems Management. IEEE Trans. On Software Engineering, Vol 25. No 6 (1999) 852-869
2. Dursun, T., Örencik, B.: POLICE: A Novel Policy Framework. Lecture Notes in Computer Science, LNCS 2869 (2003) 819-827.

3. Dursun, T., Örencik, B.: POLICE Distributed Conflict Detection Architecture. Proceedings of the IEEE International Conference on Communications (ICC04), Paris, June 20-26, 2004
4. Dursun, T., Nasır, D., Örencik, B. : Relation Based Policy Conflict Detection. Proceedings of the 3rd Asia Pacific Int'l. Symp. on Information Technology (3rd APIS), İTÜ, İstanbul, Jan. 13-14, 2004, 192-198.
5. Baliosian, J., Serrat, J.: Finite State Transducers for Policy Evaluation and Conflict Resolution. Policy Workshop 2004
6. Damianou N., Dulay, N., Lupu, E., Sloman, M.: Ponder: The Language Specification – V2.2. Research Report DoC 2000/1, Imperial College of Sci. Tech. and Medicine, London, (2000)
7. Dulay, N., Lupu, E., Sloman, M., Damianou, N.: A Policy Deployment Model for the Ponder Language. IEEE/IFIP Int..Symp. on Integrated Network Management (2001)
8. Sloman, M., Lupu, E.: Security and Management Policy Specification. IEEE Network Policy based management special issue (2002) 10-19
9. Moffett, J.D: Policy Hierarchies for Distributed Systems Management. IEEE JSAC Special Issue on Network Management, Vol 11, No. 9, (1993)
10. Sloman, M.: Policy Driven Management for Distributed Systems. Journal of Network and Systems Management, Plenum Publising Co. Vol 2, No.4 (1994)
11. Moffett J.D., Sloman M.S: Policy Conflict Analysis. Jrnl. of Org. Computing (1993)
12. Verma, D.C., Calo, S., Amiri, K.: Policy-Based Management of Content Distribution Networks. IEEE Network Policy based management special issue (2002) 34-39
13. BeanShell, http://www.beanshell.org
14. Chalvy, L., Cuppens,F.: Analyzing, Consistency of Security Policies. IEEE Symp. Security and Privacy (1997)
15. Ortalo, R.: A Flexible Method for Information System Security Policy Specification. 5th European Symposium on Research in Computer Security (ESORICS 98), Springer-Verlag, Louvain-la-Neuve, Belgium, (1998)
16. Barker, S.: Security Policy Specification in Logic. International Conference on Artificial Intelligence, Las Vegas, USA (2000)
17. Ahn, G.-J., Sandhu, R.: The RSL99 Language for Role-based Separation of Duty Constraints. Fourth ACM,Workshop on Role-Based Access Control, Fairfax, Virginia, ACM Press (1999)
18. Michael, J.B.: A Formal Process for Testing the Consistency of Composed Security Policies. Dept. of Info. and Software Sys. Eng., George Mason Univ., Fairfax, VA (1993)
19. Yavatkar, R., Pendarakis, D., Guerin, R.: A Framework for Policy-based Admission Control. RFC 2753, Intel, IBM, U. of Pensylvania (2000)
20. Wagner, T., Shapiro, J., et al: Multi-Level Conflict in Multi-Agent Systems. Proc. of AAAI Workshop on Negotiation in Multi-Agent Systems (1999)
21. Martinez, P. et al.: Using the Script MIB for Policy-based Configuration Management. IEEE NOMS (2002) 203-219
22. Pham, V.A., Karmouch, A.: Mobile Software Agents: An overview. IEEE Communication Magazine, July (1998) 26-37

A Truly Random Number Generator Based on a Continuous-Time Chaotic Oscillator for Applications in Cryptography

Salih Ergün[1] and Serdar Özoğuz[2]

[1] TÜBİTAK-National Research Institute of Electronics and Cryptology, PO Box 74, 41470, Gebze, Kocaeli, Turkey
salih@uekae.tubitak.gov.tr

[2] İstanbul Technical University, Faculty of Electrical-Electronics Eng., 34390, İstanbul, Turkey
serdar@ehb.itu.edu.tr

Abstract. A non-autonomous chaotic circuit which is suitable for high-frequency IC realization is presented. Simulation and experimental results verifying the feasibility of the circuit are given. We have numerically verified that the bit streams obtained from the stroboscopic Poincaré map of the system passed the four basic tests of FIPS-140-1 test suite. We also have verified that the binary data obtained from the hardware realization of this continuous-time chaotic oscillator in the same way pass the full NIST random number test suite. Then, in order to increase the output throughput and the statistical quality of the generated bit sequences, we propose a TRNG design which uses a dual oscillator architecture with the proposed continuous-time chaotic oscillator. Finally we have experimentally verified that the binary data obtained by this oscillator sampling technique pass the tests of full NIST random number test suite for a higher throughput speed. While the throughput data rate obtained by using continuous-time chaotic oscillator alone is effectively 488 bps, it achieves 830 Kbps for the proposed TRNG design, which uses the dual oscillator architecture.

1 Introduction

Nowadays, because of the increasing demand of electronic official or financial transactions and digital signature applications, the need for information secrecy has raised. In this manner, random number generators (RNGs) which have been used for only military cryptographic applications in the past got expanding usage for a typical digital communication equipment.

Almost all cryptographic systems require unpredictable values, therefore RNG is a fundamental component for cryptographic mechanisms. Generation of public/private key-pairs for asymmetric algorithms and keys for symmetric and hybrid crypto systems require random numbers. The one-time pad, challenges, nonces, padding bytes and blinding values are created by using truly random

P. Yolum et al.(Eds.): ISCIS 2005, LNCS 3733, pp. 205–214, 2005.

number generators (TRNGs) [1]. Pseudo-random number generators (PRNGs) generate bits in a deterministic manner. In order to appear to be generated by a TRNG, the pseudo-random sequences must be seeded from a shorter truly random sequence [2]. Random numbers are also used during the authentication procedure between two crypto equipments and initial value randomization of a crypto module that realizes an algorithm.

Even if RNG design is known, any useful prediction about the output can not be made. To fulfill the requirements for secrecy of one-time pad, key generation and any other cryptographic applications, the TRNG must satisfy the following properties: The output bit stream of the TRNG must pass all the statistical tests of randomness; the next random bit must be unpredictable; the same output bit stream of the TRNG must not be able to reproduced [3]. The best way to generate truly random numbers is to exploit the natural randomness of the real world by finding a random event that happens regularly [3]. Examples of such usable event include elapsed time during radioactive decay, thermal and shot noise, oscillator jitter and the amount of charge of a semiconductor capacitor [2].

There are few IC RNG designs reported in the literature; however fundamentally four different techniques were mentioned for generating random numbers: amplification of a noise source [4,5] jittered oscillator sampling [1,6,7], discrete-time chaotic maps [8,9,10] and continuous-time chaotic oscillators [11]. In spite of fact that, the use of discrete-time chaotic maps in the realization of RNG is well-known for some time, it was only recently shown that continuous-time chaotic oscillators can be used to realize TRNGs also. Following up in this direction, we investigated the usefulness of the proposed chaotic oscillator as the core of a RNG.

Although many chaotic oscillators exist in the literature, only a few of them are designed concerning high-performance integrated circuit (IC) design issues, such as low power consumption, high-frequency operation, operation capability at low voltage levels [12]. In this work, we present a simple non-autonomous chaotic oscillator, which is suitable for high-performance IC realization.

Initially, we have obtained random data from the stroboscopic Poincaré map of the proposed chaotic system and numerically verified that the bit streams generated from the random number generator built around the proposed circuit pass the four basic random number tests of FIPS-140-1 test suite [13]. Moreover, we have also experimentally verified that the binary data obtained from the chaotic circuit pass the tests of NIST full random number test suite [14].

External interference is a major concern in RNG design since interfered and random signals have comparable levels. To solve this problem in [15], a TRNG which mixes three of the four mentioned RNG techniques except for the continuous-time chaos method is proposed. After using the continuous-time chaotic oscillator alone, we propose a TRNG design which uses a dual oscillator architecture with the proposed continuous-time chaotic oscillator in order to increase the output throughput and the statistical quality of the generated bit sequences. In this design the chaotic oscillator output signal is used to modulate the frequency of a slower clock. Then, with the rising edge of the chaos-modulated slower clock, fast clock is sampled. Finally we have experimentally verified that the binary data obtained by this oscillator sampling technique pass the tests of full NIST random number test suite for a higher throughput speed than the one obtained by using continuous-time chaotic oscillator alone.

2 Proposed Oscillator

The proposed chaotic oscillator is shown in Fig.1. Assuming that the parasitic capacitances appearing between the collectors of the bipolar transistors and the ground are denoted by C_p, routine analysis of the circuit yields the following state equations:

$$\begin{aligned} C\dot{v}_1 &= -i_3 \\ L\dot{i}_3 &= (v_1 - v_2) \\ C_p\dot{v}_2 &= i_3 - (\tfrac{1}{R} + \tfrac{1}{R_p})v_2 + \tfrac{2}{R_p}V_p sgn(sin\Omega t) + I_0 tanh(v_1/2V_T) \end{aligned} \tag{1}$$

where $i_3 = i_R - i_L$ and $v_p(t)$ is the external periodical pulse train defined as $v_p(t) = sgn(sin\Omega t)$ and V_T is the thermal voltage ($V_T = kT/q$), which is equal to $25.8mV$ at room temperature.

The chaotic oscillator offers some considerable advantages over the existing ones. The circuit employs a differential pair to realize the required nonlinearity, which is the most widely used basic analog building block due to its high IC performance. The resistors employed in the circuit have very small values, so they can be effectively realized on IC. Moreover, the proposed chaotic oscillator is balanced; hence it offers better power supply rejection and noise immunity. Finally, the external source used to drive the circuit is a periodical pulse train, which can be very accurately and easily realized using the clock signal already available on chip.

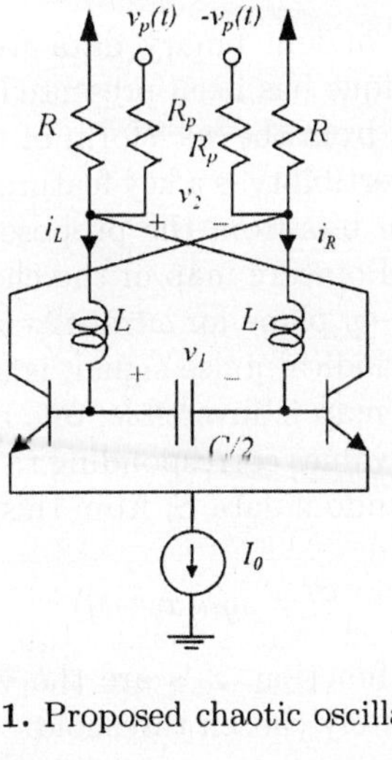

Fig. 1. Proposed chaotic oscillator

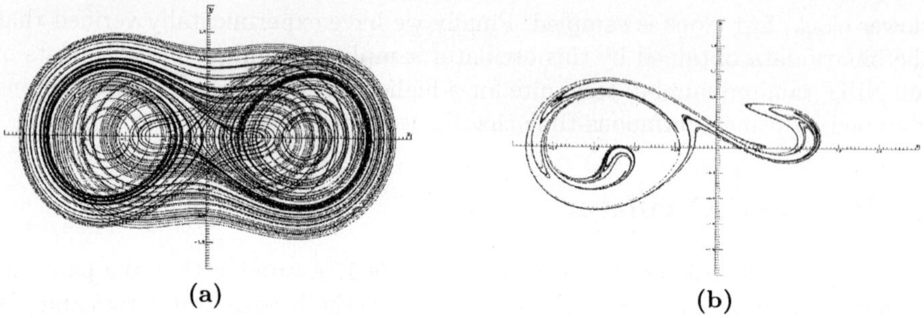

Fig. 2. a) Results of the numerical analysis of the system in (2). b) Poincaré map of the system.

Using the normalized quantities: $R_0 \equiv \sqrt{L/C}$, $x = v_1/V_s$, $y = i_3 R_0/V_s$, $z = v_2/V_s$, $c_0 = I_0 R_0/V_s$, $\alpha = R_0/R_p$, $\beta = R_0/R$, $\omega \equiv \Omega\sqrt{LC}$ and taking $V_p = 0.5V_s = V_T$ and $t_n = t/RC$, where V_S is an arbitrary scaling voltage, the equations of the system in Eqn. 1 transforms into:

$$\begin{aligned} \dot{x} &= -y \\ \dot{y} &= x - z \\ \epsilon\dot{z} &= y - (\alpha + \beta)z + \alpha sgn(sin\omega t) + c_0 tanh(x) \end{aligned} \tag{2}$$

The equations above generate chaos for different set of parameters. For example, the chaotic attractor shown in Fig.2a is obtained from the numerical analysis of the system with $c_0 = 25$, $\alpha = 4$, $\beta = 12$, $\omega = 0.27$, $\epsilon = 0.3$ using a 4th-order Runge-Kutta algorithm with adaptive step size.

3 Random Bit Generation

In [11], in order to obtain random binary data from an autonomous chaotic system, an interesting technique has been presented, which relies on generating a non-invertible binary data from the waveform of the given chaotic system. It should be noted that non-invertibility is a key feature for generating PRNGs [16].

To obtain binary random bits from the proposed chaotic attractor, we initially used the stroboscopic Poincaré map of the chaotic system of Equation 2. A Poincaré section in the $x - y$ plane for $\omega t mod 2\pi = 0$, i.e. obtained at the rising edges of the external periodical pulse signal, is shown in Fig. 2b. Note that although this 2-dimensional map is invertible, one may obtain a non-invertible map by considering only the values corresponding to one of the states, say x. We have generated the binary random data S_i from this Poincaré section according to the Equation 3:

$$S_i = sgn(x_i - q) \tag{3}$$

where $sgn(.)$ is the signum function, x_i's are the values of x at the Poincaré section and q is an appropriately chosen threshold.

However, the binary sequence thus obtained is biased. In order to remove the unknown bias in this sequence, the well-known Von Neumann's de-skewing technique [17] is employed. This technique consists of converting the bit pair 01 into the output 0, 10 into the output 1 and of discarding bit pairs 00 and 11.

Using the above procedure, a bit sequence of length 20.000 have been obtained and subjected to the four tests (monobit, poker, runs and long-run) in the FIPS-140-1 test suite. We have verified that the bit sequence passed these tests for $q = 0.28$.

After using stroboscopic Poincaré map of the chaotic system to obtain random bits, we propose a TRNG design which uses a dual oscillator architecture with the proposed chaotic oscillator. In this design, the output of a fast oscillator is sampled on the rising edge of the chaos-modulated slower clock using a D flip-flop. A voltage-controlled oscillator (VCO) is used to modulate the frequency of the slower clock with the chaotic oscillator output signal. Drift between the two oscillators provides random bit generation to be more robust. Because of the nonlinear aliasing phenomenon associated with sampling, the dual oscillator architecture achieves increased output throughput and higher statistical quality [15].

In [18], it has been reported that in order to obtain an uncorrelated random bit stream, the modulated slower oscillator period should feature a standard deviation much greater than the fast oscillator period.

4 Circuit Simulations and Experimental Verification

In order to show the high-frequency operation capability of the proposed chaotic oscillator, the circuit in Fig. 1 has been simulated using SPICE with the model parameters of AMS SiGe 0.35μ BiCMOS process. The circuit was biased with $\pm 1.5V$ power supply. The passive component values were: $L = 1\mu H$, $C = 1pF$, $R = 250\Omega$, $R_p = 120\Omega$ and the biasing current was $I_0 = 1.8mA$. The amplitude and frequency of the external square signal were $27mV$ and $43.7MHz$, respectively. The observed phase-space corresponding to i_3 versus v_1 is shown in Fig. 3a.

Due to the lack of access to a suitable fabrication facility, we have chosen to construct the proposed chaotic oscillator circuit using discrete components in order to show the feasibility of the circuit. The passive component values were: $L = 10mH$, $C = 10nF$, $R = 180\Omega$, $R_p = 120\Omega$ and $I_0 = 1.2mA$. In Fig. 1, the bipolar transistors and the current source denoted by I_0, which was realized using a simple current mirror, were implemented with CA3046 and CA3096 NPN and PNP transistor arrays. The circuit was biased with a single $5V$ power supply. The external signal $v_p(t)$ was generated by a square-wave generator, which generates a signal with an amplitude of $26mV$. We have experimentally verified that the proposed circuit had chaotic motions for the following frequency values of $v_p(t)$ (5.86 KHz, 6.23 KHz, 7.12 KHz, 13.03 KHz, 14.48 KHz, 14.91 KHz, 17.07 KHz, 17.23 KHz, 18.08 KHz) and the frequency of $v_p(t)$ was adjusted to 5.86 KHz. The observed attractor is shown in Fig. 3b.

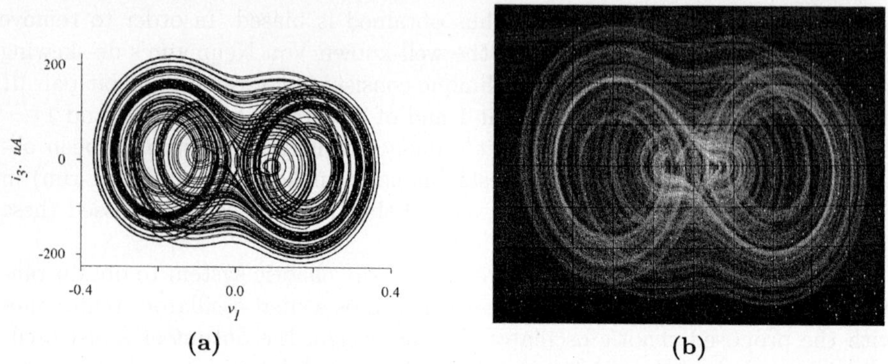

Fig. 3. a) Chaotic attractor from SPICE simulation of the high-frequency circuit. b) Experimental results of the chaotic oscillator ($Xaxis = 150mV$, $Yaxis = 100mV$).

The voltage v_1, which corresponds to the variable x, was then converted into a binary sequence according to the procedure explained in Section 3. In order to realize this procedure, the circuit shown in Fig. 4 was used. In this circuit, the comparator was implemented from LM311 chip and the voltage V_q was used to realize the threshold q in Equation 3. An FPGA based hardware, which has a PCI interface was designed to upload the binary data to the computer. With the rising edge of the external periodical pulse train, $v_p(t)$ in Fig. 1, output bit stream of the comparator was sampled and stored in binary format. Also, Von Neumann processing was implemented in the FPGA. After Von Neumann processing, candidate random numbers were uploaded to the computer through the PCI interface. Maximum data storage frequency of our FPGA based hardware is 62 Mbps.

A bit stream of length 5.000.000 was acquired for $V_q = 85.2mV$ where distribution density of v_1 on rising edge of $v_p(t)$ was maximum. The obtained bits were subjected to full NIST test suite [14]. As seen from the results in the first column of Table 1, the obtained bit stream failed in some of the tests. Then, to improve the results, we obtained a second sequence of bits by implementing a counter inside the FPGA. The output bit stream of the comparator is sampled on the second rising edges of the external periodical pulse train. Then Von Neumann

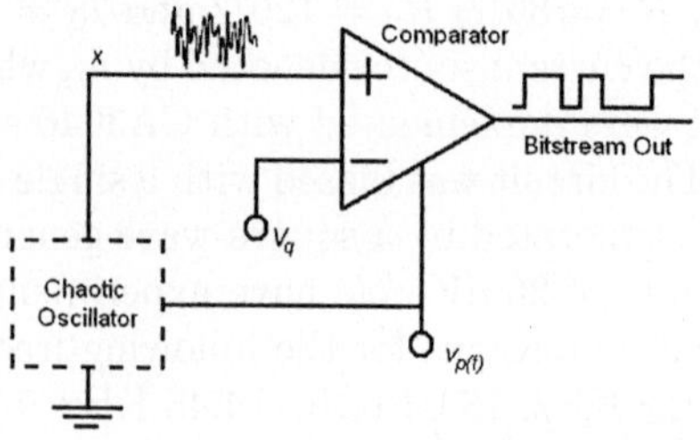

Fig. 4. Random number generation using proposed chaotic oscillator alone

Table 1. Results of the NIST test suite for RNG using proposed chaotic oscillator alone(RE: rising edge)

STATISTICAL TESTS	Each RE	2nd RE	3rd RE
Frequency	0.9902	0.9804	0.9902
Block Frequency	1.0000	1.0000	0.9902
Cumulative Sums	0.9902	0.9755	0.9902
Runs	×	×	0.9902
Longest Run	×	×	0.9804
Rank	0.9804	1.0000	0.9804
FFT	1.0000	1.0000	1.0000
Nonperiodic Templates	×	0.9794	0.9862
Overlapping Templates	0.9902	0.9608	0.9902
Universal	1.0000	1.0000	1.0000
Apen	×	×	0.9608
Random Excursions	1.0000	1.0000	1.0000
Random Excursions Variant	1.0000	1.0000	1.0000
Serial	0.9612	0.9804	0.9951
Lempel Ziv	1.0000	1.0000	1.0000
Linear Complexity	0.9902	0.9902	0.9608

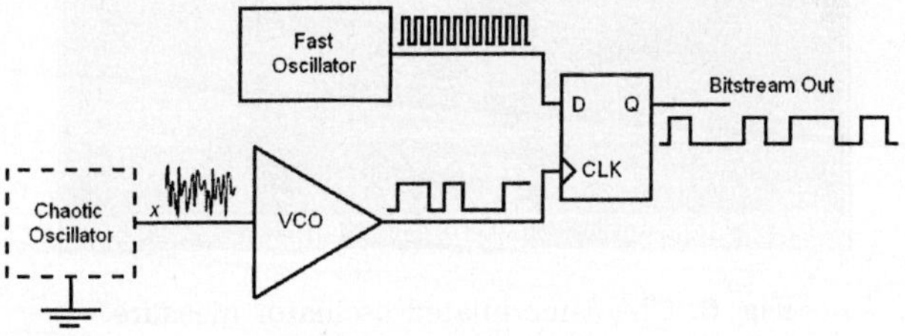

Fig. 5. Random number generation using dual oscillator architecture

processing is applied and the results of the sequence thus obtained are shown in the second column. Finally, a third sequence is obtained in the same manner. As seen from the last column of Table 1, which corresponds to the pass rates of this sequence, this binary sequence passed the tests of full NIST random number test suite. Because of sampling on the third rising edges, throughput data rate reduces to 1/3 of the external periodical pulse train ($5.86KHz/3$). As explained in Section 3, Von Neumann processing generates approximately 1 bit from 4 bits. As a result the throughput data rate obtained by using continuous-time chaotic oscillator alone is effectively 488 bps.

After realization of RNG using continuous-time chaotic oscillator alone, we propose a RNG design which uses dual oscillator architecture with the proposed chaotic oscillator as shown in Fig. 5. In this circuit, according to the procedure explained in Section 3, 74HCT4046A VCO is used to implement the modulation of the slower clock frequency with the voltage v_1, which corresponds to the variable x. Center frequency of the VCO determines the center frequency of the slower clock and can be adjusted up to 17 MHz for 74HCT4046A.

In order to remove the biasing of the output bit sequence, fast oscillator should have a balanced duty cycle. To get a satisfactory result, fast oscillator is implemented by dividing a low jitter 152MHz crystal oscillator by 8 inside the FPGA. In this way, we get a 19 MHz fast oscillator that has a guaranteed 50% duty cycle.

The slow and fast oscillators used in [1] and [18] have center frequency ratios on the order of 1 : 100. In our design, we experimentally get successful results from the full NIST test suite when the slower clock frequency is adjusted up to 830 KHz. Then, 19 MHz fast oscillator is sampled on the rising edge of the slower clock using a D flip-flop inside the FPGA. High jitter level achieved by chaos-modulated oscillator is shown in Fig. 6. Measured minimum period 261.042 ns and maximum period 1.428952μs feature a standard deviation much greater than the fast oscillator period, thus provides uncorrelated random bit stream out.

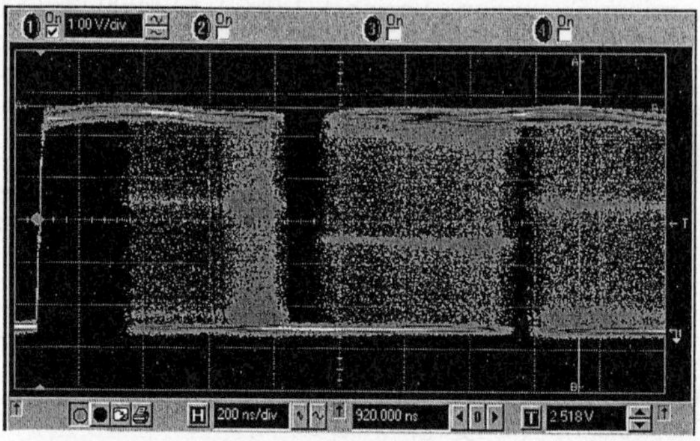

Fig. 6. Chaos-modulated oscillator measure

Table 2. Results of the NIST test suite for RNG using dual oscillator architecture

STATISTICAL TESTS / $f_{slow\ oscillator}$	790 KHz	830 KHz	905 KHz
Frequency	0.9910	0.9910	0.9791
Block Frequency	0.9970	0.9940	0.9731
Cumulative Sums	0.9955	0.9895	0.9806
Runs	0.9881	0.9821	×
Longest Run	0.9940	0.9970	0.9731
Rank	0.9881	0.9940	0.9851
FFT	0.9910	1.0000	1.0000
Nonperiodic Templates	0.9883	0.9893	0.9854
Overlapping Templates	0.9851	0.9881	0.9522
Universal	0.9881	0.9910	0.9851
Apen	0.9731	0.9940	0.9612
Random Excursions	0.9941	0.9925	0.9924
Random Excursions Variant	0.9919	0.9902	0.9954
Serial	0.9910	0.9836	0.9835
Lempel Ziv	0.9851	0.9761	0.9821
Linear Complexity	0.9970	0.9940	0.9851

A bit stream of length 920 MBytes was acquired through the PCI interface of the FPGA based hardware without Von Neumann processing. The obtained bits are subjected to full NIST test suite [14]. For different frequency values of $v_p(t)$ from 5.86 KHz to 18.08 KHz, where the proposed oscillator generates chaos as mentioned in Section 4, we have experimentally verified that the binary data obtained by this oscillator sampling technique pass the tests of full NIST test suite. The pass rates of the tests are approximately the same for the given frequency values of $v_p(t)$. The results of the tests are given in Table 2 for three different frequency values of the slower oscillator when the frequency of $v_p(t)$ and the fast oscillator are 17.07 KHz and 19 MHz, respectively. The slower clock frequency, which determines the throughput data rate is basically limited by the frequency of voltage v_1 and can be adjusted up to 830 KHz as shown in Table 2. If a balanced duty cycle can be guaranteed, the fast oscillator frequency should raise.

Finally we have experimentally verified that the binary data obtained by this oscillator sampling technique pass the tests of full NIST test suite without Von Neumann processing for a higher throughput speed while compared with the TRNG design where the proposed continuous-time chaotic oscillator is used alone.

5 Conclusions

A novel continuous-time chaotic oscillator suitable for IC realization and two novel TRNGs based on this oscillator were presented. Numerical and experimental results presented in this paper not only verify the feasibility of the proposed circuit, but also encourage its use as the core of a high-performance IC TRNG as well. In conclusion, we have experimentally verified that, the proposed TRNG which mixes the continuous-time chaos method with the dual oscillator architecture achieves increased throughput of 830 Kbps while the throughput data rate obtained by using continuous-time chaotic oscillator alone is effectively 488 bps.

References

1. Jun, B., Kocher, P.: The Intel Random Number Generator. Cryptography Research, Inc. white paper prepared for Inter Corp. http://www.cryptography.com/resources/whitepapers/IntelRNG.pdf (1999)
2. Menezes, A., Oorschot, P.van, Vanstone, S.: Handbook of Applied Cryptology. CRC Press (1996)
3. Schneier, B.: Applied Cryptography. 2nd edn. John Wiley & Sons (1996)
4. Holman, W.T., Connelly, J.A., Downlatabadi, A.B.: An Integrated Analog-Digital Random Noise Source. IEEE Trans. Circuits and Systems I, Vol. 44. 6 (1997) 521-528
5. Bagini, V., Bucci, M.: A Design of Reliable True Random Number Generator for Cryptographic Applications. Proc. Workshop Cryptographic Hardware and Embedded Systems (CHES). (1999) 204-218

6. Dichtl, M., Janssen, N.: A High Quality Physical Random Number Generator. Proc. Sophia Antipolis Forum Microelectronics (SAME). (2000) 48-53
7. Petrie, C.S., Connelly, J.A.: Modeling and Simulation of Oscillator-Based Random Number Generators. Proc. IEEE International Symp. Circuits and Systems (ISCAS), Vol. 4. (1996) 324-327
8. Stojanovski, T., Kocarev, L.: Chaos-Based Random Number Generators-Part I: Analysis. IEEE Trans. Circuits and Systems I, Vol. 48, 3 (2001) 281-288
9. Stojanovski, T., Pihl, J., Kocarev, L.: Chaos-Based Random Number Generators-Part II: Practical Realization. IEEE Trans. Circuits and Systems I, Vol. 48, 3 (2001) 382-385
10. Delgado-Restituto, M., Medeiro, F., Rodriguez-Vazquez, A.: Nonlinear Switched-current CMOS IC for Random Signal Generation. Electronics Letters, Vol. 29(25). (1993) 2190-2191
11. Yalcin, M.E., Suykens, J.A.K., Vandewalle, J.: True Random Bit Generation from a Double Scroll Attractor. IEEE Transactions on Circuits and Systems I: Fundamental Theory and Applications, Vol. 51(7). (2004) 1395-1404
12. Delgado-Restituto, M., Rodriguez-Vazquez, A.: Integrated Chaos Generators. Proc. of IEEE, Vol. 90(5). (2002) 747-767
13. National Institute of Standard and Technology, Security Requirements for Cryptographic Modules. NIST, Boulder, CO. (1994)
14. National Institute of Standard and Technology.: A Statistical Test Suite for Random and Pseudo Random Number Generators for Cryptographic Applications. NIST 800-22, http://csrc.nist.gov/rng/SP800-22b.pdf (2001)
15. Petrie, C.S., Connelly, J.A.: A Noise-Based IC Random Number Generator for Applications in Cryptography. IEEE Trans. Circuits and Systems I, Vol. 47. 5 (2000) 615-621
16. Shamir, A.: On The Generation of Cryptographically Strong Pseudorandom Sequences. ACM Transactions on Computer systems, Vol. 1. (1983) 38-44
17. Von Neumann, J.: Various Techniques Used in Connection With Random Digits. Applied Math Series - Notes by G.E. Forsythe, In National Bureau of Standards, Vol. 12. (1951) 36-38
18. Bucci, M., Germani, L., Luzzi, R., Trifiletti, A., Varanonuovo, M.: A High Speed Oscillator-based Truly Random Number Source for Cryptographic Applications on a SmartCard IC. IEEE Trans. Comput., Vol. 52. (2003) 403-409

A New Cryptanalytic Time-Memory Trade-Off for Stream Ciphers

Imran Erguler[1,2] and Emin Anarim[2]

[1] Department of Electronics & Communications Engineering, Dogus University, 34722 Acibadem, Istanbul, Turkey
ierguler@dogus.edu.tr

[2] Electrical-Electronics Engineering Department, Bogazici University, 34342 Bebek, Istanbul, Turkey
anarim@boun.edu.tr

Abstract. In 1980 M. Hellman presented a cryptanalytic time-memory trade-off which reduces computational time by distributing possible key solution space N between memory M and time T, by using a pre-computed table, for block ciphers. This method was applied to stream ciphers by A. Biryukov and A. Shamir with consideration of known output data D. Recently, P. Oechslin described a technique which makes an improvement to Hellman's original idea in computational time with introducing the rainbow chain model for block ciphers. In this paper, we present the application of the rainbow chain model as a time-memory trade-off attack for stream ciphers.

1 Introduction

As may be known there are two important classes of symmetric crypto systems that are block ciphers and stream ciphers. Each technique has different design characteristics and is used for different applications. Block ciphers tend to simultaneously encrypt groups of characters of a plaintext message, whereas stream ciphers encrypt individual characters of a plaintext message one at a time. Also for block ciphers, encryption is done by mixing plaintext with the key in an invertible way. However, for stream ciphers plaintext is XOR'ed with a stream sequence, which is produced by stream generator initiliazied by the key to realize encryption. So attacks on block ciphers may differ from those of the stream ciphers in some points. With respect to time-memory trade-off attacks, stream ciphers have different characteristics compared to block ciphers. Block ciphers take plaintext and the secret key as input and produce ciphertext as output. Since each ciphertext corresponds to a particular plaintext for block ciphers, a common pre-computed table, built up for time-memory trade-off attack, can not be used for different ciphertext. On the other hand, stream ciphers take its state as input and produce stream sequences as output. So state-stream sequence pair is independent from any plaintext (considering synchronous stream ciphers) and a common pre-computed table could be used for different plaintext blocks to analyze corresponding ciphertext blocks.

In this paper, we describe a new type of time-memory trade-off crytanalytic attack for stream ciphers. The attack consists of two parts, which are pre-computational part

P. Yolum et al.(Eds.): ISCIS 2005, LNCS 3733, pp. 215–223, 2005.

and realization of the attack. In the first part of the attack, a pre-computed table that keeps some possible stream generator states and their corresponding key streams are prepared (independent from secret key) by using the encryption algorithm. In the second part of the attack, a search is made to find a match between pre-computed table and known data. If a match is found, the initial state of stream generator is retrieved. For a known initial state, it can be very easy to obtain secret key *K*. This attack is based on the principle of time-memory tradeoff for block ciphers proposed by M. E. Hellman [1] and P. Oechslin [2]. Also the work, describing an improved time-memory tradeoff attack to stream ciphers, in [3] provided insight to our study.

In our study, *N* represents total number of solution space for stream generator internal state, *M* represents amount of required memory, *T* represents required computational time of the attack, *D* represents amount of known data available to the attacker and *P* represents the required pre-computational time of the attack. Also in this study, it is assumed that the attacker knows the internal structure of the target key stream generator.

This paper is organized as follows: In Section 2, we present some previous work. In Section 3, our proposed attack is described. Finally, Section 4 gives the concluding remarks of this study.

2 Previous Work

The idea of our attack is based on the time memory tradeoff principle of M. E. Hellman for block ciphers [1]. Hellman proposed a cryptanalytic time-memory trade-off approach which reduces cryptanalysis time by using a pre-computed table stored in memory. By defining as *M* is required amount of memory, *T* is the operations in time and *N* is possible solutions to search over, it has been showed that if the equation $mt^2=N$ is satisfied, the attack becomes successful where *m* and *t* are the parameters denoting number of rows of the pre-computed table and number of operations on the starting element of each row respectively, their functionality will be explained later. The search space is expressed in terms of *M* and *T* as:

$$M^2T = N^2 . \quad (1)$$

According to [1], if P_0 is a given a fixed plaintext and C_0 is the corresponding ciphertext, the method tries to obtain the encryption key *K* from the solution space *N* by using the encryption algorithm *S*. The relation between the plaintext and ciphertext is given as:

$$C_0 = S_K(P_0) . \quad (2)$$

If *R* is a reduction function which creates a key from a cipher text, then function *f( )* is defined as:

$$f(K) = R[S_K(P_0)] . \quad (3)$$

By successively applying the encryption algorithm *S* and the reduction function *R*, the chains of alternating keys and ciphertexts can be generated. The *f( )* function can be regarded as easy to evaluate and to iterate, however it is difficult to invert it. Hellman's principle was choosing a large number of random m start points from N, iterate f on each one of them t times and store first and the last elements in a table as shown in Fig. 1. The reason of storing only first and the last elements of the iterative chains is to save memory, because using the first key of the chain the whole chain can be regenerated. The realization of the Hellman's attack is done as searching a match between end points of the pre-computed table and the given $f(K)$ for some unknown K. It can be obtained by repeatedly applying $f(\ )$ in the easy forward direction until a match occurs with a stored end point, then going to the corresponding start point and continuing to iterate f from this starting point. The last point before the match $f(K)$ is likely to be the desired key K. In fact, finding a match does not mean that the key is in the table. Because the key may be part of a chain which has the same endpoint, it may not be in the table which is defined as a false alarm. Since a single table with m starting points and t iterations satisfying $mt^2=N$, covers only a fraction of $mt/N=1/t$ of the solution space, in [1] Hellman offered to build up t unrelated tables, each of which has m starting points iterated t times, by applying different reduction functions. In this case it is highly possible that the attack succeeds, if $mt^2=N$ is satisfied. The difference of each table stems from using different reduction R functions, so each table uses variants of $f_i(\ )$, as permuting the output bits of f. In other words, for each table the bits of $f(\ )$ is reordered by corresponding R function, so variants of $f(\ )$ function are generated. Whole pre-computational table system is shown in Fig. 2. Since there are t tables and each table has m rows with t operations Hellman's method requires $M = mt$ as memory, $T = t^2$ as computational time and $P = N$ as pre-computational time.

$$\xrightarrow{\quad\quad\quad\quad\quad t \quad\quad\quad\quad\quad}$$

$$m \downarrow \begin{bmatrix} \mathrm{SP}_1 = X_{1,0} \xrightarrow{f} X_{1,1} \xrightarrow{f} X_{1,2} \xrightarrow{f} \cdots \xrightarrow{f} X_{1,t} = \mathrm{EP}_1 \\ \mathrm{SP}_2 = X_{2,0} \xrightarrow{f} X_{2,1} \xrightarrow{f} X_{2,2} \xrightarrow{f} \cdots \xrightarrow{f} X_{2,t} = \mathrm{EP}_2 \\ \vdots \qquad\qquad\qquad\qquad\qquad\qquad\qquad\qquad \vdots \\ \mathrm{SP}_m = X_{m,0} \xrightarrow{f} X_{m,1} \xrightarrow{f} X_{m,2} \xrightarrow{f} \cdots \xrightarrow{f} X_{m,t} = \mathrm{EP}_m \end{bmatrix}$$

Fig. 1. A classic table of Hellman's attack, size $m \times t$

P. Oechslin proposed a new method based on Hellman's time-memory trade-off idea for block ciphers [2]. Oechslin showed that instead of using t different tables each of which has m starting points iterated t times, a single table can be used to reduce number of table look-ups. In this single table, variants of $f(\ )$ function are used successively for each point in the chain defined as rainbow chain. So each row or chain in the table starts with $f_1(\ )$ and ends with $f_t(\ )$ as shown in Fig. 3. The success probability of t unrelated tables of size $m \times t$ is approximately equal to that of a single rainbow table of size $mt \times t$. In both cases, the tables cover mt^2 keys with t different reduction functions [2].

$$m\downarrow\overset{t}{\longrightarrow}\begin{bmatrix} SP_1 = X_{1,0} \xrightarrow{f_1} X_{1,1} \xrightarrow{f_1} X_{1,2} \xrightarrow{f_1} \cdots \xrightarrow{f_1} X_{1,t} = EP_1 \\ SP_2 = X_{2,0} \xrightarrow{f_1} X_{2,1} \xrightarrow{f_1} X_{2,2} \xrightarrow{f_1} \cdots \xrightarrow{f_1} X_{2,t} = EP_2 \\ \vdots \qquad\qquad\qquad\qquad\qquad\qquad\qquad\qquad \vdots \\ SP_m = X_{m,0} \xrightarrow{f_1} X_{m,1} \xrightarrow{f_1} X_{m,2} \xrightarrow{f_1} \cdots \xrightarrow{f_1} X_{m,t} = EP_m \end{bmatrix}$$

$$m\downarrow\overset{t}{\longrightarrow}\begin{bmatrix} SP_1 = X_{1,0} \xrightarrow{f_2} X_{1,1} \xrightarrow{f_2} X_{1,2} \xrightarrow{f_2} \cdots \xrightarrow{f_2} X_{1,t} = EP_1 \\ SP_2 = X_{2,0} \xrightarrow{f_2} X_{2,1} \xrightarrow{f_2} X_{2,2} \xrightarrow{f_2} \cdots \xrightarrow{f_2} X_{2,t} = EP_2 \\ \vdots \qquad\qquad\qquad\qquad\qquad\qquad\qquad\qquad \vdots \\ SP_m = X_{m,0} \xrightarrow{f_2} X_{m,1} \xrightarrow{f_2} X_{m,2} \xrightarrow{f_2} \cdots \xrightarrow{f_2} X_{m,t} = EP_m \end{bmatrix}$$

$$\vdots \qquad\qquad\qquad\qquad\qquad\qquad\qquad\qquad \vdots$$

$$m\downarrow\overset{t}{\longrightarrow}\begin{bmatrix} SP_1 = X_{1,0} \xrightarrow{f_t} X_{1,1} \xrightarrow{f_t} X_{1,2} \xrightarrow{f_t} \cdots \xrightarrow{f_t} X_{1,t} = EP_1 \\ SP_2 = X_{2,0} \xrightarrow{f_t} X_{2,1} \xrightarrow{f_t} X_{2,2} \xrightarrow{f_t} \cdots \xrightarrow{f_t} X_{2,t} = EP_2 \\ \vdots \qquad\qquad\qquad\qquad\qquad\qquad\qquad\qquad \vdots \\ SP_m = X_{m,0} \xrightarrow{f_t} X_{m,1} \xrightarrow{f_t} X_{m,2} \xrightarrow{f_t} \cdots \xrightarrow{f_t} X_{m,t} = EP_m \end{bmatrix}$$

Fig. 2. Hellman's pre-computational table system

The previous two attacks defined in [1] and [2] are for block ciphers, so amount of known plaintext is considered as 1. Because incase of block ciphers, a pre-computation table can be prepared according to a fixed known plaintext, it can be only used for this known plaintext. On the other hand, for stream ciphers a pre-computational process is independent of plaintext, so different plaintext can be used with the same pre-computation table. As a result in [3], (1) is rewritten for stream ciphers as:

$$M^2TD^2 = N^2, \tag{4}$$

where D is amount of known data for stream ciphers satisfying inequality $D^2 \le T \le N$.

According to [3]; by means of D information for stream ciphers instead of using t different tables as in case of Hellman's method, using t/D different pre-computation tables is enough for success of the attack. So required memory and computational time become respectively as:

$$M = mt/D \tag{5}$$

$$T = t\frac{t}{D}D = t^2 \ . \tag{6}$$

Pre-computational time of the attack is $P = N/D$.

Also in [4] and [5] a different time-memory trade-off attack is presented for stream ciphers. In [4] J.Golic showed that using time-memory tradeoff attack, solution space N can be distributed between time T and memory M, where the inequality $TM \geq N$ and $1 \leq T \leq D$ must be satisfied for success of attack. Actually, this approach is better than Hellman's $M^2T = N^2$. However in case of large solution space, according to inequalities above, this method requires unrealistic amount of known data with regarding feasible memory M.

The work in [2] and [3] provided insight to our study and our attack is mainly based on Hellman's time-memory trade-off principle.

$$\mathrm{SP}_1 = X_{1,0} \xrightarrow{f_1} X_{1,1} \xrightarrow{f_2} X_{1,2} \xrightarrow{f_3} \cdots \xrightarrow{f_t} X_{1,t} = \mathrm{EP}_1$$

Fig. 3. A single rainbow chain

3 Proposed Attack

For stream generators; states are usually uniquely defined by the first $log_2(N)$ bits of their output sequence (key stream sequence), if the internal structure of the key stream generators are known. So with a great probability only first $log_2(N)$ bits of key stream sequences will be enough to find the internal state of the stream generator. Amount of known data, D, can be regarded as amount of known $log_2(N)$ successive output bits in the key stream sequence.

If the length of the known key stream sequence is n, this sequence provides $(n\text{-}log_2(N)\text{+}1)$ successive $log_2(N)$-bit blocks. So amount of known data D becomes as:

$$D = n - (\log_2 N) + 1 \ . \tag{7}$$

Our attack consists of two parts which are pre-computation part and realization of the attack. In the first part, a single pre-computation table will be formed rather than t/D different pre-computation tables proposed by [3] for stream ciphers. This table has mt rows with two columns and covers N/D keys as in [3].

Preparation of the table follows the procedure as: Firstly a random sample of mt different $log_2(N)$-bit blocks which are candidates for internal states of the stream generator are chosen from the solution space N as $\mathrm{SP}_1, \mathrm{SP}_2, \ldots, \mathrm{SP}_{mt}$. Then each SP_i enters random functions $f_j(\ )$'s as; firstly function $f_1(\ )$, after $f_2(\ )$ is applied to result then $f_3(\ )$ and this process goes on until $f_{t/D}(\ )$ is applied. So totally t/D operations are made to the first element of each row. This procedure is shown in Fig. 4. Notice that, for each row a rainbow chain is generated. Then only SP_i and corresponding EP_i are stored in the table as SP_i - EP_i pairs, sorted into increasing endpoint order, to use memory efficiently. This is not a problem because internal states X_{ij} can be reached by repeatedly applying $f_j(\ )$ in the correct order beginning with corresponding SP_i. The points in each chain can be defined as below:

Let $X_{i0} = SP_i$,

$$X_{ij} = f_j(X_{ij-1})\ ,\ 1 \leq j \leq t \tag{8}$$

and $f_j(X_{ij-1})$ is the random function that works as expressed below:

- It accepts X_{ij-1} as initial state of stream generator.
- Then $log_2(N)$ bits of stream sequence are produced according to encryption algorithm of the stream generator.
- Finally, it takes $log_2(N)$ bits of the produced sequence in the order depending on reduction function R (permutation function for our case) which is unique for $f_j(\ )$ and gives X_{ij} as output.

$$\overset{t}{\longrightarrow}$$

$$m\downarrow\left[\begin{array}{l} SP_1 = X_{1,0} \xrightarrow{f_1} X_{1,1} \xrightarrow{f_2} X_{1,2} \xrightarrow{f_3} \cdots \xrightarrow{f_{t/D}} X_{1,t/D} = EP_1 \\ SP_2 = X_{2,0} \xrightarrow{f_1} X_{2,1} \xrightarrow{f_2} X_{2,2} \xrightarrow{f_3} \cdots \xrightarrow{f_{t/D}} X_{2,t/D} = EP_2 \\ \vdots \qquad\qquad\qquad\qquad\qquad\qquad\qquad\qquad\qquad \vdots \\ \vdots \qquad\qquad\qquad\qquad\qquad\qquad\qquad\qquad\qquad \vdots \\ SP_{mt} = X_{mt,0} \xrightarrow{f_1} X_{mt,1} \xrightarrow{f_2} X_{mt,2} \xrightarrow{f_3} \cdots \xrightarrow{f_{t/D}} X_{mt,t/D} = EP_{mt} \end{array}\right]$$

Fig. 4. Pre-computed table of the attack

R determines in which order the produced bits is settled. Therefore each different R function generates a variant of $f(\ )$. $f_j(\ )$ can be seen as below, where C is produced $log_2(N)$ bits output by stream generator.

$$[\ X_{ij-1} \xrightarrow{\text{Stream Generator}} C_j \xrightarrow{R(C_j)} X_{ij}\ ] = [\ X_{ij-1} \xrightarrow{f_j(X_{ij-1})} X_{ij}\ ]$$

The realization of the proposed attack can be described in following steps. Since a n bit key stream sequence provides $(n\text{-}log_2(N)+1)$ successive $log_2(N)$-bit blocks, initially these $log_2(N)$ bit blocks are taken. Next, $R_{t/D}$ function, which is permutation function of $f_{t/D}(\ )$ is applied to each block. Then a search is made between this result and last column of the table (with EP_i's) to find whether a match occurs or not. If a match occurs between, for example, a $log_2(N)$-bit stream block and EP_i, then corresponding SP_i is found from the table and by repeatedly applying $f(\ )$'s beginning with $f_1(\ )$and ending with $f_{t/D-1}(\ )$, the result will be internal state of stream generator with a great probability. If a match does not occur, then firstly $R_{t/D-1}$ function and next $f_{t/D}(\ )$ function is applied to the block. The result is then searched as in the previous case. If now a match occurs with any element of the last column of the table, corresponding SP_i is found and internal state of the stream generator is obtained by repeatedly applying $f(\ )$ beginning with $f_1(\ )$ and ending with $f_{t/D-2}(\ )$. This process can be repeated at most t/D times with each $log_2(N)$ bit block until a match occurs.

The retrieval of the key given the internal state can be easily realized by running the generator backwards. If the goal of the attacker is not to find secret key K, he can run the generator forwards, produce all the later pseudo random bits and obtain rest of the plaintext (unknown part of the plaintext).

The memory and time requirements of this attack can be determined as follows: Since there is a single table with mt rows, the required words of memory is:

$$M = mt \,. \tag{9}$$

Also there are D samples from known key stream, and at most $\frac{\frac{t}{D}(\frac{t}{D}+1)}{2}$ operations are applied to each sample, so the required time is:

$$T = \frac{\frac{t}{D}(\frac{t}{D}+1)}{2} D \approx \frac{t^2}{2D} \,. \tag{10}$$

Pre-computational time of the attack is $P = N/D$.

In fact, P. Oechslin has shown that his method, which is based on rainbow chain model, is about 7 times better than classical method with respect to the required computational time, although a factor of two is explained theoretically. The reason is that there are more false alarms in classical method than in method of [2]. In Hellman's classical time-memory trade-off idea, there is a chance that chains in the same table starting at different points can collide and merge, since the function R is an arbitrary modification of space of key streams into the space of internal states of the stream generator. In the same table, each merge decreases the number of distinct internal states actually included in the table. In our attack the rainbow chain model is used, so there is no chance of merge of two collided chains unless collision appears at the same position in both chains. Since function R changes for each point in the chain, in case of collision in different points in two chains, collided points will produce different next states and so merge does not occur. Also a rainbow table is searched from the amount of calculation increases quadratically from 1 to about $t^2/2$, however in classical tables amount of calculation increases linearly to t^2. So if the key is found early, the gain may thus be much higher [2]. These extra gains mentioned above can result in a factor of about 2 and (10) can change as given below:

$$T \approx \frac{t^2}{4D} \,. \tag{11}$$

The chosen m and t must satisfy the equation below for success of the attack.

$$mt^2 = N \,. \tag{12}$$

The trade-off formula of our attack is:

$$M^2TD \approx (mt)^2 \frac{t^2}{4D} D - \frac{m^2t^4}{4} = \frac{N^2}{4} \,. \tag{13}$$

For example, if N=2^{60}, available data D=2^{27} and $t = 2^{29}$ is chosen, from (12) $m = 2^2$ is found. Using (9) required memory is $M = 2^{31}$ words of memory, the required computational time using (11) is $T = 2^{29}$ and $D \le t$ is satisfied. Required time and memory multiplication is, $MT = 2^{60}$.

If solution space N and available data D are high and available memory to the attacker is low, then a trade-off between time and memory can be done. To realize this job, in preparation of the pre-computation table, number of operations in each rainbow chain is increased and number of samples chosen from solution space is decreased. For example instead of choosing mt samples from the solution space, $\frac{mt}{D^{0.5}}$ samples can be chosen and instead of making t/D operations for each row in the table, $\frac{t}{D^{0.5}}$ operations can be done. In this case table also covers N/D keys as in the original method, however values of T and M change. Now there are $\frac{mt}{D^{0.5}}$ rows so $M = \frac{mt}{D^{0.5}}$ and $\frac{t}{D^{0.5}}$ operations for each row so $T = \frac{\frac{t}{D^{0.5}}(\frac{t}{D^{0.5}}+1)}{2} D \approx \frac{t^2}{2}$. Regarding extra gain mentioned previously T becomes $T \approx \frac{t^2}{4}$. Now lets suppose our solution space $N=2^{90}$ and available data $D=2^{38}$, $D^{0.5} \leq t$. If $t = 2^{33}$ is chosen, from (12) $m = 2^{24}$ is found. In this case required memory is $M=2^{38}$ words of memory, the required computational time is $T=2^{64}$.

In our attack, according to (9) and (11), required time and memory multiplication is $MT \approx mt^3 / 4D$. On the other hand according to [3], $MT = mt^3 / D$, so our method seems about 4 times better with respect to the multiplication of required memory and computational time for the same m, t and D values. Also, the required computational time is reduced from $T = t^2$ as presented in [3], to $T \approx t^2 / 4D$ for the same t and D values. In other words, required computational time becomes $4D$ less than the computational time in [3] for the same chosen t and available known data D. However, when we compare the tradeoff formulas (4) and (13), one can see that (4) is better than (13). The reason is obvious; for the same fixed amount of known data and for the same amount of computational time T, memory requirements of our attack become greater compared to those of [3], or for the same fixed amount of known data and for the same amount of available memory M, computational requirements of our attack become greater. So for the fixed parameters considering the time-memory-data trade-off formulas, our method is not as good as the attack in [3].

4 Conclusions

We have proposed a new way of building up pre-computed table for attack on stream ciphers, mainly based on Hellman's cryptanalytic time-memory tradeoff. The requirements of the attack are $M = mt$ as memory and $T = t^2/4D$ as computational time. Also the trade-off formula of the attack is $M^2TD = N^2/4$. Regarding the amount of solution space of the stream generator, available memory and available known data, the attacker can change number of operations in each row and number of samples inversely with covering N/D keys in the pre-computation table.

References

1. Hellman, M. E.: A Cryptanalytic Time-Memory Trade-Off. IEEE Trans. Inform. Theory 26 (1980) 525-530
2. Oechslin, P.: Making a Faster Cryptanalytic Time-Memory Trade-Off. In: Boneh, D. (eds.): CRYPTO 2003. Lecture Notes in Computer Science, Vol. 2729. Springer-Verlag, Berlin Heidelberg New York (2003) 617–630
3. Biryukov, A., Shamir, A.: Cryptanalytic Time/Memory/Data Trade-Offs for Stream Ciphers. In: Okamoto, T. (eds.): ASIACRYPT 2000. Lecture Notes in Computer Science, Vol. 1976. Springer-Verlag, Berlin Heidelberg New York (2000) 1–13
4. Golic, J.: Cryptanalysis of Alleged A5 Stream Cipher. In: Fumy, W. (eds.): EUROCRYPT 1997. Lecture Notes in Computer Science, Vol. 1233. Springer-Verlag, Berlin Heidelberg New York (1997) 239–255
5. Babbage, S.: A Space/Time Trade-Off in Exhaustive Search Attacks on Stream Ciphers. In: European Convention on Security and Detection IEE Conference Publication. 408 (1995)

SVM Approach with a Genetic Algorithm for Network Intrusion Detection*

Taeshik Shon[1], Jungtaek Seo[2], and Jongsub Moon[1]

[1] Center for Information Security Technologies/Graduate School of Information Security, Korea University, Anamdong, Sungbukgu, Seoul 138-701, Korea
{743zh2k, jsmoon}@korea.ac.kr
[2] National Security Research Institute
62-1 Hwaam-dong, Yuseong-gu, Daejeon 305-348, Republic of Korea
seojt@etri.re.kr

Abstract. Due to the increase in unauthorized access and stealing of internet resources, internet security has become a very significant issue. Network anomalies in particular can cause many potential problems, but it is difficult to discern these from normal traffic. In this paper, we focus on a Support Vector Machine (SVM) and a genetic algorithm to detect network anomalous attacks. We first use a genetic algorithm (GA) for choosing proper fields of traffic packets for analysis. Only the selected fields are used, and a time delay processing is applied to SVM for considering temporal relationships among packets. In order to verify our approach, we tested our proposal with the datasets of MIT Lincoln Lab, and then analyzed its performance. Our SVM approach with selected fields showed excellent performance.

1 Introduction

Most network attacks can be detected by state-of-the-art signature based Network Intrusion Detection System (NIDS). However, because some network attacks exhibit anomalous behavior, it is difficult to detect them. Some of the best solutions have applied machine learning algorithms [1-5]. Machine learning methods have the advantages of preparing for novel attacks and unknown attacks, but they have the problems of high false positive rates and high performance requirements. Moreover, finding appropriate features among various candidates is not easy.

Thus, in this paper, we use Genetic Algorithm (GA) for choosing network packet features, and Support Vector Machine (SVM) as the machine learning algorithm for classification. Especially, in our SVM approach, we use a time delay preprocessing method for finding temporal relationships between packets because a typical SVM doesn't receive the time variation between their inputs. In the next section we briefly review the related works of GA and SVM. In sections 3 and 4, we present our proposed method using GA for proper field selection and SVM learning methods with both soft margin SVM and one-class SVM. In section 5, we explain experimental methods including time delay preprocessing and resultant analysis. Finally, in section 6, we conclude with future works.

* This work was supported by the Ministry of Information Communications, Korea, under the Information Technology Research Center Support Program supervised by the IITA.

P. Yolum et al.(Eds.): ISCIS 2005, LNCS 3733, pp. 224 – 233, 2005.

2 Related Works

Genetic Algorithms were first developed by John Holland in the 1960s as an abstraction of biological evolution, rather than as a tool to solve a specific problem [6]. One of the aims of GA is to find an optimal solution. Most research about GA is about selecting the best parameters given a particular problem domain. A number of approaches to parameter selection have been proposed in the literature [7-9]. Yang and Honavar [10] classify many existing approaches into three groups: exhaustive search, heuristic search, and randomized search. Moreover, for gene expression data with thousands of features Manfred and Martin Schultz [11] proposed feature selection methods such as decision trees, k-nearest neighborhood, and support vector machine.

Support vector machines (SVMs) are basically a set of related supervised learning methods, applicable to both classification and regression. The basic classification SVM creates a maximum-margin hyperplane between classes in a transformed input space. The use of the maximum-margin hyperplane is inspired by Vapnik Chervonenk [12], which provides a probabilistic test error bound which is minimized when the margin is maximized. The original optimal hyperplane algorithm proposed by Vladimir Vapnik in 1963 was a linear classifier [13-15]. SVM has been successfully applied to a number of pattern recognition applications involving face detection, verification, and recognition, recognition of handwritten digits and character recognition, and so on [16]. Lately, SVM has also been applied to the field of information security. In [17-19], various SVM were applied to intrusion detection. One-class SVM and Robust SVM approach were introduced in [17-18]. Also, SVM was compared to a variety of neural network approaches [19].

3 Choosing Fields in TCP/IP Header with Genetic Algorithm

GA is a model to implement the behavior of the evolution process in nature. Initial populations in the genetic process are randomly created. GA then uses three operators to produce a next generation from the current generation: reproduction, crossover, and mutation. The reproduction operator selects from the current generation of chromosomes those that are superior to the other chromosomes. The selection uses a probabilistic survival of the fittest mechanism based on a problem-specific evaluation of the chromosomes. The crossover operator then allows the introduction of new chromosomes into the population of potential solutions by randomly combining pairs of randomly selected existing chromosomes. Finally, the mutation operator allows the random mutation of existing chromosomes so that new chromosomes may contain parts not found in any existing chromosomes. This whole process is repeated, moving from one generation to the next, until a good individual is found. When the process terminates, the best chromosome among the population of the final generation is the solution.

To apply the genetic process to our problem domain, we have to make decisions regarding the following 3-steps: individual gene presentation and initialization, evaluation function, and genetic operators and their parameters. In the first step, we present our objects (TCP/IP packets) as binary gene strings. We convert each TCP and IP header field into a bit binary gene value, 0 or 1. So, initial individuals consist of a set of randomly generated 24 bit strings including 13 bits of IP fields and 11 bits of TCP fields. It is important that our total number of individuals have a proper population size. For a population size, if the population size is too small, all gene chromosomes soon converge to the same gene string value and the genetic model cannot generate new individuals. In contrast, if the population size is too large, the model spends too much time calculating new gene strings which affects the generation of new gene strings.

The second step is to make our fitness function for evaluating individuals. The fitness function consists of an object function and its transformation function.

$$F(X) = g(f(X)) \tag{1}$$

In equation (1), the objective function's values are converted into a measure of relative fitness by fitness function, F(x), with transformation function g(x). To make our own objective function, we first analyzed anomaly attacks from MIT IST dataset [20] and then we apply each field used in the attack to the coefficients of a polynomial equation with coefficients.

$$f(X(x)) = (a_i x_i + \ldots + a_2 x_2 + a_1 x_1) \tag{2}$$

where $x_i, \ldots\ldots x_2, x_1$ mean TCP/IP header fields, and their coefficients means the frequency of being used in attacks.

While the proposed objective function (2) calculates the relative fitness, the fitness function of (1) has rank based operation. Rank-based operations helps overcomes the scaling problems of the proportional fitness assignment. Last step for genetic modeling is to decide genetic operators and their related parameters. As for the reproduction operator, a roulette wheel method selects individuals by means of n roulette "starts." The roulette wheel contains one sector per each member of the population. Reproduction probability means that current individuals can be selected in again in next generation, so a high probability means more former gene strings are inherited by the next generation. In crossover operations, one crossover point is predetermined, so that the binary string of a new chromosome consists of two parts; one from the beginning of the chromosome to the crossover point of the first parent, and the rest from the other parent. A low crossover probability prevents convergence to an optimized solution because it reduces the opportunities for crossover between individuals. Conversely, if the probability is too high, it increases the possibility which can destroy the best solution by exchanging genes too frequently. For the mutation operator, if we use a general discrete mutation operator and the mutation probability is too small, new characteristics will be accepted too late. If the probability is too high, new mutated generations cannot have a close relationship with former generations.

4 Support Vector Machines for Classification

In this section, we introduce two SVM classification approaches. Soft margin SVM is a typical supervised learning algorithm as a binary classifier. Soft margin SVM has two important variables C and ξ. Through these variables, soft margin SVM can solve non-separable problems. SVM algorithm can be also adapted into an unsupervised learning algorithm called one-class SVM which identifies outliers amongst positive examples and uses them as negative examples.

4.1 Soft Margin SVM (Supervised SVM)

SVM is a standard supervised learning algorithm with two class classifiers. This SVM classifier has slack variable and penalty function for solving non-separable problems. First, we are given a set of points $x_i \in R^d, i = 1 \ldots l$ where each point x_i belongs to either of two classes with the label $y_i \in \{-1, 1\}$. Suppose a (separating) hyper plane $\mathbf{w}^T \mathbf{x}_i + b = 0$ separates the positive from the negative examples. That is, all the training examples satisfy:

$$\mathbf{w}^T \mathbf{x}_i + b \geq 1, \text{for all } \mathbf{x}_i \in P$$
$$\mathbf{w}^T \mathbf{x}_i + b \leq -1, \text{for all } \mathbf{x}_i \in N \quad (3)$$

$\mathbf{w}$ is an adjustable weight vector, $\mathbf{x}_i$ is an input vector and b is the bias term. Equivalently:

$$y_i(\mathbf{w}^T \mathbf{x}_i + b) \geq 1, \text{ for all } i = 1 \ldots N \quad (4)$$

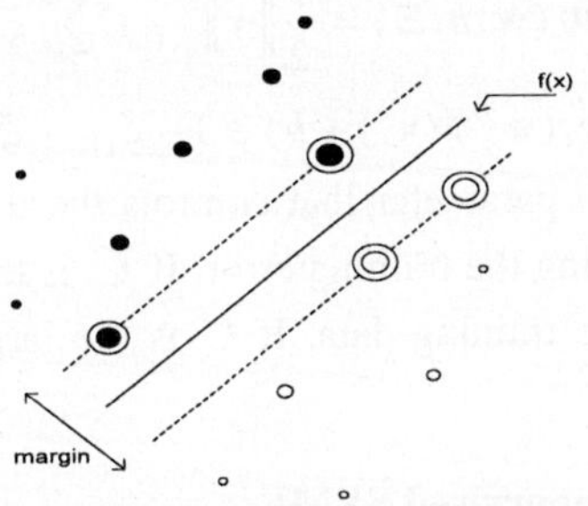

Fig. 1. Separable hyper plane between two datasets

In this case, we say the set is linearly separable. In figure 1, the distance between the hyperplane and $f(x)$ is $\frac{1}{\| w \|}$. The margin of the separating hyper plane is defined to be $\frac{2}{\| w \|}$. The learning problem is hence reformulated as: minimize $\|\mathbf{w}\|^2 = \mathbf{w}^T \mathbf{w}$ subject to the constraints of linear separability (5). This is equivalent to maximizing the distance of the hyperplane between the two classes; this maximum distance is called the support vector. The optimization is now a convex quadratic programming problem.

$$\underset{\mathbf{w},b}{\text{Minimize}} \quad \Phi(\mathbf{w}) = \frac{1}{2}\|\mathbf{w}\|^2$$
$$\text{subject to} \quad y_i(\mathbf{w}^T \mathbf{x}_i + b) \geq 1, i = 1, \ldots, l. \quad (5)$$

This problem has a global optimum because $\Phi(\mathbf{w}) = \frac{1}{2}\|\mathbf{w}\|^2$ is convex in w and the constraints are linear in w and b. This has the advantage that parameters in a QP solver will affect only the training time, and not the quality of the solution. This problem is tractable but in order to proceed to the non-separable and non-linear cases it is useful to consider the dual problem as outlined below. The Lagrange for this problem is

$$L(\mathbf{w}, b, \Lambda) = \frac{1}{2}\|\mathbf{w}\|^2 - \sum_{i=1}^{l} \lambda_i \left[y_i (\mathbf{w}^T \mathbf{x}_i + b) - 1 \right] \tag{6}$$

where $\Lambda = (\lambda_1, \ldots, \lambda_l)^T$ are the Lagrange multipliers, one for each data point. The solution to this quadratic programming problem is given by maximizing L with respect to $\Lambda \geq 0$ and minimizing with respect to $\mathbf{w}, b$. Note that the Lagrange multipliers are only non-zero when $y_i(\mathbf{w}^T \mathbf{x}_i + b) = 1$. Vectors for which this is the case are called *support vectors* since they lie closest to the separating hyperplane. However, in the non-separable case, forcing zero training error will lead to poor generalization. To take into account the fact that some data points may be misclassified we introduce c-SVM using a vector of slack variables $\Xi = (\xi_1, \ldots, \xi_l)^T$ that measure the amount of violation of the constraints (7). The problem can then be written

$$\underset{\mathbf{w}, b, \Xi}{\text{Minimize}} \quad \Phi(\mathbf{w}, b, \Xi) = \frac{1}{2}\|\mathbf{w}\|^2 + C \sum_{i=1}^{l} \xi_i^k$$

$$\text{subject to} \quad y_i(\mathbf{w}^T \phi(\mathbf{x}_i) + b) \geq 1 - \xi_i, \quad \xi_i \geq 0, \quad i = 1, \ldots, l \tag{7}$$

where C is a regularization parameter that controls the trade-off between maximizing the margin and minimizing the training error. If C is too small, insufficient stress will be placed on fitting the training data. If C is too large then the algorithm will overfit the dataset.

4.2 One-Class SVM (Unsupervised SVM)

SVM algorithm can be also adapted into an unsupervised learning algorithm called one-class SVM that identifies outliers amongst positive examples and uses them as negative examples. In anomaly detection, if we consider anomalies as outliers, one-class SVM approach can be applied to detect anomalous packets.

Figure 2 shows the relation between a hyperplane of one-class SVM and outliers.

Suppose that a dataset has a probability distribution P in the feature space and we want to estimate a subset S of the feature space such that the probability that a test point drawn from P lies outside of S is bounded by some a priori specified value $\nu \in (0, 1)$. The solution of this problem is obtained by estimating a function f which is a positive function. f takes the value of +1 in a small region where most of the data lies, and -1 elsewhere.

$$f(x) = \begin{cases} +1, & if \quad x \in S \\ -1, & if \quad x \in \overline{S} \end{cases} \tag{8}$$

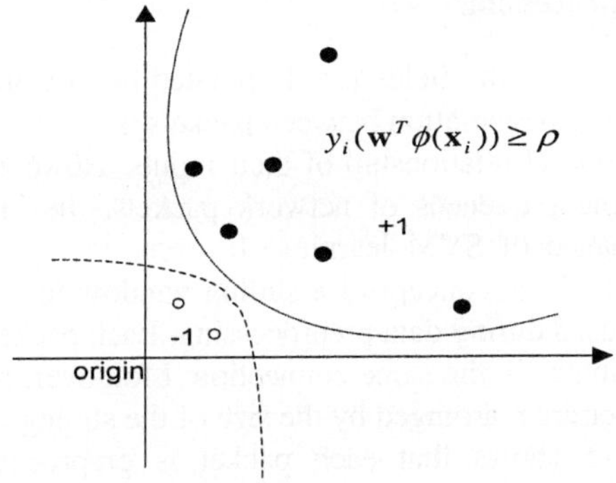

Fig. 2. One-class SVM; the origin means the only original member of second class.

The main idea is that the algorithm maps the data into a feature space H using an appropriate kernel function, and then attempts to find the hyperplane that separates the mapped vectors from the origin with the maximum margin. Given a training dataset $(x_1, y_1), \ldots, (x_1, y_1) \in \Re^N \times \{\pm 1\}$, let $\Phi : \Re^N \rightarrow H$ be a kernel map which transforms the training examples into the feature space H. Then, to separate the dataset from the origin, we need to solve the following quadratic programming problem:

$$\underset{\mathbf{w},b,\Xi}{\text{Minimize}}\Phi(\mathbf{w},b,\Xi) = \frac{1}{2}\|\mathbf{w}\|^2 + \frac{1}{\nu l}\sum_{i=1}^{l}\xi_i^k - \rho$$

$$\text{subject to} y_i(\mathbf{w}^T\phi(\mathbf{x}_i)) \geq \rho - \xi_i, \cdots \xi_i \geq 0,\ i = 1,\ldots,l \tag{9}$$

where $\nu \in (0, 1)$ is a parameter that controls the trade off between maximizing the distance from the origin and containing most of the data in the region related by the hyperplane and corresponds to the ratio of "outliers" in the training dataset. Then the decision function

$$f(x) = \text{sgn}((w \cdot \Phi(x) + b) - \rho) \tag{10}$$

will be positive for most examples x_i contained in the training set.

5 Experiments

In these experiments, we used the dataset of the Information Systems Technology Group (IST) of MIT Lincoln Laboratory. The IST of MIT Lincoln Laboratory, under Defense Advanced Research Projects Agency (DARPA) and Air Force Research Laboratory (AFRL) sponsorship, has collected and distributed the first standard corpora for evaluation of computer network intrusion detection systems [20]. In the case of the normal dataset, the attack-free datasets of the first and third week were used. In the case of the abnormal dataset, we used 212 attacks of the MIT dataset.

5.1 Time Delay Preprocessing

In our proposed approaches, the fields pre-designated by GA are used as SVM input data. In this processing, time variation between packets is not considered because SVM cannot provide the temporal relationship of their inputs. However, if we can pick out relationships among the sequences of network packets, the knowledge can deeply influence the performance of SVM learning. In order to consider the relationships between packets, we used the concept of a sliding window in accordance with the IP identification number used during data preprocessing. Each packet will be classified by an IP identification number in the same connection. Moreover, packets with the same IP identification number are rearranged by the size of the sliding window.

In figure 3, Case 1 shows that each packet is preprocessed by their arrival sequence. In contrast, Case 2 means that each packet is rearranged by their ID number regardless of their original flow. In this example, the size of the receiving window is 4.

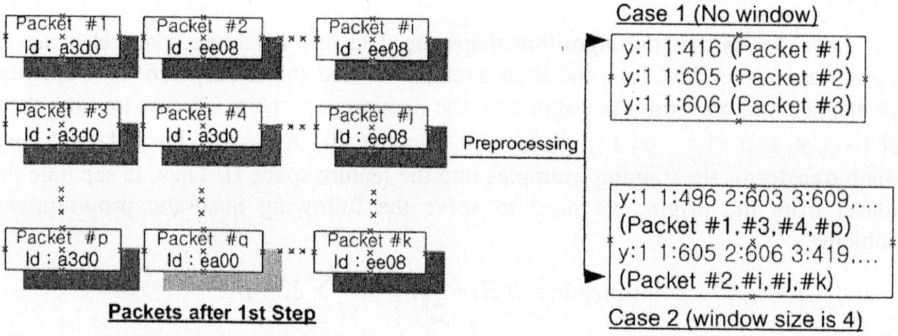

Fig. 3. The Time Delay Preprocessing based on the Packet flow

5.2 Experiment Results of GA Field Selection

Setup parameters of our evolutionary process were set to the typical values mentioned in the literature [21]. The number of Population is 100, the reproduction rate is 0.600, the crossover rate is 0.500, and the mutation rate is 0.001. Moreover, the preliminary test for deciding the optimized generation was ran on soft margin SVM with the attack-free data of the 1st week as a normal dataset, and the fragmentation/offset attacks, TCP and IP DoS attacks, forged packets and covert channel attacks, and Scan attacks as an abnormal dataset. After using soft margin SVM learning algorithm, we knew the final generation of the preliminary test was well-selected. The 91-100 generation showed the best correction rate. Moreover, less fields does not always guarantee a better correction rate. Results are described in Table 1.

5.3 Experimental Results of SVM Approaches

In this resultant analysis, two SVMs were tested as follows: soft margin SVM as a supervised method and one-class SVM as an unsupervised method. The dataset used by our SVM learning was the preprocessed fields selected by the GA process. The

Table 1. GA Fields Selection Results

Generation	No. of Field	No of Selected Fields	CR	FP	FN
01-15	19	2,5,6,7,8,9,10,11,12,13,14,15,16,17,19,21,22,23,24	96.68	1.79	7.00
16-30	15	2,5,6,7,8,9,10,11,12,16,17,20,21,23,24	95.00	0.17	16.66
31-45	15	2,5,6,7,8,9,10,11,12,16,17,20,21,23,24	95.00	0.17	16.66
46-60	18	1,2,5,6,7,8,9,10,11,12,13,14,17,19,20,22,23,24	95.12	0.00	16.66
61-75	17	2,5,6,7,8,9,10,11,12,13,14,15,16,17,19,20,21	73.17	0.00	91.60
76-90	17	2,5,6,7,8,9,10,11,12,13,14,15,16,17,19,20,21	73.17	0.00	91.60
91-100	15	3,5,6,7,9,12,13,16,17,18,19,21,22,23,24	97.56	0.00	8.33

*CR:Correction Rate(%), FP: False Positive(%), FN: False Negative(%)

Table 2. The Performance evaluation using GA schemes

Performance Measures		Correction Rate (%)		False Positive (%)		False Negative (%)	
Genetic Algorithm		GA	No GA	GA	No GA	GA	No GA
Temporal Relation	No Sliding	90.1	85.6	7.8	10.4	2.1	4.0
	Sliding	71.3	67.4	20.1	25.6	8.6	7.0

Table 3. The Experimental Results of SVM Approaches using GA and Time Delay Preprocessing

	Kernels	CR	FP	FN
Soft Margin SVM	Inner Product	90.13	10.55	4.36
	Polynomial	91.10	5.00	10.45
	RBF	98.65	2.55	11.09
	Sigmoid	95.03	3.90	12.73
One-Class SVM	Inner Product	53.41	48.00	36.00
	Polynomial	54.06	45.00	46.00
	RBF	94.65	20.45	44.00
	Sigmoid	-	-	-

verification of two SVM supplement schemes is described in Table 2. We first experimented with time variation to confirm the usefulness of considering temporal sequences. In this experiment, we fixed the kernel function of SVM as an inner product function; the function is one of the most popular kernel functions. The experimental result with packet sliding shows a correction rate of over 20% in comparison with the no sliding case, so we performed the experiments with packet sliding again according to the kind of kernel function. Among the kernel functions, the RBF kernel has the most efficient detection rate. Especially when we focus on the suitability of using a genetic algorithm, it shows better performance in all cases with a variety of conditional parameters. The average correction rate of all schemes using GA was 95.0% and the average of other cases was 89.6%.

Our SVM approach results with GA and Time Delay Preprocessing are summarized in the following Table 3. Among the experiments, soft margin SVM using RBF showed the best performance (Correction rate: 98.55%). However, when we consider that soft margin SVM depends on the pre-existed knowledge, this result is not surprising. In the case of one-class SVM, the RBF kernel provided the best performance, however, the false positive rate and false negative rate were high. Moreover, we could not obtain results from one-class SVM using sigmoid kernel because of overfitting. If we can adjust the high false rate of one-class SVM or combine the two approaches, we could provide the best performance for classifying anomalous traffic. Finally, in this experiment, we used SVMlight [22] for soft margin SVM and Libsvm [23] for one-class SVM.

6 Conclusion and Future Works

Genetic algorithms for feature selection and support vector machines for pattern classification are being used more extensively in the network security area because they are known as the best solutions for selecting appropriate values and performing binary classification. Our approach employed a genetic algorithm for selecting proper TCP/IP packet fields to be applied to support vector learning to distinguish anomaly attacks from normal packets. Moreover, time delay preprocessing based on packet flow was proposed. We also evaluated our proposed methods over normal behavior data from MIT Lincoln Lab and considered many different parameters such as SVM kernel functions and its parameters. Experiment results showed that our proposed GA and Time Delay Preprocessing were reasonable for feature selection, specifically appropriate TCP/IP header fields. Moreover, the two approaches using supervised and unsupervised SVM provide a high correction rate, but high false positive alarms of one-class SVM has to be dealt with if we apply our approaches to a real environment. Thus, future work will involve defining more realistic normal behavior and modifying SVM classifiers for decreasing high false positive rates.

References

1. Anderson D. et al.: Detecting Unusual Program Behavior Using the Statistical Component of the Next-Generation Intrusion Detection, SRI-CSL-95-06, Computer Science Laboratory, SRI International, Menlo Park, CA (1995)
2. Anderson D. et. Al.: Expert System (NIDES), Technical Report SRI-CSL-95-06, Computer Science Laboratory, SRI International, Menlo Park, CA (1995)
3. Cabrera et al.: Statistical Traffic Modeling For Network Intrusion Detection, Proc of the 8th International Symposium on Modeling, Analysis and Simulation of Computer and Telecommunication Systems, San Francisco, CA (2000) 466-476
4. Lee W., Xiang D.: Information-Theoretic Measures for Anomaly Detection, IEEE Symposium on Security and Privacy (2001)
5. Mahoney M., Chan P.: Learning Nonstationary Models of Normal Network Traffic for Detecting Novel Attacks, Proceedings of 8th International Conference on Knowledge Discovery and Data Mining (2002) 376-385
6. Holland J.: Adaptation in Natural and Artificial Systems. Michigan Press, Ann Arbor (1995)
7. Siedlecki et al.: On automatic feature selection. International Journal of Pattern Recognition, 2 (1998) 197-220
8. Langley, P.: Elements of Machine Learning, Morgan Kaufmann, Palo Alto, CA (1995)

9. Doak, J.: An evaluation of feature selection methods and their application to computer security, Technical Report CSE-92-18, Dept. of CS, UC at Davis, CA (1992)
10. Yang, J., Honavar, V.: Feature Subset Selection using a genetic algorithm, Proceedings of the Genetic Programming Conference, Stanford, CA. 380-385 (1998)
11. Lau M., Schultz M.: A Feature Selection Method for Gene Expression Data with Thousands of Features, Technical Report, CS-490, Yale University (2002)
12. Vapnik V.: the Nature of Statistical Learning Theory, Springer-Verlag, New York (1995)
13. Campbell, C., Cristianini N.: Simple learning algorithms for training support vector machines, Technical report, University of Bristol (1998)
14. Pontil, M., Verri, A.: Properties of Support Vector Machines, A.I. Memo No. 1612; CBCL paper No. 152, Massachusetts Institute of Technology, Cambridge (1997)
15. Cristianini N.: An Introduction to Support Vector Machines, Cambridge University (2000)
16. Byun H., Lee S.W.: A Survey on Pattern Recognition Applications of Support Vector Machines, International Journal of Pattern Recognition and Artificial Intelligence, Vol. 17, No. 3 (2003) 459-486
17. Heller K.A., Svore K.M., Keromytis A., Stolfo S.J.: One Class Support Vector Machines for Detecting Anomalous Windows Registry Accesses, In the proceedings of the workshop on Data Mining for Computer Security (2003) 2-9
18. Hu W., Liao Y., Vemuri V.R.: Robust Support Vector Machines for Anamoly Detection in Computer Security, International Conference on Machine Learning, Los Angeles, CA, July (2003)
19. Sung A.H. et al.: Identifying Important Features for Intrusion Detection Using Support Vector Machines and Neural Networks, Proc SAINT (2003) 209-217
20. Lincoln Laboratory, MIT, DARPA Intrusion Detection Evaluation (1999)
21. Mitchell, M.: An Introduction to Genetic Algorithms, MIT Press, MA (2002)
22. Joachmims, T.: mySVM - a Support Vector Machine, University Dortmund (2002)
23. Chang C.C.: LIBSVM : a library for support vector machines (2004)

Modeling Access Control Lists with Discrete-Time Quasi Birth-Death Processes

Sándor Palugya and Máté J. Csorba

Ericsson Hungary Ltd., Test Competence Center,
H–1117 Budapest, Irinyi J. u. 4–20, Hungary
{Sandor.Palugyai, Mate.Csorba}@ericsson.com

Abstract. This paper examines Access Control Lists (ACLs) that are used primarily in IP routers for providing network admission control and maintaining a certain level of Quality of Service. We present a method for modeling ACLs and firewall rules in various systems that use the same logic for their operation. Besides, we analyze the performance impact of ACLs on the packet forwarding capability of a router with discrete-time QBD processes.

1 Introduction

Nowadays, Internet usage is progressing at a great pace. More and more people become potential users and require faster connections. Security has also become an important issue in business and home networks, as well. As a result, such devices must be designed and created, which allow us to build and maintain a more secure network. Their operation must also be optimized. In this work a method is proposed for modeling Access Control Lists (ACLs) used in routers, which can maintain the operation of large networks in a scalable way [1]. The aim of this work is to introduce a methodology to predict performance of existing systems, rather than to give a feedback to router hardware or software designers. The models introduced in the following represent traditional ACL schemes found mainly in conventional hardware based routers. However, our QBD models readily accommodate some of the more sophisticated schemes as well. In the next section, we give a short introduction to the basics of Access Control Lists, their operation and purposes. After that, we present our models, discrete-time Quasi Birth-Death processes (QBDs). We decided to use the mathematical formalism included and build a QBD model of ACLs because QBD processes are well supported both theoretically and with tools supporting evaluation also. At the end of the paper performance indicators that can be derived from these models will be shown, and finally we summarize our results.

2 The Application of Access Control Lists

Today it is an important security issue to control or restrict TCP/IP access in IP networks. To achieve the needed control over IP traffic and to prohibit unauthorized access, ACLs are a common solution in firewall routers, border routers and in any intermediate router that needs to filter traffic.

P. Yolum et al.(Eds.): ISCIS 2005, LNCS 3733, pp. 234 – 243, 2005.

ACLs are basically criteria organized into a set of sequential conditions. Each line of such a list can permit or deny specific IP addresses or upper-layer protocols. Incoming or outgoing traffic flows can be classified and managed by a router using ACLs. There are two basic types of ACLs: standard and extended.

With standard IP access lists, a router is capable of filtering the traffic based on source addresses only. Extended access lists, on the other hand, offer more sophisticated methods for access control by allowing filtering based not only on source addresses, but also on destination addresses and other protocol properties [2].

In many cases ACLs are used for allocating the resources needed by a user at a given time of a day, or for rerouting the traffic automatically according to the varying access rates provided by Internet Service Providers (ISPs). Service Level Agreements (SLAs), negotiated in advance, can be satisfied, as well, if time ranges are also specified in an access list. However, time-based ACLs are not taken into consideration in this paper.

ACLs can be applied on one or more interfaces of the router and in both directions, but they work differently depending on which direction they are applied. When applied on outgoing interfaces, every received packet must be processed and switched by the router to the proper outgoing interface before checking against the appropriate list. And in case the rules defined in the list discard the packet, this results in a waste of processing power.

An application area for access lists is called session filtering. The main purpose of session filtering is to prevent (possibly malicious users on) outside hosts connecting to hosts inside, while still allowing users inside the protected network to establish connections to the outside world [3].

Although conventional ACLs are relatively static, dynamic access lists exist to allow the rules to be changed for a short period of time, but require additional authentication processes. In this case, exceptions are granted for the user (possibly with a higher privilege level) to access additional network elements. The current work does not consider these types of ACLs [4].

When an ACL is applied on a router's interface, the router is forced to check every packet sent or received on that interface depending on the type of the ACL (in or out). This can seriously affect the packet forwarding performance.

3 The Quasi Birth-Death Process Model

According to section 2, the behavior of ACLs can be modeled with a two-dimensional process. On one hand the model must describe the packet arrival, the buffering and serving functionalities, and on the other hand the elementary steps of ACL examination and the decision process must be described. In order to satisfy these requirements we use quasi birth-death processes to model ACLs.

In order to become acquainted with quasi birth-death processes let us consider processes N(t) and J(t), where {N(t), J(t)} is a DTMC (Discrete-Time Markov Chain). The two processes have the following meaning: N(t) is the level process and J(t) is the phase process. {N(t), J(t)} is a QBD if the transitions between levels are restricted to one level up or down, or inside the actual level. The structure of the transition probability matrix of a simple QBD is the following [5]:

$$\underline{\underline{P}} = \begin{bmatrix} \underline{\underline{A}}_1^* & \underline{\underline{A}}_0^* & & \\ \underline{\underline{A}}_2^* & \underline{\underline{A}}_1 & \underline{\underline{A}}_0 & \\ & \underline{\underline{A}}_2 & \underline{\underline{A}}_1 & \underline{\underline{A}}_0 \\ & \cdots & \cdots & \cdots \end{bmatrix}. \quad (1)$$

Matrix A_0 describes the arrivals (transitions one level up), matrix A_1 describes transitions inside each level and matrix A_2 describes departures (transitions one level down). The matrix A_1^* is an irregular transition matrix at level 0, A_0^*describes transitions one level upwards and A_2^* one level downwards. The row sum of P is equal to 1 (discrete-time model).

4 The QBD Model of ACLs

In our models the time-axis is divided into timeslots. The elementary timeslot (*dt*) is equal to the estimated duration of one single access list entry check (exactly one phase transition within a given level of the QBD). Thus *dt* is an input parameter of our models and can be predicted experimentally by means of measurements. As our current model does not incorporate the effect of incoming and outgoing interfaces it sufficient to set one global elementary timeslot.

We describe the packet arrival as a Poisson distributed process. Accordingly, the probability that *i* packets arrive in a timeslot is

$$\frac{(\lambda \cdot dt)^i}{i!} \cdot e^{-\lambda \cdot dt}, \; i = 0,1,2,\ldots \text{ and } \lambda \cdot dt << 1. \quad (2)$$

We assume that at most one packet arrival is possible in a timeslot, since the probability of more than one packet arriving in a selected timeslot is negligible. After an arrival the node maintaining the ACL immediately starts processing the packet.

In our behavior model the transitions inside a given level of the QBD process describe the functionality of the access control list of the router. The intra-level transitions represent the packet-matching mechanisms and can be described with a phase type process [5], [6]. A PH-type process has a designated state, called the drain.

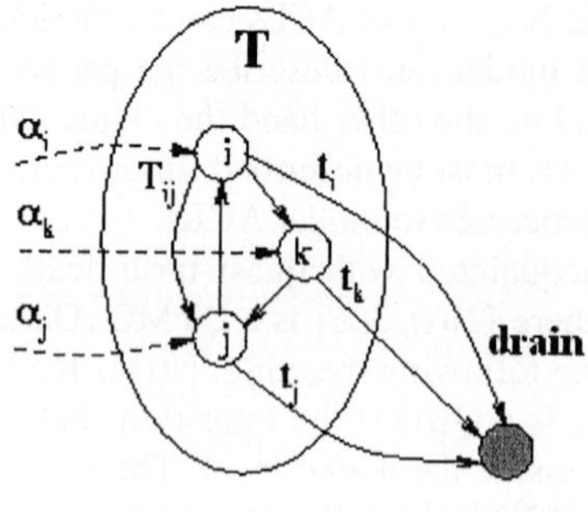

Fig. 1. A general PH-type renewal process

In Figure 1, matrix T describes transitions before entering into the drain and vector t contains the probabilities of the process entering the drain. With our model it is possible to model the original ACL conception as well as grouped lists, quick search algorithms, hashes and other ACL implementations. In this paper we present the model for the original sequential access control lists. Matrix T and vectors t and α can be seen on (3), (4), (5), independently from the general PH-type process depicted in Figure 1.

$$\underline{\underline{T}} = \begin{bmatrix} 0 & p_1 & 0 & & & \\ 0 & 0 & p_2 & 0 & & \\ & 0 & 0 & \cdots & & \\ & & 0 & 0 & p_{n-1} \\ & & & 0 & 0 \end{bmatrix} . \tag{3}$$

$$\underline{t} = \begin{bmatrix} 1 \\ . \\ . \\ 1 \\ 1 \end{bmatrix} - \underline{\underline{T}} \begin{bmatrix} 1 \\ . \\ . \\ 1 \\ 1 \end{bmatrix} = \begin{bmatrix} 1-p_1 \\ . \\ . \\ 1-p_{n-1} \\ 1 \end{bmatrix} . \tag{4}$$

$$\underline{\alpha} = \begin{bmatrix} 1 & 0 & . & . & 0 \end{bmatrix} . \tag{5}$$

The initial phase distribution (5) has the simple meaning, when a new packet arrives it is checked against the first list entry with probability of 1.

According to (3) and (4), $1\text{-}p_i$ is the probability of the examined packet matching rule number i in the access control list, so thus the PH-type process enters the drain meaning that we have a departure. To be precise, a departure in our models physically means that the examined packet is handed over to the routing process (or to the outgoing interface) and will be forwarded or is simply dropped by the router depending on the meaning of rule number i in the ACL. The routing process itself, and the routing table lookup is out of the scope of our models.

At first, we describe ACLs with an infinite QBD model for approximation. The transition matrix in this case is constructed according to (1), where the building blocks are the following:

$$\underline{\underline{A_0}} = \underline{\underline{D_1}} \otimes \underline{\underline{T}} \; ; \quad \underline{\underline{A_1}} = \underline{\underline{D_0}} \otimes \underline{\underline{T}} + \underline{\underline{D_1}} \otimes \underline{t}\underline{\alpha} \; ; \quad \underline{\underline{A_2}} = \underline{\underline{D_0}} \otimes \underline{t}\underline{\alpha} \; . \tag{6,7,8}$$

$$\underline{\underline{A_1^*}} = \underline{\underline{D_0}} \; ; \quad \underline{\underline{A_0^*}} = \underline{\underline{D_1}} \otimes \underline{\alpha} \; ; \quad \underline{\underline{A_2^*}} = \underline{\underline{D_0}} \otimes \underline{t} \; . \tag{9,10,11}$$

We describe the packet arrival with a Markov Arrival Process (MAP), where matrix D_0 describes phase transitions without arrival and matrix D_1 describes phase transitions with exactly one arrival. The $\otimes$ denotes the Kronecker product. The values of D_0 and D_1 can be calculated from the arrival intensity.

$$D_0 = (1-\lambda \cdot dt) \; ; \; D_1 = (\lambda \cdot dt) \tag{12}$$

As the arrival processes in our models are discrete Poisson processes with parameter λ, the matrices D_0 and D_1 are scalars (12).

We build the QBD depicted in Figure 2 using this mathematical formalism. Each time a packet finished its service time we have a transition to the first phase, one level back, as the router starts matching the next packet against the first rule in the list (this

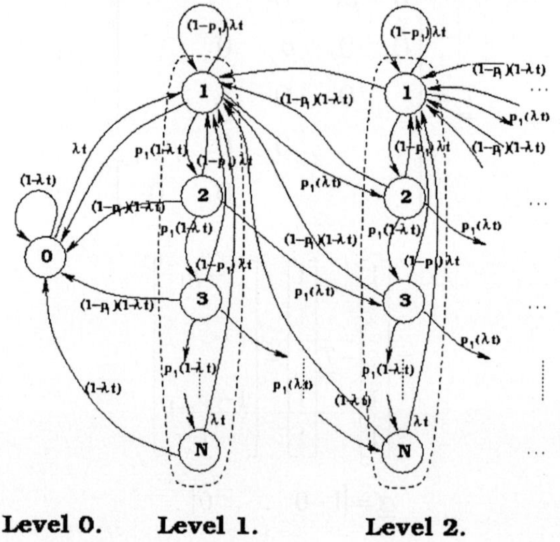

Fig. 2. The infinite QBD representing the logical behavior of ACLs

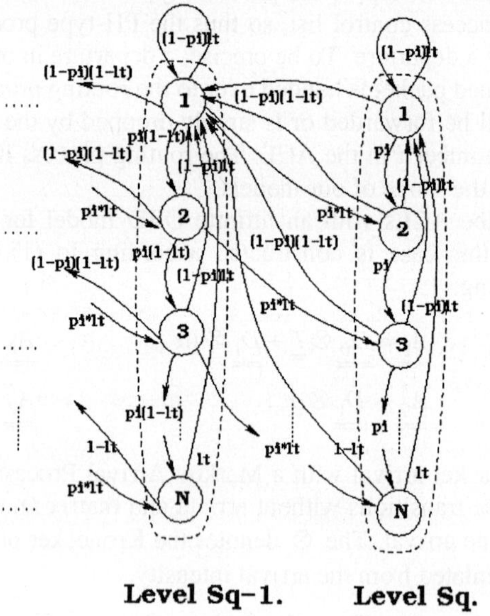

Fig. 3. The last level of the finite QBD model

behavior is described by the initial phase distribution vector α). Level 0 is irregular since we have no packets in the router waiting for service, thus no phase transitions.

Furthermore, parameter N is equal to the total number of access control list entries, which ranges between hundreds or thousands of entries, typically for ISPs.

After approximating a finite router buffer and the effect of ACLs with an infinite QBD, we developed a finite model also. However, algorithms do exist that aim to decrease the time needed for the evaluation of a finite QBD model, such as the folding algorithm from San-qi Li [7] [8], they can only be applied under certain circumstances and it is still faster to solve an infinite QBD model instead. Although calculation of a finite QBD requires more computational power, approximating with an infinite transition matrix can result in unacceptable error ratio in certain cases [9]. The finite model has the same levels, phases and overall structure as the infinite one, but the number of levels is restricted to Sq.

When there are n packets in the system, the QBD is on level n, accordingly the finite Sq represents the buffer size of the router and the QBD has a finite number of levels. In this case, the final level is depicted on Figure 3.

Consequently, the block structure of P becomes:

$$\underline{\underline{P}} = \begin{bmatrix} \underline{\underline{A}}_1^* & \underline{\underline{A}}_0^* & & \\ \underline{\underline{A}}_2^* & \underline{\underline{A}}_1 & \underline{\underline{A}}_0 & \\ & \dots & \dots & \dots \\ & & \underline{\underline{A}}_2 & \underline{\underline{A}}_1^{**} \end{bmatrix} . \qquad (13)$$

In addition to the matrices (6), (7), (8), (9), (10) and (11) the irregular matrix A_I^{**} in our transition matrix is built up as follows:

$$\underline{\underline{A}}_1^{**} = \underline{\underline{D}}_0 \otimes \underline{T} + \underline{\underline{D}}_1 \otimes (\underline{T} + \underline{t}\underline{\alpha}) . \qquad (14)$$

According to the model performance indicators like the overall delay and packet loss can be derived using existing matrix analytic methods [9].

Comparing the two models, we can estimate the applicability range of the infinite, thus the simpler and faster model. We assume that the infinite model is applicable by means of matrix-geometric methods if the relative error between the two models is below 0.001 percent. Our tests show that by comparing the computation times and results of the models regarding the delay, the applicability of the finite model is limited by the function $\frac{y(Sq)}{\lambda \cdot dt}$. Accordingly, it is reasonable to use the finite QBD process for approximation in the domain under the curve $y(Sq)$, on the other hand in the domain above the infinite model is more effective.

In Figure 4 a) the function $y(Sq)$ depends on the buffer size of the router (Sq), which is given in packets, as depicted on Figure 4 b). However, $y(Sq)$ never reaches the theoretical limit of 0.

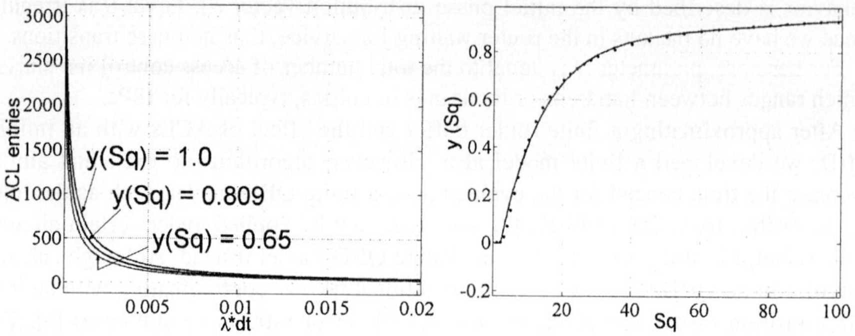

Fig. 4. The applicability domain of the finite model and y(Sq) as a function of buffer length

We also found that the function *y(Sq)* can be approximated under 150 ACL entries as (15) with a confidence bound of 95 percent.

$$y(Sq) = \left[0.843 \cdot e^{0.001 \cdot Sq} - 1.010 \cdot e^{-0.084 \cdot Sq}\right]^{+} . \tag{15}$$

5 Results

In order to validate the numerical accuracy of the computational solutions and to get a feedback whether the assumptions made in the modeling phase were right we developed a simulation of ACLs in *ns-2* [10]. The simulation was made without any assumptions or approximations and uses finite buffers to simulate real world ACL behavior. The comparison shows the same packet loss and delay values as the QBD models with a negligible variation, especially when high numbers of packets are used in the simulation.

In Figure 5 we present the relative error ratio of the results of the model, according to the equation

$$error_{relative} = \frac{value_{simulated} - value_{model}}{value_{simulated}} .$$

On both figures the x-axis represents the number of ACL entries and the y-axis the error-ratio.

The model gives approximately the same results as the simulation. The relative error is lower than 0.8 %. The approximation of packet loss values starts to be varying at lower numbers of ACL entries. However, the variation could be decreased with more extracted results. The delay is approximately 0.6 % above the simulated results, almost for any number of ACL entries.

It is possible to alter the model, thus shifting the error ratio of the delay to approximately zero, but in this case the error for low numbers of ACL entries would be out of the ±0.8 % range.

One of the important parameters that can be derived from the models is the packet loss ratio as a function of the arrival intensity (Figure 6). The models also show us the

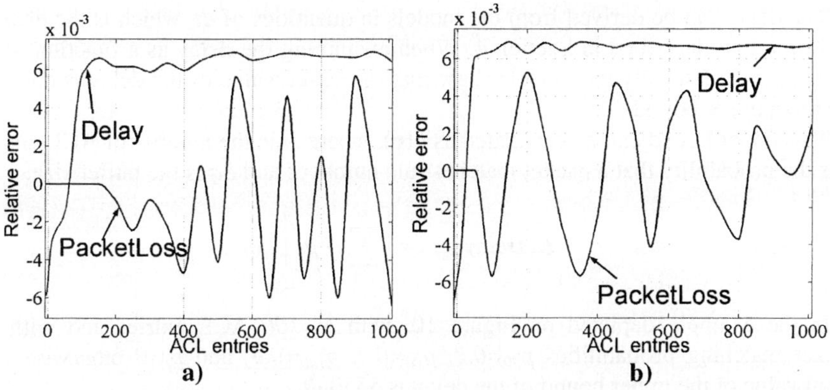

Fig. 5. The relative error of the model for intensities a) $\lambda dt = 0.005$ and b) $\lambda dt = 0.01$

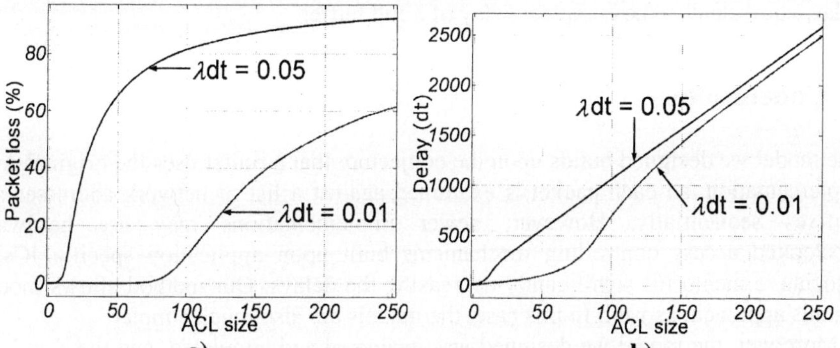

Fig. 6. Approximated packet loss (a) and delay (b) for different arrival intensities

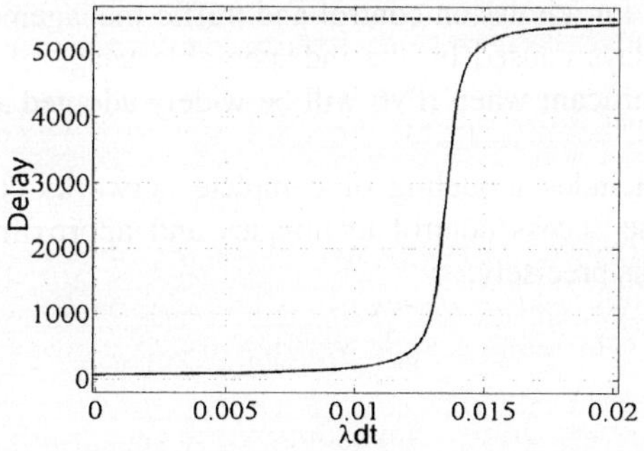

Fig. 7. The delay as a function of arrival intensity

influence of overall packet loss on the delays a packet can suffer. According to the models, for various arrival intensities, the characteristics of the delay have a soft-knee at the ACL size when the packet loss starts to be notable.

The delay can be derived from the models in quantities of dt, which is the elementary time-unit described in Section 4. When examining the delay as a function of the packet arrival intensity the models show that the actual value of the delay is converging to an upper bound.

This upper bound can be calculated as (16), where N is the number of ACL entries, p_i is the probability that a packet matches rule number i and Sq is the buffer size.

$$E(Delay_{\max}) = \left[\sum_{i=1}^{N} i \cdot p_i \right] \cdot Sq \; . \tag{16}$$

In the example depicted on Figure 10, with $N=100$ ACL entries and with the packet matching probabilities $p_{30}=0.2$, $p_{70}=0.4$, $p_{100}=0.4$, and $p_i=0$ otherwise. The mean value of the upper bound of the delay is $5550 \cdot dt$.

The physical meaning of this characteristic is that at higher arrival intensities packet loss gets more and more significant, so thus the delay parameter cannot be increasing anymore. Packets, which are not dropped by the router suffer a constant delay, equivalent to the complete delay of a full buffer.

6 Conclusions

The model we designed builds upon the conjecture that a router uses the original ACL implementation, so each packet is examined against a list of network addresses and prefixes sequentially. However, newer implementations may use hardware-accelerated access controlling mechanisms built upon application specific ICs or associative memories significantly decreasing the delays. Our method allows modeling this approach, as well. In this case, the models are also much simpler.

Moreover, the model we designed was evaluated and simulated, and the simulated results are identical to the analytic results. With the presented model, we can describe Access Control Lists both analytically and with simulation.

This way, we are able to model and approximate the delay and packet loss ratios of routers that use ACLs for admission control and traffic management in existing IPv4 networks. Possible delays caused by the indispensable usage of access control lists will be even more significant when IPv6 will be widely adopted as the network layer protocol.

Our future work includes modeling of complete networks consisting of several routers using the same access control techniques and approximating the outgoing traffic of these networks precisely.

References

1. Funke R., Grote A., Heiss H-U.: Performance Evaluation of Firewalls in Gigabit-networks, in Proc. of 1999 Symposium on Performance Evaluation of Computer and Telecommunication Systems, Chicago, (1999).
2. Catalyst 6000 Family Multilayer Switch Feature Card and Policy Feature Card Configuration Guide, Configuring Access Control Lists, Cisco Systems Inc. (2004), http://www.cisco.com/univercd/home/home.htm

3. Held G.: Working with Cisco Access Lists, Int. J. Network Mgmt. 9, John Wiley & Sons, (1999), pp. 151-154.
4. Hazelhurst S.: A Proposal for Dynamic Access Lists for TCP/IP Packet Filtering", University of Witwatersrand, Johannesburg, Technical Report TR-Wits-CS-2001-2, 2001.
5. Neuts M.F.: Matrix-Geometric Solutions in Stochastic Models, Johns Hopkins University Press, (1981), pp. 81-107, pp. 63-70, pp. 112-114.
6. Neuts M.F.: Structured Stochastic Matrices of M/G/1 Type and Their Applications, Marcel Dekker, New York, 1989, pp. 231-248.
7. Ye J., Li S.: Folding Algorithm: A Computational Method for Finite QBD Processes with Level-Dependent Transitions, IEEE Trans. Commu., Vol. 42, No. 2, (1994), 625-639.
8. Li S., Sheng H-D.: Generalized Folding Algorithm For Sojourn Time Analysis of Finite QBD Processes and its Queuing Applications, In Proc. of International Conference on Multimedia Computing and Systems, (1996), 394-398.
9. Latouche G., Ramaswami V.: Introduction to Matrix Analytic Methods in Stochastic Modeling, by the American Statistical Association and the Society for Industrial and Applied Mathematics, (1999), pp. 83-99, pp. 221-237.
10. The discrete event Network Simulator – ns-2, from the University of Southern California, Information Sciences Institute, http://www.isi.edu/nsnam/ns/

Stochastic Bounds on Partial Ordering: Application to Memory Overflows Due to Bursty Arrivals

H. Castel-Taleb, J.M. Fourneau, and N. Pekergin

[1] Institut National des Télécommunications, 9 rue C. Fourier, 91000 Evry, France
[2] PRiSM, Université de Versailles-Saint-Quentin, 78000 Versailles, France
[3] Centre Marin Mersenne, Université Paris I, 75001 Paris, France

Abstract. We apply stochastic bounding methods with a partial order on the state space to the analysis of memory overflow in a router. Usually, stochastic bounds are associated to a total order implying useless constraints and decreasing the tightness of bounds. Here we present the basic methodology of sample path comparison with a partial order and some numerical results to show the accuracy of the results. We analyze the probability of a buffer overflow with two types of packets, a Pushout access mechanism and Markov modulated batch arrivals. This problem is strongly related to the memory rejection out a Fiber Delay Loop in an all optical router using deflection routing.

1 Introduction

Bounding methods have always received considerable attention in performance evaluation. Usually QoS requirements are defined as thresholds of rewards on the steady-state or transient distributions. We advocate that it may be very efficient to compute bounds on these rewards and check if the bounds are between the exact values which are unknown and the thresholds. In this paper, we apply the sample-path stochastic ordering called also the strong stochastic ordering ($\leq_{st}$). An algorithmic theory of the "st" comparison Markov chains has been recently developed (see [4,5]). However, this theory is based on a total ordering of the state space, while many problems that we consider are based on a natural partial order. Of course, it is possible to transform this partial order into a total one. But this modification adds a lot of unnecessary constraints making bounds less accurate (see for instance [2] for the reordering problem).

Quite often, we analyze Markov chains which are specified by several components and composition. These formalisms (for instance (Stochastic Automata Networks, or Stochastic Process Algebra) generally lead to multidimensional Markov chains which are clearly associated to partial order. Similarly, when the problems involve rewards, we have a total order on the rewards but only a partial order on the states if several states have the same rewards.

In this paper, we show how stochastic comparisons are established on a partially ordered state space through an example related to memory management

P. Yolum et al.(Eds.): ISCIS 2005, LNCS 3733, pp. 244–253, 2005.

in high speed networks. Due to space limitation, we simplify the model to obtain simpler proofs and the detailed analysis is postponed in a companion paper. We consider an all optical router with some Fiber Delay Loops (FDL) for packet recirculation. Here FDL will be considered as a small memory. Deflection routing has been designed to work without storage memory [1]. In Shortest-Path Deflection Routing, switches attempt to forward packets along a shortest hop path to their destinations. Each link can send a finite number of packets per time-slot (the link capacity). Incoming packets have to be sent immediately to their next switch along the path. If the number of packets which requires a link is larger than the link capacity, only some of them will use the link they ask for and the others have to be misdirected or deflected and they will travel on longer paths. Using simulations we have shown that the average number of deflection is not that large but a significant fraction of the number of packets are heavily deflected when the traffic is unbalanced [1]. These packets constitutes a real problem: they are never physically lost due to physical errors or buffer congestion but they can be logically lost because the transport delay is larger than the timers.

Adding a small amount of optical memory (Fiber Delay Loops) will help to reduce the effect of a deflection. If a packet must be deflected, we store it in this memory instead of sending it a wrong direction and it will be sent as soon as a free slot will be available. Using fiber delay loops, is sometimes denoted as local deflection. As the memory is very small, we must add some access mechanism to give some priority to packets with high QoS requirements. In this paper, we assume that the space priority is managed according to the Pushout mechanism: when the memory is full, an arriving low priority packet is rejected while an arriving high priority packet pushes out of the memory a low priority packet if there is any in memory, otherwise it is rejected. A rejected packet is deflected in a bad direction and experience a longer travel in the network. Of course packets must be sent in the $FIFO$ order to minimize the sequencing delay. Following the ROM conclusions[6], we assume that packets have a fixed size and the network is logically time-slotted. We also consider that the arrivals of packet are bursty and we model the arrivals by a Batch process which is modulated by a 2 states Markov chain. Such a process is denoted as a Switched Bernoulli Batch Process (SBBP). Thus the models, at the packet level have to deal with queues with deterministic service times and bursty arrivals. Let B be the memory size (the number of wavelengths if we have one FDL), the state space size of the Markov chain representing $FIFO$ policy is $(2^{B+1} - 1) \times 2$ if we assume SBBP arrivals. This is too large even for small value of B. Typically, the number of wavelength is between 32 and 128.

In this paper, we are mainly concerned with the stochastic bounding methodology. So we slightly modified the system to obtain easier equations and proofs. We suppose that the service is deterministic. The comparison results we obtain can be generalized to general batches of service (a more consistent assumption to model routing) but the proofs are more complex. For the sake of readability, we simplify the model to present the methodology. We assume that we have two classes of packet with different quality of service (QoS) requirements. Both are allowed to use the memory and the Pushout mechanism gives higher priority to the packets with higher QoS need. So we model a SBBP/D/1/B queue with two classes of customers and a Pushout access mechanism. To the best of our knowledge, such a queue does not have a closed-form solution.

The paper is organized as follows: in the next section, we present the basic methods on stochastic ordering and we show that a total order implies often inaccurate results. Section 3 is devoted to the proof that the Markov chain for the *FIFO* policy is bounded by the Markov chains of Head-Of-Line (*HOL*) policies, and the inequalities are derived for the packet rejection. In section 4, we design a new bound whose complexity is linear with the memory size B. Finally we present some numerical results in section 5.

2 Stochastic Bounds on Partially Ordered Spaces

Let us now briefly introduce the key concepts about the stochastic ordering on a partially ordered space [8,7]. Let ε be a discrete denumerable state space, and $\preceq$ be at least a preorder (reflexive, transitive but not necessarily anti-symmetric) on ε. First we give the general definition of the strong stochastic ordering associated to preorder $\preceq$, that will be denoted by $\preceq_{st}$.

Definition 1. *Let X and Y be two random variables taking values on ε. $X \preceq_{st} Y$ if and only if $Ef(X) \leq Ef(Y)$, for all function $f : \varepsilon \rightarrow R$ which is not decreasing according to relation $\preceq$.*

Definition 2. *Let P and Q be two probability measures defined on ε, $P \preceq_{st} Q$ if and only if $P(\Gamma) \leq Q(\Gamma)$ for all increasing sets Γ; any subset Γ of ε is called an increasing set if $x \preceq y$ and $x \in \Gamma \Longrightarrow y \in \Gamma$.*

If the probability measures are not defined on the same state space, they can be compared by their images on a same state space [3]. Let E and F be two discrete denumerable state space, and $\alpha : E \rightarrow \varepsilon$ (resp. $\beta : F \rightarrow \varepsilon$) be a many to one mapping. Then the images of probability measures defined on E and F can be compared on G. We first give the definition of the image of a probability vector and then the comparison of the images of probability vectors on a common space.

Definition 3. *Let p be a probability vector on E, and $\alpha : E \rightarrow \varepsilon$ be a many to one mapping, the image of p on ε is defined as: $\forall u \in \varepsilon, \quad \alpha(p)[u] = \sum_{n \in E | \alpha(n)=u} p[n]$ where $p[n]$ is the probability of $n \in E$, and $\alpha(n)$ is the image of n on ε.*

Definition 4. *Let p (resp. q) be a probability vector on E (resp. F), and $\alpha : E \rightarrow \varepsilon$ (resp. $\beta : F \rightarrow \varepsilon$) be a many to one mapping, the image of p on ε is less than the image of q on ε in the sense of strong ordering ($\alpha(p) \preceq_{st} \beta(q)$), iff*

$$\sum_{n \in E | \alpha(n) \in \Gamma} p[n] \leq \sum_{m \in F | \beta(m) \in \Gamma} q[m], \quad \forall \Gamma \subset \varepsilon$$

The comparison of Markov chains is established if the stochastic ordering on the initial distributions is preserved at each step [8]. We state the following proposition to compare the images of time-homogeneous, finite discrete time Markov chains on a common space.

Proposition 1. *Let $X(i)$ (resp. $Y(i)$) be time-homogeneous discrete time Markov chains on E (resp. F) with one-step transition matrix P (resp. Q); ε be discrete denumerable space with a preorder $\preceq$, and $\alpha : E \to \varepsilon$ (resp. $\beta : F \to \varepsilon$) be many to one mapping. The image of $X(i)$ on ε is less than the image of $Y(i)$ on ε ($X(i) \preceq_{st} Y(i)$), if*

$$\alpha(X(0)) \preceq_{st} \beta(Y(0)) \Longrightarrow \alpha(X(i)) \preceq_{st} \beta(Y(i)) \ \forall i > 0$$

which is equivalent to compare the row vectors of the one-step transition matrices:

$$\alpha(P[n,*]) \preceq_{st} \beta(Q[m,*]), \quad \forall \ n \in E, m \in F \mid \alpha(n) \preceq \beta(m)$$

p where $P[n,*]$ (resp. $Q[m,*]$) is the row vector of P (resp. of Q) corresponding to state n (resp. to m).

Let us give an example to show the relation between the tightness of bounds and the state space ordering. We consider the Markov chain taking values on state space $\varepsilon = \{1,2,3,4\}$ transition matrix P. In the case of total state space order: $1 \leq 2 \leq 3 \leq 4$, the best upper bounding matrix computed by Vincent's algorithm [4] is Q. If the partial order of the state space is $1 \preceq 2 \preceq 4$ and $1 \preceq 3 \preceq 4$, it follows from proposition 1 that $P \preceq_{st} R$. Since the comparison of rows 2 and 3 are not necessary in this case, the bounds computed from matrix R are tighter. Let the performance measure of interest be the steady-state probability of being at state 4, we can see that the bound obtained from the steady-state distribution of R, $\pi_R = (0.169, 0.349, 0.333, 0.149)$ is much tighter than the bound obtained from Q: $\pi_Q = (0.153, 0.224, 0.369, 0.254)$ while $\pi_P = (0.184, 0.345, 0.342, 0.129)$.

$$P = \begin{bmatrix} 0.3 & 0.5 & 0.2 & 0 \\ 0.2 & 0.1 & 0.4 & 0.3 \\ 0.1 & 0.6 & 0.3 & 0 \\ 0.2 & 0.1 & 0.5 & 0.2 \end{bmatrix} \quad Q = \begin{bmatrix} 0.3 & 0.5 & 0.2 & 0 \\ 0.2 & 0.1 & 0.4 & 0.3 \\ 0.1 & 0.2 & 0.4 & 0.3 \\ 0.1 & 0.2 & 0.4 & 0.3 \end{bmatrix} \quad R = \begin{bmatrix} 0.3 & 0.5 & 0.2 & 0 \\ 0.2 & 0.1 & 0.4 & 0.3 \\ 0.1 & 0.6 & 0.3 & 0 \\ 0.1 & 0.2 & 0.4 & 0.3 \end{bmatrix}$$

3 Bounding the FIFO Policy by Head of Line Policies

We are interested in the packet rejection rate for packets having spatial priority. We consider two Head-Of-Line priority policies: $HOL1$ where the service priority is given to packets which do not have spatial priority and $HOL2$ where the time and the spatial priorities are given to the same class of packets. These policies are not really used for memory management They are simpler to analyze than FIFO policy and they help to establish sample-path comparisons. We now prove that by analyzing the Markov chain for Head-Of-Line priority service policy, we can provide stochastic bounds on $FIFO$ policy. It is assumed that both models are subjected to the same arrival process In order to capture the bursty nature of arrivals, a Switched Bernoulli Batch Process (SBBP) is considered. This process is represented by a two state discrete time Markov chain where state 0 is associated to the light traffic phase and state 1 represents the heavy traffic phase. We denote by r^j the probability of leaving state j in this chain. The arrival probabilities depend on the state. We assume independently identically distributed batch arrivals. Let $p^i[i]$, $0 \leq i \leq M$ be the distribution of packet arrivals at state i, where M is the maximum batch size. As we consider a discrete time model, we must define precisely the order for synchronous events. At the end of a slot, we first observe the service completion, and then the admission of packets. Because of SSBP arrivals, bounds based on total order are very bad. Indeed, bounds would correspond to the case where the arrival process is always in heavy traffic phase.

Obviously the Markov chains representing $FIFO$ and HOL policies do not have the same state space. Therefore we will project the state space of $FIFO$ policy into the state space of HOL policy. Let the state vector for HOL policy at time t_i be $\mathbf{N}_{HOL} = (Phase(t_i), NT(t_i), NH(t_i))$ where the first component is the phase of arrivals, NT is the total number of packets in buffer, NH is the number of packets having the priority for buffer. Thus the product space for HOL policy is: $\varepsilon = \{0,\ 1\} \ \times \ i \in \{0,...,B\} \ \times \ \{0,...,i\}$, and the state space size is $2 \times (B+1) \times (B+2)$. The state vector for $FIFO$ will contain one more component $\mathcal{B}(t_i)$ which is the disposition of packets in the buffer: $\mathbf{N}_{FIFO} = (Phase(t_i), NT(t_i), NH(t_i), B(t_i))$. Since the number of high priority packets can be obtained from $\mathcal{B}(t_i)$, it is not necessary, but it will be used to simplify the proofs. The state space size for $FIFO$ policy is $(2^{B+1} - 1) \times 2$.

Let φ be a many to one mapping to project the state space of $FIFO$ policy into the state space of HOL policy: all states for $FIFO$ policy having the same phase of arrivals (*phase*), the same total number (*nt*) and the same number of high priority packets (*nh*) (whatever the disposition of packets in buffer is) are aggregated to the same state (*phase, nt, nh*). We will use the following vector ordering, $\preceq$ on ε. Let $n = (n_1, n_2, n_3)$ and $m = (m_1, m_2, m_3)$ be in ε.

$$n \preceq m \Leftrightarrow n1 = m1 \text{ and } n2 = m2,\ n3 \leq m3 \tag{1}$$

Note that $\preceq$ is reflexive, transitive and antisymmetric, so it is a partial ordering on ε. The strong stochastic ordering associated to $\preceq$ on ε will be denoted by $\preceq_{st}$. Intuitively speaking, if $n \preceq m$, the number of high priority packets lost in state n will be less than that in state m. From the stochastic comparison point of view, we compare stochastic evolution of states having the same phase of arrivals and the same total number of packets. Let us remark that the same phase for arrivals implies the same arrival probabilities, and the same number of total packets is necessary because of the packet admission mechanism.

We first give the evolution equations of the considered policies and then state the theorem on the comparison of these policies. Let $AT(t_{i+1})$ (resp. $AH(t_{i+1})$ be the total number of packets (resp. high priority packets) arrived during slot i.

The indicator function $\mathbb{1}_{\{service=high\}}$ is 1, if the packet in service during slot i has high priority and 0 otherwise.

$$\mathbf{N}_{policy}(t_{i+1}) = (phase(t_{i+1}),\ \ min\{B, (NT_{policy}(t_i) - 1)^+ + AT(t_{i+1})\},\\ min\{B, NH_{policy}(t_i) - \mathbb{1}_{\{service(t_i)=high\}} + AH(t_{i+1})\}) \quad (2)$$

The evolution of the phase is modulated by the same Markov chain. Since all policies are work-conserving and are subject to the same arrivals, the total numbers of packets evolve in the same manner. But the sample-paths of the number of high priority packets depend on the service policy (indicator function).

Theorem 1. *If* $\mathbf{N}_{HOL2}(0) \preceq_{st} \varphi(\mathbf{N}_{FIFO}(0)) \preceq_{st} \mathbf{N}_{HOL1}(0)$*, then*

$$\mathbf{N}_{HOL2}(t_i) \preceq_{st} \varphi(\mathbf{N}_{FIFO}(t_i)) \preceq_{st} \mathbf{N}_{HOL1}(t_i), \quad \forall\, t_i > 0 \quad (3)$$

Proof: We only prove the right part of inequality 3. The other part which is quite similar is omitted due to space limitation. et P (resp. Q) be one-step transition matrix of the Markov chain for $FIFO$ (resp. $HOL1$) policy. We apply proposition 1 to compare the images of these time-homogeneous Markov chains on state space ε according to $\preceq$ vector ordering.

Now consider two row vectors $P[n,*]$ and $Q[m,*]$ corresponding to the states n and m respectively in $FIFO$ and $HOL1$ system, where $\varphi(n) \preceq m$. Let event e occur with probability p_e, and trigger the transition from the state n to w in $FIFO$ system and the transition from m to z in $HOL1$ system. As stated in equation 2, $n2$ and $m2$ change in the same manner. The arrivals for high priority packets are the same and if the next packet served is not a high priority one in the $HOL1$ system (it may be either a low or high priority one in $FIFO$ system), it results from the evolution equations that $\varphi(w) \preceq z$. On the other hand, if a high priority packet is served in $HOL1$ system, it means that there is not a low priority packet (i.e., $m2 = m3$). Since $\varphi(n) \preceq m$, there are two possible cases:

1) $n3 = m3$, then there is only high priority packets in the $FIFO$ system (i.e., $n3 = n2$), and the next packet to be served is a high priority packet. So $\varphi(w) \preceq z$;

2) $n3 < m3$, then the next packet which will be served in the $FIFO$ system will be a high priority or a low priority packet. Since $n3 \leq m3 - 1$, the order will be preserved even a low priority packet is served. So $\varphi(w) \preceq z$. From the definition of an increasing set, we have the following implication

$$\varphi(w) \in \Gamma \Longrightarrow z \in \Gamma \quad \forall \Gamma \subset \epsilon$$

Therefore, if the probability p_e is summed in the vector $P[n,*]$ for a particular increasing set Γ, then it is also summed in the vector $Q[m,*]$ for the same increasing set. It follows from the definition 4 that $\varphi(P[n,*]) \preceq_{st} P[m,*]$. Since this argument is valid for all couple n, m such that $\varphi(n) \preceq m$,

$$\varphi(P[n,*]) \preceq_{st} Q[m,*]), \quad \forall\ n\ , m \mid \varphi(n) \preceq m$$

and it follows from the proposition 1 that $\varphi(\mathbf{N}_{FIFO}(t_i)) \preceq_{st} \mathbf{N}_{HOL1}(t_i)\ \forall t_i > 0$.

If the steady-state distributions of the Markov chains exist, they are also ordered in the sense $\preceq_{st}$.

Corollary 1. *Let Π_{FIFO}, Π_{HOL2} and Π_{HOL1} be the steady-state distributions of the underlying Markov chains, then*

$$\Pi_{HOL2} \preceq_{st} \varphi(\Pi_{FIFO}) \preceq_{st} \Pi_{HOL1}$$

Proposition 2. *Let L_{policy} be the steady-state loss rate for high priority packets under policy. We have the following inequalities:*

$$L_{HOL2} \leq L_{FIFO} \leq L_{HOL1}$$

Proof: For all models, the number of rejected packets in a state $(phase, nt, nh)$, is $(nh + k - \mathbb{1}_{\{service=high\}} - B)^+$, if k high priority packets arrives. Thus L_{policy} can be defined as a $\preceq$ increasing function on the distribution Π_{policy}. And the inequalities on loss rates follow from the above corollary and definition 1. □

4 Bounding HOL Policy by a Linear Model

The Markov chain for $HOL1$ policy has roughly $O(B^2)$ states and the computation complexity is still important because of the eigenvalues. So we propose to compute the loss rates by using a Markov chain of $O(B)$ states which provides an upper bound on the chain representing $HOL1$ policy and which can be computed by a direct elimination algorithm. We perform an aggregation of the states of the Markov chain modeling $HOL1$ policy to obtain a new Markov chain which is stochastically greater in $\preceq_{st}$ sense than the initial one. In the aggregation process, we try to represent explicitly the states which may have large steady-state probabilities and the states with whom they are interacting. The other states are aggregated. Clearly, the selection of these states depend upon the dynamic of the considered system, which is in general difficult to foresee. Thus the aggregation partition is defined and improved heuristically. But one must prove that the aggregated chain provides a stochastic upper bound on the initial one.

Let F be the aggregation factor which takes value in the interval: $0 \dots B$. Here we only consider two values for F depending on high and low traffic phases. Note that this restriction is for the sake of simplicity and more general functions for F can be considered. In the aggregated model, only the evolution equation of the number of high priority packets denoted as NH_{agg} is different :

$$NH_{agg}(t_{i+1}) = max\{NT(t_{i+1}) - F(phase(t_{i+1})),\ \ N4(t_{i+1})\}$$
$$\text{where} N4(t_{i+1}) = min\{B, NH(t_i) - \mathbb{1}_{\{(NT(t_i)=NH(t_i))\}}\mathbb{1}_{\{NT(t_i)>0)\}} + AH(t_{i+1}\}$$

Component $N4(t_{i+1})$ gives the evolution of high priority packets with $HOL1$ policy. Due to the operation max in the previous equation, the domain of NH_{agg} is now limited. Let $n_{agg} = (phase, nt, nh_{agg})$ be an arbitrary state of the aggregated chain, and f be the aggregation factor of this state. We must have $nh_{agg} \in \{nt - f, \dots, nt\}$. Macro states gather the states which have the same values for nt, $phase$ and values of nh_{agg} which are smaller than $nt - F$. The max

operation in the second evolution equation represents the aggregation process into the macro-state. The states where nh_{agg} is strictly larger than $nt - F$ are kept unchanged. Intuitively, the states and the transitions between states are defined by the worst case for the high priority packet number. The state space size of the aggregated chain is $\sum_{i=0}^{B}(\max\{i, F(i,0)\}+1) + \sum_{i=0}^{B}(\max\{i, F(i,1)\}+1)$.

The comparison between $HOL1$ policy and the aggregated chain can be established in the aggregated state space using the same method. We only give the theorem for the sake of concision.

Theorem 2. *If* $\phi(\mathbf{N_{HOL1}}(0)) \preceq_{st} \mathbf{N}_{agg}(0)$*, then* $\phi(\mathbf{N}_{HOL1}(t_i)) \preceq_{st} \mathbf{N}_{agg}(t_i)$*,* $\forall t_i > 0$.

5 Numerical Results

We now give some typical results for the loss rates of high priority packets. We denote by c the ratio of high priority packets. The probabilities for a burst arrival and the end of a burst are assumed to be $r^0 = 10^{-6}$, and $r^1 = 10^{-2}$. Moreover, the aggregation factors $F(0)$ and $F(1)$ are chosen to be greater than the batch size (M). In the given results, we have chosen $F(1)$ greater than $F(0)$, since loss rates are more important with heavy traffic, we want to have more precision on the evolution of the system at this phase.

In the following, let us denote by *Load* the average load of the system and by Cvi^2 the squared coefficient of variation of packet arrivals. This last parameter gives some information about the burstiness of the arrival process. For some experiments, we also give all the parameters of the arrival processes in table 1 and 2. In figure 1(a), we give the buffer sizes to guarantee high priority packet rejection rates lower than 10^{-9} versus the average total load. These rates are computed using the aggregated chain which provides upper bounds on $FIFO$ and $HOL1$ policies. The input parameters are $M = 3$, $c = 0.6$, $Cvi^2 = 4$. The *Load* varies from 0.6 to 0.9. We give two curves corresponding to different aggregation factors. The aggregation factor for light traffic is chosen to be 3 ($F(0) = 3 = M$) and the aggregation factor for heavy traffic equals 3 ($F(1) =$

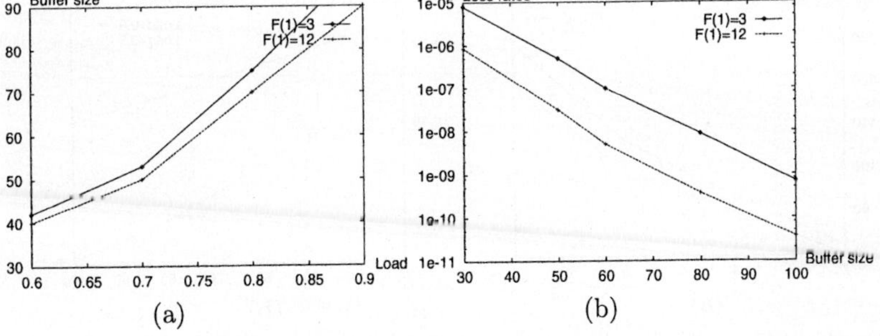

Fig. 1. High priority packets: Buffer sizes for a given QoS versus Load (a), Upper bounds on the loss rates versus buffer size (b)

$3 = M$) in the first one and 12 ($F(1) = 12 \geq M$) in the second one. In figure 1(b), we give the upper bounds on high priority packet loss rates which are computed from the aggregated chain versus buffer size. The parameters are: $r^0 = 10^{-6}$, $r^1 = 10^{-3}$, $F(0) = 3$, $M = 3$, $c = 0.6$, $Cvi^2 = 5$, $Load = 0.8$. The first curve is for $F(1) = 3$ and the second is for $F(1) = 12$. We can see from the curves the impact of the aggregation factor on the accuracy of the result. Obviously, the state space size is greater in the case $F(1) = 12$ (equal to 1174 states) than the case of $F(1) = 3$ (equal to 796 states). It results from these examples that one can improve the accuracy of the bounds by increasing the aggregation factors, but the computational complexity increases at the same time. With $F(1) = 12$,

Table 1. Packet arrival distributions for $2 \leq Cvi^2 \leq 8$

Cvi^2	ph	$p^{ph}[0]$	$p^{ph}[1]$	$p^{ph}[2]$	$p^{ph}[3]$	$p^{ph}[4]$	$p^{ph}[5]$
2	0	0.55	0	0.45	0	0	0
	1	0.74	0.06	0	0	0.1	0.1
4	0	0.7	0.1	0	0	0.2	0
	1	0.74	0.06	0	0	0.1	0.1
5	0	0.75	0	0.05	0	0.2	0
	1	0.74	0.06	0	0	0.1	0.1
7	0	0.8	0	0	0	0.1	0.1
	1	0.74	0.06	0	0	0.1	0.1
8	0	0.82	0	0	0	0	0.18
	1	0.74	0.06	0	0	0.1	0.1

Table 2. Packet arrival distributions for Load=0.5 and 0.8

$Load$	ph	$p^{ph}[0]$	$p^{ph}[1]$	$p^{ph}[2]$	$p^{ph}[3]$	$p^{ph}[4]$
0.5	0	0.825	0.05	0.025	0	0.1
	1	0.825	0.025	0	0	0.15
0.8	0	0.75	0	0.05	0.1	0.1
	1	0.75	0	0	0	0.25

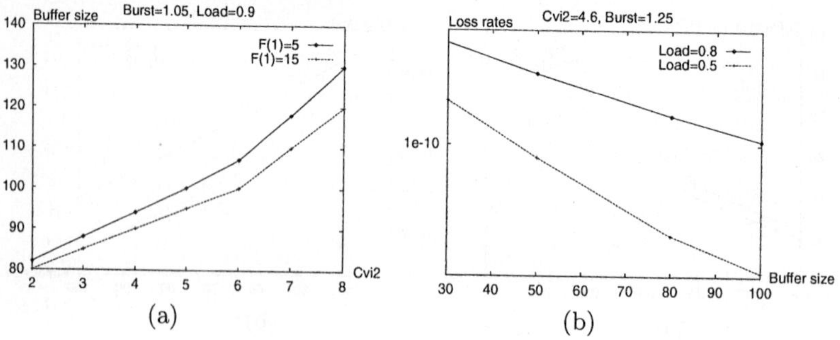

Fig. 2. High priority packets: Buffer size for a given QoS versus Cvi^2 (a), Upper bounds on the loss rates versus buffer size (b)

one can found that a FDL with 73 wavelengths provide a rejection rate smaller than 10^{-9}. If we use a smaller chain to model the system (for instance with $F(1) = 3$), this guarantee is obtained with roughly 100 wavelengths.

In figure 2(a), we give the minimal buffer sizes providing high priority packet loss rates lower than 10^{-9}, which are computed from the aggregated chain versus the squared coefficient of variation. Two curves are given with two aggregation factors at heavy load ($F(1) = 5$ and $F(1) = 15$). The other parameters are chosen as follows: $F(0) = 5$, $M = 5$, $c = 0.6$, $Load = 0.9$, $r^0 = 10^{-6}$, and $r^1 = 10^{-3}$. The arrival probabilities and the squared coefficients of variation are given in table 1. As mentioned above, Figure (2(a)) is given to show the impact of the aggregation factor versus the squared coefficient of variation. We depict in figure 2(b) the upper bounds of high priority packet rejection rate when we change the buffer size at light load (0.5) and heavy load (0.8) The parameters are chosen as follows: $Cvi^2 = 4.6$, $c = 0.6$, $F(0) = 4$, $F(1) = 8$, $M = 4$, $r^0 = 10^{-6}$, et $r^1 = 10^{-3}$ and the arrival probabilities are gathered in table 2. Due to the state space size of the $FIFO$ model, it is not possible to compare the bounds with exact results. However, one can numerically solve the $HOL1$ model and the linear bound obtained after another bounding process. The numerical results are very good because we add less constraints to bound the effects of the SBBP arrival process. Clearly, using partial order rather than a total order has several advantages: bounds are more accurate and they use less constraints to represent modulating process such as the SBBP arrivals.

References

1. Barth, D., Berthomé, P., Borrero, A., Fourneau, J.M., Laforest, C., Quessette, F., Vial, S.: Performance comparisons of Eulerian routing and deflection routing in a 2d-mesh all optical network. European Simulation Multiconference, (2001)
2. Dayar, T., Pekergin, N., Alparslan, D N.: Componentwise bounds for nearly completely decomposable Markov chains using stochastic comparison and reordering. European Journal of Operational Research **165** (2005) 810–825.
3. Doisy, M.: Comparison de Processus Markoviens. Ph-D thesis Univ. de Pau (1992)
4. Fourneau, J.M., Pekergin, N.: An algorithmic approach to stochastic bounds. Performance evaluation of complex systems: Techniques and Tools, **LNCS 2459** (2002) 64–88
5. Fourneau, J.M., Lecoz, M., Quessette, F.: Algorithms for an irreducible and lumpable strong stochastic bound. Linear Algebra and Applications **386** (2004) 167–185
6. Gravey, P., Gosselin, S., Guillemot, C., Chiaroni, D., Le Sauze, N., Jourdan, A., Dotaro, E., Barth, D., Berthomé, P., Laforest, C., Vial, S., Atmaca, T., Hébuterne, G., El Biaze, H., Laalaoua, R., Gangloff, E., Kotuliak. I.: Multiservice optical network: Main concepts and first achievements of the ROM program. Journal of Ligthwave Technology **19** (2001) 23–31
7. Massey, W.: Stochastic Ordering for Markov Processes on Partially ordered Spaces. Mathematics of operations Research, **12** (1987)
8. Stoyan, D.: Comparison Methods for Queues and Other Stochastic Models, Wiley, New York (1983)

QoS Evaluation Method in Multimedia Applications Using a Fuzzy Genetic Rule-Based System

Fabiana C. Bertoni and Sérgio D. Zorzo

Departamento de Computação (DC) - Universidade Federal de São Carlos (UFSCar),
Caixa Postal 676 - 13565-905 – São Carlos (SP) – Brasil
{fabiana, zorzo}@dc.ufscar.br

Abstract. A new method is introduced to quantify the Quality of Service (QoS) of a multimedia connection. This method uses discrete values of QoS parameters, establishing a relationship among them through the use of a Fuzzy Genetic Rule-Based System (FGRBS) to obtain a single value that expresses the QoS of the connection. This final value is classified within a predefined QoS specification standard consisting of three sets: Optimal, Acceptable and Unacceptable, resulting in a definition of the Quality of Service in a user-level language. The values obtained by the proposed method are compared with those obtained through other QoS quantification models in a multimedia connection.

1 Introduction

Multimedia applications require several levels of quality of service from the communications networks so that they can be presented satisfactorily to the user. However, the user is normally unfamiliar with specifications of low level parameters such as bandwidths and with numerical values relating to their measurement. Therefore, the system must provide a level of abstraction to enable the user to understand the quality of service the network can offer at any given moment by making a QoS Provision [1], which is the object of this study. It then behooves the user to decide whether or not to execute its application. According to refs. [2] and [3], the most relevant parameters that act decisively in multimedia applications and that were therefore analyzed in our experiments are the Network Parameters of Throughput, Delay, Jitter and Package Loss.

The literature proposes several methods to evaluate the quality of service in multimedia systems, e.g., refs. [4] and [5]. However, these methods do not give the user a reply in easily understandable language nor are they prepared for the treatment of “partial truths”, such as, for instance, classifying a service as “good, but not that good”. The use of the Fuzzy Genetic Rule-Based System will allow for these two factors. Refs. [6] and [7] develop fuzzy systems to evaluate the QoS in multimedia applications, but these systems are related to a specific application and lack the system optimization differential with the use of genetic algorithms.

The next section discusses concepts relating to a fuzzy system and its applicability in the evaluation of QoS in Multimedia Systems. Section 3 presents the experiments conducted in two case studies, a Videoconference and a Video on Demand, analyzing

P. Yolum et al.(Eds.): ISCIS 2005, LNCS 3733, pp. 254–263, 2005.

the results obtained in these experiments and comparing them with other conventional quantitative methods. Lastly, section 4 sets forth our conclusions and analyzes the approach developed in this work.

2 Evaluation of Quality of Service in Multimedia Systems

The definition of a single QoS value in a user-accessible language has become an important factor to express the quality of service the network can offer the user. Because policy rules are abstract and very close to human perception, they are difficult to map into computational rules whose very nature is absolute and exact. This difficulty lies in the fact that the definition of exact intervals of values for a variable may hinder or even invalidate a result obtained based on an analysis made in these intervals. Fuzzy Logic has the characteristic of treating semantic variables having a certain degree of vagueness. Therefore, the management policy specification rules of a Fuzzy System are based on an almost intuitive approach [6].

A Fuzzy System usually consists of the following modules: Fuzzification, Rules Base, Inference Engine, and Defuzzification, which are described below.

2.1 Fuzzification Module

The Fuzzification Module converts the system's input values (real numbers) into linguistic terms represented by given fuzzy sets. This conversion depends principally on the pertinence function, for this is the function that defines to which Fuzzy set a given value belongs and what degree of pertinence that value has in relation to the set [12].

The system's inputs are the values of the Quality of Service parameters obtained by measuring the network. After they are measured, the values of throughput, delay, jitter and package loss are transferred to the Fuzzy System, where they are converted into linguistic terms. To perform this conversion, three fuzzy sets were defined for each input variable, i.e., Unacceptable, Acceptable and Optimal. These sets are represented trapezoidally (an entire interval of maximum points can be represented) and are characterized by a pertinence function that maps the possible values of the input parameters in the interval [0,1]. The domains of the pertinence functions for each QoS parameter are defined in Table 1 in the item below, where different applications are considered.

2.2 Mapping of the QoS Parameters

To meet the user's expectations regarding a given service, it is essential that the quantified QoS parameters be transformed correctly from the end user to the transmission network. Table 1, whose definition is based on research conducted by refs. [5], [8], [9] and [4], describes the domains of the Quality of Service parameters for some applications, mapping the values directly from the User level to the Network level.

Parameters with a numerical value are mapped into a user-understandable language and vice-versa based on established policies or rules. These rules are specified according to a system command management decision.

Table 1. Mapping of the QoS Parameters – User/Network

		QUALITY		
		Unacceptable	Acceptable	Optimal
Video on demand	Delay (s)	>6	3-6	0-3
	Jitter (s)	>5	1-5	0-1
	Package Loss (%)	>3	1-3	0-1
	Throughput(Kbits/s)	0-64	64-112	>112
Videoconference	Delay (ms)	>350	150-350	0-150
	Jitter (ms)	>250	100-250	0-100
	Package Loss (%)	>2	1-2	0-1
	Throughput(Kbits/s)	0-64	64-112	>112

2.3 Rules Base

The rules base is where all the knowledge about the domain of the problem in question is stored. The rules defined for the system are presented in the following format, whose variables are only the categories of Optimal, Acceptable and Unacceptable:

IF (Throughput is Acceptable) AND (Delay is Optimal) AND (Jitter is Optimal) AND (Package Loss is Optimal) THEN (QoS is Optimal)

The initial rules bases of the fuzzy system were built with the help of a specialist in computer network performance analysis and then validated through modeling by experimentation, using the NistNet network emulator [10]. Each rule in the rules bases was emulated individually and the result observed and compared against what had been defined by the specialist, in order to validate and adjust the initial rules bases. These initial knowledge bases, albeit validated, are considered large because of the number of rules they contain. The number of rules in a rules base is defined by increasing the number of fuzzy sets to equal the number of input variables in the system. Thus, considering 3 fuzzy sets (Optimal, Acceptable and Unacceptable) and 4 input variables (throughput, delay, jitter and package loss), the number of rules is equal to 81. These 81 rules represent all the possible combinations of the system's input variables with the fuzzy sets defined here. However, some of the rules created do not represent situations that actually occur in the real world.

Therefore, the greater the number of fuzzy sets and input variables the greater the number of rules. This increases the fuzzy system's processing complexity and time exponentially due to the increase in the problem's search space. We therefore deemed it necessary to develop a mechanism that would reduce the number of rules in the rules bases and exclude non-representative rules, thereby allowing for future alterations in the initially proposed system through the insertion of new parameters for QoS analysis and of new fuzzy sets. To this end, we used the Genetic Algorithm methodology.

Selection of Fuzzy Rules by Genetic Algorithms

Presented below are the components and parameters of the Genetic Algorithm employed here. To this end, one begins with a chromosomal representation of the individuals of the population. Each individual is a possible solution for the problem. The algorithm begins by randomly developing the first population. From this point on, each individual's relative fitness for the system is calculated. Based on this calculation, the elements that will belong to the next generation are selected (by election based on probabilistic criteria). To complete the population, the selected parents are reproduced through the implementation of genetic operators such as Crossing and Mutation. Each genetic operator has a proper occurrence rate expressed as a biological metaphor. The process is repeated until a specified stop condition is met.

Codification: In this stage, the chromosomes $C_i=(c_i1,c_{i2},...c_{im})$ are encoded into sequences of binary digits and have a fixed size 'm', with 'm' representing the number of rules obtained. Each c_{ij} gene (a binary digit) is associated with a rule. If $c_{ij}=1$, the rule corresponding to this gene will be part of the selected rules base; otherwise, the rule will not be part of the base.

In the experiments conducted here, 'm' was given the value of 81, which represents the number of rules of each of the rules bases.

Population Size: The size of the population used here was 200 individuals, which allowed for a better coverage of the search space and proved efficient in our experiment.

Initial Population: The initial population is generated by introducing a chromosome that represents all the rules obtained previously, i.e., all the genes of the chromosome are given the value of 1. The remaining chromosomes are generated randomly.

Number of Generations: One hundred generations was established here as the stop criterion, which sufficed to achieve an optimized rules base, since a larger number of generations resulted in no variation in the choice of the fittest individual starting from the one hundredth generation.

Fitness Function: The fitness function evaluates each chromosome, i.e., each subset of candidate rules, based on two criteria: the number of examples it classifies correctly, and the number of rules of this subset, i.e., the number of genes of value 1 in this chromosome. The individual showing the highest value of correct classification of examples with the lowest number of rules will have the highest fitness value. Thus, the fitness function can be expressed by:

$$\text{Fitness value}(C_i) = \text{NEC}(C_i) - \text{QTDR}(C_i) \quad (1)$$

where $\text{NEC}(C_i)$ represents the number of examples classified correctly by the subset of rules represented in chromosome i and $\text{QTDR}(C_i)$ indicates the number of rules existing in the subset represented by chromosome i.

To obtain the examples to be classified, which are required to calculate the fitness value, two datasets had to be built, one for each application. These datasets were generated from the initial rules base, each set consisting of 110 examples (samples) with five variables, four of them input variables (quality of service parameters) and the fifth an output variable (value resulting from the quality of service).

Intermediate Population: Given a population in which each individual has received a fitness value, there are several methods to select the individuals upon whom the genetic algorithms of crossing and mutation will be applied. The selected individuals will make up a population called an intermediate population.

The selection method used here to separate the intermediate population was the Roulette method [11] and the Crossing and Mutation rates were defined, respectively, at 70% and 1%, as recommended in the literature [11]. An Elitism percentage [11] of 10% was also used.

After applying the Genetic Algorithm, the rules base built for the Videoconference application was reduced by about 61%, dropping from 81 to 31 rules. The base for the Video on Demand application was simplified by about 86%, ending up with only 11 rules as opposed to the initial 81.

2.4 Inference Engine

Mamdani's model was used here because its response can be a scale value and a linguistic term. The inference traditionally employed by Mamdani's model is called Max-Min Inference [12]. In this model, the inference engine receives fuzzy values from the fuzzification module, processing the rules in the rules base and aggregating the conclusions inferred from each rule. This aggregation produces a fuzzy set of outputs to the defuzzification module.

2.5 Defuzzification Module

The Defuzzification Module transforms qualitative information into quantitative information in order to obtain a non-fuzzy final output. The method used for the defuzzification was the Center of Mass Method [12], which calculates the abscissa of the mass center point corresponding to a given fuzzy set of outputs originating from a processed Rules Base, using it as the output scale value. The method's analytical implementation expression is given below:

$$Z = \frac{\sum_{i=0}^{m} \mu c(Zi) * Zi}{\sum_{i=0}^{m} \mu c(Zi)} \qquad (2)$$

In this expression, Z is the defuzzification value, 'm' is the number of output quantification intervals, Zi is the value of the output variable for the quantification interval 'i', and 'μC (Zi)' is its degree of pertinence. This defuzzified value represents the "best compromise" among the μC (Zi) values obtained [13].

3 Experiments and Results

To test and validate the QoS evaluation method developed here, various experiments were conducted using two classes of applications: Videoconference and Video on Demand.

3.1 Case Study 1: Videoconference

A videoconference is an image and voice transmission in real time between physically separate locations, using video cameras, microphones, video monitors and loudspeakers. In the application tested here, three clients connected to an ISP (Internet Service Provider) all have the same SLA (Service Level Agreements) with the ISP.

The measurements of the QoS parameters were collected using a Quality of Service Monitor, called an MQM – Multicast Quality Monitor [2], which introduces different ways of measuring parameters in a multicast network. Table 2 depicts the results of the measurements for the videoconference application.

Table 2. Videoconference – Parameter measurement results

Parameters	A-B Connection	A-C Connection
Throughput	27Mbps	1.2Mbps
Delay	20ms	150ms
Jitter	10ms	80ms
Package Loss	5%	0.1%

3.2 Case Study 2: Video on Demand

A video on demand service involves the storage of multimedia data such as images, audio and video at servers, with transmission in real time.

In the application under analysis, a video server and two clients connected to it, C1 and C2, request remote video transmissions.

Table 3 shows the results of the video on demand application.

Table 3. Video on Demand – Parameter measurement results

Parameters	C1-Server Connection	C2-Server Connection
Throughput	13Mbps	900Kbps
Delay	5s	7s
Jitter	0.6s	4s
Package Loss	2.5%	5%

3.3 Results

Considering the intervals of values that define the QoS levels (Table 1), and using the discrete values of the QoS parameters collected (Tables 2 and 3), a relationship can be established between them, using conventional numerical metrics or the methodologies of Computational Intelligence described earlier herein to obtain a single value that expresses the connection's QoS level as a whole. The metrics are differentiated, from the method used for the calculation to the format of the result obtained.

The FGRBS produced two results for each application (Tables 4 and 5), using first the initial rules base and then the rules base optimized with the application of the genetic algorithm.

Table 4. Videoconference – QoS evaluation results using a FGRBS

	A-B Connection		A-C Connection	
	Defuzzified Value	**Classification**	**Defuzzified Value**	**Classification**
Initial Rules Base	10	100% Unacceptable	90	60% Optimal
Optimized Rules Base	10	100% Unacceptable	70	40% Acceptable

In connection A-B, the results were the same for both the initial rules base and the optimized base, i.e., the QoS was found to be totally unacceptable for the videoconference application. This was expected, since the package loss, the most important parameter in this type of application, was extremely unacceptable (in the range of 5%). Moreover, the defuzzified value '10' was totally inserted into the Unacceptable fuzzy output set.

In connection A-C, the results of the initial rules base and the optimized rules based complemented each other. Another look at the Table 2, which presents the parameters measured for the videoconference application, indicates that only the delay parameter has a value between optimal and acceptable. The remaining parameters are classified as optimal. Hence, one could state that the QoS is more optimal than acceptable, as demonstrated by the two classifications. When one affirms that the QoS is 60% optimal, with a defuzzified value of 90, it is understood that the remaining ≈40% lies within a range considered acceptable and is not affected by the Unacceptable fuzzy output set.

Table 5. Video on Demand – QoS evaluation results using a FGRBS

	C1-Server Connection		C2-Server Connection	
	Defuzzified Value	**Classification**	**Defuzzified Value**	**Classification**
Initial Rules Base	≅24.6	50% Acceptable	10	90% Unacceptable
Optimized Rules Base	≅41.6	50% Acceptable	10	90% Unacceptable

An analysis of the C1-Server connection in the video on demand application reveals that the two rules bases also show the same QoS classification. The defuzzified value of approximately 41.6 represents the best QoS situation, for the values of the measurements of the most important parameters for this type of application, i.e., delay and package loss, lie within the acceptable range, although they are somewhat influenced by the Unacceptable fuzzy output set. Therefore, the QoS can be considered acceptable, albeit with a tendency toward the unacceptable.

The QoS in the C2-Server connection is considered completely unacceptable for the two rules bases. This classification was expected, for the delay and the package loss – the most important parameters in this type of application – displayed unacceptable values. Moreover, the defuzzified value of '10' lies totally within the Unacceptable fuzzy output set.

Using the conventional numerical metrics developed by refs. [4] and [5] also produces results. According to ref. [4], a connection's end-to-end QoS of depends on the aggregation of all the parameters involved in the process. Thus, the analysis of the QoS can be exemplified as shown below:

Videoconference – A-B Connection

$\mathbf{M_{Throughput}}$ = 1 (measured value and better than optimal);
$\mathbf{M_{Delay}}$ = 1 (measured value and better than optimal);
$\mathbf{m_{Jitter}}$ = 1 (measured value and better than optimal);
$\mathbf{m_{Package\ Loss}}$ = 0 (measured value and worse than the maximum tolerable);
$\mathbf{c_{AB}}$ = 1*1*1*0 = 0; which means the connection from A to B cannot be used.
$\mathbf{c_{AC}}$ = 1*1*1*1 = 1; which means the connection from A to C can be used for the service required with a guaranteed 100% QoS.
When $\mathbf{c_{AB}}$ = 1*1*1*0.5 = 0.5; (the measured values range from the maximum acceptable to the optimal): the QoS can be only partially guaranteed.

In the opinion of ref. [5], the state of the network can be defined based on its losses, i.e., Nonloaded (up to 2%), Loaded (from 2% to 4%) and Overloaded (over 4%). If the network is not loaded, the connection can be provided with a guaranteed 100% QoS; if it is loaded, there is an approximately 50% guarantee of QoS, and if it is overloaded, no QoS can be offered.

The results obtained through the numerical metrics can therefore be summarized in Tables 6 and 7, below.

Table 6. Videoconference

	A-B Connection Classification	A-C Connection Classification
DRESSLER	0	1
LUNARDI and DOTTI	0% (Overloaded)	100% (Nonloaded)

Table 7. Video on Demand

	C1-Server Connection Classification	C2-Server Connection Classification
DRESSLER	0.25	0
LUNARDI and DOTTI	≅50% (Loaded)	0 (Overloaded)

3.4 Analysis of the Results

The numerical metric developed by ref. [4] presents a final numerical value of QoS resulting from an intersection of the parameters' individual values. This value may not mean anything to a given type of user, so it should be submitted to an interpreter who defines the QoS to make it comprehensible to all users or maps it into a framework responsible for the dynamic management of the QoS. In addition, if a single parameter shows a value considered "poor", the metric simply excludes the possibility of transmission through that connection, even if the remaining parameters lie within an acceptable range. The reason for this is that no form of weighing the measured values of the parameters was defined, so they all possess the same degree of importance, which is not the case. As mentioned earlier, one of the most important factors, albeit not the only one to merit attention, is package loss.

The metric proposed by ref. [5] attempts to classify the QoS value obtained according to a linguistic term, but it is still highly technical and far from understandable for many users. Another disadvantage is that it considers only one network parameter as a form of evaluating the QoS of an entire connection, disregarding other parameters that affect the quality of the connection, albeit to a lesser extent.

These disadvantages have motivated many researchers to seek alternative non-analytical modeling techniques and to develop control systems, since the precision of a purely numerical system does not always classify a problem correctly [14].

Because they are tolerant of imprecision, uncertainty and partial truths, Fuzzy Logic and Genetic Algorithms offer an alternative for solving problems that currently cannot be solved by traditional methods or whose solutions do not offer good results, whether in terms of values or in the way they are presented, as in the case of the numerical metrics discussed here. The model presented here provides a flexible specification of the needs of an application, which is desirable, without losing performance, configurability and generality [15].

4 Conclusions

Several metrics have been developed with the purpose of analyzing the current availability of quality of service (end-to-end) in a network. This paper presented a method to evaluate the QoS in a multimedia connection using a Fuzzy Genetic Rule-Based System, comparing its results with methods of conventional quantitative models in two case studies involving applications with different characteristics: a multimedia Videoconference and a Video on Demand application.

A comparison of the results obtained with the use of the methods presented in combination with the Fuzzy Genetic System reveals very similar final values describing the QoS of the connection. This finding indicates that a Fuzzy Genetic Rule-Based System can be used to analyze the quality of service in a network connection and is extendable to any type of multimedia application. This would require only an alteration of the rules base and the pertinence functions, and would offer the advantage of providing a response with a higher degree of specificity, returning a final value of quality of service in a language understandable to every user, interpreting the system's numerical output value by associating it to a semantic term. If the user so desires, he/she can also have access to the numerical value, which can easily be supplied. The genetic-fuzzy combination is widely accepted in scientific circles, for it adheres to the principle of balancing the advantages of computational intelligence, with different methodologies working hand-in-hand and potentiating the usefulness and applicability of the resulting systems.

References

1. Kamienski, C. A., Sadok, D.: Qualidade de Serviço na Internet. Mini-curso Sociedade Brasileira de Redes de Computadores - Belo Horizonte, Minas Gerais - Brasil (2000).
2. Dressler, F.: Monitoring of Multicast Networks for Time-Synchronous Communication. Ph.D. Thesis – Computer Science Department, Erlangen-Nuremberg University (2003) http://bsd.rrze.uni-erlangen.de/~fd/publications/dissertation.pdf.
3. Dobson, G.: Quality of Service: a Service-Centric Perspective. Computing Department, Lancaster University (2004). http://www.lancs.ac.uk/ug/dobsong /qos.htm
4. Dressler, F.: A Metric for Numerical Evaluation of the QoS of an Internet Connection. ITC18 - 18th International Teletraffic Congress, Vol.5b, Berlin Germany, (2003) 1221-1230.
5. Lunardi, S., Dotti, F.: Uma Camada de Adaptação à Qualidade de Serviço na Internet para Aplicações Multimídia. 19th Simpósio Brasileiro de Redes de Computadores, Vol.1, Florianópolis, SC, Brasil (2001) 19-32.
6. Fernandez, M., Pedroza, A. C.; Rezende, J.: Implementação de Políticas de Gerenciamento através de Lógica Fuzzy visando melhoria da Qualidade de Serviço. Revista da Sociedade Brasileira de Telecomunicações, Vol.18, no.2 (2003) 171-185.
7. Koliver, C., Farines, J.; Nahrstedt, K.: QoS Adaptation Based on Fuzzy Theory. In Soft Computing for Communications, Springer-Verlag, Berlin Heidelberg New York (2004) 245-267.
8. ITU: ITU-T Study Group 12 - Workshop on QoS and user-perceived transmission quality in evolving networks. ITU Telecommunication Standardization Sector (2001).
9. Sharda, N.: Multimedia: Fundamentals and Design Principles. Computer Science and Multimedia School of Computer Science and Mathematics – Notes. Victoria University, Australia (2003).
10. Carson, M.; Santay, D.: NIST Net – A Linux-based Network Emulation Tool. ACM SIGCOMM Computer Communications Review, Vol.33, July, (2003) 111-126.
11. Mitchell, M.: An Introduction to Genetic Algorithms. The MIT Press (1996).
12. Zimmermann, H. J.: Fuzzy Set Theory and its Applications. 4th Edition. Kluwer Academic Publishers (2001).
13. Constantin, V. A.: Fuzzy Logic and Applications Explained. 1st Edition. Prentice Hall Inc, (1995).
14. Sekercioglu, Y., Ptisillides, A., Vasilakos, A.: Computational intelligence in management of ATM networks: A survey of current state of research. Soft Computing Journal, Vol.5, no.4, August, (2001) 257-263.
15. Nahrstedt, K., Li, B.: A Control-Based Middleware Framework for Quality of Service Adaptations. IEEE Journal on Selected Areas in Communications, Vol. 17, no.9, September (2000) 1632-1650.

Impact of Setup Message Processing and Optical Switch Configuration Times on the Performance of IP over Optical Burst Switching Networks

Joel J.P.C. Rodrigues[1], Mário M. Freire[1], and Pascal Lorenz[2]

[1] Department of Informatics, University of Beira Interior, Rua Marquês d'Ávila e Bolama, 6201-001 Covilhã, Portugal
{joel, mario}@di.ubi.pt
[2] IUT, University of Haute Alsace, 34, rue du Grillenbreit, 68008 Colmar, France
lorenz@ieee.org

Abstract. This paper discusses the influence of setup message processing time and optical switch configuration time on the performance of IP over optical burst switched mesh networks using one-way resource reservation protocols. It is shown that the network performance is almost independent of the optical switch configuration time for values smaller than 0.1ms. It is shown that setup message processing time does not have a significant impact on the network performance and it is shown that the five resource reservation protocols under study have a similar performance in both ring and mesh networks.

1 Introduction

In order to provide optical switching for next-generation Internet in a flexible and feasible way, a new switching paradigm called optical burst switching (OBS) [1]-[6] was proposed, which is an alternative to optical packet switching (OPS) and wavelength routing (WR). OBS combines the best of OPS and WR, and it is a technical compromise between both OPS and WR, since it does not require optical buffering or packet-level processing and is more efficient than wavelength routing if the traffic volume does not require a full wavelength channel.

In OBS networks, IP (Internet Protocol) packets are assembled into very large size packets called data bursts. These bursts are transmitted after a burst header packet, with a delay of some offset time. Each burst header packet contains routing and scheduling information and is processed at the electronic level, before the arrival of the corresponding data burst. The burst offset is the interval of time, at the source node, between the transmission of the first bit of the setup message and the transmission of the first bit of the data burst.

According to the way of reservation, resource reservation protocols may be classified into two classes: one-way reservation and two-way reservation. In the first class, a burst is sent shortly after the setup message, and the source node does not wait for the acknowledgement sent by the destination node. Therefore, the size of the offset is between transmission time of the setup message and the round-trip delay of the setup message. Different optical burst switching mechanisms may choose different offset values in this range. Tell And Go (TAG) [7], just-in-time (JIT) [3],

P. Yolum et al.(Eds.): ISCIS 2005, LNCS 3733, pp. 264 – 273, 2005.

JumpStart [4]-[6], JIT$^+$ [8], just-enough-time (JET) [1] and Horizon [2] are examples of one-way resource reservation protocols.

In the TAG protocol, a source node sends a control packet and immediately after sends a burst. At each intermediate node, the data burst has to go through with an input delay equal to the setup message processing time. If a channel cannot be reserved on a link, along the ingress-egress path, the node preceding the blocked channel discards the burst. To release the connection, a "tear-down" control signal or packet is sent [7, 9]. In this protocol a burst may need to be delayed (buffered) at each node, while waits for the processing of setup message and the configuration of the optical cross-connect (OXC) switch fabric. TAG is practical only if the switch processing time of the setup message and the optical switch configuration time are very short [10].

The offset in two-way reservation class is the time required to receive an acknowledgement from the destination. The major drawback of this class is the long offset time, which causes the long data delay. Examples of resource reservation protocols using this class include the Tell And Wait (TAW) protocol [7] and the Wavelength Routed OBS network (WR-OBS) proposed in [11]. Due to the impairments of two-way reservation class and the critical limitation of TAG, the study is focused on one-way reservation schemes, being considered the following resource reservation protocols: JIT, JumpStart, JIT$^+$, JET, and Horizon.

A major concern in OBS networks is the contention and burst loss. The two main sources of burst loss are related with the contention on the outgoing data burst channels and on the outgoing control channel. In this paper, we consider bufferless networks and we concentrate on the loss of data bursts in OBS networks.

The reminder of this paper is organized as follows. In section 2, we present an overview of one-way resource reservation protocols considered along this study. In section 3, we briefly describe the model of the OBS network under study, and in section 4 we discuss performance implications of the setup message processing time and optical switch configuration time on the performance of optical burst switched mesh networks. Main conclusions are presented in section 5.

2 One-Way Resource Reservation Protocol

This section provides an overview of one-way resource reservation protocols for OBS networks. This kind of protocols may be classified, regarding the way in which output channels (wavelengths) are reserved for bursts, as immediate and delayed reservation. JIT and JIT$^+$ are examples of immediate channel reservation, while JET and Horizon are examples of delayed reservation schemes. The JumpStart signaling protocol may be implemented using either immediate or delayed reservation.

Just-in-Time (JIT) resource reservation protocol was proposed by Wei and McFarland [3]. Under JIT, an output channel is reserved for a burst immediately after the arrival of the corresponding setup message. If a channel cannot be reserved immediately, then the setup message is rejected and the corresponding burst is lost. JIT protocol is an example of one-way resource reservation protocols with immediate resources reservation. JIT protocol uses explicit releases to set free the switch fabric resources. This message is sent either by the source node or the destination node, to tear down all OXCs along the path on an existing connection trail. Whenever any network element detects a setup failure, it sends a release message to all network elements along the path to the source node.

JumpStart [4]-[6] is a joint project supported by Advanced Research and Development Agency (ARDA) developed by the North Carolina State University (NCSU) and MCNC Research and Development Institute. The goal of JumpStart project is the definition of a signaling protocol and associated architecture for a WDM burst-switching network. Under JumpStart [4], a source edge OBS node first sends a setup message to its ingress OBS core node with information related to the burst transmission, including the source and destination addresses. If the ingress core node can switch the burst, it returns a *setup Ack* message to the edge node. Moreover, it forwards the setup message to the next node. Otherwise, the ingress core node refuses the setup message and returns a reject message to the edge node and the corresponding burst is dropped. In this case, the edge node enters in an idle period waiting for another burst. When a new burst arrives, the edge node repeats the process.

Horizon protocol was proposed by Turner in Terabit Burst Switching [2]. Horizon is considered a resource reservation protocol in the sense that it performs a delayed reservation, as mentioned in [4]-[5], [8]. This resource reservation protocol introduces the concept of Time Horizon for a given channel and it is called Horizon because every data channel has a time horizon during which it is reserved. Time horizon is defined as the earliest time to which there is no prevision to use the channel (wavelength). This concept is used in other protocols with one-way resource reservation schemes such as JET and JIT^+ that are considered in this section. In Horizon, an output channel is reserved for a burst only if the arrival of the burst happens after the time horizon for that channel; if upon the arrival of the setup message, the time horizon for that channel is later than the predicted arrival time of the first bit of the burst, then, the setup message is rejected and the corresponding burst is lost.

Just-Enough-Time (JET) resource reservation protocol was proposed in [1]. Under JET, an output channel is reserved for a burst only if the arrival of the burst (1) happens after the time horizon defined for that channel, or (2) coincides with an idle state (Void) for that channel, and the end of the burst (plus the T_{OXC}) is sooner than the end of the idle interval; if, when the Setup message arrives, it is determined that none of these conditions are met for any channel, then the setup message is rejected and the corresponding burst is lost. JET is the best-known resource reservation protocol having a delayed reservation scheme with void filling (idle state), which uses information (from the setup message) to predict the start and the end of the burst. The authors of JET made analytical and simulation studies which confirmed the good effects of delayed reservation on burst loss probability in an OBS network.

The most recently proposed resource reservation protocol is JIT^+ [8]. It was defined as an improvement of JIT and it combines JIT simplicity with the utilization of the time horizon used by delayed resource reservation protocols, such as Horizon or JET. JIT^+ is a modified version of JIT protocol, which adds limited burst scheduling (for a maximum of two bursts per channel). Under JIT^+, an output channel is reserved for a burst only if (i) the arrival time of the burst is later than the time horizon of that data channel and (ii) the data channel has at most one other reservation.

3 Network Model

In this study, we consider OBS networks with the following mesh topologies: chordal rings with nodal degrees of 3 and 4, mesh-torus with 16 and 20 nodes, the NSFNET with 14-node and 21 links [12], the NSFNET with 16 nodes and 25 links [13], the ARPANET with 20 nodes and 32 links [12], [14], and the European Optical Network (EON) with 19 nodes and 37 links [15]. For comparison purposes bi-directional ring topologies are also considered. These topologies have the following nodal degree: ring: 2.0; degree-three chordal ring: 3.0; degree-four chordal ring: 4.0; degree-five chordal ring: 5.0; degree-six chordal ring: 6.0; mesh-torus: 4.0; NSFNET with 14-node and 21 links: 3.0; the NSFNET with 16 nodes and 25 links: 3.125; the ARPANET with 20 nodes and 32 links: 3.2; and the EON: 3.89.

Chordal rings are a well-known family of regular degree three topologies proposed by Arden and Lee in early eighties for interconnection of multi-computer systems [16]. A chordal ring is basically a bi-directional ring network, in which each node has an additional bi-directional link, called a chord. The number of nodes in a chordal ring is assumed to be even, and nodes are indexed as 0, 1, 2, ..., N-1 around the N-node ring. It is also assumed that each odd-numbered node i (i=1, 3, ..., N-1) is connected to a node $(i+w) \bmod N$, where w is the chord length, which is assumed to be positive odd. For a given number of nodes there is an optimal chord length that leads to the smallest network diameter. The network diameter is the largest among all of the shortest path lengths between all pairs of nodes, being the length of a path determined by the number of hops. In each node of a chordal ring, we have a link to the previous node, a link to the next node and a chord. Here, we assume that the links to the previous and to the next nodes are replaced by chords. Thus, each node has three chords, instead of one. Let w_1, w_2, and w_3 be the corresponding chord lengths, and N the number of nodes. We represented a general degree three topology by D3T(w_1, w_2, w_3). We assumed that each odd-numbered node i (i=1, 3, ..., N-1) is connected to the nodes $(i+w_1) \bmod N$, $(i+w_2) \bmod N$, and $(i+w_3) \bmod N$, where the chord lengths, w_1, w_2, and w_3 are assumed to be positive odd, with $w_1 \leq N-1$, $w_2 \leq N-1$, and $w_3 \leq N-1$, and $w_i \neq w_j, \forall_{i \neq j \wedge 1 \leq i,j \leq 3}$. In this notation, a chordal ring with chord length w is simply represented by D3T(1,N-1,w_3).

Now, we introduce a general topology for a given nodal degree. We assume that instead of a topology with nodal degree of 3, we have a topology with a nodal degree of n, where n is a positive integer, and instead of having 3 chords we have n chords. We also assume that each odd-numbered node i (i=1,3,...,N-1) is connected to the nodes $(i+w_1) \bmod N$, $(i+w_2) \bmod N$, ..., $(i+w_n) \bmod N$, where the chord lengths, $w_1, w_2, \ldots w_n$ are assumed to be positive odd, with $w_1 \leq N-1$, $w_2 \leq N-1$, ..., $w_n \leq N-1$, and $w_i \neq w_j, \forall_{i \neq j \wedge 1 \leq i,j \leq n}$. Now, we introduce a new notation: a general degree n topology is represented by DnT(w_1, w_2,...,w_n). In this new notation, a chordal ring family with a chord length of w_3 is represented by D3T(1,N-1,w_3) and a bi-directional ring is represented by D2T(1,N-1).

We assume that each node of the OBS network supports F+1 wavelength channels per unidirectional link in each direction. One wavelength is used for signaling (carries setup messages) and the other F wavelengths carry data bursts. Each OBS node consists of two main components [8]: i) a signaling engine, which implements the OBS resource reservation protocol and related forwarding and control functions; and ii) an optical cross-connect (OXC), which performs the switching of bursts from input to output. It is assumed that each OXC consists of non-blocking space-division switch fabric, with full conversion capability, but without optical buffers. It is assumed that each OBS node requires [8]: i) an amount of time, T_{OXC}, to configure the switch fabric of the OXC in order to set up a connection from an input port to an output port, and requires ii) an amount of time, $T_{setup}(X)$ to process the setup message for the resource reservation protocol X, where X can be JIT, JET, and horizon. It is also considered the offset value of a burst under reservation scheme X, $T_{offset}(X)$, which depends, among other factors, on the resource reservation protocol, the number of nodes the burst has already traversed, and if the offset value is used for service differentiation. As in [8], in this study it is assumed the mean burst size, $1/\mu$, is equal to 50 ms (equal to $5T_{OXC}$), and the burst arrival rate λ is such that $\lambda/\mu=32$ or $\lambda/\mu=44.8$.

4 Performance Assessment

This section presents a study of the effect of the setup message processing time and the optical cross-connect (OXC) configuration time on the performance of OBS networks with ring, degree-three and degree-four chordal ring topologies for JIT, JumpStart, JIT$^+$, JET, and Horizon protocols. The topology with smallest diameter selected for degree-four chordal rings is D4T(1,19,3,9). Details about the simulator used to produce simulation results can be found in [17].

Figure 1 plots the burst loss probability as function of OXC configuration time in the last hop of D2T(1,19) and D3T(1,19,7) for the five protocols under study, with $F=64$ and $\lambda/\mu=32$. In this figure a fixed value for T_{Setup} time is assumed, which is the value defined for JIT, JumpStart, and JIT$^+$ and estimated for JET and Horizon for currently available technology [8]. T_{OXC} is assumed to range from the value estimated for a near future scenario (T_{OXC}=20µs) up to ten times the value defined for currently available technology, i.e. T_{OXC}=10*10ms=100ms. As may be seen in this figure, chordal rings clearly have better performance than rings for $T_{OXC}\leq$50ms. It may also be observed that for $T_{OXC}\leq$1ms, the performance of the chordal ring is independent of the change of the T_{OXC}, which means that a reduction of the values of T_{OXC} to ones smaller than 1ms does not improve the network performance. Moreover, it may also be observed that the relative performance of the five resource reservation protocols is similar, being JIT and JIT$^+$ slightly better than the other ones.

Figure 2 confirms results found in Figure 1. Figure 2 illustrates the burst loss probability as function of the setup message processing time (T_{Setup}) in the last hop of D2T(1,19) and D3T(1,19,7) for the five protocols under study, with $F=64$ and $\lambda/\mu=32$. Two scenarios are considered regarding T_{OXC}: it assumes the value for the

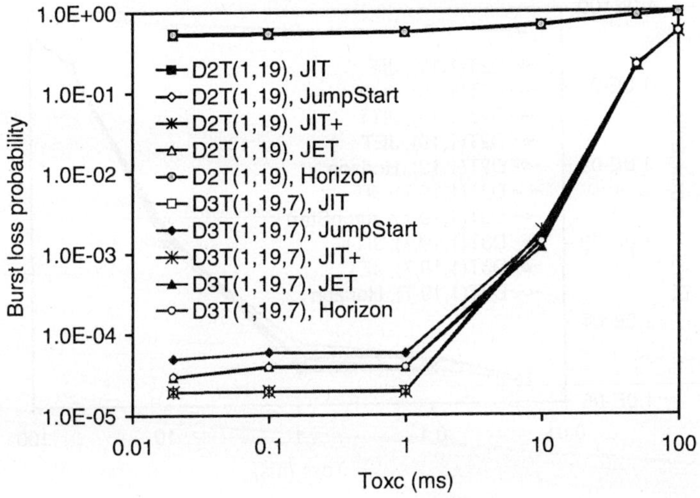

Fig. 1. Burst loss probability as function of OXC configuration time in the last hop of D2T(1,19) and D3T(1,19,7) for JIT, JumpStart, JIT$^+$, JET, and Horizon; F=64; λ/μ=32; T_{Setup}(JIT)=T_{Setup}(JumpStart)=T_{Setup}(JIT$^+$)=12.5μs; T_{Setup}(JET)=50μs; T_{Setup}(Horizon)=25μs.

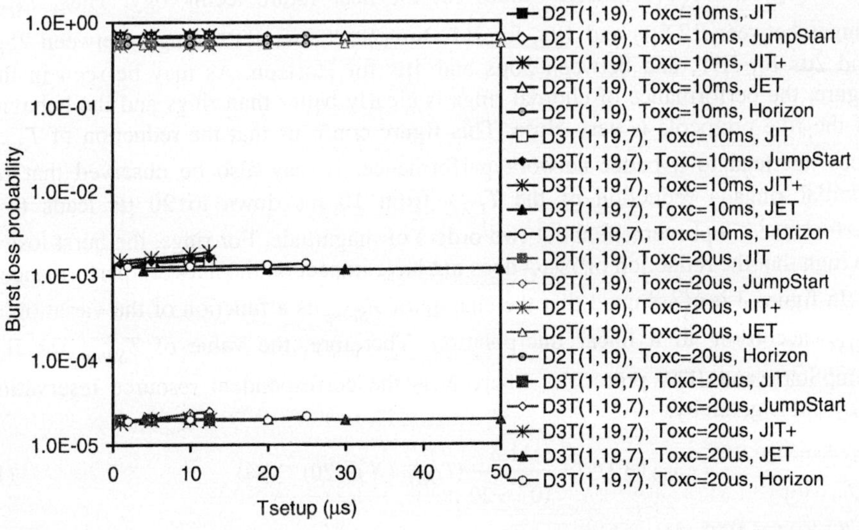

Fig. 2. Burst loss probability as function of Setup processing time in the last hop of D2T(1,19) and D3T(1,19,7) for JIT, JumpStart, JIT$^+$, JET, and Horizon; F=64; λ/μ=32

currently available technology (T_{OXC}=10ms) or an estimated value for a near future scenario (T_{OXC}=20μs). For each curve of figure 2, T_{OXC} is assumed to have a fix value while T_{Setup} ranges between the values considered for the current available

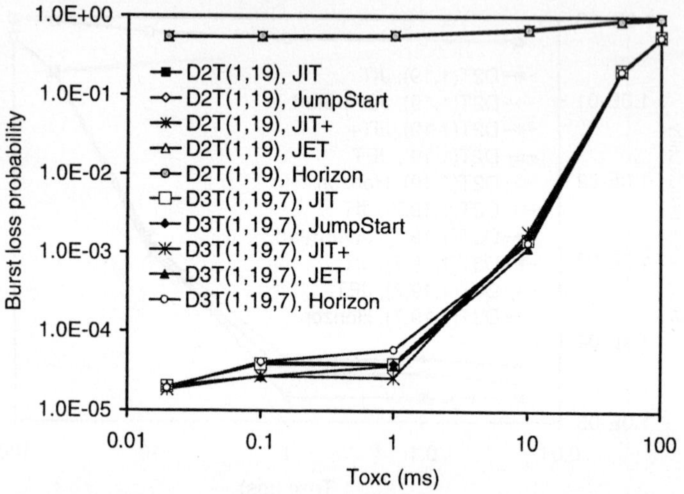

Fig. 3. Burst loss probability as function of OXC configuration time in the last hop of D2T(1,19) and D3T(1,19,7) for JIT, JumpStart, JIT$^+$, JET, and Horizon; F=64; λ/μ=32; with varied T_{Setup} according to (1), (2), and (3) for each resource reservation protocol

technology and the estimated values for the near future technology. Thus, T_{Setup} ranges between 12.5μs and 1μs, for JIT, JumpStart, and JIT$^+$, ranges between 25μs and 2μs for JET, and between 50μs and 4μs for Horizon. As may be seen in this figure, the performance of chordal rings is clearly better than rings and the behavior of the five protocols is very close. This figure confirms that the reduction of T_{Setup} does not lead to a better network performance. It may also be observed that for chordal rings a reduction of the T_{OXC} from 10 ms down to 20 μs leads to a performance improvement about two orders of magnitude. For rings, the burst loss is so high that the reduction of T_{OXC} does not have impact on the network performance.

In figure 3 it is assumed that the change of T_{Setup} is a function of the variation of T_{OXC} according to a linear interpolation. Therefore, the value of T_{Setup} for JIT, JumpStart, and JIT$^+$ protocols, where X is the correspondent resource reservation protocol is given by:

$$T_{Setup}(X) = 1 + \frac{11.5}{10^4 - 20}(T_{OXC}(X) - 20) \quad (\mu s) \tag{1}$$

T_{Setup} for JET protocol is given by:

$$T_{Setup}(JET) = 4 + \frac{46}{10^4 - 20}(T_{OXC}(JET) - 20) \quad (\mu s) \tag{2}$$

For Horizon signaling protocol, T_{Setup} is given by:

$$T_{Setup}(Horizon) = 2 + \frac{23}{10^4 - 20}(T_{OXC}(Horizon) - 20) \quad (\mu s) \tag{3}$$

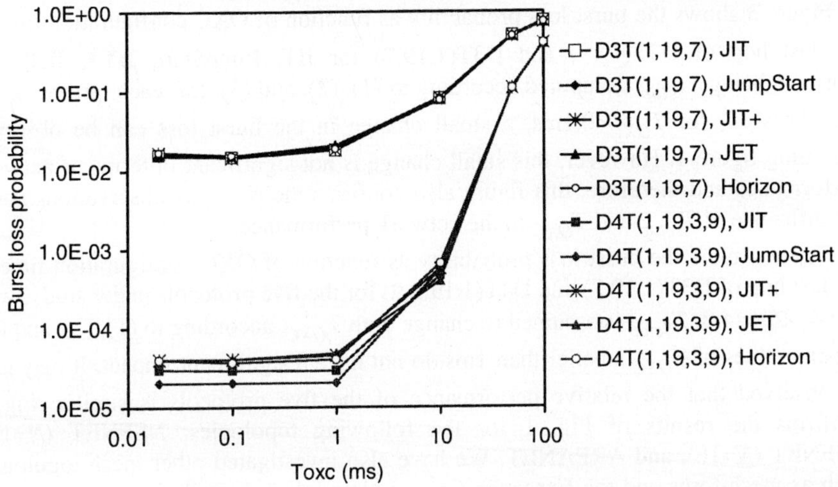

Fig. 4. Burst loss probability as function of OXC configuration time in the last hop of D3T(1,19,7) and D4T(1,19,3,9) for JIT, JumpStart, JIT^{+}, JET, and Horizon; F=64; λ/μ=44.8; with varied T_{Setup} according to (1), (2), and (3) for each resource reservation protocol

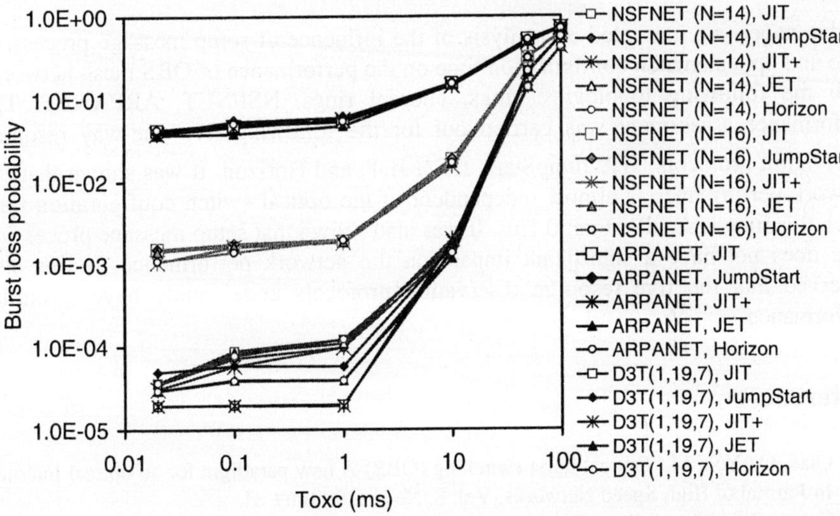

Fig. 5. Burst loss probability as function of OXC configuration time in the last hop of NSFNET (N=14), NSFNET (N=16), ARPANET, and D3T(1,19,7) for JIT, JumpStart, JIT^{+}, JET, and Horizon; F=64; λ/μ=32; T_{Setup}(JIT) = T_{Setup}(JumpStart) = T_{Setup}(JIT^{+}) = 12.5μs; T_{Setup}(JET)=50μs; T_{Setup}(Horizon)=25μs

Figure 3 shows the burst loss probability as function of OXC configuration time in the last hop of D2T(1,19) and D3T(1,19,7) for JIT, JumpStart, JIT^+, JET, and Horizon, being T_{Setup} computed according to (1), (2), and (3) for each protocol. As may be seen, for T_{OXC}<0.1ms, a small change in the burst loss can be observed regarding figure 1. However, this small change is not significant in terms of network performance and therefore, this figure also confirms the previous observations about the influence of T_{setup} and T_{OXC} in the network performance.

Figure 4 plots the burst loss probability as function of OXC configuration time in the last hop of D3T(1,19,7) and D4T(1,19,3,9) for the five protocols under study, with F=64, λ/μ=44.8. T_{Setup} is assumed to change with T_{OXC}, according to (1), (2), and (3). Again, values of T_{OXC} smaller than 1ms do not have a significant impact. It may also be observed that the relative performance of the five protocols is similar. Fig. 5 confirms the results of Fig. 1 for the following topologies: NSFNET (N=14), NSFNET (N=16), and ARPANET. We have also investigated other mesh topologies such as mesh-torus and the European Optical Network and similar results have been obtained regarding the independent network behaviour for T_{OXC}<0.1ms and the similar performance of the five resource reservation protocols under study.

5 Conclusions

In this paper, we presented an analysis of the influence of setup message processing time and optical switch configuration time on the performance of OBS mesh networks with the following topologies: rings, chordal rings, NSFNET, ARPANET. The performance assessment was carried out for the following five one-way resource reservation protocols: JIT, JumpStart, JIT^+, JET, and Horizon. It was shown that the network performance is almost independent of the optical switch configuration time when this time is smaller than 0.1ms. It was also shown that setup message processing time does not have a significant impact on the network performance. It was also observed that the five resource reservation protocols under study have a similar performance.

References

1. Qiao, C., Yoo, M.: Optical burst switching (OBS)-A new paradigm for an optical Internet. In Journal of High Speed Networks, Vol. 8, No. 1 (1999) 69-84.
2. Turner, J.S.: Terabit Burst Switching. J. High Speed Networks, Vol. 8, No. 1 (1999) 3-16.
3. Wei, J.Y., McFarland, R.I.: Just-in-time signaling for WDM optical burst switching networks. In Journal of Lightwave Technology, Vol. 18, No. 12 (2000) 2019-2037.
4. Baldine, I., Rouskas, G., Perros, H., Stevenson, D.: JumpStart: A just-in-time signaling architecture for WDM burst-switched networks. Commun. Mag., Vol. 40, No. 2 (2002) 82-89.
5. Zaim, A.H., Baldine, I., Cassada, M., Rouskas, G.N., Perros, H.G., Stevenson, D.: The JumpStart just-in-time signaling protocol: a formal description using EFSM. In Optical Engineering, Vol. 42, No. 2, February (2003) 568-585.

6. Baldine, I., Rouskas, G.N., Perros, H.G., Stevenson, D.: Signaling Support for Multicast and QoS within the JumpStart WDM Burst Switching Architecture. In Optical Networks, Vol. 4, No. 6, November/December (2003).
7. Widjaja, I.: Performance Analysis of Burst Admission Control Protocols. IEE Proceedings of Communications, Vol. 142, pp. 7-14, February (1995).
8. Teng, J., Rouskas, G. N.: A Detailed Analysis and Performance Comparison of Wavelength Reservation Schemes for Optical Burst Switched Networks, Photonic Network Communications, Vol. 9, no. 3, pp. 75-81, May (2005).
9. Detti A., Listanti M.: Application of Tell & Go and Tell & Wait Reservation Strategies in a Optical Burst Switching Network: a Performance Comparison, Proceedings of IEEE International Conference on Telecommunication (ICT), Vol. 2, Bucharest, Romania, pp. 540-548, June 4-7 (2001).
10. Xu L., Perros H. G., Rouskas G. N.: Access Protocols for Optical Burst-Switched Ring Networks, Information Sciences, Vol. 149, no. 1-3, pp. 75-81, January (2003).
11. Duser M., Bayvel P.: Analysis of a Dynamically Wavelength-Routed Optical Burst Switched Network Architecture. J. Lightwave Technol., Vol. 20, No. 4, (2002), 574-585.
12. Sridharan, M., Salapaka, M. V., Somani, A. K.: A Practical Approach to Operating Survivable WDM Networks, J. Selected Areas in Commun., Vol. 20, No. 1, (2002) 34-46.
13. Ramesh, S., Rouskas, G. N., Perros, H. G.: Computing blocking probabilities in multiclass wavelength-routing networks with multicast calls, IEEE Journal on Selected Areas in Communications, Vol. 20, No. 1, (2002) 89-96.
14. Nayak, T. K., Sivarajan, K. N.: A New Approach to Dimensioning Optical Networks, IEEE Journal on Selected Areas in Communications, Vol. 20, No. 1, (2002) 134-148.
15. O'Mahony, M. J.: Results from the COST 239 Project: Ultra-high Capacity Optical Transmission Networks, in Proc. European Conf. on Optical Communication (ECOC), Oslo, Norway, Vol. 2, (1996) 2.11-2.18.
16. Arden, B.W., Lee, H.: Analysis of Chordal Ring Networks. In IEEE Transactions on Computers, Vol. C-30, No. 4 (1981) 291-295.
17. Rodrigues, J.J.P.C., Garcia, N.M., Freire, M.M., Lorenz, P.: Object-Oriented Modeling and Simulation of Optical Burst Switching Networks, 2004 IEEE Global Telecommunications Conference Workshops (GLOBECOM'2004), Dallas, Texas, Nov. 29- Dec. 3 (2004) 288-292.

Characterizing Gnutella Network Properties for Peer-to-Peer Network Simulation*

Selim Ciraci, Ibrahim Korpeoglu, and Özgür Ulusoy

Department of Computer Engineering, Bilkent University, TR-06800 Ankara, Turkey
{selimc, korpe, oulusoy}@cs.bilkent.edu.tr

Abstract. A P2P network that is overlayed over Internet can consist of thousands, or even millions of nodes. To analyze the performance of a P2P network, or an algorithm or protocol designed for a P2P network, simulation studies have to be performed quite often, and simulation studies require the use of appropriate models for various components and parameters of a P2P network simulated. Therefore it is important to have models and statistical information about various parameters and properties of a P2P network. This paper tries to model and obtain the characteristics of some of the important parameters of one widely used P2P network, Gnutella. The methodology to derive the characteristics is based on collecting P2P protocol traces from the Gnutella network that is currently running over the Internet, and analyzing the collected traces. The results we present in this paper will be an important ingredient for studies that are based on simulation of P2P networks, especially unstructured P2P networks.

1 Introduction

Peer-to-peer (P2P) systems enable formation of huge overlay networks over Internet and allow users to become active participants in these networks. Each node is called a servent in a P2P network and acts both as a server and a client. There are several types of P2P networks, including unstructured P2P networks [2], loosely structured P2P networks, and structured P2P networks [1]. Unstructured P2P networks can further be divided into three types, which are pure, hybrid, and centralized. In pure unstructured P2P networks, each node has equal responsibilities. In other type of unstructured P2P networks [3], on the other hand, some nodes can take special responsibilities like holding an index of the resources shared by the neighboring nodes.

Unstructured P2P systems are good candidates for serving large number of Internet users due to their distributed nature. The major problem with unstructured P2P systems, however, is efficiently locating the requested resources (efficient search). The current mechanism for searching is based on flooding the query messages and therefore it is not efficient. There exists a substantial amount

* This work is supported in part by The Scientific and Technical Research Council of Turkey (TUBITAK) with Grants EEEAG-103E014 and 104E028.

P. Yolum et al.(Eds.): ISCIS 2005, LNCS 3733, pp. 274–283, 2005.

of research on improving the performance of unstructured peer-to-peer networks, including the performance of search operations, and there are many methods proposed. Evaluating the methods and their performance, however, is not easy. The number of nodes constituting a P2P network is huge and there are lots of parameters that should be considered, which make analytical approaches quite difficult to use in the evaluations. Therefore we have to resort to simulation models quite often. But building accurate and correct simulation models requires accurate modeling of the properties and workloads of real-life systems that are simulated. Therefore, it is important to characterize and model the parameters and workloads of real P2P systems that are operational in order to be able to simulate them accurately.

In this paper, we aim to characterize some of the important parameters of an operational unstructured P2P network, the Gnutella network, by examing the protocol traffic traces that we have collected from the Gnutella network. In analyzing and summarizing these traces, we have focused on the characterization of keywords (their numbers and types) in queries, time-to-live (TTL) values in query messages, peers' contribution to the network, and the characteristics of repeated queries.

The paper is organized as follows. In section 2, some of the related work is described. Then, in section 3, our Gnutella crawler that is used to collect traces from the Gnutella network is described together with our methodology in collecting the traces. In section 4, the results derived from the traces are presented, and finally in section 5 our findings are summarized.

2 Related Work

There exist several studies on the measurement and analysis of several P2P networks. The study on [4] lists some of the important parameters that should be considered when simulating a P2P file sharing network. In this study, a model for some of the parameters are derived from real world observations, and the parameters considered are separated into two groups. The first group of parameters are related with the distribution of resources in the P2P network, and the second group of parameters are related with modeling the behavior of peers. The main difference of our study from [4] is that we try to characterize P2P network parameters using traces collected by custom P2P crawlers. We also investigate some parameters that are not investigated in [4].

The authors of [5] has conducted an analysis of the Gnutella network using crawlers, like we did. They logged for an hour the query and query hit messages seen at three different points on the Gnutella network. The study of the logged messages is focused on the detailed analysis of repeated queries, the TTL values seen in the queries, and the inter-arrival times of submited queries. In this paper, we also analyze some aspects of repeated queries and the TTL values of user submited queries. But we are more focusing on the characterization of initial TTL values set in the queries, and on the characterization of inter-arrival times of repeated queries. A similar study to [5] is presented in [6]. That study, however, is more focused on content analysis of queries. It derives and lists some popular keywords that are used in submited queries. In this aspect, the work also resembles to what we did, but we are also trying to find a model for the repetition count of popular keywords.

The study presented in [7] also uses crawlers to collect message traces from Napster and Gnutella networks. It plots cumulative distributions of peer characteristics such as the number of resources shared, the uptime of peers, and the bandwidth capacity of peers. In this paper, we also focus on similar parameters such as the number of resources shared by peers, but we also try to come up with a model that can be used to generate similar values for these parameters in simulation studies.

3 Methodology

To derive information about various parameters of a Gnutella network, we followed a methodology similar to the one described in [7]. We programmed a custom Gnutella crawler to collect Gnutella network traces. Using the crawler we gathered large sets of data and logged them on a local disk. The logged data includes various Gnutella protocol messages that suit our measurement goals. After logging the Gnutella messages, we also probed numerous nodes, whose addresses are obtained from the logged messages, in order to have an idea about the duration of node uptimes.

In this section, we first briefly introduce the Gnutella architecture and its protocol messages. Then we describe beriefly our Gnutella crawler that is used to collect Gnutella protocol messages transported over a portion of the Gnuetella network. We then introduce and describe some of the P2P network parameters which we are trying to characterize and estimate using the message logs we obtained via our crawler.

3.1 Gnutella

In Gnutella network, peers form an overlay network over Internet by opening point-to-point TCP connections to each other. To join the overlay, a newcoming peer has to discover a small subset of the active overlay participants. This discovery is done by querying the hostcaches, which hold the IP addresses of some of the high-uptime participants. Each Gnutella compatible P2P client comes with a set of predefined hostcache addresses. After discovering a set of the peers to join, a newcomer initiates Gnutella handshake with a peer in that set. During this handshake, both the newcomer peer and the peer that is already part of the Gnutella network indicate to each other the Gnutella protocol version they are using and the extensions they support [2]. If the peer that is already part of the Gnutella network can accept the connection request from the newcoming peer, it indicates this by sending an `OK` message. If, on the other hand, the peer cannot accept the connection, it indicates the reason why it cannot accept the connection and provides the newcomer with a set of peers it knows. This way the newcomer can discover other peers without further querying the hostcache.

After a succsessful connection establishment, peers start exchanging Gnutella protocol messages. A Gnutella message header consists of a *global unique identifier* (*GUID*) field, a *time-to-live* (*TTL*) field, a *hops* field, a *payload type* field, and a *payload length* field. The GUID is used to overcome routing loops that may occur in the overlay. To prevent routing loops, a peer receiving two messages with the same GUID ignores the second one. Each peer receiving a Gnutella message increases the hops count value in the message by one and also decreases the TTL value by one. When the TTL value of a message reaches to zero, the message is not forwarded anymore. The payload type field is used by peers to distinguish different types of Gnutella messages. There are five types of Gnutella messages which are *Query*, *QueryHit*, *Bye*, *Ping*, and *Pong* messages.

A Query message contains the user submitted query string as its payload. A peer receiving a Query message checks its shared resources for a match to the query string included in the Query message. If the peer has resources that match the query string, it sends a Query Hit message back. The Query Hit message is set the same TTL value as the hops field of the corresponding Query message. The payload of the Query Hit message contains the physical address of the originator and the names of the resources that match the corresponding query.

The Ping and Pong messages are used to exchange topological information. When a peer receives a Ping message, it answers back with at least 10 Pong messages each containing the physical addresses of other peers that are collected again by sending Ping messages. Bye is used by a peer to indicate its disconnection from the network to its neighbors.

3.2 Gnutella Crawler

Our Gnutella crawler is written in Java and follows the Gnutella protocol specification version v0.6 [2]. First, the crawler connects to the HTTP address *gwebcache2.limewire.com:9000/gwc* to collect physical addresses of some active peers. It then starts opening connections to those peers and also builds its own hostcache from the physical addresses collected via unsuccessful connection attempts and Pong messages. After connecting to three peers successfully, the crawler starts monitoring and logging Gnutella messages considering the parameters we are going to discuss in mind.

3.3 Measured Parameters

The simulation of a Gnutella network requires consideration of a lot of parameters. We focused only a subset of all possible parameters and tried to understand the nature of the values of these parameters in the Gnutella network. We now introduce the parameters we focused on, and describe how the related traces are collected to obtain the characteristics of these parameters.

Number of keywords contained in a query: For semantic routing techniques, keywords in a query define routing rules for that query. Thus, the more keywords a query has, the more information the routing technique can extract about the query's route. It is widely believed that P2P users submit short queries consisting of one or two keywords, so its difficult to apply semantic routing techniques. To test this belief, we have programmed the crawler to collect 10 thousand queries from five different connection sets (each set consisting of different nodes). After collecting the data, the queries are tokenized with "`._*()",;:!?`" deliminators to extract the keywords and then each keyword is counted. To combine the counts from different connection sets, the averages of the counts is taken.

Repetition rate of keywords in queries: It is a fact that in P2P networks there exist some popular resources which are queried a lot. Many protocols that try to improve search quality rely on repetition rate of keywords in queries. So it is important to develop a model for popular keywords for such techniques.

To develop this model, we have used the tokenized queries of the previous parameter and hashed each keyword using Java's string class, which hashes strings by adding the integer values of each character in a string. These hashed keywords are used as a key to index the hash table holding the number of accesses made to the cells. We have given the highest rank of 1 to the mostly accessed cell, which in turn is the keyword with the highest repetition.

Initial TTL values of queries: For P2P simulations, the initial TTL values set in Query messages play an important role, since Query messages can travel longer distances with a higher TTL value which increases the chance of finding the resources requested by the query. The TTL value in a query is also important for determining the bandwidth required for various protocols. Gnutella protocol specifition [2] states that TTL values in queries should be set to 7. However, the fact that many Gnutella clients today use shorter initial TTL values makes TTL an important parameter to achive relalistic P2P simulations.

To keep track of TTL values, while collecting query data for the previous parameters we have also programmed the crawler to log the *TTL* and *hops* values of the received queries. The initial TTL values are calculated by adding these two values. Again averages of several collected data sets are used to obtain the final estimates.

Peers' contribution to the network: Distribution of resources to peers in a P2P simulation should also be handled carefully, since the query hit rate is directly affected by this parameter. Some previous studies show that %25 of the Gnutella peers do not share any files at all, and %7 of peers share 100 files [7].

To collect the required data to estimate the distibution characterictics of resources, the crawler has been programmed to collect 10 thousand Pong messages from five different connections sets. The collected Pong messages contain the total number and size of resources shared by these nodes.

Query hit to query ratio: Although peers' contribution to the network greatly affects the Query Hit messages returned to Query messages, the popularity of the shared resources is another important factor that can affect the Query Hits, since popular resources will be queried more than other ones. So it is not only important how many files a peer shares, but it is also important what kind of files the peer shares. It is hard to model the popularity of shared resources, however, collecting the number of Query messages with matching Query Hit messages in the Gnutella network may give an idea. Assuming, for example, $x\%$ of the queries in the collected data have a matching Query Hit message, we then can adjust the popularity parameter in a simulation so that the chance of getting a Query Hit to a Query message is $x\%$.

To find the Query to Query hit ratio, our crawler uses a hash table. This hash table holds the GUID of a Query message as a key and stores the corresponding Query Hit message as data. Upon receiving a Query message, the crawler inserts a null Query Hit message, which has zero as the hit-count, to the hash table. Since the Query Hit message has the same GUID as a Query message, upon receiving a Query Hit message, the crawler searches the GUID of the message in the hash table, and if found, the Query Hit message is inserted to the table. By collecting the Query Hit messages in this way, we found the chance of getting a Query Hit to a submitted Query message.

Repeated queries: When the P2P network does not return any results to a query submitted by a user, the query is re-submitted by the user or the P2P client software. Thus, it may be important to model this behaviour for simulation of caching systems.

In order to find out how many queries are repeated in a five different query sets each containing 10 thousand queries, we have hashed the query string in a Query message together with the *hops* value of the message, again by using Java's string class. If two different queries are hashed to the same cell, then that query is marked as a repeated query. Although it is impossible to know which peer has submitted the query when the hops value is greater than 1, two queries with the same query string and the same hops value have a very high probability of being repeated, thus we have used this method to recognize repeated queries.

TTL values of repeated queries: When a user of a P2P system re-submits a query, it provides some advantage for the P2P client to send the query to the network with a higher TTL value. Although Gnutella specification does not mention this, some clients may have adapted this aproach in order to increase search quality. This makes it important to analyze the TTL values in repeated queries.

4 Results

In this section we present our results about the characteristics of the parameters that we have desribed. Before that, however, we would like to mention about the overall Gnutella message traffic characteristics we observed in our setup. In our collected traces, we have observed the following distribution of the Gnutella messages monitored: 1% Query Hit messages, 8% Ping messages, and 91% Query messages. The overhead of flooding of Query messages is clearly seen from these results. Thus the need for a protocol that reduces this overhead is clear.

In Figure 1, the distribution of the number of keywords submitted in a query is shown. Our analysis of the related traces shows that 68477 queries out of 100 thousand queries contain less than 5 keywords. We found 4 as the mean

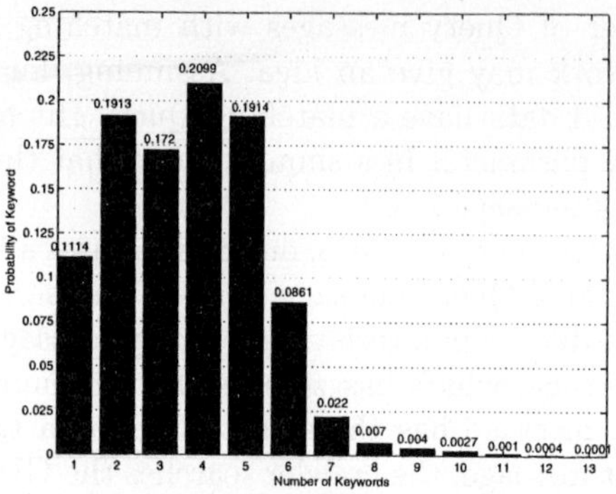

Fig. 1. Distribution of number of keywords seen in query messages

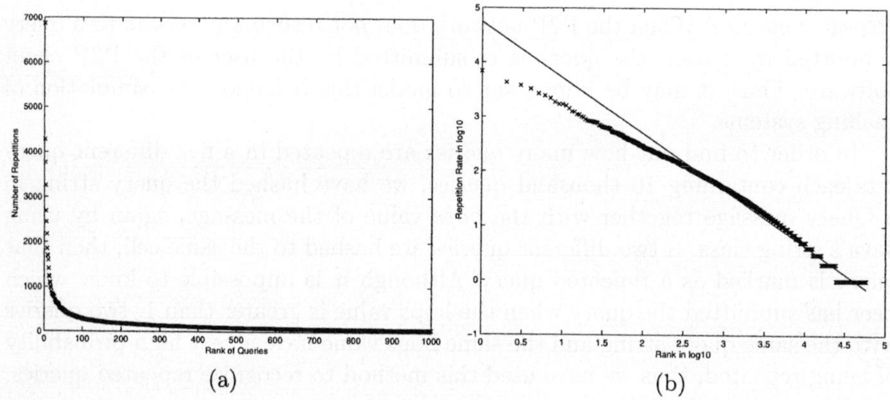

Fig. 2. Repetition count of keywords. a) Repetition count of keywords versus the rank of keywords. Keywords are ranked according their frequency of occurance in query messages. b) Log of repetition count of keywords versus log of rank of keywords.

of the number of keywords that can be seen in a query. Queries with just one keyword constitute the 10% of all queries we analyzed. The Figure 1 indicates that users tend to submit more descriptive queries instead of submitting single-keywords queries. It is also interesting to notice that 1561 queries out of 100 thousand queries contain more that 7 keywords which makes around 1.5% of all the queries analyzed.

Figure 2 shows the repetition count of keywords in user submitted queries. In plotting the graphs in the figure, we first ranked all the keywords with respect to their repetition count. In Figure 2-a, the x-axis is the rank of the keywords, and the y-axis is the repetition count of the keywords with respect to those ranks. The analysis of this plot shows that the repetition count of keywords obeys a power-law distribution with respect to the rank of keywords. We think this is due to popularity of some keywords. Since the curve on the graph is steeply decreasing, we only plotted the repetition counts up to rank 1000. Otherwise it was difficult to identify the curve on the graph. To better show that the repetition count of keywords obey a power-law distrubution, we plotted the repetition count versus rank of keywords in logarithmic scale, and fit a polynomial with degree 1 to the curve obtained in this manner. The Figure 2-b shows the plot in logarithmic scale with the fitted polynomial (in this plot we did not limit the rank). The fitted polynomial has coefficients -1.028 and 4.74 (i.e. it is the line described by equation $y = -1.028 \times x + 4.74$).

From the Gnutella messages we have collected, we have observed that majority of the Gnutella clients (89%) set the initial TTL value to 4 in a Query message. The clients setting the initial TTL value to 3 constitute around 11% of the peers. The number of clients setting the initial TTL value to something else is less than 1% and therefore negligible. We also tested what happens if a client tries to submit Query messages with larger initial TTL values than 4. For this we modified our Gnutella client so that it submits queries to the network with TTL values larger than 4. We have noticed that majority of the clients around us have lowered the TTL value to 4. We believe that Gnutella developers have taken such an action to lower the overhead introduced by the flooding mechanims used for disseminating the queries.

In Figure 3, we show the cummulative distribution function of number of files shared by a peer. On the x-axis we have the number of files shared, and on the y-axis we have the fraction of peers sharing number of files that is less than or equal to the corresponding value indicated on the x-axis. From the figure we see that 50 peers out of 420 peers share zero files. In other words, nearly 10% percent of peers do not share any files. The figure also reveals that only around 5% of peers share more than one thousand files. These are not suprising results since it is a quite well-known fact that only a small precentage of peers in a P2P network share huge numbers of files. It is also interesting to notice that although many peers indicate that they share small number of files, these shared files are quite large in size (around 2 GB). This leads us to believe that in Gnutella

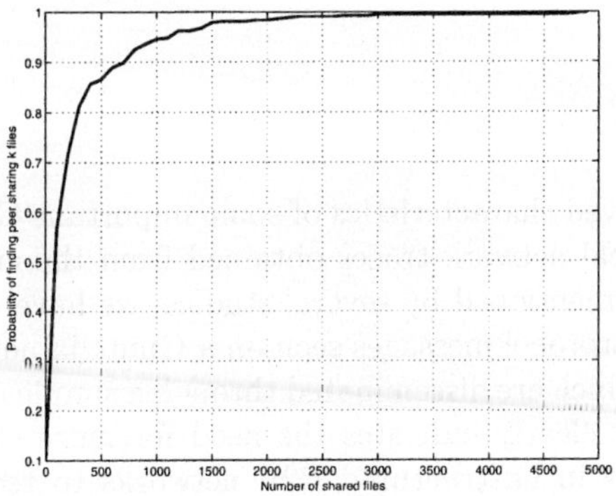

Fig. 3. Cumulative distribution function (CDF) of the number of files shared by a peer. Most of the peers (95%) share less than 1000 files.

network users tend to search and download large files which in turn causes peers to share large files.

Although Query to Query Hit ratio greatly depends on the queries submitted, as reported in the beginning of this section, our measurements indicate that Query Hit messages constitute only %1 of the overall P2P message traffic observed in the traces. This implies quite a small value for Query to Query Hit ratio.

A query string can be repeated by a peer because the results obtained in previous query submissions may not be found satisfactory by the peer. Out of the 100 thousand queries observed, we have identified 15678 queries as repeated queries. This constitutes 15% of all the queries observed. queries we have observed that the majority of the queries are repeated twice (81% of all queries). The percent of queries that are submitted three times is 14%. We have found that only 2 queries are submitted to the network more than 5 times. These two queries have all "?" as query strings, which we believe are used by peers to discover all the names of the resources shared by their neighbors, although nothing about this is mentioned in Gnutella protocol specifiction. Our inter-arrival time analysis for repeated queries shows that on average there is 21 minutes between each repeated query, which is a reasonable time, since a user re-submits a query after the arrival and inspection of the previous results. Our TTL analysis for repeated queries shows that the initial TTL values of these repeated queries are not increased by the clients submitting these queries. Given that majority of the queries are repeated only twice, we can say that a Gnutella user is statisfied with the results after a second submission that comes after a sufficient inter-arrival time (around 21 minutes). Since the mean uptime of Gnutella peers are around 60 minutes [5], we conclude that there is no need for an increase in the TTL of the repeated queries for the purpose of getting better results, and therefore we find the decision made by Gnutella developers about not to increase the TTL values in repeated queries to be correct; since by the time the query is re-submitted new nodes would join the network so there is no need to increase the TTL value of a query.

5 Conclusion

In this paper we derived characteristics of some important Gnutella network parameters based on real network traces obtained from the current live Gnutella network. As already mentioned by several studies, we have verified that a large portion of Gnutella protocol messages seen on a Gnutella network is constituted by Query messages which are disseminated through a simple and inefficient flooding mechanism. This clearly indicates the need for more clever algorithms for disseminating queries in unstructured P2P networks to reduce the messaging overhead and to provide better scalability.

Our results also indicate that most submitted queries contain query strings that consist of multiple keywords, as opposed to the common assumption in various simulations that a query consists of a single keyword. We also found that repetition count of keywords seen in a P2P network obeys a power-law distribution with respect to the rank of keywords where the keyword that is repeated the most has a rank of 1. We also verified the fact that not all peers contribute to a P2P network at the same level. A small portion of peers share a large portion of all files available in the network. Our traces also revelated the fact the same query string is not repeated too much by the same peer. Also a peer does not increase the initial TTL (time-to-live) values of repeated queries to enlarge the search horizon. We have found that most submitted queries have an initial TTL value of 4, and even though a peer submits a query with a larger TTL value, the neighboring peers immediately reduce the TTL to a value below 4.

We think that our findings can be important for P2P network simulation studies that are looking for models and information about some of the important parameters of P2P networks.

References

1. Stephanos, A. T.: A Survey of Peer-to-peer File Sharing Systems. WHP-2002-03, Athens University of Business and Economics, (2002).
2. Gnutella protocol v0.6. Available at http://rfc-gnutella.sourceforge.net/developer/testing/index.html.
3. Kazaa http://www.kazaa.com
4. Schlosser, M.T., Condie, T. E., Kamvar S.D.: Simulating a File-Sharing P2P Network. First Workshop on Semantics in P2P and Grid Computing, December, (2002)
5. Markatos, E.P.: Tracing a large scale Peer-to-Peer System: An hour in the life of Gnutella. In 2nd IEEE/ACM Int. Symp. on Cluster Computing and the Grid, (2002)
6. Zeinalipour-Yazti, D., Folias, T.: Quantitative Analysis of the Gnutella Network Traffic. TR-CS-89, Dept. of Computer Science, University of California, Riverside, June (2002)
7. Saroiu, S., Gummadi, P., K., Gribble S., D.: A Measurement Study of Peer-to-Peer File Sharing Systems. Proceedings of Multimedia Computing and Networking 2002 (MMCN'02), San Jose, CA, January (2002).

Computing Communities in Large Networks Using Random Walks

Pascal Pons and Matthieu Latapy

LIAFA – Université Paris Denis Diderot and CNRS
2 place Jussieu, F-75251 Paris Cedex 05, France
{pons, latapy}@liafa.jussieu.fr

Abstract. Dense subgraphs of sparse graphs (*communities*), which appear in most real-world complex networks, play an important role in many contexts. Computing them however is generally expensive. We propose here a measure of similarities between vertices based on random walks which has several important advantages: it captures well the community structure in a network, it can be computed efficiently, it works at various scales, and it can be used in an agglomerative algorithm to compute efficiently the community structure of a network. We propose such an algorithm which runs in time $O(mn^2)$ and space $O(n^2)$ in the worst case, and in time $O(n^2 \log n)$ and space $O(n^2)$ in most real-world cases (n and m are respectively the number of vertices and edges in the input graph).

1 Introduction

Recent advances have brought out the importance of *complex networks* in many different domains such as sociology (acquaintance or collaboration networks), biology (metabolic networks, gene networks) or computer science (Internet topology, Web graph, P2P networks). We refer to [1,2,3,4,5] for reviews from different perspectives and for an extensive bibliography. The associated graphs are in general globally sparse but locally dense: there exist groups of vertices, called *communities*, highly connected between them but with few links to other vertices. This kind of structure brings out much information about the network.

This notion of community is however difficult to define formally. Many definitions have been proposed in social networks studies [1], but they are too restrictive or cannot be computed efficiently. However, most recent approaches have reached a consensus, and consider that a partition $\mathcal{P} = \{C_1, \ldots, C_k\}$ of the vertices of a graph $G = (V, E)$ $(\forall i, C_i \subseteq V)$ represents a good community structure if the proportion of edges inside the C_i (internal edges) is high compared to the proportion of edges between them. Therefore, we will design an algorithm which finds communities satisfying this criterion.

We will consider throughout this paper an *undirected graph* $G = (V, E)$ with $n = |V|$ vertices and $m = |E|$ edges. We impose that each vertex is linked to itself by a loop (we add these loops if necessary). We also suppose that G is connected, the case where it is not being treated by considering the components as different graphs.

P. Yolum et al.(Eds.): ISCIS 2005, LNCS 3733, pp. 284–293, 2005.

1.1 Our Approach and Results

Our approach is based on the following intuition: random walks on a graph tend to get "trapped" into densely connected parts corresponding to communities. We therefore begin with a theoretical study of random walks on graphs. Using this, we define a measurement of the structural similarity between vertices and between communities, thus defining a distance. We relate this distance to existing spectral approaches of the problem. But our distance has an important advantage on these methods: it is efficiently computable, and can be used in a hierarchical clustering algorithm (merging iteratively the vertices into communities). One obtains this way a hierarchical community structure that may be represented as a tree structure called *dendrogram* (an example is provided in Figure 1). We propose such an algorithm which computes a community structure in time $\mathcal{O}(mnH)$ where H is the height of the corresponding dendrogram. The worst case is $\mathcal{O}(mn^2)$. But most real-world complex networks are sparse ($m = \mathcal{O}(n)$) and, as already noticed in [6], H is generally small and tends to the most favourable case in which the dendrogram is balanced ($H = \mathcal{O}(\log n)$). In this case, the complexity is therefore $\mathcal{O}(n^2 \log n)$.

1.2 Related Work

Community detection is related to the classical problem of *graph partitioning* that consists in splitting a graph into a given number of groups while minimizing the cost of the edge cut [7,8]. However, these algorithms are not well suited to our case because they need the number of communities and their size as parameters. The recent interest in the domain has started with a new *divisive* approach proposed by Girvan and Newman [9,10]: the edges with the largest *betweenness* are removed one by one in order to split hierarchically the graph into communities. This algorithm runs in time $\mathcal{O}(m^2n)$. Similar algorithms were proposed by Radicchi *et al* [11] and by Fortunato *et al* [12]. The first one uses a local quantity (the number of loops of a given length containing an edge) to choose the edges to remove and runs in time $\mathcal{O}(m^2)$. The second one uses a more complex notion of information centrality with a time complexity $\mathcal{O}(m^3n)$.

Hierarchical clustering is another classical approach: from a measurement of the similarity between vertices, an *agglomerative* algorithm groups iteratively the vertices into communities (different methods exist, differing on the way of choosing the communities to merge at each step). Several agglomerative methods have been recently introduced. Newman proposed in [13] a greedy algorithm that starts with n communities corresponding to the vertices and merges communities in order to optimize a function called modularity which measures the quality of a partition. This algorithm runs in $\mathcal{O}(mn)$ and has recently been improved to a complexity $\mathcal{O}(mH \log n)$ (with our notations) [6]. The algorithm of Donetti and Muñoz [14] uses the eigenvectors of the Laplacian matrix of the graph to measure the similarities between vertices. The complexity is determined by the computation of all the eigenvectors, in $\mathcal{O}(n^3)$ time for sparse matrices. Other interesting methods have been proposed, see for instance [15,16,17,18].

Random walks have already been used to infer structural properties of networks in some previous works. Gaume [19] used this notion in linguistic context. Fouss et al [20] used the Euclidean commute time distance based on the average first-passage time of walkers. Zhou and Lipowsky [21] introduced another dissimilarity index basd on the same quantity, it has been integrated in a hierarchical algorithm (*Netwalk*). *Markov Cluster Algorithm* [22] iterates two matrix operations (one corresponding to random walks) bringing out clusters in the limit state. Unfortunately the three last approaches runs in $\mathcal{O}(n^3)$ and cannot manage networks with more than a few thousand vertices. Our approach has the main advantage to be significatively faster while producing very good results.

2 Preliminaries on Random Walks

The graph G is associated with its *adjacency matrix* A: $A_{ij} = 1$ if vertices i and j are connected and $A_{ij} = 0$ otherwise. The degree $d(i) = \sum_j A_{ij}$ of the vertex i is the number of its neighbors (including itself). To simplify the notations, we only consider unweighted graphs in this paper. It is however trivial to extend our results to weighted graphs ($A_{ij} \in \mathbb{R}^+$ instead of $A_{ij} \in \{0,1\}$).

Let us consider a discrete *random walk process* (or diffusion process) on the graph G (see [23] for a complete presentation of the topic). At each time step a walker is on a vertex and moves to a vertex chosen randomly and uniformly among its neighbors. The sequence of visited vertices is a *Markov chain*, the states of which are the vertices of the graph. At each step, the transition probability from vertex i to vertex j is $P_{ij} = \frac{A_{ij}}{d(i)}$. This defines the *transition matrix* P of the random walk.

The process is driven by the powers of the matrix P: the probability of going from i to j through a random walk of length t is $(P^t)_{ij}$. In the following, we will denote this probability by P^t_{ij}. It satisfies two general properties of the random walk process which we will use in the sequel:

Property 1. When the length t of a random walk starting at vertex i tends towards infinity, the probability of being on a vertex j only depends on the degree of vertex j (and not on the starting vertex i): $\forall i, \lim_{t\to+\infty} P^t_{ij} = \frac{d(j)}{\sum_k d(k)}$.

Property 2. The probabilities of going from i to j and from j to i through a random walk of a fixed length t have a ratio that only depends on the degrees $d(i)$ and $d(j)$: $\forall i, \forall j, d(i)P^t_{ij} = d(j)P^t_{ji}$.

3 Comparing Vertices Using Short Random Walks

In order to group the vertices into communities, we will now introduce a distance r between the vertices that captures the community structure of the graph. This distance must be large if the two vertices are in different communities, and on the contrary if they are in the same community it must be small. It will be computed from the information given by random walks in the graph.

Let us consider random walks on G of a given length t. We will use the information given by all the probabilities P^t_{ij} to go from i to j in t steps. The length t of the random walks must be sufficiently long to gather enough information about the topology of the graph. However t must not be too long, to avoid the effect predicted by Property 1; the probabilities would only depend on the degree of the vertices. Each probability P^t_{ij} gives some information about the two vertices i and j, but Property 2 says that P^t_{ij} and P^t_{ji} encode exactly the same information. Finally, the information about vertex i encoded in P^t resides in the n probabilities $(P^t_{ik})_{1 \leq k \leq n}$, which is nothing but the ith row of the matrix P^t, denoted by $P^t_{i \bullet}$. To compare two vertices i and j using these data, we must notice that:

- If two vertices i and j are in the same community, the probability P^t_{ij} will surely be high. But the fact that P^t_{ij} is high does not necessarily imply that i and j are in the same community.
- The probability P^t_{ij} is influenced by the degree $d(j)$ because the walker has higher probability to go to high degree vertices.
- Two vertices of a same community tend to "see" all the other vertices in the same way. Thus if i and j are in the same community, we will probably have $\forall k, P^t_{ik} \simeq P^t_{jk}$.

We can now give the definition of our distance between vertices, which takes into account all previous remarks:

Definition 1. *Let i and j be two vertices in the graph and*

$$r_{ij} = \sqrt{\sum_{k=1}^{n} \frac{(P^t_{ik} - P^t_{jk})^2}{d(k)}} = \left\| D^{-\frac{1}{2}} P^t_{i \bullet} - D^{-\frac{1}{2}} P^t_{j \bullet} \right\| \qquad (1)$$

where $\|.\|$ is the Euclidean norm of $\mathbb{R}^n$.

One can notice that this distance can also be seen as the L^2 distance between the two probability distributions $P^t_{i \bullet}$ and $P^t_{j \bullet}$. Notice also that the distance depends on t and may be denoted $r_{ij}(t)$. We will however consider it as implicit to simplify the notations.

Theorem 1. *The distance r is related to the spectral properties of the matrix P*

$$r^2_{ij} = \sum_{\alpha=2}^{n} \lambda_\alpha^{2t} (v_\alpha(i) - v_\alpha(j))^2$$

where $(\lambda_\alpha)_{1 \leq \alpha \leq n}$ and $(v_\alpha)_{1 \leq \alpha \leq n}$ are respectively the eigenvalues and right eigenvectors of the matrix P.

This theorem relates random walks on graphs to the many current works that study spectral properties of graphs. For example, [24] notices that the modular structure of a graph is expressed in the eigenvectors of P (other than v_1) that corresponds to the largest positive eigenvalues. If two vertices i and j belong to a same community then the coordinates $v_\alpha(i)$ and $v_\alpha(j)$ are similar in all these eigenvectors. Moreover, [25,26] show in a more general case that when an eigenvalue λ_α tends to 1, the coordinates of the associated eigenvector v_α are constant in the subsets of vertices that correspond to communities. A distance similar to ours (but that cannot be computed directly with random walks) is also introduced: $d_t^2(i,j) = \sum_{\alpha=2}^{n} \frac{(v_\alpha(i)-v_\alpha(j))^2}{1-|\lambda_\alpha|^t}$. Finally, [14] uses the same spectral approach applied to the Laplacian matrix of the graph $L = D - A$.

All these studies show that the spectral approach takes an important part in the search for community structure in graphs. However all these approaches have the same drawback: the eigenvectors need to be explicitly computed (in time $\mathcal{O}(n^3)$ for a sparse matrix). This computation rapidly becomes untractable in practice when the size of the graph exceeds some thousands of vertices. Our approach is based on the same foundation but has the advantage of avoiding the expensive computation of the eigenvectors: it only needs to compute the probabilities P_{ij}^t, which can be done efficiently as shown in the following theorem.

Theorem 2. *All the probabilities P_{ij}^t can be computed in time $\mathcal{O}(tnm)$ and space $\mathcal{O}(n^2)$. Once these probabilities computed, each distance r_{ij} can be computed in time $\mathcal{O}(n)$.*

Proof. To compute the vector $P_{i\bullet}^t$, we multiply t times the vector $P_{i\bullet}^0$ ($\forall k$, $P_{i\bullet}^0(k) = \delta_{ik}$) by the matrix P. This direct method is advantageous because the matrix P is generally sparse (for real-world complex networks) therefore each product is processed in time $\mathcal{O}(m)$. The initialization of $P_{i\bullet}^0$ is done in $\mathcal{O}(n)$ and thus each of the n vectors $P_{i\bullet}^t$ is computed in time $\mathcal{O}(n+tm) = \mathcal{O}(tm)$. Once we have the two vectors $P_{i\bullet}^t$ and $P_{j\bullet}^t$, we can compute r_{ij} in $\mathcal{O}(n)$ using Equation (1).

Now we generalize our distance between vertices to a distance between communities in a straightforward way. Let us consider random walks that start from a community: the starting vertex is chosen randomly and uniformly among the vertices of the community. We define the probability P_{Cj}^t to go from community C to vertex j in t steps:

$$P_{Cj}^t = \frac{1}{|C|} \sum_{i \in C} P_{ij}^t$$

This defines a probability vector $P_{C\bullet}^t$ that allows us to generalize our distance:

Definition 2. *Let $C_1, C_2 \subset V$ be two communities. We define the distance $r_{C_1C_2}$ between these two communities by:*

$$r_{C_1C_2} = \left\| D^{-\frac{1}{2}} P_{C_1\bullet}^t - D^{-\frac{1}{2}} P_{C_2\bullet}^t \right\| = \sqrt{\sum_{k=1}^{n} \frac{(P_{C_1k}^t - P_{C_2k}^t)^2}{d(k)}}$$

This definition is consistent with the previous one: $r_{ij} = r_{\{i\}\{j\}}$ and we can also define the distance between a vertex and a community. Given the probability vectors $P_{C_1\bullet}^t$ and $P_{C_2\bullet}^t$, the distance $r_{C_1C_2}$ is also computed in time $\mathcal{O}(n)$.

4 The Algorithm

In the previous section, we have proposed a distance between vertices (and between sets of vertices) to capture structural similarities between them. The problem of finding communities is now a clustering problem. We will use here an efficient hierarchical clustering algorithm that allows us to find community structures at different scales. We present an agglomerative approach based on Ward's method [27] that is well adapted to our distance and gives very good results while reducing the number of distance computations in order to be able to process large graphs.

We start from a partition $\mathcal{P}_1 = \{\{v\}, v \in V\}$ of the graph into n communities reduced to a single vertex. We first compute the distances between all adjacent vertices. Then this partition evolves by repeating the following operations. At each step k:

- Choose two communities C_1 and C_2 in $\mathcal{P}_k$ on a criterion based on the distance between the communities that we detail later.
- Merge these two communities into a new community $C_3 = C_1 \cup C_2$ and create the new partition: $\mathcal{P}_{k+1} = (\mathcal{P}_k \setminus \{C_1, C_2\}) \cup \{C_3\}$.
- Update the distances between communities (we will see later that we actually only do this for *adjacent* communities).

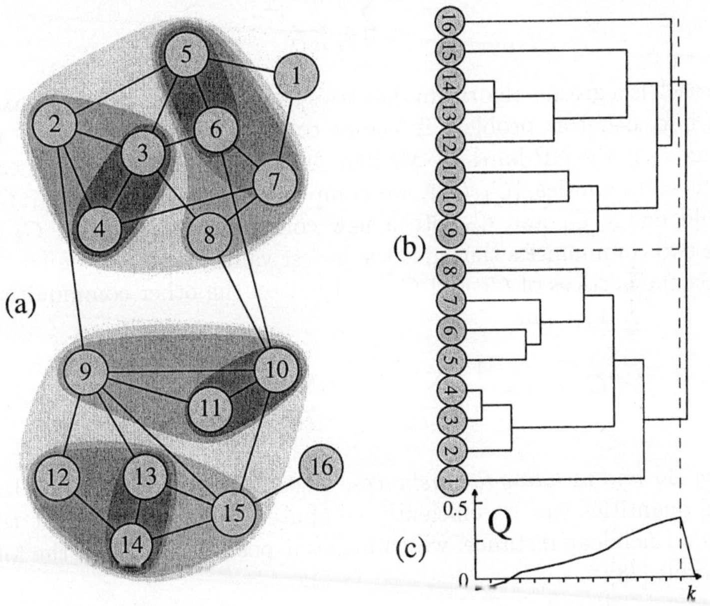

Fig. 1. (a) An example of community structure found by our algorithm using random walks of length $t = 3$. (b) The stages of the algorithm encoded as a tree (*dendrogram*). The maximum of Q, plotted in (c), shows that the best partition consists in two communities.

After $n-1$ steps, the algorithm finishes and we obtain $\mathcal{P}_n = \{V\}$. Each step defines a partition $\mathcal{P}_k$ of the graph into communities, which gives a hierarchical structure of communities called dendrogram (see Figure 1(b)). This structure is a tree in which the leaves correspond to the vertices and each internal node is associated with a merging of communities in the algorithm: it corresponds to a community composed of the union of the communities corresponding to its children. The key points in this algorithm are the way we choose the communities to merge, and the fact that the distances can be updated efficiently. We will also need to evaluate the quality of a partition in order to choose one of the $\mathcal{P}_k$ as the result of our algorithm. We will detail these points below, and explain how they can be managed to give an efficient algorithm.

Choosing the communities to merge. This choice plays a central role for the quality of the community structure created. In order to reduce the complexity, we will only merge *adjacent* communities (having at least an edge between them). This reasonable heuristic (already used in [13] and [14]) limits to m the number of possible mergings at each stage. Moreover it ensures that each community is connected. We choose the two communities to merge according to Ward's method. At each step k, we merge the two communities that minimize the mean σ_k of the squared distances between each vertex and its community.

$$\sigma_k = \frac{1}{n} \sum_{C \in \mathcal{P}_k} \sum_{i \in C} r_{iC}^2$$

This approach is a greedy algorithm that tries to solve the problem of maximizing σ_k for each k. But this problem is known to be NP-hard: even for a given k, maximizing σ_k is the NP-hard "K-Median clustering problem". So for each pair of adjacent communities $\{C_1, C_2\}$, we compute the variation $\Delta\sigma(C_1, C_2)$ of σ if we would merge C_1 and C_2 into a new community $C_3 = C_1 \cup C_2$ and we merge the two communities that give the lowest value of $\Delta\sigma$. This quantity only depends on the vertices of C_1 and C_2, and not on the other communities or on the step k of the algorithm:

$$\Delta\sigma(C_1, C_2) = \frac{1}{n}\Big(\sum_{i \in C_3} r_{iC_3}^2 - \sum_{i \in C_1} r_{iC_1}^2 - \sum_{i \in C_2} r_{iC_2}^2 \Big) \tag{2}$$

Computing $\Delta\sigma$ and updating the distances. The important point here is to notice that these quantities can be efficiently computed thanks to the fact that our distance is a Euclidean distance, which makes it possible to obtain the following classical result [28]:

Theorem 3. *The increase of σ after the merging of two communities C_1 and C_2 is directly related to the distance $r_{C_1 C_2}$ by:*

$$\Delta\sigma(C_1, C_2) = \frac{1}{n} \frac{|C_1||C_2|}{|C_1| + |C_2|} r_{C_1 C_2}^2$$

This theorem shows that we only need to update the distances between communities to get the values of $\Delta\sigma$: if we know the two vectors $P_{C_1\bullet}$ and $P_{C_2\bullet}$, the computation of $\Delta\sigma(C_1, C_2)$ is possible in $\mathcal{O}(n)$. Since we only merge adjacent communities, we only need to update the values of $\Delta\sigma$ between adjacent communities (there are at most m values). These values are stored in a balanced tree in which we can add, remove or get the minimum in $\mathcal{O}(\log m)$.

Evaluating the quality of a partition. The algorithm induces a sequence $(\mathcal{P}_k)_{1\leq k\leq n}$ of partitions into communities. We now want to know which partitions in this sequence capture well the community structure. The most widely used method is to choose the partition maximizing the modularity Q introduced in [10,13]. This quantity uses the fraction of edges e_C that are inside the community C and the fraction of edges[1] a_C bound to the community C: $Q(\mathcal{P}) = \sum_{C\in\mathcal{P}} e_C - a_C^2$. However, depending on one's objectives, one may consider other quality criterion.

Complexity. First, the initialization of the probability vectors is done in $\mathcal{O}(mnt)$. Then, at each step k of the algorithm, we keep in memory the vectors $P^t_{C\bullet}$ corresponding to the current communities (the ones in the current partition). But for the communities that are not in $\mathcal{P}_k$ (because they have been merged with another community before) we only keep the information saying in which community it has been merged. We keep enough information to construct the dendogram and have access to the composition of any community with a few more computation.

When we merge two communities C_1 and C_2 we perform the following operations:

- Compute $P^t_{(C_1\cup C_2)\bullet} = \frac{|C_1|P^t_{C_1\bullet}+|C_2|P^t_{C_2\bullet}}{|C_1|+|C_2|}$ and remove $P^t_{C_1\bullet}$ and $P^t_{C_2\bullet}$.
- Update the values of $\Delta\sigma$ concerning C_1 and C_2 using Theorem 3.

The first operation can be done in $\mathcal{O}(n)$, and therefore does not play a significant role in the overall complexity of the algorithm. The dominating factor in the complexity of the algorithm is the number of distances r computed (each one in $\mathcal{O}(n)$). We prove an upper bound of this number that depends on the height H of the dendrogram.

Theorem 4. *An upper bound of the number of distances computed by our algorithm is $2mH$. Therefore its global time complexity is $\mathcal{O}(mn(H+t))$.*

In practice, a small t must be chosen (we must have $t = \mathcal{O}(\log n)$ due to the exponential convergence speed of the random walks process) and thus the global complexity is $\mathcal{O}(mnH)$. The worst case is $H = n-1$, which occurs when the vertices are merged one by one to a large community. This happens in the "star" graph, where a central vertex is linked to the $n-1$ others. However Ward's algorithm is known to produce small communities of similar sizes. This tends to get closer to the favorable case in which the community structure is a balanced tree and its height is $H = \mathcal{O}(\log n)$.

[1] Inter-community edges contribute for $\frac{1}{2}$ to each community.

5 Conclusion and Further Work

We proposed a new distance between the vertices that quantify their structural similarities using random walks. This distance has several advantages: it captures much information on the community structure, it is well suited for approximation, and it can be used in an efficient hierarchical agglomerative algorithm. We designed such an algorithm which works in time $\mathcal{O}(mnH)$. In practice, real-world complex networks are sparse ($m = \mathcal{O}(n)$) and the height of the dendrogram is generally small ($H = \mathcal{O}(\log n)$); in this case the algorithm runs in $\mathcal{O}(n^2 \log n)$. An implementation is provided at [29].

We presented in this short paper the main principle of the algorithm. However many improvements and optimizations have been implemented, which make it possible to process very large networks (up to several hundred thousand vertices). Moreover, extensive experiments have been run to compare the different existing approaches. They show that our method provides excellent results in different conditions (graph sizes, densities, number of communities, and community size distributions) while having a time complexity among the best ones.

We are convinced that our method could be integrated in a multi-scale visualization tool for large networks. Our approach may also be relevant for the computation of *overlapping* communities (which often occurs in real-world cases and is not considered by any algorithm until now). We consider these two points as promising directions for further work. Finally, we pointed out that the method is directly usable for *weighted* networks. For directed ones (like the important case of the Web graph), on the contrary, the proofs we provided are not valid anymore, and random walks behave significantly differently. Therefore, we also consider the directed case as an interesting direction.

Acknowledgments. We thank Annick Lesne and L.S. Shulman for useful conversation and Clémence Magnien for helpful comments on preliminary versions. This work has been supported in part by the PERSI (*Programme d'Étude des Réseaux Sociaux de l'Internet*) project and by the GAP (*Graphs, Algorithms and Probabilities*) project.

References

1. Wasserman, S., Faust, K.: Social network analysis. Cambridge University Press, Cambridge (1994)
2. Strogatz, S.H.: Exploring complex networks. Nature **410** (2001) 268–276
3. Albert, R., Barabási, A.L.: Statistical mechanics of complex networks. Reviews of Modern Physics **74** (2002) 47
4. Newman, M.E.J.: The structure and function of complex networks. SIAM REVIEW **45** (2003) 167
5. Dorogovtsev, S., Mendes, J.: Evolution of Networks: From Biological Nets to the Internet and WWW. Oxford University Press, Oxford (2003)
6. Clauset, A., Newman, M.E.J., Moore, C.: Finding community structure in very large networks. Physical Review E **70** (2004) 066111

7. Pothen, A., Simon, H.D., Liou, K.P.: Partitioning sparse matrices with eigenvectors of graphs. SIAM J. Matrix Anal. Appl. **11** (1990) 430–452
8. Kernighan, B.W., Lin, S.: An efficient heuristic procedure for partitioning graphs. Bell System Technical Journal **49** (1970) 291–308
9. Girvan, M., Newman, M.E.J.: Community structure in social and biological networks. PNAS **99** (2002) 7821–7826
10. Newman, M.E.J., Girvan, M.: Finding and evaluating community structure in networks. Physical Review E **69** (2004) 026113
11. Radicchi, F., Castellano, C., Cecconi, F., Loreto, V., Parisi, D.: Defining and identifying communities in networks. PNAS **101** (2004) 2658–2663
12. Fortunato, S., Latora, V., Marchiori, M.: Method to find community structures based on information centrality. Physical Review E **70** (2004) 056104
13. Newman, M.E.J.: Fast algorithm for detecting community structure in networks. Physical Review E **69** (2004) 066133
14. Donetti, L., Muñoz, M.A.: Detecting network communities: a new systematic and efficient algorithm. Journal of Statistical Mechanics **2004** (2004) 10012
15. Wu, F., Huberman, B.A.: Finding communities in linear time: A physics approach. The European Physical Journal B **38** (2004) 331–338
16. Reichardt, J., Bornholdt, S.: Detecting fuzzy community structures in complex networks with a potts model. Physical Review Letters **93** (2004) 218701
17. Bagrow, J., Bollt, E.: A local method for detecting communities. Physical Review E (2005 (to appear))
18. Duch, J., Arenas, A.: Community detection in complex networks using extremal optimization. arXiv:cond-mat/0501368 (2005)
19. Gaume, B.: Balades alatoires dans les petits mondes lexicaux. I3 Information Interaction Intelligence **4** (2004)
20. F., F., A., P., M., S.: A novel way of computing dissimilarities between nodes of a graph, with application to collaborative filtering. In: Workshop on Statistical Approaches for Web Mining (SAWM), Pisa (2004) 26–37
21. Zhou, H., Lipowsky, R.: Network brownian motion: A new method to measure vertex-vertex proximity and to identify communities and subcommunities. In: International Conference on Computational Science. (2004) 1062–1069
22. van Dongen, S.: Graph Clustering by Flow Simulation. PhD thesis, University of Utrecht (2000)
23. Lovász, L.: Random walks on graphs: a survey. In: Combinatorics, Paul Erdős is eighty, Vol. 2 (Keszthely, 1993). Volume 2 of Bolyai Soc. Math. Stud. János Bolyai Math. Soc., Budapest (1996) 353–397
24. Simonsen, I., Eriksen, K.A., Maslov, S., Sneppen, K.: Diffusion on complex networks: a way to probe their large-scale topological structures. Physica A: Statistical Mechanics and its Applications **336** (2004) 163–173
25. Schulman, L.S., Gaveau, B.: Coarse grains: The emergence of space and order. Foundations of Physics **31** (2001) 713–731
26. Gaveau, B., Lesne, A., Schulman, L.S.: Spectral signatures of hierarchical relaxation. Physics Letters A **258** (1999) 222–228
27. Ward, J.H.: Hierarchical grouping to optimize an objective function. Journal of the American Statistical Association **58** (1963) 236–244
28. Jambu, M., M.-O., L.: Cluster analysis and data analysis. North Holland Publishing (1983)
29. Pons, P.: (`http://liafa.jussieu.fr/~pons/`)

Fame as an Effect of the Memory Size*

Haluk Bingol

Department of Computer Engineering,
Bogazici University, Istanbul 34342, Turkey
bingol@boun.edu.tr

Abstract. This paper investigates the effect of the memory size to fame. A population of individuals of the same memory size is considered. A simple recommendation model is defined based on the memory of the individuals, the social network and the population memory. Recommendation process changes the content of the memory. As the ratio of memory size to population size decreases, a self-organized pattern emerged in who-knows-who graph. Majority of the people become unknown yet a few become very famous. This could be a model for fame and memory.

1 Introduction

Suppose we need a dentist or need information about an item. What do you do? Our first approach is to check our memory whether we have any. If we do not know, then our second attempt would be to ask our friends for a recommendation. Then we would go to cataloged data such as yellow pages, search engines. A couple of concepts are involved in these processes including our memory, our social network, the cumulative memory of the social network, a recommendation process.

Suppose we are looking for S. The more S is known, the more it can be reached, since the probability of finding a person that knows it within our social network increases. Conversely, the less S is known, the more difficult to be reached. In the limit case, if nobody knows it, then there is no way to reach it. This discussion calls for fame which is the central concept of this paper.

1.1 Fame

Wikipedia.org defines fame as "the condition of being known to the general public". Popularity, which is particularly difficult concept to measure, is investigated in various contexts. One pragmatic measure is the search results in the web. A Google search returns a number of web pages that refer to an item. The assumption is that the more pages return, the more popular the item is. This measure of popularity has an

* This work was partially supported by Bogazici University Research Projects under the grant number 05A105.

P. Yolum et al.(Eds.): ISCIS 2005, LNCS 3733, pp. 294–303, 2005.

implicit problem since an item can be listed because of some other reason than what we are looking for. For example, a singer can be listed because of being a movie actor as well as being a singer.

The fame of WWI fighter-pilots are obtained using this approach [1]. It is found that the probability $p(f)$ of having fame f decreases with a power-law of f, namely $p(f) \sim f^{-\gamma}$ where $\gamma \approx 1.9$. Let a be the achievement of the person which is defined as the number of opponent aircrafts destroyed. It is found that $p(f)$ increases exponentially with achievement a, $p(f) \sim e^{\beta a}$ where $\beta \approx 0.074$.

In a similar study, the popularity of scientists in condensed matter and statistical physics is investigated [2]. The findings of this are quite different. $p(f)$ decays exponentially, rather than in power-law fashion, $p(f) \sim e^{-\eta f}$; $\eta \approx 0.00102$.

Another popularity measure proposed is the frequency of appearance in the news [3].

Popularity of a web page is another context that is crucial for search engines. The quality of a search engine is to bring the "right" pages, in the "right" order. Although there may be many web pages which covers the topic, some web pages become more famous then others. Search engines use page ranking algorithms in order to sort the pages. Google's page ranking algorithm is based on number of in-links to page and the rank of the pages that initiate the link [4]. Intuitively, if a page gets more links, it has to have more "value". Similarly, if a page gets a link from an important page, that is highly ranked page, it's "value" should be increased. Web page linking to another page forms a *network of web pages*.

Incrementing the value of someone based on the reference of a valuable one is the trust mechanism [5]. Agent A trusts agent B. Since agent B trusts agent C, agent A also trusts agent C. In this way a *trust network* is constructed.

1.2 Social Networks

Social networks are difficult to study since data collection is difficult. One of the early studies is done by Milgram which lead to *six degrees of separation* principle [6]. The basic idea is to send a letter from a source person to a destination person. The rule is that anybody who receives the letter should send it to somebody that he knows by name. This experiment establishes *who-knows-who* network and concluded that any two persons are connected by a chain of persons whose length is around 6 which is much smaller then expected. Watts and Strogotz improved this concept to "small-world" [7].

Co-authorship of scientific papers is another social network. Power-law is observed in degree distribution of these networks. Power-law degree distribution, $p(k) \sim k^{-\gamma}$ where $p(k)$ is the probability of having degree of k, seems to be quite common in many complex networks including internet router, www, e-mails, movie actors, co-authorship of scientific papers [8, 9, 10, 11, 12].

Citation of scientific papers forms a network in which power-law degree distribution is also valid [13]. Number of citations of a paper gets could be a measure of its popularity. Number of links a web page gets is another measure of fame. In who-know-who networks, the more links one gets, the more popular she becomes.

Another social network is studied in the co-occurrence in the news. Persons occur in the news are represented as vertices and there is an edge if two persons occurred in the same news article [14]. The more a person occurs in news, the more famous she becomes.

1.3 Motivation of the Model and Organization

A node should "know" the other node in order to link to it. In cases of social networks or complex networks, the number of nodes is, simply, too large. Therefore, no node should be able to "know" all the other nodes[1]. Only a small fraction of the total nodes can be known by any single node. On the other hand, there is no limit to be known. A node can be known by all of the nodes in the network. Some one discovers a new web site and starts to recommend it to his contacts. A contact that receives the recommendation evaluates it. Sometimes keeps it. Sometimes he also recommends the site to others. This behavior is the basic idea of simple recommendation model that is developed in this paper.

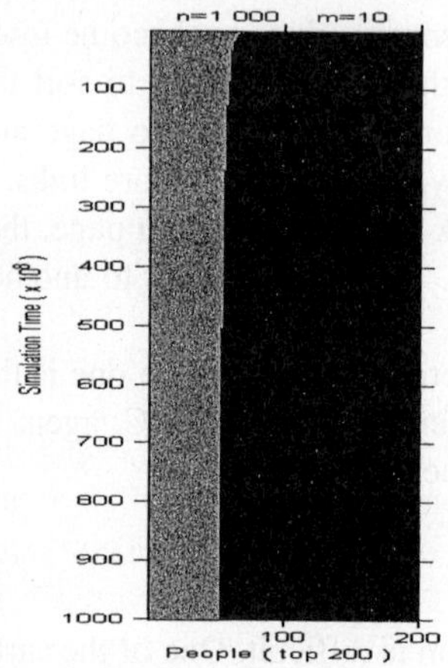

Fig. 1. For ρ=0.001 with n=10^3, m=10, 10^{11} recommendations are made. Time is on the y-axis with units of 10^8 recommendations. Peoples are on x-axis sorted according to knownness. More active 200 is shown, since majority of the people become completely unknown at the very early stages of the simulation. The system settles down quite fast. Note that after 500x10^8 there is no change. Black is unknown and white is the most known.

The concept of "to know" is the center of this paper. This paper investigates the effect of the size of memory to the fame. A model is defined. Simulation results of different memory sizes, population sizes are investigated. The findings are interpreted. A model for fame is searched. The paper is concluded by a conclusion and future work.

2 Definitions

Population is made out of persons. The *size* n of the population is defined to be the number of persons in the population. p_i is the i'th person. A person has a *memory* which is a list of persons. The *size* m of the memory is the maximum number of persons that can be stored. The *memory ratio* ρ is defined to be the ratio of the memory size to the population size, that is $\rho = m/n$.

Total memory capacity of the population is the summation of the size of memories of the individual persons that is $n \times m$. A person p_1 *knows* person p_2 if person p_2 is in the memory of person p_1. The *knownness* k_i of a person p_i is the number of persons that

[1] Some proposed models for complex networks such as prefrential attachment requires information about mostly connected nodes which is a global information.

"know" the person. If no body knows a person p_i, that is k_i=0, then person is called *completely unknown*. The *fame* f_i of a person p_i is defined as the ratio of the *knownness* to the population size, that is $f_i = k_i / n$.

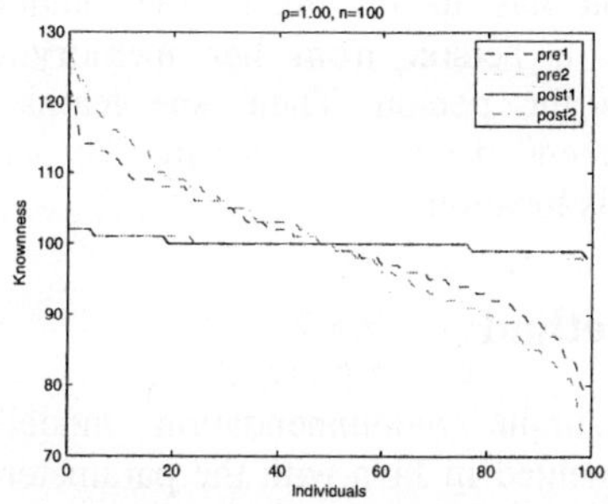

Fig. 2. This is the results of population of size n=100. All peoples are of memory size m=100. The individuals are on the x-axis and their knownness on the y-axis. Data is sorted in descending order.

In the graph, *pre1* and *pre2* are results of initial load of memories. *Post1* and *post2* are the results after 10^6 reference exchanges.

There are minor fluctuations between the two simulation runs. For *pre1* and *pre2*, the range is 79-122 and 73-128, respectively. One expects that the upper bound of knownness should be n. Knownness higher then n, such as 122 or 128, mean some persons are known by more then once by a person since duplication is allowed in the initial loading.

The ranges of *post1* and *post2* are 98-102 and 97-102, respectively. It is observed that for m=n, fluctuations are removed, the range is reduced. This is expected since duplication is not allowed during recommendation exchange.

Notice that if no duplication is allowed, then $k_i \leq$ n. Therefore $0 \leq f_i \leq 1$, that is f_i is normalized. Since it is the percentage of the population that knows the person, fame is used as a measure of famousness. As the percentage increases, the person becomes more *famous*.

Recommendation. Person *learns* if he gets a new person in his memory. A person p_1 *remembers* a person p_2, if p_1 selects p_2 among persons stored in his memory. Person *forgets* if he removes a person from his memory.

Persons interact by exchanging recommendations. Person p_1 *recommends* person p_0 to person p_2. Steps of recommendation process are i) p_1 remembers p_0, ii) p_1 gives p_0 to p_2, iii) p_2 learns p_0. Assuming that no duplication is allowed and $m<n$, the steps of learning are i) remember some person, ii) forget him therefore obtain an empty slot, iii) learn the new person using this slot. Person p_1 is called the *giver*. Person p_2 is called the *taker*. It is important to note that learning, remembering and forgetting have implicit selection processes. A model has to specify these mechanisms.

3 A Simple Recommendation Model

A simple recommendation model can be built on these concepts by defining the mechanisms based on pure random selection. Initially, the memories of the persons are filled with persons selected randomly with duplications are allowed. Any two persons are expected to have almost the same knownness, hence every one have the same fame initially. The giver and the taker are selected randomly. The giver randomly selects a person from his memory as his recommendation. This is the "remembering" process. The taker checks if she already knows the recommended

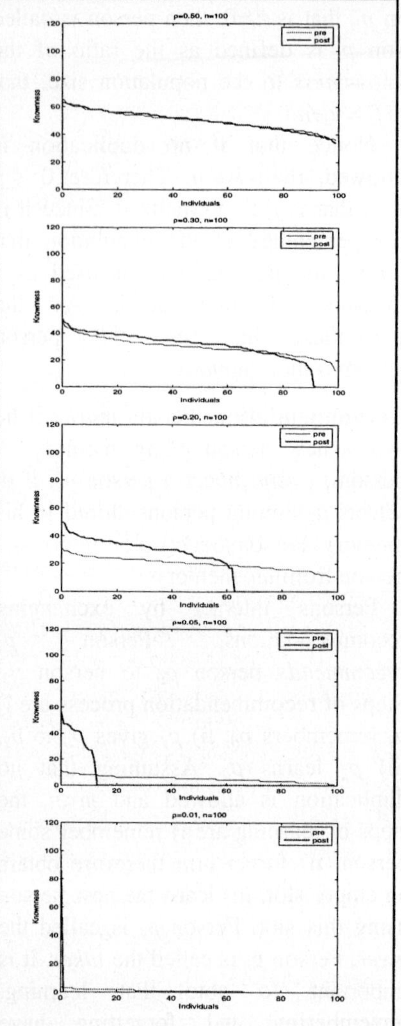

Fig. 3. Effect of memory ratio ρ=0.5, 0.3, 0.2, 0.05, 0.01 for n=100. As the memory ratio ρ decreases, some people become famous in response to that, more and more people become unknown.

person. If she remembers the person, then nothing is done. If she does not remember the recommended person, a memory location has to be freed. She randomly selects a person from her memory and forgets the person. Then, she learns the recommended person by storing the person into this location.

4 Method

This simple recommendation model is implemented in Java with the parameters n, m and the number of reference exchanges. Different combinations of values of n and ρ are used including n=100, 1000, 10000 and ρ=0.5, 0.3, 0.2, 0.1, 0.05, 0.005. The number of reference exchanges is tried to be as large as possible. As n increases, it has to increase, too. It is started from 10^6 for n=100 to 10^{10} for n=10,000 which seems to be large enough. 10 simulation runs are made for different combinations of n and ρ values. The results of these runs are visualized by Excel and Matlab. In the figures, results of two simulations runs are presented so that the fluctuations can be seen.

Random selections required by the model are implemented by random() method of java.lang.Math which is a pseudo random number generator with a uniform distribution. Java v1.5.0_02 is used.

5 Observations

System gets its steady state quite fast as seen in Figure.1. Due to short run times of simulation and the ease of visualization n=100 is used for initial observations. Then similar simulations are done for large values of n. The similar patterns are observed. Firstly, the effect of ρ is investigated. For values of ρ>1, it is not interesting. So initially the cases of $\rho\leq1$ for n=100 are studied.

5.1 Case ρ=1

The results of many simulations consistently produce similar patterns. In Figure.2, *Pre1* is the initial state and *post1* is the state at the end of the simulation of reference exchanges. In order to compare the difference between different simulations, a second data set is also given. *Pre2* and *post2* are the initial and final data for another simulation run. At any given time memory dumps of individuals provide information of about who-knows-who. The knownness of person p_i is calculated by counting the persons that know person p_i. The knownness table which consists of persons and their knownnesses is obtained. For better visualization, the data is sorted in descending order in knownness and the graph is obtained.

If everybody is of the same fame, the graph should be a horizontal line. If there are minor fluctuations in the fame, then the difference in fames of the most famous person and the least famous persons should be minor. Since the data is sorted in descending order, a small negative slope should be expected. The initial loading of the memory has some fluctuations. The recommendation exchange flattens the fluctuations by removing duplicate entries in the memories.

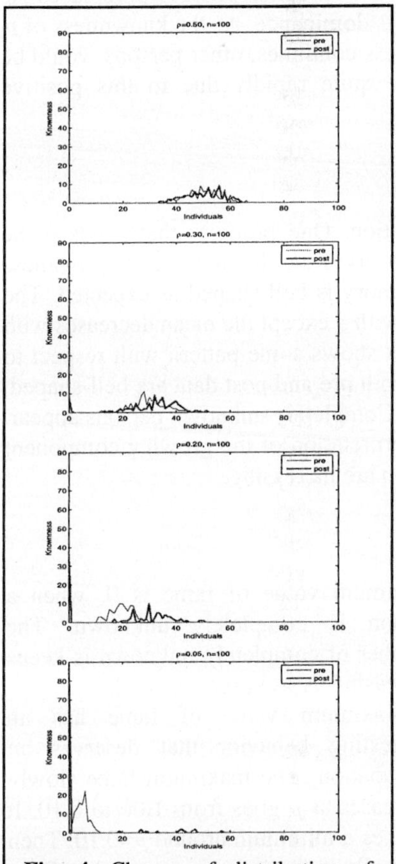

Fig. 4. Change of distribution of fame with respect to memory ratio ρ. As ρ goes to 0, the distribution of fame becomes distorted. The mean of the initial memory moves to 0 since the memory size gets smaller. A few individuals becomes very famous, while majority of the population becomes more and more unknown by the population.

5.2 Case ρ<1

An unexpected pattern forms when the memory ratio decreases. Almost uniform distribution of fame that is observed at ρ=1 disappears. Some people become more known where as some become less known. Further decreasing ρ causes some people to be completely forgotten by the population. Figure.3 gives the effect of ρ to the change in fame.

For ρ=0.5, everyone is known in varying degrees and there is no completely forgotten person. Around ρ=0.3, some people become completely unknown. The number of completely forgotten people increases as ρ decreases as seen in Table.1. It is important to notice that if a person becomes completely unknown, then there is no way for her to become known.

Table 1. Number of unknown people increases as ρ goes to 0 for population of n=*100*. In the limit case of ρ=*0.01* only one person is know and the rest of 99 people is unknown by the society.

n=100, ρ	1.00	0.50	0.30	0.20	0.10	0.05	0.01
# of unknown	0	0	7	34	79	88	99
#fame (max)	102	63	51	50	46	57	100

5.3 Case $\rho \ll 1$

As ρ decreases, it eventually reaches the extreme case in which m=1, meaning an individual can remember only one person. An interesting pattern emerges as n increases while m=1. For n=100 (ρ=0.01) only 1 person is known by the population where as for $n=10^3$ (ρ=0.001), there are around 50 known people. n=100 case can be explained by the small size of the population. Suppose this one slot is slightly dominated by a person p_i. Then p_i would be recommended more by the recommendation process. Due to the rules of recommendation process, p_i replaces the position of other people. This further increases its dominance. As the knownness of p_i increases, it is recommended more. As the process continues, other persons would be removed from the memory of the population quite rapidly due to this positive feedback.

5.4 Distribution of Fame

Individuals have different fames in the population. One property that needs to be investigated is the distribution of fame. Figure.4 gives the distribution of knownness with respect to ρ. The distribution of initial memory is bell-shaped as expected. The shape of the initial distribution does not change with ρ except the mean decreases with the memory size. The distribution of knownness shows some pattern with respect to changes in ρ. In the range of ρ=1.00 to ρ=0.50 both pre and post data are bell-shaped. Around ρ=0.30, an unexpected pattern emerges. Completely unknown persons appear. This pattern grows as ρ decreases to 0. The interpretation of the growing component near 0 is that less famous people in the population are increasing.

5.5 Change of Fame

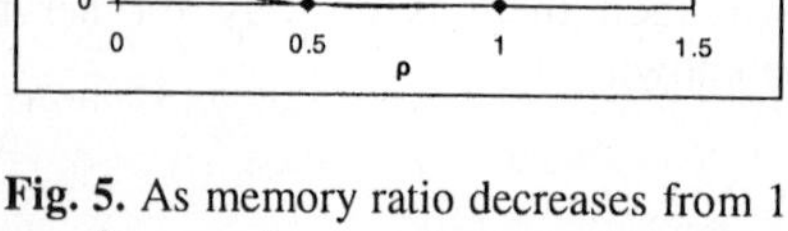

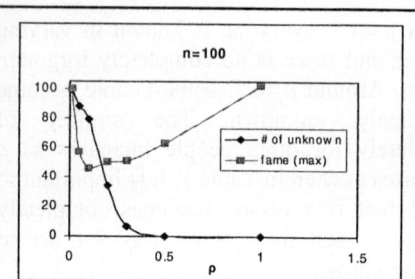

Fig. 5. As memory ratio decreases from 1 to 0, number unknown increases. Interestingly, maximum fame slowly decreases and then rapidly increases.

Minimum value of fame is 0, when a person is completely unknown. The number of completely unknown is keeps increasing as ρ approaches to 0.

Maximum value of fame has an interesting behavior that deserves an explanation. The maximum fame slowly decreases as ρ goes from 1.00 to 0.10. It reaches a minimum around ρ=0.10. Then it rapidly increases as ρ approaches from 0.10 to 0 as seen in Figure.5. This pattern can be explained. When ρ=1, that is m=100, everybody is known by everybody else so the fame is 1. As ρ decreases, the memory of the individuals decreases. Since no one dominates the memories yet, people are almost evenly distributed in the memories. So the reduction of the maximum fame is due to the decrease of the memory size. But as ρ keeps decreasing, after a certain point some people become completely forgotten and some others become the dominated ones. As

ρ approaches to the limit of 0, the more people are completely forgotten and a few people dominate the memories. Those that dominate take all the references. So the rapid increase of maximum fame can be explained due to this positive feedback.

5.6 Effect of Population Size

So far n=100 is considered. 100 is a too small size compared to complex networks that are considered for power-law or small-world properties. For larger values of n, similar observations are obtained. Table.2 gives increase of completely unknown people as ρ decreases for $n=10^3$. Figure.6 compares ρ=0.05 for $n=10^2$, 10^3 and 10^4.

Table 2. Pattern near 0 as ρ decreases for n=1,000

n= 1,000 ρ	0.50	0.15	0.10	0.05	0.03	0.01	0.005
# of unknown	0	0	16	376	661	903	958
% of unknown	0.00	0.00	0.02	0.38	0.66	0.90	0.96

6 Conclusion

The effect of the memory size m of individuals with respect to population size n is investigated. The ratio ρ of memory size to population size is used as parameter. A simple recommendation model which changes the memory of the individuals is defined.

The value of ρ is changed from 1 to 0. For ρ=1, everybody is known by everybody else. For values of ρ around 1, an individual is known by majority of the population. As ρ decreases, some individuals become unknown by the population. As ρ gets close to 0, almost everybody becomes unknown. On the other hand, as ρ decreases some people become more known by the population. As ρ gets close to 0, very few individuals become very well known.

Although in the model items stored in the memory were again people, the model is valid if some other items are stored, too. For example web pages or dentists could be the items to store. Consider persons in a country, web pages, scientific papers, radio stations, books. For all these practical situations the size of the items is much larger then the size of the memory of the individuals. Therefore, ρ values close to 0 are realistic values.

The pattern of fame, that is observed around ρ=0 in the model has corresponding counterparts in these real life cases. Very few people are famous, where as there are millions known by very few. Same is true for web pages. Google is known by almost every internet user. Nobody knows the number of unknown web pages, since only a percentage of the entire web is cataloged by the search engines.

Recommendation could be the machinery of fame. This model could be the model of fame or the dynamics of population memory.

The rapid forgetting mechanism around ρ=0 is an interesting phenomenon to look for. Once an item has small knownness, then its knownness converges to 0 quite rapidly. This can be a model of disappearing of cultural values such as languages, traditions, piece of music, a poem or the extinction of a species once the numbers become few.

One more observation is that although the memory size of the individual is small, the total memory of the population, that is, the number of items in the memory of the population is much larger. On the other hand, population memory is less than the total memory capacity of the population that is $n \times m$.

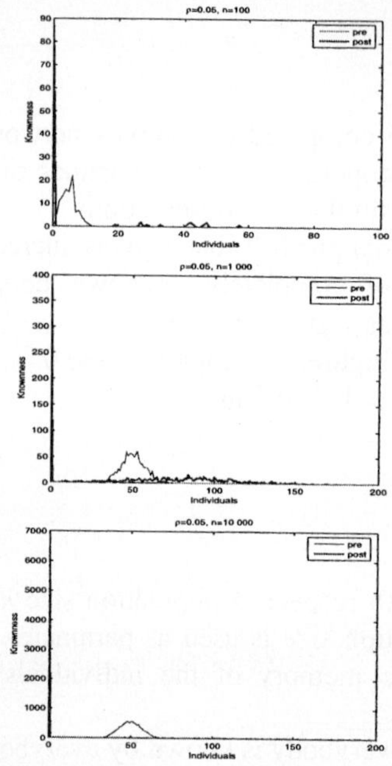

Fig. 6. Change of distribution of fame with respect to n for p=0.05 for n=100, 1,000 and 10,000. Note that the component near 0 is increasing as p decreases.

7 Future Work

It is assumed that the memory size is the same for everybody. This assumption can be relaxed to lead variation of memory sizes. For example 10% of the population has larger memory then the rest of the population.

Initially everybody has almost the same popularity. This can also be relaxed by favoring group of people to be famous initially.

"How to become popular" is another related question. Given that the population has already famous people, how do new comers become famous, that is what percentage of the population should know the person? Since to make people learn somebody is done through advertisement, this could lead to a model for advertisement campaigns.

Who-knows-who information can be represented as a directed graph called *who-knows-who graph* in which the persons are the *vertices* of the graph. There is an *arc* from person p_i to person p_j if person p_i knows person p_j. In complex networks some properties such as scale free and small world are investigated. These properties of who-knows-who graphs obtained using the reference model is investigated in the upcoming paper [15].

Acknowledgement. The author would like to thank Albert Ali Salah and Arzucan Ozgur for helping in matlab programming.

References

1. Simkin M. V., Roychowdhury V. P.: Theory of Aces: Fame by chance or merit?, (2003) cond-mat/0310049.
2. Bagrow J. P., Rozenfeld H. D., Bollt E. M., Avraham D. B.: How Famous is a Scientist? - Famous to Those Who Know Us, (2004) cond-mat/0404515.

3. Bingol H.: The frequency of appearance in the news as a popularity measure, (in preparation).
4. Brin S., Page L.: The anatomy of a large-scale hypertextual Web search engine, Computer Networks and ISDN Systems (30), (1998) 107-117.
5. Yolum P., Singh M. P.: Engineering Self-Organizing Referral Networks for Trustworthy Services Selection, IEEE Transactions On Systems, Man, And Cybernetics, 3 (2004) 396–407.
6. Milgram, S.: The small-world problem, Psychology Today, **2**, (1967) 60-67.
7. Watts, J.D., Strogatz, S.H.: Collective dynamics of 'small-world' networks, Nature **393** (1998) 440-442
8. Newman M.E.J.: The structure and function of complex networks, (2003) cond-mat/0303516.
9. Dorogovtsev, S. N., Mendes, J. F. F.: Evolution of Networks, (2001) cond-mat/0106144v2.
10. Albert, R., Barabasi, A. L.: Statistical Mechanics of Complex Networks, In Reviews of Modern Physics **73** (2002) 47-97, (cond-mat/0106096).
11. Kirlidog, M. Bingol, H.: The shaping of an electronic list by its active members, ITIRA'03 (2003) 40-48.
12. Newman M.E.J.: The structure of scientific collaboration networks, PNAS **98** 2, (2001) 404-409.
13. Redner, S.: How Popular is Your Paper? An Empirical Study of the Citation Distribution, (1998) cond-mat/9804163.
14. Ozgur, A., Bingol H.: Social Network of Co-occurrence in News Articles, LNCS 3280 (2004) 688-695.
15. Bingol H.: Graph properties of who-knows-who graphs, (in preparation).

Keeping Viruses Under Control*

Erol Gelenbe

Dennis Gabor Chair, Department of Electrical and Electronic Engineering,
Imperial College London SW7 2BT
e.gelenbe@imperial.ac.uk

Abstract. We introduce a probability model for populations of conflicting agents such as computer software (cells) and computer viruses that interact in the presence of an anti-viral agent. Cells can be infected by viruses, and their longevity and ability to avoid infection is modified if they survive successive attacks by viruses. Viruses that survive the effect of the anti-viral agent may find that their ability to survive a future encounter with molecules of the anti-viral agent is modified, as is their ability to infect a uninfected cell. Additionally, we assume that the anti-viral agent can be a cocktail with different proportions of agents that target different strains of the virus. In this paper, we give the state equations for the model and prove its analytical solution in steady state. The solution then provides insight into the approriate mix or "cocktail" of anti-viral agents that are designed to deal with the virus' ability to mutate. In particular, the analysis shows that the concentration of anti-viral agent by itself does not suffice to ultimately control the infection, and that it is important to dose a mix of anti-viral agents so as to target each strain of virus in a specific manner, taking into account the ability of each virus strain to survive in the presence of the anti-viral agent.

Keywords: Computer Viruses, Conflicts between Agents, Network Security.

1 Introduction

Mathematical models of populations [5] have been applied successfully to the study of infectious diseases [7]. Furthermore, population models [1], as well as the study of telephone calls [2] which gave rise rise to queueing theory [4,9], have had significant impact on the development of the mathematics of random processes [6].

In this paper we consider a stochastic population model which is inspired by both engineering and biological considerations. The biological context we have in mind corresponds to an environment containing a concentration of viruses, of uninfected and infected cells, and of an active anti-viral agent. The engineering context comes from computer software, where "intelligent agents" interact in accomplishing different tasks. In particular, there are harmful software agents

* Research supported by US Army ARO under Contract No. DAAD19-03-1-0135.

P. Yolum et al.(Eds.): ISCIS 2005, LNCS 3733, pp. 304–311, 2005.

which are otherwise known as computer viruses and worms. They infect and degrade the software of *bona fide* users, and can be eliminated by specific anti-viral software designed which is designed to block or destroy software viruses. In the terminology used throughout this paper, we will only refer to the biological paradigm, so as to avoid going back and forth between these motivating examples.

We show that under appropriate assumptions, a stochastic model of the size of such a biological mix of populations can lead to a steady-state solution which has a particularly simple product form, in which the joint probability distribution of the size of each sub-population is expressed as the product of the marginal distribution of each population. We then show how this result can provide insight into the manner in which the anti-viral agent should be targeted in a specific manner to each strain of the mutating virus so as to keep the viral population under control.

1.1 The Mathematical Model

We model the numbers of each of the four entities, namely the numbers of viruses and cells, and the number of molecules of anti-viral agent at some time $t \geq 0$, or their concentrations, with the following variables:

- The number of uninfected cells of type or strain i is represented by a natural number $C_i(t) \geq 0$, where $i = 0, 1, 2$ .... The strain of the cell can impact the degree to which it becomes infected, and its survivability or longevity.
- The number of infected cells (or their concentration) is also represented by a natural number $\iota(t) \geq 0$. In this paper we do not distinguish between the strains of infected cells.
- $a(t) \geq 0$ is the quantity or concentration of the anti-viral agent, and is also a natural number.
- Finally, $V_j(t) \geq 0$ is a natural number representing the number of viruses in the system that belong to strain $j \geq 0$.

uninfected cells of type 0 are those which have never encountered a virus, while viruses of strain 0 are those which have never come into contact with the anti-viral agent.

All the entities we consider enter the system at some specific rate, and diffuse through the system at specific rates. Uninfected cells of type i are added to the system (for instance via arrival into the system, or via cell division) at some rate λ_i; they diffuse through the system at rate μ_i and are eliminated from the system (e.g. as a consequence of cell death or some other form of elimination) at rate $d_i\mu_i$ where d_i can be interpreted as a probability. Infected cells result only from the infection of uninfected cells, i.e. we do not assume that infected cells enter the system from some outside source. The infected cells diffuse at rate μ, they die at rate $d\mu$, where d is a probability, and at rate $(1-d)\mu$ they leave the system before they die. Viruses belonging to strain j enter the system at some rate β_j and diffuse at rate γ_j. They are eliminated naturally at rate $b_j\gamma_j$ where $0 \leq b_j \leq 1$ is a probability. Thus different virus strains may be more or less "durable", just as certain types of cells may survive longer than others.

When an infected cell dies, we assume that it generates an additional virus of strain $j = 0$. Infected cells could potentially generate a large number of viruses; however the mathematical model is restricted to this simpler case for the time being. Furthermore, the reduced virulence of infected cells could also be attributed to the presence of the anti-viral agent. Also we could imagine that the genetic strain of the viruses generated by an infected cell should somehow mimic the strain of the viruses that infected it. Thus in both of these respects, as in other aspects, our model is a mathematical simplification of a much more complex reality.

An anti-viral agent's units (e.g. molecules) enter the medium at rate α, and diffuse in the medium at rate δ. During diffusion, they are removed from the medium with probability $0 \leq f \leq 1$. With probability $(1-f)$ a unit of the anti-viral agent will bind with some virus. With probability w_j an anti-viral agent molecule attaches itself to a virus of strain j so that $\sum_{j=0}^{\infty} w_j = (1-f)$. If, on the other hand, there are no viruses of that strain available, the unit or molecule of the anti-viral agent will be wasted. Once the anti-viral agent binds with its selected virus of type j, it will destroy it with probability r_j, or the virus will survive with probability $(1-r_j)$. If the virus survives, it is now viewed as being a virus of strain $j+1$.

Infection of uninfected cells occurs as a result of the encounter of uninfected cells and viruses. As indicated earlier, once a cell is infected, it will die at some rate μd and as a result will produce a virus. We model the infection process as follows.

Viruses belonging to strain j, when they are not naturally eliminated from the system, will diffuse at rate γ_j, and will be eliminated from the system at rate $\gamma_j b_j$. Viruses of strain j will target cells of strain i with probability z_{ji} where $\sum_{i=0}^{\infty} z_{ji} = (1-b_j)$. Thus the probability z_{ji} expresses the preference of the virus of strain j for a cell of type or strain i.

Similarly, a normal cell of type i will diffuse through the system at rate μ_i and be eliminated from the system before it encounters a virys with probability d_i. As it diffuses in the system, the cell will have preferentially bind with a viruses of type j with probability y_{ij}, $\sum_{j=0}^{\infty} y_{ij} = (1-d_i)$.

The uninfected cell of type i that is involved in either of these encounters with a virus of type i will become infected with probability p_{ji}, or with probability $(1-p_{ji})$ it remains uninfected. If it does not become infected, it will now have become a cell of type $i+1$. This model can represent either a mutation of the cell into a more resistant (or simply different) strain as a result of the encounter with the virus, or it may represent the fact that the cell's strain is being revealed by the encounter with the virus.

2 Stationary Solution

The system can be described at time $t \geq 0$ by an infinite random vector:

$$X(t) = [I(t), a(t), C_0(t), \; \dots \; C_i(t), \; \dots \;, V_0(t), \; \dots \; V_j(t), \; \dots \;], \tag{1}$$

which represents the number of infected cells, the concentration of anti-viral agent, the number of uninfected cells of each type, and the number of viruses of each strain. The total number of cells and viruses are given by:

$$C(t) = \sum_{i=0}^{\infty} C_i(t), \tag{2}$$

$$V(t) = \sum_{j=0}^{\infty} V_j(t).$$

For notational convenience we denote by c_i the infinite vector that is zero everywhere except that it is +1 in the position corresponding to $C_i(t)$, while v_j is the infinite vector which is zero everywhere except for the value +1 in the position $V_j(t)$. Similarly, let e_I be the infinite vector which is zero everywhere except that it has a +1 in its first position and e_A be the infinite vector that is zero everywhere except for its second position that is +1.

Let $x = [\iota, a, C_0, \ldots C_i, \ldots, V_0, \ldots V_j, \ldots]$ be the deterministic vector which represents some specific value taken by $X(t)$. The quantity we will examine is the probability distribution $p(x,t) = Prob[X(t) = x|X(0) = x_0]$ for some appropriate initial condition x_0. We will skip the details of the derivation for the equations satisfied by the stationary probability distribution $p(x)$.

The stationary solution of the model provides insight into the equilibria which are established between different entities. Let us define the following quantities:

$$\Lambda_{j,i}^{-} = q_j \gamma_j z_{ji}, \quad i,j \geq 0, \tag{3}$$

$$\Lambda_i = \sum_{j=0}^{\infty} \Lambda_{j,i}^{-}, i \geq 0 \tag{4}$$

$$\lambda_{i,j}^{-} = \rho_i \mu_i y_{ij}, \quad i,j \geq 0, \tag{5}$$

$$\lambda_{A,j}^{-} = q_A \delta w_j, \quad j \geq 0, \tag{6}$$

$$\Lambda_i^{+} = \lambda_i + \sum_{j=0}^{\infty} [\Lambda_{j,i-1}^{-} \rho_{i-1} + \lambda_{i-1,j}^{-} q_j](1 - p_{j,i-1}), \quad i \geq 1, \tag{7}$$

$$F_j^{-} = \lambda_{A,j}^{-} + \sum_{i=0}^{\infty} \lambda_{i,j}^{-}, \quad j \geq 0 \tag{8}$$

$$F_j^{+} = \beta_j + \lambda_{A,j-1}^{-} q_{j-1}(1 - r_{j-1}), j \geq 1. \tag{9}$$

The expressions (4) through (9) can be interpreted as follows:

- The total rate at which viruses which diffuse in the system interact with uninfected cells of type i, either resulting in an infected cell or in a uninfected cell of type $i+1$, in effect reducing each time the number of uninfected cells by 1,
- The total rate at which uninfected cells of type i join the system either from external sources or by mutation of a cell of type $i-1$ which survives an encounter with a virus,

- The total rate at which viruses of type j are removed either because they are destroyed by the anti-viral agent or because a uninfected cell that is diffusing through the system encounters the virus, becomes infected and incorporates the virus, or does not become infected and eliminates the virus,
- Finally, the total rate at which viruses of type $j \geq 1$ are replenished, either through external arrivals or by mutation after an encounter with the anti-viral agent does not result in the destruction of a virus of strain $j-1$.

Now let:

$$q_A = \frac{\alpha}{\delta} \tag{10}$$

$$\rho_0 = \frac{\lambda_0}{\mu_0 + \Lambda_0} \tag{11}$$

$$\rho_i = \frac{\Lambda_i^+}{\mu_i + \Lambda_i}, \; i \geq 1 \tag{12}$$

$$q_0 = \frac{\beta_0 + q_I \mu d}{\gamma_0 + F_0^-},$$

$$q_j = \frac{F_j^+}{\gamma_j + F_j^-}, j \geq 1, \tag{13}$$

$$q_I = \frac{\sum_{i,j=0}^{\infty} [\Lambda_{j,i}^- \rho_i + \lambda_{i,j}^- q_j] p_{ji}}{\mu} \tag{14}$$

Now consider the finite random vector:

$$X_{m,n}(t) = [\iota(t), a(t), C_0(t), \; ... \; C_m(t), V_0, \; ... \; V_n(t)], \tag{15}$$

and the deterministic vector denoting a specific set of values taken bt $X_{m,n}(t)$,

$$x_{m,n} = [\iota, a, C_0, \; ... \; C_m, V_0, \; ... \; V_n], \tag{16}$$

and let $p(x_{m,n}, t) = Prob[X_{m,n}(t) = x_{m,n}]$.

Note that $p(x_{m,n}(t)$ is a marginal distribution related to the probability distribution $p(x,t)$, *i.e.*:

$$p(x_{m,n}(t) = \sum_{m+1}^{\infty} \sum_{n+1}^{\infty} p(x,t). \tag{17}$$

Theorem. The stationary solution $p(x_{m,n}) = \lim_{t \to +\infty} p(x_{m,n}, t)$ is given by

$$p(x_{m,n}) = G_{m,n} q_A^a q_I^\iota [\prod_{i=0}^{m} (\rho_i)^{C_i}][\prod_{j=0}^{n} (q_j)^{V_j}], \tag{18}$$

provided that $0 \leq q_A, q_I, \rho_i, q_j \; < \; 1$, for all $i = 0, ..., m$, $j = 0, ..., n$, and with:

$$G_{m,n} = (1 - q_A)(1 - q_I) \prod_{i=0}^{m} (1 - \rho_i) \prod_{j=0}^{n} (1 - q_j). \tag{19}$$

From the theorem, it is easy to see that in steady state the average number:

- of infected cells is given by $q_I[1-q_I]^{-1}$, if $q_I < 1$,
- of uninfected cells of strain i is given by $\rho_i[1-\rho_i]^{-1}$, if $\rho_i < 1$,
- and of viruses of strain j is given by $q_j[1-q_j]^{-1}$, if $q_j < 1$.

2.1 A Heuristic Rule

The purpose of using the anti-viral agent is to avoid the explosive growth of the number of infected cells and viruses. Thus we are interested in finding how we can most efectively use the anti-viral agent to keep these numbers under control, or to drive them to zero.

The $i-th$ strain of uninfected cells are those which remain uninfected after i encounters with a virus. Thus we can take $\lambda_i = 0$ for $i \geq 1$ so that all new or untested cells are considered to be of strain 0. Similarly, we assume that a virus' strain is only revealed by its successive survivals to encounters with the anti-viral agent, so that $\beta_j = 0$ for $j \geq 1$. With these assumptions the expressions (11) through (14) yield:

$$q_I = \frac{\sum_{i,j=0}^{\infty} \rho_i q_j [\gamma_j z_{ji} + \mu_i y_{ij}] p_{ji}}{\mu} \tag{20}$$

so that for $j \geq 1$,

$$q_j = \frac{\lambda^-_{A,j-1} q_{j-1}(1-r_{j-1})}{\gamma_j + q_A \delta w_j + \sum_{i=0}^{\infty} \rho_i \mu_i y_{ij}} \tag{21}$$

$$= q_0 P(j) \tag{22}$$

$$P(j) = \alpha^j \prod_{l=1}^{j} \frac{w_{l-1}(1-r_{l-1})}{\gamma_l + \alpha w_l + \sum_{i=0}^{\infty} \rho_i \mu_i y_{il}} \tag{23}$$

while for $i \geq 1$,

$$\rho_i = \rho_{i-1} \frac{\sum_{j=0}^{\infty} q_j [\gamma_j z_{j,i-1} + \mu_i y_{i-1,j}](1-p_{j,i-1})}{\mu_i + \sum_{j=0}^{\infty} q_j \gamma_j z_{ji}} \tag{24}$$

$$= \rho_0 \prod_{l=1}^{i} \frac{\sum_{j=0}^{\infty} q_j [\gamma_j z_{j,l-1} + \mu_i y_{l-1,j}](1-p_{j,l-1})}{\mu_l + \sum_{j=0}^{\infty} q_j \gamma_j z_{jl}} \tag{25}$$

and

$$q_0 = \frac{\beta_0 + \sum_{i,j=0}^{\infty} \rho_i q_j [\gamma_j z_{ji} + \mu_i y_{ij}] p_{ji}}{\gamma_0 + \alpha w_0 + \sum_{i=0}^{\infty} \rho_i m y_{i0}} \tag{26}$$

$$= \frac{\beta_0}{\gamma_0 + \alpha w_0 + \sum_{i=0}^{\infty} \rho_i \mu_i y_{i0} - q_0 \sum_{i,j=0}^{\infty} \rho_i P(j)[\gamma_j z_{ji} + \mu_i y_{ij}] p_{ji}} \tag{27}$$

$$\rho_0 = \frac{\lambda_0}{\mu_0 + \sum_{j=0}^{\infty} q_j \gamma z_{j0}} \tag{28}$$

Let us now see how (23) can provide insight about the use of the anti-viral agent. First of all, notice from (27) that if we can choose αw_0 to be arbitrarily large, then we can set q_0 to a value less than 1, and in fact set it to as small a value as we wish. Obviously there will be natural limits to this since at some level of concentration, the anti-viral agent will impair the normal behaviour of uninfected cells. Once a small enough value of q_0 has been achieved using a large enough value of αw_0, we turn to (23) and see intuitively that we must also insure that $P(j)$ does not grow as j increases. An obvious way of doing this is to set $w_j > w_{j-1}(1 - r_{j-1})$, in other words the fraction of anti-viral agent which is devoted to controlling the $j - th$ viral strain should be larger than the fraction allotted to the $j - 1 - th$ strain multiplied by the probability that viruses of the $j - 1 - th$ strain survive an encounter with the anti-viral agent.

Let us now put this recomendation on a more rigorous mathematical footing. Assume first that have been able to achieve $q_0 < 1$. Then if all the $P(j) < 1$ we are sure that the $q_j < 1$ for $j \geq 1$. However, this does not suffice to guarantee that the size of the virus population is under control, i.e. that in steady state the average size of the virus population remains finite:

$$V = \sum_{j=0}^{\infty} \frac{q_j}{1 - q_j} < +\infty \,. \tag{29}$$

However, we can show that if $q_0 < 1$ and $w_j \geq w_{j-1}(1 - r_{j-1})$ so that all $q_j < 1$, then $V < +\infty$ provided that:

$$\lim_{j \to +\infty} \frac{w_j(1 - r_j)}{w_{j+1}} = 0, \tag{30}$$

Indeed, if the $q_j < 1$ for $j \geq 0$, then

$$V = \sum_{j=0}^{\infty} \frac{q_j}{1 - q_j} \leq \sum_{j=0}^{\infty} [q_j + q_j^3]. \tag{31}$$

Since each $0 \leq q_j < 1$, it follows that $\sum_{j=0}^{\infty} q_j^3 < +\infty$ whenever $\sum_{j=0}^{\infty} q_j < +\infty$, and the latter series converges if $\lim_{j \to +\infty} q_j / q_{j-1} = 0$, hence the claim.

Since the expressions obtained in the steady-state solution are non-linear, in general we should determine the existence and uniqueness of solutions to the equations we are dealing with. However, as a result of the parameter values being selected, we have $q_j < 1$ for all $j \geq 0$, we are assured in this case of existence and uniqueness of the steady-state solution.

References

1. Galton F., Watson H.W.: On the probability of extinction of families, *J. Anthr. Inst.*, 6, (1874), 138–144
2. Kolmogorov A. N.: Sur le problème d'attente, *Mat. Sbornik* 38, (1931), 101–106

3. Gelenbe E., Mitrani I.: Analysis and Synthesis of Computer Systems, Academic Press, New York and London, (1980)
4. Asmussen S.: Applied Probability and Queues, J. Wiley & Sons, Chichester, (1987).
5. May R. M., Hassell F. R.: Population dynamics and biological control, *Phil. Trans. Royal Soc. London*, B 318, (1988), 129–169
6. Medhi J.: Stochastic Processes, Second Ed., Wiley Eastern Ltd., New Delhi, (1994)
7. Bonhoeffer S., May R. M., Shaw G. M., Nowak M. A.: Virus dynamics and drug therapy, *Proc. Natl. Acad. Sci. USA*, 94, June (1997), 6971–6976
8. Gelenbe E., Pujolle G.: Introduction to Networks of Queues, 2nd Ed., J. Wiley & Sons, Chichester, (1998)
9. Gelenbe E., Fourneau J.M.: G-Networks with resets, *Performance Evaluation*, 49, 179-192, (2002), also in Proc. IFIP WG 7.3/ACM-SIGMETRICS Performance '02 Conf., Rome, Italy, October (2002)
10. Haddon M.: The Curious Incident of the Dog in the Night-Time, Vintage Random House, London, (2004)

Distributed Evaluation Using Multi-agents

Veysi Öztürk[1,2], Coşkun Sönmez[2], and Ercan Öztemel[1]

[1] Tübitak-MAM, ITRI, PK.21 41470 Gebze, Kocaeli, Turkey
{veysi.ozturk, ercan.oztemel}@bte.mam.gov.tr
[2] İTU (İstanbul Technical University) Computer Engineering Maslak, İstanbul, Turkey
sonmez@cs.itu.edu.tr

Abstract. Evaluation of systems, synthetic environments and human performance are generally complicated and time-consuming tasks. Existing evaluation systems are domain dependent and don't provide explanation on how the system reaches the evaluation results. Expertise is needed for evaluation process. Defining a model or a methodology, which simplifies and models the evaluation knowledge and speeds up the evaluation process, can obviously save cost, time and provide reusability. In this study, a knowledge representation of evaluation, which can also be used in distributed environments, was developed to handle the heuristic knowledge of experts from different domains and information from different sources for evaluation purposes. The evaluation knowledge was represented as reference model of evaluation objectives, production rules, evaluation measures, methods and parameters. Using of multiagents is proposed for evaluation in distributed environments. Different types of multiagent organizations can be designed and developed. Multi-agents can simplify the evaluation process and reduce network traffic in distributed environments and decrease security problems among the network.

1 Introduction

Evaluation is the systematic acquisition and assessment of information to provide useful feedback about a program, policy, technology, person, need, activity, synthetic environment and so on [1]. There are different levels of evaluation as follows [2]:

1. **'simple'** display of data without analysis (e.g. charts, diagrams)
2. **analysis of data**, (e.g. Number of hits, # of failure)
3. **evaluation of data**, (e.g. using Artificial Intelligence (AI) (fuzzy logic, neural networks, etc), comparison, etc)
4. **assessment:** The highest level would include the judging of the data, (e.g. 'this trainee had an excellent (or good) performance' etc.)

Some examples of evaluation are pilot evaluation [3], evaluation of event management performances of senior police officers [4], simulation based training scenarios evaluation [5], collaborative virtual environments performance evaluation [6] and High Level Architecture Run-Time Infrastructure implementations evaluation [7].

The complexity of tasks accomplished by systems, humans, and synthetic environments is increasing day by day. Evaluation is needed nearly for all engineering tasks and the obstacles related with evaluation are increased proportional with

P. Yolum et al.(Eds.): ISCIS 2005, LNCS 3733, pp. 312–321, 2005.

complexity, especially in distributed environments. It is necessary to investigate new techniques to automate manual evaluation and to overcome the obstacles related with evaluation that cannot be solved (or very difficultly solved) with conventional computing, especially in distributed environments. Some of these obstacles are as follows [8]:

- Expertise is needed for evaluation process. But there are very few Subject Matter Experts (SMEs) being able to evaluate systems and synthetic environments efficiently, especially for complex tasks and distributed environments.
- Generally, assessment is made via the subjective observations of a SME [9].
- It is important to provide evaluation results with an understanding of the source of the problem instead of only judgements on outcome [10].
- There is a need to objectively evaluate systems, trainees, simulation based training scenarios [11], trainee performance [12], synthetic environments, etc.
- Existing evaluation systems are domain dependent.
- Distributing all data across the network allows others to learn about technical and operational information of evaluated system (security problems) [13].
- High network traffic is required in distributed environments [13].
- Insuffient use of local evaluation capabilities in distributed environments [13].

In this study, *distributed evaluation* is proposed to overcome or reduce the problems and obstacles mentioned above. Distributed evaluation is a way to delegate and partition automatic evaluation between evaluated entities. Instead of shear centralized evaluation, the analysis and evaluation of data will be disseminated using an evaluation master agent (in the following just called 'master agent') and evaluation agents, referring to different levels of evaluation [13,14].

An agent is anything that can be viewed as perceiving the environment through sensors and acting upon environment through effectors [15]. Multi-agents systems are composed of multiple, interacting agents [16]. There are different application areas of multi-agents such as distributed simulation, decision support, computer games, handwritten analysis, learning, control of robots (e.g. robot soccer), telecommunications, etc [16,17,18,19,20].

The study indicates that multi-agents can be used for distributed evaluation. In distributed environments, evaluation can split into two parts:

- Overall evaluation
- Evaluation at clients (or at sub systems)

Different types of multi-agent organizations can be developed and designed. In the first type organization, user controls master agent to handle other agents and master agent collects knowledge from evaluation agents in order to do overall evaluation as shown in Fig. 1.. Master agent generates evaluation definition information, where evaluation objectives, rules, measures, methods, parameters, questionnaires, and their relationships are stored. Then master agent sends generated evaluation definition messages (or files) to the evaluation agents. Each evaluation agent is capable of doing partial evaluation at client side. Evaluation agents collect information/data from the environment, evaluate the data and send results to the master agent. The master agent analyses evaluation results from the evaluation agents and provides user final evaluation results. Both, master and evaluation agents can be referred to as evaluation environment.

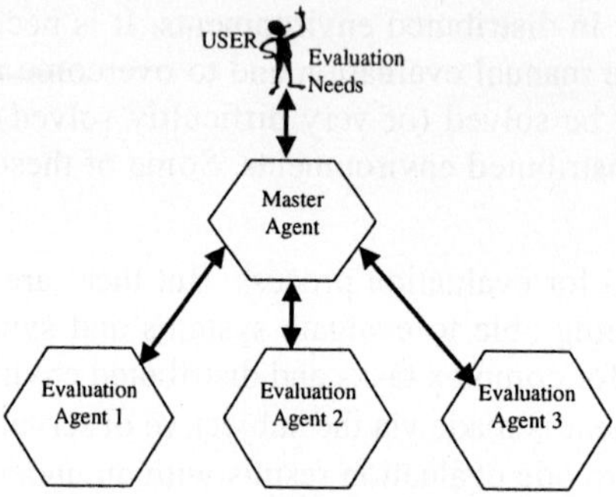

Fig. 1. Distributed evaluation using master and evaluation agents

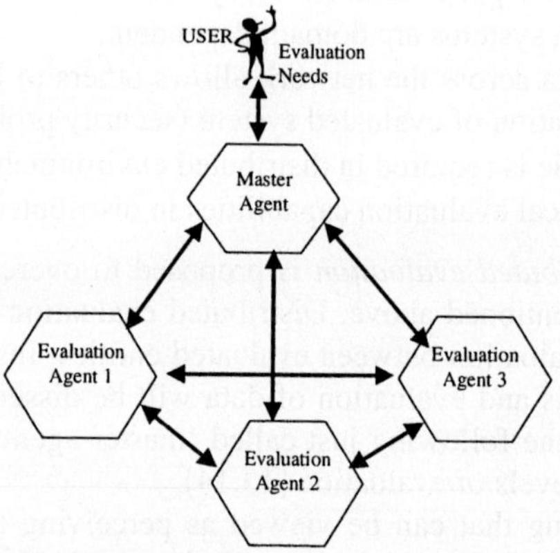

Fig. 2. Distributed evaluation using master and evaluation agents

Different types of multi-agent organizations can be designed and developed. In the first type organization, evaluation agents cannot communicate with each other. In the second type, evaluation agents can communicate with each other as shown in Fig. 2. This organization can be used in the situation, where the results generated by evaluation agents can influence the results of other agents.

The typical steps for distributed evaluation with using intelligent multi-agents are as follows [14]:

1. User (i.e. evaluator) determines what will be evaluated.
2. Master agent determines, what has to be evaluated by each evaluation agent. The master agent divides the tasks according to the evaluation agents' capabilities and the environment where the evaluation agents perform evaluation. Each task is a subset of the overall evaluation.
3. The master agent generates evaluation definition messages (or files) for each evaluation agent.
4. The master agent sends generated evaluation definition messages (or files) to the evaluation agents.

5. After or during the execution of the exercise, the master agent evaluates high level aspects and the evaluation agents evaluate low level.
6. The evaluation agents send their evaluation results to the master agent.
7. The master agent evaluates all results and generates final evaluation results and presents to the user.

2 Advantages of Distributed Evaluation

The advantages of distributed evaluation are as follows:

- It provides solutions that efficiently use information sources that are spatially distributed [17]. Delegation and partitioning of evaluation, simplifies the evaluation process.
- It reduces network traffic during exercise execution [13].
- Certain sensitive data has not to be sent across the network. Only pre-processed data, i.e. evaluation results, are distributed across the network. This reduces security issues of evaluation [13].
- It can enhance performance along the dimensions of computational efficiency, reliability, extensibility, maintainability, flexibility and reuse [17].

3 Knowledge Representation

Knowledge captured from experts and other sources must be organised in such a fashion that a computer inferencing program (master and evaluation agent) will be able to handle the captured knowledge [21]. The master agent contains all the domain evaluation knowledge and evaluation agents contain partially evaluation knowledge, which is needed for local evaluation at client side. In this study, integrated "Reference Model of Evaluation Objectives" and "Evaluation Definition Knowledge", were used to represent evaluation knowledge of the master and evaluation agents as shown in Fig. 3 [22]:

- Evaluation Objectives Hierarchical Tree (Reference Model of Evaluation Objectives) includes all evaluation objectives and their relationship including the dependencies.
- Evaluation Definition Knowledge, where evaluation objectives, rules, measures, methods, parameters, questionnaires and their relationships are stored.
  The terms used in evaluation definition are as follows:
  - *Evaluation rules:* Evaluation criteria that are used for assessments such as successful/unsuccessful.
  - *Measures:* Results of methods, which are used to simplify the evaluation rules and provide reusability.
  - *Methods:* Algorithms for analyzing the collected parameters and calculating measures used in the rules.
  - *Evaluation parameters:* Variables needed for applying rules or calculating the result of methods.

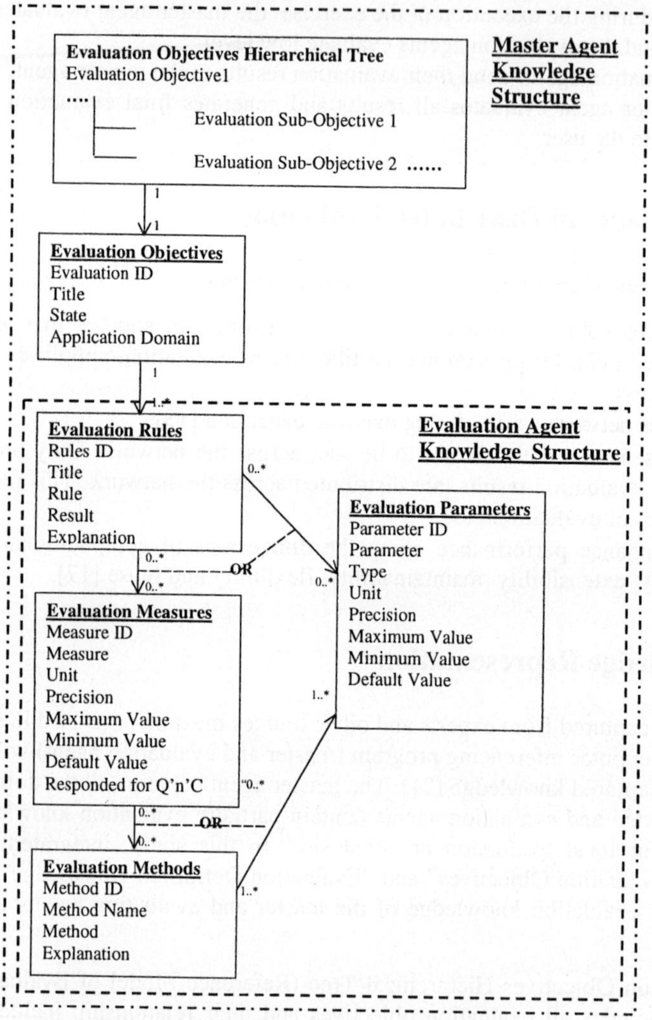

Fig. 3. Knowledge Model of Master and Evaluation Agents

In the knowledge model of master agent, each evaluation objective has related evaluation rules and different evaluation objectives can use the same evaluation rules in order to prevent duplication. In the knowledge model of master agent and evaluation agents, each evaluation rule is related with evaluation measures (or parameters) and different evaluation rules can use the same evaluation measures (or parameters) in order to prevent duplication of measures (or parameters). As similar, each evaluation measure is related with evaluation methods and different evaluation measures can use the same evaluation method in order to prevent duplication of methods. Each evaluation method or rule has one or more related evaluation parameters and different evaluation methods (or rule) can use the same related evaluation parameter in order to prevent duplication of parameters. In simple evaluations, the evaluation knowledge will be defined by using evaluation objectives, rules and parameters. In complex evaluations, the evaluation knowledge will be defined by using evaluation objectives, rules, measures, methods and parameters.

4 Modelling Evaluation Inferencing Mechanism

Inferencing mechanism of master agent was modelled to handle evaluation knowledge. The activity diagram of inferencing is shown in Fig. 4. Each activity represents the performing of a group of "actions " in a workflow. The brief explanation of activities is as follows:

Read evaluation keywords: This activity receives evaluation keywords from the user in order to present the user the possible evaluation objectives.
Search evaluation objectives tree: This activity searches evaluation keywords in the evaluation Objectives tree.
Search evaluation database for keywords: This activity searches evaluation keywords in the evaluation Database.
Generate evaluation objectives results: This activity generates and presents the result of search in hierarchical form.
Select evaluation objectives among results: This activity receives user's evaluation objectives selections from the user.
Find evaluation rules related with the selected evaluation objectives: This activity finds evaluation rules related with the selected evaluation objectives.
Check if evaluation rules use parameter directly: This activity checks if the evaluation rules are defined by evaluation measures or evaluation parameters.
Find evaluation parameters related with evaluation rules: If the evaluation rules in the KB are defined by evaluation parameters, this activity will find evaluation parameters related with evaluation rules.
Find evaluation measures related with evaluation rules: If the evaluation rules in the KB are defined by evaluation measures, this activity will find evaluation measures related with evaluation rules.
Find evaluation methods related with evaluation measures: If the evaluation rules in the KB are defined by evaluation measures, this activity will find evaluation methods related with evaluation rules.
Find evaluation parameters related with evaluation methods: If the evaluation rules in the KB are defined by evaluation measures, this activity will find evaluation parameters related with evaluation rules.
Generate and disseminate evaluation definition information: This activity generates and disseminates evaluation definition information through evaluation agents.
Put parameter values to the methods and calculate the result of measures: This activity gets common parameter values and puts these values to the related methods in order to calculate the result of measures.
Execute evaluation rules with the values of evaluation measures: This activity executes evaluation rules with the calculated the values of the evaluation measures.

Receive evaluation results from evaluation agents: This activity receives evaluation results from evaluation agents

Generate & present the results and explain the reason of inferencing: This activity generates and presents the overall results of evaluation and explains the reason of inferencing.

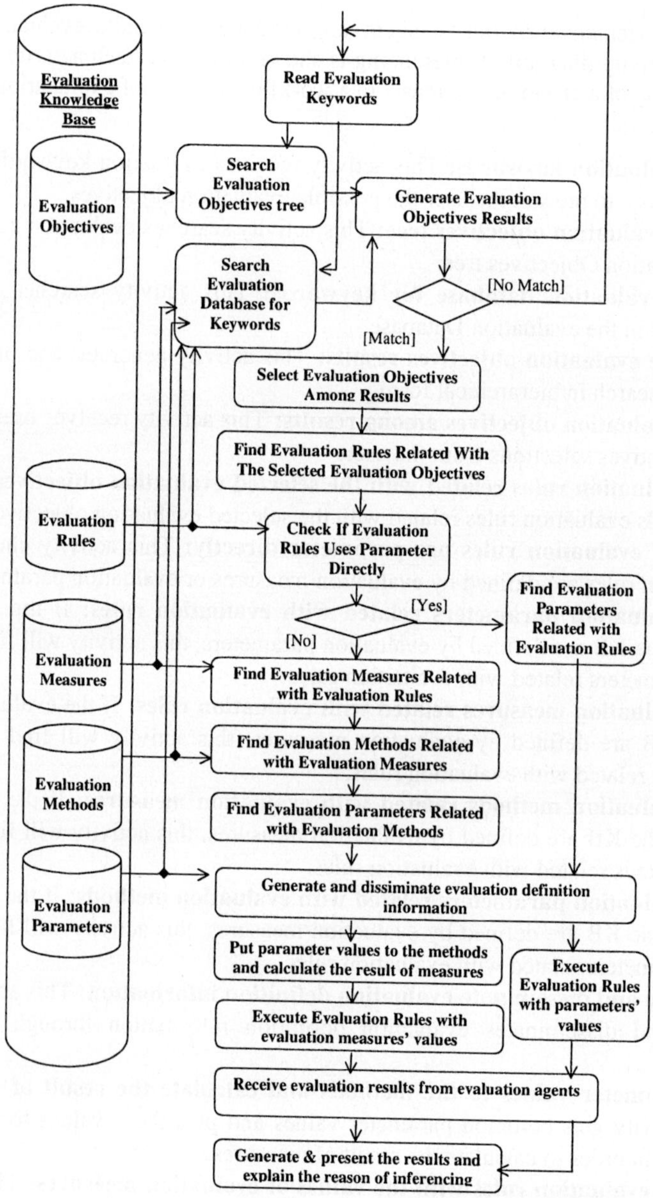

Fig. 4. Activity diagram of inferencing mechanism

5 Architecture of the Master and the Evaluation Agents

The main components of the master agent are shown in Fig. 5. The evaluation agents' structure is similar with master agent except not including a user interface.

The master agent and the evaluation agents were designed according to the knowledge representation and inferencing mechanism described in previous sections.

The main components of the master agent are as follows:

- Perception to perceive the events and information from the environment (e.g. receiving evaluation results from evaluation agents)
- Cognition to reason about perceived events. Rule-based systems such as expert system can be used for inferencing. As the evaluation includes uncertainty in some aspects, fuzzy logic can also be incorporated with expert system in the inference engines of master and evaluation agents for reasoning. Knowledge Base of agents contains the knowledge and expertise of Subject Matter Experts for performing evaluation in a structured format.
- Action to act according to the reasons produced by the cognition mechanism (e.g. sending evaluation definition information to evaluation agents).
- **User interface** to control the dialog between the user and the system and present the evaluation results to the user.

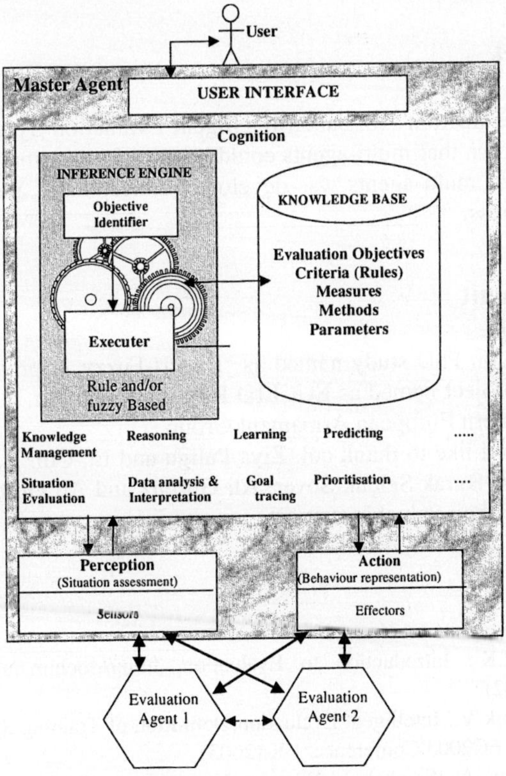

Fig. 5. The main components of master agent

6 Conclusion

Forming an evaluation definition is a complicated and time-consuming task. Finding out and formulating the required knowledge from the domain for which the evaluation is to be performed, is generally difficult due to lack of structured approach. It is not only important to formulate the knowledge, but also finding out the right source of knowledge is essential. Structured knowledge architecture is especially important in order to utilize evaluation knowledge automatically, especially in distributed environments. A methodology for forming an evaluation definition and performing evaluation according to this definition was developed in this study. The methodology was developed to handle the heuristic knowledge of experts from different domains and information from different sources for evaluation purposes. The evaluation knowledge was represented as a reference model of evaluation objectives, production rules, measures, methods and parameters.

The study highlights that multi-agents can be used for distributed evaluation and benefit users to decrease the cost and the evaluation time of synthetic environments, trainees, systems, etc for evaluation purposes. The proposed methodology is applicable to different types of multi-agent organizations. Multi-agents can simplify the evaluation process and reduce network traffic in distributed environments and decrease security problems among the network.

7 Future Work

In this study, the evaluation tool called Intelligent Evaluation System [8] was developed and it was shown that multi-agents could be used for distributed evaluation. The main architecture of multi-agents was developed conceptually and system development is under progress.

Acknowledgement

The paper is based on PhD study named as "Expert-Fuzzy Approach for Evaluation Systems" and the project named as EUCLID RTP 11.13 Project, which is carried out in CEPA 11 of Western European Armament Group.

The authors would like to thank col. Ziya Paligu and Lt. Col. K. Kiran of Turkish MoD, Savaş Öztürk, Burak Selçuk Soyer, Ali Gürbüz and Ali Görçin from Marmara Research Center for their valuable support.

References

1. Trochin, W. M.K.: Introduction to Evaluation, http://trochim.human.cornell.edu/kb/intreval.htm (2002)
2. Öztemel E., Öztürk V.: Intelligent Evaluation Definition of Training Systems in Synthetic Environments, ITEC2003 Conference, UK (2003)
3. Shub, Y., Kushnir, A., Frenkel, J.: Pilot Evaluation System Aerospace and Electronics, IEEE Proceedings of the NAECON 1994, (1994) 734–741

4. Hartley R., Varley G.: The Design And Evaluation For Development Of Complex Decision Making Skills, IEEE International Conference on Advanced Learning Technologies (2001)
5. Gregory W. H.: Evaluating Simulation Based Training Scenarios, 1998 Spring SIW (Simulation Interoperability Workshop) (1998)
6. Oliveira J.C., Shirmohammad S., Georganas, N.D.: Collaborative Virtual Environment standards: a performance evaluation Proceedings. 3rd IEEE International Workshop on Distributed Interactive Simulation and Real-Time Applications, 22-23 Oct. (1999) 14–21
7. Macannuco D., Hung J., Civinskas W.: A Test Suite to Evaluate Run-Time Infrastructure (RTI) Implementations for High Performance, Human-In-The-Loop (HITL) Simulators, 1998 Spring SIW (Simulation Interoperability Workshop) (1998)
8. Öztürk V., Sönmez C.: An Expert-Fuzzy Approach for Evaluation, International Manufacturing Symposium (IMS) 2004, Sakarya, Turkiye (2004)
9. Rigg G., Morley R., Hepplewhite R.: Themis: The Objective Assessment of CGF Performance, 9th Conference on Computer Generated Forces & Behevioral Representation (CGF-BR), SISO (2000)
10. Bass, E. J.: Architecture for an intelligent instructor pilot decision support system, IEEE International Conference on Systems, Man, and Cybernetics, Volume: 1, (1998) 891–896
11. Gregory W. H.: Evaluating Simulation Based Training Scenarios, 1998 Spring SIW (Simulation Interoperability Workshop) http://www.sisostds.org/doclib/doclib.cfm?SISO_FID_897 (1998)
12. Hemel P., Kisg W. J.: Simulation Techniques In Operator And Maintenance Training, Performance Assessment, And Personnel Selection, Comput. & Indus. Eng. Vol., No 2, UK (1981) 105-112
13. Drewer P. M.: RTP 11.13 Project Technical report, RTP11.13-CAE-WE6.1–WD1_MzD-2.0b (2001)
14. Rollesbroich B., Meyer zu Drewer P., Greiwe K. Jokipii M., Hartikainen T.: Common Evaluation Framework & Evaluation Knowledge Editor, RTP 11.13 Project Technical report, RTP11.13-CAE-WE6.1-TR-1.0 (2003)
15. Russell, S., Norvig, P.: Artificial Intelligence: A Modern Approach, Prentice Hall (1995)
16. Weiss G.: Multiagent Systems A Modern Approach to Distributed Modern Approach to Artificial Intelligence, The MIT Press Cambridge, Massachusetts London, England (1999)
17. Gokturk E., Polat F.: Implementing Agent Communication for a Multiagent Simulation Infrastructure on HLA, Proc. of the International Symposium on Computer and Information Science (ISCIS 2003), LNCS, Springer-Verlag (2003)
18. Alhajj R., Polat F.: Multiple-Agents to Identify and Separate Touching Digits in Unconstrained Handwritten Hindi Numerals, International Journal of Experimental and Theoretical Artificial Intelligence, Vol.15, No.4, (2003) 461–471
19. Ulusar, U. D., Akin H. L: Design and Implementation of a Real Time Planner for Autonomous Robots, Proceedings, TAINN 2004, Turkish Symposium On Artificial Intelligence and Neural Networks, Izmir, Turkey, (2004) 263–270
20. Sycara K. P.: Multiagent Systems, AI Magazine, American Association for Artificial Intelligence (1998)
21. Turban, E.: Expert Systems and Applied Artificial Intelligence, Macmillan Publishing Company, USA (1995)
22. Öztemel E., Öztürk V.: Intelligent Evaluation Definition of Training Systems in Synthetic Environments, ITEC2003 Conference, UK (2003)

Classification of Volatile Organic Compounds with Incremental SVMs and RBF Networks

Zeki Erdem[1,3], Robi Polikar[2], Nejat Yumuşak [3], and Fikret Gürgen[4]

[1] TUBITAK Marmara Research Center, Information Technologies Institute, 41470 Gebze - Kocaeli, Turkey
zeki.erdem@bte.mam.gov.tr

[2] Rowan University, Electrical and Computer Engineering Department, 210 Mullica Hill Rd., Glassboro, NJ 08028, USA
polikar@rowan.edu

[3] Sakarya University, Computer Engineering Department, Esentepe, 54187 Sakarya, Turkey
nyumusak@sakarya.edu.tr

[4] Bogazici University, Computer Engineering Department, Bebek, 80815 Istanbul, Turkey
gurgen@boun.edu.tr

Abstract. Support Vector Machines (SVMs) have been applied to solve the classification of volatile organic compounds (VOC) data in some recent studies. SVMs provide good generalization performance in detection and classification of VOC data. However, in many applications involving VOC data, it is not unusual for additional data, which may include new classes, to become available over time, which then requires an SVM classifier that is capable of incremental learning that does not suffer from loss of previously acquired knowledge. In our previous work, we have proposed the incremental SVM approach based on Learn^{++}.MT. In this contribution, the ability of SVMLearn^{++}.MT to incrementally classify VOC data is evaluated and compared against a similarly constructed Learn^{++}.MT algorithm that uses radial basis function neural network as base classifiers.

1 Introduction

Gas sensing systems for detection and recognition of VOCs are of significant importance for many industries and organizations. Examples include food industries for testing the quality of food products, military and humanitarian organizations for locating buried land mines, petrochemical and valve manufacturing companies for detecting and identifying hazardous gases, and airport security and customs inspection agencies for detecting illegal drugs and plastic bombs. Consequently, gas sensing systems for detection and recognition of VOCs, an important class of chemicals that can readily evaporate, have gained considerable attention, due to VOCs are encountered in many real-world applications. The VOCs classification problem is often made harder due to the irreversible behavior of the sensor array overtime such as parameter drift or just noisy data [1]. Furthermore, one of the main challenges in using gas sensing systems is to be able to increase the number of odorants that can be identified over

P. Yolum et al.(Eds.): ISCIS 2005, LNCS 3733, pp. 322–331, 2005.

time with additional data. On the other hand, the training dataset that was originally used to train the system may not be available by the time new training datasets become available.

Support Vector Machines (SVMs) have been used to recognition of VOC data in some studies [1-4]. SVMs provide good generalization performance in the context of odor detection and classification, despite the fact that it does not incorporate problem-domain knowledge [1]. As with any type of classifier, the performance and accuracy of SVMs rely on the availability of a representative set of training dataset. However, acquisition of such a representative VOC dataset is expensive and time consuming as mentioned above. Consequently, such data often become available in small and separate batches at different times. In such cases, a typical approach is combining new data with all previous data, and training a new classifier from scratch. In other words, such scenarios require a classifier to be trained and incrementally updated, where the classifier needs to learn the novel information provided by the new data without forgetting the knowledge previously acquired from the data seen earlier. Since SVMs need to be reinitialized and retrained with the combined old and new data to learn the additional information, they are not capable of incremental learning. This causes all previously acquired knowledge to be lost, a phenomenon known as *catastrophic forgetting* [5]. Therefore, SVMs require incrementally training in recognition of VOC data.

In our previous work [6], integrating the SVM classifiers into an ensemble framework using Learn^{++}.MT, we have shown that the SVM classifiers can in fact be equipped with the incremental learning capability. Learn^{++}.MT was developed in response to reduce the effect of out-voting problem, called classifier proliferation, in the ensemble of classifiers for the incremental learning [7]. In this paper, considering that the problem is caused by the nature of gas sensing system, we investigate the ability of the incremental SVM (SVMLearn^{++}.MT) to classify of VOC data, while avoiding the catastrophic forgetting problem and also reducing the effect of out-voting problem. Its performance have been compared the performance of radial basis function network used as the base classifier of the Learn^{++}.MT.

2 Gas Sensing System

Due to their ability to mimic the human olfactory system, although in a very limited sense, gas sensing systems are often referred to as *Electronic Nose (E-nose) Systems* (Figure 1). An electronic nose is an instrument, which comprises an array of electronic chemical sensors with partial specificity and an appropriate pattern recognition system, capable of recognizing simple or complex odors [8]. The sensor array is a collection of sensors exposed to the same sample and producing individual responses as well as an entire response pattern. Piezoelectric acoustic wave sensors, which comprise a versatile class of chemical sensors, are used for the detection of VOCs data used in this study [9]. For sensing applications, a sensitive polymer film is cast on the surface of the Quartz Crystal Microbalance (QCM). This layer can bind a VOC of interest, altering the resonant frequency of the device, in proportion to the added mass.

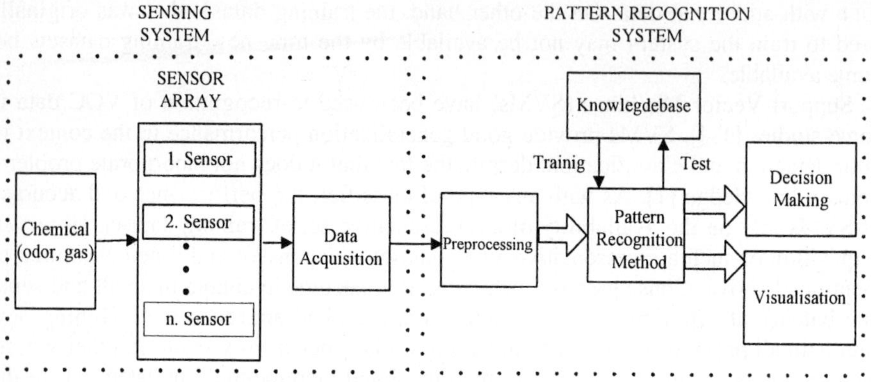

Fig. 1. An Electronic Nose System

Addition or subtraction of gas molecules from the surface or bulk of an acoustic wave sensor results in a change in its resonant frequency. The frequency change Δf, caused by a deposited mass Δm can be described as following:

$$\Delta f = -2.3\times10^{6} \cdot f^{2} \cdot \frac{\Delta m}{A} \qquad (1)$$

where f is the fundamental resonant frequency of the bare crystal, and A is the active surface area. The sensor typically consists of an array of several crystals, each coated with a different polymer. This design is aimed at improving identification, hampered by the limited selectivity of individual films. Employing more than one crystal, and coating each with a different partially selective polymer, different responses can be obtained for different gases. The combined response of these crystals can then be used as a signature pattern of the VOC detected.

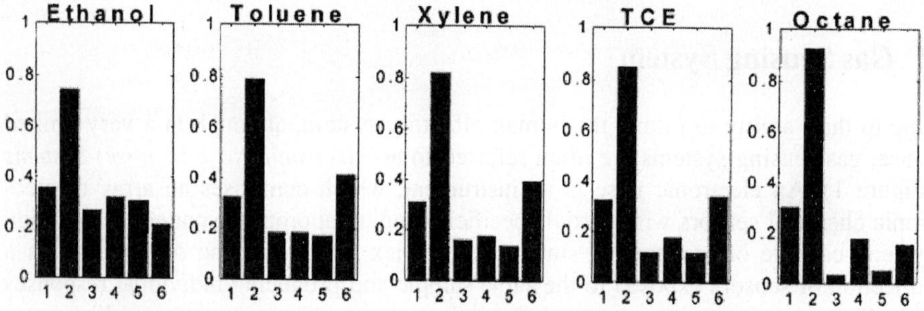

Fig. 2. Sample responses of the six-QCM sensor array to VOCs data

The gas sensing dataset used in this study consisted of responses of six QCMs to five VOCs, including ethanol (ET), xylene (XL), octane (OC), toluene (TL), and trichloroethelene (TCE). Figure 2 illustrates sample patterns for each VOC from six QCMs coated with different polymers, where the vertical axis represents normalized frequency change. Note that the patterns from toluene, xylene, and trichloroethelene look considerably similar; hence, they are difficult to distinguish from each other.

3 Incremental SVM

3.1 Learn^{++}.MT Algorithm

The Learn^{++} algorithm has been introduced as an incremental learning algorithm that is capable of learning additional information [10], even difficult learning conditions. Learn^{++} not only assumes the previous data to be no longer available, but it also allows additional classes to be introduced with new data, while retaining the previously acquired knowledge. It is an ensemble approach, inspired primarily by the AdaBoost algorithm [11]. Learn^{++} also creates an ensemble of classifiers, each trained on a subset of the current training dataset, and later combined through weighted majority voting. Training instances for each classifier are drawn from an iteratively updated distribution. The main difference is that the distribution update rule in AdaBoost is based on the performance of the previous classifier, which focuses the algorithm on *difficult instances*, whereas that of Learn^{++} is based on the performance of the entire ensemble, which focuses this algorithm on instances that carry *novel information*. This distinction gives Learn^{++} the ability to learn new data, even when previously unseen classes are introduced. As new data reach, Learn^{++} creates additional classifiers, until the ensemble learns the new information. Since no classifier is discarded, previously acquired knowledge is retained.

Learn^{++} uses weighted majority voting, where each classifier receives a voting weight based on its training performance. This works well in practice even for incremental learning problems. However, if the incremental learning problem involves introduction of new classes, then the voting scheme proves to be unfair towards the newly introduced class: since none of the previously created classifiers can pick the new class, a relatively large number of new classifiers need to be generated that recognize the new class, so that their total weight can out-vote the first batch of classifiers on instances coming from this new class. This in return populates the ensemble with an unnecessarily large number of classifiers. Learn^{++}.MT, explained below, is specifically designed to address this issue of *classifier proliferation* [7].

The main innovation in Learn^{++}.MT is the way by which the voting weights are determined. Learn^{++}.MT, also obtains a set of voting weights based on the individual performances of the classifier, however, these weights are then adjusted based on the classification of the specific instance at the time of testing, through *dynamic weight voting (DWV)* algorithm [7]. For any given test instance, Learn^{++}.MT compares the class predictions of each classifier and cross-references them with the classes on which they were trained. Essentially, if a subsequent ensemble overwhelmingly chooses a class it has seen before, then the voting weights of those classifiers that have not seen that class are proportionally reduced. The Learn^{++}.MT algorithm is given in Figure 3.

For each dataset (D_k) that becomes available to Learn^{++}.MT, the inputs to the algorithm are (i) a sequence of m training data instances x_i along with their correct labels y_i, (ii) a classification algorithm, and (iii) an integer T_k specifying the maximum number of classifiers to be generated using that database. If the algorithm is seeing its first database (*k=1*), a data distribution (D_t), from which training instances will be drawn, is initialized to be uniform, making the probability of any instance being selected equal. If *k>1* then a distribution initialization sequence initializes the data distribution. The algorithm adds T_k classifiers to the ensemble starting at $t=eT_k+1$, where eT_k denotes the current number of classifiers in the ensemble.

Input: For each dataset $\mathcal{S}_k$ *k=1,2,…,K*

- Sequence of *m* instances $S=[(x_1,y_1),\dots,(x_m,y_m)]$ with labels $y_i \in Y_k = \{1,\dots,c\}$
- Learning algorithm **BaseClassifier**.
- Integer T_k, specifying the number of iterations

Do for *k=1,2,…,K*

If k=1 **Initialize** $w_1 = D_1(i) = 1/m,\ eT_1 = 0$ for all i.

Else **Go to** Step 5 to evaluate the current ensemble on new data set $\mathcal{S}_k$, update weights, and recall current number of classifiers $eT_k = \sum_{j=1}^{k-1} T_j$

Do for $t = eT_k + 1,\ eT_k + 2, \dots,\ eT_k + T_k$:

1. Set $D_t = w_t \Big/ \sum_{i=1}^{m} w_t(i)$ so that D_t is a distribution.
2. Call **BaseClassifier** providing it with a subset of $\mathcal{S}_k$ randomly chosen using D_t.
3. Obtain a hypothesis $h_t : X \rightarrow Y$, and calculate the error $h_t : \varepsilon_t = \sum_{i:h_t(x_i)\neq y_i} D_t(i)$

   If $\varepsilon_t > ½$, discard h_t and go to step 2.

   Otherwise, compute normalized error as $\beta_t = \varepsilon_t / (1-\varepsilon_t)$.
4. $CTr_t = Y_k$, save labels of classes used in training h_t.
5. Call **DWV** to obtain the composite hypothesis H_t.
6. Compute the error of the composite hypothesis $E_t = \sum_{i:H_t(x_i)\neq y_i} D_t(i)$
7. Set $B_t = E_t/(1-E_t)$, and update the instance weights:

$$w_{t+1}(i) = w_t \times \begin{cases} B_t, & \text{if } H_t(x_i) = y_i \\ 1, & \text{otherwise} \end{cases}$$

Call **DWV** to obtain the final hypothesis, H_{final}.

Fig. 3. The Learn^{++}.MT Algorithm

For each iteration *t*, the instance weights, w_t, from the previous iteration are first normalized to create a weight distribution D_t. A classifier, h_t, is generated from a subset of $\mathcal{S}_k$ that is drawn from D_t. The error, ε_t, of h_t is then calculated; if $\varepsilon_t > ½$, the algorithm deems the current classifier, h_t, to be too weak, discards it, and returns and redraws a training dataset, otherwise, calculates the normalized classification error β_t. The class labels of the training instances used to generate this classifier are then stored. The *DWV* algorithm is called to obtain the composite classifier, H_t, of the ensemble. H_t represents the ensemble decision of the first *t* hypotheses generated thus far. The error of the composite classifier, E_t is then computed and normalized. The instance weights w_t are finally updated according to the performance of H_t such that the weights of instances correctly classified by H_t are reduced and those that are misclassified are effectively increased. This ensures that the ensemble focus on those regions of the feature space that are not yet learned, performing the incremental learning [7].

3.2 SVM Classifiers and Its Ensemble

Support vector machines (SVMs) have been successfully employed in a number of real world problems [12, 13]. They directly implement the principle of structural risk minimization [12] and work by mapping the training points into a high dimensional feature space, where a separating hyperplane (**w**, *b*) is found by maximizing the distance from the closest data points (boundary-optimization). Given a set of training samples $\boldsymbol{S}=\{(\boldsymbol{x}_i, y_i) \mid i=1,\ldots,m\}$, where $\boldsymbol{x}_i \in \boldsymbol{R}^n$ are input patterns, $y_i \in \{+1, -1\}$ are class labels for a 2-class problem, SVMs attempt to find a classifier $h(\boldsymbol{x})$, which minimizes the expected misclassification rate. A linear classifier $h(\boldsymbol{x})$ is a hyperplane, and can be represented as $h(\boldsymbol{x}) = \mathrm{sign}(\boldsymbol{w}^T\boldsymbol{x}+b)$. The optimal SVM classifier can then be found by solving a convex quadratic optimization problem:

$$\max_{w,b} \frac{1}{2}\|w\|^2 + C\sum_{i=1}^{m}\xi_i \quad \text{subject to } y_i\left(\langle w, x_i\rangle + b\right) \geq 1-\xi_i \text{ and } \xi_i \geq 0 \tag{2}$$

where *b* is the bias, **w** is weight vector, and *C* is the regularization parameter, used to balance the classifier's complexity and classification accuracy on the training set *S*. Simply replacing the involved vector inner-product with a non-linear kernel function converts linear SVM into a more flexible non-linear classifier, which is the essence of the famous *kernel trick*. In this case, the quadratic problem is generally solved through its dual formulation:

$$L(w,b,\alpha) = \sum_{i=1}^{m}\alpha_i - \frac{1}{2}\left(\sum_{i=1}^{m} y_i y_j \alpha_i \alpha_j K(x_i, x_j)\right) \text{subject to } C \geq \alpha_i \geq 0 \text{ and } \sum_{i=1}^{m}\alpha_i y_i = 0 \tag{3}$$

where α_i are the coefficients that are maximized by Lagrangian. For training samples $\boldsymbol{x}_i$, for which the functional margin is one (and hence lie closest to the hyperplane), $\alpha_i > 0$. Only these instances are involved in the weight vector, and hence are called the *support vectors* [13]. The non-linear SVM classification function (optimum separating hyperplane) is then formulated in terms of these kernels as:

$$h(x) = sign\left(\sum_{i=1}^{m}\alpha_i y_i K(x_i, x_j) - b\right). \tag{4}$$

The final composite SVM classifier is obtained using the *DWV* algorithm for Learn^{++}.MT algorithm (Figure 4), as follows. Inputs of *DWV* are (i) the current training data and corresponding correct labels, (ii) classifiers h_t (iii) β_t, normalized error for each h_t, and (iv) a vector containing the classes on which h_t has been trained. The SVMs classifier weights, $W_t = \log(1/\beta_t)$, are first initialized according to where each single SVM classifier first receives a standard weight that is inversely proportional to its normalized error β_t so that those classifiers that performed well on their training data are given higher voting weights. A normalization factor is then created as the sum of the weights of all classifiers trained with class $c=1,2,\ldots,C$. For each instance, a per-class confidence factor $0<P_c<1$ is generated. P_c is the sum of weights of all the classifiers that choose class c divided by the sum of the weights of all classifiers trained with class c. Then, for each class, the weights are adjusted for classifiers that have not been trained with that class, that is, the weights are lowered proportional to the ensemble's preliminary decision on that class. The final composite SVM classifier is then calculated as the maximum sum of the weights that chose a particular class:

$$H_{final}(x_i) = \arg\max_{c} \sum_{t:h_t(x_i)=c} W_t \,. \qquad (5)$$

Inputs:
- Sequence of i=1,…,n training instances or test instance x_i
- Classifiers h_t.
- Hypothesis error values, β_t.
- Classes, CTr_t used in training h_t.

For t=*1,2,…,T* where T is the total number classifiers.

1. Initialize classifier weights $W_t = \log(1/\beta_t)$
2. Create normalization factor, Z, for each class $Z_c = \sum_{t:c\in CTr_t} W_t$, for c=*1,2,…,C* classes
3. Obtain preliminary decision $P_c = \sum_{t:h_t(x_i)=c} W_t \Big/ Z_c$, for c=*1,2,…,C* classes
4. Update voting weights $W_{t:c\notin CTr_t} = W_{t:c\notin CTr_t}(1-P_c)$ for c=*1,2,…,C*
5. Compute final hypothesis $H_{final}(x_i) = \arg\max_{c} \sum_{t:h_t(x_i)=c} W_t$

Fig. 4. The Dynamic Weight Voting Algorithm

4 Experimental Results

A single hidden layer classical Radial Basis function (RBF) network and SVM with RBF kernel were used as the base classifier in our experiments. SVM and RBF network with Learn^{++}.MT (SVMLearn^{++}.MT and RBFLearn^{++}.MT) have been tested on VOC dataset.

RBF kernel : $$K(x_i, x_j) = \exp\left(-\left\|x_i - x_j\right\|^2 / 2\sigma^2\right) \qquad (6)$$

SVM classifier parameters are the regularization constant C, the spread σ of RBF kernel. RBF classifier parameters are the mean squared error goal and the spread of radial basis functions. The choice of classifier parameters is a form of model selection. Although the machine learning community has extensively considered model selection with SVMs, optimal model parameters are generally domain-specific [14]. Therefore, we used the cross-validation technique with 5-folds to jointly select the SVM and also RBF network parameters.

The VOC dataset consisted of 384 six dimensional signals, 220 of which were used for training, and 164 of which were used for testing (TEST). Training dataset was divided into three training subsets (DS1, DS2, DS3). DS1 had instances from ET, OC, and TL, DS2 added instances mainly from TCE and very few from the previous three,

Table 1. VOC data distribution

Class	ETHANOL (C1)	TCE (C2)	OCTANE (C3)	XYLENE (C4)	TOLUENE (C5)
DS1	20	0	20	0	40
DS2	10	25	10	0	10
DS3	10	15	10	40	10
Test	24	24	24	40	52

Table 2. SVMLearn^{++}.MT with RBF kernel ($\sigma = 3$, $C = 100$) results

	C1	C2	C3	C4	C5	Gen.	Std
DS1	94%	-	91%	-	100%	59%	1.42%
DS2	98%	97%	83%	-	93%	70%	1.24%
DS3	95%	95%	90%	100%	71%	88%	1.63%

Table 3. RBFLearn^{++}.MT ($\sigma = 0.45$, $goal = 0.5$) results

	C1	C2	C3	C4	C5	Gen.	Std.
DS1	93%	-	82%	-	98%	57%	1.18%
DS2	96%	96%	77%	-	91%	68%	1.44%
DS3	90%	92%	80%	99%	69%	85%	3.83%

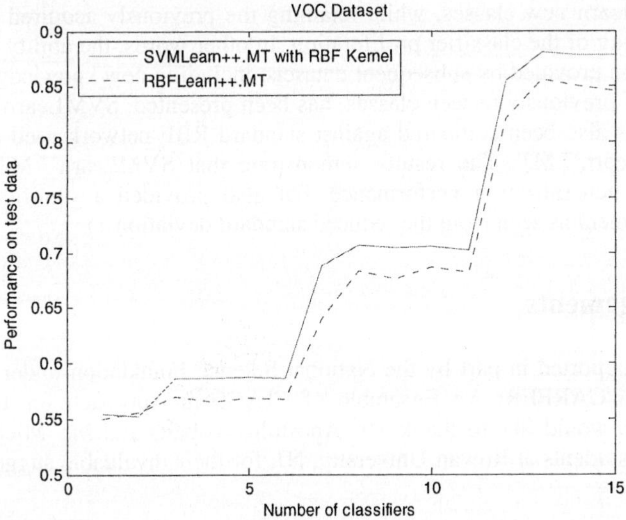

Fig. 5. Performance Results

and DS3 added instances from XL and very few from the previous four. TEST set included instances from all classes. Only DS_k was used during the kth training session. Table 1 presents the distribution of the datasets where subsequent datasets are biased toward the new class. Such a distribution results in challenge; since the algorithm will no longer have the opportunity to see adequate number of instances from previously introduced classes in the subsequent training sessions.

SVMLearn^{++}.MT and RBFLearn^{++}.MT were incrementally trained with three subsequent training datasets. They were permitted to generate as many classifiers as necessary to obtain their maximum performance. The numbers of classifiers generated were 6, 5, and 4 to achieve their best performance in three training sessions, respectively. Results from tests are shown in Tables 2 and 3 based on averages of 30 trials.

As expected, the performances of the classifiers on their own training data were very high. We note that the performance on the TEST dataset improves as incremental learning progresses and the system learns new classes. This is also expected, since TEST set had instances from all five classes, and instances from all classes were not introduced to classifiers until the last session. The performance improvement on the TEST data as new datasets are introduced demonstrates the incremental learning capability of the algorithm.

Performance results from tests are shown in Figure 5 based on mean of 30 trials. Generalization performance of SVMLearn^{++}.MT and RBFLearn^{++}.MT on the test dataset progressively improved from 59-57% to 88-85%, respectively, as new data was introduced, demonstrating its incremental learning capability even when instances of new classes are introduced in subsequent training sessions.

5 Conclusions

In this contribution, we have shown that incremental SVM (SVMLearn^{++}.MT) can incrementally learn new classes, while retaining the previously acquired knowledge and also reducing of the classifier proliferation. In other words, the ability of learning new information provided by subsequent datasets, including new knowledge provided by instances of previously unseen classes, has been presented. SVMLearn^{++}.MT with RBF kernel has also been compared against standard RBF network used as the base classifier of Learn^{++}.MT. The results demonstrate that SVMLearn^{++}.MT produced slightly better generalization performance, but also provided a significantly more stable improvement as seen from the reduced standard deviation.

Acknowledgements

This work is supported in part by the National Science Foundation under Grant No. ECS-0239090, "CAREER: An Ensemble of Classifiers Approach for Incremental Learning." Z.E. would like to thank Mr. Apostolos Topalis and Mr. Michael Muhlbaier graduate students at Rowan University, NJ, for their invaluable suggestions and assistance.

References

1. Distante, C., Ancona, N., Siciliano, P.: Support Vector Machines for Ofactory Signals Recognition. Sensors and Actuators B Vol. 88 (2003), 30-39.
2. Erdem, Z., Gürgen, F., Yumuşak, N.: Electronic Nose Data Classification using Support Vector Machines. Proceedings of IEEE 10th Turkish Signal Processing and Applications Conference (SIU'2002), Vol, 2. (2002) 1174-1179.

3. DeCoste, D., Burl, M. C., Hopkins, A., Lewis, N. S.: Support Vector Machines and Kernel Fisher Discriminations: A Case Study using Electronic Nose Data. Fourth Workshop on Mining Scientific Datasets, Seventh ACM SIGKDD International Conference on Kwowlegde Discovery and Data Mining (KDD-2001), August 26, 2001.
4. Trihaas, J., Bothe, H.H.: An application of Support Vector Machines to E-nose data. In Proceedings of ISOEN '2002 (International Symposium in Olfaction and Electronic Noses), Eds: A. D'Amico and C. Di Natale, (2003) 170-174.
5. French, R.: Catastrophic forgetting in connectionist networks: Causes, Consequences and Solutions. Trends in Cognitive Sciences, Vol. 3. No. 4. (1999)128-135.
6. Erdem, Z., Polikar, R., Gürgen, F., Yumuşak, N.: Reducing the Effect of Out-voting Problem in Ensemble Based Incremental Support Vector Machines. International Conference on Artificial Neural Networks (ICANN 2005) 11-15 September 2005, Warsaw, Poland.
7. Muhlbaier, M., Topalis, A., Polikar, R.: Learn++.MT: A New Approach to Incremental Learning. 5th Int. Workshop on Multiple Classifier Systems (MCS 2004), Springer LNCS Vol. 3077, (2004) 52-61.
8. Gardner, J.W., Bartlett, P.N.: A brief history of electronic noses. Sensors and Actuators B Vol. 18-19 (1994.), 211-220.
9. Polikar, R., Shinar, R., Honavar, V., Udpa, L., Porter, M. D.: Detection and Identification of Odorants using An Electronic Nose. Proc. of IEEE 26th Int. Conf. on Acoustics, Speech and Signal Proc., vol. 5. (2001) 3137-3140.
10. Polikar, R., Udpa, L., Udpa, S., Honavar, V.: Learn^{++}: An incremental learning algorithm for supervised neural networks. IEEE Transactions on Systems, Man, and Cybernetics. Part C: Applications and Reviews, Vol. 31, No. (2001) 497-508.
11. Freund, Y., Schapire, R.: A decision theoretic generalization of on-line learning and an application to boosting. Computer and System Sciences, vol. 57. no. 1. (1997) 119-139.
12. Vapnik, V., Statistical Learning Theory. New York: Wiley, (1998).
13. Cristianini, N., Shawe-Taylor, J.: An Introduction to Support Vector Machines and Other Kernel-based Learning Methods. Cambridge University Press (2000).
14. Duan, K., Keerthi, S.S., Poo, A.N.: Evaluation of simple performance measures for tuning SVM hyperparameters. Neurocomputing, Vol. 51. (2003) 41-59.

Agent Based Dynamic Execution of BPEL Documents

Ali Emre Arpacı and Ayşe Başar Bener

Boğaziçi University, Computer Engineering Department, İstanbul, Turkey
bener@boun.edu.tr

Abstract. Web Services are the most promising innovative solution in order to remove business and technical obstacles for e-business. They support a true service oriented architecture that is designed to securely expose business logic beyond the firewall. As the momentum around Web Services increases, there is a growing need for effective mechanisms to coordinate the interaction among them. Business Process Execution Language for Web Services (BPEL) is a good candidate, such that it satisfies the needs of the business to enable this interaction. However, BPEL still is far from fulfilling all the requirements of composition. In this research, we constructed an architecture to improve performance of parallel executions in BPEL documents. Our architecture, by the help of our controller agent, allows dynamic execution of statically designed flow with respect to customer defined issues and QoS parameters at both implementation time and runtime.

1 Introduction

Web Services is not just an interesting approach for developing software applications. It has direct business benefits. That is why; researchers and practitioners have been paying great attention to the concept of Web Services. Earlier versions of distributed object technologies failed to satisfy the business demands. Web Services, on the other hand, promises to change those disappointments in the market place. Web Services are moving from their initial "describe, publish, interact" capability to a new phase in which robust business interactions are supported [1]. Web Service Orchestration provides the ability to prescribe how Web Services are used to implement activities within a business process, how business processes are represented as Web Services, and also which business partners perform what parts of the actual business process [2]. The fundamental idea behind Web Service Orchestration specifications is to extend the basic Web Services stack with a so-called business process integration layer and make Web Services to support business operations. A general list of a variety of Web Service Composition languages can be stated as WSCI [3], BPML [4], BPEL4WS [5], BPSS [6], and XPDL [7]. Different frameworks can be constructed for comparing these process modeling languages [8] [9]. These analyses point BPEL4WS (in short BPEL) as the most promising Web Services Composition language. BPEL builds on IBM's Web Services Flow Language (WSFL) and Microsoft's Web Services for Business Process Design (XLANG). Accordingly, it combines the features of a block structured process language "XLANG" with those of a graph-based process language "WSFL". BPEL is intended for modeling two types of processes: executable and abstract processes. An abstract process is a business proto-

P. Yolum et al.(Eds.): ISCIS 2005, LNCS 3733, pp. 332–341, 2005.

col specifying the message exchange behavior between different parties without revealing the internal behavior of any of them [9]. An executable process specifies the execution order between a number of constituent activities, the partners involved, the messages exchanged between these partners, and the fault and exception handling mechanisms.

In this paper, we introduce our current effort for increasing the performance of parallel executions in BPEL documents by decreasing response time. We have been developing an architecture that allows dynamic execution of statically designed flow regarding customer defined issues at both implementation time and runtime as Figure 1 illustrates. Our proposed architecture supports the dynamic selection of sequences which are part of parallel execution with similar behavioral properties at runtime. We have designed a Controller Agent which can easily be integrated by any BPEL document for applying QoS parameters. Furthermore, our architecture allows users to obtain real-time information about server performance in order to monitor the accomplishment of assured services, giving the user an instant QoS feedback. We believe that our approach is extensible and based on Internet standards such as XML schema, SOAP, WSDL, and UDDI [10]. This ensures the independence of any particular programming model and other implementation specific semantics. It should be noted that our proposed architecture does not by itself address the problems of routing, load balancing, security, transaction, pricing and dynamic selection of Web Services. Instead, we concentrate on selecting execution paths dynamically at runtime while Web Services compositions are constructed statically. It is possible to apply QoS parameters, especially response time, through a Controller Agent. The goal of our prototype implementation that is presented in this paper is to prove the feasibility of our concept. The remainder of this paper is outlined as follows. After discussing some related work, we present the architecture of our agent based BPEL approach and discuss the specification issues in section 3. We evaluate some simulation results and clarify the performance changes in section 4. Finally, we conclude with an outlook of future work and conclusion.

2 Related Work

Web Services are starting to be deployed within organizations and being offered as paid services across organizational boundaries. Therefore, quality of service (QoS) has become one of the key issues to be addressed by providers and clients. Many important challenges stem from the quality-of-service issues in composite Web Services [11]. Efforts in the past years mainly focused on describing, advertising and signing up to Web Services at defined QoS levels. This includes HP's Web Services Management Language (WSML) [12], IBM's Web Service Level Agreement (WSLA) language [13], the Web Services Offer Language (WSOL) [14] as well as approaches based on WS-Policy [15]. WSOL provides different predefined classes of service for clients to choose from. WSML and WSLA languages have been developed to specify Service Level Agreements (SLA) for Web Services. Many scientists have conducted research for filling the gaps of stated approaches [16]. One of the works is on mapping of QoS requirements from higher layers onto the underlying network layer in terms of the Internet model [16]. SLA is an agreement regarding the guarantees of a web service which defines mutual understandings and expectations of a service between the service provider and service consumers. The service guarantees are about execution of required transactions and how well they should be executed. Any Web Service covered by an SLA must be monitored for scalability and performance. All SOAP, WSDL, and other interoperability issues must be resolved before an SLA-covered Web service is launched into a production environment. The provider offering the service may be financially liable under the terms of the SLA. In such a case, if the service does not meet certain standards, it is particularly important to make sure these kinds of problems are under control. Even though, a given business enterprise is under guarantee with SLA, there could be some problematic situations that the business can not stand These efforts enable us to describe quality metrics of services, such as response time, and the flexibility of associated service level objectives. In a way that is meaningful for the business needs of a service client. While methods to describe and advertise QoS properties have been developed, the main outstanding issue remains as how to implement a service that lives up to promised QoS properties. Especially, defining QoS properties for composite Web Services is a complex issue. Innovative solutions are needed to be able to bundle QoS properties of a service application with the properties of the provider's network, the client's network and the network connecting both. In addition, composite services may specify QoS properties dependent on the input data and the expected path of the execution. This area requires more research and novel ideas [17].

It has shown that the time spent at the slow Web Service dominates overall execution time [18]. Menascé's article provides good insights on the performance impact of a slower service that participates in an application using several Web Services. He also pointed that we can improve the application's scalability as a whole by reducing the time spent at the slow server. These mathematical derivations and insights form the basic logic of our architecture. We have tried to point out problematic and slow Web Service invocations that are part of parallel executions in BPEL document with similar behaviors. Then we ignore these branches for a specified period of time while protecting the main objective of BPEL process. User preferences also affect our selection of these slower Web Services in the parallel execution. Many respected scientific work showed that how dynamic selection of Web Services partners is critical while composing Web Services with QoS parameters in mind [16] [19] [20] [21] [22] [23]. Basically in these scenarios, partners are evaluated by their past behaviors with the help of clustered agents or by third party companies. Unfortunately, these evaluation methods can not be trusted all the time because of the difficulties behind the operation of handling evaluations accurately. Moreover, selecting new services dynamically would require us to quantify our criteria for selection. There are also challenging issues of correctness and optimality. In this respect METEOR-S is a promising tool aimed to reduce much of the service composition problem to a constraint satisfaction problem [24]. The work of these researchers also show that dynamic selection of Web Services while satisfying QoS parameters is an area where more work needs to be done. On the other hand many Web Services compositions do not necessarily need this approach for satisfying their business needs. Supply chain problems are good candidates for static composition with their close collaborations between suppliers and retailers. In our proposed approach, BPEL document is designed statically based on company's evaluation results or trust degrees on partner links. Then we evaluate all the partners in each execution of the BPEL document to reach an optimum state. Optimum state means the balance between user preferences and QoS. By this approach, one can dynamically execute a BPEL document which is constructed statically. This operation results in elimination of undesired time loss [25]. In short, we prefer to form the selection statically but execute these services dynamically or on the fly. For example, our approach can easily be adapted to middleware companies when compared to the dynamic selection and composing of Web Services partners with QoS parameters in mind. Moreover, it should be noted that there is no overhead caused by provider and requester negation on satisfying QoS parameters. Only the interaction between BPEL document and the Controller Agent cause some overhead due to the invocation of the Agent for updating information about flow executions and gathering the optimum execution path.

3 Proposed Architecture

The core logic of our proposed system (Fig. 1) is the Controller Agent integrated with BPEL document. Controller Agent Architecture is composed of three main layers (Fig. 2). At the top of the architecture, there exists Web Service Interface layer for handling the communication with BPEL documents in a standard way. By defining the agent as a Web Service, we encapsulate the Web Service advantages. Agent layer, in the middle of the architecture, decides which paths to follow in execution of flow actions composed of similar behavioral partners according to user preferences or QoS parameters. Agent mainly concentrates on broken links and Web Services that happen simultaneously. By the help of Agent layer, user preferences are balanced with business executions in BPEL in order to eliminate unnecessary and useless branches of parallel executions. In our architecture, the agent is responsible for this balance. Actually, our architecture makes a dynamic selection on statically formed Web Services. This dynamic selection concentrates on flow actions which correspond to parallel executions. We also assume that these Web Services provide overlapping or identical functionality such as in requesting a quote of some inventory items from several suppliers in a supply chain management. At the lower layer, there exits a relational database which is responsible for recording historical data gathered from each execution of BPEL documents. The database with its design structure is capable of handling historical data of many different BPEL documents. This enables agent controller to support different BPEL documents.

The Controller Agent integration with BPEL document is similar to invoking a regular synchronous Web Service. In figure 1, there exists circled numbers which correspond to a simple simulation steps of how the Controller Agent integrated BPEL document is executed. Each step, relatively circled numbers, in the figure is described briefly as follows;

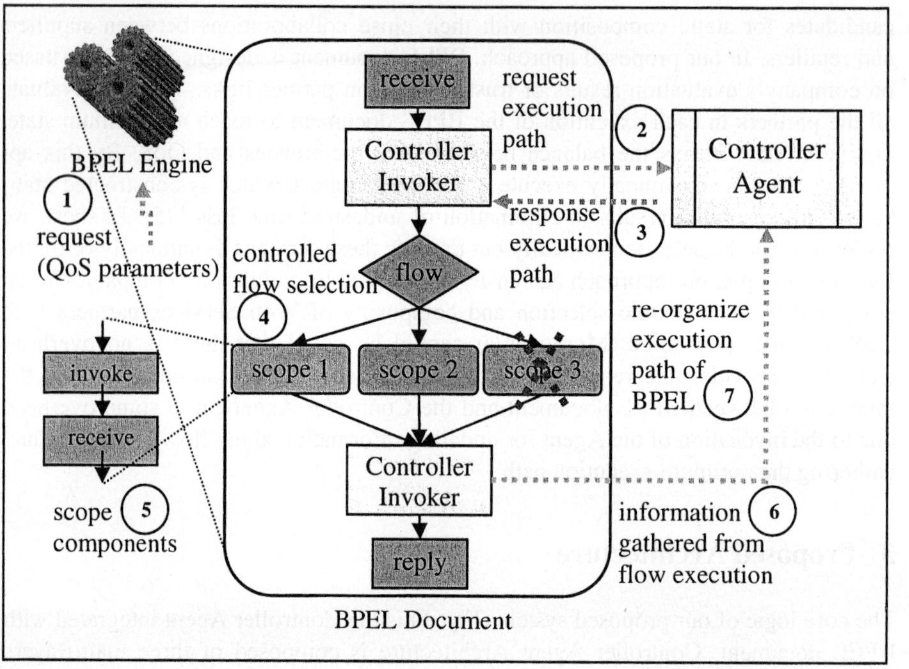

Fig. 1. Overview of the Controller Agent Integration with BPEL document

1. A requester makes a request to the Controller Agent integrated BPEL document. Since Controller Agent gives the opportunity to the requester for supporting his/her QoS parameters as input parameters, the requester can state his/her preferences for the execution. As far as the prototype is concerned, only the parameter of response time QoS in inner flow execution of BPEL document is supported.
2. The first controller invoker request that is the most suitable execution path for each parallel execution from the Controller Agent according to the user QoS parameters. This execution path is decided by the Controller Agent based on user preferences and historical data. In this decision process, the Controller Agent uses simple heuristics which are obtained through recursive executions of that BPEL document.
3. Controller Agent returns an execution path for each flow in requester BPEL document.
4. In each flow, there exists a conditional statement that decides to execute flows branches or not according to the execution path returned from Controller Agent.
5. Represents inner structure of scope, we assume that flow actions consists of invoke actions.
6. The second controller invoker sends back information about flow executions to the Controller Agent. In our prototype, since we only support response time QoS parameter in composite Web Services, the information mainly consists of start time of each flow and execution end times of each flow's branches. If a sequence is broken or if it is not responding anymore, this information is also inherited.
7. Information about how much it takes to execute a flow and its branches, and information on broken links is recorded to the relational database.

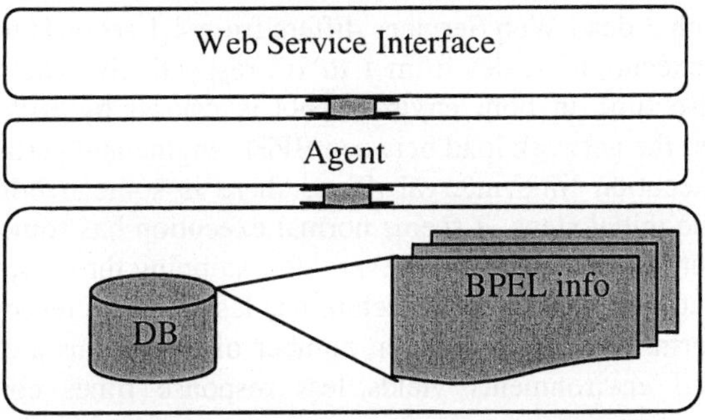

Fig. 2. Overview of the Controller Agent architecture

4 A Sample Use Case

Let us assume that a manufacturer wants to design Web Services composition with his suppliers to satisfy his business needs. In order to buy spare parts, the manufacturer obtains prices from different suppliers. The manufacturer decides to buy these parts from the supplier which gives the minimum price. Although, it is a simple scenario, it inherits basic logic behind the Web Services composition. To achieve his goal, the manufacturer designs his BPEL document including flow action (parallel execution) where available supplier Web Services provide overlapping or identical functionality. The flow action contains the suppliers as its branches. We simulate the environment variables like supplier Web Services and manufacturer Web Service. In our simulation, we do not use real data or real Web Services, since we believe that the constructed environment is sufficient enough to clarify the affects of our proposed architecture.

In composite Web Services execution it takes a lot of time to recover from Web Services that are not responding. Our architecture aims to decrease this time loss by analyzing historical data gathered from previous executions of BPEL document. After deciding that some links are not responding anymore, these branches are stated as broken links and they are not executed until the next checking procedure takes place to understand if this link restarts to respond. In our simulation, BPEL process of the manufacturers consists of one flow action which is composed of ten supplier Web Services for requesting merchandise purchases. These supplier Web Services have the same functionality and the same response time. We prepared two similar environments. First environment is a normal BPEL execution, means the Controller Agent is not integrated. The second environment is built by using our proposed architecture. Then we begin to disable supplier services one by one to see the performance changes based on average response time. For each simulation we show the obtained results as graphs illustrating how the number of disabled services for each environment affects the response time of the process (Fig. 3). In Figure 3, the y-axis denotes the average response time. The x-axis shows the number of executions of the BPEL process of the manufacturer. In Figure 3, by scaling number of executions from 1 to 10, we wanted to show that the whole system's average response time for both Controller Agent integrated and Controller Agent not integrated differs unpredictably in similar situations. For instance, average response time of the Controller Agent not integrated environment with 3 dead Web Services differs from 4.1 seconds to 4.6 seconds when the number of executions scales from 1 to 10, respectively. The reason for different average response time in both environments is caused by BPEL engine machine performance and the network load between BPEL engine and partner Web Services at that specific execution time interval. Since there is some overhead caused by the integration in the initial steps, it seems normal execution has some advantages on the Controller Agent integrated one. However, after stopping three supplier Web Services it is obvious that our proposed architecture has less average response time compared to its normal form. For instance, when number of executions are 10, the Controller Agent integrated environments yields less response times compared to normal scenario.

The simulation environment is constructed such that Web Services would have the same response time in parallel execution. However, it has been shown that BPEL process average response time changes when we manipulate the availabilities of these Web Services. One may question that although the participating Web Services have the same response time in parallel execution in a BPEL process, how come the system's response time can be affected by stopping these Web Services? It should be noted that while BPEL engine executing its operations it uses computer resources to manage its capacity through the process. When the number of operations (such as invoking participating supplier Web Services in our case) decreases/ increases the completion time of the process also decreases/ increases. Moreover, while communicating with external Web Services the network load affects the response time of each Web Services. By defining the participating Web Services in a flow activity with the same response time, we actually want to express that they have the same response time in a virtual environment with unlimited resources.

In Figure 4, we extend the Figure 3 by focusing on number of executions which are 10. In Figure 4, the y-axis denotes the average response time. The x-axis shows the number of dead branches which we disable one by one to see the performance changes of the system. The red graph represents Controller Agent not integrated environment whereas the blue graph represents Controller Agent integrated one. It is obvious that when the number of dead branches increases the gap between two environment' response time increases. Controller Agent integrated environment proves itself having better performance. By the simulation we aimed to show from a global perspective that how broken links coverage in our architecture helps to reduce response time of composite Web Services execution. Although the number of supplier Web Services is limited in our architecture, in real life it might be tens or hundreds and this would make our proposed architecture even more effective.

Moreover, the Controller Agent gives opportunity to the manufacturer to state QoS parameters. For now, only response time parameter is available. But it should be noted that this QoS parameter is not for a global execution of the BPEL process, it is only for a local flow action, since we only get information on flow actions. In our assumption, the most time consuming part of the business executions would be on parallel executions, at least for applications where concurrent Web Services invocations with the same functionality are needed. Requesting merchandise purchases from many different suppliers is a suitable example for these kinds of applications. Also, in our simulation environment, we get expected results according to QoS parameter stated by the manufacturer.

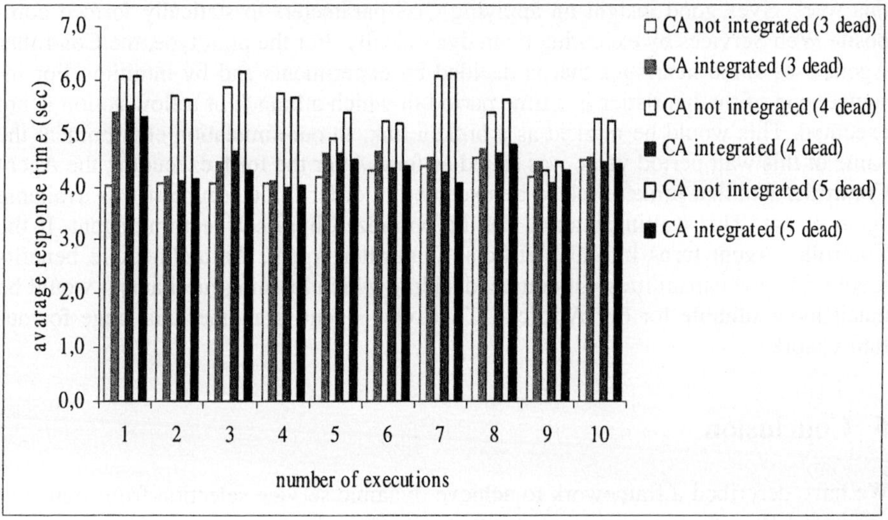

Fig. 3. Simulation results on broken link effects

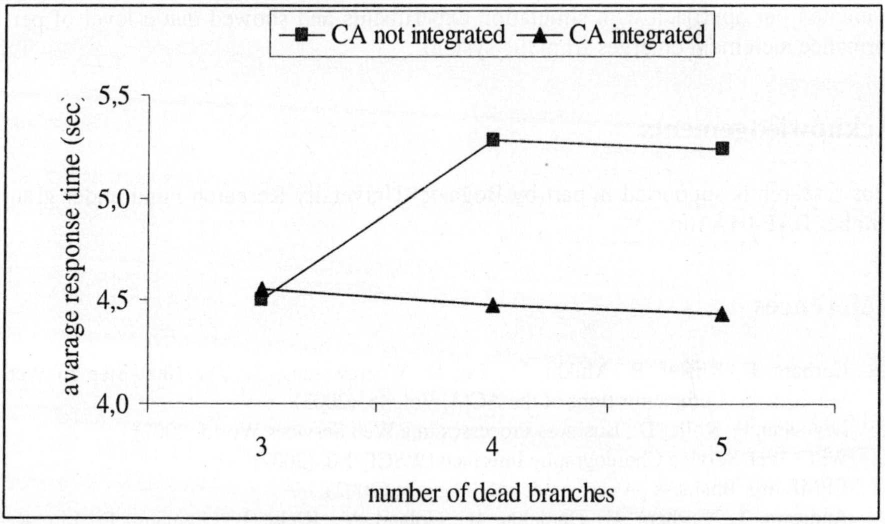

Fig. 4. Extended simulation results on broken link effects

5 Future Work

We designed and applied our proposed architecture on flow actions only where parallel executions take place. We also limited our algorithm to find optimum path on Web Services which have the same functionality. In the future, we are planning to work on removing these limitations and try to apply other QoS parameters to our architecture. Although there exists some limitations regarding the Controller Agent capabilities, this work gives good insight on applying QoS parameters to statically formed composite Web Services by executing them dynamically. For the prototype, the Controller Agent uses some heuristics that is decided by experiments and by intuition. For instance, one of the heuristics is a time period in which a branch of a flow action is not executed. This would be marked as a broken link. In our simulation environment the value of this wait period value was stated as four. After the forth execution, the Agent Controller lets that broken link to be executed in order to determine if it is available again or not. This waiting interval can be optimized by a self learning agent. If the Controller Agent turns into an Artificial Controller Agent, the architecture benefits more with new capabilities. Of course, deciding which learning mechanism would be much more suitable for our Artificial Controller Agent is another challenge for our future work.

6 Conclusion

We have described a framework to achieve dynamic service selection from statically composed Web Services in a manner that considers the optimum execution path regarding the QoS parameter: response time. We tried to optimize existing Web Services composition structure with the help of the Controller Agent Web Service. We evaluated our approach with simulation experiments and showed that a level of performance increment emerges from the system.

Acknowledgements

This research is supported in part by Boğaziçi University Research Fund under grant number BAP-04A106.

References

1. Curbera, F., Khalaf, R., Mukhi, N., Tai, S., Weerawarana, S.: The Next Step In Web Services. In: Communications of the ACM, Vol. 46. (2003)
2. Leymann, F., Roller D.: Business Processes in a Web Services World (2002)
3. W3C: Web Service Choreography Interface (WSCI) 1.0. (2002)
4. BPML.org: Business process modeling language (2002)
5. Andrews, T., Curbera, F., Dholakia, H., Goland, Y., Klein, J., Leymann, F., Liu, K., Roller, D., Smith, D., Thatte, S. *et al*: Business Process Execution Language for Web Services.(2003)
6. UN/CEFACT, OASIS: ebXML Business Process Specification Schema Version 1.01.(2001)
7. WfMC: Workflow Process Definition Interface -- XML Process Definition Language (XPDL) (2002)
8. Mendling, J., Müller, M.: A Comparison of BPML and BPEL4WS. In. Lehrstuhl Wirtschaftsinformatik Universität Trier (2003)

9. Wohed, P., Van Der Aalst, W., Dumas, M., Hofstede, A.: Analysis of Web Services Composition Languages: The Case of BPEL4WS. In. Queensland University of Technology, Brisbane (2003)
10. Curbera, F., Duftler, M., Khalaf, R., Nagy, W., Mukhi, N., Weerawarana, S.: Unraveling the Web Services Web: An Introduction to SOAP, WSDL, and UDDI. In: IEEE Internet Computing, Vol. 6. (2002) 86-93
11. Menascé, D.A.: QoS Issues in Web Services. In: IEEE Internet Computing, Vol. 6. (2002) 72–74
12. Catania, N., Kumar, P., Murray, B., Pourhedari, H., Vambenepe, W., Wurster, K.: Web Services Management Framework, Version 2.0. (2003)
13. Ludwig, H., Keller, A., Dan, A., King, R., Franck, R.: A service level agreement language for dynamic electronic services. In: Electronic Commerce Research, Vol. 3. (2003) 43-59
14. Tosic, V., Pagurek, B., Patel, K.: WSOL – A Language for the Formal Specification of Classes of Service for Web Services. In: ICWS'03 (The 2003 International Conference on Web Services). Las Vegas, USA (2003) 375-381
15. Box, D., Curbera, F., Hondo, M., Kale, C., Langworthy, D., Nadalin, A., Nagaratnam, N., Nottingham, M., VonRiegen, C., Shewchuk, J.: Web Services Policy Framework (WSPolicy) (2003)
16. Tian, M., Gramm, A., Naumowicz, T., Ritter, H., Schiller, J.: A Concept for QoS Integration in Web Services. In: Fourth International Conference on Web Information Systems Engineering Workshops (WISEW'03). Roma, Italy (2003)
17. Ludwig, H.: Web Services QoS: External SLAs and Internal Policies Or: How do we deliver what we promise? In: 4th IEEE Conf Web Information Systems Eng Workshops (2003) 115–120
18. Menascé, D.A.: Response Time Analysis of Composite Web Services. In: IEEE Internet Computing, Vol. 8. (2004) 90–92
19. Wagner, M., Balke, W.: Towards Personalized Selection of Web Services. In: Proceedings of the 12th International World Wide Web Conference (WWW 2003). Budapest, Hungary (2003)
20. Zeng, L., Benatallah, B., Ngu, A.H.H., Dumas, M., Kalagnanam, J., Chang, H.: QoS-Aware Middleware for Web Services Composition. In: IEEE Transactions on Software Engineering, Vol. 30. (2004) 311-327
21. Menascé, D.A.: Composing Web Services: A QoS View. In: IEEE Internet Computing, Vol. 8. (2004) 88–90
22. Maximilien, E.M., Singh, M.P.: A Framework and Ontology for Dynamic Web Services Selection. In: IEEE Internet Computing, Vol.8. IEEE Computer Society (2004) 84-93
23. Aggarwal, R., Verma, K., Sheth, A., Miller, J.: Dynamic QoS based Supply Chain (2004)
24. Aggarwal, R., Verma, K., Miller, J.A., Milnor, W.: Constraint Driven Web Service Composition in METEOR-S. In: Proceedings of the 2004 IEEE International Conference on Services Computing. Shanghai, China (2004) 23-30
25. Arpacı, A.E., Bener, A.B.: Web Services Orchestration with Agent Based Business Process Execution Language (BPEL). In: Proceedings of the 35th International Conference of Computers & Industrial Engineering, Vol. 1. Istanbul, Turkey (2005) 171-176

A Fair Multimedia Exchange Protocol

Cagil Can Oniz, Erkay Savas, and Albert Levi

Faculty of Engineering and Natural Sciences, Sabanci University,
Orhanli – Tuzla, TR-349656 Istanbul, Turkey
cagilo@su.sabanciuniv.edu, {erkays, levi}@sabanciuniv.edu

Abstract. In this paper, we address the problem of fair exchange of multimedia files and propose a fair multimedia exchange protocol. The protocol is fair in such a way that none of the parties obtain a significant advantage and cheat on the other party by terminating the protocol abruptly. In the application scenario that we considered two parties want to exchange some multimedia files such that neither party wants to transmit its own data in its entirety before receiving other party's data. The proposed fair multimedia exchange protocol uses a baby-step approach in which data are sent in parts and the probability of protocol completion is gradually increased over several cycles. We also implemented the proposed protocol and comparatively analyzed its performance. We observed that, in terms of execution time, the proposed protocol performs close to a secure but unfair protocol for the same amount of exchange data.

1 Introduction

The main goal of an exchange protocol is to trade data fairly between two entities. The exchanged items may differ from application to application. Below a short list of some exchange protocols is given.

- In an *e-commerce protocol* [1, 2, 3, 4, 5, 6 and 7], the customer exchanges the payment to get an electronic good (e-good) or a service.
- In a *certified mail protocol* [8, 9 and 10], an e-mail message is sent and a receipt, which shows that the receiver has obtained the e-mail, is received.
- In a *contract signing protocol* [11, 8, 12, 13 and 9], digital signatures are exchanged. These signatures bind two parties to the terms stated on a contract.

In the literature, two different types of exchange protocols are proposed: *online third-party protocols* [14, 12, 4, 6 and 7] and *baby-step protocols* [13 and 9]. In online third-party protocols, a trusted third party is employed as an active entity. Each party submits its own item to the trusted third-party and this trusted third-party passes the items to the recipient entity. In baby-step protocols, items are split into small parts. Two entities swap multiple partial items one by one. In other words, one of the entities sends one of his/her partial item to the other entity and waits for the other side to send a partial item. This swapping of partial items continues until the items are completely exchanged.

The shortcomings of online third-party protocols and baby-step protocols are discussed in [4]. Online third-party protocols require that the trusted third-party always be at service; the large amount of traffic routed to the third party may create a bottle-

P. Yolum et al.(Eds.): ISCIS 2005, LNCS 3733, pp. 342 – 351, 2005.

neck in the network. Moreover, trusted third party is a single point of failure that requires costly precautions for continuous service. On the other hand, baby-step protocols, which have peer-to-peer architecture, do not employ any central authority or party. Thus, there is no single-point-of-failure problem here. However, the protocol may impose some overheads and may be complex.

In this paper, a fair multimedia exchange protocol is proposed and its performance is comparatively analyzed. Due to the nature of the problem, a baby-step approach is taken. Some characteristics of the proposed protocol are given below:

- The protocol is fair such that even in the worst case both entities obtain approximately same amount of data from the items they expect.
- The proposed protocol also provides verification of the contents of the exchanged items in order to make sure that none of the parties try to cheat on other.
- In most of the previously proposed protocols in the literature, items are transferred multiple times, which is too costly especially for large multimedia files. In the proposed protocol, files are transferred only once during the whole protocol run.

The rest of the paper is structured as follows. We state our assumptions and give some notations in Section 2. In Section 3, we explain oblivious transfer protocol, which is necessary in order to understand our protocol description. In Section 4, we describe the proposed multimedia exchange protocol. Implementation issues and some performance figures are given in Section 5 and we conclude the paper in Section 6.

2 Assumptions and Notations

Assumptions for the proposed protocol are as follows:

- There are two entities in the protocol, Alice and Bob, who do not necessarily trust each other. Before the protocol starts, both Alice and Bob have already decided on which multimedia files to exchange.
- The public keys of Alice and Bob are securely exchanged before the protocol run.
- The integrity and authentication of the messages are provided by appending a digital signature [15, 16] to each message. For the sake of simplicity, these signatures are not shown in the protocol, but the entities are able to compute and verify digital signatures.
- An attacker may gain complete control of communications between the entities. That means, attacker may prevent messages to be sent for an indefinite period.
- Communication failures of any type and attacks that disrupt the communication may cause the protocol to stop before it comes to conclusion. In such a case, the protocol prevents violation of the fairness property. In other words, none of the parties get the exchange data that they expect.
- In order to encrypt bulk data, 128-bit Rijndael encryption is used in the protocol.
- 2048-bit RSA is used as the public-key cryptosystem.

Notations used in the protocol are given in Table 1.

Table 1. Notations

Symbol	Meaning
A	Alice
B	Bob
A → *B*: X	A sends X to B
KU	Public-Key
KR	Private-Key
‖	Concatenation Operation
$E_K(X)$	Symmetric encryption of X with key K
$D_K(X)$	Symmetric decryption of X with key K

3 Oblivious Transfer Protocol

The fair multimedia exchange protocol proposed in this paper is based on the oblivious transfer protocol described in [13]. In the oblivious transfer protocol, an entity *A* sends two messages to another entity *B*. However, only one of the messages *A* sends will be received by *B* in an intelligible format. Furthermore, *A* will not know which one of these messages is received by *B*. An oblivious transfer protocol is similar to flipping a coin and showing the result to another person without learning what the outcome was.

Figure 1 depicts the steps involved in the oblivious transfer protocol. There are two players of the protocol: *A* and *B*. First, *A* generates two public/private key pairs KU_1/KR_1 and KU_2/KR_2 and sends the public keys KU_1 and KU_2 to *B*. Second, having received the public keys, *B* chooses one of them at random, say KU_1. Subsequently, *B* creates a symmetric key K, encrypts this key with the chosen public key (KU_1 in our example case), and sends the result of encryption, $E_{KU_1}(K)$, back to *A*. Third, *A* receives this encrypted key, but does not know which one of her public keys was used as the encryption key. *A* decrypts *B*'s message twice with both of her private keys and obtains two keys. The result of one of these decryptions is the symmetric key K created by *B* since $D_{KR_1}(E_{KU_1}(K)) = K$. The other decryption is gibberish data that looks like a symmetric key since $D_{KR_2}(E_{KU_1}(K)) = K_{wrong}$. The entity *A* cannot distinguish the original symmetric key created by *B* from the gibberish data. *A* creates two messages msg_1 and msg_2 and encrypts them with the symmetric keys K and K_{wrong} as follows: $E_K(msg_1)$ and $E_{K_{wrong}}(msg_2)$ and sends them to *B*. Later, *B* decrypts these messages with his symmetric key K as follows: $D_K(E_K(msg_1))$ = msg1 and

1. A → B: $KU_1 \parallel KU_2$
2. B → A: $E_{KU_1}(K)$
3. A → B: $E_K(msg_1) \parallel E_{K_{wrong}}(msg_2)$

Fig. 1. Oblivious Transfer Protocol

$D_K(E_{K_{wrong}}(msg_2)) = msg_{wrong}$. In this way, *B* can read only one of these messages since the other cannot be decrypted correctly. Moreover, *A* does not know which message *B* can read so that she cannot cheat on *B*.

4 Fair Multimedia Exchange Protocol Description

Two entities Alice (*A*) and Bob (*B*) want to exchange their multimedia files. As the first step, each of *A* and *B* divide their multimedia files into *n* pieces grouped in pairs as in Figure 2.

Pair 1:	Piece 1	Piece 2
Pair 2:	Piece 3	Piece 4
	...	...
	...	...
Pair *n*/2:	Piece *n*-1	Piece *n*

Fig. 2. File division. *A* and *B* perform division separately so that each has *n* pieces of their files.

In the second step, each of *A* and *B* creates *n* symmetric keys grouped in pairs as in Figure 3. Both *A* and *B* perform this operation independently so that they both have different set of n keys. In step three, both *A* and *B* encrypt their *n* pieces of files with their *n* symmetric keys as in Figure 4.

Pair 1:	K_1	K_2
Pair 2:	K_3	K_4
	...	...
	...	...
Pair *n*/2:	K_{n-1}	K_n

Fig. 3. Creation and grouping of *n* symmetric keys

Pair 1:	E_{K_1}(Piece 1)	E_{K_2}(Piece 2)
Pair 2:	E_{K_3}(Piece 3)	E_{K_4}(Piece 4)
	...	...
	...	...
Pair *n*/2:	$E_{K_{n-1}}$(Piece *n*-1)	E_{K_n}(Piece *n*)

Fig. 4. Encryption of *n* pieces of files with *n* symmetric keys

In step four, both *A* and *B* send their *n* encrypted messages to each other. Please notice that the integrity and authentication of each message of the protocol are provided by appending a digital signature to that message. However, for the sake of simplicity, these signatures are not shown in the protocol.

In step five, *A* and *B* send their symmetric key pairs to each other using the oblivious transfer protocol described in Section 3. For each key pair that *A* sends to *B*, only one key will be intelligibly received by *B*. The same argument is also valid for the keys sent from *B* to *A*. Therefore, a total *n*/2 keys will be received at each side. Figure 5 shows an example of the first phase of this step in which Alice sends K1 and K2 through the Oblivious Transfer Protocol to Bob who receives, say K1. Subsequently, Bob sends K9 and K10 through the protocol in the same manner to Alice who receives, say K10. The exchange of other pairs is not shown in the figure.

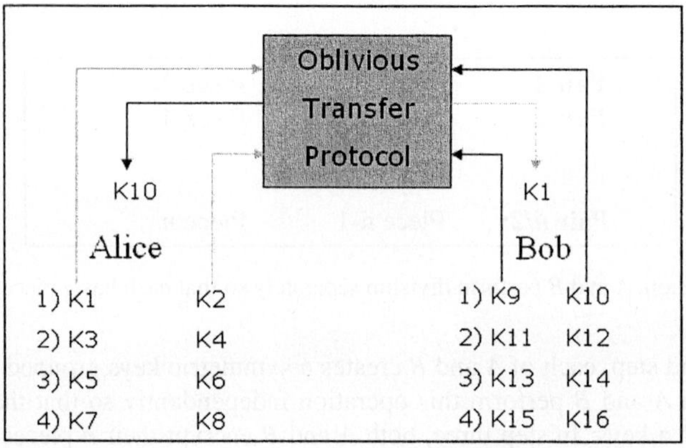

Fig. 5. Transmission of keys using oblivious transfer

In step six, *A* and *B* decrypt the pieces they can. There will be *n*/2 decrypted pieces at each party. Each party will investigate the decrypted pieces for quality control (e.g. by watching and/or listening to multimedia file pieces) and will decide whether these pieces are truly sub-parts of the multimedia files of the other party. If one of the parties is not satisfied with the quality, then this party terminates the protocol.

Step seven is for the exchange of correct keys of each pair. Here we take a baby-step approach to ensure fairness. The parties may exchange the keys one bit at a time (i.e. bit-by-bit) or several bits at a time. If both *A* and *B* exchange all keys bit-by-bit, each entity sends 128 messages (256 in total). This amount of message exchanges creates unnecessary traffic. In order to overcome this problem, instead of transmitting bit-by-bit, the first 64 bits are transferred in groups of 8 bits, the next 16 bits are transferred in groups of 2 bits and the last 48 bits are transferred bit-by-bit. Doing so, instead of transmitting 128 messages 64 messages are transmitted per entity. Let's analyze the fairness of this exchange. During this exchange of the bits, the computational power required to build a brute force attack reduces as the number of bits obtained increase. The protocol must be fair; therefore, at each baby-step and for each entity, the computational power of a brute-force attack must be approximately equal. During the transfer of first 64-bits, an unfair situation may be created since one party may know 8 bits more than the other party. However, since setting up a brute-force attack for the remaining bits of the key is not feasible at that point (e.g. compare the computational powers needed to find out 104 bits and 96 bits; both are infeasible), the unfairness caused by knowing 8 more bits does not lead to an important advantage for one party. However, after one party transmits 64 bits of all of his/her keys, he/she does not want to exchange in groups of 8 bits any more since this may cause a practical violation of the fairness property. The remaining number of bits gets smaller and relative advantage of needing less computational power to set up a brute-force attack becomes more sensitive to number of bits exchanged at each baby-step. That is why number of bits exchanged at each baby-step is gradually reduced as the protocol comes to a completion.

Due to the oblivious transfer in step five, *n*/2 correct keys have already been received; therefore, in step seven each party can check whether the other side is trying to cheat or not. Since both sides do not know which correct keys the other side has obtained, the probability of cheating by sending bits of wrong key of all pairs is $1/2^{(n/2)}$. In other words, the probability of cheating reduces exponentially as the number of pairs increases.

In the last step of the protocol, both *A* and *B* decrypt the remaining *n*/2 pieces and obtain the complete multimedia file.

5 Implementation and Performance Evaluation

The presented protocols are implemented with C# (C-sharp) programming language using Microsoft Visual Studio .Net 2003. The implementation is tested and performance figures are obtained on an Intel Celeron 1333 MHz computer with 240 MB RAM.

Table 2 shows cryptographic operation counts of the proposed Fair Multimedia Exchange Protocol. *P* represents the number of pieces that the multimedia file is divided.

Table 2. Cryptographic operation counts for the Fair Multimedia Exchange Protocol

Rijndael Encryption	Rijndael Decryption	RSA Signature Verification	RSA Signature Generation	RSA Encryption	RSA Decryption
P	2P	1 + 2P + 64	1 + 2P + 64	P/2	P

Figure 6 shows the time required to divide and encrypt a file of 600 MB. This is an offline process that is performed before transmission of any network message. As can be seen from the figure, the time required to divide and encrypt files is not affected by the number of pieces.

One of the most important parameters is the *network buffer size*. The network buffer size is the maximum amount of data to be stored in a byte array, which is subsequently sent through a network socket. If the network buffer is too large, the primary memory is overloaded. In Microsoft Windows Operating System when the memory is overloaded, the system starts paging on secondary memory (hard disk).

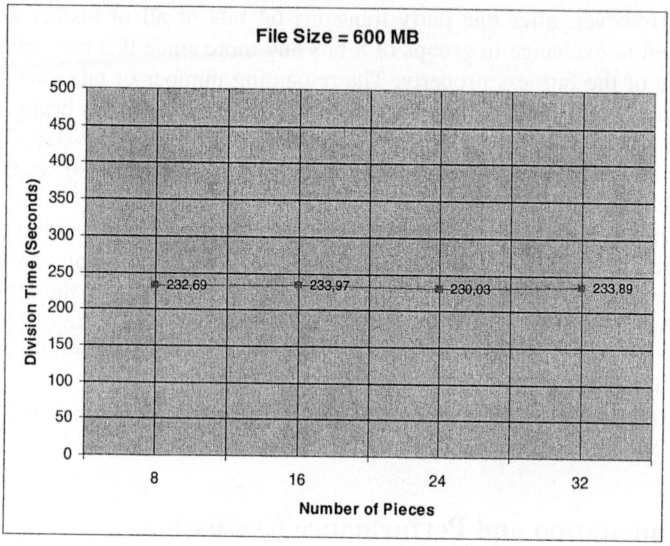

Fig. 6. File division and encryption time

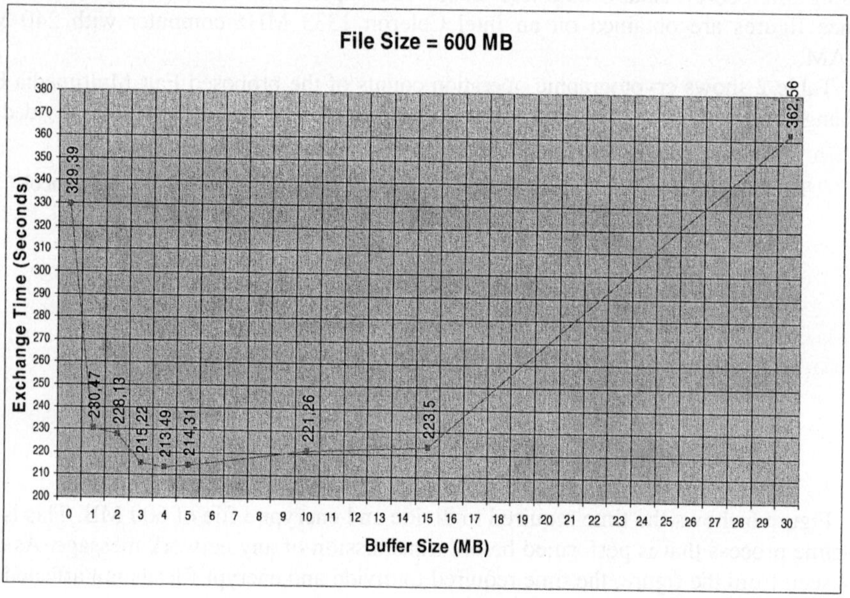

Fig. 7. File exchange (with no security) time against varying buffer sizes

Although this property provides extra memory, the execution time of an operation diminishes since secondary memory operates much slower than primary memory. If the network buffer is too small, the overhead increases because the total amount of socket operation will increase. In order to determine the optimum buffer size, we

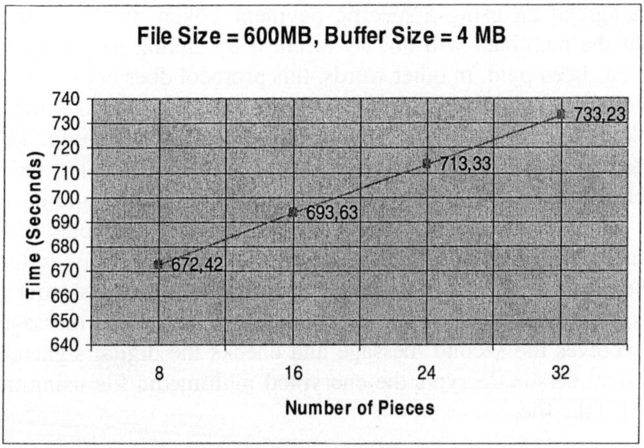

Fig. 8. Fair exchange time against different number of pieces (File Size = 600MB, Buffer Size = 4MB)

developed a simple file exchange program with no security features. Figure 7 shows the time needed to perform exchange (with no security) of a 600 MB file against varying network buffer sizes. As can be seen from the figure, the minimum network-buffer size is 4 MB.

Figure 8 shows the time needed to perform fair exchange of a 600 MB file against varying number of pieces. The network buffer size is fixed to 4 MB due to above analysis. As discussed in Section 4, if the number of pieces increases the exchange becomes more secure since the probability of cheating reduces. For example, when the number of pieces is 16, the probability of success (i.e. probability of not-cheating) becomes 99.6%, which is quite acceptable. However, when the number of pieces increases, the overhead also increases and therefore the total amount of time to finish the exchange gets larger. The overhead increases since the numbers of Rijndael encryptions/decryptions, RSA encryptions/decryptions and signature generations/verifications are directly proportional to the number of pieces as depicted in Table 2. Furthermore, an increase in the number of pieces augments the number of commands and controls due to the programming of the system.

The overhead of the fair exchange protocol is calculated as the difference between the protocol execution time (Figure 8) and the file exchange time with no security features (Figure 7). The exchange protocol, which has no security features, takes 213.49 seconds in order to barter 600 MB data using a buffer of size 4 MB. However the fair exchange protocol with 16 pieces requires 693.63 seconds in order to barter the same amount of data and with the same amount of buffer size. This shows that the overhead is 480.14 seconds and that the fair exchange of a 600 MB file is performed approximately 3.25 times slower than the exchange application with no security features.

We also compared the performance of the proposed fair multimedia exchange protocol with an ordinary e-commerce protocol in which a client pays money to a merchant in order to download a multimedia file. Figure 9 shows such an e-commerce protocol. It is assumed that the client has selected a multimedia file to download and both parties agreed on using a specific payment Token. In this protocol, the client assumes that the merchant will not try to cheat by ending the protocol prematurely, after he/she has been paid. In other words, this protocol does not ensure fairness.

Let's briefly analyze the protocol details. In the first message, the client sends a payment token, a session key encrypted with the merchant's public-key (KU_M), and the digital signature of the first message to the merchant. Having received this first message, the merchant checks the digital signature and then validity of the payment token. If all checks succeed, the merchant decrypts the encrypted session key with his/her private key and obtains the session key KS. Subsequently, in the second message, the merchant sends the multimedia file that the client has requested encrypted with the session key KS and the digital signature of the second message to the client. The client receives the second message and checks the digital signature of the message. After that, he/she decrypts the encrypted multimedia file using the session key KS and obtains the file.

1) C → M: Token || E_{KU_M}(KS) || Signature
2) M → C: E_{KS}(MMedia_File) || Signature

Fig. 9. Multimedia E-Commerce Protocol

In the fair multimedia exchange protocol, the two entities involved do not trust each other; however, in the multimedia e-commerce protocol, the client must trust the merchant. In other words, multimedia e-commerce protocol is not a fair protocol.

The multimedia e-commerce protocol, described in Figure 9, is implemented in order to compare the performance of this protocol with the performance of the fair multimedia exchange protocol. In the implementation of the Fair Multimedia Exchange Protocol, the total amount of exchanged data is 600*2 = 1200 MB since each entity transmits a multimedia file of 600 MB to the other. Since the information exchange is one-way (only one multimedia file is transmitted by the merchant) in the multimedia e-commerce protocol, the total amount of exchanged data is taken 1200 MB in order to have a fair comparison.

The implementation results show that multimedia e-commerce protocol run takes 617.29 seconds using a file of size 1200 MB. As discussed above, the fair multimedia exchange protocol with 16 pieces takes 693.63 seconds. Therefore, despite complexity of the fair multimedia exchange protocol, the time required to complete the protocol is close to the time required to complete the multimedia e-commerce protocol when the same amount of exchanged data is assumed.

6 Conclusions

In this paper, a fair multimedia exchange protocol that uses a baby-step approach has been proposed. The proposed protocol provides a method for not only fair exchange of the multimedia e-goods, but also for the verification of the contents of the exchanged e-goods for quality control purposes. Moreover, items are transferred only once per protocol run, saving both time and bandwidth. The fair multimedia exchange problem is peer-to-problem. Thus, a baby-step approach is more suitable than employing a trusted third party to ensure fairness. This makes the protocol quite complicated. We also analyzed the performance of the proposed protocol and saw that the execution time is close to a secure but unfair protocol.

References

1. Ray, I., Ray, I.: Fair Exchange in E-commerce. *ACM SIGEcomm Exchange*, volume 3, issue 2 (2002) 9 - 17
2. Ray I., Ray, I.: An Optimistic Fair-exchange E-commerce Protocol with Automated Dispute Resolution. Proceedings of the First International Conference on Electronic Commerce and Web Technologies, Greenwich, UK (2000)
3. Ray I., Ray, I.: An Anonymous Fair-exchange E-commerce Protocol. In Proceedings of the 1st International Workshop on Internet Computing and E-Commerce (2001)
4. Ray I., Ray, I.: A Fair-Exchange Protocol with Automated Dispute Resolution. In Proceedings of the 14th Annual IFIP WG 11.3 Working Conference on Database Security. Schoorl, The Netherlands, (2000)
5. Ray I., Ray, I.: Failure Analysis of an E-commerce Protocol Using Model Checking. Proceedings of the Second International Workshop on Advanced Issues of E-Commerce and Web-based Information Systems, Milpitas, CA (2000)
6. Cox, B., Tygar, J. D., Sirbu, M.: NetBill Security and Transaction Protocol. In Proceedings of the 1st USENIX Workshop in Electronic Commerce (1995) 77 – 88
7. Ketchpel, S.: Transaction Protection for Information Buyers and Sellers. In Proceedings of the Dartmouth Institute for Advanced Graduate Studies '95: Electronic Publishing and the Information Superhighway (1995)
8. Micali, S.: Simple and Fast Optimistic Protocols for Fair Electronic Exchange. Annual ACM Symposium on Principles of Distributed Computing (2003) 12 - 19
9. Even, S., Goldreich, O., Lempel, A.: A Randomizing Protocol for Signing Contracts. *Communications of the ACM*, v. 28, no. 6 (1985) 637 – 647
10. Asokan, N., Shoup, V., Waidner, M.: Asynchronous Protocols for Optimistic Fair Exchange. In proceedings of the IEEE Symp. on Res. in Security and Privacy (1998)
11. Ben-Or, M., Goldreich, O., Micali, S., Rivest, R. L.: A Fair Protocol for Signing Contracts. *IEEE Transactions on Information Theory*, v. 36, no.1 (1990) 40 - 46
12. Pfleeger, C. P.: Security in Computing. Englewood Cliffs, N.J. Prentice-Hall (1989)
13. Schneier, B.: Applied Cryptography (1996)
14. Franklin, M. K., Reiter, M. K.: Fair Exchange with a Semi-Trusted Third Party. 4th ACM Conference on Computer and Communications Security (1997) 1 - 5
15. Rivest, R., Shamir A., Adleman, L.: A Method for Obtaining Digital Signatures and Public Key Cryptosystems. *Comm. of the ACM*, vol. 21, no. 2 (1978) 120-126
16. NIST, Digital Signature Standard (DSS), FIPS PUB 186-2 (2000)

A Pervasive Environment for Location-Aware and Semantic Matching Based Information Gathering

Riza Cenk Erdur[1], Oğuz Dikenelli[1], Ata Önal[1], Özgür Gümüs[1], Geylani Kardas[2], Özgün Bayrak[1], and Yusuf Engin Tetik[1]

[1] Ege University, Department of Computer Engineering, Bornova, 35100 Izmir, Turkey
{erdur, oguzd, onal, gumus}@staff.ege.edu.tr, {bayrak, tetik}@bornova.ege.edu.tr
[2] Ege University, International Computer Institute, Bornova, 35100 Izmir, Turkey
geylani@bornova.ege.edu.tr

Abstract. The main motivation of this paper is to integrate the semantic matching capability into the pervasive computing environments. In this context, we have developed an environment that provides a semantic matching based information gathering capability for mobile users. An important feature of the developed environment is its domain independence. Domain independence is realized by first transferring the concepts of a specific domain's ontology in XML format from the server to the mobile device, and then parsing that XML file for dynamically creating a visual interface, using which users can enter requests. The generic design of the semantic matching engine also contributes to domain independence, since a generic matching engine can accept inputs and return outputs using concepts from any ontology. To show the effectiveness of the architecture, a case study was implemented in a campus area. In this case study, mobile users can find closest places to reside or eat something.

1 Introduction

Advances in the enabling technologies for pervasive computing [9] have already established the infrastructure for mobile users to access the information from anywhere and anytime. Based on this infrastructure, different applications have been developed for information access and service provisioning in pervasive environments. On the other hand, Semantic web [1] describes a new vision for web computing in which knowledge is represented and processed semantically using ontologies. An ontology defines the concepts within a domain, describes the properties of each concept, defines the relations between concepts, and rules can be constructed for reasoning about concepts. Semantic matching is kind of an ontology-based information search. A semantic matching engine takes concept(s) from an ontology as input and then it returns knowledge which semantically matches the input concepts. The advantage of semantic matching is that when an exact match is not found, semantically related results can be returned to the user. In this paper, our primary motivation is to take the advantage of semantic matching based information gathering in pervasive environments.

P. Yolum et al.(Eds.): ISCIS 2005, LNCS 3733, pp. 352 – 361, 2005.

In the pervasive computing and semantic web literature, there are pioneering studies that use semantic web technologies. For example, there are pervasive applications that use ontologies for context information modeling or semantic service discovery. Below, we will summarize the previous works by comparing them with the system that we have developed so that we can show in what ways our work is different from them.

There are studies that extend the existing service discovery infrastructures using semantic web technologies: Chakraborty, et. al. [2] implemented a semantic service discovery infrastructure that uses Darpa Agent Markup Language (DAML) to describe the services. The infrastructure contains a Prolog based reasoning engine. Masuoka at. al. [7] has taken the semantic service discovery in pervasive environments one step further and developed an application, where semantically discovered services can also be composed to achieve more complex tasks. In addition to semantic service discovery, there are studies that use ontologies for modeling context information. Wang, et. al. [10] extends the basic context information modeling by proposing an OWL (Web Ontology Modeling) encoded context ontology for pervasive environments. Chen et. al. [3] describes an ontology called as SOUPA (Standard Ontology for Ubiqutious and Pervasive Applications). Using OWL, SOUPA defines vocabularies to represent intelligent agents' beliefs, desires and intentions, time, space, events, user profiles and actions and policies for security and privacy. Although these studies use ontologies for both semantic service discovery and context information modeling, the capability of semantic matching does not exist in these systems.

On the other hand, there are many classical location-based information search services in mobile environments [4]. For example, there are systems where users with mobile phones can be directed to the nearest local restaurants, shops, etc. These systems can be considered as standard information search services for mobile users. There are two features, which make our work different from them. The first feature is being domain independent or opennes. This means that new domains can be added at any time. The visual user interfaces, which are necessary to prepare requests for querying these domains, are created dynamically at run-time by first transferring and then parsing the XML file containing the concepts belonging to that domain's ontology. Supporting semantic matching is the second feature where the system that we have developed differs from them. Using semantic matching, a result list ranked by the degree of semantic match can be presented to the user in response to his/her request so that he/she can have the option of accessing to the most semantically related information. So, we take the previous works one step further by integrating semantic matching capability into the information gathering process in pervasive environments and by modeling the system in a way that it supports domain independence.

The rest of the paper is organized as follows: Section 2 gives an example scenario to show usefulness of the proposed system. The architecture of the developed system is discussed in section 3. The semantic matching engine component is discussed in section 4. Section 5 gives an example case study, which demonstrates how the sample scenario above is realized. Section 6 includes the conclusion.

2 Motivating Example

As the motivating example, we give below an example scenario to illustrate how the system that is proposed in this paper can be useful:

John is a student who has been admitted to a university in a foreign country. In his new university campus and the nearby areas, there is a pervasive computing infrastructure where an information search service is provided for different domains such as accommodation, eating out, and shopping etc. He has not arranged an accommodation before, so when he visits the campus area for the first time, he asks his mobile device to list the available services given to mobile users around. First of all, he has to arrange an accommodation and chooses the accommodation domain. Whenever he chooses it, a visual user interface is created automatically and dynamically so that he can enter requests about accommodation. He chooses the concept of dormitory from the interface. He also enters other filtering criteria such as price or room capacity (e.g. he requests rooms for only one person). He was a bit late, so when he looked at the results presented, he saw that no dormitory could be found, but that the semantic matcher returned him names and addresses of some pensions with the desired characteristics and ranked with respect to distance from him. After visiting these pensions to see whether they are suitable to stay, he feels that he is hungry and chooses the eating domain from his mobile device, which results in the dynamic creation of a visual interface to prepare eating out requests by entering some concepts. He selects *RedMeatRestaurant* concept from the interface and the semantic matcher returns two red meat restaurants at top of the list and also one kebab restaurant since *KebabRestaurant* concept is semantically related with *RedMeatRestaurant* concept. Since the returned kebab restaurant is closer than red meat restaurants to him, he decides to go to the kebab restaurant to eat some Turkish kebab. The same way of information gathering is realized as he chooses other domains such as shopping, culture, etc. Finally, the same scenario can also be applied not only in campus area, but also for travelers arriving in a city, citizens looking for real estate to buy or hire in a specific city area, and such.

In this paper, we introduce a software architecture to develop a pervasive system that provides the requirements of above example scenario. The critical points of this scenario are that openness of the system architecture in terms of addition of new service domains, and the ability to gather semantically related services upon request.

3 System Architecture

The application that we have developed consists of three basic components. These are the mobile client component, the server component and the semantic matching engine component. The internal modules of the client and server side components, and the semantic matching engine component are shown in Fig. 1 and will be discussed in more detail in the following subsections.

3.1 Mobile Client Component

The client side component is responsible for getting the GPS data, providing the interface for specifying the user requests and displaying the results, sending the request to the server in XML format and parsing the results received in XML format. The GPS data is received using the GPS receiver. The connectivity of the mobile device and the GPS receiver is provided using a Bluetooth transceiver.

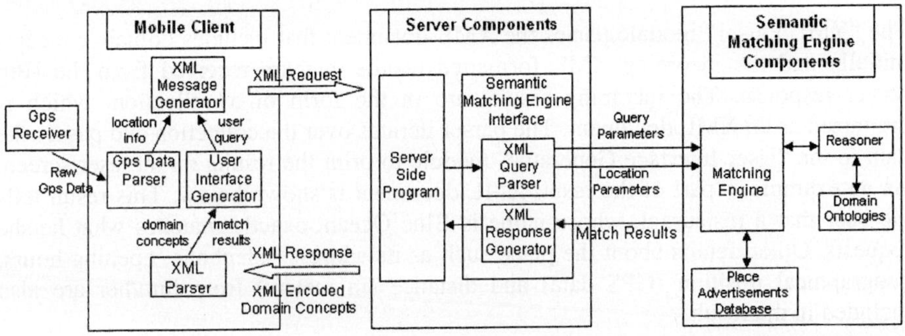

Fig. 1. Internal modules of client and server components

The "GPS Data Parser" module is responsible for parsing the location data retrieved from the GPS receiver. Connecting the GPS receiver with a mobile device using Bluetooth starts a stream of GPS data flowing over the Bluetooth serial port. To get the most current position of the client, the GPS data parser module reads periodically the GPS message strings, which are updated every second. After getting GPS data stream, this module parses it and gets the Latitude and Longitude coordinates.

"User Interface Generator" module is critical, since the creation of visual interfaces dynamically at run-time is the responsibility of this module. The XML file containing the concepts belonging to a specific domain's ontology is transferred from the server first. Then, the transferred XML file is parsed and a visual interface is created. Hence, a user interface where users can enter their requests is created independently at run-time for each different domain. In fact, the ontologies are represented in Web Ontology Language (OWL) in the semantic matcher component. However, since mobile devices are resource limited, we simplified and represented these ontologies in simple XML format to make the parsing process efficient in the mobile device. Otherwise, the mobile device should execute the code necessary to parse OWL documents.

After the user selections are collected, they are converted into XML together with the GPS location data by the "XML Message Generator" module. We preferred the requests and results to be transmitted in XML format, since it is a well-known web standard. The "XML Message Generator" module then sends the request in XML format using a GPRS Http network connection. To send the data via GPRS Http network, the client device needs to activate the GPRS settings. As an example, if the user selects *SeaFoodRestaurant* concept, corresponding request XML document is shown below:

```
<request>
   <PlaceType>SeaFoodRestaurant</PlaceType>
   <gpsData>
      <latitude>22.333E</latitude>
      <longtitude>52.444N</longtitude>
   </gpsData>
</request>
```

The "XML Parser" module parses the XML document that includes domain concepts initially and the incoming XML formatted results that are received from the Http server response. The incoming results are in the form of a collection, which is organized as an XML document. The parser iterates over the collection and passes the data to the "User Interface Generator" module to print the results on the user screen. As an example, a part of the result XML document is shown below. This result tells the user that a restaurant, whose name is Blue Ocean, exactly matches what he/she requests. Other details about the place such as its address, telephone, opening hours, geographical position (GPS data) and distance (in meters) from him/her are also included in the result.

```
<matchResults>
   <result>
      <name>Blue Ocean</name>
      <matchDegree>EXACT</matchDegree>
      <tel>+90-232-1111111</tel>
      <address>Bornova Street 1</address>
      <openingHours>08:30 AM - 11:00 PM</openingHours>
      <gpsData>
         <latitude>27.229E</latitude>
         <longtitude>38.455N</longtitude>
      </gpsData>
      <distanceToClient>350m</distanceToClient>
   </result>
   :
   :
</matchResults>
```

Mobile devices have a limited memory. For this reason, the "XML Parser" module has been designed to be small and light. The pull parser technique, in which the software drives the parsing, has been used. In this technique, only some part of a XML document is read at once; hence, it does not need a large memory size. The application drives the parser through the document by repeatedly requesting the next piece. Our application can process and display information as it is parsed after being downloaded from the server. In this case it basically iterates over the XML tree and finds the items. The parsed data is then passed to the "User Interface Generator" module to be printed on the screen of the mobile device.

3.2 The Server Component

A server side program, which in our case a Java Servlet component, meets the user request and passes it to the "Semantic Matching Engine Interface" module. The "Query Parser" sub module of this interface module decomposes the request into a format that the semantic matching engine can understand and then sends the request to the semantic matching engine as shown in Fig. 1. It then waits for the results from the semantic matching engine. The matching results are sorted by the degree of match and location knowledge and are inserted into a collection. This collection is converted into an XML message by the "XML Response Generator" sub module. The formed

XML message is then forwarded to the servlet component so that it can be sent to the requester as an Http response.

3.3 The Semantic Matching Engine

Semantic matching engine is a registry to keep records of knowledge about advertised places in a specific domain. It can be searched for the closest place to eat something, to reside, to buy some clothes etc. using domain dependent information. So, a place that gives a service in a specific domain, must advertise itself to the matching engine using concepts in predefined domain ontologies. For example, a restaurant that serves sea foods, must advertise itself using the *SeaFoodRestaurant* concept defined in eating place ontology given in Fig. 2.

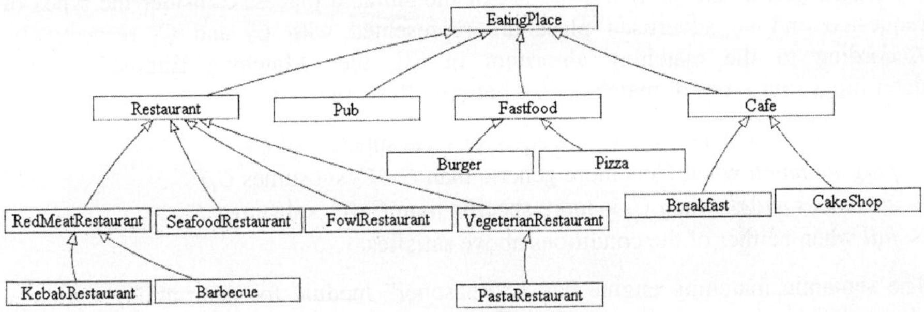

Fig. 2. An example *eating place* ontology to show the taxonomy of places in a domain

The basic idea behind the matching process is to find the advertised concepts that are identical to the requested one. However, the advertised and requested concepts can be semantically related with each other but are not directly identical. In this case, a semantic matching process is required. Semantic matching process is a matching process that can identify the semantic relationships between the advertised and requested concepts. Semantic matching engine is the software module that executes this process. For example, if a restaurant advertises itself to the matching engine using meat restaurant concept, then a request that searches a meat restaurant is matched with this advertised restaurant. With semantic matching process, a request that searches a kebab restaurant is also matched with the same advertised restaurant if there is a relationship between meat restaurant and kebab restaurant concepts.

In the literature, there are several studies [6], [8] proposing algorithms especially for discovery of semantic web services. We have adapted the matching algorithms for web services proposed in previous works and redesigned it for discovering places in a specific domain. In our system (Fig. 1), mobile users can obtain the list of the *most suitable* places based on their request and global position. Requested place type in a specific domain and global position are input to our engine to realize semantic match. Each place is advertised to the engine using predefined domain ontologies to specify its type and GPS data to specify its location.

Place types are ontology classes with defined namespace URIs. In this study, we have defined a concept named as "Place" to advertise the places in different domains to the matching engine. One of the attributes of this concept is the "Place Type" which takes value from different domain ontologies and specifies the domain dependent value of the advertised places. For example, when a restaurant that serves sea foods, wants to advertise itself to the matching engine, it fills the "Place Type" attribute with *SeaFoodRestaurant* concept from the eating place ontology shown in Fig. 2. The other critical attribute is the "GPS data" that defines the geographic position of the advertised place and it takes value from GPS ontology. The other attributes are name, address, telephone and opening hours. The "Place Advertisements Database" module of the semantic matching engine stores all the places in a particular area (e.g. campus) with their GPS Data.

The "Matching Engine" module realizes matching of mobile user's request and advertised places and produces the list of the suitable places. Consider the types of requested and an advertised place are represented with C_1 and C_2 respectively. According to the matching algorithm in [8], the "Matching Engine" module determines four types of match degree between these two concepts:

- *exact match* when C_2 and C_1 are equal or C_1 is subclass of C_2
- *plug-in match* when C_2 is more generic than C_1 (C_2 subsumes C_1)
- *subsumes match* when C_2 is more specific than C_1 (C_1 subsumes C_2)
- *fail* when neither of the conditions above satisfies

The semantic matching engine has a "Reasoner" module for determining ontology class relations. It gives the superclass distance of the two ontology classes with given URIs using the relations between them. For doing this, it parses OWL ontologies and finds subsumption relations. For example, consider the following simple ontology class tree in Fig. 2. According to the ontology model, the "Reasoner" module finds superclass distances as -1, 0, 1 and 2 in (SeaFoodRestaurant, CakeShop), (SeaFoodRestaurant, SeaFoodRestaurant), (SeaFoodRestaurant, Restaurant) and (SeaFoodRestaurant, EatingPlace) ontology class pairs respectively. In case of a multiple inheritance, there will be different paths from a subclass to its superclass. In this case, it returns the shortest distance as a result by performing a depth-first search on the ontology tree. Calculated ontology class distances are cached as instances in the "Reasoner" to optimize performance. When the same distance query is received multiple times they are all responded (excluding the first one) via it's cache.

The "Matching Engine" module determines the match degree between the requested and advertised place types using the superclass distances found between corresponding ontology classes. This is realized with the following pseudo code in the "Matching Engine" module:

```
If distance = 0 or distance = 1 then EXACT match
If distance > 1 then PLUGIN match
If distance < 0 then calculate reverse_distance
    (reverse_distance means parameters in reverse order)
    If reverse_distance > 0 the SUBSUMES match
    Else FAIL in match is determined
```

The scoring function of the "Matching Engine" is ordered as exact > plug-in > subsumes > fail. The engine sorts out advertised places according to their semantic degree of match with the given requested type. The GPS data of the places are used as tie-breaker to sort the places that have the same match degree. So, the *semantically equal* match results are sorted according to their distances to the user. To keep implementation and test simple, only latitude and longitude tags of a GPS data are evaluated and distance between two geographic points is calculated using a formula considering those points' latitude and longitude values [5].

4 Case Study

As a case study, we have implemented a scenario like the one illustrated in the section 2. To realize the test scenario, we have walked through the campus with the GPS receiver, detected the GPS data for the major places for eating and accommodation. Then, we have advertised these places to the semantic matching engine using "Place" concept. For the "Place Type" attribute of this concept, we have defined two example ontologies using OWL; one for accommodation and the other for eating places (Fig. 2). We also mapped a simplified version of these ontologies to XML format and stored in the server so that whenever a specific domain is selected, this XML file can be transferred to the mobile device for the creation of the visual interface at run-time. Finally, we have formed different requests using the mobile phone in various places of the campus and observed what the matching engine returned us.

For identifying user locations, a GPS receiver has been used. Since the application is initially implemented for campus area, which is an open area, the GPS receiver satisfied our needs. However, different location identification technologies such as cell-id based identification can be added to our system whenever a need arises. The connectivity of the mobile phone and the GPS receiver is provided via Bluetooth technology.

User screens are usually limited in mobile devices; hence, the user interfaces created are not so complex. The primary user interface window provides view of all data received along with user-selectable menu choices for controlling the application. When the user starts application, he/she first selects a domain and then a place type using the taxonomy of places within this domain. The terms representing the types of the selected place come from that domain's ontology. Then, the system will return results sorted by the degree of semantic match. Also, the system can give detailed information about returned places when the user selects a matched result.

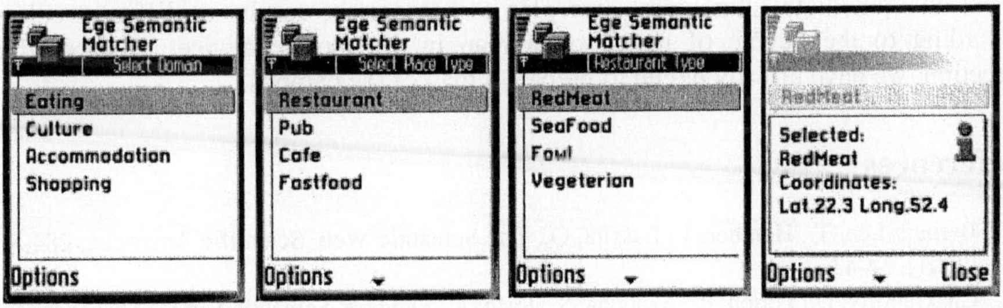

Fig. 3. Screen snapshots showing user's selection of his/her request

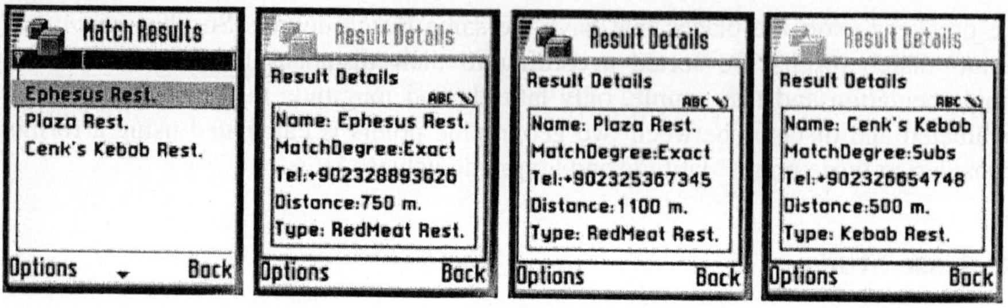

Fig. 4. Screen snapshots showing match results list and details of each returned place

First of all, the client application on mobile phone connects to the server and gets the available service domains. In parallel with the scenario, let us assume that the user selected the eating domain, then following the taxonomy of places within this domain, he/she selected *RedMeatRestaurant* concept to find places that instances of this concept. Screen snapshots showing user's selection of his/her request are given in Fig. 3. So, the *RedMeatRestaurant* concept and the position of the user send to the server and the semantic matching engine.

Again assuming that there are suitable restaurants, after the semantic matching process, the engine returns a list of three restaurants sorted by match degree and distance from the user. Then, the user selects returned results to see detailed information about them. Screen snapshots showing match results list and details of each returned place are given in Fig. 4.

As shown in Fig. 4, first two of the returned restaurants have degree of exact match with the user's requested place type. However, assume that the user is very hungry and he/she selects the third one though it has degree of subsumes match. But, it's closer to the user than the other restaurants.

5 Conclusion

We think that integrating semantic web technologies into pervasive environments will help to implement more novel services for mobile users. In this respect, we have implemented a semantic matching based information search service for mobile users. Using the application that we have developed, we have observed that having the ability of finding the most semantically related information, the semantic matching process increases the quality and relevance of the information presented to the users.

As an immediate future work, we plan to present the results in different colors according to the degree of match on a map in the mobile device. Towards this direction, we have already begun to prepare a map of the campus.

References

1. Berners-Lee, T., Hendler, J., Lassila, O.: The Semantic Web, Scientific American, 284(5), (2001), 34-43
2. Chakraborty, D., Perich, F., Avancha, S., Joshi, A.: Dreggie: Semantic Service Discovery for M-commerce Applications, in the 20th Symposiom on Reliable Distributed Systems, (2001)

3. Chen, H., Perich, F., Finin, T., Joshi, A.: SOUPA:Standard Ontology for Ubiquitous and Pervasive Applications, In the Proc. of the First Annual Conference on Mobile and Ubiqutious Systems: Networking and Services, Boston, MA, (2004)
4. Deitel, "Wireless Internet and Mobile Business: How to Program", Prentice Hall, (2002)
5. Green, R. M.: Textbook on Spherical Astronomy, 6th ed. Cambridge, England: Cambridge University Press, (1985)
6. Li, L., Horrocks, I.: A Software Framework for Matchmaking based on Semantic Web Technology, In the proc. of WWW'2003, Budapest, Hungary, (2003), 331-339
7. Masuoka, R., Labrou, Y., Parsia, B., Sirin, E.: Ontology-Enabled Pervasive Computing Applications, IEEE Intelligent Systems, Vol.18, No.5, (2003), 68-72
8. Paolucci, M., Kawamura, T., Payne, T. R., Sycara, K.: Semantic Matching of Web Services Capabilities, In the proc. of the first international semantic web conference (ISWC), Sardinia (Italy), (2002)
9. Satyanarayanan, M.: Pervasive Computing: Vision and Challenges, IEEE Personal Communications, vol.8, no.4, (2001), 10-17
10. Wang, X. H., Zhang, D. Q., Gu, T., Pung, H. K.: Ontology based Context Modeling and Reasoning using OWL, In the Proc. of Second IEEE Annual Conference on Pervasive Computing and Communications Workshops, (2004)
11. The OWL Services Coalition: Semantic Markup for Web Services (OWL-S), (2004), available at http://www.daml.org/services/owl-s/1.1/

A Web Service Platform for Web-Accessible Archaeological Databases*

Ediz Şaykol[1], Yücel Saygın[1], Aytül Erçil[1],
Andrew Willis[2], David Cooper[2], and Martha S. Joukowski[2]

[1] Faculty of Engineering and Natural Sciences, Sabancı University,
Orhanlı, 34956, Tuzla, Istanbul, Turkey
[2] Division of Engineering, Brown University,
Providence, RI, USA

Abstract. Cultural heritage has been gaining more importance in the recent years in combination with sophisticated yet effective computer vision techniques. As a consequence, archaeological data, both in textual and image forms, has been considered in the development of database models. Archaeological sites are the primary source of archaeological data, and the findings are the primary targets for storage, querying and retrieval as well as exchange through appropriate mediums. This paper introduces a Web service platform design for various archaeological resources that are available for querying through the Web. This platform also allows archaeological data exchange. The Web service platform presented in this paper can be used by both archaeologists and non-technical users to query and retrieve archaeological information through various Web-accessible archaeological databases. Our work also focuses on supporting visual content-based queries for archaeological objects stored in databases. As an initial step, similarity search facility for image-based data is developed as an additional query task within our platform.

1 Introduction

In the recent years, cultural heritage has been gaining more importance especially when considered with the perspective of computer vision and image databases. Archaeological data and archaeological sites are among the trendy applications with this respect. To establish a system to serve as an archaeological database, we have developed a framework (MIDAS) [1] for storing vast amount of information to query archaeological data and to reconstruct the objects and archaeological sites. We have decided to develop a decentralized platform to facilitate the querying of multiple heterogeneous archaeological databases through the Web. The main motivation behind this work lies in the fact that most of the archaeologists have their own databases for their findings on top of a corresponding data model. It is for sure that the archaeologists have various data

* This work was supported by National Science Foundation (NSF) under the grant number **IIS-0205477** *3D Form Models for the Representation, Manipulation, and Recovery of Shape with Applications to Archaeology and Virtual Sculpting.*

P. Yolum et al.(Eds.): ISCIS 2005, LNCS 3733, pp. 362–370, 2005.

models. Within the framework, Web services are used because they provide very useful functionalities for designing a Web-accessible platform [2].

Due to the complex nature of the archaeological data, archaeological databases are required to store wide range of complex archaeological data. The computers mainly help the excavation process. Moreover, the data stored in the archaeological databases provides a medium for reconstruction, management, and realistic visualization. In the literature, there are studies on each of these applications as well as unified frameworks aiming at modeling the management of archaeological sites. 3D Murale [3] is an important work that models a system containing recording, reconstruction, database and visualization components. Recording tools are developed for measuring terrain, stratigraphy, buildings, building blocks, pottery, pottery sherds and statues on the archaeological site.

There exist many archaeological directories and resources on the Web, which provide browsing and searching facilities based on the content of their data. Tay Project [4] is an archaeological inventory on the Web. A database is created to archive the archaeological sites and the findings. The users can search the database along with the ages. Currently, the Palaeolithic/ Epipalaeolithic, Neolithic, Chalcolithic and Early Bronze Age inventories are available for database searches. TheBan Mapping Project [5] in another archaeological resource site available on the Web. TheBan project has focused on Thebes, and decided to built a national database of pre-Islamic sites. They have built as very useful dataset and resource for Egyptologists and archaeologists in not only providing a reference and research tool, but also an aid for site management. Archaeological Resource Guide for Europe (ARGE) [6] contains a comprehensive set of resources for the European region and provides an extensive guide for European archaeology. The set of resources is handled as Web links, and searches can be made by text, date, subject, country, source, period, language. Compass is a database of around 5000 objects selected from the wide collection of the British Museum's collections [7]. The search facility provided at the site is keyword based, and the use of logical operators is allowed. Database of Irish Excavation Reports [8] contains summary accounts of all the excavations carried out in Ireland (North and South) from 1985 to 2000. It can be browsed or searched using multiple fields of the reports, e.g., name, title, etc. A Web service, called Mediolanum [9], is created to facilitate international cooperation in the planning and execution of archaeological field work all over Europe. Having selected a European region, the projects within that region can be browsed to find out a possible collaboration or information exchange.

The main contribution of this study lies in the fact that it provides a medium for archaeologists to collaborate on their individual projects as well as to facilitate information exchange on the subject matter through the Web. Besides, non-technical users can query the system and gather archaeological information from various resources located at various sites. Another contribution is the similarity search facility for image-based archaeological data. The querying module is enriched with similarity searches based on the visual content of the image-based archaeological data, as the initial step for supporting multimedia queries.

The organization of the paper is as follows: The motivation and the design principles of Web Service Platform (WSP) are presented in Section 2 along with a simple scenario. A real-life application on Petra [10] Great Temple excavation site is summarized in Section 3. Section 4 concludes the paper and presents some future work ideas.

2 Web Service Platform

There have been studies on porting archaeological databases to the Web for an extended usage in the recent years (e.g. [10]). Along with this trend, effective querying and retrieval, handling data exchange, and managing possible collaborations are one of the primary issues for the near future. Due to the complexity of archaeological data, data model variances among the archaeological resources, we have designed a Web Service Platform (WSP) for Web-accessible archaeological databases to allow effective querying and retrieval enriched with similarity search facilities.

A Web service can make itself available to potential clients by defining a Web Services Description Language (WSDL) document (a kind of signature) [2]. A WSDL description is an XML document that gives all the pertinent information about a Web service, including its name, the operations that can be called on it, the parameters for those operations, and the location of where to send requests (endpoint). XML is a markup language that makes data portable, by proving a standard way of data-exchange. A Web client can use the WSDL document to discover what the Web service offers and how to access it. In short, a Web service is a server application that implements the procedures which are available for clients to call (e.g., a database query).

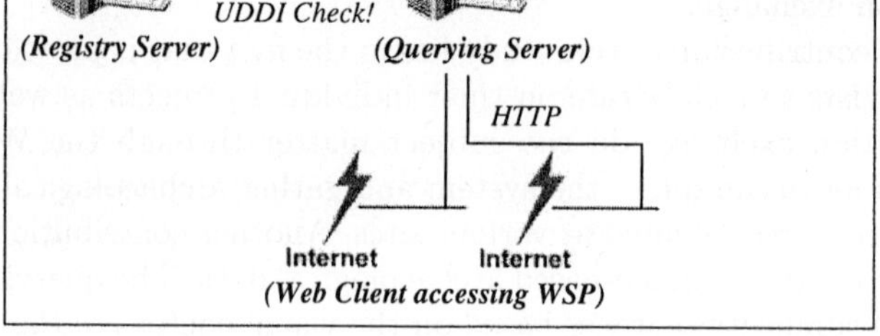

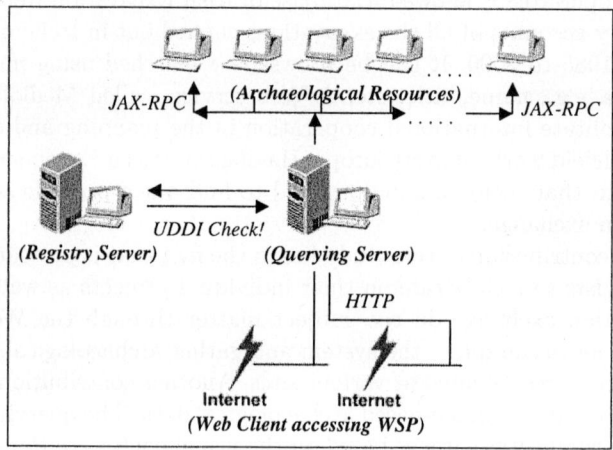

Fig. 1. Web Service Platform (WSP)

A simple illustration of WSP is shown in Figure 1. Querying Server accesses the Repositories of the Archaeologists (i.e., archaeological databases), via asking to the Registry Server for UDDI check. Each archaeologist's local computer runs a Web service that is able to retrieve information from its local database by executing query procedures. The Querying Server, via connecting to these registered Web services, retrieve information from the local archaeological databases. To submit a query to the databases, it employs (JAX-RPC) [11], which is used for developing and using Web services. The Querying Server uses *stubs* for remote procedure calls. Stubs are classes that represent a service endpoint on the client. This allows a JAX-RPC client to invoke a remote method on a service endpoint as though the method were local. To employ stubs, the signatures of the procedures available for a remote call have to be known in advance [11].

2.1 A Sample Scenario

A simple scenario to query within Web Service Platform (WSP) can be summarized as follows: Assume that a Web user initiates a querying facility at the site of the Querying Server (QS). The servlet at QS responsible for the initiated querying facility triggers a set of operations. First, QS communicates with the Registry Server (RS) to get the locations of the registered archaeological databases within WSP. Then, QS executes the database querying procedures at registered archaeological sites remotely. This communication is based on SOAP, hence the communication is paused between the two parties until the response of a request is generated. Each Web service responds to QS based on the query they received. The next operation at QS is to combine these partial results and to present them to the Web user. For the sake of simplicity, not all of the attributes of the archaeological objects are displayed at the client side. However, if the Web user wants to explore the details of a query result (e.g., a pottery found at Sagalassos excavation site), a specific servlet at QS requests the detailed information from the corresponding archaeological database, and presents it to the Web user.

3 A Real-Life Application: PETRA Web Service

Petra is a famous archaeological site in Jordan, and Great Temple excavations by Brown University have been directed by Prof. Martha Sharp Joukowsky [10]. A brief information on the Petra Great Temple Excavations can be found at `http://www.brown.edu/Departments/Anthropology/Petra/`. The archaeological database has the following catalogs: *Archaeological Fragments*, *Coin*, *Grosso Modo*, *Cat*, *Glass*, and *Image*. All of the catalogs except Grosso Modo have one level of information. Grosso Modo catalog contains two levels; Grosso Modo Items as the first level, and related materials for a selected item as the second level.

Figure 2 shows the first screen when WSP is first initiated by an HTTP connection. As seen from the figure, Petra is listed as the registered archaeological database. The querying facilities that Petra provides for the Web users are listed

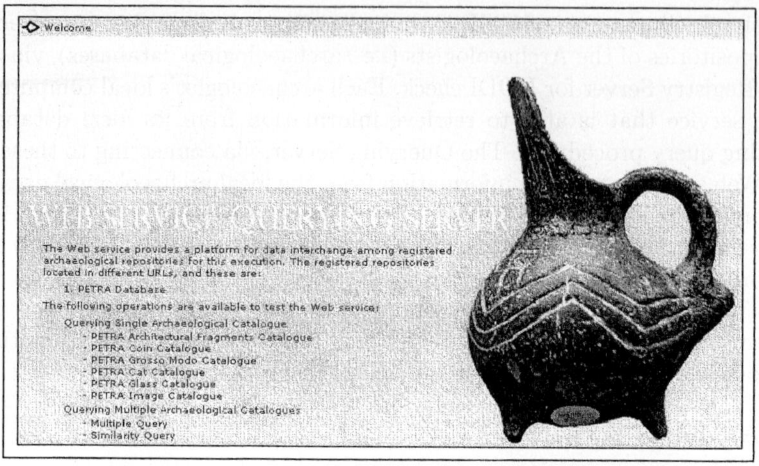

Fig. 2. The Welcome Screen of the Querying Server

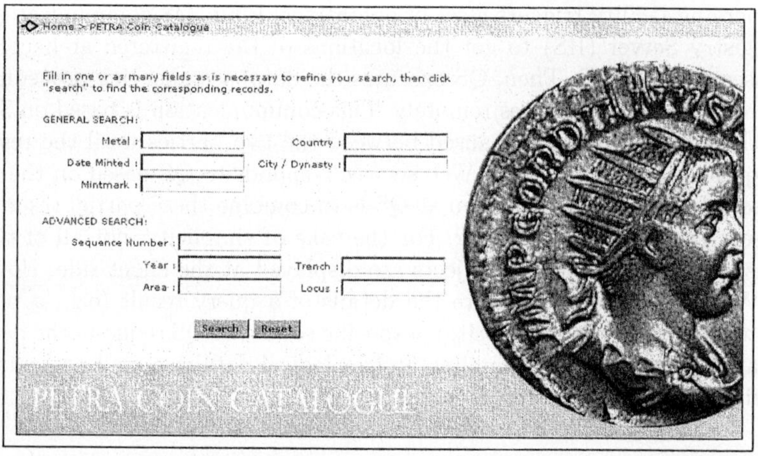

Fig. 3. The GUI of Coin Catalogue for Querying within WSP

below in the figure. Each of the six catalogues can be queried by using the specific GUIs separately (e.g., Figure 3 for Coin catalogue). Additionally, we have provided multiple query interfaces with respect to some common attributes in all of the catalogues (e.g., *year*, *trench*).

The Web service that we have developed for Petra Great Temple excavations have Web-based graphical user interfaces for querying each of the catalogs. A prototype of the system can be accessed at Brown University Web site `http://hendrix.lems.brown.edu:8080/qserver/index.html`. Each querying interface have various attribute selection parts, which can be used either separately or in combination while querying the corresponding catalogue.

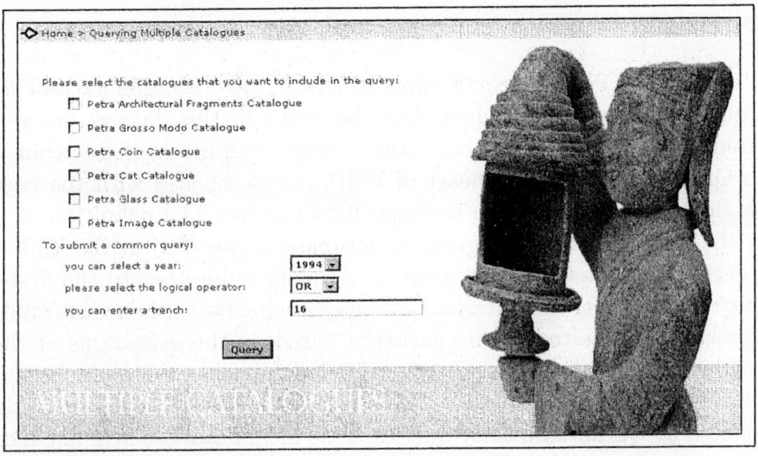

Fig. 4. Multiple Query Specification GUI among the Catalogs

Figure 4 presents the graphical user interface for the specification of multiple queries among Petra Great Temple catalogs. As shown in the figure, *year* and *trench* attributes can be combined by `AND` and `OR` logical operators for more focused queries. Year values can be selected from a combo-box, however trench values have to be entered by the Web user because of the data range and the representation of the trench values. The Web user selects the catalogs that he/she wants to query, and QS sends the multiple query to the selected catalogs only.

3.1 Evaluating WSP by Multiple Web Services

In order to evaluate the performance of the Web Service Platform (WSP) with multiple Web services, we have installed each catalogue of Petra Great Temple to a different machine. On top of each machine, we have deployed separate Web service designs, hence set up an environment of 6 Web services. In this design, the multiple query execution facility becomes more meaningful, hence gives better ideas on the performance of WSP when multiple Web services are registered to the system.

Within this environment, the six catalogs listed in Figure 2 can be queried separately by creating separate JAX-RPC connections between QS. For a single Web service search, QS sends the query formulated by the specific GUI for the catalog directly to the selected catalog. However, for multiple query by *year*, *trench*, or their combination, QS sends the query to all of the catalogs (6 Web services that are registered). QS presents the partial results in a comprehensive manner to the Web user, which is list of catalogue id's (e.g., coin no for coin catalogue, fragment no for architectural fragments catalogue) grouped by catalogue names.

3.2 Similarity Searches in Coin Catalogue

Coin Catalogue of Petra Great Temple is selected as a sample dataset for similarity queries because of the fact that the items in this dataset are generally associated with coin images whose visual content can be queried within WSP.

The QS, which lies in the heart of WSP, communicates with the registered Web services to respond to the user-specified queries. The definition of how to process the data stored in a registered database is specified at the Web service side, where the database is also located. A query submitted to the system via accessing the graphical user interface at the Querying Server is transmitted to the Web services, and the results are gathered based on the definitions at the Web service side. Although it is possible to exchange messages containing image data between the querying server and a Web service, a local database is designed and implemented at QS for similarity queries. This local database acts like a caching

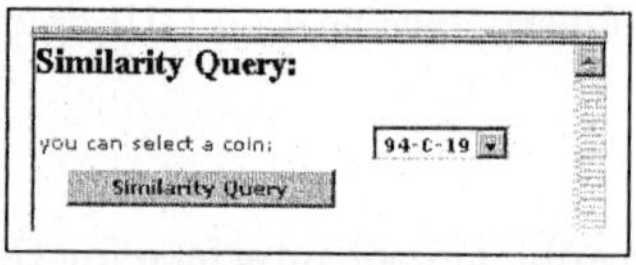

Fig. 5. The Similarity Search Window for Coin Catalogue. The coin image to be queried is selected from the combo-box to initiate the querying process.

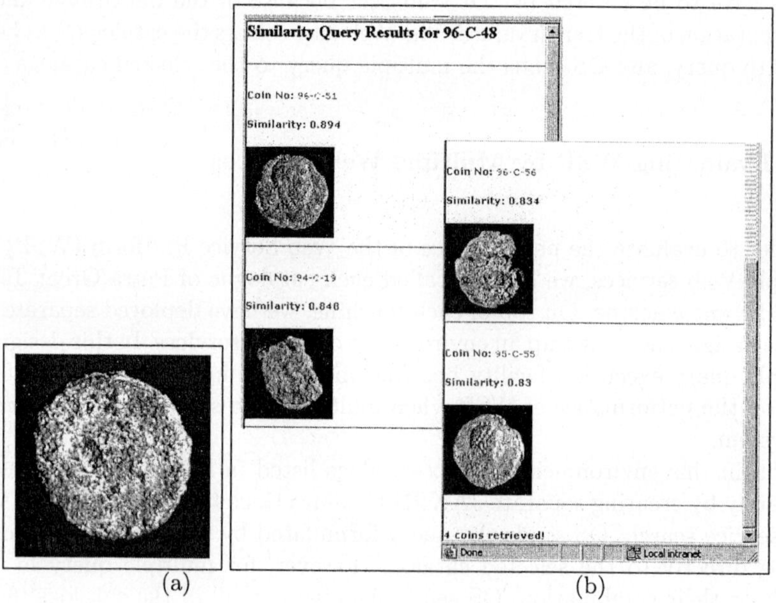

Fig. 6. The Output of Similarity Search for Coin Image 96-C-48. (a) The coin image 96-C-48. (b) The output having 4 coins retrieved, which is shown in two browser pages to the Web user.

mechanism since it stores a copy of the image data of the registered databases. A query indicating a similarity search is processed directly at the querying server, which will also reduce the transmission time significantly. This design is also more reliable for this set of queries because of being local than other types of queries requiring access to Web services.

A simple yet effective module is implemented to respond to similarity queries based on the visual content of Coin images. The coins associated with an image data are inserted in a combo box dynamically by connecting to the database at the time of the initiation of the browser window shown in Figure 5.

Having selected a coin catalogue number from the combo box and pressed the 'Similarity Query' button, QS starts processing the query. The visual content of the coin images is pre-processed at the time of the population of the local database at the querying server. Color and shape feature vectors are extracted from the visual content of the coin images [12], and the query coin image is exhaustively searched with the rest of the coin images. The relevance ordered list of coin images is returned as a result of the query.

The color vector is a probabilistically-weighted variation of color histograms. The shape vector is a combination of two vectors: the first one is based on the angular distribution of the pixels around the centroid of the object. The second vector is the accumulation of the pixels in the concentric circles centered at the centroid of the object [12]. This approach has been used for the content-based retrieval of historical Ottoman archives successfully in [13].

A sample similarity query is presented in Figure 6. The color and shape content of the query coin image (96-C-48) are compared with the color and shape content of the other coin images, and 4 coin images are retrieved. In the module, the similarity values have to pass a threshold, which is set as 0.80, to be listed in the result presentation window. The coin numbers in this final window serve as pointers to actual coin values stored in databases at Web services. By clicking on a coin no link, the system starts communicating with the corresponding Web service to present the details of the actual coin record.

4 Conclusion and Future Plans

In this paper, we have presented a Web Service Platform for Archaeological Databases having Web-access. Along with the trend in porting archaeological databases to the Web for an extended usage, effective querying and retrieval, handling data exchange, and managing possible collaborations are identified as one of the primary issues for the near future. Due to the complexity of archaeological data, data model variances among the archaeological resources, we have designed a Web Service Platform (WSP) for Web-accessible archaeological databases to provide a medium for effective querying and retrieval. The querying module is also enhanced with similarity searches based on the visual content of the image-based archaeological data.

We are planning to extend our platform by additional geometric search facilities, especially based on 3D shape model of the archaeological artifacts. Another future direction is to widen WSP by more registered archaeological databases. Our evaluations show that the performance of the system is promising when there are multiple Web services registered. We are also planning to introduce 'semantic' queries to WSP based on the data model and semantic structure of the registered databases (e.g., searching for *complete* objects).

References

1. Saykol, E., Saygın, Y., Erçil, A.: MIDAS: A multimedia database for archaeological sites. In Arnold, D., Chalmers, A., Niccolucci, F., eds.: 4th Int. Symp. on Virtual Reality, Archaeology and Intelligent Cultural Heritage (VAST 2003), Work In Progress. (2003)
2. Castro-Lean, E.: The web within the web. IEEE Spectrum **41** (2004) 42–46
3. Grabczewski et al., E.: 3D MURALE: Multimedia database system architecture. In: Int. Symp. on Virtual Reality, Archaeology and Cultural Heritage, http://www.brunel.ac.uk/project/murale/ (2001)
4. TAY Project: (http://tayproject.org/)
5. TheBan Mapping Project: (http://www.thebanmappingproject.com/)
6. Archaeological Resource Guide for Europe: (http://odur.let.rug.nl/arge_bin/w3-msql/entry.html)
7. Compass: (http://www.thebritishmuseum.ac.uk/compass/)
8. Database of Irish Excavation Reports: (http://www.excavations.ie/pages/homepage.php)
9. Mediolanum: (http://archeonet.cilea.it/archeosite)
10. Joukowsky et al., M.: Petra Great Temple Volume 1: Brown University Excavations 1993-1997. Petra Exploration Fund, Providence, RI, USA (1998)
11. Armstrong et al., E.: The Java Web Services Tutorial. (2003)
12. Saykol, E., Güdükbay, U., Ulusoy, Ö.: Integrated querying of images by color, shape, and texture content of salient objects. In Yakhno, T., ed.: Advances in Information Systems (ADVIS'04), LNCS 3261. (2004) 363–371
13. Saykol, E., Sinop, A., Güdükbay, U., Ulusoy, Ö., Çetin, A.: Content-based retrieval of historical Ottoman documents stored as textual images. IEEE Transcations on Image Processing **13** (2004) 314–325

A WSDL Extension for Performance-Enabled Description of Web Services*

Andrea D'Ambrogio

Dept. of Computer Science and Systems,
University of Roma "Tor Vergata", Roma, Italy
dambro@info.uniroma2.it

Abstract. Web services are the building blocks of the emerging computing paradigm based on service-oriented architectures. A web service is a self-describing, open component that supports rapid composition of distributed applications. Web service definitions are used to describe the service capabilities in terms of the operations of the service and the input and output messages for each operation. Such definitions are expressed in XML by use of the Web Service Definition Language (WSDL). Unfortunately, a WSDL description only addresses the functional aspects of a web service without containing any useful description of non-functional or quality of service characteristics. This paper addresses the performance attribute of quality of service and introduces a WSDL extension for the description of performance characteristics of a web service. The extension is carried out as a metamodel transformation, according to principles and standards recommended by the Model Driven Architecture (MDA). The WSDL metamodel is introduced and then transformed into the P-WSDL (Performance-enabled WSDL) metamodel. The proposed P-WSDL extension can effectively be used to specify performance requirements of web services, to describe performance data measured on given web services, to add performance-oriented characteristics when querying registries of web services, to ease the derivation of performance models of web services and to support the automated mapping from WSDL documents to P-WSDL ones and from UML models to P-WSDL web services.

1 Introduction

Service-oriented computing is becoming the prominent paradigm for distributed computing and e-commerce. Web services are the building blocks for the application of service-oriented computing on the Web [18].

A web service is a self-describing, open component that supports rapid composition of distributed applications. In a service-oriented architecture, the service provider creates a *WSDL (Web Service Description Language)* service description and publishes it to one or more discovery registries (such as UDDI), so that

* Work partially supported by funds from the FIRB project on *Performance Evaluation of Complex Systems* and from the University of Roma TorVergata CERTIA Research Center.

P. Yolum et al.(Eds.): ISCIS 2005, LNCS 3733, pp. 371–381, 2005.

service consumers can find the service using a wide variety of search criteria and then use the WSDL description to develop or configure a client that will interact with the service.

A WSDL description is an XML document that contains all the information about service capabilities and invocation mechanisms. The capabilities are described in terms of the operations of the service and the input and output messages for each operation. What is needed to invoke the service is provided by a binding implementation description that describes how messages are sent through the network to reach the service location, where the hosting environment executes the service implementation.

Unfortunately, a WSDL document only addresses the functional aspects of a web service without containing any useful description of non-functional or quality of service characteristics. Different web services may provide similar functionality, but with distinct quality of service properties. In the selection of a web service, it is important to consider both functional and quality of service properties in order to fully satisfy the needs of a service consumer [9,11].

This paper addresses the *performance* attribute of quality of service and introduces a WSDL extension for the description of performance characteristics of a web service, such as response time, throughput, utilization, etc.

The proposed extension is defined by first introducing the WSDL metamodel, derived from the WSDL XML Schema, and then transforming it into a *Performance-enabled WSDL (P-WSDL)* metamodel, from which the P-WSDL XML Schema is derived. Indeed, an XML Schema defines the WSDL language in the same respect as a metamodel is used to define a model. Representing the WSDL grammar in terms of a metamodel allows to enhance its comprehensibility and facilitate its extension.

The WSDL and P-WSDL metamodels are defined by use of the *Meta Object Facility (MOF)*, the Object Management Group's (OMG) standard for specifying technology neutral metamodels, or models used to describe other models [16]. The production of XML Schemas from MOF metamodels, and vice-versa, is specified by a further OMG's standard, the *XML Metadata Interchange (XMI)* specification. MOF and XMI are at the heart of the *Model Driven Architecture (MDA)*, the OMG's effort that focuses on models as the primary artifacts of software development, evolution and integration [15]. Applying MDA to Web services has recently received considerable attention, mainly addressing the automated generation of platform-specific implementations from web service models [1,7]. In this paper, MDA standards are also used to formally define and apply the performance-oriented extension of WSDL, in order to appropriately enrich web service descriptions with performance data.

The P-WSDL extension can be applied to serve different purposes, such as:

- to specify performance requirements of web services;
- to describe performance data measured on given web services;
- to add performance-oriented characteristics when querying registries of web services (e.g., UDDI);
- to ease the derivation of web service performance models;

- to support the automated mapping from WSDL documents to P-WSDL ones;
- to support the automated mapping from UML models to services in P-WSDL.

The paper is organized as follows. Section 2 overviews the related contributions. Section 3 describes the main steps of the extension process and clarifies the terminology used throughout the paper. Section 4 illustrates the WSDL metamodel and its performance-oriented extension, i.e., the P-WSDL (Performance-enabled WSDL) metamodel. Finally, Section 5 gives an example application of P-WSDL.

2 Related Work

Aspects that focus on describing, advertising and signing up to web services at defined levels of quality of service have also been addressed by similar and bigger efforts, such as the HPs Web Services Management Framework (WSMF) [4], the IBMs Web Service Level Agreement (WSLA) language [8], the Web Services Offer Language (WSOL) [20] and the WS-Policy [3]. Some contributions have also been given in the Semantic Web area (see OWL-S [10] and METEOR-S [21]).

All such considerable contributions consider quality of service in its broader meaning (not limited to performance attributes) and specifically target web service management activities. This paper instead proposes a lightweight WSDL extension that only addresses the performance properties of web services. This has the positive effect of reducing both the level of required expertise in the muddle of web services standards and the burden of adopting sophisticated specifications that focus on the performance properties of web services only at a very limited extent. In this respect, P-WSDL exhibits higher expressiveness and ease of use.

In addition, P-WSDL addresses some challenging issues not covered by the aforementioned contributions, such as the use of web service descriptions to seamlessly derive predictive models that assist service providers to effectively managing the levels of quality of service characteristics. The P-WSDL metamodel is an important contribution in such a direction, since methods for the automated building and evaluation of performance models based on metamodel transformations are currently being developed (see, e.g., [5] and [19]) and the P-WSDL metamodel includes the formal description of performance parameters required by such methods. Service providers can thus be endowed with methods and tools to obtain performance predictions and answer questions like: "what is the expected service performance?" or "what is a satisfactory reconfiguration of the service deployment to accomodate additional service performance?" or also "what is the acceptable response time under different workload situations?".

A further advantage of having defined the extension at metamodel level is that it is relatively easy to foresee automated transformations of both WSDL documents into P-WSDL ones and platform-independent UML models (PIMs in MDA terms) into platform-specific web services in P-WSDL (PSMs in MDA terms). The degree of automation will further be increased by the availability of a standard approach to defining and implementing metamodel and model transformations, as targeted by the MOF 2.0 Query-View-Transformation (QVT) Request for Proposals recently issued by the OMG [14].

3 Extension Process

As said in Section 1, the proposed extension has been carried out as a metamodel transformation, according to principles and standards recommended by MDA.

The set of guidelines provided by MDA strongly relies on metamodeling techniques for structuring specifications expressed as models and transformations between such models [15]. In this respect, MOF is the key standard that provides an abstract language and a framework for specifying, constructing, and managing technology neutral metamodels, or models used to describe other models [16]. In MDA terms, a *model* (e.g., an UML model) is an instance of a *MOF metamodel* (e.g., the UML metamodel), which in turn is an instance of the MOF *meta-metamodel* specified in [16] (and briefly called *MOF Model*).

A side standard of MOF is the OMG's XMI specification, which provides a set of rules to serialize models and MOF metamodels into *XML documents* and *XML Schemas*, respectively, and to derive a MOF metamodel from an XML Schema [17].

Figure 1 illustrates the metamodel-based process used to carry out the performance oriented extension of WSDL, with the relationships among the main elements in the process.

A WSDL description is basically an XML document that is produced and validated by use of the WSDL XML Schema described in [22]. The relationship between an XML document and its corresponding XML Schema is the same that links a model and its corresponding metamodel. Indeed, an XML Schema defines the WSDL language in the same respect where a metamodel is used to define

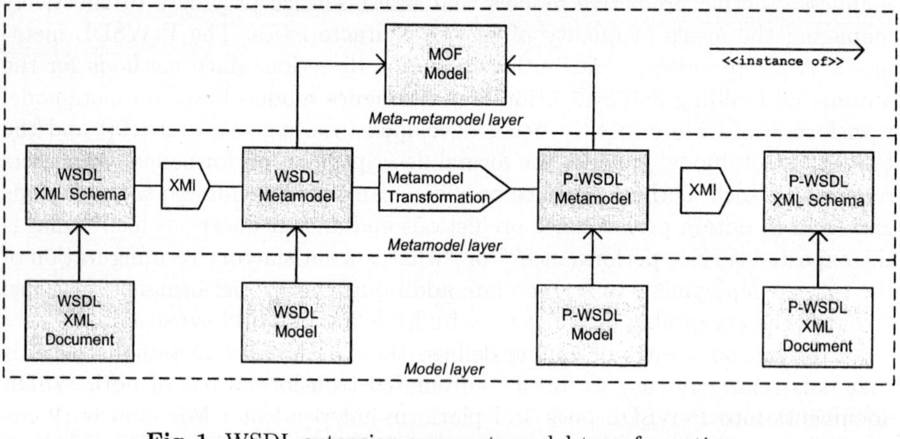

Fig. 1. WSDL extension as a metamodel transformation

a model. Restated as an `<<instance of>>` relationship, an XML document is an instance of an XML Schema in the same way a model is an instance of a metamodel.

Representing the WSDL grammar in terms of a metamodel allows to enhance its comprehensibility and facilitate its extension. A MOF metamodel is indeed expressed by use of well-known visual modeling constructs such as classes, attributes and associations, which are easy to understand and analyze compared with the verbosity and poor readability of XML Schema structures. Hence, as a first step in the process, the WSDL metamodel has been derived from the WSDL XML Schema. Such a step is based on XMI rules and can be fully automated, as described in [2].

As a second step, the WSDL metamodel has been extended by applying a metamodel transformation that maps the elements of a source metamodel (i.e., the WSDL metamodel) to the elements of a target metamodel (i.e., the P-WSDL metamodel). The transformation is inspired by the UML Profile for Schedulability, Performance and Time (hereafter SPT Profile), an OMG's contribution that extends the UML metamodel so that UML models can easily be annotated with time and performance data [13]. In a similar way, concepts stemmed from the SPT profile are here used to extend the WSDL metamodel and thus obtain the P-WSDL (Performance-enabled WSDL) metamodel, so that WSDL models (and their respective XML documents) can effectively be enriched with time and performance data.

Finally, as a third step of the extension process, the P-WSDL metamodel has been serialized to the P-WSDL XML Schema by use of XMI-based rules. The obtained P-WSDL Schema is then used to produce and validate P-WSDL XML documents, i.e. performance-enabled WSDL descriptions.

4 Performance-Enabled WSDL Metamodel (P-WSDL)

A WSDL document consists of a set of definitions that describe what a service does (the operation it provides), how a service is acceded (data formats and protocols) and where it is located (network address). Such definitions are specified in the WSDL XML Schema [22], which has been used to identify the classes and associations of the WSDL metamodel, illustrated in the portion of Figure 2 bounded by the dashed line shape[1].

Classes and associations outside the dashed line shape in Figure 2 extend the WSDL metamodel to include the description of the performance properties of a web service. The complete set of classes and association in Figure 2 (both inside and outside the dashed line shape) identifies the P-WSDL metamodel.

As said in Section 3, the extension is inspired by the SPT Profile and specifically by its performance modeling section (see chapter 7 in [13]), which provides

[1] For the sake of brevity and readability, only relevant classes are illustrated in Figure 2. Specialized classes (e.g., classes for operations of type *one-way*, *request-response*, *solicit-response* and *notification-response*) have been omitted, as well as classes related to specific documenting and extensibility features of XML.

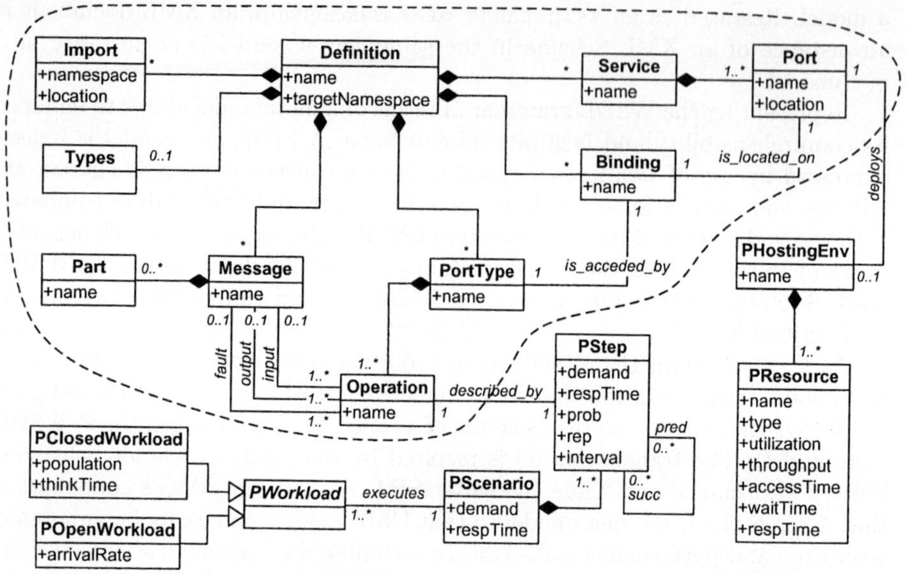

Fig. 2. The P-WSDL metamodel as an extension of the WSDL metamodel (dashed line shape)

mechanisms for expressing performance related QoS characteristics and associating them to a UML model.

In the SPT profile, a scenario defines response paths through a system, and can have performance requirements in terms of, e.g., response time or throughput. Scenarios are executed by workloads, which can be either closed or open workloads. Each scenario is composed of steps or activities that can be joined in sequence, loops, branches, forks and joins. Each step is deployed onto a host device that executes it. Resource demands by a step include the host execution demand (i.e., the execution time taken on the host device) and may include demands to additional resources (such as network or I/O resources).

In the paper case, the concepts introduced in the SPT profile have been adapted and used to derive the following classes of the P-WSDL metamodel[2]:

- `PScenario`: class that models a sequence of one or more scenario steps that conform to a general precedence/successor relationship;
- `PStep`: class that models a scenario step with attributes including `demand` (step execution time) and `respTime` (step response time);
- `PHostingEnv`: class that models the hosting environment that executes scenarios or steps;

[2] The P character (as in Performance) is added as a prefix to the name of classes introduced in the P-WSDL metamodel. Classes already present in the WSDL metamodel have not been modified, to maintain backward compatibility.

- `PResource`: class that models a resource of the hosting environment with attributes including `utilization` (expressed as percentage) and `throughput` (the rate at which the resource performs its function);
- `PWorkload`: abstract class that specifies the intensity of demand for the execution of a specific scenario;
- `PClosedWorkload`: class that models a workload characterized by a fixed number of active or potential users who cycle between executing the scenario and spending a *think time* between the end of one response and the next request;
- `POpenWorkload`: class that models a workload characterized by a stream of requests that arrive at a given rate in some predetermined pattern (e.g., Poisson arrivals).

Figure 2 describes how the newly introduced classes have been associated to selected classes of the WSDL metamodel. It is easily seen that each `Operation` object is associated to the `PStep` object that specifies its performance properties. A `PScenario` object groups the set of `PStep` objects associated to a set of operations invoked by a service consumer according to a predecessor-successor pattern. The attributes of a `PScenario` object refer to client-side performance properties (i.e., as seen by the service consumer). As an example, the `respTime` value specifies the total time required to execute the scenario and thus includes the time spent on the network that connects the service consumer site to the service provider site. On the other hand, the attributes of a `PStep` object refer to server-side properties, and thus the `respTime` value specifies the total time required to execute a single operation of the web service, without including the time to transfer requests and responses from and to the service consumer. The intensity of demand for the execution of a specific scenario is captured by the association between the `PScenario` class and the `POpenWorkload` or `PClosedWorkload` class that implements the abstract `PWorkload` class. The hosting environment that executes the operations of a web service is described by the association between a `Port` object and a `PHostingEnv` object, which is composed of a set of `PResource` objects. It is worth noting that the multiplicity `0..1` in the association between classes `PHostingEnv` and `Port` denotes that such association is optional. Indeed, there is no need to introduce `PHostingEnv` and `PResource` objects if P-WSDL is only used to specify constraints on the performance properties of web service operations without reference to a specific deployment, as better illustrated in next section.

The attributes of classes introduced in the P-WSDL metamodel include resource utilizations, waiting times, execution demands (in terms of CPU cycles or seconds) and response time (the actual time to execute a scenario step or scenario). Each attribute may be specified as an *assumed* value, based on experience (e.g., for an execution demand or an external delay), a *required* value, to denote a constraint on performance, a *predicted* value, calculated by a performance tool or a *measured* value, obtained by a monitoring tool. Moreover, the specified value can represent an average, a maximum, a *i-th* percentile or a distribution, according to the general structure for performance values specified in [13].

An appropriate trade-off between completeness and usability has driven the derivation of the P-WSDL metamodel in Figure 2. As an example, additional classes, attributes and associations could be introduced to describe more details about the service consumer's client application or the network connection characteristics, although it is likely that the introduction of additional details would result in adding excessive complexity to a relatively simple but powerful language like WSDL, thus preventing an effective use of P-WSDL.

5 P-WSDL Example Application

As said in Section 1, the proposed P-WSDL metamodel can be applied to serve different purposes. This section gives two example applications of P-WSDL, namely to the specification of performance requirement of a web service and to the description of performance data measured on a given web service.

Specific P-WSDL documents are here represented as P-WSDL models (see Figure 1), or object diagrams instantiated from the P-WSDL metamodel. Objects in the object diagram are directly translated into XML elements, according to XMI rules for XML document production. P-WSDL XML documents can then be validated by use of the P-WSDL XML Schema, that is produced by applying XMI rules for XML Schema production to elements of the P-WSDL metamodel.

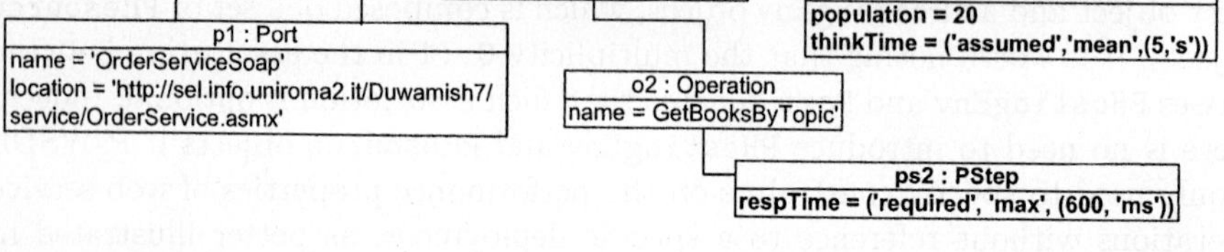

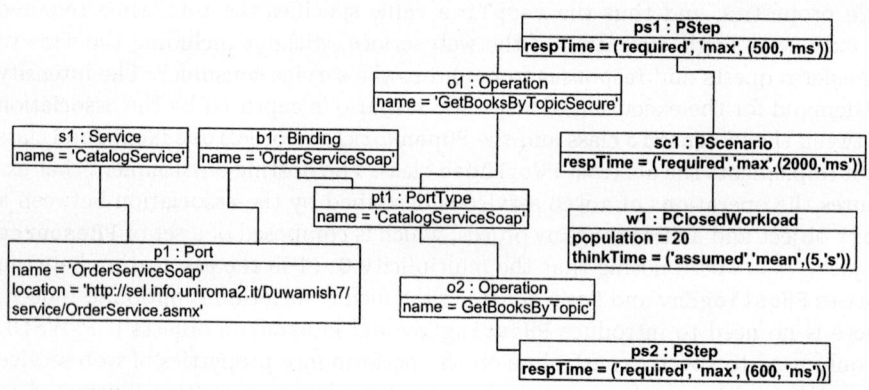

Fig. 3. P-WSDL example application to the specification of performance requirements

Figure 3 illustrates the example application to the specification of performance requirements[3]. To this purpose, the *Duwamish7* web application has been considered [12]. Such application includes a web service implementation that

[3] For the sake of clarity, object diagrams of this section only consider WSDL objects relevant to the P-WSDL extension and objects specific to P-WSDL are shown in bold characters.

provides two operations to select books from a catalog (i.e., `getBooksByTopic` and `getBooksByTopicSecure`). The example describes a usage scenario that assumes a population of 20 users executing a single step, i.e., the one associated to the `getBooksByTopicSecure` operation. `PStep` objects specify constraints on the performance properties of web service operations, while the PScenario object specifies a requirement of maximum 2 seconds to complete the described scenario (without regard to type and capacity of the network linking service consumer to service provider). The example does not specify any assumption or requirement about the web service hosting environment, and thus no objects are instantiated from classes `PHostingEnv` and `PResource`.

The performance measure specified by the `respTime` attributes of `PScenario` and `PStep` objects in Figure 4 is a maximum value expressed as *required* value.

Figure 4 illustrates the example application to the description of performance data obtained from measurement. To this purpose, the *Duwamish7* code has been instrumented to monitor web service invocations and collect actual performance data on both client and server side [6]. The obtained data can directly be expressed in P-WSDL and used to check if the web service implementation meets the performance requirements specified in Figure 3 (under the specified workload and deployment). In addition, they could also be stored into registries of P-WSDL web services, and eventually returned to service consumers submitting queries that include performance properties.

Figure 4 shows that the web service operation is invoked by a (simulated) population of 20 users invoking the `getBooksByTopicSecure` operation. The web service is deployed on a hosting environment composed of a Pentium IV processor, a Microsoft Windows Server 2003 operating system, an IIS 6.0 (Internet Information Services) web server and a SQL Server 2000 database server. The performance measures specified by `respTime` attributes of `PScenario` and `PStep` objects in Figure 4 are average values expressed as *measured* values.

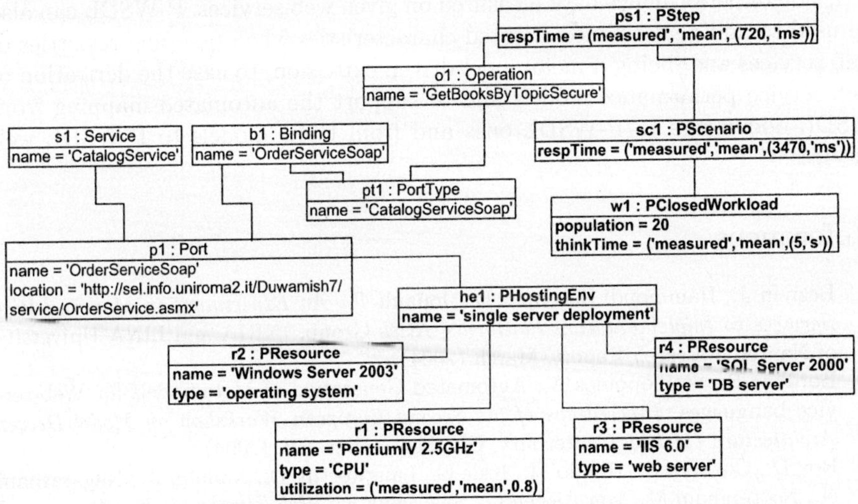

Fig. 4. P-WSDL example application to the description of measured performance data

The `respTime` attribute of the `PStep` object gives the average time measured by monitoring the executions of the `getBooksByTopicSecure` operation. On the other hand, the `respTime` attribute of the `PScenario` object gives the average time, measured at client-side, to execute the specified scenario and includes the time taken for request and response to pass through the network. In the example case, the average times are greater than the maximum times specified as a requirement in Figure 3 and thus the actual performance does not meet the required one. Such a result could endorse the development of a performance model to carry out what-if studies and predict which alternative solution (e.g., in terms of different deployments) would satisfy the required performance constraints. As said in Section 2, this is an additional circumstance where P-WSDL proves to be beneficial.

6 Conclusions

Web services are the building blocks of the emerging computing paradigm based on service-oriented architectures. Web service capabilities are expressed in XML by use of the Web Service Definition Language (WSDL). Unfortunately, a WSDL description only addresses the functional aspects of a web service without containing any useful description of non-functional or quality of service characteristics.

This paper has introduced a WSDL extension that allows to describe the performance properties of a web service. The extension, called P-WSDL (Performance-enabled WSDL), is inspired by the SPT profile and has been carried out as a metamodel transformation, according to MDA principles and standards.

Example applications of the proposed P-WSDL extension have been shown to the specification of performance requirements of web services and to the description of performance data measured on given web services. P-WSDL can also be used to add performance-oriented characteristics when querying registries of web services and, being a metamodel-driven extension, to ease the derivation of web service performance models and to support the automated mapping from WSDL documents to P-WSDL ones and from UML models to P-WSDL web services.

References

1. Bezivin J., Hammoudi S., Lopes D., Jouault F.: *An Experiment in Mapping Web Services to Implementation Platforms*, Atlas Group, INRIA and LINA University of Nantes, Research Report, March (2004)
2. Bordbar B., Staikopoulos A.: Automated Generation of Metamodels for Web service Languages, *Proceedings of the Second European Workshop on Model Driven Architecture (MDA)*, Canterbury, UK, September 7–8, (2004)
3. Box D., Curbera F., Hondo M., Kale C., Langworthy D., Nadalin A., Nagaratnam N., Nottingham M., von Riegen C., Shewchuk J., *Web Services Policy Framework (WS-Policy)*, `http://www.ibm.com/developerworks/library/ws-policy`, (2003)

4. Catania N., Kumar P., Murray B., Pourhedari H., Vambenepe W., Wurster K.: *Web Services Management Framework*, Version 2.0, Hewlett-Packard, `http://devresource.hp.com/drc/specifications/wsmf/WSMF-WSM.jsp`, (2003)
5. D'Ambrogio A.: A Model Transformation Framework for the Automated Building of Performance Models from Software Models, *Proc. of the 5th International Workshop on Software and Performance (WOSP 2005)*, Palma de Mallorca, Spain, July (2005)
6. D'Ambrogio A., Conticelli L., Fondi A.: *An Environment for Measuring the Performance of Web Services*, Technical Report RI.05.04, Software Engineering Lab., Dept. Computer Science, University of Roma TorVergata, Roma, Italy, Feb. 2005.
7. Frankel D., Parodi J.: *Using Model-Driven Architecture to Develop Web Services*, IONA Technologies PLC White Paper, 2nd Ed., April (2002)
8. Ludwig H., Keller A., Dan A., King R., Franck R. , *Web Service Level Agreement (WSLA) Language Specification*, Version 1.0, IBM Corporation, `http://www.research.ibm.com/wsla/WSLASpecV1-20030128.pdf`, Jan. (2003)
9. Ludwig H.: Web Services QoS: External SLAs and Internal Policies - Or: How do we deliver what we promise?, *4th IEEE International Conference on Web Information Systems Engineering*, WISE 2003 Workshops, Roma (Italy), 13 December (2003)
10. Martin D., Burstein M., Lassila O., Paolucci M., Payne T., McIlraith S., *Describing Web Services using OWL-S and WSDL*, `http://www.daml.org/services/owl-s/1.1/owl-s-wsdl.htm`, 2004.
11. Menascé D.A.: QoS Issues in Web Services, *IEEE Internet Computing*, pp. 72–75, Nov./Dec. 2002.
12. Microsoft: The Duwamish 7.0 Enterprise Application, `http://msdn.microsoft.com`.
13. OMG: *UML Profile for Scheduling, Performance and Time*, v. 1.0, (2003)
14. OMG: *Request for Proposal: MOF 2.0 Query / View / Transformations*, (2002), `http://www.omg.org/docs/ad/02-04-10.pdf`.
15. OMG: *MDA Guide*, version 1.0.1, June (2003)
16. OMG: *Meta Object Facility (MOF) Specification*, version 1.4, April (2002)
17. OMG: *XML Metadata Interchange (XMI) Specification*, version 2.0, May (2003)
18. Papazoglou M.P., Georgakopoulos D.: Service-oriented computing, *Communications of the ACM*, vol. 46, no. 10, October (2003), 25-28
19. Petriu D.B., Woodside M.: A Metamodel for Generating Performance Models from UML Designs, *Proceedings of UML2004*, Lecture Notes in Computer Science 3273, Lisbon, Portugal, October 11-15, (2004)
20. Tosic V., Pagurek B., Patel K.: WSOL A Language for the Formal Specification of Classes of Service for Web Services, *Proceedings of the 2003 International Conference on Web Services*, Las Vegas, USA, (2003), 375-381
21. Verma K., Sivashanmugam K., Sheth A., Patil A., Oundhakar S., Miller J.: METEOR-S WSDI: A scalable P2P infrastructure of registries for semantic publication and discovery of web services, *Inf. Tech. and Management*, 6(1):1739, (2005)
22. WWW Consortium, *Web Services Description language (WSDL)*, version 2.0, W3C Working Draft, August (2004), `http://www.w3.org/TR/wsdl20/`
23. WWW Consortium, *XML Schema*, W3C Recommendation, `http://www.w3.org/XML/Schema`.

A Novel Authorization Mechanism for Service-Oriented Virtual Organization*

Hai Jin, Weizhong Qiang, Xuanhua Shi, and Deqing Zou

Cluster and Grid Computing Lab.
Huazhong University of Science and Technology, Wuhan 430074, China
{hjin, wzqiang, xhshi, deqingzou}@hust.edu.cn

Abstract. There are more challenges for authorization in service-oriented virtual organization. In this paper we propose a novel authorization mechanism for virtual organization, which uses the threshold signature scheme for authorization management and voting mechanism for decision-making. We design three protocols in the authorization mechanism: authorization acquisition protocol, authorization revocation protocol, and secure interaction protocol. Our solution can satisfy the dynamic coalition requirement of virtual organization, and also guarantee the autonomous characteristic of participant organizations and service entities. Privacy preservation is also provided for service entities to interact with authorized entities.

1 Introduction

Service-oriented architecture (SOA) is the next wave in networked computing. As a well-adopted SOA paradigm, web services has some advantages on interoperability, simplified programming model for networked program and loose coupling. In SOA, designers must apply service-oriented security architecture concepts to build a new trust management web that can be federated across security domains.

The existing service-oriented security mechanism, such as WS-Security, WS-Policy and WS-Federation, only provides the capabilities for interoperability and integration. The mechanism is lack of a security architecture that enables security relationships among service entities to be established and managed. We specially study the security relationship for virtual organization in SOA.

The *virtual organization* (VO) concept in web service technology is defined as a group of service entities (e.g., services and users) from different administration and security domains collaborating in order to complete some cross-organization cooperative tasks. More skillful, flexible and complex security mechanism must be presented to support scalable, dynamic, autonomous VOs.

Considering a hypothetical research project, which may consist of several research teams from different universities or institutes, they collaborate to work on some complicated physical problems that involve some laboratorial instruments and experiment data that belong to respective teams or researchers. The access to the instrument and data must be controlled in order to guarantee security.

* This paper is supported by National Science Foundation under grant 90412010 and ChinaGrid Project from Ministry of Education.

P. Yolum et al.(Eds.): ISCIS 2005, LNCS 3733, pp. 382–391, 2005.

The example above is a typical service-oriented application based on virtual organization. Because each member domain (each research team) is *autonomous*, a centralized administrator for the virtual organization is not appropriate. The access control policies for virtual organization must be jointly administrated by all of the member domains. Some research teams may depart from the virtual organization, and new research teams may also join in the virtual organization. Therefore, how to make the security administration adapt to the *dynamic* characteristic of the virtual organization is great challenge. Also, the research project seems to be a large project and includes many participant research teams, which means that the joint authorization management framework of the virtual organization must be *scalable* with the increase of members.

The paper is organized as follows. Section 2 introduces some related works about security solutions in service systems and coalition applications. We then analyze the challenges for authorization mechanism in virtual organization. In Section 4 we present the authorization mechanism for service-oriented virtual organization. In Section 5, we describe the authorization acquisition protocol, authorization revocation protocol and secure interaction protocol. We conclude this paper in Section 6.

2 Related Works

There are some works focusing on security in VO-based grid computing [1][9]. In *Community Authorization Service* (CAS) [9], the owners of resources grant the access to a community account as a whole. The CAS server is responsible for managing the policies that govern access to a community's resources. It maintains fine-grained access control information and grants restricted GSI proxy certificates to the users of the community. *Virtual Organization Management System* (VOMS) [1] is similar to CAS. The difference between CAS and VOMS is that CAS directly assigns low-level access rights to users, but VOMS specifies the role and VO membership attribute to users. Both CAS and VOMS are based on centralized management for access control policies, which violates the autonomous of virtual organization.

There are also some efforts trying to integrate the existing distributed access control systems with virtual organization systems, such as integrating Akenti and PERMIS with Globus Toolkit. Akenti [10] is an access control architecture that is applicable in the situation that all the resources are controlled by multiple authorities. PERMIS [4] is a policy-driven RBAC *Privilege Management Infrastructure* (PMI), in which the policies are written in XML and stored in X.509 *attribute certificates* (AC), which may be widely distributed. Both Akenti and PERMIS can incorporate multiple stakeholders' access control policies, which means polices are autonomously managed by the stakeholders. In fact, these two systems only provide policy-decision engine and police repository; they do not provide the actual policy management mechanism.

Some researches on coalition applications are similar to our research. Khurana [8] presents a method for joint management of the access policies in coalition resources. Threshold RSA signature techniques are used in order to provide threshold signature for each operation request. But threshold RSA method can not adapt to the dynamic coalition situation, because dynamic coalition requires re-keying the RSA keys, and the generation of RSA keys requires high computation overhead that can not satisfy the scalability requirement of dynamic coalitions.

3 Authorization Challenges in Virtual Organization

Figure 1 is an illustration for a virtual organization. Several research teams from different organizations (Org A, Org B, and Org C) provide services or users and compose the hypothetical research project, which is a representative virtual organization. In general, the participant organizations compose an organization federation and jointly manage the authorization inside the federation.

Some service entities (services or users, both of them are treated equally as service entity) that respectively belong to these participant organizations compose virtual organizations. The access privilege of service entities must be jointly controlled by all the participant organizations.

Participant organizations possess membership (it proves that they are valid members of the organization federation) and authorization (it proves that they have some privilege of the organization federation). The service entities in a virtual organization also possess authorization that proves some privilege possession, but membership is not required. Actually, membership is a special type of authorization.

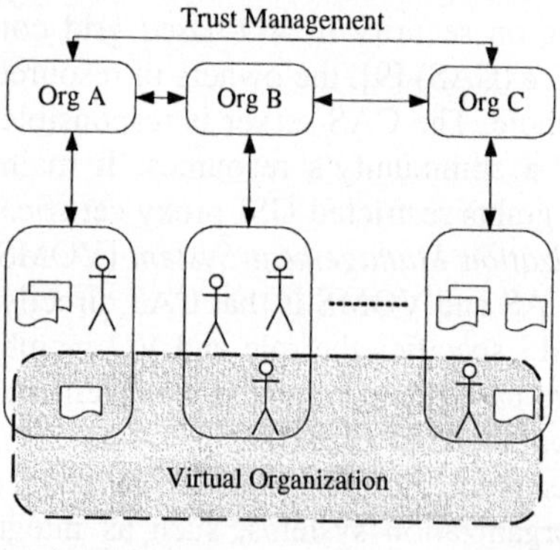

Fig. 1. An illustration of a virtual organization

The general requirements of virtual organization are autonomy, dynamic and scalability. In this section, we discuss the detailed challenges in service-oriented virtual organization applications.

- Centralized administrative point must be avoided. The federation and collaboration of service entities are jointly controlled by different organizations. Each participant may have its own policies on membership and authorization for new participant organizations, and also on authorization for new service entities.
- The same service entities may play different roles in different contexts (such as different task sessions). Different security policies must be enforced.
- Some service entities may take part in a task session without previous knowledge and access control polices on each other. Trust relationship between service entities must be established online in a peer-to-peer mode.

- Privacy preservation must be provided for service entities. The service entities in a virtual organization must be protected from each other. The virtual organization must also be protected from outsiders, such as service entities from original participant organizations and other unrelated service entities.
- Organizations may dynamically join in or depart from the organization federation; and service entities may dynamically join in or depart from a virtual organization. So the membership and authorization of organizations, or the authorization of service entities must be maintained timely and effectively.
- Membership and authorization revocation mechanism must be provided in case maliciousness or compromise would happen. Renewal mechanism must be provided in order to regenerate membership and authorization.
- Some security risks resistance function must be integrated in the virtual organization security scheme, such as impersonation resistance and collusion resistance.
- The management of membership and authorization must be scalable with the augmentation of the organization federation and virtual organizations.

4 A Novel Authorization Mechanism

In this paper, we provide a suitable method for the management of membership and authorization, which can satisfy the requirements above in some respects.

4.1 Trust Model of Dynamic Virtual Organization

In the scenario above, the trust model must be defined in order to restrict the trust relationship between grid entities in the virtual organization, the trust relationship between participant organizations, and the trust relationship between grid entities and participant organizations. The relationship definition is as follows:

- Trust relationship between grid entities. The authorization of each grid entity in the virtual organization is the combination of the authorization from original organization and the authorization from virtual organizations in which it participates. There is not direct authorization relationship (such as entity A authorizes entity B *Read* privilege) between grid entities in a virtual organization. All the authorization relationship is indirectly controlled by the attribute definition (such as role definition) that is jointly managed by the participant organizations (certain grid entity which wants to take part in a virtual organization must get enough approvals from the participant organizations).
- Trust relationship between participant organizations. The participant organizations compose the authorization decision-making layer for grid entities in the virtual organization. The join and departure of a participant organization is dynamic. The membership and authorization of each participant organization are both jointly decided by the existing organizations. When some organizations depart from the organization federation, the authorization of the grid entities that belong to the organization must be revoked.
- Trust relationship between grid entities in the virtual organization and participant organizations. As discussed above, the federation of participant organizations jointly decides the authorization of each grid entity in a virtual organization.

4.2 System Architecture of the Authorization Scheme

Figure 2 presents the membership acquisition process that a new organization acquires the membership from the existing participant organizations. Org_{new} initiates the membership protocol by sending a membership request to all the existing participants. Then they vote for the membership request and send back the decision. If the request organization collects enough approval votes (e.g. k out of n), it generates the membership for itself.

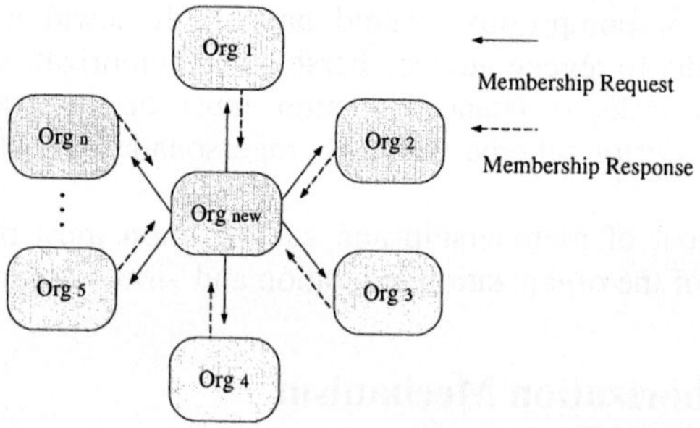

Fig. 2. Membership acquisition for new organization

Once the participant organization gets the membership of the organization federation, the next step is to try to acquire authorization. Figure 3 presents the authorization acquirement process for participant organization, which is similar to the membership acquirement process. We differentiate the membership and authorization for organizations in this paper. The details about membership and authorization acquisition protocol will be discussed in the latter section.

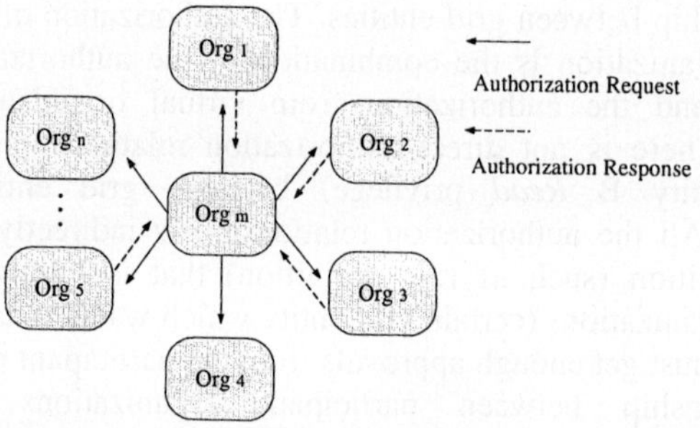

Fig. 3. Authorization acquisition for participant organization

Actually, a virtual organization is an aggregation of service entities. The participant organizations are the controllers of the aggregation, but they do not belong to the virtual organization. Figure 4 shows the authorization acquisition process for service entities. The service entity that belongs to one existing participant organization independently chooses an interested virtual organization controlled by the organizations federation, and makes authorization request to the target virtual organization. Then the participant organizations make decisions about the request. If enough approval votes collected, the service entity can extract the authorization. Once the service entities get the authorization, they can interact with each other inside the virtual organization.

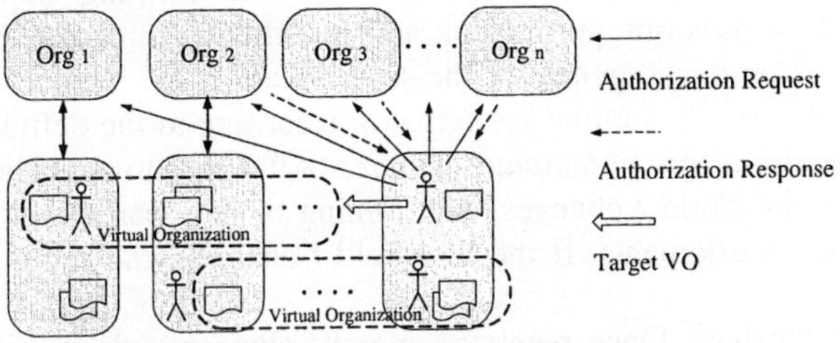

Fig. 4. Authorization acquisition for service entities

4.3 Threshold Signature Scheme

A threshold signature scheme is proposed in this paper. The scheme is based on pairing-based cryptography and threshold signature technique.

- Threshold signature technique

In our threshold signature scheme, the master key s is divided into n parts and each of them possesses a share s_i. Each part can sign a request *req* using its share of master key. The signature of the request *req* can only be constructed by collecting at least t (threshold) partial signatures.

A central authority (trust dealer) selects a random polynomial with t-1 degree, $w(z)=w_0+ w_1z+\cdots+ w_{t-1}z^{t-1}$ ($z \in \mathbb{Z}_q$, $w_0=s$). Then the share key s_i can be computed as $s_i= w(i)$ (i=1, ⋯,n). And witnesses $W_i=w_iP$ (i=0, ⋯, t-1) are also computed and published in order to enable verifiable secret sharing [5].

- Pairing-based cryptography

The pairing-based cryptography is based on bilinear maps over groups of large order.

Definition 1: If $\mathbb{G}_1$, $\mathbb{G}_2$ are two cyclic groups of some large prime order q, then $\hat{e}$: $\mathbb{G}_1\times\mathbb{G}_1\rightarrow\mathbb{G}_2$ is called a bilinear map if the three properties exist [2]:

1. Bilinear: $\hat{e}(aP, bQ) =\hat{e}(P, Q)^{ab}$ for all $P, Q \in \mathbb{G}_1$ and $a, b \in \mathbb{Z}_q$.
2. Non-degenerate: The map $\hat{e}$ does not send all pairs in $\mathbb{G}_1\times\mathbb{G}_1$ to element in $\mathbb{G}_2$.
3. Computable: For any P, Q$\in\mathbb{G}_1$, $\hat{e}(P, Q)$ can be computed by an efficient algorithm.

We use pairing-based cryptography for the signature scheme in this paper [3]. $H_1:(0,1)^*\rightarrow G_1^*$ is the hash function that maps binary strings to non-zero points in G_1. $sH_1()$ is the signature on $H_1()$. $\hat{e}$ is some particular map that is Tate pairing on super-singular elliptic.

4.4 Basic Operations

We now present the basic operations for participant organizations and grid entities. The operations for participant organization include threshold setup and renewal, assertion service, creation of virtual organizations, modification of access control policies and voting policies, and proactive secret share enhancement. The operations for grid entities include the secure interaction besides the authorization request.

- **Secret share setup and renewal.** Before the forming of the organization federation, a random participant acts as the trust dealer of the threshold signature scheme and generates the secret share s_i and membership assertion M_i for at least t_0 ($t_{min} \geq t_0$) initial participants according to the definition of threshold signature parameters in *template policies*. After that trust dealer is not required unless the threshold t changes. The joining of new participant can be dealt by the existing participants. If the threshold t changes, the setup process must be renewed.
- **Assertion services.** Once receiving membership or authorization request, each participant organization makes a decision and provides requestor a partial signature signed by the secret share. The requestor can combine t partial signature into a security assertion.
- **Creating virtual organizations.** As illustrated in Figure 4, the organization federation can generate and control a series of virtual organizations. Participants with special privilege can create a new virtual organization. The organization federation can represent the collaboration of some research organizations, and the virtual organization can represent various virtual research teams controlled by the federation.
- **Modifying authorization policies and voting policies.** Each virtual organization has its own authorization policies definition. Participant organizations with special privilege can tune or modify the authorization policies for each virtual organization. The participant organizations can just control the role-to-user assignment relationship. Permission-to-role assignment relationship is controlled by the service provider. Moreover, each participant can modify its own voting policies respectively.
- **Proactive secret share enhancement.** Our identity-based threshold signature scheme can tolerate t-1 revealment of secret share. In order to resist share secret disclosure over a long time period, the secret share for each participant must be updated periodically.
- **Secure interaction.** Grid entities get the authorization assertions and interact with each other. The interaction is based on the concept in [6][7], and privacy preservation is provided.

4.5 Assertion Service

The authorization assertion services for participant organizations and grid entities are the same.

4.5.1 Authorization Assertion Service

An authorization assertion attests the possession and validity of authorization. Figure 5 shows a typical authorization assertion. It includes the *ID* of the assertion carrier, the *Role* assigned to carrier, the *SecretToken* providing the authorization, the *StartTime* and *LifeTime* of the assertion, and the *ValidityToken* providing the validity of the assertion.

ID	Role	SecretToken	StartTime	LifeTime	ValiditvToken

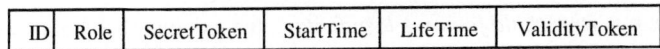

Fig. 5. Assertion format

The *ID* is the distinguished name of the participant organizations or service entities, e.g. "*/O=CHINASERVICE/OU=HUST/*" for the organization "*HUST*", "*/O=CHINASERVICE/OU=HUST/GE=HEP_Service*" for the service entity "*HEP_Service*" in "*HUST*". The *Role* is the authorization assigned to the carrier. *StartTime* and *LifeTime* defines the validity period of the assertion.

The *SecretToken* and *ValidityToken* represent possession and validity of authorization, respectively, and must be conjugated, which means that for each *SecretToken*, there exists a *ValidityToken*.

SecretToken is the signature on "*ID*||*Role*". Here, H_1(ID||Role) is computed, and $SecretToken_i = sH_1(ID_i||AuthZ)$. *SecretToken* will be kept by the carrier and not shown to anyone else.

Each participant organization possesses two *SecretTokens*, *SecretToken* for membership and *SecretToken* for other authorization. Each service entity only possesses one *SecretToken* for authorization.

ValidityToken is a signature on "*ID*||*StartTime*||*LifeTime*", and $ValidityToken_i = sH_1(ID_i||StartTime||LifeTime)||StartTime||LifeTime$. *ValidityToken* will be shown to others in order to confirm the validity. The verification of *ValidityToken* is: $\hat{e}(P_{pub}, H_1(ID_i||StartTime||LifeTime) = \hat{e}(P, ValidityToken_i)$.

4.5.2 Secret Share Acquisition

A grid entity in a virtual organization must only possess the authorization assertion. A participant organization must simultaneously possess the membership and authorization assertions. Membership assertion is also a special authorization assertion, and the format of membership assertion is the same as authorization assertion, so we treat both of them as authorization assertion. But for a new organization, the authorization assertion service results in the secret share acquisition and the secret share renewal.

If a new organization gets the membership assertion, it gets its secret share and makes voting decisions as the other existing participants. Each existing participant that approves the membership request sends the partial secret share to the requestor.

If a new organization gets the membership assertion and the secret share, it tries to get authorization assertion.

4.5.3 Secret Share Renewal

We adopt dynamic threshold in this paper, the threshold factor is fixed and the threshold *t* varies with new organizations joining or existing organizations. The secret share of each participant will also be renewed with the threshold changing dynamically. All the authorization assertion of the participant organizations and grid entities will be updated.

But updating the threshold and the following operations are expensive, so it is not practical to update the threshold when the organization federation changes. In this paper, we use a lazy-updating mechanism. In detail, if the threshold *t* ranges between the two values $n \times$ *(threshold factor ± lazy factor)*, the existing threshold t will still be used for the signature scheme, and also the existing secret shares for each participant organization will not need to be renewed. Otherwise a new threshold $t_{new} = n \times$ *threshold factor* will be applied and secret shares will be renewed.

In fact, the participant organizations join in or depart infrequently, so there is no need to update the threshold frequently. The lazy factor and the infrequency characteristic make the updating cost sustainable.

4.5.4 Assertion Renewal and Revocation

Each authorization assertion is stamped with *StartTime* and *LifeTime*. If necessary, a new authorization assertion must be issued once the old one is to be expired. Assertion renewal is initiated by the holder of the old assertion. Renewal process is the same as the process of new assertion acquisition.

Revoking assertion via expiration is an implicit mechanism to guarantee security. In addition, an explicit mechanism is also provided in this paper.

LifeTime of grid entities' authorization assertion is shorter than that of participant organizations. Moreover, participant organizations' authorization assertion is much more important than those of grid entities. So we only apply explicit revocation mechanism for participant organizations.

5 Conclusions

In this paper, we propose an authorization mechanism for service-oriented virtual organization. First, we analyze the challenges of authorization management in virtual organization applications. Then, we present the authorization mechanism for service-oriented virtual organization, which is based on threshold signature scheme and voting mechanism. We also describe the assertion service for virtual organization.

The proposed system design can satisfy the requirements related to the challenges analyzed in Section 3.2. Here, we list some advantages of our scheme.

- Voting mechanism avoids the centralized administration point, and also the autonomous characteristic is attained.
- A service entity can take part in different virtual organizations inside the organization federation, and each virtual organization can be mapped into a task session.
- The role-based authorization divides the security responsibility. The service provider can control the permission-to-role assignment relationship, and the participant organizations can control the role-to-user assignment relationship.
- By secure interaction mechanism, privacy of each service entity is preserved.
- By authorization assertion revocation and secret share renewal mechanism, the dynamic characteristic is guaranteed.
- The verifiable secret sharing mechanism provided by our threshold signature scheme can resist impersonation, and threshold scheme can essentially resist collusion.

References

1. Alfieri, R. et al.: VOMS: an authorization system for virtual organizations, DataService Project, http://service-auth.infn.it/docs/VOMS-Santiago.pdf, (2003)
2. Boneh, D., Franklin, M.: Identity-Based Encryption from the Weil Pairing, *Proc. Crypto 2001*, LNCS 2139, Springer-Verlag, (2001) 213-229
3. Boneh, D., Lynn, B., Shacham, H.: Short signatures from the weil pairing, *Journal of Cryptology*, 17(4): 297-319, (2004)
4. Chadwick, D., Otenko, A.: The Permis X.509 role based privilege management infrastructure, *Proc. the 7th ACM Symposium on Access Control Models and Technologies*, Monterey, (2002) 135-140
5. Feldman, P.: A Practical Scheme for Non-interactive Verifiable Secret Sharing, *Proc. 28th Symposium on Foundations of Computer Science (FOCS)*, (1987) 427-437
6. Qiang, W., Jin, W., Shi, X., Zou, D.: VO-Sec: An Access Control Framework for Dynamic Virtual Organization, *Proceedings of the 10th Australia Conference on Information Security and Privacy (ACISP'05)*, (2005)
7. Qiang, W., Jin, W., Shi, X., Zou, D.: Joint Management of Authorization for Dynamic Virtual Organization, *Proceedings of the 5th International Conference on Computer and Information Technology (CIT'05)*, (2005)
8. Khurana, H., Gligor, V., Linn, J.: Reasoning about joint administration of access policies for coalition resources, *Proc. the 22nd International Conference on Distributed Computing Systems*, pp.429-443, Vienna, (2002)
9. Pearlman, L., Welch, V., Foster, I., Kesselman, C., Tuecke, S.: A community authorization service for group collaboration, *Proc. the 3rd International Workshop on Policies for Distributed Systems and Networks*, Monterey, (2002)
10. Thompson, M., Johnston, W., Mudumbai, S., Hoo, G., Jackson, K., Essiari, A.: Certificate-based access control for widely distributed resources, *Proc. the Eighth Usenix Security Symposium*, (1999)

Metrics, Methodology, and Tool for Performance-Considered Web Service Composition

Hyung Gi Song[1], Yeonseung Ryu[2], Taesun Chung[2], Wooseok Jou[3], and Kangsun Lee[3,*]

[1] R &D Institute, Netville Co., Ltd., 161-7 Yeomni Mapo, Seoul, 121874 South Korea
[2] Dept. of Computer Software
[3] Dept. of Computer Engineering, Myongji University, San 38-2 Namdong Yongin, Kyungki, 449728 South Korea
Tel: +82-31-330-6444; Fax: +82-31-330-6432
ksl@mju.ac.kr

Abstract. Web service is a promising technology to efficiently integrate disparate software components over various types of systems and to exchange various business artifacts across business organizations. As many web services are available on Internet, performance becomes increasingly important to distinguish different service providers. Performance is a difficult property to assess, since it involves non-deterministic networks, frequent changes on workload and unexpected usage patterns. In this work, we propose a performance analysis methodology for web services, and introduce sPAC (Web Services Performance Analysis Center) that implements our methodology for performance-considered web service composition. sPAC 1) graphically describes web services and the flow between them, 2) automatically generates test codes for the web process and executes them for performance analysis under low load intensity, 3) automatically generates a simulation model for the web process, and conducts extensive simulations for heavy load intensity, and 4) reports analysis and estimation results to help service customers verify timeliness of their web services.

Keywords: Web Services Composition, Performance Analysis.

1 Introduction

Web service is a technology that allows applications to communicate with each other in a platform- and programming language-independent manner. A group of Web services interacting together defines a particular Web service application (or Web process) in a Service-Oriented Architecture (SOA). [1] As many web services with similar functionalities are available on the Internet, performance will distinguish service providers from each other [2] when service customers select a suitable web service to create a new web process.

Performance of web services is a difficult property to assess, since it involves non-deterministic networks, abrupt changes on load intensity, and unexpected usage patterns. While mathematical methods [3-4] are efficient by solving well-defined

[*]Corresponding author.

P. Yolum et al.(Eds.): ISCIS 2005, LNCS 3733, pp. 392 – 401, 2005.

performance equations, they make explicit assumptions on usage patterns and work loads. Test-based analysis actually invokes web services in real environments, and analyzes the resulting data to determine the overall operational properties. While these methods can provide accurate analysis results, they cost significant time and cannot be used when a given test load exceeds resource capability of the test-host computer [5-6]. Simulation-based analysis is another alternative. Most simulation-based analysis methods represent a given web process with a discrete event simulation model first, and then virtually execute the model with various simulation conditions to determine the performance of the given web process [7-8]. They can provide fairly accurate performance properties cost-effectively. However, the analysis may become totally wrong unless the simulation model and experimental parameters are validated against the real world. Combining simulation-based analysis with test-based analysis might be the best way to produce accurate performance estimation and to save cost, at the same time.

In this work, we propose a performance analysis methodology for web services. Our methodology combines test- and simulation-based performance analysis methodology to save cost and time; test codes are automatically generated for the web services and executed for performance analysis under low load intensity. Also, the web services and the flow between them are automatically translated into a simulation model. The simulation model is then used to estimate the performance under heavy load intensity. Increased accuracy can be achieved by carrying out simulations based on test results; Test-based analysis records how the web process behaves on low load conditions in terms of response time and throughput. These historical data are then used to set up simulation parameters. `sPAC` (Web Services Performance Analysis Center) is a performance analysis and estimation tool to enable our methodology. We introduce useful facilities of `sPAC` and show how a customer uses `sPAC` to design, reengineer, verify their web services and finally produce a new web process with guaranteed performance. The methodology of `sPAC` can be the foundation of SLA automation [9] (i.e., automatic SLA creation, SLA monitoring and control) if SLAs are mainly described by performance requirements as in the case of mission-critical services.

This paper is organized as follows. In Section 2, we present our simulation-based performance analysis methodology and metrics for web services and their composition. Section 3 demonstrates `sPAC` with an example and shows how users can benefit from `sPAC` to design, reengineer and verify their new web process. Section 4 concludes this paper with future works to achieve.

2 Performance Analysis Methodology for Web Services

In this section, we present our performance analysis methodology for web services with detailed explanations on performance metrics.

2.1 Performance Metrics

DRT (Dissected Response Time) and TRT (Traced Response Time) are our performance metrics. DRT divides response time into three factors: *Network Time* (`N`), *Messaging Time* (`M`) and *Service Time* (`S`). The response time, `T`, for a single web service, `s`, is defined in Equation 1.

$$T(s) = N(s) + M(s) + S(s) \quad (1)$$

Network Time is the amount of delay determined by bandwidth of network path between customers and the providers of web services, network traffic and performance of network equipments. *Messaging Time* is the amount of time taken by service providers to process SOAP messages. SOAP is an XML-based protocol. Therefore, the size of the exchanging message is usually bigger than other binary-based protocols, and the time to process SOAP messages is not negligible. *Service Time* is the amount of time for a web service to perform its designated task. It depends on efficiency of business logic, hardware capability, framework for web services and/or operating system of web services.

When a web process is commercialized with packaged software or in the form of web application, each web service is expected to experience heavy load intensity. TRT performance analysis creates *virtual* users with `Java threads`, lets them invoke web services simultaneously, and collects DRT for various load conditions. While TRT tests can answer how the composed web process performs in various user load conditions, it costs time and system resources. Moreover, the maximum testable load always has a limit; the testable load is determined by physical memory size, operating system's memory management policy, network conditions, and/or framework for web services of the test host computer. We use simulation to tear this barrier away; A simulation model is automatically generated and then used for testing out heavy load conditions without actually invoking web services through physical resources and networks. To achieve better accuracy, the real test results are normalized and fed into the simulation parameters. Detailed explanations on performance analysis are found in the next section.

2.2 Methodology

As shown in Figure 1, our methodology conducts performance analysis in dual mode in order to save time and cost: test-based analysis for low load intensity and simula tion-based analysis for heavy load intensity. Web services are automatically translated into a discrete event simulation model, while the results from test-based analysis are fed into the simulation parameters to increase estimation accuracy.

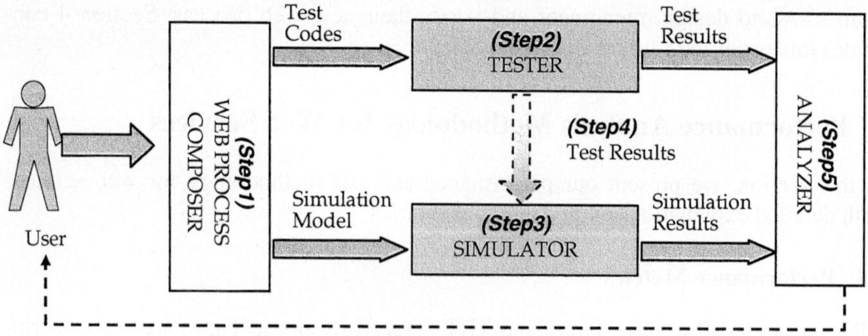

Fig. 1. Performance Analysis Methodology

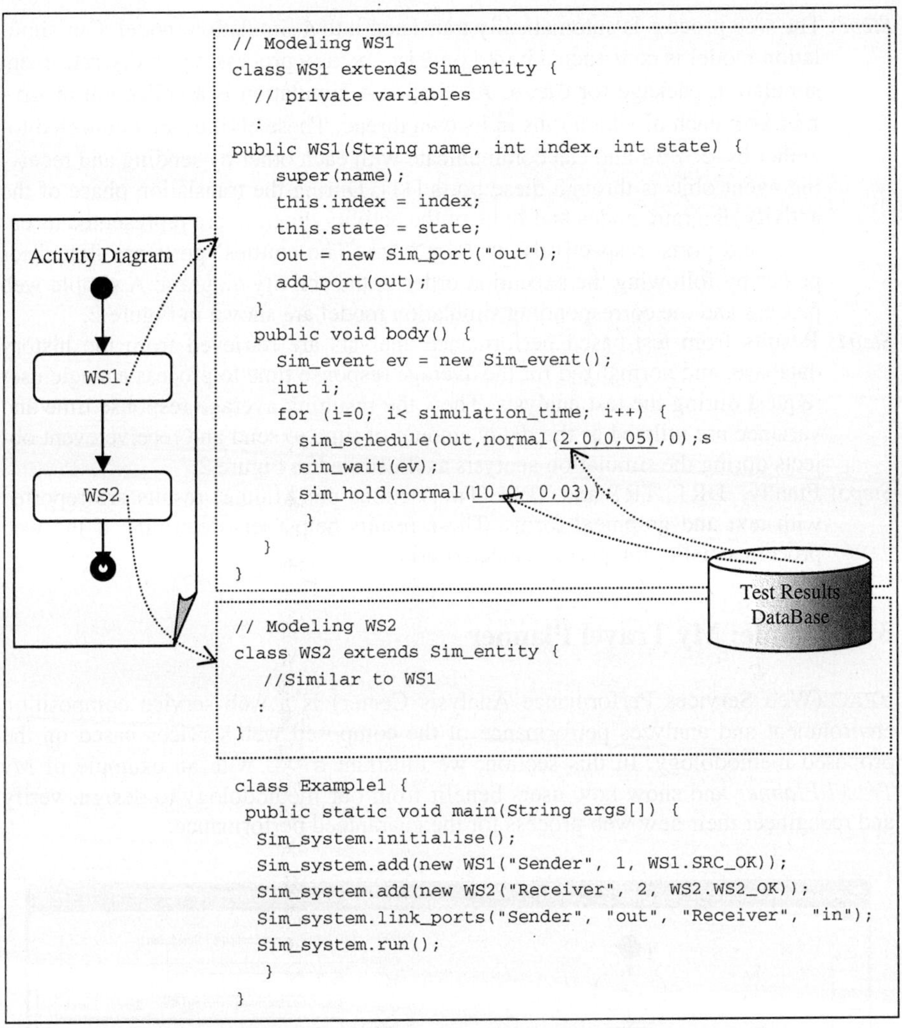

Fig. 2. A web process and the corresponding simulation model

Followings are detailed explanations on our methodology:

Step1: A customer defines how web services are formed into a new web process using UML's activity diagram [10]. With activity diagrams, web services are represented as *nodes*, while the flow between them is represented as *links* with decorations to specify *fork*, *join*, execution types (*parallel* or *serial*), and other various conditions.

Step2: Web services are dynamically invoked and executed for test-based performance analysis. DRT (Dissected Response Time) and TRT (Traced Response Time) are analyzed under low load intensity, and recorded in history database.

Step3: The web process is automatically translated into a simulation model. Our simulation model is constructed based on `Simjava`, a process-based discrete event simulation package for `Java`. A `Simjava` simulation is a collection of `entities` each of which runs in its own thread. These entities are connected together by `ports` and can communicate with each other by sending and receiving event objects through these ports [11]. During the translation phase of the activity diagram, nodes and links of the activity diagram are represented as entities and ports, respectively, in `SimJava`. The entities' ports are linked together by following the execution order in the activity diagram. A simple web process and the corresponding simulation model are shown in Figure 2.

Step4: Results from test-based performance analysis are retrieved from the history database, and normalized for the average response time to process a single user request during the test analysis. Then, the resulting average response time and variance are utilized as the *delay* amount of time to send and receive event objects during the simulation analysis as illustrated in Figure 2.

Step5: Finally, DRT, TRT and TPM (Transactions per Minute) results are reported with text and graphical forms. These results help users determine if the web process satisfies the performance criteria.

3 Example: My Travel Planner

`sPAC` (Web Services Performance Analysis Center) is a web service composition environment and analyzes performance of the composed web services based on the proposed methodology. In this section, we illustrate `sPAC` with an example of *My Travel Planner* and show how users benefit from our methodology to design, verify and reengineer their new web process for the guaranteed performance.

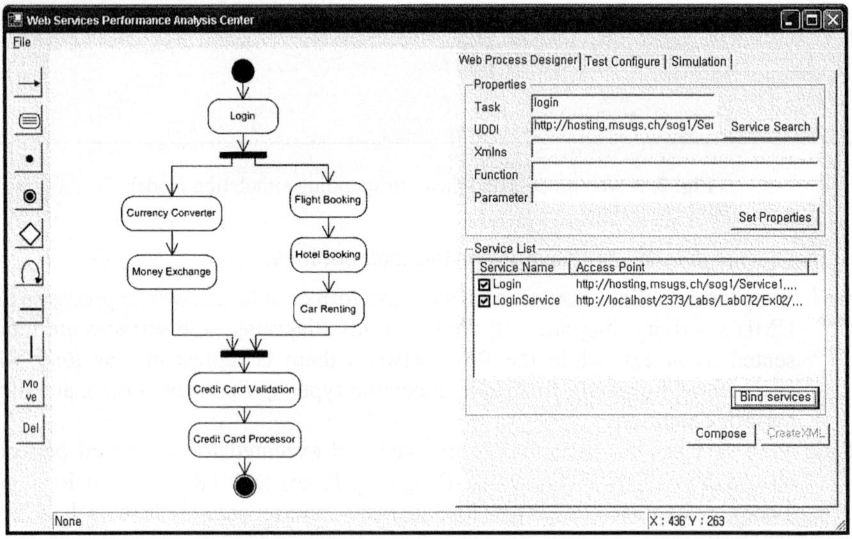

Fig. 3. Web Process Specification

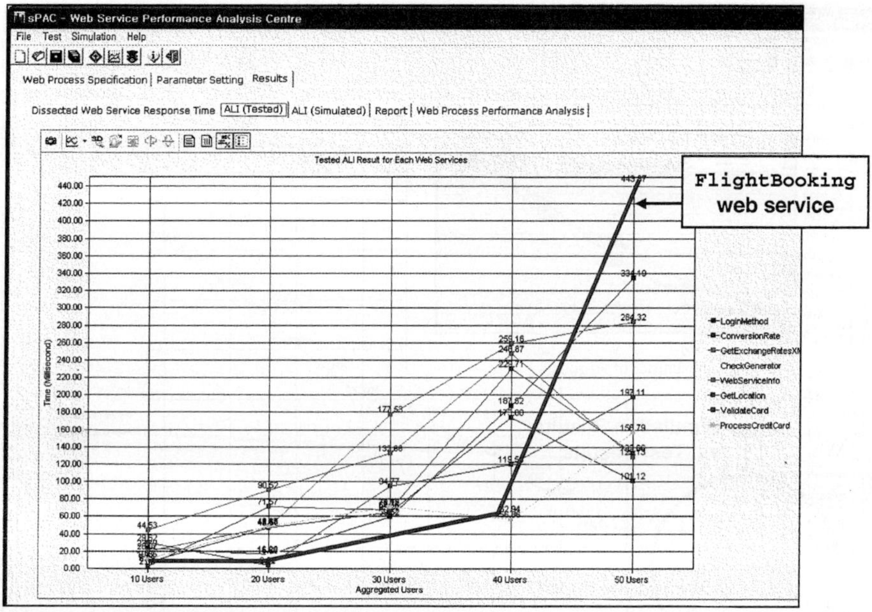

Fig. 4. TRT test results

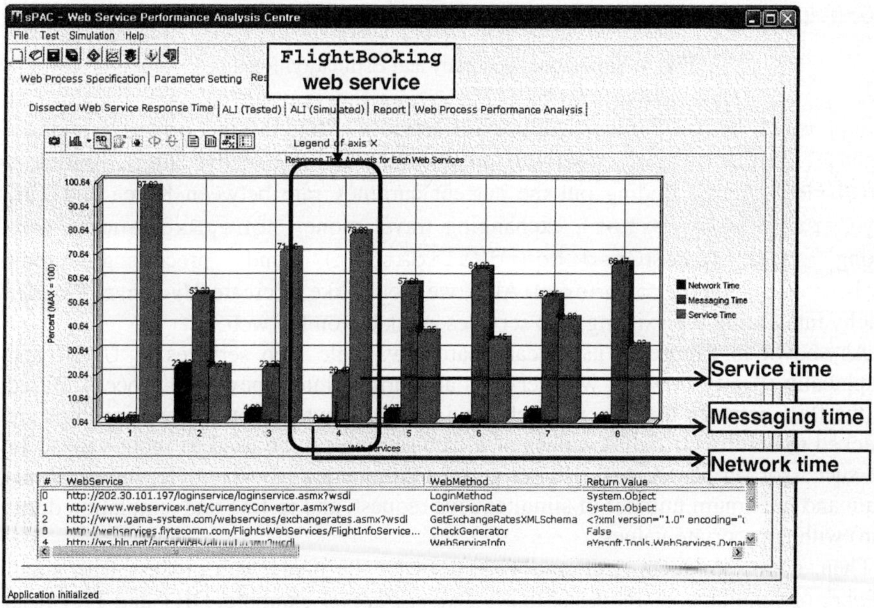

Fig. 5. DRT test results

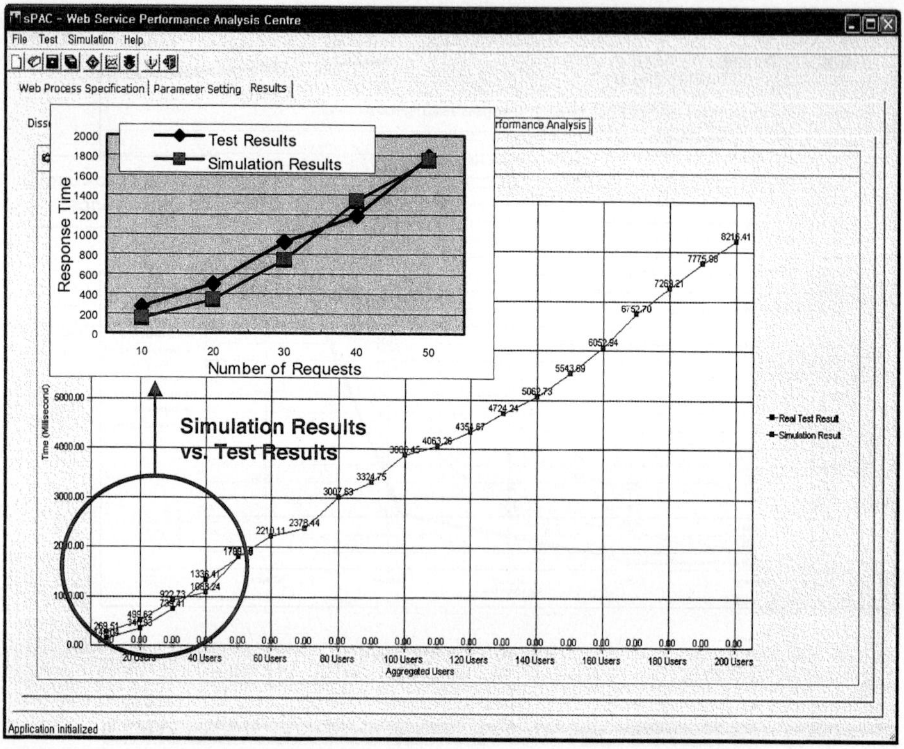

Fig. 6. Simulation Accuracy and Estimation Results

Suppose *My Travel Planner* will provide services of logging-in(`LogIn`), booking a flight(`FlightBooking`), reserving an accommodation(HotelBooking), renting a car(`CarRenting`), finding out the current currency rate between Korea and Turkey(`CurrencyConverter`), exchanging travel money(`MoneyExchange`), validating credit cards(`CreditcardValidation`), and processing credit cards(`CreditcardProcessor`). Also, we would like to create *My Travel Planner* just by integrating the existing web services available on the web.

As shown in Figure 3, users can search available web services in UDDI and graphically specify how the web services are formed into a new web process. Based on the flow between the selected web services, the input and output relationships are checked to confirm if output values of a web service can be used as input values for the successor service. Users also set various parameters (for example, inputs, minimum and maximum number of simultaneous request, and testing and simulation duration) with appropriate values.

Then, `sPAC` conducts DRT and TRT tests for the given web process with small number of simultaneous requests. In *My Travel Planner* example, DRT and TRT tests are conducted with 10 – 50 numbers of simultaneous users, and take 40 seconds to complete. Figure 4 and Figure 5 show DRT and TRT test results, respectively, for *My Travel Planner* example. Followings are some interesting performance properties indicated by DRT and TRT tests in Figure 4 – 5.

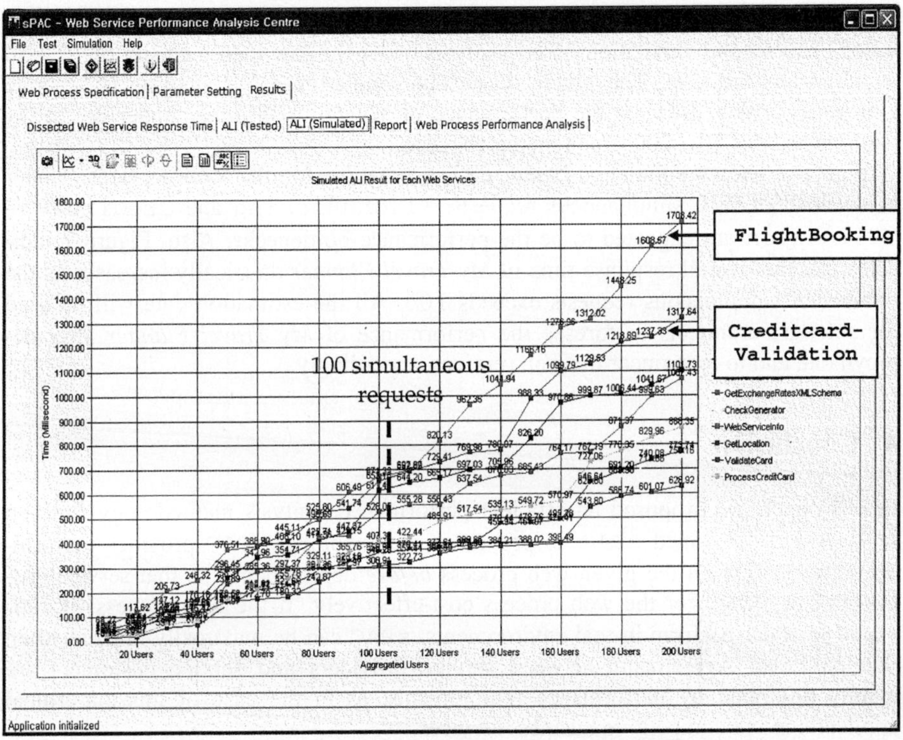

Fig. 7. Simulation-based TRT estimation

- `FlightBooking` web service becomes the performance bottleneck of *My Travel Planner* as the number of simultaneous requests increases as shown in Figure 4. According to DRT tests in Figure 5, the response time of `Flight-Booking` web service is mainly dominated by service time (78.89% of the response time) compared to messaging time (20.46 %) and network time (0.64%). This observation suggests us to reengineer the business logic of `FlightBooking`, or to increase hardware capability, or to find other alternatives for better performance.
- `CurrencyConverter` (53.33%), `HotelBooking` (57.68%), `Car-Renting` (64.02%), `CreditcardValidation` (52.45%) and `CreditcardProcessor` (66.17%) require significant amount of time to process SOAP messages comparing to other service-intensive web services (`FlightBooking`(20.48%), `MoneyExchange`(23.26%), `LogIn(1.6%)`). This observation suggests us to consider other service alternatives that might require less messaging overheads or to reengineer message formats.

Meanwhile, `sPAC` translates the activity diagram into a `SimJava`-based simulation model as described in Section 2. Also, DRT and TRT test results of each web service are analyzed for the average response time to process a single request. The average values are utilized in a simulation model as the amount of delay to send and receive event objects as illustrated in Figure 2. Figure 6 shows the difference between test-based analysis and simulation-based analysis under the low load intensity of 10 – 50 simultaneous requests. The graph shows our simulation-based analysis is accurate enough to further estimate the performance of *My Travel Planner* under the heavy load intensity of 50 – 200 simultaneous requests.

Figure 7 shows simulation-based TRT estimation for the web services. Under heavy load of 200 simultaneous requests, FlightBooking and Creditcard-Validation are expected to be the performance bottlenecks. Also, Figure 7 indicates that the overall response time of *My Travel Planner* drastically increases as the number of simultaneous requests exceeds 100. All the estimation data will be used for software architects to foresee the performance of *My Travel Planner* after deployment, and to reengineer the web services, accordingly.

4 Conclusion

In this paper, we proposed an efficient performance analysis methodology for web services and developed sPAC to prove our methodology. sPAC provides performance information on the given web process *before* deployment, so that service customers can reengineer the web process cost-effectively if the web process is estimated to under-perform in real environments. sPAC can be maximally utilized when Service Level Agreements between service providers and service customers are mainly described by performance requirements, as in the case of mission-critical applications and competitive business services.

We will extend our methodology to consider other dynamic QoS(Quality of Service) properties, such as, availability, reliability, security and their combinations for future works. Reference [12] is part of our achievement for this research direction. Also, we would like to continue our efforts to increase the simulation accuracy by employing well-known learning mechanisms.

Acknowledgement

This work was supported by grant No. R05-2004-000-11329-0 from Korea Research Foundation.

References

1. IBM, *SOA and Web Services*, http://www-130.ibm.com/developerworks/webservices/
2. Shuping R.: *A model for Web services discovery with QoS*, ACM SIGecom Exchanges, Volume 4, Issue 1, Spring, (2003), pp. 1-10
3. Menasce D.A., Almeida V.A.F.: *Capacity Planning for Web Services: Metrics, Models, and Methods*, Prentice-Hall, (2002)
4. Zeng L, et. al: Quality Driven Web Services Composition Proceedings of WWW 2003, (2003), Budapest, Hungary
5. Meise J.D., Vasireddy S., Babbar A, Mackman A.: *How to: Use ACT to Test Web Services Performance*, Microsoft Developer Network, Microsoft Corporation, (2004)

6. Davidson N.: Web Services Testing: (2005) http://www.red-gate.com/dotnet/more/web_services_testing.htm, Red-Gate Software,
7. Silver G., Miller J.A., Gardoso J., Sheth A. P.: Web service technologies and their synergy with simulation, In Proceedings of the Winter Simulation Conference, pp. 606 – 615, (2002)
8. Silver G., Maduko A., Jafri R., Miller J.A., Sheth A.P.: *Modeling and Simulation of Quality of Service for Composite Web Services*, Proceedings of the 7th World Multiconference on Systems, Cybernetics, and Informatics (SCI'03), Orlando, Florida, pp. 420-425., July (2003)
9. Jin L., Machiraju V., Sahai A.: *Analysis on Service Level Agreement of Web services*, Software Technology Laboratory, HP Laboratories, Palo Alto, HPL-2002-180, Hewlett Packard Company, (2002), June
10. Object Management Group, *UML (Unified Modeling Language)* ™ *Resource Page*, http://www.uml.org/, January 2005
11. Howell F., McNab R.: *Simjava Library,* http://www.dcs.ed.ac.uk/home/hase/simjava, 1996
12. Chang H. et. al: *Simulation-Based Web Service Composition: Framework and Performance Analysis*, Lecture Notes in Computer Science, Springer Verlag, vol. 3398/2005, Feb. (2005), pp. 352-361

Brazilian Software Process Reference Model and Assessment Method

Kival C. Weber[1], Eratóstenes E.R. Araújo[1], Ana Regina C. da Rocha[2], Cristina A.F. Machado[3], Danilo Scalet[3], and Clênio F. Salviano[4]

[1] SOFTEX – Associação para Promoção da Excelência do Software Brasileiro
{kival.weber, eratostenes}@nac.softex.br
[2] COPPE/UFRJ – Universidade Federal do Rio de Janeiro
darocha@cos.ufrj.br
[3] CELEPAR – Companhia de Informática do Paraná
{cristina, danilo}@pr.gov.br
[4] CenPRA – Centro de Pesquisas Renato Archer
clenio.salviano@cenpra.gov.br

Abstract. This paper presents the MR-MPS Process Reference Model and the MA-MPS Process Assessment Method. They were created according to the Brazilian reality in the MPS.BR Project, aiming at improving software process mainly in small to medium-size enterprises (SMEs). They are compatible with CMMI[SM] and conformant with ISO/IEC 15504 and ISO/IEC 12207. This paper describes three MPS documents: a general guide, an assessment guide and an acquisition guide. The initial project outcomes are presented. The MPS Model has a great potential to be replicated in other countries with similar characteristics related to the software industry.

1 Introduction

Studies have shown the need of a significant effort to improve software process maturity in Brazilian software companies and that a concern with process has emerged in the country over the past few years, but local firm have favored the ISO 9001 [5] instead of the ISO/IEC 12207 [6] and ISO/IEC 15504 [7] standards, and models such as CMM[SM] or CMMI[SM] [9, 13]. In 2003, there were 214 software companies in Brazil with an ISO 9000 certificate, whereas only 30 companies reached a CMM[SM] certificate: 24 CMM[SM] level 2, five CMM[SM] level 3, one CMM[SM] level 4 and none CMM[SM] level 5, most of these are branches of foreign firms.

In December 2003, the Association for Promoting the Brazilian Software Excellence (SOFTEX) has begun a nationwide project to improve software process in Brazil, known as MPS.BR Project [14, 15]. SOFTEX is a private not-for-profit organization aiming at promoting competitiveness of the Brazilian software industry, which holds a network of 31 SOFTEX agents (in 23 cities of 13 estates). There are almost 1100 SOFTEX affiliated firms – 11% large, 13% medium, 36% small and 40% micro-size companies (see www.softex.br).

This paper presents the MR-MPS Process Reference Model and the MA-MPS Process Assessment Method. Section 2 introduces the MPS.BR Project. Section 3 describes MR-MPS and MA-MPS, which are documented in three guides: a General

P. Yolum et al.(Eds.): ISCIS 2005, LNCS 3733, pp. 402 – 411, 2005.

Guide, an Assessment Guide, and an Acquisition Guide. Section 4 presents the initial project outcomes, from December 2003 to March 2005. Section 5 concludes this paper highlighting its main points and addressing future work.

2 MPS.BR – The Brazilian Software Process Improvement Project

Organizations and industry associations that perceive a strategic competitive advantage in their business processes, now have the option to create their own Process Reference Model or use an existing process model they already have. They can then create a Process Assessment Model based on this reference model. However, the effort needed to ensure that the models are compliant or conformant with ISO/IEC 15504 should not be underestimated. It is likely that only large organizations will undertake the step. The European space and automotive industries are taking this step through their industry associations [11].

In Brazil, this step was taken by SOFTEX in December 2003 with the MPS.BR Project (MPS.BR from 'Melhoria de Processo do Software Brasileiro', in Portuguese). This project aims at improving software process in the Brazilian software companies, with a focus on the small to medium-size enterprises (SMEs). It has two goals: i) to develop and improve the MPS Model, compatible with CMMI[SM] and conformant with ISO/IEC 12207 and ISO/IEC 15504; ii) to implement and assess the MPS Model in Brazilian software companies in all regions of the country. The MPS.BR Project does not aim to define something new related to standards and models. What is new in the project is its implementation strategy, created according to the reality of the Brazilian firms [14, 15].

The MPS.BR Project is managed by: (i) a Project Team coordinated by SOFTEX, with representatives from University-Industry-Government; (ii) a Model Team coordinated by COPPE/UFRJ, which documents the MPS Model in three guides and also deals with mps professional training and certification; (iii) an Accreditation Forum, which deals with SOFTEX authorized organizations that provide MPS Process Implementation service and MPS Process Assessment service.

3 MPS Model Description

The MPS Model is a software process improvement and assessment model, mainly oriented to the small and medium-size enterprises (SMEs). This model aims at: i) to fulfill the 'business need' of these firms; ii) to be recognized, locally and internationally, as an applicable model to organizations which develop or acquire software. The theoretical bases used to create the MPS Model are the international standards ISO/IEC 12207 and ISO/IEC 15504 – with which it is conformant. Additionally, the MPS Model covers other software process models content, such as CMMI[SM] [3] – with which it is compatible. The MPS Model also defines rules to implement and assess itself, so it supports and assures a coherent use according to its definitions.

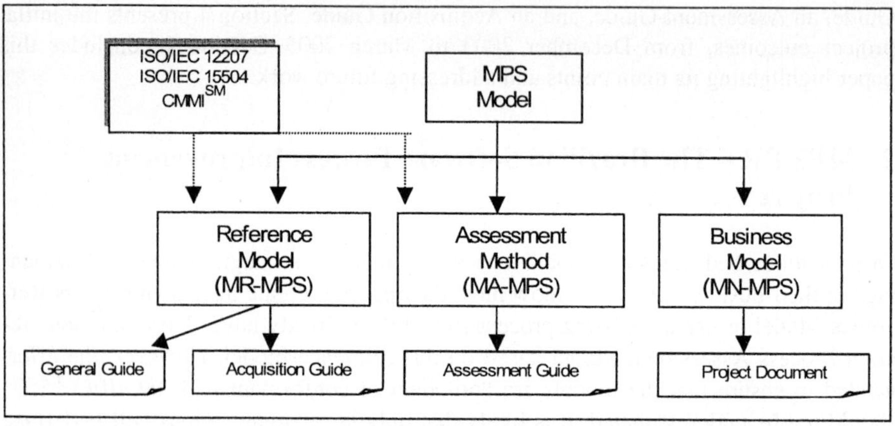

Fig. 1. MPS Model

It has three components, as shown in Figure 1: the MR-MPS Process Reference Model (MR-MPS from 'Modelo de Referência para Melhoria de Processo de Software', in Portuguese), the MA-MPS Process Assessment Method (MA-MPS from 'Método de Avaliação para Melhoria de Processo de Software') and the MN-MPS Business Model (MN-MPS from 'Modelo de Negócio para Melhoria de Processo de Software'). Each model component is described in a specific document, such as the three guides.

MR-MPS contains the requirements that organizations must implement to be compliant with the MPS Model. It contains definitions of the maturity levels, process capabilities and software processes. MR-MPS is strongly aligned with ISO/IEC 12207 and ISO/IEC 15504, and it is compatible with CMMI^{SM}. MR-MPS is described in the MPS General Guide.

The MPS Acquisition Guide is a complementary document which describes an acquisition process for software and related service acquisition. The acquisition process is defined by subprocesses and activities, and it conforms to international standards and recommended practices.

MA-MPS describes process assessment, assessor requirements and the requirements for ISO/IEC 15504 compliance. MA-MPS is described in the MPS Assessment Guide. MN-MPS describes business rules in three domains: (i) the mps Br Project domain, coordinated by SOFTEX; (ii) the domain of the SOFTEX authorized organizations that provide MPS Process Implementation service and MPS Process Assessment service; (iii) the domain of the companies that are using the MPS Model for software process improvement, both group of firms in the MPS Cooperative Business Model (CBM) and specific firms in the MPS Specific Business Model (SBM). MN-MPS is described in a MPS.BR Project document.

3.1 MPS General Guide

The document MPS General Guide contains a MPS Model general description, the common definitions to all guides and details on MR-MPS Process Reference Model. MR-MPS is defined through seven maturity levels, sequential and accumulative. Each maturity level is a joint of two dimensions – software processes and process capabilities, so comprising a set of processes in a certain capability level.

MR-MPS describes each process by its purpose and outcomes. Each process has a unique identification in conformance with ISO/IEC 12207 and ISO/IEC 15504-5. The process purpose and outcomes are indicators that demonstrate whether the organization's processes are being achieved. Each capability level is described by one or more generic goals. Each generic goal comprises a set of generic practices that are indicators that demonstrate whether the organization's capabilities are being achieved. This framework is shown in Figure 2.

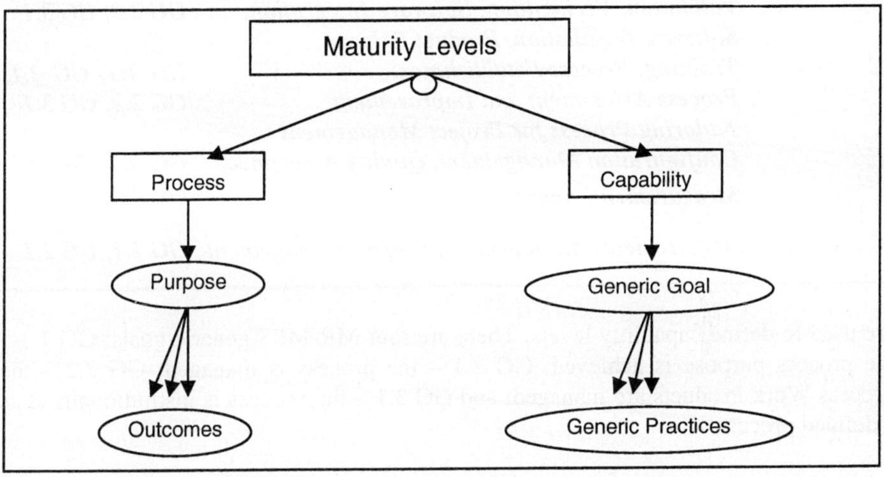

Fig. 2. MR-MPS Process Reference Model

MR-MPS Process Reference Model defines seven maturity levels: A (Optimizing), B (Quantitatively Managed), C (Defined), D (Largely Defined), E (Partially Defined), F (Managed) and G (Partially Managed). MR-MPS level G is the lowest – the most immature, and level A is the highest – the most mature. The MR-MPS maturity levels are based on the four maturity levels of the CMMI^{SM} staged representation (level 2 to 5), where MR-MPS levels F, C, B and A correspond respectively to CMMI^{SM} levels 2, 3, 4 and 5. MR-MPS level G is one intermediary level between the CMMI^{SM} levels 1 and 2, and MR-MPS levels E and D are two intermediary levels between the CMMI^{SM} levels 2 and 3. This seven levels grading makes possible a more gradual implementation and recognition of the software process improvements with better visibility in a shorter term, making MR-MPS easier to adopt and suitable to adapt in Brazilian SMEs.

Table 1 shows the MR-MPS processes and generic goals that shall be added to the process capability profile for each maturity level. MR-MPS processes are a combination of the ISO/IEC 12207 Amd 1 & Amd 2 processes (purpose and outcomes) and the CMMI^{SM}-SE/SW process areas. MR-MPS generic goals are combinations of the CMMI^{SM}-SE/SW generic goals and the ISO/IEC 15504-2 process attributes, which

Table 1. MPS maturity levels, processes and generic goals

Level	Process	Generic Goal
A (highest)	*Organizational Innovation and Deployment, Causal Analysis and Resolution*	*GG 1.1, GG 2.1, GG 2.2, GG 3.1*
B	*Organizational Process Performance, Quantitative Project Management*	*GG 1.1, GG 2.1, GG 2.2, GG 3.1*
C	*Risk Management, Decision Analysis and Resolution*	*GG 1.1, GG 2.1, GG 2.2, GG 3.1*
D	*Requirements Development, Technical Solution, Validation, Verification, Software Integration, Software Installation, Product Release*	*GG 1.1, GG 2.1, GG 2.2, GG 3.1*
E	*Training, Process Establishment, Process Assessment and Improvement, Tailoring Process for Project Management*	*GG 1.1, GG 2.1, GG 2.2, GG 3.1*
F	*Configuration Management, Quality Assurance, Measurement, Acquisition*	*GG 1.1, GG 2.1, GG 2.2*
G (lowest)	*Requirements Management, Project Management*	*GG 1.1, GG 2.1*

are used to define capability levels. There are four MR-MPS generic goals: GG 1.1 – the process purpose is achieved; GG 2.1 – the process is managed; GG 2.2 – the process Work Products are managed; and GG 3.1 – the process is institutionalized as a defined process.

3.2 MPS Assessment Guide

Ideally, the organizations should consider its performance against its competitors and peers in its market, and against peers in related markets – in other words its overall 'business successes'. It should relate this performance to the processes (and technology) it uses to determine how those processes contribute to business success. It should also consider its absolute performance (or lack of performance) and attempt to calculate the cost of failure. Process assessment provides an accepted, independent measurement framework for assessment of processes. The ISO/IEC 15504 standard has been developed as an international view of 'best practice' in process assessment. Using ISO/IEC 15504 allows organizations to assess whether their processes are capable of helping them achieve organizational success [12].

According to ISO/IEC 15504-1 and ISO/IEC 12207 Amd 1, the purpose of process assessment is to determine the extent to which the organization's standard processes contribute to the achievement of its business goals and to help the organization focus on the need for continuous process improvement. The document MPS Assessment Guide describes the MA-MPS Process Assessment Method. Basically, it contains assessment requirements, assessment activities, assessment indicators and assessors requirements. MA-MPS makes possible to carry out assessment activities in a given organizational unit through authorized competent assessors. MA-MPS requirements are aligned with ISO/IEC 15504-2 assessment requirements, CMMI^{SM} ARC Class A requirements (except appraisal team leader requirements) and MPS.BR specific requirements. So, it is ISO/IEC 15504 conformant, CMMI^{SM} ARC Class A compatible and suitable to SMEs.

MA-MPS assessment activities are mainly based on SCAMPI^{SM} [10], with parts of QUICK [8] and MARES [2] methods. SCAMPI^{SM} (Standard CMMI^{SM} Appraisal Method for Process Improvement) has three classes of assessments: Class A is more rigorous and time consuming, providing basis for improvement plan, while Class B and Class C are less rigorous and time consuming. The need to be able to achieve translation to ISO/IEC 15504 Process Profiles is only required for SCAMPI^{SM} Class A. QUICKLocus is a Brazilian process assessment method suitable for software organizations with less than 50 employees, low time consuming, which provides basis for software development process improvement. MARES is another Brazilian process assessment method in SMEs, ISO/IEC 15504 conformant, which focus on process improvement.

The MA-MPS Process Assessment Method is described in Figure 3 by: i) its four sequential activities; ii) its six major Work Products; iii) relationships between activities and input/output Work Products; iv) relationships between activities and the five minimum activities required by ISO/IEC 15504-2 for process assessment; v) relationships between activities and the three phases of SCAMPI^{SM} method.

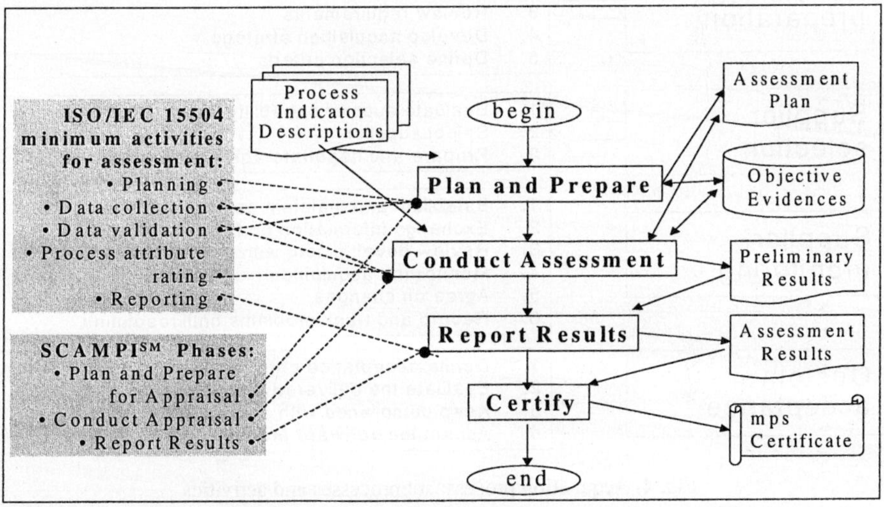

Fig. 3. MA-MPS Process Assessment Method

The set of Work Products (WP) satisfies the requirements of ISO/IEC 15504 and are based on SCAMPI^{SM}. For example, the Assessment Plan WP satisfies the six minimum requirements for ISO/IEC 15504 assessment plan (required inputs, activi ties to be performed, resources and schedule, identity and defined responsibilities of the participants, criteria for verification, and description of the planned assessment outputs). As another example, the Process Indicator Descriptions WP satisfies the assessment indicator requirements of ISO/IEC 15504-2 and is based on the Practice Implementation Indicators Descriptions (PIID) of SCAMPI^{SM}.

3.3 MPS Acquisition Guide

The acquisition of software and related service is a complex process, mainly to characterize acquisition requirements and acquisition outcomes such as software quality, product acceptance, change request management, products release, responsibilities and liability. The acquisition process involves risks to both parts and it is common to occur serious conflicts in the supplier-customer relationship. So some initiatives to turn the acquisition process more predictable, with better outcomes for the parts, are being considered in international standards and practices [1].

According to ISO/IEC 12207 Amd 1, the purpose of the acquisition process is to obtain the product and/or service that satisfy the need expressed by the customer. The process begins with the identification of a customer need and ends with the acceptance of the product and/or service by the customer.

As shown in Figure 4, the acquisition process contains four subprocesses: acquisition preparation, supplier selection, supplier monitoring and customer acceptance. Therewith each sub-process is deployed in activities aligned with ISO/IEC 12207 Amd 1.

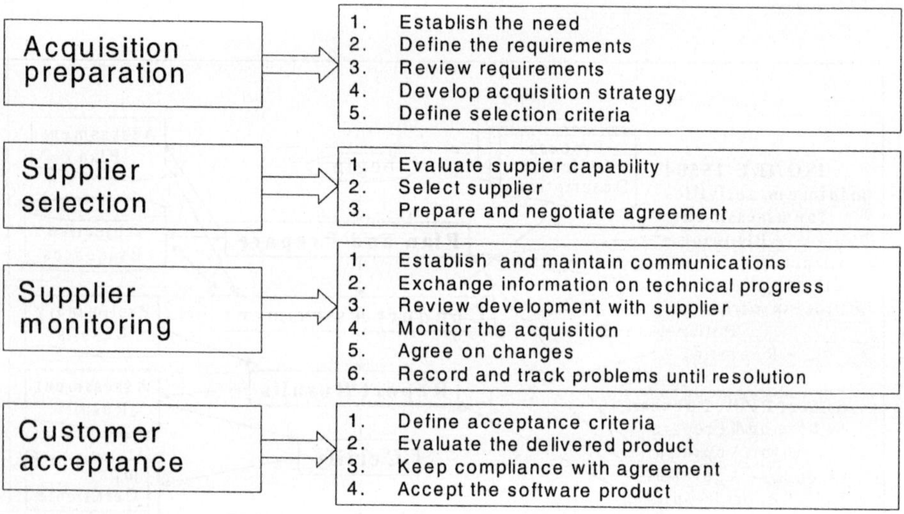

Fig. 4. Acquisition process: subprocesses and activities

The document MPS Acquisition Guide maps all these subprocesses and activities to the phases and steps of the IEEE STD 1062 recommended practice for software acquisition [4]. MPS Acquisition Guide describes a software and related services acquisition process to be used both by software acquirers and suppliers. It is useful to organizations that are looking for improving their software acquisitions, especially when the suppliers are using the MR-MPS Process Reference Model to improve software process. Of course, it is also useful for software suppliers that are looking for improving their software and related service.

MPS Acquisition Guide is aligned with ISO/IEC 12207 Amd 1 acquisition process and subprocesses, IEEE STD 1062 recommended practices, and MPS.BR specific requirements. It details each acquisition subprocess considering: i) required activities; ii) required products; iii) deliverable products; iv) contract agreements with a certified supplier, such as MPS certified or an equivalent certification. It also describes common problems that occur in the acquisition process, aspects relating to the acquisition of free software/open source and the acquisition of software components, as well as the evolution of the acquisition process in the capability dimension.

4 Initial MPS.BR Project Outcomes (Dec.2003–Mar.2005)

The following outcomes are related to the first project goal - to develop and improve the MPS Model: (i) Dec.2003-Jul.2004: MPS Model preliminary version, compatible with CMMI^{SM}; (ii) Aug.2004-Mar.2005: MPS Model version 1.0, compatible with CMMI^{SM} and conformant with ISO/IEC 12207 and ISO/IEC 15504, documented in three guides – general guide, assessment guide and acquisition guide; (iii) May-Dec.2004: 12 Courses on Introduction to MPS Model, in 11 cities, with 637 participants. 3 Exams for MPS Process Implementers, in 12 cities, with 137 approved; (iv) Nov.2004-Mar.2005: 4 organizations authorized to provide MPS Process Implementation service.

The following outcomes are related to the second project goal - to implement and assess the MPS Model in Brazilian software companies in all regions of the country: (i) Dec.2003-Mar.2005: Pilot experience on MPS Process Implementation in groups of firms; (ii) Sep.2004-Mar.2005: First international activities, with presentations on MPS.BR Project and MPS Model in Argentina, Peru and Portugal.

5 Conclusions

This paper presented the MR-MPS Process Reference Model and the MA-MPS Process Assessment Method. They were created according to the Brazilian reality, aiming at improving software process mainly in small to medium-size enterprises (SMEs) with feasible costs. They are compatible with CMMI^{SM} and conformant with ISO/IEC 15504 and ISO/IEC 12207.

The MPS Model has a great potential to be replicated in other countries with similar characteristics related to the software industry. In April 2005, it was announced that the MPS.BR project also will be supported by the Inter-American Development Bank (IDB). According to an IDB representative, "having two other countries accompanying Brazil in this experience sets the stage for promoting partnerships as well as a common space among firms in the different countries involved".This paper also described how has been tested the step taken by SOFTEX - a Brazilian software industry association, in December 2003, with the MPS.BR Project. There is a strong interaction among University-Industry-Government in this project. The MPS.BR Project is very important to the Brazilian software sector, whereas it is promoting significant cultural changes.

The initial project outcomes were presented in this paper. Up to now the main results are: i) an ample debate on the MPS.BR Project and MPS Model, with an extraordinary receptivity in all regions of the country and in organizations of different sizes – governmental and private enterprises; ii) the involvement of a large team in the project and model, with representatives of several Brazilian regions; iii) the development and improvement of the MPS Model, documented by three guides, with a great value-added and technological impact; iv) the qualification of hundreds of professionals in the MPS Model; v) the first four organizations authorized to provide mps Process Implementation service; vi) the pilot experiences on MPS Process Implementation in groups of firms in three important cities.

In 2005, the main challenges are: i) to commit more qualified people, experienced institutions and interested firms in the MPS.BR Project and MPS Model; ii) to improve continuously the three MPS guides; iii) to carry out the MPS Professional Training and Certification Plan; iv) to authorize new organizations to provide MPS Process Implementation service and also MPS Process Assessment service; v) to carry out pilot experiences on MPS Process Assessment in firms in Rio de Janeiro, Recife and Campinas from May to July, and regular MPS Process Assessment in several cities from August to December; vi) to create new groups of firms for MPS Process Implementation.

Acknowledgements

We would like to acknowledge to all participants in the MPS.BR Project. From 2005 on the project is supported by FNDCT/CT-INFO/VERDE-AMARELO/FINEP/MCT. CMM^{SM}, CMMI^{SM} and SCAMPI^{SM} are SEI/CMU service marks. MR-MPS, MA-MPS, MN-MPS and MPS.BR are SOFTEX service marks.

References

1. Alves, A. M., Guerra, A.: Aquisição de Produtos e Serviços de Software. Rio de Janeiro, Elsevier (2004) (in portuguese)
2. Anacleto, A., von Wangenheim, C. G., Salviano, C. F., Savi, R.: A Method for Process Assessment in Small Software Companies. In: Proceedings of SPICE 2004: The Fourth International SPICE Conference, Lisbon Portugal (2004) 69–76
3. Chrissis, M. B., Konrad, M., Shrum, S.: CMMI^{SM}: Guidelines for Process Integration and Product Improvement. Addison-Wesley (2003)
4. IEEE STD 1062:1998. IEEE Software Engineering Standards Collection. IEEE Recommended Practice for Software Acquisition, IEEE STD 1062 Edition, New York NY USA (1998)
5. ISO 9001:2000. Quality Management Systems. Requirements (2000)
6. ISO/IEC 12207:1995/Amd 1:2002/Amd 2:2004. Information Technology – Software Life Cycle Processes (2004)
7. ISO/IEC 15504. Information Technology – Process Assessment. Part 1 – Concepts and vocabulary (2004); part 2 – Performing an assessment (2003); part 3 – Guidance on performing an assessment (2004); part 4 – Guidance on use for process improvement and process capability determination (2004); and part 5 – An exemplar process assessment model (1999)
8. Kohan, S.: QuickLocus: Proposta de um método de avaliação de processo de desenvolvimento de software em pequenas organizações. Dissertação de mestrado, Instituto de Pesquisas Tecnológicas do Estado de São Paulo – IPT (2003) (in portuguese)

9. MCT/SEPIN – Ministério da Ciência e Tecnologia, Secretaria de Política de Informática. Qualidade e Produtividade no Setor de Software Brasileiro 2001, Brasília Brasil (2001) (in portuguese)
10. SEI – Software Engineering Institute, Carnegie Mellon University. Standard CMMI^{SM} Appraisal Method for Process Improvement (SCAMPI^{SM}), Version 1.1: Method Definition Document, CMU/SEI-2001-HB-001 (2001)
11. van Loon, H.: Process Assessment and ISO/IEC 15504: a reference book. The Kluwer International Series in Engineering and Computer Science, Vol. 775, Springer (2004a)
12. van Loon, H.: Process Assessment and Improvement: a practical guide for managers, quality professionals and assessors. The Kluwer International Series in Engineering and Computer Science, Vol. 776, Springer (2004b) 10–11
13. Veloso, F., Botelho, A. J., Tschang, A., Amsden, A.: Slicing the Knowledge-based Economy in Brazil, China and India: a tale of 3 software industries. Report, MIT – Massachusetts Institute of Technology, Massachusetts USA (2003)
14. Weber, K. C. *et al.*: Modelo de Referência para Melhoria de Processo de Software: Uma Abordagem Brasileira. In: Proceedings of the XXX Conferencia Latinoamericana de Informatica (CLEI 2004), Arequipa Peru (2004) (in portuguese)
15. Weber, K. C., *et al.*: Uma Estratégia para Melhoria de Processo de Software nas Empresas Brasileiras. In: Proceedings of the Fifth Conference for Quality in Information and Communications Technology (QUATIC'2004), Porto Portugal (2004) (in portuguese)

A Secure Communication Framework for Mobile Agents

Suat Ugurlu and Nadia Erdogan

Istanbul Technical University, Computer Engineering Department,
Ayazaga, 34390 Istanbul, Turkey
suat@suatugurlu.com, erdogan@cs.itu.edu.tr

Abstract. Communication, a fundamental concept in computing, allows two pieces of software to interact and to exchange information. It is an important aspect of mobile agent systems because mobile agents generally need to coordinate their activities through some type of communication. Using mobile agent technologies provides potential benefits to distributed applications; however, an agent's ability to move introduces significant security risks. Consequently, a mobile agent system should provide a safe and secure communication infrastructure along with other security management and maintenance activities. This paper describes the communication framework of a new mobile agent platform, Secure Mobile Agent Platform (SECMAP) that provides mobile agents a flexible and secure communication environment with both synchronous and asynchronous messaging facilities.

1 Introduction

Intelligent agents and multi-agent systems bring in a new approach to the design and implementation of complex distributed systems. Several multi-agent systems have been implemented either as commercial products or in various research projects, with varying success [1] [2] [3] [4] [5] [6] [7]. Reasons for the growing recognition of agent technology are the innovative solutions it provides to problems of more traditionally designed distributed systems through mobility of code, machine based intelligence, and improved network and data-management possibilities.

Using mobile agent technologies provides potential benefits to applications, however, an agent's ability to move introduces significant security risks. Both mobile agents during their life times and hosts executing mobile agents are under security threats [8], [9]. The attacks against mobile agent security can be divided into three categories: attacks by hosts against agents, attacks by agents against hosts and attacks between agents. There may also be more complex attacks that agents and hosts may be exposed to. Consequently, a secure mobile agent system is a firm requirement especially when designing and implementing industrial or e-business applications. Mobile agents generally need to coordinate their activities, and do so by passing messages between them in a location transparent manner. Therefore, a mobile agent system should provide a safe and

P. Yolum et al.(Eds.): ISCIS 2005, LNCS 3733, pp. 412–421, 2005.

secure communication infrastructure along with other security management and maintenance activities.

This paper describes the secure communication framework of a new mobile agent platform, Secure Mobile Agent Platform (SECMAP). Unlike other agent systems, SECMAP proposes a new agent model, the *shielded agent model*, for security purposes. A shielded agent is a highly encapsulated software component that ensures complete isolation against unauthorized access of any type. SECMAP provides mobile agents a flexible, location transparent communication environment with both synchronous and asynchronous secured messaging facilities.

2 SECMAP Approach to Security

SECMAP treats every agent as a distinct principal and provides protection mechanisms that isolate agents. The system differs from other mobile agents systems in the abstractions it provides to address issues of agent isolation.

SECMAP agents are light-weight implementations as threads instead of processes. Each agent is an autonomous object with a unique identification and agents communicate via asynchronous message passing. A Secure Mobile Agent Server (SMAS) resident on each node presents a secure execution environment on which new agents may be created or to which agents may be dispatched. SMAS provides functionalities that meet security requirements and allow the implementation of the *shielded agent model.* A shielded agent is a highly encapsulated software component that ensures complete isolation against unauthorized access of any type. On a request to create a new agent, SMAS instantiates a private object of its own, an instance of predefined object *AgentShield*, and uses it as a wrapper around the newly created agent by declaring the agent to be a private object of AgentShield object. This type of encapsulation ensures complete isolation, preventing other agents to access the agent state directly. An agent is only allowed to communicate with its environment over the SMAS engine through the methods defined in a predefined interface object, *AgentInterface*, which is also made the private object of the agent during the creation process. The interface provides limited yet sufficient functions for the agent to communicate with SMAS. All variables of agents are declared as private and they have corresponding accessor methods. Agents issue or receive method invocation requests through asynchronous messages over the secure communication facility of SMAS. Thus, a source that is qualified for a particular request, for example, that has received the rights to communicate with a target agent, is granted to pass its message.

SECMAP employs cryptographic techniques to meet security constraints. Each SMAS owns a certificate which is used to identify its identity and to encrypt and decrypt data. A requests from a SMAS is not processed until the validity of the SMAS identitiy is verified. A SECMAP agent's code and state information are kept encrypted during its life time using Data Encryption Standard (DES) algorithm. They are decrypted only when the agent is in running state on the host's memory. To protect agents during migration over the network, agent code and state data are encrypted as well while in transfer and can only be decrypted on the target host after retrieving the appropriate DES key from the security manager. SECMAP employs a policy based authorization mechanism to permit or restrict agents to carry out certain classes of actions. SECMAP also monitors, time stamps and logs all agent activity in a file, in order to be later analyzed to determine the actions an agent carried out on the host.

2.1 SECMAP Architecture

A brief overview of SECMAP architecture is necessary before the description of the secure communication framework. We have used Java for the implementation of the execution environment because it offers several features that ease the development process. Figure 1 shows the SECMAP architecture. The main component of the architecture is a Secure Mobile Agent Server (SMAS) that is responsible of all agent related tasks such as creation, activation, communication, and migration. The system comprises of several SMAS executing on each node which acts as a host for agents. A SMAS may operate in three modes according to the functionality it exhibits. It can be configured to execute in any of the three modes on a host through a user interface. A SMAS on a node can also operate in all three modes at the same time.

Standard Mode (S-SMAS): S-SMAS provides standard agent services such as agent creation, activation, inactivation, destruction, communication, and migration. It also includes a policy engine that checks agent activity and resource utilization according to the rules that are present in a policy file, which has been received from a Security Manager SMAS. In addition, S-SMAS maintains a list of all active agents resident on the host and notifies the Master Browser SMAS anytime an agent changes state. Keeping logs of all agent activities is another important task S-SMAS carries out. Log content may be very useful in the detection of certain kinds of attacks which are difficult to catch instantly.

Master Browser Mode (MB-SMAS): When agents are mobile, location mappings change over time, therefore agent communication first requires a reference to the recipient agent to be obtained. In addition to supporting all functionalities of S-SMAS, MB-SMAS also maintains a name-location directory of all currently active agents in the system. This list consists of information that identifes the host where an agent runs and is kept up to date as information on the identities and status (active/inactive) of agents from other SMAS is received.

Security Manager Mode(SM-SMAS): In addition to supporting all functionalities of S-SMAS, SM-SMAS performs authentication of all SMAS engines, handles policy management, and maintains security information such as DES keys and certificates. Any SMAS engine in the system has to be authenticated before it can start up as a trusted server. SM-SMAS holds an IP address and key pair for each of SMAS engine that wants to be authenticated. If the supplied key and the IP address of the requesting SMAS engine is correct then it is authenticated. The authenticated SMAS engine gets a ticket from the

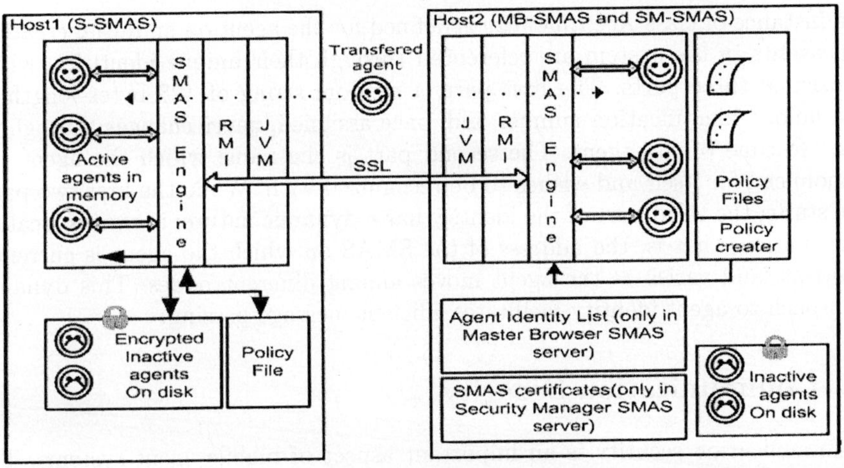

Fig. 1. SECMAP Architecture

SM-SMAS and uses this ticket when communicating with other SMAS engines. A SMAS that receives a request from another SMAS refers to SM-SMAS to verify the validity of its ticket before proceeding with the necessary actions to fulfill the request. Every SMAS, regardless of its mode, creates a private-public key pair once. Next, it creates its certificate and sends it to the SM-SMAS. Any SMAS can receive the certificate list from SM-SMAS before authentication and store it in its key store in order to use SSL communication with other SMAS engines in the system. From then on, all agent-to-agent and SMAS-to-SMAS communication is established through SSL.

2.2 SECMAP Agents

SECMAP requires agents to conform to a software architectural style, which is identified by a basic agent template. The agent programmer is provided a flexible development environment with an interface for writing mobile agent applications. He determines agent behavior according to the agent template given and is expected to write code that reflects the agent's behavior for each of the public methods. For example, code for the *OnCreate()* method should specify initial actions to be carried out while the agent is being created, or code for the *OnMessageArrive()* method should define agent reaction to message arrival.

```
public class Main extends Agent{
public void OnMessageArrive(){...}
public void OnCreate(){ ... }
public void OnActivate(){...}
public void OnInactivate(){... }
public void OnTransfer(){... }
public void OnEnd(){... }}
```

An instance of class *AgentIdentity* is defined for the agent on an initial creation. All agents in the system are referenced through their unique identities, which consist of three parts. The first part, a random string of 128 bytes length, is the unique identification number and, once assigned, never changes throughout the life time of the agent. The second part is the name which the agent has announced for itself and wishes to be recognized with. While the first two parts are static, the third part of the identity has a dynamic nature: it carries location information, that is, the address of the SMAS on which the agent is currently resident, and varies as the agent moves among different nodes. This dynamic approach to agent identity facilitates efficient message passing.

3 Communication Security

Communication security is an important aspect of mobile agent systems. The messages exchanged between agents or between an agent and its owner may be confidential, or can contain sensitive information. It should be possible to detect if messages are tampered with. Also, it should be possible to verify the target entity to which a message is being directed and to verify if a message received really originates from a given entity. Therefore, the communication framework of an agent system should provide facilities for the fulfillment of the following security requirements [10]:

- *Confidentiality*
- *Data integrity*
- *Authentication of origin*
- *Non-repudiation of origin*
- *Non-repudiation of receipt*

SECMAP meets the first three requirements through application of the SSL protocol and cryptographic techniques. All SMAS engines are authenticated before their requests are processed. The implementation relies on Java RMI and it is enhanced to support SSL communication. Non-repudiation of origin and receipt ensures that agents can not deny their actions. SECMAP keeps logs of all agent activity, which can later be analyzed for execution tracing if need arises on conflicts or denial of certain actions.

4 SECMAP Secure Communication Framework

SECMAP agents communicate via messages. SMAS supports asynchronous message exchange primitives through methods of *AgentInterface*. Agent communication is secured by transferring encrypted message content through SSL. Agents are provided with a flexible communication environment where they can question the results of send message requests, wait for responses for a specified period of time, and receive messages or replies when it is convenient for them. Figure 2 shows the communication framework and how a request to send a message proceeds. During agent creation, SMAS, while instantiating a shield object for the

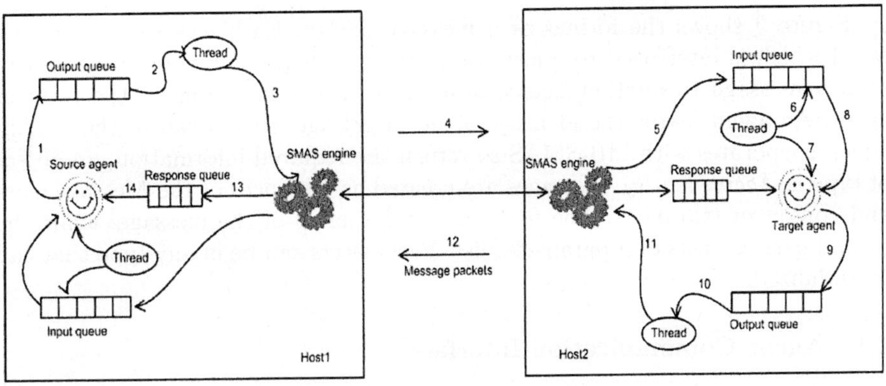

Fig. 2. SECMAP Communication Framework

agent, also creates three queues: one for outgoing messages, one for incoming messages and one for reply messages. The input and output queues are monitored by two threads which are spawned on agent activation. The thread monitoring the input queue alerts the agent if a message arrives, while the thread monitoring the output queue alerts the SMAS engine to route messages to their destination.

When an agent issues a send message call through the *AgentInterface*, the message is placed into the output queue by the agent shield and the call returns. From then on, the agent may continue with its operations. It may question the result of the send request, or, if it expects a response, it may retrieve the reply message at any point suitable in its execution path. The thread monitoring the output queue alerts the SMAS engine to route the message. After the SMAS on the recipient host places the message into the input queue of the target agent, the input queue thread alerts the agent of the arrival of a new message via a call to its *OnMessageArrive()* method,using Java Reflection feature. Subsequent to being alerted, the receiver agent can issue a call to receive the message at any time. Reply messages are also routed as regular messages are. The only difference is that the SMAS engine sending the reply sets the acknowledgement field at the end of the message packet object to true so that the message can be placed in the reply queue of the agent to which the call returns a result. The reply can be retrieved at any time.

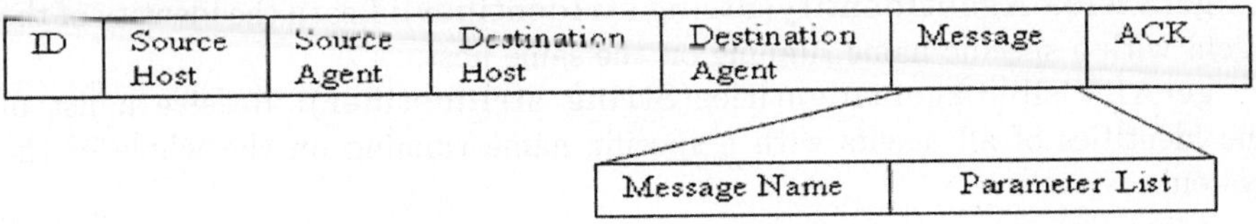

Fig. 3. Message Packet

Figure 3 shows the format of a message packet. Each message is assigned an id which is later used to query the result of a request. Before an agent can send a message to another agent, it needs to learn the name of the receiver agent. An agent learns the identity of the target agent via a call to the SMAS, which cooperates with MB-SMAS to return the required information, an object of type is *AgentIdentity*. Messages are created as instances of the Message class and consist of two parts. The first part is the name of the message, while the second part consists of a parameter list. Parameters can be of any type that can be serialized.

4.1 Agent Communication Interface

SECMAP provides communication security transparently at a lower level and agents are not aware of it. An agent is only allowed to communicate with its environment over the SMAS engine through the methods defined in a predefined interface object, AgentInterface. The methods of AgentInterface related to agent communication are listed below.

sendMessage(String strAgentHostName, AgentIdentity agentidentity, Message message): Send a message to an agent whose identity is known. The call returns the identifier of the message packet, which the agent can later use to query the result of the send operation.

sendBroadcastMessage(Message message): Send a broadcast message to all agents running on the same host. **receive() :** Read and then remove a message packet from the input queue.

sendReply(Packet packet, Object reply): Send the reply of a message which has been received before.

Sent(PIdentifier id): Returns true if a message send request has been carried out successfully, that is the message has been placed into the input queue of the receiver.

ReplyReady(PIdentifier id): Query to learn if the reply of the message has arrived. An agent may not always expect a reply. As communication is asynchronous, in case a reply is expected, the agent queries its arrival at a time convenient for it.

waitForMessage(long ms): Make a blocking call to listen on the input message queue for a specifed period of time.

waitForReply(PIdentifier id, long ms): Make a blocking call to listen on the reply message queue for a specifed period of time and returns true if the reply is ready. If issued right after a send, it leads to synchronous messaging.

getVisibleAgentIdentity(String strIdentifier): Learn the identity of the agent with a specific name running on the same host.

getAllVisibleAgentIdentities(String strIdentifier): Receive a list of the identities of all agents with a specific name running on the whole of the system.

Below are the code fragments of two agents. One of the agents has announced itself with the name *"calculator"* and, on receiving a message with the name *"cal-*

culate" and a parameter list in the form of an arithmetic expression, computes the result and sends it as the reply message. The second agent, a client, wishes to have the result of an arithmetic expression to be computed. In its *OnActivate* method, it constructs a request message, inquires if any *"calculator"* agents are currently active on the system and, if it receives identities of "calculator" agents, scans the list to send its request until a result is obtained.

"calculator" agent:

```
public void OnMessageArrive(){
Packet packet =getAgentInterface().receive();
Message message=(Message)packet.getObject();
if (message.getMessageName().equals("Calculate")) {
Object[]parameters = message.getParameters();
String par1 =(String)parameters[0];
Calc calculator = new Calc(); String result = "";
try\\
{result = calculator.calculate(par1);}
//details of calculator class not included here.
catch (Exception ex){ }
getAgentInterface().sendReply(packet, result);}}
public void OnActivate(){
getAgentInterface().setVisibleOn("calculator");}
```

"client" agent:

```
Enumeration calcagentlist=
agentinterface.getAllVisibleAgentIdentities ("calculator");
//acquire identities of all agents on the system
//who have announced themselves with the name "calculator"
while (calcagentlist.hasMoreElements()){
AgentIdentity agentidentity = (AgentIdentity)
                              calcagentlist.nextElement();
Message message = new Message
                    ("Calculate",CalculateInput.getText());
PIdentifier id = agentinterface.sendMessage
  (agentidentity.getAgentHostName(),agentidentity,message);
if (!agentinterface.waitForReply(id,5000))
   System.out.Println("Timed out.."+"\n");
else{ String result = (String) agentinterface.getReply(id);
System.out.println(CalculateInput.getText()+" = "+result+"\n");
break();}}
```

4.2 Location Transparence

The system is managed with a decentralized control; several MB-SMAS and SM-SMAS may currently be active and they cooperate for a smooth execution.

They share their data and communicate messages to keep it coherent. When initializing an S-SMAS on a node, the programmer specifies the addresses of the MB-SMAS and the SM-SMAS it should register itself to. Next, S-SMAS sends its agent list to MB-SMAS and, in return, receives the identities of all other agents active on the system. All MB-SMAS and SM-SMAS in the system share their data. We call those S-SMAS that a MB-SMAS or a SM-SMAS cooperates with as its partners. When a MB-SMAS gets a request to return an agent identity, it cooperates with its partners to obtain the current agent identities. A similar mode of processing is true for SM-SMAS. If an SM-SMAS can not authenticate a request, it directs it to its partners for possible authentication. Additionally, when an S-SMAS communicates with its MB-SMAS and SM-SMAS, it obtains the addresses of their partners and saves them, in order to use as a contact address in case its communication to its MB-SMAS or SM-SMAS fails. This approach adds robustness against network or node failures. Figure 4 shows MB-SMAS integration to allow location transparent agent messaging.

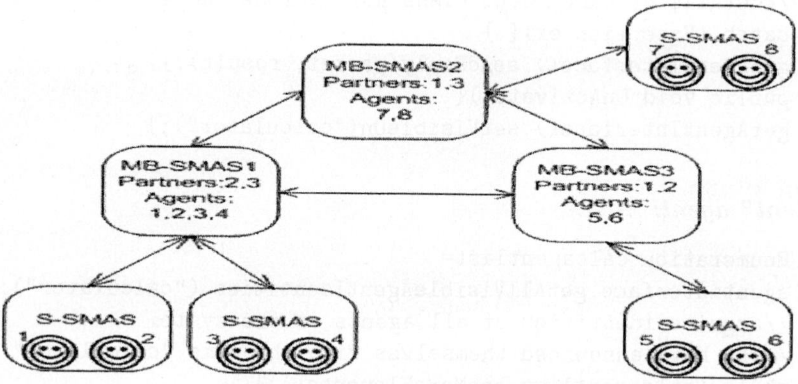

Fig. 4. MB-SMAS integration

5 Related Work

Several mobile agent systems have been proposed and developed up to now. They all have their software agent specific features. These agent systems allow agents to communicate with each other and some have better and more flexible features over the others. SECMAP has the advantage of having a scalable, secure and location transparent messaging architecture. SSL provides message privacy while origion of the message are provided to be safe by authenticating SMAS servers installed on each agent server on the network. Using queues and managing agent queues with agent shields also provides a scalable messaging architecture. Alerting the agent when a message arrives for the agent gives the programmer to write the agent code in an easier way.

6 Conclusions and Future Work

This paper describes the secure communication infrastructure of SECMAP. Mobile agents are provided with a flexible and secure communication environment where they can benefit both synchronous and asynchronous messaging facilities. Confidentiality, integrity, authentication of origin and non-repudiation of messages are assured through security techniques. SMAS are authenticated by several SM-SMAS through certificates, thus introducing trusted nodes to which mobile agents can migrate when required, or send sensitive information. Location tranparency is provided by integrating more than one MB-SMAS into the system, which, at the same time, adds to the robustness of the system. SECMAP keeps logs of all agent activity, such as creation, activation, migration, and message exchange, which can later be used for execution tracing, either for debugging purposes or analysing agent behaviour. Currently, the system does not possess a message buffering feature. Our future work includes adding such a feature into the system so that while an agent is in transit from one host to another, all messages sent to the agent can be kept in the system and the agent be alerted immediately when it is activated on the destination host. Additionally, remote broadcasting support is another feature we plan to add into the system. At its present state, SECMAP supports local broadcasting, that is, a message can only be broadcast to all agents running on the same host as the sender.

References

1. Voyager, http://www.recursionsw.com/products/voyager/voyager.asp
2. Aglets, http://www.trl.ibm.com/aglets/
3. http://www.genmagic.com/technology/odyssey.html
4. JATLite, http://www-cdr.stanford.edu/ProcessLink/papers/JATL.html
5. http://www.cs.dartmouth.edu/ dfk/papers/gray:security-book.ps.gz
6. Bryce C., Vitek J.: The JavaSeal Mobile Agent Kernel, Autonomous Agents and Multi-Agent Systems, 4, 359-384, (2001)
7. Concordia, http://www.merl.com/projects/concordia
8. Sander T., Tschudin C.: Protecting Mobile Agents Against Malicious Hosts, in: Giovanni Vigna (Ed.), Mobile Agent Security, LNCS 1419, (1998), Springer, 44–60
9. Varadharan V., Foster D.: A Security Architecture for Mobile Agent Based Applications, World Wide Web:Internet and Web Information System, 6, (2003), 93–122
10. Borselius N.: Mobile Agent Security, Electronics & Communication Engineering Journal, October (2002), Volume 14, no 5, IEE, London, UK, 211

A Novel Algorithm for the Coordination of Multiple Mobile Robots

Nusrettin Gulec and Mustafa Unel

Sabanci University, Faculty of Engineering and Natural Sciences,
Orhanli-Tuzla, 34956 Istanbul, Turkey
nusrettin@su.sabanciuniv.edu, munel@sabanciuniv.edu

Abstract. The coordinated motion of a group of autonomous mobile robots performing a coordinated task has been of high interest in the last decade. Previous research has shown that one of the main problems in the area is to avoid collisions of the robots with obstacles and other members of the group. In this work, we develop a novel coordination scheme along with a new online collision avoidance algorithm. In the proposed algorithm, reference trajectories for a group of autonomous mobile robots are generated in terms of linear and angular velocities of the robots. Several coordinated tasks have been presented and the results are verified by simulations.

1 Introduction

The interest in modeling groups of autonomous mobile robots engaged in coordinated behavior has been growing recently [1] - [10]. Most of the previous research is devoted to define coordinated behavior on the basis of mutual forces among the members of the group [2]. In 1995, Vicsek proposed the simple "neighbors" method [4]. In [5], coordination among the group is achieved by the effect on each member of the group due to its closest neighbors. Yamaguchi defined "formation vectors" for coordination and repulsive forces for collision avoidance to achieve coordinated motion for mobile robot troops [7].

For holonomic (omnidirectional) mobile robots, the definition of appropriate forces might be sufficient to achieve coordination. Since these robots can move in any direction, the problem of achieving coordination is reduced to solving the dynamics of masses according to Newtonian mechanics under the effect of conveniently defined forces. However, for nonholonomic robots; such as unicycle robots or car-like vehicles, the generated reference trajectories should satisfy the nonholonomic constraint (no side way motion). Generating reference trajectories for the robots using a "*virtual reference robot*" that satisfies the nonholonomic constraint guarantees the generation of nonholonomic reference trajectories [11]. Modeling coordinated behavior of a group of autonomous nonholonomic mobile robots has become an active research area in recent years [12] - [13]. Yamaguchi used "formation vectors" that take care of the nonholonomic constraint to define coordination [14].

P. Yolum et al.(Eds.): ISCIS 2005, LNCS 3733, pp. 422–431, 2005.

There has also been a growing interest in decentralized systems in the last decade [18] - [21]. Achievement of a goal by multiple autonomous mobile robots in coordination is an example of a decentralized system. Failure of a single member in centralized systems results in system failure, whereas in decentralized systems the remaining members can still achieve the goal even if some members of the group fail. Economic cost of a decentralized system is usually lower than a centralized system that could carry out the same task [20]. A huge single robot, no matter how powerful it is, is spatially limited while smaller robots could achieve a given goal more efficiently. Flocking birds, schooling fish and bees building a honeycomb in the beehive are examples of decentralized natural groupings, where each member works in coordination with the others. Decentralized systems outclass centralized systems where the task is exploration of an area for some task such as a search and rescue action [21].

Manipulation of a given coordinated task by a group of autonomous mobile robots requires certain formations. Moreover, the necessary formation may vary based on the definition of the coordinated task [22]. It could be better to carry a heavy rectangular object by multiple robots in a rectangular formation, while a circular formation of the robots might be better for capturing and enclosing an invader to provide security in surveillance areas.

2 Problem Formulation

We consider a group of n mobile robots, namely $R_1, R_2, \ldots, R_{n-1}, R_n$, and an object, T, that will serve as a target for the group on the same plane. In the sequel, R_i denotes the ith robot in the group.

By coordination among a group of robots, we mean the group's achievement of a given coordinated task in certain formations. In this work, we consider a coordinated task scenario as follows:

- $R_1, R_2, \ldots, R_{n-1}, R_n$ should form a circle of radius d_{target} with T at the center.
- The robots should be uniformly distributed on the final formation circle.
- Each R_i should orient itself towards T once it maintains a certain distance d_{near} from its closest neighbors and d_{target} from T.

Aforementioned scenario is a general one that would be the basis for a sequence of coordinated tasks. In other words, we can think of complicated coordinated tasks in terms of simple coordinated tasks. The above scenario might serve as the first phase in other complicated coordinated tasks. Manipulation of a heavy object, T, by a mobile robot group could be one example. Once they achieve the desired formation described above, they can grasp and move the object in a coordinated manner. Another example could be enclosing and catching a prisoner, T, in a surveillance area by decreasing the distances d_{target} and d_{near} after the desired formation has been achieved. Depending on the nature of the coordinated task, R_i might need to check if all other robots have accomplished the task in the current phase before it goes on with the task of the next phase.

During each phase of the coordinated motion, autonomous robots must avoid collisions with other members of the group and any possible static obstacles. Collision is one of the most essential problems in the context of coordinated motion [23]. In this scenario, we assume there are no static obstacles, except T itself.

In this work, we assume a stationary target, T, the position of which is known by all robots before coordinated motion is initiated. We are also assuming that each robot, R_i, perceives its environment by some sensor. Visual sensing by cameras or ultrasonic sensing are most common examples in the literature.

3 Computing Desired Velocities

Coordination between a group of wheeled mobile robots is usually defined on the basis of forces. In this approach, the desired linear and angular velocities are derived from the desired position and orientation obtained by solving the dynamic equations of the system. The desired kinematics of a "*virtual reference robot*" [11] so obtained is given as a reference to the actual robot. This approach fails to take the nonholonomic constraint into consideration when generating the reference pose. The actual robot might not be able to follow the virtual reference robot if abrupt changes in the reference position and orientation occur.

In this work, we are defining coordination among the group by proper selection of the linear and angular velocities of the virtual reference robot. This approach automatically satisfies the nonholonomic constraint. Hence, the regulation of the errors between the virtual reference robot's pose and the actual robot's pose to zero are guaranteed with an appropriate feedback controller [11]. Once the desired velocities that will yield coordinated motion are obtained, they are integrated to get the desired positions and orientations of the robots.

3.1 Coordination and Target Velocities

We consider a biologically inspired coordination algorithm where R_i is in coordination only with its closest two neighbors. The second closest neighbor loses effect on the desired velocity of R_i when the distance between R_i and T falls below a predefined value, d_{relax}.

Coordination is defined by mutual distances between the robots. In other words, R_i should maintain a certain distance d_{coord} from its closest neighbors. The desired velocity vector of R_i due to coordination, $\mathbf{v}_{coord}$, that forces a distance of d_{coord} between R_i and its neighbors is given as follows:

$$\mathbf{v}_{coord} = k_{lin}(d_{i2cl1} - d_{coord})\mathbf{n}_{i2cl1} + \left\{ \begin{array}{ll} k_{lin}(d_{i2cl2} - d_{coord})\mathbf{n}_{i2cl2}, & d_{i2T} \geq d_{relax} \\ 0, & d_{i2T} < d_{relax} \end{array} \right\}, \tag{1}$$

where k_{lin} is a proportionality constant, d_{i2cl1} and d_{i2cl2} are the distances between R_i and its closest and second closes neighbors respectively, $\mathbf{n}_{i2cl1}$ and $\mathbf{n}_{i2cl2}$ are the unit vectors from R_i to its closest neighbors, d_{coord} is the specified coordination distance to be maintained between the robots, d_{relax} is the critical distance of R_i to T below which it loses contact with its second closest neighbor, and d_{i2T} is the distance between R_i and T.

Similarly, a desired velocity vector due to T is defined, for each robot R_i to move it towards T until it maintains the given distance d_{target} between itself and T, as:

$$\mathbf{v}_{target} = k_{lin}(d_{i2T} - d_{target})\mathbf{n}_{i2T} , \quad (2)$$

where d_{i2T} is the distance between R_i and T, $\mathbf{n}_{i2T}$ is the unit vector from R_i to T.

The desired velocity vector of R_i, namely $\mathbf{v}_{des}$ is formed by taking a linear combination of the velocities $\mathbf{v}_{coord}$ and $\mathbf{v}_{target}$ by appropriate coefficients as follows:

$$\mathbf{v}_{des} = k_{target}\mathbf{v}_{target} + k_{coord}\mathbf{v}_{coord} , \quad (3)$$

where k_{target} is the coefficient of the velocity due to T and k_{coord} is the coefficient of the velocity due to the closest neighbors of R_i. These coefficients define the effect of the neighbors and T on the generated reference velocity of R_i.

The desired position and orientation of R_i is then obtained by integration of the computed desired velocity.

Successful manipulation of coordinated tasks by certain formations might require changes in the above parameters. In our scenario, we split the coordinated task into two main phases:

- (A) Approaching T starting from an initial setting.
- (B) Achieving a circular formation with radius d_{target} with T at the center to which all robots head towards.

3.2 Switching Parameters Around Target

In phase (A), the priority is given to coordination. In other words, $\mathbf{v}_{coord}$ is dominant in this case so the robots move together. However, $\mathbf{v}_{target}$ still contributes to the desired velocity so all robots approach T. To achieve the dominance of $\mathbf{v}_{coord}$ on $\mathbf{v}_{des}$, we choose $k_{coord} > k_{target}$ in (3). In this phase, d_{coord} in (1) is set to the initially defined value d_{far} while k_{coord} is set to the predefined value k_{far}. R_i is in this phase as long as $d_{i2T} \geq d_{relax}$; i.e. R_i is far from T.

If d_{i2T} gets lower than d_{relax}, R_i enters phase (B). In this phase, the priority is given to maintaining the distance d_{target} from T. Hence, $\mathbf{v}_{target}$ is dominant. To achieve this, we set $k_{target} > k_{coord}$ in (3). In this phase, k_{coord} is set to the predefined value k_{near}. To achieve a uniform distribution on the formation circle, d_{coord} in (1) should also be changed to a new value, d_{near}, possibly different from the initial coordination distance, d_{far}. It follows from *Law of Cosines* that for a uniform distribution of n robots on a circle with radius d_{target}, d_{near} is given as follows:

$$d_{near} = d_{target}\sqrt{2(1 - cos(2\pi/n))} . \quad (4)$$

When R_i maintains distance d_{target} from T and d_{near} from its closest neighbor, the last maneuver it does is to orient itself towards T, hence complete phase (B).

The last parameter that affects desired velocities is k_{target} in (3) which defines the dependency of $\mathbf{v}_{des}$ on $\mathbf{v}_{target}$. For dominance in both phases to be significant, we also switch k_{target}.

k_{coord} and k_{target} are switched as continuous sigmoid functions of d_{i2T}, namely:

$$k_{coord} = k_{near} + \frac{k_{far} - k_{near}}{1 + exp(\mu(d_{relax} - d_{i2T} + \phi))}, \qquad k_{target} = 1 - k_{coord} \,, \quad (5)$$

where $\mu > 0$ and $\phi > 0$ are constants and $0 \leq k_{coord} \leq 1$. The continuous switchings of k_{coord} and k_{target} are depicted in Fig. 1.

Similarly, d_{coord} is defined as k_{coord} in (5), with k_{near} and k_{far} replaced by d_{near} and d_{far}, respectively.

3.3 Velocity Update to Avoid Collisions

Collision avoidance is the last factor contributing to the generation of the desired velocities for the robots. In this paper, we are not considering either any static obstacles or T as an obstacle because $\mathbf{v}_{target}$ is dominant in phase (B) and it keeps the robot at distance d_{target} from T.

Our algorithm uses sensory information coming from robots to predict collisions ahead of time. For each R_i, we define a *virtual collision prediction region(VCPR)*, Ω_i, given by a circular arc of radius r_{coll} and angle θ_{coll}, symmetric with respect to its velocity as depicted in Fig. 2(a).

Since R_j hits the virtual arc, Ω_i, R_i predicts a collision in Fig. 2(b). In this case, disregarding $\mathbf{v}_{des}$ given by 3, the orientation of R_i is changed according to the relative velocity of R_j with respect to R_i. The easiest way of avoiding the predicted collision in this case is to change the orientation of R_i in counter-clockwise direction until R_j loses contact with Ω_i. This would be useful if R_j were stationary. However, since R_j is moving to the left, it will be hitting Ω_i again just after the predicted collision is avoided. To avoid this occurrence, the orientation of R_i is changed in clockwise direction, taking the relative velocity of

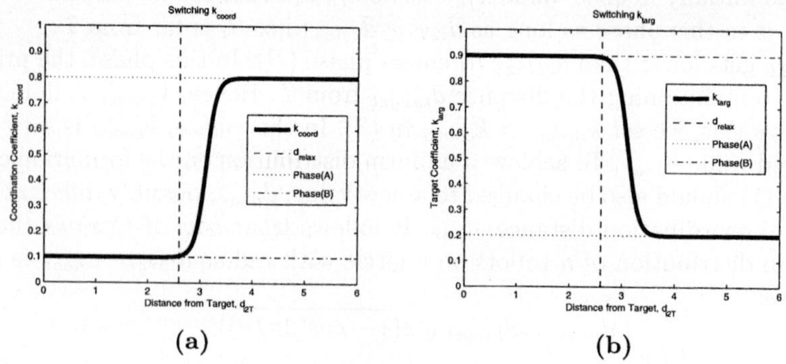

Fig. 1. Continuous switching of coefficients (a)Coordination coefficient vs distance from T (b)Target coefficient vs distance from T

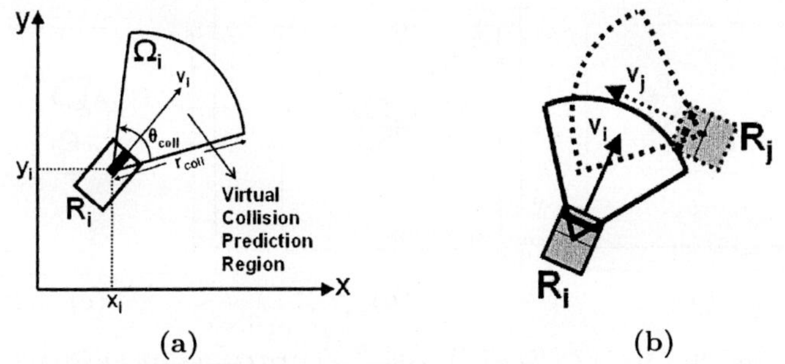

Fig. 2. (a) *VCPR*, Ω_i, for the robot, R_i (b) R_i predicts a collision with R_j

R_j with respect to R_i into account. The orientation of R_j is not changed since R_j doesn't predict a collision at the given instant.

4 Simulation Results

Simulations and animations were carried out for the verification of both the collision avoidance and the coordination algorithms. In the simulations, maximum linear speed of the robots was set to $1.0m/sec$ and maximum rotational speed was set to $(\pi/3)rad/sec$. The parameters for Ω_i of each R_i were set to be $r_{coll} = 0.9m$ and $\theta_{coll} = (\pi/2)rad$.

4.1 Collision Avoidance Simulations

The simulations were run with $\mathbf{v}_{coord} = \mathbf{v}_{target} = 0$ to see the performance of the collision avoidance algorithm. In both scenarios, the robots start moving with constant and equal initial speeds and different initial orientations.

In the first scenario, two robots are moving towards each other as seen in Fig. $3(a)$. As they approach each other and each robot touches the *VCPR* of the other, they both predict a collision. The snapshot of this moment is given in Fig. $3(b)$. Since they both carry out collision prediction, they both change their orientations and the final situation is depicted in Fig. $3(c)$. The result proves the success of the algorithm for head-to-head collisions.

In the second scenario, three robots are headed towards each other as given in Fig. $4(a)$. At the moment shown in Fig. $4(b)$, B predicts collisions with both of the other robots. On the other hand, the others predict collision with one of its neighbors. In each mutual pair, only the velocity of the robot that predicts the collision is updated. It was observed that they manage to avoid collisions and the resulting situation is given in Fig. $4(c)$.

4.2 Coordinated Motion Simulations

The novel coordinated motion algorithm and the coordinated task explained throughout the paper was simulated for groups of three, four and five robots. The following values were used in simulations: $k_{lin} = 0.5$, $d_{relax} = 1.3d_{target}$ in (1); $k_{far} = 0.8$, $k_{near} = 0.1$, $\mu = 10$ and $\phi = 0.5$ in (5).

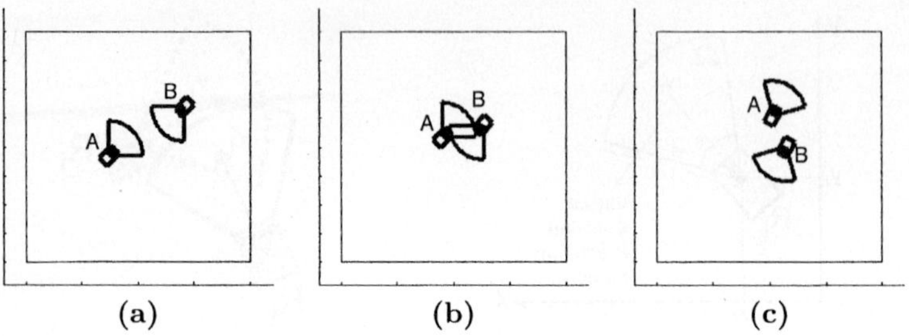

Fig. 3. Head-to-Head Collision Avoidance (a)Before (b)Prediction (c)After

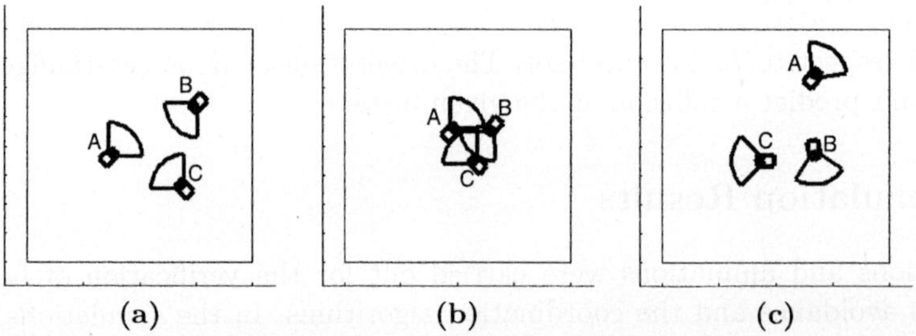

Fig. 4. Three Robots Simultaneous Collision Prediction (a)Before (b)Prediction (c)After

Three Robots. In the initial setting, the robots are placed on one corner of the room while T is at the opposite corner. It was observed that they approach each other and form an equilateral triangle with sides d_{far}. Once they are close enough to T, to achieve mutual distances of d_{near}, and they spread around on the circle since they should stay on the circle due to $\mathbf{v}_{target}$. Finally, the group achieves the desired formation. Snapshots from this animation are given in Fig. 5.

This result proves that the algorithm suffices to define coordinated motion and coordinated task manipulation for a group of three autonomous robots.

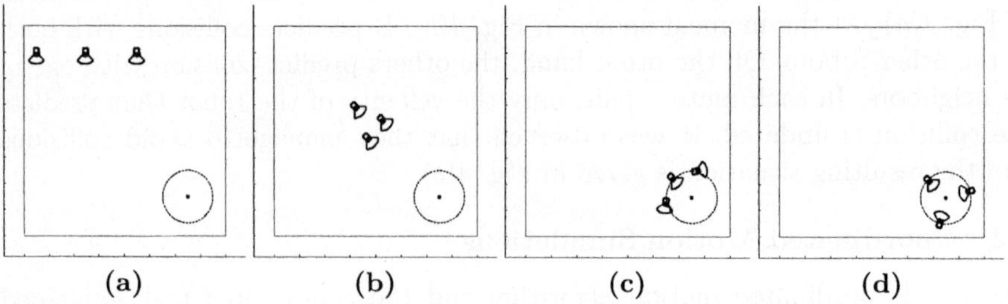

Fig. 5. 3 Robots (a)Initial Situation (b)Coordinated Motion (c)Distribution on the circle (d)Final Situation

Four Robots. The case with four robots has the initial setting as depicted in Fig. 6(a). Since coordination is dominant in phase (A), the robots approach each other, instead of going directly towards T, and form a square with sides d_{far} as shown in Fig. 6(b). The result is a circular formation with the robots on the corners of a square of sides d_{near} as depicted in Fig. 6(d).

These simulation results prove the validity of the proposed coordination algorithm for a group of four mobile robots.

Five Robots. The given scenario with five robots is shown in Fig. 7(a). They take the form of a pentagon while going to T as seen in Fig. 7(b). As there are more robots, the risk of collisions around T increases. As depicted in Fig. 7(c), some collisions were predicted around the formation circle, but they were successfully avoided and the final formation is satisfactory as shown in Fig. 7(d).

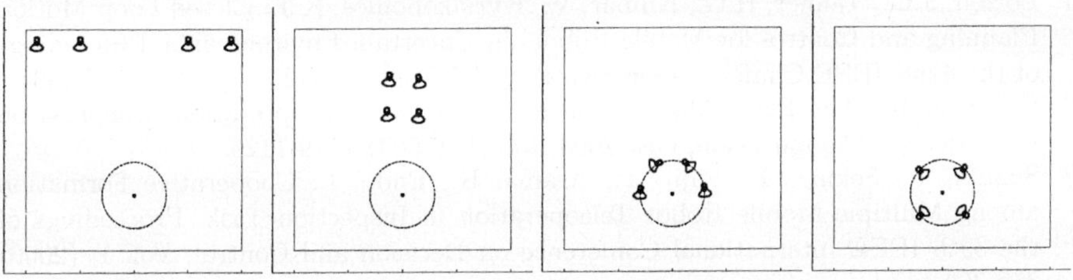

(a) (b) (c) (d)

Fig. 6. 4 Robots (a)Initial Situation (b)Coordination Achieved (c)Distribution on the circle (d)Final Situation

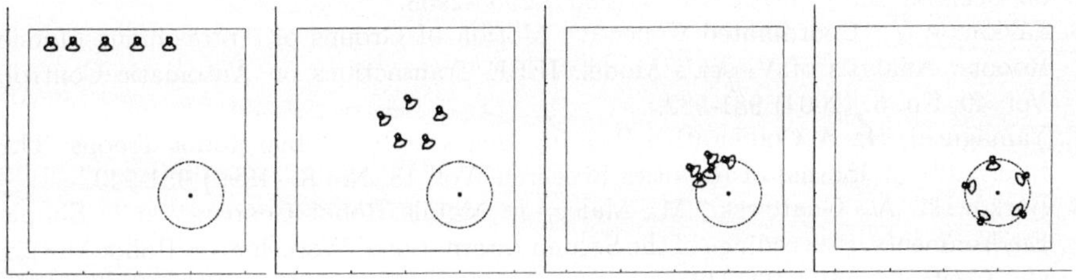

(a) (b) (c) (d)

Fig. 7. 5 Robots (a)Initial Situation (b)Coordination Achieved (c)Collisions Predicted (d)Final Situation

5 Conclusions

In this paper, we have developed a decentralized coordination algorithm for a group of wheeled mobile robots by introducing a virtual reference robot, the linear and angular velocities of which are designed to achieve coordinated motion.

Possible collisions are predicted by virtual collision prediction regions and the reference velocities are updated when a collision risk is detected.

Simulation results are promising. Both collision avoidance and coordinated motion algorithms for groups of 3, 4 and 5 robots are successful in achieving coordinated motion and coordinated task manipulation. Since the proposed algorithm is modular, the success of the system would not be affected by increasing the number of robots.

We are working on the physical implementation of the proposed coordination scheme with two-wheeled mobile robots equipped with vision sensors. We are also considering to employ visual sensing to develop a knowledge-based scheme for detecting mobile targets.

References

1. Loizou, S.G., Tanner, H.G., Kumar, V., Kyriakopoulos, K.J.: Closed Loop Motion Planning and Control for Mobile Robots in Uncertain Environments. Proceedings of the 42nd IEEE Conference on Decision and Control, Vol. 3. (2003) 2926-2931.
2. Salomon, R.: The Force Model: Concept, Behavior, Interpretation. Congress on Evolutionary Computation, CEC2004, Vol. 1. (2004) 1119-1126.
3. Suzuki, T., Sekine, T., Fujii, T., Asama, H., Endo, I.: Cooperative Formation among Multiple Mobile Robot Teleoperation in Inspection Task. Proceedings of the 39th IEEE International Conference on Decision and Control, Vol. 1. (2000) 358-363.
4. Vicsek, T., Czirk, A., Ben-Jacob, E., Cohen, I., Shochet, O.: Novel Type of Phase Transition in a System of Self-Driven Particles. Phys. Rev. Lett., Vol. 75, No. 6. (1995) 1226-1229.
5. Jadbabaie, A., Lin, J., Morse, A.S.: Coordination of Groups of Mobile Autonomous Agents Using Nearest Neighbor Rules. Proceedings of the 41st IEEE Conference on Decision and Control, Vol. 3. (2002) 2953-2958.
6. Savkin, A.V.: Coordinated Collective Motion of Groups of Autonomous Mobile Robots: Analysis of Vicsek's Model. IEEE Transactions on Automatic Control, Vol. 49, No. 6. (2004) 981-982.
7. Yamaguchi, H.: A Cooperative Hunting Behavior by Mobile-Robot Troops. The International Journal of Robotics Research, Vol. 18, No: 8. (1999) 931-940.
8. Borkowski, A., Gnatowski, M., Malec, J.: Mobile Robot Cooperation in Simple Environments. Proceedings of the Second International Workshop on Robot Motion and Control. (2001) 109-114.
9. Gold, T.B., Archibald, J.K., Frost, R.L.: A Utility Approach to Multi-Agent Coordination. Proceedings of the 2000 IEEE International Conference on Robotics and Automation, ICRA '00, Vol. 3. (2000) 2052-2057.
10. Weigel, T., Gutmann, J.S., Dietl, M., Kleiner, A., Nebel, B.: CS Freiburg: Coordinating Robots for Successful Soccer Playing. IEEE Transactions on Robotics and Automation, Vol. 18, No. 5. (2002) 685-699.
11. Samson, C.: Trajectory tracking for non-holonomic vehicles: overview and case study. Proceedings of the Fourth International Workshop on Robot Motion and Control, RoMoCo'04. (2004) 139-153.
12. Marques, C., Lima, P.: Avoiding Obstacles - Multisensor Navigation for Nonholonomic Robots in Cluttered Environments. IEEE Robotics and Automation Magazine, Vol. 11, No. 3. (2004) 70-82.

13. Shen, J., Schneider, D.A., Bloch, A.M.: Controllability and Motion Planning of Multibody Systems with Nonholonomic Constraints. Proceedings of the 42nd IEEE Conference on Decision and Control, Vol. 5. (2003) 4369-4374.
14. Yamaguchi, H.: A Cooperative Hunting Behavior by Multiple Nonholonomic Mobile Robots. 1998 IEEE International Conference on Systems, Man, and Cybernetics, Vol. 4. (1998) 3347-3352.
15. de Sousa, J.B., Pereira, F.L.: Specification and design of coordinated motions for autonomous vehicles. Proceedings of the 41st IEEE Conference on Decision and Control, Vol. 1. (2002) 101-106.
16. Seiler, P., Pant, A., Hedrick, K.: Analysis of Bird Formations. Proceedings of the 41st IEEE Conference on Decision and Control, Vol. 1. (2002) 118-123.
17. Souissi, S., Defago, X., Katayama, T.: Decomposition of Fundamental Problems for Cooperative Autonomous Mobile Systems. Proceedings of the 24th International Conference on Distributed Computing Systems. (2004) 554-560.
18. Sweeney, J.D., Li, H., Grupen, R.A., Ramamritham, K.: Scalability and Schedulability in Large, Coordinated, Distributed Robot Systems. Proceedings of the 2003 International Conference on Robotics and Automation, ICRA '03, Vol. 3. (2003) 4074-4079.
19. Baras, J.S., Tan, X., Hovareshti, P.: Decentralized Control of Autonomous Vehicles. Proceedings of the 42nd IEEE Conference on Decision and Control, Vol. 2. (2003) 1532-1537.
20. Spletzer, J., Das, A.K., Fierro, R., Taylor, C.J., Kumar, V., Ostrowski, J.P.: Cooperative Localization and Control for Multi-Robot Manipulation. Proceedings of the 2001 IEEE/RSJ International Conference on Intelligent Robots and Systems, Vol. 2. (2001) 631-636.
21. Sheng, W., Yang, Q., Tan, J., Xi, N.: Risk and Efficiency: A Distributed Bidding Algorithm for Multi-robot Coordination. Proceedings of the Fifth World Congress on Intelligent Control and Automation, WCICA 2004, Vol. 5. (2004) 4671-4675.
22. Hur, Y., Fierro, R., Lee, I.: Modeling Distributed Autonomous Robots using CHARON: Formation Control Case Study. Sixth IEEE International Symposium on Object-Oriented Real-Time Distributed Computing, ISORC '03. (2003) 93-96.
23. Rabie, T., Shalaby, A., Abdulhai, B., El-Rabbany, A.: Mobile Vision-based Vehicle Tracking and Traffic Control. Proceedings of the Fifth IEEE International Conference on Intelligent Transportation Systems. (2002) 13-18.

Multiagent Elite Search Strategy for Combinatorial Optimization Problems

SeungGwan Lee

School of Computer Science and Information Engineering, Catholic University,
43-1, Yeokgok 2-Dong, Wonmi-Gu, Bucheon-Si, Gyeonggi-Do 420-743, Korea
leesg@catholic.ac.kr

Abstract. Ant Colony System is a new meta heuristics algorithms to solve hard combinatorial optimization problems. It is a population based approach that uses exploitation of positive feedback as well as greedy search. In this paper, we propose a multi colony interaction ant model that achieves positive·negative interaction through an elite strategy divided by intensification strategy and diversification strategy to improve the performance of original ACS. Positive interaction makes agents belonging to other colony to select the high frequency of the visit of edge, and negative interaction makes to escape the selection of relevant edge. And, we compares with original ACS method for the performance. This multi colony interaction ant model can be applied effectively in occasion that problem regions are big and complex, parallel processing is available, and can improve the performance ACS model.

1 Introduction

In this paper, we introduce about Ant Colony System(ACS) that is meta heuristics method to solve optimal solution through an local updating and global updating method that is first proposed by Colorni, Dorigo and Maniezzo to solve Traveling Salesman Problems(TSP) [1], [2]. And, we suggest a multi colony ant model that achieve interaction between the colonies to improve the performance of ACS, through an intensification and diversification strategy. This is method that ACS colonies which are consists of some agent colonies solve TSP through an elite strategy.

Proposed a multi colony interaction ant model is consist of several agent colonies which accomplish independent searching process, and each agent colony searches the optimal solution through an elite strategy that is divided by positive interaction by intensification strategy and negative interaction by diversification strategy. Positive interaction makes agents belonging to other colony to select the high frequency of the visit of a edge, and negative interaction makes to escape the selection of relevant edge.

Therefore, in this paper, we apply an elite strategy divided by intensification strategy and diversification strategy between the colonies to TSP, and compares with original ACS method for the performance.

P. Yolum et al.(Eds.): ISCIS 2005, LNCS 3733, pp. 432–441, 2005.

The remainder of the paper is organized as follows. In section2, we introduce previous the multi colony ant algorithms. Section3 describes new a multi colony intensification and diversification strategy by an elite strategy. Section 4 presents experimental results. Finally, Section 5 concludes the paper and describes directions for future work.

2 Ant Algorithms

2.1 Ant Colony System

Ant Colony System(ACS) algorithm has emerged recently as a relatively novel meta-heuristic for hard combinatorial optimization problems. It is designed to simulate the ability of ant colonies to determine shortest path to food [1], [2], [3], [4], [5].

Informally, ACS works as follows: m agents are initially positioned on n nodes chosen according to some initialization rule (e.g., randomly). Each agent builds a tour (i.e., a feasible solution to the TSP) by repeatedly applying a stochastic greedy rule (the state transition rule). While constructing its tour, an agent also modifies the amount of pheromone on the visited edges by applying the local updating rule. Once all agents have terminated their tour, the amount of pheromone on edges is modified again (by applying the global updating rule). In the following we will discuss the state transition rule, the local updating rule, and the global updating rule.

Let k be an agent whose task is to make a tour: visit all the nodes and return to the starting one. Associated to k there is the list $J_k(r)$ of nodes still to be visited, where r is the current node. An agent(k) situated in node(r) moves to node(s) using the follow rule, called pseudo-random proportional action choice rule(or state transition rule):

$$s = \begin{cases} \arg\max_{u \in J_k(r)} \left\{ [\tau(r,u)]^{\delta} \cdot [\eta(r,u)]^{\beta} \right\} & , if\ q \leq q_0\ (exploitation) \\ S & , otherwise\ (exploration) \end{cases} \tag{1}$$

Where, $\tau(r,u)$ is the amount of pheromone trail on the edge between nodes. $\eta(r,u)$ is a heuristic function which is the inverse of the distance between nodes r and u, β is a parameter which weighs the relative importance of pheromone trail agents, q is a value chosen randomly with uniform probability in [0,1], $q_0(0 \leq q_0 \leq 1)$ is a parameter, and S is a random variable selected according to the distribution given by Eq.(2) which gives the probability with which an agent in node r choose the node s to move to.

$$p_k(r,s) = \begin{cases} \frac{[\tau(r,s)] \cdot [\eta(r,s)]^{\beta}}{\sum_{u \in J_k(r)} [\tau(r,u)] \cdot [\eta(r,u)]^{\beta}} & , if\ s \in J_k(r) \\ 0 & , otherwise \end{cases} \tag{2}$$

While building a solution of the TSP, agents visit edges and change their amount of pheromone trail by applying the following local updating rule:

$$\tau(r,s) \leftarrow (1-\rho) \cdot \tau(r,s) + \rho \cdot \Delta\tau(r,s) \tag{3}$$

Where, $\rho(0<\rho<1)$ is the pheromone decay parameter. $\Delta\tau(\mathrm{r,s})=\tau_0=(n * L_{nn})^{-1}$ is the initial pheromone level, where L_{nn} is the tour length produced by the nearest neighbor heuristic and n is the number of nodes.

Global updating is performed after all agents have completed their tours. The pheromone amount is updated by applying the follow global updating rule:

$$\tau(r,s) \leftarrow (1-\alpha)\cdot\tau(r,s) + \alpha\cdot\Delta\tau(r,s)$$
$$where\;\; \Delta\tau(r,s) = \begin{cases} (L_{gb})^{-1} & ,if(r,s) \in global\,best\,tour \\ 0 & ,otherwise \end{cases} \tag{4}$$

$\alpha(0<\alpha<1)$ is the pheromone decay parameter, and L_{gb} is the length of the globally best tour from the beginning of the trail.

2.2 Multi Colony Ant Algorithms

A multi colony ant algorithm is method that solve problem through an ACS between the colonies special interaction which is consists of some agent colonies to solve TSP.

Middendorf et al. [6] proposed a parallelization where an information exchange between several colonies of ants. They investigated four strategies for information exchange differing in the degree of coupling that is enforced between the colonies through this exchange. The four strategies are Exchange of globally best solution, Circular exchange of locally best solutions, Circular exchange of migrants and Circular exchange of locally best solutions plus migrants.

Talbi et al. [7] implemented a parallel ant algorithm for a Quadratic Assignment Problem. They used a fine grained master-worker approach, were every worker holds a single ant that produces one solution. Every worker then sends its solution to the master. The master computes the new pheromone matrix and sends it to the worker.

Jong et al. [8] developed an algorithm called Multiple Ant Colony Systems(MACS) to solve the Busstop Allocation Problem(BAP) consists of a collection of buslines and each busline consists of a sequence of a sequence of busstops. This algorithm is based on the workings of the ACS but is developed in such a way that each busline is represented by a separate ACS. This means that the pheromone levels of each ACS are updated separately.

Kawamura et al. [9] proposed the Multiple Ant Colonies Algorithm, in which several ant colonies interact with one another, thus keeping exploration while intensification is accelerated in each colony level. Moreover, two kinds of pheromone effect, positive and negative pheromone effect, are introduced as the colony level interaction.

3 Multi Colony Intensification and Diversification Strategy by an Elite Strategy

3.1 Multi Colony Interconnection Network Structure

In this paper, we suggest a multi colony agent structure that has several multi agents that accomplish independent searching process by an elite strategy. This structure has been by some independent ACS colonies, and interaction achieves search according to an elite strategy between the colonies.

An elite strategy is divided into intensification strategy and diversification strategy. Intensification strategy enables to select of good path to use heuristic information of other agent colony. This makes to select the high frequency of the visit of an edge by agents through an positive interaction of between the colonies. Diversification strategy makes to escape selection of the high frequency of the visit of an edge by agents achieve negative interaction by search information of other agent colony.

The interconnection network structure by an elite strategy is consisted of multi colony structure in a multi colony interaction ant model. Figure 1.A displays Mesh structure, this can be applied effectively in case of problem area is small(That is, the number of nodes are less than 100). Figure 1.B displays Double Mesh structure, this can be applied effectively in case of problem area is complex and more(That is, the number of nodes are more than 100).

In Queen1 group, positive interaction by intensification strategy achieves between (C1,C5), (C2,C5), (C3,C5), and (C4,C5) colonies and negative interaction by diversification strategy is achieved between other colonies. In Queen2 group, positive interaction achieves between (C6,C10), (C7,C10), (C8,C10), and (C9,C10) colonies and negative interaction is achieved between other colonies. Here, C5 and C10 are center agent colony(Queen Colony) and other colony are ergate colonies. And center colonies(C5, C10) achieve exchange of locally best solution. This means that achieve different duty between each colonies.

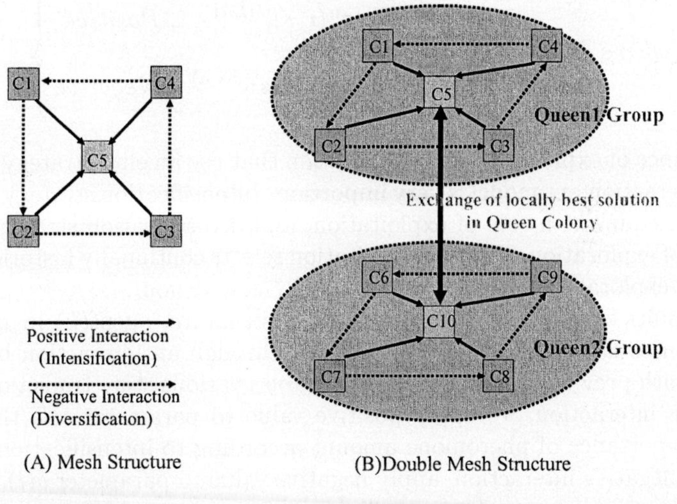

Fig. 1. An elite strategy interaction in a multi colony interconnection network structure (C5 and C10 are queen colony, others are ergate colony. Solid line express positive interaction (Intensification) and dotted line express negative interaction (Diversification)).

3.2 Multi Colony Intensification and Diversification Strategy

All colonies independently achieve search each other in a multi colony interaction ant model. First, examining the action of ergate colonies, agent(k) in colony(l) uses following Eq.(5) to move to node(u) at node(r).

$$s = \begin{cases} \arg \max\limits_{u \in J_k^l(r)} \left\{ \left[\tau^l(r,u)\right]^{\delta(l)} \cdot \left[\eta^l(r,u)\right]^{\beta(l)} \right\}, & if\ q \le q_0 (exploitation) \\ S & , otherwise(exploration) \end{cases} \tag{5}$$

$\tau^l(r,u)$ is the amount of pheromone trail on edge $E(r,u)$ between node(r) and node(u) in colony(l), $\eta^l(r,u)$ is a heuristic function which is the inverse of the distance between node(r) and node(u) in colony(l), $J_k^l(r)$ associated to k there is the list of nodes still to be visited, where r is the current node in colony(l). And $\delta(l)$ and $\beta(l)$ is a parameter which weigh the relative importance of pheromone trail agents. q is a value chosen randomly with uniform probability in [0,1], $q_0(0 \le q_0 \le 1)$ is a parameter, and S is a random variable selected according to the distribution given by Eq.6 which gives the probability with which an agent in node(r) choose the node(s) to move to.

$$p_k^l(r,s) = \begin{cases} \dfrac{\left[\tau^l(r,s)\right]^{\delta(l)} \cdot \left[\eta^l(r,s)\right]^{\beta(l)}}{\sum\limits_{u \in J_k^l(r)} \left[\tau^l(r,u)\right]^{\delta(l)} \cdot \left[\eta^l(r,u)\right]^{\beta(l)}} & , if\ s \in J_k^l(r) \\ 0 & , otherwise \end{cases}$$

$$where\ [\tau^l(r,s)]^{\delta(l)} = \left\{ \begin{matrix} \sum\limits_{n=1}^{M} [\tau^n(r,s)]^{\delta(l,n)} & , Positive \\ \sum\limits_{n=l-1}^{l} [\tau^n(r,s)]^{\delta(l,n)} & , Negative \end{matrix} \right\} \tag{6}$$

Here, balance of exploration and exploitation that use an elite strategy in a multi colony interaction ant model is very important. Intensification strategy in an elite strategy is equal with role of exploitation, and diversification strategy is equal with role of exploration. That is, exploitation selects continually historically good path, and exploration extends path search by new region.

In a multi colony interaction ant model structure, agent(k) in node(r) of colony(l) uses Eq.(6) to select next node(s) through an interaction by an elite strategy with previous colony(*l-1*). This enables various state transition. In case of positive interaction, we apply positive value to parameter $\delta(l)$ that decide relative importance of pheromone amount according to intensification strategy, in case of negative interaction, apply negative value to parameter $\delta(l)$ according to diversification strategy. This enables various searching of new region, and also intensification role for specification edges.

Where M is the total number of colony, $\delta(l,n)$ displays degree of interaction that colony(l) receives from colony(n).

Once, Interaction between the ergate colonies achieves negative interaction by diversification strategy. In case of negative interaction, it is influenced by total of the reciprocal value of negative of the frequency of the visit to relevant edge in previous colony and the reciprocal value of negative of the frequency of the visit to relevant edge on present colony. Through this negative interaction, agents of ergate colonies achieve various searching by new region. And agents of each colonies achieve local updating that use Eq.(7) and global updating that use Eq.(8).

And, Interaction between ergate colonies and center colony achieve positive interaction by intensification strategy. In case of positive interaction, center colony is influenced by the reciprocal value of positive of the frequency of the visit of relevant edge from all ergate colonies. Therefore, agents of center colony select good edge with search result of all ergate colonies, and intensify relevant edge. This differs with that assign foundation of a degree of interaction by fixing value [9], we dynamically allocate using the frequency of the visit.

Also, in Double Mesh structure, interaction between center colony(C5) of Queen1 group and center colony(C10) of Queen2 group select strategy that global updating about excellent solution, compares local best solution of two colonies.

While building a solution of the TSP, agents of each colonies visit edges and change their amount of pheromone trail by applying the following local updating rule:

$$\tau(r,s)^l \leftarrow (1-\rho)\cdot\tau^l(r,s) + \rho\cdot\Delta\tau^l(r,s) \tag{7}$$

Where, $\rho(0<\rho<1)$ is the pheromone decay parameter. $\Delta\tau^l(r,s)=\tau_0=(n*L_{nn})^{-1}$ is the initial pheromone level, where L_{nn} is the tour length produced by the nearest neighbor heuristic and n is the number of nodes.

Global updating is performed after all agents have completed their tours. The pheromone amount is updated by applying the follow global updating rule:

$$\begin{aligned} &\tau^l(r,s) \leftarrow (1-\alpha)\cdot\tau^l(r,s) + \alpha\cdot\Delta\tau^l(r,s) \\ &where\ \ \Delta\tau^l(r,s) = \begin{cases} (L^l_{gb})^{-1} & ,if E(r,s) \in best\,of\,colony\,l \\ 0 & ,otherwise \end{cases} \end{aligned} \tag{8}$$

$\alpha(0<\alpha<1)$ is the pheromone decay parameter, and L^l_{gb} is the length of the globally best tour from the beginning of the trail in colony(l).

4 Experiments and Results

We experimented the proposed a multi colony interaction ant model by using TSPLIB [10] which is a famous TSP example.

The valuc of used parameters were set to the following:. The number of colony M was set to 10, $\beta(l)$=2, $\alpha=\rho$=0.1, q_0=0.9, $\delta(l$,n)=±(1/the frequency of tho visit of a edge) and $\tau_0=(n*L_{nn})^{-1}$. If the number of nodes are less than 100, we use Mesh structure. On the other hand, if the number of nodes are more than 100, we use Double Mesh structure. The number of agent used in each colonies m was set to 10, the initial position of agents assigned one agent in an each node at randomly.

The original ACS and proposed a multi colony interaction ant model in this paper were tested as comparative experiments with the same parameter setting as above setting. The termination condition is that a fixed number of cycles or the value known as the optimum value was found.

Figure 2 is search performance result by size of colony using Eil51 and St70 problem. The Search performance appeared variously according to size of colony in a multi colony interaction ant model. When the number of iterations are 2000, colony number(4,1) was seen excellent performance.

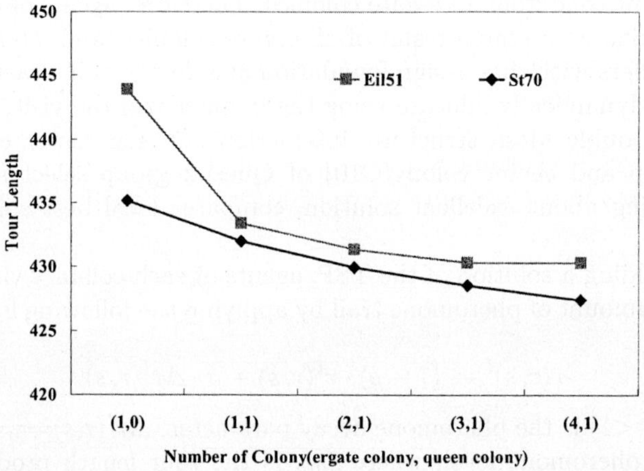

Fig. 2. Experiment result by colony number(using Eil51.tsp and St70.tsp in the TSPLIB)

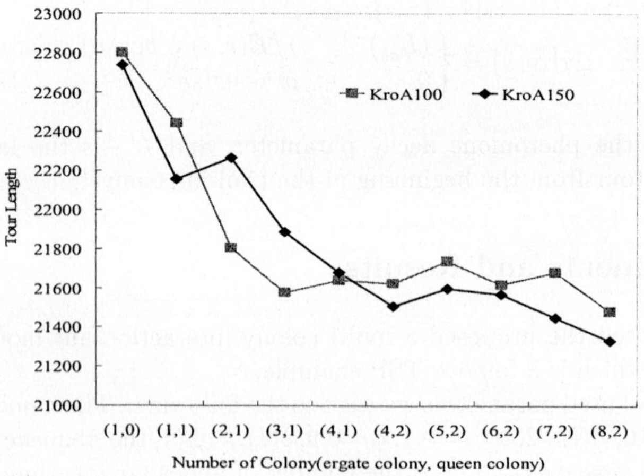

Fig. 3. Experiment result by colony number(using KroA100.tsp and KroA150.tsp in the TSPLIB)

Figure 3 is search performance result by size of colony using KroA100 and KroA150 problem. When the number of iterations are 2000, colony number(8,2) was seen excellent performance. Therefore, colony number decision in a multi colony interaction ant model gave a lot of influences in search performance. Here, so that we express two problems in uniformity graph, KroA100 problem displays original value and KroA150 problem displays 79% value of result.

Table 1 shows the results of the experiments in which original ACS [5], Middendorf et al. [6] and a multi colony interaction ant model were tested as comparative experiments in Mesh structure. In this table, "Best Length" and "Average Length" represent the shortest tour length and the average tour length after 5000 iterations and 10 trials respectively.

Here, Used City Set(1∼5) are node sets that are consisted of 50 random coordinate values, and other sets are node set that select in TSPLIB.

Table 2 shows the results of the experiments in which original ACS [5], Middendorf et al. [6] and a multi colony interaction ant model were tested as comparative experiments in Double Mesh structure after 20000 iterations and 10

Table 1. Multi Colony Interaction Ant Model Performance (Experiment in Mesh structure. ACS by M.Dorigo et al.[5] and Circular exchange of locally best solutions by Middendorf et al.[6]).

Node	ACS[5]		Circular Exch.[6]		Multi Colony	
	Average length	Best length	Average length	Best length	Average length	Best length
City Set1	47.30	45.42	46.95	43.62	46.12	43.02
City Set2	51.88	48.98	50.14	47.48	49.36	46.32
City Set3	45.19	42.17	45.12	41.87	43.61	41.16
City Set4	49.54	48.46	47.52	45.73	47.63	45.73
City Set5	49.20	47.52	47.31	43.48	46.59	43.09
Eil51	431.82	426.31	429.85	426.73	428.45	426.42
St70	684.35	677.14	682.49	676.47	682.12	675.35

Table 2. Multi Colony Interaction Ant Model Performance (Experiment in Double Mesh structure.ACS by M.Dorigo et al.[5] and Circular exchange of locally best solutions by Middendorf et al.[6]).

Node	Optimum	ACS[5]		Circular Exch.[6]		Multi Colony	
		Average length	Best length	Average length	Best length	Average length	Best length
KroA150	26524	28908.8	27824	28115.3	26857	26891.36	26524
Rat195	2323	2571.63	2461	2497.87	2342	2443.61	2338
Gil262	2378	2636.75	2526	2567.08	2459	2459.82	2415
A280	2579	2892.58	2768	2701.46	2678	2632.17	2602
Pr299	48191	53497.8	51395	50101.3	48913	48419.75	48336
Lin318	42029	46244.4	44837	44749.6	43027	43425.31	42963

trials respectively. This result indicates the multi colony interaction ant model by an elite strategy is effective with better qualities against the original ACS.

Usually, the early convergence of original ACS that do not accomplish various searching process is fast. But, because of characteristic to search by edge with good heuristic information as time passes, the convergence of the solution happens since some improvement of solution.

But, the proposed method achieves various searching in ergate colonies and intensification process in center colony converges more faster.

5 Conclusion and Future Work

In this paper, we suggested the multi colony interaction ant model by an elite strategy to improve the performance of original ACS.

The proposed the multi colony interaction ant model is consist of the multi colony agent structure(Mesh structure and Double Mesh structure) that have several agent group which accomplish each other independent searching process, and searches optimal solution through an elite strategy that is divided by positive interaction by intensification strategy and negative interaction by diversification strategy between the colonies. This is method that agent colony exchanges heuristic information mutually and solves problem, positive interaction prefers the selection of specification edge by agents belonging to other colony, and negative interaction makes to escape selection of the edge.

Therefore, this structure offers to agents belonging to other colony good heuristic information and share searching region each other.

This multi colony interaction model can be applied effectively in occasion that problem region is big and complex, parallel processing is available, and can improve the performance ACS model.

Forward, we will need study for new additional factor for balance of intensification and diversification in the multi colony ant model based on these results. And we will need study about new standardized network structure except proposed network structure.

References

1. Colorni, A., Dorigo, M., Maniezzo, V.: An investigation of some properties of an ant algorithm. Proceediings of the Parallel Parallel Problem Solving from Nature Conference(PPSn 92), R.Manner and B.Manderick (Eds.), Elsevier Publishing, (1992) 509-520
2. Colorni, A., Dorigo, M., Maniezzo, V.: Distributed optimization by ant colonies. Proceedings of ECAL91 - European Conference of Artificial Life, Paris, France, F.Varela and P.Bourgine(Eds.), Elsevier Publishing, (1991) 134-144
3. Gambardella, L.M., Dorigo, M.: Ant Colony System: A Cooperative Learning approach to the Traveling Salesman Problem. IEEE Transactions on Evolutionary Computation, vol. 1, No. 1, (1997)
4. Dorigo, M., Maniezzo, V., Colorni, A.: The ant system: optimization by a colony of cooperation agents. IEEE Transactions of Systems, Man, and Cybernetics-Part B, vol. 26, No. 2, (1996) 29-41

5. Dorigo, M., Gambardella, L.M.: Ant Colonies for the Traveling Salesman Problem. BioSystems, (1997) 73-81
6. Middendorf, M., Reischle, F., Schmeck, H.: Information Exchange in Multi Colony Ant Algorithms. In Proceedings of the Workshop on Bio Inspired Solutions to Parallel Processing Problems, LNCS 1800, Springer-Verlag, (2000) 645-652
7. Talbi, E.G., Roux, O., Fonlupt, C., Robillard, D.: Parallel ant colonies for combinatorial optimization problems. in J. Rolim et al. (Eds.) Parallel and Distributed, Processing, 11 IPPS/SPDP'99 Workshops, LNCS 1586, Springer-Verlag, (1999) 239-247
8. Jong, J.de., Wiering, M.: Multiple Ant Colony Systems for the Busstop Allocation Problem. BNAIC'01: Proceedings of the Thirteenth Belgium-Netherlands Conference on Artificial In telligence, (2001) 141-148
9. Kawamura, H., Yamamoto, M., Suzuki, K., Ohuchi, A.: Multiple Ant Colonies Algorithm Based on Colony Level Interactions. IEICE Transactions, Vol. E83-A, No.2, (2000) 371-379
10. http://www.iwr.uni-heidelberg.de/groups/comopt/software/TSPLIB95/

Managing Theories of Trust in Agent Based Systems

Ji Ma and Mehmet Orgun

Department of Computing, Macquarie University, Sydney, NSW 2109, Australia
{jma, mehmet}@ics.mq.edu.au

Abstract. A theory of trust for a given system is a set of rules that describes trust of agents in the system. In a certain logical framework, the theory is generally established based on the initial trust of agents in security mechanisms of the system. Such a theory provides a foundation for reasoning about agent beliefs as well as security properties that the system may satisfy. However, trust changes dynamically. When agents lose their trust or gain new trust, the theory established based on the initial trust of agents must be revised, otherwise it can no longer be used for any security purpose. This paper proposes a methodology for revising and managing dynamic theories of trust for agent based systems.

1 Introduction

Trust is an important issue for agent-based systems [1,2]. It influences not only the specification of security policies but also the techniques needed to manage and implement security policies for systems.

In a simple trust model proposed in Liu and Ozols [3], it is assumed that for security consideration initially agents may not trust anyone but the security mechanisms (as special agents) of a system whose trustworthiness has been verified based on required evaluation criteria. The initial trust or meta-beliefs of agents in the system can be encapsulated in a notion of trust and represented as a set of rules (axioms) in a chosen logical framework. These rules with the logic together form a theory, called a *theory of trust* (or a *trust theory*) for the system [2]. However, trust changes dynamically. When agents lose their trust or gain new trust in a dynamic environment, the theory established based on the initial trust of agents in the system must be revised, otherwise it is no longer valid. So dynamic theories of trust is an important topic in trust management, but there are not many papers focusing on it, although some researchers, e.g., Jonker and Treur [4] and Liu *et al.* [5], have been involved in the investigation of trust changes; Liu *et al.* give a principle regarding theory revision but do not discuss how to revise a theory and how to manage the theory in dynamic environments. The motivation of our work is to provide a formal approach for obtaining and managing evolving theories of trust for agent-based systems.

P. Yolum et al.(Eds.): ISCIS 2005, LNCS 3733, pp. 442–451, 2005.

Regarding theory revision, generalizations of theory revision have become known as base change [6,7]. In the view of base changes, revising a theory can be usually conducted by defining appropriate base change operations. Theories of trust discussed in this paper can also be regarded as theory bases. Such a theory is a "basic set" describing meta-beliefs of agents, and revising a theory of trust is in fact the revision of the base of the theory. Differing from general studies of theory revision, we focus on investigating the methods for modelling trust changes and the formalization of theory changes.

The main contributions of this work include: (1) we provide a method for modelling the dynamics of trust for agent-based systems; (2) we propose a methodology for revising theories of trust for agent-based systems; and (3) we also discuss a framework for managing evolving theories of trust in dynamic environments. Our methods developed for modelling trust changes, acquiring information from trust changes to formalize theory changes, and revising a theory based on trust changes are very general. They could be used for any agent-based systems where the notion of trust is essential.

In the next section, we give a brief introduction to the logic TML (Typed Modal Logic) [2], and present a practical theory as an example to show how to establish a trust theory for a given system. Section 3 presents a method for modelling trust change. Section 4 proposes a formal approach for revising theories of trust, and discusses the framework for managing theories of trust in dynamic environments and degrees of trust. Section 5 concludes the paper with a discussion about future work.

2 Theories of Trust

We choose the logic TML (Typed Modal Logic) [2] to construct theories of trust for agent-based systems. TML is an extension of first-order logic with typed variables and multiple modal operators. In TML, one can express agent beliefs in a natural way. For example, assume "Alice believes that John believes that Bob has the key k to open the room B where a document f_1 is stored, and she also believes that John believes that anyone who has the key k may read any document d stored in that room." In TML, this assumption can naturally be formalized by two formulas as follows:

$$(1)\quad \mathbf{B}_{\mathrm{alice}}(\mathbf{B}_{\mathrm{john}}\ \mathrm{Has}(\mathrm{bob}, \mathrm{k}, \mathrm{roomB}) \wedge \mathrm{IsStored}(\mathrm{f}_1, \mathrm{roomB})).$$

$$(2)\quad \mathbf{B}_{\mathrm{alice}}(\mathbf{B}_{\mathrm{john}}\ (\forall x \forall d\ (\mathrm{Has}(x, \mathrm{k}, \mathrm{roomB}) \wedge \mathrm{IsStored}(d, \mathrm{roomB}) \rightarrow \mathrm{Mayread}(x, d)))).$$

Here $\mathbf{B}_a(\varphi)$ means agent a believes that property φ is true. In formula (2) variable x represents a person ranging over the set of people that includes anyone in the world, and d represents a document ranging over the set of documents.

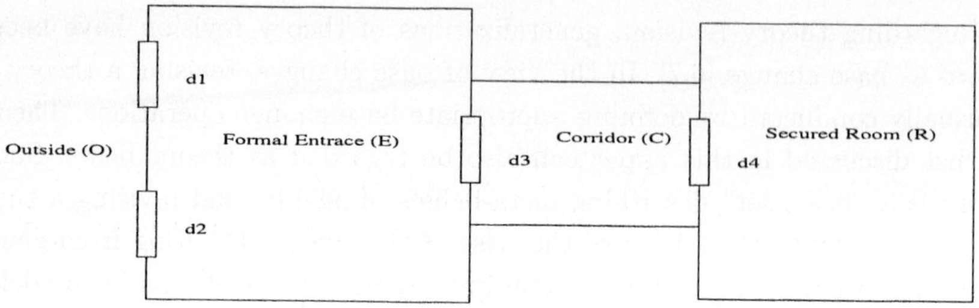

Fig. 1. A secured room

From formulas (1) and (2), the following conclusion can be derived: Alice believes that John believes that Bob may read the document f_1, i.e., we have the formula

(3) $\mathbf{B}_{alice}(\mathbf{B}_{john}\ \text{Mayread}(bob, f_1))$.

From this example, we can see that these expressions regarding agent beliefs and the reasoning process are very natural and precise. It should be kept in mind that every variable in TML is typed. (i.e., it ranges over a suitable domain.)

A theory of trust for a given system consists of a set of formulas (rules) that specify the functions (behaviour) of the security mechanisms. Therefore, for reasoning about agent beliefs, the key is to obtain such a theory. In the following, we show how to establish a theory of trust for a given system based on the logic TML through a simple example.

Example 1. Suppose that there is a secured room of an organization. To enter the room, anyone who is currently at outside (O) must first pass through the doors d_1 or d_2 to get into the formal entrance (E), then pass through the door d_3 to get into the corridor (C), and finally pass through the door d_4 to get into the room (R), as shown in Figure 1. Doors d_1, d_2, d_3, and d_4 are controlled by agents a_1, a_2, a_3 and a_4, respectively. The methods of authentication adopted for d_1, d_2, d_3, and d_4 are assumed to be m_1, m_2, m_3, and m_4, respectively. Each agent allows a person pass through the door it controls only if the agent believes that the identity of the person is authenticated. The security mechanisms of the system, include the physical security environment (consisting of doors and walls, denoted by pse) can be represented as $H = \{a_1, a_2, a_3, a_4, m_1, m_2, m_3, m_4, pse\}$.

In order to establish a theory of trust for the system, we now define three predicates as follows:

- $\text{At}(x, l, t)$: x is at the location l at time t, where x represents a person ranging over the set of agents, l represents a location ranging over {O, E, C, R} and t represents a point in time ranging over the set of natural numbers.
- $\text{RequestsToEnter}(x, l)$: x requests to enter the location l.
- $\text{AuthenticatedBy}(x, m)$: the identity of x is authenticated by m, where m represents the authentication method ranging over $\{m_1, m_2, m_3, m_4\}$.

Thus, we can have the following rules that describe the functional (behavioural) properties of the authentication system. Here x and t are assumed to be universally quantified over agents and points in time respectively:

$$(\mathrm{I}_1)\quad \mathrm{At}(x,\mathbf{O},t)\wedge \mathrm{RequestsToEnter}(x,\mathbf{E})\rightarrow(\mathrm{At}(x,\mathbf{E},t+1)\leftrightarrow (\mathbf{B}_{\mathrm{a}_1}\mathrm{AuthenticatedBy}(x,\mathrm{m}_1)\vee \mathbf{B}_{\mathrm{a}_2}\mathrm{AuthenticatedBy}(x,\mathrm{m}_2))).$$

$$(\mathrm{I}_2)\quad \mathrm{At}(x,\mathbf{E},t)\wedge \mathrm{RequestsToEnter}(x,\mathbf{C})\rightarrow (\mathrm{At}(x,\mathbf{C},t+1)\leftrightarrow \mathbf{B}_{\mathrm{a}_3}\mathrm{AuthenticatedBy}(x,\mathrm{m}_3)).$$

$$(\mathrm{I}_3)\quad \mathrm{At}(x,\mathbf{C},t)\wedge \mathrm{RequestsToEnter}(x,\mathbf{R})\rightarrow (\mathrm{At}(x,\mathbf{R},t+1)\leftrightarrow \mathbf{B}_{\mathrm{a}_4}\mathrm{AuthenticatedBy}(x,\mathrm{m}_4)).$$

$$(\mathrm{I}_4)\quad \mathrm{At}(x,\mathbf{O},t)\rightarrow \mathrm{At}(x,\mathbf{O},t+1)\vee \mathrm{At}(x,\mathbf{E},t+1).$$

$$(\mathrm{I}_5)\quad \mathrm{At}(x,\mathbf{E},t)\rightarrow \mathrm{At}(x,\mathbf{E},t+1)\vee \mathrm{At}(x,\mathbf{O},t+1)\vee \mathrm{At}(x,\mathbf{C},t+1).$$

$$(\mathrm{I}_6)\quad \mathrm{At}(x,\mathbf{C},t)\rightarrow \mathrm{At}(x,\mathbf{C},t+1)\vee \mathrm{At}(x,\mathbf{E},t+1)\vee \mathrm{At}(x,\mathbf{R},t+1).$$

$$(\mathrm{I}_7)\quad \mathrm{At}(x,\mathbf{E},t)\wedge \mathrm{At}(x,\mathbf{E},t+1)\wedge \mathrm{At}(x,\mathbf{E},t+2)\rightarrow \mathrm{At}(x,\mathbf{O},t+3).$$

$$(\mathrm{I}_8)\quad \mathrm{At}(x,\mathbf{C},t)\wedge \mathrm{At}(x,\mathbf{C},t+1)\wedge \mathrm{At}(x,\mathbf{C},t+2)\rightarrow \mathrm{At}(x,\mathbf{E},t+3).$$

The meanings of these rules are easily understood. For example, the rule I_1 says that, if a person currently requests to enter the location E, then the person is at location E at the next moment in time if and only if agent a_1 believes that the identity of the person is authenticated by method m_1 or agent a_2 believes that the identity of the person is authenticated by method m_2. Now we have established a trust theory $\mathrm{T} = \{\mathrm{I}_1,\mathrm{I}_2,\mathrm{I}_3,\mathrm{I}_4,\mathrm{I}_5,\mathrm{I}_6,\mathrm{I}_7,\mathrm{I}_8\}$ for this agent based system. Based on the theory T, if none of agents believes a person's identity is authenticated, then the person can never enter the secured room. The proof can be done as follows: assume a person x is currently at the location O and requests to get into the location E, but none of agents a_1 and a_2 believes the identity of this person is authenticated by method m_1 or method m_2, respectively. Then according to I_1, the person x cannot get in location E at the next moment, furthermore, by I_4, x is still at location O.

This example has shown a methodology of establishing a theory of trust for a given system. This methodology involves the following steps:

1. Analysing the system to identify trusted agents in it, and finding what kind of trust is involved in the system;
2. Defining appropriate predicates used to express agent beliefs; and
3. Defining rules that describe functions (behaviour) of the trusted agents.

3 Modelling Trust Changes

The theory of trust for a given system is built based on the initial trust of agents in the security mechanisms of the system. As we mentioned before, trust changes dynamically. When agents lose their trust or gain new trust in a dynamic environment, the theory established based on the initial trust of agents in the system must be revised, otherwise it is no longer valid. Several major factors that influence trust of agents include: modifications of the security policy, adopting new mechanisms instead of the old ones to enforce a policy, accidents occurring within the system, *etc.* These factors directly lead to trust changes.

Jonker and Treur [4] call an event that can influence the degree of trust of an agent a *trust-positive experience* or a *trust-negative experience* of the agent. if it is a trust-positive experience then the agent may gain his trust to some degree; If the event an agent experiences is a trust-negative experience then the agent may loose his trust to some degree. The dynamics of trust addressed in [8] is as "there is a circular relation, and more precisely a positive feedback, between trust in reciprocal delegation-adoption relations (from commerce to friendship)."

For modelling trust changes, we adopt a different approach. Let Ω be the set of agents involved in the system (e.g., users, operators, managers *etc*) and Θ be the set of binary trust relations over Ω. That is, Θ consists of pairs of agents such that $(x, y) \in \Theta$ if and only if x *trusts* y. We give the formal definition of a trust state as follows: A *trust state* of a system, denoted by S, is defined as the pair $\mathrm{S} = (\Omega, \Theta)$.

Trust changes to a trust state S involve two cases: agents lose their trust in some agents (security mechanisms) in the current state S, and agents gain new trust in some agents (e.g., some new security mechanisms are adopted). We view a trust change to trust state S as consisting of two classes of operations: deleting a relation (x,y) from S, and adding a relation (x,y) to S. Therefore, we express a trust change to state S as a pair of sets: one set contains all relations of the form (x,y) that will be added to state S; and the other set contains all relations of the form (x,y) that will be deleted from state S. Formally, we say that

- $\delta = (\mathrm{IN}, \mathrm{OUT})$ is a *trust change* to state $\mathrm{S} = (\Omega, \Theta)$, if IN and OUT satisfy the following conditions: (1) $\mathrm{OUT} \subseteq \Theta$, and (2) $\mathrm{IN} \cap \Theta = \emptyset$. IN and OUT are called the *in set* and *out set* of this change, respectively.

For simplifying the discussion, we assume the set of agents Ω is static. Thus, from state $\mathrm{S} = (\Omega, \Theta)$ and trust change $\delta = (\mathrm{IN}, \mathrm{OUT})$, we have the new trust state $\mathrm{S}' = (\Omega, \Theta')$, where Θ' is obtained by the formula

- $\Theta' = \Theta \cup \mathrm{IN} - \mathrm{OUT}$

where '$-$' is the "difference" operation on sets.

4 Theory Revision

In Section 2, we have established a theory $\mathrm{T} = \{\mathrm{I}_1, \mathrm{I}_2, \mathrm{I}_3, \mathrm{I}_4, \mathrm{I}_5, \mathrm{I}_6, \mathrm{I}_7, \mathrm{I}_8\}$, where each rule describes the functions (behaviour) of one or more agents. e.g., rule

I_1 is related to agents a_1, a_2, m_1, and m_2. To emphasize this, we redefine $T = \{I_1(a_1, a_2, m_1, m_2), I_2(a_3, m_3), I_3(a_4, m_4), I_4(pse), I_5(pse), I_6(pse), I_7(pse), I_8(pse)\}$

In general, we assume that a theory T describes trust of agents at the current trust state S. A trust change, say δ, causes a transition from the current trust state S to the new trust state S′. In this case, the theory T must be changed corresponding to the trust change δ. We denote this theory change by σ. Thus, at the new (or next) trust state S′, we shall have a new theory T′ that describes the trust of agents at the new state S′.

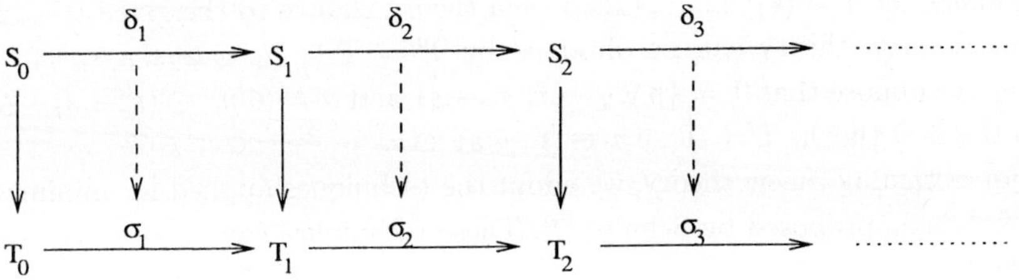

Fig. 2. Relationships between trust states, trust changes and theory changes

Thus, there are three questions we need to answer. They are: (1) how to find the theory change corresponding to a trust change at a given state? (2) how to express a theory change? (3) how to obtain the new theory from an existing theory and the theory change to it? We now answer these questions.

For question 1, let $H = \{x \in \Omega \mid \text{there exists a rule } r \in T,\ r = r(\ldots, x, \ldots)\}$ be the set of trusted agents. Assume $\delta = (IN, OUT)$ is a trust change to S, the corresponding theory change σ to T can be obtained by the following:

- For any $x \in H$, if there exists a pair $(y, x) \in OUT$, indicating that agent x is no longer trusted by agent y, then we must delete x from H. Thus, if there is a rule $r = r(\ldots,\ x, \ldots)$, then $\ominus r$ is added to σ, and rule r will be retracted from T. However, at the same time, we may need to add some formulas to T due to the retraction of r, till there are no conflicts between rules.
- For any agent x, $x \notin H$, but $(y, x) \in IN$ for all $y \in \Omega$, we add x to H, since this fact means that all agents have trust in x although it does not belong to H at state S. Thus, there must be some rule (rules) to specify the behaviour of x. If $r = r(\ldots,\ x, \ldots)$ is such a rule, we add $\oplus r$ to σ, then rule r will be added to T. In this case, similarly, at the same time we may need to retract some rules due to the addition of r, till there are no conflicts between rules.

With the method described above, we can obtain the theory change to a theory from a trust change to the trust state at which the theory holds.

Now, we discuss the question of how to express a theory change. A *theory change* to a given theory T can be viewed as consisting of two types of activities:

adding a formula to, and retracting a formula from, T. Therefore, we define a theory change as a sequence of formulas with the sign $\oplus$ or $\ominus$, where signs $\oplus$ and $\ominus$ are regarded as the operations "addition" and "retraction", respectively. Formally, we say that $\sigma = \langle *_1\varphi_1, \ldots, *_n\varphi_n\rangle$ is a *theory change* to a given theory T, where each $*_i$ is $\oplus$ or $\ominus$, $\varphi_1, \ldots, \varphi_n$ are formulas, and if $*_i$ is $\ominus$ then φ_i must belong to T, if $*_i$ is $\oplus$ then φ_i must not be in T.

In theory revision, given a theory T and a formula φ, we say that T′ adds the formula φ to T, written $\mathrm{T}' = \mathrm{T} \oplus \varphi$, iff $\mathrm{T} \nvdash \varphi$ and $\mathrm{T}' \vdash \varphi$; and T′ retracts the formula φ from T, written $\mathrm{T}' = \mathrm{T} \ominus \varphi$, iff $\mathrm{T} \vdash \varphi$ and $\mathrm{T}' \nvdash \varphi$.

Finally, let $\sigma = \langle *_1\varphi_1, \ldots, *_n\varphi_n\rangle$ be a theory change to the given theory T. Then, the new theory can be obtained by $\mathrm{T}' = \mathrm{T} *_1 \varphi_1 *_2 \varphi_2, \ldots *_n \varphi_n$. For example, suppose that $\mathrm{T} = \{p \vee q \rightarrow r,\ r \rightarrow s\}$ and $\sigma = \langle \oplus p,\ \ominus (r \rightarrow s),\ \oplus s\rangle$, then the new theory $\mathrm{T}' = \mathrm{T}\ \oplus p\ \ominus (r \rightarrow s)\ \oplus s$.

For obtaining a new theory, we adopt the techniques applied for minimizing belief change, proposed by Schulte [7]. These techniques can be summarized as follows:

- $\mathrm{T} \oplus \varphi$: the revision of T by adding formula φ can proceed in two steps: first remove from T all formulas inconsistent with φ to obtain a theory T′; then add φ to T′.
- $\mathrm{T} \ominus \varphi$: the revision of T by retracting formula φ can proceed in this way: take out the formula from T to get T′ such that $\mathrm{T}' \nvdash \varphi$ and T′ is exactly the subset of T that cannot be expanded without entailing φ.

The following example shows how to obtain an evolving theory of trust based on the analysis of the dynamics of trust.

Example 2. Recall the example theory given in Section 2. We have the trust theory $\mathrm{T} = \{\mathrm{I}_1, \mathrm{I}_2, \mathrm{I}_3, \mathrm{I}_4, \mathrm{I}_5, \mathrm{I}_6, \mathrm{I}_7, \mathrm{I}_8\}$. Let $\mathrm{T}_0 = \mathrm{T}$ and the initial trust state be S_0. Then T_0 is the theory that specifies trust of agents in the set of security mechanisms $\mathrm{H}_0 = \{\mathrm{a}_1, \mathrm{a}_2, \mathrm{a}_3, \mathrm{a}_4, \mathrm{m}_1, \mathrm{m}_2, \mathrm{m}_3, \mathrm{m}_4, \mathrm{pse}\}$ at the trust state S_0.

Assume it is found that the authentication method m_2 is not reliable, so the organization replaces it by m_1. Thus, m_2 is deleted from H_0, and we therefore have a theory change $\sigma = \langle \ominus \mathrm{I}_1\rangle$. But, after retracting I_1 from T_0, we have to add the following formula to it.

$$(\mathrm{I}_9)\quad \mathrm{At}(x, \mathbf{O}, t) \wedge \mathrm{RequestsToEnter}(x, \mathbf{E}) \rightarrow (At(x, \mathbf{E}, t+1) \leftrightarrow (\mathbf{B}_{\mathrm{a}_1}\mathrm{AuthenticatedBy}(x, \mathrm{m}_1) \vee \mathbf{B}_{\mathrm{a}_2}\mathrm{AuthenticatedBy}(x, \mathrm{m}_1))).$$

Therefore, we have the new theory $\mathrm{T}_1 = \{\mathrm{I}_2, \mathrm{I}_3, \mathrm{I}_4, \mathrm{I}_5, \mathrm{I}_6, \mathrm{I}_7, \mathrm{I}_8, \mathrm{I}_9\}$, and T_1 is based on the new trust state S_1, where $\mathrm{H}_1 = \{\mathrm{a}_1, \mathrm{a}_2, \mathrm{a}_3, \mathrm{a}_4, \mathrm{m}_1, \mathrm{m}_3, \mathrm{m}_4, \mathrm{pse}\}$.

The second revision of this theory is made when the organization changes the security policy to let people freely enter the formal entrance. Due to this change,

a_1, a_2, and m_1 are no longer part of the security mechanisms for the authentication system. Thus, a_1, a_2, and m_1 will be deleted from H_1. Therefore at the new trust state, the set of mechanisms that agents trust is $H_2 = \{a_3, a_4, m_3, m_4, pse\}$. We also have to note that the function of the agent pse changes a bit since the new location E consists of old locations O and E. Corresponding to this trust change, there is a need to retract rules I_9, I_4 and I_7 from T_1 and to add a new rule as follows to T_1:

(I_{10}) $\mathrm{At}(x, \mathbf{E}, t) \rightarrow \mathrm{At}(x, \mathbf{E}, t+1) \vee \mathrm{At}(x, \mathbf{C}, t+1)$.

Therefore we have the theory change $\sigma = \langle \ominus I_9, \ominus I_4, \ominus I_7, \oplus I_{10} \rangle$, and the new theory $T_2 = T_1 \ominus I_9 \ominus I_4 \ominus I_7 \oplus I_{10}$. Noting that before adding I_{10} to T_1, we need to retract I_5 from it. Thus, we finally obtain the new theory $T_2 = \{I_2, I_3, I_6, I_8, I_{10}\}$.

Furthermore, the organization notes that there is a problem with door d_4 (assuming that agent a_4 is a card reader): one who does not have a valid card may enter the secured room when the door d_4 is open for others. For preventing this, the organization decides to add a new security mechanism to check whether the corridor is empty before letting a person pass through door d_3. We assume that agent a_5 will play this role. At this time, a_5 is added to H_2, and we have a theory change $\sigma = \langle \oplus I_{11} \rangle$, where I_{11} is as follows:

(I_{11}) $\mathrm{At}(x, \mathbf{E}, t) \wedge \mathrm{RequestsToEnter}(x, \mathbf{C}) \rightarrow (\mathrm{At}(x, \mathbf{C}, t+1) \leftrightarrow$
$(\mathbf{B}_{a_5} \mathrm{Empty}(\mathbf{C}, t) \wedge \mathbf{B}_{a_3} \mathrm{AuthenticatedBy}(x, m_3)))$.

For adding I_{11} to T_2, we have to retract rule I_2 from T_2. Therefore, we obtain the new theory $T_3 = \{I_3, I_6, I_8, I_{10}, I_{11}\}$, which is based on the new trust state S_3 where $H_3 = \{a_3, a_4, a_5, m_3, m_4, pse\}$.

From the above discussion, our framework for managing a theory of trust can be formulated as follows: Let T be a theory of trust based on a trust state S, where H is the set of trusted agents. It is obvious that H should contain all those agents who have at least one formula in T related to them. Thus, if there are no trust changes to the trust state S, then there is no need to revise the theory T. If there is a trust change δ to S, the revision process must be performed as follows:

1. Based on the trust change δ, identify those agents who belong to H but are no longer trusted by one or more agents, and those agents who are not in H but trust all agents in H and are trusted by all agents.
2. Compute the theory change σ that corresponds to the trust change δ.
3. Obtain the new theory T′ from T and σ by using revision operations.

Since systems change and evolve, there is a need to monitor trust relationships, to determine whether the criteria (policy) on which they are based still apply and whether the security mechanisms can still satisfy security requirements.

The proposed methodology for revising and analysing theories of trust is based on a binary valued trust relation model, which has only two trust values or two different trust degrees, 1 (*trust*) or 0 (*no trust*). The advantage of using this model is that we do not need to assign or compute a value for each trust relation, so that theory revision can be easily handled. However, in some applications, we need to consider other models, for which trust degrees can be any number between 0 and 1. With the consideration of trust degrees, here we outline the general idea as follows: given a system, we redefine the trust relation of a trust state $\mathrm{S} = (\Omega, \Theta)$ by defining $\Theta = \{(x, y, g) \mid x, y \in \Omega \ \wedge \ 0 \leq g \leq 1\}$, where Ω is the set of agents involved in the system, g is the trust degree, (x, y, g) is read as "x trusts y at the rate g", and if $(x, y, g) \in \Theta$ and $(x, y, g') \in \Theta$, then $g = g'$.

For a given system, a number t $(0 \leq t \leq 1)$ is chosen as the *trust threshold* based on its security requirements. Then, we partition Θ into two sets, $\Theta_{\mathrm{u}} = \{(x, y, g) \mid x, y \in \Omega \ \wedge \ t \leq g \leq 1\}$ and $\Theta_{\mathrm{l}} = \{(x, y, g) \mid x, y \in \Omega \ \wedge \ 0 \leq g \leq t\}$. It is obvious that $\Theta = \Theta_{\mathrm{u}} \cup \Theta_{\mathrm{l}}$ and $\Theta_{\mathrm{u}} \cap \Theta_{\mathrm{l}} = \emptyset$. Thus, for any $x, y \in \Omega$, there is a unique g, such that (x, y, g) is $\in \Theta_{\mathrm{u}}$ or $\in \Theta_{\mathrm{l}}$. The trust theory at the state S describes trust of agents in those agents who belong to the set $\mathrm{H} = \{y \mid (x, y, g) \in \Theta_{\mathrm{u}}$ for all $x \in \Omega\}$; we called H the *trusted agent set* at the trust state S.

As in the binary valued trust relation model, we model trust changes and find theory changes corresponding to trust changes. The new theory can be obtained in the same way as it is proposed for the binary valued trust model. With this new model, we need to employ some new methods and techniques, such as the trust evolution and update functions in [4] for timely updating trust of agents.

5 Concluding Remarks

We have proposed a formal approach to revising a theory of trust, which includes a technique for modelling trust changes, a method for computing the new trust state from an old one and its changes, a method to express theory changes, and a technique for obtaining a new theory based on given trust changes. Like in Blaze's work [9], we focus on the system trust rather than interpersonal trust. Our approach is very general, and all these methods and techniques could be used in the management of trust theories for agent-based systems where the notion of trust is essential.

Revising a theory of trust is in fact the revision of the base of the theory. Therefore, many existing methods and techniques for belief revision [10,6,7] are helpful for revising theories of trust. In the future, we may further investigate a variety of belief revision techniques that can be applied for revision of trust theories. Also, an evolving theory can be applied to the analysis of temporal security properties that a system may satisfy in dynamic environments. How to express and analyse such kind of security properties with evolving theories would be considered in the future work.

Acknowledgements

This research has been supported in part by an Australian Research Council (ARC) grant.

References

1. Grandison, T., Sloman., M.: A survey of trust in Internet applications. In: IEEE Communications Surveys and Tutorials. (Fourth Quarter, 2000)
2. Liu, C.: Logical foundations for reasoning about trust in secure digital communication. In: Proceedings of AI2001: Advances in Artificial Intelligence. Volume 2256 of LNAI., Springer (2001) 333–344
3. Liu, C., Ozols., M.A.: Trust in secure communication systems – the concept, representations, and reasoning techniques. In: Proceedings of AI2002: Advances in Artificial Intelligence. Volume 2557 of LNAI., Springer (2002) 60–70
4. Jonker, C.M., Treur., J.: Formal analysis of models for the dynamics of trust based on experiences. In: Multi-Agent System Engineering, Proceedings of MAAMAW'99. Volume 1647 of LNAI., Springer (1999) 221–231
5. Liu, C., Ozols, M.A., Orgun., M.: A temporalised belief logic for specifying the dynamics of trust for multi-agent systems. In: Proceedings of the Ninth Asian Computer Science Conference 2004. Volume 3321 of LNCS., Springer (Dec. 2004) 142–156
6. Meyer., T.: Basic infobase change. In: Proceedings of AI'99. Volume 1747 of LNAI., Springer-Verlag (1999) 156–167
7. Schulte, O.: Minimal belief change and pareto-optimality. In: Proceedings of AI'99. Volume 1747 of LNAI., Springer-Verlag (1999) 144–155
8. Castelfranchi, C., Falcone., R.: Social trust: Cognitive anatomy, social importance, quantification, and dynamics. In: Proceedings of the First International Workshop on Trust. (1998) 35–49
9. Blaze, M., Feigenbaum, J., Lacy., J.: Decentralized trust management. In: Proceedings of the 1993 IEEE Computer Society Symposium on research in Security and Privacy. (1993) 164–173
10. Alchourron, C.E., Gardenfors, P., Makinson., D.: On the logic of theory change: Partial meet functions for contraction and revision. In: Journal of Symbolic Logic. Volume 50. (1985) 510–530

Applying Semantic Capability Matching into Directory Service Structures of Multi Agent Systems

Geylani Kardas[1], Özgür Gümüs[2], and Oğuz Dikenelli[2]

[1] Ege University, International Computer Institute, 35100 Bornova, İzmir, Turkey
geylani@bornova.ege.edu.tr
[2] Ege University, Department of Computer Engineering, 35100 Bornova, Izmir, Turkey
{gumus, oguzd}@staff.ege.edu.tr

Abstact. In this paper, we introduce a semantically enriched capability matching model for agent services. Our vision is to integrate both agent and semantic web services and provide the interoperability of agents under the semantic web extension. In multi agent system architectures, there is a specific agent or service called directory facilitator which is responsible to keep knowledge about the services given by the agents within the system. Other agents query in directory facilitator to identify agents that provide the required services. Hence, automated service discovery in multi agent systems is a critical issue. Here, we propose a matching engine architecture in which capabilities of agent services are handled semantically and it replies agent service requests with *most suitable* service advertisements. The paper includes formal basics and design details of this engine and also discusses its implementation with a proper case study.

1 Introduction

Semantic Web [2] evolution has doubtlessly brought a new vision into agent research. This *Second Generation Web* aims to improve WWW (World Wide Web) such that web page contents are interpreted by using ontologies. It is apparent that the interpretation in question will be realized by autonomous computational entities –so agents- to handle semantic content on behalf of their human users.

Semantic Web vision obviously effects the current mainstream research directions in agent technologies [16] especially considering agent modeling, multi agent system (MAS) architectures and MAS methodologies.

Various studies on semantic web and agent systems integration have already produced new artifacts like new agent systems, agent development frameworks, etc. For example, in [3] a smart meeting room system is introduced in which agents provide relevant services and information to the meeting participants based on their contexts. Another system offers access to information about activities such as talks or seminars [6]. This system uses DAML+OIL (DARPA Agent Markup Language + Ontology Inference Layer) [4] for knowledge representation and lets agents to retrieve and manipulate information stored in a proper knowledge base.

Those above mentioned systems use multi agent development frameworks like Jackal [5] and Jade [1] in their underlying infrastructure. However those frameworks do not have a built-in support for semantic web and system developers encounter

P. Yolum et al.(Eds.): ISCIS 2005, LNCS 3733, pp. 452–461, 2005.

difficulties in supporting basic semantic web functionalities such as automated discovery and dynamic invocation of agent services.

We believe that semantic web enabled multi agent systems can only be developed by using frameworks which will internally support basic semantic web functionalities and facilitate integration of semantic web and agents. We introduced such a framework in [7] and called it *SEAGENT*. SEAGENT is FIPA-compatible [8] and it looks like other existing agent development frameworks such as DECAF [10] and JADE [1]. However it includes several built-in features that the existing agent frameworks and platforms do not have.

Agents created using SEAGENT can handle their internal knowledge base using semantic web standards. Directory facilitator of SEAGENT is implemented in a way that it supports semantic matching of the agent capabilities.

In this paper, we introduce design basics and give implementation details of SEAGENT's semantic matching engine which will improve directory services in multi agent systems. We believe that agent platforms developed with SEAGENT will have more powerful yellow page services and easily realize semantic capability matching on agent services which will be a must in future's semantically enriched environments.

The rest of the paper is organized as follows: Section 2 gives our motivation and idea behind semantically enriched MAS directory services. This section also exposes our capability matching model and formal basics of the developed semantic matching engine. Section 3 explains the internal architecture and software design of the matching engine. A case study on proposed semantic capability matching is discussed in Section 4. Section 5 includes the conclusion and future work.

2 Semantic Matching for MAS Directory Services

Members of a multi agent platform need services offered by other members during execution of their plans and doing the jobs on behalf of their users. So, they inevitably look for those requested services in a predefined service registry. No matter it is FIPA-compliant [8] or not, a MAS owns one or more registries which provides yellow page services for system's agents to look for proper agent services. Of course registries mentioned above are not simple structures and mostly implemented as directory services and served by some platform specific agents. For example there is a mandatory agent called *directory facilitator (DF)* in FIPA abstract architecture specification on which agent services are registered. When an agent looks for a specific agent service, it gathers supplier data (agent's name, address, etc.) of the service from the DF and then it begins to communicate with this service provider agent to complete its task.

Matchmaking could be defined as the process of verifying whether a capability specification *"matches"* the specification of a request (e.g, a task to be solved) [9]. Two specifications "match" if their specifications verify some matching relation, where the matching relation is defined according to some criteria (e.g. a capability being able to solve a task). This matching may consider semantic relation(s) between these two specifications (advertised and requested). Therefore, in case of agent service discovery, we should define semantic matching criteria of service capabilities and design registration mechanisms (directory services) of agent service specifications according to those criteria. That makes matching of requested and advertised services more efficient by not only taking into consideration of identical service matching: New capability matching will determine type and degree of relation between two services (requested and advertised) *semantically*.

Capability matching of services is not a new idea and several studies exist in literature, proposing algorithms especially for discovery of semantic web services. For example studies in [12] and [14] introduce a capability matching on semantic web services which are modeled in DAML-S (DAML Services) [15]. Service profiles of both requested and advertised services are processed and a match between these profiles is determined when the advertised service could be used in place of the requested service.

On the other hand, [9] aims extending matchmaking on MAS environments in order to maximize the reuse of capabilities and tasks over new domains. To achieve this goal, the use of a knowledge modeling framework as the basis of an agent capability description language is proposed.

However, according to our vision; new generation multi agent environments will be semantically enriched by all means of agent interactions. These environments will be open to semantic web services in addition to existing agent services. Depending of its kind and needs, a service may be implemented as stand-alone (semantic web services) or an autonomous structure (an agent) as traditionally serves it. An agent may use a semantic web service and/or a service provided by another agent during its plan execution. So, middle agents of such platforms should realize matching on all those kind of services. At this point of view; our proposal on capability matching of services differentiates from the others mentioned above. We also take this semantically improved MAS vision into automated composition and interaction of services as proposed in [7] but those issues are beyond the scope of this paper.

Before discussing capabilities of the proposed semantic matching engine, it is worth for giving the formal basics of the match process in question:

Let;

O be an ontology defined using an ontology language (such as OWL [13]) and
C_1 and C_2 are classes (concepts) defined in O.

Definition 1: For all $C_X \in O$; C_1 is a direct subclass of C_2 if:

$(C_X \neq C_1) \wedge$
$(C_X \neq C_2) \wedge$
$((C_X \supset C_1) \wedge (C_X \subset C_2)) \Rightarrow C_X = \varnothing$

Definition 2: C_1 is a distant subclass of C_2 if:

$(C_2 \supset C_1)$ and C_1 is not direct subclass of C_2

Definition 3: $DoM(C_1, C_2)$ is a degree of match function which determines semantic match degree between concepts C_1 and C_2 such that:

$DoM(C_1, C_2) =$ *exact* if C_1 is a direct subclass of C_2 or $C_1 = C_2$
$DoM(C_1, C_2) =$ *plug-in* if C_1 is a distant subclass of C_2
$DoM(C_1, C_2) =$ *subsumes* if C_2 is a direct or distant subclass of C_1
$DoM(C_1, C_2) =$ *fail* otherwise

We have used those relation and function definitions to design and implement the capability matching engine which works on agent services. In addition to other properties, an agent's service has a type which is a concept (or class) predefined in a domain ontology. Matching engine of the agent platform takes the above defined relations into account and determines the *suitability* of the advertised agent services with the requested one.

3 Seagent Matching Engine

We designed and implemented a capability matching engine for multi agent platforms in which directory services are semantically enriched. This matching engine -called *Seagent Matching Engine*- receives service requests and matches "semantically right" agent services with given service requests.

The engine stores agent service definitions in a database. Actually this database is an ontology model of the agent services in which agent service ontology individuals are included. Each agent service that is registered to the directory facilitator is also represented in this ontology with an individual. The matching engine uses those individuals and compares them with given service requests semantically.

The fact that a reasoning mechanism is needed to find out conceptual relations between individuals, a simple reasoner called *Ontolog* is developed within the engine. In our implementations, Ontolog is used by the matching engines to determine how the given two ontology concepts are related to each other and obtain the degree of the relationship if it exists. To perform its operations, Ontolog uses domain ontologies which may be web or locally enabled.

We implemented above proposed matching engine as a software package which can be used by directory service providers of any multi agent system (FIPA-compliant or not) to enhance their yellow page services with semantic capability matching. Fig. 1 shows the object model of the developed engine software.

DescriptionDB class is the database component of the software in which agent service descriptions are stored in an ontology model. For example, by using OWL we

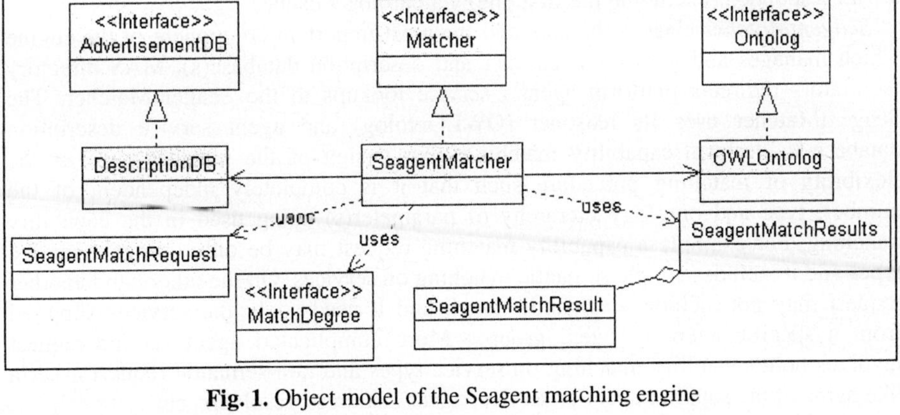

Fig. 1. Object model of the Seagent matching engine

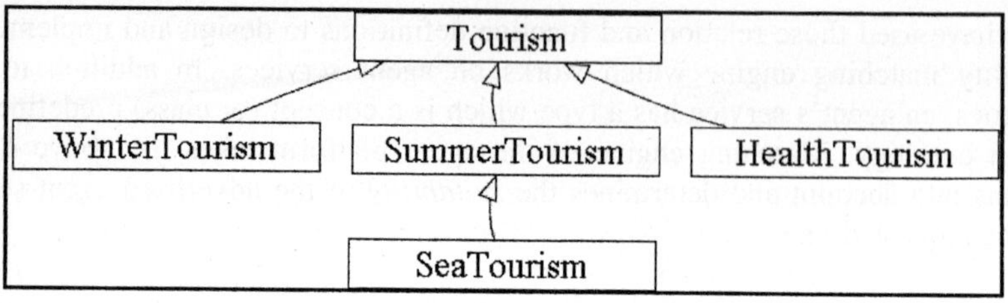

Fig. 2. A fragment of tourism ontology

prepare an Agent Management Ontology in proper to FIPA Agent Management Specification (AMS) [8] so that the database stores directory facilitator agent descriptions as individuals. Each individual also includes its service description with a service type. Service types come from a predefined service ontology so that the engine can perform capability matching on requested and advertised services. Sample service ontology for a tourism domain is given in Fig. 2.

Ontolog is the generic interface that represents the above mentioned primitive reasoner of the matching engine. We implemented this engine component's various implementations in our studies and those were formerly dealing with DAML ontologies. The new version called *OwlOntolog* has been designed to process on OWL ontologies. It parses OWL documents and finds ontology concept distances.

Basically, OwlOntolog gives the superclass distance of the two ontology class with given URIs by determining "subClassOf" relations on the ontology. Consider the simple ontology class tree given in Fig. 2. Nodes of the ontology tree are service types of agents serving in a simple tourism domain. According to the ontology model, OwlOntolog finds superclass distances as -1, 0, 1 and 2 in (SeaTourism, HealthTourism), (SeaTourism, SeaTourism), (SeaTourism, SummerTourism), (SeaTourism, Tourism) ontology class pairs respectively. In case of a multiple inheritance, there will be different paths from a subclass to its superclass(es). At this condition OwlOntolog returns the shortest distance as a result of performing a depth-first search on the ontology tree.

Calculated ontology class distances are cached as instances in OwlOntolog to optimize performance. When the same distance query is received multiple times, they are all responded (excluding the first one) via ontolog's cache.

SeagentMatcher class is the core and the most important component of the engine which manages and uses both reasoner and description database(s). MAS directory facilitators redirects platform agent's service lookups to the SeagentMatcher. The SeagentMatcher uses its reasoner (OWLOntolog) and agent service description database to perform capability matching. Our design of the matcher gave us the flexibility of matching procedure such that it is completely independent of the number, type and ontology hierarchy of parameter(s) being used in the capability matching. For example a capability matching request may be only on agent service types and it includes simple semantic matching on services. On the other hand another request may not include a semantic match and it needs only the services supplied from a specific agent or agent group. More complicated agent service request involves both capability matching on service types and non-semantic request criteria like name of the supplier agent or service, agent's address, resolvers, etc.

The proposed engine meets all the requirements given above and enriches lookup services by providing matching for any level of match complexity. During its execution, it first performs an RDF (Resource Description Framework) query on individuals of the database model by RDQL (RDF Data Query Language) [11] filtering to find out proper individuals according to the given non-semantic parameters. Then the engine realizes a semantic capability matching on those filtered individuals and determines the result set of the match request. Such a filtering mechanism both supplies the management of complicated match requests and improves the performance by reducing number of database members to be processed by the reasoner. Of course the above pre-filtering will not be performed in a case of request in which only semantic match on database members is needed.

Each match request is encapsulated by a *SeagentMatchRequest* object which is given to matching engine to be processed on. A SeagentMatchRequest stores a match request in RDF triples. Sentences belong to semantic and non-semantic queries are given as form of RDF triples and those triples are stored in proper collections in the object. The request object also includes the desired match degree of the requester.

SeagentMatcher determines the semantic match degree between the requested and advertised service descriptions by calling appropriate OwlOntolog's method with service types of those descriptions. Calculated ontology class distance will be evaluated in the SeagentMatcher as follows:

```
If distance = 0 or distance = 1 then EXACT match is determined
If distance > 1 then PLUGIN match is determined
If distance < 0 then look for a reverse distance calculation
  (call finder with parameters in reverse order)
  If reverse_distance > 0 then SUBSUMES match is determined
  Else FAIL in match is determined
```

Each match result is encapsulated in a *SeagentMatchResult* including its degree of match. In software design, each match result implements a programming language specific "Comparable" interface to be easily and quickly sorted so agent service requester can retrieve service descriptions in order - from semantically most exact to least one.

Due to its proper API (Application Program Interface) design, use of the above given matching engine inside Java based multi agent development frameworks is so easy. One such implementation has been tested on SEAGENT [7] and will be discussed later. However it should be noted that integration of the engine to the directory service(s) is an important issue and it needs an appropriate communication mechanism to realize semantic service discovery. Directory structures –e.g. directory facilitators in FIPA-compliant MASs- retrieve service discovery requests of the agents in MAS platform specific language structures –such as ACL (Agent Communication Language) in FIPA MASs- and so, those requests should be pre-processed and transformed into the language of the semantic matching engine. In our design, the semantically enriched directory facilitator parses ACL content of an incoming service discovery request and prepares the appropriate semantic matching engine input (SeagentMatchRequest). After its execution, the engine outputs the matchmaking results in a predefined collection (SeagentMatchResults). Finally the directory facilitator puts those results into the outgoing ACL reply message and sends this message back to the requester agent. All those message conversions are performed inside the directory facilitator's communication module. During those message conversions, the module uses ontology mappings of the domain to generate OWL representations of the service requests and results to be used in message contents.

4 A Case Study on Semantic Capability Matching

To give ideas in a more concrete way, a case study on the proposed semantic capability matching is discussed in this section. We have tested the matching engine on a MAS that is developed by using SEAGENT [7] framework. The agent environment is about "Tourism" domain in which customer agents try to reserve hotel rooms on behalf of their users while some other agents are offering hotel services for those ones. For our simple scenario, four agents were created using SEAGENT framework and these agents registered their services to the semantically enriched directory facilitator (DF) of the system. For each service advertisement; the servicing agent's name and service type is given in Table 1.

Table 1. Four agent services registered into the directory facilitator

DFAgentDescription	Agent's Name	Service Type (from Tourism.owl)
D1	health@agents.com	HealthTourism
D2	summer@agents.com	SummerTourism
D3	sea@agents.com	SeaTourism
D4	tourism@agents.com	SummerTourism

Service type of each description is a concept defined in the domain ontology given in Fig. 2. Actually, service database of the DF is also an *ontology model* in which each agent service is represented with an individual. For example the DF description for the service offered by the agent called "health@agents.com" has a description on the model as follows (xml namespace definitions for RDF and OWL are omitted due to space limitations):

```
<rdf:RDF xmlns:j.0="http://.../~aegeants/ont/fipa-agent-management.owl#">
 <rdf:Description rdf:nodeID="D1">
   <rdf:type rdf:resource="fipa-agent-management.owl#DFAgentDescription"/>
   <j.0:name rdf:nodeID="A1"/>        <j.0:service rdf:nodeID="S1"/>
 </rdf:Description>
 <rdf:Description rdf:nodeID="A1">
   <rdf:type rdf:resource="fipa-agent-management.owl#AgentIdentifier"/>
   <j.0:name>health@aegeants.com</j.0:name>
   <j.0:addresses rdf:nodeID=" "/>      <j.0:resolvers rdf:nodeID=" "/>
 </rdf:Description>
 <rdf:Description rdf:nodeID="S1">
   <rdf:type rdf:resource=" fipa-agent-management.owl#ServiceDescription"/>
   <j.0:name>Health Tourism</j.0:name>
   <j.0:type>http://.../~aegeants/ont/Tourism.owl#HealthTourism</j.0:type>
 </rdf:Description>      </rdf:RDF>
```

"fipa-agent-management.owl" is an ontology that involves the concepts given in FIPA AMS [8]. It makes the DF descriptions fully compliant with FIPA specifications. Service types of the descriptions come from the "Tourism" domain ontology.

Then we developed a customer agent which has a simple plan looking for a hotel with "SummerTourism" service. However, in addition to exactly matched agent services, it requests other services semantically related with this type. Here is the OWL representation of the request parsed by the communication module and transmitted in a SeagentMatchRequest object to the engine (again namespace definitions are omitted):

```
<rdf:RDF xmlns:j.0="http://.../~aegeants/ont/seagent-match-ontology.owl#">
 <rdf:Description rdf:nodeID="R1">
  <rdf:type rdf:resource="seagent-match-ontology.owl#MatchRequest"/>
  <j.0:hasQuery rdf:nodeID="Q1"/>
  <j.0:hasSemanticMatch rdf:nodeID="S1"/>
  <j.0:hasPremise rdf:nodeID="P1"/>     <j.0:hasPremise rdf:nodeID="P2"/>
  <j.0:mustBindVariable>?x</j.0:mustBindVariable>
  <j.0:matchDegree>1</j.0:matchDegree>
 </rdf:Description>
 <rdf:Description rdf:nodeID="P1">
  <rdf:type rdf:resource="seagent-match-ontology.owl#Premise"/>
  <j.0:subject>?s</j.0:subject>
  <j.0:object>fipa-agent-management.owl#ServiceDescription</j.0:object>
  <j.0:predicate>http://www.w3.org/1999/02/22-rdf-syntax-ns#type</j.0:predicate>
 </rdf:Description>
 <rdf:Description rdf:nodeID="P2">
  <rdf:type rdf:resource="seagent-match-ontology.owl#Premise"/>
  <j.0:subject>?x</j.0:subject>
  <j.0:object>fipa-agent-management.owl#DFAgentDescription</j.0:object>
  <j.0:predicate>http://www.w3.org/1999/02/22-rdf-syntax-ns#type</j.0:predicate>
 </rdf:Description>
 <rdf:Description rdf:nodeID="Q1">
  <rdf:type rdf:resource="seagent-match-ontology.owl#Query"/>
  <j.0:subject>?x</j.0:subject>     <j.0:object>?s</j.0:object>
  <j.0:predicate>fipa-agent-management.owl#service</j.0:predicate>
 </rdf:Description>
 <rdf:Description rdf:nodeID="S1">
  <rdf:type rdf:resource="seagent-match-ontology.owl#SemanticMatch"/>
  <j.0:subject>?s</j.0:subject>
  <j.0:object>Tourism.owl#SummerTourism</j.0:object>
  <j.0:predicate>fipa-agent-management.owl#type</j.0:predicate>
 </rdf:Description>  </rdf:RDF>
```

Service discovery request is obviously an individual of the "seagent-match-ontology.owl" with the type of "MatchRequest". It both contains semantic matching and filtering query parameters which are given in RDF triple format. "Premise" properties of a request list RDF type of query variables while "Query" properties define relations between those variables. They may also include non-semantic query sentences those to be used in RDQL query. Every "SemanticMatch" property of the request defines a semantic query. "mustBindVariable" and "matchDegree" gives return type and desired match degree of the request respectively. Above "Premise" and "Query" descriptions tell that "?s" is a "ServiceDescription" and "?x" is a "DFDescription" and "?s" is a service of "?x". Finally, "SemanticMatch" property says that the request need a semantic query on *type* of the "?s": Find advertised agent services (ServiceDescriptions) whose types has a semantic relation with the type "SummerTourism". Match results will be of type "?x" (so DFDescription) and desired match degree is 1 (so SUBSUMES).

We examined that when the matching engine received this request; it first performed an RDQL query on the advertised agent services and filtered them according to the non-semantic parameters. Then, it used its reasoner (OWLOntolog) to determine semantic relationship between the given request and recently filtered service advertisements. The requester agent had asked for the services those have at least a "subsumes" relationship between the given request service type ("SummerTourism" in case). So, the engine matched the service descriptions D2, D3 and D4 with the given request as we expected and it sorted the match results starting from the most exact one(s) in the following order: D2, D4, D3 with EXACT, EXACT and SUBSUMES match degrees respectively. Each match result was returned to the communication module in a SeagentMatchResult object. According to our design, the DF used OWL representations of those results to put them into the ongoing ACL message and sent this result message to the requester agent. Then, the customer agent parsed the content and de-serialized each result object to proceed on its task. During this de-serialization it used "seagent-match-ontology.owl" to have an idea on ontology concepts those describes each match result due to match results are also semantically defined in the seagent-match-ontology likewise match requests. After all, the customer agent successfully retrieved *appropriate* services and it was ready to communicate agents offering those matched services.

5 Conclusion

Capability matching on agent services is a big challenge especially taking into consideration of future's semantic web enabled multi agent platforms. The main contribution of this study is to present a working model for semantic service matching on multi agent systems by indicating requirements to deal with that challenge. It introduces basics and design details of a semantic matching engine which is fully operational on MASs. Its integration into directory service structures is discussed with a working example given in this paper.

The engine is currently in use. However, we believe that it needs improvements on its capabilities taking into account of near future's platform requirements. Currently we are working on the Ontolog component of the engine and trying to enhance its reasoning system by adding support for extra ontology class relations such as "intersection" and "union". So, matching engine will be able to response more complex service discovery requirements (e.g. identifying composite agent services that owns two or more semantic types).

Our future work is to bring an abstraction to inner software design of the engine via a container mechanism such that it permits use of other semantic web tools in addition to (or in place of) Jena [11]. So, changes in these tools will not affect the core structure and it will need no or less modification on matching software.

References

1. Bellifemine, F., Poggi, A., Rimassa, G.: Developing Multi-agent Systems with a FIPA-compliant Agent Framework, Software Practice and Experience, 31 (2001) 103-128
2. Berners-Lee, T., Hendler, J. and Lassila, O.: The Semantic Web, Scientific American, 284(5), (2001), pp:34-43
3. Chen, H., et al.: Intelligent Agents Meet Semantic Web in a Smart Meeting Room, in the proc. of Autonomous Agents and Multi Agent Systems 2004 (AAMAS'04), NY, USA
4. Connolly, D., et al.: DAML+OIL (March 2001) Reference Description, available at: http://www.w3.org/TR/daml+oil-reference
5. Cost, R. S., et al.: Jackal:A Java-Based Tool for Agent Development, in the proc. workshop tools for Developing Agents (AAAI98), AAAI Press, Calif., (1998), pp:73-82
6. Cost, R. S., et al.: Ittalks: A Case Study in the Semantic Web and DAML+OIL, IEEE Intelligent Systems, January-February, (2002), pp:40-46
7. Dikenelli, O., et al.: SEAGENT: A Platform for Developing Semantic Web Based Multi Agent Systems, accepted to be presented in Fourth International Joint Conference on Autonomous Agents and Multi Agent Systems 2005 (AAMAS'05), Utrecht, The Netherlands
8. FIPA (Foundation for Intelligent Physical Agents): FIPA Specifications, available at: http://www.fipa.org
9. Gomez, M., Plaza, E.: Extending matchmaking to maximize capability reuse, in the proc. of Autonomous Agents and Multi Agent Systems 2004 (AAMAS'04), NY, USA
10. Graham, J. R., Decker, K. S., Mersic, M.: DECAF – A Flexible Multi Agent Systems Infrastructure, Journal of Autonomous Agents and Multi-Agent Systems,7 (2003), 7-27
11. JENA - A Semantic Web Framework for Java, available at: http://jena.sourceforge.net
12. Li, L., Horrocks, I.: A Software Framework for Matchmaking based on Semantic Web Technology, in the proc. of WWW'2003, Budapest, Hungary, pp. 331-339
13. McGuiness, D. L., van Harmelen, F.: OWL Web Ontology Language Overview, (2004), available at: http://www.w3.org/TR/owl-features/
14. Sycara, K., Paolucci, M., Ankolekar, A., Srinivasan, N.: Automated discovery, interaction and composition of Semantic Web Services, Journal of Web Semantics, Elsevier 1, (2003) pp. 27-46
15. The DAML Services Coalition: DAML-S 0.9 (May 2003): Semantic Markup for Web Services, available at: http://www.daml.org/services/daml-s/0.9/daml-s.html
16. Zambonelli, F., Omicini, A.: Challenges and Research Directions in Agent-Oriented Software Engineering, Journal of Autonomous Agents and Multi-Agent Systems, Vol. 9, No. 3, (2004)

Self-organizing Distribution of Agents over Hosts

Gabriel Ciobanu[1] and Dănuţ Rusu[2]

[1] Romanian Academy, Institute of Computer Science
and Research Institute IeAT, Timişoara, Romania
gabriel@iit.tuiasi.ro
[2] "A.I. Cuza" University of Iaşi, Faculty of Mathematics
drusu@uaic.ro

Abstract. In this paper we present a self-organizing system of agents able to move agents over the hosts to offer their services with an increase of the access speed, and decrease of the network traffic. We refer to a service layer represented by the agents, and a network layer of hosts and routers. We use a formal coordination model defining how agents interact and how their interactions can be controlled. This includes dynamic creation and destruction of agents, control of communication flows among agents, control of spatial distribution of agents, as well as synchronization of actions over time. We use various distances and topological relations in order to explain our self-organizing mechanism. We provide a good approximation of stability depending only on the moment of the first requests of agents by hosts. Finally we provide a visualization of the services evolution using Kohonen self-organizing maps, and presenting a service clustering structure.

1 Introduction

An important issue in a distributed systems is to locate the required resources such that the global performance of the system can be improved. In this paper we present a self-organizing system of agents able to modify their locations on network hosts in order to offer their services in a better way. We refer to a network layer of hosts and routers, and a service layer represented by the agent system. According to [8], our agents interoperate with each other, and an external observer could consider the whole community a structured agent offering multiple services. From a software engineering point of view, an agent can be defined as a process able to interoperate with other processes running on the same, or on a separate machine [5]. Clever relocations of services on hosts increase the access speed, and decrease the network traffic. A similar form of self-organization appears in society, particularly in business. It is easy to imagine a commercial company having a strategy of location/relocation of its shops or offices based on the balance between supply and demand. Such a market-oriented strategy provides a self-organization structure of the whole system. We get a form of self-organization achieved by the arrangement of parts of a system in a

P. Yolum et al.(Eds.): ISCIS 2005, LNCS 3733, pp. 462–471, 2005.

coordinated way. We use a coordination model defining how agents interact and how their interactions can be controlled. This includes dynamic creation and destruction of agents, control of communication flows among agents, control of spatial distribution of agents, as well as synchronization of actions over time. Communication among the agents is governed by a coordinator process able to establish the propagation of events, dynamic (re)configurations, creation and activation of various processes. Coordination rules define the actions between the agents and coordination media (locations, channels).

We formalize the notions used in this paper (hosts, routers, network manager, agents, agent manager, service, requests, answers), and use various distances and topological relations in order to explain our self-organizing distribution of services over network hosts. The topological results are based on general notions presented in any textbook, for instance [4]. A certain metric is used in studying the difficult problem of stability for an agent system, namely of placing the agents in an optimal way on the hosts such that they respond promptly to the requests. We define a weak form of stability, and we give a condition for this stability. Finally we provide a visualization of the services evolution using Kohonen self-organizing maps [6], presenting the dynamics of service clustering process.

2 Network Layer

The activities of agents take place in an environment provided by a network of hosts and routers, working under a specific routing protocol.

We consider a network, and a set $\mathcal{H}$ of connected hosts (at a certain moment of time). If an IP address of a host h is $A.B.C.D$, where $A, B, C, D \in \{0, 1, ..., 255\}$, then we can define a function $i : \mathcal{H} \to \mathbb{N}$ by $i(h) = A \cdot 2^{32} + B \cdot 2^{16} + C \cdot 2^8 + D$.

We define a binary relation $\overset{t}{\hookrightarrow} \subseteq \mathcal{H} \times \mathcal{H}$, and by $h_1 \overset{t}{\hookrightarrow} h_2$ we denote the fact that we have a direct connection from a host h_1 to a host h_2 at a certain time t. The inverse relation is denoted by $\overset{t}{\hookleftarrow}$; $\overset{t}{\hookleftarrow} \overset{def}{=} \left(\overset{t}{\hookrightarrow}\right)^{-1}$. We use t to emphasize the evolution in time of the network. From an algorithmic point of view, t describes the periodic updates of the routing tables.

Definition 1. *Let h_1, h_2 be hosts of $\mathcal{H}$. A t-connection of length $n > 0$ from h_1 to h_2 is a function $c_t : \{1, ..., n\} \to \mathcal{H}$, where $h_1 = c_t(1) \overset{t}{\hookrightarrow} c_t(2) \overset{t}{\hookrightarrow} \ldots \overset{t}{\hookrightarrow} c_t(n) = h_2$. The length of a connection c_t is denoted by $\lambda(c_t)$, and the set of hosts involved in such a connection is in fact the image of c_t, and it is denoted by $Im(c_t)$.*

It is easy to note that $\lambda(c_t) \geq card(Im(c_t))$.

We denote by $C_t(h_1, h_2)$ the set of all t-connections from h_1 to h_2. We assume that for each h there is a unique connection $c_t \in C_t(h, h)$, and $\lambda(c_t) = 0$.

Definition 2. *Considering $h_1, h_2 \in \mathcal{H}$, we say that h_1 is connected to h_2 at moment t if $C_t(h_1, h_2) \neq \emptyset$; we denote this by $h_1 \overset{t}{\rightsquigarrow} h_2$. We say that h_1 is* *biconnected to* h_2 *at moment* t *if* h_1 *is connected to* h_2 *at moment* t*, and* h_2 *is connected to* h_1 *at moment* t*; we denote this by* $h_1 \overset{t}{\leftrightsquigarrow} h_2$.

Proposition 1.

(i) $\overset{t}{\rightsquigarrow}$ *is a quasi-order relation on* $\mathcal{H}$.
(ii) $\overset{t}{\leftrightsquigarrow}$ *is an equivalence relation over* $\mathcal{H}$.

Network is an essential support for our system of agents. The key aspects are network performance, stability and security. Network performance is determined by its bandwidth and latency. Since latency is closely related to bandwidth, we consider the functions $l_t : \mathcal{H} \rightarrow [0, \infty)$, as well as $istab_t, isec_t : \mathcal{H} \rightarrow [0,1]$ representing the average latency, degree of stability, and degree of security, respectively. All these functions depend on a certain moment of time t. We can aggregate these aspects into a function $E_t : \mathcal{H} \times \mathcal{H} \rightarrow [0, \infty)$ defined by $E_t(h) = \sqrt{l_t(h)^2 + istab_t(h)^2 + isec_t(h)^2}$ for all $h \in \mathcal{H}$. As a distance over $\mathcal{H}$, we use a function $d_t : \mathcal{H} \times \mathcal{H} \rightarrow [0, \infty)$ defined by $d_t(h_1, h_2) =$

$$= \sqrt{(l_t(h_1) - l_t(h_2))^2 + (istab_t(h_1) - istab_t(h_2))^2 + (isec_t(h_1) - isec_t(h_2))^2}$$

for all $h_1, h_2 \in \mathcal{H}$.

Proposition 2. d_t *is a pseudo-metric over* $\mathcal{H}$.

This function d_t represents the cost of connecting two hosts. This cost is used in the routing tables of the network. Among the existing protocols, we are thinking of the OSPF (Open Shortest Path First) TCP/IP routing protocol for the Internet [9]. OSPF has two characteristics. The first is that the protocol is open, and the second characteristic is that OSPF is based on the Dijkstra algorithm. OSPF is a link-state routing protocol based on the communication with all other routers within the same hierarchical area. As OSPF routers accumulate link state information, they use the Dijkstra algorithm to calculate the shortest path to each node.

OSPF domain is represented by an autonomous network system divided into areas.An area is a collection of hosts and routers. Routers inside an area dissipate routing information. The OSPF protocol allows the administrators to assign a cost to each route. The cost is based on a type of service (minimum delay, maximum throughput, etc.); a router can have multiple routing tables, each based on a different type of service. In OSPF terminology, a connection is called a link. OSPF uses link state routing, and in this way a router can have the whole picture of the hosts, being able to calculate the shortest path between itself and each host. A link state database is a tabular representation of the network topology inside an area. Each router applies the Dijkstra algorithm to its link state database.

We can imagine a new routing protocol, where we determine the cost of the paths $C_t(h_1, h_2)$ between two hosts h_1, h_2 based on the cost of each point-to-point link given by our previous d_t. Considering that $C_t(h_1, h_2) \neq \emptyset$, we define $\mu_t : C_t(h_1, h_2) \to [0, \infty)$ by $\mu_t(c_t) = \sum_{i=1}^{\lambda(c_t)} d_t(c_t(i), c_t(i+1))$ for all $c_t \in C_t(h_1, h_2)$. Considering a given large constant $K > 0$ (larger than any other number involved in our computation), we can define $D_t : \mathcal{H} \times \mathcal{H} \to [0, \infty)$ by

$$D_t(h_1, h_2) = \begin{cases} \min\limits_{c_t \in C_t(h_1,h_2)} (\mu_t(c_t) \wedge K), & \text{if } C_t(h_1, h_2) \neq \emptyset \\ K & \text{if } C_t(h_1, h_2) = \emptyset \end{cases}, \forall h_1, h_2 \in \mathcal{H}$$

In this definition, $\min\limits_{c_t \in C_t(h_1,h_2)} (\mu_t(c_t) \wedge K)$ is determined by the Dijkstra algorithm.

Proposition 3. *D_t is a pseudo-metric over $\mathcal{H}$.*

We describe now the topology of $\mathcal{H}$ based on the minimal costs at a certain moment of time, by defining a function $T_t : \mathcal{H} \times \mathcal{H} \to \left(\bigcup\limits_{h_1,h_2 \in \mathcal{H}} C_t(h_1, h_2) \right) \cup \{\emptyset\}$

$$T_t(h_1, h_2) = \begin{cases} c_t \in C_t(h_1, h_2), \text{if } D_t(h_1, h_2) = \mu_t(c_t) < K \\ \emptyset \qquad \text{otherwise} \end{cases}, \forall h_1, h_2 \in \mathcal{H}$$

$\mathcal{I}m(T_t) = \{T_t(h_1, h_2) \mid h_1, h_2 \in \mathcal{H},\ h_1 \neq h_2\}$ is called the t-topology of $\mathcal{H}$. We note that this network topology has certain dynamics in time. We describe here a possible self-organizing procedure of determining the network topology at each moment t.

We consider a network manager NM. At the installation of an agent system $\mathcal{A}$, such a network manager surveys the networks, and activate a copy of itself on each router. Each NM has four threads. Let us consider a host $h \in \mathcal{H}$ at a moment t. Initially $istab_t(h) = 0$, and $isec_t(h) = 0$.

The first thread of NM is responsible to update $l_t(h)$, $istab_t(h)$, and $isec_t(h)$ at certain moments of time t. It sends testing packages to h, and records the reply time $t(h)$. If $t(h) \geq T$ where T is a predefined time constant, then sets $t(h) = T$, $istab_t(h) = 1$, and $isec_t(h) = 1$. It can eventually determine the average latency of h at t, and goes to another host.

The second thread takes care of the requests received from other hosts. These requests are placed into a queue. If the waiting time of a request is greater than a given period of time, then the corresponding request is removed from the queue. For each removed request, NM increases $istab_t(h)$ according to a penalty algorithm. On the other hand, if $istab_t(h)$ remains constant for a certain period of time, NM decreases $istab_t(h)$ according to a rewarding algorithm.

The third thread deals with the security degree of h at time t, and records it in $isec_t(h)$. There exist various mothods of calculating the security degree; it depends on the designers choice. Finally, the fourth thread calculates $E_t(h)$, and eventually modifies the network topology of $\mathcal{H}$. This happens periodically, using a self-organizing algorithm. By this self-organization, the hosts can be organized in areas. Let us suppose that at a certain moment t, $\mathcal{H} = \{h_1, h_2, ..., h_N\}$, and $E_t(h_1) \leq E_t(h_2) \leq ... \leq E_t(h_N)$. We associate a representation vector to each host by using an injective function $f_t : \mathcal{H} \to \mathbb{C}$. We consider initially $m_0(h) =$

$(l_t(h), istab_t(h), isec_t(h))$ for all $h \in \mathcal{H}$. A number *iter* of iterations are then executed:

```
for (int τ = 0; τ < iter; τ++)
{
  build an arbitrary vector x_τ ∈ [0,∞) × [0,1] × [0,1];
  determine a host h_c in which d(x_τ, m_τ(h_c)) = min_{j∈1,N} d(x_τ, m_τ(h_j));
  for (int j = 1; j ≤ N; j++)
      m_{τ+1}(h_j) ← m_τ(h_j) + h_cj(τ) [x_τ − m_τ(h_j)];
}
```

where $h_{cj}(\tau) = \alpha(\tau) \cdot \exp\left(-\frac{|f_t(h_c) - f_t(h_j)|}{2\sigma^2(\tau)}\right)$ is a "smoothing" function, with learning factor $\alpha(\tau)$, and $\sigma(t)$ represents the dimension of h_{cj} kernel.

This algorithm provides a map based on the representation vector $f_t(h)$, where a certain map area puts together hosts with similar properties. The network topology at a certain moment t is related to this map.

3 Agents and Their Dynamics

Let $\mathcal{A}$ be a set of agents distributed on the hosts of $\mathcal{H}$. We use a coordination mechanism by considering an agent manager *AM*. *AM* coordinates the agents interaction, including dynamic creation and destruction of agents, control of communication flows among agents, control of spatial distribution of agents over network hosts. *AM* is able to localize the agents, and contains a history of each service (agent). There are two agent managers: an active agent manager, and a passive one. Whenever the active manager is collapsing, the passive manager is becoming active, and creates dynamically a passive manager. Then inform the agents that it is the new agent manager.

First we present a topological result regarding the agents system.

Definition 3. *Considering $a \in \mathcal{A}$ and $h \in \mathcal{H}$, we say that $a \overset{t}{\in} h$ iff the agent a is on the host h at the moment t.*

We denote by $A_h^t = \left\{a \in \mathcal{A} \mid a \overset{t}{\in} h\right\}$ the set of agents on h at time t, and by $\tau_t = \{A_h^t \mid h \in \mathcal{H}\}$ the agents topology at a certain moment t.
Let $ATop$ be $\{\tau_t \mid t \in Time\}$; we define $d : ATop \times ATop \rightarrow \mathbb{R}_+$ by $d(\tau_t, \tau_{t'}) = \sum_{h\in\mathcal{H}} card\left(A_h^t \Delta A_h^{t'}\right)$ for all $\tau_t, \tau_{t'} \in ATop$. We use discrete time, i.e. $Time = \mathbb{N}$.

Proposition 4. *d is a metric over $ATop$.*

Proof. $d(\tau_t, \tau_{t'}) = 0 \Leftrightarrow card\left(A_h^t \Delta A_h^{t'}\right) = 0$, for all $h \in \mathcal{H}$. This means that $A_h^t \Delta A_h^{t'} = \emptyset$ for all $h \in \mathcal{H}$, namely $\tau_t = \tau_{t'}$. It is obvious that $d(\tau_t, \tau_{t'}) = d(\tau_{t'}, \tau_t)$ for all $\tau_t, \tau_{t'} \in ATop$. Finally, we prove that $d(\tau_t, \tau_{t'}) \leq d(\tau_t, \tau_{t''}) + d(\tau_{t''}, \tau_{t'})$, $\forall \tau_t, \tau_{t'}, \tau_{t''} \in ATop$. Since $A_h^t \Delta A_h^{t'} \subset (A_h^t \Delta A_h^{t''}) \cup (A_h^{t''} \Delta A_h^{t'})$, then we have

$card\left(A_h^t \Delta A_h^{t'}\right) \leq card\left(A_h^t \Delta A_h^{t''}\right) + card\left(A_h^{t''} \Delta A_h^{t'}\right)$ for all $h \in \mathcal{H}$. Therefore $d\left(\tau_t, \tau_{t'}\right) \leq d\left(\tau_t, \tau_{t''}\right) + d\left(\tau_{t''}, \tau_{t'}\right)$.

This metric can measure the dynamics of agents in time. It could be useful to observe the stability of the whole system after a certain time. It is therefore interesting to find a good approximation of $d\left(f\left(\tau_t\right), \tau_t\right)$.

In order to describe the changes of the agent topology, we introduce the functions $cr, rm, id : \tau_t \times \mathcal{A} \rightarrow \tau_t$ defined by $cr\left(A_h^t, a\right) = A_h^t \cup \{a\}$, $rm\left(A_h^t, a\right) = A_h^t \setminus \{a\}$, and $id\left(A_h^t, a\right) = A_h^t$ for all $A_h^t \in \tau_t$ and $a \in \mathcal{A}$. $cr\left(A_h^t, a\right)$ represents the process of creating an agent a on host h, and $rm\left(A_h^t, a\right)$ represents the removing of an agent a from host h. We define $\varphi_t : \mathcal{H} \times \mathcal{A} \rightarrow \{0, 1\}$ by

$$\varphi_t\left(h, a\right) = \begin{cases} 1, & \text{if } h \text{ requests the service of } a \text{ at time } t \\ 0, & \text{if } h \text{ does not request } a \text{ at time } t \end{cases}$$

We need a history in time of the services requests on each host. We use the functions $\alpha, \omega : \mathcal{H} \times \mathcal{A} \rightarrow \mathbb{N}$, where $\alpha\left(h, a\right)$ represents the moment of the first requests of a by the host h, and $\omega\left(h, a\right)$ is the moment of the last requests of a by the host h. We suppose that initial $\alpha\left(h, a\right) = \omega\left(h, a\right) = 0$ for all $\left(h, a\right) \in \mathcal{H} \times \mathcal{A}$. If $\varphi_t\left(h, a\right) = 1$ and $\alpha\left(h, a\right) = 0$, then $\alpha\left(h, a\right) = t$. If $\varphi_t\left(h, a\right) = 1$, $\omega\left(h, a\right) = t'$ and $t' < t$, then $\omega\left(h, a\right) = t$.

We define $hist_t : \mathcal{H} \times \mathcal{A} \rightarrow \mathbb{N}$ by $hist_t\left(h, a\right) = \sum_{u=\alpha(h,a)}^{t} \varphi_u\left(h, a\right)$.

We define also an "update function" $F : \tau_t \times \mathcal{A} \rightarrow \tau_t$ by $F\left(A_h^t, a\right) =$

$$= \begin{cases} cr\left(A_h^t, a\right), & \text{if } a \notin A_h^t, \text{ and } hist_t\left(h, a\right) \geq nr \\ rm\left(A_h^t, a\right), & \text{if } a \in A_h^t, t - \omega\left(h, a\right) \geq ns, \text{ and } hist_t\left(h, a\right) = hist_{\omega(h,a)}\left(h, a\right) \\ id\left(A_h^t, a\right), & \text{otherwise} \end{cases}$$

In this definition nr and ns are two working constants of AM. nr represents the number of requests triggering the necessity of having a certain agent on a host, and ns is the number of steps without any request for a certain agent on a host, triggering its removal. We should add that $\alpha\left(h, a\right) = 0$ whenever $F\left(A_h^t, a\right) = rm\left(A_h^t, a\right)$. Based on this "update function", we can define a more general function $f : \tau_t \rightarrow \tau_t$ defined by $f\left(A_h^t\right) = \bigcup_{a \in \mathcal{A}} F\left(A_h^t, a\right)$ for all $A_h^t \in \tau_t$. We can extend this function to $f : ATop \rightarrow ATop$ defined by $f\left(\tau_t\right) = \left\{f\left(A_h^t\right) \mid h \in \mathcal{H}\right\}$. At a certain moment t, f transforms A_h^t and makes it available for the next step; therefore $f\left(A_h^t\right) = A_h^{t+1}$ for all $h \in \mathcal{H}$, and $f\left(\tau_t\right) = \tau_{t+1}$.

The previous defined metric d is able to measure how much different is $\tau_{t'}$ than τ_t. Let us assume $t < t'$. The number of changes on a host h is given by $card\left(A_h^t \Delta A_h^{t'}\right) = card\left(A_h^t \setminus A_h^{t'}\right) + card\left(A_h^{t'} \setminus A_h^t\right)$, where $card\left(A_h^t \setminus A_h^{t'}\right)$ represents the number of agents removed from h, and $card\left(A_h^{t'} \setminus A_h^t\right)$ represents the number of agents added to h between t and t'. The dynamics of the agent system is related to the evolution in time of $d\left(\tau_t, \tau_{t+1}\right)$. Let us analyze this evolution for the whole system.

We have $d\left(f\left(\tau_t\right), \tau_t\right) = \sum_{h \in \mathcal{H}} card\left(A_h^{t+1} \Delta A_h^t\right)$, where $card\left(A_h^{t+1} \Delta A_h^t\right) = card\left(A_h^{t+1} \setminus A_h^t\right) + card\left(A_h^t \setminus A_h^{t+1}\right)$.

On the other hand,

$$card\left(A_h^{t+1}\backslash A_h^t\right) = \sum_{a\notin A_h^t}\left[\frac{hist_t(h,a)}{nr}\right], \text{ and}$$

$$card\left(A_h^t\backslash A_h^{t+1}\right) = \sum_{a\in A_h^t}\left[\frac{t-\omega(h,a)}{ns}\right]\cdot\left[1-\frac{hist_t(h,a)-hist_{\omega(h,a)}(h,a)}{t-\omega(h,a)}\right].$$

Our metric d is important in studying the difficult problem of reaching the stability of an agent system, namely of placing the agents in an optimal way on the hosts such that they respond promptly to the requests. The stabilization depends mainly on the number of modifications in the system; however there are many parameters, and reaching the stability is an open problem. On the other hand, the stability of an agent system is an ideal situation. We define a weak form of stability.

Definition 4. *Given a constant $\varepsilon > 0$, we say that a system $\mathcal{A}$ is ε-stable if there is a time t_0 such that $d(\tau_t,\tau_{t+1}) \leq \varepsilon$ for each $t \geq t_0$.*

Therefore we look now for a certain upper bound of $d(\tau_t,\tau_{t+1})$. Let $p_{h,a,\delta} \in [0,1]$ be the probability of having a request of a on a host h in a temporal interval of length δ. Then $hist_t(h,a) = (t-\alpha(h,a))\,p_{h,a,\delta}$, and

$$card\left(A_h^{t+1}\backslash A_h^t\right) = \sum_{a\notin A_h^t}\left[\frac{t-\alpha(h,a)}{nr}p_{h,a,\delta}\right] = \sum_{a\in\mathcal{A}}\left[\frac{t-\alpha(h,a)}{nr}\chi_{\mathcal{A}\backslash A_h^t}(a)\,p_{h,a,\delta}\right],$$

$$card\left(A_h^t\backslash A_h^{t+1}\right) = \sum_{a\in A_h^t}\left[\frac{t-\omega(h,a)}{ns}\right]\cdot\left[1-\frac{(t-\omega(h,a))\,p_{h,a,\delta}}{t-\omega(h,a)}\right] =$$

$$= \sum_{a\in\mathcal{A}}\left[\frac{t-\omega(h,a)}{ns}\chi_{A_h^t}(a)\right]\cdot\left[1-p_{h,a,\delta}\right].$$

Thus $d(\tau_{t+1},\tau_t) =$

$$= \sum_{h\in\mathcal{H},\,a\in\mathcal{A}}\left(\left[\tfrac{t-\alpha(h,a)}{nr}\chi_{\mathcal{A}\backslash A_h^t}(a)\,p_{h,a,\delta}\right]+\left[\tfrac{t-\omega(h,a)}{ns}\chi_{A_h^t}(a)\right]\cdot\left[1-p_{h,a,\delta}\right]\right).$$

We have $\left[\frac{t-\alpha(h,a)}{nr}\chi_{\mathcal{A}\backslash A_h^t}(a)\,p_{h,a,\delta}\right]+\left[\frac{t-\omega(h,a)}{ns}\chi_{A_h^t}(a)\right]\cdot\left[1-p_{h,a,\delta}\right] \leq$

$$\leq \frac{t-\alpha(h,a)}{nr}p_{h,a,\delta}+\frac{t-\omega(h,a)}{ns}\left(1-p_{h,a,\delta}\right).$$

Since $\frac{t-\alpha(h,a)}{nr}p_{h,a,\delta}+\frac{t-\omega(h,a)}{ns}\left(1-p_{h,a,\delta}\right) =$

$$= \frac{1}{\min(nr,ns)}\left[(t-\omega(h,a))+(\omega(h,a)-\alpha(h,a))\,p_{h,a,\delta}\right],$$

then we have

$$\frac{t-\alpha(h,a)}{nr}p_{h,a,\delta}+\frac{t-\omega(h,a)}{ns}\left(1-p_{h,a,\delta}\right) \leq \frac{t-\alpha(h,a)}{\min(nr,ns)}.$$

Therefore $d(\tau_{t+1},\tau_t) \leq \frac{1}{\min(nr,ns)}\left[card\mathcal{H}\cdot card\mathcal{A}\cdot t - \sum_{h\in\mathcal{H},\,a\in\mathcal{A}}\alpha(h,a)\right].$

This last inequality provides a way to find a good approximation of stability depending only on function α.

Proposition 5. *Given a constant* $\varepsilon > 0$*, if there is a time* t_0 *such that*
$$\sum_{h \in \mathcal{H},\, a \in \mathcal{A}} \alpha(h,a) \geq card\mathcal{H} \cdot card\mathcal{A} \cdot t - \varepsilon \cdot \min(nr, ns) \text{ for every } t \geq t_0,$$
then $\mathcal{A}$ *is* ε*-stable.*

The agent manager $AM \in \mathcal{A}$ should relate the topology of the agent system $\mathcal{A}$ to the network topology of $\mathcal{H}$. We define such a topology, describing a self-organizing distribution of agents over network hosts.

A service s is the class of agents able to offer this service. AM contains the whole set of services. AM keeps a map of the agents, and it is able to identify the location of a certain agent by a pair $(service, IPhost)$. AM creates and moves agents, as well as it removes the agents according to a set of coordination rules.

The removal of the agents is given periodically by a garbage collector controlled by AM. It considers each service s. We denote by $H(s)$ the set of hosts having agents offering s. For each $h \in H(s)$ where we have an agent a offering s, it computes the sphere B of radius r depending on the distance D_t, i.e. $B = \{h' \in \mathcal{H} \mid D_t(h', h) < r,\ h' \text{ asks for } s\}$. For each $h' \in B$, $\theta_s(h')$ represents time of the last request of s sent by h'. If $\underset{h' \in \mathcal{H}}{max} > const$, then the garbage collector remove agent a from host h.

Let us consider that a host h asks for a service s; its request $req(s)$ is given by $(IPh, s, param)$, where $param$ represents specific parameters of s. We have a general situation when $req(s)$ is sent to a router which redirects it to AM. AM updates the corresponding $\theta_s(h)$, and determines a set $H(s)$ of hosts offering s ($H(s) \neq \emptyset$ because at least $AM \in H(s)$). Then it computes $\underset{h' \in \mathcal{H}}{min} D_t(h', h)$. Let us assume that this minimum is given by h'; then AM sends $req(s)$ to h'. h' solves this request, producing an answer $ans(s)$ sent then to IPh. Moreover, if $\underset{h' \in \mathcal{H}}{min} D_t(h', h) > 0$, then AM increments a counter $c(s)$ representing the number of requests for s from a different host (i.e. $h = h'$). If $c(s) > k$, where k is a constant of the agent system, then AM follows a procedure regarding the re-organization of $\mathcal{A}$. For each host h' asking for a service s,

- AM computes the sum of distances from h' to all h'' requesting s;
- it determines a host h_{min} which minimizes this sum;
- AM copies its agent a providing s on host h_{min}.

4 Agents Clustering by Self-organizing Maps

This distribution of services over hosts shows a self-organization which could be visualized by the help of Kohonen self-organizing maps. We can imagine a 2D map where the hosts providing various services are represented by small white squares. Around these hosts are many colored points representing the services they provide. We associate three attributes to each service, and these attributes are represented by numbers between 0 and 255. A service is characterized by a 5-uple (x, y, r, g, b), where x and y indicate the position of the service on the map, and $r, g, b \in N_{255} \times N_{255} \times N_{255}$ represent its attributes ($N_{255} = \{0, 1, ..., 255\}$).

We can describe by $s(x,y) = (r,g,b)$ a service s on a host localized at (x,y) on the map.

We can cluster the services distributed over various hosts by using Kohonen self-organizing maps. Moreover, by using these maps we can relate and order the services by considering various similarities among them. We can use different measures of similarity. Let r be a positive number. We select initially an arbitrary set $M = \{m_1, m_2, ..., m_k\} \subset N^3_{255}$ of models. For each model m_i, we determine a ball of radius r with respect to a similarity metric d, namely $B(m_i, r) = \{s(x,y) \,|d(m_i, s(x,y)) < r\}$. We determine a vector from $B(m_i, r)$ which is the closest, according to d, to all other vectors. For each $s(x,y) \in B(m_i, r)$ we compute the sum of distances from $s(x,y)$ to all other vectors of $B(m_i, r)$. Then we select a vector $s(x,y)$ for which this sum is minimal. If there are more than one such a vector, we select an arbitrary one of them.

Since these vectors are three-dimensional, it is also possible to calculate their average for each dimension, and then to determine the closest vector of $B(m_i, r)$ to this average. Independent of the used method, let us assume that for model m_i we determine a vector $s(x', y') \in B(m_i, r)$. Then we follow the following steps:

1. we modify each vector $s(x,y) \in B(m_i, r)$ by
$s(x,y) \leftarrow [s(x,y) + f(x,y)(m_i - s(x,y))]$,
where $f(x,y) = \exp\left(-\alpha\sqrt{x^2+y^2}\right)$;
2. we substitute m_i with $s(x', y')$, and iterate the process.

After a certain number of iterations, the whole process becomes stable. However, the convergence of this algorithm is proved only for special similarity distances. Such a result is presented in [3].

Fig. 1. Kohonen self-organizing maps

Figure 1 is generated by an applet simulating the distribution of services according to the method described in this section. In this applet, $s(x, y)$ is represented by the color generated by the numbers r, g, and b.

5 Conclusion

Self-organization refers to the evolution of a structure resulting from internal mechanisms, due mainly to local interactions between components. The system evolves dynamically in time or space, and it can finally reach a stable structure. We present a self-organizing system of distributing software agents over network hosts, with increase of service supply speed, and decrease of network traffic. We use a formal description of the network and the agent system, providing some topological results relevant to the self-organizing algorithms. We use a coordination model popular in self-organizing systems. This model uses interaction between hosts and between agents, and it is based on specific coordinators both at the network level and the services level. Starting from the fact that various services of the agents need to cope with requirements and constraints stemming from the increased dynamism and sophisticated network control, we introduce a self-organization mechanism for services. We analyze the stability of the system, and provide a new result regarding a weak form of stability. Finally we provide a visualization of the services evolution using Kohonen self-organizing maps.

References

1. Alboaie, S., Ciobanu G.: Designing and Developing Multi-Agent Systems, Proceedings Int'l Symposium on Parallel and Distributed Computing, Scientific Annals "A.I.Cuza" University **XI** (2002) 142–153
2. Cheng, Y.: Clustering with competing self-organizing maps. In Int'l Joint Conf on Neural Networks, Vol.IV (1992) 785–790
3. Cheng, Y.: Convergence and ordering of Kohonen's batch map. Neural Computation **9** (1997) 1667–1676
4. Engelking, R.: General Topology. 2nd edn. Sigma Series in Pure Mathematics, Vol. 6, Heldermann (1989)
5. Genesereth, M.R., Ketchpel, S.P.: Software Agents. Communications ACM **7** (1994) 48–53
6. Kohonen, T.: Self-Organizing Maps. 3rd edn. Springer-Verlag, Berlin Heidelberg New York (2001)
7. Kohonen, T.: Exploration of very large databases by self-organizing maps. In Proceedings Int'l Conference on Neural Networks. IEEE Press (1997) 1–6
8. Minski, M.: The Society of Mind. Simon and Schuster (1985)
9. Moy, J.T.: OSPF Anatomy of An Internet Routing Protocol. Addison-Wesley (1998)

Evolutionary Design of Group Communication Schedules for Interconnection Networks

Jiří Jaroš, Miloš Ohlídal, and Václav Dvořák

Brno University of Technology, Faculty of Information Technology,
Department of Computer Systems, Božetěchova 2, 612 66 Brno, Czech Republic
Phone: +420-541141149, fax: +420-541141270
{Jarosjir, Ohlidal, Dvorak}@fit.vutbr.cz

Abstract. As chip multiprocessors are quickly penetrating new application areas in network and media processing, their interconnection architectures become a subject of optimization. Group communications are frequently used in many parallel algorithms and if their overhead is excessive, performance degrades rapidly with a processor count. This paper deals with the design of a new application-specific Bayesian Optimization Algorithm (BOA) and the use of BOA and HSGA (Hybrid parallel Genetic Simulated Annealing) to design optimal communication algorithms for an arbitrary topology of the interconnection network. Each of these algorithms is targeted for a different switching technique. The group communication schedules were designed for an asymmetrical AMP network on one hand and for the benchmark hypercube network on the other, using SF (Store-and-Forward) and WH (Wormhole) switching.

1 Introduction

With parallel and distributed computing coming of age, multiprocessor systems are more frequently found not only in high-end servers and workstations, but also in small-scale parallel systems for high performance control, data acquisition and analysis, image processing, networking processors, wireless communication, and game computers. The design and optimization of hw and sw architectures for these parallel embedded applications have been an active research area in recent years. For many cases it is better to use several small processing nodes rather than a single big and complex CPU. Nowadays, it is feasible to place large CPU clusters on a single chip (multiprocessor SoCs, MSoCs), allowing both large local memories and the high bandwidth of on-chip interconnect.

One of the greatest challenges faced by designers of digital systems is optimizing the communication and interconnection between system components. As more and more processor cores and other large reusable components have been integrated on single silicon die, a need for a systematic approach to the design of communication part has become acute. One reason is that buses, the former main means to connect the components, could not scale to higher numbers of communication partners. Recently the research opened up in Network on Chip (NoC) area, encompassing the interconnection/communication problem at all levels, from physical to the architectural to the OS and application level [1].

P. Yolum et al.(Eds.): ISCIS 2005, LNCS 3733, pp. 472 – 481, 2005.

At the present time, there are many different interconnection network topologies for multiprocessors and new networks for specific parallel applications can still be created. While the lower bounds on the time complexity of various group communications (in terms of required number of communication steps) can be mathematically derived for any network topology and the given communication pattern, finding a corresponding schedule of communication is more difficult and in some cases it is not known as yet. The rest of the paper addresses the quest for an optimal communication schedule based on evolutionary algorithms, provided that network topology and a specific communication pattern are given.

2 Models of Communications

Communications between two partners (p2p) or among all (or a subset) of partners engaged in parallel processing have a dramatic impact on the speedup of parallel applications. Performance modeling of p2p and group communications is therefore important in design of application-specific systems. A p2p communication may be random (input data dependent) as far as source-destination pair or a message length is concerned. However, in many parallel algorithms we often find certain communication patterns, which are regular in time, in space, or in both time and space; by space we understand spatial distribution of processes on processors. Communications taking place among a subset or among all processors are called group or collective communications. Examples of these may serve one-to-all broadcast (OAB), all-to-all broadcast (AAB), one-to-all scatter (OAS, a private message to each partner), all-to-one gather (AOG), all-to-all scatter (AAS), permutation, scan, reduction and others. Provided that the amount of computation is known, as is usually true in case of application-specific systems, the only thing that matters in obtaining the highest performance are group communication times.

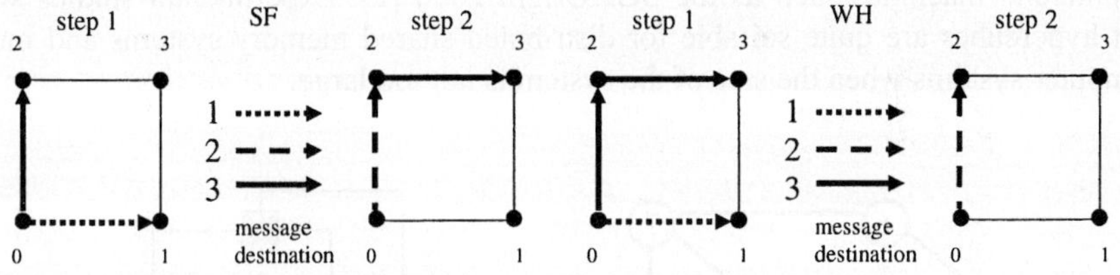

Fig. 1. OAS using SF and WH switching

The simplest time model of communication uses a number of communication steps (rounds): point-to-point communication takes one step between adjacent nodes and a number of steps if the nodes are not directly connected. Each step includes start-up (head) latency t_0 and then the serialization latency that is proportional to the message length m (in bytes) and to per byte transfer time t_l. For distance-sensitive store-and-forward (SF) switching, the serialization latency is incurred in every hop between neighbor nodes, $h\ x\ (m\ t_l)$ in total, where h is the distance (in hops) of source and destination nodes. For distance-insensitive wormhole (WH) switching or virtual cut-through (CT) switching several p2p messages between source-destination pairs, not necessarily neighbors, can proceed concurrently and can be combined into a single step if their paths are disjoint. The head latency t_0 is slightly dependent on the distance h, but the serialization latency is incurred only once. Of course, for simplicity, we assume no contention for channels and no resulting delays. An example of these switching techniques is shown in fig. 1.

Further, we have to distinguish between unidirectional (simplex) channels and bidirectional (half-duplex, full-duplex) channels. The number of ports that can be engaged in communication simultaneously (1-port or all-port models of routers) has also an impact on number of communication steps and communication time, as well as if nodes can combine/extract partial messages with negligible overhead (combining model) or can only retransmit/consume original messages (non-combining model). Finally we have to take into account a switching technique (store-and-forward SF, wormhole WH or cut-through CT) and network topology. Thus complexity of every group communication pattern (permutation, OAB, ABB, OAS, AOG, AAS) can be investigated in at least 3×2×2×3 = 36 modes for a single topology, so that we would have to deal with 180 cases. We therefore limit ourselves to the analysis of only all-port models, non-combining nodes, full-duplex channels, SF and WH switching and only OAB, OAS (OAG – a reverse operation to OAS), AAB and AAS communication patterns.

In our experimental runs hypercube and AMP network topologies were tested. The goal was to find communication algorithms whose time complexity corresponds to mathematically derived lover bounds on number of communication steps.

2.1 Hypercube and a Minimum Path Topology (AMP)

An n-dimensional hypercube is a node symmetric, direct interconnection network that has 2^n processors (or nodes). Any processor has n bidirectional connections to the neighbor processors. The hypercube network found its applications in the recent commercial machines such as the SGI Origin 2000 [2]. Experimental studies show that hypercubes are quite suitable for distributed shared memory systems and multi-computer systems when the size of the system is not too large.

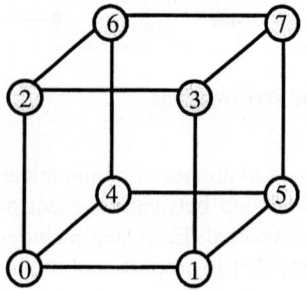

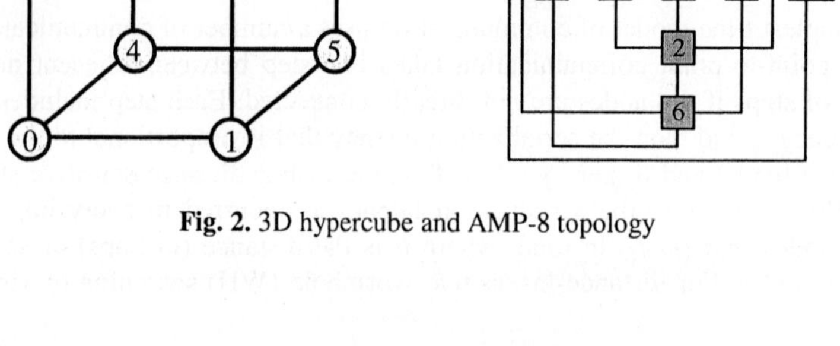

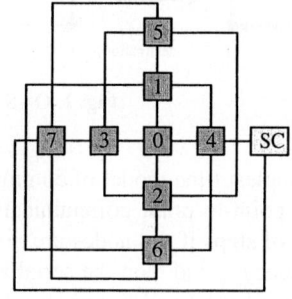

Fig. 2. 3D hypercube and AMP-8 topology

The AMP topology is a result of genetic graph optimization. It is an asymmetrical network that minimizes the network diameter and the average inter-processor distance. Optimum graphs with 4 bidirectional links and one extra node (a system controller SC) were found for 5, 8, 12, 13, 14, 32, 36, 42, 53, 64, 128, 256 processors. Here we will consider a modified version without the system controller, where one out of P compute nodes will act accordingly [6]. The example of AMP topology is at fig.2.

3 Discrete Optimization Algorithms

Combinatorial search and optimization techniques in general are characterized by looking for a solution to a problem from among many potential solutions. For many search and optimization problems, exhaustive search is infeasible and some form of guided search is undertaken instead. In addition, rather than only the best (optimal) solution, a good non-optimal solution is often sought.

An optimization part of the algorithms described below is based on genetic algorithm (GA), which is a powerful, domain-independent search technique. GA is any population based computational model that uses selection and recombination operators to generate a new sample in the search space. A chromosome (individual), consisting of genes, represents one encoded solution from the search space. The values of genes are referred to as alleles. The chromosomes form population, which changes through the evolution process. The reproduction process is performed in such a way that chromosomes, which represent a better solution, are given more chances to reproduce than those chromosomes, which represent poorer solutions. The fitness function (a measure of quality) of chromosomes is defined in the frame of the population. The fitness function is applied to genotype (chromosomes) for evaluating phenotype (decoded form of the individual /chromosome). While the fitness function operates with phenotype, genetic operators are defined on the genotype.

3.1 Mixed Bayesian Optimization Algorithm (MBOA)

MBOA algorithm is based on Bayesian Optimization Algorithm (BOA). The general procedure of BOA algorithm [3], [4] is similar to that of GA, but the classical recombination operators (crossover and mutation) are replaced by probability estimation followed by probability sampling. These algorithms use advantageously the statistical information contained in the set of promising solutions to discover the linkage between genes. A new feature of these algorithms is a global usage of the whole population in the process of model construction. One of the basic advantages is the capability to discover nonlinear interaction between genes, which allows solving complex nonlinear problems.

The probabilistic model of MBOA is a set of binary decision trees/graphs. The MBOA differs from BOA also in the heterogeneous model parameters. The decision trees can be used also for continuous or mixed domains. MBOA uses variance adaptation for scaling variance in continuous domains. This algorithm was proposed and implemented for coarse-grained type of parallelism.

3.2 Hybrid Parallel Genetic Simulated Annealing (HGSA)

HGSA is a hybrid method and it uses parallel SA with the operations that are used in standard genetic algorithms [7]. The flow of the evolution is shown in fig. 3. In the proposed algorithm, there are sequential SA processes running in parallel. After a number of steps (after one hundred of iterations of Metropolis algorithm), the crossover is used to produce new solution.

During communication, which is activated each 100th iteration of Metropolis algorithm, each process sends its solution to a master. The master keeps one solution for himself and sends one randomly chosen solution to each slave. These activities are based on the roulette wheel, where the biggest probability of selection has the individual with the best value of the fitness function.

After communication phase, all processes have two individuals. Now the phase of genetic crossover starts. We used double-point crossover. From two parent solutions two children solutions are generated. Then the solution with the best value of the fitness function is selected and mutation is performed: always in case of the parent solution, otherwise only with a predefined probability. Mutation is performed by randomly selecting genes and by randomly changing their subjects. A new solution is selected from the actual solution provided by SA process and from the solution, which was obtained after genetic mutation. It is selected using the well-known Metropolis criterion.

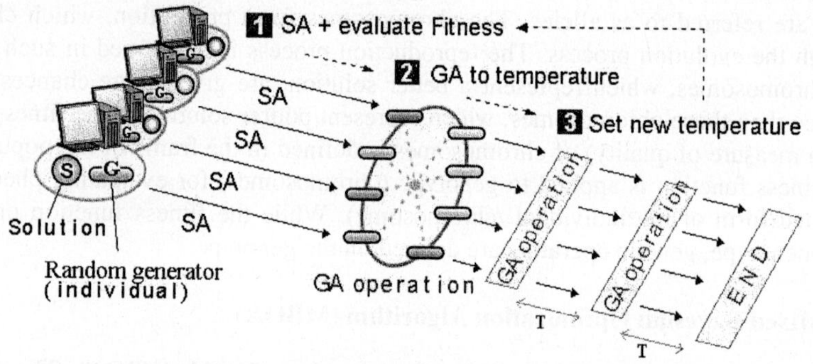

Fig. 3. Hybrid parallel genetic simulated annealing

4 Problem Definition

A multiprocessor topology can be seen as graph $G=(V, E)$, where $V=\{P_i\}$, $i=1,2,..,P$ represents a set of processor cores or discrete computers. $E=\{e_{ij}\}$ is the set of interconnection links between these processors. In our case, because links are bidirectional and full-duplex, the edges are undirected. Each vertex has the same degree d (number of communication links). A path from the source to destination is a sequence of vertices (processor indices), in which every two adjacent vertices are connected by a direct edge (link). The length of this path is defined as number of edges in the path.

Now we will discuss the collective communication patterns, which are most frequently found in parallel algorithms. If their overhead is excessive, performance degrades rapidly with the processors count. The lower bounds on the number of communication steps for the hypercube and for AMP topology are shown in Tab.1.

Table 1. Lower bounds on number of communication steps (all-port models)

	SF hypercube	WH hypercube	SF AMP	WH AMP
OAB	$D (= d)$	$\lceil d/\log(d+1) \rceil$	D	$\lceil \log_{d+1} P \rceil$
AAB	$\lceil (P-1)/d \rceil$	$\lceil (P-1)/d \rceil$	$\lceil (P-1)/d \rceil$	$\lceil (P-1)/d \rceil$
OAS	$\lceil (P-1)/d \rceil$	$\lceil (P-1)/d \rceil$	$\lceil (P-1)/d \rceil$	$\lceil (P-1)/d \rceil$
AAS	$P/2$	$P/2$	Pd_a/d	$P^2/(2B_C)$

Network parameters in Tab.1 are: processor count P, network diameter D, node degree d, bisection width B_C, and average distance d_a.

5 Design of Algorithms

The goal of proposed algorithms is to find a schedule of a group communication with the number of steps as close to the above lower bounds as possible.

The solution of this optimization problem using evolutionary algorithms may be decomposed into several phases. In the first phase, it is necessary to choose a suitable encoding of the problem into a chromosome. The second step is a definition of the fitness function, which determines quality of a chromosome. The next phase is a design of the input data structure for the evolutionary algorithm. The last phase is experimental runs of the evolutionary algorithm and search for the best set of its parameters. The choice of parameters should speed-up the convergence of the algorithm and simultaneously minimize a probability of getting stuck in local minima.

5.1 Solution Encoding

Very simply encoding, different for each OAB/OAS/OAG (generally OAX) and AAB/AAS (AAX) communication pattern, has been chosen. In the case of OAX communication, every chromosome consists of P genes, where P is a number of processors in a given topology. The gene's index represents the destination processor for a message. The gene consists of two integer components. The first component is an index of one of the shortest path from source to destination. The second component is a communication step sequence number. Fig. 4 illustrates an example of encoding for 2D-hypercube and OAS communication pattern. The source processor has index 0. Note also in this picture that the chromosome includes communication from source to source processor, but this communication is not realized. This gene is included only for the easier evaluation of the fitness function. The chromosome is extended from vector to matrix in case of AAB/ AAS communication. It contains P OAX chromosomes (every processor performs OAX).

The main advantage of this encoding is a short chromosome and absence of inadmissible solutions (every message is transmitted from the source to a destination). The main disadvantage is a large number of values of the first gene component. The number of values rapidly increases with the distance from source to destination as there are more shortest paths.

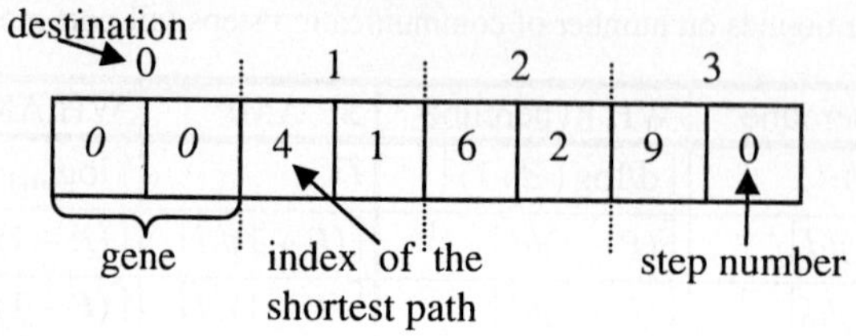

Fig. 4. Encoding for OAB/OAS/OAG

5.2 The Fitness Function

Having solution encoding defined, we can describe the main idea of fitness function evaluation. The main idea is based on the testing of conflict-freedom. We say that two communications are in a conflict if and only if they use the same communication link in the same time and in the same direction (see fig. 5).

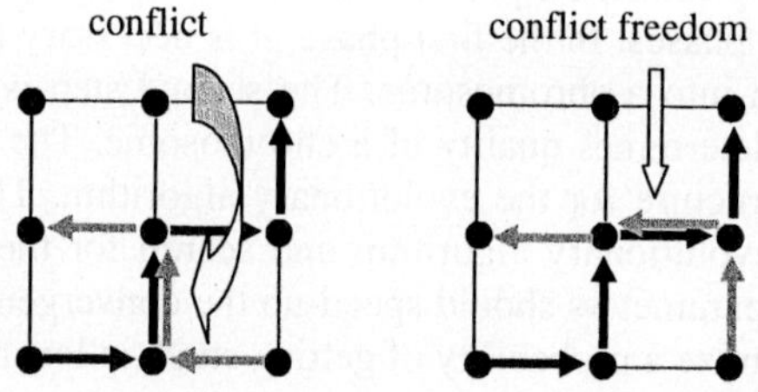

Fig. 5. Conflict freedom of a communication schedule

The optimal schedule of communication for the given number of communication steps does not contain any conflict. If the conflict occurs, the schedule is of no use. This is true for MBOA and HGSA as well, however HGSA tries to achieve, moreover, the minimal number of steps in group communication. It means that HGSA not only counts the number of conflicts, but also the number of communication steps.

5.3 The Search for the Shortest Path

The breadth-first search algorithm is applied to the topology graph. A tree is gradually constructed, one level at a time, from a root that is assigned an index of a source node. When a new level of the tree is generated, every node at the lowest level (leaf) is expanded. When a node is expanded, its successors are determined as all its direct neighbors except those, which are already located at higher levels of the tree (this is necessary to avoid cycles). Construction of the tree is finished when a value of at least one leaf is equal to the index of a destination node. Destination leaves' indices determine identity of found paths, which are then stored as sequences of node indices.

5.4 Heuristics

In HGSA two heuristics are used to speed up convergence to a sub-optimal solution. They decrease the probability of being trapped in local optima during the execution. The idea of these heuristics is a reduction of the path length. The first heuristics is used after initialization of HGSA and then after each application of Metropolis algorithm. The length of the path from the source to a destination node has some value. If these end nodes occur in another gene with a smaller length, than the length and the path in the original gene are changed accordingly.

The second heuristics is used in the case when the number of conflicts between genes of a chromosome is zero. This heuristics performs the analysis of chromosome. It looks for the longest path in some gene in the chromosome. If the number of the longest paths doesn't exceed some defined value, it tries to reduce the size of these longest paths by performing the mutation on them. In case that the size of the path is reduced, the new gene replaces this gene; otherwise the gene is not changed.

6 Experimental Results

Scheduling of OAB, AAB, OAS and AAS collective communications for two different architectures, a hypercube and AMP, has been done. The number of processors in the target architectures varied from 8 to 128 for OAB, OAS and AAS; AAB communication was tested only on 8-processor architecture. A hypercube has been chosen because of its regular topology with known optimal scheduling so that it can serve as a convenient benchmark. The lover bounds on number of communication steps are shown in Tab. 2. Each configuration of both the networks underwent 10 optimization runs, see Tab. 3. We counted only the number of successful completions, i.e. reaching the global optimum.

Table 2. Lower bounds on number of comm. steps for the given topology and processor count

Hypercube				AMP			
P	OAB	OAS	AAS	P	OAB	OAS	AAS
8	3	3	4	8	2	2	4
16	4	4	8	23	3	6	14
32	5	7	16	32	3	8	22
64	6	11	32	42	4	11	31
128	7	19	64	53	3	13	46

Scheduling of AAB communication was tested only for 8-processors architectures (hypercube, AMP). We obtained a sub-optimal solution, 3 steps for AMP and 4 steps for hypercube. But optimal solutions are 2 steps for AMP and 3 steps for hypercube. However, model of AAB communication is still in development.

Table 3. Success rate in achieving the optimum schedule for OAB, OAS, AAS

P	OAB (HSGA)		OAS (MBOA)		AAS (MBOA)	
	AMP	Cube	AMP	Cube	AMP	Cube
8	100	100	70	100	70	60
16	-	100	-	100	-	30
23	100	-	70	-	70	-
32	100	100	100	90	50	10
42	100	-	90	-	20	-
53	100	-	100	-	20	-
64	-	100	-	90	-	0
128	-	100	-	90	-	0

7 Conclusion

Optimization of communication schedules by means of evolutionary algorithms has been successful. Optimal schedules achieve the lower bounds of communication steps derived from graph-theoretical properties of interconnection networks. Optimum schedules can speed-up execution of many parallel programs that use collective communication as a part of their algorithm. Because finding of the optimum schedule is very hard combinatorial problem if it cannot be obtained by analytical means, two types of evolutionary algorithms have been tested. The first one (MBOA) is derived from Bayesian optimization algorithm and the second one HSGA is a composition of parallel simulated annealing and the standard genetic algorithm. Both the presented algorithms are able to find a schedule of the given communication pattern for arbitrary network topology, each one with different efficiency, and give the required number of communication steps.

Future work will be oriented to other communication patterns like OAB, AAB for MBOA and OAS, AAS for HGSA. Our future experiments will also target other networks like Midimew, Octagon, 2D mesh etc. Another way to improve these algorithms may be to implement the multicriterial optimization for MBOA (without the need not to enter the number of communication steps) and to design and implement more efficient heuristics for HGSA.

Acknowledgement

This research has been carried out under the financial support of the research grant GA 102/02/0503 "Parallel system performance prediction and tuning" (Grant Agency of Czech Republic).

References

1. Jantsch, A., Tenhunen, H.: Networks on Chip, Kluwer Academic Publ., Boston, 2003, ISBN 1-4020-7392-5
2. URL: www.sgi.com

3. Larrañaga P., Lozano J. A.: Estimation of Distribution Algorithms, A New Tool for Evolutionary Computation, Kluwer Academic Publishers, 2002
4. Ocenasek J.: Parallel Estimation of Distribution Algorithms, PhD. Thesis, Faculty of Information Technology, Brno University of Technology, Brno, Czech Rep., 2002
5. Duato, J., Yalamanchili, S.: Interconnection Networks – An Engineering Approach, Morgan Kaufman Publishers, Elsevier Science, 2003
6. Staroba J.: Parallel Performance Modelling, Prediction and Tuning, PhD. Thesis, Faculty of Information Technology, Brno University of Technology, Brno, Czech Rep., 2004
7. Ohlídal, M., Schwarz, J.: Hybrid parallel simulated annealing using genetic operations, Brno, 2004

Memetic Algorithms for Nurse Rostering

Ender Özcan

Yeditepe University, Department of Computer Engineering,
Kayışdağı, İstanbul, Turkey
eozcan@cse.yeditepe.edu.tr

Abstract. Nurse rostering problems represent a subclass of scheduling problems that are hard to solve. The goal is finding high quality shift and resource assignments, satisfying the needs and requirements of employees as well as the employers in healthcare institutions. In this paper, a real case of a nurse rostering problem is introduced. Memetic Algorithms utilizing different type of promising genetic operators and a self adaptive violation directed hierarchical hill climbing method are presented based on a previously proposed framework.

1 Introduction

Timetabling problems are well known NP complete problems [15]. As a timetabling problem, shift scheduling is concerned with the arrangement of employee timetables, considering the constraints provided by employees, employers and even customers. A nurse roster is a timetable consisting of shift assignments and rest days of nurses working at a hospital. In nurse rostering, the ultimate aim is to create high quality timetables, taking well-being of nurses as a basis without discarding the concerns of employers.

There is variety of approaches used for solving nurse rostering problems ([10], [12], [23]). Increasing number of researchers applies Genetic Algorithms (GAs) or other metaheuristic approaches, such as, Simulated Annealing, Tabu Search and their hybrids to tackle timetabling problems ([5], [6], [14], [17]). Ahmad et. al. [1] applied a modified version of a GA, named as population-less cooperative genetic algorithm on a 3-shift problem. Kawanaka et. al. [21] used GA to obtain optimal nurse schedules satisfying absolute and desirable constraints. Aickelin et. al. [2] utilized a coevolutionary pyramidal GA for solving nurse rostering. Each subpopulation attempts to solve nurse rostering for a set of nurses having either the same grade or a predetermined combination of them, organized in a hierarchical way as a pyramid for mate selection. Aickelin et. al. [3] proposed an indirect representation in GA for NRP and three different decoders. Recently, research on timetabling started to move towards finding a good hyper-heuristic ([9], [11], [20]); a heuristic for selecting a heuristic among a set of them to solve an optimization problem.

Details about nurse rostering, such as, constraint categorizations, models and approaches can be found in [7], [16] and [27]. In this paper, a set of memetic algorithms (MAs), combining GAs utilizing a set of genetic operators and a self adaptive violation directed hierarchical hill climbing method (VDHC) are introduced. MAs are based on the very same framework proposed by Alkan et. al. [4]. Extensive experiments are performed using randomly generated data and a real one retrieved from a major hospital. VDHC is a promising approach.

P. Yolum et al.(Eds.): ISCIS 2005, LNCS 3733, pp. 482–492, 2005.

2 Nurse Rostering Problem

Nurse rostering problems (NRPs) are constraint optimization problems that can be represented by a 3-tuple <*V*, *D*, *C*>. *V* is a finite set of variables, possibly each representing a shift of a nurse at a hospital, $V = \{v_1, v_2, \ldots, v_i, \ldots, v_N\}$, $D=\{ d_1, d_2, \ldots, d_i, \ldots, d_N\}$, is a finite set of domains of variables, where d_i is the domain of the variable v_i. Let $T=\{ t_1, \ldots, t_j, \ldots, t_M\}$ represent a set of start times for a shift, then a possible domain of each variable: $d_i \subseteq T$. *C* is a set of constraints to be satisfied, $C=\{ c_1, c_2, \ldots, c_L\}$. NRP can be described as a search for finding the best assignment (v_i, t_j) for each variable $v_i \in V$, such that, all constraints are satisfied. The assignment implies that the ith shift of a nurse at v_i starts at t_j. Constraints are categorized as *hard* or *soft*, where hard constraints must be satisfied and soft ones represent preferences.

2.1 Nurse Rostering Problem at Memorial Hospital

Shift schedules in Memorial Hospital (İstanbul, Turkey) are generated manually for all the departments in the hospital. There are two shift periods per day: *day* and *night.* In order to simplify the timetabling process, the hospital authorities produce a weekly schedule manually, although a biweekly schedule is preferred. Since the preferences of nurses are essential and might change in time, schedules are acyclic. There are three departments and about twenty nurses in the hospital. In some cases, a nurse from a different department is allowed to work at another department for support. Nevertheless, this type of cross duty does not occur often. Each nurse is considered to be independent belonging to a department. A nurse has a rank assigned from {0, 1, 2} indicating the level of experience (from lowest to highest). Rank 2 implies an experienced nurse. There are one or two nurses with rank 2 at each department. During the analysis a set of hard and soft constraints are determined. Hard Constraints:

- *Presets* (PRC): Presets represent the predetermined shift schedules of nurses.
- *Shift Constraint* (SHC): At a department, during each shift there must be at least one nurse.
- *Successive Night Shifts Constraint* (SNC): A nurse can not be assigned to more than two successive night shifts.
- *Successive Day Shifts Constraint* (SDC): A nurse can not be assigned to more than three successive day shifts.
- *Successive Shifts Constraint* (SSC): A nurse can not be assigned to two successive shifts. A day shift in one day and a night shift in the following day are considered as successive shifts.
- *Exclude Night Shifts Constraint* (ENC): Night shifts can not be assigned to an experienced nurse with rank 2.
- *On-duty Constraint* (ODC): Each nurse can not be assigned less than eight shifts per two weeks.

Soft Constraints:

- *Off-duty Constraint* (RDC): Nurses can define at most 3 rest day preferences.

3 Memetic Algorithms for Solving Nurse Rostering Problems

Genetic Algorithms (GAs) were introduced by J. Holland [19], and have been used to solve many difficult problems [18]. Usefulness of hill climbing in population based algorithms is emphasized by many researchers ([24, 28, 29]).

The problem described in Section 2 is chosen, due to the similarities with the university course scheduling problem, which is described in [25]. Memetic Algorithms (MAs) are presented for solving nurse rostering problems, based on a violation directed hierarchical hill climbing (VDHC). In most of the timetabling problem instances, variables are arranged hierarchically. Let a *classifier* be a subset of variables, then at each level in the hierarchy; a set of classifiers, representing logical groupings can be formed. In most of the cases, classifiers at a hierarchy level are collectively exhaustive in *V*. Classifiers form a basis for designing of a rich set of operators, discussed in the following sections. Arrangements can be formed statically or dynamically. A *static* arrangement is used during the experiments (Fig. 1). This study is a part of an attempt to provide a framework for solving different type of timetabling problems using a single tool based on Memetic Algorithms. Ozcan proposed an XML standard for timetabling problems in [27]. The goal is to represent different classes of timetabling problems using a single format. There are some developers already supporting the XML standard; schoolTool (http://www.schooltool.org), tablix (http://www.tablix.org).

3.1 Representation

The direct representation is used. Assuming *S* denotes the total number of nurses in a hospital, there is a subset of nurses available for duty at each department. Each nurse has a timetable, having *R* slots (days) to be filled with a shift type. *R* is set to 14 for producing bi-weekly acyclic schedule for each nurse. Each gene denotes the start time of a shift for a nurse in a day. Additional to day shift (**1**) and night shift (**2**), off-duty (**0**) allele is used in the individual representation. The representation scheme allows implementation of different sets of genetic operators.

Shifts of all nurses (variables) are arranged hierarchically in the individual representation (Fig. 1). Top hierarchy level, denoted as H-level contains a single classifier;

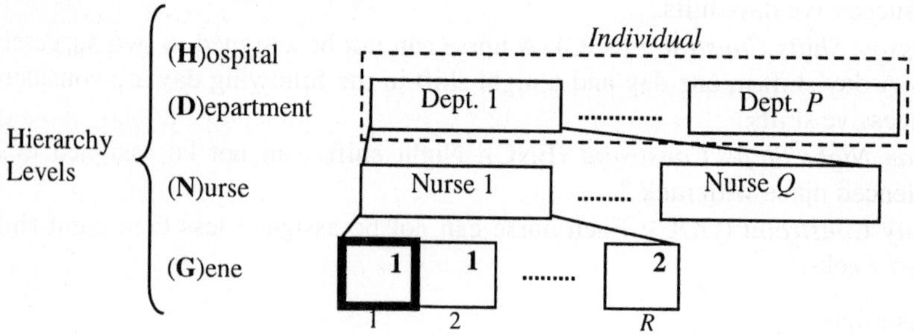

Fig. 1. Individual representation used in MA for solving NRP

V. There are three more hierarchy levels. D-level, N-level and G-level contain *P*, *S* and $N=S\text{x}R$ number of classifiers, respectively, as demonstrated in Fig. 1. Furthermore, each classifier at a level is a partition of *V*.

3.2 Fitness Function

An optimum nurse roster is the one with no violations. Let *NR* represent a proposed schedule of all nurses in the hospital, $T_i \in NR$ represent the nurse roster of the ith nurse, $p_j(.)$ represent the violation penalties due to the jth constraint for a given nurse roster and w_j to be the associated weight for the corresponding type of constraint. Fitness accumulates each weighted violation penalty with respect to its constraint type.

$$f(NR) = \sum_{\forall i \forall j} w_j p_j(T_i) \tag{1}$$

3.3 Mutation

Mutation can be applied on all classifiers at the same level, independently. For example, at D-level, the same mutation operator can be applied within all the departments using an appropriate mutation rate, as if each department is an individual. Similarly, at N-level, the mutation operator can be applied on each nurse. Swap mutation can be extended and a part (or whole) of the hierarchy level component can be replaced by a same size component at the same level. This set of mutations is straightforward to implement, if hierarchy level components are partitions. Behave as if each partition is a gene and swap it. For example, two nurse rosters or 3 days of the two nurse rosters can be swapped using an appropriate mutation rate. Similarly, two department rosters, or the same number of several nurse rosters in two departments can be swapped. Representation allows designing violation directed mutations as well:

- At a hierarchy level, select a classifier (partition or subset) based on the violations
- Apply mutation operator only on the selected classifier

As a different approach, the same or an adaptively selected mutation operator can be applied on each classifier, separately. Traditional mutation operator (M0) is used in the experiments. M0 randomly perturbs an allele with a *mutation rate* of *1/length_of_the_part_to_be_mutated*. Furthermore, two *smart* mutation operators are implemented. M1 and M2 operate in a similar manner on nurses and departments, respectively. Two randomly selected classifiers enter into a tournament. The one causing higher number of violations is selected for mutation. M0 is applied on the selected classifier (part of the chromosome). More disruptive mutations are implemented as well. M3 and M4 apply M0 on each nurse and department, respectively.

3.4 Crossover

Traditional one point crossover (1PTX) and uniform crossover (UX) are used to design a set of modified crossover operators. Boundary based crossover operators are applied on the classifiers defined at a hierarchy level. For example, 1PTX_N works at the N-level and 1PTX is applied as if the set of genes forming a nurse classifier is itself a gene. Hence, 6 different types of crossover operators are implemented: 1PTX (X1), UX (X2), 1PTX_D (X3), UX_D (X4), 1PTX_N (X7), and UX_N (X8).

Less disruptive and *smart* crossovers can be created to operate in two steps:

- Select one of the classifiers based on a strategy
- Apply crossover only within that classifier

As a result, four more crossover operators are implemented, utilizing tournament selection strategy with a tour size of two. A classifier is selected by comparing the total number of violations in each classifier at a level. 1PTX or UX is used on the selected classifier: 1PTX_SD (X5), UX_SD (X6), 1PTX_SN (X9), UX_SN (X10).

Additionally, highly disruptive crossover operators are created, applying crossover on all classifiers at a level, one by one. 1PTX_AD (X11) applies 1PTX on all departments, while 1PTX_AN (X12) applies 1PTX on all nurses. More crossover techniques can be generated allowing different crossovers to be operational at each classifier in the same level. For example, while 1PTX can be applied on the first and fourth nurse schedules, UX can be applied on the second and third nurse schedules, assuming four nurses and a single department. Ultimately, this type of strategies might require an adaptive method to decide which crossover to apply.

3.5 Hill Climbing

Timetabling problems are also formulated as multi-criteria optimization problems. This formulation would be very useful, especially in the existence of different types of soft constraints. Several solutions might be obtained having comparable qualities. Obviously, while attempting to reduce the violations due to a constraint, overall quality of a suggested solution might worsen. Applying a hill climbing method as a part of a hybrid algorithm is computationally expensive in timetabling problems. After each step is applied, the new configuration has to be evaluated in order to determine whether an improvement is provided or not. Yet, if the quality of solution increases, a hill climbing approach might be preferred. A violation directed hierarchical hill climbing method, denoted as VDHC is proposed as a part of a Memetic Algorithm for solving timetabling problems. Hill climbing is applied after mutation. VDHC provides cooperation of a set of hill climbers.

4 Self Adaptive Violation Directed Hierarchical Hill Climbing

VDHC represents a self adaptive approach which requires iterative application of a hill climbing method for a selected type of constraint as shown in Fig. 2. First, hierarchy levels to be used in VDHC are determined with an uppermost level chosen as a starting level to operate on. VDHC stays at a level as long as current candidate solution improves. It applies a selected hill climbing method, evaluating violations due to each constraint type, to a selected classifier at a level. If no improvement is confirmed, then VDHC reduces the area of concern to classifiers at one level down in the hierarchy. Hence, hierarchy level changes and the same steps of the algorithm repeat. VDHC terminates whenever a maximum number of steps is exceeded. Violation based selection methods are suggested.

```
1. Mark the hierarchy levels to be used
2. Set current level to the top hierarchy level
3. while (terminationCriteria-1 are not satisfied) do
   a. while (terminationCriteria-2 are not satisfied)
      do
        i. Start the traversal from the top until to
           the current level and select a classifier
       ii. Select a constraint type
      iii. Apply hill climbing for the selected con-
           straint type within the selected classifier
   b. end while
   c. Lower the hierarchy level
4. end while
```

Fig. 2. Pseudo-code of the VDHC approach

4.1 VDHC for Nurse Rostering

Three hierarchy levels are marked: H-level, D-level and N-level. As a classifier and constraint selection method a tournament selection is used. At the H-level classifier selection method always returns the whole chromosome. At the D-level, classifier selection method computes the violation contribution of each department to the overall fitness and selects one of them using tournament. Similarly, at the N-level, classifier selection method computes the violation contribution of each nurse to the overall fitness and selects one of them. In order to select a classifier from the N-level, a department has to be determined. Hence, D-level classifier selection is done first. Then the violations caused by each constraint type are distinguished. One of the constraint types is selected, giving a higher chance to the hill climbing step of the related constraint type causing more violations. Selected hill climbing is applied to the predetermined classifier to get rid of all the violations due to the related constraint type, producing a new individual.

Seven constraint based hill climbing methods are developed corresponding to each constraint type; SHC_HC, SNC_HC, SDC_HC, SSC_HC, ENC_HC, ODC_HC, RDC_HC. PRCs are handled by fixing assignments of related nurse shifts; hence, this constraint does not require application of a hill climbing method. SHC_HC checks departmental rosters and locates shifts without a nurse assignment. Then a nurse in the department is selected randomly and assigned to that shift. SNC_HC checks whether three consecutive shifts are night shifts or not. If they are, one of the shifts is changed to a day shift or marked as off-duty. SDC_HC checks whether four consecutive shifts are day shifts or not. If they are, one of the shifts is modified to a night shift or marked as off-duty. SSCs are partially satisfied by the use of the representation. If a candidate solution contains a successive two day pattern night shift-day shift, SSC_HC modifies the second day shift as either a night shift or off-duty. ENC_HC transforms a night shift assigned to a nurse with rank 2 to a day shift or off-duty. ODC_HC modifies required number of off-duty assignments to either a day or a night shift. RDC_HC attempts to realize nurse preferences. All choices and modifications in each hill climbing method are carried out randomly. In the tests the maximum number of hill climbing steps is a factor of chromosome length.

5 Experiments

A random nurse rostering problem instance generator (RNR) is implemented. 9 problem instances, produced by RNR, and a real data obtained from Memorial Hospital, labeled as *rnd#id* and *mhtr*, respectively, are used in the experiments. Characteristics of the data set are summarized in Table 1. All runs are repeated 50 times. Pentium IV 2 GHz. machines with 256 MB RAM are used. Experiments are performed in three stages. In the first stage crossover operators are compared using *rnd*1-6 data. Operators are compared based on their ranks considering the number of violations of best achieved solutions averaged over runs. In the second stage, mutation operators are tested with the top crossover operator on the same data. In the final stage, all the data set is tested using the best MA. Experimental data can be reached at http://cse.yeditepe.edu.tr/~eozcan/TTML.

Population is initialized randomly, and its size is a factor of the chromosome length. As a mate selection method linear ranking strategy is preferred, giving four times higher chance for the best individual than the worst one to be selected. All the runs are terminated whenever a fitness value of 0 is achieved, or whenever a maximum number of generations is exceeded. It is known that an optimal schedule is possible for the data used in the experiments. Hence, soft and hard constraints are not distinguished. Weight of each penalty is set to 1. Define *success rate* (*s.r.*) indicate the proportion of the successful runs yielding optimal solutions. As a replacement strategy, trans-generational MA (TGMA) with weak elitism is preferred, based on our previous experience ([4], [25], [26], [28]). Two best individuals are inherited to the next generation and the rest of them are obtained from the offspring pool.

In the first stage of experiments M0 is fixed as a mutation operator. According to the results, 1PTX performs better than the rest of the crossover operators (Table 2). UX is the second best. All crossover operators, other than 1PTX and UX fail to find the optimal solution. Considering boundary based and smart crossover methods,

Table 1. Characteristics of the data set used in the experiments. Number of departments and nurses are denoted as *ndep* and *nnur*, respectively. Percentage of nurses from each rank and average number of off-duty preferences of each nurse is denoted as *pnr* and *avrpr*, respectively.

label	*mhtr*	*rnd*1	*rnd*2	*rnd*3	*rnd*4	*rnd*5	*rnd*6	*rnd*7	*rnd*8	*rnd*9
ndep	4	3	3	3	4	4	4	6	8	6
nnur	20	21	21	21	21	21	21	34	51	66
*pnr*0	0.33	0.42	0.18	0.28	0.14	0.19	0.13	0.18	0.19	0.36
*pnr*1	0.48	0.32	0.51	0.42	0.47	0.46	0.47	0.47	0.47	0.35
*pnr*2	0.19	0.28	0.32	0.32	0.42	0.37	0.42	0.38	0.35	0.30
avrpr	0.55	1.95	0.67	2.19	1.67	2.33	0.95	1.97	1.88	2.09

Table 2. Results of the first stage experiments, indicating the rank of each crossover operator

Label	X1	X2	X3	X4	X5	X6	X7	X8	X9	X10	X11	X12
*rnd*1	1	2	11	12	9	4	10	8	7	3	6	5
*rnd*2	1	1	10	11	8	3	9	7	5	2	4	6
*rnd*3	1	1	10	11	8	3	9	7	6	2	5	4
*rnd*4	1	2	11	12	9	4	10	8	7	3	5	6
*rnd*5	1	2	11	12	9	4	10	6	8	3	5	7
*rnd*6	1	2	11	12	9	4	10	6	7	3	5	8

Table 3. Results of the 2nd stage experiments, indicating *s.r.* of each mutation operator

Label	M0	M1	M2	M3	M4
*rnd*1	**0.99**	0.96	0.56	0.00	0.48
*rnd*2	**1.00**	**1.00**	**1.00**	0.08	0.90
*rnd*3	**1.00**	**1.00**	**1.00**	0.00	0.84
*rnd*4	**0.98**	**0.98**	0.66	0.00	0.52
*rnd*5	**1.00**	**1.00**	0.94	0.00	0.72
*rnd*6	**1.00**	**1.00**	0.98	0.00	0.86
avr	**0.99**	0.96	0.56	0.00	0.48

Table 4. Results obtained using MA with the best set of operators on the data set

Label	*s.r.*	Avr.Gen./Run	*std.*	Avr.Eval./Gen.	*std.*
mhtr	0.72	1,736	2,881	1,176	1,178
*rnd*1	0.99	219	660	1,293	1,293
*rnd*2	1.00	42	44	1,333	1,333
*rnd*3	1.00	51	53	1,302	1,302
*rnd*4	0.98	265	787	1,306	1,306
*rnd*5	1.00	148	301	1,299	1,299
*rnd*6	1.00	61	62	1,330	1,330
*rnd*7	0.99	181	857	2,092	2,092
*rnd*8	1.00	96	99	3,155	3,155
*rnd*9	1.00	145	167	3,928	3,928

the ones operating on N-level perform better. X3 and X4 are the worst crossover methods. X10, X6, X11, X12 and X9 are the top five crossovers in the given order following the traditional operators. Whenever these top crossover operators are used, on average less than 21 violations are left unresolved.

In the second stage experiments 1PTX is fixed as a crossover operator. According to the experimental results, performance of operators are from the best towards the worst is M0, M1, M2, M4 and M3 (Table 3). M0 and M1 perform approximately the same, while M3 is the worst mutation operator, failing to find the optimal solution in most of the cases. In the last generations, a single violation is left to be resolved for all mutations, except M3. Violation directed smart mutation operators turn out to be more effective than the crossover operators.

TGMA performs best whenever M0 and X1 are used. TGMA reduces the number of violations rapidly in few hundreds of generations on average as established in Table 4. A run of the best MA takes less than 3 minutes on average for all data. Real data turns out to be the hardest problem instance of all. Genetic Algorithm version of the best MA without VDHC is applied to the real data. MA outperforms the GA version.

6 Conclusions

Timetabling is an interdisciplinary research area, containing many subclasses, such as, nurse rostering, course timetabling, examination timetabling. As an attempt to propose a general solver for timetabling problems ([4], [25], [26], [27]) a nurse rostering problem is investigated. A real world data obtained from Memorial Hospital and randomly generated data set are used as a test bed. Various mutation and crossover operators, including boundary oriented and smart genetic operators are presented to be used in timetabling problems. Several of these operators and proposed self adaptive violation directed hierarchical hill climbing operator (VDHC) are experimented within Memetic Algorithms. These operators can be used in other approaches as well.

VDHC and suggested operators exploit the underlying structure of problem instances. VDHC boosts the performance of the GA for nurse rostering as expected. Using a hierarchy of levels provides means to correct conflicts once and for all, or for a group of events, or for a single event. Violation directed operators; especially smart mutations achieve promising performances.

Proposed framework enables researchers to design a variety of operators. Such operators are already used by some researchers. For example, the shake operators suggested in [10] are a subset of genetic operators described for the MAs in Section 3. Other than static arrangement of data, *dynamic* arrangement is also possible. For example, considering a nurse rostering problem, shift assignments of nurses in the same period forms a dynamic arrangement. List of nurses might change from one candidate solution to another. More operators can be designed to work on these dynamic arrangements in a similar manner as discussed for static arrangements. Combining these operators underneath a hyper-heuristic might yield good solutions. As a future work, different combinations of hill climbing methods and genetic operators will be investigated. MA with VDHC will be compared to a multimeme strategy [22].

Acknowledgement

Author thanks Özgür Kelemci for modifying GAlib and obtaining the real data.

References

1. Ahmad, J., Yamamoto, M., Ohuchi, A.: Evolutionary Algorithms for Nurse Scheduling Problem. Proc. of IEEE Congress on Evolutionary Computation (2000) 196-203.
2. Aickelin, U., Bull, L.: On the Application of Hierarchical Coevolutionary Genetic Algorithms: Recombination and Evaluation Partners. JASS, 4(2) (2003) 2-17
3. Aickelin, U., Dowsland, K.: An Indirect Genetic Algorithm for a Nurse Scheduling Problem. Computers & Operations Research, 31(5) (2003) 761-778
4. Alkan, A., Ozcan, E.: Memetic Algorithms for Timetabling. Proc. of IEEE Congress on Evolutionary Computation (2003) 1796-1802
5. Berrada, I., Ferland, J., Michelon, P.: A Multi-Objective Approach to Nurse Scheduling eith both Hard and Soft Constraints. Socio-Economic Planning Science. vl. 30(1996)183-193
6. Burke, E.K., De Causmaecker, P., Vanden Berghe, G.: A Hybrid Tabu Search Algorithm For the Nurse Rostering Problem, Proc. of the Second Asia-Pasific Conference on Simulated Evolution and Learning, vol. 1, Applications IV (1998) 187-194
7. Burke, E.K., De Causmaecker, P., Vanden Berghe, G., Van Landeghem, H.: The State of the Art of Nurse Rostering, Journal of Scheduling, 7 (2004) 441-499
8. Burke, E.K., Cowling, P.I., De Causmaecker, P., Vanden Berghe, G.: A Memetic Approach to the Nurse Rostering Problem, Applied Intelligence, vol 15 (2001) 199-214
9. Burke, E., Kendall, G., Newall, J., Hart, E., Ross, P., Schulenburg, S.: Handbook of metaheuristics, chapter 16, Hyper-heuristics: an emerging direction in modern search technology, Kluwer Academic Publisher (2003) 457-474
10. Burke, E.K., De Causmaecker, P., Petrovic, S., Vanden Berghe G.: Variable Neighbourhood Search for Nurse Rostering Problems, in Metaheuristics: Computer Decision-Making (edited by M.G.C. Resende and J. P. de Sousa), Chapter 7, Kluwer (2003) 153-172
11. Burke, E., Soubeiga, E.: Scheduling Nurses Using a Tabu-Search Hyperheuristic, Proc. of the 1st MISTA, vol. 1 (2003) 197-218
12. Chun, A.H.W., Chan, S.H.C., Lam, G.P.S., Tsang, F.M.F., Wong, J., Yeung, D.W.M.: Nurse Rostering at the Hospital Authority of Hong Kong, Proc. of 17th National Conference on AAAI and 12th Conference on IAAI (2000) 951-956
13. Downsland, K.: Nurse Scheduling with Tabu Search and Strategic Oscillation, European Journal of Operations Research. Vol. 106, 1198 (1998) 393-407
14. Duenas, A., Mort, N., Reeves, C., Petrovic, D.: Handling Preferences Using Genetic Algorithms for the Nurse Scheduling Problem, Proc.of the 1st MISTA, vol.1(2003)180-195
15. Even, S., Itai, A., Shamir, A.: On the Complexity of Timetable and Multicommodity Flow Problems, SIAM J. Comput., 5(4) (1976) 691-703
16. Fang, H.L.: Genetic Algorithms in Timetabling and Scheduling, PhD thesis, Department of Artificial Intelligence, University of Edinburgh, Scotland (1994)
17. Gendrau, M., Buzon, I., Lapierre, S., Sadr, J., Soriano, P.: A Tabu Search Heuristic to Generate Shift Schedules, Proc. of the 1st MISTA, vol.2 (2003) 526-528
18. Goldberg, D. E.: Genetic Algorithms in Search, Optimization, and Machine Learning, Addison-Wesley, Reading (MA) (1989)
19. Holland, J. H.: Adaptation in Natural and Artificial Systems, Univ. Mich. Press (1975)
20. Han, L., Kendall, G.: Application of Genetic Algorithm Based Hyper-heuristic to Personnel Scheduling Problems, Proc. of the 1st MISTA, vol.2 (2003) 528-537
21. Kawanaka, H., Yamamoto, K., Yoshikawa, T., Shinogi, T., Tsuruoka, S.: Genetic Algorithms with the Constraints for Nurse Scheduling Problem, Proc. of IEEE Congress on Evolutionary Computation (CEC), Seoul (2001) 1123-1130

22. Krasnogor, N.: Studies on the Theory and Design Space of Memetic Algorithms, PhD Thesis, University of the West of England, Bristol, United Kingdom (2002)
23. Li, H., Lim, A., Rodrigues, B.: A Hybrid AI Approach for Nurse Rostering Problem, Proc. of the 2003 ACM Symposium on Applied Computing (2003) 730-735
24. Moscato, P., Norman, M. G.: A Memetic Approach for the Traveling Salesman Problem Implementation of a Computational Ecology for Combinatorial Optimization on Message-Passing Systems, Parallel Computing and Transputer Applications (1992) 177-186
25. Ozcan, E., Alkan, A.: Solving Time Tabling Problem using Genetic Algorithms, Proceedings of the 4th International Conference on the Practice and Theory of Automated Timetabling (2002) 104-107
26. Ozcan, E., Ersoy, E.: Final Exam Scheduler - FES, 2005 IEEE CEC, (2005) to appear
27. Ozcan, E.: Towards an XML based standard for Timetabling Problems: TTML, Multidisciplinary Scheduling: Theory and Applications, Springer Verlag (2005) 163 (24)
28. Ozcan, E., Onbasioglu E.: Genetic Algorithms for Parallel Code Optimization, Proc. of 2004 IEEE Congress on Evolutionary Computation, vol. 2 (2004) 1775-1781
29. Radcliffe, N. J., Surry, P.D.: Formal memetic algorithms, Evolutionary Computing: AISB Workshop, LNCS, vol. 865, Springer Verlag (1994) 1-16
30. Ross, P., Corne, D., Fang, H-L.: Improving Evolutionary Timetabling with Delta Evaluation and Directed Mutation, Proc. of PPSN III (1994) 556-565
31. Ross, P., Corne, D., Fang, H-L.: Fast Practical Evolutionary Timetabling, Proc. of AISB Workshop on Evolutionary Computation (1994) 250-263
32. De Werra, D.: An introduction to timetabling, European Journal of Operations Research, 19:151-162 (1985)

Discretizing Continuous Attributes Using Information Theory

Chang-Hwan Lee

Department of Information and Communications, DongGuk University,
Seoul, Korea 100-715
chlee@dgu.ac.kr

Abstract. Many classification algorithms require that training examples contain only discrete values. In order to use these algorithms when some attributes have continuous numeric values, the numeric attributes must be converted into discrete ones. This paper describes a new way of discretizing numeric values using information theory. The amount of information each interval gives to the target attribute is measured using Hellinger divergence, and the interval boundaries are decided so that each interval contains as equal amount of information as possible. In order to compare our discretization method with some current discretization methods, several popular classification data sets are selected for discretization. We use naive Bayesian classifier and C4.5 as classification tools to compare the accuracy of our discretization method with that of other methods.

1 Introduction

Discretization is a process which changes continuous numeric values into discrete categorical values. It divides the values of a numeric attribute into a number of intervals, where each interval can be mapped to a discrete categorical or nominal symbol. Most real-world applications of classification algorithm contain continuous numeric attributes. When the feature space of data includes continuous attributes only or mixed type of attributes (continuous type along with discrete type), it makes the problem of classification vitally difficult. For example, classification methods based on instance-based measures are generally difficult to apply to such data because the similarity measures defined on discrete values are usually not compatible with similarity of continuous values. Alternative methodologies such as probabilistic modelling, when applied to continuous data, require an extremely large amount of data.

In addition, poorly discretized attributes prevent classification systems from finding important inductive rules. For example, if the ages between 15 and 25 mapped into the same interval, it is impossible to generate the rule about the legal age to start military service. Furthermore, poor discretization makes it difficult to distinguish the non-predictive case from poor discretization. In most

P. Yolum et al.(Eds.): ISCIS 2005, LNCS 3733, pp. 493–502, 2005.

cases, inaccurate classification caused by poor discretization is likely to be considered as an error originated from the classification method itself. In other words, if the numeric values are poorly discretized, no matter how good our classification systems are, we fail to find some important rules in databases.

In this paper, we describe a new way of discretizing numeric attributes. We discretize the continuous values using a minimum loss of information criterion. Our discretization method is supervised one since it takes into consideration the class values of examples, and adopts information theory as a tool to measure the amount of information each interval contains. A number of typical machine learning data sets are selected for discretization, and these are discretized by both other current discretization methods and our proposed method. To compare the correctness of the discretization results, we use the naive Bayesian classifier and C4.5 as the classification algorithms to read and classify data.

The structure of this paper is as follows. Section 2 introduces some current discretization methods. In Section 3, we explain the basic ideas and theoretical background of our approach. Section 4 explains the brief algorithm and correctness of our approach, and experimental results of discretization using some typical machine learning data sets are shown in Section 5. Finally, conclusions are given in Section 6.

2 Related Work

Although discretization influences significantly the effectiveness of classification algorithms, not many studies have been done because it usually has been considered a peripheral issue. Among them, we describe a few well-known methods in machine learning literature.

A simple method, called equal distance method, is to partition the range between the minimum and maximum values into N intervals of equal width. Another method, called equal frequency method, chooses the intervals so that each interval contains approximately the same number of training examples; thus, if $N = 10$, each interval would contain approximately 10% of the examples. However, with both of these discretizations, it would be very difficult or almost impossible to learn certain concepts.

Some classification algorithms such as C4.5 [11] and PVM [13] take into account the class information when constructing intervals. For example, in C4.5, an entropy measure is used to select the best attribute to branch on at each node of the decision tree. And that measure is used to determine the best cut point for splitting a numeric attribute into two intervals. A threshold value, T, for the continuous numeric attribute A is determined, and the test $A \leq T$ is assigned to the left branch while $A > T$ is assigned to the right branch. This cut point is decided by exhaustively checking all possible binary splits of the current interval and choosing the splitting value that maximizes the entropy measure.

Fayyad [6] has extended the method of binary discretization in and C4.5 [11], and introduced multi-interval discretization, called Entropy Minimization Discretization(EMD), using minimum description length(MDL) technique. In this method, the data are discretized into two intervals and the resulting class information entropy is calculated. A binary discretization is determined by selecting the cut point for which the entropy is minimal amongst all candidates. The binary discretization is applied recursively, always selecting the best cut point. A minimum description length criterion is applied to decide when to stop discretization. This method is implemented in this paper, and used in our exprimental study.

Fuzzy discretization(FD), proposed by Kononenko [8], initially forms k equal-width intervals using equal width discretization. Then it estimates $p(a_i < X_i \leq b_i|C = c)$ from all training instances rather than from instances that have value of X_i in (a_i, b_i). The influence of a training instances with value v of X_i on (a_i, b_i) is assumed to be normally distributed with the mean value equal to v. The idea behind fuzzy discretization is that small variation of the value of a numeric attribute should have small effects on the attribute's probabilities, whereas under non-fuzzy discretization, a slight difference between two values, one above and one below the cut point can have drastic effects on the estimated probabilities. The number of initial intervals k is a predefined parameter and is set as 7 in our experiments. This method is also implemented and used in our experimental study.

Khiops [3] proposes a discretization method using chi-square statistic. This method optimizes the chi-square criterion in a global manner on the whole discretization domain. It is a bottom-up method which starts with the discretization from the elementary single value intervals. It then evaluates all merges between adjacent intervals and selects the best one based on the chi-square criterion, and iterates.

Even though some algorithms use dynamic discretization methods, it might still be preferable to use static discretization. Using static discretization as a preprocessing step, we can see significant speed up for classification algorithm with little or no loss of accuracy [4]. The increase in efficiency is due to that the dynamic algorithm, such as C4.5/CART, must re-discretize all numeric attributes at every node in the decision tree while in static discretization all numeric attributes are discretized only once before the classification algorithm runs.

3 Hellinger-Based Discretization

It is seldom possible to verify that a given discretization is reasonable because a classification algorithm can hardly distinguish a non-predictive case from a poorly discretized attribute. In general, it is seldom possible to know what the correct or optimal discretization is unless the users are familiar with the problem domain. Another problem which complicates evaluation is that discretization quality depends on the classification algorithms that will use the discretization. Even though it is not possible to have an optimal discretization with which to compare results, some notion of quality is needed in order to design and evaluate a discretization algorithm.

The primary purpose of discretization, besides eliminating numeric values from the training data, is to produce a concise summarization of a numeric attribute. An interval is essentially a summary of the relative frequency of classes within that interval. Therefore, in an accurate discretization, the relative class frequencies should be fairly consistent within an interval(otherwise the interval should be split to express this difference) but two adjacent intervals should not have similar relative class frequencies(otherwise the intervals should be combined to make the discretization more concise). Thus, the defining characteristic of a high quality discretization can be summarized as: maximizing intra-interval uniformity and minimizing inter-interval uniformity.

Our method achieves this notion of quality by using an entropy function. The difference between the class frequencies of the target attribute and the class frequencies of a given interval is defined as *the amount of information* that the interval gives to the target attribute. The more different these two class frequencies are, the more information the interval gives to the target attribute. Therefore, defining an entropy function which can measure the degree of divergence between two class frequencies is crucial in our method and will be explained in the following.

3.1 Measuring Information Content

The basic principle of our discretization method is to discretize numeric values so that each discretized interval has as equal amount of information as possible. In other words, we define the amount of information that a certain interval contains as the degree of divergence between a priori distribution and a posteriori distribution of the target attribute. Therefore, the critical part of our method is to select or define an appropriate measure of the amount of information each interval gives to the target attribute.

In our approach, the interpretation of the amount of information is defined in the following. For a given interval, its class frequency distribution is likely to differ from that of the target attribute. The amount of information an interval provides is defined as the dissimilarity(divergence) between these two class frequencies. We employ an entropy function in order to measure the degree of divergence between these two class frequencies.

Some entropy functions have been used in this direction in machine learning literature. However, the purpose of these functions is different from that of ours. They are designed to decide the most discriminating attributes for generating decision trees [11]. Suppose X is the target attribute and it has k discrete values, denoted as $x_1, x_2, \ldots, x_k$. Let $p(x_i)$ denote the probability of x_i. Assume that we are going to discretize an attribute A with respect to the target attribute X. Suppose $A = a_i$ and $A = a_{i+1}$ are boundaries of an interval, and this interval is mapped into a discrete value a. Then the probability distribution of X under the condition that $a_i \leq A < a_{i+1}$ is possibly different from a priori distribution of X. We will introduce several studies for measuring divergence from machine learning literature and information theory literature.

In machine learning literature, C4.5 [11], which generates decision trees from data, has been widely used for rule induction. It uses the following formula, called information gain, for estimating the information given from $A = a$ about X.

$$H(X) - H(X|a) = \sum_t p(t) \log \left(\frac{1}{p(t)} \right) - \sum_t p(t|a) \log \left(\frac{1}{p(t|a)} \right) . \quad (1)$$

It takes into consideration both a priori and a posteriori probabilities. It calculates the difference between the entropy of a priori distribution and that of a posteriori distribution, and uses the value to determine the most discriminating attribute of decision tree. However, it sometimes fails to calculate the divergence between two distributions correctly. Calculating the average value of each probability, it cannot detect the divergence of the distributions in the case that one distribution is a permutation of the other.

In information theory literature, several studies are done about divergence measure. Kullback [9] derived a divergence measure, called I-measure, defined as

$$\sum_i p(x_i|a) \log \frac{p(x_i|a)}{p(x_i)}. \quad (2)$$

Another group of divergence measure, widely used in information theory, includes Bhattacharyya divergence [2] and Renyi divergence [12].

However, since these measures are originally defined on continuous variables, there are some problems when these are applied to discrete values. These measures are not applicable in case one or more than one of the $p(x_i)$ are zero. Suppose that one class frequency of a priori distribution is unity and the rest are all zero. Similarly, one value of a posteriori distribution is unity and the rest are all zero. Then Kullback divergence, Renyi divergence and Bhattacharyya divergence are not defined in this case, and we cannot apply these directly without approximating the original values.

In this paper, we adopt Hellinger divergence [7] which is defined as

$$\left| \sum_i (\sqrt{p(x_i)} - \sqrt{p(x_i|a)})^2 \right|^{1/2} . \quad (3)$$

It was originally proposed by Beran [1], and unlike other divergence measures, this measure is applicable to any case of probability distribution. In other words, Hellinger measure is continuous on every possible combination of a priori and a posteriori values. It can be interpreted as a distance measure where distance corresponds to the amount of divergence between a priori distribution and a posteriori distribution. It becomes zero if and only if both a priori and a posteriori distributions are identical, and ranges from 0 to $\sqrt{2}$. Therefore, we employ Hellinger divergence as a measure of divergence, which will be used as the information amount of intervals. The entropy of an interval I described above is defined as follows.

Definition 1. *The entropy of an interval I is defined as follows:*

$$E(I) = \left| \sum_i \left(\sqrt{p(x_i)} - \sqrt{p(x_i|I)} \right)^2 \right|^{1/2} . \tag{4}$$

4 Discretizing Algorithm

The algorithm consists of an initialization step and a bottom up combining process. As part of the initialization step, the training examples are sorted according to their values for the attribute being discretized and then each example becomes its own interval. The midpoint between each successive pair of values in the sorted sequence is called a potential *cutpoint.* Each cutpoint associates two adjacent intervals(or point values), and its corresponding entropy is defined as follows.

Definition 2. *The entropy of a cutpoint C, adjacent to interval a and b, is defined as follows.*

$$E(C) = E(a) - E(b). \tag{5}$$

If the class frequency of these two intervals are exactly the same, the cutpoint is called *in-class cutpoint,* and if not, the cutpoint is called *boundary cutpoint.* In other words, if two adjacent point values or intervals have different class frequencies, their midpoint(cutpoint) is defined as boundary cutpoint. Intuitively, discretization at in-class cutpoints are not desirable because it separates examples of one class. Therefore, boundary cutpoint must have high priority to be selected for discretization.

In combining process, the amount of information that each interval gives to the target attribute is calculated using Hellinger divergence. For each pair of two adjacent intervals, the system computes the informational difference between them. The least value of difference will be selected and its corresponding pair of intervals will be merged. Merging process continues until the system reaches the maximum number of intervals(k) usually given by users. The value of k, maximum number intervals, is determined by selecting a desired precision level the user wants. The standard recommended value of k is to set the value between 3 to 10 depending on the domain to prevent an excessive number of intervals from being created. Figure 1 shows the abstract algorithm of the discretization method.

We have the following theorem which shows the correctness of our discretization algorithm.

Theorem 1. *The in-class cutpoints are not to be selected for discretization unless all boundary cutpoints are exhausted for discretization.*

The proof is omitted due to space limit. This theorem implies that in our algorithm discretization keeps occurring only at boundary cutpoints unless it exhausts all boundary cutpoints. By doing so, it prevents the in-class cutpoints from being selected for discretization.

Input : $a_1, a_2, \ldots, a_N$ (sorted and distinct numeric values)

$a_0 = a_1$; $a_{N+1} = a_N$;
K:=maximum number of interval;
/* Initialization step */
for i=1 **to** N **do**
  INTVL= $\{I_i = (p_i, q_i) | p_i = (a_{i-1} + a_i)/2, q_i = (a_i + a_{i+1})/2\}$;
end
/* Entropy of each interval */
for each $I_i \in$ INTVL **do**
  $E(I_i) = \left| \sum_j (\sqrt{P(a_j)} - \sqrt{P(a_j|I_i)})^2 \right|^{1/2}$;
end
/* Entropy of each cutpoint */
for i=1 **to** N-1 **do**
  $E(p_i) = E(I_i) - E(I_{i+1})$;
end
repeat N-K times **do**
  MERGE=cutpoint with least value of E;
  merge two intervals of MERGE;
end
return INTVL;

Fig. 1. Discretization Algorithm

The computational complexity of our discretization method is given as $O(n)$, where n is the number of examples.

Lemma 1. *Suppose n is the number of examples. The complexity of the proposed discretization method is given as*

$$O(n) \tag{6}$$

The proof of the lemma is trivial based on the pseudo code in Figure 1.

5 Empirical Results

Because our discretization method is not itself a classification algorithm it cannot be tested directly for classification accuracy, but must be evaluated indirectly in the context of a classification algorithm. Therefore, our discretization method will be used to create intervals for two well-known classification systems: naive Bayesian classifier and C4.5 [11].

In our experimental study, we compare our proposed method with Fuzzy Discretization(FD) [8], as a preprocessing step to the C4.5 algorithm and naive-Bayes classifier. C4.5 algorithm is a state-of-the-art method for inducing decision trees. The naive Bayes classifier computes the posterior probability of the classes given the data, assuming independence between the features for each class.

For the test data set, we have chosen eight datasets. Table 1 shows the datasets we chose for our comparison. These datasets are obtained from the

UCI repository [10] such that each had at least one continuous atribute. We used 10-fold cross-validation technique and, for each experiment, the training data are separately discretized into seven intervals by Fuzzy Discretization(FD) [8] and our proposed discretization method, respectively. The intervals so formed are separately applied to the test data. The experimental results are recorded as average classification accuracy that is the percentage of correct predictions of classification algorithms in the test across trials.

Table 2 shows the classification results of naive Bayes classifier using the different discretization methods. As we can see, our discretization method shows

Table 1. Description of datasets

Dataset	Size	Numeric	Categorical	Classes
Anneal	898	6	32	6
Breast	699	10	0	2
Glass	214	9	0	3
Hepatitis	155	6	13	2
Horse-colic	368	8	13	2
Hypothyroid	3163	7	18	2
Iris	150	4	0	3
Vehicle	846	18	0	4

Table 2. Classification results using naive Bayesian method

Dataset	FD	Proposed method
Anneal	92.3	89.2
Breast	96.3	97.2
Glass	64.8	68.1
Hepatitis	87.7	88.3
Horse-colic	81.5	78.4
Hypothyroid	97.2	97.0
Iris	94.7	96.6
Vehicle	59.6	62.8

Table 3. Classification results using C4.5

Dataset	FD	Proposed method
Anneal	89.2	87.3
Breast	91.5	95.8
Glass	69.2	70.1
Hepatitis	85.4	87.2
Horse-colic	81.5	82.7
Hypothyroid	98.8	97.3
Iris	95.6	96.3
Vehicle	62.7	66.4

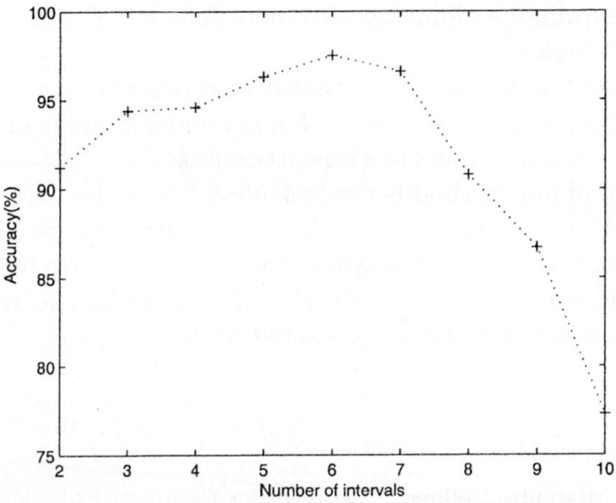

Fig. 2. Classification accuracy versus number of intervals

better results than other method in most data sets. In five cases among eight datasets, our method showed better classification accuracy.

Table 3 shows the results of classification for each data set using C4.5, and we can easily see that our discretization method shows the better classification accuracy in most cases. In six cases among eight datasets, our method showed the better classification accuracy.

Determining the right value of maximum number of intervals significantly effects the correctness of discretization. Too small number of intervals prevents important cutpoints from being discretized while too many cuts produce unnecessary intervals. In order to see the effect of the number of intervals, we applied naive Bayesian classifier to iris data set with different number of intervals, and the results are shown in Figure 2. For iris data set, when the attribute is discretized into 5-7 intervals, its classification result shows better accuracies while the number of intervals is greater than 7 or less than 5, the classification accuracy drops significantly.

6 Conclusion

In this paper, we proposed a new way of discretizing numeric attributes, considering class values when discretizing numeric values. Using our discretization method, the user can be fairly confident that the method will seldom miss important intervals or choose an interval boundary when there is obviously a better choice because discretization is carried out based on the information content of each interval about the target attribute. Our algorithm is easy to apply because all it requires for users to do is to provide the maximum number of intervals.

Our method showed better performance than other traditional methods in most cases. Our method can be applied virtually to any domain, and is applicable to multi-class learning(i.e. domains with more than two classes–not just positive and negative examples).

Another benefit of our method is that it provides a concise summarization of numeric attributes, an aid to increasing human understanding of the relationship between numeric features and the class attributes.

One problem of our method is the lack of ability to distinguish between true correlations and coincidence. In general, it is probably not very harmful to have a few unnecessary interval boundaries; the penalty for excluding an interval is usually worse, because the classification algorithm has no way of making a distinction that is not in the data presented to it.

References

1. Beran R. J.: Minimum Hellinger Distances for Parametric Models, *Ann. Statistics*, Vol. 5 (1977) 445-463
2. Kadota T., Shepp L. A.: On the Best Finite Set of Linear Observables for discriminating two Gaussian signals, *IEEE Transactions on Information Theory*, Vol. 13 (1967) 278-284
3. Boulle M.: Khiops: A Statistical Discretization Method of Continuous Attributes, *Machine Learning*, Vol. 55 (2004) 53-69
4. Catlett J.: On changing continuous attributes into ordered discrete attributes. In *European Working Session on Learning* (1991)
5. Dougherty J., Kohavi R., Sahami M.: Supervised and Unsupervised Discretization of Continuous Features, 12th Int'l Conf. on Machine Learning (1995)
6. Fayyad U. M., Irani K. B.: Multi-Interval Discretization of Continuous-Valued Attributes for Classification Learning, *13th International Joint Conference of Artificial Intelligence* (1993) 1022-1027
7. Ying Z.: Minimum Hellinger Distance Estimation for Censored Data, *The Annals of Statistics*, Vol. 20, No. 3 (1992)
8. Kononenko I.: Inductive and Bayesian Learning in Medical Diagnosis, *Applied Artificial Intelligence*, Vol. 7 (1993) 317-337
9. Kullback S.: *Information Theory and Statistics*, New York: Dover Publications (1968)
10. Murphy P. M., Aha D. W.: UCI repository of machine learning databases. http://www.ics.uci.edu/ mlearn (1996)
11. Quinlan J. R.: *C4.5: Programs for Machine Learning*, Morgan Kaufmann Publisher (1993)
12. Renyi A.: On Measures of Entropy and Information, *Proceedings of Fourth Berkeley Symposium*, Vol. 1 (1961) 547-561
13. Weiss S. M., Galen R. S., Tapepalli P. V.: Maximizing the predictive value of production rules, *Artificial Intelligence*, Vol. 45 (1990) 47-71

System Identification Using Genetic Programming and Gene Expression Programming

Juan J. Flores and Mario Graff

División de Estudios de Posgrado, Facultad de Ingeniería Eléctrica,
Universidad Michoacana de San Nicolas de Hidalgo

Abstract. This paper describes a computer program called ECSID that automates the process of system identification using Genetic Programming and Gene Expression Programming. ECSID uses a function set, and the observed data to determine an ODE whose behavior is similar to the observed data. ECSID is capable to evolve linear and non-linear models of higher order systems. ECSID can also code a higher order system as a set of higher order equations. ECSID has been tested with linear pendulum, non-linear pendulum, mass-spring system, linear circuit, etc.

1 Introduction

System identification (SID) is concerned with building a model from input-output observations. The model is represented as a mathematical formula. Linear system identification methods have been widely studied (e.g. [1]). However, these methods involve a complicated process that usually can only be followed by an expert. Nonlinear system identification remains a difficult task because, frequently there is not enough information about the system (i.e. the structure's system is unknown).

This article introduces a system called ECSID (Evolutionary Computation based System Identification). ECSID is a system that creates a model from observed data using evolutionary techniques; it uses GP (Genetic Programming [2]) and GEP (Gene Expression Programming [3]).

In order to find a model ECSID only needs the observed data and a function set. ECSID represents the evolve system as an ordinary differential equation (ODE). it has the following features.

- Evolve higher order ODEs.
- Evolve linear highor order ODEs.
- Only needs the maximum order of the system.
- Use GP or GEP to discover the model.

Section 2 presents related work. Section 3 briefly introduces Genetic Programming and Gene Expression Programming. Section 4 presents the methodology used in ECSID. Section 5 presents the results. Section 7 presents the conclusions and proposes some ideas for future work.

P. Yolum et al.(Eds.): ISCIS 2005, LNCS 3733, pp. 503–511, 2005.

2 Related Work

Bradley et al [4] built a system called PRET for system identification. PRET automates the system identification process by building a layer of artificial intelligence techniques around a set of traditional formal engineering methods. PRET builds models using meta-domain information about the system and hypotheses given by the user.

Gray et al [5] used GP to model a system of fluid flow through pipes. They used GP to find the system's structure and Nelder-Simplex and Simulated Annealing to optimize the system's parameters. Their program can evolve only first-order systems of ordinary differential equations.

Weinbrenner [6] used genetic programming to model a helicopter engine. Genetic Programming was used to find the system structure and a search procedure (Nelder-Simplex and Simulated Annealing) to optimize the system parameters. He used automatically defined functions (ADFs) [2] to incorporate dynamic behavior to the system. His procedure was not able to produce a system of ordinary differential equations.

Cao et al [7] modeled a system of ordinary differential equations, using genetic programming and genetic algorithms. Genetic Programming was used to discover the system's structure while genetic algorithms were used to optimize its parameters. Cao evolved a higher order system, expressed as a set of first order equations (SODE) and higher order ordinary differential equations. Cao cannot evolve a system of higher order differential equations, but only a higher order differential equation (HODE). They always evolve equations of the same order, and the order has to be provided by the user.

Hinchliffe [8] models a system from observed data, but his models were not ODEs instead were based on previous values of their inputs.

The conclusion section enumerates some of the characteristics presented by ECSID, which are not contained in the works mentioned in this section.

3 Genetic Programming and Gene Expression Programing

Genetic Programming [2] and Gene Expression Programming [3] are evolutionary tools inspired in the Darwinian principle of natural selection and survival of the fittest individual. These methods use an initial random population and apply genetic operators to this population until the algorithm finds an individual that satisfies some termination criteria.

GP and GEP are evolutionary tools which evolve computer programs. GP represents the computer program as a tree structure, while GEP uses a string. Each string represents a tree structure (Figure 1 shows this representation).

The genetic operators generally used by GP are: crossover and mutation. Crossover choose two individuals in the population and merges them to build other two individuals. The procedure used by crossover is to select a sub-tree from each individual and swap these sub-trees. Mutation chooses an individual

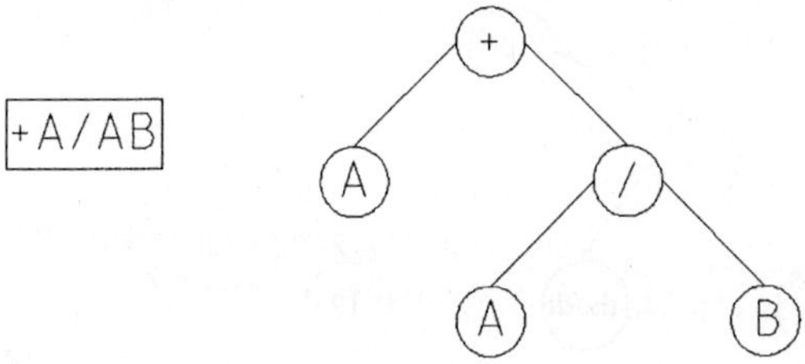

Fig. 1. Convert a chromosome to a tree expression

from the population and randomly changes a node in the tree structure by another. These operators are better described in [2].

The genetic operators used by GEP are: Mutation, Root transposition, Gene transposition, one-point recombination, two-point recombination, and gene recombination. These operators are deeply described in [3].

4 ECSID

ECSID can use either GP or GEP to determine ODEs, it can evolve higher-order differential equation and higher-order differential equation system. ECSID can evolve linear equations with constant or variable coefficients. The system is represented in GEP by a multi-chromosome where each chromosome represents an equation. In GP each individual has a list of s-expressions, where each s-expression represents an equation. All the equations evolved by ECSID have the following form:

$$y^{(n)} = f(t, y, y', y'', \cdots, y^{(n-1)}) \tag{1}$$

ECSID evolves only the right part of the Equation 1. The order of the system is determined by the higher order element. Figure 2 shows the 0DE $\frac{d^2x}{d^2t} = 7\frac{dx}{dt} + 10x + 12$ represented in ECSID. In this figure it is observed that ECSID evolves only the right part of the Equation 1. In order to integrate Equation 1 ECSID needs to build a system with the form of Equation 2.

$$\begin{cases} y_1' &= y_2 \\ y_2' &= y_3 \\ \vdots & \\ y_n &= f(t, y_1, y_2, \cdots, y_n) \end{cases} \tag{2}$$

Equation 2 is formed by replacing the following variables $y_1 = y, y_2 = y', y_3 = y'', \cdots, y_n = y^{(n-1)}$.

There are some experiments in which is necessary to evolve linear systems, in order to evolve a linear model we introduced an operator called "coefficient". This operator receives any s-expression and a constant, then "coefficient" multiplies the s-expression with the constant. Alternatively we introduce a method

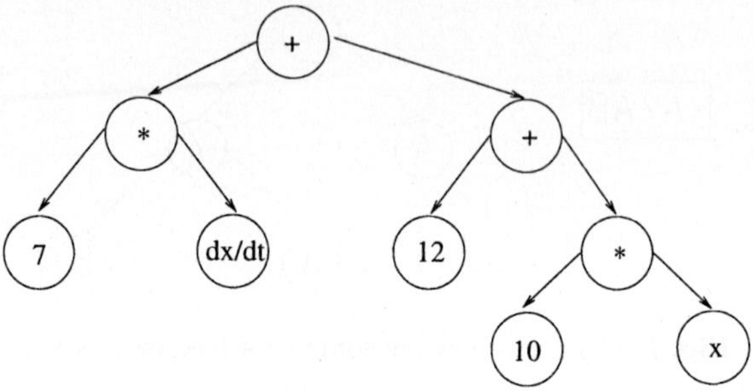

Fig. 2. ODE represented in ECSID

that checks if the equation is linear. If it is not, the fitness function will be decreased. This is useful when we do not want to use the "coefficient" method but we want to evolve only linear equations.

ECSID is capable to find the order of the system, the user sets the maximum order and ECSID evolves systems up to this.

ECSID uses the standard evolutionary computation procedure, random population, fitness proportional selection and elitism. The fitness function is the absolute difference of the errors $\Sigma|e|$. The table 1 shows the parameters used in ECSID.

In order to compare experiments from different domains, we use the correlation coefficient (Equation 3). The correlation coefficient gives a number between -1 and 1 where 1 means that the curves are equal.

$$r = \frac{n\sum xy - \sum x \sum y}{\sqrt{[n\sum x^2 - (\sum x)^2][n\sum y^2 - (\sum y)^2]}} \quad (3)$$

The evaluation method used by ECSID is shown below (*Evaluation*). This method receives an individual to be evaluated and a list t , where each element of t represents time. *CreateTrees* builds trees from the individual. *Order* identifies the system's order. Each equation of the system can be of different order therefore it returns a list. Lines 3 and 4 punish non-linear individuals in the case of a linear assumption. *Eval* evaluates the equations using the system order and an integration method (4th order Runge-Kutta). *Evaluation* returns the values of the individual in t.

Table 1. Genetic operators' parameters

Genetic Operator	Probability
Mutation	0.2
Crossover	0.8
is-transposition	0.1
ris-transposition	0.1
gene-transposition	0.1
one-point recombination	0.3
two-point recombination	0.3
gene-recombination	0.1

```
EVALUATION(individual, t)
trees ← CREATETREES(individual)
n ← ORDER(trees)
if EVOLVELINEAR() and ISLINEAR(trees) = NIL
   then return ∞
return EVAL(n, trees, t)
```

5 Modeling Experiments

This section presents the results obtained using ECSID; these results were obtained running the experiments 20 times and the best individual of all is selected. Each experiment was run for 500 generations and the population size is 500. The termination criteria is when the correlation coefficient is $r \geq 0.99$.

5.1 Example 1

This example identifies a model for a linear pendulum. Equation 4 shows the system to identify with the initial conditions $f(0) = 1, f'(0) = 0$.

$$\frac{d^2\theta}{d^2t} = -19.6\theta \tag{4}$$

Equations 5 and 6 show the result using GEP and GP respectively. Figure 3 shows Equation 4, 5 and 6, the equations obtained by ECSID are good. You can see that ECSID found the structure of the system but could not find the exact parameters. Table 2 shows the correlation coefficient.

$$\frac{d^2\theta}{d^2t} = -19.335010\theta \tag{5}$$

$$\frac{d^2\theta}{d^2t} = -20\theta \tag{6}$$

5.2 Example 2

This example is a non-linear pendulum with friction. Equation 7 shows the model, the initial conditions are the same than those of the previous example.

$$\frac{d^2\theta}{d^2t} = -2\frac{d\theta}{dt} - 19.6sin(\theta) \tag{7}$$

Equations 8 and 9 show the result using GEP and GP respectively. Both methods find a good model; the correlation coefficient is above $r \geq 0.99$ (Table 2). These equations (8 and 9) do not have the same structure that the system but they are good models. Figure 4 shows the behavior exhibited by those models.

$$\frac{d^2\theta}{d^2t} = -2\theta\frac{d\theta}{dt} - 2\frac{d\theta}{dt} - 20\theta \tag{8}$$

$$\frac{d^2\theta}{d^2t} = -2.3048492976\frac{d\theta}{dt} - 19.3437292976\theta \tag{9}$$

5.3 Example 3

In this example we model a coupled mass-spring system Equation 10 shows the system with the initial conditions $f(0) = 1, f'(0) = 0, g' = 2, g'(0) = 0$. This system is different than the other examples because it has two second order equations.

$$\begin{aligned} \frac{d^2x}{d^2t} &= -5x + 2y \\ \frac{d^2y}{d^2t} &= 2x - 2y \end{aligned} \tag{10}$$

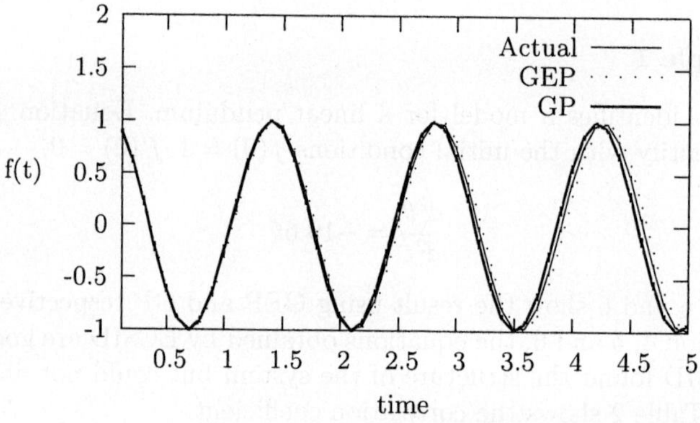

Fig. 3. Linear pendulum

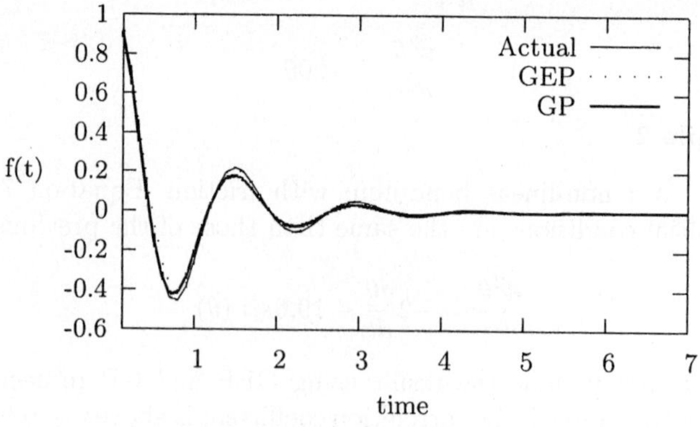

Fig. 4. Pendulum with friction

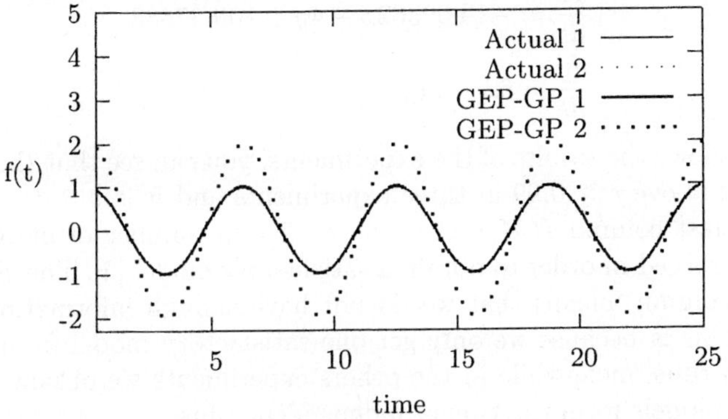

Fig. 5. Mass springs coupled

GEP and GP gave the same Equation 11, the correlation coefficient is $r = 1$, you can see that neither the structure nor the parameters are the same that Equation 10. Figure 5 shows the behavior exhibited by those models (each model has two equations).

$$\begin{aligned} \frac{d^2x}{d^2t} &= -x \\ \frac{d^2y}{d^2t} &= -y \end{aligned} \tag{11}$$

6 Example 4

This example shows a linear circuit Equation 12 presents the system with the initial conditions $f(0) = 0, g(0) = 0$. This system is different than the other examples because it is linear, therefore ECSID needs to find a linear model.

$$\begin{aligned} \frac{dx}{dt} &= -20x + 10y + 100 \\ \frac{dy}{dt} &= 10x - 20y \end{aligned} \tag{12}$$

Equations 13 and 14 show the results using GEP and GP respectively. Both methods find a good model and both models are linear. GP found the structure of the model but it did not found the exact same coefficients. Figure 6 shows the behavior exhibited by those models.

$$\begin{aligned} \frac{dx}{dt} &= \frac{1424}{25} - 8x \\ \frac{dy}{dt} &= \frac{1399}{50} - 4x \end{aligned} \tag{13}$$

$$\begin{aligned} \frac{dx}{dt} &= -19.09362x + 4y + 109.37688 \\ \frac{dy}{dt} &= 6x - 11y \end{aligned} \tag{14}$$

Table 2 shows the results of the experiments, you can see that the correlation coefficient is above $r \geq 0.99$ in three experiments and it is $r = 1$ in one experiment. The last column $I(M, i, z)$ is the minimum number of individuals that need to be proceed in order to obtain a satisfactory model [2]. The symbol N/A, in the last column, means that we do not have enough information to obtain $I(M, i, z)$. This is because we only get one satisfactory model from the twenty independent runs, meanwhile in the others experiments we obtain at least five satisfactory models from the twenty independent runs.

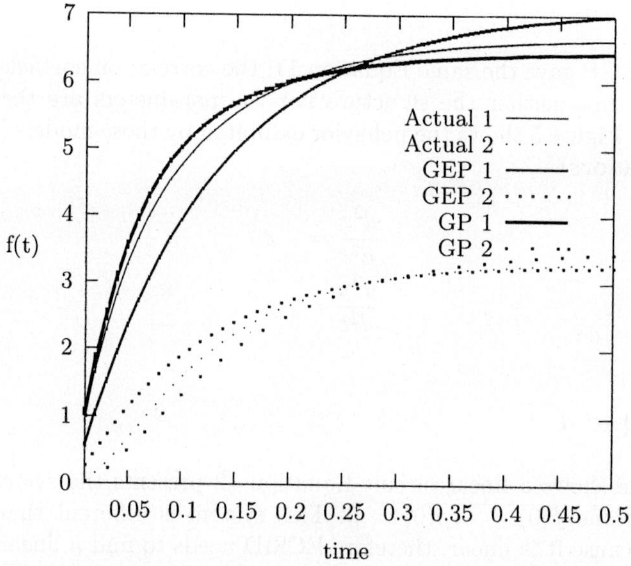

Fig. 6. Linear circuit

Table 2. Results using GP and GEP

Method	Problem	r	$I(M,i,z)$
GEP	Linear pendulum (Eq. 5)	$r = 0.99635$	N/A
GP	Linear pendulum (Eq. 6)	$r = 0.99201$	N/A
GEP	Pendulum with friction (Eq. 8)	$r = 0.99822$	154783
GP	Pendulum with friction (Eq. 9)	$r = 0.99697$	278609
GEP	Coupled mass-springs (Eq. 11)	$r_1 = 1, r_2 = 1$	41276
GP	Coupled mass-springs (Eq. 11)	$r_1 = 1, r_2 = 1$	42761
GEP	Circuit (Eq. 13)	$r_1 = 0.98623$, $r_2 = 0.99753$	N/A
GP	Circuit (Eq. 14)	$r_1 = 0.99579$, $r_2 = 0.99491$	N/A

7 Conclusions

We presented the results obtained with ECSID. ECSID found good models for linear pendulum, non-linear pendulum with friction, coupled mass-spring, and linear circuit.

ECSID has the following advantages compared to related work.

- ECSID can model higher order system expressed as as a set of higher order equations (Example 5.3).
- ECSID is capable to determine the order of the system, the user sets the maximum order and it evolves systems up to that limit. Cao's system can only evolve equations of the same order.
- ECSID can evolve a linear model.

In our work we have not found the necessity to use genetic algorithms or a search procedure to optimize the system's parameters. GP by itself does a good work on finding a good model.

ECSID has proved to be useful in system identification, but it needs to be improved. Below there is a list of the future work.

- Test ECSID with noisy data and with real experiments.
- Explore the differences between GP and GEP and to identify which one of them is better.
- Improve the usability of ECSID

ECSID can be downloaded from [9].

References

1. Ljung, L.S.: System Identification: Theory for the User. Prentice Hall (1987)
2. Koza, J.R.: Genetic Programming: On the Programming of Computers by Means of Natural Selection (Complex Adaptive Systems). The MIT Press (1992)
3. Ferreira, C.: Gene expression programming: A new adaptive algorithm for solving problems. In: Complex Systems. Number 2 (2001) 87–129
4. Bradley, E., Stolle, R.: Automatic construction of accurate models of physical systems. Technical report, (University of Colorado, Department of Computer Science)
5. Gray, G.J., Murray-Smith, D.J., Li, Y., Sharman, K.C.: Nonlinear model structure identification using genetic programming. In Koza, J.R., ed.: Late Breaking Papers at the Genetic Programming 1996 Conference Stanford University July 28-31, 1996, Stanford University, CA, USA, Stanford Bookstore (1996) 32–37
6. Weinbrenner, T.: Genetic programming techniques applied to measurement data. Diploma Thesis (1997)
7. Cao, H., Kang, L., Chen, Y., Yu, J.: Evolutionary modeling of systems of ordinary differential equations with genetic programming. Genetic Programming and Evolvable Machines **1** (2000) 309–337
8. Hinchliffe, M.: Dynamic Modelling Using Genetic Programming. PhD thesis, University of Newcastle upon Type (2001)
9. Graff, M., Flores, J.J.: (2005) http://sourceforge.net/projects/ecsid.

ARKAQ-Learning: Autonomous State Space Segmentation and Policy Generation

Alp Sardağ and H. Levent Akın

Boğaziçi University, Department of Computer Engineering, 34342 Bebek, Istanbul, Turkey
akin@boun.edu.tr

Abstract. A real world environment is often partially observable by the agents either because of noisy sensors or incomplete perception. Autonomous strategy planning under uncertainty has two major challenges. First, autonomous segmentation of the state space for a given task; Second, emerging complex behaviors that deal with each state segment. This paper suggests a new approach that handles both by utilizing combination of various techniques, namely ARKAQ-Learning (ART 2-A networks augmented with Kalman Filters and Q-Learning). The algorithm is an online algorithm and it has low space and computational complexity. The algorithm was run for some well known partially observable Markov decision process problems. World Model Generator could reveal the hidden states, mapping non-Markovian model to Markovian internal state space. Policy Generator could build the optimal policy on the internal Markovian state model.

1 Introduction

Traditional learning approaches deal with models that define an agent and its interactions with the environment via its perceptions, actions, and associated rewards. The agent tries to maximize its long term reward when performing an action. This would be easier if the world model was fully observable, namely the underlying process was a Markov Decision Process (MDP). However, in many real world environments, it will not be possible for the agent to have complete perception. When designing agents that can act under uncertainty, it is convenient to model the environment as a Partially Observable Markov Decision Process (POMDP). This model incorporates uncertainty in the agent's perceptions, actions and feedback which is an immediate or delayed reinforcement. POMDP models contain two sources of uncertainty; stochasticity of the controlled process, and imperfect and noisy observations of the state.

In POMDP's, a learner interacts with a stochastic environment whose state is only partially observable. Actions change the state of the environment and lead to numerical penalties/rewards, which may be observed with an unknown temporal delay. The learner's goal is to devise a policy for action selection that maximizes the reward. Although, the POMDP framework embraces a large range of practical problems useful in modeling, it has the disadvantage of being hard to solve, where previous studies have shown that computing the exact optimal policy is intractable for problems with more

P. Yolum et al.(Eds.): ISCIS 2005, LNCS 3733, pp. 512–523, 2005.

than a few tens of states, observations and actions. The complexity of POMDP algorithms grows exponentially with the number of state variables, making it infeasible for large problems [1,2].

Most of the methods dealing with POMDP's assume that the underlying POMDP parameters are known. However, collecting such information is impossible for most of the real world cases. Additionally, past work has predominately studied POMDP's in discrete worlds. Discrete worlds have the advantage that distributions over states (so called "belief states") can be represented exactly, using one parameter per state. The optimal value function (for finite planning horizon) has been shown to be convex and piecewise linear, which makes it possible to derive exact solutions for discrete POMDP's.

In this study we aim to use POMDP as a model of the real environment in which an agent exists. Consequently, this brings two complications which do not exist in previous studies. First we assume that the POMDP parameters are not known, and we expect our agent to discover them as the world model is generated. This makes the task extremely difficult. Second, since a large number of real world problems are continuous in nature, we are interested in POMDP's with continuous parameters. In general, such POMDP's cannot be solved exactly, and little is known about the special cases that can be solved. We propose ARKAQ-Learning algorithm, an approximate approach consisting of two layers, which can accommodate real valued spaces and models. The first layer is responsible for the generation of the world model and the second is responsible for deciding the next action that maximizes the expected discounted reward.

In Section 2 we formally describe conventional POMDP solution techniques. In Section 3 we describe ARKAQ-Learning algorithm in detail. In section 4 we present the application of ARKAQ to some of the well-known POMDP problems. We conclude the paper with the summary of the result obtained.

2 Conventional POMDP Solution Techniques

The methods for learning within the POMDP [3] framework may be classified as exact methods, which are intractable and approximate methods. There exist two versions of the POMDP training problem: learning when a model of the POMDP is known, and the much harder problem learning when a model is not available. Since we have assumed the world model is not known we will be not referring to techniques with a world model.

The methods used to solve POMDP's are referred to as reinforcement learning algorithms since the only feedback to the agent is a scalar reinforcement signal. Q-learning [4] is an online reinforcement learning algorithm, which estimates the values of state-action pairs. The value $Q(s, a)$ is defined to be the expected discounted sum of future rewards obtained by taking action a from state s and following an optimal policy thereafter. The optimal action from any state is the one with the highest Q value.

The simplest agents using Q-learning and acting believing its current observation, and ignoring noise and incomplete perception do not maintain past observations, they are memoryless. In [5], it has been shown that these agents mostly performed worse than a randomly acting agent, i.e. a deterministic policy can do arbitrarily worse than a stochastic policy.

In summary, the Q-learning algorithm is successful in Markovian environments. It is important to realize an architecture that learns the correct action while constructing a state identification mechanism which also realizes Markovian state representation from continuous and non-Markovian perceptual input.

Most of the algorithms in the literature use a certain amount of past observations. For discrete observations, these can be arranged into a suffix tree. The *Utile Suffix Memory* [6] uses a suffix tree with variable depth. The *U-Tree* algorithm is a slight extension where the observation is treated as a vector, and different branches can be created depending on the value of the "utility test". *Window-Q* uses a neural network to learn Q-values where the inputs are the last k observations and actions [7]. *Recurrent-Q* augments the output of a neural network with continuous state outputs which are fed back into a previous layer of network [7]. The network has a continuous internal-state space allowing a POMDP to be controlled by presenting observations as inputs and interpreting the outputs as action distributions. Training algorithms include back-propagation through time [8] which has difficulty in learning long-term memory because the back propagated error signals tend to blow up or shrink to nothing depending on the feedback weights.

3 Proposed Approach

We aim to use POMDP as a model of the real environment in which an agent exists. We have further assumed that POMDP parameters are not known, indeed they will be discovered by the agent and that these parameters are continuous. These two assumptions make the problem even harder and such POMDP's cannot be solved exactly.

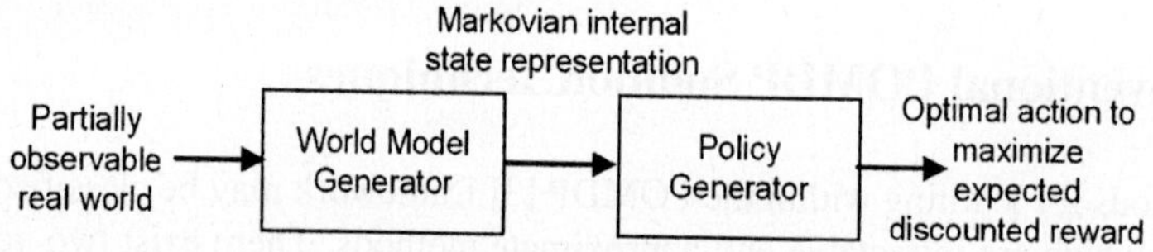

Fig. 1. The proposed architecture

The proposed architecture shown in Fig.1 consists of two layers. The first layer is a world model generator that incrementally segments real world Markovian states for a given task [19]. The second layer is a policy generator that proposes actions that deal with each state segment in order to maximize expected discounted reward. Conversion of non-Markovian states into Markovian internal world model representation in the first layer makes it possible to use Q-learning at this layer.

3.1 World Model Generator

Although the real world has the Markovian property, an agent can observe it partially due to noisy and incomplete perception. In order to achieve its goal, the agent must learn the underlying real world states related to its task(s), i.e. construct an internal state-representation that interprets continuous and non-Markovian perception into Markovian states.

The second layer takes the current action $a(t)$, observation $o(t)$, current belief of state $b(t)$ and the reward $r(t)$ as inputs. Then it incrementally segments and distinguishes current internal world representation of Markovian states $b(t)$, which in turn is recursively conditioned current estimate on all of past measurements. As a result, history is implicitly maintained, which is important for successfully building an internal world model in a POMDP environment. The world model generator is a hybrid architecture composed of a state representation network augmented with state estimation. It makes use of Kalman filtering and ART2-A networks. This section will briefly introduce these components.

Kalman Filtering. The Kalman filter [9,10] addresses the general problem of trying to estimate the state of the agent. As shown in Fig.1, it is governed by a nonlinear stochastic equation consisting of the past history $b(t)$, current observation $o(t)$imperfectly measured with a measurement noise function $v(t)$, the immediate reward $r(t)$, and action $a(t)$ disturbed by a Gaussian noise $w(t)$.

$$b(t) = F(b(t-1), a(t-1), o(t-1), r(t-1), w(t)) \tag{1}$$

$$o(t) = H(b(t), v(t)) \tag{2}$$

The equations for the Kalman filter fall into two groups: time update equations and measurement update equations. The time update equations are responsible for projecting forward (in time) the current state and error covariance estimates to obtain the *a priori* estimates for the next time step.

The measurement update equations are responsible for the feedback—i.e. for incorporating a new measurement into *the a priori* estimate to obtain an improved *a posteriori* estimate.

The observation noise represented by a covariance matrix is then used to update the Kalman gain matrix, which in turn is the weighting factor used to combine the a *priori* state estimate and the observation. Gain matrix also depends on the state error covariance matrix which is continuously updated. In short, Kalman filter first predicts the state

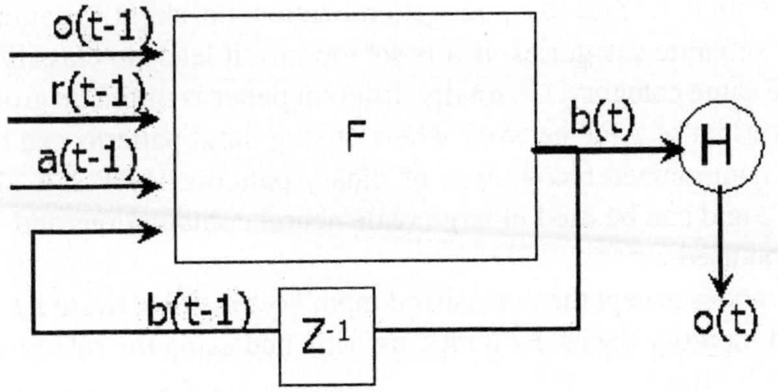

Fig. 2. Sketch of the Kalman filter

and then corrects the prediction using the observation by recursively reconditioning the current estimate on all of the past measurements.

ART2-A: State. A learning system must be able to respond to significant changes while staying stable upon irrelevant events. This is called the *stability-plasticity dilemma*. Although Kalman filter is good in tuning the current estimate by recursively reconditioning the current estimate on all of the past measurements, it has drawbacks in stability-plasticity dilemma at the prediction phase. Prediction phase, formulated by the nonlinear Eq.1 is modified and calculated by ART2-A network.

The issue is to let the agent know how to switch between its stable and plastic modes, ensuring that as the agent acts keeping the state space stable it avoids rigidity, and as it allows plasticity of the state space it avoids chaos. To overcome this problem, either the total number of input patterns needs to be restricted, or the learning process itself must be shut off. Shutting off the world is not possible in many real time applications. In the absence of a self-stabilization mechanism, an external teacher must act as the system's front end to independently recognize the inputs and make the decision. In this case, the external teacher must be able to carry out the recognition tasks that the learning system was supposed to carry out. Hence, non-self-stabilizing learning systems are not capable of functioning autonomously in stochastic environments. In learning systems that need an external teacher to supply the correct representation to be learned, the learning process is driven by the mismatches between desired and actual outputs. Such schemes must learn slowly, or risk unstable oscillations in response to the mismatch. These learning models also tend to be trapped in a local minima, or globally incorrect solutions.

Since an Adaptive Resonance Theory (ART) [11,20] network with short-term memory models recognition of unexpected patterns and can remember these patterns where needed and is designed to learn quickly and stably in response to a possibly non-stationary world, it is used to incrementally segment and distinguish real world Markovian states. Approximate matches, rather than mismatches, drive the learning process in ART. Learning in the approximate match mode enables rapid and stable learning to occur while buffering the system's memory against external noise. The hypothesis testing cycle replaces internal system noise as a scheme for discovering a globally correct solution. It does not use an external teacher. A vigilance parameter ρ determines the maximum tolerable difference between two patterns in the same category. If this parameter is set too high, it leads to a poor generalization, i.e. slight variations of the same pattern become separate categories. If it is set too low, it leads to classifying dissimilar patterns into the same category, i.e. totally different patterns might be grouped together.

ART2 is a variant of ART network where analog input patterns can be categorized compared to self-organized recognition of binary patterns. ART 2-A [12] is a faster version of ART2 and can be used in large scale neural computations and was chosen as the network to be used.

In Fig.3, F1 nodes accept the normalized input vector and activate F2 nodes according to long term memory traces. F2 nodes are activated using the rule given in Eq.3.

$$T_i = \begin{cases} \alpha \sum_t I_i & \text{if j is an uncommitted node} \\ I \cdot z_j^* & \text{if j is a commited node} \end{cases} \quad (3)$$

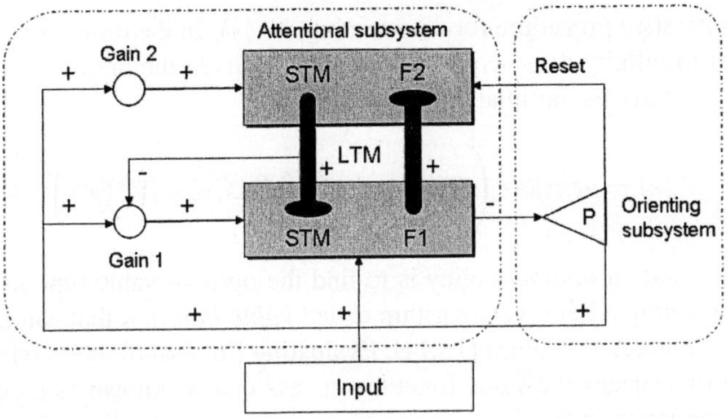

Fig. 3. Sketch of ART2A architecture. F1 is the input representation field whereas F2 is the category representation field.

Initially all F2 nodes are uncommitted. The set of committed F2 nodes are the scaled LTM vectors z_j defined iteratively. The initial choice denoted by j at F2 is one of which satisfying the maximum T value. j remains constant if it is uncommitted or it has a higher value than ρ. If j is committed then j is reset to the index of an arbitrary uncommitted node. The input is then transformed to z_j^{new} defined by Eq.4,

$$\begin{array}{ll} I & \text{if j is an uncommitted node} \\ \left(\beta\Psi + (1-\beta)\, z_j^{*(old)}\right) & \text{if j is a commited node} \end{array} \quad (4)$$

where ψ is given in Eq.5

$$\Psi_i \equiv \begin{cases} I_i \;\; z_j^{*(old)} > 0 \\ 0 \;\; otherwise \end{cases} \quad (5)$$

The concept of our hybrid network can be summarized as follows:

- ART updates the state space and predicts the current state.
- Kalman recursively conditions the current estimate on all of the past measurements and fine tune the current state estimate. This helps to keep history (which is important for POMDP solutions) in an implicit manner.

4 Policy Generator

We used a method of determining the long-term value of acting in each state. Using this information, an agent that knows the state can act optimally by the definition of a Markov process. Bellman describes a procedure known as Dynamic Programming [13], which allows us to determine the long-term value $V(s)$ for each state s. Dynamic Programming is summarized by the Bellman Equation, where $0 \leq \gamma \leq 1$.

$$V(s) = \max_a \left(R(s,a) + \gamma \sum_{s' \in S} T(s,a,s')V(s') \right), \forall s \in S \quad (6)$$

This is an iterative procedure for determining, $V^*(s)$. In the limit, as the number of iterations goes to infinity, $V(s)$ converges to $V^*(s)$. Given the optimal value function $V^*(s)$, we can specify the optimal policy as

$$\pi^*(s) = \arg\max_a \left(R(s,a) + \gamma \sum_{s' \in S} T(s,a,s')V^*(s') \right) \tag{7}$$

One way to find an optimal policy is to find the optimal value function. It can be determined by a simple iterative algorithm called *value iteration* that can be shown to converge to the correct V^* values [13,14]. Evaluating Eq. 6 until the maximum difference between two successive value functions is less than ε, known as ε-convergence, and forming a policy from Eq. 7 is the basis of value iteration [15]. Eq. 6 has complexity order $O(|A||S|^2)$ for each iteration, and becomes intractable for very large state spaces. In addition, the transition probabilities, T, may not always be available. These two observations motivate Monte-Carlo methods for computing V^*. These methods learn by interacting with the world and gathering experience about the long-term rewards from each state. Q-learning is an algorithm for learning value functions $Q(s,a) : s \times a \rightarrow \Re$, which represent the value of taking action a in state s and than acting optimally. It is summarized by the following update rule [16], which introduces a learning rate $0 \leq \alpha < 1$.

$$Q_t(s,a) = Q_t(s,a) + \alpha_t \left(r_{t+1} + \gamma \max_{a'} Q_{t+1}(s',a') - Q_t(s,a) \right) \tag{8}$$

Since a Markovian internal world model is constructed, Q-leaning is used to generate the optimum policy. The world model generator reduces the complexity of $Q(s,a)$ by aggregating states into cluster centers. The optimal action or actions from any cluster center is the one with the highest Q-value. Closer Q-values may result in more than one optimal action from a state.

This layer is activated after the world model layer has converged. The final architecture is given in Fig. 4.

5 Sample Runs

The resulting architecture was used to solve several known POMDP problems. The results are classified according to the chosen vigilance parameter (ρ).

5.1 A Basic POMDP Problem

The basic problem is a one dimensional 4-cell hallway where the goal is one of the cells. A sketch is given in Fig.5(a). The agent, represented with a circle can move EAST and WEST. The goal state is marked by a star. The reward is inversely proportional to the distance to the goal cell. The agent, which is a robot, has two range finders disturbed with Gaussian noise. Note that the region is closed so that the agent cannot move outside the region.

The resulting state space with vigilance parameters 0.9 is sketched in Fig.5(b). Since the vigilance parameter has a higher value, each cell is mapped to a different state. The optimum actions for states 1, 2 and 3 is *WEST* and the optimum action for state 4 is *EAST* according to the $Q(s,a)$ values. The agent could classify each cell separately and the optimum policy has been successfully found.

5.2 4x4 Maze Problem

This problem is a two dimensional maze, where the sketch is given in Fig.6. The goal state is the lower right corner. The agent can move *EAST, WEST, LEFT and SOUTH*. The reward is 1 for the goal state and 0 for the others. The agent can only sense the reward and the region is bounded. Since the agent is almost blind and the reward is delayed, this is a challenging problem.

If the vigilance parameter is low two clusters were established, namely *Goal* and *Non-Goal* states. If the vigilance parameter was chosen to have a higher value, four clusters were established. They are classified according to the optimum action from them and their distance to the goal. The agent could classify the goal cell from the others no matter what the vigilance parameter is chosen. The optimum policy for vigilance parameter 0.9 is; *EAST* for state 3, *SOUTH* for state 0, *EAST* or *SOUTH* for state 1 (with *EAST* favored) and *EAST* or *SOUTH* for the goal state.

5.3 Load-Unload Problem

In this very challenging problem [17] shown in Fig.7, the agent has a cart that must be driven from an *Unload* location to a *Load* location, and then back to *Unload*. This problem is a simple POMDP with a hidden variable that makes it partially observable (the agent cannot see whether it is loaded or not): If the agent had memory it would remember its latest *Load* or *Unload* action, and it would go left or right correspondingly. The actions the agent can make are *EAST* and *WEST*. Note that the goal state dynamically changes. If the cart is loaded the goal is the unload station or vice versa. Since our agent does not have any prior information and has implicit memory this problem becomes challenging.

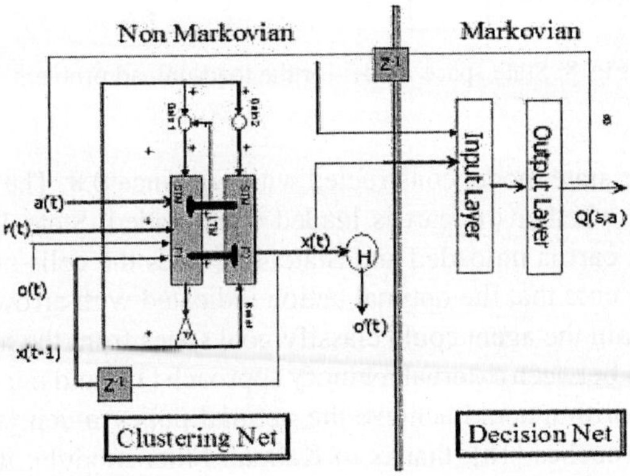

Fig. 4. The ARKAQ architecture. a denotes the action, r denotes the reward, o denotes the observation and x is the state

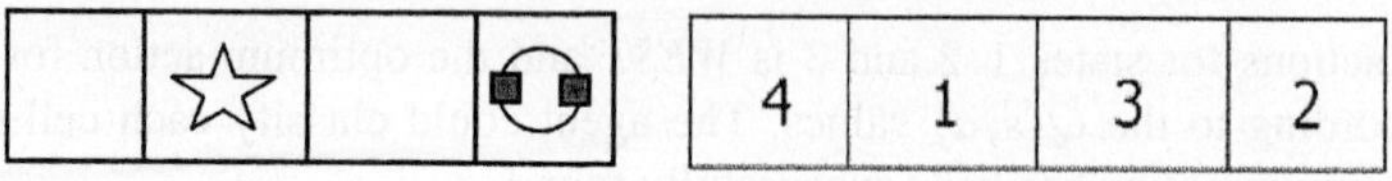

Fig. 5. (a) Classical POMDP Problem with 4 cells and one goal state. (b) The resulting assigned states to each cell.

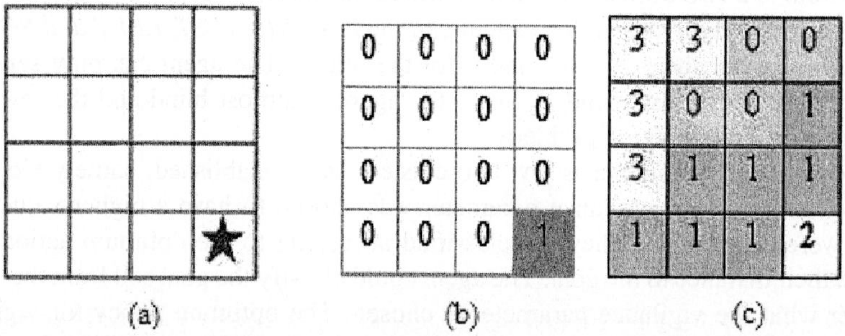

Fig. 6. (a) 4x4 maze problem (b) State space with ρ=0.1 and (c) State space with ρ=0.9.

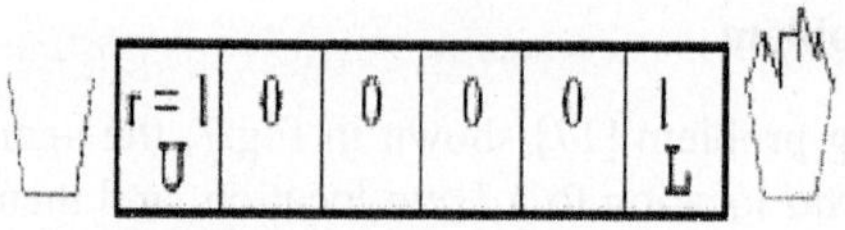

Fig. 7. Load-Unload problem [17]

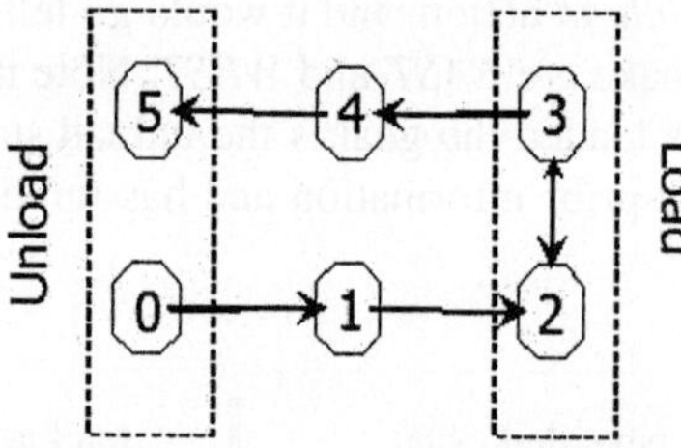

Fig. 8. State space model for the load-unload problem

Fig. 8 shows the state model constructed with vigilance 0.8. The world model generator has revealed whether the cart is loaded or unloaded. State 1 denotes the cells marked 0 when the cart is unloaded and State 4 denotes the cells marked 0 when the cart is loaded. Also note that the optimal action indicated with arrows differs for these two states. Once again the agent could classify goal states from the non-goal states.

The comparison between external memory approach [18] and our algorithm is given in Table 1. Our algorithm could achieve the optimal policy much faster than external memory based approaches [18], thanks to Kalman Filter module. It needs 50 runs to discover states and another 30 runs for generating the optimal policy. Although it discovers the task oriented states by itself, it is still 20 percent faster than external memory approach. Another advantage of our algorithm is that it does not need to know how

Table 1. Comparison of the external memory approach [18] and ARKAQ-Learning

	Autonomous State Segmentation and Aggregation	Hint given about how to reveal hidden state	Problem Definition changed by Adding new actions	Number of Runs
External Memory Approach	No	Yes	Yes	100
ARKAQ-Learning	Yes	No	No	80

much memory should be used or what to store in the memory. Instead the agent will find this information itself.

5.4 5x5 Grid Multi Station Load-Unload Problem

In this variation of the standard Load-Unload problem proposed in this paper, there are two "load" stations namely L1, L2, and two "unload" stations, U1, U2, placed in a 5x5 grid world. When the agent loads at station L1 it has to unload at U1, or visa versa. The agent can move *EAST, WEST, LEFT and SOUTH*. The reward is 1 for the goal state and 0 for the others. Note the goal state changes, depending on the loaded station. Fig. 9 shows the sketch of the 5x5 world.

As shown in Fig. 10, ART successfully preserved the previously learned knowledge despite of the new learned things, as defined by the stability-plasticity dilemma.

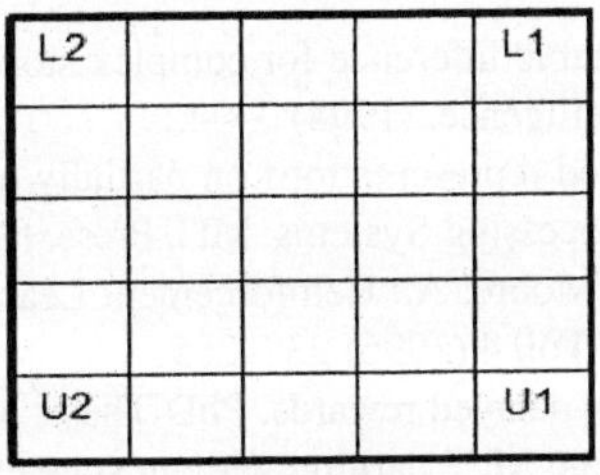

Fig. 9. 5x5 Grid Multi Station Load – Unload Problem. The agent has to unload the widgets to the right station among the U1 and U2.

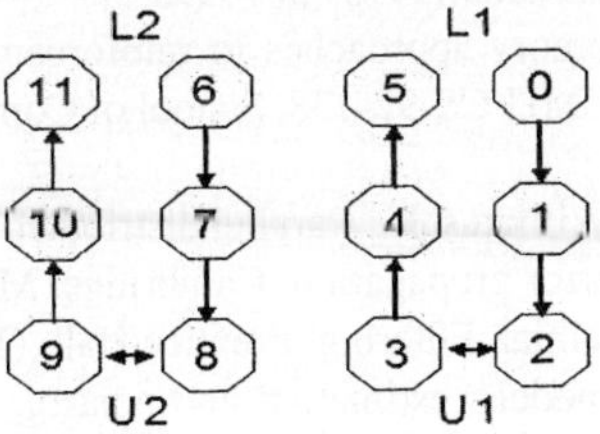

Fig. 10. The agent stabilizes its path between only one Load Unload stations depending on the point of start

6 Conclusion

ARKAQ inherits best features of ART (stability – plasticity) and Kalman Filters (conditioning the current estimate on all of the past measurements). It successfully discovers the task specific Markovian states for the given problems. Our algorithm does not need a prior hint or a change to the problem definition by addition of new actions (e.g. how to reveal the hidden state in external memory approaches) to discover Markovian states. It also aggregates the revealed states into clusters and computes the optimal policy. Moreover, our approach does not keep a history window, instead, each state estimate is recursively built on all past measurements. The world model generator reveals all hidden states by mapping non-Markovian perceptual input to Markovian states, thus making it possible to use Q-Learning, which is an online learning algorithm. Moreover, the space and computational complexity of this approach is very low compared to the mentioned alternative solutions.

The vigilance parameter has a very important role on the outcome. The state space segmentation depends on the vigilance parameter, if set too high, similar states may become separate categories, resulting in too many states, and if set too low dissimilar states may be classified into the same category, resulting in misclassification. As the policy is built on the world states, the vigilance parameter affects indirectly also the policy generated. The whole system performance depends on the choice of the vigilance parameter. Therefore, further work on estimation of the vigilance parameter using evolutionary algorithms when not given will be investigated.

References

1. Boyen, X., Koller, D.: Tractable inference for complex stochastic processes. Conference on Uncertainty in Artificial Intelligence. (1998) 33–42
2. Sallans, B.: Learning factored representations on partially observable Markov decision process. Neural Information Processing Systems. MIT Press. (2000) 1050–1056.
3. Kaelbling, L., Littman, M., Moore, A.: Reinforcement Learning: A Survey, Journal of Artificial Intelligence Research, Vol. 4 (1996) 237–285
4. Watkins, C.J.: Learning with delayed rewards. PhD Thesis, Cambridge University, (1989)
5. Singh, S., Jaakkola, T., Jordan, M.: Learning without state estimation in partially observable Markov decision processes. International Conference on Machine Learning. (1994) 284–292
6. McCallum, R.A.: Instance-based util distinctions for reinforcement learning with hidden state. In Proceedings of the Twelfth International Conference on Machine Learning, San Francisco, CA. Morgan Kaufmann. (1995) 387–395
7. Lin, L., Mitchell, T.M.: Memory approaches to reinforcement learning in non-Markovian domains. Technical Report CMU-CS-92-138, School of Computer Science, Carnegie Mellon University. (1992)
8. Rumelhart, D., Hinton, G., Williams, R.: Parallel distributed processing, chapter 8: Learning internal representations by error propagation. Cambridge, MA. MIT Press. (1986)
9. Grewal, A., Andrews, C.: Kalman Filtering. Prentice Hall. (1993) 80–102
10. Maybeck, P.S.: Stochastic models, estimation and control, Academic Press. Vol 1. (1979) 1–15
11. Carpenter, G. A., Grossberg, S.: ART2. Self-Organization of Stable Category Recognition Codes for Analog Input Patterns. Applied Optics. (1989) 4919–30

12. Carpenter, G. A., Grossberg, S., Rosen, D. B.: ART 2-A: An Adaptive Resonance Algorithm for Rapid Category Learning and Recognition. Neural Networks, Pergamon Press. Vol 4. (1991) 493–504
13. Bellman, R.: Dynamic Programming. Princeton University Press, Princeton, NJ, USA. (1957)
14. Bertsekas, D.: ynamic Programming: Deterministic and Stochastic Models. Prentice-Hall, Englewood Cliffs, NJ. (1987)
15. Howard, R.A.: Dynamic Programming and Markov Processes. The MIT Press, Cambridge MA. (1960)
16. Sutton, R., Singh, S., Precup, D., Ravindran, B.: Improved switching among temporally abstract actions. Proceedings of Neural Information Processings Systems, MIT Press. (1999) 1066–1072
17. Peshkin, L., Shelton, H.: Learning from scarce experience. Proceedings of the Nineteenth International Conference on Machine Learning. (2002) 498–505
18. Peshkin, L., Meuleau, N., Kaelbling,L. P.: Learning Policies with External Memory, Proceedings of the Sixteenth International Conference on Machine Learning. (1999) 307–314
19. Tesauro, G.: Programming Backgammon Using Self-Teaching Neural Nets. Artificial Intelligence. (2002) 181–199
20. Carpenter, G. A., Grossberg, S.: A massively parallel architecture for a self-organizing neural pattern recognition machine. Computer Vision, Graphics, and Image Processing. (1987) 3754

Signature Verification Using Conic Section Function Neural Network

Canan Şenol[1] and Tülay Yıldırım[2]

[1] Department of Electronic Eng., Kadir Has University, Cibali, 34230, Istanbul, Turkey
canan@khas.edu.tr
[2] Department of Electronics and Communication Eng., Yildiz Technical University, Besiktas, 34349, Istanbul, Turkey
tulay@yildiz.edu.tr

Abstract. This paper presents a new approach for off-line signature verification based on a hybrid neural network (Conic Section Function Neural Network-CSFNN). Artificial Neural Networks (ANNs) have recently become a very important method for classification and verification problems. In this work, CSFNN was proposed for the signature verification and compared with two well known neural network architectures (Multilayer Perceptron-MLP and Radial Basis Function-RBF Networks). The proposed system was trained and tested on a signature database consisting of a total of 304 signature images taken from 8 different persons. A total of 256 samples (32 samples for each person) for training and 48 fake samples (6 fake samples belonging to each person) for testing were used. The results were presented and the comparisons were also made in terms of FAR (False Acceptance Rate) and FRR (False Rejection Rate).

1 Introduction

Signature is a special case of handwriting in which special characters and flourishes are available. Signatures can be handled as an image, and hence, it can be verified using computer vision and neural network techniques.

Signature verification problem is concerned with determining whether a particular signature truly belongs to a person, so that forgeries can be detected. In signature recognition problem, a signature database is searched to establish identity of a given signature. Depending on the need, signature recognition and verification problems are often categorized in two major classes: online signature recognition and verification systems (SRVS) and offline SRVS. Online SRVS requires some special peripheral units (like electronic tablet) for measuring hand speed and pressure on the human hand when it creates the signature. In offline SRVS, systems rely on image processing and feature extraction techniques. [1, 9]

During the last few years some online SRVS are developed [1, 3, 7]. There are so many studies of offline SRVS. [1, 2, 4, 6, 8, 9]

In this work, a hybrid neural network approach (Conic Section Function Neural Network-CSFNN) for off-line signature verification was presented. Sample signatures

P. Yolum et al.(Eds.): ISCIS 2005, LNCS 3733, pp. 524 – 532, 2005.

formed were verified by using CSFNN and comparisons were made using two well known neural network architectures, Multilayer Perceptron (MLP) and Radial Basis Function (RBF).

2 Preprocessing

Signature samples are required to be preprocessed before training and testing. In SRVS problems, similar preprocessing steps are used for different methods. The preprocessing stage is divided into three parts: Noise Reduction, Signature Normalization and Signature Skeletonization. [2]

2.1 Noise Reduction

The goal of noise reduction is to eliminate single black pixels on white background. In this work, a 3×3 mask is applied to the image. If the colour of the centre pixel is different from the same coloured 8 pixels around, the colour of the centre pixel is converted to opposite (if it is white it is made black, or vice versa).

2.2 Signature Normalization

Height and width of signatures vary from the person to person or sometimes same person may use different size signatures. Therefore these size differences need to be eliminated. During the normalization process the signature size is adjusted so that the width reaches to a default value while the height to width ratio is kept constant.

2.3 Signature Skeletonization

Skeletonization is to remove unnecessary pixels, without destroying signature characteristics. Some genuine sample signatures are shown in Figure 1 and Figure 2 shows some fake sample signatures.

Used signature in further processings is the picture of skeletonized signature.

Fig. 1. Some genuine signature samples

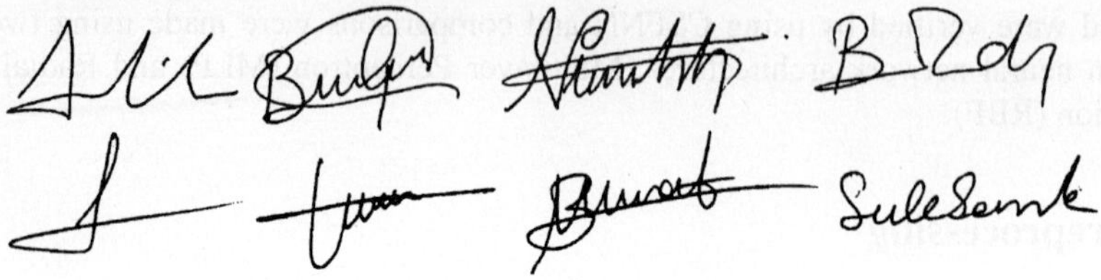

Fig. 2. Some fake signature samples

3 Feature Extraction

The choice of a convenient set of features is crucial at signature recognition and verification problems. In the work presented here, two groups of features which are categorized as global and grid information features were used.

3.1 Global Features

Global features give information about the structure of a signature sample. Some of these features are image area, signature height, baseline shift, vertical center of the signature, horizontal center of the signature, global slant angle, number of edge points, number of cross points, number of closed loops, maximum vertical and horizontal projection vertical and horizontal projection peaks etc...

Only baseline shift, vertical and horizontal center of the signature, global slant angel, maximum vertical and horizontal projection vertical and horizontal projection peaks features were used in this work. Baseline shift feature is the difference between the vertical centers of gravity of the left and the right parts of the signature [2]. These eight features give us eight input values for training and testing of the neural networks.

3.2 Grid Information Features

The skeletonization image is divided into 384 (16×24) segments, and the sum of foreground pixels (area) for each segment is calculated. Results are normalized as the

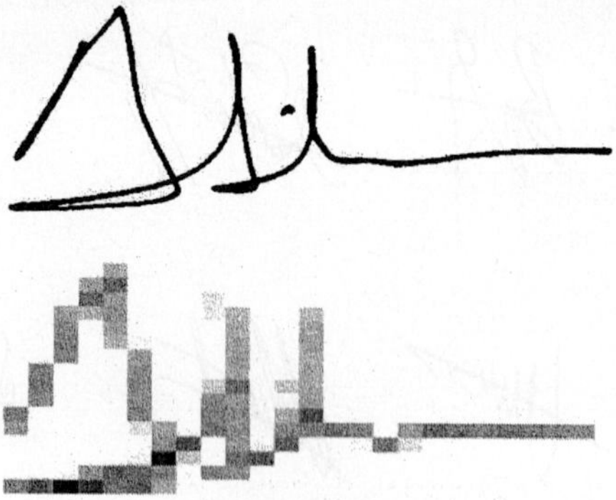

Fig. 3. Grid vector of a signature

lowest value would be zero and the highest value would be one. This feature gives us 384 input values for training and testing of the neural networks. Figure 3 shows the grid vector of a signature.

At the end of feature extraction processes, the total size of our input vector is 392×304. The input vector varies between 0 and 1.

4 Applied Neural Network Structures

In this work, a new approach for off-line signature verification using a hybrid neural network (CSFNN) is presented and compared with two well known (MLP and RBF) neural network architectures. Sample signatures formed and preprocessed were recognized and verified using CSFNN, MLP and RBF.

4.1 Multilayer Perceptron (MLP) Neural Networks

In general modelling, the MLP consist of an input layer, one or more hidden layers and an output layer. The input signal propagates through the network in a forward direction. Therefore it is commonly referred to as feed forwarded network. The neuron number of the input layer depends on the input number of problem to be solved. Number of hidden layers and the number of neurons in the hidden layer can be changed. The neuron number of the output layer depends on the problem. Figure 4 shows the architectural graph of a MLP with one hidden layer. The network shown here is fully connected, which means that a neuron in any layer of the network is connected to all the nodes/neurons in the previous layer.

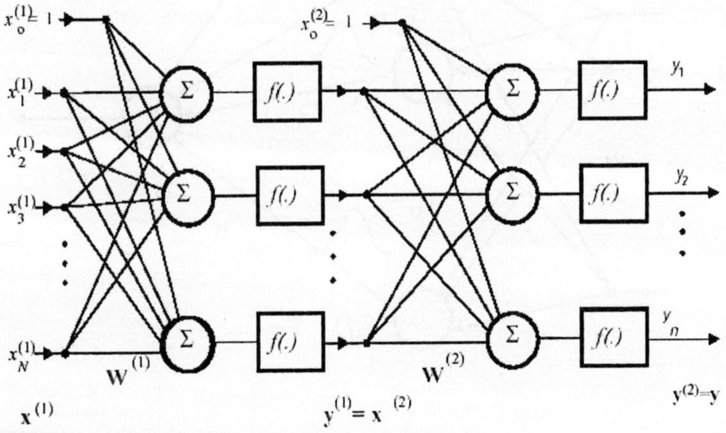

Fig. 4. Architectural graph of MLP

4.2 Radial Basis Function (RBF) Neural Networks

A different approach by viewing the design of a neural network as a curve-fitting approximation problem in a high-dimensional space is taken. According to this viewpoint, learning is equivalent to finding a surface in a multidimensional space that provides a best fit to the training data. The input layer is made up of source nodes. The second layer is a hidden layer of high enough dimension, which serves a different purpose from than in a multilayer perceptron. The output layer supplies the response of the network to the activation patterns applied to the input layer. The transformation from the input space to the hidden-unit space is nonlinear, whereas the transformation from the hidden-unit space to the output space is linear. The mathematical expression of an RBF is given as

$$y = \sum_i w_i g_i(x) = \sum_i w_i g(\|x - c_i\|) \tag{1}$$

where w_i is the weight from the ith neuron of the hidden layer to the output layer. $g_i(x)$ is an activation function and in general Gaussian Function. In Gaussian Function, x denotes input vector, c_i denotes center, where $\|x-c_i\|$ standard Euclidean distance, and σ_i as spread. Gaussian Function's mathematical expression is

$$g(\|x - c_i\|) = \exp\left(-\frac{\|x - c_i\|^2}{2\sigma_i^{\,2}}\right) \tag{2}$$

Figure 5 shows the architectural graph of a RBF.

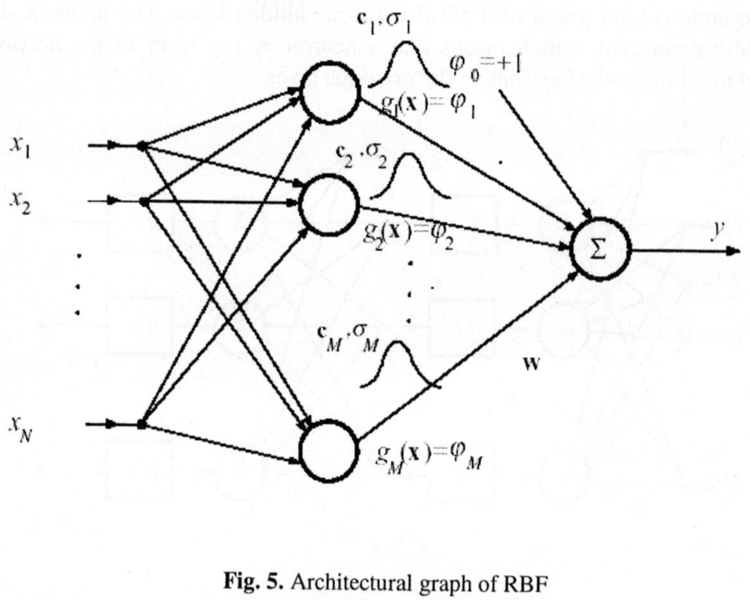

Fig. 5. Architectural graph of RBF

4.3 Conic Section Function Neural Network (CSFNN)

The idea of the conic section function neural network is to provide unification between RBF and MLP networks. The new propagation rule (which will consist of RBF and MLP propagation rules) can be derived using analytical equations for a cone.

Let x be any point on the surface of the right circular cone. ω can be any value in the range [-π/2,π/2], v vertex of the cone and a the unity vector defining the axis of the cone. Thus the equation of the circular cone is

$$(\vec{x}-\vec{v})\vec{a} = \cos w\|\vec{x}-\vec{v}\| \tag{3}$$

If the coordinates of the points and vectors are defined by $x=(x_1,x_2)$, $v=(v_1,v_2)$ and $a=(a_1,a_2)$ for two dimensional space, Eq. 3. can be written as below

$$(x_1-v_1)a_1+(x_2-v_2)a_2=\cos w\sqrt{(x_1-v_1)^2+(x_1-v_2)^2} \tag{4}$$

The propagation rule of conic section function network is described using Eq.4. First of all the following form is obtained for n-dimensional input space.

$$\sum_{i=1}^{n+1}(x_i-v_i)a_i = \cos w\sqrt{\sum_{i=1}^{n+1}(x_i-v_i)^2} \tag{5}$$

The center coordinate of the circle, c, can be used instead of the coordinate of vertex v since the distance between the x point and the vertex v equals to the radius of the circle when the opening angle, 2ω, is 90 degrees. Subtracting the right hand side from the left hand side, the propagation rule of the CSFNN is obtained as

$$y_j = \sum_{i=1}^{n+1}(x_i-c_{ij})a_{ij} - \cos w_j\sqrt{\sum_{i=1}^{n+1}(x_i-c_{ij})^2} \tag{6}$$

where a_{ij} refers to the weights for each connection between the input and hidden layer units in an MLP network, and c_{ij} refers to the center coordinates in an RBF network, i and j are the indices referring to the units in the input and hidden layer, respectively, and y_j are the activation values of the CSFNN neurons. As can be seen easily, this

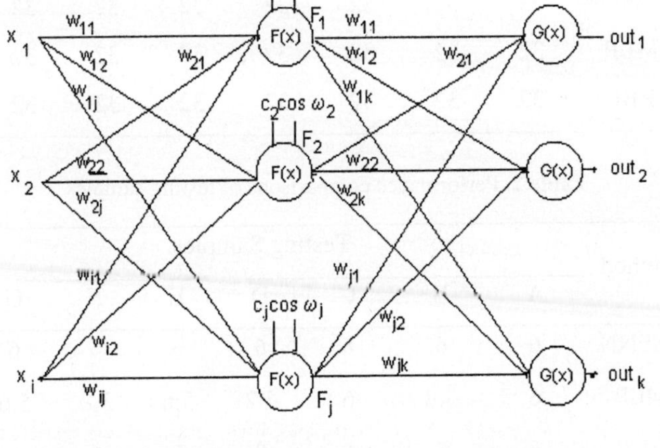

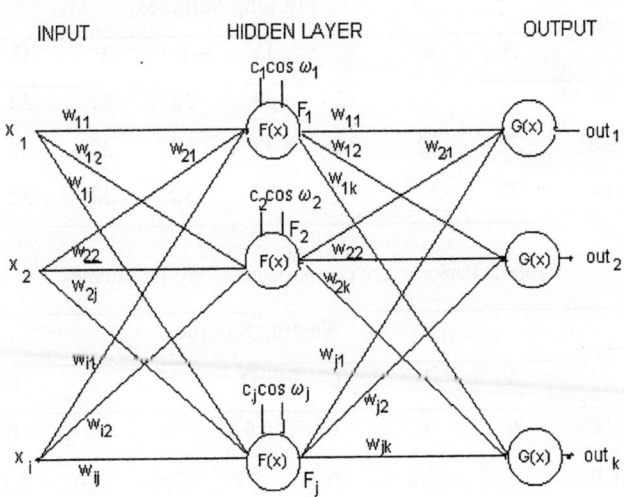

Fig. 6. Conic Section Function Neural Network Structure

equation consists of two major parts analogous to the MLP and the RBF. The equation simply turns into the propagation rule of an MLP network, which is the dot product when the ω is $\pi/2$. Second part of the equation gives the Euclidean distance between the inputs and the centers for an RBF network. Figure 6 illustrates the structure of a Conic Section Function Neural Network. [12]

5 Simulation Results

The proposed signature verification system was trained and tested on a signature database consisting of a total of 304 signature images. A, B, C, D, E, F, G, and H denote the signatures of different persons. After the preprocessing and feature extraction, an input vector sized 392×304 was formed. 256 signatures (32 samples for each person) for training and 48 fake samples (6 fake samples belonging to each person) for testing are used.

An MLP with an input layer (with 392 inputs), two hidden layers (with 250 and 100 neurons, respectively) and an output layer with 8 neurons was formed. MLP was trained by standard error back propagation using Matlab 7.0. Training process was repeated 10 times since it gives different results depending on random initialization of weights in the algorithm. Then, the average of the results was taken. The most appropriate learning rate was found as 0,05.

RBF structure was trained by Orthogonal Least Square algorithm using Matlab 7.0 Toolbox. RBF structure reached to 240 neurons in the hidden layer after the training. Suitable spread value was found as 8.

The CSFNN was formed by using only one hidden layer with 30 neurons and output layer with 8 neurons. Suitable spread value was found as 1.

Table 1. Performance comparisons of training samples

Method	Training Samples							
	A	B	C	D	E	F	G	H
CSFNN	32	32	32	32	32	32	32	32
MLP	32	32	32	32	32	32	32	32
RBF	32	32	32	32	32	32	32	32

Table 2. Performance comparisons of testing samples

Method	Testing Samples							
	A	B	C	D	E	F	G	H
CSFNN	6	6	6	6	6	6	6	4
MLP	6	5.8	6	5.2	5.6	5.8	5.6	3
RBF	6	5	6	6	5	6	6	6

Table 3. Results of signature verification using CSFNN, MLP and RBF

Method	Training Samples	Testing Samples
CSFNN	%100	%95.83
MLP	%100	%89.58
RBF	%100	%95.83

The results were given in the following tables. Table 2 shows the number of test samples correctly classified as fake, whereas Table 1 demonstrates the training samples correctly classified as genuine signatures.

In general, two types of error rates are useful in describing accuracy of signature verification systems. The first is the FAR – False Acceptance Rate (fakes that were accepted as genuine) and the second is FRR – False Rejection Rate (genuine signatures that were flagged as fakes). Table 4 shows these rates and accuracies of proposed methods for signature verification.

Table 4. FAR and FRR data comparisons

Method	FAR	FRR	Accuracy
CSFNN	4.16	0	%95.84
MLP	11.25	0	%88.75
RBF	4.16	0	%95.84

6 Conclusions

An off-line signature verification based on Conic Section Function Neural Network was presented in this paper. Two well known neural network architectures, MLP and RBF, were used to compare the results. CSFNN and RBF give a good accuracy in terms of FRR and FAR rates. The size of CSFNN structure is quite small compared to those standard ones. It needs only 38 (30+8) neurons while MLP needs 358 (250+100+8) and RBF needs 248 (240+8) neurons for training. This result gives superiority to CSFNN for neural network hardware implementations in practice.

References

1. Bajaj, R., Chaudhury, S.: Signature Verification Using Multiple Neural Classifiers, Pattern Recognition Society, (1996), 30:1-7.
2. Baltzakis, H., Papamarkos, N.: A new signature verification technique based on a two-stage neural network classifier, Engineering Applications of Artificial Inteligence, (2001), 14:95-103.

3. Brault, J., Plamondon, R.: Segmenting handwritten signatures at their perceptually important points, IEEE transactions on Pattern Analysis and machine Inteligence, Vol. 15. (1993) 953–957.
4. Hanmandlu, M., Madasu, V.K., Madasu, S.: Neuro-Fuzzy Approaches to Signature Verification, 2nd National Conference on Document Analysis and Recognition (NCDAR-2003), 11-12 July 2003, Mandya, India, (2003).
5. Haykin, S.: Neural Networks: A Comprehensive Foundation, Macmillan College Publishing, New York, (1994).
6. Huang, K., Yan, H.: Off-line Signature Verification Based on Geometric Feature Extraction and Neural Network Classification, Pattern Recognition Society, (1996), 30:9-17.
7. Keit, T.H., Palaniappan, R., Raveendran, P., Takeda, F.: Signature Verification System using Pen Pressure for Internet and E-Commerce Application, ISSRE2001 International Symposium on Software Reliability Engineering, 27-30 November, Hong Kong, (2001).
8. Murshed, N.A. Bortolozzi, F., Sabourin, R.: Off-Line Signature Verification using Fuzzy ARTMAP Neural Network, IEEE International Conference on Neural Networks, 27 November-1st December 1995, Perth, Australia, (1995).
9. Öz, C., Ercal, F., Demir, Z.: Signature Recognition and Verification with ANN, ELECO'2003 International Conference on Electrical and Electronics Engineering, 3-7 December 2003, Bursa, (2003).
10. Parizeu, M., Plamondon, R.: A Comparative analysis of regional correlating dynamic time warping and skeletal tree matching for signature verification, IEEE transactions on Pattern Analysis and machine Inteligence, Vol. 12. (1990) 710–717.
11. Yıldırım, T., Özyılmaz, L.: Dimensionality reduction in Conic Section Function Neural Network, Sadhana-Academy Proceedings in Engineering Sciences, Vol 27, Part 6, (2002), 675-683.
12. Yıldırım,T.: Development of Conic Section Function Neural Networks in Software and Analogue Hardware, Ph.D. Thesis, Liverpool University, UK, May (1997).

Fusion of Rule-Based and Sample-Based Classifiers – Probabilistic Approach

Marek Kurzynski

Wroclaw University of Technology, Faculty of Electronics, Chair of Systems and Computer Networks, Wyb. Wyspianskiego 27, 50-370 Wroclaw, Poland
marek.kurzynski@pwr.wroc.pl

Abstract. The present paper is devoted to the pattern recognition methods for combining heterogeneous sets of learning data: set of training examples and the set of expert rules with unprecisely formulated weights understood as conditional probabilities. Adopting the probabilistic model two concepts of recognition learning are proposed. In the first approach two classifiers trained on homogeneous data set are generated and next their decisions are combined using local weighted voting combination rule. In the second method however, one set of data is transformed into the second one and next only one classifier trained on homogeneous set of data is used. Presented algorithms were practically applied to the computer-aided diagnosis of acute renal failure in children and results of their classification accuracy are given.

1 Introduction

The design of the classifier in statistical pattern recognition generally depends on what kind of information is available about the probability distribution of classes and features. If this information is complete, then the Bayes decision scheme can be used. If such information is unknown or incompletely defined, a possible approach is to design a system which will acquire the pertinent information from the actually available data for constructing a decision rule. Usually it is assumed that available information on the probability characteristics is contained in a learning set consisting of a sequence of observed features of patterns and their correct classification. In such a case many learning procedures are known within empirical Bayes decision theory, which lead to the different sample-based pattern recognition algorithms (e.g. [3], [5]).

Another approach, interesting from both theoretical and practical point of view, supposes that appropriate information is contained in expert knowledge. A typical knowledge representation consists of rules of the form IF A THEN B with the weight (uncertainty measure) α. These rules are obtained from the expert as his/her conditional beliefs: if A is known with certainty then the expert's belief into B is α. In this case numerous inference procedures are proposed and very well investigated for different formal interpretations of the weight α ([4], [6], [16]).

P. Yolum et al.(Eds.): ISCIS 2005, LNCS 3733, pp. 533–542, 2005.

In this paper we shall focus our attention on decision algorithms for the case in which both the learning set and expert rules are available. Additionally, adopting the probabilistic interpretation of weight coefficients, we suppose that expert rules are not provided with exact value of α (i.e. conditional probability), but only an interval is specified (by its upper and lower bounds), into which this probability belongs.

We may expect that the quality of the recognition algorithm will improve when both kinds of information are concurrently utilized. The concept of pattern recognition for considered case requires that both kinds of information have unified formal interpretation. In this paper the probabilistic model is adopted and hence we assign probabilistic meaning to both the information obtained from experts and the numerical data. According to general principles of this model we assume that the classes and features are observed values of appropriate random variables for which the joint probability distribution exists but is unknown. We treat expert-acquired information (rules) and numerical data as a source of knowledge about the unknown probability characteristics.

This paper is a sequel to the author's earlier publications [10], [11], [12], [13], [14], [15] and it yields an essential extension of the results included therein.

The contents of the work are as follows. Section 2 introduces necessary background and provides the problem statement. In section 3 we present two different concepts of pattern recognition algorithms for the problem in question. In the first approach two classifiers trained on homogeneous data set are generated and next their decisions are combined using local voting and linear combination rules. In the second method however, one set of data is transformed into the second one and next only one classifier trained on homogeneous set of data is used. The proposed algorithms were practically implemented in the computer-aided diagnosis of acute renal failure in children and results of classification accuracy obtained on the real data are given in section 4.

2 Preliminaries and the Problem Statement

Let us consider the pattern recognition problem with probabilistic model. This means that vector of features describing recognized pattern $x \in \mathcal{X} \subseteq \mathcal{R}^d$ and its class number $j \in \mathcal{M} = \{1, 2, ..., M\}$ are observed values of a couple of random variables $(\mathbf{X}, \mathbf{J})$, respectively. Its probability distribution is given by *a priori* probabilities of classes

$$p_j = P(\mathbf{J} = j),\ j \in \mathcal{M} \tag{1}$$

and class-conditional probability density function (CPDFs) of $\mathbf{X}$

$$f_j(x) = f(x/j),\ x \in \mathcal{X},\ j \in \mathcal{M}. \tag{2}$$

Pattern recognition algorithm Ψ maps the feature space $\mathcal{X}$ to the set of class numbers $\mathcal{M}$, viz.

$$\Psi : \mathcal{X} \to \mathcal{M}, \tag{3}$$

or equivalently, partitions $\mathcal{X}$ into decision regions:

$$C_x^{(i)} = \{x \in \mathcal{X} : \Psi(x) = i\},\quad i \in \mathcal{M}. \tag{4}$$

If probabilities (1) and CPDFs (2) are known, i.e. in the case of complete probabilistic information, the optimal (Bayes) recognition algorithm Ψ^*, minimizing the probability of misclassification, makes decision according to the following rule:

$$\Psi^*(x) = i \text{ if } p_i(x) = \max_{k \in \mathcal{M}} p_k(x), \tag{5}$$

where *a posteriori* probabilities $p_j(x)$ can be calculated from the Bayes formula.

Let us now consider the interesting from practical point of view, novel concept of recognition. We assume that *a priori* probabilities (1) and CPDFs (2) are not know, whereas the only information on the probability distribution of $\mathbf{J}$ and $\mathbf{X}$ is contained in the two qualitatively different kinds of data.

1. Learning set:

$$S = \{(x_1, j_1), (x_2, j_2), ..., (x_N, j_N)\}, \tag{6}$$

where x_i denotes the feature vector of the i-th learning pattern and j_i is its correct classification.

Additionally, let S_i denotes the set of learning patterns from the i -th class.

2. Expert rules:

$$R = \{R_1, R_2, ..., R_M\}, \tag{7}$$

where

$$R_i = \{r_i^{(1)}, r_i^{(2)}, ..., r_i^{(L_i)}\}, \quad i \in \mathcal{M}, \quad \sum L_i = L \tag{8}$$

denotes the set of rules connected with the i-th class. The rule $r_i^{(k)}$ has the following general form:

IF $w_i^{(k)}(x)$ **THEN** $\mathbf{J} = i$ **WITH** probability greater than $\underline{p}_i^{(k)}$ and less than $\overline{p}_i^{(k)}$, where $w_i^{(k)}(x)$ denotes a predicate depending on the values of the features x.

These rules obtained from an expert are a cosequence of his experience and competence and furthermore, they reflect the common regularities resulting from the general knowledge. Experiences have proved that an expert is very frequently not able to formulate the logical rules describing the dependences between the observed and internal values of the system and he cannot describe his way of reasoning. What is relatively easy to obtain is a kind of input-output description of the expert decision making process.

We will continue to adopt the following equivalent form of the rule $r_i^{(k)}$:

$$\underline{p}_i^{(k)} \le p_i^{(k)} \le \overline{p}_i^{(k)} \text{ for } x \in D_i^{(k)}, \tag{9}$$

where

$$D_i^{(k)} = \{x \in \mathcal{X} : w_i^{(k)}(x) = true\} \tag{10}$$

will be called rule-defined region and

$$p_i^{(k)} = \frac{\int_{D_i^{(k)}} p_i(x)dx}{\int_{D_i^{(k)}} dx} \tag{11}$$

is the mean *a posteriori* probability of the i-th class in the set $D_i^{(k)}$.

Let

$$\mathcal{X}_R = \cup_{i,k} D_i^{(k)} \text{ and } \mathcal{X}_R^{(i)} = \cup_k D_i^{(k)} \qquad (12)$$

denote feature subspaces covered by rules R and R_i respectively.

Let introduce additionally families of sets $\mathcal{B}_i = \{B_i^{(1)}, B_i^{(2)}, ...B_i^{(l_i)}\}$, $i \in \mathcal{M}$ and $\mathcal{B} = \{B^{(1)}, B^{(2)}, ...B^{(l)}\}$, where $B_i^{(m)}$ and $B^{(m)}$ denote not empty constituents of families $\mathcal{D}_i = \{D_i^{(k)}, k = 1, 2, ..., L_i\}$, $i \in \mathcal{M}$ and $\mathcal{D} = \{D_i^{(k)}, k = 1, 2, ..., L_i, i \in \mathcal{M}\}$, respectively. It is clear, that sets from family $\mathcal{B}_i$ and $\mathcal{B}$ are disjoint and furthermore $\mathcal{X}_R = \cup\mathcal{B}$ and $\mathcal{X}_R^{(i)} = \cup\mathcal{B}_i$, i.e. families $\mathcal{B}$ and $\mathcal{B}_i$ form partitions of feature subspaces $\mathcal{X}_R$ and $\mathcal{X}_R^{(i)}$, respectively ([17]).

Now our purpose is to construct the recognition algorithm

$$\Psi(S, R, x) = \Psi_{SR}(x) = i, \qquad (13)$$

which using information contained in the learning set S and the set of expert rules R recognizes a pattern on the basis of its features x. Some propositions of the rule (13) will be presented in the next section.

3 Pattern Recognition Algorithms

In the sample-based classification, i.e. when the only learning set S is given, one obvious and conceptually simple method is to estimate *a priori* probabilities and CPDFs and then to use these estimators to calculate *a posteriori* probabilities (let say $p_i^{(S)}(x)$), i.e. discriminant functions of the optimal (Bayes) classifier (5).

On the other hand, using this concept in the case when only the set of rules R is given, we obtain the so-called GAP (the Greatest Approximated *a posteriori* Probability) rule-based algorithm, which originally was introduced in [10]:

$$\Psi_R(x) = i \text{ if } p_i^{(R)}(x) = \max_{k \in \mathcal{M}} p_k^{(R)}(x). \qquad (14)$$

$p_i^{(R)}(x)$ denotes approximated *a posteriori* probability of i-th class, which - for $x \in B^{(m)}$ - is calculated from the set R according to the following formulas:

– for $i \in \mathcal{M}^{(m)} = \{i : I_i^{(m)} = \{k : B^{(m)} \subseteq D_i^{(k)}\} \neq \oslash\}$:

$$\hat{p}_i(x) = \frac{\underline{\underline{\hat{p}}}_i^{(m)} + \overline{\overline{\hat{p}}}_i^{(m)}}{2}, \quad \overline{\overline{\hat{p}}}_i^{(m)} = \min_{k \in I_i^m} \overline{p}_i^{(k)}, \quad \underline{\underline{\hat{p}}}_i^{(m)} = \min_{k \in I_i^m} \underline{p}_i^{(k)}, \qquad (15)$$

– for $i \in \mathcal{M} - \mathcal{M}^{(m)}$:

$$\hat{p}_i(x) = [1 - \sum_{j \in \mathcal{M}^{(m)}} \hat{p}_j]/[M - \mid \mathcal{M}^{(m)} \mid]. \qquad (16)$$

The final value of $p_i^{(R)}(x)$ should be normalized to 1, i.e.

$$p_i^{(R)}(x) = \hat{p}_i(x) / \sum_{i \in \mathcal{M}} \hat{p}_i(x). \tag{17}$$

When both sets S and R are given we propose two concepts of recognition algorithms, which are presented in next subsections. In our propositions information included in sets S and R is submitted to processing and fusion. Difference consists in order of both activities.

3.1 Mixed Algorithm

In so-called mixed algorithm decision is made according to the following rule:

$$\Psi_{SR}(x) = i \text{ if } p_i^{(SR)}(x) = \max_{k \in \mathcal{M}} p_k^{(SR)}(x), \tag{18}$$

where

$$p_i^{(SR)}(x) = \gamma(x)\, p_i^{(R)}(x) + [1 - \gamma(x)]\, p_i^{(S)}, \quad 0 \leq \gamma(x) \leq 1. \tag{19}$$

It means, that first we calculate approximated (estimated) values of *a posteriori* probabilities separately from both sets, and next we use their weighted sum in the Bayes algorithm (5).

In the mixed algorithm (18) a mixing coefficient $\gamma(x)$ plays the crucial role. Assuming that $\gamma(x)$ is constant in set $B^{(m)}$ and equal to $\gamma^{(m)}$, $m = 1, 2, ..., l$, we propose three methods of calculating it.

1. The first method takes into account intuitively obvious character of dependence between $\gamma^{(m)}$ and the number of learning patterns in $B^{(m)}$ (let say $N^{(m)}$) and the accuracy of determining *a posteriori* probabilities $p_i(x)$ in rules R for $x \in B^{(m)}$ (let say $\Delta^{(m)}$). Namely, $\gamma^{(m)}$ should be a decreasing function of $N^{(m)}$ and $\Delta^{(m)}$. In the practical example presented in section 4 the following formula was applied:

$$\gamma^{(m)} = \frac{1 - \Delta^{(m)}}{(1 - \Delta^{(m)}) + (1 - e^{-N^{(m)}})}. \tag{20}$$

2. In the second approach, for a particular $B^{(m)}$ such value $\gamma^{(m)} \in [0, 1]$ is applied which maximizes the number of correctly classified learning patterns from $B^{(m)}$.
3. As previously, but now $\gamma^{(m)} \in \{0, 1\}$. It means that we always use a simple algorithm Ψ_R or Ψ_S, which for each set $B^{(m)}$ is selected independently to obtain the better local result of recognition.

3.2 Unified Algorithms

Now, in order to find (13) we will transform one set of data into the second set and next, having the homogeneous form of information, we can simply use either the GAP algorithm (for transformation $S \to R'$) or recognition algorithm with learning (e.g. NN - nearest neighbour decision rule [3], [5]) for transformation $R \to S'$.

Our proposition of procedures for "the unification of information" leads to the following algorithms.

Algorithm $R \to S'$

```
Input data: N'_i^(m) -the number of generated patterns for region B_i^(m)
for i = 1 to M
    for m = 1 to l_i
        for k = 1 to N'_i^(m)
            generate random class number j ∈ 𝓜 with probabilities
            if j = i
            then
                (variant 1) p(j) = (p̲_i^(m) + p̄_i^(m))/2
                (variant 2) p(j) randomly (uniformly) selected
                from the interval [p̲_i^(m), p̄_i^(m)]
            else
                p(j) = [1 - p(i)]/(M - 1)
            fi
            generate random feature vector x uniformly distributed
            in B_i^(m)
        endfor
    endfor
endfor
```

In order to obtain algorithm for transformation $S \to R'$, let first note that for Bernoulli distribution on the base of observation k successes in n trials, we can determine for given confidence level $\alpha = \underline{\beta} + \overline{\beta}$ the confidence interval

$$P(p_1(\underline{\beta}, k, n) \leq p \leq p_2(\overline{\beta}, k, n)) = 1 - (\underline{\beta} + \overline{\beta}), \tag{21}$$

where the endpoints in (21) (confidence limits) are equal ([18]):

$$p_1(\underline{\beta}, k, n) = \frac{k}{k + (n-k+1)F(\underline{\beta}, 2(n-k+1), 2k)}, \tag{22}$$

$$p_2(\overline{\beta}, k, n) = \frac{(k+1)F(\overline{\beta}, 2(k+1), 2(n-k))}{n-k+(k+1)F(\overline{\beta}, 2(k+1), 2(n-k))}, \tag{23}$$

and $F(\beta, k, n)$ is quantile in the range of β of a Snedecor's F distribution with k and n degrees of freedom.

Hence, we can propose the following algorithm

Algorithm $S \to R'$

```
Input data: α - conficence level for created rules
            L'_i - number of rules for i-th class (i ∈ 𝓜)
            D'_i^(k) - feature regions for rules k = 1, 2, ..., L'_i
```

```
for i = 1 to M
      for k = 1 to L'_i
         find N^(k) - number of learning patterns belonging to D'_i^(k)
         find N_i^(k) - number of learning patterns belonging to D'_i^(k)
         calculate p_i'^(k)((1-α)/2, N_i^(k), N^(k)) and p̄_i'^(k)((1-α)/2, N_i^(k), N^(k))
         according to (22) and (23), respectively
      endfor
endfor
```

In order to determine regions $D_i^{'(k)}$ we can use methods known in procedures of generating fuzzy rules from numerical data, e.g. based on cluster analysis, graph theory or decomposition of CPDFs ([2]).

4 Practical Example: Computer-Aided Diagnosis of Acute Renal Failure

In order to investigate the quality of recognition for proposed combining methods and to compare them with simple algorithms (i.e. GAP and sample-based algorithm), several experiments were made on the real data dealing with problem of diagnosis of acute renal failure (ARF) in children.

ARF is a syndrome of clinical symptoms caused by the adverse action of factors of the urinary tracts. In view of character of the disease a quick and proper diagnosis of ARF is mandatory which is of essential importance for appropriate therapy and prognosis. Unfortunately, the cause of ARF, particularly in the initial phase of the disease is very often difficult to be established, hence a need for computer-aided diagnosis process is clearly evident.

The diagnosis of ARF as a pattern recognition task includes the following ten classes (etiologic types of ARF) ([8]): 1) Toxicosis, 2) Nephrotic syndrome, 3) Sepsis, 4) Circulatory failure, 5) Acute gromeluronephritis, 6) Uremic-haemolytic syndrome, 7) Renal vain thrombosis, 8) Andrenogenital syndrome, 9) Others (prerenal or intrarenal), 10) Postrenal failure.

The vector of features contains the values of 33 items of clinical data presented in Table 1.

In the Department of Pediatric Nephrology of Wroclaw Medical Academy the set of 380 case records of children suffering from ARF were collected, which constitute the learning set (6). Each case record contains administrative data, values of 33 clinical features and a firm diagnosis. Most of the diagnoses were made during the period of hospitalization according to the generally accepted criteria. 25 children had died and the anatomopathologic findings provided a definite diagnosis.

Furthermore, the knowledge base for the diagnostic problem in question contains 65 rules (7) which connect the observed values of clinical data with etiologic type of ARF. For example:

IF 24-hours amount < 100 ml AND specific weight > 1.035 g/ml THEN uremic-haemolytic syndrome PROBABILITY $0.5 - 0.6$

Table 1. Clinical features considered

GENERAL: Age, Weight
PHYSICAL EXAMINATIONS: Blood pressure (systolic and diastolic), Pulse, Body temperature, Urine in bladder
LABORATORY EXAMINATIONS: Sedimentation rate (after 1 hour and 2 h.)
GASOMETRIC EXAMINATIONS OF THE BLOOD: pO_2, pCO_2, pH, Stand. HCO_3, Actual HCO_3, BE
MORPHOLOGY OF THE BLOOD: Leucocytes, Reticulocytes, Trombocytes, Erythrocytes, Hemoglobin
SERUM: Urine level, Creatinine level, Uric acid level, Total protein level SERUM IONOGRAM: Na^+ , K^+ , Ca^+
URINE: 24-hours amount, Specific weight, Protein, Leucocytes, Erythrocytes, Cylinders

`IF sed. rate (1 h.)` > 25 `mm AND` $7.2 <$ `pH` < 7.7 `AND` $125 <$ `blood pressure (syst.)` > 150 `mm Hg THEN toxicosis PROBABILITY` $0.65 - 0.8$
`IF urine level` > 8 `mmol AND` $120 <$ `creatinine level` < 200 `micromol AND` $50 <$ `p` $CO_2 < 80$ `mm Hg THEN renal vain thrombosis PROBABILITY` $0.6 - 0.85$

In computer investigations and experimental comparative analysis 4 recognition procedures were tested: Empirical Bayes, GAP, Mixed algorithm with different concepts of mixing coefficient and Unified algorithm for both methods of unification of information. The outcome of experiments is shown in Table 2.

All the experiments show that algorithms which use the both sets of data are much more effective as far as the correct decision frequency is concerned than algorithms which include only one set of data. This testifies that the proposed concepts are correct, and demonstrates effectiveness of the presented algorithms in such classification problems in which both the learning set and expert rules are available.

Table 2. Results of empirical tests

No	Algorithm	Accuracy [%]
1	GAP algorithm with the set R	83.2
2	Empirical Bayes algorithm with the set S	90.6
3	Mixed algorithm (Method 1 for γ)	87.3
4	Mixed algorithm (Method 2 for γ)	92.1
5	Mixed algorithm (Method 3 for γ)	88.5
6	GAP algorithm with sets $R + R'$ ($\alpha = 0.99$ in procedure $S \to R'$)	87.2
7	GAP algorithm with sets $R + R'$ ($\alpha = 0.95$ in procedure $S \to R'$)	86.8
7	GAP algorithm with sets $R + R'$ ($\alpha = 0.90$ in procedure $S \to R'$)	85.4
8	EB algorithm with sets $S + S'$	93.8

5 Conclusions

During the past decade the fusion of various sources of knowledge was firmly established as a practical and effective solution for difficult pattern recognition tasks ([1], [7]). This idea is established using classifier combination approach, which in the literature is known under many names: hybrid methods, decision combinations, classifier fusion, mixture of experts, modular systems, to name only a few ([9]).

Most of the research on classifier ensambles is concerned with generating ensambles by using a single learning model. Different classifiers are received by manipulating the training set, or the input features, and next their decisions are combined in some way (typically by voting) to classify new patterns. Another approach is to generate classifiers by applying different learning algorithms to a single data set ([19]).

The present paper is devoted to the methods for combining heterogeneous sets of learning data: set of training examples and the set of expert rules with unprecisely formulated weights. Adopting the probabilistic model of classification, we discussed two different concepts of pattern recognition algorithms in which the both sets of data are treated as a source of information about the probability distribution of features and classes. In the first approach two classifiers trained on homogeneous data set are generated and next their decisions are combined using local weighted voting combination rules. In the second method however, one set of data is transformed into the second one. This procedure of unification of information allows to generate only one classifier trained on homogeneous set of data.

References

1. Chen, D., Cheng, X.: An Asymptotic Analysis of Some Expert Fusion Methods. Pattern Recognition Letters **22** (2001) 901 - 904
2. Czabanski, R.: Self-Generating Fuzzy Rules from Numerical Data. Techn. Report, Silesian Technical Univ. Gliwice, PhD Thesis (2002) (in Polish)
3. Devroye, L., Gyorfi, P., Lugossi, G.: A Probabilistic Theory of Pattern Recognition. Springer-Verlag, Berlin Heidelberg New York (1996)
4. Dubois, D., Lang, J.: Possibilistic Logic. In: Handbook of Logic in Artificial Intelligence and Logic Programming. Oxford Univ. Press (1994) 439-513
5. Duda, R., Hart, P., Stork, D.: Pattern Classification. John Wiley and Sons, London (2001)
6. Halpern, J.: Reasoning about Uncertainty. MIT Press (2003)
7. Jacobs, R.: Methods for Combining Experts Probability Assessments. Neural Computation **7** (1995) 867-888
8. James, J.A.: Renal Disease in Childhood. The C.V. Mosby Comp., London (1996)
9. Kuncheva, L.: Combining Classifiers: Soft Computing Solutions. In: Pal, S., Pal, A. (eds.): Pattern Recognition: from Classical to Modern Approaches. World Scientific (2001) 427-451
10. Kurzynski, M., Sas, J., Blinowska, A.: Rule-Based Medical Decision-Making with Learning. Proc. 12th World IFAC Congress, Vol. 4, Sydney (1993) 319-322

11. Kurzynski, M., Sas, J.: Rule-Based Classification Procedures Related to the Unprecisely Formulated Expert Rules. Proc. SIBIGRAPI Conference, Rio de Janeiro (1998) 241-245
12. Kurzynski, M.: The Application of Combined Recognition Decision Rules to the Multistage Diagnosis Problem. 20th Int. Conf. of IEEE EMBS, Hong-Kong (1998) 1194-1197
13. Kurzynski, M., Wozniak, M.: Rule-Based Algorithms with Learning for Sequential Recognition Problem. Proc. 3rd Int. Conf. Fusion 2000, Paris (2000) 10-13
14. Kurzynski, M., Puchala, E.: Hybrid Pattern Recognition Algorithms Applied to the Computer-Aided Medical Diagnosis. In: Crespo, J., Maojo V. (eds.): Medical Data Analysis. Lecture Notes in Computer Science, Vol. 2199, Springer-Verlag, Berlin Heidelberg New York (2001) 133-139
15. Kurzynski, M.: Consistency Conditions of the Expert Rule Set in the Probabilistic Pattern Recognition. In: Zhang F., Hu, X. (eds.): Computer Information Systems. Lecture Notes in Computer Science, Vol. 3314 Springer-Verlag, Berlin Heidelberg New York (2004) 831-836
16. Mitchell, T.: Machine Learning. McGraw-Hill Science, London (1997)
17. Kuratowski, K., Mostowski, A.: Set Theory. Nort-Holland Publishing Co, Amsterdam (1986)
18. Sachs, L.: Applied Statistics: A Handbook of Techniques. Springer-Verlag, New York, Berlin, Tokyo (1982)
19. Woods, K., Kegelmeyer, W.: Combination of Multiple Classifiers Using Local Accuracy Estimates. IEEE Trans. on PAMI **19** (1997) 405-410

Construction of a Learning Automaton for Cycle Detection in Noisy Data Sequences

Aleksei Ustimov and Borahan Tümer

Marmara University Faculty of Engineering, Göztepe Campus MB Building 4th floor, 81040 Kadiköy, İstanbul, Turkey
{austimov, bora}@eng.marmara.edu.tr

Abstract. This paper investigates the problem of cycle detection in periodic noisy data sequences. Our approach is based on reinforcement learning principles. A constructive approach is used to devise a variable structure learning automaton (VSLA) that becomes capable of recognizing the potential cycles of the noisy input sequence. The constructive approach allows for VSLAs to analyze sequences not requiring *a priori* information about their cycle and noise. Consecutive tokens of the input sequence are presented to VSLA, one at a time, where VSLA uses data's syntactic property to construct itself from a single state at the beginning to a topology that is able to recognize an unknown cycle of the given data. The main strength of this approach is applicability in many fields and high recognition rates.

1 Introduction

Pattern recognition receives attention in many applications for analysis of one-dimensional signals such as ECG based automatic diagnosis [1,2,3,4], voice and speech recognition [5] and two-dimensional signals such as image recognition [6,7]. Several researches focused on analysis of data using minimum (if any) a priori information [8,9]. Using correlation integral the authors attempt to reduce the number of possible template matching tasks from exponential to polynomial order in [8]. The same approach is used in [9] to detect the presence of any repetitive pattern in noisy data sequences. Analysis on statistical frequency of separate tokens is performed manually in all these works [10,8,9].

In this work, we devise a variable structure learning automaton (VSLA) using a constructive approach based on reinforcement learning principles. During the construction of VSLA, a noisy input sequence undergoes an automatic analysis where the frequency of tokens and token pairs are studied in an attempt to detect the cycle of the sequence presented. A sequence generator produces these periodic sequences with a desired amount of noise randomly injected to the sequence. VSLA is progressively constructed from a single state at the beginning to a topology that is able to recognize the unknown cycle of the noisy sequence presented. The property of VSLA that the current state is dependent on the previous state only, establishes the necessary background for modeling our work as a first degree Markov process.

P. Yolum et al.(Eds.): ISCIS 2005, LNCS 3733, pp. 543–552, 2005.

This paper is organized into five sections. In section 2 we introduce the sequence generator and define the production of an input sequence used in constructing and testing VSLAs. Section 3 is where the methodology is briefly discussed. A detailed discussion about VSLA and its construction process is provided in section 4. Finally in Section 5, we show the results of our study and provide conclusions.

2 Input Sequence

In this section we explain the way an input sequence used in this work is generated. We use periodic sequences produced by a sequence generator that randomly injects noise in the sequence. We call a generated data unit *token*, τ. Let the set of tokens $\Sigma = \{\tau_k | k \in [1, K] \wedge \tau_i \neq \tau_j, \text{for } i \neq j\}$, define an *alphabet*, and let a *cycle* be $C = \tau_1 \cdots \tau_P$, with $\tau_p \in \Sigma$ and $p \in [1, P]$ a short sequence of alphabet tokens. Further, *noise* is defined to be any token or sequence of tokens that distort any cycle within the random sequence. We distinguish between three types of noise: missing, replaced or inserted token. Then we define a noisy sequence as $Q = \bigcup_i D_{1,i} C D_{2,i}, i = 1, 2, \ldots$ with $\bigcup$ standing for the concatenation operation, where $D_{1,i}$ and $D_{2,i}$ denote any two sequences (including the empty sequence) of alphabet tokens other than C before and after the ith cycle in the sequence, respectively. The generator has five parameters: (1) the token alphabet, (2) the length of the cycle, (3) the length of the sequence in numbers of cycles, (4) the ratio in percent of noisy tokens to all tokens in the sequence, and (5) the percent distribution of the three types of noise. With the first three parameters presented, the generator forms the cycle starting from its first token by randomly selecting their tokens in sequential order. The last two parameters describe how

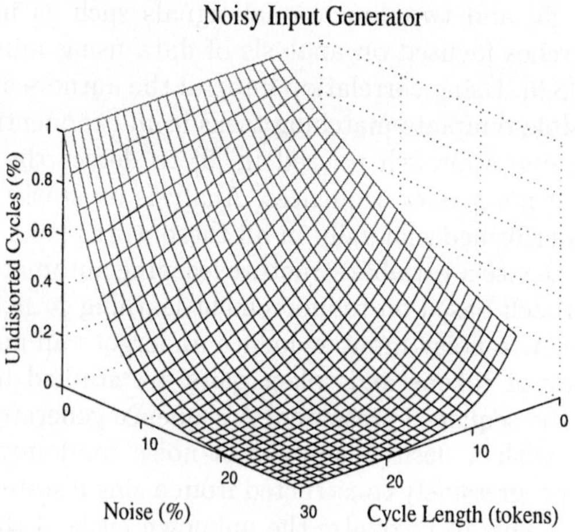

Fig. 1. Average values of non-distorted cycles in a generated sequence depending on the noise injected and cycle lengths $|C|$

noise is added to the "clean" sequence. The fourth parameter specifies the percent amount of noise within the entire sequence that is to be randomly injected. The last parameter specifies the distribution of three noise types during the random injection. The noisy sequence produced by the generator is then used in the process of constructing a VSLA that discovers the possible cycle(s) after a second pass of the input sequence. In Fig. 1, the statistics of the input generator are provided. Fig. 1 illustrates the percentage of the non-distorted cycles as a function of the cycle length and the percent random noise in the sequence. The percent of non-distorted cycles in the sequence tends to fall for increasing noise. This tendency to fall is dramatic in longer cycles while it is relatively slower for shorter cycles.

3 Methodology

In this section we discuss our method. A diagram in Fig. 2 illustrates the processes, how they are inter-related. Once the input generator produces the noisy periodic sequence, the VSLA starts to progressively construct with the presentation of consecutive tokens, one at a time. During its construction, VSLA incorporates states and transitions in its structure that originate from the noise in the sequence. To discover the potential cycle of the sequence, VSLA undergoes a noise removal process where the states and transitions that represent noise

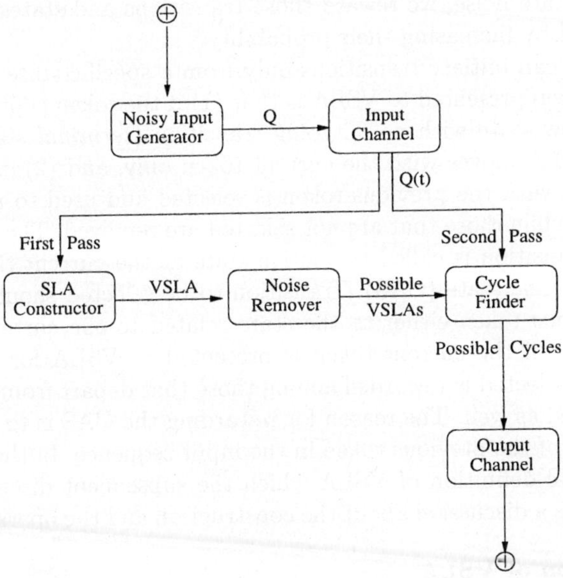

Fig. 2. Process flow diagram of the method. The input sequence generated is used in the construction of VSLA. VSLA obtained undergoes a noise removal process where structural components representing noise are eliminated. After a second pass of the input sequence through each VSLA potential cycles of the sequence are listed.

are eliminated. This process elicits several possible VSLAs, each capable of accepting a potential cycle. At this point at which the construction is over and the structure of the automaton is not subject to modification (i.e., not variable) anymore, the learning automaton changes to a fixed structure learning automaton [11]. Finally, each fixed structure learning automaton is presented the input sequence a second time, again one token at a time in sequential order, whereby candidate cycles are cast.

4 Variable Structure Learning Automaton (VSLA)

This work is a constructive approach to building a variable structure learning automaton composed of a single state at the beginning. The construction of VSLA is based on two principles: (1) each input token presented should carry VSLA from one state to another via transitions with adjustable probabilities, and (2) the transitions initiated by non-distorted tokens of a noisy and periodic sequence are more frequently used than transitions initiated by noise. Based upon the first principle, structural components of VSLA (i.e., states and transitions) are inserted as necessary during the presentation of consecutive tokens. This constructive approach provides for an automaton architecture that is capable of detecting the potential cycle of the sequence presented. The second principle is exploited to identify transitions and states that are initiated by noisy tokens. To distinguish between the transitions initiated by the real tokens of the cycle and those that are noise, we reward those transitions and states that are more frequently used by increasing their probability.

Each token can initiate transitions only from a specific state. The contribution of each token presented to VSLA is that (1) if the token is presented for the first time, a new state with no outgoing transition (*terminal* state) is inserted from which VSLA moves with the current token only, and (2) one of the transitions inserted with the previous token is selected and used to move VSLA to the next state while those that are not selected are removed. The source state of the selected transition is called the active state at the current time instant, or the *currently active* state (CAS). Transition to be selected should move VSLA with the previous token either to the state related to the current token or to a terminal state if the current token is presented to VSLA for the first time. The transition selected is rewarded among those that depart from the CAS. The CAS is rewarded as well. The reason for rewarding the CAS is to emphasize the temporal order of the previous token in the input sequence. In the following, we provide a formal definition of VSLA which the subsequent discussion is based on. Then follows a discussion about the construction and the operation of VSLA.

4.1 Definition of VSLA

VSLA is a quintuple $< \Sigma, \Phi, \alpha, \mathcal{F}, \mathcal{L}_\delta >$, where

- $\Sigma = \{\tau_1, \ldots, \tau_K\}$ is a set of tokens, the *token alphabet*
- $\Phi(n) = \{\phi_1, \ldots, \phi_S\}$ is a set of states, representing temporal positions within the token sequence

- $\mathcal{F}(.,.)$:$\Phi \times \Sigma \rightarrow \Phi$ is the stochastic transition relation mapping the current state and token to the next set of states
- $\Delta(n) = \bigcup_{\tau_k \in \Sigma} \bigcup_{\phi_i \in \Phi(n)} \bigcup_{\phi_j \in \Phi(n)} \delta^{\tau_k}_{\phi_i \phi_j}$ is a set of transitions $\delta^{\tau_k}_{\phi_i \phi_j}$ where a transition $\delta^{\tau_k}_{\phi_i \phi_j}$ defines a move of VSLA initiated by k^{th} alphabet token τ_k from the source state ϕ_i to the destination state ϕ_j.
- $\mathcal{L}_\delta$ is the learning algorithm used to update the probability of each relevant state and transition upon receipt of each token.

Learning during the construction of VSLA occurs based on reinforcement learning. VSLA considers each token as a response produced by an environment. Each token is regarded as a reward for both the state that is able to move the VSLA with the current token and the transition that has moved VSLA with the previous token to the next active state. The value of each transition and state is their probability. We use temporal difference learning in adjusting probabilities. The learning algorithm, $\mathcal{L}_\delta$, is defined as follows:

Let $\phi_i, i \in [1, S]$ be the state to be rewarded. Further, $\delta^{\tau_k}_{ij}$ be the transition deserving rewarding. Then the probability adjustments are accomplished based on linear reward-inaction scheme (L_{R-I}) [11] as follows:

$$\begin{aligned} f^{\tau_k}_{ij}(n+1) &= f^{\tau_k}_{ij}(n) + \alpha[1 - f^{\tau_k}_{ij}(n)] \\ f^{\tau_k}_{lj}(n+1) &= [1-\alpha] f^{\tau_k}_{lj}(n), \qquad \forall \phi_l \neq \phi_i \\ f^{\tau_m}_{lj}(n+1) &= f^{\tau_m}_{lj}(n), \qquad \forall \phi_l \neq \phi_i \quad \text{and/or} \quad \tau_m \neq \tau_k \end{aligned} \tag{1}$$

where $\alpha \in (0, 1)$ is a constant learning parameter.

4.2 Construction of VSLA

The algorithm of the construction of VSLA is given in Fig. 3. We discuss the construction of the VSLA following an example. We construct a VSLA that recognizes a cycle $C = (1\ 2\ 3\ 2\ 4\ 4)$ in the example where we use a simple token alphabet, $\Sigma = \{1, 2, 3, 4\}$. VSLA initially consists of a single state, the start state, $\phi_0(0) = a$ as in Fig. 4, which represents the machine at the time $n = 0$ prior to the receipt of the first token $\tau_1 = 1 \in \Sigma$. Received by VSLA at $n = 1$ at step 2 in Fig. 3, 1 cannot move VSLA anywhere. Therefore, a becomes the next active state (NAS) at step 3. Steps 4-6 are skipped since a CAS does not exist. Since a is not improbable, nothing is performed at step 7, either. At this point, VSLA still has a single state a as in Fig. 4. Step 8 is, where a is marked as the CAS. At step 9(a), a new currently improbable terminal state b is inserted. In part (b), δ^1_{ab} is added to VSLA along with δ^1_{aa} also with 0 probability. With the next token 2 received, b is identified as NAS, since no states in VSLA can move with 2. The CAS is a from the previous turn of the loop. At step 4, we select δ^1_{ab}. At step 5, we reward a and δ^1_{ab}. Step 6 is where we remove δ^1_{aa}. The resulting VSLA is illustrated in Fig. 5. Next, b is marked to be the CAS. A new currently improbable terminal state c is inserted and the transition set is updated by adding the currently improbable transitions with token 2 from b to all states: $\Delta(2) = \Delta(1) \bigcup_{i=a}^{c} \{\delta^2_{bi}\}$. Upon receipt of the next token 3, c is selected

Algorithm

1. initialize
   (a) VSLA by a start state with probability 1 prior to the receipt of first token
   (b) currently active state: none
2. receive token
3. identify the state from which transitions originate with current token only, or, if not, the terminal state (next active state)
4. if a currently active state exists, select the transition between currently active state and next active state (selected transition)
5. if a currently active state exists, generate reward to
   (a) currently active state among all states
   (b) selected transition among transitions originating from currently active state
6. remove all improbable transitions from currently active state
7. remove all inaccessible improbable states
8. mark next active state as currently active state
9. perform temporary structure modification
   (a) insert a currently improbable terminal state
   (b) insert new currently improbable transitions from currently active state to all states (including the terminal state)
10. loop back to step 2 as long as there are tokens left in the sequence

Fig. 3. The algorithm for the construction of VSLA

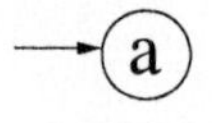

Fig. 4. The initial topology of VSLA. VSLA is a single state with probability 1 prior to the receipt of the first token. After the presentation VSLA still maintains its topology until insertions of necessary structural components are performed.

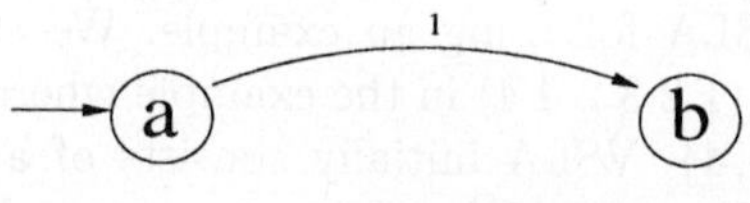

Fig. 5. Structure of VSLA after processing first token 1. At this point, 2 is presented to VSLA. This is the point right after the removals but before the insertions related to 2.

as the NAS, and δ^2_{bc} the transition to be rewarded. Following the probability adjustment of both b and δ^2_{bc}, the removal of unused transitions originating from b are accomplished. The topology of VSLA at this point is shown in Fig. 6. Finally, the terminal state d is inserted and the transitions stemming from c are added to all states including c: $\Delta(3) = \Delta(2) \bigcup_{i=a}^{d} \{\delta^3_{ci}\}$. The next token presented is 2. This time, the NAS is again b since 2 has already been presented to VSLA and b is the state VSLA moves from with 2. Further $\delta^3_{c,b}$ is selected to be rewarded. After the probability adjustment of c and δ^3_{cb} is made, all improbable transitions from c but the one going to b are removed. Further, d is removed since

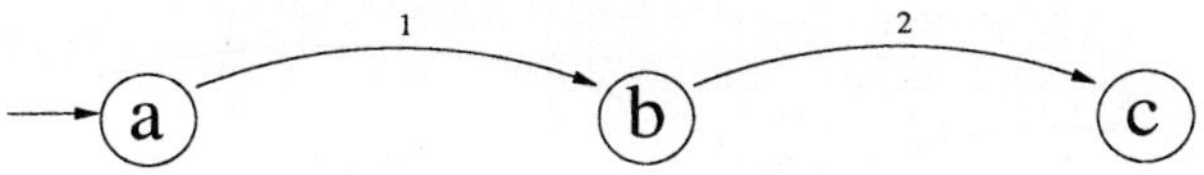

Fig. 6. VSLA's structure after 2 has been processed and 3 received

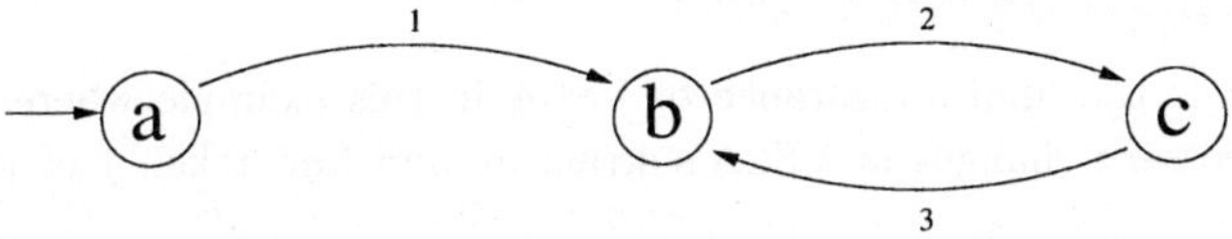

Fig. 7. VSLA topology follows after the first three tokens have been processed and 2 presented a second time

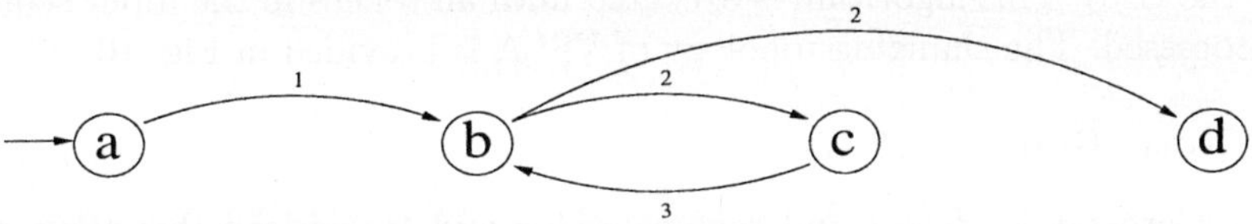

Fig. 8. Structure of VSLA following the process of the second 2. At this point VSLA knows the first 4 is the next token but has not processed it yet.

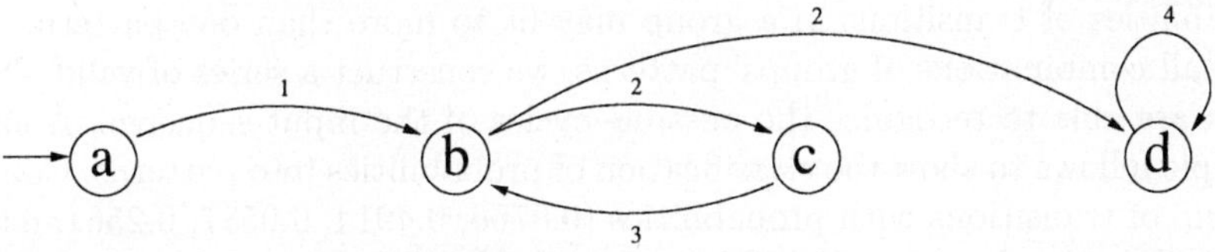

Fig. 9. VSLA after making necessary changes in its structure after the first 4. VSLA is also presented the second 4, but has not processed it, yet.

it becomes inaccessible. Now, VSLA is as shown in Fig. 7. Following the removals, the insertions are performed: the state d is added and the set of transitions is modified as follows: $\Delta(4) = \Delta(3) \bigcup_{i=a i \neq c}^{d} \{\delta_{bi}^2\}$. The CAS is b. Upon receipt of the next token 4, the only terminal state, d, becomes the NAS since 4 is a new token presented to VSLA and δ_{bd}^2 is selected to be rewarded. Following the probability update of rewarded components b and δ_{bd}^2, improbable transitions $\bigcup_{i=a}^{b} \{\delta_{bi}^2\}$ are removed. VSLA then appears as in Fig. 8. Next, d is marked as the CAS. A new terminal state e and an improbable transition from d to all other states are added: $\Delta(5) = \Delta(4) \bigcup_{i=a}^{e} \{\delta_{di}^4\}$. With the next token 4 received, d is found to be the NAS, since 4 has already been presented to VSLA and d is the state VSLA moves from with 4. The CAS is also d from the previous turn of the loop, and δ_{dd}^4 is selected. d and δ_{dd}^4 are rewarded. Following the probability

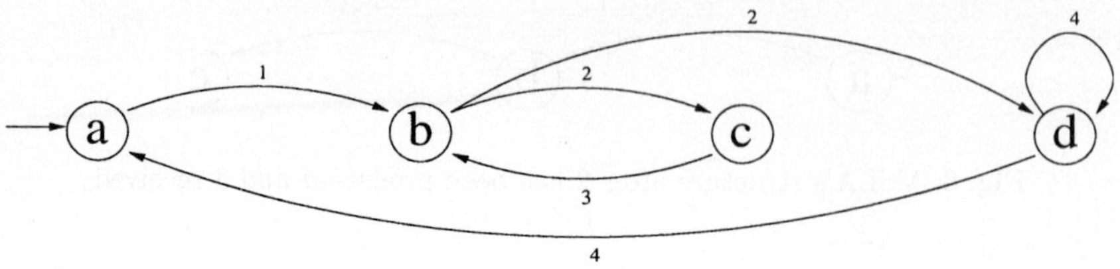

Fig. 10. This is the final appearance of VSLA in this example where the second 4 has made necessary changes in VSLA's structure and first token 1 of the next cycle presented.

update of rewarded components d and δ^4_{dd}, improbable transitions $\bigcup^e_{i=a,i\neq d}\{\delta^4_{di}\}$ are removed. The resulting VSLA is illustrated in Fig. 9. Next, d is again marked to be the CAS. This algorithm is executed until all tokens in the input sequence are processed. The changing topology of VSLA is provided in Fig. 10.

4.3 Noise Removal (NR)

NR is a process to detect and remove states and transitions that have close-to-zero probability and potentially represent noise in the sequence. Transitions are grouped by their source states and the probabilities within each group are sought for classification into some suitable pattern by their ratios. Classification may result in more than one pattern in each group. In other words, the ratios of probabilities of transitions in a group may fit to more than one pattern. Then using all combinations of groups' patterns, we construct a series of valid VSLAs which are able to recognize the possible cycles of the input sequence. A simple example follows to show the classification of probabilities into patterns: Consider a group of transitions with probabilities (0.0766, 0.4914, 0.0587, 0.2561, 0.0631, 0.0481, 0.0060). Suppose that this group may have at most 3 transitions: then we have to try patterns with a total number of transitions from 1 to 3: Possible patterns are $1 = \{1\}$, $2 = \{2, 1 : 1\}$, $3 = \{3, 2 : 1, 1 : 1 : 1\}$. Strongest match is $2 : 1$. Weaker matches may be 1, 2, 3. Match $2 : 1$ means that probability 0.4914 is 2, 0.2561 is 1 and all others are 0 (i.e., noise).

5 Results and Conclusions

To assess the performance of VSLA in discovering the cycle of noisy periodic sequences, we have run 15400 experiments with cycle lengths ranging within [5, 22], using sequences with noise percent ranging within [0, 30] and have observed the average recognition probability of VSLA. The test results of our method are shown in Fig. 11. For each point in the mesh in Fig. 11, we have conducted 200 experiments. At all experiments, we used a 9-element token alphabet, and a quite small learning parameter $\alpha = 0.01$ to approach to expected transition probabilities as close as possible. VSLAs constructed by our method display almost a full recognition capability (i.e., within [0.97,1]) for all cycle lengths within

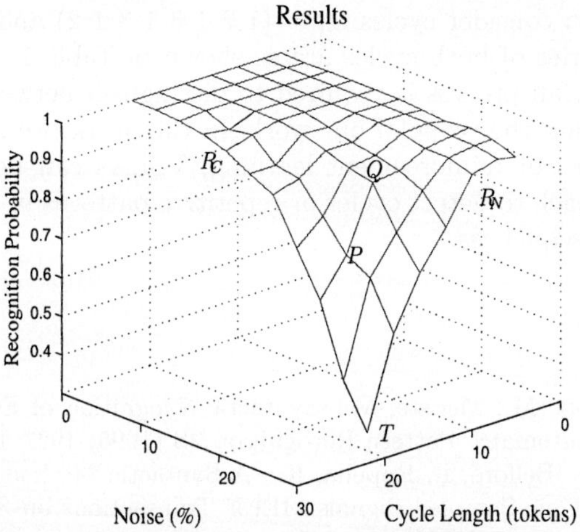

Fig. 11. Illustration of results. The probability that VSLA constructed finds the cycle of the noisy input sequence is shown as a function of noise added and cycle length. The coordinates of the tip representing the worst case are $|C| = 22, Noise = 30\%$ and $P_{recog} = 0.38$.

Table 1. An example to two different sequences displaying the same frequency summary

Tokens	Probabilities
1	0.5
2	0.25
3	0.25

Tokens pairs	Probabilities
1 2	0.25
2 1	0.25
1 3	0.25
3 1	0.25

the given range up to a level of 12% of noise (i.e., in Fig. 11 to a plane at R_C parallel to the cycle length-recognition probability plane). Further, VSLAs are able to discover cycles of sequences with $|C| \leq 10$ (i.e., to a plane at R_N parallel to the noise-recognition probability plane) for all experimented noise levels with a probability of not worse than 0.97. We note in Fig. 11, that Q establishes the starting corner of a dramatic fall that ends up at the lowest tip T of the mesh pointing out the worst-case recognition probability of 0.38 for $|C| = 22$ with a maximum noise level of 30%. It is worth further noting that the coordinates of P, a representative point of the fall, are $(C = 19, N = 24\%, P_{recog} = 0.77)$, meaning that, in a set of experiments with sequences in which five cycles can fit in 100 tokens, and, in average, one of four tokens is noisy, constructed VSLAs are expected to correctly discover the cycles of three of every four sequences. A final word on the size of token alphabet is that as token alphabets shrink, VSLA complexity grows. Furthermore, in certain cases, use of a smaller number of alphabet tokens enhances the probability that two sequences with different cycles may display the same frequency summary of token pairs. We provide an example to show this below: consider cycles $C_1 = (1\ 2\ 1\ 3\ 1\ 3\ 1\ 2)$ and $C_2 = (1\ 2\ 1\ 3)$. Frequency summaries of both cycles are as shown in Table 1. In these cases, a 2nd-degree Markovian process is required to distinguish between these two cycles, which is beyond the scope of our work. In this work, we have shown that, using the principles of reinforcement learning, VSLAs can be devised with a constructive approach to detect cycles or repetitive patterns in noisy periodic or partially periodic sequences.

References

1. Koski, A., Juhola, M., Meriste, M.: Syntactic recognition of ECG signals by attributed finite automata. Pattern Recognition **28** (1995) 1927–1940
2. Tümer, M.B., L. Belfore, I., Ropella, K.: A Syntactic Methodology for Analysis of Continuous Time-Sampled Signals. IEEE Transactions on Systems, Man and Cybernetics, Part:B **45** (2003) 951–965
3. Tümer, M.B.: A Fuzzy Syntactic Approach to Fault Diagnostics by Analysis of Time Sampled Signals. PhD thesis, Marquette University (1998)
4. Udupa, J.K., Murthy, I.S.N.: Syntactic approach to ECG rhythm analysis. IEEE Transactions on Biomedical Engineering **27** (1980) 370–375
5. Fu, K.S.: Syntactic Methods in Pattern Recognition. Springer-Verlag (1974)
6. Charalampidis, D., Kasparis, T., Georgiopoulos, M.: Classification of noisy signals using fuzzy ARTMAP neural networks. IEEE Transactions on Neural Networks **12** (2001) 1023–1036
7. He, Q., Debrunner, C.: Individual recognition from periodic activity using hidden markov models. Proceedings of the IEEE Workshop on Human Motion (2000) 47–52
8. Christen, M., Kern, A., Nikitchenko, A., Steeb, W.H., Stoop, R.: Fast spike pattern detection using the correlation integral. Physical Review E **70** (2004) (011901)1–7
9. Christen, M., Kern, A., van der Vyver, J.J., Stoop, R.: Pattern detection in noisy signals. IEEE Proceedings on International Symposium on Circuits and Systems **IV** (2004) 669–672
10. Buckley, J.P., Seitzer, J.: A paradigm for detecting cycles in large data sets via fuzzy mining. IEEE Proceedings on Knowledge and Data Engineering Exchange (1999) 68–74
11. Narendra, K., Thathachar, M.A.L.: Learning Automata: An Introduction. Prentice Hall, Inc. (1989)

A New Trend Heuristic Time-Variant Fuzzy Time Series Method for Forecasting Enrollments

Melike Şah and Konstantin Degtiarev

Computer Engineering Department, Eastern Mediterranean University,
Mersin 10, PO Box-95, Turkey
{melike.sah, konstantin.degtiarev}@emu.edu.tr

Abstract. In this paper, we have proposed a new modified forecasting method based on time-variant fuzzy time series. It uses trend heuristics in addition to high-order fuzzy logical relations and enhances the average forecasting accuracy significantly. To illustrate the whole forecasting process, we use actual enrollments (historical data for 22 years) of the University of Alabama (UA) and compare results obtained through other well-known fuzzy time series-based approaches described up to date in the literature. As a result, for all examined cases, the new time-variant method yields better forecasting accuracy as compared with alternative methods.

1 Introduction

Virtually everywhere and incessantly forecasting plays an important role in human activities and making decisions about the future – for instance, weather and natural phenomena prediction, university enrollment forecasting, production, sales and financial planning are amongst those examples, where more accurate forecasts both determine to a considerable degree a shape of the further steps to take and contribute positively to the development of more efficient plans of actions. With this end in view, a variety of qualitative and quantitative forecasting approaches were proposed to date with a clear purpose of increasing the accuracy of prediction as far as possible [5]. However, such methods cannot tackle problems, in which historical data take the form of linguistic constructs rather than precise numerical values. Fuzzy time series allows to compensate for such deficiency [4] clearing the way to process both linguistic and numeric data.

Forecasting based on fuzzy time series attracts substantial attention of researchers over the last decade; cf. [1]-[4], [8,9,11]. Song and Chissom [7]-[9] introduced time-invariant (TI) and time-variant (TV) models for forecasting with fuzzy time series. Section 2 of the present paper provides all principal definitions related to fuzzy time series, but at the moment we define in passing what is entailed by time-invariant and time-variant fuzzy time series. If for any moment of time t, fuzzy time series $F(t)$ is caused by $F(t-1)$ only, i.e. $F(t)=F(t-1)\circ R(t,t-1)$, and fuzzy relationship R does not depend on time t, then $F(t)$ is called *time-invariant*; otherwise, it is called a *time-variant* fuzzy time series [3],[4]. In the ongoing studies, we proposed time-invariant method [11] having average student enrollment forecast error (a.f.e.) close to

P. Yolum et al.(Eds.): ISCIS 2005, LNCS 3733, pp. 553 – 564, 2005.

2.42%. Also, Chen [1] worked on time-invariant fuzzy time series for forecasting enrollments and obtained the average prediction error around 3.23%. Results of experiments with both time-invariant models are shown in Fig. 1 (Matlab® 6.5).

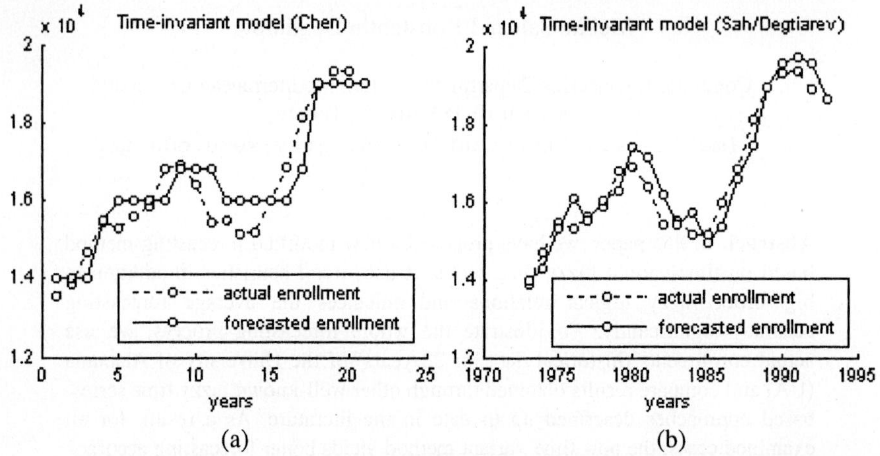

Fig. 1. Experimental forecast results – TI models proposed by *(a)* Chen (a.f.e. is 3.23 %) [1], and *(b)* Şah-Degtiarev (a.f.e. is 2.42 %, 6 fuzzy sets) [11]

For the time-invariant model, Song and Chissom [8] obtained 3.18% average error. Based on UA enrollment data (the most commonly cited example in the literature) that cover a period of more than 20 years (see Table 1), same authors [9] also studied time-variant model that is expressed as

$$F(t) = F(t-1) \circ R^{w}(t,t-1) \; , \tag{1}$$

where $F(t-1)$ denotes the enrollment of the year $t-1$, $F(t)$ is the forecasted enrollment of the year t expressed by fuzzy sets, symbol $\circ$ denotes a max-min composition operator. Besides, $R^{w}(t,t-1)$ is a union of first-order fuzzy relations within the forecasting window (with a length) of w years prior to year t, i.e. the value of fuzzy time series at the moment t is forecasted by "combining" time series values at moments $(t-1),\ldots,(t-w)$, where $w>1$. The average prediction error of this time-variant model turned out to be 4.37% when the data window w is 4 [9]. Although a certain dispersion of forecast error measures exist, nevertheless all of them appear to outnumber those results that use traditional models [4].

Along with Song and Chissom, Hwang, Chen and Lee [4] proposed a new time-variant forecasting model, which was tested on the same enrollment data of the University of Alabama (UA). Fig. 2 shows Matlab® 6.5 simulation results attained – the model uses variations of enrollments and derives relations between these variations. In compliance with the suggested approach, the highest significance is set to variations of current and previous years, i.e. the variation of the last year serves as a criterion. The authors used a model basis w (window) that indicates the number of years of enrollment data used in the forecasting. Enrollment variations from the last (previous) year to wth year in the past form so-called *operation matrix* $O^{w}(t)$ on $F(t)$.

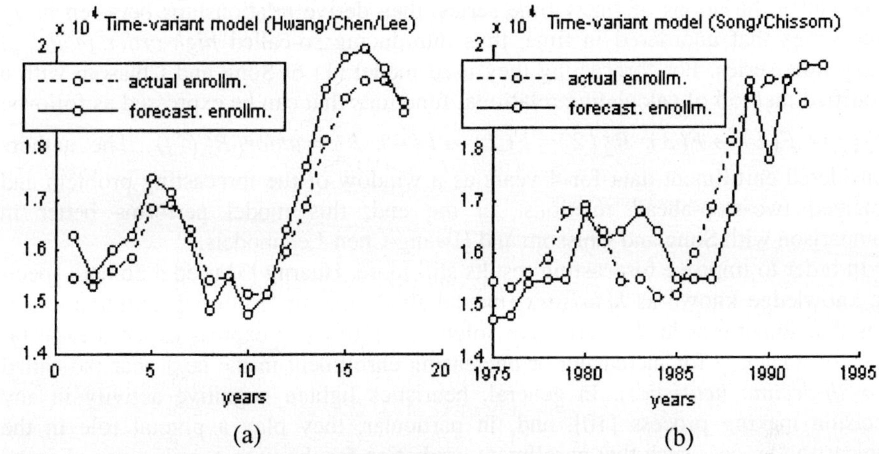

(a) (b)

Fig. 2. Experimental forecast results – TV models proposed by *(a)* Hwang-Chen-Lee (a.f.e. is 3.12%) [4], and *(b)* Song-Chissom (a.f.e. is 4.37%, window w is 4) [9]

As a result, the model of Hwang, Chen and Lee $R(t) = O^{w}(t) \times C(t)$ uses a criterion vector $C(t)$ (last year variation) and operation matrix $O^{w}(t)$ to calculate a relation $R(t) = [R_{ij}]$, $i = \overline{1,w}$, $j = \overline{1,m}$ (m is the number of intervals universe of discourse is partitioned to); symbol $\times$ represents the matrix multiplication. Finally, the forecasted variation of the year t (fuzzy set) is calculated as $F(t) = [\,max(R_{11}, R_{21}, \ldots, R_{w1}), \ldots, \ max(R_{1m}, R_{2m}, \ldots, R_{wm})\,]$. Hence, fuzzy set $F(t)$ (fuzzified enrollment variation between successive years t and $t-1$) is calculated by taking maximum values from each column of the relation $R(t)$. The model of Hwang, Chen and Lee turns out to be quite effective on account of use of simple matrix multiplications. In addition, it results in better forecasting as compared with Song and Chissom time-invariant and time-variant models – average forecast error of the time-variant model constitutes 3.12% under the window w equal to 4 [4].

Chen and Hwang continued working on fuzzy time series, and subsequently they put forward another model for temperature prediction, which is *two-factors time-variant fuzzy time series* [2]. With the aim to improve accuracy, this method uses two factors in the forecasting process, namely, daily average temperature as a main-factor and daily average cloud density as a second-factor. In this model, criterion and operation matrix are used in the same way as described above, at that, they are calculated from main-factor (daily average temperature) fuzzy time series. The relationship matrix is calculated as $R(t)=O^{w}(t)\times S(t)\times C(t)$. Both $O^{w}(t)$ and $C(t)$ are obtained from main-factor fuzzy time series $F(t)$, whereas $S(t)$ is a second-factor fuzzy time series generated from daily average cloud density.

Another original approach to enrollment forecasting that utilizes high-order fuzzy time series was introduced by Tsai and Wu [12]. Instead of using relations between consecutive variations of fuzzy time series, they derive relationships between fuzzy time series that unordered in time, thus introducing so-called *high-order model* of fuzzy time series. For forecasting they used model (1) of Song and Chissom with a modified method of calculating relational functions that can be expressed as follows: $R_2^2(1)=F(1)\rightarrow F(3)$, $R_2^2(2)=F(2)\rightarrow F(4)$, $R_2^2=union(R_2^2(i))$. The authors considered enrollment data for 4 years as a window of the forecasting problem and obtained two-step-ahead relations. In the end, this model performs better in comparison with Song and Chissom and Hwang-Chen-Lee models.

In order to improve forecasting results still more, Huarng [3] used a domain specific knowledge known as *heuristics* (mental short-cuts, or "informal, intuitive strategies that sometimes lead to effective solutions" [10]) that express expert's expectations of tendency for increasing or decreasing enrollment in the next year (so-called *growth-decline heuristics*). In general, heuristics lighten cognitive activity in any decision making process [10], and, in particular, they play a pivotal role in the forecasting process such that enrollment prediction for the year t makes use of fuzzy time series of the previous (last) year $t-1$. Following the proposed model, all first-order relations between fuzzy time series of consecutive years are generated, and those of them, which have the same left-hand-side, are grouped together. Heuristic model studies revealed better results as compared to both non-heuristic models and methods proposed by Song-Chissom and Chen.

In this paper, we introduce a new modified time-variant fuzzy time series approach to enrollment forecasting, which, in general, can be equally applied to various forecasting problems such as foreign exchange rate prediction. The proposed approach uses variations of disposable historical enrollments in place of raw numeric values as fuzzy time series. The forecasting procedure makes use of historical enrollment data of the University of Alabama (UA) for the period of 1971-1992. Major peculiarities of the proposed approach lie in the use of high-order relations and trend heuristics that provides information (subjective expectations) about future enrollments. In addition, the model is checked up for the purpose of effect of different number of fuzzy time series on forecasting process. It is shown that the average forecasting error for 6 fuzzy time series with the window basis w equal to 4 comes close to 1.51%. Concurrently, results obtained are compared with fuzzy time series models studied up to date with the object of forecasting accuracy.

We organize the paper as follows. In Section 2, brief review of basic fuzzy time series concepts is given. Trend heuristic time-variant fuzzy time series method is introduced in Section 3. In Section 4, the effect of different number of fuzzy time series on forecasting results is studied and comparison with existing time-variant fuzzy time series methods is done. Finally, concluding remarks and observations are drawn in Section 5.

2 Basic Fuzzy Time Series Definitions

In this section, we provide a summary of basic fuzzy time series concepts needed for the subsequent text; cf. [2], [4], [7]-[9].

Definition 1. Let $U = \{u_1, u_2, ..., u_n\}$ be a universe of discourse (universal set); a fuzzy set A of U is defined as $A = \{f_A(u_1)/u_1 + ... + f_A(u_n)/u_n\}$, where f_A is a membership function of a given set A, $f_A : U \to [0,1]$.

Definition 2. Assume $Y(t) \subset \mathbf{R}$ (real line), $t = ..., 0, 1, 2, ...$, to be a universe of discourse defined by the fuzzy set $f_i(t)$. $F(t)$ consisting of $f_i(t)$, $i = 1, 2, ...$, is a fuzzy time series on $Y(t)$. At that, function of time $F(t)$ is understood as a *linguistic variable*, whereas $f_i(t)$ are *linguistic values* of $F(t)$.

Definition 3. If there exists a fuzzy relation $R(t, t-1)$ such that $F(t) = F(t-1) \circ R(t, t-1)$, then $F(t)$ is said to be caused by $F(t-1)$. The relationship between $F(t)$ and $F(t-1)$ can be denoted by the expression $F(t-1) \to F(t)$; $R(t, t-1)$ is called the *first-order model* of fuzzy series.

Definition 4. If solution of forecasting problem uses only $F(t)$, then it is called *one-factor time series.*

Definition 5. If $F(t)$ is caused by $F(t-1)$, $F(t-2)$, ... , $F(t-n)$, i.e. $F(t-1) \to F(t)$ $F(t-2) \to F(t-1)$ ... $F(t-n) \to F(t-n+1)$, then the *n-th order fuzzy logical relationship* can be represented as $\mathrm{F(t-1) \to F(t) \cup F(t-2) \to F(t-1) \cup ... \cup F(t-n) \to F(t-n+1)}$.

Definition 6. If $F(t)$ is caused by $F(t-1)$, $F(t-2)$, ... , $F(t-n)$ simultaneously, that is $F(t-1) \to F(t)$ $F(t-2) \to F(t)$ ... $F(t-n) \to F(t)$, then so-called *high-order fuzzy logical relationship* can be represented as follows: $F(t-1) \to F(t) \cup F(t-2) \to F(t) \cup ... \cup F(t-n) \to F(t)$.

Definition 7. If there exists a fuzzy relation $R(t, t-w)$, such that

$R(t, t-w) = F(t-1) \to F(t) \cup F(t-2) \to F(t) \cup ... \cup F(t-w) \to F(t)$, then $R(t, t-w)$ is a union of high-order logical relations.

3 A New Modified Trend Heuristic Time-Variant Fuzzy Time Series Method

The fundamental aim of this study is to improve the forecasting accuracy of the method based on time-variant fuzzy time series. For this purpose we state three primary provisions, namely:

(a) variations of historical enrollments are used in place of raw numeric values as fuzzy time series,

(b) trend heuristics that summarize opinions on what changes will be take place in enrollment activities in the year to come in terms of linguistic values (terms) "de-crease", "no change" or "increase" guides next year estimates, and

(c) calculation of R is based on high-order fuzzy logical relations.

It should be stressed that the latter corresponds to the core distinctive feature of the method proposed in this paper, ensuring better forecasting results. Among other things, a new peculiarity of the proposed method is grounded on using trend heuristics. In line with a generally recognized thesis asserting that better forecasting results can be obtained when more factors are added to the process under study, we suggest to use trend heuristics in addition to historical enrollment data. The former can be provided by domain experts and other recruited highly skilled individuals who have a specific knowledge on economic/political situation and academic-related developments.

Thus, the forecasting process based on UA enrollment data can be described in a step-by-step manner as follows (as an example, we consider 6 fuzzy sets to be used in the model).

Step 1: Definition of the universe of discourse U based on variations of the enrollment data.

Set U is defined on the yearly variations of the enrollments for the period of 1971-1992. Actual data and corresponding variations are listed in Table 1 (second and sixth columns; minimum and maximum variations are $V_{min} = -955$ and $V_{max} = 1291$, respectively). To simplify the division of U into equally length intervals, we assume a closed interval $[V_{min} - V_1, V_{max} + V_2]$ in the capacity of U, where V_1 and V_2 are positive integers 45 and 109, accordingly. As a result, $U = [-1000, 1400]$.

Step 2: Partitioning universe of discourse into equally length intervals.

Universal set U is partitioned into six equivalent (400 units each) intervals, namely, they are $u_1 = [-1000, -600]$, ..., $u_6 = [1000, 1400]$. Additionally, we denote mid-points of these intervals as m_i, $i = \overline{1,6}$, i.e. $m_1 = -800, \ldots, m_6 = 1200$.

Step 3: Definition of fuzzy sets A_i, $i = \overline{1,6}$.

We assume that the linguistic variable "variations of enrollments" is characterized by terms (values) A_1 (big decrease), A_2 (decrease), A_3 (no change), A_4 (increase), A_5 (big increase), and A_6 (too big increase). In general, as the number of fuzzy sets is changing, linguistic variables are re-determined accordingly.

Each $u_i \in U$ is an element of a particular set A_i, $i = \overline{1,6}$, and the membership degree $\mu(u_i)$ of element u_i is expressed by the real value from the closed interval $[0,1]$ as shown below (elements u_i not displayed explicitly are assumed to have zero membership degrees):

$$A_1 = \{1/u_1 + 0.5/u_2\} \qquad A_2 = \{0.5/u_1 + 1/u_2 + 0.5/u_3\}$$
$$A_3 = \{0.5/u_2 + 1/u_3 + 0.5/u_4\} \qquad A_4 = \{0.5/u_3 + 1/u_4 + 0.5/u_5\}$$
$$A_5 = \{0.5/u_4 + 1/u_5 + 0.5/u_6\} \qquad A_6 = \{0.5/u_5 + 1/u_6\}$$

Step 4: Fuzzification of variations of historical data (finding an appropriate fuzzy set for each year's variation).

This step is eliminated when historical data are already expressed in linguistic form. However, for the enrollment forecasting process, which is the subject of the present paper, both absolute data of actual enrollments and variations are set in the integer format. Therefore, this step stipulates for conversion of numeric variations to fuzzy sets following the rule: if variation of the year t is $p \in u_i$, and there is a term repre-sented by a fuzzy set A_i with the maximum membership value falling on the same interval u_i, then p is fuzzified as A_i. Results of fuzzification are summarized in Table 1 (fourth and eighth columns).

Table 1. Actual data and fuzzified historical enrollments based on variations

Years	Actual enrollments	Variations	Fuzzified variations	Years	Actual enrollments	Variations	Fuzzified variations
1971	13055			1982	15433	– 955	A_1
1972	13563	+ 508	A_4	1983	15497	+ 64	A_3
1973	13867	+ 304	A_4	1984	15145	– 352	A_2
1974	14696	+ 829	A_5	1985	15163	+ 18	A_3
1975	15460	+ 764	A_5	1986	15984	+ 82	A_5
1976	15311	– 149	A_3	1987	16859	+ 875	A_5
1977	15603	+ 292	A_4	1988	18150	+ 1291	A_6
1978	15861	+ 258	A_4	1989	18970	+ 820	A_5
1979	16807	+ 946	A_5	1990	19328	+ 358	A_4
1980	16919	+ 112	A_3	1991	19337	+ 9	A_3
1981	16388	– 531	A_2	1992	18876	– 461	A_2

Step5: Determination of trend heuristics (formulated by experts) to be used in forecasting process.

At this step, trend heuristics are settled by experts in definite terms – actually, these are verbally expressed statements that "put into shape" subjective assumptions on tendencies towards enrollment changes in the next year, e.g. "no change", "increase", or "decrease". We use these pieces of information to generate heuristic trend fuzzy time series denoted as h_j, $j = \overline{1,3}$. With that end in view, midpoints of defined intervals u_i, $i = \overline{1,6}$, are used to obtain fuzzified values of h_j as follows:

tendency "decrease": $\forall u_i$, $i = \overline{1,6}$: if $m_i < 0$ then $\mu(u_i) = 1$,

tendency "no change": $\forall u_i$, $i = \overline{1,6}$: if $m_i = 0$ then $\mu(u_i) = 1$,

tendency "increase": $\forall u_i$, $i = \overline{1,6}$: if $m_i > 0$ then $\mu(u_i) = 1$.

Corresponding intervals and their midpoints for all six fuzzy sets determined at the step 2 are now used for calculation of membership degrees of set h_j elements. For example, assume that trend heuristic indicator for the next year is "decrease". Midpoints of the intervals u_1 and u_2 are less than 0 (zero), namely, they are $m_1 = -800$ and $m_2 = -400$, therefore both $\mu(u_1)$ and $\mu(u_2)$ become equal to 1; on the contrary, midpoints m_i, $i = \overline{3,6}$ are greater than or equal to 0, thus giving $\mu(u_i) = 0$ ($i = \overline{3,6}$). In the end, membership degrees $\mu(u_i)$ of elements that constitute heuristic trends h_1, h_2 and h_3 are

"decrease": $h_1 = \{1/u_1 + 1/u_2\}$ "no change": $h_2 = \{1/u_3\}$
"increase": $h_3 = \{1/u_4 + 1/u_5 + 1/u_6\}$.

<u>Step 6:</u> Calculation of $R^w(t,t-1)$, $w > 1$, using fuzzy high-order logical relations.

To calculate relation $R^w(t,t-1)$, we use window w equal to 4 – later on in the paper (Section 4), we will discuss the effect of different values of w, $w = \overline{2,8}$, in aggregate with varying number of fuzzy sets (from 5 to 9) on the average forecasting errors (a.f.e.).

To make use of 4 previous years of variations, the forecasting process starts to consider data from the year of 1976. Fuzzified variations of four consecutive years are taken outright from Table 2 – they are as follows: (years 1972 and 1973) - A_4, (years 1974 and 1975) - A_5.

Calculation of $R^w(t,t-1)$ requires to determine (high-order) fuzzy relations, which are generated through fuzzified variations within w years, viz $A_{t-1} \to A_t$, $A_{t-2} \to A_t$, …, $A_{t-w+1} \to A_t$. For data under study those relations are $A_4 \to A_5$ and $A_5 \to A_5$. In general case, some relations may appear in the list more than once, so such duplicates are simply eliminated. Relation $R^w(t,t-1)$ for the present forecasting problem has the form: $R^4(t,t-1) = A_4^T \times A_5 \cup A_5^T \times A_5$.

The forecasting procedure implies regeneration of the relation $R^w(t,t-1)$ on the basis of corresponding fuzzified variations each time window basis w is changed.

<u>Step 7:</u> Forecasting and defuzzification of the output (variations).

Forecasting model in use is as follows:

$$A_i = A_{i-1} \times R^w(i,i-1) \times h_j \ , \tag{2}$$

where A_i is a forecasted variation of the year i in terms of fuzzy set, A_{i-1} is a fuzzified variation of the year $i-1$, $R^w(i,i-1)$ is the union of high-order fuzzy logical relations within w years, h_j is a trend heuristics (change tendencies stated by domain experts). Fuzzy outputs calculated using (2) are summarized in Table 2 (third column).

Table 2. Forecasted fuzzy outputs and enrollments (1976 – 1989), window $w = 4$

Year	Actual enrollments	Fuzzy Outputs	Forecasted Enrollments	Relative (percentage) error
1976	15311	0 0 0 0 0 0	15460	0.97 %
1977	15603	0 0 0 0.25 0 0	15711	0.69 %
1978	15861	0 0 0 1 0.25 0	16003	0.89 %
1979	16807	0 0 0 1 0.25 0	16261	3.25 %
1980	16919	0 0 0 0.25 1	17607	4.06 %
1981	16388	0 0.25 0 0 0 0	16519	0.79 %
1982	15433	0.25 1 0 0 0 0	15988	3.59 %
1983	15497	0 0 0 0 0 0	15433	0.41 %
1984	15145	0 0.25 0 0 0 0	15097	0.31 %
1985	15163	0 0 0.25 0 0 0	15145	0.11 %
1986	15984	0 0 0 0.25 0 0	15563	2.63 %
1987	16859	0 0 0 0.25 1	16784	0.44 %
1988	18150	0 0 0 0.25 1	17659	2.70 %
1989	18970	0 0 0 0 0.25 1	19350	2.00 %

Step 8: Calculation of forecasted enrollments (actual numeric values).

This step envisages conversion of fuzzy outputs obtained above to crisp integers. In general, this *defuzzification* process is "context- and problem-dependent" to a high degree, and one of the criteria to select a defuzzification method is the value of its computational simplicity [6]. In the problem under study we suggest to use defuzzification approach proposed by Song and Chissom [8],[9]. It takes proper account of both principal characteristic properties of the problem and specificity of fuzzy process output. Well known mean-max (MoM) membership/height and centroid methods underlie it, thus resting on a rational enough combination of procedures that put emphasis on membership function peak points and its shape depending on the output result. Consequently, relative simplicity, robustness and reasonable accuracy of defuzzification scheme is achieved.

Core regulations of Song and Chissom defuzzification procedure can be brought to the following: **(a)** if all membership values of the output are 0 (zeros), then the forecasted variation is set to null as well, **(b)** if the membership function of output has exactly one maximum (single peak), the midpoint of interval, on which this value is attained, is recognized as a forecasted variation, **(c)** if the output membership function has two or more consecutive maximums, the midpoint of corresponding conjunct intervals is regarded as a forecasted variation, **(d)** under all other cases, standardize the fuzzy out-put and use the midpoint of each interval to apply centroid method for calculation of defuzzified forecasted variation.

When the fuzzy variation of the year under consideration is obtained, it is summed up with actual enrollment of the last (previous) year. For instance, if calculated variation (year 1977) is 300, and the actual enrollment (year 1976) is 15311, then the forecasted enrollment estimate (year 1977) becomes 15711. Forecasted results for the University of Alabama are shown in Table 2 (fourth column).

4 Test for Different Number of Fuzzy Sets and Discussion

In general, the number of fuzzy sets (N_{FS}) affects the forecasting accuracy – animo we tested the developed model on different values of N_{FS} in the range from 5 to 9 (such choice is mainly governed by a commonly cited 7 ± 2 information span of human short-term memory). Depending on N_{FS} value, intervals u_i and corresponding linguistic values undergo applicable change as well. Table 3 shows results obtained, and it can be noticed that better forecasting accuracy is achieved when N_{FS} is equal to 6, as also shown in Fig. 3(b). Simultaneously, our results were compared with the ones produced by Song-Chissom and Hwang-Chen-Lee methods – Table 4 puts together all these cases. Our simulations show that the proposed time-variant method outperforms existing fuzzy time series models significantly on the same set of UA historical data.

Table 3. Average forecasting errors (%) for different values of N_{FS} ranging from 5 to 9

Window →	2	3	4	5	6	7	8
5 fuzzy sets	1.96 %	1.82 %	1.88 %	1.94 %	2.00 %	2.10 %	1.90 %
6 fuzzy sets	1.51 %	1.43 %	1.51 %	1.54 %	1.59 %	1.64 %	1.52 %
7 fuzzy sets	1.74 %	1.71 %	1.76 %	1.81 %	1.84 %	1.91 %	1.66 %
8 fuzzy sets	1.86 %	1.78 %	1.81 %	1.86 %	1.88 %	1.98 %	1.86 %
9 fuzzy sets	1.86 %	1.78 %	1.81 %	1.86 %	1.88 %	1.98 %	1.87 %

Table 4. Average forecasting errors (%) of different fuzzy time series models

Song-Chissom time-variant (TI) model (window $w = 4$)	4.17 %
Hwang-Chen-Lee time-variant (TV) model (window $w = 4$)	3.12 %
Song-Chissom time-invariant (TI) model	3.18 %
Chen time-invariant (TI) model	3.23 %
Şah-Degtiarev time-invariant (TI) method ($N_{FS} = 6$)	2.42 %
Proposed time-variant (TV) method ($w = 4$, $N_{FS} = 6$)	~1.51 %
	average forecasting errors (a.f.e.)

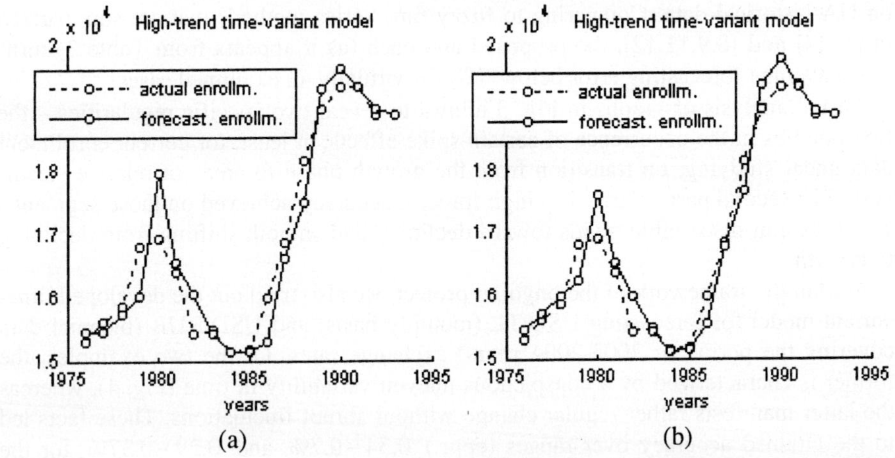

Fig. 3. Forecasting results: *(a)* $N_{FS} = 5$ (a.f.e. is 1.88 %, window $w = 4$), and *(b)* $N_{FS} = 6$ (a.f.e. is 1.51 %, window $w = 4$) based on high-trend TV model

5 Conclusions

In this paper, we presented a new modified time-variant fuzzy time series method for forecasting university enrollments. The key particularity of this approach is in joint use of trend heuristics and high-order fuzzy logical relations; here, from a computational perspective, it remains allowably simple. The forecasting process is illustrated

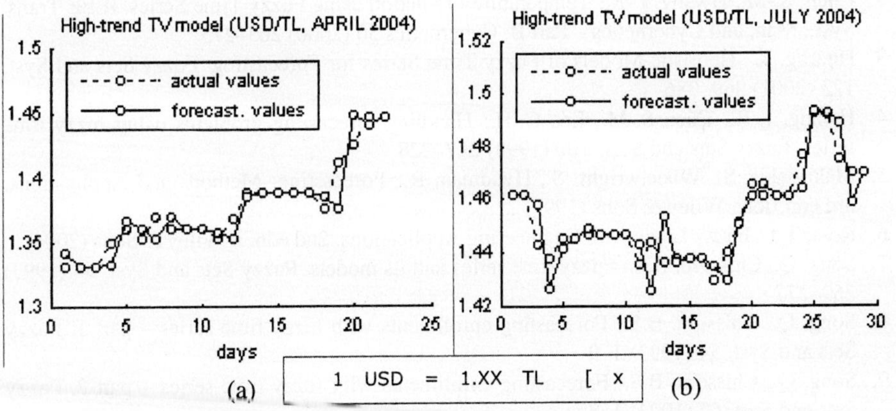

Fig. 4. Experimental forecast results – high-trend time-variant model USD/TL: *(a)* $N_{FS} = 9$ (a.f.e. is 0.57 %, window w is 8), and *(b)* $N_{FS} = 6$ (a.f.e. is 0.36 %, window w is 2). With the object of interval length narrowing, USD/TL exchange rate was regarded as 1USD = 1.XX TL, i.e. the actual rate (for the year 2003) should consider "casted away" factor of 1,000,000.

on UA historical data. Comparing to fuzzy time series methods that are summarized in [1]-[4] and [8,9,11,12], the proposed approach (as it appears from Table 3) turns down average forecasting error below 2% for virtually all examined cases.

Visual analysis of graphs in Fig. 3 allows to reveal two specific regularities – the first one lies in the occurrence of certain spike effects, at least, for current enrollment data under studying, on transition from the growth phase to areas of relative steadiness. The second particularity is a high forecast accuracy achieved on those segments, which exhibit discernible trends toward declining and smooth shifting from declining to growth.

Within the framework of the ongoing project, we also tried out the developed time-variant model for forecasting USD/TL (monthly basis) and USD/RUB (biennial data covering the period of 2003-2004 years) exchange rates. Of the two examples, the former is characterized by a conspicuous uneven variability in time (Fig. 4), whereas the latter manifests rather regular change without abrupt fluctuations. These facts led to the attained accuracy over ranges (appr.) $0.34-0.7\%$ and $0.29-0.37\%$ for the first and second exchange rate problems, correspondingly (examination of million strong values of TL leads to substantial widening of intervals of U partitioning and to respective sharp decline of forecast accuracy down to (appr.) $3.18-6.95\%$). Notwithstanding vague difference between results, for both of problems mentioned above, the proposed trend heuristic time-variant approach shows noticeably good performance reckoning with specialities of actual processed data.

References

1. Chen, S.-M.: Forecasting Enrollments Based on Fuzzy Time Series. Fuzzy Sets and Syst. 81 (1996) 311–319
2. Chen, S.-M., Hwang, J.-R.: Temperature Prediction using Fuzzy Time Series. IEEE Trans. Syst., Man, and Cybernetics – Part B: Cybernetics 30 (2000) 263–275
3. Huarng, K.: Heuristic Models of Fuzzy Time Series for Forecasting. Fuzzy Sets and Syst. 123 (2001) 369–386
4. Hwang, J.-R., Chen S.-M., Lee C.-H.: Handling forecasting problems using fuzzy time series. Fuzzy Sets and Syst. 100 (1998) 217–228
5. Makridakis, S., Wheelwright, S., Hyndman, R.: Forecasting: Methods and Applications. 3rd edn. John Wiley & Sons (1997)
6. Ross, T.J.: Fuzzy Logic with Engineering Applications. 2nd edn. J. Wiley & Sons (2004)
7. Song, Q., Chissom, B.S.: Fuzzy time series and its models. Fuzzy Sets and Syst. 54 (1993) 269–277
8. Song, Q., Chissom, B.S.: Forecasting enrollments with fuzzy time series – part 1. Fuzzy Sets and Syst. 54 (1993) 1–9
9. Song, Q., Chissom, B.S.: Forecasting enrollments with fuzzy time series – part 2. Fuzzy Sets and Syst. 62 (1994) 1–8
10. Sternberg, R.J. : Cognitive Psychology. 3rd edn. Thomson Wadsworth (2003)
11. Şah, M., Degtiarev, K.Y.: Forecasting Enrollment Model Based on First-Order Fuzzy Time Series. Proc. Int. Conf. Comp. Intelligence (ICCI) (2004) 375–378
12. Tsai, C.-C., Wu, S.-J.: Forecasting enrollments with high-order fuzzy time series. Proc. IEEE (2000) 196–200

Using GARCH-GRNN Model to Forecast Financial Time Series

Weimin Li, Jianwei Liu, and Jiajin Le

College of Computer Science and Technology of Donghua University,
1882 West Yan'an Road, Shanghai, China 200051

Abstract. Recent researches in forecasting with generalized regression neural network (GRNN) suggest that GRNN can be a promising alternative to the linear and nonlinear time series models. It has shown great abilities in modeling and forecasting nonlinear time series. Generalized autoregressive conditional heteroscedastic (GARCH) model is a popular time series model in forecasting volatility of financial returns. In this paper, a model combined the GARCH and GRNN is proposed to make use of the advantages of both models in linear and nonlinear modeling. In the GARCH-GRNN model, GARCH modeling aids in improving the combined model's forecasting performance by capturing statistical and volatility information from the time series. The relative tests testify that the combined model can be an effective way to improve forecasting performance achieved by either of the models used separately.

1 Introduction

One of the basic problems of economy and finance is the predictability of future events. Within a large scale of uncertainty predictions are indeed possible. The analysis of financial time series from the point of predictability has attracted a lot of interest. Because of financial time series' inherently noisy, non-stationary, and chaotic characteristics, it is difficult to obtain complete information from history data and to capture the relation between the future prices and the past records.

Volatility of financial returns is an important aspect of many financial decisions. For example, volatility of exchange rates is a determinant for pricing currency options that are used for risk management. Hence, there is a need for better forecasting in volatility. GARCH modeling builds on advances in the understanding and modeling of volatility [1, 2, 3]. It provides accurate forecasts of variances and covariances of asset returns through its ability to model time-varying conditional variances. As a consequence, GARCH models are applied to such diverse fields as risk management, portfolio management and asset allocation, option pricing, foreign exchange, and the term structure of interest rates [4].

Even so, GARCH models do have limitations [5]. Firstly, they are only part of a solution. Although GARCH models are usually applied to return series, financial decisions are rarely based solely on expected returns and volatilities. Another limitation is that parametric specifications of GARCH models operate best under relatively stable market conditions. Although GARCH models are explicitly designed to model time-varying conditional variances, they often fail to capture highly irregular

P. Yolum et al.(Eds.): ISCIS 2005, LNCS 3733, pp. 565 – 574, 2005.

phenomena, and other highly unanticipated events that can lead to significant structural change. The third drawback in the GARCH models is that they often fail to fully capture the fat tails observed in asset return series.

Financial time series is a nonstationary series, so it is difficult to construct a suitable time series model for it. Thus, the forecasting, based on time series model like GARCH, can't be satisfying. Many alternative approaches are proposed through a range of nonlinear models that are widely available such as artificial intelligence models [6, 7]. Neural networks represent a promising technology with a wide scope of potential applications. There is a growing interest in using neural networks to forecast the future changes in prices of stocks, exchange rates, commodities, and other financial time series.

GRNN is a branch of radial basis function (RBF) neural network. RBF network not only has better computation precision than back propagation (BP) network but also converge faster than BP network [8]. Therefore, the GRNN has been considered as an alternative to the popular back-propagation training algorithm for feed-forward neural network. And it is a good means to construct a model based on GRNN for forecasting financial time series [9].

Because of highly irregular phenomena and many potential non-stationary factors, the real-world financial time series isn't absolutely linear or nonlinear. Thus, a single model isn't the best way for forecasting [10, 11]. Linear and nonlinear patterns can be captured by combining different methods. To some extent, improving performance in forecasting is equal to capturing more information from the given time series. Therefore, using GARCH technology in GRNN model is proposed to improve the accuracy of the forecasting value. The proposed model GARCH-GRNN forecasting integrates the GARCH and GRNN in prediction and mapping nonlinear system. Especially, GARCH model effectively captures the volatility of financial time series.

2 Forecasting Models

In this paper, three models including GARCH, GRNN and GARCH-GRNN are employed in forecasting Shanghai comprehensive index. In the following subsections, GARCH and GRNN models are described.

2.1 GARCH Models

GARCH models, first proposed by Bollerslev [12], who extended the simpler ARCH models previously suggested by Engle [13], specify current conditional variance as a function of past conditional variances and past squared observations. ARCH models are used to study and forecast the conditional variances. The specification of ARCH models is given as follows:

$$y_t = f(t-1, X) + \varepsilon_t \tag{1}$$

$$\sigma_t^2 = \omega + \sum_{i=1}^{p} \alpha_i \varepsilon_{t-i}^2 \tag{2}$$

Eq. (1) represents a univariate model of an observed time series y_t, $f(t-1, X)$ represents the deterministic component of the current return as a function of any information known at time t-1, and any other relevant explanatory time series data X. ε_t is the random component. It represents the innovation in the mean of y_t. Eq. (2) is referred to as an ARCH (p) variance model. p is non-negative, scalar integer representing a model order of the ARCH process, and it is the number of lags of the conditional variance. When p=0, the variance process is simply white noise with variance ω. ái is the real valued parameters. σ_t^2 is the conditional variance at time t. If given the value of statistical variable $\varepsilon_{t-1}^2, \varepsilon_{t-2}^2, \cdots, \varepsilon_{t-p}^2$, $\sigma_t^2 = E(\varepsilon_t^2 \mid \varepsilon_{t-1}^2, \varepsilon_{t-2}^2, \cdots, \varepsilon_{t-p}^2)$. ARCH models are the basic models in the class of GARCH models. Other models are basically generalized by them.

GARCH (p,q) model will be gotten through adding lag item of conditional variance in ARCH models.

$$\sigma_t^2 = \omega + \sum_{i=1}^{p} \alpha_i \varepsilon_{t-i}^2 + \sum_{j=1}^{q} \beta_j \sigma_{t-j}^2 \tag{3}$$

In the Eq. (3), the variance forecast, σ_t^2, consists of a constant plus a weighted average of last period's forecast, σ_{t-j}^2, and last period's squared disturbance, ε_{t-i}^2. This implies a correlation in the variance process, and indicates that the data is a candidate for GARCH modeling. The usual GARCH restrictions for non-negativity and stationarity are imposed, such as non-negativity of variances, the real valued parameters ù, âj and ái satisfying ù>0, âj≥0, ái≥0, and $\sum_{i=1}^{p} \alpha_i + \sum_{j=1}^{q} \beta_j < 1$.

2.2 GRNN Model

Specht[14] has proposed the GRNN model that is capable of estimating any arbitrary function from historical data. The theory of kernel regression is the foundation of GRNN operation. GRNN can be equivalent to a nonlinear regression expression as follows:

$$E[Y \mid X] = \int_{-\infty}^{\infty} Yf(X, Y)\,dY \Big/ \int_{-\infty}^{\infty} f(X, Y)\,dY \tag{4}$$

where *Y* is the predicted value of GRNN, *X* the input series ($X_1, X_2, \cdots, X_m$), which consists of m predictable variables, *E*[*Y* |*X*], the expected value of the output *Y* given an input vector *X*, and *f*(*X*, *Y*) the joint probability density function of *X* and *Y*.

The GRNN model [15] has four layers of processing unit. Each layer of processing units is assigned with a specific computational function when non linear regression is performed. The first layer of the network is responsible for the reception of information. There is a unique input neuron for each predictable variable in the input vector *X*. The input neurons then feed the data to the second layer. The number of neurons in the second layer is equal to the number of cases in the training set. Therefore, the neurons in the second layer are called pattern neurons. A pattern neuron is employed to process the data in a systematic way so that the relationship between the input and the proper response is "memorized". A multivariate Gaussian function is expressed as follows:

$$a_i = e^{-b_{1j} \|dist\|_j / 2\sigma_j^2} = e^{-b_{1j} \sqrt{\sum_{i=1}^{m} (x_i - IW_{j,i})^2} / 2\sigma_j^2} \quad (j = 1,2,\cdots n) \tag{5}$$

where b1 is set to a column vector of 0.8326/SPREAD. The SPREAD is the distance between an input vector and a neuron's weight vector. The data from the input neurons are used to compute an output a_i by a typical pattern neuron i, where $IW_{j,i}$ is a specific training vector represented by pattern neuron i, and σ_j is the smoothing parameter. The shape of basic function figure in No.j latent layer is decided by σ_j. The neurons of the third layer, namely the summation neurons, receive the outputs of the pattern neurons. In the third layer, the outputs from all pattern neurons are augmented. Simple and weighted summations are conducted in neurons of the third layer. The outputting of the network can be represented as Eq.6:

$$y_k = \sum_{j=1}^{n} LW_{k,j} a_j, (k = 1,2 \cdots S) \tag{6}$$

where $LW_{k,j}$ is the pattern neuron j connected to third layer of weights, a_i would be gotten through Eq. (5).

3 Proposed Model GARCH-GRNN

Predicting financial time series is an important yet difficult task. Many kinds of linear and nonlinear theoretical models have been developed in forecasting financial time series, but few of them are satisfying for the given time series. The technology of neural networks was proposed to yield more accurate results. One significant advantage of the GRNN model over other classes of nonlinear models is that GRNN is a universal approximator which can approximate a large class of functions with a high degree of accuracy. GRNN has high time complexity, and its power comes from the parallel processing of the information from the data. In the following study, GRNN exceeds GARCH model in forecasting time series which can improve the accuracy of the prediction, but it can't map to any type of data exactly. It is almost universally agreed in the forecasting literature that no single method is best in every situation [16]. The advantages of the two kinds of models may be utilized. Hence, a proposed model that contains both can be a good methodology for practical use. The two models in the combined model may bring different information from the given time series. The given time series would be better described by the proposed model.

The model GRNN performs a nonlinear functional mapping from the past observations $(X_{t-1}, X_{t-2}, \cdots, X_{t-k})$ to the future value X_t, that is,

$$X_t = F(X_{t-1}, X_{t-2}, \cdots, X_{t-k}, \omega) \tag{7}$$

where ω is a vector of all parameters and F is a function produced by the GRNN network and connection weights. In this study, a model GARCH-GRNN is proposed whose framework is described in Fig.1. The input and aim data include innovation series inferred from the GARCH model. The relationship between the ouput vector (Y_i) and the input vector (Y_{i-1}) has the following mathematical representation:

$$Y_i = F(Y_{i-1}, \omega), i = t, t+1, \cdots t+l; \tag{8}$$

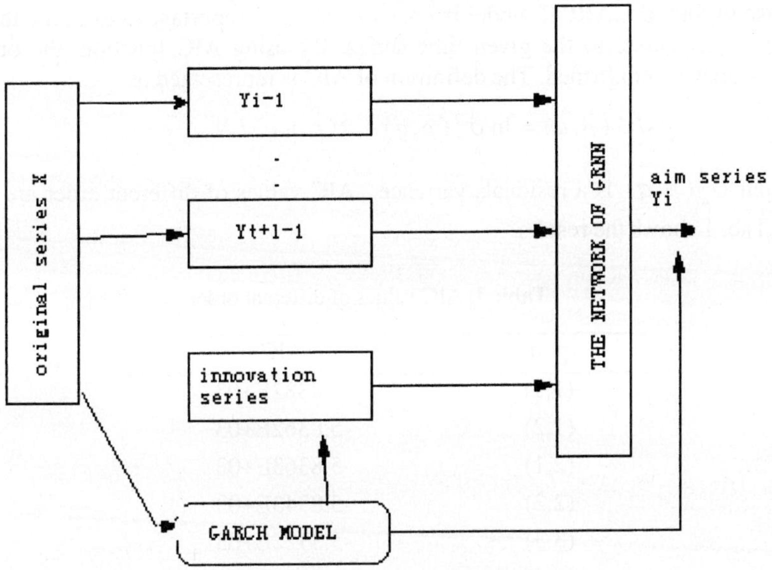

Fig. 1. The architecture of proposed model GARCH-GRNN

Though vector (Y_{i-1}) is equal to $(X_{i-1}, X_{i-2}, \cdots, X_{i-k})$, it not only contains the past observations, but also includes the innovation series. Thus, the GARCH-GRNN network is equivalent to a nonlinear autoregressive model with a component capturing volatility and statistical information from the financial time series. If vector (Y_{i-1}) is an m-dimension, an m-step-ahead forecasting will be obtained.

In order to construct suitable model, a suitable GARCH model must be constructed firstly. By using the forecasting return series from GARCH, we get the innovation series of the given time series. The innovation series contains much statistical and volatility information about the time series. It is taken into account the input and aim data in GRNN architecture. The function of innovation series in the framework is lowering the noise level and aims in improving the performance of forecasting.

4 Experimental Results

4.1 Experimental Data

This study gives 1020 data points that contain the Shanghai exponent observations from January 1999 to March 2003. The data are divided into two parts to serve different purposes: the training data set (from January 1999 to January 2003) and the testing data set (from February 2003 to March 2003).

4.2 Parameters Selection of Three Models

It is difficult to identify whether the return series is suitable to the GARCH process. Because of this, if GARCH model is constructed, it is important to examine the suitability of the model to the given time series. By using AIC function, the order of GARCH may be confirmed. The definition of AIC is represented as:

$$AIC\ (p,q) = \ln \hat{\sigma}_a^2(p,q) + 2(p+q)/N \tag{9}$$

in which $\hat{\sigma}_a^2(p,q)$ is a residuals variance. AIC values of different order are calculated. Tab. 1 shows the results.

Table 1. AIC values of different order

(p, q)	AIC
(1,1)	-5.8382E+03
(1,2)	-5.8362E+03
(2,1)	-5.8363E+03
(2,2)	-5.8343E+03
(3,3)	-5.8322E+03
(4,4)	-5.8318E+03
(5,5)	-5.8378E+03
(6,6)	-5.8303E+03

The suitable model is confirmed by the minimum AIC value. From the table 1, the most suitable model for the given time series is GARCH(1,1). The equation is described as follows:

$$y_t = 0.000090054 + \varepsilon_t \tag{10}$$

$$\sigma_t^2 = 8.427e - 006 + 0.77879\sigma_{t-1}^2 + 0.20949\varepsilon_{t-1}^2 \tag{11}$$

After the GARCH(1,1) model has been constructed, it is necessary to test its fitness to the given time series. Namely, the innovation series inferred by the GARCH(1,1) model must be examined. The autocorrection function (ACF) and the partial autocorrection function (PACF) are used to check the innovation and indicate that the innovation is white noise approximately. The values of ACF and PACF are showed in Fig.2.

From Fig.2, we can see that the ACF and PACF of innovation series are in the reliability bound. Therefore, the GARCH(1,1) constructed above is suitable. The innovation series is shown in Fig.3.

In GRNN model [17, 18], there are few parameters to determine. A larger spread leads to a large area around the input vector where layer 1 neurons will respond with significant outputs. Therefore if spread is small the radial basis function is very steep. As spread gets larger the radial basis function's slope gets smoother and several neuron's may respond to an input vector. As spread gets larger more and more neurons contribute to the average with the result that the network function becomes smoother. Through selecting different value of spread, a better result will be obtained if spread is 0.7288. The second layer has many neurons as input/target vectors.

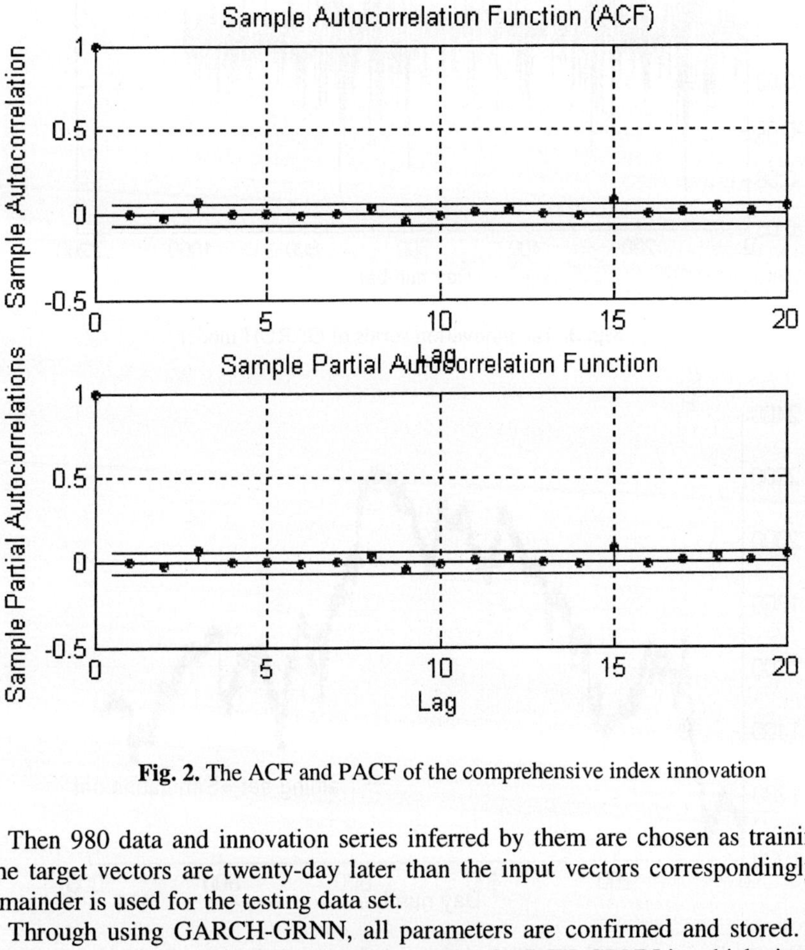

Fig. 2. The ACF and PACF of the comprehensive index innovation

Then 980 data and innovation series inferred by them are chosen as training set. The target vectors are twenty-day later than the input vectors correspondingly. The remainder is used for the testing data set.

Through using GARCH-GRNN, all parameters are confirmed and stored. Fig. 4 shows the simulating results by using the model GARCH-GRNN in which simulating values basically accord with the training set.

In this way, the suitable parameters of different models are confirmed. Then these three models are used in ten-step-ahead forecasting. In this study, three indices, namely mean absolute error (MAE), root mean square error (RMSE), mean absolute percent error (MAPE), are used as measures for forecasting accuracy. The results are displayed in Tab. 2.

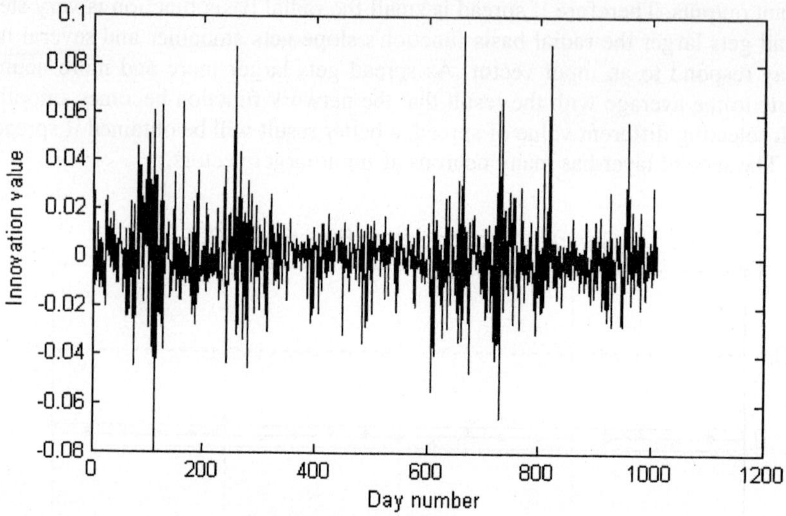

Fig. 3. The innovation series of GARCH model

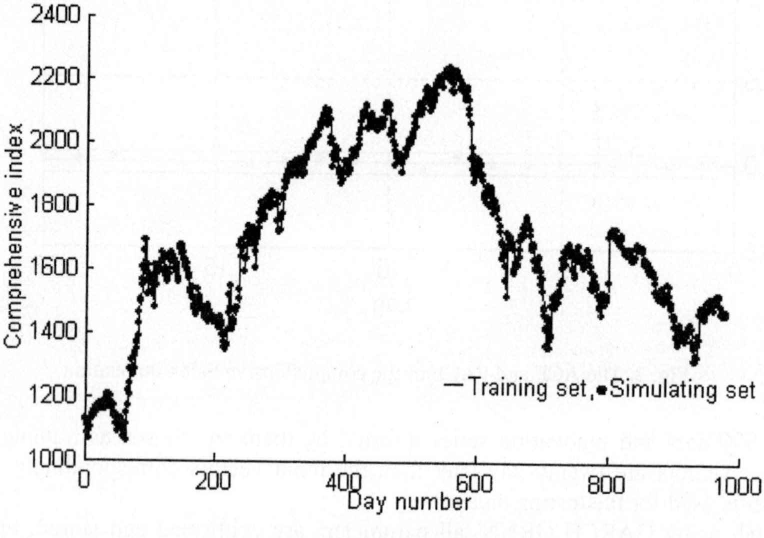

Fig. 4. The result of the stimulating Shanghai comprehensive index by using GARCH-GRNN model

Table 2. Forecasting results based on forecasting indices

	MAE	RMSE	MAPE
GARCH	56.8	67.994	0.0373
GRNN	42.03	46.358	0.0238
GARCH -GRNN	31.4	34.413	0.0199

5 Conclusions

In theory, both GRNN and GARCH-GRNN models can map any nonlinear system. However, the error they cause is inevitable, because a financial time series is influenced by many factors, including wild market fluctuations (e.g., crashes and subsequent rebounds). From Tab. 2, we can see that the forecasting results from GRNN are satisfying generally, and the results from GRNN are more accurate than that from GARCH. In this paper, a proposed forecasting technique is employed to examine its feasibility in forecasting financial time series. Experimental results indicate that the GARCH -GRNN outperforms the former two approaches in terms of foresting accuracy. We also conclude that innovation series inferred from GARCH model can capture volatility and statistical information of the financial time series. The proposed model takes advantage of the virtue of each model.

References

1. Nelson D.: Conditional Heteroscedasticity in asset returns: A new approach. Econometrica. 59 (1991) 347–370.
2. Nelson, D.B.: ARCH Models as Diffusion Approximations. Journal of Econometrics. 45 (1990) 7–38.
3. Andersen TG, Bollerslev T: Answering the skeptics: Yes, standard volatility models do provide accurate forecasts. International Economic Review. 39 (1998) 885–905.
4. Bollerslev, T., Chou R.Y., Kroner K.F.: ARCH Modeling in Finance: A Review of the Theory and Empirical Evidence. Journal of Econometrics. 52 (1992) 5–59.
5. Gourieroux. C.: ARCH Models and Financial Applications, Springer-Verlag (1997).
6. Cao LJ, Tay Francis EH: Financial forecasting using support vector machines. Neural Computing & applications. 10 (2001) 184–192.
7. Qai M, GP Zhang: An investigation of model selection criteria for neural network time series forecasting. European Journal of Operational Research. 132 (2001) 188–102.
8. Pei-Yan Zhang, Tian-Sheng LU, Li-Bo Song: RBF networks-based inverse kinematics of 6R manipulator. Int J Adv Manuf Technol . 26 (2005) 144–147.
9. Leung M T, Chen A S, Daouk H: Forecasting exchange rates using general regression neural networks. Computers & Operations Research. 27 (2000) 1093–1110.
10. Tang Z., Almeida C., Fishwick P.A.: Time series forecasting using neural networks vs Box–Jenkins methodology. Simulation . 57 (1991) 303–310.
11. Palit AK, Popovic D.: Nonlinear combination of forecasts using artificial neural network, fuzzy logic and neurofuzzy approaches. In: Proceedings of the 9th IEEE International Conference on Fuzzy Systems, Melbourne, Australia (2001).
12. Bollerslev T.: Generalized autoregressive conditional heteroskedasticity. Journal of Econometrics. 31 (1986) 307–327.
13. Engle RF: Autoregressive conditional heteroskedasticity with estimates of the variance of U.K. inflation. Econometrica. 50 (1982) 987–1008.
14. Specht, D. F.: A general Regression Neural Network. IEEE Transactions on Neural Networks. 2 (1991) 568–576.
15. Ping-Feng Pai, Chih-Sheng Lin: Using support vector machines to forecast the production values of the machinery industry in Taiwan. Int J Adv Manuf Technol (2005).

16. G. Peter Zhang: Time series forecasting using a hybrid ARIMA and neural network model. Neurocomputing. 50 (2004) 159–175.
17. Wasserman, P.D.: Advanced Methods in Neural Computing, New York: Van Nostrand Reinhold (1993) 155–61.
18. http://www.mathworks.com/access/helpdesk/help/toolbox/nnet/radial79.html.

Boosting Classifiers for Music Genre Classification*

Ulaş Bağcı and Engin Erzin

Multimedia, Vision and Graphics Laboratory,
College of Engineering, Koç University, Sarıyer, İstanbul 34450, Turkey
{ubagci, eerzin}@ku.edu.tr

Abstract. Music genre classification is an essential tool for music information retrieval systems and it has been finding critical applications in various media platforms. Two important problems of the automatic music genre classification are feature extraction and classifier design. This paper investigates discriminative boosting of classifiers to improve the automatic music genre classification performance. Two classifier structures, boosting of the Gaussian mixture model based classifiers and classifiers that are using the inter-genre similarity information, are proposed. The first classifier structure presents a novel extension to the maximum-likelihood based training of the Gaussian mixtures to integrate GMM classifier into boosting architecture. In the second classifier structure, the boosting idea is modified to better model the inter-genre similarity information over the mis-classified feature population. Once the inter-genre similarities are modeled, elimination of the inter-genre similarities reduces the inter-genre confusion and improves the identification rates. A hierarchical auto-clustering classifier scheme is integrated into the inter-genre similarity modeling. Experimental results with promising classification improvements are provided.

1 Introduction

Music genre classification is crucial for the categorization of bulky amount of music content. Automatic music genre classification finds important applications in professional media production, radio stations, audio-visual archive management, entertainment and recently on the Internet. Although music genre classification is done mainly by hand and it is hard to precisely define the specific content of a music genre, it is generally agreed that audio signals of music belonging to the same genre contain certain common characteristics since they are composed of similar types of instruments and having similar rhythmic patterns. These common characteristics motivated recent research activities to improve automatic music genre classification [1,2,3,4]. The problem is inherently challenging as the

* This work has been supported by the European FP6 Network of Excellence SIMILAR (http://www.similar.cc). The authors would like to thank George Tzanetakis for sharing his music genre database with us.

P. Yolum et al.(Eds.): ISCIS 2005, LNCS 3733, pp. 575–584, 2005.

human identification rates after listening to 3s samples are reported to be around 70% [5].

Feature extraction and classifier design are two important problems of the automatic music genre classification. Timbral texture features representing short-time spectral information, rhythmic content features including beat and tempo, and pitch content features are investigated throughly in [1]. Another novel feature extraction method is proposed in [3], in which local and global information of music signals are captured by computation of histograms on their Daubechies wavelets coefficients. A comparison of human and automatic music genre classification is presented in a recent work [4]. Mel-frequency cepstral coefficients (MFCC) are also used for modeling and discrimination of music signals [1,6]. Various classifiers are employed for automatic music genre recognition including K-Nearest Neighbor (KNN) and Gaussian Mixture Models (GMM) classifiers as in [1,3], and Support Vector Machines (SVM) as in [3]. In a recent study, Boosting is used as a dimensionality reduction tool for audio classification [7].

In this study, we designed discriminative classifiers to improve the automatic music genre classification rates. Two alternative classifier structures are proposed: i) Boosting of the Gaussian mixture model based classifiers, and ii) Classifiers that are using the inter-genre similarity information. These classifier structures are described in detail in Sections 3 and 4, and they are experimentally tested with promising performance improvements in Section 5.

2 Feature Extraction

Timbral texture features, which are similar to the proposed feature representation in [1], are considered in this study to represent music genre types in the spectral sense. Short-time analysis over 25ms overlapping audio windows are performed for the extraction of timbral texture features for each 10ms frame. Hamming window of size 25ms is applied to the analysis audio segment to remove edge effects. The resulting timbral features from the analysis window are combined in a 17 dimensional vector including the first 13 MFCC coefficients, zero-crossing rate, spectral centroid, spectral roll-off and spectral flux.

3 Boosting Gaussian Mixture Model Classifiers

Boosting is a method of training many simple classifiers, and combining them into a single strong classifier [8]. The main approach is to generate a sequence of weak classifiers on a weighted set of training samples, and to adapt the training sample weights such that in each new classifier the hard-to-classify samples are weighted more than easy-to-classify samples. The outputs of the weak classifiers are then combined to guarantee certain bounds on error rate [8,9]. Many variations of the boosting algorithms exist, and they are used successfully in a wide range of problems. In this paper, we used the first multi-class extension of widely used **AdaBoost** algorithm [9].

Gaussian mixture density modeling has been widely used in various disciplines that require signal characterization for classification and recognition, as well as estimation of unknown probability densities. In this study, the Gaussian Mixture Models (GMM) are used for the class-conditional probability density function, $p(f|\lambda)$, estimation, where f and λ are respectively the feature vector and the genre class model. Let $\lambda_1, \lambda_2, \ldots, \lambda_N$ be the N different genre models in the database. In the music genre classification process, given a sequence of features, $\{f_1, f_2, \cdots, f_K\}$, which are extracted from a decision window of music signal, one can find the most likely music genre class, λ^*, by maximizing the joint class-conditional probability,

$$\lambda^* = \arg\max_{\lambda_n} \sum_{k=1}^{K} \log p(f_k|\lambda_n). \quad (1)$$

The maximum-likelihood method has been one of the most commonly used techniques to estimate the parameters of the mixture densities [10]. In this study, we propose a modification to the expectation-maximization (*EM*) [10] based training of mixture densities to adapt the weighting approach of the boosting algorithm. The following subsection describes the modified *EM* algorithm for boosting GMMs.

3.1 Modified *EM* Algorithm

Let us have an input sequence of N samples $\{x_1, \ldots, x_N\}$ with the associated sample weights $\{\omega_1, \ldots, \omega_N\}$. The underlying density function for K mixtures is given as,

$$f(x) = \sum_{k=1}^{K} P(k)\mathcal{N}_k(\mu_k, \Sigma_k), \quad (2)$$

where $P(k)$ values are the mixture weights, μ_k and Σ_k are the respectively mean vector and covariance matrix of the k-th Gaussian mixture density $\mathcal{N}_k$. The modified *EM* algorithm to train the mixture densities over our sample data is given as:

Initialize: mixture weights, means and variances. Repeat the following E-step and M-step until achieving convergence.
E-step: Calculate the weighted responsibility $p(k|x_n)$ of each Gaussian mixture $\mathcal{N}_k$ for each training data point x_n as,

$$p_{kn} = \omega_n p(k|x_n) = \omega_n \frac{p(x_n|k)P(k)}{p(x_n)}, \quad (3)$$

where $p(x_n)$ can be calculated as, $p(x_n) = \sum_{k=1}^{K} p(x_n|k)P(k)$.
M-step: Re-estimate mixture weights, means and variances,

$$\hat{P}(k) = \frac{\sum_n p_{kn}}{\sum_k \sum_n p_{kn}}, \quad \hat{\mu}_k = \frac{\sum_n p_{kn} x_n}{\sum_n p_{kn}}, \quad \hat{\sigma}_{ik}^2 = \frac{\sum_n p_{kn}(x_n - \hat{\mu}_k)(x_n - \hat{\mu}_k)'}{\sum_n p_{kn}}. \quad (4)$$

Note that, sample weights ω_n are determined by the first extension of AdaBoost [9]. Since, AdaBoost adjusts the sample weights to de-emphasize the easy-to-classify samples, the hard-to-classify samples are better modeled by the resulting Gaussian mixture density function.

4 Boosting with Inter-genre Similarity Information

The music signals belonging to the same genre contain certain common characteristics as they are composed of similar types of instruments with similar rhythmic patterns. These common characteristics are captured with statistical pattern recognition methods to achieve the automatic music genre classification [1,2,3,4]. The music genre classification is challenging problem, especially when the decision window spans a short duration, such as a couple of seconds. One can also expect to observe similarities of spectral content and rhythmic patterns across different music genre types, and with a short decision window misclassification and confusion rates increase. Two novel approaches are proposed to build discriminative musical genre classifiers that are aware of the similarities across genre models. The first approach addresses capturing the inter-genre similarities to decrease the level of confusion across similar music genre types. The inter-genre similarity modeling is closely related with the boosting idea, where in boosting the main motivation is to better model the hard-to-classify samples, and in inter-genre similarity modeling, the main motivation is to cluster the hard-to-classify samples to form the inter-genre similarity. The later approach presents an automatic clustering scheme to determine similar music genre types in a hierarchical classifier architecture.

4.1 Inter-genre Similarity Modeling

The timbral texture features represent the short-term spectral content of music signals. Since, music signals may include similar instruments and similar rhythmic patterns, no sharp boundaries between certain different genre types exist. The inter-genre similarity modeling (IGS) is proposed to capture the similar spectral contents among different genre types. Once the IGS clusters are statistically modeled, the IGS frames can be captured and removed from the decision process to reduce the inter-genre confusion.

Let $\lambda_1, \lambda_2, \ldots, \lambda_N$ be the N different genre models in the database. In this study, the Gaussian Mixture Models (GMM) are used for the class-conditional probability density function estimation, $p(f|\lambda)$, where f and λ are respectively the feature vector and the genre class model. The construction of the IGS clusters and the class-conditional statistical modeling can be achieved with the following steps:

i. Perform the statistical modeling of each genre in the database using the available training data of the corresponding music genre class.
ii. Perform frame based genre identification task over the training data, and label each frame as a true-classification or mis-classification.

iii. Construct the statistical model, λ_{IGS}, for the IGS cluster over all the misclassified frames among all the music genre types.
iv. Update all the N-class music genre models, λ_n, over the true-classified frames.

The above construction creates N-class music genre models and a single-class IGS model. In the music genre identification process, given a sequence of features, $\{f_1, f_2, \ldots, f_K\}$, which are extracted from a window of music signal, one can find the most likely music genre class, λ^*, by maximizing the weighted joint class-conditional probability,

$$\lambda^* = \arg\max_{\lambda_n} \frac{1}{\sum_k \omega_{kn}} \sum_{k=1}^{K} \omega_{kn} \log p(f_k|\lambda_n) \tag{5}$$

where the weights ω_{kn} are defined based on the class-conditional IGS model as following,

$$\omega_{kn} = \begin{cases} 1 & \text{if } p(f_k|\lambda_n) > p(f_k|\lambda_{IGS}), \\ 0 & \text{otherwise.} \end{cases} \tag{6}$$

The proposed weighted joint class-conditional probability maximization eliminates the IGS frames for each music genre from the decision process. The inter-genre confusion decreases and the genre classification rate increases with the resulting discriminative decision process. Experimental results, which are supporting the discrimination based on the IGS elimination, are presented in Section 5.

4.2 Hierarchical Classification with Auto-clustering

Hierarchical music genre classification avails easier and flexible music browsing, increases classification efficiency by lowering the number of classes, and decreases the confusion between music genre types of different hierarchies. Recently, the hierarchical classification is studied and found promising for music genre classification [11,12]. Similar to the music genre interpretation, the music signals belonging to the same hierarchy contain common characteristics, such as common types of instruments and common rhythmic patterns. The structure of the music genre hierarchy could be human determined for the flexible browsing or automatically determined for maximizing the classification performance. It is expected to extract similar hierarchy structures for both human and machine determined systems, however the structures may differ due to the different objectives, where in the human determined system ease of browsing and in the machine determined system classification performance are favored.

In this section, a new auto-clustering algorithm for the hierarchical structure extraction is proposed. The auto-clustering algorithm is iterative and depends on the confusion matrix, where it generates an hierarchy tree by combining the most confused two clusters in each iteration. Let $C = \{c_{ij}\}$ be the $N \times N$ confusion matrix, which is calculated over the training data, for N-class music genre classification, and c_{ij} is the confusion rate of i-th music genre to the j-th one. Then, the auto-clustering algorithm is defined as,

i. Find the most confused two genre clusters i^* and j^*,

$$(i^*, j^*) = \arg \max_{ij \text{ s.t. } i \neq j} c_{ij}.$$

ii. Combine the genre clusters i^* and j^* into a new genre cluster, estimate the class-conditional pdf models for each cluster using the training data, and compute the confusion matrix of the new $(N-1)$-class structure using the same training data.
iii. Repeat steps (i) and (ii) to further reduce the number of clusters to M in the hierarchical structure, where $M < (N-1)$.

The classification task starts with an M-class identification system, then the identification process is repeated within the identified cluster until reaching the lowest level in the hierarchy.

In the experimental studies, hierarchical music genre classification is tested with human and machine determined hierarchy structures, and also with the integration of discriminative IGS clustering. The experimental results are promising with significant classification gains.

5 Experimental Results

Evaluation of the proposed classification algorithms is performed over a music genre database that includes 9 different genre types: classical, country, disco, hiphop, jazz, metal, pop, reggae and rock. The database includes 20 different representative audio segments of duration 30s for each of the 9 music genre types, resulting a total duration of $9 \times 20 \times 30 = 5400$ seconds. All the audio files are stored mono at 22050Hz with 16-bit words. The resulting timbral texture feature vectors are extracted for each 10ms audio frame with an overlapping window of size 25ms. The music genre classification is performed based on the maximization of the class-conditional probability density functions, which are modeled using the Gaussian mixture models (GMM). Two training and testing scenarios are employed. In the first scenario (TTA), the training and testing are repeated for 10 independent data partitions and the average performances are reported. Each data partition includes respectively 18 and 2 audio segments for each music genre type in training and testing. Hence, after 10 independent tests, all the data is employed in the tests. In the second scenario (TTB), the database is split into two equal partitions, where each partition includes 10 different audio segments from each genre type. These two partitions are used in alternating order for training and testing of the music genre classifiers. The main difference between TTA and TTB scenarios is, TTA scenario has significantly more training data compared to TTB scenario that improves classification performance for TTA scenario. The average performances over these training and testing scenarios are reported in the following subsections.

5.1 Results on Boosting GMM Classifiers

The average correct classification rates of the two testing scenarios over all music genre types for varying number of Gaussian mixtures are given in Table 1.

Table 1. Average identification rates (%) for varying number of Gaussian mixture densities over three different decision window sizes (one audio frame (10ms), 1s and 3s windows)

Average Identification Rates (%)					
Classifier	TTA			TTB	
	10 ms	1 s	3 s	1 s	3 s
GMM(8)	34.85	61.90	65.15	55.56	57.45
GMM(16)	36.89	65.76	68.71	57.90	60.12
GMM(32)	38.46	67.53	70.13	57.69	59.25
GMM(64)	39.75	69.54	72.64	-	-
GMM(128)	39.95	69.69	71.85	-	-

Each classification decision is given for a decision window whose size is picked to be 10ms, 1s or 3s. The class conditional probability of a decision window is calculated by multiplying all class conditional frame probabilities in the specific decision window as described in (1). The average identification rates are comparable with the rates that are presented in [1], where the best identification rates in [1] are reported as 61% for 5-mixture GMM classifier with 1s decision window. However, we observed significant improvements on the correct classification rates for longer decision window sizes and for increasing number of Gaussian mixtures. Note that the training and testing scenario TTB suffers from the lack of available training data and the identification performances for the TTB results lower than the TTA training and testing scenario. In TTB case available training data is lower than in TTA, since increasing the training data improves the classification performance. Also, the classification performances with TTA and TTB saturate for GMM classifiers with more than 64 and 16 mixtures, respectively.

Boosting the GMM classifiers are implemented as described in Section 3. The GMM(64) and GMM(8) classifiers are boosted respectively with the two different training and testing scenarios, TTA and TTB, to observe the possible performance gain of boosting GMM classifiers. The correct identification rates for 1s and 3s decision windows upto 5 boosting iterations are given in Table 2.

Table 2. Average identification rates for 1s and 3s decision windows with boosting of 64-mixture and 8-mixture GMM classifiers, respectively with TTA and TTB training and testing scenarios

Average Identification Rates (%)				
Iteration	TTA GMM(64)		TTB GMM(8)	
	1 s	3 s	1 s	3 s
1	69.54	72.64	55.56	57.45
2	69.54	72.64	56.31	58.46
3	70.53	73.64	56.36	58.25
4	70.57	73.40	56.43	58.26
5	70.56	73.75	56.43	58.17

After the second iteration of boosting GMM(64) classifiers, a performance gain, which is better than GMM(128) classifier provides, is achieved. A similar performance gain is also observed with the GMM(8) classifiers under TTB training and testing. Especially, when the challenging automatic music genre classification task is considered with 70% human identification rate over 3s decision windows and 61% identification rate reported in [1], the incremental gain in identification performance is significant.

5.2 Results on Inter-genre Similarity

The experimental results of this section is generated using TTB training and testing scenario over the music genre classifiers that are employing flat or hierarchical structures with or without the discriminative IGS clustering. The structure of the best hierarchical auto-clustering is given in Fig. 1.

The performance comparisons of the flat and hierarchical classifiers with and without the discriminative IGS clustering for varying decision window sizes are given in Table 3. Note that as expected the correct classification rates are increasing with the increasing decision window size for all classifiers. The discriminative IGS clustering over the nine music genre types results with some incremental classification gain over the flat classifiers as presented in the IGS column in Table 3. The performance of the hierarchical auto-clustering without and with IGS are given in the last two columns with some additional identification improvements.

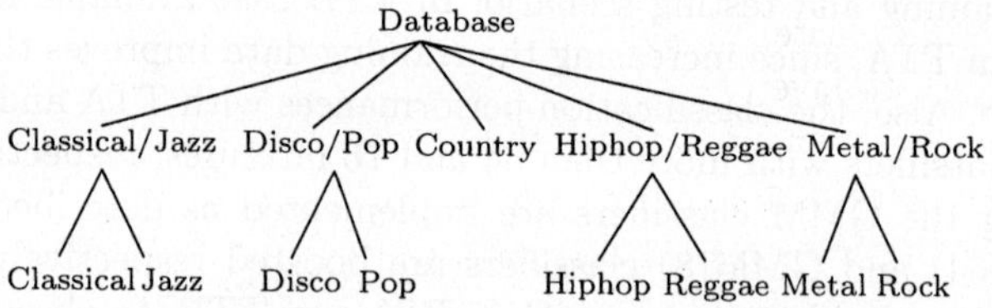

Fig. 1. The best hierarchical auto-clustering structure

Table 3. The average correct classification rates of the flat (F), IGS clustering, hierarchical auto-clustering (HAC), and hierarchical auto-clustering with IGS classifiers using 16-mixture GMM modeling for varying decision window sizes under TTB training and testing scenario

Decision Window	Correct Classification Rates (%)			
	F	IGS	HAC	HACIGS
10ms	37.96	34.76	39.54	42.87
5s	55.58	59.72	61.67	65.88
1s	57.91	63.67	65.30	67.83
3s	60.14	69.86	67.98	73.93
20s	63.33	74.18	71.18	78.00

Table 4. The average correct classification rates of the flat (F), IGS clustering, hierarchical auto-clustering (HAC), and hierarchical auto-clustering with IGS classifiers using 3s and 20s decision windows for varying number of GMM mixtures

Dec Win	# of Mix	Correct Classification Rates (%)			
		F	IGS	HAC	HACIGS
3s	8	57.47	62.83	66.64	70.74
	16	60.14	69.86	67.98	73.93
	32	59.26	71.16	69.33	72.92
20s	8	61.67	72.65	68.63	74.94
	16	63.33	74.18	71.18	78.00
	32	61.11	76.20	70.03	80.83

The human determined hierarchical classifier differs from the hierarchical auto-clustering structure only by combining disco, pop and country into one cluster.

The average classification rates of human determined hierarchical classifier without and with IGS is measured respectively as 68.70% and 75.35% for 20s decision window size. Note that these rates are slightly worse than the hierarchical auto-clustering classifier in Table 3. Although the human and machine determined hierarchical structures are quite similar, the classification performance of the auto-clustering has incremental gains for all decision window sizes. The structural closeness and the better performance of the auto-clustering to the human determined hierarchical classifier is a verification of the proposed hierarchical auto-clustering approach.

In Table 4, the average correct classification rates for 3s and 20s decision window sizes are given for varying number of GMM mixtures. The correct classification rates increase by increasing number of Gaussian mixtures. However, the classification performance saturates with the 32 mixture Gaussian models. Note that, 13.79% and 14.67% improvements on classification rates are observed with 16 mixture GMM classifiers, respectively for 3s and 20s decision windows. These improvements are significant when compared with the recently presented hierarchical classifier improvements, which are less than 3%, in [11]. Note that, these identification rates are also superior to the performances of the boosting of GMM classifiers that are presented in Table 2.

6 Conclusions

Automatic music genre classification is an important tool for music information retrieval systems. In this paper, we investigate two novel classifier structures for discriminative music genre classification. Classification error rates are reduced using the proposed modified EM algorithm for boosting GMM classifiers. It is encouraging that boosting GMM classifiers yields performance gain, which is not attainable with increasing number of Gaussian mixtures. In the second proposed classifier structure the inter-genre similarities are captured and modeled over the mis-classified feature population for the elimination of the inter-genre confusion, and an auto-clustering scheme for hierarchical classification is devised. Experimental results with promising identification improvements, which are superior than the recent literature, are provided. Although, the proposed hierarchical auto-clustering with IGS classifier achieves significant identification improvements and results close to the human identification rates for 3s decision windows, we should note that the automatic music genre classification still has a big room for possible improvements. Discriminative feature selection and iterative inter-genre similarity modeling are planned as the extension of this study.

References

1. Tzanetakis, G., Cook, P.: Musical genre classification of audio signals. Speech and Audio Processing, IEEE Transactions on **10** (2002) 293–302
2. Pye, D.: Content-based methods for managing electronic music. In: Proc. of the Int. Conf. on Acoustics, Speech and Signal Processing 2000 (ICASSP 2000). (2000)
3. Li, T., Ogihara, M., Li, Q.: A comparative study on content-based music genre classification. In: Proceedings of the 26th annual international ACM SIGIR conference on Research and development in information retrieval. (2003) 282–289
4. Lippens, S., Martens, J., Mulder, T.D., Tzanetakis, G.: A comparison of human and automatic musical genre classification. In: Proc. of the Int. Conf. on Acoustics, Speech and Signal Processing 2004 (ICASSP 2004). Volume 4. (2004) 233–236
5. Perrot, D., Gjerdigen, R.: Scanning the dial: An exploration of factors in identification of musical style. In: Proc. Soc. Music Perception Cognition. (1999) 88
6. Logan, B.: Mel frequency cepstral coefficients for music modeling. In: In Proc. Int. Symposium on Music Information Retrieval, ISMIR. (1997) 138–147
7. Ravindran, S., Anderson, D.: Boosting as a dimensionality reduction tool for audio classification. In: Circuits and Systems, 2004. ISCAS '04. Proceedings of the 2004 International Symposium on. Volume 3. (2004) 465–468
8. Schapire, R.E.: A brief introduction to boosting. In: In Proceedings of the Sixteenth International Joint Conference on Artificial Intelligence. (1999)
9. Freund, Y., Schapire, R.E.: A decision-theoretic generalization of on-line learning and an application to boosting. Journal of Computer and System Sciences **55** (1997) 119–139
10. Redner, R.A., Walker, H.F.: Mixture densities, maximum likelihood and the EM algorithm. SIAM Rev. **26** (1984) 195–239
11. Li, T., Ogihara, M.: Music genre classification with taxonomy. In: Proc. of the Int. Conf. on Acoustics, Speech and Signal Processing 2005 (ICASSP 2005). Volume V., Philadelphia (2005) 197–200
12. Xu, C., Maddage, N., Shao, X., Cao, F., Tian, Q.: Musical genre classification using support vector machines. In: Proc. of the Int. Conf. on Acoustics, Speech and Signal Processing 2003 (ICASSP 2003). Volume V. (2003)

Discriminating Biased Web Manipulations in Terms of Link Oriented Measures

Wookey Lee

Department of Computer Science, Sungkyul University,
Anyang 430-742, Republic of Korea
wook@sungkyul.edu

Abstract. In this paper, we present a link oriented measuring method to discriminate the manipulated web pages effectively. We define the label of an edge as having a link context and a similarity measure between link context and target page. By suggesting an assessing measure based on singular value decomposition, it is explained that our proposed method can effectively detect the manipulated web pages. We, however, extend the SVD as an assessment measure to detect the rank-manipulated pages. In the experiment, the LOD method reduced about 17% amount of the rank that is minimum 209.4% higher than not manipulated web pages. Using this proposed approach, the chance of manipulated web pages getting high ranks than deserved can be discriminated effectively.

1 Introduction

The organization of the web is progressively more being used to improve search and analysis of information on the web as a large collection of heterogeneous documents. Most people begin at a web search engine to find information, but the user's pertinent search results are often greatly diluted by irrelevant data or sometimes appear on target but still mislead the user in an unwanted direction. One of the intentional, sometimes vicious manipulations of web databases is a deliberately manipulated web page. The web manipulation refers to web page contents and hyperlinks that are created with the intention of misleading search engines. Traditional search engines based on the information retrieval techniques are well known to weaknesses for manipulations on body, title, meta tag, anchor text, and URL so that the added keywords can be invisible to persons through ingenious use of color representations, but can mislead the search engines. Another web manipulation technique is the creation of a large number of fake web pages, attenuating the page rank. Since many search engines take into account the number of incoming links in ranking pages, the rank of the target page is likely to increase, and appear earlier in query result sets. We call this manipulation pages as a manipulated web page that can use various techniques to achieve higher-than-deserved rankings in a search engine's results [1].

A web structuring technique in terms of the number of incoming links is widely put to use and is expected to minimize these weakness [2]. However, the results of many web search engines are equally hard to assay since search engines usually return huge lists of URLs, most of which can be judged almost irrelevant to the query [3].

P. Yolum et al.(Eds.): ISCIS 2005, LNCS 3733, pp. 585 – 594, 2005.

Though the link structure of the web contains important implied information, and can help in filtering or ranking web pages [4], and while there are several web search engines using web structuring techniques, Google being the most popular example, web structuring techniques still endures hardships because they still have several weak points. For example, the PageRank can easily be manipulated by generating of a large number of bogus web pages and then all the pages point a single target web page. In identifying the reason for the weaknesses we can look to the inaccuracy of the algorithm on one hand, and web pages that are deliberately composed to manipulation the search engine, on the other. Like traditional information retrieval techniques, web content mining alerts the discovery of useful information on the basis of match percentages gathered by scanning web contents, related data, and uploaded documents [2, 14]. Google bombing [1, 5] uses this weak point of the PageRank algorithm.

In this paper, we will recognize the weak points of the web structuring algorithm and suggest an alternative for that. With this algorithm, web search engines can filter the intentionally manipulated web pages effectively and offer the correct information to users. This work is organized as follows. Section two presents a review of web structuring and hypertext information. In section three, we define the problem that is focused upon and will be solved in this paper and constitutes the similarity measures. Section four describes the method and section five pertains performance analysis to solve the link based structuring problem and we work through a brief example to show how the algorithm can solve the problem. Then we put forth some concluding remarks and suggestions for the future works.

2 A Graph Based Web Structuring

2.1 Web Schema

A web site can be defined as a set of web nodes $N_w = \{N_1, ..., N_n\}$, a directed graph $G_w = (N_w, E_w)$, an arc function $x_{ij} : N^k \rightarrow \{0, 1\}$, $\forall (i, j) \in E_w$ consisting of a finite web node set N_w, a finite web arc set E_w of ordered pairs of web nodes, and the web arc elements (i, j) respectively, where $i, j \in \{0, 1, 2, 3, ..., n\text{-}1\}$, and $n = |N_w|$ the cardinality of web pages. There is a mapping system for the nodes corresponding to web pages and the arcs to Uniform Resource Identifiers [4]. The web node (N_W) can be defined as follows:

$$N_w = [N_i, \{\forall i, w_i, (i,j) \in E_w\}] \tag{2-1}$$

The N_i represents a web node corresponding to an HTML file whose node identifier is denoted simply by i. Where the homepage is defined as a default page (index.html) predetermined by the web server. For all i, $\{ w_i, (i, j) \in E_w, \forall i, j \in N_w\}$ is the set of web arcs having hypertext links to which the web page indicates, and corresponding w_i represent hypertext information that describes the link.

2.2 Related Works

Web structuring tries to discover the model underlying the link structures of the web. The model is based on the topology of the hyperlink with or without the link description. This model can be used to categorize the web pages and is useful to generate information such as similarity and relationships between web sites [2]. And the link structure of the web contains important implied information, and can help in filtering or ranking web pages. In particular, a link from page A to page B can be considered a recommendation of page B by the author of A. Some new algorithms have been proposed that exploit this link structure—not only for keyword searching, but other tasks like automatically building a Yahoo-like hierarchy or identifying communities on the web. The qualitative performance of these algorithms is generally better than the IR algorithms since they make use of more information than just the contents of the pages. While it is indeed possible to influence the link structure of the web locally, it is quite hard to do so at a global level. So link analysis algorithms that work at a global level possess relatively robust defenses against manipulation [1, 4].

There are two major link-based search algorithms, HITS (Hypertext Induced Topic Search) and PageRank. The basic idea of the HITS algorithm is to identify a small sub-graph of the web and apply link analysis on this sub-graph to locate the authorities and hubs for the given query. The sub-graph that is chosen depends on the user query. The selections of a small sub-graph (typically a few thousand pages), not only focus the link analysis on the most relevant part of the web, but also reduce the amount of work for the next phase. The main weaknesses of HITS are known to non-uniqueness and nil-weighting [5]. THESUS suggested a domain based PageRank algorithm, but its limitation depends on the usefulness of the ontology and the thesaurus that the system tries to include semantics among web documents [6].

The PageRank algorithm [7] can be used to severely advance the quality of results from web search engines. The fundamental idea of PageRank is to use the stationary distribution of a Markov chain on the web graph in order to assign relative ranks to the web pages. While this method has demonstrated to be outstandingly effective in practice as Google, it leaves extensive opportunity for improvement to reflect promising web characteristics.

There are three approaches to investigate the web digraph domain as (1) the whole web [1, 15], (3) a set of web sites [2, 16], and (2) a set of strongly coupled components [7, 9]. The first one is utilized to measure the whole WWW or growing ratio, but it is inappropriate to derive a web structure. The second is inclined to practical implementation, and the third focuses a mathematical model. We adopt the third for tackling to enhance PageRank by discriminating manipulated web pages theoretically.

3 Comparison and Assessment Measures

3.1 Similarity Measures

In order to generate the web structure, we have to introduce a weight measure for quantifying web pages and links between them. There are three representative measures such as *cosine* measure and *tf-idf* measure from Vector Space Model (VSM), and *PageRank*. The similarity measure in this paper is the weight of web node. We investigate the *cosine* measure, *tf-idf* measure, and *PageRank* measure as the weight measure which can be used to determine the topological ordering of web sites.

A popular measure of similarity for text, which normalizes the features by the covariance matrix, clustering is the *cosine* of the angle between two vectors. It captures a scale invariant understanding of similarity. An even stronger property is that the cosine similarity does not depend on the length. This allows documents with the same composition, but different totals to be treated identically which makes this the most popular measure for text documents. Also, due to this property, samples can be normalized to the unit sphere for more efficient processing. In the *tf-idf* measure, the *tf* factor itself is sometimes normalized by dividing it by the frequency of the most-frequent non-stop term in the document as, $tf_{norm} = tf/tf_{max}$. The *idf* factor is typically computed by $[df(w_i)/N]^{-1}$, and most often the $log_2[N/\ df(w_i)]$ is used, where, N, is the total number of documents and, $df(w_i)$, is the number of documents containing the ith word [6].

The *PageRank* measure is that, if source page, *i*, has a link to target page, *j*, then the author of source page, *i*, is implicitly conferring some importance to page, *j*. Let N_j be the out-degree of page, *i*, and let *Rank*(*p*) represents the importance of page, *p*. Then, the link (*i*, *j*) confers a certain number of units of rank to, *j*. This simple idea leads to the following iterative fix-point computation that yields the rank vector over all of the pages on the web. If, *n*, is the number of pages, assign all pages the initial value 1/n. Let, B_j represent the set of pages pointing to *j*. Links between web pages propagate the ranks [9]. We continue the iterations until the rank is stabilized to within some defined threshold. The final rank vector contains the *PageRank* vector over the web. This vector is computed only once after each crawl of the web; the values can then be used to influence the ranking of search results [6]. Guaranteeing the rank vector to converge, *PageRank* algorithm uses the following equation with a damping factor (*d*). Google usually set the value of the damping factor to 0.85 [7, 8] so that we can see that the *PageRank* vector converges either slowly or quickly in terms of the magnitude of the damping factor.

$$\forall i, Rank^{(k+1)}(i) = (1-d)E + d(\sum_{i \in B_j} Rank^{(k)}(j)\,/\,N_j) \quad where,\ E = \left[\frac{1}{n}\right]_{n \times 1} \tag{3.1}$$

The prototype system has been experimentally tested to search for the structure of the test web site. The link structure of the site is shown in reference Fig. 3.1. The circle in the figures represents a web node and the arrow represents a hyperlink or a web arc. For example, by (3.3) we can get the weights in Table 3.1 and derived weights as Fig. 3.1. The node weights by *PageRank* are: <1.1029, 0.9693, 0.5213, 0.5213, 1.5593, 0.7495>.

Table 3.1. *PageRank* values for Fig. 3.1

N0	N1	N2	N3	N4	N5	N6
1.0000	1.0000	1.0000	1.0000	1.0000	1.0000	1.0000
0.9797	0.7247	0.4414	0.4414	1.7164	1.8297	0.8664
1.2267	1.0250	0.5387	0.5387	1.3424	1.6019	0.7263
1.0335	0.9334	0.5531	0.5531	1.6533	1.4914	0.7820
1.1318	0.9752	0.5068	0.5068	1.5352	1.6019	0.7418
1.0947	0.9719	0.5369	0.5369	1.5812	1.5255	0.7523
1.1029	0.9693	0.5213	0.5213	1.5756	1.5593	0.7495

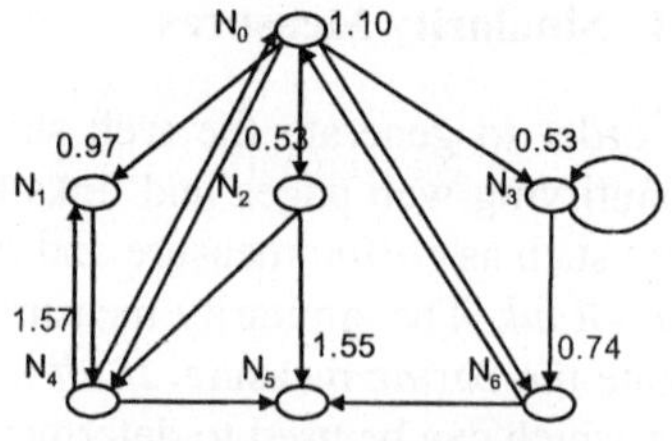

Fig. 3.1. The example site

3.2 Assessment Measure

After deciding all web structures, we need to assess and examine that whether the intentionally biased web page is hidden and distorts the web structure or not. When specifying a manipulation page in terms of context based PageRank algorithm, the criteria to determine which pages that the rank value indicates can be decided by the SVD (Singular Value Decomposition) method [12, 13]. The SVD has been adopted to reduce matrix dimensions or to utilize possibly to derive a hidden semantics in the keyword by document matrix. We, however, adopt the SVD to detect the rank-manipulated pages.

The SVD decomposes the transition matrix as *U*, *V*, and *S* matrix as following equation (3.2). This method has an advantage that can analyze the matrix within a predetermined error range with giving arbitrary values, and a disadvantage that it is not applicable to nonsingular matrix even though it is unrealistically rare case.

$$M = USV \tag{3.2}$$

Where *U*: $m*m$ orthogonal matrix with left singular vectors of *M*, *V*: $n*n$ orthogonal matrix with left singular vectors of *M*, and *S*: m*m diagonal matrix with positive singular value of *M*, for diagonal elements $\sigma_1, \sigma_2, ..., \sigma_r (\sigma_1 \geq \sigma_2 \geq ... \geq \sigma_r \geq 0)$, where rank($M$) = r.

The explicit and implicit QR algorithms are based on the same idea as the QR algorithm for the eigenvalue problem, but they are direct rather than iterative in nature, since the eigenvalues to be assigned are used as shifts [14]. In the single-input case, there exist RQ implementations of both the explicit and implicit QR algorithms. We can derive the rank value from the Frobenius norm as following equation (3.3) that analyze the matrix *M* and the approximated matrix M_k that gives lower ranking selecting *k* maximum values and replacing the other values 0's [13].

$$\| M - M_k \|_F = \min_{rank(A) \leq k} \| M - A \|_F = \sqrt{\sigma_{k+1}^2 + \sigma_{k+2}^2 + ... + \sigma_r^2} \tag{3.3}$$

If we specify a web node as the manipulated node, then we can measure the possible error to delete the node. A low rank approximation error has been used the approximated matrix M_k over the Frobenius norm, we adopt it as the web node deletion error in the following equation (3.4):

$$\text{Node deletion error} = \|M_k\|_F \,/\, \|M\|_F \tag{3.4}$$

There respectively is a relative ratio over the sum of all weights. The relative error is defined as the individual eigenvalue square term over the sum of the eigenvalue squares:

$$\text{Relative error} = \sigma_i^2 \,/\, \| M \|_F \tag{3.5}$$

4 Link Oriented Discrimination Method

The web is modeled by a directed graph $G = (V, E)$, and the rank x_i of each for the n pages $i \in V$ is defined recursively in terms of the pages which point to it.

$$x_i = \sum_{(i,j)\in E} a_{ij} x_j \tag{4.1}$$

Where the coefficient a_{ij} consists a Markov transition matrix, and x_i should be an eigenvector. The PageRank assumes that the web graph G is strongly coupled component and set a damping factor (d) for the error term ($1/n$) of the recurrent nodes. Google usually set the value of the damping factor to 0.85 [7, 8], by which the vector converges either slowly or quickly with respect to the magnitude of the damping factor. One caveat is that the convergence of PageRank is only guaranteed if transition matrix T is irreducible (i.e. graph is strongly connected) and aperiodic [13]. The latter is guaranteed in practice for the web, while the former is true only if all of the nodes in the graph are accessible; hence, we 1) add a complete set of outgoing edges to nodes in G with out-degree 0 and 2) damp the rank propagation by a factor of $(1-d)$ by adding a complete set of outgoing edges, with weight $1/n$, to all nodes [6]. So, we add the matrix D , which is made by following equation (3.7). It is the coefficient a_{ij} which triggers so many questions, including those considered here.

$$x_i = (1-d)\left[\frac{1}{n}\right]_{n\times 1} + d\left(\sum_{(i,j)\in E} a_{ij} x_j\right) \tag{4.2}$$

We set the normalized coefficient a_{ij} from the hypertext information such that the target page for $(i, j) \in E$. We normalize the weight values of the coefficient. It is the way to guarantee the convergence of the sum of the elements of the rank vector. If the sum of a row of the transition matrix is larger than 1, the sum of the elements of the rank vector will diverge. In contrast, if the sum is less than 1, the sum of the elements of the rank vector converges to 0. Thus, we must normalize the weight values to set the sum of a row of transition matrixes to 1. Since this is very easy to prove, we will not expound upon this assertion.

In order to produce mechanism for discriminating manipulated web pages, the following simplified (by the space limit) procedural steps, call the LOD (Link Oriented Discrimination) method, are recommended as follows:

- Step 1. Derive the web nodes and links on the given specified domain (SCC).
- Step 2. Generate link measures according to equation (4.2)
- Step 3. Normalize the measure, and make a transition matrix in terms of the link structure from Step 1.
- Step 4. Calculate the matrix and decide the manipulated node from assessing errors by the equation (3.2) to (3.5).

5 Performance Analyses

Fig. 3.1 explains how the proposed method finds the manipulated link and reduces the importance of the manipulation page. The Page 5 in the example is assumed a manipulation page and links (2, 5), (4, 5), and (6, 5) are manipulated links. Table 5.1 shows the information of each page including title, link and initial rank. Like simple example, initial rank value of each page was set to 1 for preventing page rank from being influenced by initial value.

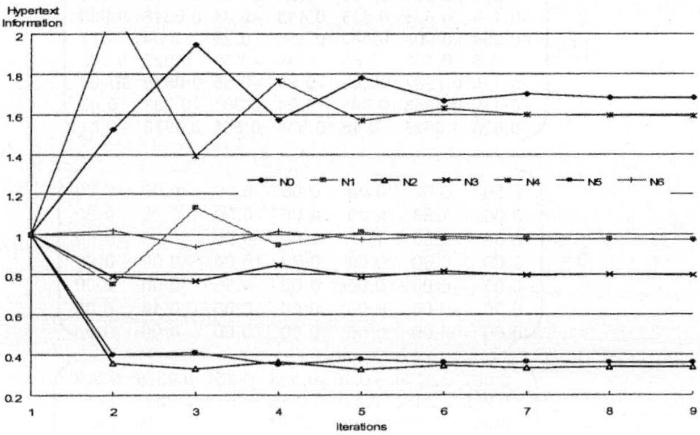

Fig. 5.1. Converged Values for LOD method

Table 5.1 shows the synthetically analyzed results that each node begins with weight 1 having links to each node, and finalized by PageRank method and by the LOD method respectively. The left column represents weight values and the right column represents corresponding percentage by RageRank respectively. By the result of PageRank, each node gets different value according to its node topology. Note that the weight of Page 5 is increased from 14.3% to 22.3%, which means that the manipulation would be successful. In other words, the discrimination by PageRank failed on the spot. The results of LOD method, however, represent that the weight of manipulated page decreased from 14.3% to 5.1% so that the weight to the page 5 have the smallest weight value. Thus, we can say that the discrimination is successful.

Table 5.1. The results of PageRank and LOD method

Page	Link to	Initial	PageRank		LOD method		difference
0	1,2,3,4,6	1	1.103	15.8%	1.68	23.9%	-0.08185
1	4	1	0.969	13.8%	0.97	13.8%	1.97E-05
2	4, 5	1	0.521	07.4%	0.34	04.8%	0.026384
3	3, 6	1	0.521	07.4%	0.79	11.4%	-0.03904
4	0, 1, 5	1	1.576	22.5%	1.59	22.7%	-0.00146
5	No	1	1.559	22.3%	0.36	5.1%	0.171401
6	0, 5	1	0.75	10.7%	0.97	14.9%	-0.01166

We normalized weight values and made stochastic transition matrices U, S, and V of the SDV assessment measure described in section 3. With this transition matrix, we can calculate each page's rank value. Figure 5.2 shows the change of the LOD method value in the each iteration by the SDV. We can find that the weight value converges on certain value of the assessment measure and can get eigenvalues in matix S as follows.

$$U=\begin{pmatrix} -0.836 & -0.026 & 0.265 & -0.29 & 0.354 & 0.1452 & -0.01 \\ -0.114 & -0.005 & 0.538 & 0.446 & -0.31 & 0.0318 & 0.635 \\ -0.094 & -0.004 & 0.442 & 0.365 & -0.26 & -0.04 & -0.77 \\ -0.5 & -0.182 & -0.65 & 0.38 & -0.39 & -0.027 & 0.003 \\ -0.115 & 0.7287 & -0.01 & -0.39 & -0.55 & 0.0675 & 3E-04 \\ -0.119 & 0.0963 & 0.045 & -0.04 & 0.061 & -0.983 & 0.05 \\ -0.028 & 0.6527 & -0.15 & 0.538 & 0.506 & 0.0678 & -0.01 \end{pmatrix}$$

$$S=\begin{pmatrix} 2.59 & 0.00 & 0.00 & 0.00 & 0.00 & 0.00 & 0.00 \\ 0.00 & 1.63 & 0.00 & 0.00 & 0.00 & 0.00 & 0.00 \\ 0.00 & 0.00 & 1.18 & 0.00 & 0.00 & 0.00 & 0.00 \\ 0.00 & 0.00 & 0.00 & 0.72 & 0.00 & 0.00 & 0.00 \\ 0.00 & 0.00 & 0.00 & 0.00 & 0.35 & 0.00 & 0.00 \\ 0.00 & 0.00 & 0.00 & 0.00 & 0.00 & 0.14 & 0.00 \\ 0.00 & 0.00 & 0.00 & 0.00 & 0.00 & 0.00 & 0.00 \end{pmatrix}$$

$$V=\begin{pmatrix} -0.062 & 0.9126 & -0.16 & 0.334 & 0.161 & 0.0316 & 0.007 \\ -0.299 & 0.3452 & 0.175 & -0.75 & -0.39 & 0.2061 & 0.065 \\ -0.219 & -0.002 & 0.153 & -0.27 & 0.686 & -0.325 & 0.527 \\ -0.546 & -0.096 & -0.14 & -0.1 & 0.407 & 0.1166 & -0.7 \\ -0.38 & -0.011 & 0.818 & 0.409 & -0.14 & 0.0056 & 0.002 \\ -0.016 & 0.11 & 0.003 & -0.09 & -0.25 & -0.913 & -0.29 \\ -0.645 & -0.163 & -0.48 & 0.252 & -0.33 & -0.067 & 0.386 \end{pmatrix}$$

Fig. 5.2. Assessment Results for LOD method

Table 5.2 shows the result and each page's error terms. In table 4, the error terms deleting the last singular value from matrix S is 0.002 that is about relatively 0.09% of total errors. And if we delete the page 5, then the singular value is 0.137 that is about relatively 2.1% of total errors. With this we can see that the node 5 is included discarding criteria, that is stochastically significant level so that the information loss by discriminating the node 5 is about 5.6%. This represents the same result with the LOD in the above table 5.1. The assessment by SVD, however, represents an exceptional result that our method detects the normal node 2 is also included. Thus we can say that it shows the transition matrix converges low weight result to the unimportant pages, but it is not always a manipulation page.

Table 5.2. Frobenius norm and related errors for LOD method

deleted node	0	4	6	1	3	5	2
$\sum \sigma_i^2$	2.595	1.627	1.185	0.716	0.353	0.137	0.002
Frobenius norm	1.611	1.276	1.088	0.846	0.595	0.374	0.047
Node deletion error	0.2435	0.1928	0.1645	0.1279	0.0899	0.056	0.0072
Relative error	0.3922	0.246	0.1791	0.1082	0.0534	0.021	0.0003

As a conclusion, the LOD method reduced about 17% amount of the rank value of Page 5 that is minimum 209.4% higher than normal (not manipulated) web page changes. In the example, web page which is suspected as a manipulation page has the smallest rank value but in this complex example, we can not make page 5 have the smallest value. But we can reduce the rank value significantly.

6 Conclusions and Future Works

The web manipulation refers to hyperlinked pages on the web that are created with the intention of misleading search engines. It is one of the most significant problems in the web search engine that can generate the best output to the user's submitted query and can effectively avoid the intentionally biased web pages. We discovered that the intentionally biased web page was exploiting the limitations of the PageRank based search engine's algorithm. In order to solve the problem originating from link based manipulation, we modified the PageRank algorithm to the filtering algorithm that incorporates the similarity between link contexts and hypertext information that can be generalized to the context based measure. The SVD has been adopted to reduce matrix dimensions or to utilize possibly to derive a hidden semantics in the keyword by document matrix. We, however, extend the SVD as an assessment measure to detect the rank-manipulated pages. It can be measured by the traditional transition matrix method as well as the SVD method; so that the LOD method reduced about 17% amount of the rank that is minimum 209.4% higher than normal (not manipulated) web page changes. Using this proposed approach, the chance of manipulated web pages getting high ranks than deserved can be detected, and we can reinforce search accuracy significantly.

References

1. Gyöngyi, Z., Garcia-Molina, H., and Pedersen, J.: Combating web Spam with TrustRank, In: Proc. *VLDB,* (2004) 576-587
2. Lee, W., Shin, K., Kang, S.: Structuring Web with Semantic Hypertext Algorithm, In: Proc. *CITSA*, Florida, (2004) 257-262
3. Halkida, M., Nguyen, B., Varlamis, I., Vazirgiannis, M.: THESUS: Organizing web document collections based on link semantics, *The VLDB Journal* (12), (2003) 320-332
4. Arasu, A., Cho, J., Garcia-Molina, H., Paepcke, A. and Rachavan, S.: Searching the web, *ACM Transactions on Internet Technology*, Vol.1, No.1, (2001) 2-43
5. Miller, J., Rae, G. and Schaefer, F.: Modifications of Kleinberg's HITS Algorithm Using Matrix Exponentiation and web Log Records, In: Proc. *ACM SIGIR*, (2001) 444-445
6. Haveliwala, T.: Topic-Sensitive PageRank: A Context-Sensitive Ranking Algorithm for web Search, *IEEE TKDE*, Vol. 15, No. 4, (2003) 784-796
7. Brin, S., Page, L.: The Anatomy of a Large-Scale Hypertextual web Search Engine, In Proc. *WWW*, (1998) 107-117
8. Wang, Y., DeWitt, D.: Computing PageRank in a Distributed Internet Search Engine System, In Proc. *VLDB*, (2004) 420-431
9. Caldo, P., Ribeiro-Neto, B., Ziviani, N.: Local versus Global Link Information in the web, *ACM TOIS*, Vol. 21, No. 1, (2003) 42–63
10. Phelps, T. and Wilensky, R.: Robust Hyperlinks: Cheap, Everywhere, Now, In Proc. *DDEP/PODDP*, (2000) 28-43

11. Lu, W., Chien, L. and Lee, H.: Anchor Text Mining for Translation of web Queries, In Proc. *ICDM*, (2001) 401-408
12. Gentle, J.: Singular Value Factorization, *Numerical Linear Algebra for Applica-tions in Statistics*, Springer-Verlag, (1998) 102-103
13. Castelli, V., Thomasian, A. and Li, C.: CSVD: Clustering and Singular Value Decomposition for Approximate Similarity Search in High-Dimensional Spaces, *IEEE TKDE*, Vol. 15, No. 3, (2003) 671-685
14. Elmroth, E., Gustavson, F.: Applying recursion to serial and parallel QR factorization leads to better performance. *IBM Journal of R&D*, 44(4) (2000) 605-624
15. Pandurangan, G., Raghavan, P. and Upfal, E.: Using PageRank to Characterize Web Structure. COCOON (2002) 330-339
16. Lee, W., Kim, J., Structuring the Web to Cope with Dynamic Changes, In: ICWS, (2005)

ORF-NT: An Object-Based Image Retrieval Framework Using Neighborhood Trees

Mutlu Uysal and Fatos Yarman-Vural

Middle-East Technical University, 06530 Ankara, Turkey
{uysal, vural}@ceng.metu.edu.tr

Abstract. This study proposes an object-based image retrieval framework, called, ORF-NT, which trains a discriminative feature set for each object class and introduces a neighborhood tree for object labelling. For this purpose, initially, a large variety of features are extracted from the regions of the pre-segmented images. These features are, then, fed to a training module to select the `important` features, suppressing relatively less important ones for each class.

ORF-NT (**O**bject-based Image **R**etrieval **F**ramework using **N**eighborhood **T**rees) defines a neighborhood tree for identifying the whole object from over-segmented regions. The neighborhood tree consists of the nodes corresponding to the neighboring regions as its children and merges the regions through a search algorithm. Experiments are performed on Corel database using MPEG-7 features in order to observe the power and the weakness of ORF-NT. The training phase, is tested by using Fuzzy ARTMAP [1], Euclidean distance and Adaboost algorithms [2]. It is observed that Fuzzy ARTMAP yields better retrieval rates than Euclidean distance and Adaboost algorithms.

1 Introduction

In most of the image retrieval systems, the images in the database are compared to the query image with a common set of features, which are used to represent all the objects and/or classes in the database. For large number of classes, the power of separation of the image collection with the same set of features decreases, especially in large databases [3], [4]. As the number and the diversity of images in the database increase, the fixed-feature set methods fail to give satisfactory results.

As an alternative approach, a CBIR system, which uses different set of features for each query class, is proposed in [5]. The `best set of features` for each query class is estimated in a training module. Then, the similar objects are retrieved by using the best feature set for that query object, applied on the pre-segmented image database. The performance of this method is much better than the systems, which use any combinations of fixed features for all the objects.

In a recent study [6], rather then using the `best set of features`, we represent each object class by a different weighted mixture of a large feature set and query that class with the corresponding weight vector [6]. The weights of the mixture are obtained by training a fuzzy neural network architecture, called fuzzy ARTMAP [1], which

P. Yolum et al.(Eds.): ISCIS 2005, LNCS 3733, pp. 595–605, 2005.

computes a membership value depending on the relevance of each feature for each object class. The major problem of the system in [6], was to use a greedy algorithm for merging all possible combinations of neighboring regions. The greedy algorithm could sometimes stop without finding the whole object, but only a part of it.

In this study, we improve the system proposed in [6] by introducing a neighborhood tree for representing the contiguous regions having the same label. Then, object localization by region merging becomes an optimization problem which can be solved by a search algorithm over the tree. ORF-NT is compared to the system in [6]. The training phase of the system is implemented using Fuzzy ARTMAP, Adaboost and simple Euclidean Distance methods. As an expected result, fuzzy ARTMAP and Adaboost are much better than Euclidean distance. The experiments indicate that fuzzy ARTMAP is slightly better than the Adaboost algorithm in content based image retrieval problems.

1.1 Related Work

Well-known popular region based image retrieval systems work with a fixed feature space defined over regions. For example, NeTra [7] uses color, texture, shape and spatial location information in segmented image regions to search and retrieve similar regions from the database. A distinguishing aspect of this system is its incorporation of a robust automated image segmentation algorithm that allows object or region-based search.

On the other hand, Blobworld [8] is based on finding coherent image regions, which roughly correspond to objects. The image is segmented into regions by fitting a mixture of Gaussians to the pixel distribution in a joint color-texture-position feature space. Each region ("blob") is then associated with color and texture descriptors. Querying is based on the user specifying attributes of one or two regions of interest, rather than a description of the entire image.

SIMPLIcity [9] is another image retrieval system, which uses semantics classification methods, a wavelet-based approach for feature extraction, and integrated region matching based upon image segmentation. A measure for the overall similarity between images is developed using a region-matching scheme that integrates properties of all the regions in the images.

In [10], the authors propose an automatic approach for annotating and retrieving images based on a training set of images. They assume that regions in an image can be described using a small vocabulary of blobs, which are generated from image features using clustering. In [11], object recognition is considered as the translation of images to words. The "lexicon" for the translation is learned from large annotated image collections, which consist of images that are associated with text. The correspondences between the regions and words are learned using a method based on the Expectation Maximization algorithm.

In [12], a statistical approach to automatic image annotation problem is introduced using two-dimensional multi-resolution hidden Markov models. Categorized images are used to train a dictionary of hundreds of statistical models each representing a concept. To measure the extent of association between an image and the textual description of a concept, the likelihood of the occurrence of the image based on the characterizing stochastic process is computed. A high likelihood indicates a strong association.

ORF-NT, introduced in this paper, describes an algorithm that uses the notion of neighborhood trees to limit the search space of an object retrieval system. Objects are first segmented and object recognition is performed on these segmented pieces. The algorithm limits the possible combinations of object pieces that are labelled by training algorithm based on the neighborhood information.

2 The ORF-NT

There are three major phases in ORF-NT: 1-Training, 2-Labelling and 3- Querying. In the training phase, firstly, the images in the training set are segmented. Then, features of the segmented regions are extracted. These features are, then, fed to the training module of ORF-NT. In the labelling phase, output regions of the segmentation are labelled using neighborhood trees and training component. In the querying layer, user performs a query where the results are shown to the user from highest to lowest membership values. Figure-1 shows the block diagram of ORF-NT. In the next sub-sections the modules in these phases will be explained.

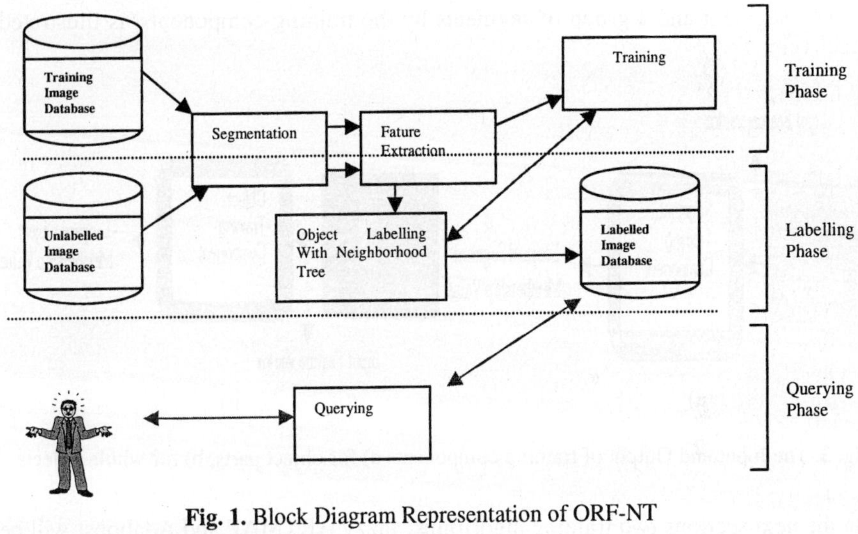

Fig. 1. Block Diagram Representation of ORF-NT

2.1 Segmentation and Feature Extraction

The images in the database are segmented into regions using the N-cut segmentation algorithm of [13]. It is well known that this algorithm performs over-segmentation, which mostly yields objects or parts The images in the database are stored as a set of regions obtained from the segmentation process for further processing steps.

Initially, a crisp feature space is formed by selecting a large variety of features from the MPEG7 descriptors. Dominant Color (4 features), Color Structure (32 features), Scalable Color (16 features), Edge Direction Histogram (80 features) and Region-based Shape (35 features) are chosen from [14]. The features are normalized to analogue [0-1] scale and concatenated to form the feature vectors, which are then fed to training module of the framework.

2.2 Training

The aim of the training is to find a discriminative feature set for each object class. For this purpose, a training set is formed by entering the objects from each class. There are two different components of training module. In the first component, the whole objects, which are selected by the user in a minimum bounding rectangle are trained, whereas in the second one, the parts of the selected object which are obtained from the output of the segmentation algorithm are trained.

The training component used for the whole object, receives a feature vector, which is formed by concatenation of color, texture and shape features. The input to the training component for the sub regions excludes the region based shape feature, since the shape is not a characteristic feature of the sub regions of the objects.

The training components, which are trained by segments and whole objects separately, are used to label an unknown segment or a group of neighboring segments. The training schema is indicated in Figure 2-a and 2-b, where labelling of an unknown segment and a group of segments by the training components, is illustrated respectively.

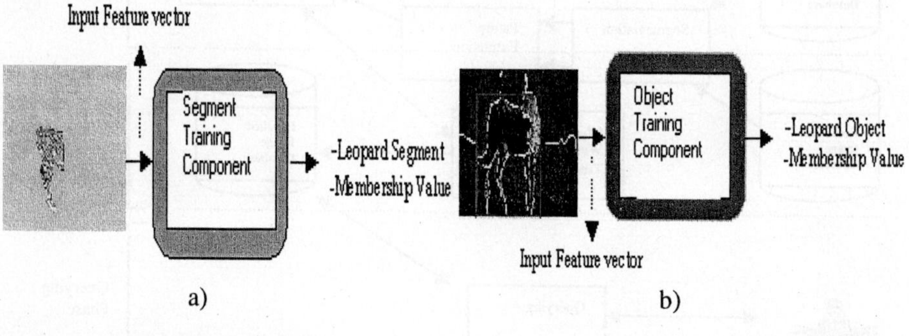

Fig. 2. The Input and Output of training components a) for object parts, b) for whole objects

In the next sections two training algorithms: fuzzy ARTMAP and Adaboost will be explained briefly. These algorithms will be used in our experiments.

2.2.1 Fuzzy ARTMAP Training

It is well known that, ARTMAP is a class of Neural Network architecture that performs incremental supervised learning of recognition categories. The fuzzy ARTMAP system includes a pair of Adaptive Resonance Theory modules (ART_a and ART_b) that create stable recognition categories in response to arbitrary sequences of input patterns (Figure-3). Input features are the feature vectors of the input class. Target prediction is the corresponding label of each input class. Map field module maps the input features to the corresponding target predictions. Such a mapping can be performed by finding the appropriate weight vector (w_j) for each input feature class.

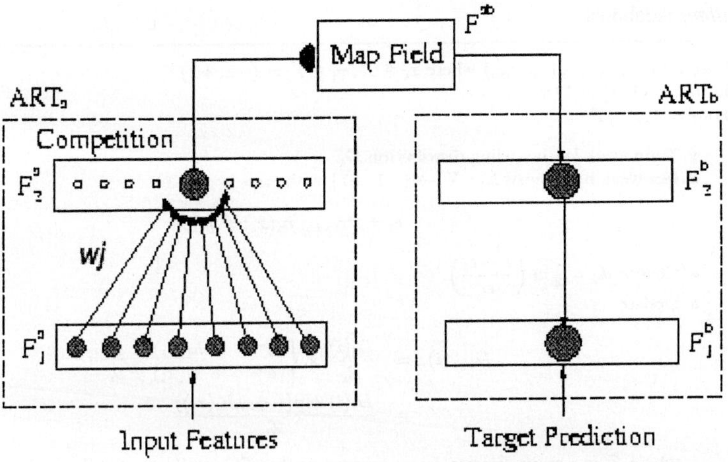

Fig. 3. Fuzzy ARTMAP Architecture

The details of the training algorithm of fuzzy ARTMAP are given in [1]. The main point is to find the weight vector (w_j) for each training object group j. The weight vector shows the relevance of each feature for a particular training class. In the labelling phase, a membership value is calculated using this vector to identify the unknown object by fuzzy ARTMAP, using the formula:

$$\text{MEMBERSHIP} = \frac{\| \mathbf{A} \wedge \mathbf{w}_J^a \|}{\| \mathbf{A} \|}$$

where A denotes the input vector , $\wedge$ denotes the fuzzy AND operation and $\|$ denotes the norm operation.

2.2.2 Adaboost Training

Adaboost is a well-known algorithm to obtain a strong classifier from a set of weak classifiers. Each weak classifier performs slightly better than the random guessing. The input to the algorithm is a set of features and their labels $(x_1,y_1),\ldots(x_m,y_m)$ extracted from a training set. The main idea of the algorithm is to maintain a set of weights over the training set. The strong classifier is then defined as a linear combination of the weak classifiers using the weights. Initially all weights are equally likely, but on each round, the weights of incorrectly classified examples are increased so that the weak learner is forced to focus on the hard examples in the training set. The final hypothesis H is a weighted majority vote of the T weak hypothesis where α_t is the weight assigned to h_t. The weight on training example i on round t is denoted as $D_t(i)$. The pseudo-code of the algorithm is given bellows. Details about the algorithm can be found in [2].

Algorithm: Adaboost

Given: $(x_1, y_1), \ldots, (x_m, y_m)$ where $x_i \in X, y_i \in Y = \{-1, +1\}$
Initialize $D_1(i) = 1/m$.
For $t = 1, \ldots, T$:

- Train weak learner using distribution D_t.
- Get weak hypothesis $h_t : X \to \{-1, +1\}$ with error

$$\epsilon_t = \Pr_{i \sim D_t}\left[h_t(x_i) \neq y_i\right].$$

- Choose $\alpha_t = \frac{1}{2} \ln\left(\frac{1 - \epsilon_t}{\epsilon_t}\right)$.
- Update:

$$D_{t+1}(i) = \frac{D_t(i)}{Z_t} \times \begin{cases} e^{-\alpha_t} & \text{if } h_t(x_i) = y_i \\ e^{\alpha_t} & \text{if } h_t(x_i) \neq y_i \end{cases} = \frac{D_t(i) \exp(-\alpha_t y_i h_t(x_i))}{Z_t}$$

where Z_t is a normalization factor (chosen so that D_{t+1} will be a distribution).

Output the final hypothesis:

$$H(x) = \text{sign}\left(\sum_{t=1}^{T} \alpha_t h_t(x)\right).$$

T value is selected as 20 in our experiments. The membership value is obtained by normalizing $\alpha_t h_t(x)$ value by the possible minimum and maximum values of $\alpha_t h_t(x)$.

2.3 Object Labelling with Neighborhood Tree

In this section, we propose an algorithm to extract and label an object in the image database. There are two inputs to the algorithm:

i) the regions obtained from the segmentation component,
ii) labels and membership values for segmented regions and objects obtained from the training component.

The Output of the algorithm yields the label, membership value and rectangular coordinates of each object in the unlabelled image database.

In order to find and label the set of regions, which correspond to the query object, *neighborhood trees* are formed. The neighborhood tree is a directed acyclic graph, whose nodes are contiguous regions of the pre-segmented image. The neighborhood tree is constructed from the segmented image as follows: For each region in the segmented image, a label and a membership value is obtained by the trained segment component. Then, separate sets are formed by collecting the regions with the same label. For each of the set, a separate neighborhood tree is constructed. The starting node of the tree is selected as the region with maximum membership value in the set. The tree grows downward adding neighboring regions at each level.

One of the major problems in construction of the neighborhood tree is the complexity introduced by each additional layer. To solve this problem, a pruning algorithm is developed after the first level neighbors of the starting node. When a new node is formed in the tree, the fuzzy ARTMAP relabels the collection of the regions representing this node. If the label does not match to the label of the starting node, the path is pruned. Figure-4 illustrates the construction of the neighborhood tree with a pre-segmented sample image.

As the next step, the neighborhood tree is traversed from starting node to the bottom. The membership of each node is obtained using the trained object component. At the end of the search, the node having the maximum membership is labelled as the query object. This algorithm is given by the following pseudo-code:

Algorithm: Neighborhood Tree Construction and Object Labeling

Step 1: Find the label and membership value of each segmented region of the unlabelled image by using trained segment component.

Step 2: Form a set for the regions having the same label. For each set, select the region with maximum membership value as the starting node of the neighborhood tree.

Construction of the neighborhood tree

Step 3: For each of the starting node, repeat

Step 4: For each neighboring region of the starting node, add a child node to the tree. (These are first level child nodes).

Step 5: For each of the first level child node, repeat

Step 6: For each neighboring region of the child node, merge the regions in the child node and the neighboring region. If the label of the merged region and the label of the starting node are the same, add this node to the neighborhood tree, else prune this node.

Step 7: Go to Step 6 until all neighboring regions are added to the tree or pruned.

Step 8: Go to Step 5 until all first level child nodes are processed.

Traversing neighborhood tree for labelling

Step 9: Starting from the starting node of the neighborhood tree, search for the node having maximum membership value obtained from trained object component.

Step 10: Save label, membership and rectangular coordinates calculated in Step 9.

Step 11: Go to Step 3 until all starting nodes are processed.

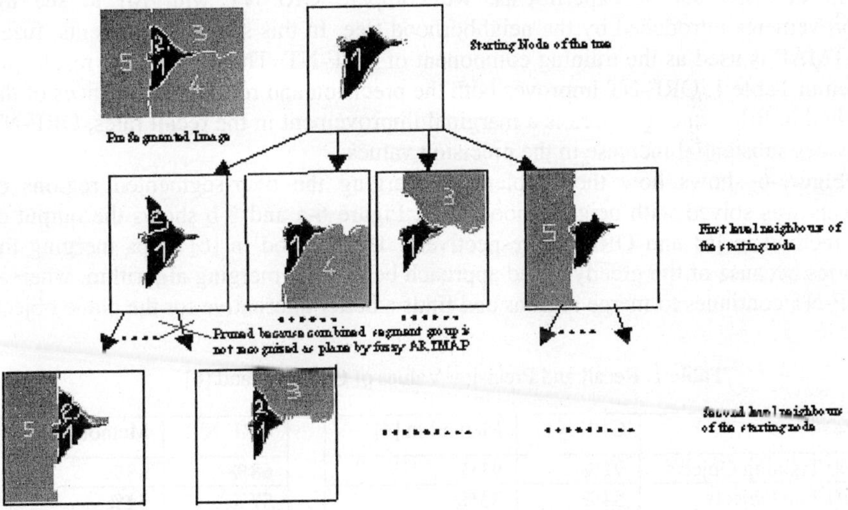

Fig. 4. Construction of the neighborhood tree for a pre-segmented image

2.4 Querying

The output of the labelling algorithm provides us a set of labelled regions and their membership values. In the querying process, the user selects a query object among the test set and the object in the database are shown to the user from highest to lowest membership values. Figure-5 shows the first 5 query results and corresponding membership values for the query object "plane" where fuzzy ARTMAP is used in training phase.

0.9996 0.9991 0.9989 0.9986 0.9985

Fig. 5. First 5 query results and corresponding membership values

3 Experimental Results

The proposed content-based image retrieval framework is developed in C++ Builder and tested over a subset of Corel Draw image database. 10 object classes, namely, *Antelope, Bear, Cheetah, Horse, Fish, Fox, Penguin, Plane, Sun Set, and Train,* are selected from the images of Corel Draw. In order to form the training set, 30 images are selected for each object class, from Corel Draw image database. Test set for the queries are formed by randomly selecting additional 30 images for each class from the same data set. Total of 600 images for the training and test stages are segmented using the N-cut segmentation algorithm, yielding 3154 and 2605 unlabelled regions for the training and test data, respectively. This data set was also used in [6].

In the first set of experiments, we compare ORF-NT with [6] to see the improvements introduced by the neighborhood tree. In this set of experiments, fuzzy ARTMAP is used as the training component of ORF-NT. The comparison results are given in Table 1. ORF-NT improves both the precision and recall performances of the method in [6]. Although there is a marginal improvement in the recall rates, ORF-NT provides substantial increase in the precision values.

Figure-6 shows how the problem of merging the over-segmented regions of objects was solved with neighborhood trees. Figure 6-a and 6-b shows the output of the method in [6] and ORF-NT respectively. The method in [6] stops merging the regions because of the greedy based approach behind the merging algorithm, whereas ORF-NT continues to merge regions and finds a better alternative for the plane object.

Table 1. Recall and Precision Values of ORF-NT and [6]

	ORF-NT	Method in [6]		ORF-NT	Method in [6]
300 Training Objects	**92%**	**91%**		**68%**	**65%**
300 Test Objects	**84%**	**83%**		**57%**	**54%**

a) Recall Values b) Precision Values

a) b)

Fig. 6. Example labellings of [6] and proposed method for plane object

In the second set of experiments, we tested the performance of ORF-NT with two different training algorithms which are fuzzy ARTMAP and AdaBoost algorithms. The results are then compared to plain Euclidean distance for image retrieval. In our experiments we have seen that fuzzy ARTMAP is more suitable than Adaboost and Euclidean distance algorithms for object-based image retrieval for Corel database and Mpeg-7 features.

In the Euclidean distance experiments, two feature vectors are simply compared to each other using the Euclidean distance between them. For each of the feature vector in the training set, the nearest 10 feature vectors are retrieved. Among these, the label, which appears the most frequently, is selected as the label of the query feature vector. If the number of occurrence of two labels are the same, then the minimum ranked label is selected as the label of the query feature. Fuzzy ARTMAP and Adaboost methods are implemented from the references given in Section 2.2.1 and 2.2.2 respectively. The comparison results are presented in Table 2.

Table 2. Performance of ORF-NT with Fuzzy ARTMAP, Adaboost and Euclidean distance training algorithms. Numbers correspond to the percentage of correctly recognized samples.

	FUZZY ARTMAP	ADABOOST	EUCLIDEAN
300 Training Objects	**92%**	**88%**	**71%**
300 Test Objects	**84%**	**79%**	**61%**

Table 2 indicates the retrieval rates of ORF-NT for the fuzzy ARTMAP, Adaboost and Euclidean distance training algorithms. As it is expected, the fuzzy ARTMAP and Adaboost provides a very significant increase in the performance of content based image retrieval system. Additionally, for this particular dataset and feature space, fuzzy ARTMAP yields better results than Adaboost.

4 Conclusion

In this study, an object retrieval framework called ORF-NT, which uses neighborhood tree is proposed. Rather than merging the N Cut segments in an image using a greedy based algorithm as in [6], the Neighborhood Tree is introduced and used for object detection. The systematic merging of the search algorithm applied on the neighborhood tree, facilitates extracting the query object from a set of over segmented regions.

In our experiments, ORF-NT is run to compare two different training methods, namely, Fuzzy ARTMAP and Adaboost. We have seen that fuzzy ARTMAP outperformed the Adaboost method. The superiority of Fuzzy ARTMAP compared to the Adaboost method in the image retrieval problems is due to two major reasons: First of all, Adaboost selects the most salient features and weights them to form a strong classifier from the weak classifiers, whereas Fuzzy ARTMAP weights all the features and use almost all of them.

Secondly, fuzzy ARTMAP architecture introduces new nodes to split an object class in case it has `dissimilar` features. Therefore, the Fuzzy ARTMAP method can assign dissimilar vectors into the same object class. This structure allows to assign, for example, different birds to the class of birds. Such property does not exist in the Adaboost method. Since the segmentation may results in many different regions for the same object, we need to deal with large within class variances. Adaboost can not cope with distinct representations of the same class.

References

1. Carpenter G. A., Grossberg S., Markuzon N., Reynolds J. H., Rosen D. B.: Fuzzy ARTMAP: A Neural Network Architecture for Incremental Supervised Learning of Analog Multidimensional Maps. IEEE Transactions on Neural Networks, Vol. 3, No :5. (1992)
2. Freund Y., Schapire R. E.: A Short Introduction to Boosting. Journal of Japanese Society for Artificial Intelligence (1999)
3. Berchtold,Bohm C., Keim D., Kriegel H.: A cost Model for nearest neighbor search in high-dimensional data space. In Proc. ACM Symp. On Principles of Database Systems, Tuscon, Arizona, (1997) 78-86
4. Ravi Kant K.V., Agrawal D.,Abbadi A. E.,Singh A.: Dimensionality Reduction for Similarity Searching In Dynamic Databases. Computer Vision and Image Understanding. CVIU, (1998)
5. Uysal M.,Vural F. Y.: Selection of The Best Representative Feature And Membership Assignment For Content-Based Fuzzy Image Database. CIVR (2003)
6. Uysal M., Vural F. Y.: A Content Based Image Retrieval Based On The Fuzzy ARTMAP Architecture. ACM International Conference on Multimedia (2004)
7. Ma W.Y. , Manjunath B.: NeTra: A Toolbox for Navigating Large Image Databases. Proc. IEEE Int. Conf. Image Processing, (1997) 568-571
8. Carson C., Thomas M., Belongie S.,Hellerstein J.M., Malik J.: Blobworld: A System for Region-Based Image Indexing and Retrieval. Proc. Visual Information Systems, (1999) 1355-1360.
9. Wang J.Z., Li J., Wiederhold G.: SIMPLIcity: Semantics-Sensitive Integrated Matching for Picture Libraries. IEEE Trans. Pattern Anal. Machine Intell., vol. 23, no. 9. (2001) 947-963.
10. Mori Y, Takahashi H., Oka R. Image-to-word transformation based on dividing and vector quantizing images with words. In Proceedings of the International Workshop on Multimedia Intelligent Storage and Retrieval Management, (1999)
11. Duygulu P., Barnard K., N de Fretias, Forsyth D.: Object recognition as machine translation: Learning a lexicon for a fixed image vocabulary. In Proceedings of the European Conference on Computer Vision, (2002) 97-112
12. Li J., Wang J.Z.: Automatic Linguistic Indexing of Pictures By a Statistical Modeling Approach. IEEE Trans. Pattern Anal. Machine Intell., vol. 25, (2003)

13. Shi J., Malik J.: Normalized Cuts and Image Segmentation. IEEE Transactions and Pattern Analysis and Machine Intelligence,(1997)
14. Cieplinski L., Kim W., Ohm J.-R., Pickering M., Yamada A.: MPEG-7 Visual part of eXperimentation Model Version 12.0. International Organisation for standardization ISO/IEC JTC1/SC29/WG11 (2001)

Text Categorization with Class-Based and Corpus-Based Keyword Selection

Arzucan Özgür, Levent Özgür, and Tunga Güngör

Department of Computer Engineering, Boğaziçi University,
Bebek, İstanbul 34342, Turkey
{ozgurarz, ozgurlev, gungort}@boun.edu.tr

Abstract. In this paper, we examine the use of keywords in text categorization with SVM. In contrast to the usual belief, we reveal that using keywords instead of all words yields better performance both in terms of accuracy and time. Unlike the previous studies that focus on keyword selection metrics, we compare the two approaches for keyword selection. In corpus-based approach, a single set of keywords is selected for all classes. In class-based approach, a distinct set of keywords is selected for each class. We perform the experiments with the standard Reuters-21578 dataset, with both boolean and tf-idf weighting. Our results show that although tf-idf weighting performs better, boolean weighting can be used where time and space resources are limited. Corpus-based approach with 2000 keywords performs the best. However, for small number of keywords, class-based approach outperforms the corpus-based approach with the same number of keywords.

Keywords: keyword selection, text categorization, SVM, Reuters-21578.

1 Introduction

Text categorization is a learning task, where pre-defined category labels are assigned to documents based on the likelihood suggested by a training set of labelled documents. Many learning algorithms such as k-nearest neighbor, Support Vector Machines (SVM) [1], neural networks [2], linear least squares fit, and Naive Bayes [3] have been applied to text classification. A comparison of these techniques is presented in [4].

Text categorization methods proposed in the literature are difficult to compare. Datasets used in the experiments are rarely same in different studies. Even when they are the same, different studies usually use different portions of the datasets or they split the datasets as training and test sets differently. Thus, as Sebastiani [5] and Yang and Liu [4] argue, most of the results in the literature are not comparable. Some recent studies consider different classification methods by using standard datasets [4,5,6,7], which enable us to compare these.

We use the standard Reuters-21578 dataset in our study. We have used ModApte split, in which there are 9,603 training documents and 3,299 test documents. We have used all the classes that exist both in the training and the test

P. Yolum et al.(Eds.): ISCIS 2005, LNCS 3733, pp. 606–615, 2005.

sets. Our dataset thus consists of 90 classes and is highly skewed. For instance, seven classes have only one document in the training set, and most of the classes have less than ten documents in the training set.

SVM, which is one of the most successful text categorization methods, is a relatively new method that evolved in recent years [4,7]. It is based on the Structural Risk minimization principle and was introduced by Vapnik in 1995 [8]. It has been designed for solving two-class pattern recognition problems. The problem is to find the decision surface that separates the positive and negative training examples of a category with maximum margin. SVM can be also used to learn linear or non-linear decision functions such as polynomial or radial basis function (RBF). Pilot experiments to compare the performance of various classification algorithms including linear SVM, SVM with polynomial kernel of various degrees, SVM with RBF kernel with different variances, k-nearest neighbor algorithm and Naive Bayes technique have been performed [7]. In these experiments, SVM with linear kernel was consistently the best performer. These results confirm the results of the previous studies by Yang and Liu [4], Joachims [1], and Forman [6]. Thus, in this study we have used SVM with linear kernel as the classification technique. For our experiments we used the SVM^{light} system, which is a rather efficient implementation by Joachims [9] and has been commonly used in previous studies [1,4,6].

Keyword selection can be implemented in two alternative ways. In the first one, which we name as *corpus-based keyword selection*, a common keyword set for all classes that reflects the most important words in all documents is selected. In the alternative approach, named as *class-based keyword selection*, the keyword selection process is performed separately for each class. In this way, the most important words specific to each class are determined. This technique has been implemented in some recent studies. One of these studies involves the categorization of internet documents [10]. A method for evaluating the importance of a term with respect to a class in the class hierarchy was proposed in that study. Another study is about clustering the documents [11]. Main focus of that paper is to increase the speed of the clustering algorithm. For this purpose, the authors have tried to make the method of extracting meaningful unit labels for document clusters much faster by using class-based keywords. In both studies, class-based keyword selection approach has been considered, but it was not compared with all words approach or with the corpus-based keyword selection approach.

In SVM-based text categorization, generally all available words in the document set are used instead of limiting to a set of keywords [1,4,7]. In some studies, it was stated that using all the words leads to the best performance and using keywords is unsuccessful with SVM [6,12]. An interesting study by Forman covers the keyword selection metrics for text classification using SVM [6]. While this study makes extensive use of class-based keywords, it naturally does not cover some of the important points. The main focus of the study is on the keyword selection metric; there does not exist a comparison of the class-based and corpus-based keyword selection approaches. Also, all the experiments were performed using boolean weighting algorithm and the study lacks a time complexity comparison between the results.

The aim of this paper is to evaluate the use of keywords for SVM-based text categorization. The previous studies focus on keyword selection metrics such as chi-square, information gain, tf-idf, odds ratio, probability ratio, document frequency, and bi-normal separation [6,13,14]. In this study we use tf-idf and, instead of the keyword selection metric, we focus on the comparison of the two keyword selection approaches, corpus-based keyword selection approach and class-based keyword selection approach. Unlike most studies, we also perform time complexity analysis. We aim to reach better results in less time and space complexity, which enables us to achieve good classification performance with limited machine capabilities and time. There are many situations in which only a small number of words are essential to classify the documents. Our research in this paper involves the inquiry of the optimal number of keywords for texts in text categorization.

The paper is organized as follows: Section 2 discusses the document representation and Section 3 gives an overview of the keyword selection approaches. In Section 4, we describe the standard Reuters-21578 dataset we have used in the experiments, our experimental methodology, evaluation metrics, and the results we have obtained. We conclude in Section 5.

2 Document Representation

Documents should first be transformed into a representation suitable for the classification algorithms to be applied. In our study, documents are represented by the widely used vector-space model, introduced by Salton *et al.* [15]. In this model, each document is represented as a vector **d**. Each dimension in the vector **d** stands for a distinct term in the term space of the document collection. We use the bag-of-words representation and define each term as a distinct word in the set of words of the document collection. To obtain the document vectors, each document is parsed, non-alphabetic characters and mark-up tags are discarded, case-folding is performed (i.e. all characters are converted to the same case-to lower case), and stopwords (i.e. words such as "an", "the", "they" that are very frequent and do not have discriminating power) are eliminated. We use the list of 571 stopwords used in the Smart system [15,16]. In order to define words that are in the same context with the same term and consequently to reduce dimensionality, we stem the words by using Porter's Stemming Algorithm [17], which is a commonly used algorithm for word stemming in English. We represent each document vector **d** as

$$\mathbf{d}=(w_1, w_2, \ldots, w_n)$$

where w_i is the weight of ith term of document **d**.

There are various term weighting approaches studied in the literature [18]. Boolean weighting and tf-idf (term frequency-inverted document frequency) weighting are two of the most commonly used ones.

In boolean weighting, the weight of a term is considered to be 1 if the term appears in the document and it is considered to be 0 if the term does not appear in the document:

$$w_i = \begin{cases} 1, & \text{if } tf_i > 0 \\ 0, & \text{otherwise} \end{cases} \quad (1)$$

where tf_i is the raw frequency of term i in document d.

tf-idf weighting scheme is defined as follows:

$$w_i = tf_i \cdot \log\left(\frac{n}{n_i}\right) \quad (2)$$

where tf_i is the same as above, n is the total number of documents in the document corpus and n_i is the number of documents in the corpus where term i appears. tf-idf weighting approach weights the frequency of a term in a document with a factor that discounts its importance if it appears in most of the documents, as in this case the term is assumed to have little discriminating power. Also, to account for documents of different lengths we normalize each document vector so that it is of unit length.

In his extensive study of feature selection metrics for SVM-based text classification, Forman used only boolean weighting [6]. However, the comparative study of different term weighting approaches in automatic text retrieval performed by Salton and Buckley reveals that the commonly used tf-idf weighting outperforms boolean weighting [18]. On the other hand, boolean weighting has the advantages of being very simple and requiring less memory. This is especially important in the high dimensional text domain. In the case of scarce memory resources, less memory requirement also leads to less classification time. Thus, in our study, we used both the boolean weighting and the tf-idf weighting schemes.

3 Keyword Selection

Most of the previous studies that apply SVM to text categorization use all the words in the document collection without any attempt to identify the important keywords [1,4]. On the other hand, there are various remarkable studies on keyword selection for text categorization in the literature [6,13,14]. As stated above, these studies mainly focus on keyword selection metrics and employ either the corpus-based or the class-based keyword selection approach, do not use standard datasets, and mostly lack a time complexity analysis of the proposed methods. In addition, most studies do not use SVM as the classification algorithm. For instance, Yang and Pedersen use kNN and LLSF [13], and Mladenic and Grobelnic use Naive Bayes in their studies on keyword selection metrics [14]. Later studies reveal that SVM performs consistently better than these classification algorithms [1,4,6].

In this study, we focus on the two keyword selection approaches, corpus-based keyword selection and class-based keyword selection. These two approaches have not been studied together in the literature. We also compare these keyword selection approaches with the alternative method of using all words without any keyword selection. Our focus is not on the keyword selection metric, thus we use the most commonly used tf-idf metric. In the corpus-based keyword selection approach, the terms that achieve the highest tf-idf score in the overall corpus are selected as the keywords. This approach favors the prevailing classes and gives penalty to classes with small number of training documents in document corpora where there is high skew. In the class-based keyword selection approach, on the other hand, distinct keywords are selected for each class. This approach gives equal weight to each class in the keyword selection phase. So, less prevailing classes are not penalized. This approach is also suitable for the SVM classifier as it solves two class problems.

4 Experiment Results

4.1 Document Data Set

In our experiments, we used the Reuters-21578 document collection, which is considered as the standard benchmark for automatic document categorization systems [19].

The documents in Reuters-21578 have been collected from Reuters newswire in 1987. This corpus consists of 21,578 documents. 135 different categories have been assigned to the documents. The maximum number of categories assigned to a document is 14 and the mean is 1.24. This dataset is highly skewed. For instance, the "earnings" category is assigned to 2,709 training documents, but 75 categories are assigned to less than 10 training documents. 21 categories are not assigned to any training documents. 7 categories contain only one training document and many categories overlap with each other such as "grain", "wheat", and "corn".

In order to divide the corpus into training and test sets, mostly the modified Apte (ModApte) split has been used [19]. With this split the training set consists of 9,603 documents and the test set consists of 3,299 documents. For our results to be comparable with the results of other studies, we also used this splitting method. We also removed the classes that do not exist both in the training set and in the test set, remaining with 90 classes out of 135. The total number of distinct terms in the corpus after preprocessing is 20,307. We report the results for the test set of this corpus.

4.2 Evaluation Metrics

To evaluate the performance of the keyword selection approaches we use the commonly used F-measure metric, which is equal to the harmonic mean of recall (ρ) and precision (π) [4]. ρ and π are defined as follows:

$$\pi_i = \frac{TP_i}{TP_i + FP_i}, \quad \rho_i = \frac{TP_i}{TP_i + FN_i} \tag{3}$$

Here, TP_i (True Positives) is the number of documents assigned correctly to class i; FP_i (False Positives) is the number of documents that do not belong to class i but are assigned to class i incorrectly by the classifier; and FN_i (False Negatives) is the number of documents that are not assigned to class i by the classifier but which actually belong to class i.

The F-measure values are in the interval (0,1) and larger F-measure values correspond to higher classification quality. The overall F-measure score of the entire classification problem can be computed by two different types of average, *micro-average* and *macro-average* [4].

Micro-averaged F-Measure. In micro-averaging, F-measure is computed globally over all category decisions. ρ and π are obtained by summing over all individual decisions:

$$\pi = \frac{TP}{TP+FP} = \frac{\sum_{i=1}^{M} TP_i}{\sum_{i=1}^{M}(TP_i + FP_i)}, \quad \rho = \frac{TP}{TP+FN} = \frac{\sum_{i=1}^{M} TP_i}{\sum_{i=1}^{M}(TP_i + FN_i)} \tag{4}$$

where M is the number of categories. Micro-averaged F-measure is then computed as:

$$F(\text{micro-averaged}) = \frac{2\pi\rho}{\pi+\rho} \tag{5}$$

Micro-averaged F-measure gives equal weight to each document and is therefore considered as an average over all the document/category pairs. It tends to be dominated by the classifier's performance on common categories.

Macro-averaged F-Measure. In macro-averaging, F-measure is computed locally over each category first and then the average over all categories is taken. π and ρ are computed for each category as in Equation 3. Then F-measure for each category i is computed and the macro-averaged F-measure is obtained by taking the average of F-measure values for each category as:

$$F_i = \frac{2\pi_i\rho_i}{\pi_i+\rho_i}, \quad F(\text{macro-averaged}) = \frac{\sum_{i=1}^{M} F_i}{M} \tag{6}$$

where M is total number of categories. Macro-averaged F-measure gives equal weight to each category, regardless of its frequency. It is influenced more by the classifier's performance on rare categories. We provide both measurement scores to be more informative.

4.3 Results and Discussion

Tables 1 and 2 display the micro-averaged and macro-averaged F-measure results for boolean and tf-idf document representations for all words and for keywords ranging in number from 10 to 2000, respectively. From Table 1, we can conclude that class-based keyword selection achieves higher micro-averaged F-measure performance than corpus-based approach for small number of keywords. In text categorization, most of the learning takes place with a small but crucial portion of keywords for a class [2]. Class-based keyword selection, by definition, focuses on this small portion; on the other hand, corpus-based approach finds general keywords concerning all classes. So, with few keywords, class-based approach achieves much more success by finding more crucial class keywords. Corpus-based approach is not successful with that small portion, but has a steeper learning curve that reaches the peak value of our study (86.1%) with 2000 corpus-based keywords, which exceeds the success scores of recent studies with standard usage of Reuters-21578 [4,5].

Boolean class-based approach performs always worse than tf-idf class-based approach for all number of keywords. This is an expected result, previous studies show parallel results with boolean approach [18].

Table 1. Micro-averaged F-measure results

# of keywords	Boolean (class-based)	tf-idf (corpus-based)	tf-idf (class-based)
10	0,738	0,425	0,780
30	0,780	0,543	0,814
50	0,802	0,628	0,831
70	0,802	0,671	0,833
100	0,806	0,697	0,838
200	0,811	0,761	0,838
300	0,819	0,786	0,839
400	0,823	0,804	0,842
500	0,821	0,813	0,848
1000	0,820	0,845	0,854
1200	0,818	0,850	0,855
1500	0,818	0,859	0,853
2000	0,818	0,861	0,855
All words	0,817	0,857	0,857

Table 2. Macro-averaged F-measure results

# of keywords	Boolean (class-based)	tf-idf (corpus-based)	tf-idf (class-based)
10	0,481	0,010	0,500
30	0,469	0,030	0,515
50	0,472	0,051	0,519
70	0,466	0,082	0,510
100	0,443	0,091	0,508
200	0,398	0,162	0,511
300	0,384	0,207	0,492
400	0,385	0,242	0,494
500	0,377	0,263	0,494
1000	0,349	0,373	0,498
1200	0,345	0,388	0,494
1500	0,332	0,425	0,492
2000	0,328	0,431	0,492
All words	0,294	0,439	0,439

Table 3. Classification time in seconds

# of keywords	Boolean (class-based)	tf-idf (class-based)
10	5	3
30	5	5
50	7	7
70	9	6
100	10	14
200	11	14
300	17	17
400	18	22
500	20	31
1000	25	40
1200	27	41
1500	31	42
2000	35	44
All words	43	66

From Table 2, we can conclude that class-based keyword selection achieves consistently higher macro-averaged F-measure performance than corpus-based approach. The high skew in the distribution of the classes in the dataset affects the macro-averaged F-measure values in a negative way because macro-average gives equal weight to each class instead of each document and documents of rare classes tend to be more misclassified. By this way, the average of correct classifications of classes drops dramatically for datasets having many rare classes. Class-based keyword selection is observed to be very useful for this skewness. As stated above, with even a small portion of words (50-100-200), class-based tf-idf method reaches 50% success which is far better than the 43.9% success of tf-idf with all words. Rare classes are characterized in a successful way with class-based keyword selection, because every class has its own keywords for the categorization problem. Corpus-based approach shows worse results because most of the keywords are selected from prevailing classes which prevents rare classes to be represented fairly by their keywords.

Table 3 shows the classification times for class-based boolean and class-based tf-idf approaches. We do not display the results for the corpus-based tf-idf approach as its time-complexity is similar to that of the class-based tf-idf approach. We observe that when we use a small number of keywords in the class-based tf-idf approach we gain a lot from time without losing much from performance. For instance, when we use 70 keywords, the classification phase is 10 times faster than the classification phase in the case where all words are used. In addition, the macro-averaged F-measure performance for 70 keywords is better than the case where all words are used and the micro-averaged F-measure performance is not much worse. Another observation is that time complexity of boolean class-based approach is better than tf-idf class-based approach. This is an expected result because boolean approach consumes less space and performs less operations than tf-idf approach. In situations where we have limited time and space resources, we may sacrifice from performance by using class-based boolean approach, which gives around 82% success rate and can be deemed as satisfying.

5 Conclusion

In this paper we investigate the use of keywords in text categorization with SVM. Unlike the previous studies that focus on keyword selection metrics, we study the performance of the two approaches for keyword selection, corpus-based approach and class-based approach. We use the standard Reuters-21578 dataset and both boolean and tf-idf weighting schemes. We analyze the approaches in terms of micro-averaged F-measure, macro-averaged F-measure and classification time.

Generally all of the words in the documents were used for categorization with SVM. Keyword selection was not performed in most of the studies; even, in some studies, keyword selection was stated to be unsuccessful with SVM [6,12]. In contrast to these studies we reveal that keyword selection improves the performance of SVM both in terms of F-measure and time. For instance, corpus-based approach with 2000 keywords performs the best in much less time than the case where all words are used. In the corpus-based approach the keywords tend to be selected from the prevailing classes. Rare classes are not represented well by these keywords. However, in the class-based approach, rare classes are represented equally well as the prevailing classes because each class is represented with its own keywords for the categorization problem. Thus, the class-cased tf-idf approach with small number of keywords (50-100) achieves consistently higher macro-averaged F-measure performance than both the corpus-based approach and the approach where all the words are used. It also achieves higher micro-averaged F-measure performance than corpus-based approach when a small number of keywords is used. This is important as there is a lot of gain from classification time when small number of keywords is used.

When we compare the tf-idf and boolean weighting approaches we see that class-based tf-idf approach is more successful than class-based boolean approach. However, in situations where we have limited time and space resources, we may sacrifice from performance by using class-based boolean approach, which gives around 82% success rate and can be deemed as satisfying.

Acknowledgment

This work has been supported by the Boğaziçi University Research Fund under the grant number 05A103.

References

1. Joachims, T.: Text Categorization with Support Vector Machines: Learning with Many Relevant Features. European Conference on Machine Learning (ECML) (1998)

2. Özgür, L., Güngör, T., Gürgen, F.: Adaptive Anti-Spam Filtering for Agglutinative Languages. A Special Case for Turkish, Pattern Recognition Letters, **25** no.16 (2004) 1819–1831
3. McCallum, A., Nigam, K.: A Comparison of Event Models for Nave Bayes Text Classification. Sahami, M. (Ed.), Proc. of AAAI Workshop on Learning for Text Categorization (1998), Madison, WI, 41–48
4. Yang, Y., Liu, X.: A Re-examination of Text Categorization Methods. In Proceedings of SIGIR-99, 22nd ACM International Conference on Research and Development in Information Retrieval, Berkeley, US (1996)
5. Sebastiani, F.: Machine Learning in Automated Text Categorization. ACM Computing Surveys **34** no. 5 (2002) 1–47
6. Forman, G.: An Extensive Empirical Study of Feature Selection Metrics for Text Classification. Journal of Machine Learning Research **3** (2003) 1289–1305
7. Özgür, A.: Supervised and Unsupervised Machine Learning Techniques for Text Document Categorization. Master's Thesis (2004), Bogazici University, Turkey
8. Burges, C. J. C.: A Tutorial on Support Vector Machines for Pattern Recognition. Data Mining and Knowledge Discovery Vol. 2 No. 2 (1998) 121–167
9. Joachims, T.: Advances in Kernel Methods-Support Vector Learning. chapter Making Large-Scale SVM Learning Practical MIT-Press (1999)
10. Lin, S-H., Shih C-S., Chen, M. C., Ho, J-M.: Extracting Classification Knowledge of Internet Documents with Mining Term Associations: A Semantic Approach. In Proc. of ACM/SIGIR (1998), Melbourne, Australia 241–249
11. Azcarraga, A. P., Yap, T., Chua, T. S.: Comparing Keyword Extraction Techniques for Websom Text Archives. International Journal of Artificial Intelligence Tools **11** no. 2 (2002)
12. Aizawa, A.: Linguistic Techniques to Improve the Performance of Automatic Text Categorization. In Proceedings of 6th Natural Language Processing Pacific Rim Symposium (2001), Tokyo, JP 307–314
13. Yang, Y., Pedersen J. O.: A Comparative Study on Feature Selection in Text Categorization. In Proceedings of the 14th International Conference on Machine Learning (1997) 412–420
14. Mladenic, D., Grobelnic, M.: Feature Selection for Unbalanced Class Distribution and Naive Bayes. In Proceedings of the 16th International Conference on Machine Learning (1999) 258–267
15. Salton, G., Yang, C., Wong, A.: A Vector-Space Model for Automatic Indexing. Communications of the ACM **18** no.11 (1975) 613–620
16. ftp://ftp.cs.cornell.edu/pub/smart/ (2004)
17. Porter, M. F.: An Algorithm for Suffix Stripping. Program **14** (1980) 130–137
18. Salton, G., Buckley, C.: Term Weighting Approaches in Automatic Text Retrieval. Information Processing and Management **24** no. 5 (1988) 513–523
19. Lewis, D. D.: Reuters-21578 Document Corpus V1.0. http://kdd.ics.uci.edu/databases/reuters21578/reuters21578.html

Aligning Turkish and English Parallel Texts for Statistical Machine Translation

İlknur D. El-Kahlout and Kemal Oflazer

Faculty of Engineering and Natural Sciences, Sabancı University,
Istanbul 34956, Turkey
ilknurdurgar@su.sabanciuniv.edu, oflazer@sabanciuniv.edu
http://www.hlst.sabanciuniv.edu

Abstract. This paper presents a preliminary work on aligning Turkish and English parallel texts towards developing a statistical machine translation system for English and Turkish. To avoid the data sparseness problem and to uncover relations between sublexical components of words such as morphemes, we have converted our parallel texts to a morphemic representation and then used standard word alignment algorithms. Results from a mere 3K sentences of parallel English–Turkish texts show that we are able to link Turkish morphemes with English morphemes and function words quite successfully. We have also used the Turkish WordNet which is linked with the English WordNet, as a bootstrapping dictionary to constrain root word alignments.

1 Introduction

Availability of large amounts of so-called parallel texts has motivated the application of statistical techniques to the problem of machine translation starting with the seminal work at IBM in the early 90's [1,2]. Statistical machine translation views the translation process as a noisy-channel signal recovery process in which one tries to recover the input "signal" e, from the observed output signal f.[1] Thus given some output sequence f one tries to find

$$e^* = \arg\max_e P(e|f)$$

as that (English) sentence that maximizes the probability of giving rise to the specific output (French) sentence f. Using Bayes' law, this probability is expanded into

$$e^* = \arg\max_e P(e|f) = \arg\max_e \frac{P(f|e)P(e)}{P(f)} = \arg\max_e P(f|e)P(e)$$

since f is constant for all candidate e's. This formulation has two components: the first component called the *translation model* gives the probability of translating e

[1] Denoting *English* and *French* as used in the original IBM Project which translated from French to English using the parallel text of the Hansards, the Canadian Parliament Proceedings.

P. Yolum et al.(Eds.): ISCIS 2005, LNCS 3733, pp. 616–625, 2005.

into f and the second component called the *language model* assigns the sentence e, a certain probability among all possible sentences in the source language.

Early statistical machine translation systems used a purely word-based approach without taking into account any of the morphological or syntactic properties of the languages [2]. Later approaches exploited morphology and/or syntactic properties in one way or the other, to increase the quality of parameters for the translation model and also to rely on smaller parallel texts [1,3,4,5].

The translation model relies on model parameters that are estimated from sentence-aligned parallel texts [2]. Obviously, for accurate estimation of parameters, one needs large amounts of data which for some language pairs may not be easy to obtain. This can be further complicated by the nature of the languages involved as may be the case for the Turkish and English parallel texts. Even a cursory analysis of sentence aligned Turkish and English texts indicates that translations of certain English words to surface as various morphemes embedded into Turkish words. Thus for accurate estimation of parameters, one needs to consider sublexical structures.

In this paper, we present results from aligning Turkish and English parallel texts towards developing a translation model from English to Turkish for use in a statistical machine translation system. We use morphology in a similar way to Lee [4], but with further exploitation of allomorphy to get more accurate statistics and use a Turkish WordNet [6] that is aligned with the English WordNet [7] as a dictionary for root word alignment.

This paper is organized as follows: we start with a short overview of Turkish morphology to motivate its impact on alignment with English texts for deriving translation model parameters. We then present results from aligning Turkish texts with English texts, followed by the use of the aligned Turkish and English WordNets as a constraining dictionary to improve translation model parameters. We conclude by discussing future work that will make use of this translation model.

2 An Overview of Turkish Morphology

Turkish is an Ural-Altaic language, having agglutinative word structures with productive inflectional and derivational processes. Turkish word forms consist of morphemes concatenated to a root morpheme or to other morphemes, much like “beads on a string”. Except for a very few exceptional cases, the surface realizations of the morphemes are conditioned by various regular morphophonemic processes such as vowel harmony, consonant assimilation and elisions. The morphotactics of word forms can be quite complex when multiple derivations are involved. For instance, the derived modifier `sağlamlaştırdığımızdaki`[2] would be broken into surface morphemes as follows:

[2] Literally, “(the thing existing) at the time we caused (something) to become strong”. Obviously this is not a word that one would use everyday. Turkish words (excluding noninflecting frequent words such as conjunctions, clitics, etc.) found in typical running text average about 10 letters in length. The average number of bound morphemes in such words is about 2.

`sağlam+laş+tır+dığ+ımız+da+ki`

Starting from an adjectival root *sağlam*, this word form first derives a verbal stem *sağlamlaş*, meaning "to become strong". A second suffix, the causative surface morpheme *+tır* which we treat as a verbal derivation, forms yet another verbal stem meaning "to cause to become strong" or "to make strong (fortify)". The immediately following participle suffix *+dığ*, produces a participial nominal, which inflects in the normal pattern for nouns (here, for 1st person plural possessor which marks agreement with the subject of the verb, and locative case). The final suffix, *+ki*, is a relativizer, producing a word which functions as a modifier in a sentence, modifying a noun somewhere to the right.

However, if one further abstracts from the morphophonological processes involved one could get a lexical form

`sağlam+lAş+DHr+DHk+HmHz+DA+ki`

In this representation, the lexical morphemes except the lexical root utilize meta-symbols that stand for a set of graphemes which are selected on the surface by a series of morphographemic processes which are rooted in morphophonological processes some of which are discussed below, but have nothing whatsoever with any of the syntactic and semantic relationship that word is involved in. For instance, `A` stands for back and unrounded vowels *a* and *e*, in orthography, `H` stands for high vowels *ı*, *i*, *u* and *ü*, and `D` stands for *d* and *t*, representing alveolar consonants. Thus, a lexical morpheme represented as `+DHr` actually represents 8 possible allomorphs, which appear as one of *+dır, +dir, +dur, +dür, +tır, +tir, +tur, +tür* depending on the local morphophonemic context. Thus at this level of representation words that look very different on the surface, look very similar. For instance, although the words *masasında* 'on his table' and *defterinde* 'in his notebook' in Turkish look quite different, the lexical morphemes except for the root are the same: *masasında* has the lexical structure `masa+sH+ndA`, while *defterinde* has the lexical structure `defter+sH+ndA`.

The use of this representation is particularly important for the quality of translation models. Allomorphs almost always correspond to the same components in English in translation. If they are considered by themselves as the units of alignment, the statistics get fragmented and the model quality suffers. When however allomorphs are abstracted to their lexical forms, the statistics combine and the data sparseness problem is less acute.

3 Aligning English–Turkish Parallel Texts

The collection of parallel texts that we have used for this work were a 3K sentence segment of about 300K sentence parallel texts mostly from the legal and international relations domain collected from various sources. Table 1 presents some statistics on the Turkish side of the 3K sentence fragment used.

If one computes a word-level alignment between the components of parallel Turkish and English sentences one obtains an alignment like the one shown

Table 1. Statistics on Turkish texts used

Type	Count
Total tokens	58,498
Unique tokens (incl. punctuation, etc.)	11,058
Unique forms (excl. punctuation, etc)	4,078
Unique root words	1,925
Average Morphological Ambiguity	1.98

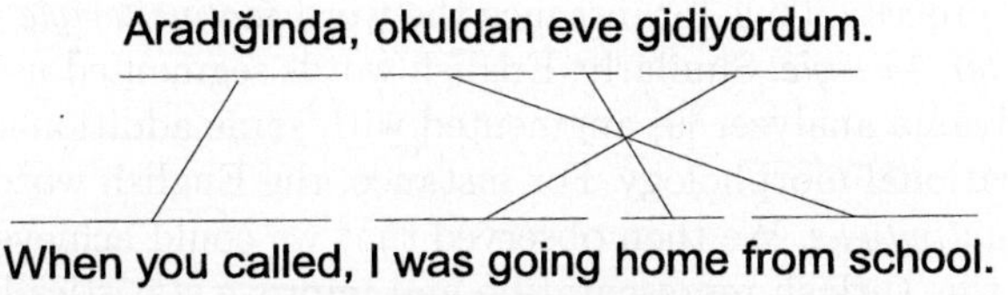
Aradığında, okuldan eve gidiyordum.
When you called, I was going home from school.

Fig. 1. Alignment between Turkish and English sentences

in Figure 1, where we can easily see Turkish words may actually correspond to whole phrases in the English sentence. One major problem with that this situation hints at is that, with a word-level alignment, one could get a situation in which when even a word occurs many times in English part, the actual for Turkish equivalent could be either missing from the Turkish part, or occur with a very low frequency, but many inflected variants of the form could be present. For example, Table 2 shows the occurrences of different forms for the root word *faaliyet* 'activity' in the parallel texts we experimented with. Although, many

Table 2. Occurrences of forms of the word *faaliyet* 'activity'

Wordform	Count	Gloss
faaliyet	3	'activity'
faaliyete	1	'to the activity'
faaliyetinde	1	'in its activity'
faaliyetler	3	'activities'
faaliyetlere	6	'to the activities'
faaliyetleri	7	'their activities'
faaliyetlerin	7	'of the activities'
faaliyetlerinde	1	'in their activities'
faaliyetlerine	5	'to their activities'
faaliyetlerini	1	'their activities (accusative)'
faaliyetlerinin	2	'of their actlvltles'
faaliyetleriyle	1	'with their activities'
faaliyette	2	'in (the) activity'
faaliyetteki	1	'that which is in activity/active'
Total	41	

forms of the root word appear, none of the forms appear very frequently and one may even have to drop occurrences of frequency 1 depending on the word-level alignment model used, further worsening the sparseness problem.

To overcome this problem, we decided to perform morphological analysis of both the Turkish and the English texts to be able to uncover relationships between root words, suffixes and function words while aligning them. First we extracted the surface morphemes of each word using a version of the morphological analyzer [8] that segmented the Turkish words along morpheme boundaries and normalized the root words in cases they were deformed due to a morphographemic process. Thus for instance the word *faaliyetleriyle* was segmented into *faaliyet +ler +i +yle*. Similarly, English words segmented using the University of Pennsylvania analyzer [9] augmented with some additional processing for handling derivational morphology. For instance, the English word *activities* was segmented as *activity+s*. We then observed that we could achieve a further normalization on the Turkish representation and improve statistics by using lexical morphemes discussed earlier.

Employing this representation on the Turkish side and conflating the statistics of the allomorphs allowed us to improve the alignments. Table 3 provides

Table 3. Counts of some surface and lexical morphemes in Turkish text

Surface Morpheme	English	Count	Lexical Morpheme	Total Count
+ler	+s	1419	+lAr	3346
+lar	+s	1927		
+da	in	193	+DA	724
+de	in	215		
+te	in	135		
+ta	in	121		
+den	from	63	+DAn	194
+dan	from	49		
+ten	from	37		
+tan	from	45		

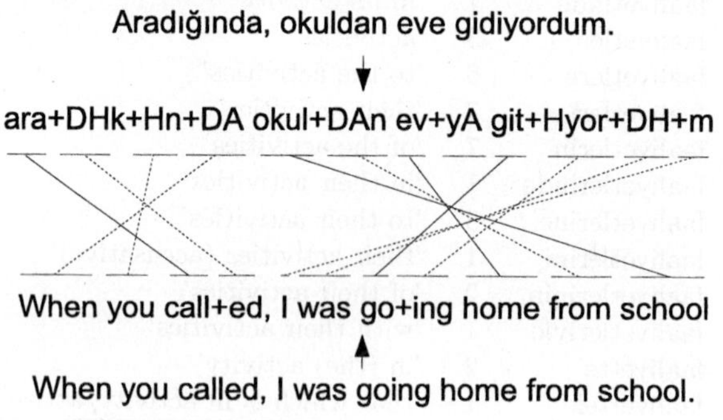
Aradığında, okuldan eve gidiyordum.
ara+DHk+Hn+DA okul+DAn ev+yA git+Hyor+DH+m
When you call+ed, I was go+ing home from school
When you called, I was going home from school.

Fig. 2. Morpheme alignment between Turkish and English sentences

the counts of some very frequent surface morphemes in Turkish text (along with their most likely English glosses), and provides the counts of the lexical meta-morphemes to which the surface morphemes are abstracted.

We morphologically analyzed and disambiguated the Turkish text and converted each word into their lexical representation so that lexical morphemes on the Turkish side were treated as "words" for the purposes of alignment. Morphological analysis was applied to English text also to segment English words into their morphemes. The alignments we expected to obtain are depicted in Figure 2 for the example sentence given earlier in Figure 1. We obtained alignments using the GIZA++ tool [10] which also gave us the translation probabilities. Table 4 shows the translation probabilities for some of the English function words and affixes with some Turkish function words and suffixes. It can be seen that even with such a small amount of parallel text, the top alignment for most cases is usually the most likely one. Of particular interest is the alignment of *will* to

Table 4. Alignments for various Turkish morphemes and English suffixes and function words

e	t	$p(t\|e)$
+ation	+mA	0.731
+ation	+Hn	0.269
be	+Hl	0.573
be	+nHn	0.185
by	+ndAn	0.342
by	taraf	0.287
+ed	+Hl	0.640
+ed	+mHş	0.274
+ed	+yAn	0.040
has	+mHş	0.776
has	+ndA	0.117
has	+mHş	0.075
in	+ndA	0.640
in	,	0.302
in	+DA	0.041
into	+yA	0.603
into	+ndA	0.148
is	+mAktA	0.605
is	+Hn	0.243
must	+lH	0.282
must	için	0.212
must	+mAlH	0.212
no	+mA	0.625
no	bir	0.315
not	+mA	0.675
not	+nA	0.116
of	+nHn	0.995
on	+ndA	0.392

e	t	$p(t\|e)$
on	+nA	0.333
pre	önce	0.542
pre	nA	0.141
pre	ilişkin	0.117
+s	+lAr	0.992
+s	,	0.005
+ship	+lHk	0.589
+ship	'	0.157
should	+mAlH	0.487
should	+nHn	0.283
should	gerek	0.162
the	+sH	0.816
the	,	0.161
under	+ndA	0.548
under	+yAn	0.343
were	+mHş	0.523
were	+Hl	0.413
which	+yAn	0.632
which	ol	0.269
while	+yken	0.399
while	+Hr	0.276
while	+ki	0.201
who	+yAn	0.881
will	+yAcAk	0.872
with	ile	0.3095
with	+ylA	0.219
with	+yA	0.200
would	+yAcAk	0.537

the Turkish future tense marker lexical morpheme *+yAcAk*[3] which is usually surrounded by other morphemes marking other relevant morphological features when it appears in a verb. Also of interest are alignments of *should* to *+mAlH*, the Turkish necessitative mood marker, of *while* to *+yken*, the adverbial derivation suffix with the semantics 'while'.

4 Wordnet as a Dictionary

Dictionaries and similar resources comprise an additional resource for obtaining more accurate alignments. Dictionaries provide possible correct word translation pair biases to the EM (expectation maximization) algorithm used in generating word-level alignments. Such biases then decrease fertility probabilities and increase translation probabilities. Conventional dictionaries such as Harper-Collins Robert French Dictionary have been used for the French-English translation developed by IBM [11].

Table 5. Best translation probabilities for word *brain*

Word t	*p(t|brain)* w/o WordNet	*t*	*p(t|brain)* with WordNet
gör	0.499	beyin	0.999
önem	0.499		

Table 6. Translation probabilities for word *basket*

t	*p(t|basket)* w/o WordNet	*t*	*p(t|basket)* with WordNet
belirle	0.199	sepet	0.999
dış	0.199		
endeks	0.199		
tüket	0.199		
+yHcH	0.199		

Another interesting resource that can be used to help alignment, in place of a dictionary, is a WordNet [7], a hierarchical network of lexical relations (such as synonymity) that words in a language are involved in. The Turkish WordNet [6] was built earlier, and is actually linked to the English WordNet using interlingual indexes, so that words in Turkish are indirectly linked to words in English that describe the same concept via these indexes. We used these relationships as a bootstrapping dictionary for the GIZA++ alignment process.

[3] This morpheme has 4 allomorphs that differ in the selection of the vowels and the elision of the initial consonant depending on the morphographemic context.

Table 7. Translation probabilities for word *credit*

t	$p(t\|credit)$ w/o WordNet	t	$p(t\|credit)$ with WordNet
kredi	0.625	kredi	0.923
sağla	0.156	sağla	0.077
ki	0.110		
+yA	0.056		
miktar	0.052		

Tables 5, 6 and 7 show improvement in translation probabilities after including dictionary with 3K sentences. One can see that the use of the WordNet as a bootstrapping dictionary significantly reduces noisy alignments – either the bogus alignments (usually stemming from the fact that there are not enough sentences to robustly estimate the alignment stastistics) are weeded out by constraining possible root word alignments, or correct alignments are boosted.

5 Future Work

Our aim in this line of work is to develop a comprehensive model of statistical machine translation from English to Turkish. The details of the model have to at least take into a probabilistic model of the morpheme morphotactics in addition to models of higher level word order. This will certainly require certain non-trivial amendments to the translation models developed so far for various other language pairs. Nevertheless, we can still use some of the basic models for translation such as the IBM Model 4, and obtain some very crude translations using the ISI ReWrite Decoder [12,13]. Table 8 shows the two very preliminary

Table 8. Very crude statistical translation results

Input: international terrorism also remain +s to be an important issue .
Statistical Translation: terörizm +nHn uluslararası aynı kal +yAcAk önem +lH bir sorun +DHr .
Surface Form: terörizmin uluslararası aynı kalacak önemli bir sorundur .
Reference Translation: uluslararası terörizm de önemli bir sorun olmaya devam etmektedir .

Input: structural reform +s in the economy are already bear +ing fruit .
Translation: yapısal reform +sH ekonomi +nHn ön sağla +mAktA meyve .
Surface Form: yapısal reformu ekonominin ön sağlamakta meyve .
Reference Translation: ekonomideki yapısal reformların meyvelerini vermeye başladığı görülmektedir .

examples of translations that are obtained using the standard models (containing no Turkish specific models) developed with only 3K sentences.

Once the basic statistical translation model for Turkish is developed, we expect to incorporate phrase level modeling and translation [14] and [15].

6 Conclusions

This paper presents the very first exploration of the issues in statistical machine translation between Turkish and English. Statistical machine translation needs substantial amounts of aligned texts from which probabilistic translation models can be trained. We have used a morphological preprocessing to identify lexical morphemes on both the Turkish and the English words to alleviate the data sparseness problem but more importantly to uncover relationships between the morphemes on the Turkish side with morphemes and function words on the English. Our results indicate that even with a very modest amount of parallel texts, the alignment we have obtained are very reasonable. We have used Turkish and English WordNets which are aligned via the interlingual index as a bootstrapping dictionary to improve root word alignments.

References

1. Brown, P.F., Della Pietra, S.A., Della Pietra, V.J., Lafferty, J.D., Mercer, R.L.: Analysis, statistical transfer, and synthesis in machine translation. In: Proceeding of TMI: Fourth International Conference on Theoretical and Methodological Issues in MT. (1992) 83–100
2. Brown, P.F., Della Pietra, S.A., Della Pietra, V.J., Mercer, R.L.: The mathematics of statistical machine translation: Parameter estimation. Computational Linguistics **19** (1993) 263–311
3. Yamada, K., Knight, K.: A syntax-based statistical translation model. In: Proceedings of the 39th Annual Meeting of the Association for Computational Linguistics, Toulouse (2001) 00–00
4. Lee, Y.S.: Morphological analysis for statistical machine translation. In: Proceedings of HLT-NAACL 2004 - Companion Volume. (2004) 57–60
5. Niessen, S., Ney, H.: Statistical machine translation with scarce resources using morpho-syntatic information. Computational Linguistics **30** (2004) 181–204
6. Bilgin, O., Çetinoğlu, O., Oflazer, K.: Building a Wordnet for Turkish. Romanian Journal of Information Science and Technology **7** (2004) 163–172
7. Fellbaum, C., ed.: WordNet, An Electronic Lexical Database. MIT Press (1998)
8. Oflazer, K.: Two-level description of Turkish morphology. Literary and Linguistic Computing **9** (1994) 137–148
9. Karp, D., Schabes, Y., Zaidel, M., Egedi, D.: A freely available wide coverage morphological analyzer for english. In: Proceedings of the 14th International Conference on Computational Linguistics. (1992)
10. Och, F.J., Ney, H.: Improved statistical alignment models. In: Proceedings of the 38th Annual Meeting of the Association for Computational Linguistics, Hong Kong (2000) 440–447

11. Brown, P.F., Della Pietra, S.A., Della Pietra, V.J., Goldsmith, M., Hajic, J., Mercer, R.L., Mohanty, R.: But dictionaries are data too. In: Procedings of the ARPA Human Language Technology Workshop, Princeton, NJ (2003) 202–205
12. Germann, U., Jahr, M., Knight, K., Marcu, D., Yamada, K.: Fast decoding and optimal decoding for machine translation. In: Procedings of ACL-01, Toulouse, France (2001)
13. Ulrich, G.: Greedy decoding for statistical machine translation in almost linear time. In: Procedings of HLT-NAACL-2003, Edmonton, AB, Canada (2003)
14. Och, F.J., Ney, H.: The alignment template approach to statistical machine translation. Computational Linguistics **30** (2004) 417–449
15. Koehn, P., Och, F.J., Marcu, D.: Statistical phrase-based translation. In: Proceedings of HLT/NAACL. (2003)

The Effect of Windowing in Word Sense Disambiguation

Ergin Altintas[1], Elif Karsligil[2], and Vedat Coskun[1]

[1] Turkish Naval Academy, Naval Science and Engineering Institute, PK 34942 Tuzla, Istanbul
{ealtintas, vedatcoskun}@dho.edu.tr
[2] Yildiz Technical University, Computer Engineering Department, Pk 34349 Yildiz, Istanbul
elif@ce.yildiz.edu.tr

Abstract. In this paper, the effect of different windowing schemes to the success rate of word sense disambiguation is probed. In these windowing schemes it is considered that the impact of a neighbor word to the correct sense of the target word should be somewhat related to it's distance to the target word. Several weighting functions are evaluated for their performance in representing this relation. Two semantic similarity measures, one of which is introduced by the authors of this paper, are used in a modified version of Maximum Relatedness Disambiguation algorithm for the experiments. This approach yielded improvements up to 4.24% in word sense disambiguation accuracy.

1 Introduction

Word sense disambiguation (WSD) is one of the most critical and widely studied Natural Language Processing (NLP) tasks, which makes NLP applications like machine translation, language understanding, information retrieval, parsing etc. more successful. In a general view, WSD can be defined as the assignment of a meaning (sense) or a definition to a target word (the word to be disambiguated) in a context (text or discourse), which is distinguishable from other meanings of this word.

Semantic similarity is a kind of semantic relatedness defining a resemblance. It is an important topic in NLP. It has also been subject to studies in Cognitive Science and Artificial Intelligence. Application areas of semantic similarity include WSD, information retrieval (IR), malapropism detection etc. There are mainly two approaches to semantic similarity. First approach is making use of a large corpus and gathering statistical data from this corpus to estimate a score of semantic similarity. Second approach makes use of the relations in the hierarchy of a thesaurus, which is generally a hand-crafted lexical database such as WordNet [1]. As in many other NLP studies, hybrid approaches that make benefit from both techniques also exist in semantic similarity.

In this work we have analyzed the performance of different windowing schemes using two conceptual hierarchy based semantic similarity metrics in a modified version of the Maximum Relatedness Disambiguation algorithm.

P. Yolum et al.(Eds.): ISCIS 2005, LNCS 3733, pp. 626–635, 2005.

The remainder of this paper is organized as follows: The similarity metric of Leacock and Chodorow and the Maximum Relatedness Disambiguation algorithm [2] is presented in Section 2. Our similarity metric is introduced in Section 3. The windowing schemes we have used in our tests are defined in Section 4. Experimental results are presented and evaluated in Section 5. Some discussion topics are probed in Section 6 and the paper is concluded in Section 7.

2 Related Work

To quantify the concept of similarity between words, some ideas have been put forth by researchers, most of which rely heavily on the knowledge available in lexical knowledge bases like WordNet. First studies in this area date back to Quilian's semantic memory model [3] where the number of hops between nodes of concepts in the hierarchical network specifies the similarity or difference of concepts.

Wu and Palmer's semantic similarity metric [4] was based on the path length between the concepts located in a hierarchical structure. Resnik introduced a new factor of relatedness called information content (IC) in [5], which is defined as the negative logarithm of the probability of a concept (c) based on its frequency in a large enough corpus:

$$IC_{res}(c) = -logP(c). \quad (1)$$

Similarity metrics of Resnik [5] , Jiang and Conrath [6] and Lin [7] all rely on the IC values assigned to the concepts in an is-a hierarchy, but their interpretations of the IC values have little differences. Using a different approach Hirst G. and St-Onge assigns relatedness scores to words instead of word senses [8]. They set different weights for different kinds of links in the semantic network and uses those weights for edge counting.

2.1 Leacock and Chodorow's Similarity Metric

The similarity metric of Leacock and Chodorow (*LCH*) is also based on the path length between two concepts (c_1, c_2) in an is-a hierarchy [9] like Wu and Palmer's. Although it is a relatively simple approach it's precision and recall are competitive to others'. The formulation is as follows:

$$Sim_{LCH}(c_1,c_2) = max\left(-log\frac{PathLength(c_1,c_2)}{2*TaxonomyDepth}\right). \quad (2)$$

The path length between the concepts is rated by twice the taxonomy depth[1]. In this way the difference between the estimations derived from different kind of taxonomies is minimized. Then the negative logarithm of this ratio is considered to be the value of similarity. If there is more than one path between the concepts, the maximum similarity value is used.

[1] This is the longest possible length between two concepts in the taxonomy.

2.2 Maximum Relatedness Disambiguation

In this paper we have used a relatively simple algorithm of WSD which is introduced in [2]. This algorithm uses a quantitative measure of similarity[2] between word senses as a metric to disambiguate them in a context. The algorithm is described in Fig.1. In this algorithm it is assumed that, the sense of a target word having the highest collective relatedness (hence similarity) value with the senses of other words in its window of context, is more likely to be the correct sense. We will test our approaches using a slightly modified version of this algorithm.

1. Select a window of n-word size context that contains the target word in the middle (as much as possible).
2. Identify candidate senses of each word in the context.
3. For each candidate sense of the target word:
   3.1. Measure the relatedness of the candidate sense of the target word to those of the surrounding words in the context.
   3.2. Sum the highest relatedness scores for each combination of senses
   3.3. Assign this sum to the candidate sense of the target word.
4. Select the candidate sense that has the highest score of relatedness.

Fig. 1. Maximum Relatedness Disambiguation Algorithm

3 Our Similarity Metric

Our similarity metric (*OUR*) is also based on the shortest path length between two concepts in an is-a hierarchy like *LCH*, but we have tried to improve over *LCH* by adding another factor which is derived from the specificities (*Spec*) of the compared senses in the hierarchy. We have formulated specificity of a concept (*c*) as follows:

$$Spec(c) = \frac{Depth(c)}{ClusterDepth(c)}. \tag{3}$$

ClusterDepth is the depth of the deepest concept which is in the same cluster with the concept *c*. We have defined our similarity metric according to two different factors. *LenFactor* is the first one of them:

$$LenFactor = \frac{ShortestLen(c_1, c_2)}{2 * TaxonomyDepth}. \tag{4}$$

LenFactor is calculated just as in *LCH* except for the negative logarithm. Our second factor makes the difference from *LCH* which is defined as follows:

$$SpecFactor = |Spec(c_1) - Spec(c_2)|. \tag{5}$$

[2] This algorithm may also use measures of semantic relatedness, but we have only used similarity metrics in our work.

SpecFactor is briefly the difference between the specificities of the two concepts. And the formulation of our similarity metric is as follows:

$$Sim_{OUR}(c_1,c_2)=\frac{1}{1+k_{\text{len}}*LenFactor+k_{\text{spec}}*SpecFactor}. \qquad (6)$$

Our metric produces results in the range [0, 1]. k_{len} and k_{spec} are the constant values to adjust the impacts of the two factors to the results. In our experiments we have used $k_{len} = 0.8$ and $k_{spec} = 0.2$.

4 Our Windowing Schemes

Windowing is used in many NLP applications. It is sometimes used for the sake of performance needs, but sometimes the necessity comes from the nature of the problem. In case of WSD both assertions are valid.

In our windowing schemes we have followed the general approach of considering the target word to be in the center of the window. For example by a window of length 11, we mean ±5 words to either side of the target word. In our experiments we only considered nouns in the WordNet hierarchy. So our window of length 11 should include 11 words which have noun forms in WordNet including the target word it self. If one side of the target word doesn't have enough words meeting this criterion then the window is expanded to the other side, until the criterion is met. If this criterion can't be met, because of the limitations of the context, then the window will contain as many words as possible.

Considering the words having different distances from the target word should have different impacts to target words correct sense, we calculated different weights to every position in a window of context according to their distance from the target word. We have defined 10 reasonable weighting functions (numbered from 0 to 9) to see, how much the different weighting functions will affect the results, and which of them will act better.

To define the weighting functions in an easier way, we first denote three functions: *Dist*(i), *Limit*(i) and *Imp*(i). i is the index of neighbor word whose weight we want to calculate. We assume target words index is zero (i_{target}=0), the words preceding the target word have negative index values and the words subsequent to target word have positive index values. We also assume that the distance of nearest (i=±1) neighbors to be 0 instead of 1. According to these assumptions we denote *Dist*(i) (distance of i to target word) as:

$$Dist(i)=|\ i\ |-1. \qquad (7)$$

And *Limit(i)* is defined as follows:

$$Limit(i)\begin{cases} max(i), & i>0 \\ \text{-1}, & i=0 \text{ (corresponds to undefined)} \\ \text{-}min(i), & i<0 \end{cases} \qquad (8)$$

For example if we have a window of size 15, which ranges from -11 to +3, our *Limit*(*i*) function will return 11 for negative *i* values and 3 for positive *i* values.

We can now define the *Imp*(*i*) (impact of *i* th neighbor to target word) as:

$$Imp(i) = \frac{Limit(i) - Dist(i)}{Limit(i)}. \tag{9}$$

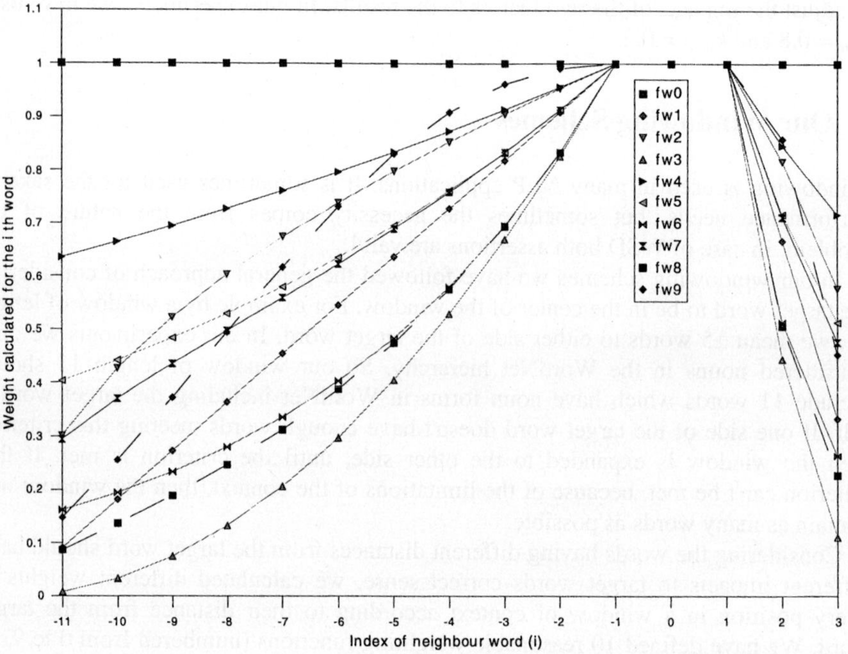

Fig. 2. All of the weighting functions ($f_{w0} - f_{w9}$) plotted together

According to these definitions we define our weighting functions as follows:

$$f_{w0}(i) = 1.$$

$$f_{w1}(i) = Imp(i).$$

$$f_{w2}(i) = \sqrt{Imp(i)}.$$

$$f_{w3}(i) = Imp(i)^2.$$

$$f_{w4}(i) = e^{\frac{Imp(i)-1}{2}}.$$

$$f_{w5}(i) = e^{Imp(i)-1}.$$

$$f_{w6}(i) = e^{2(Imp(i)-1)}.$$

$$f_{w7}(i) = \frac{1}{1 + |\ln Imp(i)|}.$$

$$f_{w8}(i) = \frac{1}{(1 + |\ln Imp(i)|)^2}.$$

$$f_{w9}(i) = \frac{1}{1 + (\ln Imp(i))^2}.$$

f_{w0} is meant to represent the case of using no weighting functions, f_{w1} is the plain impact function, f_{w2} increases[3] the impact of distance by square rooting, f_{w3} decreases the impact of distance by squaring etc. With all these functions we aimed to increase diversity. The graphical representation of these functions can be seen in Figure 2 and sample weights calculated using these weighting functions can be seen in Table 1.

Table 1. Sample weights for a window of size 15 (ranging from -11 to +3) calculated with different weighting functions (f_{w0} - f_{w9})

f_w	Index of the Neighboring Word														
	-11	**-10**	**-9**	**-8**	**-7**	**-6**	**-5**	**-4**	**-3**	**-2**	**-1**	**T[4]**	**1**	**2**	**3**
f_{w0}	1	1	1	1	1	1	1	1	1	1	1	-	1	1	1
f_{w1}	0.09	0.18	0.27	0.36	0.45	0.55	0.64	0.73	0.82	0.91	1	-	1	0.67	0.33
f_{w2}	0.3	0.43	0.52	0.6	0.67	0.74	0.8	0.85	0.9	0.95	1	-	1	0.82	0.58
f_{w3}	0.01	0.03	0.07	0.13	0.21	0.3	0.4	0.53	0.67	0.83	1	-	1	0.44	0.11
f_{w4}	0.63	0.66	0.7	0.73	0.76	0.8	0.83	0.87	0.91	0.96	1	-	1	0.85	0.72
f_{w5}	0.4	0.44	0.48	0.53	0.58	0.63	0.7	0.76	0.83	0.91	1	-	1	0.72	0.51
f_{w6}	0.16	0.19	0.23	0.28	0.34	0.4	0.48	0.58	0.7	0.83	1	-	1	0.51	0.26
f_{w7}	0.29	0.37	0.43	0.5	0.56	0.62	0.69	0.76	0.83	0.91	1	-	1	0.71	0.48
f_{w8}	0.09	0.14	0.19	0.25	0.31	0.39	0.47	0.58	0.69	0.83	1	-	1	0.51	0.23
f_{w9}	0.15	0.26	0.37	0.49	0.62	0.73	0.83	0.91	0.96	0.99	1	-	1	0.86	0.45

5 Experiments and Results

We did our WSD experiments using a subset of the noun data in English lexical sample task of Senseval-2 (training portion). In this data source, each instance was made up of three or four sentences containing a single tagged target word. Our subset contains the first 914 noun instances of this data source which includes 5 different target words (*art*, *authority*, *bar*, *bum*, and *chair*). They are used with an average of 15.42 senses per target word in our test data, which is quite a high value.

To access WordNet, we have made use of a Perl interface called *WordNet::QueryData* [10]. We have implemented our similarity metric on our own but we have used *WordNet::Similarity* [11] for *LCH* in which it was already implemented. We have modified *WordNet::SenseRelate* in order to handle our weighted windowing schemes. Since taxonomies other than the noun taxonomy are not deep enough for the similarity metrics we used, to differentiate between word senses, we have taken only nouns as our target for disambiguation. We didn't POS tag our input text, instead we followed Patwardhan et.al.'s approach [12], selecting the nearest words to our target word into our context, which have noun forms in WordNet, regardless of if they are used as a noun or not.

[3] Since the impact function's values are in the range [0, 1] square rooting increase them.

[4] There is no need to calculate weights for the target word.

Table 2. Disambiguation accuracy (%) of *OUR* using different window sizes and different weighting functions

f_w	Window Size						
	3	**5**	**7**	**9**	**11**	**13**	**15**
f_{w0}	19.04	19.31	19.86	18.87	18.05	17.40	16.41 *
f_{w1}	19.26	19.20	20.57	20.08	19.47	18.71	18.27
f_{w2}	19.31	19.09	20.30	19.31	18.49	17.94	17.40
f_{w3}	19.58	18.87	19.47	19.69	20.24	19.69	19.69
f_{w4}	19.20	19.31	19.97	19.53	18.16	17.94	16.74
f_{w5}	19.31	19.42	19.97	19.75	18.49	18.16	17.61
f_{w6}	19.04	18.87	19.80	20.08	19.80	19.15	18.27
f_{w7}	19.17	19.42	21.01 #	20.58	19.79	19.23	18.82
f_{w8}	19.04	18.84	19.80	19.91	19.58	19.69	19.85
f_{w9}	19.13	19.42	19.71	20.11	20.17	20.88	20.65 *

Table 3. Disambiguation accuracy (%) of *LCH* using different window sizes and different weighting functions

f_w	Window Size						
	3	**5**	**7**	**9**	**11**	**13**	**15**
f_{w0}	19.60	20.19	20.73	19.58	19.15	18.60	17.40 *
f_{w1}	19.88	20.35	21.83	20.95	21.11	20.34	19.91
f_{w2}	19.49	20.51	21.99	20.73	19.80	19.15	18.82
f_{w3}	19.88	19.58	20.57	20.90	21.33	21.01	21.12 *
f_{w4}	19.49	21.12	21.55	20.40	19.47	18.71	18.05
f_{w5}	19.68	20.30	21.88	20.95	20.13	18.93	18.71
f_{w6}	19.82	20.13	21.01	21.33	20.68	20.68	20.13
f_{w7}	19.71	20.30	22.10 #	20.95	20.24	19.47	19.15
f_{w8}	19.82	19.91	21.01	21.12	20.68	20.68	20.35
f_{w9}	19.60	20.40	21.55	20.95	20.13	19.47	19.47

We have done 7 tests for all the weighting functions represented in Section 5, with different window lengths ranging from 3 to 15. The results of our experiments regarding *OUR* and *LCH* can be seen in Table 2 and Table 3.

In Table 2 and Table 3 the best results are marked by '#' and the two result in the same window size which have the biggest difference is marked with '*'. We see that the best results are in window size 7 and the biggest differences are in window size 15. From the second result, we can conclude that when the window size increases the difference that the weighting functions can make also increases. The biggest differences in *OUR* and *LCH* are 4.24% and 3.72% respectively. Both of the best results were archived by f_{w7} which is an exponential function. Improvements of the best results over f_{w0} are 1.16% and 1.37% for *OUR* and *LCH* respectively.

In our experiments we have seen that using different weighting functions affect the disambiguation time slightly, but as you can see in Fig. 3, increasing the window size also increases the disambiguation time, nearly proportional.

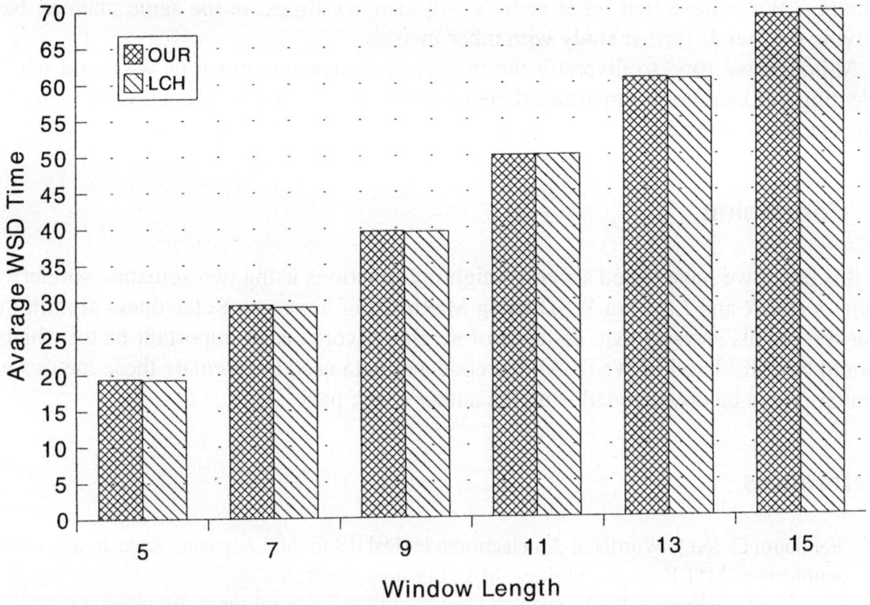

Fig. 3. Average WSD times of the metrics (*OUR* and *LCH)* for the window sizes 5 to 15

In Table 4 it can be seen that the 3 best average success rates are archived by f_{w3}, f_{w9}, f_{w8} and the worst performing function is f_{w0}, which represents the case of using no weighting functions. This result shows that using a reasonable weighting function will usually give better results than using none.

Table 4. Average success rates of weighting functions

f_{w0}	f_{w1}	f_{w2}	f_{w3}	f_{w4}	f_{w5}	f_{w6}	f_{w7}	f_{w8}	f_{w9}
18.87	20.00	19.45	20.12	19.26	19.52	19.91	20.00	20.02	20.08

In Table 5 we see that the best performing window size on average is 7.

Table 5. Average success rates of window sizes

3	5	7	9	11	13	15
19.45	19.73	20.71	20.29	19.75	19.29	18.84

6 Discussions

The correlation (%79.1) of WSD results in Table 2 and Table 3 is high enough to say that success rates of these two metrics reacts nearly the same to different windowing schemes. We believe that other metrics will also act almost in the same manner, but proving this needs further study with other metrics.

Although we tried to diversify the impact of distance as much as we could while selecting our weighting functions, there could be other weighting functions which can improve the test results.

7 Conclusion

In this paper we have tested several weighting functions using two semantic similarity metrics (*OUR* and *LCH)* in WSD using Maximizing Semantic Relatedness algorithm. Our test results showed that, distance of neighbor words is an important factor which, should be considered in WSD. All the code and data used to calculate these metrics of similarity can be downloaded from the author's web page[5].

References

1. Fellbaum C. (ed.): WordNet: An electronic lexical database. Language, Speech, and Communication. MIT Press, Cambridge, MA (1998)
2. Banerjee S., Pedersen T.: An adapted Lesk algorithm for word sense disambiguation using WordNet. In: Proceedings of Intelligent Text Processing and Computational Linguistics, Mexico City (2002)
3. Quillian, M.R.: Semantic memory. In: Minsky, M. (ed.): Semantic Information Processing. MIT Pres, Cambridge, MA (1968) 227-270
4. Wu Z., Palmer M.:Verb Semantics and Lexical Selection. In: Proceedings of the 32nd Annual Meeting of the Association for Computational Linguistics. Las Cruces, New Mexico (1994)
5. Resnik P.: Using information content to evaluate semantic similarity. In: Proceedings of the 14th International Joint Conference on Artificial Intelligence, Montreal (1995) 448-453
6. Jiang J., Conrath D.: Semantic similarity based on corpus statistics and lexical taxonomy. In: Proceedings of International Conference on Research in Computational Linguistics. Taiwan (1997) 19-33

[5] Http://www.ergin.altintas.org

7. Lin D.: An information-theoretic definition of similarity. In: Proceedings of the 15th International Conference on Machine Learning. Madison, Wisconsin (1998)
8. Hirst G., St-Onge D.: Lexical Chains as representations of context for the detection and correction of malapropisms. In: Fellbaum C. (ed.): WordNet: An electronic lexical database. Language, Speech, and Communication. MIT Press, Cambridge, MA (1998) 305-332
9. Leacock C., Chodorow M.: Combining local context and WordNet similarity for word sense identification. In: Fellbaum C. (ed.): WordNet: An electronic lexical database. Language, Speech, and Communication. MIT Press, Cambridge, MA (1998) 265-283
10. Rennie, J.: WordNet::QueryData: a Perl module for accessing the WordNet database (2000) http://search.cpan.org/dist/WordNet-QueryData
11. Pedersen, T., Patwardhan, S., Michelizzi, J.: WordNet::Similarity - Measuring the Relatedness of Concepts. AAAI (2004) 1024-1025
12. Patwardhan S., Banerjee S., Pedersen T.: Using Semantic Relatedness for Word Sense Disambiguation. In: Proceedings of the Fourth International Conference on Intelligent Text Processing and Computational Linguistics, Mexico City (2002) 241-257

Pronunciation Disambiguation in Turkish

M. Oğuzhan Külekci[1,2] and Kemal Oflazer[1]

[1] Faculty of Engineering and Natural Sciences, Sabancı University
Tuzla, Istanbul, Turkey 34956
[2] TÜBİTAK-UEKAE, Gebze, Kocaeli, Turkey 41470
kulekci@su.sabanciuniv.edu, oflazer@sabanciuniv.edu

Abstract. In text-to-speech systems and in developing transcriptions for acoustic speech data, one is faced with the problem of disambiguating the pronunciation of a token in the context it is used, so that the correct pronunciation can be produced or the transcription uses the correct set of phonemes. In this paper we investigate the problem of pronunciation disambiguation in Turkish as a natural language processing problem and present preliminary results using a morphological disambiguation technique based on the notion of *distinguishing tag sets.*

1 Introduction

Words typically have different pronunciations depending on their syntactic, and semantic properties in context. In Turkish, differences in pronunciation stem from differences in the phonemes used, the length of the vowel and the location of the primary stress [1]. The selection of the correct pronunciation requires a disambiguation process that needs to look at local morphosyntactic and semantic information to determine the correct pronunciation among alternatives. Disambiguating morphology serves a good starting basis for disambiguating of pronunciations, although it by itself, does not disambiguate all ambiguous cases of pronunciation. For example, determining the correct morphological analysis of the word *okuma* in Turkish, distinguishes between the possible pronunciations of this word in the sentences *Okuma kitabı belirlendi.* 'Reading book has been determined.' and *Saçma sapan şeyleri okuma.* 'Don't read those silly things.' In the former, *okuma* is an infinitive form derived from verb *okumak* (to read) and corresponds to phonetic representation /o-ku-"ma/ in SAMPA representation.[1,2] In the latter case the same word functions as an imperative form of the same verb, and pronunciation is represented with /o-"ku-ma/ where the primary

[1] SAMPA(Speech Assessment Methods Pronunciation Alphabet) is an international machine-readable pronunciation alphabet. For further information, please refer to www.phon.ucl.ac.uk/home/sampa. See http://www.phon.ucl.ac.uk/home/sampa/turkish.htm for the set of Turkish SAMPA phoneme representations. We use the SAMPA notation to represent pronunciations in the text, where necessary.

[2] "Indicates the stressed syllable, and - indicates a syllable boundary.

P. Yolum et al.(Eds.): ISCIS 2005, LNCS 3733, pp. 636–645, 2005.

stress is on the second syllable. A text-to-speech system would have to take this into account for proper prosody.

Morphological disambiguation has employed stochastic, knowledge-based, and hybrid methods ([2,3,4,5,6]). Morphological disambiguation for Turkish has experimented with various alternatives: Oflazer and Kuruöz [7] have used a symbolic approach using handcrafted rules. Oflazer and Tür [3] have proposed a similar scheme with rules learned automatically. Oflazer and Tür also have used voting constraints [8]. Recently, statistical morphological disambiguation of Turkish has been studied by Tür *et al.* [6]. None of these however have been applied to the problem of disambiguating pronunciation. We should also mention in passing that full morphological disambiguation is an *overkill* for disambiguating pronunciations, since in general words have less pronunciation ambiguity than morphological ambiguity.

2 Pronunciation Ambiguities in Turkish

Turkish orthography, uses 29 letters to encode its orthography but phonologically there are 34 phonemes: the 8 vowels /i, y, e, 2, a, o, 1, u/ which correspond to *i, ü, e, ö, a, o, ı,* and *u* in orthography and the 26 consonants: /p, t, tS, k, c, b, d, dZ, g, gj, f, s, S, v, w, z, Z, m, n, N, l, 5, r, j, h, G/. Orthography uses only 21 letters for consonants: /g/ and its palatal counterpart /gj/ are written as *g*, while /k/ and and its palatal counterpart /c/ are written as *k*, /5/ and its palatal counterpart /l/ are written as *l*, /v, w/ are written as *v*, and /n/ and its nasal counterpart /N/ are written as *n*. Palatalized segments (/gj, c, l/) contrast with their nonpalatalized counterparts only in the vicinity of back vowels (thus *sol* is pronounced /so5/ when used to mean 'left' vs. /sol/ when used to mean 'note in scale'). In the neighborhood of front vowels, palatality is predictable (*lig* /ligj/ 'league').[3] /G/, written as *ğ*, represents the velar fricative or glide corresponding to the historical voiced velar fricative that was lost in Standard Turkish. When it is syllable-final, some speakers pronounce it as a glide and others just lengthen the preceding vowel. We treat it as a consonant for the purposes of this work and explicitly represent it. This inventory does not include long vowels – such phonemes are indicated with a vowel length symbol.[4]

Statistics in Table 1 from Oflazer and Inkelas [1] over a 1 million corpus indicate that approximately 90% of the words in running Turkish text have single, 9% have two and only 1% has more than two distinct pronunciations. Thus, a Turkish TTS synthesizer would have to resolve ambiguities in 10% of the words in an input text.

[3] In conservative spellings of some words, contrastive velar or lateral palatality is indicated with a circumflex on the adjacent vowel, though this convention actually ambiguous and because circumflexes are also used in some words, equally sporadically, to indicate vowel length.

[4] It is certainly possible to come up with a finer set of phonemes especially for text-to-speech purposes, so that the effects of palatal consonants, etc., can be distributed to the neighboring vowels.

Table 1. Statistics about the pronunciation ambiguity observed in Turkish

Average Morphological Parse-Pronunciation Pairs / Token	1.86
Average Distinct Morphological Parses / Token	1.84
Average Distinct Pronunciations / Token	1.11
Average Distinct Pronunciations (ignoring stress) / Token	1.02

There are three types of pronunciation ambiguities in Turkish arising from (i) the phonemes used, (ii) the position of the primary stress, and (iii) differences in vowel length. The numbers in Table 1 indicate that the main source of ambiguity to be resolved in Turkish pronunciation is the position of the primary stress and if we ignore the position of the stress only 2% of the tokens has ambiguities such as differences in vowel length and consonant palatality in the root portions of the words.

These differences in pronunciations manifest themselves in various combinations, and different techniques have to be applied to resolve the resulting ambiguities:

1. The root words are homographs but have different parts-of-speech: *ama*(/"a-ma/, `ama+Conj`, 'but') vs. *ama* (/a:-"ma:/, `ama+Adj`, 'blind'). Morphological disambiguation would be able to resolve such ambiguities.
2. The root words are homographs *and* have the same part-of-speech; and further they inflect in exactly the same way: *kar* (/"kar/ 'snow') vs. *kar* (/"car/ 'profit') or *yar* (/"jar/ 'ravine') versus *yar* (/"ja:r/ 'lover'). This is akin to the disambiguation in English of *bass* ('fish') vs. *bass* ('musical instrument'). Morphological disambiguation would not be of much use here and one would have to resort to techniques used in word sense disambiguation.
3. The root words are homographs and have the same part of speech and pronounced the same, but under certain inflections, the root word with a certain sense undergoes further changes: For example for the word *hal* (/"hal/ 'fruit market' or 'state'), with the dative case marker suffix we get *hale* (/ha-"le/ `hal+Noun...+Dat`) with the first sense vs. *hale* (/ha:-"le/ `hal+Noun...+Dat` with the second sense (and an additional reading *hale* (/ha:-"le/ `hale+Noun...+Nom` 'halo')). We need to first disambiguate morphology here. If we predict that the word has nominative case, then we know the pronunciation and we are done. However, if we predict that the word has dative case, we now have to resort to word sense disambiguation to select the appropriate pronunciation depending on the sense of the root *hal* is used.
4. The words are homographs but morphological analysis produces multiple segmentations giving rise to free and bound morphemes with different semantics, morphosyntactic functions and stress marking properties: Here are some interesting examples:
   - *ajanda* (/a-"Zan-da/, `ajanda+Noun...+Nom`, 'agenda') vs. *ajanda* (/a-Zan-"da/, `ajan+Noun...+Loc` 'on the agent'). Here the first parse has a root word with exceptional root stress.
   - *fazla* (/faz-"5a/ `fazla+Adverb` 'much') vs. *fazla* (/"faz-5a/ `faz+Noun...+Ins` 'with the phase'). Here, the instrumental case marking morpheme

(*-la*) is prestressing, but happens to surface as the last two phonemes of the first root word.
- *uyardı* (/u-"jar-d1/ `uy+Verb...+Aor+Past+A3sg` 's/he/it used to fit') vs. *uyardı* (/u-jar-"d1/ `uyar+Verb...+Past+A3sg` 's/he warned'). In the first interpretation, the morpheme marking past tense is prestressing when preceded by the aorist aspect morpheme, but not otherwise.
- *attı* (/"at-t1/ `at+Noun...^ DB+Verb+Past+A3sg` 'it was a horse') vs. *attı* (/at-"t1/ `at+Verb...+Past+A3sg` 'he threw'). Similar to above, in the first interpretation, the morpheme marking past tense is prestressing when applied to a noun or adjective root (through an implicit verbal derivation.)

Most such cases can be resolved with morphological disambiguation.

5. Proper nouns especially those denoting place names that are homographs with common nouns (inflected or otherwise) usually have non-final stress in the root affecting the stress properties of their inflected versions: e.g., *Ordu* (/"or-du/ 'name of a city') versus *Ordu* (/or-"du/ 'army').[5] Although it may be possible to disambiguate whether a noun is a proper noun or not using orthographical cues such as initial capitalization and/or suffix separation characters, this may not always be possible and one may have to use again techniques akin to word sense disambiguation.
6. The problem above is further complicated in cases where a proper noun is stressed differently when it denotes a place than when it denotes person, e.g., *Aydın* (/"aj-d1n/ 'city') vs. *Aydın* (/aj-"d1n/ 'person'). To disambiguate such cases one would have to resort to named-entity recognition techniques.

Since morphological disambiguation is one of the major pronunciation disambiguation tools, in the rest of the paper we present a morphological disambiguation scheme that is based on the concept of *distinguishing tags* – that subset of morphological feature tags in a morphological analysis that is sufficient to uniquely identify that analysis, and apply it to pronunciation disambiguation. The use of word sense disambiguation and named entity recognition techniques are outside the scope of this paper.

3 Morphological Disambiguation

Morphological analysis is a prior step to be performed in many natural language processing applications. A morphological analyzer produces all the possible morphological parses of an input word. An ambiguity arises if more than one analysis are generated for one word.[6] Given a sequence of words, selecting the correct analysis among alternatives for each is defined as morphological disambiguation.

Let $W = w_1, w_2, \ldots, w_n$ be a sequence of n words. The set of morphological parses of w_i will be denoted by $M_i = \{m_{i,1}, m_{i,2}, \ldots m_{i,a_i}\}$, where a_i denotes

[5] For example, *3. Ordu Futbol Şenliği* (Third Ordu Soccer Festival) vs. *3. Ordu Futbol Takımı* (Third Army Soccer Team).

[6] In a typical running Turkish text, every word has on the average close to 2 morphological interpretations but about 60% actually have a single interpretation.

Table 2. Possible morphological parses and pronunciations of the word `karın`

Morphological Analysis	*Pronunciation*	*English Translation*
`kar+Noun+A3sg+P2sg+Nom` (m_1)	/ca:-"r1n/ (s_1)	your profit
	/ka-"r1n/ (s_2)	your snow
`kar+Noun+A3sg+Pnon+Gen` (m_2)	/ca:-"r1n/ (s_1)	of the profit
	/ka-"r1n/ (s_2)	of the snow
`kar+Verb+Pos+Imp+A2sg` (m_3)	/"ka-r1n/ (s_3)	mix it
`karı+Noun+A3sg+P2sg+Nom` (m_4)	/ka-"r1n/ (s_2)	your wife
`karın+Noun+A3sg+Pnon+Nom` (m_5)	/ka-"r1n/ (s_2)	belly

number of distinct parses for w_i. Morphological disambiguation aims to select the correct $m_{i,j}$ for each w_i in the given context. Associated with each morphological analysis m_j, are one or more possible pronunciations of the word, s_k[7] under that morphological interpretation. For example, Table 2, shows all morphological parses of word `karın` in Turkish with the corresponding pronunciations in SAMPA format, and the English gloss. There are five distinct morphological analyses but only three different pronunciations. Pronunciations 1 and 2 are associated with morphological parses 1 and 2, since the sense of the word is not in the morphological analysis. If the morphological disambiguation process for an occurrence of the word `karın` in a context results in m_3, the pronunciation would be s_3. Otherwise, if m_4 or m_5 is selected, then the reading is s_2. On the other hand, word sense disambiguation would be required to select the pronunciation in the cases of m_1 or m_2.

3.1 Modeling with Distinguishing Tags

Turkish is an agglutinative language with a highly productive inflectional and derivational morphology. Morphosyntactic analyses of words in the language require large number of tags to indicate all the morphosyntactic and morphosemantic tags encoded in a word. Statistical disambiguation methods that rely on n-gram statistics of all the tags suffer from data sparseness problem, since the tags set is very large. Tür *et al.* [6] have split up the morphological analyses across any derivational boundaries into inflectional groups (IGs) to partially overcome the problem and proposed to model each morphological parse via these IGs, each of which is actually a shorter sequence of feature tags.

This work proposes to use distinguishing tag sets of the final IG and major POS of the first IG. The *distinguishing tag sets* (DTS) of a morphological parse are defined as follows: Given a morphological analysis, let α represent the set of all subsets of the features used in its final IG. The distinguishing tag sets of the analysis are the elements from α with the smallest size, such that if we determine that the correct analysis has those features, then we can uniquely identify the complete parse.

[7] We will avoid using multiples indices to denote morphological parses pronunciations and just refer to them with m_j and s_k respectively when the word index is obvious from the context.

For example, the word `çalışmaları` has the following parses:

1. `çalış+Verb+Pos^DB+Noun+Inf2+A3pl+P3sg+Nom`
2. `çalış+Verb+Pos^DB+Noun+Inf2+A3pl+Pnon+Acc`
3. `çalış+Verb+Pos^DB+Noun+Inf2+A3pl+P3pl+Nom`
4. `çalış+Verb+Pos^DB+Noun+Inf2+A3sg+P3pl+Nom`

The `^DB` symbols mark the derivation boundaries. Every morphological parse of the word is split up into inflectional groups (IG) across any derivation boundaries. Note that, if no derivation boundaries exist in an analysis, then its first and final IG is the same. The second column of below shows the distinguishing tag sets for each analysis of the word *barışmış*.

Parse	*Possible Sets of Distinguishing Tags*	*Major POS of first IG*
1	{ +P3sg }	+Verb
2	{ +Pnon } , { +Acc }	+Verb
3	{ +A3pl,+P3pl }	+Verb
4	{ +A3sg }	+Verb

So if we determine during disambiguation that the correct parse is {+P3sg} , then that is sufficient to deduce that the correct analysis is the first one. Similarly {+A3pl,+P3pl} and {+A3sg} imply the third and fourth parses. There are two distinct DTS for the second morphological analysis and either {+Pnon} or {+Acc} identifies it.

We model each $m_{i,j}$ by the DTS and the major part-of-speech tag[8] of the first IG. Note that, a morphological analysis may have more than one DTS, but only one root major POS. Following the notation used in statement of the problem, for each $m_{i,j}$, let $O_{i,j}$ be the major POS tag of the first IG and $DTS^l_{i,j}$ be one of its DTS. The set $R_{i,j} = \{(O_{i,j}, DTS^1_{i,j}), (O_{i,j}, DTS^2_{i,j}), \ldots, (O_{i,j}, DTS^q_{i,j})\}$ contains all distinct representations of $m_{i,j}$, assuming there are q different DTS identifying the analysis. For the example word w_i `çalışmaları`; $R_{i,1}$= {(Verb, P3sg)}, $R_{i,2}$= {(Verb, Pnon), (Verb, Acc)}, $R_{i,3}$= {(Verb, (A3pl,P3pl))}, and $R_{i,4}$= {(Verb, A3sg)}. Remembering that a_i was the number of distinct analyses of word w_i, $R_i = R_{i,1} \cup R_{i,1} \cup \ldots \cup R_{i,a_i}$ contains all representations of all morphological parses for w_i, where each element $(O_{i,j}, DTS^1_{i,j})$ of the set uniquely selects an analysis.

Finally, let us define t_i as the element selected from R_i by the morphological disambiguator. The $t_i \in R_i$ determines the morphological parse. If $t_i \in R_{i,1}$ then $m_{i,1}$ is selected; if $t_i \in R_{i,2}$ then $m_{i,2}$ is selected. Similarly, $m_{i,3}$ and $m_{i,4}$ are selected if $t_i \in R_{i,3}$ and $t_i \in R_{i,4}$ respectively.

[8] This study is performed on the outputs of the Turkish morphological analyzer [9], which assigns following tags as major POS to every IG: `+Noun`, `+Adj` (adjective), `+Adverb`, `+Verb`, `+Det` (determiner), `+Conj` (conjunction), `+Pron` (pronoun), `+Dup` (duplication), `+Interj` (interjection), `+Ques` (question), `+Postp` (postposition), `+Num` (number), `+Punc` (punctuation), `+BSTag` (beginning of sentence), `+ESTag` (end of sentence).

The disambiguation of a given sequence of words begins with the identification of $O_{i,j}$ and $DTS^l_{i,j}$ for all possible values of i,j, and l in the word sequence. A Hidden Markov Model is then constructed to compute for the sequence $T = t_1, t_2 \cdots t_i \cdots t_n$, where each t_i denotes a root POS and DTS combination referring to a unique morphological analysis $m_{i,j}$. The sequence T is computed in the usual way using Equation (1) by maximizing the probability $P(T \mid W)$:

$$\underset{T}{\operatorname{argmax}}\, P(T \mid W) = \underset{T}{\operatorname{argmax}}\, \frac{P(T) \times P(W \mid T)}{P(W)} = \underset{T}{\operatorname{argmax}} P(T) \times P(W \mid T) \quad (1)$$

since $P(W)$ is constant for every selection of T.

Turkish does not have morphological generation ambiguity[9] so that the word formed by the given set of tags is unique. This implies $P(W \mid T) = 1$ all the time, and hence the equation simplifies to:

$$\underset{T}{\operatorname{argmax}}\, P(T \mid W) = \underset{T}{\operatorname{argmax}}\, P(T) \quad (2)$$

The trigram approximation for P(T)

$$P(T) = \prod_{i=1}^{n} P(t_i \mid t_{i-1}, t_{i-2}) \quad (3)$$

can now be written as

$$P(T) = \prod_{i=1}^{n} P(\, (O_{i,x}, DTS^{l_i}_{i,x}) \mid (O_{i-1,y}, DTS^{l_{i-1}}_{i-1,y}),\ (O_{i-2,z}, DTS^{l_{i-2}}_{i-2,z})\,) \quad (4)$$

where $t_i \in R_i$, $t_{i-1} \in R_{i-1}$, and $t_{i-2} \in R_{i-2}$; and x, y, z range over the respective number of ambiguous parses – $1 \le x \le a_i$, $1 \le y \le a_{i-1}$, $1 \le z \le a_{i-2}$.

The Viterbi algorithm can now be used on the expanded trigram model to find the highest scoring path, which makes up the sequence T. As an example, Figure 1 illustrates the distinguishing tag modeling used in the morphological disambiguation of the utterance "`Sadece doktora çalışmaları tartışıldı.`" (*Only the Ph.D. studies were discussed.*). The morphological parses of the words along with their ($O_{i,j}$,$DTS^l_{i,j}$) pairs are as:

1. `sadece+Adverb` : $t_{1,1}$=(Adverb,Adverb)
   `sadece+Adj^DB+Adj+Asif` : $t_{1,2}$=(Adj,Adj)[10]
2. `doktor+Noun+A3sg+Pnon+Dat` : $t_{2,1}$=(Noun,Dat)
   `doktora+Noun+A3sg+Pnon+Nom` : $t_{2,2}$=(Noun,Nom)
3. `çalışmaları` : $t_{3,1}$, $t_{3,2}$, $t_{3,3}$, $t_{3,4}$, and $t_{3,5}$ were given in the previous example.
4. `tartış+Verb^DB+Verb+Pass+Pos+Past+A3sg` : $t_{4,1}$=(Verb,Verb), $t_{4,2}$=(Verb,Pass), $t_{4,3}$=(Verb,Pos), $t_{4,4}$=(Verb,Past), $t_{4,5}$=(Verb,A3sg)

[9] Refer to Tür *et al.* [6] for a few rarely seen words that have this ambiguity.
[10] `+Asif` is a semantic marker and thus not included in the DTS generation.

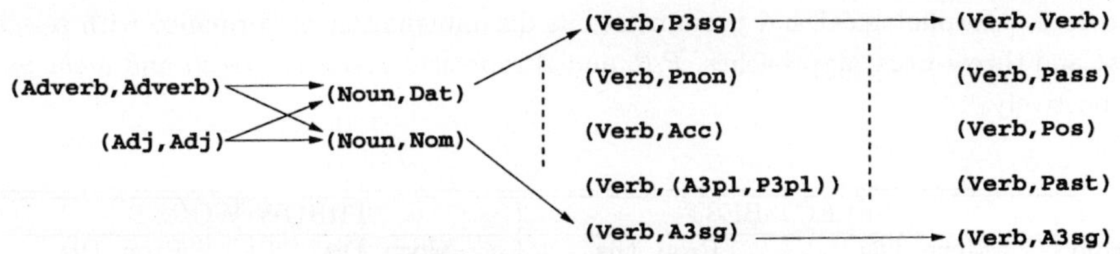

Fig. 1. Sample sentence modeled with distinguishing tags

It should be noted that we can also use a formulation using *argmin* instead of *argmax* to find the worst scoring parses and remove them to *reduce* morphological ambiguity. This may also be meaningful in pronunciation disambiguation that does not need full-fledged morphological disambiguation.

4 Implementation and Results

We have used the same 1 million-word corpus used by Tür *et al.* [6]. The morphological analysis of each word was generated by the Turkish morphological analyzer [9]. The current analyzer produces 116 feature tags of which 28 are used to label the semantic features. Throughout the study those semantic tags were discarded and our model considered only the inflectional tags while computing the DTS. If two or more parses of a word differ only in semantic tags, then they are assumed to be the same analysis.

Before any disambiguation, the precision was 55.9% and the morphological ambiguity was 1.8 parses per word. A preprocessing step which does not reduce the recall, was run on the test set before the actual disambiguator is run. The preprocessor performs some rule-based reductions to eliminate analyses that can only be seen in very restricted domains or are very infrequent or obsolete root words. At this stage the morphological ambiguity becomes 1.45 while precision rises to 68%.

The morphological parses selected by the disambiguator by Tür *et al.* ([6]) were used to train the statistical model using of the CMU-Cambridge statistical language modeling toolkit[10]. The corpus was split into 10 approximately equal pieces and a 10-fold cross validation scheme was used. In each of the tests, 9 of the segments were used as the training set from which the trigram statistics were trained, and one segment was used as the test set.

No disambiguation was performed on the ambiguous proper names because selecting their correct pronunciations require special processing beyond the morphosyntactic analysis as described in Section 2. They were left with all their morphosyntactic parses and corresponding pronunciations. Although this lowers precision a little bit, it lets further named entity recognition tasks to be performed on the corpus without loss of recall.

As described earlier, there are two choices for the disambiguation process. The first is to run the model with *argmax* and select the best scoring tag sequence and the second is to run with *argmin* to select the worst scoring tag sequence

Table 3. Morphological and pronunciations disambiguation performance with select-best and throw-worst approaches. *P*,*R*, and *A* represent *precision*, *recall* and *ambiguity* respectively.

Fold	SELECT-BEST						THROW-WORST					
	Morp. Dis.			Pron. Dis.			Morp. Dis.			Pron. Dis.		
ID	% of P	% of R	A	% of P	% of R	A	% of P	% of R	A	% of P	% of R	A
1	84.97	92.80	1.09	98.28	99.13	1.01	80.88	96.05	1.18	98.06	99.58	1.01
2	84.20	92.30	1.09	98.29	99.10	1.01	80.06	95.86	1.20	97.96	99.53	1.02
3	84.26	92.81	1.10	98.23	99.17	1.01	80.36	95.95	1.19	97.96	99.55	1.02
4	84.95	92.93	1.09	98.28	99.09	1.01	80.88	95.89	1.18	98.02	99.55	1.01
5	84.24	92.87	1.10	98.04	99.16	1.01	80.37	96.05	1.19	97.72	99.54	1.01
6	84.66	92.90	1.09	98.11	99.10	1.01	80.74	96.02	1.19	97.75	99.49	1.02
7	83.91	92.97	1.11	98.13	99.25	1.01	80.13	95.97	1.20	97.84	99.60	1.02
8	84.21	92.99	1.10	98.12	99.22	1.01	80.40	96.02	1.19	98.70	99.58	1.02
9	84.15	93.04	1.10	97.90	99.11	1.01	80.60	96.10	1.19	97.64	99.57	1.02
10	82.60	90.80	1.09	98.11	99.01	1.01	77.97	92.99	1.19	97.81	99.45	1.02
AVG	**84.22**	**92.64**	**1.10**	**98.15**	**99.13**	**1.01**	**80.24**	**95.69**	**1.19**	**97.95**	**99.54**	**1.02**

and discard the parses on that sequence away (unless the only parse for a word). The results of each experiment are summarized in Table 3 that lists both the morphological disambiguation and pronunciation disambiguation results.[11] The evaluations are done by *precision*, *recall* and *ambiguity* metrics.

5 Conclusions

We presented our results for pronunciation disambiguation in Turkish using only restricted morphological disambiguation. The morphosyntactic disambiguator was based on distinguishing tag sets which was formulated as a solution to the data sparseness problem. The number of distinct distinguishing tag sets used in the study is 374. Note that Tür *et al.* [6] reported 2194 distinct inflectional groups on the same corpus. Using a 10-fold validation experiment we found that with the throw-worst approach (using *argmin*), our approach disambiguates the pronunciations with 99.54% recall and 97.95% precision. Although this approach does not fully disambiguate the morphological ambiguities, it performs well on the disambiguation of pronunciations. The more aggressive select-best approach (using *argmax*) gives better precision values, but the recall gets lower. The remaining pronunciation ambiguities need additional techniques such as named entity recognition and word sense disambiguation.

[11] In Table 3, note that *A* is a little bit higher than its expected exact value of 1 in select-best strategy. The reason is that although the analyses of a word that differ only in their semantic tags are considered to be the same for disambiguation purposes as mentioned in Section 4, they are counted separately while extracting the statistics.

References

1. Oflazer, K., Inkelas, S.: The architecture and the implementation of a finite state pronunciation lexicon for Turkish. To appear in Computer Speech and Language (2005)
2. Brill, E.: A simple rule-based part-of-speech tagger. In: Proceedings of the third Applied Natural Language Processing, Trento, Italy (1992)
3. Oflazer, K., Tür, G.: Combining hand-crafted rules and unsupervised learning in constraint-based morphological disambiguation. In Brill, E., Church, K., eds.: Proceedings of the ACL-SIGDAT Conference on Empirical Methods in Natural Language Processing. (1996)
4. Ezeiza, N., Alegria, I., Arriola, J., Urizar, R., Aduriz, I.: Combining stochastic and rule-based methods for disambiguation in agglutinative languages. In: Proceedings of the 36th Annual Meeting of the Association for Computational Linguistics and 17th International Conference on Computational Linguistics, Montreal, Quebec, Canada (1998) 379–384
5. Hajic, J., Krbec, P., Kveton, P., Oliva, K., Petkevic, V.: Serial combination of rules and statistics: A case study in Czech tagging. In: Proceedings of ACL'01, Toulouse, France (2001)
6. Tür, D.Z.H., Oflazer, K., Tür, G.: Statistical morphological disambiguation for agglutinative languages. Computers and the Humanities **36** (2002) 381–410
7. Oflazer, K., Kuruöz, I.: Tagging and morphological disambiguation of Turkish text. In: Proceedings of the 4th Applied Natural Language Processing Conference, ACL (1994) 144–149
8. Oflazer, K., Tür, G.: Morphological disambiguation by voting constraints. In: Proceedings of ACL'97, Madrid, Spain (1997)
9. Oflazer, K.: Two level description of Turkish morphology. Literary and Linguistic Computing **9** (1994) 137–148
10. Clarkson, P., Rosenfeld, R.: Statistical language modeling using the CMU-Cambridge toolkit. In: Proceedings of Eurospeech'97, Rhodes, Greece (1997) 2707–2710

Acoustic Flow and Its Applications

Yusuf Sinan Akgul[1] and Chandra Kambhamettu[2]

[1] Department of Computer Engineering,
Gebze Institute of Technology,
Cayirova, Gebze,
Kocaeli 41400, Turkey
[2] Department of Computer and Information Sciences,
University of Delaware, Newark,
Delaware 19716, USA

Abstract. This paper introduces a new ultrasound technique called acoustic flow which is the flow of the echoed acoustic signal amplitudes in time. Acoustic flow can be used for a wide variety of medical tasks that require analysis of structures in motion. Since it is designed specifically for ultrasound, we expect acoustic flow to be robust and efficient for the analysis of ultrasound image sequences. Estimation of the acoustic flow is performed by a novel method which is based on the optimization of a deformable mesh energy. This estimation method can impose both spatial and temporal smoothness on the extracted flow vectors. It is also efficient, intuitive, and fully automatic. We applied acoustic flow to echocardiographic image sequences. We used the variance of the acoustic flow vectors to visually validate our results. The extracted flow vectors were also used to estimate the distance of the heart center from the ultrasound transducer, which showed the effectiveness of the technique. Other application areas of acoustic flow are also proposed.

1 Introduction

Ultrasound technology provides a number of unique medical investigation and imaging techniques that are either impossible or impractical with other technologies such as MRI or X Rays. Ultrasound can visualize the moving structures inside a patient's body in real-time, which helps obtaining crucial information about the dynamics of the structure. In addition, ultrasound images are produced by significantly smaller and less expensive equipment compared to other modalities. It is also painless, harmless and non-invasive. As a result, ultrasound has become a valuable medical imaging technique and it is widely employed in many different medical areas.

Popularity and significance of ultrasound makes the computerized processing of ultrasound images a very desirable task. However, this task faces challenging problems such as high levels of corrupting noise, acoustic shadowing, and mirror artifacts [1]. Most of the above problems are unique to ultrasound because ultrasound images are formed very differently from the traditional images. For this

P. Yolum et al.(Eds.): ISCIS 2005, LNCS 3733, pp. 646–655, 2005.

reason, we argue that systems based on traditional computer vision techniques to analyze ultrasound images will not be robust. In order to be able to address ultrasound-specific-problems and to take advantage of the modality, we need to develop techniques specific to ultrasound imaging.

One such technique is by Herlin and Ayache [2], who developed a spatial smoothing method for ultrasound images. Spatial smoothing is a common technique to deal with image noise. However, a direct application of a classical smoothing filter to ultrasound images represented in cartesian coordinates does not account for the varying density of the image data. To avoid the varying data density problem, Herlin and Ayache [2] construct the rectangular ultrasound images after the application of desired level of smoothing to the polar data. This kind of ultrasound-specific approach produced better tracking results.

The above method utilizes the knowledge of how the ultrasound images are produced to address known problems or to develop new techniques specific for ultrasound. Following this research trend, in this paper, we introduce a new ultrasound technique called *acoustic flow* that can be used for a wide variety of medical tasks that require analysis of structures in motion.

Ultrasound images are formed by propagating an acoustic wave from a transducer through the patients body and measuring the time-of-return and amplitude of the signals echoed off the tissue interfaces. The process is repeated about 25 to 30 times a second, producing a real-time image sequence for the moving structure. We define *acoustic flow* as the flow field of echoed acoustic signal amplitudes in time. In other words, given an echo signal amplitude for time frame f for a local image area, we try to find the most similar echo signal amplitude caused by the same transducer at time frame $f+1$. Since similar echo amplitudes are likely to be caused by the same tissue interfaces, to some degree, we expect the flow vectors to mimic the motion of the structure. In section 3, we provide a more precise definition for acoustic flow.

Once it is estimated, acoustic flow can be used to extract crucial information about the structure in motion. In order to show an example application, in section 6, we apply our technique to echocardiology where the extracted acoustic flow field is used to obtain depth of the heart center using the short axis view image sequences.

2 An Introduction to Ultrasound Visualization

In this section we will describe how different types of ultrasound images are produced. We will also introduce our formulations for each visualization type, which will later be used for the formal definition of acoustic flow.

As mentioned in the previous section, ultrasound images are formed by propagating an ultrasound wave through the patients body (Figure 1(a) shows a transducer pointing through the patient's liver.) The ultrasound images are then compiled from the echoes returned off the tissue-tissue, tissue-bone, and tissue-air interfaces [1]. There are different ways of visualizing the compiled data.

$$Corr(f,i,j,v) = \frac{\sum_{k=i-w/2}^{i+w/2} \sum_{l=j-w/2}^{j+w/2} (B_f(k,l) - M_1)(B_{f+1}(k,l+v) - M_2)}{\left[\sum_{k=i-w/2}^{i+w/2} (B_f(k,l) - M_1)^2\right]^{\frac{1}{2}} \left[\sum_{k=i-w/2}^{i+w/2} (B_{f+1}(k,l+v) - M_2)^2\right]^{\frac{1}{2}}}. \tag{1}$$

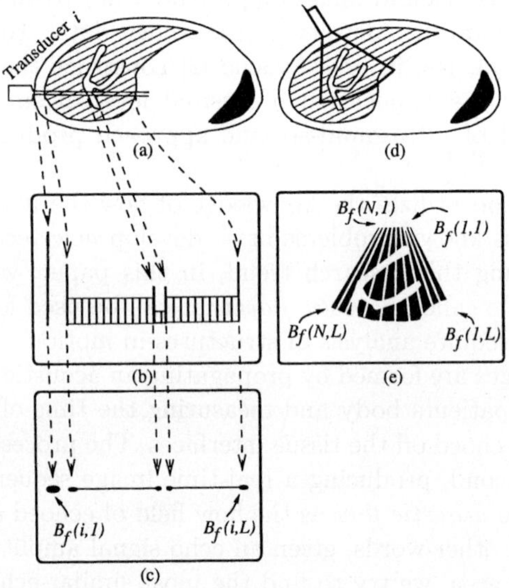

Fig. 1. (a) An ultrasound transducer pointing through the liver. (b) A-Mode display. (c) B-Mode Display: larger spots represent higher brightness (d) An array of transducers pointing through the liver. (e) 2D B-Mode display.

In time-amplified or A-mode visualization (Figure 1(b)), the data is displayed as a graph of time of return versus amplitude of the returned signal. For a transducer i emitting an ultrasound wave at time step f, we define a discrete amplitude function $A_f(i,j)$ as the amplitude of the returned signal sensed at j units of time after the time step f. Note that j is directly proportional to the distance between the transducer and the structure causing the echo. Therefore, we will use the term *depth* to refer to this index. We will assume that L is the maximum value for depth. For simplicity, the minimum value of depth can be 1.

In brightness or B-Mode display (Figure 1(c)), the amplitude of A-mode display is visualized as brightness on a line called a *B-Mode line* which is actually a 1D image. Similar to the function $A_f(i,j)$, we define a discrete brightness function $B_f(i,j)$ as the brightness amount proportional to the value of $A_f(i,j)$. In other words, the higher the value of $A_f(i,j)$ and $B_f(i,j)$, the brighter the corresponding position on a B-Mode line. In this paper, we will use the terms image intensity and echo signal amplitude interchangeably because $A_f(i,j)$ and $B_f(i,j)$ are actually linearly dependent.

If a one dimensional array of transducers, $i = 1..N$, are employed in a fan-like configuration, the resulting B-Mode lines can be displayed to form a 2D fan-like image, which is called a 2D B-Mode view(Figure 1(d-e)). In other words, if given N B-Mode lines produced by a fan-like-configured N transducers are used to form a polar image P_f, where $P_f(i,j)$ is $B_f(i,j)$, the 2D B-Mode view for time frame f is obtained by converting P_f to rectangular coordinates.

2D B-Mode views are very useful in observing the motion of the organs in real time, which is an important feature especially for cardiology and fetal measurements. We will use polar representations of 2D B-Mode views to estimate the acoustic flow for given ultrasound image sequences.

3 Formal Definition of Acoustic Flow

At the end of acoustic flow estimation process, each pixel on an ultrasound image will be assigned a flow vector. Formally, given the position of $B_f(i,j)$ on a B-Mode line produced by transducer i at time frame f, the flow vector for $B_f(i,j)$ will point to the image location of $B_{f+1}(i,j+v)$ at time frame $f+1$, where $|v|$ is the magnitude of the flow velocity per time frame. Since we are searching for the flow on images produced by the same transducer i, the flow vectors will be one dimensional. The vector valued acoustic flow function AF will assign flow vectors to given image positions. For example, if the flow vector for $B_f(i,j)$ points to the image location of $B_{f+1}(i,j+v)$, then $AF(f,i,j) = v$. Since vectors of AF are one-dimensional, we will treat them as scalar numbers.

In order to have similar image intensities or echo amplitudes at $B_f(i,j)$ and $B_{f+1}(i,j+v)$ on a 2D B-Mode image, the image regions around $B_f(i,j)$ and $B_{f+1}(i,j+v)$ are also expected to be similar. We can test the similarity between image regions by running a cross-correlation operation. Given two w by w image regions centered around positions of $B_f(i,j)$ and $B_{f+1}(i,j+v)$, the similarity between these areas can be calculated using the Equation (1), where M_1 and M_2 are the intensity averages of the regions centered around $B_f(i,j)$ and $B_{f+1}(i,j+v)$, respectively. Equation (1) will produce values closer to 1 if the image regions are similar and it will produce values closer to 0 if the image regions do not match.

In order to estimate the acoustic flow robustly, we also use a global smoothness constraint. In other words, we force the values of $AF(f,i,j)$ to change smoothly and gradually if we change any of the three indices. The way we impose the global smoothness is specifically developed for acoustic flow and it is fundamentally different from the techniques of optic flow as explained in the next section.

4 Estimation of Acoustic Flow

We use a deformable mesh approach to estimate the flow vectors of the function AF. Given the B-Mode lines $B_f(i,j)$ of a sequence of 2D B-Mode ultrasound images, for each time frame f, we form a deformable mesh M_f, which is a set of horizontally and vertically connected points in a mesh form with N columns and L rows in 3D space.

$$M_f = \begin{bmatrix} m_{11}^f & m_{12}^f & \cdots & m_{1N}^f \\ m_{21}^f & m_{22}^f & \cdots & m_{2N}^f \\ \vdots & \vdots & \vdots & \vdots \\ m_{L1}^f & m_{L2}^f & \cdots & m_{LN}^f \end{bmatrix}$$

where m_{ij}^f represents the element at the ith column and j^{th} row. The columns of M_f will correspond to transducers or the index i of $B_f(i,j)$ and the rows will correspond to depth or the index j of $B_f(i,j)$.

For each time frame, we also form a 3D volume filled with correlation values.

$$V_f(i,j,v) = Corr(f,i,j,v). \tag{2}$$

Given a set of ultrasound images for time frames $f = 1..F$, the values of AF are assigned by letting the meshes M_f deform in volumes V_f. During the mesh deformations, the mesh elements can move only in the v dimension of the volume $V_f(i,j,v)$. At the end of the mesh deformations, the v position of the m_{ij}^f will show the acoustic flow vector for the image position of $B_f(i,j)$. Figure 2 shows the initial position of M_f inside volume V_f. Note that for the initial position of M_f, the v position of m_{ij}^f is 0 for all i and j.

Each mesh M_f is associated with a mesh energy functional and the deformation of the meshes are actually the minimization of the mesh energies. The energy associated with a deformable mesh is written as

$$E_{Mesh}(M_f) = \sum_{i=1}^{N}\sum_{j=1}^{L} \alpha E_{Smo}(m_{ij}^f) + \beta E_{Time}(m_{ij}^f) + \gamma E_{Ext}(m_{ij}^f) \tag{3}$$

where α, β, and γ are the weighting parameters. For the experiments, we fixed these parameters as $\alpha = 0.25$, $\beta = 0.25$, and $\gamma = 0.5$.

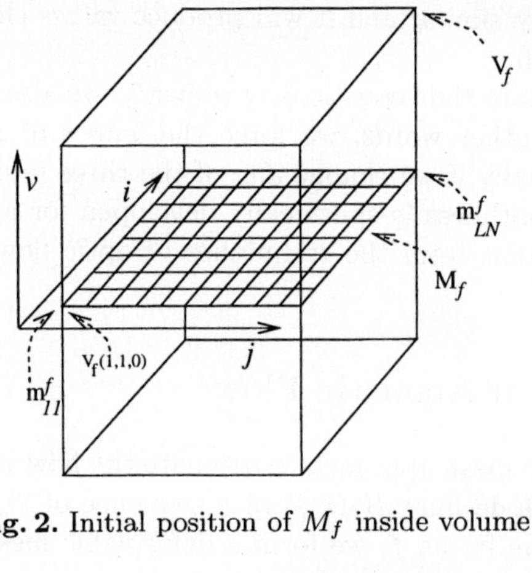

Fig. 2. Initial position of M_f inside volume V_f

The smoothness term $E_{Smo}(m_{ij})$ is responsible for the spatial smoothness of the mesh M_f. It is based on the summation of 3D dot vector products in both horizontal and vertical mesh directions and it is proportional to the angles between these 3D vectors in 3D space V_f. Formally,

$$E_{Smo}(m_{ij}^f) = \left(1 - \frac{\overrightarrow{m_{i-1j}^f m_{ij}^f} \cdot \overrightarrow{m_{ij}^f m_{i+1j}^f}}{|\overrightarrow{m_{i-1j}^f m_{ij}^f}|\,|\overrightarrow{m_{ij}^f m_{i+1j}^f}|}\right) + \left(1 - \frac{\overrightarrow{m_{ij-1}^f m_{ij}^f} \cdot \overrightarrow{m_{ij}^f m_{ij+1}^f}}{|\overrightarrow{m_{ij-1}^f m_{ij}^f}|\,|\overrightarrow{m_{ij}^f m_{ij+1}^f}|}\right).$$

The time term $E_{Time}(m_{ij}^f)$ is responsible for making the meshes of the adjacent time frames change smoothly. In other words, it imposes temporal smoothness on the estimated flow vectors. It is measured by

$$E_{Time}(m_{ij}^f) = \left(1 - \frac{\overrightarrow{m_{ij}^{f-1} m_{ij}^f} \cdot \overrightarrow{m_{ij}^f m_{ij}^{f+1}}}{|\overrightarrow{m_{ij}^{f-1} m_{ij}^f}|\,|\overrightarrow{m_{ij}^f m_{ij}^{f+1}}|}\right).$$

The external energy is the only mechanism that links the deformation of the meshes to the ultrasound images. Given the position of m_{ij}^f in 3D space V_f, if we represent the v position of m_{ij}^f by $\mathbf{vOf}(m_{ij}^f)$, a smaller value of $E_{Ext}(m_{ij}^f)$ indicates that $\mathbf{vOf}(m_{ij}^f)$ is likely to be the acoustic flow vector for the image position $B_f(i,j)$.

$$E_{Ext}(m_{ij}^f) = 1 - V_f(i, j, \mathbf{vOf}(m_{ij})). \tag{4}$$

The Equation (4) resembles the original snake energy formulation by Kass *et al.* [3]. The terms E_{Smo} and E_{Time} can be compared to the internal energy of a snake. Unlike snakes, we do not measure continuity of the deformable structure because it is satisfied by the definition of the mesh.

5 Minimization of the Mesh Energy

Given a set of ultrasound images for time frames $f = 1..F$, acoustic flow vectors are estimated by minimizing the total energy of a set of deformable meshes.

The technique we use for minimization is based on steepest-gradient-descent search. Since the mesh elements of M_f can move only along the v dimension, the gradient values along the i and j dimensions of the 3D space V_f vanish. Therefore, the gradient direction for the minimization search affects only the v positions of each m_{ij}^f, which is represented by $\mathbf{vOf}(m_{ij}^f)$. Intuitively, a one-dimensional direction vector is assigned for each mesh element. The vectors can be towards the positive or negative v directions or they can be 0.

We execute the following steps to minimize the total energy and get the values of the function AF.

1. Given a set of 2D B-Mode ultrasound images for time frames $f = 1..F$, obtain the B-Mode lines, form corresponding volumes V_f using Equation (2), construct corresponding deformable meshes M_f, and initialize the meshes M_f in volumes V_f as described in section 4.

2. Calculate the search direction D.
3. Move the mesh elements m_{ij}^{f} along the direction assigned by D until E_{Total} does not decrease.
4. If the position of the mesh elements are the same as in step 2, then go to next step. Otherwise, go to step 2.
5. The meshes are stabilized. Now, we can assign the values of AF by

$$AF(f,i,j) = \mathbf{vOf}(m_{ij}^{f})$$

For the initial iteration of the above steps, we use a higher γ value for the Equation (4) to push the meshes towards the high correlation areas. Later, we decrease γ to obtain smooth flow vectors.

Our method of minimizing the total energy resembles our previous work [4], which uses a dual-mesh approach to recover and track 3D surfaces from stereo data.

6 Application to Echocardiography

Ultrasound plays a major role in diagnostic cardiology. One of the main uses of ultrasound for cardiology is to produce real-time 2D B-Mode images of left-ventricle(LV) during the cardiac cycle. These image sequences can be used to obtain crucial information about various cardiac functions such as ejection fraction and regional wall thickening [5]. [6] decribes a recent method for this task.

We applied acoustic flow to short axis echocardiographic image sequences. Figure 3 shows a short axis echocardiogram with acoustic flow vectors superimposed. The flow vectors are magnified for visibility and only non-zero vectors are shown. At this cardiac cycle instant, the heart is deforming from diastole, where it is at the largest volume, to systole, where it is at the smallest volume. In other words, the heart is contracting to decrease its size. For the upper parts of the echocardiogram, the flow vectors are pointing mostly downwards, and for the lower part, the vectors are pointing upwards. This is exactly what is expected during heart contractions.

In order to validate our results, we calculated the variance of the acoustic flow vectors for each time frame. The flow vector variance will be small for structures under translation or no motion. It will be high if the structure is in a non-rigid motion. Figure 4-a shows the variance of each time frame versus the frame number. As expected, at systole (frame 14) and diastole (frame 37), the variance is small because heart deformation is relatively small at these cardiac cycle instants. The deformations are high immediately before and after the systole, which is typical for a normal heart cycle.

Acoustic flow can be used to measure the distance between LV center and the transducer for image frames with a flow variance above some threshold. Such an estimation is valuable for systems that need the LV center to detect the cardiac borders such as Hunter *et al.* [7].

We observe from the flow fields of the high variance frames that the flow vectors are mostly towards the depth (or j position) of the LV center for a

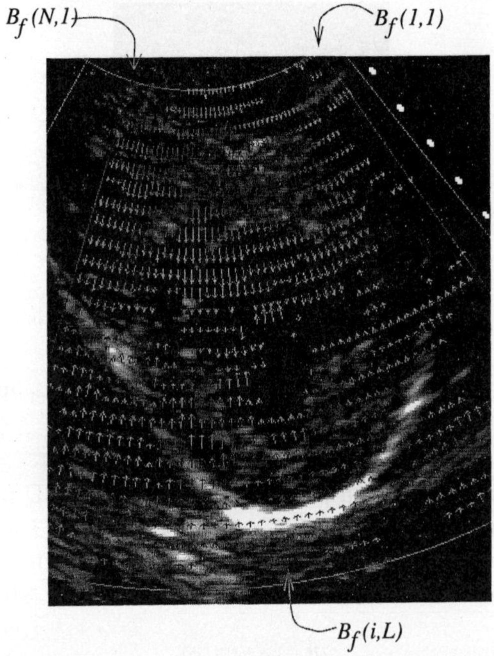

Fig. 3. Acoustic flow vectors for an image frame while the heart is deforming from diastole to systole

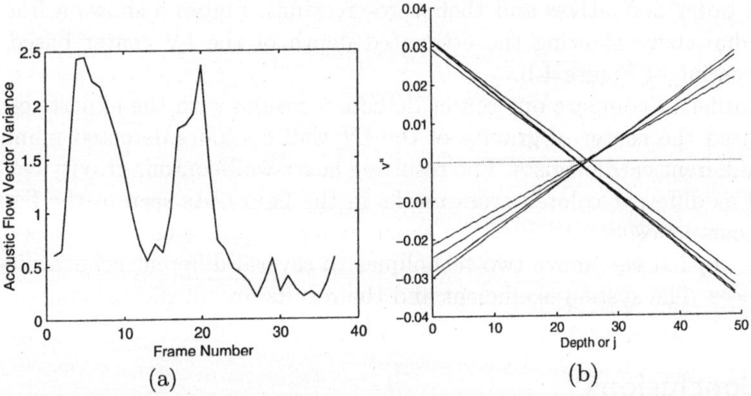

Fig. 4. (a) Acoustic flow vector variance versus frame number for a cardiac cycle. The cycle is at systole at frame number 14 and it is at diastole at frame number 37. (b) Second order derivatives of the polynomials.

contracting heart. The directions are reversed for an expanding heart. We can estimate the depth of LV center by detecting the average depth position where the flow vectors change their signs. If we assume that there is no global translation of the heart, this depth position will give us the approximate depth position of the LV center.

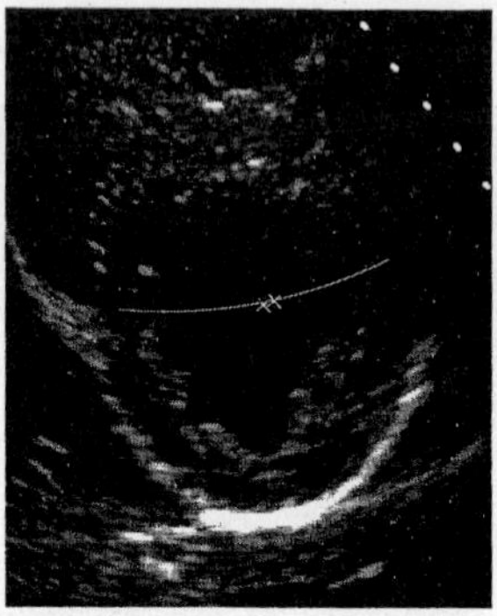

Fig. 5. Radial curve showing the estimated depth of the LV center. The marks represent the expert detected LV centers.

In order to detect this depth position, we project the 3D positions (i, j, v) of each mesh element m^f_{ij} to the j–v plane by ignoring the i positions. This will produce LN number of 2D points. Using least squares estimation, for each time frame, we then fit a third order polynomial to these points, which has the second order derivative

$$v'' = 6aj + 2b. \tag{5}$$

Zero-crossing of Equation (5) is the point where the third order polynomial changes from concave to convex or vice versa. Figure 4-b shows the corresponding second order derivatives and their zero-crossings. Figure 5 shows a frame with the radial curve showing the estimated depth of the LV center based on the zero-crossing of Figure 4-b.

In order to compare our center detection results with the expert results, we calculated the center of gravity of the LV wall contours detected manually by three different cardiologists. The resulting heart-wall-contour gravity centers are placed as different colored cross marks in the figure. As seen in the figure, our depth curve closely estimates the expert detected positions.

We applied the above two techniques to several different echocardiographic sequences. The system is efficient and the results are all encouraging.

7 Conclusions

We presented a novel ultrasound specific technique called acoustic flow, which is the flow of the echoed acoustic signal amplitudes in time. It can be used for a wide variety of medical applications that require analysis of structures in motion. It closely parallels the image formation process of ultrasound and it is fully automatic.

The experiments performed on echocardiographic image sequences showed the effectiveness of acoustic flow in producing useful information about the dynamics of the moving structures. We successfully used acoustic flow to detect the distance between the LV center and the transducer. A comparison with the expert detected centers validated the accuracy of the technique.

The main power of acoustic flow is due to the fact that it is specifically designed for the analysis of ultrasound image sequences. It takes advantage of the knowledge of how ultrasound images are produced and hence incorporates more information about the images. The newly introduced estimation technique for acoustic flow is also specifically designed for this task.

Acknowledgments

This work is supported by Grant No. R01 DC01758 from NIH and Grant No. IRI 961924 from NSF. Yusuf Akgul completed this work while he was at University of Delaware.

References

1. Meire, H., Farrant, P.: Basic Ultrasound. Wiley (1994)
2. L.H., H., Ayache, N.: Features extraction and analysis methods for sequences of ultrasound images. Image and Vision Computing **10** (1992) 673–682
3. Kass, M., Witkin, A., Terzopoulos, D.: Snakes: Active contour models. International Journal of Computer Vision (1988) 321–331
4. Akgul, Y.S., Kambhamettu, C.: Recovery and tracking of continuous 3d surfaces from stereo data using a deformable dual-mesh. In: International Conference on Computer Vision. (1999) 765–772
5. Chalana, V., Linker, D., Haynor, D., Kim, Y.: A multiple active contour model for cardiac boundary detection on echocardiographical sequences. IEEE Transactions of Medical Imaging **15** (1996) 290–298
6. Zhou, X.S., Gupta, A., Comaniciu, D.: An information fusion framework for robust shape tracking. IEEE Transactions on Pattern Analysis and Machine Intelligence **27** (2005) 115–129
7. Hunter, I., Soraghan, J., McDonagh, T.: Fully automatic left ventricular boundary extraction in echocardiographic images. Computers In Cardiology **22** (1995) 741-744

A DCOM-Based Turkish Speech Recognition System: TREN – Turkish Recognition ENgine

Hasan Palaz, Alper Kanak, Yücel Bicil, and Mehmet Uğur Doğan

The Scientific and Technical Research Council of Turkey-National Research Institute of Electronics and Cryptology, TÜBİTAK-UEKAE, Gebze, Kocaeli, PO Box 74, 41470, Turkey
akustiklab@uekae.tubitak.gov.tr

Abstract. Turkish Recognition ENgine (TREN) is a modular, Hidden Markov Model based (HMM-based), speaker independent and Distributed Component Object Model based (DCOM-based) speech recognition system. TREN contains specialized modules that allow a fully interoperable platform including a Turkish speech recognizer, a feature extractor, an end-point detector and a performance monitoring module. TREN deals with the interaction between two layers constituting the distributed architecture of TREN. The first layer is the central server, which applies some speech signal preprocessing and distributes the recognition calls to the appropriate remote servers according to their current CPU load of the recognition process. The second layer is composed of the remote servers performing the critical recognition task. In order to increase the recognition performance, a Turkish telephony speech database with a very large word corpus is collected and statistically the widest span of triphones representing Turkish is examined. TREN has been used to assist speech technologies which require a modular and multithreaded recognizer with dynamic load sharing facilities.

1 Introduction

Since speech processing technologies have a wide variety of application areas among Turkic language speaking countries with a total population of more than 200 million people, developing a robust recognition engine for Turkish language, accepted as the *language of the silk road*, is a promising field in the next generation information systems. When developing a speech recognition engine for Turkish, the recognition system must be adapted by means of vocabulary, acoustic parameters, language models and the dialog structure of Turkish.

With the rapid growth of distributed systems and speech technologies, distributed speech recognition (DSR) applications have become very attractive. In particular, the increasing use of component objects in speech processing makes DSR compatible to Personal Computers (PCs), Personal Digital Assistants (PDAs), wired and wireless network architectures or even World Wide Web (WWW) applications [1,2].

In the past decade, organizations have been moving from mainframe-based systems toward open and distributed computing environments where multiple

P. Yolum et al.(Eds.): ISCIS 2005, LNCS 3733, pp. 656–667, 2005.

computers are networked together and allowed to share data and processing responsibilities. Recently, component-based software engineering has been very popular for the large-scale speech processing system development. Distributed Component Object Model (DCOM), which is one of the industrial criteria for component-based software development, is accepted as a robust software architecture that allows applications to be built from binary software components [3]. DCOM offers many advantages, including location transparency to users, scalability, fault tolerance, load balancing, programming language independency and object orientation. Object orientation makes it easier to maintain software modules and re-use existing software objects. Thus, DCOM interoperability architecture is rapidly utilized in designing software systems for speech recognition systems. Remote communication established through DCOM makes the design and implementation of a DSR easy [3]. Generally there are three alternative strategies in the design of DSR architectures: server-only, client-only and client-server processing. In server-only processing, all speech processing are implemented at the server side. Most of the telephony speech applications or web-based speech recognition tools are good examples for server-only systems. In client-only strategy, most of the speech processing is utilized at the client side and the results are transmitted sequentially to the server. Since this approach requires powerful machines at the client side, it is not a practical solution for DSR systems. Finally, the client-server mechanism concentrates on simple and low power client devices which quantize and packetize the speech data (usually in the form of speech feature vectors) and transmit it over the communication channel to a remote speech recognition server [4,5].

One of the oldest DSR systems with client-server architecture is presented in [6] which combines three different speech recognition systems working in parallel. The system consists of one computer serving as the experimenter's station and a master of three slave computers hosting to three different speech recognition systems. Networked computers are connected with RS-232 serial communication links. The master is responsible for presenting words to be recognized and transmitting the recognition results along an algorithm based on "Enhanced Majority Rules". The overall results have shown that the distributed system performs better than the individual recognition systems.

Another good example for client-server processing is reported in [7] which examines alternative architectures for a client-server model of speech-enabled applications over the WWW. In this study, a server-only processing model is compared to a client-server model where the recognition front end runs locally at the client side and encodes the speech signal and transmits the cepstral coefficients to the recognition server over the Internet. Carrying speech features instead of pure voice, makes the system more efficient.

In [8], a hybrid approach is implemented for DSRs which is based on ability to choose arbitrary feature vectors without changing the amount of data sent to the recognition engine. The hybrid recognizer can include context in the recognition process, it is trained in a discriminative way and the client side can be adapted to specific conditions without changing the server side. Results have shown that the recognizer performs better than the traditional DSR systems under different noise conditions and the performance can be adjusted if the different features are combined.

A recent project, named *Project54*, integrates electronic devices in police cruisers into a single system [9]. *Project54* is a modular, component-based and practical speech processing system with which officers interact through a voice interface. The system is designed by considering the in-car conditions (such as noise, reverberation, microphone direction, etc.). *Project54* is COM-based and includes specialized speech recognition and text-to-speech (TTS) modules. The communication between the modules is implemented by one-to-one text messages.

Due to the emphasized advantages of distributed component objects, a multithreaded speech recognition engine for Turkish with client-server processing, namely Turkish Recognition ENgine (TREN), is proposed as an efficient solution, especially for telephony speech applications. TREN could also be adapted to a wide range of speech technologies including DSR, Voice-to-Voice (VTV) applications, Interactive Voice Response (IVR) systems, speech translators, etc. The database used to train TREN, a Turkish Telephony speech database - TURTEL (TURkish TELephony), which is a collection of spoken word sets and the most widely used triphones are examined in this set, to obtain better recognition results, as well as better utilization scores.

The organization of the paper is as follows: Section 2 discusses DCOM-based, modular and layered structure of TREN. Details of the modular software architecture and algorithms are given in Section 3. Information about TURTEL, recognition and load sharing performance of TREN are examined by giving detailed results in the experimental framework presented in Section 4. Finally, Section 5 concludes the paper.

2 TREN Modular Structure

For the complex speech processing systems, a layered architecture, which is a natural outgrowth of the client-server model, could be an effective solution concerning the problems, such as lack of scalability and portability. Compared with the traditional client-server model, layered architecture of TREN offers a natural way to separate user interface from the background of the hard work performed by the recognizer. TREN is composed of two layers: Central Server (CS) constitutes the first layer of the system, which is subjected to apply some speech processing routines (feature extraction and end-point detection) to the audio files collected as an input from third party applications or environments. CS is also responsible for the authorization of a Remote Server (RS) with the least CPU load of the recognition process (L_{PCPU}) as compared to the other RSs, all of which constitute the second layer of TREN. Once this authorization is accomplished the selected RS will become ready to serve as a recognizer. This two-layered architecture allows RSs work in a parallel and distributed manner. Note that this architecture also gives a flexibility to install or uninstall any number of machines according to the application requirements. TREN supports up to 64 simultaneous recognitions, resembling a 64-channel system.

2.1 Modules of TREN

To implement TREN, the facilities of DCOM are heavily considered and an interface-based software architecture is developed. If TREN is examined in a procedural point of view it could be separated into two folds: tasks running on the CS and on one of the RSs.

TREN is composed of 3 service-type modules waiting to be invoked by Object Remote Procedure Calls (ORPCs). These awaiting services are the core of CS and RSs, Dynamic Load Monitoring Service (DLMS), which blinks by reporting L_{PCPU} values on each RS, simultaneously. Additionally there exists 3 non-service-type modules: Feature Extraction Module (FEM), End-Point Detection Module (EPDM) and Recognition Engine (TRENCore) (See Fig. 1). As presented in Fig 2, the procedure begins with attaining of a raw file which will be processed and recognized at CS. The first front end process applied to the pure raw file is cropping the nonspeech regions of the waveform by EPDM. FEM then converts the cropped speech data to a Mel-Frequency Cepstral Coefficients based (MFCC) audio feature and stores in a file. Now the feature file to be recognized is ready to be sent to the least-loaded RS. Meanwhile, each RS computes its corresponding L_{PCPU}. CS collects current L_{PCPU} values on each RS by simple ORPCs and executes a selection algorithm to identify the least-loaded engine. After the least loaded RS is determined, the feature file is sent to the selected server via an FTP link. This lucky server is invoked by a message and it is guaranteed to transmit the coming MFCC file. On the other hand, lexicon and word network structure which is antecedently

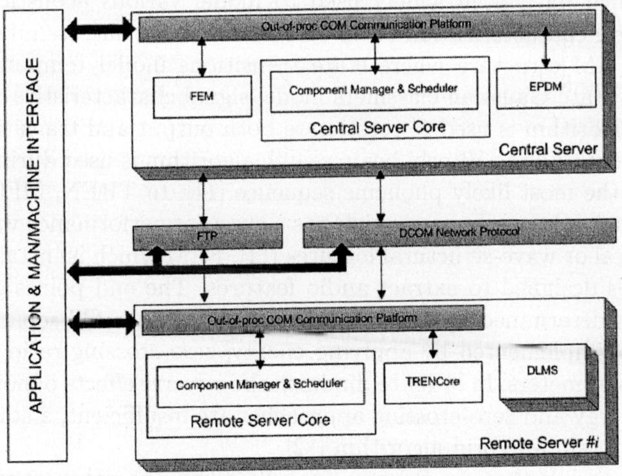

Fig. 1. Software architecture of TREN

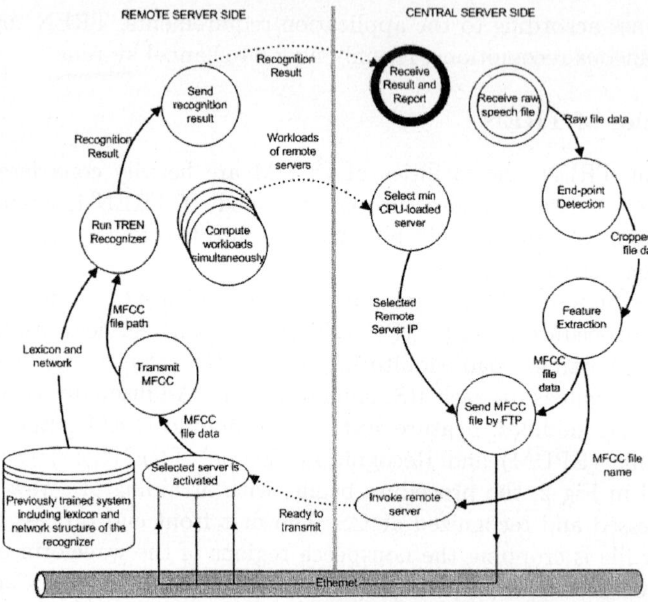

Fig. 2. Data Flow Diagram of TREN

obtained after a training procedure, is already loaded on each RS. The transmitted MFCC file is then recognized by TRENCore according to the lexicon and word network file stored as a distinct file. Finally, the recognition result is reported to CS by an ORPC and the task is accomplished. Note that, by changing the lexicon file, the recognition engine could be adapted to a different recognition space.

TRENCore is based on a very common method of Hidden Markov Models (HMM) which have been widely used to model various acoustic phenomena. The temporal characterization of an audio stream can successfully be modelled using an HMM structure where state transitions model temporal correlation and in each state Gaussian classifiers model signal characteristics. The forward-backward algorithm is used to reestimate both output and transition probabilities iteratively, and the Viterbi beam search algorithm is used during recognition to find out the most likely phoneme sequence [11]. In TREN, MFCC is used as the parametrization technique which has a superior performance with respect to other spectral or wave-structural features [11]. FEM which is installed to the CS separately is designed to extract audio features. The end points of an isolated utterance is determined by EPDM which is installed to CS separately. EPDM algorithm is implemented by applying energy, zero-crossing ratio and duration modelling parameters. In order to diminish the adverse effects of noisy conditions in which energy and zero-crossing approaches are insufficient, a state machine is applied to obtain a hybrid algorithm [12].

DLMS ensures that no RS remains idle when the other servers are heavily loaded. As reported in [13] since so-called Dynamic Load Sharing (DLS) approaches react to the system state instead of estimating the average behavior of system, they perform better than the static policies. In TREN, a separate DLS module is designed and this module is installed as a service (DLMS) to each RS to report the corresponding L_{PCPU} simultaneously. DLMS uses the Performance Data Helper (PDH) library which is an enhancement to the performance-monitoring capabilities of Windows NT-based systems.

3 Software Architecture

To implement TREN, the facilities of DCOM are heavily considered and an interface-based software architecture is developed. Since both the CS and the RSs are designed as Windows services, they are kept alert for any call. Whenever a call is detected by the service, a thread is activated and the sequence of corresponding tasks is executed through the thread procedure. As depicted in Table 1, after the validation of the speech waveform path on the CS, the method `Central_Server_Core` creates a thread and invokes the `ThreadFunc` procedure. Similarly, a RS validates the feature file path and invokes the corresponding `ThreadFunc` after the thread is created as presented in Algorithm 1.

The `ThreadFunc`of the CS first initializes the COM library. Meanwhile, each RS computes its corresponding CPU load of the recognition process. CS collects current loads on each registered RS by simple ORPCs through the DLMS interface pointer, `*iDLMS`. The least loaded RS is selected by `Select_Min_PCPU`, a method of `*iDLMS`, and the IP of the lucky RS is returned as `MinIP` . Since the sequential tasks may overload CS only, T_{max}recognition tasks are allowed. As presented in Fig 2, the speech processing front end begins with attaining of an audio file (in raw format) which will be processed and recognized at CS. First, the pure non-speech regions of the speech waveform file is discarded by EPDM. EPDM is utilized by the interface pointer `*iEPDM`. The end points (`crop_coordinates`) of the speech waveform (`path_wave`) are detected by the method `End_Point_Detect` of `*iEPDM` . After the end points are detected, removal of the silent regions of the speech waveform by `Silence_Removal` , a method of `*iEPDM` , is straightforward and the path of the cropped speech waveform (`path_EP`) is returned. The cropped speech data is then converted to a MFCC-based speech feature and stored in a file by activating `*iFEM` , an interface of FEM. Feature extraction is implemented by `Extract_Feature`, a method of `*iFEM`, and the path of MFCC file (`path_MFCC`) is returned. Now the feature file to be recognized is ready to be sent to the least-loaded RS. After the least loaded RS is determined, the feature file is sent to the selected server via an FTP link by the function `SendbyFTP`. The critical recognition tasks will then be executed on the selected RS. This lucky server is invoked by `Remote_Server_Core`, a method of the interface `*iRemoteServer`. `Remote_Server_Core`is the core procedure of the RS service which manages the components and schedules the recognition task. When a recognition request call is taken, as similar to the `Central_Server_Core`, a thread is activated and the full path of the feature file on the RS is passed as an argument to the `ThreadFunc`. On the other hand, lexicon and word network structure which are antecedently

Algorithm 1 Central_Server_Core(void)

```
output: boolean S_OK or S_{error message}
var:string path_wave, path of the wave file to be sent to RS
     integer t, time required for an object to become signaled
     Timeout, 5-second timeout interval
begin
wait until RS is invoked by the receipt of path_wave
if path_wave is not valid
     return S_{invalid path}
else
     Create a thread for the corresponding wave file
if thread is successfully created
     t = wait for the specified object to become signaled
     if t >Timeout
          return S_{timeout}
          exit thread
     else
          Invoke the ThreadFunc by passing path_wave as an argument
return S_OK
end
Procedure ThreadFunc
input:  string path_wave path of the wave file to be sent to RS
var:    *iEPDM, EPDM interface pointer
     *iFEM, FEM interface pointer
     *iRemoteServer, RS interface pointer
     *iDLMS, DLMS interface pointer
     N, number of registered RS
     MinIP, RS IP with the least load
     NumOfActiveTask, number of active recognition tasks requested by the CS
     T_max, maximum number of active recognition tasks
     crop_coordinates, frame-wise coordinates of the spoken word boundaries
     path_EP, path of the cropped speech file
     path_MFCC, path of the MFCC feature file
     path_MFCC_on_RS, MFCC feature file path on the selected least loaded RS
     RecognitionResult, recognition result of path_wave
Initialize the COM library on the current thread
LABEL1 Compute the workloads on RS_j where j = 1,···,N
MinIP = iDLMS → Select_Min_PCPU(RS_j, j = 1,···,N)
if NumOfActiveTask > T_max
     NumOfActiveTask−−
     goto LABEL1
else
     NumOfActiveTask++
     crop_coordinate = iEPDM → End_Point_Detect(path_wave)
     path_EP = iEPDM → Silence_Removal(crop_coordinates)
     path_MFCC = iFEM → Extract_Feture(path_EP)
path_MFCC_on_RS = SendbyFTP(path_MFCC, MinIP)
RecognitionResult = iRemoteServer → Remote_Server_Core(path_MFCC_on_RS)
Pass RecognitionResult to the client
end
```

obtained after a training procedure is already loaded on each recognizer and passed as an argument to the `Remote_Server_Core`. After the COM library on the current thread is initialized, the transmitted MFCC file is recognized by `Recognize`, a method of the interface `*iTRENCore`. Finally, the recognition result is reported to the CS by an ORPC and the whole task is accomplished. The details of `Remote_Server_Core`are presented in Algorithm 2.

Algorithm 2 Remote_Server_Core(path_MFCC_on_RS, lexicon, word_network)

```
input:path_MFCC_on_RS, path of the MFCC feature file on the corresponding RS
      binary file lexicon, lexicon file in binary format
      binary file word-network, word network structure for the previously trained recognizer
output: boolean S_OK or S_ {error message }
var:    integer t, time required for an object to become signaled
      Timeout, 5-second timeout interval
begin
Initialize lexicon and word_network
wait until RS is invoked by the receipt of path_MFCC_on_RS
if path_MFCC_on_RS is not valid
      return S_{invalid path}
else
      Create a thread for the corresponding feature file
if thread is successfully created
      t = wait for the specified object to become signaled
      if t >Timeout
            return S_{timeout}
            exit thread
      else
            Invoke the ThreadFunc by passing path_MFCC_on_RS as an argument
return S_OK
end
Procedure ThreadFunc
input: string path_MFCC_on_RS path of the feature file to be recognized on this selected RS
var: *iTRENCore, TRENCore interface pointer
      RecognitionResult, recognition result of path_MFCC_on_RS
begin
Initialize the COM library on the current thread
RecognitionResult = iTRENCore → Recognize(path_MFCC_on_RS)
Pass RecognitionResult to the CS
end
```

4 Experimental Framework

4.1 TURTEL Speech Database

The triphones (context-dependent phones) are widely used units for speech recognition because of their capability to better represent the acoustic characteristics of speech. In this view, TURTEL is collected by considering statistically the widely used triphones in Turkish. The probable number of triphones in Turkish is nearly 27000. Yet, this number of triphones increases the database size and inflates the search space. Thus triphones should be either clustered or reduced in number. In order to collect samples of TURTEL, it is assumed that there is a text group which models the target language extensively and is used to extract the most frequent triphones. This method has two main advantages: First, since the vocabulary has built in control, phonetically balanced vocabularies can be achieved. Second, the selected triphones can model the language extensively and no more clustering is needed. However, the building period of this vocabulary is computationally loaded and requires more effort.

The procedure followed to collect TURTEL is as follows: In order to determine the words that will form the database, a 2.2 million-word corpus is examined and the most frequent 1000 triphones, which span 88% of Turkish,are selected. 25 female and 40 male speakers utter phonetically balanced 373 words and 15 sentences in terms of triphones. These speakers' ages are in between 15 and 55 and they used 3 kinds of telephones: landline with handset, GSM and hands-free. All the utterances are collected at the multimedia laboratory of TÜBİTAK-UEKAE.

4.2 Experimental Results

In order to evaluate the performance of TREN, some adverse conditions are simulated by applying various background noises to the test set and the resulting recognition performances are measured in terms of true recognition rates. Training consists of 2 stages. First, TREN is trained by considering the whole database and this whole set is used again as the test set to identify the outlier speakers. After the speakers with an average personal word error rate are specified, they are used to determine the system's performance in a more realistic manner. The speakers with the best and the worst rate are eliminated from the test set. At the second stage 5 male and 5 female speakers whose recognition rates are in the nearest neighborhood of average recognition rate, are isolated from the whole database and used as the test set. The utterances acquired from the rest of the speakers (35 male and 20 female) is then used for the second training stage. Note that each speaker utters 373 words which are widely used in Turkish telephony speech.

In TREN, each triphone is represented by a 3-state left-to-right HMM structure. The audio stream has an 8 kHz sampling rate. The acoustic noises, which are added to the speech signal to observe the recognition performance under adverse conditions, are selected as: office, in-car, white and pink noise. The audio stream is processed over 10 msec frames, centered on 20 msec Hamming window. The MFCC feature vector is formed from 13 cepstral coefficients, including the 0th gain coefficient using 26 mel frequency bins. The resulting audio feature vector of size 26, includes the MFCC vector along with the first delta MFCC vectors.

Recognition Performance. In order to examine the recognition performance of TREN, 4 noisy conditions (office, in-car, white and pink noise) and 2 triphone statistical models (continuous and tied-mixture) are considered. In experiments the acoustic noise is applied in three different levels (6 dB SNR, 12 dB SNR and

Table 1. Recognition performance under adverse conditions

Statistical Model	Noise Type	Quiet	Noise 12 dB SNR	Noise 6 dB SNR
Continuous	Office	96.76	68.46	35.66
	In-car		85.04	78.01
	White		54.19	33.71
	Pink		60.13	30.04
Tied-mixture	Office	93.49	65.32	27.44
	In-car		81.70	70.35
	White		60.90	36.57
	Pink		61.65	27.03

Quiet). The quiet conditions may also include minor telephony speech environmental adverse effects. The true recognition rates for each test are presented in Table 1.

The results have shown that as the noise level increases the recognition performance significantly decreases. The best recognition rates are obtained under quiet conditions, as expected. However, in-car conditions do not significantly affect the overall recognition as compared with the other noisy conditions. Thus, it could be said that TREN performs well for both standard telephony speech and mobile communication purposes. On the other hand, the continuous model performs better than the tied-mixture model in all cases, except for the white noise case.

Load Sharing Performance. In order to evaluate the load sharing performance of TREN, three RSs are used (RS1 and RS3 are two identical machines with Intel Pentium 4-1.4 Ghz CPU and 512 MB RAM while RS2 is a weaker one with Pentium 3-0.8 GHz CPU and 256 MB RAM). Since L_{PCPU} is the dominating load factor on a utilized processor, it is measured as the percentage of elapsed time that the processor has used for the recognition threads. The main purpose of the simulation is to present the gain of the load sharing strategy of TREN, by comparing the cases with multi-RS versus the cases with a single RS. In order to simulate the real time execution of TREN, a fixed number of audio files (300), each of which takes approximately 1 second in length are used. The tests consist of four cases, considering the combination of two statistical models, tied-mixture and continuous, and two different network sizes with N = 373 and N = 40 words. The experiments have shown that using multiple RSs significantly decreases the total recognition time of 300 audio files in all cases. As depicted in Fig. 3, the total recognition time of multi-RS case is less than half of the single case. On the other hand, the network size significantly influences the total recognition time as expected. As the network size increases the search space increases, and this makes the recognition process more complex. For larger network sizes, the tied-mixture model performs better than the continuous model. However, due

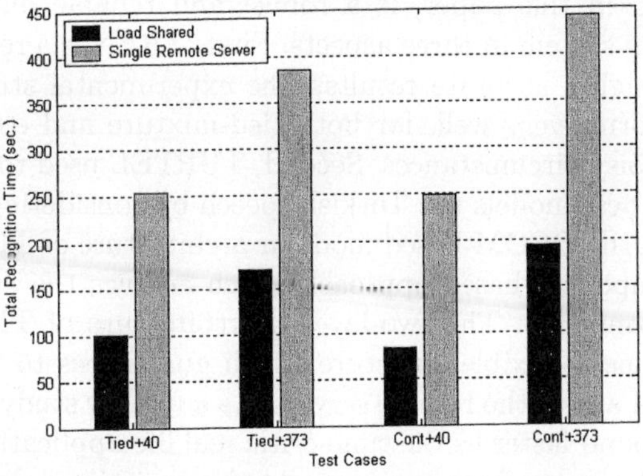

Fig. 3. Total recognition time in seconds for the single and multiple use of RSs

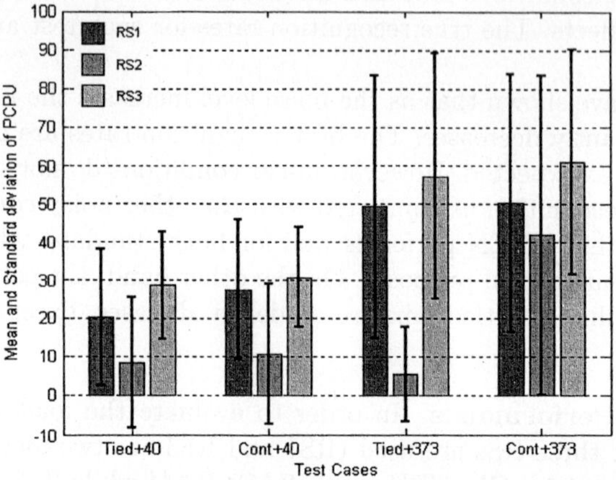

Fig. 4. Mean and standard deviation of L_{PCPU} values

to its preprocessing stage where the tied-mixture triphone pool is constructed the tied-mixture model is not efficient for small network sizes in contrast with the continuous model as presented in Fig. 3.

The mean and standard deviation of L_{PCPU} usage for each RS is depicted in Fig. 4. According to the mean and standard deviation values, RS1 and RS3 often share a large portion of L_{PCPU} while RS2 only answers the urgent recognition calls. RS2 is recoursed only when RS1 and RS3 are heavily loaded. Since the last case (the continuous model with a 373-word network) is very complex and requires much computation, the load on RS2 significantly increases.

5 Conclusion

TREN, presented in this paper, is a robust and reliable distributed Turkish speech recognition system in three aspects. First, TREN is a reliable recognition engine with its highly accurate results. The experimental studies have shown that TREN performs very well, for both tied-mixture and continuous models, under different noisy circumstances. Second, TURTEL used to train the HMM-based recognizer best models the Turkish speech by considering the widely used triphones. Third, the DCOM-based modular architecture of TREN is an object-oriented and component-based approach which enables the system to work in distributed environments. The two-layered architecture of TREN, including a CS and RSs, forms a flexible structure which guarantees to serve whenever a problem occurs in any of the remote servers. As a further study, TREN might be revisioned to respond faster as the time-critic real life applications are becoming more popular. The recognition engine could also be improved to get lower error rates for larger databases.

References

1. Goddeau, D.: Deploying Speech Application over the Web, *Proceedings of Eurospeech*, Rhodes, Greece, September (1997), 685-688
2. Sokolov, M.: Speaker Verification over the World Wide Web, *Proceedings of Eurospeech*, Rhodes, Greece, September (1997), 847-850
3. Microsoft Corp., "DCOM technical Overview," (1996)
4. "The Aurora Project," announced at Telecom 95, http://gold.ity.int/TELECOM/wt95, Geneva, October (1995)
5. Stallard, D.: The BBN SPIN System, *Voice on the Net Conference*, Boston MA, September (1997)
6. Barry, T., Solz, T., Reising, J., Williamson, D.: The Simultanous Use of Three Machine Speech Recognition Systems to Increase Recognition Accuracy, *Proceedings of IEEE National Aerospace and Electronics Conf. (NAECON)*, Vol 2., May 23-27, (1994), 667-671
7. Digalakis, V., Neumeyer, L., Perakakis, M.: Quantization of Cepstral Parameters for Speech Recognition over the World Wide Web, *IEEE Journal on Selected Areas in Communcations*, Vol. 17, Num.1, Jan (1999), 82-90
8. Stadermann, J., Righoll, G.: Flexible Feature Extraction and HMM Design for a Hybrid Speech Recognition System in Noisy Environments, *International Conference on Acoustics, Speech, Signal Processing*, Vol.3, April 6-10, (2003), 332-335
9. Kun, A. L., Miller III, W. T., Lenharth, W. H.: Modular System Architecture for Electronic Device Integration in Police Cruisers, *Proceedings of the 2002 IEEE Intelligent Vehicle Symposium*, Versailles, France, June 18-20, (2002)
10. Yapanel, Ü., Doğan, M. U., Arslan, L. M.: "Türkçe Anahtar Sözcük Yakalama Sistemi için farklı Atık Modellerinin Karşılaştırılması (Comparison of Garbage Modeling Techniques for a Turkish Keyword Spotting System)," *SIU proc.*, Gazimagusa, April (2001), 122-127
11. Rabiner, L. R., Juang, B.: *Fundamentals of Speech Recognition* P. Hall Signal Processing Series, N.Jersey, (1993)
12. Rabiner, L. R., Sambur, M. R., "An algorithm for determining the endpoints of isolated utterances," *Bell Syst. Tech. J.*, vol. 54, February (1975), 297-315
13. Karatza, H. D.: A Comparison of Load Sharing and Job Scheduling in a Network Of Workstations, *International Journal of Simulation: Systems, Science, Technology*, Vol. 4, No 3-4, (2003), 4-11

Speaker Recognition in Unknown Mismatched Conditions Using Augmented PCA

Ha-Jin Yu

School of Computer Science, University of Seoul,
Dongdaemungu, Seoul 130-743, South Korea
hjyu@venus.uos.ac.kr

Abstract. Our goal was to build a text-independent speaker recognition system that could be used under any conditions without any additional adaptation process. Unknown mismatched microphones and noise conditions can severely degrade the performance of speaker recognition systems. This paper shows that principal component analysis (PCA) can increase performance under these conditions without reducing dimension. We also propose a PCA process that augments class discriminative information sent to original feature vectors before PCA transformation and selects the best direction between each pair of highly confusable speakers. In tests, the proposed method reduced errors in recognition by 32%.

1 Introduction

Ubiquitous speech processing involves inputting speech from any environment into a recognition system. The microphones used during speaker recognition [1] may differ greatly from the ones used in the enrolment process, and noise conditions may be totally unknown. These situations can severely degrade system performance. Many researchers have studied such mismatched environments, and have found numerous useful solutions, such as cepstral subtraction and signal-to-noise ratio (SNR)-dependent cepstral normalization algorithms [2][3]. Many of these solutions require some prior knowledge of conditions, such as the type of headset or SNR; however, real situations may not allow enough time to acquire such information. This study involves speaker identification without prior knowledge of the environment. We used clean speech to enroll speakers and tested the system with speech data using different types of microphones and recorded in a moving car without any additional adaptation session.

Our goal was to build a system that could perform in any unknown environment without an additional adaptation session. In the first step, we used principal component analysis (PCA) to extract robust features for speaker modeling. Many researchers have successfully used principle component analysis to reduce the dimension of original feature vectors and cost of computation [4-6]. This research emphasized PCA characteristics that find uncorrelated directions of maximum variances in data space, which are invariant to mismatched headsets and noisy conditions. We also proposed augmented PCA, which augments feature vectors with

P. Yolum et al.(Eds.): ISCIS 2005, LNCS 3733, pp. 668–676, 2005.

class discriminative information; this allows us to add useful directions to the transformed feature space to aid in recognition.

The next section of this paper introduces the Gaussian mixture model and PCA, which are very well known to most speaker recognition researchers. Section 3 describes the proposed pairwise-augmented PCA, which improved the performance and the architecture of our speaker recognition system. Section 4 describes our experiment and its results, and finally Section 5 provides a summary and conclusions.

2 Speaker Identification Using GMM and PCA

We used Gaussian mixture models (the most common method) to build our speaker models, and applied PCA to extract robust features.

2.1 Gaussian Mixture Model (GMM) [7]

Gaussian mixture models (GMMs) are the most prominent modeling approach used in text-independent speaker recognition applications. In GMM, the acoustic parameter distribution of each speaker is represented by a speaker-dependent mixture of Gaussian distributions:

$$p(\mathbf{x} \mid \lambda) = \sum_{i=1}^{M} w_i g_i(\mathbf{x}), \quad \sum_{i=1}^{M} w_i = 1 \tag{1}$$

where M represents the number of mixtures, w_i represents mixture weight, and the Gaussian density, g_i, is given by:

$$g_i(\mathbf{x}) = \frac{1}{(2\pi)^{D/2} \mid \Sigma_i \mid^{1/2}} \exp\left\{ -\frac{1}{2} (\mathbf{x} - \boldsymbol{\mu}_i)^T \Sigma_i^{-1} (\mathbf{x} - \boldsymbol{\mu}_i) \right\}. \tag{2}$$

We can estimate maximum likelihood parameters using the expectation maximization (EM) algorithm. For speaker identification, we can compute the log-likelihood of a model given an utterance $X = \{x_1, ..., x_T\}$ and choose the speaker associated with the most likely model for the input utterance as the recognized speaker $\hat{S}$:

$$\hat{S} = \arg\max_{1 \le k \le S} \sum_{t=1}^{T} \log p(\mathbf{x}_t \mid \lambda_k) \tag{3}$$

2.2 Principal Component Analysis (PCA)

Principal component analysis is a linear orthogonal transform that can remove correlations among vector components. Researchers use it to reduce the feature vector dimension, which results in reduced processing time and space. It processes training feature vectors using the following steps:

Step 1. Subtract the mean from each data dimension.
Step 2. Calculate the covariance matrix.
Step 3. Calculate the eigenvectors and eigenvalues of the covariance matrix, using unit eigenvectors (i.e., their lengths are all one) such that the eigenvectors are perpendicular to each other.
Step 4. Choose components and form a transformation matrix ***w***. The eigenvector with the highest eigenvalues is the direction with the greatest variance. Order them by eigenvalue; take *k* eigenvectors with the highest eigenvalues; and form matrix ***w*** with these eigenvectors in the columns. (In this study, since we were not interested in reducing the original feature space dimension, we used all of the components.)
Step 5. Transform the feature vectors using the transformation matrix formed in Step 4:

$$TransformedData = \mathbf{w} \times RowData \tag{4}$$

3 The System Using the Proposed Augmented PCA

Researchers mainly use PCA to reduce the feature space dimension and to find uncorrelated directions of maximum variance. However, maximum variance does not always correspond to maximum discriminative capability. Consider the following artificial sets of two-dimensional points from two classes (see Fig. 1).

Class 1: (1,4), (2,0), (3,-4).
Class 2: (-1,-4), (-2,0), (-3,4).

The first component, x_1, is very useful for class discrimination, while the second one is not, although it has greater variation. If PCA transforms the points, we can obtain the points that show the direction with the maximum variance (Figure 2), but this information is useless for discrimination.

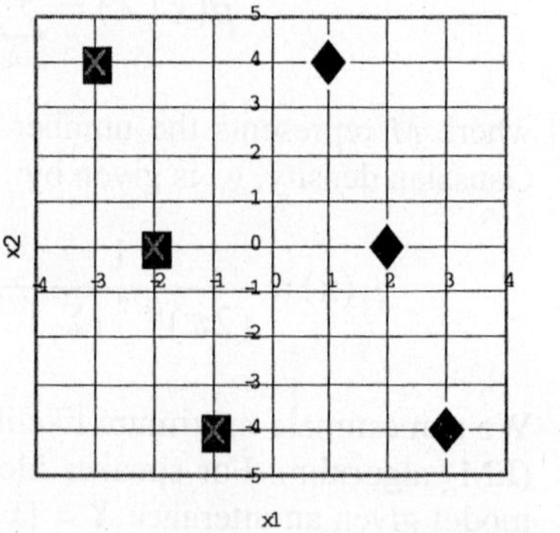

Fig. 1. Two-dimensional artificial data

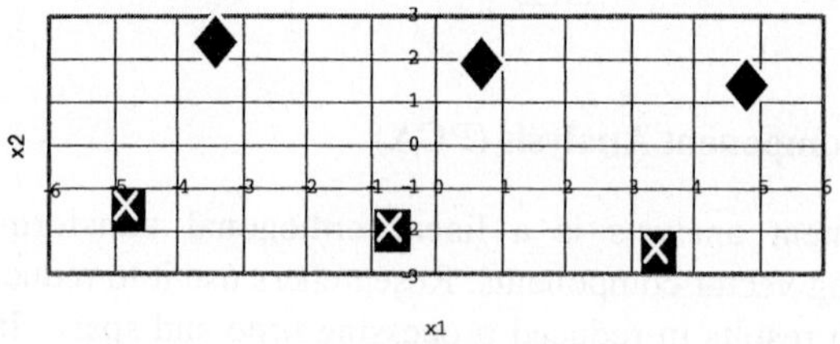

Fig. 2. PCA-transformed data from Figure 1

Now, consider the following three-dimensional data points; we produce these by positing an axis at the heads of the original two-dimensional vectors:

Class 1: (3,1,4), (3,2,0), (3,3,-4).
Class 2: (-3,-1,-4), (-3,-2,0), (-3,-3,4).

In the vectors, the new axis is supervised information that tells us to which classes the points belong. If we analyze the points using PCA, we can get an orthogonal three-dimensional feature space. For new data points, the augmented components are all zeros because class information is not known in the recognition phase. We obtain the following augmented data representation:

Class 1: (0,1,4) , (0,2,0) , (0,3,-4).
Class 2 : (0,-1,-4) , (0,-2,0) , (0,-3,4).

If we transform the zero-augmented data using the same transformation matrix, we get the following data points:

(1.2535663, 3.5741005, 1.6292263)
(-1.1396058, 0.2166122, 1.6292262)
(-3.5327779, -3.1408761, 1.6292261)
(-1.2535663, -3.5741005, -1.6292263)
(1.1396058, -0.2166122, -1.6292262)
(3.5327779, 3.1408761, -1.6292261)

Note that the values of the third component are highly concentrated within classes. Figure 3 shows the points projected on three planes. This process does not reduce the data dimension, and we can get a new direction, which is very useful for class discrimination. Components correlated with class information should be projected to the new directions. To examine the proposed augmented PCA effect, we applied it to each speaker pair; using the following process:

Step 1. Augment each feature vector in the entire training set as follows:

$$(x_1, x_2, \ldots, x_d, a_1, a_2, \ldots, a_n)$$

Here, d represents the dimension of the original feature vectors, n is the number of classes, x_i is the i-th component of the original feature vector, and a_j is the augmented component in which:

$a_j = \alpha$ if the vector belongs to class j
$a_j = -\alpha$ if the vector does not belongs to class j.

Here, α is a constant. (We set α as the maximum value of all the components in the raw feature vectors.)

Step 2. Form transformation matrix **w'** with augmented vectors using Steps 1 through 4 described in Section 2.2.

Step 3. Remove the last n rows in transformation matrix **w'**. This is equivalent to augmenting n zeros to the raw vectors before transformation. We augment zeros instead of class information (as we did in Step 1) because the classes of the new input vectors are unknown.

Step 4. Transform all training data using transformation matrix **w'** to get $(n+d)$ dimensional vectors.

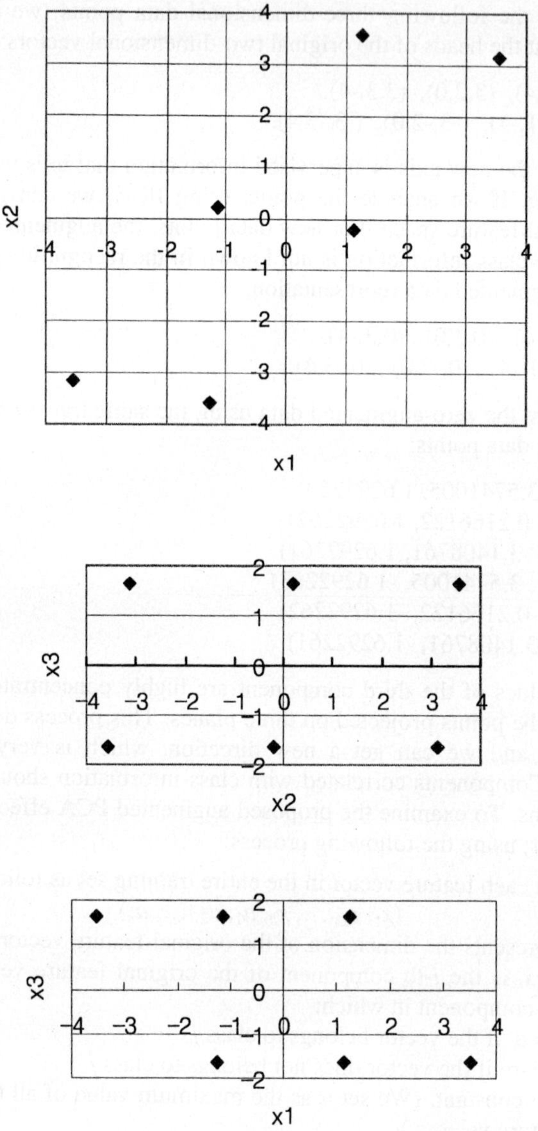

Fig. 3. Two-dimensional projections of the augmented PCA-transformed data from Figure 1

Step 5. For training vectors in each pair of confusable classes, select d components from $(n+d)$ dimensional transformed vectors. Select the directions most highly correlated to the augmented components used in Step 1 (i.e., the class information before transformation). Calculate the covariance between each component and augmented components and select the component with the highest covariance. Now, the new feature space should have the same order as the original feature space.

Step 6. Train GMMs for each pair, using vectors with components selected in Step 5.
Step 7. Apply Steps 4 and 5 to all the test data and use the result vectors for recognition using the GMMs trained in Step 6.

Figure 4 depicts this process and Figure 5 diagrams the training and recognition flow. We can use the same training data set used for PCA transformation matrix generation, GMM training, and to augment the PCA process for each pair of confusable speakers. In the recognition phase, we follow the normal PCA GMM recognition with augmented PCA GMM recognition using the top n candidates.

4 Experimental Evaluation of the Proposed System

We used the corpus for speaker recognition (CarSpkr01) collected by SITEC (Speech Information Technology & Industry Promotion Center, South Korea). They recorded speech in a moving car with its windows closed and no music playing, driving on roads in good condition at speeds of 30 to 60 kilometers per hour. They used a dynamic microphone (head-worn SHURE SM-10A, Uni-Cardioids), condenser microphones (AKG B400-BL, Cardioids), and an inexpensive hands-free microphone, each placed in eight different positions in the car.

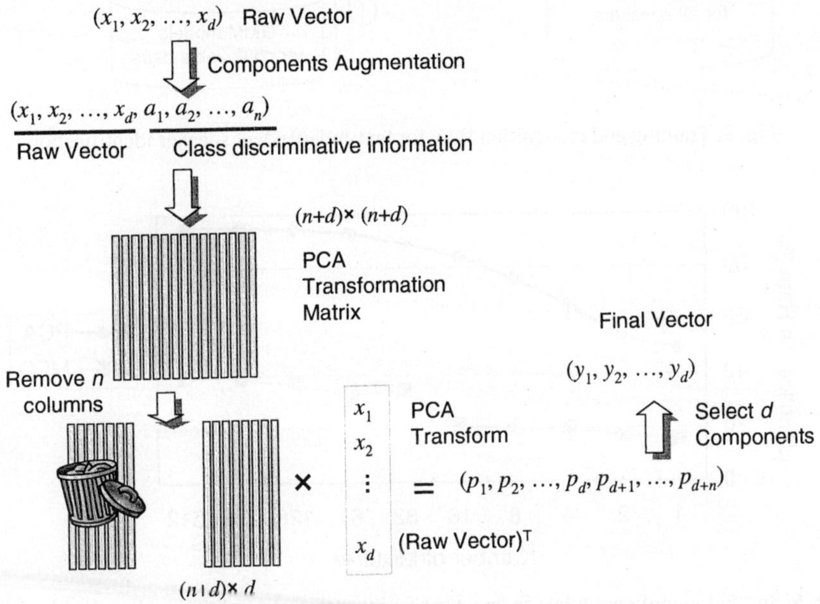

Fig. 4. Augmented PCA feature extraction process

In this experiment, we used data recorded using the dynamic microphone located about three centimeters from the speaker's mouth as the training set, and data recorded using the condenser microphone positioned on a sun visor as the test set. We intentionally used different types of microphones to evaluate performance in mismatched conditions. Moreover, the speech used in the test set had a low SNR because we recorded it using a condenser microphone relatively far from the mouth, whereas the speech in model training had a high SNR because we recorded it using a dynamic microphone located relatively close to the mouth.

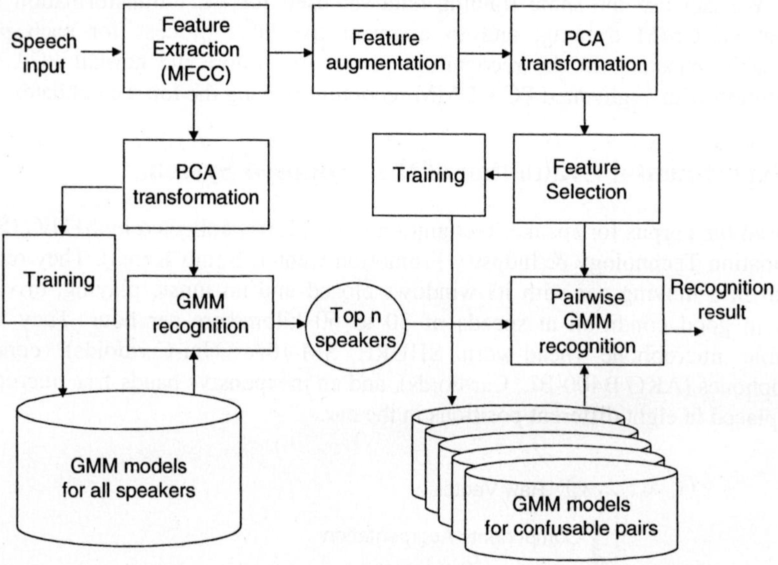

Fig. 5. Training and recognition flow for text-independent speaker identification

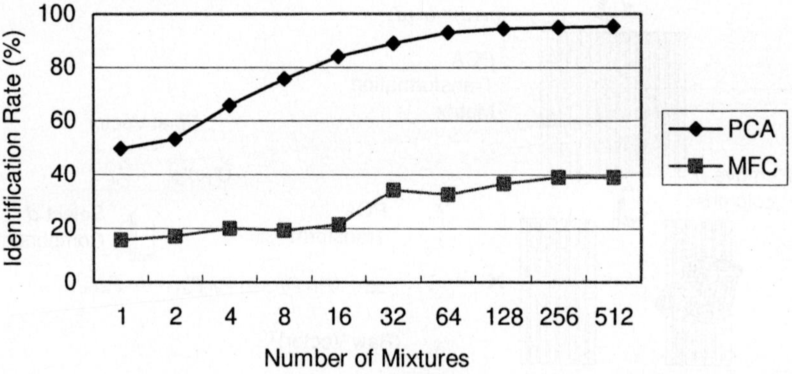

Fig. 6. Speaker identification rate in an unknown mismatched condition with and without PCA

Phrases recorded included a phoneme-balanced sentence, a set of phoneme-balanced words, and a set of four-digit numbers, all in Korean. In each of five sessions, we recorded 250 utterances made by 30 speakers. There were one-day, one-week, one-month, and two-month intervals between sessions. We used data recorded during the first session for model training, and data recorded during the third session (a week after the first session) for the test. We used 20 first-order mel-frequency cepstral coefficients (MFCC) [3] and their first and second derivatives as the basis feature.

Figure 6 shows that PCA greatly increased the identification rates using mismatched microphones with noise at a satisfactory level. Figure 7 illustrates the error reduction for the most confusable pair of speakers using the proposed augmented PCA GMM with 128 mixtures; the error rate was obtained by considering only two speakers as candidates. Finally, when we used augmented PCA GMM in addition to PCA GMM with 128 mixtures, we were able to reduce the total identification error rate for all 30 speakers from 5.59% to 3.82%, a relative reduction of 32% (see Figure 8).

When we increase the number of mixtures to 256 without using the augmented PCA process, the error rate dropped to 5.03%, providing a relative error reduction of only 10%. This indicates that it is impossible to increase recognition rates to the same levels as in our proposed method by simply increasing the number of mixtures.

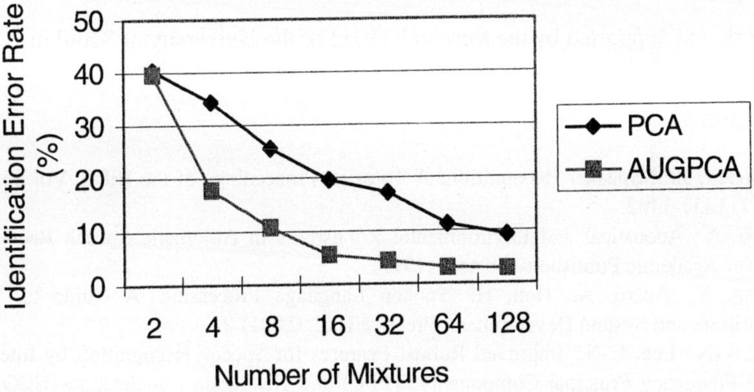

Fig. 7. Identification error rates for the most confusable pair of speakers using the proposed augmented PCA

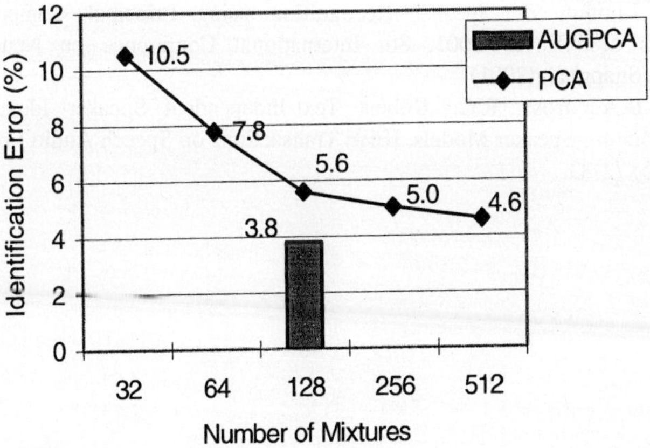

Fig. 8. Identification error rates for all speakers using augmented PCA

5 Conclusions

This paper presented a text-independent system for recognizing speakers under unknown mismatched conditions. Our goal was to build a system that could perform moderately well in such conditions without an additional adaptation process or any prior knowledge of the situation. We first showed that using principal component analysis without dimension reduction could increase performance under unknown conditions. We then proposed a PCA process that augments class discriminative information to the feature vectors. As a result, we were able to reduce the relative error rates by a further 32%. We plan to apply this method to speaker verification, and to compare its performance with other linear or non-linear transformations, such as linear discriminative analysis and independent component analysis.

Acknowledgement

This work was supported by the Research Grant of the University of Seoul in 2004.

References

1. Campbell, J.P.: Speaker Recognition: A Tutorial, Proceedings of the IEEE, Vol 85, No 9, (1997) 1437-1462.
2. Acero, A.: Acoustical and Environmental Robustness in Automatic Speech Recognition, Kluwer Academic Publishers, Boston, (1993)
3. Huang, X., Acero, A., Hon, H.: Spoken Language Processing, A Guide to Theory, Algorithm, and System Development, Prentice Hall, (2001)
4. Tsai, S.-N., Lee, L.-S.: Improved Robust Features for Speech Recognition by Integrating Time-Frequency Principal Components (TFPC) and Histogram Equalization (HEQ), 2003 IEEE Workshop on Automatic Speech Recognition and Understanding, (2003) 297 – 302.
5. Wanfeng, Z., Yingchun, Y., Zhaohui, W., Lifeng, S,: Experimental Evaluation of a New Speaker Identification Framework using PCA, IEEE International Conference on Systems, Man and Cybernetics, Volume 5, (2003) 4147 – 4152.
6. Ding, P., Liming, Z.: Speaker Recognition using Principal Component Analysis, Proceedings of ICONIP 2001, 8th International Conference on Neural Information Processing, Shanghai, (2001)
7. Reynolds, D.A., Rose, R.C.: Robust Text-Independent Speaker Identification Using Gaussian Mixture Speaker Models, IEEE Transactions on Speech Audio Processing, vol. 3, no. 1, (1995) 72-83.

Real Time Isolated Turkish Sign Language Recognition from Video Using Hidden Markov Models with Global Features

Hakan Haberdar and Songül Albayrak

Yildiz Technical University, Department of Computer Engineering,
34349 Istanbul, Turkey
hakan@haberdar.org, songul@ce.yildiz.edu.tr

Abstract. This paper introduces a video based system that recognizes gestures of Turkish Sign Language (TSL). Hidden Markov Models (HMMs) have been applied to design a sign language recognizer because of the fact that HMMs seem ideal technology for gesture recognition due to its ability of handling dynamic motion. It is seen that sampling only four key-frames is enough to detect the gesture. Concentrating only on the global features of the generated signs, the system achieves a word accuracy of 95.7%.

1 Introduction

Researchers study on designing new intelligent interfaces to provide easier and more comfortable interaction between human and computer. The interfaces generally analyze body motion and decide what to do according to the motion. Gestures, which are generated by hands and arms, are special case of the body motion [1]. Recognition of the gestures is an important step for the human-computer interaction [2]. If a system that recognizes sign language (SL) gestures can be designed, deaf-dumb people will have chance of communicating with the others.

SL, which consists of hand postures and dynamic gestures with facial expressions, is a visual language used by deaf-dumb people. Each gesture corresponds to a word or a letter in spoken language. Most of the countries have their own SL that is different from the others [3]. TSL consists of gestures for common words and the letters in Turkish alphabet. Facial expressions may modify meaning of the signs in TSL, but we discard this effect. Although SL is affected by spoken language, it has a different grammatical structure. It is not required that there must be relation between TSL and Turkish [4]. SLs are characterized by manual and non-manual features [1]. The non-manual features include facial expressions and body direction. The manual features can be divided into 2 categories; global features (hand movement, location) and local features (hand shape, orientation). SL recognition system (SLRS) is required to use both the global features and the local features [2].

In this paper, we present an easily extensible SLRS that uses a single CCD camera to track hands. Output of the camera can be thought as a sequence of images called frames. Signer, who performs SL gestures, doesn't have to wear a data-glove or any kind of colored glove. Hands and face in the frames are found by features of skin-tone [5].

P. Yolum et al.(Eds.): ISCIS 2005, LNCS 3733, pp. 677 – 687, 2005.

After detecting start and end moments of the generated gesture, we select four frames, called key-frames, to extract feature vectors. In the experiments, we see that sampling only the key-frames for a gesture is enough to recognize the sign word.

In the last decade, HMM has demonstrated its ability of dynamic gesture recognition. HMMs have unique features that make it desired method for SLRS [6]. We use location information of the hands in the key-frames as inputs of HMMs.

Our study does not aim to be a large lexicon SLRS, but the system can be easily modified to work with the local features to enlarge the vocabulary size. A commercial product that recognizes related words can be used in banks or hospitals.

The organization of this paper is as follows. In section 2, we discuss the previous work. Section 3 describes our system architecture. In section 4, we present HMMs. Section 5 is about feature extraction. The principles of training are given in section 6. In section 7, we show the experimental results. Section 8 concludes the paper.

2 Related Work

Studies about sign language recognition have begun to be seen in the literature for 15 years. To date, many systems have been designed for recognition of sign languages. These systems can be categorized into two main groups: data glove based systems and vision based systems. Previously, most work on SLRS is based on expensive data gloves [7, 8]. Signer must wear the data glove, so it is not comfortable and it limits the signer's motions. In the last decade, because of disadvantages of the data gloves, several systems have been designed by using the vision based approach. The vision based systems are subdivided into two groups such as motion based systems [6] and posture based systems [2]. The motion based systems, like us, handle only the global features. The posture based systems only concentrate on hand postures at a discrete time. Naturally, it is required to use both the hand motion and the hand posture to design a large lexicon SLRS.

Starner and Pentland [6] demonstrate a system for recognition of short sentences in American Sign Language. They use a single camera and signer wears solid color gloves for each hand. Grobel and Assan [1] use HMMs to recognize 262 isolated signs. They extract the features from video recordings of signers who must wear different colorful gloves for each hand.

In the literature, we can see sign language recognition systems for American SL, Netherlands SL, and Japanese SL etc. [6, 1, 9]. Unfortunately, there is not a comprehensive work on Turkish SL.

3 System Architecture

The aim of our study is to design a vision based system that recognizes gestures of TSL from the global features. A single CCD camera is used to track hands. First of all, the system finds the hands and face in a frame using a skin-tone detection algorithm [5]. Then, we segment the face, the right hand, and the left hand by using connected component labeling [10]. As we use features of skin-tone to segment the hands from background, our system has some limitations such as hands should not be in contact and the right hand should always be on the right side of the left hand.

We examine all the sign words in [4], and because the scope of this work is limited to the global features, the gestures are selected so that they do not have similar global features. There are some short signs in TSL, so we try to choose an optimum frame rate that does not miss the global features of the signs and is small enough for real time considerations. To recognize the gestures, HMMs are used.

4 Hidden Markov Models

Before using HMMs technology, we briefly summarize the fundamentals of HMMs.

4.1 Theory of Hidden Markov Models

A system, that at any time is one of a set of N distinct states, has a Markov property if the conditional probability of the current state, given all present and past states, depends on the i-th most recent states. For the special case of a first order Markov process, the current state depends solely on the previous state [11]. Although the order of gestures in TSL has not really a first order, we assume it to simplify the model. Determining the topology of the HMM can be performed by estimating how many states are required to represent a gesture in TSL. Fig. 1 shows the topology of the HMM that has been used in our experiments. It contains only four states including the start and final states that do not emit observations.

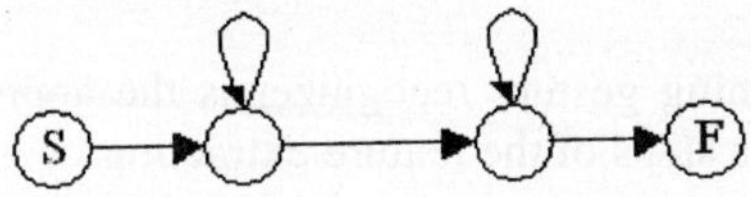

Fig. 1. The HMM topology used in our experiments

There are 3 basic problems in HMM: evaluation, decoding, and estimation. If we can evaluate $P(O|\lambda_i)$, for all present candidate models, then the model with the highest probability can be chosen for recognition. We use an efficient algorithm called forward-backward procedure to evaluate $P(O|\lambda_i)$.

The decoding problem concerns the state sequence Q having the highest probability of generating the observation sequence O. The Viterbi algorithm is used to evaluate the probability $P(Q|O, \lambda)$ [11].

The goal of the last problem is to estimate HMM parameters from training data. Baum-Welch algorithm, which is an expectation maximization procedure, is used to find the most suitable λ.

Although we concentrate on discrete observations in our discussion, the features that constitute the observations are usually continuous. Typically, a vector quantization method can be used to convert continuous value to discrete index [11]. However, the actual probability density functions for the observations may be used instead of using vector quantization. In this case, forward-backward, Viterbi, and Baum-Welch algorithms should be updated to handle continuous observation densities [12]. We assume that the observation probability densities are Gaussins with different means and variances. Initial values for the parameters are calculated by making some approximate assignment of feature vectors to states. If $L_j(t)$ denotes the probability of being in state j at time t, then adapted forms of the parameters are:

$$\mu_j = \frac{\sum_{t=1}^{T} L_j(t) o_t}{\sum_{t=1}^{T} L_j(t)_t} \tag{1}$$

$$\Sigma_j = \frac{\sum_{t=1}^{T} L_j(t)(o_t - \mu_j)(o_t - \mu_j)'}{\sum_{t=1}^{T} L_j(t)} \tag{2}$$

A similar but slightly more complex formula can be derived for the state transition probabilities. Formulations and very detailed information can be found in [11, 12].

4.2 Application of Hidden Markov Models in Gesture Recognition

Yamato et. al. [13] introduce firstly HMM approach to recognize image sequences of six tennis strokes with a rate of 90%. This experiment is very important because it used a 25x25 pixel sub-sampled video image as the feature vector. Although the information is so low-level, HMMs can learn these six motions to achieve respectable recognition results. We use the global features of each hand as an input of HMMs. For each word we train a distinct model, so we have 50 different HMMs.

5 Feature Extraction

A vital aspect of designing gesture recognizer is the appropriate choice of features. This section summarizes steps of the feature extraction.

5.1 Turkish Sign Language Recognition

The exact number of the gestures in TSL is not known, but it is being searched. The only published material for TSL is a manual prepared by Turkish Ministry of Education [14]. There are about 2000 gestures in the manual. In the literature, there is not a comprehensive study on TSL recognition. We select 50 gestures (given in Table 1) to show the performance of our TSL recognizer by using the global features.

Table 1. List of the recognized gestures

	1	2	3	4	5
a	hurt	mean	some	bicycle	sentence
b	open	take	city bus	finish	not
c	heavy	mother	shopping	large	disco
d	short	throw	ayran	live	baker
e	president	banker	leave	error	two-way
f	wear	hear	cloth	architect	hard
g	right	fault	frog	normal	love
h	rise	closed	row	pay	later
i	retainer	dirty	argue	wind	hat
j	twin	coke	press	choose	follow

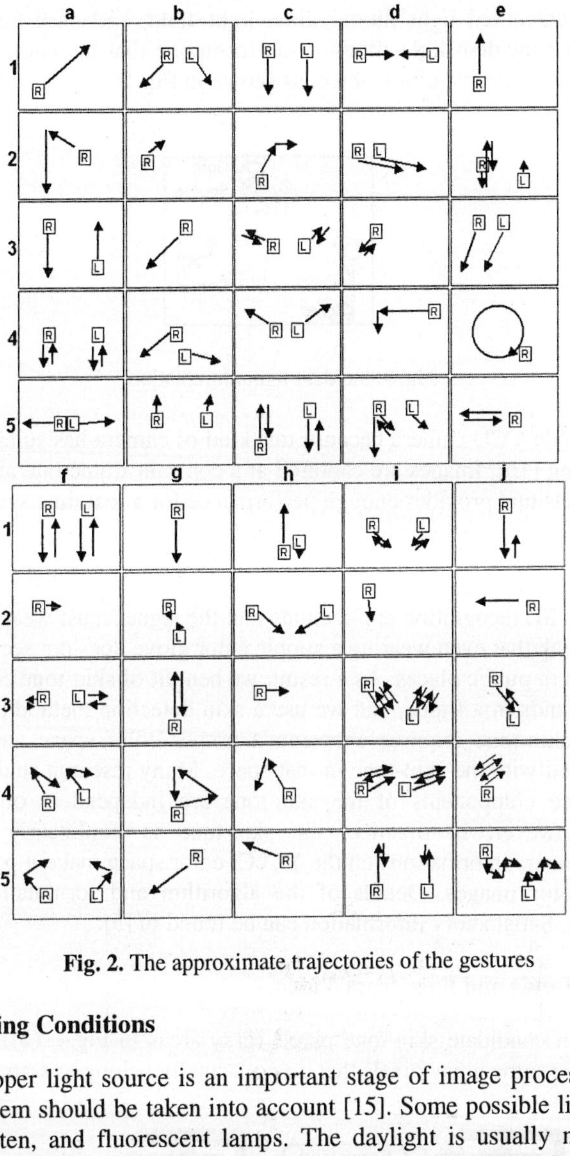

Fig. 2. The approximate trajectories of the gestures

5.2 Illuminating Conditions

Choosing a proper light source is an important stage of image processing. Working area of the system should be taken into account [15]. Some possible light sources are daylight, tungsten, and fluorescent lamps. The daylight is usually not suitable for image processing because the color and the intensity of the light change during the day. In fact, it does not seem ideal to place a recognizer outside. The tungsten light sources are very cheap but not very well suited for image processing. They get very hot due to operating with direct current which causes a non-uniform illumination field. The fluorescent lamps have a large homogenous illumination field, and they do not get very hot [15]. As a result, a possible commercial SL recognizer is probably used inside a building like a hospital or a bank, and the fluorescent lamps are used to illuminate the imaging environment.

Positions of the camera and the light source are also important for designing a recognizer. There are four fundamental ways of lighting a scene: incident light illumination, transmitted light illumination, light–field, and dark–field illumination [15]. We use the incident light illumination technique that the camera and the light source are on the same side of the object as shown in Fig. 3.

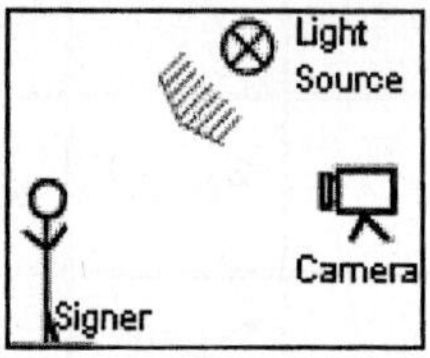

Fig. 3. Incident light illumination

We use a single CCD camera because this kind of camera has suitable features for image processing [16]. Images are captured at a constant frame rate and resolution of 160 by 120 pixels that provides enough performance for a real time system.

5.3 Skin Detection

There are many SL recognition applications that the signer must wear colorful gloves [1, 6, 9]. We think that even wearing a simple color glove does not seem suitable for a recognizer used in public places. As a result, we benefit of skin-tone characteristics to find face and hands in a frame, and we use a skin detection method proposed in [5]. Modeling the skin-tone requires choosing a proper color space and identifying a cluster associated with the skin-tone in that space. Many research studies assume that the chrominance components of the skin-tone are independent of the luminance component. However, in practice, the skin-tone is nonlinearly dependent on luminance. Some transformations on the YCbCr color space make it possible to detect skin-tone in color images. Details of the algorithm and formulation will not be mentioned here. Satisfactory information can be found in [5].

5.4 Finding Hands and Face from Video

When we detect candidate skin-tone pixels (gray areas in Fig.4. (b)) in a frame, we see that there are some noisy pixels that do not actually belong to skin regions.

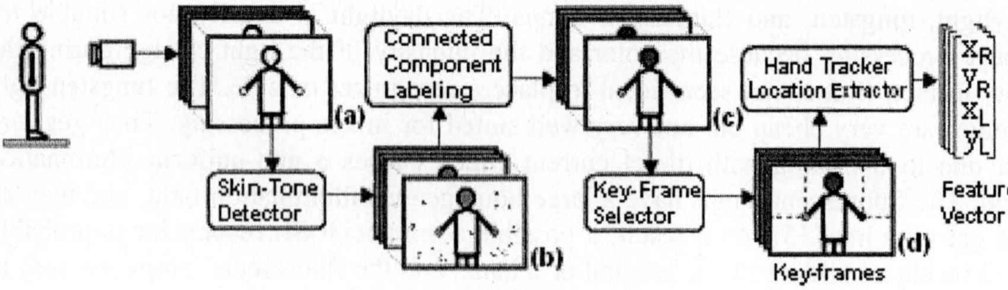

Fig. 4. Feature extraction steps

We use some basic image enhancement filters to remove the noisy pixels, then we try to segment face and hands by applying connected component labeling algorithm which can find all the connected components in the frame [10]. The largest component C1 is assumed as the face, and the second and third components C2, C3 are assumed as the hands. In addition, we make a control that if sizes of the three components are suitable for a face or a hand. At 160 by 120 resolution image, F_{min}–F_{max} and H_{min}–H_{max} pairs are minimum and maximum possible sizes for a face and for a hand respectively. These thresholds are obtained from training images.

- Component C_1 is face if $F_{min} \leq S_1 \leq F_{max}$
- Components C_2 and C_3 are hands if $H_{min} \leq S_2 \leq H_{max}$ and $H_{min} \leq S_3 \leq H_{max}$

We assign C_1 as the face and C_2 and C_3 are the hands if the conditions shown above are true where S_1, S_2 and S_3 are the sizes of the components. The leftmost hand component is the left hand, and the other is the right hand as shown in Fig. 5.

Fig. 5. View from the camera, and the three components

Our system has some limitations due to working with skin-tone: Hands shouldn't be in contact during a gesture, the right hand should always be on the right side of the left hand, and the face and the hands of the signer should be in the view of the camera. When the hands are initially found, the center pixels of the hands can be given as seeds for the consecutive frame [6]. The hands can be obtained faster by checking the eight neighbors of the seeds for the skin-tone. If the hands are lost, they can be recovered by detecting skin-tone pixels. In the scope of this work, we do not use the face information, although we find it, but our systems can be modified to work with face information in the future.

5.5 Motion Extraction

SL gestures can be classified as two-handed and one-handed signs. For the one-handed signs, the action of only one hand is required, where the signer generally takes the same hand, known as the dominant hand. For the two-handed signs, the other hand, called the non-dominant hand, performs the sign together with the dominant hand [1]. We can make further classification for the two-handed signs such as symmetric and asymmetric two-handed signs shown in Fig. 6.

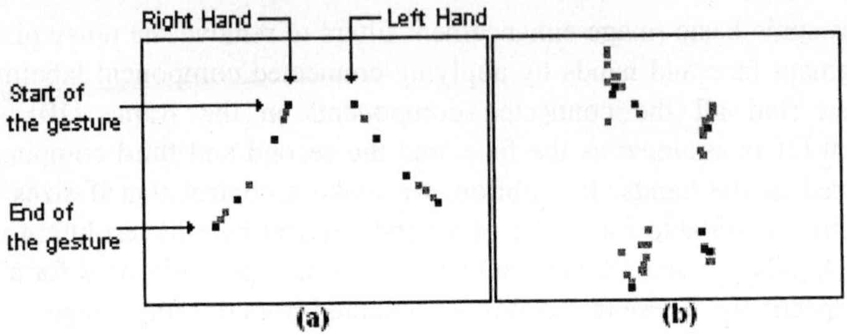

Fig. 6. (a) Symmetric two-handed sign (b) Asymmetric two-handed sign

For the symmetric signs, which the both hands make similar motion, it can be thought that it is enough to track only the dominant hand. However, our experiments show that the dominant and the non-dominant hand generate the same motion differently. Of course, hands should be tracked separately for the asymmetric signs. As a result, we have 2 distinct trackers for each hand. Position of a hand is defined by the center of the rectangle as shown in Fig. 7 (a).

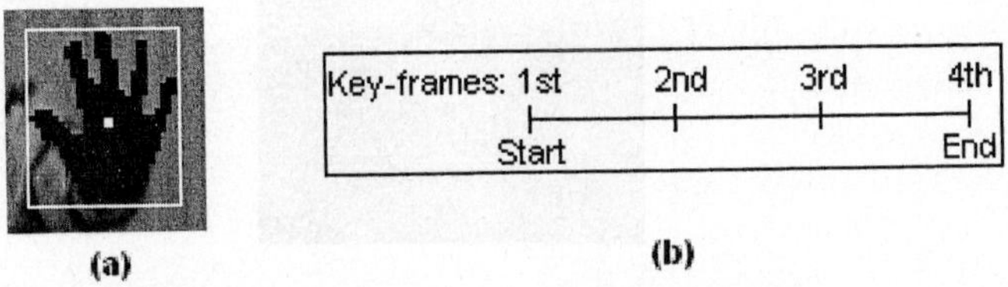

Fig. 7. (a) Position of the hand (b) Key-frames

If the position of the hand changes larger than a threshold between consecutive frames, we assign that frame as the start frame. After the gesture has started, if the position of the hand stays the same, we assign that frame as the end frame.

5.6 Key Frame Selection

Signs vary in time and space. When a signer tries to perform the same gesture twice, different lengths of frame sequences for the gesture will occur [1]. A HMM topology with skip transitions may handle with it [2]. However, a fixed number of states for all signs is not suitable since our training samples contain short signs and long signs. As a result, we choose four frames, called key-frames, instead of using all the frames in order not to deal with problems due to the length of the gestures.

After obtaining the start and end frame of the gesture, we see that sampling only four key-frames for each hand is enough to detect the gesture. We divide the whole duration of the gesture into 3 equal segments as shown in Fig.7 (b) to select the key-frames. In Fig. 6 (a) and (b), the gray squares show the positions of the hands in each frame, and the key-frames are marked as the black squares.

We use a four-element feature vector that consists of each hand's x and y positions in a key-frame. As a result, we achieve expressing a TSL gesture with 4 key-frames.

6 Training

Our gesture database consists of 22 one-handed and 28 two-handed signs representing words in Turkish Sign Language. It is aimed to choose signs having different global features. A signer, who learned the gestures in the database, performed 15 samples for each of the 50 signs–750 samples overall. 500 samples are used to train 50 distinct HMMs. The Baum-Welch algorithm is operated to train HMMs and to find best λ_i for i=1,2,...,50. Basic steps of the algorithm are as follows:

- Step 1: Initialize HMM parameters.
- Step 2: Calculate forward-backward variables by current parameters.
- Step 3: Update HMM parameters using the forward-backward variables.

Step 2 and step 3 are repeated until the HMM parameters are converged [12].

7 Experimental Results

Our experimental platform consists of a CCD (Charge Coupled Device) camera, and a personal computer with an Intel Pentium® IV 1.9GHz CPU.

In the experiments, the signs are tested at 160 by 120 pixels resolution. JAVA® programming platform is used to generate HMM algorithms and graphical user interface of the Turkish Sign Language recognition system.

Three different tests are performed. For one-handed gesture test, we use features of only the dominant hand, and train 22 distinct HMMs by using 220 one-handed training samples. For two-handed gesture test, we use both the features of the dominant and non-dominant hand, and train 28 distinct HMMs by using 280 two-handed training samples. Although the non-dominant hand doesn't move during a one-handed sign, we take it into account to be able to test all gestures together as a final test.

For the recognition task, the forward algorithm is used to evaluate the probability that a test gesture is generated by the model corresponding to word i, $P(O|\lambda_i)$ for i=1,2,...,50. The gesture is assigned to the word having the highest probability. The results are shown in Table 2.

Table 2. The test results

Vocabulary	One-handed (110 gestures)	Two-handed (140 gestures)	Final Test (250 gestures)
Results	96.3 %	95.3 %	95.7%

Our system recognizes with 96.3% accuracy out of the 110 one-handed test gestures and with 95.3% accuracy out of the 140 two-handed test gestures. In the final test, the recognition rate is 95.7% out of the 250 test gestures.

We see that recognizing one-handed and two-handed signs together, in other words adding the location information of non-dominant hand in the feature vector for a one-handed sign, does not affect the system performance. The recognition rate for the two-handed signs is a little bit lower than one-handed signs. This is an expected result because the two-handed signs have more complex structure than the one-handed signs have. When we examine the second highest probability P(O|λ) for the test gestures, we see that the system can find the gestures that have similar global features.

8 Conclusions and Feature Work

Our system is a starting step for a large lexicon and signer independent Turkish Sign Language (TSL) recognizer. Sign language is mainly recognized from the global features that is why we prefer to handle them for the first step and obtain satisfactory results. We will use the local features for the selected candidates that are previously derived from the global features, and improve the performance of TSL recognition system.

The limitations of the system due to skin-tone based hand tracking can be achieved by adding information about the joint points between hands and arms. The results show that the system meets the requirements of signer dependent recognition, but a system working in public places must be user independent. Because of having no TSL gesture database, we have to learn and perform the signs. Learning phase, which takes too much time, makes difficult to design the signer independent system, so we plan to work with TSL course instructors. We will concentrate on continuous sign language recognition after obtaining large vocabulary size.

References

1. Grobel, K., Assan, M.: Isolated Sign Language Recognition using Hidden Markov Models. International Conference on Computational Cybernetics and Simulation Vol. 4. IEEE (1997) 3081–3084
2. Imagawa, K., Matsuo, H., Taniguchi, R., Arita, D., Lu, S., Ilgi, S.: Recognition of Local Features from Camera-based Sign Language Recognition System. Proceedings of the 15th International Conference on Pattern Recognition, Vol. 4. (2000) 849–853
3. Hai, W., Sutherland, A.: Irish Sign Language Recognition Using PCA, Multi-scale Theory, and Discrete Hidden Markov Models. Proceedings of the Irish Machine Vision Conference (2004) 66–73
4. Özyürek, A., İlkbaşaran, D., Arık, E.: Turkish Sign Language Gestures. Koç University, http://turkisaretdili.ku.edu.tr (2005)
5. Hsu, R. L., Abdel-Mottaleb, M., Jain, A. K.: Face Detection in Color Images. IEEE Trans. on Pattern Analysis and Machine Intelligence, No. 5 Vol. 2. (2002) 696–706
6. Starner, T., Pentland, A.: Real-Time American Sign Language Recognition from Video Using HMMs. Technical Report No 375. MIT Cambridge, Media Laboratory (1995)
7. Takahashi, T., Kishino, F.: Hand Gesture Coding Based on Experiments Using a Hand Gesture Interface Device. SIGCHI Bulletin, Vol. 23-2 (1991) 67–73
8. Liang, H., Ouhyoung, M.: A Sign Language Recognition System Using HMM and Context Sensitive Search. ACM VRST (1996)

9. Yoshino, K., Kawashima, T., Aoki, Y.: Recognition of Japanese Sign Language from Image Sequence Using Color Combination. Proceedings of the International Conference on Image Processing, Vol. 3. (1996) 511–514
10. Gonzales, R. C., Woods, R. E.: Digital Image Processing. Addison Wesley (1993)
11. Alpaydın, E.: Introduction to Machine Learning. The MIT Press (2004) 305–326
12. Young, S.: The Hidden Markov Model Toolkit Book Version 3.2.1. Cambridge University Eng. Dept. Speech Group and Entropic Research Lab. Inc., Washington DC (2002)
13. Yamato, J., Ohta, J., Ishii, K.: Recognition Human Action in Time-Sequential Images Using HMM. Proceedings of the Conference on Computer Vision and Pattern Recognition. IEEE (1992) 379–385
14. Turkish Sign Language Manual for Adults. Turkish Ministry of Education, Ankara (1995)
15. Erhardt-Ferron, A.: Theory and Applications of Digital Image Processing. University of Applied Sciences Offenburg (2000)
16. Russ, J. C.: The Image Processing Handbook 3rd edn. CRC Press LLC (1999)

An Animation System for Fracturing of Rigid Objects*

Ayşe Küçükyılmaz and Bülent Özgüç

Department of Computer Engineering, Bilkent University, 06800 Ankara, Turkey
{aysek, ozguc}@bilkent.edu.tr

Abstract. This paper describes a system for the animation of fracturing brittle objects. The system combines rigid body simulation methods with a constraint-based model to animate fracturing of arbitrary polyhedral shaped objects under impact. The objects are represented as sets of masses, where pairs of adjacent masses are connected via a distance-preserving linear constraint. Lagrange multipliers are used to compute the forces exerted by those constraints, where these forces determine how and where the object will break. However, a problem with existing systems is that the initial body models exhibit well-defined uniformity, which makes the generated animations unrealistic. This work introduces a method for generating more realistic cracks without any performance loss. This method is easy to implement and applicable on different models.

1 Introduction

Realistic animation of fracture is a difficult one, because in order to generate a convincing animation, we need to understand the physical properties of the objects in a scene, rather than considering them as merely geometric shapes. These bodies should be thought of as real objects that have mass, elasticity, momentum, etc., and they display certain material properties. Another difficulty of fracture animation is that the scenes change dynamically during the animation. The bodies are fragmented to create new bodies which are again subject to the same effects. Physically precise animations cannot be realized successfully by computation, not only because they are time consuming and hard, but also the real motions and the fragmentation of objects require an extensive amount of calculations. However, such great accuracy is not a requisite for animation purposes. By using physically based animation techniques, we can create realistic-looking shatters and breaks with much less effort, yet with as much visual precision as necessary.

In this paper we discuss a system for computer animation that is implemented for generating animations of rigid objects that involve fracturing. This implementation combines the methods for simulating the fracturing of brittle

* This work is supported by EC within FP6 under Grant 511568 with the acronym 3DTV.

P. Yolum et al.(Eds.): ISCIS 2005, LNCS 3733, pp. 688–697, 2005.

objects with the rigid body simulation techniques in order to generate realistic-looking fracturing animations. Additionally, an improvement to this system is made through some techniques used for generating and modifying the object models more realistically.

The organization is as follows: In Sect. 2, we give a description of the object model that is proposed by Smith, Witkin and Baraff [14], which forms the basis for the simulation of the fracturing process. The process of generating each animation frame, which combines the rigid body and the fracture simulation techniques, are described in Sect. 3. Finally, some example animations generated by our system and conclusions are provided in Sect. 4 and 5, respectively.

2 Object Models

For the simulation of the fracturing of rigid objects, each object is modeled as a system of particles connected by distance-preserving constraints. The object models are constructed in tetrahedral mesh representation, using a tetrahedral mesh-generation software package such as NETGEN [10]. For each tetrahedron in the mesh, a particle is located at its center of mass, where the mass of each particle is a function of the volume of the tetrahedron it represents, and the density of the material at that point. For each pair of tetrahedra with a shared face, the corresponding particles are connected with a rigid constraint, which has strength proportional to the area of the shared face. The usage of distance-preserving constraints realistically models the inflexible nature of the objects that we are trying to animate by preventing the neighboring particles to change their positions relative to each other.

Although these constraints model the fracturing behavior successfully, the effects generated by using them alone are not satisfactorily realistic. This is due to the fact that the generated mesh, which characterizes the models' density, is uniform. Thus the cracks are developed deterministically.

In order to achieve user control on the fracturing behavior of the objects, some modification heuristics can be applied on their initial models. This might be useful for defining the overall crack pattern of the final models. Cleaving

Fig. 1. The cleaving effect

planes are used for systematically modifying the connection strengths along a cross-section of the objects. Fig. 1 illustrates the cleaving effect on a sample animation.

In addition, three-dimensional noise functions provide a way to change the connection strength of the objects procedurally to achieve different fracturing behavior for the same object geometry.

However, these methods are done as preprocessing on the models. Further randomization can be achievable by modifying the connection strengths during the fracture process. The idea depends on the fact that, in real life, when an object shatters, its inner material properties change due to the cracks occurring on it. This technique will be explained in Sect. 3.

3 Generating the Animation

The animation frames are generated by calculating the motion paths of the objects in the scene and determining their updated positions and orientations for each frame by the bisection technique. In the case of a contact between two objects, the motion paths of the objects are updated accordingly and fracture calculations are performed. If these calculations result in the shattering of the object, the resulting shards are modeled as new objects and they are included in the animation calculations. This process is repeated until either all the desired frames of animation are generated or the system finally comes to rest.

3.1 Rigid Body Simulation

The states of the objects in the space can be represented by their positions, orientations, and angular and linear velocities. Therefore, given the initial states, finding the states at any given time is simply an initial value problem. An ODE integrator using the Fourth-Order Runge-Kutta method with adaptive step sizing is implemented to solve this initial value problem and calculate the motion of the objects (see [9]). By applying an adaptive step-sizing algorithm, an upper bound for error is maintained in motion calculations.

However, when there is collision between objects, these unconstrained motion calculations fail to give realistic results. Thus, by applying appropriate responses on the objects when they are in contact, the impenetrability constraints can be enforced throughout the animation, letting the objects continue their unconstrained motion paths.

A contact between two objects is defined by the contact normal and a contact point extracted from contacting features of the two objects. In the case of multiple contact points between two objects, each contact point is considered as a separate contact.

After the contact points and the corresponding contact normals of a contact are determined, the appropriate response for the contact is calculated by looking at the projection of the relative velocity of the objects at the contact points over the contact normal.

The vector E, which is the impulse that acts on an object that is in contact, can be defined as:

$$E = \int F(t)dt \tag{1}$$

where, $F(t)$ is the vector function that defines the contact force acting on the object during the course of the contact. The required change in the velocity of the object due to this collision can be achieved by applying the changes $\Delta P(t)$ and $\Delta L(t)$ to the linear and angular momentums of the object respectively. $\Delta P(t)$ and $\Delta L(t)$ are defined as:

$$\Delta P(t_c) = E, \tag{2}$$

$$\Delta L(t_c) = (p - x(t_c)) \times E. \tag{3}$$

Here, p is the contact point, $x(t)$ is the position of the center of mass of the object and t_c is the time of the collision.

Even though the contacting objects are neither moving towards each other nor moving apart at the contact point (i.e. a resting contact), the impenetrability constraint can still be violated if the contacting objects are accelerating towards each other. In this case, contact forces must be calculated and applied to the objects in order to prevent them from accelerating into each other.

Besides requiring the relative acceleration of the objects, a_{rel}, to be nonnegative, two other conditions must be satisfied while calculating the contact forces. Firstly, the contact forces should never be attractive; and secondly, the contact forces must remain as long as the corresponding contact remains and no more. By combining these conditions together, we can formulate the problem of finding the contact forces as a quadratic programming (QP) problem as follows:

$$\min f^T(Af + b) \text{ subject to } \begin{cases} (Af + b) \geq 0 \\ f \geq 0 \end{cases} \tag{4}$$

Here $(Af + b)$ is the concatenation of all the a_{rel} values for all of the resting contacts and f is the concatenated vector of contact forces that are required for enforcing the impenetrability constraints. The concatenated vector is separated into its force dependent and force independent parts in order to be able to formulate it as a QP problem.

3.2 Fracture Simulation

The simulation of the fracturing process makes use of the lattice model representation of the objects. The crack initialization is invoked due to some external force applied to a point on the outer surface or in the inner region of the object. Upon the application of such a force, in response, constraint forces are calculated for connections in the lattice model in order to preserve the distances on the lattice of particles. In case the constraint force for a connection is greater than the current connection strength, that connection is removed. Otherwise, the existing connection strength is weakened by the amount of the constraint force applied on it. Any connection for which the resulting connection strength is weaker than a predefined threshold is removed.The process of modifying the connection strengths will be explained in detail after providing the details on how to calculate the constraint forces.

For calculating the constraint forces that act on the system of particles of the object, the positions of the particles are placed in a vector named q, such that, for an n particle system, q is a $3n \times 1$ vector defined as:

$$q = \begin{bmatrix} q_1 \\ \vdots \\ q_n \end{bmatrix}. \quad (5)$$

A mass matrix M is defined in such a way that it holds the particles' masses on the main diagonal, and 0's elsewhere. So a mass matrix for n particles in 3D is a $3n \times 3n$ matrix with diagonal elements $\{m_1, m_1, m_1, m_2, m_2, m_2, ..., m_n, m_n, m_n\}$.

Finally, a global force vector Q is obtained by joining the forces on all particles, just as we did for the positions. From Newton's Second Law of Motion, the global equation on the particle system is as follows:

$$\ddot{q} = M^{-1}Q, \quad (6)$$

where M^{-1} is the inverse of the mass matrix, M.

A similar global notation will be used for the set of constraints: Concatenating all scalar constraint functions form the vector function $C(q)$. In 3D, for n particles subject to m constraints, this constraint function has an input of a $3n \times 1$ vector, and an output of an $m \times 1$ vector. In our case, this constraint function consists of the scalar distance-preserving constraints in the form:

$$C_i(p_a, p_b) = \|p_a - p_b\| - d_i, \quad (7)$$

where p_a and p_b are the positions of two particles connected to constraint i, and d_i is the distance between the particles that needs to be preserved.

Assuming initial positions and velocities are legal, we try to come up with a feasible constraint force vector $\hat{Q}$ such that the distance preserving constraints are held. In other words, for the initial conditions that satisfy $C(q) = \dot{C}(q) = 0$, we are trying to find the constraint force vector $\hat{Q}$, such that, when added to Q, guarantees $\ddot{C}(q) = 0$. Taking the derivative of $C(q)$, we get:

$$\dot{C} = \frac{\partial C}{\partial q}\dot{q}. \quad (8)$$

$\frac{\partial C}{\partial q}$ is called the Jacobian of C, and will be denoted by J. Differentiating the above formula once again with respect to time gives

$$\ddot{C} = \dot{J}\dot{q} + J\ddot{q}. \quad (9)$$

Replacing $\ddot{q}$ according to relation 6 and adding the constraint forces gives

$$\ddot{C} = \dot{J}\dot{q} + JM^{-1}(Q + \hat{Q}). \quad (10)$$

where $\hat{Q}$ is the unknown constraint force vector. Setting $\ddot{C}(q) = 0$ gives

$$JM^{-1}\hat{Q} = -\dot{J}\dot{q} - JM^{-1}Q. \tag{11}$$

In order not to break the balance of the system, it has to be assured that no work is done by the constraint forces in system, for all valid position vectors:

$$\hat{Q}.\dot{q} = 0, \quad \forall \dot{q} | J\dot{q} = 0. \tag{12}$$

All vectors that satisfy this requirement can be written as

$$\hat{Q} = J^T \lambda, \tag{13}$$

where λ is a vector with the same dimensions as C. The components of λ are known as Lagrange multipliers and they tell how much of each constraint gradient is mixed into the constraint force. From 11 and 13:

$$JM^{-1}J^T\lambda = -\dot{J}\dot{q} - JM^{-1}Q. \tag{14}$$

Note that the above formula is a system of linear equations of the form $Ax = b$ where A is a matrix and x and b are vectors. By calculating the λ vector from equation 14 and placing it in equation 13, the constraint force vector $\hat{Q}$, which satisfies the given rigidity constraints can be calculated.

Additionally, to ensure that the λ vector is a physically realizable solution for the system, the conjugate gradient method [11], which gives the minimum norm solution of the system, is used since the minimum norm solution of the system is also the physically realizable one.

Once a crack is invoked at some point of the model, due to some external or internal force, the connection strengths are modified procedurally. Obviously, the connections that are close to the crack region will be affected more than the connections that are far away from it. The strengths are modified gradually as given in the following algorithm. However, weakening the connection strengths uniformly produces cracks that are visually artificial. Hence, in order to introduce a randomness into the crack pattern, some connections are made weaker than the others. These connections, and the amount of weakening are selected randomly (lines 9-11). This operation introduces no performance loss, yet it is very successful in generating crack patterns. Moreover, even though two geometrically same objects are broken under the same conditions, the system produces distinct final cracks. In addition, with this modification, formation of longer cracks is achieved.

Fig. 2 compares the effect of modifying the connections with and without the given technique. The object in (a) is broken with the original algorithm, while (b), (c), and (d) are broken with our modified one. It is easily observable how the crack patterns change every time the algorithm is run. In addition, with the technique used here, not only a successful randomization in cracks is achieved, but also the cracks formed after the fracture are longer.

Algorithm: modifying the connection strengths

changeConnectionStrengths(*latticeNode*1, *latticeNode*2, −*change*)
decrease the connection strength between *latticeNode*1 and *latticeNode*2 by *change*
change ← $\alpha \times$ *change* where $0 < \alpha < 1$
for *latticeNode* ∈ {*latticeNode*1, *latticeNode*2}
    select *selNeighborNode* ∈ neighbors of *latticeNode* randomly
    str ← connection strength between *selNeighborNode* and *latticeNode*
    str ← *str* − $\beta \times$ *change* where $0 < \beta < 1$ and $\beta > \alpha$
    connection strength between *selNeighborNode* and *latticeNode* ← *str*
    for (*neighborNode* ∈ neighbors of *latticeNode*) ∧ (*neighborNode* ≠ *selNeighborNode*)
        if *change* $\geq \tau$ where τ is a predefined threshold
            changeConnectionStrength(*latticeNode*, *neighborNode*, *change*)
        endif
    end
end

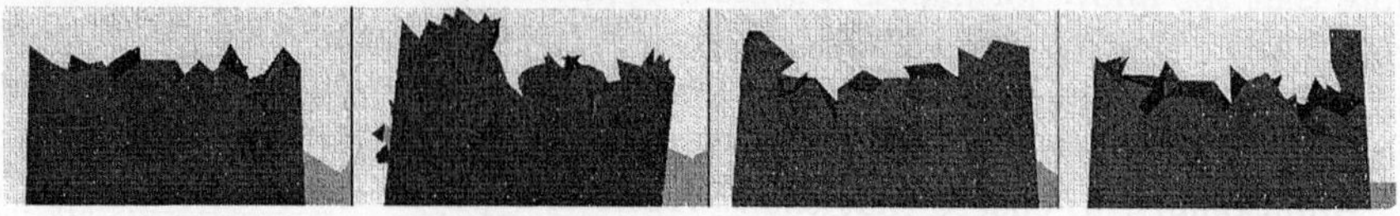

(a) (b) (c) (d)

Fig. 2. A comparison of the crack patterns generated by modifying the connection strengths (a) uniformly (b-d) with the given algorithm

4 Results

This section presents the important results generated by our system. The movies for the animations given in the figures, are accessible through the Internet. For viewing these, please visit the web page:
`http:\\www.cs.bilkent.edu.tr\~aysek\research.php`.

Fig. 3 shows an adobe wall struck by a heavy weight. The wall, which consists of 4080 tetrahedra with 8897 shared faces, is fixed to the ground and experience collision only with the heavy ball. In addition, since it is the only breakable object in the scene, the fracture calculations are done only for it.

In Fig. 4, cleaving is used to make the connections passing through the middle of the table's surface weaker than the rest of the surface to give a more realistic look.

Three major steps take place during the creation of an animation. The first step, generation of the object models, is performed once for an animation scene, and the results are stored in a file. This is a very fast process, taking only a few

Fig. 3. An adobe wall breaking under the impact of a heavy ball

Fig. 4. Glass table breaking under the impact of a heavy ball

seconds even for very large numbers of tetrahedra. The second step, creation of the animation, is the most time consuming one. The time required in this step for the animation shown in Fig. 3 was 4437 seconds, giving an average calculation speed of 61.7 seconds/frame. As it can be seen from the performance graph in Fig. 5, the generation of the frames that are created just after the shattering occurs took significantly more time than the average. The main reason for this is the big number of contacts that occurred between the newly created fragments. After a few frames, the calculation durations stabilize near 55 seconds. The time required for the third step, visualization of the results, greatly depends on the material qualities of the object in the animation scene.

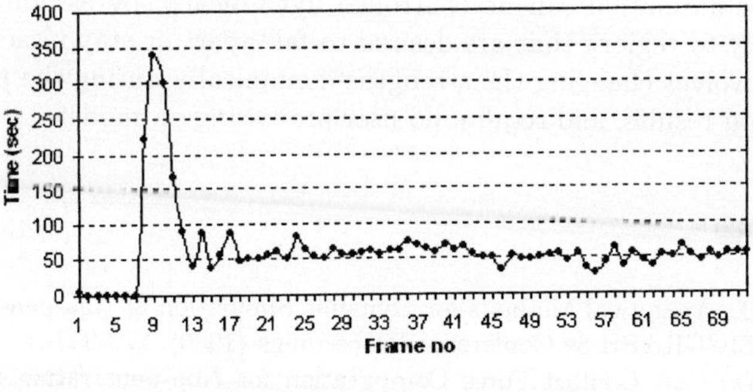

Fig. 5. Calculation times for the breaking wall animation on a 1.6 GHz Pentium4 machine

5 Conclusion

This study explores and implements a method for animating brittle fracture realistically. The implementation follows the method explained in [12]: The objects are represented as tetrahedral mesh and lattice models as explained in Sect. 2. In our implementation, as an improvement to the existing model, the constraint strengths are further modified by some heuristics in order to simulate the irregularity in the material properties.

Naturally, the number of the tetrahedra increases with respect to the complexity of the object geometry, and for generating visually improved animations. However, the time required for generating the animation increases as this number increases. Another limitation stems from the space requirements. The files describing the geometry of a high-resolution tetrahedral object are quite large. As a result of this drawback, the tetrahedron meshes for the samples illustrated in Sect. 4 were generated just as dense to illustrate the breaking behavior. However, higher-quality animations could have been generated.

The animation generated by the formulation presented in previous sections outputs a fracture effect where there are several fragments consisting of single tetrahedron. Although, Smith et. al. suggest in [12] that particles consisting of a single tetrahedron can be eliminated without loss of visual effects, this approach results with gaps around the cracks that seem to originate from nowhere. Therefore, in this study, single tetrahedron objects are left as is. However, this resulted with identical looking fragments, which can be seen in the results section.

As explained in previous sections, the constraint-based model is not sufficient on its own to mimic real world. Since the lattice construction assigns masses to tetrahedra according to their volumes, the density of objects stay uniform at every point of their bodies. This imposes that an object is never weak at some parts of its body, and this results in a uniform shattering effect, which seems dull. Since it is desirable to have irregularities in objects' mass distributions; some techniques are implemented in order to eliminate such uniformities by modifying the constraint strengths. The first class of these techniques, which are done as preprocessing, include applying noise function on an object that assigns different strengths to different parts of a body in a random manner, and using a cleaving function, which modifies the strengths at given regions. With cleaving, the animation can be controlled dynamically, by assigning strengths appropriately to regions that are desired to fall apart or stay intact. The other technique involves changing the strengths dynamically during the process. This presents good results, and require no user processing on models.

References

1. Baraff, D.: Analytical Methods for Dynamic Simulation of Non-penetrating Rigid Bodies. SIGGRAPH 89 Conference Proceedings (1989), 223-237
2. Baraff, D.: Fast Contact Force Computation for Non-penetrating Rigid Bodies. SIGGRAPH 94 Conference Proceedings (1994), 23-34

3. Baraff, D.: Non-Penetrating Rigid Body Simulation. Eurographics'93 State of the Art Repors (1993)
4. Baraff, D.: Physically Based Modeling: Principles and Practice, Chapter Rigid Body Simulation. SIGGRAPH 2001 Course Notes, ACM SIGGRAPH (2001)
5. Mirtich, B.: Impulse-based Dynamic Simulation of Rigid Body Systems, Ph.D. Thesis, University of California, Berkeley (1996)
6. Moore, M., Wilhelms, J.: Collision Detection and Response for Computer Animation. ACM Computer Graphics (1998), 22-4:289-298
7. O'Brien, J. F., Hodgins, J.: Animating Fracture. Communications of the ACM, Vol. 43 No. 7 (2000)
8. O'Brien, J. F., Hodgins, J.: Graphical Modeling and Animation of Brittle Fracture. SIGGRAPH 99 Conference Proceedings (1999), 33:287-296
9. Press, W. H., Flannery, B. P., Teukolsky, S. A., Vetterling, W. T: Numerical Recipes in C; The Art of Scientific Computing, 1st edn. Cambridge University Press, Cambridge, NY, USA (1992)
10. Shcberl, J.: NETGEN - 4.3. www.sfb013.uni-linz.ac.at/ joachim/netgen/, (2003)
11. Shewchuk, J. R.: An Introduction to the Conjugate Gradient Method Without the Agonizing Pain. Computer Science Tech. Report 94-125, Carnegie Mellon University, Pittsburgh, PA (1994) see also http://www.cs.cmu.edu/ quake/papers.html
12. Smith, J., Witkin, A., Baraff, D.: Fast and Controllable Simulation of the Shattering of Brittle Objects. Graphical Interface, Montreal, Canada (2000)
13. Terzopoulos, D., Fleischer, K.: Modeling Inelastic Deformation: Viscoelasticity, Plasticity, Fracture. SIGGRAPH 88 Conference Proceedings (1988), 22:287-296
14. Witkin, A., Baraff, D.: Physically Based Modeling: Principles and Practice, Chapter Differential Equation Basics. SIGGRAPH 2001 Course Notes, ACM SIGGRAPH (2001)

2D Shape Tracking Using Algebraic Curve Spaces

Burak Yöndem, Mustafa Unel, and Aytul Ercil

Sabancı University, Faculty of Engineering and Natural Sciences,
Istanbul-Turkey
burakyondem@su.sabanciuniv.edu
{munel, aytulercil}@sabanciuniv.edu

Abstract. Tracking free form objects by fitting algebraic curve models to their boundaries in real-time is not feasible due to the computational burden of fitting algorithms. In this paper, we propose to do fitting once offline and calculate an algebraic curve space. Then, in every frame, algebraic curves from the search region of curve space are evaluated with the extracted edge points. The curve that has the smallest error according to some error metric is chosen to be the fit for that frame. The algorithm presented is for tracking a free-form shaped object, moving along an unknown trajectory, within the camera's field of view (FOV). A discrete steady-state Kalman filter estimates the future position and orientation of the target object and provides the search area of curve space for the next frame. For initialization of the Kalman filter we used the "related points" extracted from the decomposition of algebraic curves, which represent the target's boundary, and measured position of target's centroid. Related points undergo the same motion with the curve, hence can be used to initialize the orientation of the target. Proposed algorithm is verified with experiments.

1 Introduction

Implicit algebraic curves have proven very useful in many model-based applications in the past two decades. Implicit models have been widely used for important computer vision tasks such as single computation pose estimation, shape tracking, 3D surface estimation and indexing into large pictorial databases [1-8].

Tracking techniques are based on matching tokens from the image. They are extracted along the sequence and are used as measurements for the tracking algorithm. There are several tracking approaches in the literature. Most of them can be divided into four groups:

1. 3D based methods use precise geometrical representation of known objects. These type of methods present a considerable computational load that can not be justified by a real-time system most of the time. However, they have been applied for tracking individual vehicles in traffic scenes by using expensive hardware [9].

2. *Feature-based methods* track individual tokens such as points, lines or curves [10]. These methods present two main disadvantages [11]: they do not provide explicit grouping of tokens moving with coherent motion and are quite sensitive to occlusion.

P. Yolum et al.(Eds.): ISCIS 2005, LNCS 3733, pp. 698 – 707, 2005.

3. Deformable model-based methods fit models to the contours of the moving objects of the scene [11]. They exhibit initialization problems [12]. When moving objects are partially occluded in the scene, initialization fails, since models can not be adapted to the real objects.

4. Region-based methods define groups of connected pixels that are detected as belonging to a single object that is moving with a different motion from its neighboring regions [13]. Region tracking is less sensitive to occlusion due to the extensive information that regions supply. Characteristics such as size, shape, or intensity can directly be obtained from them.

In this paper, we are interested in tracking a free-form object whose boundary can be described by a planar algebraic curve. We will only consider rigid motion of the object along an unknown trajectory. An implicit curve will be fitted to the target once and curve space covering all the translations and orientations for that algebraic curve will be calculated offline. We will use a unique decomposition [2,8] of algebraic curves to obtain feature points for initialization of position and orientation. Decomposition represents such curves as a unique sum of products of (possibly) complex lines. The real intersection points of these lines are so called "related-points", which map to one another under affine transformations. The block diagram of Fig. 1 summarizes the steps involved in the proposed scheme.

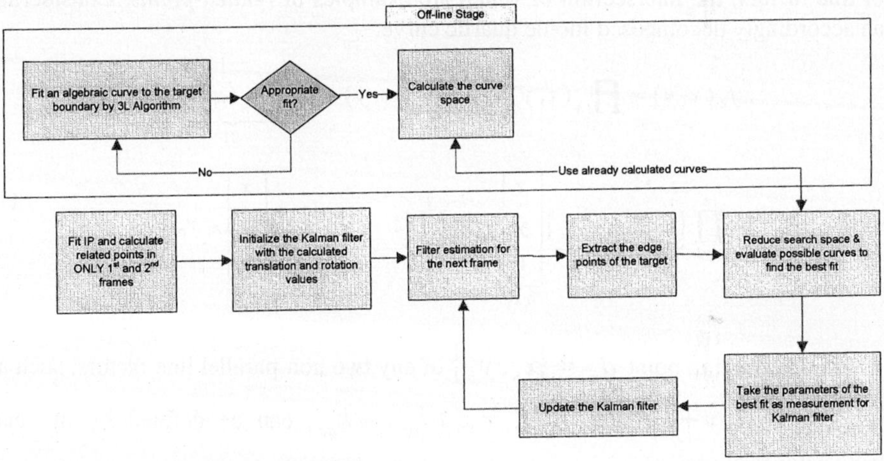

Fig. 1. The complete diagram for target tracking algorithm

2 Planar Algebraic Curves

2D curves can be modelled by implicit algebraic equations of the form, where $f_n(x, y)$ is a polynomial in the variables x, y, i.e. $f_n(x, y) = \sum_{ij} a_{ij} x^i y^j$ where $0 \leq i + j \leq n$ (n is finite) and the coefficients a_{ij} are real numbers [1]. Algebraic curves of degree 1, 2, 3, 4... are called lines, conics, cubics, quartics...etc. Fig. 2

shows some objects with their outlines modelled by a 3L curve fitting procedure detailed in [14].

In the sequel, we will focus on the tracking of quartics and note that results can easily be extended to higher degree algebraic curves.

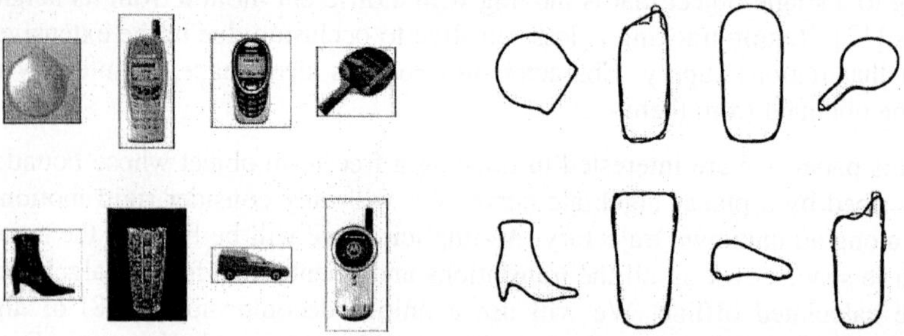

Fig. 2. Objects and their free form 3L curve models

2.1 Decomposed Quartics and Related Points

It has been shown in [2,3] that algebraic curves can be decomposed as a unique sum of line factors, the intersection of which are examples of *related-points.* Considering an accordingly decomposed monic quartic curve:

$$f_4(x,y) = \prod{}_4(x,y) + \gamma_2 \prod{}_2(x,y) + \gamma_0 \underbrace{\prod{}_0(x,y)}_{\square 1}$$

$$= \prod_{i=1}^{4} \underbrace{\begin{bmatrix} 1 & l_{4i} & k_{4i} \end{bmatrix}}_{\square L_{4i}^T} \underbrace{\begin{bmatrix} x \\ y \\ 1 \end{bmatrix}}_{\square X} + \gamma_2 \prod_{i=1}^{2} \underbrace{\begin{bmatrix} 1 & l_{2i} & k_{2i} \end{bmatrix}}_{\square L_{2i}^T} \begin{bmatrix} x \\ y \\ 1 \end{bmatrix} + \gamma_0 = 0 \quad (1)$$

The intersection point $d_p = \{x_p, y_p\}$ of any two non-parallel line factors, such as $L_{ij}^T X = x + l_{ij} y + k_{ij}$ and $L_{qr}^T X = x + l_{qr} y + k_{qr}$, can be defined by the matrix/vector relation:

$$\begin{bmatrix} 1 & l_{ij} & k_{ij} \\ 1 & l_{qr} & k_{qr} \end{bmatrix} \begin{bmatrix} x_p \\ y_p \\ 1 \end{bmatrix} = \begin{bmatrix} 0 \\ 0 \end{bmatrix} \Rightarrow \begin{bmatrix} x_p \\ y_p \end{bmatrix} = \begin{bmatrix} l_{ij} k_{qr} - l_{qr} k_{ij} \\ k_{ij} - k_{qr} \end{bmatrix} \div (l_{qr} - l_{ij}) \quad (2)$$

In the case of closed-bounded quartics, we have two pairs of complex-conjugate lines, i.e. $L_{42} = L_{41}^* \; L_{44} = L_{43}^*$, the intersection points of which are real. For tracking, we will be using the centroid of the bounding curve and these two related points.

For the robust calculation of the orientation of the free-form curve, we follow [16] and form two vectors originating from the center of mass to the two related points. The sum of these two vectors is a new vector that is quite robust against noise throughout the whole trajectory. The angle between this sum vector and the positive x-axis is defined to be the orientation of the curve (see Fig. 3).

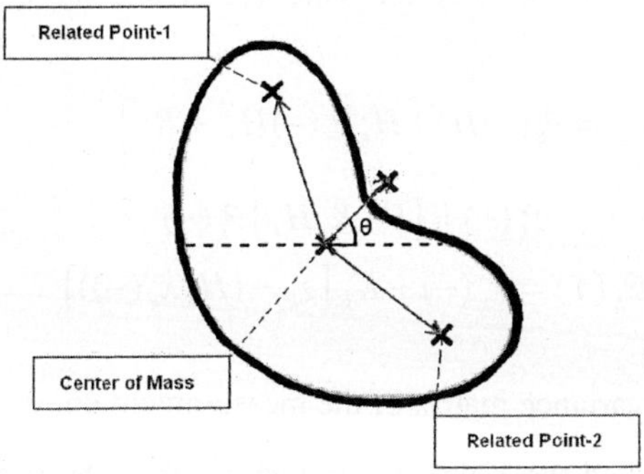

Fig. 3. Shows the tracked object with the center of mass, two related points and the corresponding point used for orientation

3 Tracking Using Kalman Filter

Kalman filters are recursive filters which provide an unbiased, minimum-variance and consistent estimate $\hat{x}_k$ of a state vector x_k. In this section the index k represents the discrete time. Kalman filtering consists of a three-steps strategy named prediction, measurement and update. The prediction computes a first estimate of the state vector $\hat{x}_{k+1}(-)$ and of the covariance matrix defined as $P_k = E\left[\tilde{x}_k \tilde{x}_k^T\right]$, where $\tilde{x} = x_k - \hat{x}_k$ and E[.] is the average operator. $\hat{x}_k(-)$ denotes the prediction vector before measurement and $\hat{x}_k(+)$ refers to the updated vector after the measurement. Prediction equations are based on previous realizations of the updated vector $\hat{x}_k(+)$ and the updated matrix $P_k(+)$:

$$\hat{x}_{k+1}(-) = f(\hat{x}_k(+)) + w'_k \,, \quad P_{k+1}(-) = P_k(+) + Q_k \tag{3}$$

where Q_k is the covariance matrix of the noise w'_k, i.e. $Q_k = E\left[w'_k w'^T_k\right]$. Q_k reflects the adequacy of the model to describe the underlying physical system. The measurement step consists of the computation, through image processing routines, of visual features named the measurements: z_k. Measurements are related to the state vector through the observation equation:

$$z_k = H\hat{x}_k + v_k \tag{4}$$

where H is the observation matrix and v_k is a measurement error, modelled as an uncorrelated noise. The final update step modifies the state vector according to the measurement z_k, thus providing an updated estimate $\hat{x}_k(+)$. The equations describing the update step modify the state vector and the covariance through the following equations:

$$\begin{aligned} K_k &= P_k(-)H_k^T\left[H_k P_k(-)H_k^T + R_k\right]^{-1} \\ P_k(+) &= \left[I - K_k H_k\right]P_k(-) \\ \hat{x}_k(+) &= \hat{x}_k(-) + K_k\left[z_k - (H_k\hat{x}_k(-))\right] \end{aligned} \tag{5}$$

R_k represents the covariance matrix of the measurement noise v_k, i.e. $R_k = E\left[v_k v_k^T\right]$. The matrix K_k is called the Kalman gain and has the role of modulating the update of the state vector $\hat{x}_k(-)$ into $\hat{x}_k(+)$ by appropriately weighting the measurement error v_k.

3.1 Target Model

In order to create a Kalman filter, an appropriate linear model of the target must be created. The model must describe the x and y coordinates of the target centroid and the orientation of the target. All three parameters are independent of each other. The x and y models are the same and based on Newton's second law. The orientation is based on a moment equation.

The state space representation of the model for the x and y coordinates and orientation in discrete time takes the form:

$$\begin{bmatrix} x_{k+1} \\ v_{k+1} \\ a_{k+1} \end{bmatrix} = \begin{bmatrix} 1 & T & T^2 \\ 0 & 1 & T \\ 0 & 0 & 1 \end{bmatrix} \begin{bmatrix} x_k \\ v_k \\ a_k \end{bmatrix} + \overline{w}_k, \quad \begin{bmatrix} \theta_{k+1} \\ \omega_{k+1} \\ \alpha_{k+1} \end{bmatrix} = \begin{bmatrix} 1 & T & T^2 \\ 0 & 1 & T \\ 0 & 0 & 1 \end{bmatrix} \begin{bmatrix} \theta_k \\ \omega_k \\ \alpha_k \end{bmatrix} + \overline{w}_k \tag{6}$$

where T is the sampling period of the system and w_k is the disturbance applied to the object.

Clearly, the state matrix and input vector are identical to the translational models. Therefore it is sufficient to use one model for all three parameters. Corke has used the Kalman filter as a solution to the visual servoing problem [15]. He used the filter to have an end-effector tracks an object, using a velocity based control scheme. He employed the recursive form of the filter and his target model was second order. In this work, we used the steady-state form of the Kalman filter in order to estimate the position and orientation of the object between measurements. Since the system is at steady-state, a single equation is used to determine the filter:

$$x_{k+1} = \underbrace{[A - KH]}_{\triangleq \bar{A}} x_k + Kz_k = \bar{A}x_k + Kz_k \tag{7}$$

4 Algebraic Curve Spaces

Instead of fitting an algebraic curve to the boundary of the target at each frame, selecting a suitable curve among possible candidates decreases the computational complexity drastically. A curve space for the given target can found by first fitting an algebraic curve to the target's boundary offline and computing all possible Euclidean transformations, rotations and translations, of that polynomial.

4.1 Euclidean Equivalent Algebraic Curves

A Euclidean transformation, E is defined by both a rotation R and a linear translation T ; i.e.

$$\begin{bmatrix} x \\ y \end{bmatrix} = \underbrace{\begin{bmatrix} \cos\theta & -\sin\theta \\ \sin\theta & \cos\theta \end{bmatrix}}_{\triangleq R} \begin{bmatrix} \bar{x} \\ \bar{y} \end{bmatrix} + \underbrace{\begin{bmatrix} t_x \\ t_y \end{bmatrix}}_{\triangleq T} \Rightarrow \underbrace{\begin{bmatrix} x \\ y \\ 1 \end{bmatrix}}_{X} = \underbrace{\begin{bmatrix} \cos\theta & -\sin\theta & t_x \\ \sin\theta & \cos\theta & t_y \\ 0 & 0 & 1 \end{bmatrix}}_{\triangleq E} \underbrace{\begin{bmatrix} \bar{x} \\ \bar{y} \\ 1 \end{bmatrix}}_{\bar{X}} \tag{8}$$

The mathematical relationship defined by (9) will be abbreviated as $X \xrightarrow{E} E\bar{X}$, where R is an orthogonal(rotation) matrix, so that $R^T R = RR^T = I$.

In general, any two n-th degree curves, defined by a monic $f_n(x, y) = 0$ and a monic $\bar{f}_n(\bar{x}, \bar{y}) = 0$, which outline the boundary of the same object in two different configurations will be Euclidean equivalent if:

$$f_n(x, y) = 0 \xrightarrow{E} f_n(\cos\theta\,\bar{x} - \sin\theta\,\bar{y} + p_x, \sin\theta\,\bar{x} + \cos\theta\,\bar{y} + p_y) = s_n \bar{f}_n(\bar{x}, \bar{y}) = 0 \tag{9}$$

Instead of using the whole curve space as the search region for the next frame, estimated translation and orientation values from the Kalman filter is used to reduce the search region.

4.2 Error Metrics

For the evaluation of algebraic curves within the search region of our curve space, we use the sum of squared distances from the data points to the algebraic curves. For a collection of data points Γ, error is calculated as

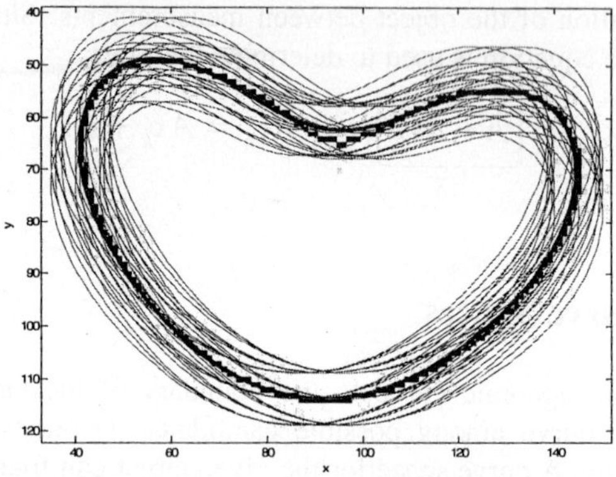

Fig. 4. Algebraic curves in the search region for frame 50 and the selected curve with smallest error term

$$\sum_{(x,y)\in\Gamma} f^2(x,y) \tag{10}$$

Other distance measures can also be employed for the evaluation of curves. For example, the sum of absolute distances from data points to the implicit curve is given as

$$\sum_{(x,y)\in\Gamma} |f(x,y)| \tag{11}$$

Yet another distance measure which approximates the true geometric distance can be calculated as follows:

$$\sum_{(x,y)\in\Gamma} \frac{|f(x,y)|}{\|\nabla f(x,y)\|} \tag{12}$$

5 Experimental Results

For experiments we have used a Boomerang shaped object undergoing a rigid motion with a relatively complex trajectory. Object boundaries have been modelled by quartic curves. For the initialization of the Kalman filter, related points of curves are obtained from the decomposition of the curve. Figure 5 shows the ability of the filter to predict the x-coordinate of the target's centroid. There is an overshoot when tracking fast changes in the x direction. A better illustration of the performance can be seen in an error comparison. The objective is to track the measured signal, so it is assumed that the measure is the true coordinate position. So, the error is the difference between the predicted and measured value. The error values are low and within a band of (-/+)0.5 pixels when the target performs relatively uniform motion. When the target makes a maneuver, error values shows rapid increases, however the values converge to normal error values when the maneuver is over.

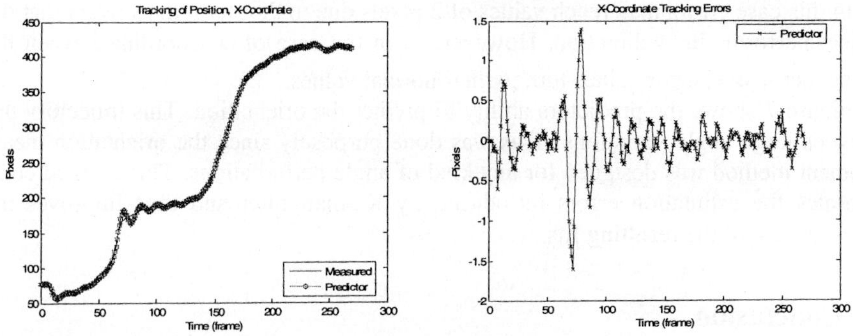

Fig. 5. X-Coordinate tracking of the target

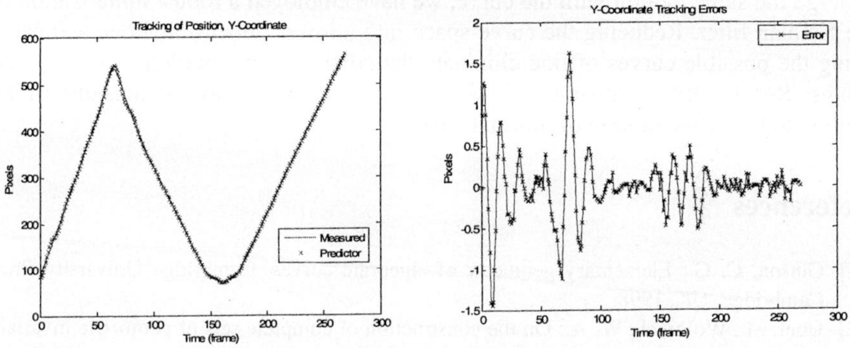

Fig. 6. Y-Coordinate tracking of the target

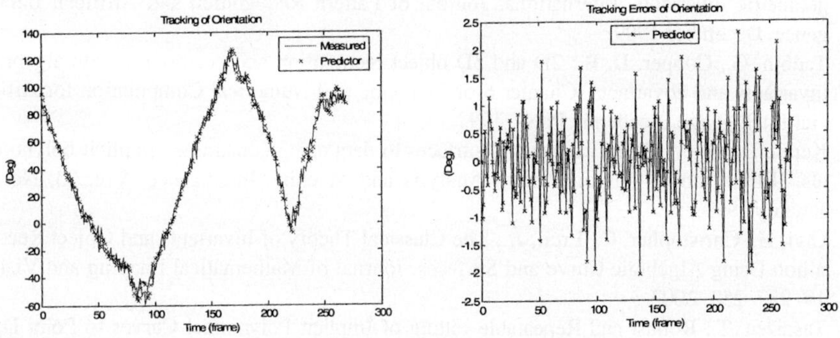

Fig. 7. Orientation tracking of the target

The y-coordinate, on the other hand was exposed to higher speeds and sharp maneuvers. Figure 6 shows the y-coordinate position as a function of time, and it shows the predictor's ability to track this trajectory.

In this case errors may reach values of 2 pixels due to the sharp maneuvers that the object performs in y direction. However, as in the case of x-coordinate when the manevuer is over error values turn to their normal values.

Figure 7 shows the predictors ability to predict the orientation. This trajectory undergoes large angle variations. This was done purposely since the orientation measurement method was designed for any kind of angle perturbations. This method compensates the estimation errors introduced by Kalman filter and thus improves the performance of the resulting fits.

6 Conclusion

We have now presented a method for tracking the position and the orientation of 2D free-form objects undergoing rigid motion. By using the fact that the related points undergo the same motion with the curve, we have employed a robust initialization for the Kalman filter. Reducing the curve-space into a lower dimensional one and calculating the possible curves offline eliminate the computational burden of fitting algorithms. Results are promising and we are working on possible extensions of our method to the affine motion of lips and hands.

References

[1] Gibson, C. G.: Elementary geometry of algebraic curves. Cambridge University Press, Cambridge, UK, 1998.

[2] Unel, M., Wolovich, W. A.: On the construction of complete sets of geometric invariants for algebraic curves. Advances in Applied Mathematics Vol. 24, No. 1, pp. 65-87, January 2000.

[3] Unel, M., Wolovich, W. A.: A new representation for quartic curves and complete sets of geometric invariants. International Journal of Pattern Recognition and Artificial Intelligence, December 1999.

[4] Taubin, G., Cooper, D. B.: 2D and 3D object recognition and positioning with algebraic invariants and covariants. Chapter 6 of Symbolic and Numerical Computation for Artificial Intelligence, Academic Press, 1992.

[5] Keren, D., et al.: Fitting curves and surfaces to data using constrained implicit polynomials. IEEE Transactions on Pattern Analysis and Machine Intelligence, Vol. 23, No. 1, January 1999.

[6] Civi, H., Christopher, C., Ercil, A.: The Classical Theory of Invariants and Object Recognition Using Algebraic Curve and Surfaces. Journal of Mathematical Imaging and Vision 19: 237–253, 2003.

[7] Tasdizen, T.: Robust and Repeatable Fitting of Implicit Polynomial Curves to Point Data Sets and to Intensity Images. PhD Thesis, Brown University, Providence, RI 02912, September 2000.

[8] Wolovich, W. A., Unel, M.: The determination of implicit polynomial canonical curves. IEEE Transactions on Pattern Analysis and Machine Intelligence, Vol. 20, No. 10,pp. 1080-1089, October 1998.

[9] Frank, T., Haag, M., Kollnig, H., Nagel, H-H.: Tracking of occluded vehicles in traffic scenes. 7th European Conference on Computer Vision, pages 485-494,Cambridge,April 1996, Springer Verlag.

[10] Deriche, R., Faugeras, O.: Tracking Line Segments. Image and Vision Computing, 8(4): 261-270, 1990

[11] Mitiche, A., Bouthemy, P.: Computation and analysis of image motion: a synopsis of current problems and methods. International Journal of Computer Vision, 19(1):29-55, 1996

[12] Blake, A., Curwen, R., Zisserman, A.: A framework for spatio-temporal control in the tracking of visual contours. International Journal of Computer Vision, 11(2): 127-145, 1993.

[13] Kottke, D. P., Sun, Y.: Motion estimation via cluster matching. IEEE Transactions on Pattern Analysis and Machine Intelligence, 16:1128-1132, 1994

[14] Lei, Z., Blane, M. M., Cooper, D. B.: 3L Fitting of Higher Degree Implicit Polynomials. In proceedings of 3rd IEEE Workshop on Applications of Computer Vision, pp. 148-153, Florida 1996

[15] Corke, P. I., Good, M. C.: Dynamic effects in high performance visual servoing. Proc. IEEE Int. Conf. Robotics and Automation, pages 1838-1843, 1992

[16] Unel, M.: Polynomial Decompositions for Shape Modeling, Object Recognition and Alignment. PhD Thesis, Brown University, Providence, RI 02912, May 1999.

A Multi-camera Vision System for Real-Time Tracking of Parcels Moving on a Conveyor Belt

Hüseyin N. Karaca and Cüneyt Akınlar

Department of Computer Engineering, Anadolu University, Eskisehir, Turkey
{hnkaraca, cakinlar}@anadolu.edu.tr

Abstract. We consider the problem of designing a vision system for tracking parcels moving on a conveyor belt. After computing parcels dimensions, i.e., length, width and height, at the entrance of the conveyor belt using a stereo camera pair, the vision system incorporates 30fps grayscale image input from 4 cameras equally spaced over the conveyor belt, and computes in real-time the location of each parcel over the belt. The corner points of the tracked parcels are then sent to a controller, which arranges the parcels into a single line at the output. We use Lucas-Kanade-Tomasi (LKT) feature tracking algorithm as the base of our tracking algorithm: Corner points of a parcel from the previous frame are fed into the LKT algorithm to get the new corner coordinates of the parcel in the current frame. Although this approach tracks a parcel for a few frames over the belt, it is not enough for long-term successful tracking of a parcel. To achieve successful parcel tracking, an edge mapping is added as a refinement step following LKT corner tracking. In this paper we detail the design and implementation of our tracking software and show that the proposed algorithms are novel and are able to track parcels in real-time.

1 Introduction

We consider the problem of designing a vision system for real-time tracking of parcels moving on a conveyor belt. The goal of the vision system is to compute the corner points of all parcels and send them to a controller, which arranges the parcels into a single line at the output. Thus the machine is called a "singulator", as it arranges incoming parcels into a single line at the output.

As shown in Figure 1, the singulator is made up of four parts. The first part is the gapper. It has a length of 1500 mm. at the start and 1650 mm. at the end. Gapper consists of several small parallel belts. When parcels come across the gapper, they are separated from each other. This would enable the vision system to detect each individual parcel easily. The second part of the singulator is the 2000 x 1650 mm transition belts, which are observed by two cameras. As the parcels move over these belts in constant speed, their dimensions, i.e., length, width, and height, are computed. The third part of the singulator is the singulator bed that performs the actual parcel singulation. The singulator bed consists of several parallel conveyer belts. There are 12 rows and 7 columns of belts for total of 84 belts. The belts are connected to a controller system, which can change the speed of each belt between 0 to 2.5 meter/sec by the help of servo motors. The job of the controller is to arrange the incoming parcels into

P. Yolum et al.(Eds.): ISCIS 2005, LNCS 3733, pp. 708 – 717, 2005.

a single line at the output by intelligently adjusting the belt speeds. The final parcel output should be similar to the one depicted in Figure 1, where incoming parcels form a single line at the output and are also parallel to the x-axis. The last part of the singulator is the roller junction or the diverter, which is used to direct parcels toward one of two takeaway belts.

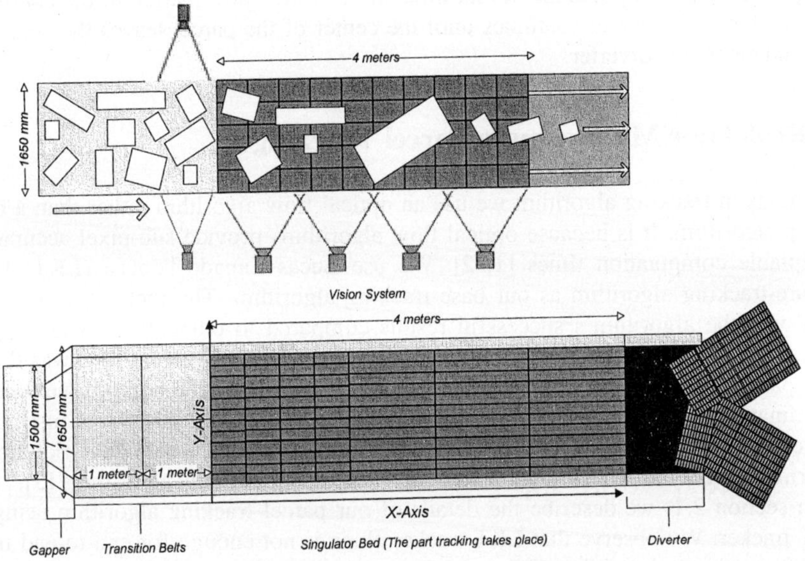

Fig. 1. Different views of the singulator

For the controller to perform proper singulation of parcels, it must know parcels' locations at all times. So there is a need for a system that would perform parcel location computation in real-time and feed this information to the controller. This is the job of the vision system.

In the design of the vision system, we use 6 cameras as shown in Figure 1. Each camera captures grayscale images at 30 fps. The first 2 cameras are positioned side-by-side over the transition belts. Inputs from these cameras are used for initial parcel dimension computation. That is, the length, width and height of all incoming parcels are computed using the input from these two cameras. Since the parcels move at constant speed along the x-axis over these belts, parcel tracking over the transition belts is not a problem. The actual tracking of a parcel starts when the center of a parcel enters the singulator bed. Since a parcel can rotate and translate over the singulator bed, tracking in this area is a formidable job. We use 4 equally-spaced cameras over this area for tracking purposes. Each camera's view intersects with the one that comes before and after it. This makes it possible to view a parcel in more than one camera when it crosses camera boundaries, which makes tracking easier. The whole conveyer belt is calibrated with the vision system. This calibration enables conversion of pixel values on the images to the real life millimeter coordinates and vice versa.

In this paper we discuss the part of the vision system that performs real-time tracking of the parcels as they move over the singulator bed. We do not address the detection and height computation of parcels, which is performed using the input from the first two cameras. We assume that when the parcels arrive at the tracking area, that is the singulator bed, we already know their dimensions, i.e., length, width, height. The tracking software then uses these initial coordinates and inputs from 4 cameras to compute new parcel positions in real-time and feed this information to the controller. The tracking of a parcel continues until the center of the parcel leaves the singulator bed and enters the diverter.

2 Real-Time Multi-camera Parcel Tracking

As the main tracking algorithm we use an optical flow algorithm rather than a block match algorithm. It is because optical flow algorithms provide sub-pixel accuracy in acceptable computation times [1, 2]. We use Lucas-Kanade-Tomasi (LKT) [5, 8] feature-tracking algorithm as our base tracking algorithm. The motivation for using LKT was the algorithm's successful results compared to other block matching and optical flow algorithms in some previous studies [6, 7]. Our general idea was to feed in a parcel's known "corner" coordinates to LKT and get the parcel's new corner coordinates in the current images. The tracked corners are then used to reconstruct the parcel's 3D coordinates using the camera calibration. Since corners have rich texture information, they are more suitable to be tracked by optical flow algorithms [3].

In section 2.1, we describe the details of our parcel tracking algorithm using the LKT tracker. We observe that LKT tracker alone is not enough for end-to-end tracking of parcels. So in sections 2.2 and 2.3 we describe refinements that were added for end-to-end successful tracking of parcels. In section 3, we present running time results of our algorithms.

2.1 Using LKT for Parcel Tracking

When parcels arrive at the tracking area, i.e., the singulator bed, their initial corner coordinates are known. So when the tracking starts, the 3D corner coordinates of a parcel and its height are assumed to be given to the tracker. The tracker's job then boils down to the following: Given the corner coordinates of a parcel at time t, compute the new corner coordinates of the parcel at time $t + 33$ ms, that is, at the current frame. As a first attempt to solve this problem, we use the following algorithm:

1. Back-project the 3D corner coordinates of parcels to 2D pixel coordinates in the given image using the camera calibration
2. Feed the back-projected parcel corner coordinates into LKT and get the new corner coordinates in the current image
3. Compute the parcels' new 3D coordinates using the corners tracked by LKT

The idea is simple: To compute the new 3D corner coordinates of a parcel, we first back-project the current 3D corner coordinates to obtain the parcel's 2D, i.e., image, corner coordinates in a given image. Recall that the system is fully calibrated, so the back-projection gives precise results. We then feed these coordinates into LKT along with the current image and get a parcel's new 2D corner coordinates in the current image. Finally, the new 3D corner coordinates are computed from the tracked 2D corner coordinates with the help of camera calibration. This is possible since the height of the parcel is known.

Although all four corners of a parcel are fed into LKT for tracking, it is possible for LKT to lose tracking of some corners. But observe that 2 corners are enough to reconstruct the parcel since the dimensions of the parcel is already known. To handle such cases we have a detailed algorithm that computes the parcel's new location given a set of tracked corner points. Clearly we need at least 2 corners to reconstruct the parcel.

The above algorithm is repeated for each image. An additional consideration exists when a parcel is viewed by two cameras. This happens during transition times when a parcel moves from the view of one camera to the view of the next. We handle such cases as follows: If a corner is viewed with more than one camera, it is tracked by both cameras. We then select the best feature point as the new corner, where the best feature is defined to be the feature that has the bigger eigenvalue.

Figure 2 shows the tracking results of the above algorithm. The top two images are from the stereo cameras observing transition belts, where the parcel dimension computation is performed. The image below these two cameras is from the first camera looking at the entrance of the singulator bed, where the tracking starts. The 3 images displayed from top to bottom on the right are from the other 3 cameras that observe the singulator bed. A parcel entering the singulator will first be observed by the stereo cameras on the left. It will then move downward and will be seen by the camera below these two cameras. The parcel will then appear on the top-most camera on the right and will move downward until it exits the singulator. In the figure we display the top-face of a parcel. If the tracking is successful, the back-projection will exactly fit on the parcel's boundaries. Otherwise, the back-projection will show up at an irrelevant place on the belt.

As both figures above show the algorithm is able to track a parcel for a few frames, but end-to-end tracking of a parcel cannot be sustained. This is clear on both figures

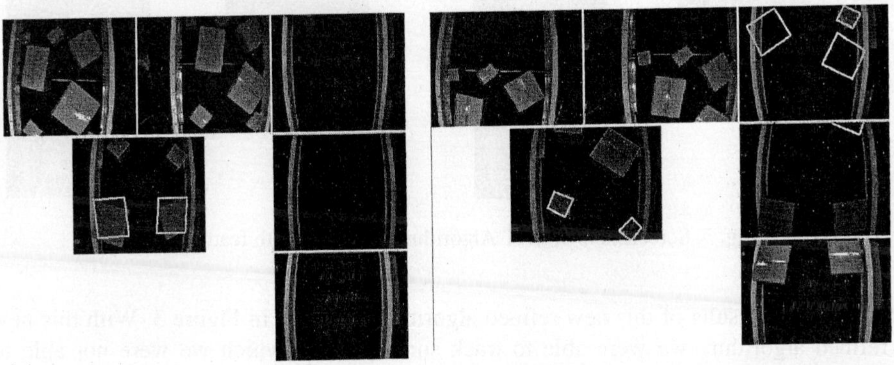

Fig. 2. Screenshots parcels tracked by the LKT algorithm

above: When the tracking starts with the first camera, the parcels are almost tracked as evidenced by the back-projected top-face on the first camera. But as parcels have moved along the singulator bed, the tracking is lost as the back-projections show up at irrelevant places on the singulator. The failure is a result of insufficient image quality, lighting problems and color intensities of the conveyer: The LKT tracker is not able to track the corners of a parcel with high precision, which causes corner errors to compound after several frames leading to tracking failure.

2.2 Supporting LKT with Feature Detection

With the observation that LKT is not able to successfully track all corner coordinates of a parcel, which leads to tracking failure, our next idea was to refine the LKT tracking results before reconstructing the parcel's 3D coordinates. Specifically, after LKT returns the new corner coordinates, we run the feature detection algorithm of [3] around each tracked corner. We then move the tracked feature to this new detected feature if the detected feature is better than the tracked feature, where better is defined to be the feature that has the bigger eigenvalue. Notice that feature detection is run around each tracked corner rather than the entire image, which results in fast computation of relevant features. Here is the new algorithm:

1. Back-project the 3D corner coordinates of parcels to 2D pixel coordinates in the given image using the camera calibration information
2. Feed the back-projected parcel corner coordinates into LKT and get the new corner coordinates in the current image
3. Apply a feature detection algorithm around the tracked features, pick the best feature and move the tracked feature to the detected feature if necessary
4. Compute the parcels' new 3D coordinates using the tracked and refined corners

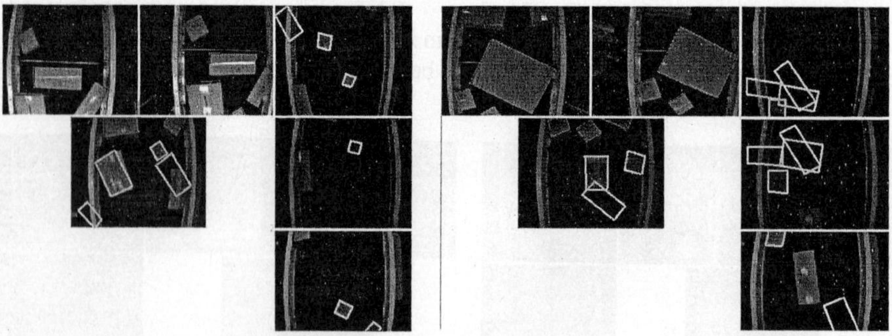

Fig. 3. Screenshots of LKT Algorithm supported with feature detection

Tracking results of this new refined algorithm is shown in Figure 3. With this new refined algorithm, we were able to track some parcels, which we were not able to track using just the LKT algorithm. But overall, the tracking failed for most of the parcels. Our conclusion was that parcel tracking solely based on parcel corners will not be sufficient for successful tracking of parcels.

2.3 Supporting LKT with Edge Detection and Mapping

Armed with the conclusion from the previous section that parcel tracking solely based on parcel corners is not sufficient for successful tracking of parcels, we turned our attention to the other available feature of a parcel: Parcel edges. Our idea is first to run LKT as before to compute the *approximate* location of the parcel, and then try to find the *real* location of the parcel by mapping the parcel's edges to the edges extracted from the images. Observe that the parcel's real location will be around the vicinity of its approximate location as computed by the algorithm presented in section 2.2. The new algorithm is outlined below:

1. Back-project the 3D corner coordinates of parcels to 2D pixel coordinates in the given image using the camera calibration information
2. Feed the back-projected parcel corner coordinates into LKT and get the new corner coordinates in the current image
3. Apply a feature detection algorithm around the tracked features, pick the best feature and move the tracked feature to the detected feature if necessary
4. Compute the parcels' new 3D coordinates using the tracked and refined corners
5. Extract edge information from the images and fix the parcels' coordinates using an edge mapping algorithm

The first 4 steps of the algorithm are the same as the algorithm presented in section 2.2. The only difference is the last step, which refines the computed parcel location using the edge information of the parcel. This step can be implemented in one of two ways: (1) Use an edge finding algorithm and extract possible edges from all images. Map the extracted edges to parcels' edges and refine parcels' locations with the mapped edge information, (2) Form a search space for possible parcel locations. Then test the validity of each hypothesis and pick the one that is the best.

Although an algorithm that is based on (1) would be more robust, edge extraction is an expensive operation. Since our tracker needs to run in real-time, we use the second approach. To implement this approach we proceed as follows: After approximate parcel location is computed using the algorithm in section 2.2, we form a small search space in 3D. We hypothesize that the center of the parcel in x-direction can be off by -20, 0, 20, 40 mm, can be off in the y-direction by -20, 0, 20 mm, and the parcel orientation can be off by -15, 0, 15 degrees. So there are 36 different parcel location hypotheses to be tested.

To test each hypothesis, we back-project the hypothesized 3D parcel corner coordinates back to the 2D image coordinates. We then go over the back-projected edges of the parcel and test whether the virtual line fits any real edges within the image. Notice that this test must be very fast. So we use the famous line tracing algorithm by Bresenham [9, 10, 12]. This algorithm computes the pixels of an ideal line between two end points, and is known to use only integer arithmetic, which makes the implementation run very fast. Since there are 4 edges of a parcel, we take each edge of the parcel and use Bresenham's algorithm to find the ideal pixels that the edge goes over the image. We then test whether each pixel on the line is an edge pixel for some parcel by comparing the intensity of 3 pixels above and below the current pixel. If the

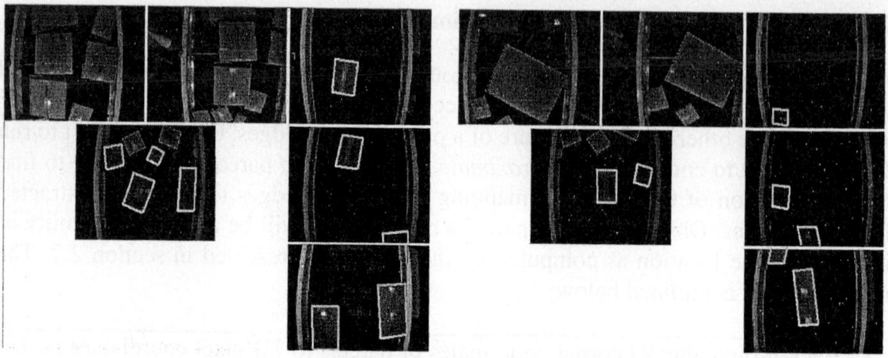

Fig. 4. Screenshots of LKT Algorithm supported with edge mapping

difference is bigger than some threshold, the pixel is assumed to be an edge pixel. For each hypothesis we count the number of edge pixels and pick the hypothesis that gives the biggest number of edge pixels as the parcel's new location.

Tracking results of this new refined algorithm is shown in Figure 4. It should be clear from the figures that we were able to track all parcels successfully. We ran the algorithm for a 25 seconds video sequence and observed that the algorithm successfully tracked *all* parcels without losing a single one.

2.4 Edge Mapping Alone

Edge mapping played a key role in the whole tracking system and led us to think what happens if we use only the edge mapping algorithm without LKT tracker. To use the edge mapping algorithm alone, it is clear that we need a larger search space. So we extended the search space as follows: (1) Change the center of the parcel in +x direction between 0 to 120mm in 20mm increments, (2) change the center of the parcel in y direction between –60 to 60mm in 20mm increments, and (3) change the orientation of the parcel between –15 to 15 degrees in 3 degrees increments. This search space corresponds to 539 different hypotheses.

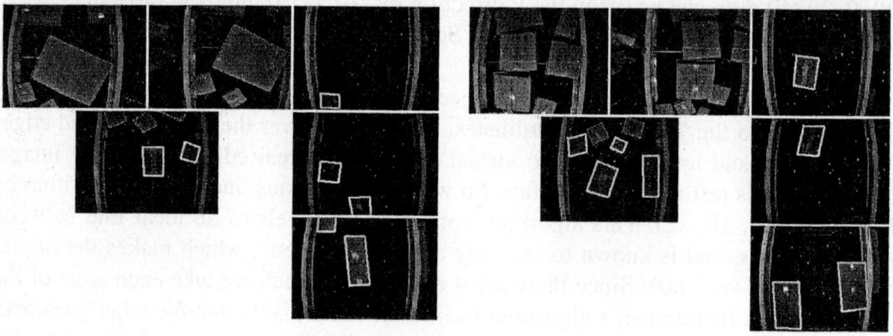

Fig. 5. Screenshots of using only an edge mapping algorithm

Tracking results of this algorithm is shown in Figure 5. Similar to the algorithm in section 2.3, this algorithm was able to track all parcels successfully without any miss. The problem with this algorithm turns out to be the running time as it is impossible to run this algorithm in real-time as discussed in section 3.

3 Time Evaluations and Results

In section 2.3 and 2.4 we presented two algorithms that successfully track parcels as the parcels move over the singulator bed. To test the feasibility of running these algorithms in real-time, and compare them to each other, we run the algorithms on a 25 seconds video sequence. As our testbed we use an Intel Pentium IV 1.90 GHz PC with 1 GB RAM. Since the video capture rate is 30 fps, a tracking algorithm must finish the computation of all parcel locations within 33ms to be real-time.

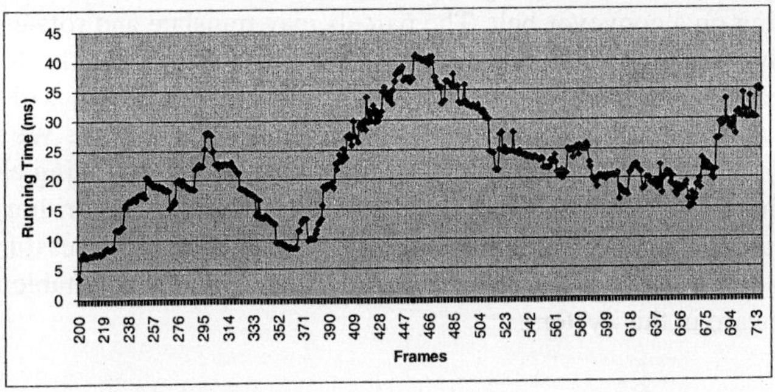

Fig. 6. Running time of the algorithm in section 2.3 based on LKT

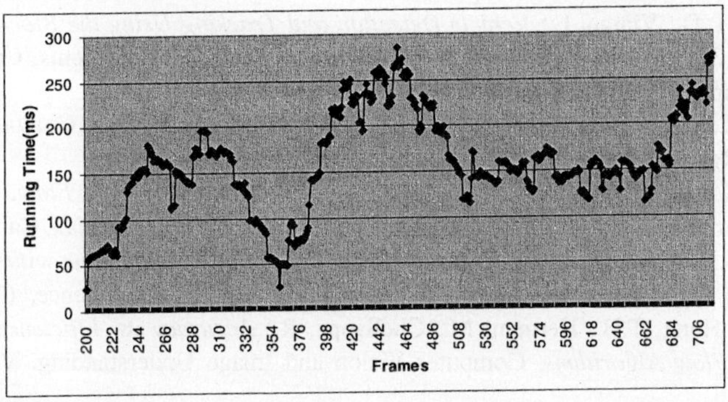

Fig. 7. Running time of the algorithm in section 2 4 based on edge mapping

Figure 6 shows the total running time of the algorithm presented in section 2.3 for each frame in the sequence. Recall that this algorithm first runs LKT to compute an approximate location of the parcel and then uses edge-mapping to refine the parcel's location. As seen, total computation time is below 33ms for a majority of the frames.

Only around frame 450, where a lot of parcels enter the tracking area, does the algorithm take more than 33ms. But we argue that by simply using a more powerful PC, or a PC with dual processors the algorithm can easily run in real-time for all frames. Observe that the algorithm is embarrassingly parallel in nature: LKT for each frame can be run on a different processor in a multi-processor system. Also edge mapping for each parcel can be done in separate processors.

Figure 7 shows the total running time of the algorithm presented in section 2.4. Recall that this algorithm runs edge mapping alone. As seen, total computation time is well beyond 33ms for almost all frames. So we conclude that this algorithm is not suitable for use in a real-time system.

4 Conclusions

In this paper we address the design and implementation of a vision system to track parcels moving on a conveyor belt. The parcels may translate and rotate as they move over the belts. The job of the tracking software is to compute the location of all parcels in real-time and send it over to a controller system, which will then use this information to arrange the parcels into a single line at the output. We presented an algorithm that is based on the famous Lucas-Kanade-Tomasi tracking algorithm, and uses Bresenham's line tracing algorithm as an edge mapping algorithm to refine the computed parcel locations. We showed that the algorithm successfully tracks all parcels for a given video sequence and runs in real-time. So it is suitable for use as the tracking software in this system.

References

1. Eltoukhy, H. , Salama K.: *Multiple Camera Tracking*, Project Report, (2002)
2. Stefano, L.D., Viarani E.: *Vehicle Detection and Tracking Using the Blocking Algorithm*, Proc. of 3rd IMACS/IEEE Int'l Multiconference on Circuits, Systems, Communications and Computer" Athens, Greece, Vol. 1, (1999), 4491-4496
3. Shi, J., Tomasi, C.: *Good Features to Track*, IEEE Conference on Computer Vision and Pattern Recognition, (1994), 593-600
4. Wong, K.Y., Spetsakis, M.E.: *Tracking, Segmentation and Optical Flow*, Proceedings of 16th International Conference on Vision Interface, 57-64, S1.5, Halifax, Canada (2003)
5. Lucas, B.D., Kanade, T.: *An Iterative Image Registration Technique with an Application to Stereo Vision,* International Joint Conference on Artificial Intelligence, (1981), 674-679
6. Liu, H., Hong, T.H., Herman, M., Chellappa, R.: *Accuracy vs. Efficiency Trade offs in Optical Flow Algorithms,* Computer Vision and Image Understanding, Vol. 72, (1998), 271 – 286
7. Barron, J. L., Fleet, D.J., Beauchemin, S.S.: *Performance of Optical Flow Techniques*, Int J Comp Vis, vol. 12, no. 1, (1994), 43-77
8. Tomasi, C., Kanade, T.: *Detection and Tracking of Point Features,* Carnegie Mellon University Technical Report CMU-CS-91-132, (1991)
9. Bresenham, J.E.: "Algorithm for Computer Control of a Digital Plotter", IBM Systems Journal, 4(1), (1965), 25-30

10. Bresenham, J.E.: "A linear Algorithm for Incremental Digital Display of Circular Arcs", Communications of the ACM, 20(2), February (1977), 100-106
11. Baker, S., Gross, R., Matthews, I.: *Lucas-Kanade 20 years on: A unifying frame work* Part 4, Technical Report CMU-RI-TR-04-14, Robotics Institute, Carnegie Mellon University, Pittsburgh, PA, (2004)
12. Pitteway, M.L.V.: "Algorithm for Drawing Ellipses or Hyperbolae with a Digital lotter", Computer J., 10(3), November (1967), 282-289

Selection and Extraction of Patch Descriptors for 3D Face Recognition

Berk Gökberk and Lale Akarun

Boğaziçi University, Computer Engineering Department, Turkey
{gokberk, akarun}@boun.edu.tr

Abstract. In 3D face recognition systems, 3D facial shape information plays an important role. 3D face recognizers usually depend on *point cloud representation* of faces where faces are represented as a set of 3D point coordinates. In many of the previous studies, faces are represented holistically and the discriminative contribution of local regions are assumed to be equivalent. In this work, we aim to design a local region-based 3D face representation scheme where the discriminative contribution of local facial regions are taken into account by using a subset selection mechanism. In addition to the subset selection methodology, we have extracted patch descriptors and coded them using Linear Discriminant Analysis (LDA). Our experiments on the 3D_RMA database show that both the proposed floating backward subset selection scheme and the LDA-based coding of region descriptors improve the classification accuracy, and reduce the representation complexity significantly.

1 Introduction

Despite two decades of intensive study, the challenges of face recognition remain: changes in the illumination and in-depth pose problems make this a difficult problem. Recently, 3D approaches to face recognition have shown promise to overcome these problems [1]. 3D face data essentially contains multi-modal information: *shape* and *texture*. Initial attempts in 3D research have mainly focused on *shape* information, and combined systems have emerged which fuse shape and texture information.

Surface normal-based approaches use facial surface normals to align and match faces. A popular method is to use the EGI representation [2]. *Curvature-based* approaches generally segment the facial surface into patches and use curvatures or shape-index values to represent faces [3]. *Iterative Closest Point-based (ICP)* approaches perform the registration of faces using the popular ICP algorithm [4], and then define a similarity according to the quality of the fitness computed by the ICP algorithm [5]. *Principal Component Analysis-based (PCA)* methods first project the 3D face data into a 2D intensity image where the intensities are determined by the depth function. Projected 2D depth images can later be processed as standard intensity images [6]. *Profile-based* or *contour-based*

P. Yolum et al.(Eds.): ISCIS 2005, LNCS 3733, pp. 718–727, 2005.

approaches try to extract salient 2D/3D curves from face data, and match these curves to find the identity of a person [7]. *Point signature-based* methods encode the facial points using the relative depths according to their neighbor points [8].

In this paper, we present a framework to represent faces locally by surface patches. The motivations of employing local patches are twofold: 1) we can analyze the contribution of local facial regions to the recognition accuracy of a 3D face recognizer, and 2) we can obtain a more compact face representation using sparse feature sets. For the first case, we formulate the recognition problem as a floating feature selection problem, and for the second case, we extract patch descriptors, and code them using statistical feature extraction methods. The face representation part is based on a novel variation of an ICP-based registration scheme. Designed registration algorithm is very fast, and it makes use of a generic average face model. As features, we have used the 3D coordinates and surface normals of the registered faces.

The organization of the paper is as follows: Section 2.1 explains the registration algorithm. In Section 2.2, we provide our face description method and the similarity measures. Detailed explanation of the patch-based representation schemes are given in Section 2.3. The application of feature selection and extraction methods are explained in Section 2.4. Experimental results are presented in Section 3.

2 The Proposed System

2.1 3D Face Registration and Dense Correspondence Establishment

Registration of facial data involves two steps: a preprocessing step and a transformation step. In the preprocessing step, a surface is fitted to the raw 3D facial point data. Surface fitting is carried out to sample the facial data regularly. After surface fitting, central facial region is cropped and only the points inside the cropped ellipsoid are retained. In order to determine the central cropping region, nose tip coordinates are used. Cropped faces are translated so that the nose tip locations are at the same coordinates. In the rest of the paper, we refer to the cropped region as the facial data. After preprocessing of faces, a transformation step is used to align them. In the alignment step, our aim is to rotate and translate faces such that later on we can define acceptable similarity measures between different faces. For this purpose, we define an *average face model* in a specific position in the 3D coordinate system. Average face model is defined as the average of the training faces. Each face is rigidly rotated and translated to fit the template. Iterative Closest Point (ICP) algorithm is used to find the rotation and the translation parameters. The correspondences found between the template face and two arbitrary faces F_i and F_j by the ICP algorithm are then used to establish point-to-point dense correspondences. The ICP algorithm basically determines the nearest point on F_i to an arbitrary point on the average face model. Therefore, for each point on the average face model, the corresponding point on F_i is selected. If there are m points on the average face model $F_A = \{p_1^A, p_2^A, ..., p_m^A\}$, we represent face F_i by the nearest m points on F_i, i.e $\Phi_i = \{p_1^i, p_2^i, ..., p_m^i\}$. Here, Φ_i denotes the registered face. This methodology allows the ordering of 3D points on faces which is necessary to define similarity between two faces.

2.2 Facial Features

Let Φ_i be the registered 3D face of the ith individual. In *point cloud-based* representation, 3D coordinates of a facial point cloud are used as features. We can represent Φ_i in *point cloud representation* as $\Phi_i^P = \{p_1^i, p_2^i, ...p_m^i\}$, where p^is are the (x, y, z) coordinates of each 3D point the face and m is the number of points in the face. In *surface normal-based representation*, surface normals of all m points are used as features: $\Phi_i^N = \{n_1^i, n_2^i, ...n_m^i\}$ where n^is are unit surface normal vectors. Since the dense point correspondence algorithm produces an ordering of facial points, we define the distance between two faces Φ_i and Φ_j in point-cloud representation as: $D(\Phi_i^P, \Phi_j^P) = \sum_{k=1}^{n} ||p_k^i - p_k^j||$ where $||.||$ denotes Euclidean norm. The same distance function is used for the surface normal-based representation technique. As a pattern classifier, 1−nearest neighbor algorithm is used.

2.3 Local Patch-Based Representation of Faces

In this paper, we propose to use local patches for 3D face representation. Instead of using all facial features extracted from every point on the facial surface, we divide the face region into rectangular patches. Figure 1 depicts the patches on a sample face.

We use two different patch representation techniques. The first technique uses all the features extracted from each point inside the patches. Suppose that there are k patches over the facial surface. In the first technique, the patch Γ_i is

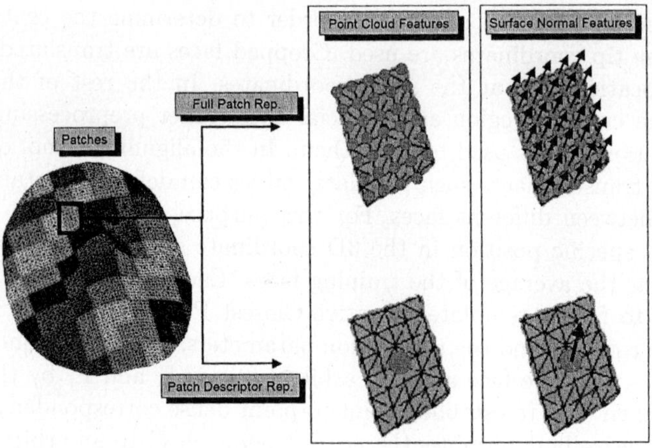

Fig. 1. Illustration of *full patch representation* and *patch descriptor representation* for point cloud and surface normal features

represented by $\Gamma_i = \{p_1^i, p_2^i, ..., p_q^i\}$ where p's are point cloud features, and there are q points on the Γ_i. If all k patches are used to define a face Φ, then Φ can be written as: $\Phi = \cup_{i=1}^{k} \Gamma_i$.

The second patch representation technique is based on patch descriptors. Instead of using all features, we compute a patch descriptor, and use this descriptor to represent the patch. Formally, let d_i be the descriptor calculated from patch Γ_i, then $\Gamma_i = d_i$. In this work, we use two patch descriptors. In point cloud representation, average 3D coordinate of the patch points are used as d_i, and in surface-normal representation, average surface normal of every point on the patch is used as d_i.

The difference between the two patch representation techniques is that in the first one, all surface features are stored in representing patch Λ_i, whereas in the second, only one surface feature is stored. In the rest of the paper, we refer to the first technique as *full patch representation*, and the second technique as *patch descriptor representation*. The *full patch representation* technique is used for floating feature selection, and the *patch descriptor representation* is used for statistical feature extraction.

2.4 Feature Selection and Extraction Methodology

Subset Selection. We use near-optimal feature selection techniques to find the most discriminating patch subsets for identification. Our aim is to find the patch subset $\Omega = \cup_{i=1}^{c} \Gamma_i$ where $c << k$ (k = the number of patches over the facial surface). In this method, *full patch representation* is used.

Formulating a local feature-based 3D face recognition problem as a subset selection methodology has three important advantages: 1) Floating backward elimination algorithm takes into account the dependencies between features, 2) Regions which are not selected can be discarded from the representation, thus allowing to reduce the representation complexity 3) Floating backward elimination is a supervised procedure which uses the class information in determining the subsets. A similar approach was previously proposed for 2D face recognition problem where floating forward selection algorithms and genetic algorithms are used to determine 2D Gabor wavelets in [9]. In feature selection, the goal is to find a subset maximizing a selected criterion. This criterion can be inter–class distance measure or the classification rate of a classifier. The optimal solution could be found by using exhaustive search. However, for higher dimensional problems, this solution is unusable. Alternative to optimal algorithms, several fast sub–optimal algorithms can be used. In order to find the most discriminative image locations of faces for recognition, we have used floating backward search (SFBS). SFBS tries to remove a feature from the initial set, and then tries to add previously removed features to the current set if the inclusion is beneficial. Nested removal and addition operators in SFBS increases the run-time complexity of the search process, however this methodology produces near-optimal subsets.

Statistical Feature Extraction. Feature subset selection method can be viewed as a dimensionality reduction technique. It selects the most useful features according to some criteria such as classification rate. An alternative would be to use statistical feature extraction techniques for dimensionality reduction. For this purpose, we propose to use Principal Component Analysis (PCA) and Linear Discriminant Analysis (LDA) to extract features. For these methods, we use *patch descriptor representation* of faces. Formally, let the face Φ be represented by k patch descriptors: $\Phi = \{d_1, d_2, ...d_k\}$. d_i's can be 3-vectors for point coordinates or surface normals. By applying PCA or LDA we form a new subspace of dimensionality s, $(s << k \times 3)$, and represent any face using PCA or LDA coefficients: $\Phi = \{c_1, c_2, ...c_s\}$.

3 Experimental Results

In our experiments, we have used the `3D_RMA` dataset [7]. Specifically, a subset of the automatically prepared faces, which consists of 106 subjects each having five or six shots, were used in the experiments. The data is obtained with a stereo vision assisted structured light system. On the average, faces contain about 4,000 3D points, and they cover different portions of the faces and the entire data is subject to expression and rotation changes. To be able to statistically compare the algorithms, we have designed five experimental sessions. Training and test set configurations of each experimental session are: $S_1 = Tr : \{1,2,3,4\}, Ts : \{5,6\}$, $S_2 = Tr : \{1,2,3,5\}, Ts : \{4,6\}$, $S_3 = Tr : \{1,2,4,5\}, Ts : \{3,6\}$, $S_4 = Tr : \{1,3,4,5\}, Ts : \{2,6\}$, $S_5 = Tr : \{2,3,4,5\}, Ts : \{1,6\}$. Numbers in Tr and Ts sets denote which images of each subject are placed into the training and test set, respectively. At each session, there are 193 test shots. In order to determine the best subset Ω_{best}, we have to use only training instances, and then test the accuracy of Ω_{best} on the test instances. For this purpose, four cross-validation sets have been formed from training examples.

3.1 Subset Selection Results

Suppose that at the ith iteration of the SFBS algorithm, we have a subset Ω_i containing several patches. The recognition performance of Ω_i is calculated as the average of the four cross-validation experiments. We have divided the whole facial region into 93 non-overlapping rectangular patches. Each face contains 3,389 points which are densely registered to the average face model. On the average, central patches contain 36 points. Let Ω_{ALL} be the set containing all 93 patches. The average recognition performance of Ω_{ALL}^{PC} for *point cloud representation* in five experiments is found to be 95.96 percent (See *PC-All regions* entry in the *Non-overlapping* part of the Table. 1). In *surface normal representation*, the average recognition accuracy of all regions, Ω_{ALL}^{SN}, is 99.17 percent. By applying the SFBS algorithm, we have found best subsets, Ω_{BEST}^{PC} and Ω_{BEST}^{SN} for point cloud, and surface normal representations, respectively. The average recognition performances of Ω_{BEST}^{PC} and Ω_{BEST}^{SN} in the test set are 96.79 and 98.14 percent.

The selected patches of Ω_{BEST}^{PC} and Ω_{BEST}^{SN} are shown in Figure 2 as dark regions. These results confirm that by using SFBS method, we can reduce the dimensionality of the face representation by half, an still have a comparable

Table 1. Average classification accuracies of 1) floating backward selection of non-overlapping regions, and 2) feature extraction of overlapping region descriptors (PC = Point cloud rep., SN = Surface normal rep.)

Non-overlapping (93 regions)		
Method	Dimensionality	Accuracy
PC - All regions	3,389	95.96
PC - Best Subset	53 × 36	96.79
SN - All regions	3,389	99.17
SN - Best Subset	48 × 36	98.14
Overlapping (327 regions)		
Method	Dimensionality	Accuracy
PC - All regions	327 × 3	96.06
PC - PCA	70	90.88
PC - LDA	60	99.69
SN - All regions	327 × 3	99.28
SN - PCA	70	94.51
SN - LDA	40	99.69

Fig. 2. Selected regions (in dark color) using, Left: point cloud, and Right: Surface normal representations

recognition accuracy. Note that the recognition performance of Ω_{BEST}^{PC} is better than Ω_{ALL}^{PC}.

3.2 Statistical Feature Extraction Results

For PCA and LDA-based face representation methods, we use a different patch formation scheme. In this scheme, we have formed overlapping regions over the face, thus increased the number of patches. In these experiments, 327 overlapping regions are formed, where the size of each patch is the same as in the non overlapping scheme. In the non-overlapping case, each region is described by the 3D points lying on that region. In the overlapping case, each patch is represented by a *patch descriptor*. In point cloud representation, the mean of the 3D coordinates of each patch's point cloud is used as a patch descriptor. In surface normal representation, the mean of the surface normals of a patch is used as a patch descriptor.

The mean recognition accuracies of the point cloud and surface normal representations using patch descriptors are found to be 96.06 and 99.28 percent respectively (See *PC-All regions* and *SN-All regions* entries in the *Overlapping* part of Table. 1). These are the classification accuracies of using all patch descriptors without applying PCA or LDA. The use of patch descriptors in the overlapping division scheme improved the classification accuracy when compared to the non-overlapping case. It is found that dimensionality reduction using PCA decreases the recognition performance to 90.88 and 94.51 percent for point cloud and surface normal-based representations, respectively (See *PC-PCA* and *SN-PCA* entries in Table. 1). However, LDA is found to be very beneficial in reducing the dimensionality of patch descriptor-based face representation scheme. LDA obtained 99.69 percent accuracy in both point cloud and surface normal representations, using 60 and 40 features, respectively.

3.3 The Effect of Patch Resolution

In the previous section, we have presented the results of the classification experiments where a fixed patch resolution is used for both overlapping and non-overlapping patch division strategy. The patch height and width are selected to be $H/10$ and $W/10$, where H and W denote the height and width of the cropped

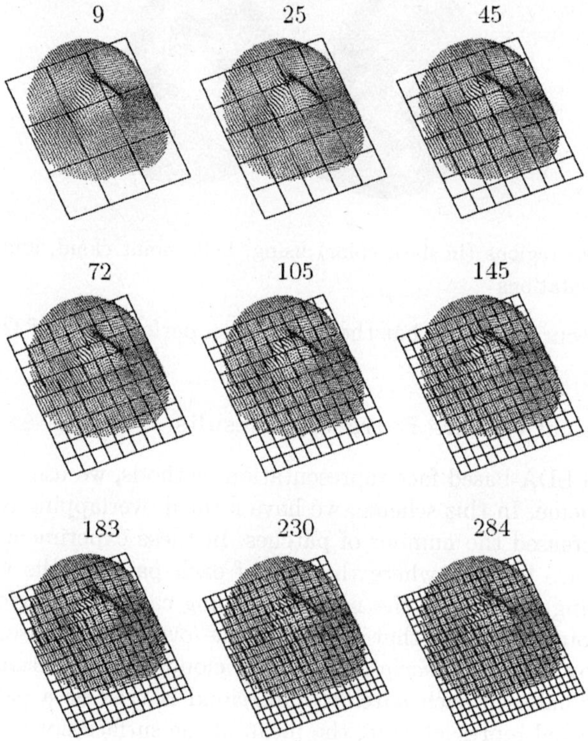

Fig. 3. Different patch resolutions and the total number of patches found over a facial surface

mean face. We have shown that the use of 327 patch descriptors is slightly better than using raw point clouds and surface normals, where patch-based classification accuracies are $d_{depth} = 96.06, d_{normals} = 99.28$ and raw recognition accuracies are 95.96 and 99.17 percent for 3,389 point clouds and surface normals, respectively. This finding motivates us to analyze the effect of patch resolution on the classification performance. For this purpose, we have used different patch resolutions for segmenting the whole facial region. Figure 3 depicts a subset of various patch resolutions that we have used. From coarse to fine scale, we have extracted different face segmentations where the numbers of patches used are : 4, 9, 16, 25, 34, 45, 60, 72, 88, 105, 124, 145, 166, 183, 211, 230, 260, 243 and 207.

Table 2 displays the classification accuracies of surface normal-based and point cloud-based patch descriptors on different patch resolutions. The first column shows the number of local patches formed over the face region and the second column shows the average number of 3D points at each local patch. Patch descriptors form a feature vector, and as in previous experiments, 1-nn algorithm is used as a pattern classifier. Figure 4 graphically displays the recognition rates found in Table 2.

It is evident by analyzing Table 2 that significant dimensionality reduction is possible without a significant loss in classification accuracy. Recognition system

Table 2. Classification accuracies of surface normal and point cloud representations for different patch resolutions. First column denotes the number of patches over the facial surfaces and the second column shows the average number of 3D points in each patch.

Number of Patches	Patch Density	Surface Normal Accuracy	Point Cloud Accuracy
4	866	65.80	39.59
9	375	92.64	72.64
16	225	94.61	86.01
25	136	95.96	91.81
34	99	97.62	92.64
45	84	97.62	94.82
60	64	97.93	95.34
72	47	98.86	95.34
88	39	98.86	95.75
105	32	99.17	96.17
124	27	99.17	95.86
145	24	99.28	96.37
166	26	99.07	96.17
183	19	99.28	96.37
211	18	99.17	96.48
230	15	99.17	96.06
260	13	99.17	96.06
243	12	99.07	96.58
207	12	99.17	96.27

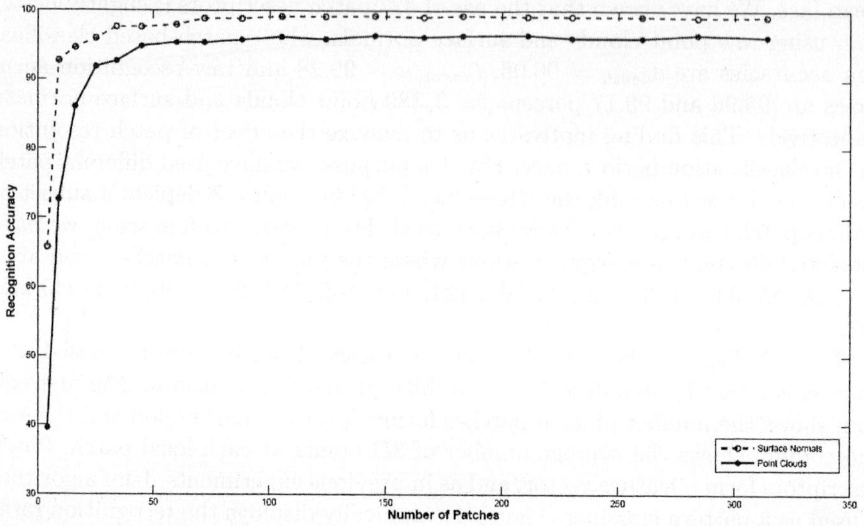

Fig. 4. Recognition accuracy versus patch number plot for surface normal and point cloud-based face representations

can obtain a very good accuracy using approximately 100 patch descriptors. Using only 105 non-overlapping patches, the system obtains 99.17 and 96.17 percent recognition accuracies, and using more patches does not improve the accuracy significantly. These results indicate that the local patch idea which can be considered as a local averaging operator, helps to filter out redundant information. Another advantage would be the de-noising characteristic of local averaging operation. However, in our experimental face database, since we have no local perturbations or noise, this behavior is not visible.

4 Conclusion and Future Work

In this work, we have proposed a local patch-based 3D face representation and recognition system. The motivations behind the patch-based representation scheme are i) to find out the important facial regions for identity recognition and ii) to use a more compact representation. The registration of faces is accomplished by establishing a dense point-to-point dense correspondence between a given face and an average face model. ICP-based registration with the average face model allows an ordering of face vertices. Thus we can define an acceptable similarity measure between any two face.

Two different patch representation schemes are devised where the first scheme uses all feature points over the patch (*full patch representation*) and the second scheme extracts descriptors and uses them to represent patches (*patch descriptor representation*). Floating backward search algorithm is used to find out the useful local regions over the faces in full patch representation. Experimental results on the 3D_RMA dataset show that using nearly half of the 3D surface points, we can get a better recognition accuracy when compared to using the whole facial structure. We also showed that it is very effective to represent faces using patch descriptors in combination with LDA. Experiments related to the patch resolutions indicate that it is useful to code facial features using sparse patch descriptors without a significant classification accuracy loss.

We are currently extending our methodology to include different feature selection methods, and to use other surface descriptors other than 3D point coordinates and surface normals. As future work, we plan to include a unifying framework of feature selection and statistical feature extraction methods using a multi-resolution scheme where the patch sizes are selected dynamically.

References

1. Bowyer, K.W., Chang, K., Flynn, P.J.: A survey of 3D and multi-modal 3D+2D face recognition. In: International Conference on Pattern Recognition. (2004)
2. Tanaka, H.T., Ikeda, M., Chiaki, H.: Curvature-based face surface recognition using spherical correlation principal directions for curved object recognition. In: International Conference on Automated Face and Gesture Recognition. (1998) 372–377
3. Moreno, A.B., Sanchez, A., Velez, J.F., Diaz, F.J.: Face recognition using 3D surface-extracted descriptors. In: Irish Machine Vision and Image Processing Conference. (2003)
4. Besl, P., McKay, N.: A method for registration of 3D shapes. IEEE Transactions on Pattern Analysis and Machine Intelligence **14** (1992) 239–256
5. Irfanoglu, M.O., Gokberk, B., Akarun, L.: 3D shape based face recognition using automatically registered facial surfaces. In: International Conference on Pattern Recognition. (2004) 183–186
6. Xu, C., Wang, Y., Tan, T., Quan, L.: Automatic 3D face recognition combining global geometric features with local shape variation information. In: International Conference on Automated Face and Gesture Recognition. (2004) 308–313
7. Beumier, C., Acheroy, M.: Face verification from 3D and grey level cues. Pattern Recognition Letters **22** (2001) 1321–1329
8. Y.Wang, Chua, C., Ho, Y.: Facial feature detection and face recognition from 2D and 3D images. Pattern Recognition Letters **23** (2002) 1191–1202
9. Gokberk, B., Irfanoglu, M.O., Akarun, L., Alpaydin, E.: Optimal Gabor kernel selection for face recognition. In: IEEE International Conference on Image Processing. (2003)

Implementation of a Video Streaming System Using Scalable Extension of H.264

Aylin Kantarcı

Computer Engineering Department, Ege University, 35100 Bornova, İzmir, Turkey
aylin.kantarci@ege.edu.tr

Abstract. Scalable video coding (SVC) offers flexible adaptation of video bitrate through spatial, temporal and SNR scalability. Recently, it has been shown that SVC can achieve comparable coding performance with the state of the art nonscalable codec H.264 and since then, SVC has regained its popularity among researchers. In this work, a streaming system for scalable H.264 videos has been implemented. In the system, a flexible rate adaptation module selects an appropriate bitstream by considering motion dynamics of video in cases of packet loss in the network and buffer drain at the receiver. In this paper, the developed system has been introduced and the performance results of the implementation have been reported. Experimental results show that the system reacts to congestion and buffer drains in a flexible way and maintains interrupt-free display througout the whole video.

1 Introduction

The goal of current research in the field of video coding is to develop flexible compression approaches to support video services in heterogeneous environments. Scalability, which allows for partial decoding of a single bitstream depending on the availability of system resources such as bandwidth, memory and display resolutions, is the expected functionality to fulfill this requirement. In 2003, to promote the research on scalable coding, MPEG initiated a standardization activity known as Scalable Video Coding (SVC). Since then, scalability has been the main topic of many research groups and the volume of information on scalability in literature has increased tremendously [1].

For video data, there are three dimensions of scalability: *Temporal scalability* means that frame rate of the video can be adjusted. *Spatial scalability* refers to the capability of decoding video frames at different resolutions. *SNR scalability* allows adjusting the target data rate by changing the quantization parameter [2].

Scalability can be attained by a layered coding approach which distributes the video information over a number of layers. The most fundamental information to reconstruct the video is placed on a layer which is called the *base layer*. Other layers, i.e. the *enhancement layers*, provide additive information to increase video quality. An enhancement layer requires a base layer and lower enhancement layers to be able to be decoded. The more layers the decoder receives, the better qualities it will receive [2].

P. Yolum et al.(Eds.): ISCIS 2005, LNCS 3733, pp. 728–738, 2005.

Nonscalable coding schemes are based on a hybrid structure given in Fig. 1. Hybrid structures are difficult to be incorporated in scalable coding schemes based on a layered architecture. This is because of the fact that hybrid architectures maintain the state of an assumed decoder within a predictive feedback loop to minimize prediction errors [1, 3, 4]. However, in layered coding, some enhancement layers may be dropped due to network congestion and end system capability limits. Hence, the decoded video at the encoder and at the receiver will not be the same. As a result, a *drift* occurs between the encoder and the decoder. Various methods have been proposed to eliminate the drifts [4]. Among these methods, motion compensated temporal filtering (MCTF) is commonly agreed to be the best solution to this problem [5].

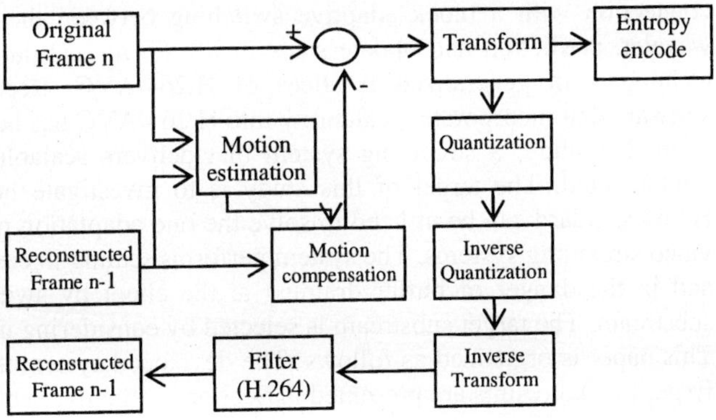

Fig. 1. A nonscalable encoder

MCTF based codecs perform motion compensation through the lifting properties of filter banks, which are cascaded sequences of prediction and update steps (Fig. 2). Because lifting is invertible, any motion compensation technique can be incorporated into the prediction and update states of the filter bank. As shown in Fig. 2, unlike traditional codecs with closed loop architectures given in Fig. 1, MCTF based codecs have an open loop structure of a temporal subband representation. Open loop architectures offer the possibility to efficiently incorporate spatial and SNR scalability. The recent results have shown that MCTF scheme with scalability support can achieve comparable coding performance with the state of the art nonscalable H.264 codec, and even sometimes it outperforms H.264 [6].

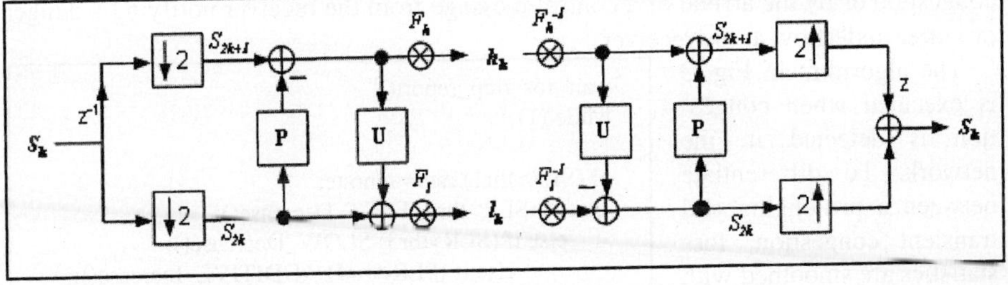

Fig. 2. A scalable encoder: Lifting scheme (Analysis Filterbank) and Inverse Lifting Scheme (Synthesis FilterBank)

With their inherent properties to support temporal, spatial and SNR scalability, MCTF schemes have attracted the attention of JVT experts. JVT initiated an activity to investigate how H.264/AVC can be extended to include scalability aspects. For many reasons, H.264/AVC is a suitable candidate to be implemented in a scalable manner. For example, by using the highly efficient motion model of H.264/AVC in connection with a block adaptive switching between the Haar and the 5/3 spline wavelet, prediction and update steps in MCTF are similar to motion compensation techniques in generalized B slices of H.264/AVC. Recently, a reference codec software that incorporates scalability into H.264/AVC has been prepared [7].

In this study, a streaming system that delivers scalable H.264 videos has been implemented. The target of this study is to investigate how scalable extension of H.264 standard can be utilized to solve the rate adaptation problem that is inherent in video streaming systems. The system performs scaling in cases of network congestion and in the danger of buffer draining at the client by switching to a lower quality substream. The target substream is selected by considering motion dynamics of video. This paper is organized as follows: The developed system is introduced in Section 2. Experimental results are presented in Section 3. Finally, Section 4 is the conclusion.

2 The Developed System

The developed system has client/server architecture. The server software accepts connection requests from clients, streams videos to clients and performs content adaptive QoS adaptation considering network status and buffer level at the client site. Client software receives video packets, places them into a buffer and consumes them from the buffer on a GOP basis. In relation to buffer management, it also tracks the buffer occupancy and notifies the server in case of an undesired change in buffer level. Detailed information about the building blocks of the system is given in [2].

The developed system uses RTP for unicast data transfer. Network statistics are fed back to the server via an accompanying protocol called RTCP. For the exchange of control messages, UDP is used. Scalable H.264 videos are packetized according to the guidelines given in the related Internet draft [9].

Rate adaptation module is an important component of the streaming server. This module is invoked either by the arrival of an RTCP report indicating the existence of congestion or by the arrival of a control message from the receiver notifying a danger of buffer underflow at the receiver.

The algorithm in Fig. 3 is executed when congestion is detected in the network. To differentiate between a prolonging and transient congestion, loss statistics are smoothed with a low pass filter. The system adjusts its data rate according to the level of congestion. The more

```
wait_for_rtcp_report();
while (1)
{
 if (SLR>thr1) rate=minrate;
 else if (SLR>thr2) FAST_Decrease();
      else if (SLR>thr3) SLOW_Decrease();
           else if (SLR<thr4) ADDITIVE_Increase();
 wait_for_rtcp_report()
}
```

Fig. 3. Rate adaptation algorithm for packet losses

severe the congestion, at the higher rate the video quality is reduced. Currently; thr1, thr2, thr3 and thr4 values are 30%, 15%, 5% and 2% respectively. A smoothed loss rate (SLR) value greater than thr1 means the network is SEVERELY congested and video quality is decreased to the minimum level. When the SLR is between thr1 and thr2, the congestion level is considered to be HIGH and video rate is reduced sharply imitating a multiplicative decrease policy. If the SLR value is between thr2 and thr3, the congestion is at MEDIUM level and the video quality is decreased in smaller steps. The prevailing quality is maintained for SLR values between thr3 and thr4. Finally, the network is considered to be LIGHTLY_LOADED when the SLR value is below thr4. In this case, video quality is increased in additive manner.

Another event that invokes the adaptation module is the arrival of notification messages about an important change in buffer level. Client buffers incoming packets to reorder the packets that have arrived out of order, to compensate the effects of jitter and to accumulate a sufficient amount of video data prior to playback to decrease the likelihood and frequency of buffer drains. Experiments show that a prebufferring period of 15 sec. is adequate for the system.

Buffer occupancy drops when consumption rates from the buffer is greater than the input rate to the buffer. This occurs when the sender remains slow to send packets in time or when the delay in the network causes the input rate to the buffer to decrease.

```
wait_for_buffer_notification_message()
{
if (buffer level <10 sec)
  {
   if (network_lightly_loaded)
      Decrease_packet_interval()
   else SLOW_Decrease();
  }
if (buffer level>30 sec) ADDITIVE_Increase();
wait_for_buffer_notification_message();
}
```

Fig. 4. Outline of the buffer management algorithm

In general, delay statistics increase prior to congestion periods. Tracking buffer occupancy may be a practical way of commenting on network delay. When a control message indicating that the buffer level is below 10 sec. is received from the client, it is assumed that the buffer will drain in short time. Provided that there is no packet loss, the first action is to decrease the sending interval between two consecutive packets by a small amount with the expectation that the drop in the buffer level is due to a slow sender. If this does not help, the decrease in buffer level is considered to have resulted from a delay prior to congestion and video quality is decreased to alleviate the network load. If the buffer completely drains, the consumer thread pauses for 5 secs. On the other hand, if the buffer level has risen above 30 sec, it is assumed that there is no delay and video quality is increased in additive manner. If buffer notifications and RTCP reports indicating congestion arrive at the same time, the algorithm in Fig. 3 takes precedence over the algorithm in Fig. 4 since losses have more crucial effects than the delay.

There are two important points to be emphasized in the adaptation algorithm. The first one is that frequent rate switches are avoided not to disturb the viewer. This is achieved by keeping the interval between consecutive quality decreases (increases) at least 10 (20) sec. This also lets the effects of the last adaptation operation have taken place in the network. Secondly, when there is no loss and delay, video quality is increased in additive manner because a sudden large increase in quality may itself result in congestion.

An important property of the rate adaptation module is that it is content-aware. Motion dynamics of video segments is taken into account to select the most appropriate bitstream during rate adaptation decisions. Motion content of videos can be practically determined by an analysis at macroblock level [8]. H.264 videos consist of I, B and P macroblocks. I macroblocks are coded independently of other macroblocks. They are also used as reference for other macroblock types. P and B macroblocks are obtained by prediction from one or more reference pictures. The difference between the two is that P macroblocks are predicted from pictures of one reference list whereas B macroblocks are predicted from pictures from one or two reference lists. Skipped macroblocks are a special kind of predicted macroblocks. The target block is skipped in case where there is little or no difference between the macroblock(s) in the reference frame(s).

Counting the number of different types of macroblocks in video scenes is a practical method to distinguish segments with different motion dynamics [10, 11]. In the case of H.264 videos, motion compensated prediction is performed on submacroblocks with sizes of 16x16, 16x8, 8x16 and 8x8 samples. 8x8 submacroblocks are further divided into partitions with sizes of 8x4, 4x8 and 4x4 blocks. Similarly, intra-prediction is performed on blocks with sizes of 16x16 or 4x4 samples. Therefore, it is more appropriate to analyze the motion content by counting the number of 4x4 blocks of each macroblock type on GOP basis. Our motion analysis module concludes that, a GOP is said to have high motion dynamics if the intracoded content exceeds 20% in that GOP. If the sum of the number skipped blocks and the number of blocks predicted from more than one reference picture is higher than 45%, that GOP has low motion content. Otherwise, that GOP is considered to have motion content of medium level.

When a new video is added to the system, motion analysis is performed and the video is segmented considering motion dynamics. Motion type and location of each segment are stored in a metafile to use during content-aware rate adaptation process.

As given in Fig. 3, video rate is reduced at a fast or slow rate. In the case of congestion at HIGH level; to imitate a multiplicative decrease strategy, the fast rate reduction policy is followed by dropping all FGS layers, one quality layer and one temporal layer at once. In the case of congestion at MEDIUM level, video rate is reduced in smaller steps, imitating an additive decrease policy. At first, FGS layers are dropped one by one. If this does not help, video rate is reduced further by dropping layers or temporal levels. Scaling dimension is determined by considering motion dynamics to maximize perceptual visual quality. In segments with high motion content, details within a frame may not be important because, frame contents change rapidly. Therefore, quality layers are dropped one by one during dynamic scenes. On the other hand, temporal scaling may be more appropriate for scenes with low motion content, since there is little or no change between successive frames, which makes details more visible and dropping frames does not degrade the perceptual quality a lot. In the scenes with medium level of motion, a balance between the two types of scalability is tried to be maintained.

Rate adaptation module increases video rate when the network is lightly loaded and there is no problem with the buffer space at the client. As previously mentioned, quality increases are performed in additive manner. A temporal level is added during scenes with high motion content where as a quality layer is added when the content is static. More detailed explanation about the rate adaptation algorithm is given in [2].

3 Experimental Work

The streaming system introduced in the previous section has been implemented on Sun Ultra Sparc workstations running Solaris 2.8 operating system. RTP library has been obtained from Lucent Technologies. POSIX4 and Pthread libraries have been used to provide realtime support and concurrency, respectively.

The developed system has been tested on an Ethernet LAN network with a client workstation, a server workstation and a PC running CLOUD™ software between them. CLOUD™ enables the PC to act as a router by forwarding packets sent from one workstation to the other one. It also simulates actual WAN environment by dropping and delaying packets in accordance with a given loss and queuing delay pattern.

Various experiments have been carried out to observe the behavior of the system in various congestion scenarios. Loss rates conveyed with RTCP reports have been smoothed with a low pass filter to avoid unnecessary rate regulations due to transient increases of loss rate values. During congestion periods, loss values are associated with queuing delay values, which refer to the amount of time the CLOUD™ software keeps the video packets in its buffer. Another delay type that has affected the behavior of the system in the experiments is the transmission delay which is a function of the bandwidth demand and the bit rate of the channel. Unlike queuing delay, transmission delay can not be configured with CLOUD™. Transmission delay can be calculated by dividing the amount of data to be transmitted by the channel bit rate.

In the following subsections, we will present the experimental results for a scenario in which the rate adaptation module is excluded from the system and for another one in which the rate adaptation module is integrated into the system. In both of the experiments, the system has been tested with two videos one of which has significantly higher bandwidth demand than the other one. The properties of these videos have been presented in Table 1. These videos have been encoded with the recently implemented JSVM 1.0 reference codec for scalable H.264 videos [7]. In the experiments, CLOUD™ has been configured to generate congestion for a period of approximately 60 secs. The queuing delay during congestion is configured to vary within the range [2000-4000] msec. For better simulation of the actual WAN environment, CLOUD™ is configured to drop and delay a small fraction of video packets throughout the experiment.

Table 1. Properties of video sequences used in the experiments

	Layer No	Resolution	Frame rate	Min bit rate	Max bitrate
VIDEO 1	0	176x144	3.75, 7.5 fps	49.06 kbit/s	229.73 kbit/s
	1	176x144	0.9375, 1.875, 3.75, 7.5, 15 fps	43.25 kbit/s	348.67 kbit/s
	2	352x288	0.9375, 1.875, 3.75, 7.5, 15 fps	84.65 kbit/s	939.63 kbit/s
	3	352x288	0.9375, 1.875, 3.75, 7.5, 15 fps	85.26 kbit/s	2046.88 kbit/s
	4	352x288	0.9375, 1.875, 3.75, 7.5, 15, 30 fps	85.61 kbit/s	3137.51 kbit/s
VIDEO 2	0	176x144	7.5,15 fps	217.29 kbit/s	951.63 kbit/s
	1	176x144	1.875, 3.750 , 7.5 ,15 fps	194.60 kbit/s	1341.80 kbit/s
	2	352x288	1.875, 3.750 , 7.5 ,15, 30 fps	462.08 kbit/s	4583.42 kbit/s
	3	352x288	1.875, 3.750 , 7.5 ,15, 30 fps	463.03 kbit/s	8494.76 kbit/s
	4	704x576	1.875, 3.750 , 7.5 ,15, 30 fps	597.36 kbit/s	15628.82 kbit/s
	5	704x576	1.875, 3.750 , 7.5 ,15, 30, 60 fps	598.83 kbit/s	31402.10 kbit/s

1. EXPERIMENT 1: System Behavior without the Rate Adaptation Module

It is adequate to examine the buffer statistics to understand the behavior of the system when the rate adaptation module is omitted. In this experiment, video quality is kept at the highest level throughout streaming. When the initial buffering period is over, buffer level remains constant for 30 sec and declines due to the large transmission delay induced by the high bandwidth demand.

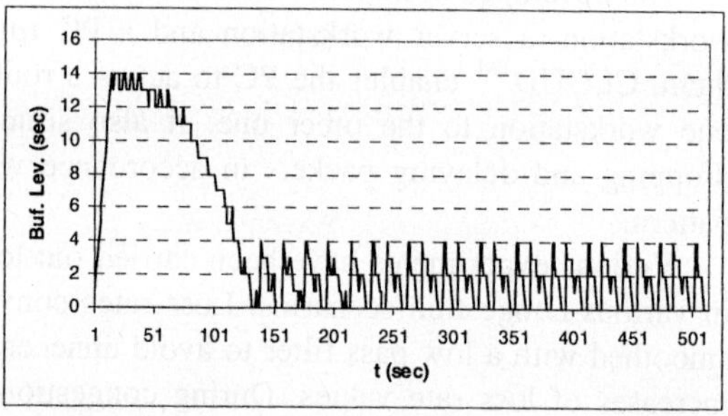

Fig. 5. Buffer statistics when rate adaptation module is omitted

Buffer level drops below 10 sec at t=90 sec. Since adaptation module is omitted, no action is taken to increase the buffer level. Therefore, buffer drains at t=130 sec and the consumer thread pauses for 5 secs. to accumulate new packets in the buffer. When the consumer thread wakes up, 4 secs. of video has been stored in the buffer. Due to the large transmission delay, buffer quickly drains again. As a consequence, the consumer thread pauses again. This cycle is repeated throughout streaming. The graph in Fig. 5 has been obtained in the experiment with Video1 when there is no loss and delay in the network. It has been observed that buffer status has worsened when congestion is applied to the system. In the experiments with Video2, the first buffer drain occurred earlier and buffer drains were more frequent.

2. EXPERIMENT 2: System Behavior with the Rate Adaptation Module

Fig. 6 shows the states of system variables during the experiment with Video1. In this experiment, congestion occurs between t=480 sec. and t=545 sec. Therefore, rate adaptation decisions are based only on buffer status throughout the experiment except during this interval. Rate adaptation module considers both congestion level and buffer status within the interval [480 sec.- 545 sec.]. Streaming starts with the initial quality settings *Layer*=2; *Temp. Lev.* = 2 and *FGS Layer* = 0. The system switches to better qualities after probing experiments that indicate the availability of sufficient network capacity. Buffer level increases during prebuffering period and remains constant until t=50 sec., where *Layer*=3, *Temp.Lev.*=4 and *FGS Layer*=0. The corresponding quality increase introduces higher network load and higher transmission delay. Therefore, a small decline in buffer occupancy is observed at t=50 sec. At t=75 sec., the *Layer* variable is set to the highest possible value, increasing the network load and transmission delay further. As a consequence, buffer level falls below 10 sec. quickly. In sequence, the consumer thread increases its consumption interval by 10 % for approximately 20 secs. and notifies the server about the decrease in buffer level. The server responds by decreasing the transmission interval by 10%. The effects of these actions are observed as an increase in buffer level. As buffer level has been rising above 10 sec., video quality is enhanced with the addition of FGS layers. It should be noted that the server invalidates the trick with the transmission rate when the video quality is changed. At t=130 sec., video quality reaches the highest level with the settings *Layer*=4, *Temp.Lev.*=5 and *FGS Layer*=2. This quality level increases the network load and transmission delay, resulting in a drop of buffer level below 10 sec at t=140 sec. It has been observed that the tricks with consumption and transmission rates have not been helpful at that quality level. Therefore, the server responds to the drop in buffer level by dropping FGS layers. As FGS layers are dropped, the decrease in buffer level stops. After all FGS layers have been dropped, buffer level starts to rise again. At t=195 sec., buffer level is above 10 sec. Consequently, quality is increased by adding FGS layers. At t=225 sec., video quality reaches the highest level, increasing the network load and transmission delay. Buffer level drops below 10 sec again. The server takes the necessary actions to increase the buffer level and this cycle repeated until t=480 sec, when the congestion starts. CLOUD™ software has been configured such that queuing delay values significantly increase before packet loss starts. This is reflected in buffer status as a quick drops in buffer level. It has been observed that buffer level falls down to 5 sec. during congestion. While configuring CLOUD™ software, the loss percentages have been selected in such a way that the congestion level would be HIGH or MEDIUM during congestion period. As explained in the previous section, rate adaptation module drops all FGS layers, one quality layer and one temporal level when RTCP reports indicate the existence of heavy congestion. When the congestion is at medium level, quality is decreased by dropping FGS layers, if there are any. If all FGS layers have been dropped, a temporal layer or a quality layer is dropped in accordance with the motion dynamics of the current scene. As shown in Fig. 6, the adaptation module decreases the quality down to the level with the settings *Layer*=1, *Temp. Lev*=1 and *FGS Layer*=0. After t=525 sec., packet losses start to decrease and congestion is completely removed at t=540 sec. After this point, there is no packet loss and queuing delay. The transmission delay introduced by the current quality level is low due to the low bandwidth demand with the prevailing settings *Layer*=1, *Temp. Lev.*=1 and *FGS Layer*=0. Therefore, buffer level starts to increase at a high rate. After buffer level exceeds 10 sec., the rate of increase in buffer level gets smaller. It has been observed that the buffer level increases up to 18 sec. As the buffer level increases, rate adaptation module increases video quality since there is no congestion. As a consequence, network load and transmission delay increase and buffer level starts to decrease at t=575 sec. It falls below 10 sec. at t=700 sec after the video quality has been switched to the best level. The same behavior that is observed before the congestion period repeats until the end of the experiment.

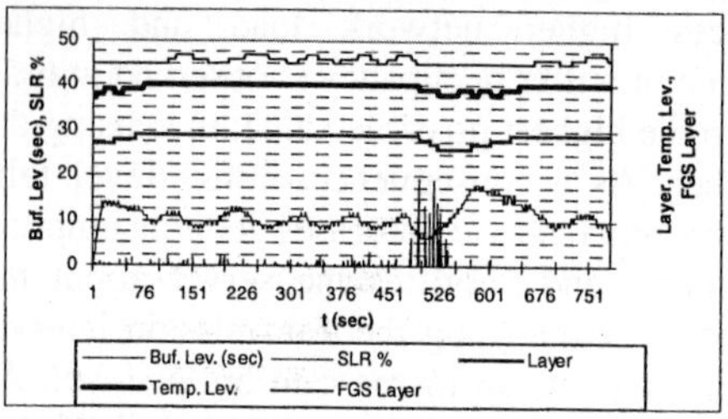

Fig. 6. Experiment with Video1 when the rate adaptation module is included

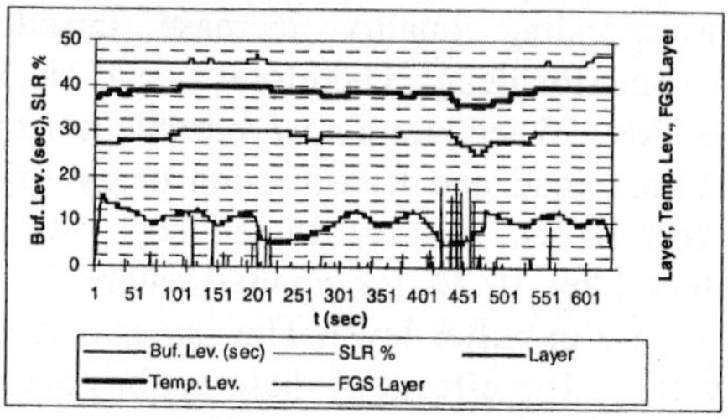

Fig. 7. Experiment with Video2 when the rate adaptation module is included

Fig. 7 shows the states of system variables during the experiment with Video2. As explained previously, Video2 imposes higher bandwidth demand than Video1. Although the same congestion pattern in the previous experiment has been applied, the graph in Fig. 7 depicts momentarily increase in congestion at t=110 sec., t=145 sec and a congestion period of MEDIUM level has been observed between t=180 sec. and t=220 sec. When the graph is carefully examined, it is seen that packet losses occur in a short time period after FGS layers are started to be added. This shows that addition of a FGS layer increases the network load such that the available bandwidth becomes insufficient to meet the bandwidth requirement. As a consequence, the application itself causes congestion. During the congestion interval [180 sec.- 220 sec], buffer level falls quickly below 10 sec. due to packet losses and high transmission delays. In this experiment, it has been observed that dropping only FGS layers has not been adequate to increase the buffer level above 10 sec. as in the experiment with Video1. Both quality layers and temporal layers have been dropped in order to increase the buffer level by reducing the transmission rate even if there is no congestion. At t=420 sec., the configured congestion period starts. Due to the heavy congestion, video quality is quickly reduced down to the level with the settings *Layer*=0, *Temp. Lev.*=1 and *FGS Layer*=0. At t=480 sec., both packet loss and queuing delay have been removed. Due to the prevailing low quality levels, network load and transmission delay is low. Consequently, buffer level rises above 10 sec. quickly and video quality is increased. As the network load increases, transmission delay starts to increase and buffer level starts to decrease. At t=520 sec., it falls below 10 secs. The tricks with consumption and transmission rates help to increase the buffer level above 10 sec. without reducing video quality. After *Layer* and *Temp. Lev.* settings reach the highest values, quality is enhanced with the addition of FGS layers. However, in a short time after the first FGS layer has been added at t=550 sec., the bandwidth demand increases above the network capacity and a momentarily increase in packet loss is observed. In sequence, adaptation module drops the currently added FGS layer to relieve the network status.

When the graphs in Fig. 6 and Fig. 7 are compared, it is seen that *Layer* and *Temp. Lev.* settings have been managed to be kept at the highest values (*Layer*=5, *Temp. Lev.*=5) throughout the experiment with Video1 as long as no congestion exists. Dropping only FGS layers has been adequate to keep buffer level around 10 sec. During the experiment with Video2, a video stream with much higher bandwidth demand than that of Video1, rate adaptation module had to drop quality layers and temporal layers in addition to FGS layers to keep buffer level above 10 sec. Secondly, due to the excessive network load introduced with FGS layers, we observed that the application itself caused congestion which was not configured with CLOUD™ software.

Finally, when the results of *EXPERIMENT1* and *EXPERIMENT2* are compared, it is seen that the rate adaptation module responded to the congestion properly and prevented the buffer from getting emptied throughout the experiment. In *EXPERIMENT1*, buffer has drained frequently resulting in gaps during display. During *EXPERIMENT2*, gaps due to buffer drain have been eliminated by the actions of the rate adaptation module, resulting a much more better perceptual quality and higher satisfaction of viewers.

4 Conclusion

In this study, a streaming system for scalable H.264 videos has been implemented. The system reacts to congestion in the network and drops in buffer level at the client side by switching to a lower quality substream. The system is content adaptive in the sense that it considers motion dynamics during rate adaptation process. The system has been tested with various network conditions. The experimental results show that the system properly reacts to changes in congestion level and buffer occupancy. The system is suitable to be used for Internet video streaming where losses occur any time unpredictably.

Currently, the reference software JSVM1.0 is at the stage of development. New features that will be useful in streaming applications are continuing to be added to the codec. As a future work, we plan to reflect the effects of the new features to our streaming system for more effective streaming. Another goal is to extend the system to be used in video multicast applications to investigate the benefits of scalable codecs in supporting clients with different resolutions.

References

1. Santa_Cruz D., Maestroni D., Zilliani F., Reichel J., Tubara S.: Improved Scalable MCTF Video Codec Using a H.264/AVC Base Layer, Proceedings of the Picture Coding Symposium (PCS-2004), USA (2004).
2. Kantarcı A.: Content Adaptive Streaming of Scalable H.264/AVC Videos, submitted to Signal Processing- Image Communications, (2005).
3. Sun X., Wu F., Li S., Gao W., Zhang Y.: Seamless Switching of Scalable Video Bitstreams for Efficient Streaming, IEEE Transactions on Multimedia, Special Issue on Video Streaming, vol. 6, no. 2, pp 291-303 (2004).

4. Taubman D., Zakhor A.: Multirate 3-D Subband Coding of Video, IEEE Transactions on Image Processing, Vol. 3, No. 5, (1994).
5. Schwarz H., Maupe D., Wiegand T.: MCTF and Scalability Extension of H.264/AVC, Proceedings of the Picture Coding Symposium (PCS-2004), USA, (2004).
6. Song L., Xu J., Xiong H., F. W.: Content Adaptive Update Steps for Lifting-Based Motion Compensated Temporal Filtering , Proceedings of the Picture Coding Symposium (PCS-2004), USA, (2004).
7. Reference software for JSVM software, JVT-N024, http://ftp3.itu.int/av-arch/jvt-site/2005_01_HongKong, February, (2005).
8. Reichel H. J., Schwarz H., Wien M.: Joint Scalable Video Model: JSVM1, JVT-N023.doc, JVT Documentation, January (2005).
9. Wenger S., Hasnnuksela M. M., Stockhammer T., Westerlund M., Singer D.: Request for Comments: 3984, RTP Payload Format for H.264 Video, February, (2005).
10. Triphathi A., Claypool M.: Adaptive Content-aware Scaling for Improved Video Streaming, Proceedings of the 2nd International Workshop on Intelligent Multimedia Computing and Networking (IMMCN), USA, (2002).
11. Katou K., Zhao L., Sakauzowa S., Yamamato H.: An Adaptive Content-Aware Scaling for Receiver Driven Layered Video Multicast, Proceedings of International Conference on Circuits, Systems, Computers and Communications, Korea (2003).
12. Kantarcı A., Özbek N., Tunalı T.: Rate Adaptive Video Streaming Under Lossy Network Conditions, Signal Processing- Image Communications, Vol. 19, pp. 479-497 (2004).

Blotch Detection and Removal for Archive Video Restoration

M. Kemal Güllü, Oğuzhan Urhan, and Sarp Ertürk

Kocaeli University, Faculty of Engineering, Department of Electronics & Telecommunications Engineering, 41040, İzmit, Kocaeli, Turkey
{kemalg, urhano, sertur}@kou.edu.tr

Abstract. Blotch detection and removal are important subjects for archive video restoration. In this work, spatial segmentation based post-processing has been proposed to increase the detection performance of the SDIa blotch detector. Furthermore a novel pixel based correction method that determines the new values of blotched pixels from spatio-temporal correlation is developed. Experimental results show that the proposed approach gives significant detection and correction performances and outperforms previously proposed techniques.

1 Introduction

Archive film materials are particularly degraded by blotch, scratch, flicker and noise. Blotches are significant degradations that mainly originate from the loss of film gelatine and dirt particles covering the film surface. Blotch is basically impulsive noise and leads to discontinuity because it appears randomly in the image sequence and hence the probability of existence of blotch at the same place in succeeding frames is very low.

It is possible to consider the removal of blotches from image sequences as a two stage process, firstly detecting the missing locations, and then correcting the detected regions using spatio-temporal methods. Several techniques have been proposed for the detection stage in the literature [1-4]. The simplest method SDIa (Spike Detection Index) that detects blotch regions, using motion compensated preceding and following frames, by thresholding the minimum of backward and forward squared pixel differences has been proposed in [1]. SDIa is capable of achieving a high correct detection rate however usually results in too many false alarms. To reduce the false alarms that arise from edges, morphological post-processing has been proposed in [2]. This post processing improves the detection rate of SDIa but false alarms caused from local object motion or incorrect global motion compensation are not eliminated adequately. In [3], a ROD (Ranked Order Difference) detector that arranges pixels from motion compensated previous and subsequent image regions and applies a three stage thresholding to them has been proposed. These three thresholds control the number of correct detections and false alarms but the difficulty of determining these three thresholds constraints the effectiveness of this method. Therefore, a simplified ROD detector (S-ROD) that uses only one threshold has been proposed in [4].

In the correction stage, a multi-stage median filter (MMF) that is a concatenation of median filtering operations can be used to correct the missing data regions as

P. Yolum et al.(Eds.): ISCIS 2005, LNCS 3733, pp. 739–747, 2005.

proposed in [5]. A texture synthesis method for computer vision applications has been proposed in [6], which models texture as a Markov Random Field (MRF) and finds a new pixel value for each unfilled pixel according to the squared difference matching criteria. In [7], long-range correlation based image information restoration has been proposed to recover lost image blocks using a long search region according to the luminance transformation based MSE criterion for a given block.

None of the aforementioned detection methods is able to detect blotches that occur at the same spatial location in subsequent frames (i.e. occluded blotches). This is the main drawback of these methods. In our work, segmentation based post processing is enforced to the SDIa detector output in order to improve correct detection rate while reducing false alarms. In the correction stage, a new pixel based correction method that determines the new values of blotched pixels from temporal correlation based on [6] and [7] is proposed.

2 Blotch Detection and Removal

The degraded image $I(x)$ can be modelled as

$$I(x) = [1 - b(x)] \times y(x) + b(x) \times c(x) \tag{1}$$

where $b(x)$ is a detection variable that determines degraded ($b(x)=1$) or clean ($b(x)=0$) pixels, and $c(x)$ is the observed intensity value of blotched pixels. The detection stage intends to estimate $b(x)$ for each pixel. The aim of the correction stage is to find the new value $y(x)$ for blotched pixels (i.e. pixels for which $b(x)=1$).

2.1 Blotch Detection

The SDIa detector calculates the intensity value of each pixel from corresponding pixels of neighbouring frames and if the squared difference values of both differences are larger than a predetermined threshold, the pixel is flagged as a blotch. This method can be expressed as in (2).

$$\begin{aligned} e_b(i) &= \left(I_n(i) - I_{n-1}^{mc}(i)\right)^2 \\ e_f(i) &= \left(I_n(i) - I_{n+1}^{mc}(i)\right)^2 \\ b(i) &= \begin{cases} 1, & \text{if } e_b(i) \rangle T \text{ and } e_f(i) \rangle T \\ 0, & \text{otherwise} \end{cases} \end{aligned} \tag{2}$$

where $e_b(i)$ is the backward, and $e_f(i)$ is the forward squared pixel difference and T is the threshold that determines whether the pixel is a blotch or not.

This method gives comparably high correct detection rates but results in too many false alarms and is furthermore highly sensitive to global motion compensation accuracy. Another problem is that occluded blotches cannot be detected. To overcome these problems, segmentation based post processing is proposed in this paper to improve performance as shown in Fig. 1.

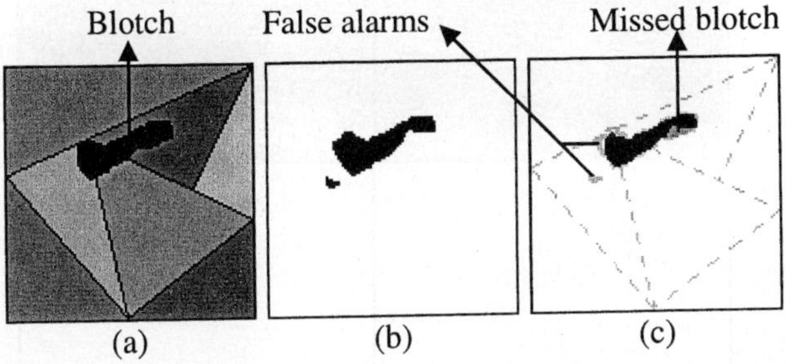

Fig. 1. a) Observed (blotched) image frame, b) blotch detected pixels and, c) determining the blotch region using spatial segmentation

In Fig. 1-a, a synthetic image that contains 7 real image regions and one blotch is given. The binary detection image obtained with SDIa, which contains missed pixels as well as incorrectly detected pixels in the detection process, is shown in Fig 2-b. The proposed segmentation based post-processing that uses spatial segmentation and detection is shown to enforce accurate blotch detection. Controlled segmentation is performed in place of segmenting whole image frame to reduce the computational load. Segmentation is enforced around each detected pixel to establish its correct shape according to a segmentation threshold (T_S). If the absolute difference between the detected pixel and any pixels around the detected pixel is smaller than T_S, these pixels are labelled as part of the segment. This operation goes on recursively along the labelled pixels until there are no pixels that satisfy the condition. If any detected pixel has already been labelled along the process, that pixel is skipped and the process continues with the other detected and unlabeled pixel. In the proposed approach, missed blotch regions are decided if the ratio of the sum of blotch detected pixels to the total number of pixels within the segment is larger than a given completeness threshold (T_c). Otherwise, i.e. if this ratio is smaller than the threshold, a false alarm is given and detected pixels in the segment are marked as clear. Furthermore, to eliminate false detections resulting from noise, each segments size is checked and if any segment size is equal to one pixel only, that pixel is marked as non-blotched.

Artificial white and black blotches are introduced to image sequences randomly in order to test the detection performance of the methods. Example original and randomly blotched frames, as well as SDIa blotch detection and segmentation based post processed detection results for the "Silent" test sequence are given in Fig. 2 and Fig. 3 to show the benefit of post processing. False detections in SDIa arising from local motion and the effect of post processing are shown in Fig. 2-c and Fig. 2-d, respectively.

In Fig. 3-c, missed detection occurring as a result of occluded blotch regions is shown. Segmentation based post-processing helps to improve the correct detection rate of the detector and provides correct detection results (See Fig. 3-d).

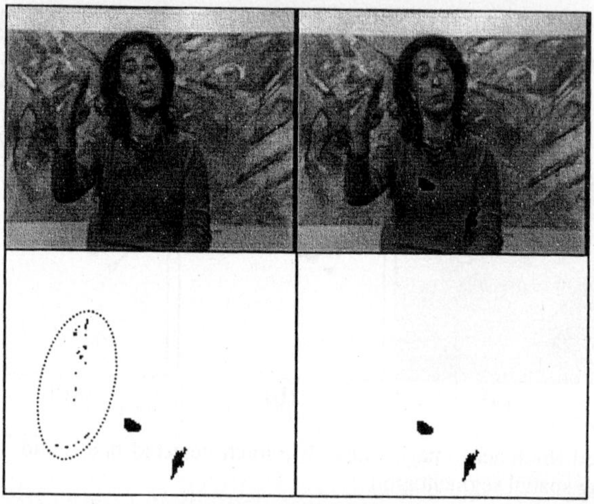

Fig. 2. a) Original frame, b) Blotched frame, c) SDIa detection and d) segmentation based post processing results for frame #32 of the "Silent" sequence

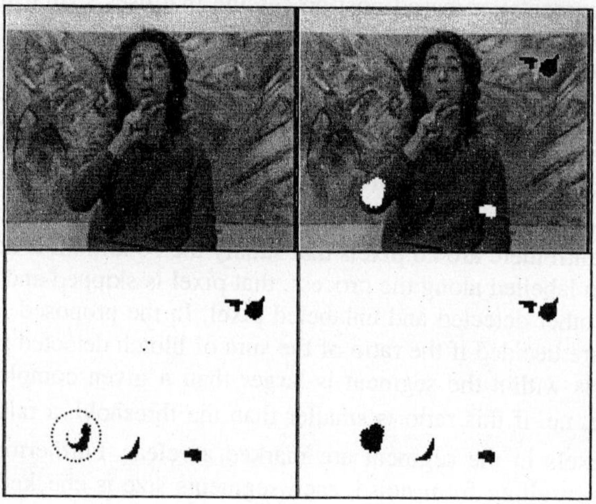

Fig. 3. a) Original frame, b) Blotched frame, c) SDIa detection and d) segmentation based post processing results for frame #93 of "Silent" sequence

2.2 Blotch Removal

In this paper a new pixel based correction method that determines blotched pixels new values using spatio-temporal correlation is proposed. Our method uses a contour based correction strategy similar to [6] and uses luminance transformation based matching criteria as given in [7]. The proposed method is operating as follows:

If $b'(x)=1$ for the current image (Note that $b'(x)$ shows the post-processed $b(x)$);

1. Take a square window around position x (local window).
2. Find the best matching luminance transformed remote window from large search windows of preceding and succeeding image frames for the local window; skipping all blotched regions. Note that the centre pixel of the remote window should be non-blotched.
3. Put the centre pixel of the best matched luminance transformed remote window to the corrected image ($y'(x)$).

In this work, MSE is used as a matching criterion in the form of

$$MSE=\frac{1}{p_u}\sum_{i=1}^{M}\sum_{j=1}^{M}\left[1-m^r(i,j)\right]\times\left[1-m^l(i,j)\right]\times\left[l(i,j)-v(r(i,j))\right]$$
$$p_u=\sum_{i=1}^{M}\sum_{j=1}^{M}\left[1-m^r(i,j)\right]\times\left[1-m^l(i,j)\right] \tag{3}$$

where p_u is the total number of used pixels, M is the window size, $m^r(i,j)$ is the remote window blotch mask, $m^l(i,j)$ is the local window blotch mask, $l(i,j)$ is the local window pixel, $r(i,j)$ is the remote window pixel, and $v(\ )$ is the luminance transform. The best matched remote window searching procedure is executed as shown in Fig. 4. To match the remote window to the local window using the *MSE* criterion, a first-order polynomial function given in (4) is used as the luminance transform similar to [7].

$$v(r(i,j))=\alpha_0+\alpha_1\times r(i,j),\qquad \begin{array}{l}\partial MSE/\partial\alpha_0=0\\ \partial MSE/\partial\alpha_1=0\end{array} \tag{4}$$

In this equation α_0 and α_1 can be denoted as additive and multiplicative luminance transform coefficients, respectively and these coefficients are computed as given in (5).

$$a_1=\frac{p_u\sum_{i=1}^{M}\sum_{j=1}^{M}(1-m^r(i,j))\times(1-m^l(i,j))\times r(i,j)\times l(i,j)-\left[\sum_{i=1}^{M}\sum_{j=1}^{M}(1-m^r(i,j))\times(1-m^l(i,j))\times r(i,j)\right]\times\left[\sum_{i=1}^{M}\sum_{j=1}^{M}(1-m^r(i,j))\times(1-m^l(i,j))\times l(i,j)\right]}{p_u\sum_{i=1}^{M}\sum_{j=1}^{M}(1-m^r(i,j))\times(1-m^l(i,j))\times r^2(i,j)-\left[\sum_{i=1}^{M}\sum_{j=1}^{M}(1-m^r(i,j))\times(1-m^l(i,j))\times r(i,j)\right]}$$
$$a_1=\frac{1}{p_u}\left[\sum_{i=1}^{M}\sum_{j=1}^{M}(1-m^r(i,j))\times(1-m^l(i,j))\times l(i,j)-a_1\times\sum_{i=1}^{M}\sum_{j=1}^{M}(1-m^r(i,j))\times(1-m^l(i,j))\times r(i,j)\right] \tag{5}$$

The new value of a blotched pixel is then computed as

$$y'(i,j)=v(r_{bm}((M+1)/2,(M+1)/2)),\quad M \text{ is odd number} \tag{6}$$

where $y'(i,j)$ is the corrected pixel value, and r_{bm} is the best matched remote window.

Correction results for a part of frame #22 of the "Hall Monitor" sequence are shown in Fig. 5 to give an idea about the visual performance of the proposed correction method.

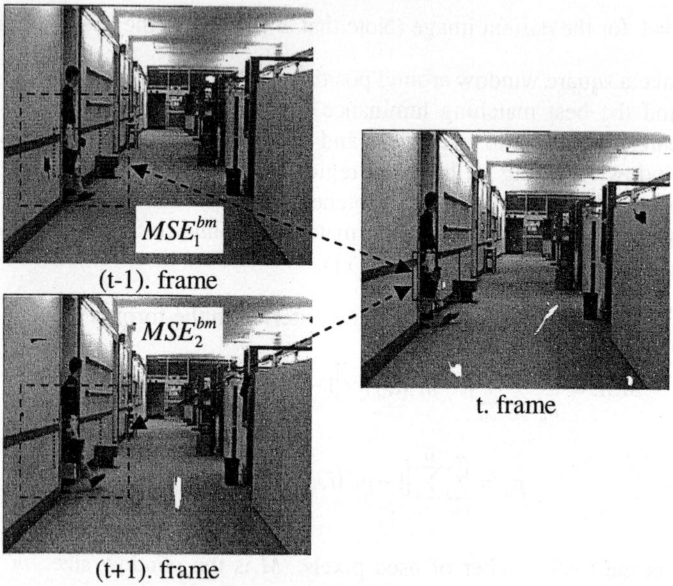

$$MSE^{bm} = \min\left(MSE_1^{bm}, MSE_2^{bm}\right)$$

Fig. 4. Best matched remote window searching strategy from preceding and succeeding image frames

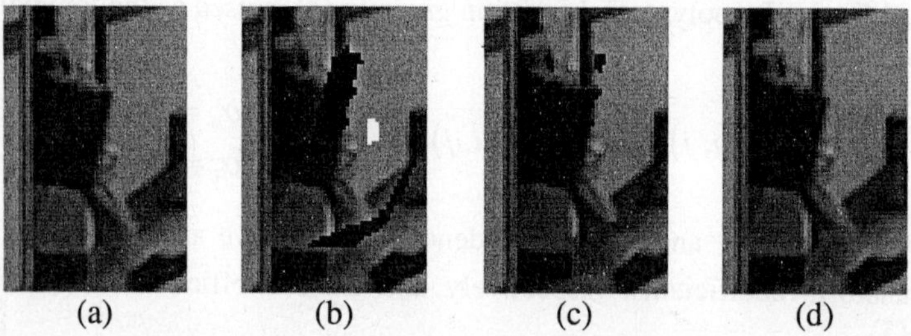

Fig. 5. a) Original, b) artificially blotched, c) MMF [5] corrected, and d) proposed correction of the image part of frame #22 of the "Hall Monitor" sequence

It is shown in Fig. 5-c that MMF can not correct occluded blotch areas (the black blotch region) and gives unsatisfactory results in cases of local motion. The proposed method presents superior performance in this manner.

3 Experimental Results

Fig. 6 shows ROC (Receiver Operator Characteristics) curves obtained for the "Silent" test sequence using SDIa [1], SDIa with post-processing method proposed in [2], S-ROD [5] and SDIa with our segmentation based post-processing method. It is seen in Fig. 6 that our segmentation based post processing highly improves the correct detection rate of the SDIa and reduces the false detection rate, significantly outperforming all other methods.

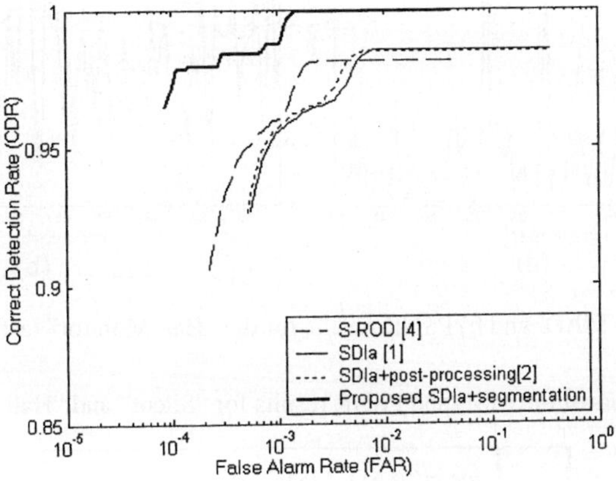

Fig. 6. ROC curves results for blotch detection methods

For the correction stage, MAD (Minimum Absolute Difference) and PSNR (Peak Signal to Noise Ratio) results for original and corrected "Silent" and "Hall Monitor" test sequences are given in Fig. 7 and Fig. 8, respectively. These figures show that our correction method gives enhanced results in the overall.

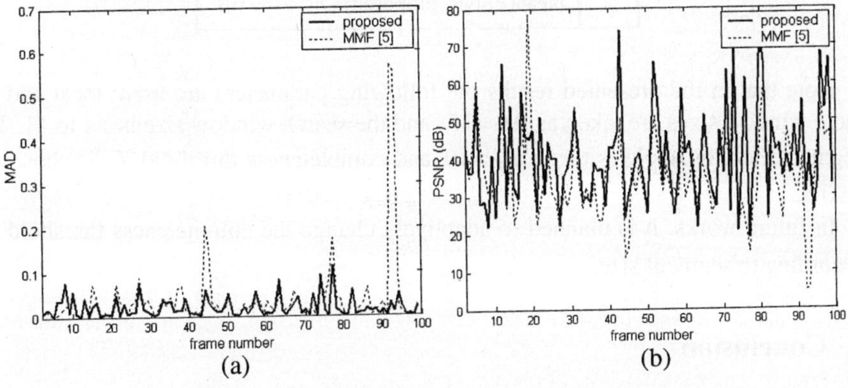

Fig. 7. a) MAD, and b) PSNR results for the "Silent" test sequence

In Table 1, average MAD and PSNR results for the "Silent" and "Hall Monitor" sequences are shown. These results also confirm that the proposed method outperforms MMF based correction.

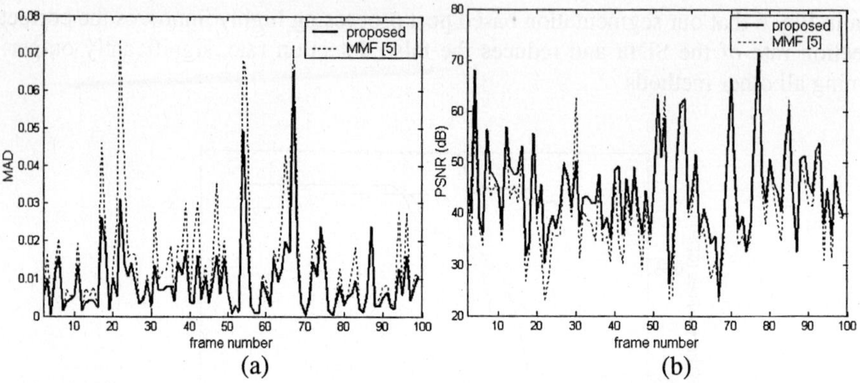

Fig. 8. a) MAD, and b) PSNR results for the "Hall Monitor" test sequence

Table 1. Mean values of the MSE and PSNR results for "Silent" and "Hall Monitor" sequences

Silent	mean(MAD_MMF)=0.0392 mean(PSNR_MMF)=35.2878 dB
	mean(MAD_proposed)=0.0197 mean(PSNR_proposed)=40.2828 dB
Hall Monitor	mean(MAD_MMF)= 0.0143 mean(PSNR_MMF)=41.2092 dB
	mean(MAD_proposed)=0.0092 mean(PSNR_proposed)= 44.0769 dB

Note that in the presented results the following parameters are used: local and remote window sizes are taken as $M = 15$, and the search window size is set to 41. The segmentation threshold is taken $T_S = 10$ and completeness threshold T_c is chosen to be 0.5.

In future works, it is planned to adaptively change the completeness threshold T_c according to segment size.

4 Conclusion

New methods for the detection and removal of blotches are proposed in this paper to improve the visual quality of archive film sequences that are degraded as a result of blotches. Initially, a segmentation based post-processing approach has been proposed to increase the detection performance of the SDIa detector in this paper. Additionally a new pixel based correction method that determines the new value of blotched pixels using spatio-temporal correlation is implemented. Experimental results demonstrate that the proposed detection and correction methods outperform previously proposed techniques.

Acknowledgement

This work was supported by the Turkish Scientific and Technical Research Council (Tübitak), under grant EEEAG/103E007.

References

1. Kokaram A.C., Morris R.D., Fitzgerald W.J., Rayner P.J.W.: Detection of Missing Data in Image Sequences. IEEE Trans. on Image Processing, Vol. 4, No. 11, (1995) 1496-1508
2. Ghaderi M., Kasaei S.: Novel Post-Processing Methods used in Detection of Blotches in Image Sequences. AEÜ Int. J. Electron. Comm., Vol. 58, (2004) 58-64
3. Nadenau M.J., Mitra S.K.: Blotch and Scratch Detection in Image Sequences based on Rank Ordered Differences. in Time-Varying Image Processing and Moving Object Recognition, V. Cappelini ed., Elsevier (1997)
4. Roosmalen P.M.B., Lagendijk R.L., Biemond J.: Improved Blotch Detection by Postprocessing. Proc. of IEEE Signal Processing Symposium SPS'98, Leuven, Belgium (1998), 223-226
5. Kokaram A.C., Morris R.D., Fitzgerald W.J., Rayner P.J.W.: Interpolation of Missing Data in Image Sequences. IEEE Trans. on Image Processing, Vol. 4, No. 11, (1995) 509-519
6. Efros A.A., Leung T.K.: Texture Synthesis by Non-parametric Sampling. Proc. of IEEE Int. Conf. on Computer Vision (ICCV'99), Corfu, Greece (1999), Vol. 2, 1033-1038
7. Zhang D., Wang Z.: Image Information Restoration Based on Long-Range Correlation. IEEE Trans. on Circuits and Systems for Video Technology, Vol. 12, No. 5, (2002) 331-340

Performance Study of an Image Restoration Algorithm for Bursty Mobile Satellite Channels

Fatih Alagöz[1], Gürkan Gür[1], and Mohammed AbdelHafez[2]

[1] NETLAB, Department of Computer Engineering, Boğaziçi University, TR
{alagoz, gurgurka}@boun.edu.tr

[2] Department of Electrical Engineering, United Arab Emirates University, UAE
mhafez@uaeu.ac.ae

Abstract. Error-concealment techniques provide a simple framework to compensate transmission distortions without incurring additional delays and wasting bandwidth resources which are crucial for real-time applications over networks with limited resources. In [1], we have presented an error concealment technique utilizing discrete wavelet transform (DWT) for embedding macroblock-based best-neighborhood-matching (BNM) information into the original image in order to utilize spatial redundancy. In this paper, we investigate the performance of Best-neighborhood-matching and Wavelets based Error-Concealment (BWEC) algorithm in bursty mobile satellite channels. We show that this technique is specifically promising for bursty mobile satellite channels suffering a wide range of packet losses, at the expense of some degradation in the perceptual quality of the original image and computational burden.

1 Introduction

The problem of error control and concealment in image and video communication is becoming increasingly important because of the growing interest in multimedia delivery over unreliable channels such as wireless networks and the Internet.

When transmitting image and video data over satellite channels, the transmitted data may suffer from losses or errors due to fading, propagation anomalies, intentional jamming, or other user interference [2]. The lore in the wireless environment is that if the propagation delay is small and latency requirements are not stringent, automatic repeat request (ARQ) techniques may become a feasible solution for the error recovery as compared to forward error correction (FEC) mechanisms [3,4]. FEC, ARQ and hybrid FEC/ARQ schemes may fail especially for the realtime applications with high propagation delay, and subject to transmission over channels with high error rates [5]. Alternatively, error concealment (EC) approach is a relatively new yet an effective way to recover the lost information at the decoder. Compared to other error control mechanisms, error concealment has the advantages of not consuming extra bandwidth as in FEC mechanisms and not introducing retransmission delay as in ARQ mechanisms. Fortunately, error concealment techniques can be used to supplement FEC and ARQ when both FEC and ARQ fail to overcome the transmission errors [6].

P. Yolum et al.(Eds.): ISCIS 2005, LNCS 3733, pp. 748–758, 2005.

The main purpose of EC techniques is to obtain a close approximation of the original signal or attempt to make the output signal at the decoder least objectionable to human eyes. Human eyes can tolerate a certain degree of distortion in image and video signals, unlike the case in data transmission where lossless delivery is absolutely required. Various approaches have been proposed for image and video EC [7, 8].

In previous work, we have proposed BWEC algorithm, an error concealment technique utilizing discrete wavelet transform for embedding macroblock-based BNM information into the original image in order to utilize spatial redundancy [1]. In this work, we show that BWEC algorithm is specifically promising for bursty mobile satellite channels suffering a wide range of packet losses. Our paper is organized as follows: The next section describes BWEC algorithm and land mobile satellite (LMS) channel model employed in our work. Experimental results and performance analysis are presented in Section III. Finally, we conclude with discussions and future work in Section IV.

2 Background

2.1 BWEC Algorithm

DWT is widely used in signal processing for signal analysis, denoising, compression and it is also the basis of JPEG2000 image compression standard. DWT decomposes a signal into lowpass and highpass components by using filter banks. These subbands vary in spatial frequency and orientation. Two-dimensional DWT leads to a decomposition of approximation coefficients at level j in four components: the approximation (lowpass signal) at level j+1, and the details (highpass signals) in three orientations (horizontal, vertical, and diagonal). This process can be further repeated to construct higher-order decompositions. DWT has advantages such as space-frequency localization, hierarchical multi-resolution presentation, superior human visual system (HVS) modelling and adaptivity [9]. In our algorithm, BNM information is embedded into DWT level 2 and 1 detail coefficients of host image, excluding the LL_2 subband to limit visual degradation. Traversal order of coefficients is determined by a shared-key dependent pseudo-random permutation of the wavelet coefficient addresses. This is an oblivious method since this embedding scheme allows the encoder to extract the watermark without the original image by using the shared key.

The dissimilarity measure, Δ, for two macroblocks is simply the total absolute difference of all pixel values from those compared macroblocks, i.e.,

$$\Delta_t = \sum_{i,j}^{N_s,N_s} \left|\alpha_{ij}^t - \tilde{\alpha}_{ij}^{t,m}\right| \qquad (1)$$

where α_{ij}^t is the pixel value of the tth reference macroblock and $\tilde{\alpha}_{ij}^{t,m}$ is the mth checked macroblock in the neighborhood of $N_s \times N_s$ pixels, where the reference macroblock is the tth reference macroblock.

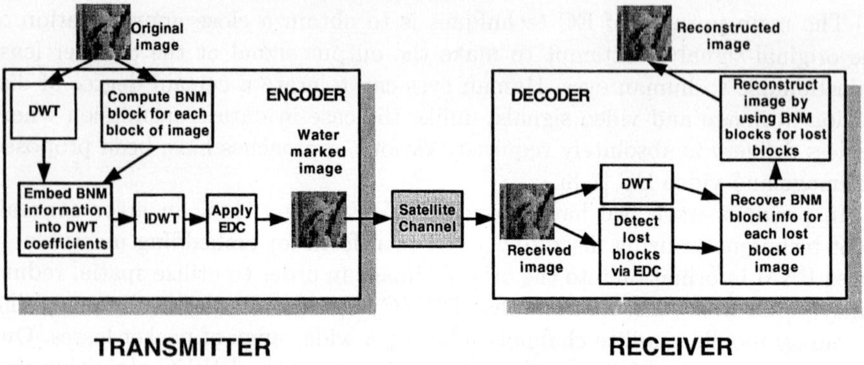

Fig. 1. Block diagram of BWEC algorithm

BWEC algorithm, depicted in Fig. 1, can be stated in steps as follows:

At the encoder,

1. Read in the original image, $\tilde{N}$, with size of $N_1 \times N_2$ pixels.
2. Find the BNM macroblock address for each macroblock, with size $N_b \times N_b$ pixels, in its neighborhood of $N_s \times N_s$ pixels. Thus, there are $\frac{N_1 \times N_2}{{N_b}^2}$ macroblocks in the image and $(\frac{N_s}{N_b})^2$ domain macroblocks in each neighborhood mask.
3. Take DWT of the original image.
4. Our data embedding scheme is a modified version of the wavelet based method, studied by Chang *et al.* in [10].
   It works by changing position of DWT coefficients with the following condition:

   if W[j] = 1,
   Exchange C[i] with max(C[i], C[i+1],
   C[i+2], C[i+3], C[i+4])
   else
   Exchange C[i] with min(C[i], C[i+1], C[i+2],
   C[i+3], C[i+4]).

   where *C[i]* is the ith DWT coefficient of host image and i is j^{th} element of *A[j]*, the shared-key dependent pseudorandom permutation of the wavelet coefficient addresses. *W[j]* is the jth element of binarized BNM address vector constituting the watermark. This scattered selection of host coefficients allows the scheme to embed watermark in a spatially-distributed manner. Therefore, this aspect increases the robustnesss of our scheme against macroblock losses and localized artifacts.
5. Take IDWT (inverse discrete wavelet transform) of the modified multiresolution representation.

6. Apply error-detection-coding (EDC) into the watermarked image, which is simply to convert first and last N_{edc} pixel values of each macroblock to the nearest even or odd value. This is a simple method of least-significant-bit (LSB) fragile watermarking.

Then, the image is transmitted through the error-prone channel and macroblocks are lost according to the channel statistics.

At the decoder,

1. Determine the lost macroblocks of the received image via utilizing the embedded EDC pattern. If the pattern is not detected, mark that macroblock as lost.
2. Take DWT of the received image.
3. Determine BNM macroblock addresses for the lost macroblocks using the embedded watermark:

   if CR[i] > median (CR[i], CR[i+1], CR[i+2], CR[i+3], CR[i+4])

   WR[j] = 1

   else

   WR[j] = 0.

   where *CR[i]* is the ith DWT coefficient of received image and i is j^{th} element of *A[j]*, the shared-key dependent pseudorandom permutation of the wavelet coefficient addresses. Please note that since both parties share the same key, they are able to generate exactly the same coefficient address sequence. *WR[j]* is the jth element of extracted binarized BNM address vector constituting the watermark.
4. Reconstruct the image by replacing each lost macroblock with BNM block of the extracted address. If that neighbor is lost as well, replace with the average of healthy neighbors in the BNM window.

2.2 LMS Channel Model Based on Lutz's Model

The congestion of radio spectrum in the lower L/S band (1-2 GHz) and the maturing of *Ka*-band (20/30 GHz) technologies are creating a lot of interest in the *Ka*-band for satellite communications [11]. Therefore, we have adopted a Ka-band LMS model based on Lutz's model [12], which is a special case of the multistate channel model applicable for a nonuniform propagation environment, for evaluation of BWEC algorithm. The *Ka*-band mobile satellite transmission mainly includes the following propagation impairments: effects related to the troposphere (or weather) and the effects due to the environment in the vicinity of the receiver. The former denoted as ω includes rain attenuation, gaseous absorption, cloud attenuation, scintillation etc. The later denoted as β is the same as in other frequency bands (L/S), and basically consists of shadowing/blockage and multipath fading effects. These two effects represented by ω and β are assumed

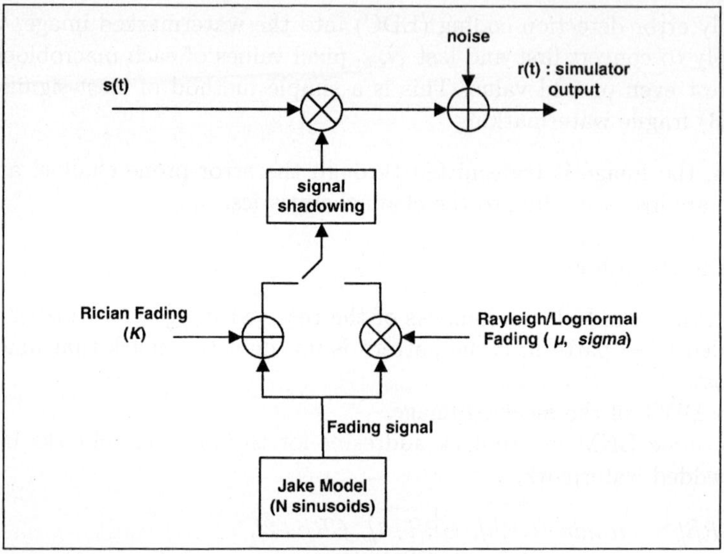

Fig. 2. Lutz's simulation model for satellite channels. The signals s(t), r(t), and the fading process a(t) are complex valued.

to be statistically independent because the underlying mechanisms are independent. The received signal amplitude can be interpreted as $r = \beta\omega$, assuming that the transmit signal amplitude is normalized to unity.

The *Ka*-band propagation studies show that when weather impairments are not considered, the basic concept for L/S band LMS channel modeling is also applicable to the *Ka*-band, except for more severe shadowing and faster multipath fluctuations encountered in the *Ka*-band. In this work, based on the data collected by Rice, Lutz's model is adopted [12] in the case of no weather impairments. The following analysis has been done in [11] and adopted here. According to Lutz's model, the LMS channel is a two-state (good and bad states, namely nonshadowing and shadowing states) Markov model. In the nonshadowing state, the received signal amplitude follows a Rician distribution.

$$p_{good}(r) = 2kre^{-k(r^2+1)}I_0(2kr) \tag{2}$$

where k is a Rice factor. In the shadowing state, no direct signal path exists and the multipath fading has a Rayleigh characteristic with its envelope s_0 following a lognormal distribution. The probability density functions (pdfs) of the multipath fading and its envelope are

$$p_{bad}(r|s_0) = \frac{2r}{s_0}\exp\left(-\frac{r^2}{s_0}\right) \tag{3}$$

and

$$f_{lg}(s_0) = \frac{10}{\sqrt{2\pi}\sigma\ln 10}\frac{1}{s_0}\exp\left[-\frac{(10\log s_0-\mu)^2}{2\sigma^2}\right] \tag{4}$$

respectively. Evidently in the bad state, the channel is actually a Suzuki distribution, and its pdf is

$$p_{bad}(r) = \int_0^\infty p_{bad}(r|s_0) f_{lg}(s_0) ds_0. \quad (5)$$

The two states (good and bad) are time-sharing and can be modeled as a Gilbert model. Assuming that A is the average duration of the bad state, the pdf of the received signal amplitude can be represented by

$$p_\beta(r) = (1 - A)p_{good}(r) + Ap_{bad}(r). \quad (6)$$

Ω follows a Gaussian distribution when combining all tropospheric factors according to empirical data [11]

$$p_\omega(r) = \frac{1}{\sqrt{2\pi}\sigma_\omega} \exp\left[-\frac{(r - m_\omega)^2}{2{\sigma_\omega}^2}\right]. \quad (7)$$

Among all the weather impairments, rain attenuation is the most serious especially in tropical heavy rain zones. The long term statistics of the rain attenuation can be modeled by a lognormal process

$$p_L(L) = \frac{1}{\sqrt{2\pi}\sigma_d L} \exp\left[-\frac{(\ln L - m_d)^2}{2{\sigma_d}^2}\right], L \geq 0 \quad (8)$$

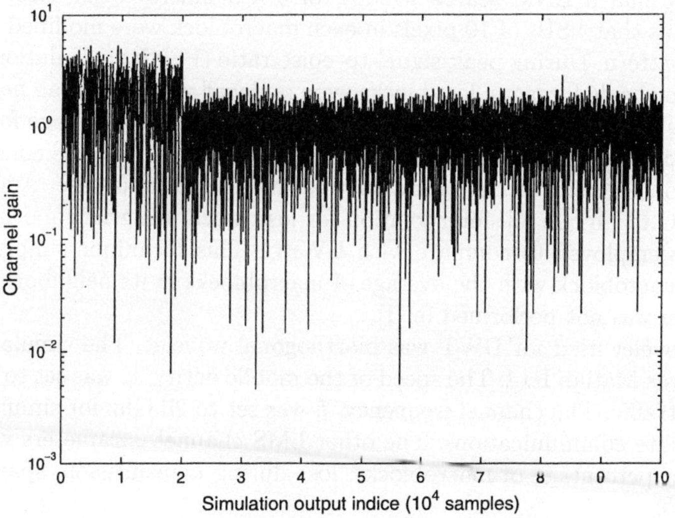

Fig. 3. Channel simulation output (10k samples) of Lutz's model: $K = 5$ dB, $\overline{K} = 5$ dB, $\mu = 10$ dB, $\sigma = 2$ dB, $N = 10$, $f = 20$ Ghz, $v = 50$ km/hr

where L is in decibels, m_d and σ_d are also in decibels. Considering the relation of rain attenuation between fixed systems and mobile systems, the probability distribution of the envelope of a mobile receiver can be obtained from that of the fixed system, by multiplying a factor which approximately varies between 0.5 and 2.0 and is independent of rain attenuation [11]. Fig. 2, adapted from [12], shows the dynamic model of the implemented LMS Lutz channel model. The fading process a(t) is "switched" between Rician fading, representing unshadowed areas with high received signal power (good channel state) and Rayleigh/lognormal fading, representing shadowed areas with low received signal power (bad channel state). When data packets are transferred over channels with bursty errors, packet error statistics are more important than bit error statistics to analyze the communication performance [13]. Thus our model generates the channel statistics based on packet errors. This is a reasonable approximation resulting in a simplified LMS channel model [12].

3 Performance Analysis

To show the performance of BWEC algorithm, we have conducted comprehensive sets of simulation experiments using a discrete event simulator. In our simulations, we have used grayscale "Lena", "Baboon" and "Peppers" images of size 512×512 pixels. The macroblock size lost during transmission, N_L, and used for BNM calculations, N_b, were both 8×8 pixels. Therefore, there were 4096 macroblocks in each image during experiments. The window of neighbouring macroblocks searched for best match, N_s, was of size 40×40 pixels. Consequently, we had a BNM search window of 5×5 macroblocks. N_{edc} was five, which means that LSBs of 10 pixels in each macroblock were modified to embed the EDC pattern. During peak-signal-to-noise-ratio (PSNR) calculations and for constructing healed images, lost blocks were replaced with Gaussian noise rather than pixels of zero value (black macroblocks) in the erroneous image for a realistic simulation. "Gaussian noise injection" into lost blocks may be considered as an error concealment technique rather than mere erroneous case. Additionally, another EC technique [6], interpolation for lost block using neighborhood averaging, was employed to compare with BWEC. This technique simply replaces each lost macroblock with the average of macroblocks in its neighborhood. This comparison was not performed in [1].

The wavelet used for DWT was biorthogonal wavelet. The simulation environment was Matlab R14. The speed of the mobile entity, v, was set to 50 km/hr as in-city traffic. The channel frequency, f, was set to 20 Ghz for simulating *Ka*-band satellite communications. The other LMS channel parameters were set in a way that percentage of macroblocks, lost during transmission, spanned from 10% to 75%.

For the performance evaluation of our technique, we used PSNR as the performance metric. PSNR is used to measure the difference between two images and defined as

$$PSNR(dB) = 20 \log_{10}(\frac{p}{RMSE}) \tag{9}$$

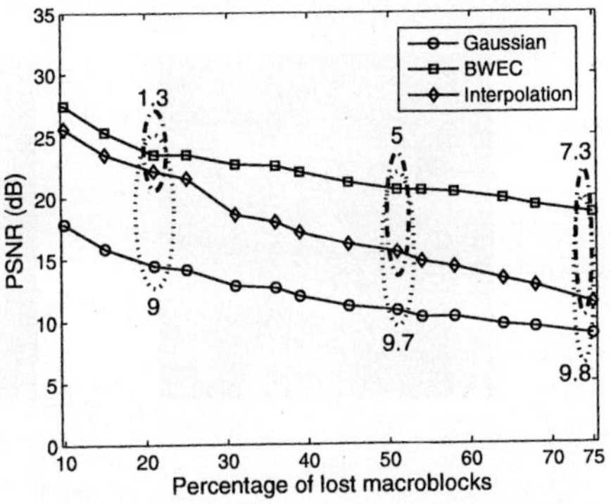

Fig. 4. PSNR (dB) for *Lena* image with various packet loss levels

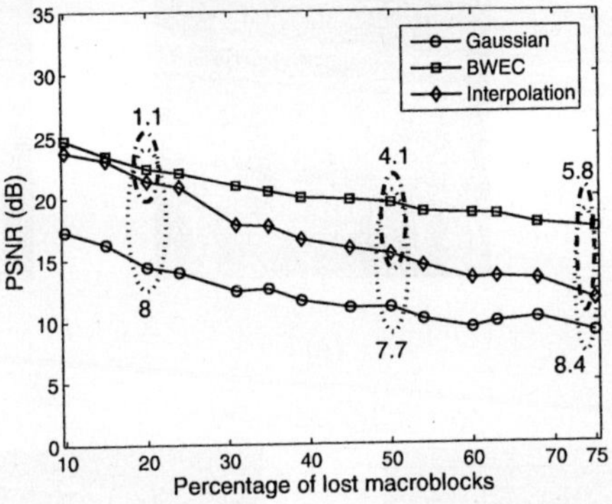

Fig. 5. PSNR (dB) for *Peppers* image with various packet loss levels

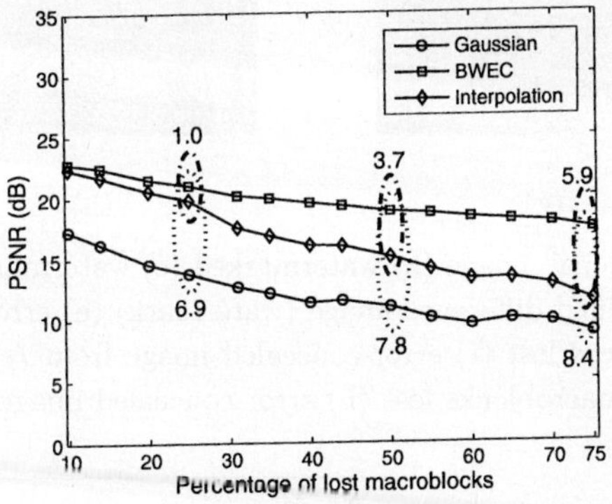

Fig. 6. PSNR (dB) for *Baboon* image with various packet loss levels

where p is the largest possible value of the signal (255 for grayscale images), and $RMSE$ is the root mean square error between two images which are denoted as $I(m,n)$ and $\tilde{I}(m,n)$, respectively. $RMSE$ is given by

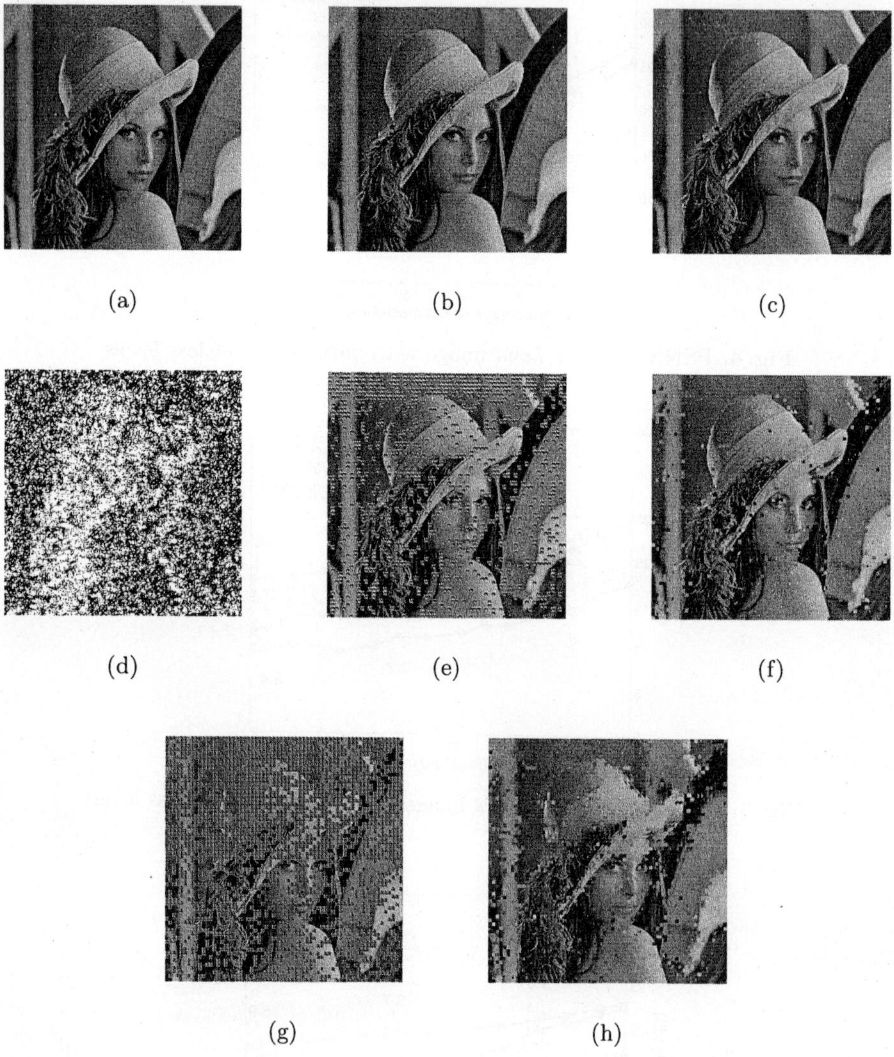

Fig. 7. (a) Original "Lena" image (b) watermarked (c) watermarked with EDC before transmission (d) amplified difference image (watermark) (e) erroneous image received with 20% of macroblocks lost (f) error-concealed image from *(e)* (g) erroneous image received with 50% of macroblocks lost (h) error-concealed image from *(g)*.

$$RMSE = \sqrt{\frac{1}{NM}\sum_{n}^{N}\sum_{m}^{M}[I(m,n) - \tilde{I}(m,n)]^2} \quad (10)$$

where N, M are the row and column sizes of the images. The PSNR is given in decibel units (dB), which measures the ratio of the peak signal and the difference between two images.

For visual evaluation, the original, watermarked and two reconstructed *Lena* images for 20% and 75% packet losses are given in Fig. 7. BWEC technique seems to improve substantially the perceptual quality of the distorted images, especially for the bursty, high-error rate conditions. The numerical results for all three images, elucidated in Fig. 4, 5 and 6, show that as packet loss gets more severe, PSNR for the received image decreases as expected. The same trend is also valid for the reconstructed image. However, the error-concealment method manages to keep an enhancement gap of 9.8 dB on average (min. 9 dB, max. 10.3 dB), depicted in Fig. 4. For "Baboon" and "Peppers" images, the results are similar: an improvement of 7.5 dB on average (min. 7.2 dB, max. 8.7 dB) and 8.2 dB on average (min. 7.2 dB, max. 9.2 dB), respectively. The specific gaps for 20%, 50% and 75% packet loss rates are marked on those graphs. BWEC performs better than interpolation for all packet loss levels and images. The non-centralized distribution of BNM macroblocks strengthens BWEC scheme against bulky macroblock losses due to deep-fading phenomena encountered in LMS channel. These achieved PSNR values for LMS channel are close to the results for general Gilbert-Elliot channel, obtained in [1]. However, the enhancement gap in this work is 2-3 dB narrower than in [1], due to the fact that in this simulation, for our reference PSNR, we replace lost blocks with Gaussian noise instead of pixels of zero value (black blocks). The latter scheme implies a lower PSNR for erroneous case, and thus a wider enhancement gap in [1].

4 Conclusions

In this paper, we have evaluated the performance of Best-neighborhood-matching and Wavelets based Error Concealment (BWEC) algorithm for use in land mobile satellite systems. First, we have presented background information both for the algorithm and land mobile satellite channels. For the former, we consider that the algorithm should be backward compatible. That is, an incompatible receiver should be able to operate with a BWEC-enabled transmitter without any glitches. For the latter, the satellite channel model should support real system parameters, and a time-critical and content valuable image is being transmitted over the channel and the receiver station may be a hand-held device with low-power. Given that the background, we have described the simulator setup, and provided the simulation results for the BWEC algorithm in a land mobile satellite system. The results indicate that the proposed scheme is a promising image restoration tool which may enable satellite systems to cope with bursty error channel conditions. Implementation of BWEC has provided substantial improvements in PSNR values of corrupt images.

Unfortunately, this profound improvement comes at the expense of some computational burden and visual degradation. Currently, we are working to further minimize the visual degradation. This leads to the necessity of better utilization of HVS and wavelet domain as well as incorporating the inherent characteristics of satellite channels.

References

1. Gür, G., Alagöz, F., Abdel-Hafez, M.: A novel error concealment method for images using watermarking in error-prone channels. In: 16th Annual IEEE International Symposium on Personal Indoor and Mobile Radio Communications (PIMRC'05), Berlin, DE (2005)
2. Alagöz, F., Walters, D., AlRustamani, A., Vojcic, B., Pickholtz, R.: Adaptive rate control and QoS provisioning in direct broadcast satellite networks. ACM Wireless Networks **7** (2001) 269–281
3. Pejhan, S., Schwartz, M., Anastassiou, D.: Error control using retransmission schemes in multicast transport protocols for real-time media. IEEE/ACM Transactions on Networking **4** (1996)
4. Zorzi, M.: Performance of FEC and ARQ error control in bursty channel under delay constraints. In: Proc. VCT'98, Ottawa, Canada (1998)
5. Zhu, J., Roy, S.: Performance of land mobile satellite communication (LMSC) channel with hybrid FEC/ARQ. In: Proc. GLOBECOM'02, Taipei, Taiwan (2002) 2851–2854
6. Lam, W., Reibman, A.: An error concealment algorithm for images subject to channel errors. IEEE Transactions on Image Processing **4** (1995) 533–542
7. Wang, Y., Zhu, Q.F.: Error control and concealment for video communication: A review. Proc. IEEE **86** (1998) 974–997
8. Atzori, L., Ginesu, G., Raccis, A.: JPEG2000-coded image error concealment exploiting convex sets projections. IEEE Transactions on Image Processing **14** (2005) 487–498
9. Meerwald, P., Uhl, A.: A survey of wavelet-domain watermarking algorithms. In: Proc. SPIE, Electronic Imaging, Security and Watermarking of Multimedia Contents III. Volume 4314., San Jose, CA, USA (2001)
10. Chan, P., Lyu, M.R.: A DWT-based digital video watermarking scheme with error correcting code. In: Proc. 5th Int. Conf. on Information and Communications Security (ICICS'03), Inner-Mongolia, China (2003)
11. Li, W., Law, C.L., Dubey, V.K., Ong, J.T.: *Ka*-Band land mobile satellite channel model incorporating weather effects. IEEE Communications Letters **5** (2001) 194–196
12. Lutz, E., Cygan, D., Dippold, M., Dolainsky, F., Papke, W.: The land mobile satellite communication channel - recording, statistics, and channel model. IEEE Transactions on Vehicular Technology **40** (1991) 375–386
13. Jiao, C., Schwiebert, L., Xu, B.: On modeling the packet error statistics in bursty channels. In: Proc. 27th Annual IEEE Conf. on Local Computer Networks (LCN'02), Florida, USA (2002) 534–541

Polymorphic Compression

U. Topaloglu[1] and C. Bayrak[2]

[1] Applied Science Department, University of Arkansas at Little Rock,
Little Rock, AR 72204
umtopaloglu@ualr.edu

[2] Computer Science Department, University of Arkansas at Little Rock,
Little Rock, AR 72204
cxbayrak@ualr.edu

Abstract. Compression is an economical and efficient way of data handling in not only communication, but also storage purposes. We aimed to implement a compression application based on frequent use of English letters, digraphs, trigraphs and tetragraphs without sacrificing memory and/or the other resources. Despite its conceptual simplicity, the approach achieves promising results. The system is tested for several data and the result was compared with LZW, Huffman Coding, and arithmetic coding. The system can be applied to either small or large files, and it can be seen that the result is still stable.

1 Introduction

Nowadays, computer users are managing gigabytes or terabytes of data with their computation equipments. This usage contains file exchange through a network or storing them in a local storage media. Even though current technology allows us to deal with that large size of files, having capability of reducing the size becomes more economical and often improve the performance [1]. Video, picture and documents are the files frequently exchanged between groups of people, and compression gives ability to transfer those in comparably very short times.

Text compression is substituting the representation of data into another form using one of the lossless techniques because loosing one or more characters might cause the totally opposite meaning or meaningless text. After compression, it requires less space to store, and less time to transmit the text along the network [2].

PC (Polymorphic Compression) is a text compression technique and implemented as a part of secure communication framework study LEAD (Layered Encoding and Decoding) [12]. It's a dictionary based symbolic substitution with low computational resource requirements. Substituting frequent English symbols with the least number of bits is the idea behind the PC. A predefined static dictionary contains the repeatedly used letters, digraphs, trigraphs and tetragraphs.

Compression easiness and having the compression rate of almost 50% are the two advantages of the system. Use of statistics in the technique is still under development. With the help of usage statistics of letters, digraph, trigraphs and tetragraphs, the dictionary will be updated after pre-defined attempt. So the system will have semi-adaptive behavior, which is believed to be the best approach [13].

P. Yolum et al.(Eds.): ISCIS 2005, LNCS 3733, pp. 759 – 767, 2005.

2 Background

Compression is possible where data representation is more frequent than others in a document [3]. There are three different main classes for the compression algorithms; Finite context modeling, finite state modeling, and dictionary modeling [1]. Under those classes several approaches were proposed. Some of those are LZ77, LZ78, LZW, Huffman Coding, Arithmetic Coding, Run-Length Coding and Dynamic Markov Chain.

Lempel and Ziv (LZ) developed a system which is based on adaptive dictionary scheme [2]. Some other researchers added new features on LZ's algorithm and proposed as a new method, at least 11 LZ variation algorithms available. The most common ones are LZ77, LZ78 and LZW. LZ77 is an easy to implement, sliding window type approach. Main idea is to use part of previous symbol as the dictionary [6]. According Sayood [8], in summarizing the differences between LZ77 and LZ78, "the LZ77 approach implicitly assumes that like patterns will occur close together. However, this means that any pattern that recurs over a period longer than that covered by the coder window will not be captured." LZW (Lempel-Ziv-Welch) is another dictionary-based compression method based on LZ. It maps a variable number of symbols to a fixed length code. It is a patented well known approach. The disadvantage of such adaptive models is that compression can not be applied to the beginning, so it is not useful for small files [10]. Another disadvantage of LZW is that a more sophisticated data structure is needed to handle the dictionary.

Huffman coding maps fixed length symbols to variable length codes and optimal only when symbol probabilities are powers of 2 [8]. One disadvantage to Huffman coding is that input file needs to be read twice; one for building the tree and the second for coding the file. Another disadvantage is necessity of sending the header so that the decompressor knows what the codes is [6]. According to the NIST [7], having the frequency distribution that follows the Fibonacci numbers is the worst case for Huffman encoding.

In arithmetic coding one codeword which has half-open subintervals, is assigned to the each possible set. Shorter codes correspond to larger subintervals, so more probable input data sets are represented by less code [5]. According to Howard and Vitter [4] arithmetic coding tends to be slow and some operations like the model lookup and update are also deliberate, which are the main disadvantages. Another disadvantage, it is unable to produce a prefix code [4].

Run Length encoding finds the redundant samples, and sends the lengths of the redundant runs that occur between non-redundant samples [9]. The results are not satisfying on regular type text files which have fewer repetitions. Moreover, it can not compress the large files well.

DMC (Dynamic Markov Chain) is also another commonly used algorithm. Markov modeling is essentially a method to predict the probability of a given character based on what has come before it. In practice, the DMC often consumes outrageous memory [11].

To address the deficiencies of the aforementioned approaches, a symbolic substitution based a polymorphic compression is developed. When compared with some of the currently available compression approaches, early version's result of the system is satisfying and proves its easiness and performance as well.

In PC, the classic three med (medical), cisi (computer science), and cran (cranfiled), and the time set were used as a test data. For the test, randomly chosen texts from the four data sets are used for the 10 test files, named p1 to p10. The file sizes are between 86 to 14044 bytes. The table 1 represents the comparison of the compression ratios of PC, LZW, Huffman, and Arithmetic coding for the four different data sets. As can be seen from the Fig. 1, PC has stable results, while the other's varying by the file size. In other words, when the file size is getting smaller, the compression result is decreasing or even greater than the original. The compression ratio is the gain achieved. I.e. the file p6 is 10312 bits (S_o), PC can compress into 5649 bits (S_r). So;

$$Compression\,ratio = 1 - \frac{S_r}{S_o} \tag{1}$$

Table 1. Comparison table

(%)	p1	p2	p3	p4	p5	p6	p7	p8	p9	p10
File (bytes)	86	262	457	942	1246	1289	2843	5072	9647	14044
PC	41.42	47.81	46.01	45.33	45.43	45.23	46.79	47.75	47.53	46.79
LZW	3.49	21.37	25.16	30.68	37.56	35.61	42.42	51.12	53.87	50.95
Huffman	-391.86	-114.89	-8.75	20.06	25.36	29.87	26.42	38.72	44.07	41.83
Arith cod	13.95	27.10	29.32	34.29	38.36	37.86	40.03	45.21	47.33	42.64

In another test, the Calgary corpus is used and the results are given in Table 2.

2.1 Test in German

In regard to other languages, German is chosen for another test case to prove the system works by adapting the dictionary to the language. Two tetragraphs ("sche", "isch") as well as 17 trigraphs ("der", "che", "die") are used. Moreover, 18 digraphs ("en", "er", "un") are adapted along with the most frequent letters in German "e, n, i, r, s, a, t" into the dictionary.

After the changes are employed, two German texts are used for the test. The first file has the size of 20,344 bits and is reduced to the 12,183 bits (~41%). The size of the second test file is 42,608 bits and compressed into 24,053 bits (~44%).

The aforementioned results show that PC works well with the languages other than English by adjustment in the dictionary.

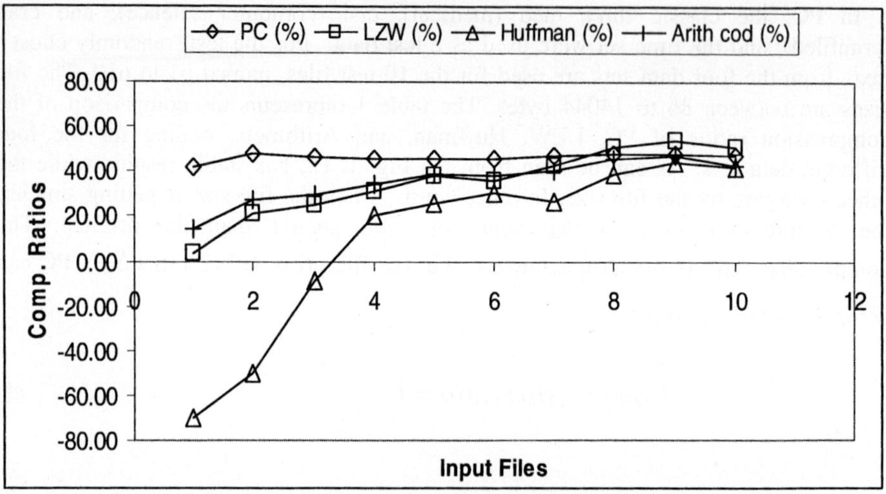

Fig. 1. Different approaches compression results vs. different file sizes

Table 2. Calgary corpus results

File	Org size (bytes)	Reduced size (bits)	Ratio (%)
bib	117,543	532,475	43.37
book1	785,395	3,413,123	45.67
book2	626,492	2,840,998	43.31
news	387,170	1,881,859	39.24
paper1	54,413	261,632	39.89
paper2	83,932	375,098	44.13
progc	41,100	218,404	33.57
progl	73,892	406,952	31.15
progp	51,347	258,347	37.10
trans	90,726	536,028	26.14

3 Design

The system consists of the compression module and the decompression module. Both modules interact with the dictionary. The system overview can be seen in Fig. 2.

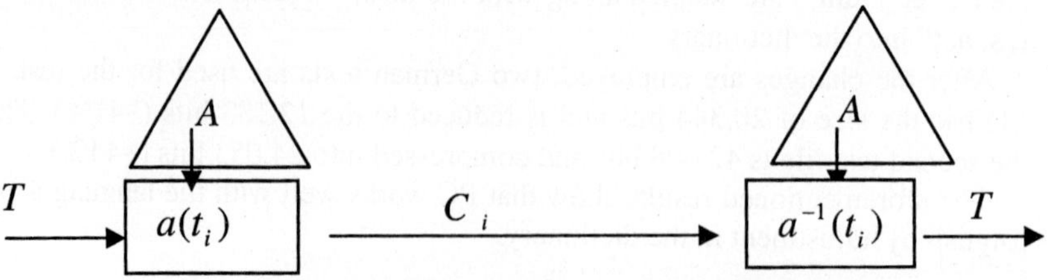

Fig. 2. The system overview

PC designed considering Shannon's [3] theory of source coding, which is;

$$-\sum p_i \log p_i \tag{2}$$

where p_i is the expected probability of the symbol i. The theory says that the symbol with the higher probability needs to be represented with fewer bits, while lower probability symbols can be represented with more bits.

PC uses predefined dictionary, in which tetragraphs, trigraphs, digraphs, letters, numbers and special characters are kept. After a number of statistical studies and tests, the dictionary was created based on 6 different symbol categories.

a) Tetragraphs

Tetragraphs are four letters symbols (i.e. "tion") and some of them can be found more than others in English. The tetragraphs are normally represented in 32 bits, in the dictionary common tetragraphs are represented with 8 bits.

b) Trigraphs

Three letter symbols are called as trigraphs (i.e. "the", "ing", "ive"). 17 trigraphs were used in the dictionary. Trigraphs normally reside in 24 bits, in the dictionary the first 8 represented with 7 bits and 8 bits were used for the rest.

c) Digraphs

Character couples are named as digraph (i.e. "ed", "ca", "re"). 18 digraphs were selected to be used. Normally they are 16 bit symbols, but in the system 7 of them are represented with 7 bits and for the rest 8 bits were dedicated.

d) Letters

As known, single letters use 8 bits to be represented. Based on the English letter frequencies, (Table 3) the first 7 of them were represented with 3 bits, the remaining 16 were represented with 7 bits and for the rest 8 bits were used. Fortunately, according to the research [14], the four vowels "a, e, i, o" and the four consonants "n, r, s, t" form 2/3 of the normal English plain text. Besides, the space character has an approximate frequency of 10% in a text, so 3 bits were used for the representation.

e) Numbers and Special Characters

The numbers and special characters like "?, !, @, " , +, >, ..." were also used in the dictionary. There is no reduction possible for this category in the system. They were represented with 8 bits.

f) Other ASCII Characters

The system allows use of the characters which are not in the dictionary, for example, the characters whose ASCII values are above 128. If the input symbol is not in the dictionary, PC uses its original ASCII value with an identifier to prevent the mix with the other substitutions.

Table 3. English Letter frequencies

e 12.31	l 4.03	b 1.62
t 9.59	d 3.65	g 1.61
a 8.05	c 3.20	v 0.93
o 7.94	u 3.10	k 0.52
n 7.19	p 2.29	q 0.20
i 7.18	f 2.28	x 0.20
s 6.59	m 2.25	j 0.10
r 6.03	w 2.03	z 0.09
h 5.14	y 1.88	

4 Reducing the Text Size

Let $M = \{T, C\}$ be a compression system, where T is plaintext, C is compressed output. And it has at least two nodes; compression and decompression.

4.1 Compression

Definition 1; the representation of source document is defined as $T = Z_{255}$, $t_i \in T$ where Z_{255} denotes a domain with 255 ASCII characters, t_i is possible plaintext between any ASCII characters, and i is the symbol number.

Definition 2; the compressed out symbolized as C is binary output file and $c_i \in C$ is member of C domain.

Definition 3; the system uses predefined alphabet A which has frequently used tetragraphs, trigraphs, digraphs, letters, numbers, and special characters. The function $a(x) \in A$ and $a(t_i) = (w_i)$ where $x = 1,2,\ldots,103$ is an integer, and w represents the binary value for input text t_i.

Based on the definitions, the compression can be denoted as;

$$c_i = \begin{cases} a(t_i) & \text{if } t_i \in A \\ ASC(t_i) & \text{if } t_i \notin A \end{cases} \tag{3}$$

where $ASC(t_i)$ is the ASCII converter function of input t_i.

Based on the given definitions PC's algorithm can be seen in Fig. 3.

```
READ = input file
WHILE there are still input characters DO
     CHARACTER = get input character
     CHARACTER1 = input character + 1st neighbor
     CHARACTER2 = CHARACTER1 + 2nd neighbor
     CHARACTER3 = CHARACTER2 + 3rd neighbor
      IF CHARACTER (), (1), (2), (3) is in the
        dictionary then
         STRING = dictionary value
     ELSE
        STRING = identifier + ASCII value
     END of IF
END of WHILE
output code
```

Fig. 3. PC's compression algorithm

The system reads the first character, and than 2nd, 3rd, and 4th following characters. After that, PC check for the tetra graph first, trigraphs second, digraphs third and finally the letters. If any symbol pattern is matched with the one in the dictionary, the substitution occurs and next character is read until the end of the input file.

4.2 Decompression

At the decompression end, the definitions 1, 2, and 3 are valid and applicable. The decompressing is the reverse function of compression. It can be represented as;

$$t_i = \begin{cases} a^{-1}(t_i) & \text{if } c_i \in A \\ ASC^{-1}(t_i) & \text{if } c_i \notin A \end{cases} \tag{4}$$

When the compression process is started, the system reads the first three bits from the stream. If it matches with the one of single letters in the dictionary, the associated letter is substituted. If it is not in the dictionary, the system reads 3 more bits then 1 more bit until it finds the dictionary entry of the stream. If it was an identifier, the next 8 bits is the ASCII value of the character (Fig. 4).

```
READ = input bit stream
WHILE there are still input bits DO
    BIT = get the first three bits.
    IF BIT is in the dictionary then
       STRING = dictionary value
    ELSE
       BIT =BIT + get four more bits.
       IF BIT is in the dictionary then
          STRING = dictionary value
          ELSE
             BIT =BIT + get one more bits.
         IF BIT is in the dictionary then
             STRING = dictionary value
         ELSE
                 STRING = Char. value of the
following 8 bits
               END of IFs
END of WHILE
output text
```

Fig. 4. PC's decompression algorithm

5 Conclusion

The proposed system achieves very satisfying results. In terms of compression ratio, it accomplishes the ratio range of 42% to 50%. The scalability and performance is also promising. In addition, it can attain the same results for both small and large size files, which is the disadvantage of the adaptive approaches. Moreover, it is easy to run and does not require outrageous computational resource.

The only disadvantage of the system is language limitations. If it is to be used in other languages, the dictionary needs to be adapted, which may cause different results.

As a future work, semantic analysis of the text is being performed to study its effects on compression.

References

1. Bell, T., Witten, I., Cleary, J.:Modeling for Text Compression. ACM Computing surveys, Vol: 21, No: 4 (1989)
2. Witten, I., Bell, T., Moffat, A.:Managing Gigabytes; Compressing and Indexing Documents and Images. 2nd edn. Morgan-Kaufman (1999)

3. Shannon, C. E.:A Mathematical Theory of Communication. Bell Syst. Tech. J. 27 (July 1948), 398-403.
4. Howard ,P., Vitter,J.:Practical Implementations of Arithmetic Coding: Image and Text Compression. James A. Storer, ed., Kluwer Academic Publishers, Norwell Massachusetts (1992) 85-112
5. Howard ,P., Vitter,J.: Arithmetic Coding for Data Compression. Proceedings of the IEEE, 82(6) (June 1994) 857-865
6. Salomon, D.:Data Compression; The complete Reference. 2nd edn. Springer- Verlag (2000)
7. NIST (National Institute of Standards and Technology) http://www.nist.gov/dads/HTML/huffmanEncoding.html (March 2005)
8. Sayood, K.:Introduction to Data Compression. 2nd edn. Morgan-Kaufman (2000)
9. Lynch, T.: Data Compression techniques and Applications. Van Nostrand Reinhold Company (1985)
10. Krone, J.: TRACS project: http://www.denison.edu/mathsci/tracs/ (October 2004)
11. Bunton, S.: The structure of DMC [dynamic Markov compression]. Data Compression Conference 1995. DCC '95 Proceedings
12. Topaloglu, U., Bayrak, C.:Secure Information Exchange With Layering (Six L). Submitted to the IEEE Transactions on Dependable and Secure Computing
13. Plantinga, H.: An Asymmetric, Semi-adaptive Text Compression Algorithm. IEEE Data Compression Conference 1994
14. Friedman, W., Callimahos, L.:Military Cryptanalytics Part I - Volume 1, Aegean Park Press, Laguna Hills California (1985)

Efficient Adaptive Data Compression Using Fano Binary Search Trees

Luis Rueda[1,*] and B. John Oommen[2,**]

[1] School of Computer Science, University of Windsor,
401 Sunset Ave., Windsor, ON N9B 3P4, Canada
Phone +1-519-253-3000 Ext. 3780, Fax +1-519-973-7093
lrueda@uwindsor.ca

[2] School of Computer Science, Carleton University,
1125 Colonel By Dr., Ottawa, ON K1S 5B6, Canada
oommen@scs.carleton.ca

Abstract. In this paper, we show an effective way of using adaptive *self-organizing* data structures in enhancing compression schemes. We introduce a new data structure, the *Partitioning Binary Search Tree* (PBST), which is based on the well-known *Binary Search Tree* (BST), and when used in conjunction with Fano encoding, the PBST leads to the so-called *Fano Binary Search Tree* (FBST). The PBST and FBST can be maintained adaptively and *in a self-organizing manner* by using new *tree*-based operators, namely the Shift-To-Left (STL) and the Shift-To-Right (STR) operators. The encoding and decoding procedures that also update the FBST have been implemented, and show that the adaptive Fano coding using FBSTs, the Huffman, and the greedy adaptive Fano coding achieve similar compression ratios.

1 Introduction

Adaptive lists have been investigated for more than three decades, and schemes such as the Move-to-Front (MTF), Transposition, Move-k-Ahead, the Move-to-Rear families [14], and randomized algorithms [3], and their applicability in compression has also been acclaimed, for example, of the MTF in block sorting [9], and by Albers *et al.* in [2]. As opposed to this, Binary Search Trees (BSTs) have been used in a wide range of applications that include storage, dictionaries, databases, and symbol tables. In our case, we assume that the (adaptive) BST is dynamically changed while the records are searched for. Heuristics to maintain an adaptive BST include *move-to-root* heuristic [4], the *simple exchange rule* [4], *splaying* [18], the *monotonic tree* [7], *biasing* [6], *dynamic binary search* [13], *weighted randomization* [5], *deepsplaying* [16], and the technique that uses *conditional rotations* [8].

* *Member of the IEEE.*
** *Fellow of the IEEE.*

P. Yolum et al.(Eds.): ISCIS 2005, LNCS 3733, pp. 768–779, 2005.

On the other hand, adaptive coding is important in many applications that require online data compression and transmission. The most well-known adaptive coding technique is Huffman coding [17], *arithmetic coding* [10], *interval* and *recency rank encoding* [10], and the *Elias omega codes* [1]. Adaptive methods for Fano coding have been recently introduced (for the binary and multi-symbol code alphabets) [15], which have been shown to work faster than adaptive Huffman coding, and consume one-sixth of the resources required by the latter. Although these methods are efficient, they need to maintain a *list* of the source symbols and the respective probabilities from which the Fano coding tree can be *partially* reconstructed at each encoding step. In this paper, we show how we can effectively use results from the field of adaptive *self-organizing* data structures in enhancing compression schemes. We introduce a new data structure, the Fano BST (FBST), and the corresponding updating operators. Afterwards, we show that by incorporating the FBST into an adaptive encoding algorithm leads to faster compression while achieving comparable compression ratios to its counterpart, the Huffman coding.

2 Fano Binary Search Trees

The basis for the particular "species" of binary search trees introduced in this paper, the FBST, comes from the structure used in the *conditional rotation heuristic* [8]. Consider a (complete) BST, $\mathcal{T} = \{t_1, \ldots, t_{2m-1}\}$. If t_i is any internal node of $\mathcal{T}$, then: P_i is the parent of t_i, L_i is the left child of t_i, R_i is the right child of t_i, B_i is the sibling of t_i, and P_{P_i} is the parent of P_i (or the grandparent of t_i). Using these primitives, B_i can also be L_{P_i} if t_i is the right child of P_i, or R_{P_i} if t_i is the left child of P_i.

Let $\alpha_i(n)$ is the total number of accesses to node t_i up to time n. $\tau_i(n)$ is the total number of accesses to $\mathcal{T}_i$, the subtree rooted at t_i, up to time n, and is calculated as follows:

$$\tau_i(n) = \sum_{t_j \in \mathcal{T}_i} \alpha_j(n) . \tag{1}$$

$\kappa_i(n)$ is the Weighted Path Length (WPL) of $\mathcal{T}_i$, the subtree rooted at t_i, at time n, and is calculated as follows:

$$\kappa_i(n) = \sum_{t_j \in \mathcal{T}_i} \alpha_j(n)\lambda_j(n) , \tag{2}$$

where $\lambda_j(n)$ is the path length from t_j up to node t_i.

By using simple induction, it can be shown that:

$$\kappa_i(n) = \sum_{t_j \in \mathcal{T}_i} \tau_j(n) . \tag{3}$$

In order to simplify the notation, we let α_i, τ_i, and κ_i be the corresponding values (as defined in the conditional rotation heuristic) contained in node t_i at time n, i.e. $\alpha_i(n)$, $\tau_i(n)$, and $\kappa_i(n)$ respectively.

Broadly speaking, an FBST is a BST in which the number of accesses of all the internal nodes are set to zero, and the number of accesses of each leaf represents the number of times that the symbol associated with that leaf has appeared so far in the input sequence. The aim is to maintain the tree balanced in such a way that for every internal node, the weight of the left child is as nearly-equal as possible to that of the right child.

Definition 1. *Consider the source alphabet* $\mathcal{S} = \{s_1, \ldots, s_m\}$ *whose probabilities of occurrence are* $\mathcal{P} = [p_1, \ldots, p_m]$, *where* $p_1 \geq \ldots \geq p_m$, *and the code alphabet* $\mathcal{A} = \{0, 1\}$. *A* PBST *is a binary tree,* $\mathcal{T} = \{t_1, \ldots, t_{2m-1}\}$, *whose nodes are identified by their indices (for convenience, also used as the keys* $\{k_i\}$*), and whose fields are the corresponding values of* τ_i. *Furthermore, every PBST satisfies:*

(i) Each node t_{2i-1} *is a leaf, for* $i = 1, \ldots, m$, *where* s_i *is the* i^{th} *alphabet symbol satisfying* $p_i \geq p_j$ *if* $i < j$.
(ii) Each node t_{2i} *is an internal node, for* $i = 1, \ldots, m-1$.

Remark 1. Given a PBST, $\mathcal{T} = \{t_1, \ldots, t_{2m-1}\}$, the number of accesses to a leaf node, α_{2i-1}, is a counter, and p_i refers to either α_{2i-1} (the frequency counter) or the probability of occurrence of the symbol associated with t_{2i-1}. We shall use both these representation interchangeably. In fact, the probability of occurrence of s_i can be estimated (in a maximum likelihood manner) as follows:

$$p_i = \frac{\alpha_{2i-1}}{\sum_{j=1}^{m} \alpha_{2j-1}} . \quad (4)$$

We now introduce a particular case of the PBST, the *FBST*. This tree has the added property that each partitioning step is performed by following the principles of the Fano coding, i.e. the weights of the two new nodes are as nearly equal as possible. This is formally defined below.

Definition 2. *Let* $\mathcal{T} = \{t_1, \ldots, t_{2m-1}\}$ *be a PBST.* $\mathcal{T}$ *is an* FBST, *if for every internal node,* t_{2i}, *the following conditions are satisfied:*

(a) $\tau_{R_i} - \tau_{L_i} \leq \tau_{2i+1}$ *if* $\tau_{L_i} < \tau_{R_i}$,
(b) $\tau_{L_i} - \tau_{R_i} \leq \tau_{2i-1}$ *if* $\tau_{L_i} > \tau_{R_i}$, *or*
(c) $\tau_{L_i} = \tau_{R_i}$.

The algorithm for constructing an FBST from the source alphabet symbols and their probabilities of occurrence can be found in [15]. Each time a partitioning is performed, two sublists are obtained, and two new nodes are created, t_{n_0} and t_{n_1}, which are assigned to the left child and the right child of the current node, t_n. This partitioning is recursively performed until a sublist with a single symbol is obtained.

In order to ensure that $\mathcal{T}$ satisfies properties (i) and (ii) of Definition Structure_PBST, and also the conditions of Definition Structure_FBST, the FBST generated by procedure FanoBST(...) must be rearranged as if each node were accessed in a traversal order, from left to right [15]. The sorted FBST is generated by invoking procedure FanoBSTSort(...), which produces a list of nodes in the desired order, $\mathcal{T} = \{t_1, \ldots, t_{2m-1}\}$.

Remark 2. The structure of the FBST is similar to the structure of the BST used in the conditional rotation heuristic introduced in [8]. The difference, however, is that since every internal node does not represent an alphabet symbol, the values of α_{2i} are all 0, and the quantities for the leaf nodes, $\{\alpha_{2i-1}\}$, are set to $\{p_i\}$ or to frequency counters representing them.

Clearly, the total number of accesses to the subtree rooted at node t_{2i}, τ_{2i}, is obtained as the sum of the number of accesses to all the leaves of $\mathcal{T}_{2i}$. This is given in the lemma below, whose proof can be found in [15].

Lemma 1. *Let $\mathcal{T}_{2i} = \{t_1, \ldots, t_{2s-1}\}$ be a subtree rooted at node t_{2i}. The total number of accesses to $\mathcal{T}_{2i}$ is given by:*

$$\tau_{2i} = \sum_{j=1}^{s} \alpha_{2j-1} = \tau_{L_{2i}} + \tau_{R_{2i}} \,. \tag{5}$$

We now present a result that relates the WPL of an FBST and the average code word length of the encoding schemes generated from *that* tree. For any FBST, $\mathcal{T}$, κ is calculated using (3). By optimizing on the relative properties of κ and τ, we can show that the average code word length of the encoding schemes generated from $\mathcal{T}$, $\bar{\ell}$, can be calculated from the values of κ and τ that are maintained at the root. Note that this is done with a single access – without traversing the entire tree. This result is stated in Theorem 1 given below.

This is quite an "intriguing" result. The issue at stake is to compute the expected value of a random variable, in this case, the *expected code word length.* In general, this can be done if we are given the values that the random variable assumes, and their corresponding probabilities. The actual computation would involve the summation (or an integral in the case of continuous random variables) of the product of the values and their associated probabilities. Theorem 1, whose proof can be found in [15], shows how this expected code word length can be computed quickly – without *explicitly* computing either the product or the summation. However, this is done *implicitly*, since κ and τ take these factors into consideration. Since the FBST is maintained adaptively, the average code word length is also maintained adaptively. Invoking this result, we can obtain the average code word length by a single access to the root of the FBST.

Theorem 1. *Let $\mathcal{T} = \{t_1, \ldots, t_{2m-1}\}$ be an FBST constructed from the source alphabet $\mathcal{S} = \{s_1, \ldots s_m\}$ whose probabilities of occurrence are $\mathcal{P} = [p_1, \ldots, p_m]$. If $\phi : \mathcal{S} \to \{w_1, \ldots, w_m\}$ is an encoding scheme generated from $\mathcal{T}$, then*

$$\bar{\ell} = \sum_{i=1}^{m} p_i \ell_i = \frac{\kappa_{root}}{\tau_{root}} - 1 \,, \tag{6}$$

where ℓ_i is the length of w_i, τ_{root} is the total number of accesses to $\mathcal{T}$, and κ_{root} is as defined in (2).

From Theorem 1, we see that the WPL and $\bar{\ell}$ are closely related. The smaller the WPL, the smaller the value of $\bar{\ell}$. Consequently, the problem of minimizing the WPL of an FBST is equivalent to minimizing the average code word length of the encoding schemes obtained from that tree.

3 Shift Operators in Partitioning Binary Search Trees

The aim of our on-line encoding/decoding is to maintain a structure that maximally contains and utilizes the statistical information about the source. Using this structure, the current symbol is encoded and the structure is updated in such a way that the next symbol is expected to be encoded as optimally as possible. We propose to use our new structure, namely the FBST defined in Section 2, which is adaptively maintained by simultaneously encoding, and learning details about the relevant statistics of the source[1]. The learning process requires that two separate phases are sequentially performed. The first consists of updating the frequency counters of the current symbol, and the second involves changing the structure of the PBST so as to maintain an FBST. Other adaptive encoding techniques, such as Huffman coding or arithmetic coding, utilize the same sequence of processes: encoding and then learning.

After the encoder updates the frequency counter of the current symbol and the corresponding nodes, the resulting PBST may need to be changed so that the FBST is maintained consistently. To achieve this, we introduce two new *shift* operators which can be performed on a PBST : the *Shift-To-Left (STL)* operator and the *Shift-To-Right (STR)* operator[2]. Broadly speaking, these operators consist of removing a node from one of the sublists obtained from the partitioning, and inserting it into the other sublist, in such a way that the new partitioning satisfies the properties of Definition Structure_PBST. For the sake of brevity, we exclude the definition of the STR operator, which can be found in [15], and which operates in a similar manner to the STL.

The STL operator, performed on an internal node of a PBST, consists of removing the *left*-most leaf of the subtree rooted at the *right* child of that node, and inserting it as the *right*-most leaf in the subtree rooted at the *left* child of that node. The relation between the STL operator and the Fano code construction procedure is the following. Suppose that a list $\mathcal{P} = [p_1, \ldots, p_m]$ has already been partitioned into two new sublists, $\mathcal{P}_0 = [p_1, \ldots, p_k]$ and $\mathcal{P}_1 = [p_{k+1}, \ldots, p_m]$. The equivalent to the STL operator for this scenario consists of deleting p_{k+1} from $\mathcal{P}_1$ and inserting it into the last position of $\mathcal{P}_0$, yielding $\mathcal{P}_0' = [p_0, \ldots, p_k, p_{k+1}]$ and $\mathcal{P}_1' = [p_{k+2}, \ldots, p_m]$.

[1] The structure that we introduce here, namely the FBST, could also be combined with other structure models, such as Markov models, dictionary-based compression, PPM schemes, etc., to achieve much more efficient compression. In this paper, we consider the zeroth-order model. The use of FBSTs with higher-order models is currently being investigated.

[2] We have defined these operators in terms of various cases, which is, conceptually, similar to the zig-zig and zig-zag cases of the tree-based operations already introduced in the literature [11,12,18].

Notation STL: Consider a PBST, $\mathcal{T} = \{t_1, \ldots, t_{2m-1}\}$, in which the weight of each node, t_l, is τ_l, and the key for each internal node is k_l, for $l = 1, \ldots, m$. Let

- t_i be an internal node of $\mathcal{T}$,
- R_i be also an internal node of $\mathcal{T}$,
- t_j be the left-most leaf of the subtree rooted at R_i,
- B_j be the sibling of t_j, and
- t_k be the right-most leaf of the subtree rooted at L_i.

Using this notation, we can identify three mutually exclusive cases in which the STL operator can be applied. These cases are listed below, and the rules for performing the STL operation and the corresponding examples are discussed thereafter.

STL-1 : $P_{P_j} = t_i$ and L_i is a leaf.
STL-2 : $P_{P_j} \neq t_i$ and L_i is a leaf.
STL-3 : L_i is *not* a leaf.

The STL operator performed in the scenario of Case STL-1 is discussed below.

Rule 1 (STL-1). *Consider a PBST, $\mathcal{T}$, described using* **Notation STL**. *Suppose that the scenario is that of Case STL-1. The STL operator applied to the subtree rooted at node t_i consists of the following operations:*

(a) the value $\tau_k - \tau_{B_j}$ is added to τ_{P_j},
(b) k_i and k_{P_j} are swapped[3]*,*
(c) B_j becomes the right child of t_i,
(d) P_j becomes the left child of t_i,
(e) t_k becomes the left child of P_j, and
(f) t_j becomes the right child of P_j.

Remark 3. The node on which the STL operator is applied, t_i, can be any internal node or the root satisfying the **Notation STL**. The tree resulting from the STL-1 operator is a PBST. This is stated for the operator, in general, in Lemma 2 given below. The complete proof of the lemma can be found in [15].

Lemma 2 (STL-1 validity). *Consider a PBST, $\mathcal{T} = \{t_1, \ldots, t_{2m-1}\}$, specified as per* **Notation STL**. *If an STL operation is performed on the subtree rooted at node t_i as per Rule 1, then the resulting tree, $\mathcal{T}' = \{t'_1, \ldots, t'_{2m-1}\}$, is a PBST.*

The weights of the internal nodes in the new tree, $\mathcal{T}'$, are consistently obtained as the sum of the weights of their two children. This is achieved in only *two* local operations, as opposed to re-calculating *all* the weights of the tree in a bottom-up fashion.

We now provide the mechanisms required to perform an STL operation when we are in the scenario of Case STL-2.

[3] In the actual implementation, the FBST can be maintained in an array, in which the node t_l, $1 \leq l \leq 2m-1$, can be stored at position l. In this case, and in all the other cases of STL and STR, swapping these two keys could be avoided, and searching the node t_l could be done in a single access to position l in the array.

Rule 2 (STL-2). *Consider a PBST, $\mathcal{T} = \{t_1, \ldots, t_{2m-1}\}$, described using* ***Notation STL****. Suppose that we are in the scenario of Case STL-2. The STL operator performed on node t_i involves the following operations:*

(a) $\tau_k - \tau_{B_j}$ *is added to* τ_{P_j},
(b) τ_j *is subtracted from all the* τ*'s in the path from* P_{P_j} *to* R_i,
(c) k_i *and* k_{P_j} *are swapped,*
(d) B_j *becomes the left child of* P_{P_j},
(e) t_j *becomes the right child of* P_j,
(f) t_k *becomes the left child of* P_j, *and*
(g) P_j *becomes the left child of* t_i.

Note that the resulting tree is a PBST. The general case is stated in Lemma 3, whose proof can be found in [15].

Lemma 3 (STL-2 validity). *Consider a PBST, $\mathcal{T} = \{t_1, \ldots, t_{2m-1}\}$, as per* ***Notation STL****. The resulting tree, $\mathcal{T}' = \{t'_1, \ldots, t'_{2m-1}\}$, obtained after performing an STL-2 operation as per Rule 2 is a PBST.*

The corresponding rule for the scenario of Case STL-3 satisfying **Notation STL** is given below in Rule 3.

Rule 3 (STL-3). *Consider a PBST, $\mathcal{T} = \{t_1, \ldots, t_{2m-1}\}$, specified using the notation of* ***Notation STL****, and the scenario of Case STL-3. The STL operator performed on the subtree rooted at t_i consists of shifting t_j to the subtree rooted at L_i in such a way that:*

(a) $\tau_k - \tau_{B_j}$ *is added to* τ_{P_j},
(b) τ_j *is subtracted from all the* τ*'s in the path from* P_{P_j} *to* R_i,
(c) τ_j *is added to all the* τ*'s in the path from* P_k *to* L_i,
(d) k_i *and* k_{P_j} *are swapped,*
(e) B_j *becomes the left child of* P_{P_j},
(f) t_j *becomes the right child of* P_j,
(g) t_k *becomes the left child of* P_j, *and*
(h) P_j *becomes the right child of* P_k.

Observe that in the STL-3 operation, all the nodes in the entire path from P_k to the left child of t_i have to be updated by adding τ_j to the weight of those nodes. As in the other two cases, the weight of t_i is not changed. We show below an example that helps to understand how the STL-3 operator works.

Example 1. Let $\mathcal{S} = \{a, b, c, d, e, f, g\}$ be the source alphabet whose frequency counters are $\mathcal{P} = [8, 3, 3, 3, 3, 3, 3]$. A PBST, $\mathcal{T}$, constructed from $\mathcal{S}$ and $\mathcal{P}$ is the one depicted on the left of Figure 1. After applying the STL operator to the subtree rooted at node t_i (in this case, the root node of $\mathcal{T}$), we obtain $\mathcal{T}'$, the tree depicted on the right. Observe that $\mathcal{T}'$ is a PBST. The general result is stated in Lemma 4 given below, and proved in [15].

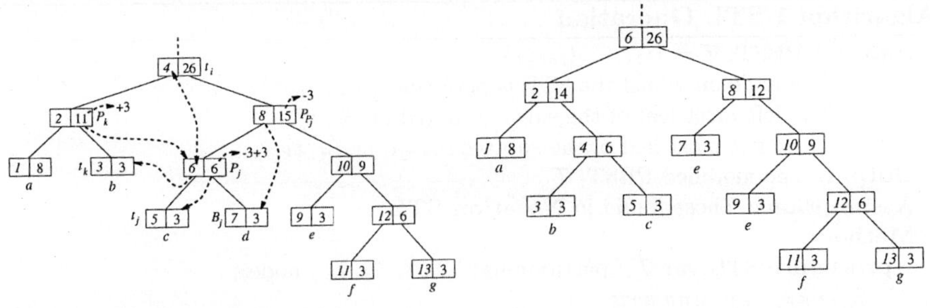

Fig. 1. A PBST, $\mathcal{T}$, constructed from $\mathcal{S} = \{a, b, c, d, e, f, g\}$ and $\mathcal{P} = [8, 3, 3, 3, 3, 3, 3]$, and the corresponding PBST, $\mathcal{T}'$, after performing an STL-3 operation. The top-most node can be a left child, a right child, or the root.

Lemma 4 (STL-3 validity). *Let $\mathcal{T} = \{t_1, \ldots, t_{2m-1}\}$ be a PBST in which an STL-3 operation is performed as per Rule 3, resulting in a new tree, $\mathcal{T}' = \{t'_1, \ldots, t'_{2m-1}\}$. Then, $\mathcal{T}'$ is a PBST.*

In order to facilitate the implementation of the STL operator, we present the corresponding algorithm that considers the three mutually exclusive cases discussed above. This procedure is depicted in Algorithm **STL_Operation**. When performing an assignment operation by means of the left arrow, "$\leftarrow$", the operand on the left is the new value of the pointer or weight, and the operand on the right is either the value of the weight, or the value of the actual pointer to a node. For example, $L_{P_{P_j}} \leftarrow B_j$ implies that the value of the pointer to the left child of P_{P_j} acquires the value "B_j"[4].

4 Fano Binary Search Tree Coding

Using the PBST and the underlying tree operations (discussed in Section 3), we now apply them to the adaptive data encoding problem. Given an input sequence, $\mathcal{X} = x[1] \ldots x[M]$, which has to be encoded, the idea is to maintain an FBST at all times - at the encoding and decoding stages. In the encoding algorithm, at time 'k', the symbol $x[k]$ is encoded using an FBST, $\mathcal{T}(k)$, which is identical to the one used by the decoding algorithm to retrieve $x[k]$. $\mathcal{T}(k)$ must be updated in such a way that at time '$k+1$', both algorithms maintain the same tree $\mathcal{T}(k+1)$.

To maintain, at each time instant, an FBST, i.e. the tree obtained after the updating procedure, $\mathcal{T}(k+1)$, must satisfy the conditions stated in Definition Structure_FBST. Since the PBST structures are maintained at both the encoder and decoder sides, it is up to the updating procedure to ensure that the resulting tree satisfies the conditions stated in Definition Structure_FBST.

[4] In the actual implementation, "B_j" contains the memory address of the node B_j, or the position of B_j in a list if the tree is stored in an array.

Algorithm 1 STL_Operation

Input: A PBST, $\mathcal{T} = \{t_1, \ldots, t_{2m-1}\}$.
The node on which the STL is performed, t_i.
The left-most leaf of the subtree rooted at R_i, t_j.
The right-most leaf of the subtree rooted at L_i, t_k.
Output: The modified PBST, $\mathcal{T}$.
Assumptions: Those found in **Notation STL**.
Method:

```
procedure STL(var T : partitioningBST; t_i, t_j, t_k : node);
  k_i ↔ k_{P_j}   // swap keys
  τ_{P_j} ← τ_{P_j} + τ_k − τ_{B_j}
  for l ← P_{P_j} to R_i step l ← P_l do
    τ_l ← τ_l − τ_j
  endfor
  for l ← P_k to L_i step l ← P_l do
    τ_l ← τ_l + τ_j
  endfor
  if t_i = P_k then   // Move P_j to the subtree on the left
    L_i ← P_j   // STL-1 and STL-2
  else
    R_{P_k} ← P_j   // STL-3
  endif
  if t_i = P_{P_j} then   // B_j remains in the right subtree
    R_i ← B_j   // STL-1
  else
    L_{P_{P_j}} ← B_j   // STL-2 and STL-3
  endif
  R_{P_j} ← t_j   // t_j becomes the right child of its parent
  L_{P_j} ← t_k; P_k ← P_j   // P_j becomes the parent of t_k
  P_{B_j} ← P_{P_j}   // Update the parent of B_j
  P_{P_j} ← P_k   // New parent of P_j is now old parent of t_k
endprocedure
end Algorithm STL_Operation
```

The updating procedure is based on a *conditional shifting heuristic*, and used to transform a PBST into an FBST. The conditional shifting heuristic is based on the principles of the Fano coding – the nearly-equal-probability property [15]. This heuristic, used in conjunction with the STL and the STR operators defined in this paper, are used to transform a PBST into an FBST. Details of the heuristic, as well as the encoding and decoding algorithms are provided in [15].

5 Empirical Results

To analyze the speed and compression efficiency of our newly introduced adaptive coding schemes, we report the results obtained after running the scheme on files of the Canterbury corpus. Similar results are also available for the Calgary corpus, which can be found in [15]. We also run the greedy adaptive Fano coding presented in [15], and the adaptive Huffman coding algorithm introduced in [17] on the same benchmarks. The results obtained from the tests are shown in Table 1. The first column contains the name of the file. The second column, labeled $l_{\mathcal{X}}$, represents the size (in bytes) of the original file. The next columns correspond to the speed and compression ratio for the *Adaptive Huffman Coding* (AFC), the *adaptive Greedy Fano Coding* (GFC), and the adaptive Fano coding that uses FBSTs (FBSTC). Each of the two groups of three columns contains the compression ratio, ρ, calculated as $\rho = \left(1 - \frac{\ell_{\mathcal{Y}}}{l_{\mathcal{X}}}\right) 100$, the time (in seconds) required to compress the file, and the time (in seconds) needed to recover the original file.

The compression ratio obtained after running GFC and FBSTC are, as expected, similar. We observe that the FBSTC obtains compression ratios slightly higher (only 0.15%) than the AHC. In terms of compression speed, on small files, GFC is faster than FBSTC, and the latter is significantly faster than AHC. On large files (e.g. *kennedy.xls*), however, FBSTC is faster than GFC. In fact, the reason why GFC is faster on *ptt5* is due to the fact that a high compression ratio is achieved, and the input file contains only a few different symbols, which makes the FBST look like a list. Consequently, its behavior is similar to that of the GFC, with the additional burden of maintaining a complex structure, the FBST. Observe that to compress the file *kennedy.xls*, GFC takes more than 2.5 times as much time as that of FBSTC. In terms of decompression speed, FBSTC is slower than AHC. However, the former achieves similar speed values for both compression and decompression, which implies an advantage when the entire process has to be synchronized.

Table 1. Speed and compression ratio obtained after running the adaptive Huffman coding, the greedy adaptive Fano coding, and the adaptive coding that uses FBST on files of the Canterbury corpus. Similar results are available for the Calgary corpus.

File Name	$l_{\mathcal{X}}$ (bytes)	AHC ρ (%)	AHC T.Enc. (sec.)	AHC T.Dec. (sec.)	GFC ρ (%)	GFC T.Enc. (sec.)	GFC T.Dec. (sec.)	FBSTC ρ (%)	FBSTC T.Enc. (sec.)	FBSTC T.Dec. (sec.)
alice29.txt	148,481	42.84	2.49	0.48	42.59	1.20	0.99	42.59	1.44	1.33
asyoulik.txt	125,179	39.21	2.37	0.42	39.05	1.25	0.89	39.06	1.31	1.23
cp.html	24,603	33.27	1.87	0.10	33.19	0.30	0.19	33.19	0.88	0.82
fields.c	11,150	35.31	1.77	0.05	34.92	0.14	0.08	34.89	0.52	0.49
grammar.lsp	3,721	37.70	1.70	0.02	37.29	0.05	0.02	37.24	0.32	0.29
kennedy.xls	1,029,744	55.04	6.71	2.90	54.66	11.72	5.76	54.81	4.50	3.86
lcet10.txt	419,235	41.74	4.18	1.41	41.72	3.83	2.84	41.72	2.41	2.19
plrabn12.txt	471,162	43.43	4.40	1.52	43.32	4.20	3.08	43.32	2.33	2.16
ptt5	513,216	79.18	2.57	0.67	79.16	1.68	1.29	79.16	1.86	1.60
sum	38,240	32.48	1.93	0.18	31.50	0.66	0.30	31.42	0.92	0.88
xargs.1	4,227	34.77	1.74	0.02	34.81	0.06	0.03	34.79	0.42	0.38
Total	2,788,958	53.53	31.73	7.77	53.33	25.09	15.47	53.38	16.91	15.23

6 Conclusions

We have shown that we can effectively use results from the field of adaptive *self-organizing* data structures in enhancing compression schemes. Unlike *adaptive* lists, which have already been used in compression, to the best of our knowledge, adaptive *self-organizing* trees have not been used in this regard. To achieve this, we have introduced a new data structure, the *Partitioning Binary Search Tree* (PBST), which leads to the so-called *Fano Binary Search Tree* (FBST) by incorporating the required Fano coding (nearly-equal-probability) property. We have introduced the updating procedure that performs the two new *tree*-based operators, namely the Shift-To-Left (STL) operator and the Shift-To-Right (STR) operator.

The encoding and decoding procedures that also update the FBST have been implemented and rigorously tested. Our empirical results on files of the Canterbury Corpus show the salient advantages of our strategy. An open problem that deserves investigation is that of combining the adaptive self-organizing BST methods and other statistical and/or dictionary-based methods, which, undoubtedly would lead to more efficient compression schemes implied by the higher-order models. The resulting advantage can be obtained as a consequence of the additional speed-enhanced updating procedure provided by the adaptive self-organizing *tree*-based principles.

Acknowledgements. This research work has been partially supported by NSERC, the Natural Sciences and Engineering Research Council of Canada, CFI, the Canadian Foundation for Innovation, and OIT, the Ontario Innovation Trust.

References

1. Ahlswede, R., Han, T. S., Kobayashi, K.: Universal Coding of Integers and Unbounded Search Trees. *IEEE Trans. on Information Theory*, 43(2):669–682, (1997)
2. Albers, S., Mitzenmacher, M.: Average case analyses of list update algorithms, with applications to data compression. *Algorithmica*, 21:312–329, (1998)
3. Albers, S., Westbrook, J.: Self-organizing data structures. In Amos Fiat and Gerhard Woeginger, editors, *Online Algorithms: The State of the Art*, pages 13–51. Springer LNCS 1442, (1998)
4. Allen, B.,Munro I.: Self-organizining Binary Search Trees. *J. Assoc. Comput. Mach.*, 25:526–535, (1978)
5. Aragon, C., Seidel, R.: Randomized Search Trees. *Proceedings 30th Annual IEEE Symposium on Foundations of Computer Science*, (1989) 540–545
6. Bent, S., Sleator, D., Tarjan, R.: Biased Search Trees. *SIAM Journal of Computing*, 14, (1985) 545–568
7. Bitner, J.: Heuristics that Dynamically Organize Data Structures. *SIAM Journal of Computing*, 8:82–110, (1979)
8. Cheetham, R., Oommen, B.J., Ng, D.: Adaptive Structuring of Binary Search Trees Using Conditional Rotations. *IEEE Transactions on Knowledge and Data Engineering*, 5(4):695–704, (1993)

9. Deorowicz, S.: Second step algorithms in the burrows-wheeler compression algorithm. *Software - Practice and Experience*, 32(2):99–111, (2002)
10. Hankerson, D., Harris, G., Johnson Jr, P.: *Introduction to Information Theory and Data Compression.* CRC Press, (1998)
11. Iacono, J.: Alternatives to splay trees with o(log n) worst-case access times. In *Proceedings of the 12th Annual ACM-SIAM Symposium on Discrete Algorithms (SODA-01)*, (2001), 516–522
12. Lai, T., Wood, D.: Adaptive Heuristics for Binary Search Trees and Constant Linkage Cost. *SIAM Journal of Computing*, 27(6):1564–1591, December (1998)
13. Mehlhorn, K.: Dynamic Binary Search. *SIAM Journal of Computing*, 8:175–198, (1979)
14. Oommen. B.J., Zgierski, J.: A Learning Automaton Solution to Breaking Substitution Ciphers. *IEEE Transactions on Pattern Analysis and Machine Intelligence*, PAMI-15:185–192, (1993)
15. Rueda, L. : *Advances in Data Compression and Pattern Recognition.* PhD thesis, School of Computer Science, Carleton University, Ottawa, Canada, April (2002). Electronically available at http://www.cs.uwindsor.ca/~lrueda/papers/PhdThesis.pdf.
16. Sherk, M.: Self-adjusting k-ary Search Trees and Self-adjusting Balanced Search Trees. Technical Report 234/90, University of Toronto, Toronto, Canada, February (1990)
17. Vitter, J.: Design and Analysis of Dynamic Huffman Codes. *Journal of the ACM*, 34(4):825–845, (1987)
18. Williams, H., Zobel, J., Heinz, S.: Self-adjusting trees in practice for large text collections. *Software - Practice and Experience*, 31(10):925–939, (2001)

Word-Based Fixed and Flexible List Compression

Ebru Celikel[1], Mehmet E. Dalkilic[1], and Gokhan Dalkilic[2]

[1] Ege University International Computer Institute, 35100 Bornova, Izmir, Turkey
{celikel, dalkilic}@ube.ege.edu.tr
[2] Dokuz Eylul University Computer Engineering Department, 35100 Bornova, Izmir, Turkey
dalkilic@cs.deu.edu.tr

Abstract. We present a dictionary based lossless text compression scheme where we keep frequent words in separate lists (list_n contains words of length n). We pursued two alternatives in terms of the lengths of the lists. In the "fixed" approach all lists have equal number of words whereas in the "flexible" approach no such constraint is imposed. Results clearly show that the "flexible" scheme is much better in all test cases possibly due to the fact that it can accommodate short, medium or long word lists reflecting on the word length distributions of a particular language. Our approach encodes a word as a prefix (the length of the word) and the body of the word (as an index in the corresponding list). For prefix encoding we have employed both a static encoding and a dynamic encoding (Huffman) using the word length statistics of the source language. Dynamic prefix encoding clearly outperformed its static counterpart in all cases. A language with a higher average word length can, theoretically, benefit more from a word-list based compression approach as compared to one with a lower average word length. We have put this hypothesis to test using Turkish and English languages with average word lengths of 6.1 and 4.4, respectively. Our results strongly support the validity of this hypothesis.

1 Introduction

The techniques used in compression algorithms today utilize various data characteristics to compress better. Text compression requires lossless compression to make recovery possible.

The Shannon-Fano Algorithm [1] is one of the first lossless compression algorithms using the symbol frequencies to assign varying length encodings to the symbols belonging to the source alphabet. Huffman [2] based his technique on Shannon-Fano Algorithm and exploited the symbol frequencies to obtain shorter encodings of the original data. More frequent symbols are represented with shorter encodings and the less frequent symbols are represented with longer encodings. Diri [3] has generated Huffman trees based on the character, stem-root or syllabus-suffix types on Turkish texts and compressed Turkish texts using these codings. Another scheme called Arithmetic Coding [2] used for text compression takes a stream of text to represent it as a floating point number between 0 and 1.

Bentley et al. [4] developed a data compression scheme that exploits locality of reference. This scheme performs better than Huffman Coding because a word will have a short encoding when it is used frequently and a long encoding when it is used rarely.

P. Yolum et al.(Eds.): ISCIS 2005, LNCS 3733, pp. 780 – 790, 2005.

Teahan employed a statistical model to exploit symbol statistics and used these statistics to compress data. The model he used is Prediction by Partial Matching (PPM) and provides compression around 2 bits per character (*bpc*) which is among the best rates provided by many compression tools today [5]. Teahan expanded the PPM technique with *bigraph coding*, where the subsequent character pairs (*bigraphs*) existing among the most frequent digrams of the source language are encoded with a single symbol to improve the compression performance of the PPM model. Celikel and Dincer [6] have developed a Turkish PoS (Parts of Speech) tagger and obtained considerable compression performance improvements by compressing the PoS tagged Turkish texts with the word and tag based PPM model.

In this paper, we present a new text compression scheme using the word statistics of the source language. For that we use full words or n-grams if corresponding words are not found in our dictionary (which is represented as a union of lists) instead of only digrams, to determine the encoding of a specific word encountered throughout the source text. In our scheme, a word contains the space character following it. Hence, we encode the succeeding space symbol while encoding each word.

Within the introduced system, we employed two different encoding schemes as *fixed* length encoding and *flexible* (varying) length encoding: The former using fixed number of bits to encode each word and the latter using variable number of bits - like that of Shannon-Fano's and Huffman's – for words having different levels of occurrences. The performances of the fixed and flexible length schemes are then compared.

The following section (Section 2) introduces the general aspects of the word based list compression algorithm. Section 3 presents the results obtained for sample English and Turkish text files and the performance differences of various schemes employed for both languages. In Section 4, we present the comparison of the compression performance of our scheme with standard GZIP and another text based compression algorithm called WBDH. In the last section (Section 5), conclusion is given.

2 Word Based List Compression

The motivation behind our idea relies on the fact that, we can represent frequent longer words with shorter codes and hence provide compression on the average. The word length statistics gathered from English and Turkish Corpora support this motivation (Tables 2.1 and 2.2). Carefully organized dictionaries of natural language words can be useful for text compression. Furthermore, languages with a greater average word length can benefit more from this approach. Because, each bit of encoding corresponds to more bits as compared to an encoding in a language with lower average word length. Each natural language has its own statistics and may significantly differ from those of the others. A fixed approach may not be suitable for all languages.

Suppose we have two artificial languages both containing only 16 words consisting of ASCII characters. Also assume that words have the length from 1 through 4. The distribution of 16 words for languages, say A and B is as follows:

Language / Word length	1	2	3	4
Language A	6	6	2	2
Language B	2	2	6	6

Suppose we have two separate texts, one for each language. Each word occurs once in the corresponding text. Ignoring the white spaces, each word is coded with 4 bits but text in language A is of length $6\times1+6\times2+2\times3+2\times4=32$ characters while text in language B is of length $2\times1+2\times2+6\times3+6\times4=48$ characters. Therefore, a bit of encoding in language A represents 32 chars / 64 bits = 4 bits and in language B represents 48 chars / 64 bits = 6 bits. Hence, a word based compression algorithm would have a higher performance potential for a language with a greater average word length.

The average word length is 4.43 symbols for English and 6.14 symbols for Turkish as shown in Tables 2.1 and 2.2, respectively. These statistics can well be exploited to encode the text written in these languages into shorter length codes. Given these percentages, the main concern is to figure out an encoding scheme that would represent the original data with the least number of bytes.

Table 2.1. English word length statistics [7]

English Word Statistics								
Word-length	1	2	3	4	5	6	7	8
Ratio (%)	3.86	16.30	23.06	18.70	11.66	7.78	6.67	4.77
Word-length	9	10	11	12	13	14	15	16 and +
Ratio (%)	3.30	1.95	0.97	0.56	0.22	0.13	0.04	0.03

Table 2.2. Turkish word length statistics [7]

Turkish Word Statistics								
Word-length	1	2	3	4	5	6	7	8
Ratio (%)	0.72	8.10	10.69	10.83	16.74	12.04	11.82	9.05
Word-length	9	10	11	12	13	14	15	16 and +
Ratio (%)	7.16	5.07	3.21	2.16	1.13	0.65	0.33	0.31

In the algorithm we introduced, the input text is read word by word and each word is searched within the corresponding word list, i.e. the dictionary. The dictionary is a pre-constructed combination with 15 different lists: Each list –except for the length-one list- contains the most frequent 256 words of the corresponding length. Hence, in the dictionary, there exists one list for the single symbol lists having all symbols of the source alphabet (26 symbols for English and 29 symbols for Turkish), another list for the most frequent 256 digrams, another list for the most frequent 256 trigrams, .. and the last list for the most frequent 256 15-grams of the source language. The reason why we used only 15 different lists is that, we limit the maximum word length for both source languages (English and Turkish) to 15 characters. The words longer than this, which would rarely be the case, are divided at length 15 and are considered to be two separate words. By choosing only 256 most frequent words for each list, we guarantee to use at most 8 bits to encode each word, since $256=2^8$.

2.1 The Corpora

The dictionary for English is constructed by gathering the statistics of the 11MB English Corpus composed of the stories of Huckleberryfinn together with the text files of the standard Calgary and Canterbury Corpora. For generating the Turkish dictionary, an 11MB Turkish Corpus containing the corpus compiled by Diri [8], the daily articles of various journalists at Turkish daily newspaper Hurriyet, and the corpus compiled by Koltuksuz [9] were used. Our corpora were filtered to contain only the lower case letters of the language, i.e. 26 for English and 29 for Turkish and the space symbol. We implemented our scheme on eight sample text files, four in English and four in Turkish. We have deliberately chosen two text files as in-Corpus and the other two as out-Corpus for each source language. This is because we intend to see the effect of being in (or out) -Corpus on the performance of our scheme.

Table 2.3. English sample text files

English Sample Texts			
Filename	**File size (bytes)**	**Explanation**	**In Dictionary's Corpus?**
Eng1	785,393	The novel "*Far from the Madding Crowd*" by Thomas Hardy	Yes
Eng2	1,963,426	The novel "*The Brothers Karamazov*" by Dostoyevsky	Yes
Eng3	171,461	The novel "*The Battle of Life*" by Charles Dickens	No
Eng4	2,054,730	The novel "*Democracy in America*" by Alexis de Tocqueville	No

Table 2.4. Turkish sample text files

Turkish Sample Texts			
Filename	**File size (bytes)**	**Explanation**	**In Dictionary's Corpus?**
Trk1	232,967	The novels by Furuzan	Yes
Trk2	251,607	The novels by Omer Seyfettin	Yes
Trk3	113,545	The theatre text "*Galilei Galileo*" by Bertolt Brecht	No
Trk4	746,010	The novel "*Son Antlasma*" by Can Eryumlu	No

2.2 Encoding

Within the word based list compression scheme, lists of words are categorized according to their length *len* (where $1 \leq len \leq 15$), and each word list is sorted in decreasing order of frequency. Word based compression exploits the idea of processing words of the original text individually by encoding each word with its index at the corresponding word list. In this manner, each word including the following space character is encoded with a new, and probably shorter, code. The performance of the scheme relies on the fact that, most of the words encountered in the source text are found within the corresponding word list.

According to our scheme, the length of words encountered in the source text may be in the range 1 to 15. Hence, there should be a way of indicating the length of word currently being encoded. For that, we employ a two-part encoding: The first part called the *prefix*, indicating the length of the current word encoded and the second part called the *encoding* indicating the index of the current word within the corresponding word list. The scheme is called either *fixed* or *flexible* according to the way we encode the second part.

In *fixed* encoding, the *prefix* bits are either predetermined, or encoded with the corresponding Huffman codes generated using the word statistics within the source text. The number of *encoding* bits are fixed. Knowing that the average word length is 4.43 for English and 6.14 for Turkish, using shorter prefixes for shorter length words is better as far as compression is concerned. Following that rule, we used the predetermined *prefix* codes throughout our study as shown in Table 2.5:

Table 2.5. Predetermined Prefix Codes for the Word Based List Encoding

Word Length	Prefix Code	Word Length	Prefix Code
1	000	9	111001
2	001	10	111010
3	010	11	111011
4	011	12	111100
5	100	13	111101
6	101	14	111110
7	110	15	111111
8	111000		

In *flexible* encoding, *encoding* bits are generated by using the corresponding Huffman codes of the words. For that, two different statistics are used: One being the language statistics of the words and the other being the statistics of the file being compressed. During *flexible* encoding, the number of bits to be used for the *encoding* part is $\lceil \log_2 len \rceil$, where *len* is the list size. We adjusted list sizes when a small reduction from the raw size allowed us to save one bit during encoding phase. For instance, if a particular list contains say 550 words, to avoid using 10 bits to encode a word in this list, we reduce the list size to 2^9=512 and use 9 bits. The algorithm below summarizes the encoding procedure:

```
do
{
 ch ← read character;
 current_word ← NULL;
 word_length ← 0;
 //Construct the current_word
 while (ch ≠ eof AND ch ≠ space_character AND word_length <= 15) do
 {
   current_word[word_length] ← ch;
   word_length ← word_length + 1;
   ch ← read character;
 }

 //Search the current_word within the corresponding dictionary
 found = search_word(current_word, word_length);
 if (found) then encode_word(current_word, word_length)
 else {
        while (NOT found) do
        {
         // Construct the reduced_word by dropping the last character of
         // the current_word
         for (i ← 0; i < word_length; i ← i+1)
         {
          reduced_word[i] ← current_word[i];
         }
         word_length ← word_length - 1;
```

```
        // Search the reduced_word within the corresponding dictionary
        found = search_word(reduced_word, word_length);
       } //while
       //Encode the reduced_word
       encode_word(reduced_word, word_length);
 } //else
} while (NOT eof) //while
```

During implementation, the original text file is read character by character to construct a word. A word is generated by either reading a *space character* or by reaching the maximum word length, which is chosen to be 15, and its length is determined. Then, this word is searched within the appropriate word list. If the word is found within the corresponding list, then its index in the word list is encoded to the output.

If the current word is not in the dictionary, its length is decreased by one and a new search is made to find the new word in the list of appropriate size. Dropping of the last symbol continues until the current word is found within the corresponding word list.

The worst case for reduction process is the case when only a single character remains as the word, which is guaranteed to be found within the monograms list. In case a word is encoded not directly but with a reduction process, the encoding should be followed by a special encoding called the *cancel_space* to inform the decoder that the last word encoded was not an individual word, but only a part of it.

The performance of the word based scheme mainly depends on the following factors: The type of encoding used, i.e. whether *fixed* or *flexible* length. The rate of success of finding the words within the corresponding word lists, i.e. the *hit rate*. This rate can only be increased if the sample text where statistics are collected from is the same as the one where frequency distributions of various word lists having different word lengths are constructed.

3 Implementation and Results

We implemented the word based list compression algorithm for both *fixed* and *flexible* schemes on sample texts from English and Turkish Corpora. The two fundamental criteria used to measure the performance of a compression scheme are throughput and compression rate. In general, there exists a tradeoff between the two, i.e. the higher the throughput is, the lower the compression rate and vice versa. The compression algorithms available today typically either focus on high throughput or better compression rates. Our work falls into the latter category. Therefore, our basic performance measure used in this section is compression rate expressed in bits per character – *bpc*. Throughput of our current implementation (where no effort to optimize the throughput was made) is quite low at 6.67 KB/sec.

3.1 Word Based List Compression for English

We employed the word based list compression algorithm for both fixed and flexible encoding on English as well as Turkish texts. Compression rates obtained by applying the introduced scheme with *fixed encoding* on the four sample English texts are given in Table 3.1. In the table, static and dynamic represent the cases where *prefix* encoding is made with predetermined length and with using the corresponding Huffman codes of the word frequencies, respectively.

Table 3.1. *Fixed* Word Based List Encoding for English

File		Fixed				
		Static			Dynamic	
	Encoding Cost (Bytes)	Prefix Cost (Bytes)	bpc		Prefix Cost (Bytes)	bpc
Eng1	1,878,545	848,271	3.73		658,439	3.47
Eng2	4,329,481	1,933,764	3.39		1,593,316	3.20
Eng3	413,436	185,817	3.76		144,142	3.49
Eng4	5,071,172	2,330,559	3.76		1,831,511	3.51

As Table 3.1 indicates, compression rates obtained with in-Corpus texts (*Eng1* and *Eng2*) are better than that of the out-Corpus texts (*Eng3* and *Eng4*). The table also shows that using dynamic instead of static encoding, decreases the *prefix* costs.

Running the word based list compression algorithm by employing the *flexible* encoding on the same set of English texts, we obtained the values in Table 3.2:

Table 3.2. *Flexible* Word Based List Encoding for English

File		Flexible				
		Static			Dynamic	
	Encoding Cost (Bytes)	Prefix Cost (Bytes)	bpc		Prefix Cost (Bytes)	bpc
Eng1	1,547,183	436,197	2.71		435,373	2.71
Eng2	3,942,394	1,112,006	2.73		1,109,497	2.73
Eng3	353,897	103,323	2.87		101,173	2.85
Eng4	4,060,826	1,230,711	2.69		1,202,005	2.67

In Table 3.2, static and dynamic are for the cases where prefix encoding is made using the corresponding Huffman codes obtained from each word's frequency in the language and in the source file itself, respectively. The *bpc* results for dynamic case are slightly better than that of static case in Table 3.2. Hence, employing the word frequencies gathered from source files yields better compression rates. Each of the figures in Table 3.2 is better than that of the corresponding values in Table 3.1. This indicates that using the *flexible* scheme for word list compression on English texts is better than employing the *fixed* scheme.

3.2 Word Based List Compression for Turkish

We repeated the experiments with *fixed* and *flexible* word based list compression algorithm on sample texts in Turkish. Applying the *fixed* version of the introduced scheme on the four text files of the Turkish Corpus, we obtained the results given in Table 3.3.

Results in Table 3.3 are highly in accordance with the values in Table 3.1: For Turkish also, using the corresponding Huffman coding (dynamic case) instead of predetermined codes (static case) for *prefix* encoding, decreases the *prefix* costs. This is reflected in the overall compression performance as lower *bpc* rates. Although the text file *Trk4* is out-Corpus, the compression rate is lower than the in-Corpus files. This might be due to the characteristic of that file: Words might be coincidentally occurring in the corresponding word lists.

Table 3.3. *Fixed* Word Based List Encoding for Turkish

File		Fixed				
		Static			Dynamic	
	Encoding Cost (Bytes)	Prefix Cost (Bytes)	bpc		Prefix Cost (Bytes)	bpc
Trk1	741,637	343,656	4.86		233,964	4.37
Trk2	751,119	348,021	4.79		236,758	4.30
Trk3	329,180	153,624	4.94		101,995	4.41
Trk4	2,091,378	957,987	4.51		688,074	4.08

Implementing our scheme with flexible encoding, we obtained the results in Table 3.4:

Table 3.4. *Flexible* Word Based List Encoding for Turkish

File		Flexible				
		Static			Dynamic	
	Encoding Cost (Bytes)	Prefix Cost (Bytes)	bpc		Prefix Cost (Bytes)	bpc
Trk1	386,135	109,527	2.22		108,831	2.22
Trk2	412,691	112,939	2.29		112,746	2.29
Trk3	209,567	84,799	3.01		66,346	2.82
Trk4	1,395,866	527,737	2.83		440,507	2.70

Using source file statistics (dynamic case) to generate the corresponding Huffman codes for *prefix* codes yields lower prefix costs than using language statistics (static case) according to Table 3.4.

4 Analysis and Comparisons

We compared the compression performance of our scheme with that of a well-known lossless compression tool GZIP. The comparison results for dynamic prefix coding are listed in Tables 4.1 and 4.2. A positive value in the "Improvement over GZIP" columns indicates that our scheme outperforms GZIP while a negative value means GZIP outperforms ours.

The fixed scheme does not provide any improvement while the flexible scheme outperforms GZIP for each sample file in English. The average rate of improvement is more for the text files that are in-Corpus, which was quite expected.

We repeated the above comparison for Turkish and obtained the values in Table 4.2. Our scheme does behave similar on Turkish as well: The word list flexible compression yields better results than GZIP while the fixed scheme is worse than GZIP. Looking at the average improvement levels of flexible scheme in Tables 4.1 and 4.2, we see that the average level of improvement for Turkish is better than that of English, 16.83% and 1.78%, respectively. These results support our hypothesis that a language with higher average word length (Turkish) can benefit more from a word-list based compression approach as compared to one with a lower average word length (English).

Table 4.1. Performance Comparison of English Texts

Filename	In Corpus?	GZIP	Fixed		Flexible	
			bpc	Improvement over GZIP	bpc	Improvement over GZIP
Eng1	Yes	2.93	3.47	-18.43%	2.71	7.51%
Eng2	Yes	2.69	3.20	-18.96%	2.73	-1.49%
Eng3	No	2.85	3.49	-22.46%	2.85	0.00%
Eng4	No	2.70	3.51	-30.00%	2.67	1.11%
Avg		*2.79*	*3.42*	*-22.46%*	*2.74*	*1.78%*

Table 4.2. Performance Comparison of Turkish Texts

Filename	In Corpus?	GZIP	Fixed		Flexible	
			bpc	Improvement over GZIP	bpc	Improvement over GZIP
Trk1	Yes	3.13	4.37	-39.62%	2.22	29.07%
Trk2	Yes	3.10	4.30	-38.71%	2.29	26.13%
Trk3	No	2.95	4.41	-49.49%	2.82	4.41%
Trk4	No	2.90	4.08	-40.69%	2.70	6.90%
Avg		*3.02*	*4.29*	*-42.13%*	*2.51*	*16.63%*

The compression technique we introduced is a general tool. So, we cannot expect new source texts to be in-Corpus. For this reason, analyzing the out-Corpus figures in Tables 4.1 and 4.2 is more convenient. Calculating the average rate of improvement for both in-Corpus and out-Corpus files in both Tables, we get 2.72 bpc average for English in-Corpus files, 2.76 bpc average for English out-Corpus files while the corresponding values on Turkish files are 2.26 bpc and 2.76 bpc, respectively. Hence, Turkish has more potential for improvement in terms of finding a way to boost out-Corpus text compression rates to the level of in-Corpus compression rates.

We also compared the compression performance of our scheme with another word based compression tool called Word Based Dynamic Huffman Coding (WBDH), which was introduced by Diri [8]. We used the same Turkish data set containing 14 text files as in [8] and the results are given in Table 4.3.

Our scheme with flexible encoding outperforms each of GZIP and WBDH techniques for the first sample text file *1*. In terms of the average *bpc* rates, GZIP is the best algorithm with 2.82 bpc, our technique employing *flexible* encoding where statistics are gathered on sample texts is the second best with 3.37 bpc, which is followed by WBDH with 3.61 bpc, then comes our technique with *fixed* encoding where *prefix* codings are made using corresponding Huffman codes with 3.95 bpc, then *flexible* word based list encoding using statistics gathered from language and lastly comes the fixed word based list encoding employing predetermined *prefix* length with 4.62 bpc.

Table 4.3. Comparison with WBDH on Turkish Texts

Filename	GZIP-9	WBDH	Word Based List Compression			
			Fixed		Flexible	
			Static	Dynamic	Static	Dynamic
	bpc	bpc	bpc	bpc	bpc	bpc
1	3.41	4.02	4.62	4.01	2.31	2.31
2	2.76	3.90	4.64	3.96	4.13	3.43
3	2.94	4.04	4.92	4.14	4.24	3.51
4	2.48	3.82	4.71	4.01	3.95	3.32
5	2.98	3.84	4.75	4.03	4.12	3.41
6	2.18	3.62	5.06	4.22	5.01	3.95
7	2.80	3.76	4.61	3.92	4.17	3.42
8	3.08	3.74	4.66	3.96	4.24	3.47
9	3.04	3.78	4.68	3.98	4.15	3.42
10	2.74	3.27	4.50	3.87	4.02	3.37
11	2.73	2.96	4.51	3.87	4.13	3.44
12	2.69	3.19	4.48	3.85	3.98	3.33
13	2.74	3.18	4.46	3.84	4.11	3.42
14	2.90	3.39	4.12	3.57	4.09	3.39
Average	*2.82*	*3.61*	*4.62*	*3.95*	*4.05*	*3.37*

5 Conclusions

We have introduced a novel concept for compressing text files in a word based manner. For that, we utilized word frequencies of source languages being English and Turkish. The results we obtained showed that Turkish having a higher average word length benefits more from our word-list based compression approach as compared to English with a lower average word length with 16.83% and 1.78% improvements over standard GZIP, respectively.

The compression performance of our scheme is comparable to and in some cases even better than that of the conventional compression tool GZIP. We also compared our results with another word based compression algorithm called Word Based Dynamic Huffman (WBDH) Coding. Our scheme again outperforms this algorithm for some individual texts on the average.

References

1. Witten, I., Moffat, A., Bell, T.C.: Managing Gigabytes – Compressing and Indexing Documents and Images, San Francisco, CA, USA, (1999)
2. Nelson M.: The Data Compression Book. Ch. 3., NewYork, USA, (1996)
3. Diri, B.: A Text Compression System Based on the Morphology of Turkish Language, International Symposium on Computer and Information Sciences (ISCIS) XV, 11-13 October, Yildiz Technical University, Istanbul (2000)
4. Bentley, J. L., Sleator D. D., Tarjan R. E. and Wei, V. K: A Locally Adaptive Data Compression Scheme, Communications of the ACM, April, vol. 29, no. 4, pp. 320-330, (1986)
5. Teahan, W.J: Modelling English Text. Ch.8: The Entropy of English Using PPM Based Models, p.140. (1998)

6. Celikel, E., Dincer, B. T.: Improving the Compression Performance of Turkish Texts with PoS Tags, pp. 519-523, International Conference on Information and Knowledge Engineering (IKE'04), Las Vegas, NV, USA, (2004)
7. Dalkılıç, M. E. and Dalkılıç, G.: Some Measurable Language Characteristics of Printed Turkish, International Symposium on Computer and Information Sciences (ISCIS) XVI, 5-7 November, Antalya (2001)
8. Diri, B.: A System for Turkish Texts Based on the Analysis of Turkish Language Structure and Providing Dynamic Compression with Word-based Lossless Recovery, (in Turkish) PhD thesis, Yildiz Technical University, Istanbul (1999)
9. Koltuksuz, A. H.: Cryptanalitic Measures of Turkish for Symmetrical Cryptosystems, (in Turkish) PhD Thesis, Ege University Department of Computer Engineering, Izmir, Turkey (1995)

Effective Early Termination Techniques for Text Similarity Join Operator*

Selma Ayşe Özalp[1] and Özgür Ulusoy[2]

[1] Department of Industrial Engineering, Uludag University, 16059 Gorukle Bursa, Turkey
ayseozalp@uludag.edu.tr
http://www20.uludag.edu.tr/~ayseozalp

[2] Department of Computer Engineering, Bilkent University, 06800 Bilkent Ankara, Turkey
oulusoy@cs.bilkent.edu.tr

Abstract. Text similarity join operator joins two relations if their join attributes are textually similar to each other, and it has a variety of application domains including integration and querying of data from heterogeneous resources; cleansing of data; and mining of data. Although, the text similarity join operator is widely used, its processing is expensive due to the huge number of similarity computations performed. In this paper, we incorporate some short cut evaluation techniques from the Information Retrieval domain, namely Harman, quit, continue, and maximal similarity filter heuristics, into the previously proposed text similarity join algorithms to reduce the amount of similarity computations needed during the join operation. We experimentally evaluate the original and the heuristic based similarity join algorithms using real data obtained from the DBLP Bibliography database, and observe performance improvements with continue and maximal similarity filter heuristics.

1 Introduction

The text similarity join operator, as its name implies, joins two relations if their join attributes, which consist of pure text, are highly similar to each other. The similarity between join attributes is determined by well-known techniques such as *tf-idf* weighting scheme [1] and *cosine similarity* measure from the Information Retrieval (IR) domain. The text similarity join operator has various application domains. Cohen [2], Gravano et al. [3], and Schallehn et al. [4] use this operator for the integration of data from distributed, heterogeneous databases that lack common formal object identifiers. For instance, in two Web databases listing research institutions, to determine whether the two names "AT&T Labs" and "AT&T Research Labs" denote the same institution or not, text similarity join operator may be employed.

Meng et al. [5] use the text similarity join operator to query a multidatabase system that contains local systems managing both structured data (e.g., relational database) and unstructured data (e.g., text). As an example let's assume that we have two global relations: *applicants* containing information about job applicants and their resumes,

* This research is supported by a joint grant from TÜBİTAK (grant no. 100U024) of Turkey and the National Science Foundation (grant INT-9912229) of the USA.

P. Yolum et al.(Eds.): ISCIS 2005, LNCS 3733, pp. 791 – 801, 2005.

and *positions* including the description of each job; then the text similarity join operator is used to answer queries like "for each position, find *k* applicants whose resumes are most similar to the position's description". Jin et al. [6] employ similarity join operator for solving the problem of record-linkage in the context of data cleansing. In [7, 8], we describe similarity join operator to facilitate metadata based web querying [9].

We classify the text similarity join operators as top-k, threshold, and directional similarity join operators [8] such that the *top-k similarity join* takes two relations *R* and *S*, and an integer *k* as input, then joins tuple pairs from *R* and *S* according to the similarity of their textual join attributes, and returns *k* joined tuples having the highest similarity values. The *threshold similarity join* also takes two relations *R* and *S*, and a real *threshold value* in the range [0..1] as input, and joins tuples from *R* and *S* if the similarity of their textual join attributes is greater than or equal to the threshold value. The last similarity join operator, called *directional similarity join*, joins each tuple from relation *R* with *k* most similar tuples from relation *S*, and returns at most $|R|*k$ joined tuples where $|R|$ is the number of tuples in relation *R*. In this study, we focus on the directional similarity join operator, and we try to reduce the amount of similarity comparisons executed by employing some early termination heuristics (e.g., Harman, quit, continue, and maximal similarity filter) from the IR domain. These heuristics improve the performance of the join operation by considering only the tuple pairs that have high similarity to each other and ignoring the ones having small or no similarity. We also show through experimental evaluation that early termination heuristics improve the performance of the similarity join operator considerably in terms of the number of disk accesses made and the amount of similarity computations performed.

The rest of the paper is organized as follows. In the next section, we describe the related work. A brief summary of the previously proposed directional join algorithms and the early termination heuristics are presented in sections 3 and 4. In Section 5, we experimentally evaluate and compare all the algorithms in terms of the CPU time required for processing, the number of tuple comparisons and the number of disk accesses made. Finally, we conclude our discussion in Section 6.

2 Related Work

Recently, similarity join operator for both low and high dimensional data has become a popular research topic as it is used in variety of applications such as data integration, data cleansing, data mining, and querying. Different techniques have been used for the similarity join of low dimensional (e.g., text) and high dimensional data (e.g., multimedia, biological data). Among the text similarity join proposals, the works presented in [3, 4, 6] describe processing techniques for the threshold similarity join operator. In [2, 10, 11, 12, 13, 14], algorithms for the top-k similarity join operator are described.

Although numerous proposals exist for the threshold and the top-k similarity join operators, only Meng et al. [5] study the directional similarity join operator. They propose and experimentally evaluate three join algorithms namely, Horizontal-Horizontal Nested Loop (HHNL), Horizontal-Vertical Nested Loop (HVNL), and Vertical-Vertical Merge (VVM), which use the well-known similarity measure, *tf-idf* weighting scheme and cosine similarity measure for similarity comparisons. As the names of the algorithms imply, HHNL and HVNL algorithms are nested loops based join algorithms such that HHNL algorithm compares each document (tuple) pairs in the collections (relations), and HVNL algorithm, on the other hand, uses the documents in one collection and the inverted file for the other collection to compute the similarities. Algorithm VVM, which is not nested loops based, uses inverted files on both collections to compute the similarities. The details of these similarity join algorithms and the early termination heuristics applied to these algorithms are given in the subsequent sections.

The similarity measure employed in [5] and also in this study is the *cosine similarity measure* with *tf-idf* weighting scheme [1] in which, each document (join attribute in the similarity join operator) is represented as a vector consisting of *n* components, *n* being the number of distinct terms (i.e., stemmed words) in the document collection, such that each component of a vector for a document gives the weight of the term *i* for that document. Weight of a term for a particular document is computed according to *tf-idf* value, where *tf* (term frequency) is the number of occurrences of term *i* within the document; and *idf* (inverse document frequency) gives more weight to scarce terms in the collection. The similarity measure is the cosine of the angle between the two document vectors such that the larger the cosine, the greater the similarity. Other measures such as Hamming distance, and longest common subsequence (LCS) for determining the similarity between short strings have also been developed. In [2, 3, 5] *tf-idf* weighting scheme and cosine similarity measure are preferred as the vector space model gives quite good matches even for short strings. Also, the vector space model allows the use of inverted indices, which makes possible for us to integrate some early termination heuristics from the IR domain during the similarity comparisons of tuples.

3 Directional Text Similarity Join Algorithms

The only study that has appeared in the literature for the directional similarity join operator were developed by Meng et al. [5] who presented three algorithms namely HHNL, HVNL, and VVM for the join operator. The HHNL (Horizontal-Horizontal Nested Loops) algorithm is a blind nested loops join algorithm, in which each tuple *r* in relation *R* is compared with every tuple in relation *S*, and *k* most similar tuples from *S* are joined with tuple *r*. In [5], the input relations *R* and *S* are read from disk. After reading *X* tuples from *R* into the main memory, the tuples in *S* are scanned; and while a tuple in *S* is in the memory, the similarity between this tuple and every tuple in *R* that is currently in the memory is computed. For each tuple *r* in *R*, the algorithm keeps track of only those tuples in *S*, which have been processed against *r* and have the *k* highest similarities with *r*. In the HHNL algorithm, and also in all other algorithms described in [5], a heap structure is used to find the smallest of the *k*-largest similarities.

The HVNL (Horizontal-Vertical Nested Loops) [5] algorithm is an adaptation of the ranked query evaluation techniques in the IR domain to the join operation. In an IR system, the aim is to find the *k* documents in the system which are most similar to the user query. For that purpose, most of the IR systems employ inverted files. In these systems, for each term t in the user query, the term is searched from the inverted index and the ids of documents containing term t are found. Then, the similarity calculations are performed only for those documents that have at least one common term with the user query. Algorithm HVNL is a straightforward extension of this method such that for each tuple r in R, the algorithm calculates the similarity of r to all tuples in S having at least one common term with r, and selects the k most similar tuples from S. The advantage of HVNL algorithm is that, it does not perform similarity calculations for all tuples in S as in the case of the HHNL algorithm. In the HVNL algorithm, the *inverted file* consists of (i) an *inverted index* which includes the index term (t), the number of tuples in S containing the index term (f_t), and a pointer to its corresponding inverted list entry, and (ii) an *inverted list* which stores tuple id having the index term t, and the frequency of the term in that tuple ($f_{s,t}$). In the HVNL algorithm the inverted index is stored in the memory, the inverted list entries, and the relations R and S are read from disk.

The algorithm VVM (Vertical-Vertical Merge) employs sorted inverted indices with respect to the index terms on both of the input relations R and S [5]. The VVM algorithm scans both inverted files on the input relations at the same time. During the scan of the inverted indices, if both index entries correspond to the same index term, then similarities are accumulated between all tuples in the inverted lists of the indices. The VVM algorithm assumes that, both inverted files as well as relations R and S are read from disk. In order to store intermediate similarities between every pair of tuples in the two relations, the algorithm needs $|R|*|S|$ accumulators[1] that are stored in main memory. The strength of the algorithm is that it scans the inverted files only once to compute similarities between every pair of tuples. However, the memory requirement for the accumulator is so large that it cannot be run for relations having large number of tuples. As an example, let's assume that both relations R and S consist of 100,000 tuples, and each similarity value requires 4 bytes (size of float), so the memory allocated for the accumulator should be at least 100,000*100,000*4 bytes = 40Gb. In this study, we do not consider the algorithm VVM due to its huge memory requirement.

4 Heuristic Based Directional Similarity Join Algorithms

In the subsequent sections, we first describe early termination heuristics [15] from the IR domain that we use to improve the performance of directional similarity join operation, and then we briefly introduce directional similarity join algorithms employing these heuristics.

4.1 Harman Heuristic

Harman et al. [16] proposed a heuristic to decrease the number of similarity computations performed during the search of similar documents to a user query. We apply this heuristic to the HVNL algorithm as it employs an inverted index over the relation S. The HVNL algorithm extended with Harman heuristic is called HVNL-Harman in which, for each tuple r in relation R, weights of the terms in r are

---

[1] Accumulator is a set of real numbers (A_{rs}) each stores an accumulated similarity between tuples r and s.

examined, and the inverted index is accessed only for these terms having a weight greater than the 1/3 of the highest weighted term in r. This heuristic is implemented by modifying the original HVNL algorithm as presented in Figure 1. The HVNL-Harman algorithm considers S tuples which have high weighted terms in tuple r, and does not perform similarity computations for other S tuples that do not contain high weighted terms.

```
1.  for each tuple r in R
2.     {compute weights (w_t) of each term in r and sort the terms with
       respect to w_t in descending order;
3.     for each term t in r having weight w_t > (max{w_t for all t in r}/3)
4.        if t also appears in S
5.           if the inverted file entry of t on S (I_1^t) is in the memory
6.              accumulate similarities;
7.           else (if the inverted file entry of t on S (I_1^t) is not in the memory)
8.              if the available memory space can accommodate I_1^t
9.                 read in I_1^t;
10.             else
11.                find the inverted file entry in the memory with the lowest
                   term frequency and replace it with I_1^t ;
12.             accumulate similarities;}
13. find the tuples in S which have the k largest similarities with r;
```

Fig. 1. HVNL algorithm with Harman heuristic (HVNL-Harman)

4.2 Quit and Continue Heuristics

Moffat et al. [17] also suggested to sort the terms in the user query with respect to their weights in descending order, and to access the inverted index with respect to this order. They place an a priori bound (i.e., accumulator bound) on the number of candidate documents that can be considered for the similarity calculation. New documents are compared until this bound is reached. The idea behind this heuristic is that, terms of high weight are permitted to contribute to the similarity computation, but terms of low weight are not. When the bound is reached; in the *quit* approach, the cosine contribution of all unprocessed terms are ignored, and the accumulator contains only partial similarity values for documents. In the *continue* strategy, documents that do not have an accumulator are ignored, but documents for which accumulators have already been created continue to have their cosine contributions accumulated. When the processing ends, the computation of full cosine values for a subset of the documents becomes completed.

As the quit heuristic allows only the partial similarity computation, it is not suitable for the directional similarity join operator. To find top-k similar tuples for a given tuple r, we need to have full cosine values and thus, we use the continue heuristic with the HVNL algorithm (HVNL-Continue). In this variation of the HVNL algorithm, for each tuple r of R, only s tuples from S which have high weighted terms in r are considered for similarity computations until the accumulator bound on the number of tuples that can be considered for similarity computations is reached. When the accumulator bound is reached, the full cosine similarities between tuple *r* and *s* tuples become computed and the k-most similar tuples to *r* are selected. In the HVNL-Continue algorithm, we need document vectors (term weights) for tuples in relation *S* to compute the full cosine similarity values. Term weights for each *s* tuple can be computed prior to the join operation by just passing over the relation only once as a one time cost. For the implementation of the HVNL-Continue algorithm, we modify the 3rd line of the algorithm in Figure 1 as "for each term *t* in (sorted terms list of) *r*". Also, in the 6th and 12th lines of the algorithm, for each tuple *r* in relation *R*, we increase the value of a counter variable by 1 each time a new *s* tuple is considered for similarity computation, and when the value of the counter becomes equal to the predetermined accumulator bound, the for loop in line 3 is exited, and the counter is reset.

4.3 Maximal Similarity Filter Heuristic

"Maximal similarity filter" [7] is another technique that may be used to reduce the number of tuple comparisons made during the directional text similarity join operation. Let $\boldsymbol{u_s} = <u_1\ u_2\ \ldots\ u_n>$ be the term vector corresponding to the join attribute of tuple *s* of *S*, where u_i represents the weight of the term *i* in the join attribute. Assume that the *filter vector* $\boldsymbol{f_R} = <w_1\ \ldots\ w_n>$ is created such that each value w_i is the maximum weight of the corresponding term *i* among all vectors of *R*. Then, if $cos\_sim\ (\boldsymbol{u_s}, \boldsymbol{f_R}) < V_t$ then *s* can not be similar to any tuple *r* in *R* with similarity above V_t. The value $cos\_sim\ (\boldsymbol{u_s}, \boldsymbol{f_R})$ is called the *maximal similarity* of a record *s* in *S* to any other record *r* in *R*.

In the HVNL algorithm with maximal similarity filter (HVNL-Max-Filter), the inverted list entries are accessed with respect to descending order of maximal similarity values of *s* tuples. For each term *t* in tuple *r* of *R*, the inverted index is entered and the similarity comparisons are stopped at the point when the maximal similarity value ($cos\_sim\ (\boldsymbol{u_s}, \boldsymbol{f_R})$) for the tuple *s* is less than the smallest of the k-largest similarities computed so far for tuple *r*, since it is not possible for *s* to be in the top-k similar tuples list. The maximum weight of a term for a given relation is determined while creating the vectors for the tuples, and the filter vector for each relation may be formed as a one-time cost. To apply this heuristic, we need to sort the inverted list entries with respect to maximal similarity values of tuples just once during the preprocessing step. The HVNL-Max-Filter algorithm is also very similar to the HVNL-Harman algorithm (Figure 1). One difference is, the 3rd line of HVNL-Harman is changed as "for each term *t* in *r*". Also, in lines 6 and 12, similarity computations for *s* tuples having term *t* are performed if the maximal similarity value for the tuple *s* is greater than the smallest of the k-largest similarities computed so far for tuple *r*, otherwise the for loop in line 3 is exited.

We also apply the maximal similarity filter heuristic to the HHNL algorithm (i.e., HHNL-Max-Filter), in which we sort the tuples in relation *S* in descending order of their maximal similarity filter values as a preprocessing step, and we terminate the inner loop when the maximal similarity filter for the *s* tuple that is being processed is less than the smallest of the k-largest similarities computed so far for the tuple *r*.

5 Experimental Results

We compared the performance of HHNL, HVNL, HVNL-Harman, HVNL-Continue, HVNL-Max-Filter, and HHNL-Max-Filter in terms of the number of tuple comparisons made, the number of disk accesses required, and the CPU time needed. For the experimentation, we implemented these algorithms in C programming language under MS WindowsXP operating system. We did not include VVM since it requires huge amount of memory to keep intermediate similarities between tuple pairs. In the implementation, the relations *R* and *S* are stored on disk and each block read from the relations contain 10000 tuples. For the HVNL and its variations, the inverted index is in-memory, however the inverted list entries are stored on disk and up to 5000 inverted list entries are kept in the cache. An inverted list entry that is not in the cache is retrieved from disk by making random disk access, and when the cache is full, the entry for the term having the least term frequency is replaced with the new entry.

In the experiments, we used a real dataset that consists of the bibliographic information of journal and conference papers obtained from the DBLP Bibliography database [18]. In the implementation of the directional text similarity join, the relations *R* and *S* do not contain any common tuple, and the relation *R* consists of bibliographic information of approximately 91,000 journal papers, and the relation *S* contains bibliographic information of 132,000 conference papers. The paper title attribute is chosen as the join attribute, and for each journal paper *r* in relation *R*, we try to find *k* conference papers from relation *S* having the most similar titles to the title of *r*. We created the vectors and the maximal similarity filters for the join attribute of each tuple in the relations *R* and *S*, and the inverted index on relation *S* in advance as the preprocessing step. We assumed that we have enough main memory to store the inverted index and the accumulators used for similarity calculations. The experiments were performed on a PC having Pentium III 450 MHz CPU and 320 MB of main memory.

In Figure 2, the results in terms of the number of tuple comparisons (i.e., similarity computations) performed by the implemented algorithms for different *k* values are presented. As displayed in the figure, the HHNL algorithm needs to make around 12 billion comparisons for each different *k* values to join *R* and *S*, while all versions of the HVNL algorithm do less than 900 million tuple comparisons for the same join operation. HVNL, and all variations of the HVNL algorithm perform much better than the HHNL algorithm, because of the fact that these algorithms employ inverted index on the input relation *S*, and they compare similarity of tuples which are guaranteed to have a similarity value greater than 0. The HHNL algorithm, on the other hand, makes similarity computation for all tuple pairs regardless of whether the tuples contain any common term or not.

The maximal similarity filter heuristic reduces the number of tuple comparison about 25% for both the HHNL and the HVNL algorithms. We use continue and Harman heuristics with the HVNL algorithm only, as these heuristics are applicable when an inverted index is employed. The continue heuristic, in which accumulator bound is set to 5000 tuples, provides more improvement on the performance of the HVNL algorithm by decreasing the number of tuple comparisons by 50%. The Harman heuristic, on the other hand, does not improve the performance of the HVNL algorithm, because term weights for our input data are quite close to each other. Changing the value of *k* does not affect the number of tuple comparisons except for the maximal similarity filter heuristic. As the *k* value increases, maximum similarity filter heuristic needs to make more tuple comparisons to find top *k* similar tuples.

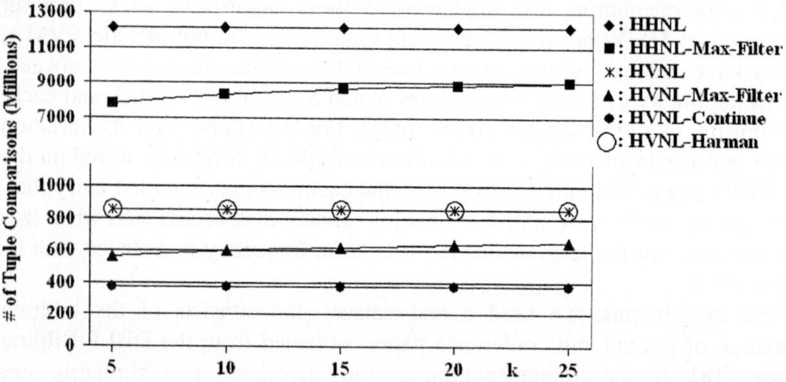

Fig. 2. Number of tuple comparisons for all algorithms vs. *k* values

We also computed the number of disk accesses (Table 1) required by all algorithms when the relations *R* and *S*, and the inverted list entries on the join attribute of relation *S* are stored on disk. In the disk access computation, we ignored the number of disk accesses made for writing the joined tuples to the disk. According to Table 1, the number of disk accesses performed by the HHNL algorithms, which is approximately 150 disk accesses, is quite less than those obtained with the HVNL algorithms since for each term *t* considered during the similarity comparisons, the HVNL based algorithms read inverted list entries of term *t* (i.e., I_t) by making a disk access if it is not in the memory. According to the Table 1, the continue heuristic reduces the number of disk accesses of the HVNL algorithm by 50%. The Harman and maximal similarity filter heuristics, on the other hand, do not lead to any reduction on the number of disk accesses required. This result is due to the fact that, the term weights in our dataset are close to each other and the Harman heuristic considers almost all terms in a tuple *r* during the similarity computations. The maximal similarity filter heuristic on the other hand, needs to access all the inverted list entries for all terms in a tuple *r* to find the *s* tuples having high maximal similarity values. Therefore, the maximal similarity filter heuristic only reduces the number of tuple comparisons performed when the inverted list entries are sorted with respect to the maximal similarity value of tuples.

Table 1. Number of disk accesses performed by all the algorithms for all *k* values

k	HHNL	HHNL-Max-Filter	HVNL	HVNL-Harman	HVNL-Continue	HVNL-Max-Filter
5-25	150	150	26282	26198	14176	26282

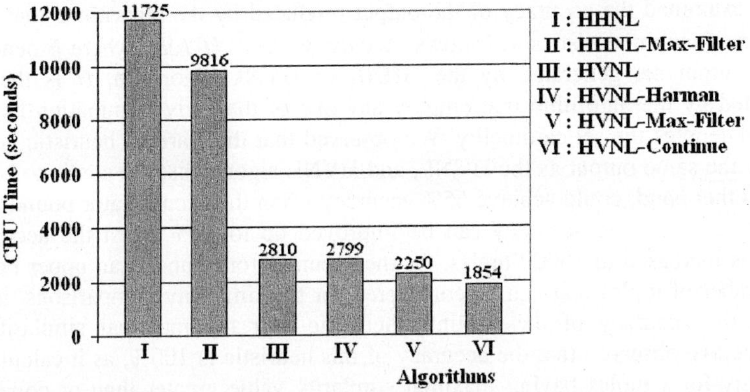

Fig. 3. CPU time required by all algorithms for the directional similarity join

Although the number of disk accesses performed by the HHNL based algorithms is quite less, the number of tuple comparisons is considerably higher than the HVNL based algorithms. To determine which group of algorithms is more efficient, we measured the CPU time required by all of the join algorithms for k=10 and reported the results in Figure 3. As presented in Figure 3, the CPU time required to execute the join operation is 11725 seconds for the HHNL algorithm, and 2810 seconds for the HVNL algorithm, which implies that similarity computations take much longer CPU time than making disk accesses for retrieving inverted list entries. The maximal similarity filter heuristic reduces the CPU time by 16% for the HHNL and 20% for the HVNL algorithms. The continue heuristic makes 35% reduction in the processing time when the accumulator bound is set to 5000 tuples. The Harman heuristic, on the other hand, does not provide any improvement since it also does not make any reduction in the number of tuple comparisons and disk accesses.

For the continue heuristic, the accumulator bound is an important factor on the performance of the join algorithm. To show the effect of the accumulator bound on the join operation, we run the HVNL-Continue algorithm with different accumulator bounds and present the results in Table 2. We observed that, as the accumulator bound is decreased, the number of tuple comparisons falls, due to the fact that, the accumulator bound is an upper bound on the number of tuples that can be considered for similarity comparisons. The number of tuple comparisons made remain the same for different k values.

Table 2. The effect of accumulator bound for the continue heuristic

Accumulator Bound	# of Tuple Comparisons	# of Disk Accesses	CPU Time (sec)	Accuracy
5,000	372,448,481	14,176	1854	65%
10,000	604,454,778	20,001	2595	84%
15,000	732,112,934	22,678	2801	91%

We examined the accuracy of the output produced by the algorithms that employ early termination heuristics as follows: *Accuracy*= $|B \cap H| / |B|$, where B denotes the actual output set generated by the HHNL or HVNL algorithm, H is the output generated by the algorithm that employ any one of the early termination heuristics, and $| . |$ denotes the set cardinality. We observed that the Harman heuristic generates exactly the same output as the HHNL, and HVNL algorithms; the continue heuristic, on the other hand, could achieve 65% accuracy when the accumulator bound is set to 5000 tuples, and the accuracy can be improved up to 91% when the accumulator bound is increased to 15000 tuples. As the accumulator bound is an upper bound on the number of tuples that can be considered for the similarity comparisons, it highly affects the accuracy of the continue heuristic. For the maximal similarity filter heuristic, we observed that the accuracy of this heuristic is 100%, as it calculates the similarity for s tuples having maximal similarity value greater than or equal to the smallest of the k largest similarities computed so far for tuple r. Therefore, the heuristic considers all s tuples that can be in the result set by eliminating the ones that are not possible to be in the result.

6 Conclusion

Similarity based text join is a very useful operator to be employed in a variety of applications. In this study, we incorporate some early termination heuristics from the Information Retrieval domain to achieve performance improvement for the text similarity join algorithms. We have demonstrated through experimental evaluation that nested loops based similarity join algorithm performs the best in terms of the number of disk accesses required; however, it compares every tuple pairs from the relations to be joined and leads to a huge amount of expensive similarity computations. Inverted index based join algorithm, on the other hand, achieves very small number of similarity computations while requiring large number of disk accesses. When we compare the processing time of the algorithms, we have demonstrated that the index based algorithm is superior to the nested loops based one, and we have observed further performance improvement by applying the maximal similarity filter and the continue heuristics to the index based join algorithm.

References

1. Salton, G.: Automatic Text Processing. Addison-Wesley (1989).
2. Cohen, W.: Data Integration Using Similarity Joins and a Word-Based Information Representation Language. ACM Trans. on Inf. Sys., Vol. 18, No. 3 (2000) 288-321.
3. Gravano, L., Ipeirotis, P. G., Koudas, N, Srivasta, D.: Text Joins in an RDBMS for Web Data Integration. In Proc. of WWW2003 (2003).
4. Schallehn, E., Sattler, K. U., Saake, G.: Efficient Similarity-Based Operations for Data Integration. Data & Knowledge Engineering, Vol. 48 (2004) 361–387.
5. Meng, W., Yu, C., Wang, W., Rishe, N.: Performance Analysis of Three Text-Join Algorithms. IEEE Trans. on Knowledge and Data Eng., Vol. 10, No. 3 (1998) 477-492.
6. Jin, L., Li, C., Mehrotra, S.: Efficient Record Linkage in Large Data Sets. In Proc. of the 8th Int. Conf. on Database Systems for Advanced Applications (DASFAA'03) (2003).

7. Özsoyoğlu, G., Altıngövde, I. S., Al-Hamdani, A., Özel, S. A., Ulusoy, Ö., Özsoyoğlu, Z.M.: Querying Web Metadata: Native Score Management and Text Support in Databases. ACM Trans. on Database Sys., Vol. 29, No. 4 (2004) 581-634.
8. Özel, S. A.: Metadata-Based and Personalized Web Querying. PhD Thesis, Dept. of Computer Engineering, Bilkent University, Ankara (2004).
9. Özel, S. A., Altıngövde, İ. S., Ulusoy, Ö., Özsoyoğlu, G., Özsoyoğlu, Z. M.: Metadata-Based Modeling of Information Resources on the Web. JASIST, Vol. 55, No. 2 (2004) 97-110.
10. Fagin, R., Lotem A, Naor, M.: Optimal Aggregation Algorithms for Middleware. In Proc. of PODS 2001 (2001).
11. Bayardo, R. J., Miranker, D. P.: Processing Queries for First Few Answers. In Proc. of Conference on Information and Knowledge Management (1996) 45-52.
12. Chang, K. C., Hwang, S.: Minimal Probing: Supporting Expensive Predicates for Top-k Queries. In Proc. of SIGMOD 2002 (2002) 346-357.
13. Natsev, A, Chang, Y. C., Smith, J. R., Li, C. S., Vitter, J. S.: Supporting Incremental Join Queries on Ranked Inputs. In Proc. of VLDB 2001 (2001) 281-290.
14. Ilyas, I. F., Aref, W. G., Elmagarmid, A. K.: Supporting Top-k Join Queries in Relational Databases. In Proc.of VLDB 2003 (2003).
15. Vo, A. N., Krester, O., Moffat, A.: Vector-Space Ranking with Effective Early Termination. In Proc. of ACM SIGIR 2001 (2001) 35-42.
16. Harman, D. K., Candela, G.: Retrieving Records from a Gigabyte of Text on a Minicomputer Using Statistical Ranking. JASIS, Vol. 41, No. 8 (1990) 581-589.
17. Moffat, A., Zobel, J.: Self Indexing Inverted Files for Fast Text Retrieval. ACM Trans. on Inf. Sys., Vol. 14, No. 4 (1996) 349-379.
18. Ley, M.: DBLP Bibliography. At http://www.iformatik.uni-trier.de/~ley/db/ (2001).

Multimodal Video Database Modeling, Querying and Browsing*

Nurcan Durak and Adnan Yazici

Dept. of Computer Engineering, Middle East Technical University, Ankara, Turkey
{nurcan, yazici}@ceng.metu.edu.tr

Abstract. In this paper, a multimodal video indexing and retrieval system, MMVIRS, is presented. MMVIRS models the auditory, visual, and textual sources of video collections from a semantic perspective. Besides multimodality, our model is constituted on semantic hierarchies that enable us to access the video from different semantic levels. MMVIRS has been implemented with data annotation, querying and browsing parts. In the annotation part, metadata information and video semantics are extracted in hierarchical ways. In the querying part, semantic queries, spatial queries, regional queries, spatio-temporal queries, and temporal queries have been processed over video collections using the proposed model. In the browsing parts, video collections are navigated using category information, visual and auditory hierarchies.

1 Introduction

With the developments in data capturing, storing and transferring technologies, video usage has increased in different applications. Video data is different from textual data since video has image frames, sound tracks, visible texts, speech texts, temporal, and spatial dimensions. For handling all video semantics coming from different data sources, an efficient and effective video data model is necessary. Besides the data model, functional query interfaces and efficient querying algorithms are crucial issues.

There are visual, auditory, and textual modalities in video. The *visual modality* contains everything that can be seen in the video. The *auditory modality* contains everything that can be heard in the video, such as speech, music, and environmental sounds. The auditory modality can provide valuable information when analyzing video programs [1, 2, 3, 4]. The *textual modality* contains everything that can be converted into text streams in the video document [5, 3, 6, 7, 8]. Texts give illuminating information to watchers of the video. Considering all information sources in the video, Snoek and Worring [9] define *multimodality* as expressing video data using at least two modalities. Different video modalities are used corporately for automatic scene detection [2, 3, 5, 7].

To model the huge content of video and to return video segments to asked questions are the main focuses of *semantic based video modeling and retrieval* studies [4, 10, 11, 12, 13]. In semantic based video modeling [4, 10, 11, 12], video is

* This work is supported in part by Turkish State Planning Organization (DPT) under grant number 2004K120720.

P. Yolum et al.(Eds.): ISCIS 2005, LNCS 3733, pp. 802–812, 2005.

segmented into meaningfully manageable portions, then semantically rich entities and relationships are extracted and indexed. Relationships between semantic entities can be temporal [12, 13] or spatial [11, 12, 13, 14]. Spatio-temporal relations consider changing object positions in time and provide querying object trajectories [11, 12, 14]. The *hierarchical video model* provides many semantic levels that facilitate the understanding of video content. Visual events are modeled in a hierarchy at [6, 11, 13] and visual, auditory, and textual sources are considered in physical hierarchies in [7]. Petkovic and Jonker [4] model audio primitives beside visual primitives. Video querying is used by users who know what they want, while video browsing is used by users who want to figure out the video content. Besides semantic entities, video collections and video clips can be modeled using metadata and querying the video database can be done by using metadata information [8, 11].

The main purpose of this study is as follows: modeling video collections using all kinds of semantic entities with space and time dimensions; getting results to different kinds of queries more effectively and efficiently; and finally browsing video collections. The MMVIRS has the following properties and contributions:

1. It supports modeling the video semantics using *auditory, visual,* and *textual* information and spatio-temporal dimensions altogether. Our main differences from previous works [4, 10, 11, 12] is modeling all modalities and dimensions altogether.
2. Our model is constructed over *semantic hierarchies* in visual modality and auditory modality. We separate from previous works [6, 7, 11, 13] by combining semantic visual hierarchies with semantic auditory and speech hierarchies.
3. Based on our model, we introduce *multimodal semantic queries* that enable various query combinations of visual, auditory, and textual semantics. Considering all modalities, users can access desired information more quickly and redundant results are minimized. We support *hierarchical queries* that are usable in querying visual, auditory and speech hierarchies. Our model considers video collections and keeps video metadata information in addition to semantic entities. Semantic, spatial and spatio-temporal queries are processed on video collections. In previous works, there are no multimodal queries and hierarchical queries.
4. We support browsing of video collections according to categories of video, visual semantic hierarchies, and auditory semantic hierarchies. We combine metadata information and semantic hierarchies. Our difference video browsing is supporting multimodal and hierarchical browsing. Studies in [8,11] consider metadata information and visual semantic entities in browsing.
5. We have developed compact *MMVIRS* tool that covers data annotation, querying and browsing parts. In the annotation part, metadata information, visual entities, and auditory entities are annotated and stored in a database. In the querying part, semantic queries, temporal queries, fuzzy spatial queries, fuzzy regional queries, and fuzzy trajectory queries have been implemented. We have also implemented *conjunctive queries* that contain multiple query sentences in the same type. In the browsing part, videos are navigated using category information, visual hierarchies, and auditory hierarchies. In querying and browsing, proposed multimodal video model is used.

The rest of this paper is organized as follows: section 2 describes the proposed data model, section 3 shows supported query types, section 4 describes MMVIRS architecture, and the conclusion and future research directions are given in Section 5.

2 MMVIRS Architecture

In MMVIRS architecture, there are annotator, video model, query processor, and browser parts as shown in Figure 1. In annotator part, video metadata, visual semantic entities, auditory semantic entities, speech, and visible texts are annotated and placed in the proposed video model. The annotated data and model structure are stored in a database. Annotator allows update the previously annotated video data. The video data model consists of time interval trees, data structures and their relations. The model is constructed using information in the database. In query processor part, there are query algorithms, which use the proposed data model, for answering users' query specifications coming from user interfaces. In query user interfaces, user can specify the query by selecting semantic entities, typing text, drawing region, or drawing path. The results of the queries can be played on the raw video files. The browser is connected to the video model and provides users to navigate video collections via their categories and semantic hierarchies. Browser opens the navigated raw video and plays the selected events.

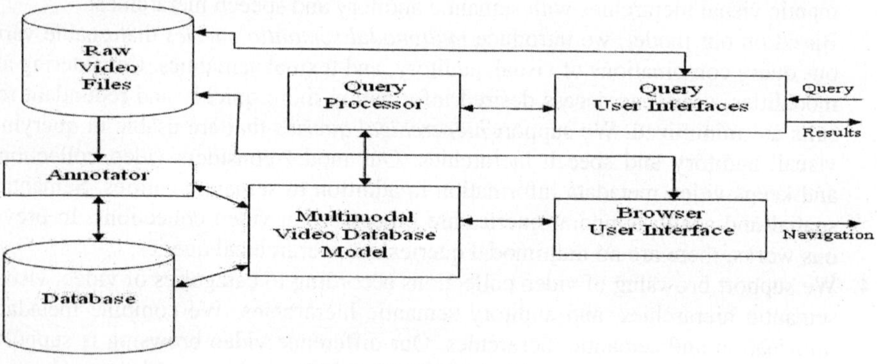

Fig. 1. MMVIRS Architecture

3 Multimodal Video Database Model

In video data, each video source has different characteristics. Time boundaries of visual semantics and auditory semantics can be different. While visual semantics are changing, the audio part can still give the same meaning or vice versa. Thus, auditory and visual data sources should be segmented separately. Written texts are part of image frames, so "text appearing" can be modeled as one of the visual events. Speech is one type of auditory event and is suitable for modeling with auditory information.

Considering all differences and similarities among different modalities, we propose the multimodal video model. In our approach, video is segmented into time intervals logically. After segmentation, semantic entities in each time interval are extracted and associated to the time interval. The semantic entities are annotated manually and labeled using free text.

3.1 Video Segmentation

We use semantic hierarchies in auditory and visual semantic segmentation. Our hierarchy has two levels. At the first level, video is segmented into big chunks containing semantically related and temporally adjacent events. These big chunks do not overlap with each other. At the second level, big chunks are divided into atomic semantic segments. These atomic chunks can overlap with each other.

The *visual content* is segmented by considering visual happenings. The levels of visual content hierarchy are:

1. *Sequences:* Temporally adjacent and semantically related events can be gathered under a *sequence*. Generally sequences have more general and wide titles such as party, street, war, night, wedding, and so on.
2. *Scenes:* Each sequence can be partitioned into atomic sub-events which are called *scenes*. A scene's time interval is bound with its sequence time interval. There must be one visual event in each scene. For example, the wedding sequence has scenes such as "groom kissing bride" and "audience applauding". The applauding and kissing events can overlap. Text keywords are extracted at this level.

The *auditory content* of the video is segmented into coherent time intervals having distinct audio characteristics. The levels of auditory content hierarchy are:

1. *Background intervals:* Audio content can be segmented into big chunks listening background sounds. Background sounds give a general feeling of the ambiance in the time intervals. Some examples of background sounds are bar ambience, street sounds and so on. If there is a long speech given by one speaker, such as prime minister is speaking, we label this speech at the background level and we divide this background interval into sub-sections according to varying speech subjects.
2. *Foreground intervals:* Each background interval is divided into *foreground intervals*, which are more distinguishable and distinct audio happenings, such gunshot, screaming, explosion etc. Foreground interval characteristics resemble scenes' characteristics. In speech events, speech keywords are extracted at the foreground level.

After segmentation the visual content and the auditory content, we get a time interval tree as shown in Figure 2. In a video, there are two hierarchy trees: visual and auditory. In the visual tree, there are sequence and scene levels. Objects and events are connected to time intervals. At the scene level, visual objects are related with region and text events are related with keywords and text region. In the auditory tree, there are background and foreground intervals. Events and objects are connected to time intervals. Speech keywords are extracted at the foreground level. There can be many videos in the database, and each video has the same structure.

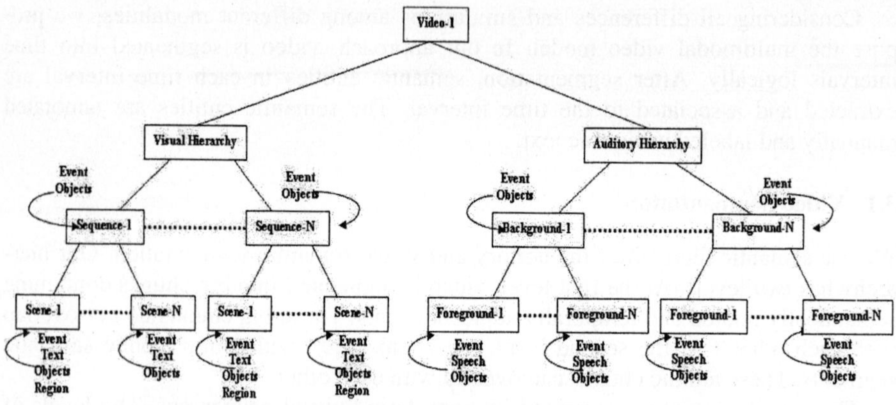

Fig. 2. Video hierarchies and their relations with semantic entities

3.2 Multimodal Video Model

Considering video metadata information and all semantic entities, we propose a generic video model that is shown in Figure 3. Metadata information is kept in video-metadata class that is associated with other classes with 'VideoId' attribute. Semantic

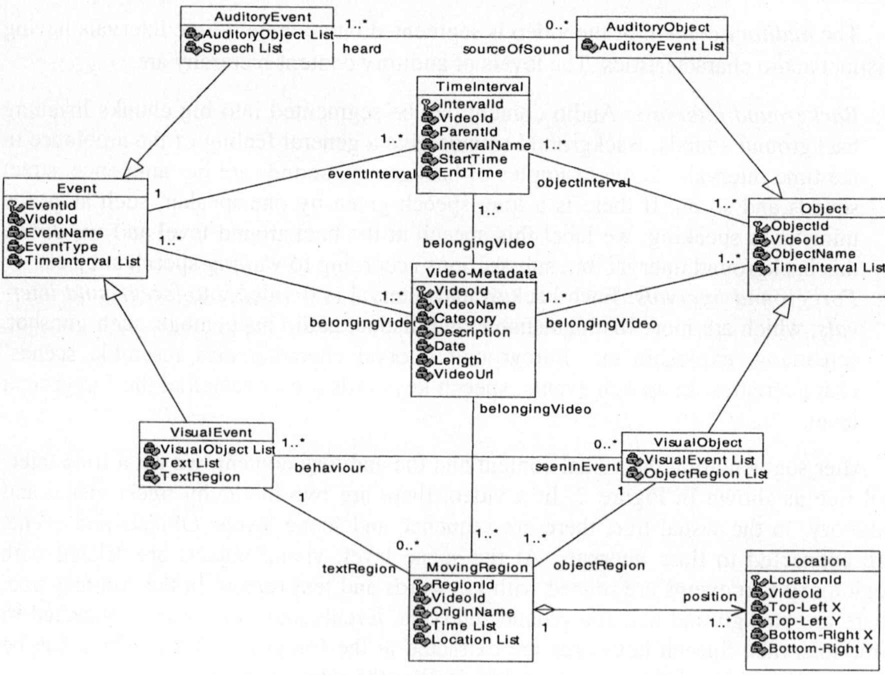

Fig. 3. Generic model in UML

entities in video are events and objects. Events may have zero or more objects. Each event and each object are related with at least one time interval. Auditory events and visual events have common and different features, so common features are generalized in event class, different features are specialized events in inherited classes. A similar way, the auditory object and the visual object inherit from the object class. Visual objects can be seen in different regions in different time intervals. "Visual-Text" events have spatial regions. The moving region is composed of locations. List keywords represent linked-list data structure. All classes will be described in sub-sections.

3.2.1 Video Metadata

We propose a model that considers video collections so video metadata information must be kept. Metadata information can be extended according to application requirements. Each video has a unique video identity number that is given from the database automatically. Formally, we describe video metadata as *video-metadata = {VideoId, VideoName, Category, Description, Date, Length, VideoUrl}*.

3.2.2 Time Interval

There are two levels in both auditory and visual semantic hierarchy. At the first level, big chunks may have multiple atomic segments, so these two levels construct a multi-way tree structure. A multi-way tree structure is constructed through 'ParentId' attribute. If the time interval is at the first level, then there is no parent of this interval, hence we give 0 for 'ParentId'. If the time interval is at the second level, then we give parent's 'IntervalId' for 'ParentId' of the interval. Each time interval must be labeled with one event as 'IntervalName' and must be between the start time and end time. Formally, we describe video metadata as *time-interval = {IntervalId, VideoId, ParentId, IntervalName, StartTime, EndTime}*.

3.2.3 Event

Events are visual or auditory happenings. They happen in a time interval, so they are related with time intervals. One event can happen in different time intervals and in different videos. Each event must have a unique event-id in a video. Each event must have name and type. Formally, the event is described as, *event = {EventId, VideoId, EventName, EventType, TimeInterval List}*.

3.2.3.1 Visual Event. The visual event is inherited from the event class. We categorize events at the sequence level with "Visual-Sequence" type. At the scene level, there are text appearing events in "Visual-Text" type and normal events in "Visual-Normal" type. Events in "Visual-Text" type do not contain objects, but contain text keywords and text region. All visual events in "Visual-Text" type are named with "text appearing". There can be more than one visible text in the vidco. They differ from each other with their keywords and their time intervals. Events in "Visual-Normal" type can contain visual objects. Formally, the visual event is described as *visual-event = {VisualObject List, Text List, TextRegion}*.

3.2.3.2 Auditory Even. The auditory event is inherited from the event class. The "Auditory-Ambiance" type is given to events in background intervals. At the foreground level, all aural happenings except speech are in the "Auditory-Normal" type. A speech event is different from other events because it contains speech text. So we separate speech events from other auditory events with the "Auditory-Speech" type. In the speech events, speech keywords are associated with the event and the speaker is associated with the object of the speech event. All speech events are labeled with "speech". Different speech events vary from each other with their time interval, speaker, and speech keywords. Formally, the auditory event is described as *auditory-event = {AuditoryObject List, Speech List}.*

3.2.4 Object

Objects are can be seen or heard in events. There are a lot of real world objects in a video, but we consider only salient objects. One object can be seen or heard in different time intervals, and in different videos. Each object must have name and a unique id in a video. Formally, the object is described as *object= {ObjectId, VideoId, ObjectName, TimeInterval List}.*

3.2.4.1 Visual Object. One visual object can be seen in different visual events and in different spatial positions. Visual events, in which the object is seen, are kept in the 'VisualEvent List'. The visual objects have spatial positions which are extracted at the scene level. One object can be seen in different regions in different time intervals. Formally, the visual object is described as *visual-object = {VisualEvent List, TimeInterval List, ObjectRegion List}.*

3.2.4.2 Auditory Object. Auditory objects are sources of sound. Sometimes finding the sound source can be difficult. Background intervals have this kind of mixed sound, so we do not label the objects at the background level except from the long speeches. However objects are more distinguishable in foreground intervals, so we label the sound sources at the foreground level. Formally, the auditory object is described as *auditory-object = {AuditoryEvent List}.*

3.2.5 Moving Region

Moving region is concerned with visual objects and visual events in text type. The object position or text position is taken in every considerable movement. We kept changing positions and their taken times in the moving-region class described formally as *moving-region = {RegionId, VideoId, OriginName, TimeList, Location List}.*

3.2.6 Location

The positions of the object or the text are annotated manually using a minimum bounding rectangular that covers the object's top-left point and bottom-right point. These two points are stored in the location class that is described formally as *location = {LocationId, VideoId, Top-Left X, Top-Left Y, Bottom-Right-X, Bottom-Right Y}.*

4 Querying and Browsing

In addition to covering all video modalities and dimensions, our model considers video collections; consequently, we have very rich query types. Supported queries are semantic queries, regional queries, fuzzy spatial queries, temporal queries, and fuzzy spatio-temporal queries. Metadata information can be queried with these queries.

In *semantic queries*, semantic entities are queried over a video or a video collection. We support conjunctive semantic queries. We collect all semantic queries in four categories: auditory, visual, multimodal, and hierarchical queries.

Auditory Queries: This type of queries contains auditory clues such as auditory events, auditory objects or speech keywords; therefore, auditory data structures are searched for retrieving the query results. An example is: "Find all intervals where *Bush* is speaking about *Turkey* in all news videos between 2003 and 2005".
Visual Queries: These queries contain visual clues such as visual events, visual objects, and visible text keywords. Therefore visual data structures are searched for retrieving the query results. Examples are "Find all intervals in which *Tom Hanks is eating* and *Burger King text is appearing* in terminal film" and "Find all videos having *plane* and *tower* objects".
Multimodal Queries: Queries in this type contain both auditory clues and visual clues. With multimodal queries, users can search the video collections from different aspects. Using different data modalities, users can express their queries more detailed and richly, and they reach to exact results more quickly. Each subpart of the multimodal query is processed separately, then results of each part are combined. Some multimodal query examples are: "Find all intervals that *'Gool keyword is appearing'* and *'Speaker is speaking about Zidane and penalty'* in soccer videos" or "Find all videos in which *'America text appears'* and *'crashing is heard'* ".
Hierarchical Querying: In this type of queries, the hierarchical structure of video content is queried. We can search events in "Visual-Sequence" or "Auditory-Ambience" types via their sub-events or sub-objects. Some examples are: "Find all sub-events in *Party* visual event" or "Find all objects in *Accident* auditory event".

In *fuzzy spatial queries*, spatial relationships between two objects are queried with a membership value. Our approach differs from previous studies [11,12] by processing queries over video collections. Fuzzy values are computed with membership functions defined in the study [12]. An example query for this type can be "Find all intervals in which *'player-1 is left of ball with 0.6 certainty level'* and *'ball is right of goalpost with 0.5 certainty level'* in all videos".

In *fuzzy regional queries*, visual objects or texts are queried according to their position over the video frames. In addition to this query type, text and visual object locations can be queried. Some query types are: "Find all locations, in which *assassin* is seen between 4th and 9th minutes in news videos" or "Find all intervals *Cola Coca* text is seen in center with a threshold value of 0.8 in soccer videos".

In *fuzzy trajectory queries*, whether given object follows given path is queried over video collections. Trajectory queries are processed using formulas in [12]. We can process the trajectory queries over video collections instead of a single video file as in [12]. One query example is: "Find all *ball* trajectories from the location L1 and to location L2 with uncertainty level of 0.5 in news videos".

In *temporal queries*, temporal relations between events in either the auditory type or the visual type are queried in a specified video. We do not support this query processing over video collections, because temporal orders of events are meaningful in own video. We also support conjunctive temporal queries. Some temporal query examples are: "Find all time intervals when *'fighting is seen'* overlaps with *'ambulance is heard'* ".

In video browsing, all videos in the system can be navigated via auditory and visual semantic hierarchies. We use tree format for showing these hierarchies. At the first level of the tree, videos are grouped as their categories hence users can navigate the desired video category. Under each video, there are auditory semantic hierarchy and visual semantic hierarchy. In the visual hierarchy, sequences are listed and under each sequence its scenes are listed. In the auditory hierarchy, background intervals are listed and under each background interval its foreground intervals are listed. Besides browsing, users can play the desired semantic event.

In Figure 4, MMVIRS tool is shown with semantic query user interface and query results user interface. Tool provides annotation, querying, and browsing facilities on video collections.

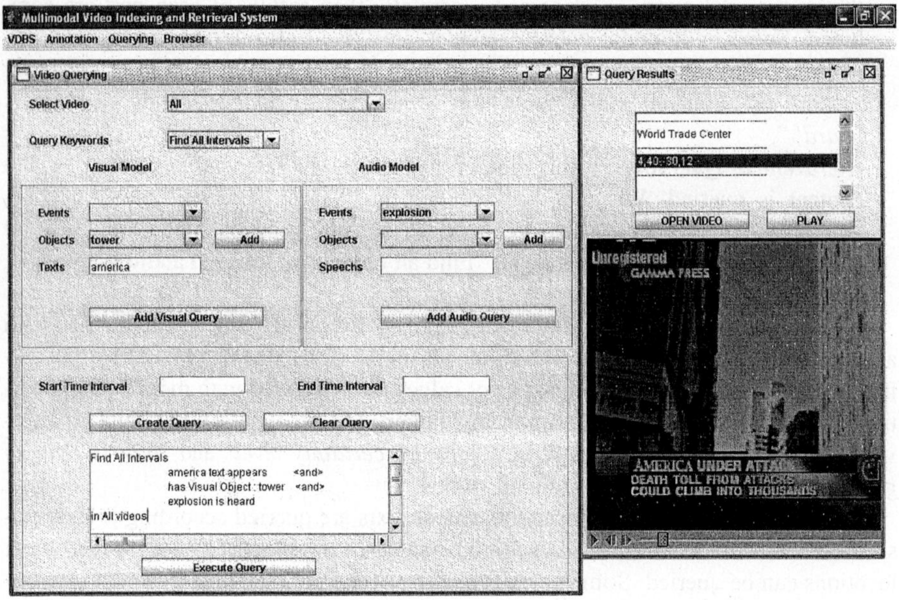

Fig. 4. Screenshot of MMVIRS tool

5 Conclusion

In this paper, we present a multimodal video model that considers visual, auditory, and textual sources with spatial and temporal dimensions. By covering all data sources of video, we capture all types of semantic entities that complement each other. Besides semantic entities, the model considers video collections and keeps metadata information. Thus, it constitutes a full video database system. The model is constructed on visual and auditory hierarchies. Using semantic hierarchies, users can query or browse the video collections roughly or in detail. A variety of query types can be processed using the proposed model such as semantic, spatial queries, regional queries, temporal queries, and fuzzy queries. Our multimodal queries enable users to query different data sources altogether, thus users can reach desired information more quickly. Our proposed model can be applied in different video applications and variety of video domains such as news, sports, films, talk-shows, and so on. The MMVIRS has been implemented in Java as a compact tool. Due to space limitation, the details of the implementation, query algorithms and all user interfaces of the system are not included in this paper. They can be found at [15].

In our hierarchy, there are two semantic hierarchy levels. Under the second level, the physical shots can be added. Thus low level features and high level features can be handled in one model. Another topic for a future study is to develop a query processor supporting answering people's daily questions that can be developed using natural language techniques. Online querying and browsing of the video collections could be another improvement.

References

1. Moncrieff, S., Dorai, C., Venkatesh, S.: Detecting indexical signs in film audio for scene interpretation. IEEE ICME 2001, Tokyo, Japan, (2001) 1192-1195
2. Nam, J., Alghoniemy, M., Tewfik, A.H.: Audio-visual content-based violent scene characterization. In IEEE Int. Conf. on Image Processing, vol. 1,(1998) 353-357
3. Petkovic, M., Mihajlovic, V., Jonker, W.: Multi-Modal Extraction of Highlights from TV Formula 1 Programs. IEEE ICME, Lausanne, Switzerland, (2002), 817 - 820
4. Petkovic, M., Jonker, W.: A framework for video modeling. Eighteenth IASTED Int. Conf. Applied Informatics, Innsbruck, Austria, (2000)
5. Informedia-II Digital Video Library, Web Site: http://www.informedia.cs.cmu.edu/
6. Agius, H.W., Angelides, M.C.: Modeling content for semantic-level querying of multimedia, Multimedia Tools and Applications 15(1), 2001, 5-37
7. Huang, Q., Puri, A., Liu, Z.: Multimedia search and retrieval: new concepts, system implementation, and application, IEEE Trans.on Circ. and Syst. for Video Tech., Vol. 10, No. 5 (2000) 679-692
8. Gibbon, D., Bejeja, L., Liu, Z., Renger, B., Shahraray, B.: Creating Personalized Video Presentations using Multimodal Processing. Handbook of Multimedia Databases, Edited by Borko Furht, CRC Press (2003), 1107-1131
9. Snoek, C.G.M., Worring, M.: Multimodal video indexing: A review of the state-of-the-art. Multimedia Tools and Applications, (2005), 5-35
10. Adalı, S., Candan, K. S., Chen, S., Erol, K., Subrahmanian, V.S., The advanced video information system: data structures and query processing, Mult. Syst., vol. 4, (1996) 172-186

11. Dönderler, M.E., Saykol, E., Arslan, U., Ulusoy, O.: BilVideo: Design and Implementation of a Video Database Management System. Multimedia Tools and Applications, (to appear)
12. Köprülü, M., Cicekli, N.K., Yazici, A.: Spatio-temporal querying in video databases, Inf. Sci. 160(1-4) (2004) 131-152
13. Ekin, A., Tekalp, A. M., Mehrotra, R.: Integrated semantic-syntactic video modeling for search and browsing. IEEE Trans. on Multimedia, vol. 6, no. 6 (2004) 839-851
14. Li, J.Z., Özsu, M.T., Szafron, D.: Modeling of moving objects in a video database. Proc. of IEEE Int. Conf. on Multimedia Computing and Systems, Ottawa, Canada (1997) 336-343
15. Durak N., Yazıcı A.: Semantic Video Modeling And Retrieval with Visual, Auditory, Textual Sources, MS. Thesis, Metu, Ankara, 2004

Semantic Load Shedding for Prioritized Continuous Queries over Data Streams*

Jaeseok Park and Haengrae Cho

Department of Computer Engineering, Yeungnam University,
Gyungsan, Gyungbuk 712-749, Republic of Korea
hrcho@yu.ac.kr

Abstract. A data stream management system (DSMS) has to handle high-volume and bursty data streams with large number of continuous queries. When an input rate of any data stream exceeds the system capacity, the DSMS has to shed load by dropping some fraction of unprocessed data items. In this paper, we propose a new load shedding algorithm for continuous queries over data streams. Unlike previous algorithms assuming that all queries are equally important, we consider the priority of each query so that more important queries make more convincing outputs. As a result, the proposed algorithm can support differentiated quality of services by exploiting semantics inherent to applications. We also report the experiment results confirming the benefits of the proposed algorithm.

Keywords: data stream, load shedding, continuous query, quality of service, performance evaluation.

1 Introduction

There has been a surge of interest recently in query processing over data streams [2,4,8]. A *data stream* is a real-time, continuous, and ordered sequence of data items. In many of the relevant applications - network monitoring, sensor processing, web tracking, telecommunication, and so on - data streams are typically queried using long-running continuous queries rather than the traditional one-time queries. A *continuous query* is a query that is logically issued once but runs forever. For example, continuous queries over network packet streams can be used to monitor network behavior to detect anomalies (e.g., link congestion) and their cause (e.g., hardware failure, intrusion, denial-of-service attack) [2]. We will abbreviate continuous query to query throughout the paper.

A data stream management system (DSMS) processes large number of queries over data streams and stored relations. Example DSMSs are Aurora [1], PSoup [6], and STREAM [4]. The online nature of data streams and their potentially high input rates impose high resource requirements on the DSMS [7]. Especially, for data streams with high input rates, the CPU might not be fast enough to process all incoming data items in a timely manner. Under these conditions, the DSMS may *shed load* by dropping some fraction of unprocessed data items to

* This research was supported by University IT Research Center Project.

P. Yolum et al.(Eds.): ISCIS 2005, LNCS 3733, pp. 813–822, 2005.

continue to provide up-to-date query response. The current state of the art consists of two main approaches [5,7,11]. The first relies on *random* load shedding, where data items are removed with a random manner based on input rates. The second relies on *semantic* load shedding that drops data items based on the importance of their content.

In this paper, we propose a new semantic load shedding algorithm for queries over data streams. The goal of the proposed algorithm is to support differentiated quality of services by exploiting semantics inherent to applications. To achieve this goal, we adopt the following approaches.

- We consider the *priority* of each query so that more important queries can make more convincing outputs. This is contrary to the previous semantic load shedding algorithms. They assumed that all queries are equally important and then tried to reduce the average deviation of the estimated answers of all queries.
- We also consider the *quality of data* (QoD) by prioritizing data items accessed by multiple queries. Data items with high value of QoD have lower probability of being dropped.

The rest of this paper is organized as follows. Sect. 2 reviews the related work, and Sect. 3 proposes our load shedding algorithm. Sect. 4 presents the experiment results to evaluate the performance of the proposed algorithm. Sect. 5 summarizes our work and provides future research directions.

2 Related Work

Aurora system introduces a representative semantic load shedding algorithm [11]. The work is similar to our algorithm in the sense that it considers the quality of service (QoS) specifications which assign priorities to data items and then shed those with low-priority first. It is important to note that the QoS specifications are attached to a single query not between queries. Then Aurora system drops part of data items which are the least important for a query. On the other hand, our algorithm tries to drop data items accessed by the least important queries.

Das et al. [7] also consider the problem of how to effectively shed load in overloaded data streams. They consider join queries between data streams, and the metric being optimized is the number of data items produced in the approximate answer. Load shedding for join query is also considered at [9], but the goal is to optimize the output rate of data items. The algorithms in [7,9] are not applicable to our problem setting where each query has its own priority.

Babcock et al. [5] propose a load shedding algorithm for aggregation queries in STREAM system. Most of their work considers a random load shedding for queries with same importance. Specifically, they deal with the optimum placement of random filters for multiple aggregation queries sharing operators and resources over data streams. They also present a basic idea to modify their algorithm to allow the prioritized queries, which motivated our work. We extend the idea to the semantic load shedding and propose a new idea of QoD by assigning priorities to data items.

3 Load Shedding Algorithm

In this section, we first describe our model of load shedding. Then we propose a semantic load shedding algorithm on the model.

3.1 The Model

Fig. 1 shows our model of load shedding. The load shedder performs the load shedding algorithm. Note that the load shedder is placed at the start of data streams before data items are processed by the query processor. This is the optimal position for queries with no shared operations since it minimizes wasted work [3,11]. The statistics manager provides the necessary information to the load shedder. Specifically, the input to the load shedding algorithm consists of *query information* and *data region information.* Suppose that there is a set of queries $q_1, \ldots, q_n$ over a set of data streams. The query information of a query q_i consists of:

- $P(q_i)$: priority of q_i
- $C(q_i)$: cost of q_i to process a data item
- $R(q_i)$: set of data regions accessed by q_i

The load shedder drops data items accessed by queries with lower priority first. The cost of a query means the processing overhead for a data item. The load shedder considers the cost of each query to determine the amount of load shedding when the system is in overload state. We consider queries with arithmetic comparisons and optional aggregation over a data stream. Join queries between multiple data streams are not considered in this paper, since they are comparatively rare in practice [5].

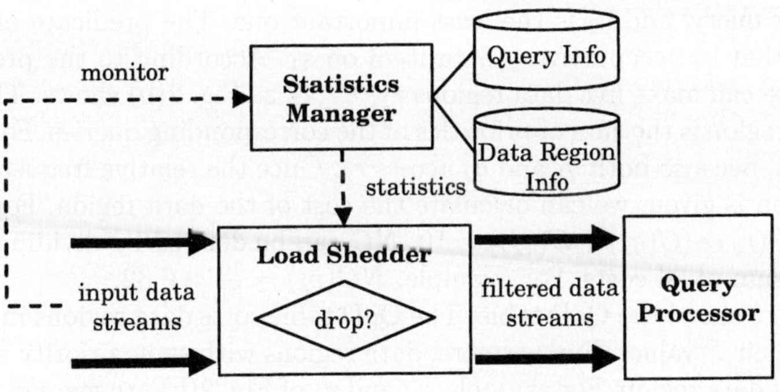

Fig. 1. The model of load shedding

We define several *data regions* for a data stream. Each data region represents a non-overlapping value interval of the data stream. The data region is created with the selection predicates of queries. For example, suppose that there are two queries q_1 and q_2 over a data stream with a single field a. Suppose also that the selection predicate of q_1 is $a > 0$ and that of q_2 is $a < 100$. Then we can define three data regions r_1, r_2, and r_3 with predicates of $r_1 : a \leq 0$, $r_2 : 0 < a < 100$, and $r_3 : a \geq 100$. As a result, $R(q_1) = \{r_2, r_3\}$ and $R(q_2) = \{r_1, r_2\}$.

Suppose that there is a set of data regions $r_1, \ldots, r_m$ over a set of data streams. The statistics manager provides the following data region information of each data region r_i to the load shedder.

- $P(r_i)$: priority of r_i, $P(r_i) = \sum P(q_k)$, for all q_k where $r_i \in R(q_k)$
- $F(r_i)$: relative frequency of r_i, $\sum F(r_i) = 1$
- $C(r_i)$: cost of r_i, $C(r_i) = F(r_i) * \sum C(q_k)$, for all q_k where $r_i \in R(q_k)$
- $NC(r_i)$: normalized cost of r_i, $NC(r_i) = \frac{C(r_i)}{\sum C(r_i)}$
- pred(r_i): predicate of r_i to specify values in r_i

The priority of a data region is defined as a sum of priorities of queries accessing the data region. Suppose that there are two data regions, r_i and r_j. If $P(r_i) > P(r_j)$, r_i should be accessed by more important queries or by larger number of queries. This means that the quality of data (QoD) of r_i is higher than that of r_j. Then the load shedder has to drop a data region with the lowest QoD first. To select the data region easily, the load shedder maintains a QoD table which is a sorted list of data regions in ascending order of their P values. If two data regions r_i and r_j have same priority, the QoD table stores only one of them, say r_k. Then $NC(r_k)$ is changed to $NC(r_i) + NC(r_j)$, and pred(r_k) is set to 'pred(r_i) OR pred(r_j)'. In what follows, we assume that in the QoD table $P(r_i) < P(r_j)$, if $i < j$. Example 1 illustrates the creation of a QoD table with query information and data region information.

Example 1: Suppose that there are two queries q_1 and q_2 on a data stream s_1, and q_3 and q_4 are defined on another data stream s_2. s_1 has a single field a, and s_2 has a single field b. Fig. 2(a) shows the query information. q_4 is the most important query, and q_2 is the least important one. The predicate of q_2 is 'all' meaning that q_2 accepts every data item on s_1. According to the predicates of queries, we can make five data regions $r_1, \ldots, r_5$ as Fig. 2(b) shows. The priority of a data region is the sum of priorities of the corresponding queries. For example, $P(r_2) = 4$, because both q_1 and q_2 access r_2. Once the relative frequency of each data region is given, we can calculate the cost of the data region. For example, $C(r_2) = F(r_2) * (C(q_1) + C(q_2)) = 10$. NC can be derived by dividing each cost with the sum of all costs. For example, $NC(r_2) = \frac{10}{31} = 0.32$.

Fig. 2(c) shows the QoD table. The QoD table sorts data regions in ascending order of their P values. Furthermore, data regions with same priority are merged into a new data region. For example, r_2 and r_3 of Fig. 2(b) are merged into a new r_3 at the QoD table. The predicate of the new r_3 integrates the old predicates with OR operation. The new NC value is the sum of old NC values. □

	Predicate	P	C	R
q_1	$a > 0$	3	40	$\{r_2\}$
q_2	all	1	10	$\{r_1, r_2\}$
q_3	$b < 50$	2	20	$\{r_4, r_5\}$
q_4	$b > 0$	4	40	$\{r_3, r_4\}$

(a) Query information

	Predicate	P	F	C	NC
r_1	$a \le 0$	1	0.3	3	0.10
r_2	$a > 0$	4	0.2	10	0.32
r_3	$b \ge 50$	4	0.2	8	0.26
r_4	$0 < b < 50$	6	0.1	6	0.19
r_5	$b \le 0$	2	0.2	4	0.13

(b) Data region information

	Predicate	P	NC
r_1	$a \le 0$	1	0.10
r_2	$b \le 0$	2	0.13
r_3	$a > 0$ OR $b \ge 50$	4	0.58
r_4	$0 < b < 50$	6	0.19

(c) QoD table

Fig. 2. Example of quereies, data regions, and a QoD table

3.2 The Algorithm

The load shedder starts to drop data items when the system is in overload state. To determine the amount of drop operations, the load shedder calculates the overload ratio $\mathcal{L}$, where $\mathcal{L}$ = (current load − system capacity) / current load. When the load shedder drops a data region r_i, the current load will be reduced about the fraction of $NC(r_i)$. This means that if $\mathcal{L} > 0$, the load shedder has to drop at least k data regions so that $\sum_{i=1}^{k} NC(r_i) \ge \mathcal{L}$. Furthermore, the selected k data regions have to be the least important ones. Since the QoD table stores data regions in ascending order of their priorities, data regions $r_1 \dots r_k$ in the QoD table are the least important k ones. Specifically, the load shedder performs the following algorithm when $\mathcal{L} > 0$.

1. In the QoD table, find a tuple r_k with the smallest k that satisfies the following inequality: $\sum_{i=1}^{k} NC(r_i) \ge \mathcal{L}$.
2. For each $r_i, i < k$, insert a drop operator with a predicate of 'pred(r_i)' at the start position of a data stream of r_i.
3. Then calculate the remaining load $\mathcal{R} = \mathcal{L} - \sum_{i=1}^{k-1} NC(r_i)$.
4. Insert a drop operator with a predicate of 'p AND pred(r_k)' at the start position of a data stream of r_k. p is a random boolean variable that becomes 1 with the probability of $\frac{\mathcal{R}}{NC(r_k)}$.

There are some comments on the algorithm. First, the predicate of the kth drop operator includes an additional random filter p. This compensates for the potential loss of the last data region r_k. Specifically, p has a role to drop data items of r_k with the probability of $\frac{\mathcal{R}}{NC(r_k)}$. Second, there may be several drop operators on a data stream. The order of drop operators is not important, however, since each operator drops non-overlapping data items. Third, suppose that

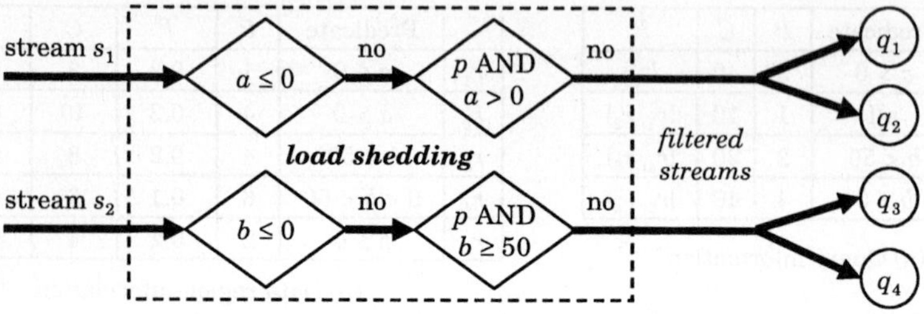

Fig. 3. Example of data flow diagram

a data region r_i in the QoD table results from merging different data regions. If pred(r_i) consists of predicates on multiple data streams, then pred(r_i) has to be split into multiple drop operators, one for each data stream. Note that a drop operator has to be attached to only a single data stream. Finally, we assume that the overhead of drop operator itself is negligible. The same assumption is also hold at [5]. While we believe this assumption holds at most applications, there might be other applications where the relative cost of load shedding is larger. In that case, step 1 and 3 have to be modified to consider the effect of k drop operators.

The load shedder keeps the number k indicating which tuples in the QoD table were used last. Later on, if additional load needs to be shed, the search on the QoD table can begin at the tuple. On the other hand, if the current load is determined to be under the system capacity, then the load shedder removes the drop operations by searching the QoD table in the reverse direction.

Example 2 illustrates the process of load shedding with the same information of Example 1. Assume that the load shedder has the QoD table of Example 1.

Example 2: Suppose the overload ratio $\mathcal{L}$ is 0.4. Then the load shedder searches the smallest k such that $\sum_{i=1}^{k} NC(r_i) \geq 0.4$. k is 3 in the QoD table of Fig. 2(c). So two drop operators, drop($a \leq 0$) and drop($b \leq 0$), are inserted at the start of data stream s_1 and s_2, respectively. The remaining load $\mathcal{R} = 0.4 - 0.23 = 0.17$. Since pred($r_3$) includes predicates of s_1 and s_2, it has to be split as 'p AND $a > 0$' for s_1 and 'p AND $b \geq 50$' for s_2. The random filter p becomes 1 with the probability of $\frac{0.17}{0.58}$. Fig. 3 shows the result data flow diagram. □

4 Experiments

We evaluate the performance of our algorithm by simulation. In this section, we first describe the experiment methodology. Then we present the experiment results and analyze their meanings.

4.1 Experiment Methodology

To the best of our knowledge, there are not any semantic load shedding algorithms that consider the priority of queries. So it is not possible to compare the performance of our algorithm with others. Instead, we concentrate on determining the performance behavior of our algorithm itself. Specifically, the goals of experiments are (a) to validate if our algorithm can support differentiated quality of services according to the query priority and (b) to determine the performance behavior when we change the access pattern of queries and the frequency of data regions.

We implement the simulator of a data stream using the CSIM18 Simulation Engine [10]. There are three types of queries, q_l, q_m, and q_h, where $P(q_l) = 1$, $P(q_m) = 2$, and $P(q_h) = 4$. Their costs to process a data item are assumed to be equal. We also model the data stream with four equal-sized data regions, $r_1, \ldots, r_4$. Fig. 4 shows the access relationship between queries and data regions. Then the priority of data regions are $P(r_1) < P(r_2) < P(r_3) < P(r_4)$.

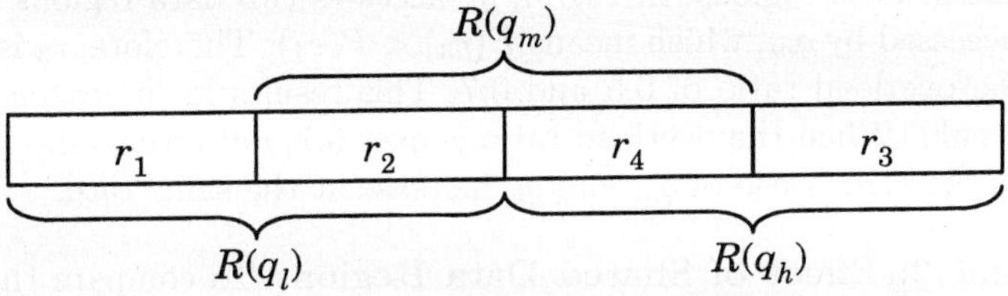

Fig. 4. The access relationship between queries and data regions in a data stream

The input parameters of the simulator are an *overload ratio* and a *relative frequency* of data region. The overload ratio is defined as (current load − system capacity) / current load. We change the overload ratio from 0.1 to 0.8, representing the excess load between +11% to +400% of the system capacity. We make three types of frequency settings:

- **Low-major** $F(r_1) : F(r_2) : F(r_3) : F(r_4) = 8 : 4 : 2 : 1$
- **Uniform** $F(r_1) : F(r_2) : F(r_3) : F(r_4) = 1 : 1 : 1 : 1$
- **High-major** $F(r_1) : F(r_2) : F(r_3) : F(r_4) = 1 : 2 : 4 : 8$

The low-major setting represents a case where most of data items have low-priority, while the high-major setting models the reverse case. The uniform setting models the evenly distributed case. Note that every query has same processing cost, but data regions r_2 and r_4 are accessed by two queries. So the cost rate of data regions is $1 : 2 : 1 : 2$. We can calculate the rate of normalized cost by multiplying the frequency rate and the cost rate. For example, the rate of normalized cost at the low-major setting becomes $8 : 8 : 2 : 2$.

The performance metric of experiments is an *error ratio* of each query. Suppose that for a query q, A = number of data items satisfying the predicate of q with an original data stream, and A' = number of data items satisfying the predicate of q after load shedding. While A should not be calculated in practice at the overload state, we can get the value by assuming the infinite system capacity at the simulation. Then the error ratio of q is defined as $\frac{A-A'}{A}$.

4.2 Experiment Results

Experiment 1: Comparison with Random Algorithm. We first compare the performance of our algorithm with the random load shedding algorithm. Fig. 5(a) shows the experiment results. The uniform frequency setting is used.

As expected, the high-priority query (q_h) performs best and can output exact answers until the overload ratio is 0.5. The error ratio of medium priority query (q_m) is between q_l and q_h. The low-priority query (q_l) performs worst. When the overload ratio is over 0.5, q_l cannot output any answers. This is contrary to the random algorithm, where the error ratio of every query is same and increasing as the overload ratio increases.

In the overload ratio interval between 0.5 and 0.7, an interesting observation is that the error ratio of q_h increases while that of q_m is fixed. This is due to the effect of shared data regions. In Fig. 4, q_h accesses two data regions r_3 and r_4. r_4 is also accessed by q_m, which means $P(r_3) < P(r_4)$. Therefore, r_3 is shed first between the overload ratio of 0.5 and 0.7. This results in increasing the error ratio of q_h only. When the overload ratio is over 0.7, data items in r_4 begins to shed. Then the error ratio of q_m and q_h increase at the same rate.

Experiment 2: Effect of Shared Data Region. To compare the effect of shared data regions in detail, we change the access relationship between queries and data regions as follows: $R(q_l) = \{r_1\}, R(q_m) = \{r_2\}, R(q_h) = \{r_3\}$. Each query accesses a disjoin data region. The frequency setting is uniform, hence $F(r_1) : F(r_2) : F(r_3) = 1 : 1 : 1$. Fig. 5(b) shows the experiment results.

Compared to Experiment 1, the performance difference of each query becomes more distinguished. A query can output exact answers until the load of queries with lower priorities are completely shed. For example, q_m can output exact answers until the overload ratio is 0.3, because all the load shedding performs at r_1 only. Similarly, q_h starts to make errors from the overload ratio of 0.7, where the error ratio of q_l and q_m are 1.

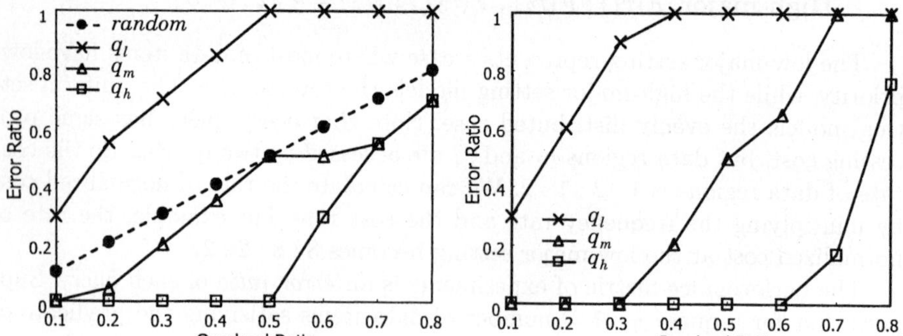

(a) Experiment 1 (b) Experiment 2

Fig. 5. Results of Experiment 1 and Experiment 2

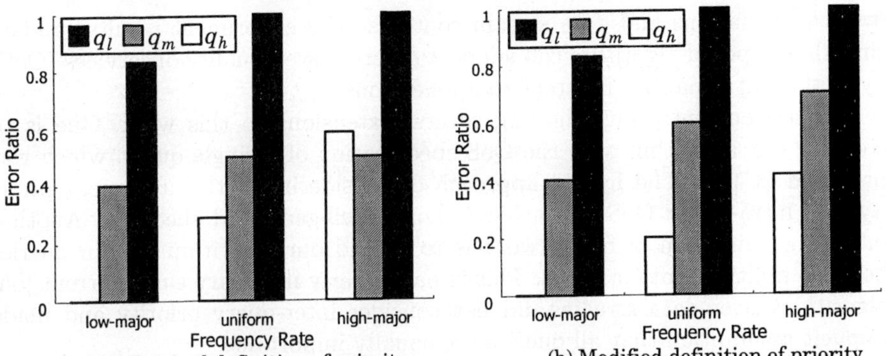

(a) Original definition of priority

(b) Modified definition of priority

Fig. 6. Results of Experiment 3

Experiment 3: Effect of Frequency and Priority. Our last experiment changes the frequency setting from low-major to uniform and high-major. The access relationship of Fig. 4 is used. The overload ratio is set to 0.6. Fig. 6(a) shows the experiment results. At the low-major setting, shedding low-priority data regions is enough to remove the excess load. So the error ratio of q_h is 0. However, at uniform and high-major settings, low-priority data regions occupy only a small fraction of total load. This means that data regions accessed by q_h need to be shed also. As a result, the error ratio of q_h increases.

An important observation of Fig. 6(a) is that the error ratio of q_h is higher than q_m at the high-major setting. This is not strange since we define the priority of a data region as a *sum* of priorities of queries accessing the data region. Specifically, at Fig. 4, $P(r_3) < P(r_4)$ and r_3 is shed first before r_4. If shedding r_3 drops larger portion of data items accessed by q_h than shedding r_2 of q_m, then the error ratio of q_h would be higher than that of q_m. We can modify the priority definition of a data region as the *maximum* priority among queries accessing the data region. Fig. 6(b) shows the result of our algorithm using this definition. The error ratio of q_h is always lower than q_m. There are tradeoffs between these two priority definitions of a data region. In case of sum, we can prioritize data items accessed by multiple queries. So it is well matched to applications where the priority has a role to the weighted vote. In case of maximum, we can support real-time applications where high-priority queries always have to be processed with best effort. Note that our algorithm can support both applications by adapting the priority definition of a data region.

5 Concluding Remarks

In this paper, we proposed a semantic load shedding algorithm for continuous queries over data streams. The proposed algorithm is novel in the sense that it considers the priority of queries. Specifically, the proposed algorithm sheds load from the less important queries before affecting the more important queries. We also explored the performance of the proposed algorithm under a wide variety of overload situations and data stream contents. The experiment results validate that the proposed algorithm can support differentiated quality of services (QoS) by exploiting semantics inherent to applications.

We are currently investigating several extensions to this work. One is to combine our algorithm with the QoS specification of a single query, which was proposed at [11]. The hybrid approach of considering both inter-query priority and intra-query QoS can achieve more intelligent load shedding. Another interesting direction of future work is to extend our algorithm to join queries between multiple data streams. This is particularly necessary since current join algorithms over data streams did not consider inter-query priority and made implicit assumption that all queries are equally important.

References

1. Abadi, D., Carney, D., Cetintemel, U., Cherniack, M., Convey, C., Lee, S., Stonebraker, M., Tatbul, N., Zdonik, S.: Aurora: A New Model and Architecture for Data Stream Management. VLDB J. 12(2) (2003) 120-139
2. Arasu, A., Babcock, B., Babu, S., McAlister, J., Widom, J.: Characterizing Memory Requirements for Queries over Continuous Data Streams. ACM Trans. Database Syst. 29(1) (2004) 162-194
3. Ayad, A., Naughton, J.: Static Optimization of Conjunctive Queries with Sliding Windows over Infinite Streams. In: Proc. ACM SIGMOD (2004) 419-430
4. Babcock, B., Babu, S., Datar, M., Motwani, R., Widow, J.: Models and Issues in Data Stream Systems. In: Proc. ACM PODS (2002) 1-16
5. Babcock, B., Datar, M., Motwani, R.: Load Shedding for Aggregation Queries over Data Streams. In: Proc. 20th ICDE. (2004) 1-12
6. Chandrasekaran, S., Franklin, M.: PSoup: A System for Streaming Queries over Streaming Data. VLDB J. 12(2) (2003) 140-156
7. Das, A., Gehrke, J., Riedewald, M.: Approximate Join Processing over Data Streams. In: Proc. ACM SIGMOD (2003) 40-51
8. Gehrke, J. (ed.): Special Issue on Data Stream Processing. IEEE Data Eng. Bull. (2003)
9. Kang, T., Naughton, J., Viglas, S.: Evaluating Window Joins over Unbounded Streams. In: Proc. 19th ICDE. (2003) 341-352
10. Schwetmann, H.: User's Guide of CSIM18 Simulation Engine. Mesquite Software, Inc. (1996)
11. Tatbul, N., Cetintemel, U., Zdonik, S., Cherniack, M., Stonebraker, M.: Load Shedding in a Data Stream Manager. In: Proc. 29th VLDB Conf. (2003) 309-320

Probabilistic Point Queries over Network-Based Movements

Utku Kalay and Oya Kalıpsız

Computer Engineering Department,
Faculty of Electrical-Electronics Engineering,
Yıldız Technical University, 34349 Beşiktaş, Istanbul

Abstract. Spatial-temporal environments contain large number of continuously moving objects on which variety of queries are executed, preferably within a real time. In such a dynamic system, processing location-based queries is a challenging problem. In this paper, the dynamic system has objects moving over a road of network. This paper proposes a new uncertainty model for this type of dynamic system. We applied this model on the indexing scheme that has recently been proposed, namely MON-tree. With our uncertainty model, we also explored a probabilistic query execution algorithm. For the purpose of an experimental evaluation, we set up a simulation environment that visualizes the movements and also provides a query processing capability. To achieve a better index storage utilization and query execution performance, we decreased the location update frequency of the dataset.

1 Introduction

The mobility is the most distinguishing feature for the mobile computing applications. The primary difficulty in mobile computing arises from the nature of the dynamic attributes. In literature, designing robust indexing structures for such dynamic attributes has been extensively studied recently. There are many research sub-areas distinguishing each other based on the constraints such as the dimension size, shape of objects, motion types and topology. These constraints are important while modeling the system; on the other hand, query types (range query, k-NN query i.e.) applied to the system is another important decision parameter while designing the index structures.

In this paper, we are going to deal with the objects that are moving in a 2-dimensional space, especially moving on a predefined network of lines. Handling with the range queries about the past location information of the moving points over a network of roads is originally done in [1] under the name of MON-tree. Since the network nodes and connectivity bound the motion vector, this constraint can be efficiently exploited during the design of the indexing scheme. This is actually the motivation for designing the MON-tree. In this paper, based on a simple motion vector model under the assumption of an uncertainty, we set up a simulation test bed to generate the moving objects over a network. Then, we implemented MON-tree structure indexing the locations of this dynamic set. We focused on executing point location queries such that we are interested with the objects that are going to reach the query

P. Yolum et al.(Eds.): ISCIS 2005, LNCS 3733, pp. 823 – 832, 2005.

point within a predefined time. As a contribution in this paper, we developed a variant of a probabilistic query execution approach which is originally defined in [2]. Our probabilistic solution is for querying over the network movements.

In section 2, we briefly explain the network and movement models that we used in our experiments. MON-tree and our observations on this structure are studied in Section 3. In section 4, we propose the probabilistic point query execution. Section 5 presents the experimental results. Section 6 concludes the paper.

2 Modeling

We have two models implemented, one for the network and the other for the movement of objects.

2.1 The Network Model

The network, representing a roadmap, consists of nodes that are connected to each other with a line-segment. We define edges between any of two *cross-points* or open-ended points. The cross-point is the intersecting point of more than two line-segments.

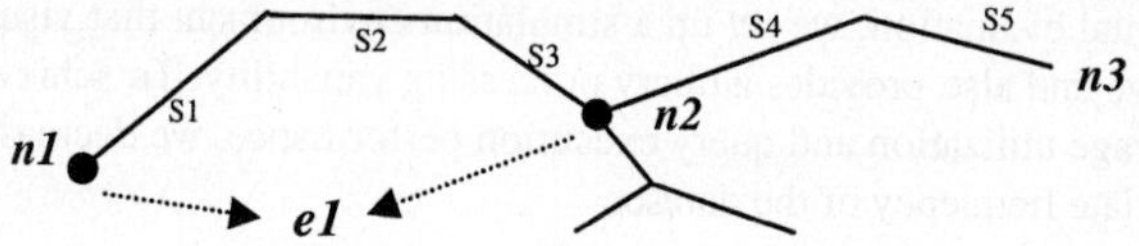

Fig. 1. A small portion of a road-network. ***e1***, an edge between the nodes ***n1*** and ***n2***, consists of 3 line-segments, namely, *s1, s2,* and *s3.* Note that *n1* is an open-ended point, whereas *n2* is a cross-point.

2.2 The Uncertainty Model

Due to the fact that the future locations of moving points are naturally imprecise, we need to define an uncertain motion model. In [3], the *uncertainty* is defined as the size of the area in which the object can possibly be at a specific time, *t*. Additionally; the *deviation* of a moving object *m* at a particular point in time *t* is defined as the distance between the actual location and its database location at time *t*.

Before discussing the uncertainty, consider the case that there has no uncertainty. In that case, the exact speed and direction of the movement are known. This model requires updates at the database when the motion vector changes; in other words when the direction and/or velocity changes. Based on the assumption of a motion vector that is linear with constant speed, the location between two reported positions can easily be found with linear functions. Having said this, applying the certain movement model would produce high number of updates, because this model requires strict synchronization with the objects motion updates. Additionally, in our network model, large number of small length segments is the other factor that causes frequent updates. Thus, to keep up with more realistic scenarios that have high agility, it is inevitable to use the uncertainty model.

Of the uncertainty models in literature, the most common one is that, at any point in time, the location of the object is within a certain distance of its last reported position. Therefore, this model requires updating when the object leaves the predefined threshold distance.

As a minor modification to this model, we used predefined update interval time in our implementation rather than using a threshold distance. In the simulation, a ***m***aximum ***u***pdate ***i***nterval *(mui)* time value is the threshold value to update the locations of the objects. We fixed the *mui* value for each moving object. Thus, an object reports a location update either when its *mui* value is up or it is at end of an edge. It is important to note that the object does not send an update at the end of a segment even though its motion vector changes. We defer discussing the advantages/disadvantages of this model until inserting the movements into the index structure (at section 3).

Note that the uncertainty region starts to expand after the time of update until it reaches its maximum at the end of *mui*. Since the object moves on a network, the uncertainty region is a group of connected segments. (See Fig.2 for an example)

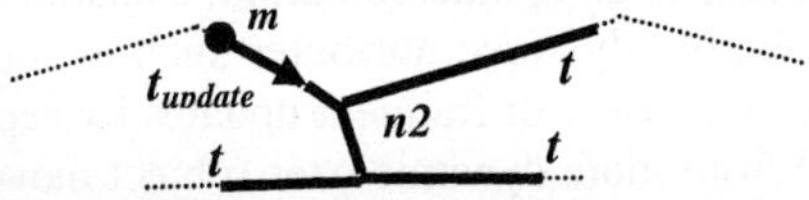

Fig. 2. The thick lines depict the uncertainty region of object, ***m*** traveling towards node ***n2***. t_{update} is the time of last update while t is the time of observation, such that $t_{update} \leq t \leq t_{update}+mui$. Note that there 3 are possible paths, each of which has a length of $[v_{max}*(t - t_{update})]$, that is, v_{max} is the highest allowable velocity of ***m*** for this *mui* period.

In fact, we are unable to say the exact location of the object between two consecutive update times, due to the fact that the velocity is not stable between two consecutive update points. As defined at the beginning of this section, it is the *deviation* that gives the distance between the actual location and the database location at time *t*. We used Gaussian random variable *(r.v.)* to represent the velocity of each object. Actually, this leads the object locations to follow the Gaussian distribution inside the uncertainty region. It is a good idea to choose Gaussian distribution because it is a good mathematical model for many types of physically observed random phenomena including our case.

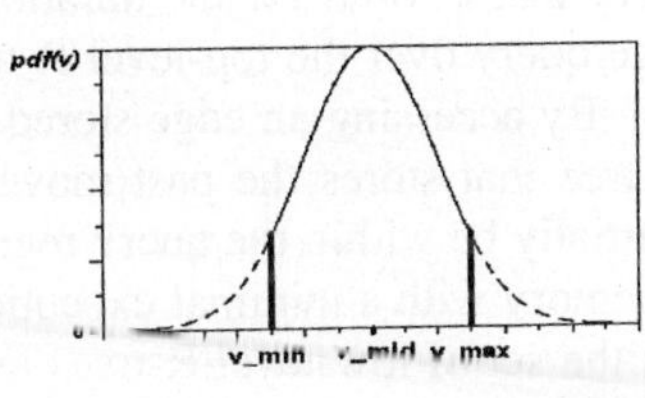

Fig. 3. Velocity of a moving object following Gaussian distribution. In our environment, the object velocity is between a lower and upper limit values, i.e. v_{min} and v_{max}. This introduces the modified ***pdf*** of velocity *r.v.* (and object location *r.v.*) that has Gaussian characteristics.

3 Network-Based Spatial-Temporal Indexing

MON-tree is an efficient organization of a group of R-tree [4], which is a widely used spatial index structure. (See Fig.4)

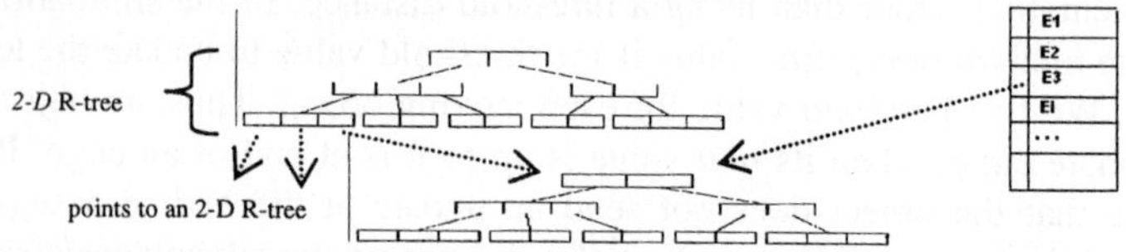

Fig. 4. MON-tree is a 2-level organization of a set of 2D R-trees. Hash table is an auxiliary structure to directly access the movements on a specific edge by hashing an edge, E_i to the corresponding low-level R-tree.

When indexing dynamic attributes, the main problem is the frequent update on the index. Due to the high cost of an update operation; a spatial index structure can not be directly used to index highly dynamic attributes such as location. The MON-tree index eliminates the negative effect of frequent updates by separating the stable characteristics (like the edge) from more dynamic ones (object movements). Basically, it consists of an R-tree at the upper level indexing the edges of the network that had traffic on it, and a number of lower level R-trees, each of which stores the movements along the corresponding edge. Thus, the number of low-level R-trees is equal to the total number of edges at leaves of the top level R-tree. It is important to note that top-level R-tree does not contain all edges of the network so that insertion to top-level R-tree occurs only when any object enters an edge that has not been visited before by any of the objects. This approach makes the top-level R-tree relatively small depending on the size of the dataset and/or the duration of the simulation length. In addition to the R-tree set, a hash table is used to map the edges inserted in the top-level R-tree to the lower R-tree in order to avoid searching the top-level R-tree for each object movement insertion. The top-level R-tree is in fact used for the purpose of the range query.

An object movement is represented as a rectangle *(p1, p2, t1, t2)*, which means an object motion starts at *p1* part of an edge, E_i at time t1, and ends its movement at *p2* part of E_i at time *t2*.

Now, think of a spatial-temporal range query, $Q\ (q_{spatial}, t1, t2)$, where $q_{spatial}$ is a traditional spatial range query that is valid for the duration from *t1* to *t2*. At the first step, $q_{spatial}$ is the static range query over the top-level R-tree that finds the edges that are covered by query region. By accessing an edge stored in the top-level, we get the corresponding low-level R-tree that stores the past movements on this edge. Moreover, since the edge may partially be within the query region, the covered parts of the edge are selected in main memory with a minimal execution overhead. Therefore, the output from the first step is the set of low-level R-trees and a query set that contains the part of edges covered by the query region, ***w***. Then, the second step is to find the moving objects of which past movement regions are intersecting with any query region in ***w***. That is actually done by another range query executions over the low-level R-trees found in the first step. Detailed explanation on this range query execution and performance improvements can be found in [1] for more interested readers.

We implemented MON-tree index structure as it is originally described in [1]. MON-tree originally keeps movements based on the motion vector updates. This results in many updates when the objects mostly travel on small-length line-segments. In our experiments, we figured out that most updates occur at the end-of-segment points in the network rather than on the segment-lines. This is a valid indication especially for the road-networks that have many small line-segments (i.e. city roads). In addition, when we increase the *mui (maximum update interval)* parameter; the number of updates on the segment lines decreases dramatically, while the number of updates at the end-of-segment points shows minor decreases. In other words, increasing the *mui* does not alleviate the high update rate resulting from end-of-segment points. Table 1 shows the number of updates at the critical locations for a sample simulation with a length of $T=100$.

Table 1. Number of updates at the critical locations for a sample simulation with a length of $T=100$. Last column shows the execution time for a sample range query. As expected, while the number of insertions decrease, the index becomes more compact resulting in better execution overhead.

mui (timeunits)	# of onSegment updates	# of end-of-segment updates	# of end-of-edge updates	Execution Time*(msec)*
1	5903	3400	553	31
5	628	3116	473	31
15	69	2906	462	15

Instead of recording movements based on the motion vector change, we applied the uncertainty model that we presented in the Section 2 in our MON-tree implementation. With this uncertainty model, we propose to select longer movements to construct the low-level R-tree of the MON-tree as opposed to having small movements inserted into low-level R-tree.

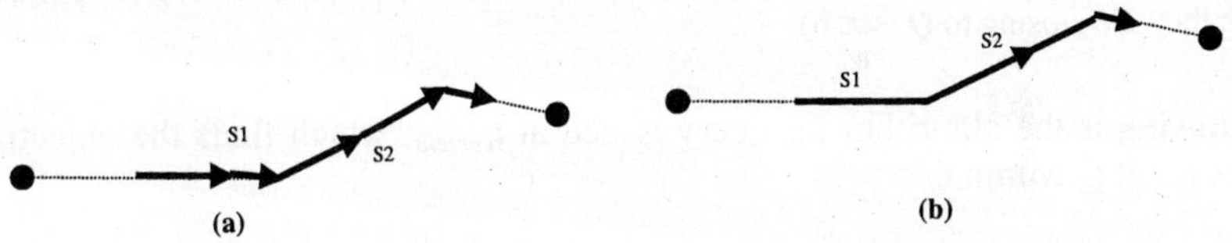

Fig. 5. Trace recordings of a moving object, which are inserted into MON-tree. (a) shows the traces with low ***mui*** value with updates at the end of segment. (b) shows the traces with high ***mui*** value without updates at the end of line-segments.

At this point, another important issue is the precision. The process of making movements coarser essentially brings the crucial concept of correctness of the result set. To tackle this drawback, we propose a probabilistic range query approach for the network-based movements. Applying uncertainty model (while increasing the *mui*) not only affects the query results on future events, it is also required to use probability model for executing queries about past recordings. However, we will handle the first case in this paper, which is about finding the objects that are expected to reach a query point within a given time in future.

4 Probabilistic Point Query

Probabilistic Range Query *(PRQ)* is generally defined in the literature [2],[3]:

Definition. Probabilistic Range Query (PRQ): Given a closed region R and a set of n objects O_1, O_2, ...O_n with uncertainty regions and probability density functions at time t_0, a PRQ returns a set of tuple in the form of (O_i, p_i), where p_i is the nonzero probability that O_i is located inside R at time t_0.

In this paper, instead of the region query, we will take the query as a point. We are interested with the moving objects, m_i, within the distance so that m_i has a non-zero probability to reach the query point within the predefined time units, t_q. For example, suppose that we are searching the ambulances that will arrive at the place of an accident within the next 20 time units (see Fig6 for an example). To execute this kind of query, we followed a 2-step procedure. At first step, namely *QueryExec&Filter* step, we need to find the result set that contains the possible set of moving objects having a non-zero probability of being in the place of the accident on time. Then, in the second step, we determine the probability of each element in the result set based on the uncertainty model.

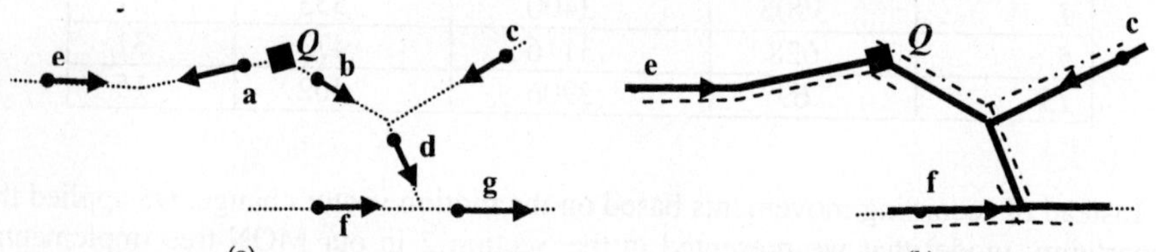

(a) (b)

Fig. 6. A scenario that has a query point, ***Q*** and a number of moving points (see a). After executing the first step of query execution, we eliminate the elements that are getting far away from ***Q*** *(eliminate a,b,d,g)* and that are too far so that they are unable to reach ***Q*** in t_q*(eliminate f)*, even they are closing to ***Q*** (see b).

Following is the algorithm for query issued at $t_{current}$, which finds the objects that reaches point ***Q*** within t_q.

Algorithm: FindObjectsReachingToPoint (Q, t_q)
Step1: *(QueryExec & Filter)*
(1a). Issue a point query E_i := **PointLocation**(Q) that finds the edge that Q is on.
(1b). Determine the maximum distance d_{max}:=(V_{max} * t_q).
(1c). Traverse form E_i to find the nearest segments that are within the distance (d_{max}) from Q. Let this list of segment be *seg_list*.
(1d). Select the list of moving objects that are currently on the *seg_list*. Let it be *S1*.
(1.e). Eliminate the objects from *S1* that are getting far away from Q to construct the *S*.
Step 2: *(Finding Probabilities)*
(2a). for i←1 to | *S* | do
i.) A ← $U_i(t_{current}) \cap seg\_list$
ii.) if (A ≠ 0) then
p_i←***Prob***(following the correct path) * ***Prob***(reach)

In the algorithm above, *PointLocation* (*Q*) at *(1a)* is a typical range query algorithm that finds the edge intersecting with point ***Q***. This query is executed on the first level of the MON-tree. At *(1b)*, we find maximum possible distance that an object can be away from the position at the time of its last update. Note that at *(1c)*, we find the nearest edges based on the network distance by using network connectivity. It is also important to observe that ***S*** contains the objects that have a possible set of objects having a non-zero probability to reach point ***Q***.

In Fig.6(b), the bold region on the network shows the ***seg_list*** in the Algorithm. Additionally, the dashed lines distinctly shows each object's uncertainty region, which is represented with $U_i(t_{current})$ in the Algorithm. At step *(2ai)*, ***A*** is not always greater than zero, because set ***S*** has only those objects of which are able to reach ***Q*** in case of moving with V_{max}. We use V_{max} as a global system parameter that defines a maximum velocity that any object can have, while v_{max} denotes the maximum velocity of the object during a *mui* period. Observe that object *f*, even within d_{max}, has an uncertainty region that does not expand to ***Q*** at the time of query, $t_{current}$. It means that object *f* with its current motion characteristics is unable to reach ***Q*** on time, even though this situation may change in future.

At *(2aii)*, we calculate $\mathbf{p_i}$, which is the probability of each object to reach ***Q***. The first multiplier, the probability to follow the path reaching ***Q*** is *Prob*(following the correct path). Assuming the objects at the end of a segment choose the next segment with a uniform distribution, following is the probability to follow the path that takes the object to ***Q***.

$$Prob(\text{following the correct path}) = \prod_{i=1}^{u} 1/ki \tag{1}$$

***u**: # of decision points,* $\mathbf{k_i}$ *: # of possible selections at the* i^{th} *decision point*

Assume that an object requires number of ***u*** independent decisions until it reaches ***Q***, each of which has a probability of $(\mathbf{1/k_i})$ to select the correct path to reach ***Q***. We chose the shortest path to ***Q*** and ignored the longer paths in our implementations.

The second multiplier of $\mathbf{p_i}$, ***Prob(reach)***, is a typical probability calculation on the Gaussian distribution. Derived from Fig3 that shows *pdf* of velocity, the *pdf* of an object location, ***X*** for the following time units is shown in Fig.7 below. Note that ***X*** is a random variable denoting the distance from the last reported location of the object. Additionally, let d_o denote the network distance of the object from its last reported position to ***Q***. It is important to note that, d_{max} is always between $(t_q{*}V_{min})$ and $(t_q{*}V_{max})$. Therefore, d_o is always between $(t_q{*}v_{min})$ and $(t_q{*}v_{max})$. Thus, the probability of being at ***Q*** is found by taking the integral of $f_X(x)$ from d_o to $(t_q{*}v_{max})$ as following:

$$Prob(\text{reach}) = \int_{d_0}^{t_q * v_{max}} f_X(x)dx\,, \quad f_X(x)\text{: Normal distribution with } (t_q * \bar{v}) \tag{2}$$

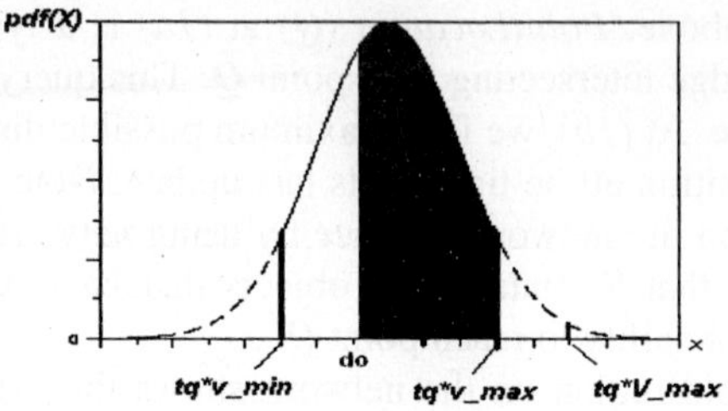

Fig. 7. *pdf* of distance from the object's last reported position at the time, $t_{current} + t_q$

Since we assume that the distribution of selecting the new segment on its way is independent from each of other path selections and from the distribution of the velocity, at last we calculate the probability of each object in **S** as the following:

$$p_i = Prob(\text{following the correct path}) * Prob(\text{reach}) \quad (3)$$

5 Experiments

Based on the models discussed in the previous sections, we implemented a simulation environment so that we could visualize the moving objects traveling over a network of roads and query results on this dynamic dataset. Each object in the system has a simple shape of point. Consequently, our dynamic system corresponds to a 3-dimensional coordinate system, 2-axes for the location and 1 for the time. Visualization seems to be a natural way of verifying the query results over a large number of moving objects. Once the traffic generator generators the traffic over the predefined network, it is possible to execute many types of queries over this series of movements. At the time of issuing this paper, we completed our studies on range queries about the past events and point location queries over the near-future events.

We developed the simulation program executing within time duration of *T*. As seen in Fig. 8, in the simulation architecture, we have two generators, *Road Network Generator (RNG)* and *Network Traffic Generator (NTG)*. *RNG* is a static generator that generates a network connectivity based on the model discussed in the modeling section by reading this information from a text file. In our simulation environment, we assumed that the network is completely in main memory. We used appropriate main memory data structures that reflect the connectivity of the network. In fact, for large networks, our assumption is not applicable. Partitioning the network appropriately to store each partition in the disk page requires clustering algorithms, which is beyond the scope of this paper.

NTG randomly generates objects moving over the network for duration of time, *T*. *NTG* updates the motion vectors of a group of objects at each time step based on the initialization parameters, such as agility and maximum update interval *(mui)*. While the motion vector of each object at each time step is stored in a text file, the trajectory of each point is updated in the index structure. After completion of the generating data set and constructing the corresponding index, the visualization module reads the text file to show the trace of movements. At the same time, query processing module use the index structure to execute the queries in a real time manner.

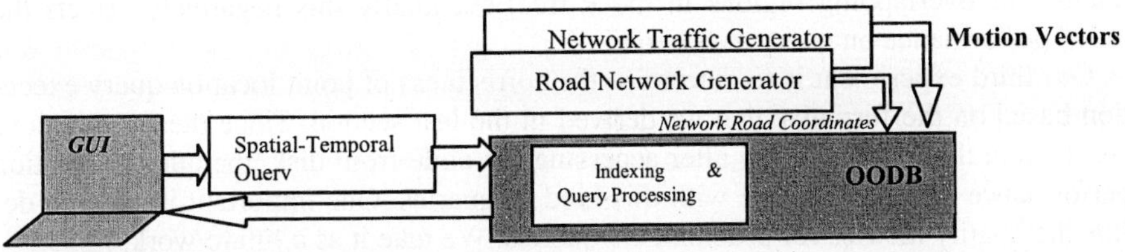

Fig. 8. Simulation system architecture. *Indexing* module supports R-tree index and its variants. We used spatial index implementations in Java programming language[5], with minor modifications to coordinate our simulation scenario to run queries on MON-tree.

Table 2. Parameters used in the Experiments

Parameters	Meaning	Values
mui	maximum update interval	1 to 20
V_{max}	overall maximum velocity for any object	3.2 miles/minute
v_{min}, v_{max}	min/max velocity of an object during a *mui* interval	$v_{max} \leq V_{max}$
T	simulation length in time steps	200
ds	dataset size	400

Recall that by increasing the *mui* value, sampling rate decrease and we get more compact index structure. Fig.9(a) shows the number of total nodes at the MON-tree, while we change the *mui* value.

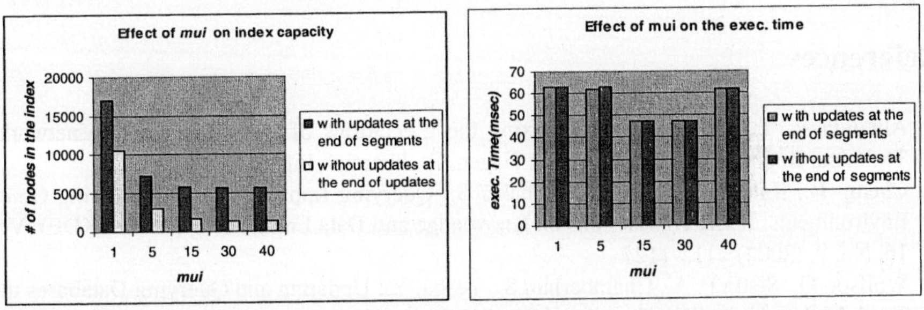

Fig. 9. (a)The effect of *mui* on the size of index. Index nodes corresponds to 4096-byte disk pages. (b) The effect of *mui* on the execution time of a sample query.

Note that after a threshold *mui* value, for both cases, the capacity is no longer diminishing. This threshold value actually indicates the expected value of traveling duration over the edges over the network. Thus, larger *mui* values than this does not affect the index size, because reaching the end of edge causes insertions to index.

Our second experiment is to study how the index size affects the execution performance of sample range queries. Fig.9(b) shows that around the same threshold values of *mui* that we found at Fig.9(a), executing a sample range query gives best results. After that value (i.e. when *mui* is 40), the execution time increases. In our opinion, this is because of larger movements (represented with rectangles) inserted in the low-level R-trees due to high value of *mui*. Since larger rectangles results in high number of overlapping regions in the R-tree, eventually this negatively affects the index performance on query execution.

Our third experiment is to determine the correctness of point location query execution based on the formulas that we derived in the last section. Since these executions are done in the main memory after accessing the node from disk, the query execution performance does not change with this kind of queries. One important issue is to define the quality metrics for probabilistic queries. We take it as a future work.

6 Summary

In this study, we analyze the network-based index structure, MON-tree, with regard to its capacity and query execution performance. In order to decrease the index capacity for better storage efficiency, we propose a motion model that keeps up with the dynamic objects with a lower sampling rate. Additionally, since less sampling results in imprecision on the object locations, we proposed an uncertainty model which leads us to define probabilistic execution model for network-based queries.

Of various types of queries, we studied range query over past movements on the network, which is already done in [1] without an uncertainty model. With our uncertainty model while decreasing the number of insertions into index, we achieved better storage utilization. In addition to that, we derived probabilistic point query formulas based on the studies done in [2] and basic calculations in probability theory.

In future, we plan to study on probabilistic k-NN query execution over the network-based moving objects.

References

1. Almeida V. T., Güting R. H.: Indexing the trajectories of moving objects in networks. Technical Report 309, Fernuniversitat Hagen, Fachbereich Informatik. (2004)
2. Cheng R., Kalashnikov D. V., Prabhakar S.: Querying Imprecise Data in Moving Object Environments. IEEE Transactions on Knowledge and Data Engineering (IEEE TKDE), Vol. 16, No. 9. (2004) 1112-1127
3. Wolfson O., Sistla P. A., Chamberlain S., Yesha, Y.: Updating and Querying Databases that Track Mobile Units. Distributed and Parallel Databases, vol.7, no.3. (1999) 257-387
4. Guttman A.: R-trees: A Dynamic Index Structure for Spatial Searching. Proceedings of the ACM SIGMOD. (1984)
5. Spatial Index Library. http://www.cs.ucr.edu/~marioh/spatialindex/index.html, (2005)

Effective Clustering by Iterative Approach

Tansel Özyer[1] and Reda Alhajj[1,2]

[1] Department of Computer Science, University of Calgary, Calgary, Alberta, Canada
{ozyer, alhajj}@cpsc.ucalgary.ca

[2] Department of Computer Science, Global University, Beirut, Lebanon

Abstract. In this study, we present multi-objective genetic algorithm based iterative clustering approach. Two objectives are employed in the process: minimizing the within cluster similarity and maximizing the difference between the clusters: inter-cluster distance (average linkage, centroid linkage, complete linkage and average to centroid linkage) versus intra-cluster distance (total within cluster variation). The proposed approach is iterative in the sense that it basically tries possible partitioning of the dataset for the given range of clusters one by one; the result of the previous partitioning n favors that of the current solution *n+1*. In order to achieve this, we identified a global k-means operator and we do "what if" analysis in the aspect of the objectives to see the better initialization in case the number of clusters is increased by one. After evaluating all, a feedback mechanism is supplied at the back-end to analyze the partitioning results with different indices. The entire system has been tested with a real world dataset: glass. The reported results demonstrate the applicability and effectiveness of the proposed approach.

Keywords: data mining, clustering, multi-objective optimization, validity analysis, alternative partitioning.

1 Introduction

Clustering refers to methods for grouping unlabeled data. Several clustering approaches have been proposed so far [1] for different types of data such as web data, documents, biological data, financial data, etc. The motto behind clustering is to partition the data into homogeneous subgroups with less variability; clustering algorithms intuitively favor these two criteria. It would be more suitable to take into account these two criteria leading to all possible optimal solutions. So, a good framework for cluster validation is needed for the assessment of the number of clusters. Our motivation is that clustering is based on two famous objectives, namely homogeneity and separateness. During the clustering process, the intention is to find homogeneous (less variable) instance groups and separate the clusters as much as possible to clarify the distinction between them [1].

Despite the fact that clustering is explained with two objectives, in general the outcome of the clustering process is based on error minimization, such that a

P. Yolum et al.(Eds.): ISCIS 2005, LNCS 3733, pp. 833–842, 2005.

model is improved with respect to Error(Model, Data) where Model is described by the mean, standard variance, maximum likelihood, residual analysis, etc. Homogeneity and separateness may be the two criteria to be taken into account. Awareness of these two objectives all the time leads to many possible solutions automatically without any need for justifying the weight of the criteria.

The work described in this paper is the second phase of our ongoing project to improve the utilization of multi-objectivity in clustering. During the first phase, we tested different objectives and achieved promising results [2,3,4]; Euclidean distance was used for the hard clustering, where an object is a member of one and only one cluster. The obtained results were also validated with different internal assessment criteria from the R-Project fpc and cclust packages(traceW, rubin, c-index, db, silhouette, hubertgamma, dunn). On the other hand, we used for the second phase described in this paper an iterative model that does evaluate the partitioning one by one. By doing so, it is aimed at having accurate results given the possible optimal number of clusters to be tested. The contributions of the work described in this paper are: 1) applying an iterative clustering process that uses the results for number of clusters n as initialization to the next step $n+1$; 2) trying the new objective functions: homogeneity (total within cluster variation) and separateness (average linkage, centroid linkage, complete linkage and average to centroid linkage); 3) using the validity indices scott, friedman, ball, ratkowsky, calinski, hartigan, mariott, tracecovW, traceW, rubin, Hubert, db, ssi, dunn, silhouette to give a feedback to suggest the best possible partitioning. Finally, the entire system has been tested with a real world dataset: glass. The reported results demonstrate the effectiveness of the proposed approach.

The rest of the paper is as follows. The proposed system is described in Section 2. The experiments and the results are reported in Section 3. Section 4 is summary and conclusions.

2 Alternative Clustering by Multi-objective Iterative Approach

Our system is composed of two components. The first is multi-objective, which uses a list of parameters to drive the evaluation procedure as in the other genetic types of algorithms, including population size (number of chromosomes), number of comparison set (t_dom) representing the assumed non-dominated set, crossover, mutation probability and the number of iterations needed to obtain the result. The second part involves applying validity analysis to decide on the appropriate clustering from the alternatives produced by the first part.

Sub-goals can be defined as fitness functions; and instead of scalarizing them to find the goal as the overall fitness function with the user defined weight values, we expect the system to find the set of optimal solutions, i.e., the pareto-optimal front. By using the specified formulas, at each generation, each chromosome in the population is evaluated and assigned a value for each fitness function. As discussed above, we have two main criteria: homogeneity and separateness. For the separateness we used the inter-cluster separability formulas given next:

$$\textbf{Average Linkage}: d(C,D) = \frac{1}{|C|.|D|}\sum_{\substack{x\in C,\\ y\in D}} d(x,y) \qquad (1)$$

(Note that the cardinality of C and D may be omitted to reduce the scaling factor).

$$\textbf{Complete Linkage:}\mathrm{d(C,D)} = \max_{\substack{x\in C,\\ y\in D}} d(x,y) \qquad (2)$$

$$\textbf{Centroid Linkage:}\mathrm{d(C,D)} = d(v_C, v_D) \qquad (3)$$

where v_C and v_D are the centroids of the two clusters.

$$\textbf{Average to Centroid:} d(C,D) = \frac{1}{|C|+|D|}\left[\sum_{x\in C} d(x,v_D) + \sum_{y\in D} d(y,v_C)\right] \qquad (4)$$

For the homogeneity we used the the intra-cluster distance formula given next:

$$TWCV = \sum_{n=1}^{N}\sum_{d=1}^{D} X_{nd}^2 - \sum_{k=1}^{K}\frac{1}{Z_k}\sum_{d=1}^{D} SF_{kd}^2 \qquad (5)$$

where $X_1, X_2,..,X_N$ are the N objects, X_{nd} denotes feature d of pattern X_n (n= 1 to N). SF_{kd} is the sum of the dth features of all the patterns in cluster $k(G_k)$ and Z_k denotes the number of patterns in cluster $k(G_k)$ and SF_{kd} is:

$$SF_{kd} = \sum_{\overrightarrow{x_n}\in G_k} X_{nd}\ , \quad (d = 1, 2, ...D). \qquad (6)$$

We modified both objectives into minimization: the separateness value is multiplied by -1 for the minimization. After that both are normalized by dividing the values by their maximum corresponding values.

Individual coding in the population is a chromosome of length n; the number of instances in the data set is given in Table 1. Every gene is represented by an allele where allele i is the corresponding cluster value of instance i in the data set. In other words, each allele in the chromosome takes a value from the set $\{1, 2, \ldots, K\}$, where K is the maximum number of clusters for which we try to get an optimal partitioning.

Each individual suggests a partitioning in the population. If the chromosome should have k clusters, then each gene a_n (n=1 to N) takes different values from

Table 1. Chromosome Representation

Allele#	1	2	3	4	5	....	*n*
Cluster#	2	3	1	3	2	....	2

[1..k]. The employed process is as follows: For every optimal number of clusters value tried in ascending order:

Initially, *current generation* is assigned to zero. Each chromosome takes *number of clusters* parameter within the range 1 to the current optimal number of clusters k. At the very beginning, for the lowest number of clusters, a population with the specified number of chromosomes is created with an equal probability. In order to do this, we used the ordered initialization first. In round order, each allele takes values 1 to k in order, and then those allele value assignments are shuffled within the chromosome randomly by processing the random pairwise swap operation inside the chromosome. By using this method, we can avoid generating illegal strings, which means some clusters do not have any pattern in the string.

Following the first step, the next generation is the selection using pareto domination tournament. In this step, two candidate items picked among (*population size*-t_{dom}) individuals participate in the pareto domination tournament against the t_{dom} individuals for the survival of each in the population. In the selection part, t_{dom} individuals are randomly picked from the population. With two randomly selected chromosome candidates in (*population size*-t_{dom}) individuals, each of the candidates is compared against each individual in the comparison set, t_{dom}. If one candidate has larger total within-cluster variation fitness value and larger number of cluster values than all of the chromosomes in the comparison set, then it is dominated by the comparison set already and will be deleted from the population permanently. Otherwise, it resides in the population.

After the pareto domination tournament, crossover operator is applied on randomly chosen two chromosomes. The crossover operation is carried out on the population with the crossover rate p_c.

The mutation operator on the current population is employed after the crossover. During the mutation, we replace each gene value a_n by a_n' with respect to the probability distribution; for n =1 *to* N simultaneously. a'_n is a cluster number randomly selected from {1, ..., K} with the probability distribution $\{p_1, p_2, \ldots, p_K\}$ defined using the following formula:

$$p_i = \frac{e^{-d(X_n, c_k)}}{\sum_{j=1}^{k} e^{-d(X_n, c_j)}} \tag{7}$$

where $i \in [1..k]$ and $d(X_n, \quad C_k)$ denotes Euclidean distance between pattern X_n and the centroid C_k of the kth cluster; p_i represents the probability interval of mutating gene assigned to cluster i (e.g., Roulette Wheel). Eventually k-means operator [5] is applied to reorganize each object's assigned cluster number. After all the operators are applied, we have twice the number of individuals after having the pareto dominated tournament. We can not give an exact number as equal to the number of initial population size because at each generation candidates are randomly picked for the survival test leading to deletion of one, in case dominated. To halve the number of individuals, having the number of individuals we had, the ranking mechanism proposed in [6] is employed. So, the individuals obtained after crossover, mutation and k-means operator are ranked, and we pick the best individuals for the population in the next generation. Our approach picks the first l individuals by considering the elitism and diversity among $2l$ individuals. Pareto fronts are ranked. Basically, we find the pareto-optimal front and remove the individuals of the pareto-optimal front from $2l$ set and place them in the population to be run in the next generation. In the remaining set, again we get the first pareto-optimal front and we put it in the population and so on. Since we try to get the first l individuals, the last pareto-optimal front may have more individuals required to complete the number of individuals to l; we handle the diversity automatically. We rank them and reduce the objective dimension into one. Then, we sum the normalized value of the objective functions of each individual. We sort them in increasing order and find each individual's total difference from its individual pairs, the one with the closest smaller summed values and the one with the closest greater summed values. After sorting the individuals in terms of each one's total difference in decreasing order, we keep placing from the top as many individuals as we need to complete the population size to l. The reason for doing this is to take the crowding factor into account automatically, so that individuals occurring closer to others are unlikely to be picked. Solutions far apart from the others will be considered for the necessity of diversity. Further details are given in [6]. This method was also suggested as a solution for the elitism and diversity for improvement in NSGA-II. Finally, if the maximum number of generations is reached, or the pre-specified threshold is satisfied then exit; otherwise the next generation is produced.

Eventually, after finding the solution set for the current number of clusters k, we rerun it again for the next number of clusters $(k+1)$; the same sequence of operators is followed but in this case, with a variation. We expect the current solution set to favor in the next round. The individuals ending up with the optimal number of clusters k are tested with what-if analysis such that we experiment the case after making one of the instances as an additional new cluster centroid. That is, the cluster number is incremented by 1 and in this case, we try to see the minimization of homogeneity and maximization of inter-cluster distance objectives result. For the results, we apply the NSGA-II ranking to see which one is the best. The best one is selected as the individual at the initialization for the next round, number of clusters is $k+1$. The idea of finding the possible cluster by incrementing the number of clusters is based on the assumption that the resulting individuals are the optimal solutions obtained. For the next round, if the number of clusters is incremented, the new cluster should be located somewhere to maximize the difference between the total sum of cluster within square of the objects of the current solution k and the separateness of all the points to the possible cluster to be located. That is, the tendency of instances to dismember from their current cluster to be members of the $(k+1)^{st}$ cluster. Here we suggest two ways to follow: 1) put all instances as the new cluster location and try them all to pick the minimum for all the solutions in straightforward manner; 2) randomly pick a number of instances to check with, and pick the minimum.

We adopted the idea of using the second way for our algorithm. We want to look into more diverse and less biased cases within a shorter period. Otherwise, for the individuals ending up with less than the optimal number of clusters k, we perform this analysis more than once. For example, if k=4 and the individual has at most 2 clusters, do this analysis 2 times in order, for 3 and 4. To avoid the premature convergence and adding randomness, we apply the default initialization for this individual, the same as described above, to assign allele values 1,2,..,k+1 and shuffle them.

At the end we used the clustering validation schema described in [7]; the same authors also implemented the cclust package. Instead of picking the maximum and minimum, it is claimed to find a local peak, and positive or negative jump in the index results would be the better case [7]. The maximum difference to the cluster at the left side (scott, ball,$TraceW^{-1}B$):

$$\max_n(i_n - i_{n-1}) \tag{8}$$

The curve has its maximum increase. The maximum difference to the cluster at the right side (ratkowsky)

$$\max_n(i_n - i_{n+1}) \tag{9}$$

The curve has its maximum decrease. The minimum value of the second differences (calinski, hartigan, -marriott, trace covW, $-|T|/|W|$(rubin), -traceW, -hubert).

$$\max_n((i_{n+1} - i_n) - (i_n - i_{n-1})) \tag{10}$$

minimum of DB, wb.ratio, maximum of ssi, dunn and silhouette value closer to one are the best.

3 Experiments and Results

We conducted our experiments on Intel 4, 2.00 GHz CPU, 512 MB RAM, running Windows XP Dell PC. The proposed algorithm has been implemented based on the integrated version of GAlib(A C++ Library of Genetic Algorithm Components 2.4.6) [8] and NSGA-II source code(Compiled with g++). Necessary or needed parts have been (re)implemented for the multi-objective case; and NSGA-II ranking mechanism has been included in after it was transformed to C++. The approach and the utilized cluster validity algorithms have been conducted by using the cclust and fpc packages of the R Project for Statistical Computing [9]. We have run our implementation 20 times with parameters: *population size*=100; t_{dom} *for the selection*=10; *tournament size during the increment, the no of clusters*= approximately the $noofitems/5$ (20% of the entire data set); *p(crossover)* for the selection=.9; we tried single and two point crossover in order; two point crossover gave better results; *p(mutation)*= 0.05 and for the mutation itself the allele number is not changed randomly but w.r.t Equation 7.

Table 2. Converged Result with iterations run for each cluster

Glass	c	Iterations	Homogeneity	Separateness
Complete L.	2	4.7	820	-231
	3	3.6	685	-526
	4	4.1	567	-820
	5	5.3	465	-1214
	6	3.8	402	-1671
	7	3.2	342	-2047
Average L.	2	5.2	830	-51
	3	3.8	619	-194
	4	4.7	496	-470
	5	5.2	419.95	-802
	6	5.6	364	-1274
	7	5.8	340	-1691
Avg. T. Centr.	2	4.8	838	-98
	3	3.2	722	-290
	4	5.4	599	-368
	5	4.6	457	-620
	6	7.2	355	-1122
	7	3.6	344	-1598
Centroid L.	2	4.8	838	-25
	3	4.2	737	-63
	4	8.6	618	-224
	5	4.6	443	-393
	6	-9.4	373	-917
	7	-8.7	334	-1238

Table 3. Average Linkage

	avg.silwidth	hubertgamma	dunn	wb.ratio
3	0.73229179	-0.04746083	0.010079678	0.147598565
4	**0.749239025**	-0.105643855	0.009530867	0.118047505
5	0.675532037	**0.059459555**	0.010490812	0.112423819
6	0.655052066	-0.040064514	**0.01944298**	**0.104230977**
7	0.532479211	-0.477436742	0.004323585	0.104418821

We used a real world data set[1] in the evaluation process: **Glass:** Glass classification, with 9 features, 214 examples and 6 classes. (Class 1:70, Class 2:76, Class 3:17, Class 4:13, Class 5:9, Class 6:29).

We executed the clustering process for the cluster range of 2-7 for different homogeneity and separateness choices. Our termination criteria was chosen as the average of the population for which each objective is no more minimized. After running the algorithms, we obtain the average of the population objectives for Glass as in Table 2. The process converged in smaller number of iterations.

[1] http://sci2s.ugr.es/keel-dataset/index.php

Table 4. Average Linkage and TWCV for number of clusters= 3 to 7

	calinski	Db	hartigan	ratkowsky	scott	marriot	ball	trcovw	tracew	Friedman	Rubin	ssi
3	2458	**0.23**	0.03	-0.03	202.68	-32059447	-6.16	9026	**86**	1.96	34.87	**0.12**
4	559	0.30	0.00	0.01	**234.25**	**57061667**	-3.34	2624	43	1.97	28.22	0.07
5	279	0.30	0.04	0.01	153.84	-21782633	-1.97	1142	16	2.68	183.30	0.06
6	**56**	0.29	**-0.04**	**0.02**	219.23	35567201	-1.58	842	30	**4.55**	86.25	0.06
7	17	0.31	0.04	0.01	136.26	19109385	**-0.90**	**-3184**	-3	3.01	**-366.60**	0.10

Table 5. Average to Centroid Linkage

	avg.silwidth	hubertgamma	dunn	Wb.ratio
3	**0.7303171**	-0.199946695	0.01058622	0.15089338
4	0.613542167	0.071099559	0.004817699	0.142378532
5	0.604399545	-0.089583093	0.004175417	0.118750272
6	0.495793099	**0.149888863**	**0.005503966**	**0.070512979**
7	0.472953701	-0.499344329	0.001304799	0.107284916

Table 6. Average To Centroid L. and TWCV for number of clusters= 3 to 7

	calinski	db	hartigan	ratkowsky	scott	Marriot	ball	trcovw	tracew	Friedman	rubin	ssi
3	2219	0.26	**-0.05**	0.00	240.20	**103562116**	-6.54	8949	**113**	3.11	2.56	0.11
4	780	**0.25**	0.09	-0.01	119.30	-135867395	-2.78	3091	8	1.10	119.30	**0.15**
5	167	0.28	-0.02	**0.01**	**296.20**	95929190	-2.43	1066	44	**4.01**	68.87	0.07
6	**56**	0.29	-0.04	0.01	165.30	19592540	-1.49	**212**	9	3.12	51.66	0.08
7	57	0.31	0.08	0.01	113.30	9690128	**-0.80**	559	9	2.73	**-179.20**	0.11

Table 7. Complete Linkage

	avg.silwidth	hubertgamma	dunn	wb.ratio
3	0.725549149	-0.08333936	0.008465874	0.15089338
4	**0.736960447**	-0.078051222	**0.012021079**	0.142378532
5	0.628093293	**0.0871833**	0.007225859	0.118750272
6	0.713034566	-0.065111408	0.005806125	**0.070512979**
7	0.521031234	-0.453084421	0.003771547	0.107284916

Table 8. Complete Linkage and TWCV for number of clusters= 3 to 7

	calinski	Db	hartigan	ratkowsky	scott	marriot	ball	trcovw	tracew	Friedman	Rubin	ssi
3	2639	**0.28**	0.06	-0.02	177.04	-87623772	-5.45	201	-6	2.22	13.17	0.13
4	582	0.31	0.02	0.00	186.35	38627234	-3.32	**-6460**	-72	1.04	17.69	**0.16**
5	330	0.31	0.10	0.00	147.53	-82373555	-2.14	9826	**103**	2.30	279.43	0.09
6	**-4**	0.29	**-0.07**	**0.01**	**344.40**	**119212373**	-2.12	536	32	**5.75**	**-50.12**	0.09
7	37	0.34	-0.02	0.01	120.70	-4528527	**-1.10**	-484	-17	3.10	751.17	0.08

Table 9. Centroid Linkage

	avg.silwidth	hubertgamma	dunn	wb.ratio
3	0.722569489	**0.220524922**	0.000611231	0.299867636
4	**0.778992645**	-0.046499816	0.000696145	0.189345662
5	0.618693278	-0.028301898	0.001707514	0.107757942
6	0.702749364	-0.13982855	**0.001757835**	**0.102788534**
7	0.546218942	-0.226882347	0.00064492	0.123924566

Table 10. Centroid Linkage and TWCV for number of clusters= 3 to 7

	calinski	db	hartigan	ratkowsky	scott	marriot	ball	trcovw	tracew	friedman	rubin	ssi
3	2048	0.25	**-0.06**	-0.03	308.30	110891711	-7.02	**-121**	24	**4.34**	**12.69**	0.08
4	750	**0.16**	0.06	0.00	144.10	-54191257	-2.70	5693	**48**	0.83	70.21	0.08
5	199	0.26	-0.02	**0.01**	207.30	44534577	-2.09	1782	39	2.81	70.82	0.07
6	**119**	0.17	0.00	0.01	**139.30**	4663213	**-1.27**	566	14	3.06	143.00	0.06
7	125	0.29	0.05	0.01	132.50	**14746903**	-1.40	362	13	3.17	105.52	**0.11**

Reported in Tables 3 to 10 are the convex clustering index results of the cclust, average silhouette width, hubert, dunn and wb.ratio results from fpc. In average linkage, dunn and wb.ratio indices found the right optimal number of clusters as 6. For the convex clustering indices of clust, friedman, ratkowsky, hartigan and calinski ended up with 6. In average to centroid, hubert index also found 6 as well as the dunn and wb.ratio. Also, traceW and calinski found the right answer among the convex clustering indices. In complete linkage, wb.ratio found the right answer. Also hartigan, ratkowsky, scott, marriott, friedman and rubin got the right answer. At the same time, silhouette index got closer to find the value 6 and ranked third among the indices. In centroid dunn, wb.ratio; ball, scott and calinski had the outcome as 6.

4 Summary and Conclusions

Clustering as a fundamental data mining task can be applied in several areas. Researchers, mostly considered only one objective whereas clustering is naturally multi-objective process. At the same time, clustering of the instances may depend on the judgement of human experts. From this point of view, our clustering algorithm tries to find more than one feasible solution by taking into account more than one objective; the process has been automated and there is no need to keep the objective weights at a fixed value. Besides, it works iteratively within a given range of the number of clusters. It uses the immediate previous run's solutions as an input to the next run. During this process, there are two challenges to consider: 1) the scalability for large datasets 2) complexity and trial of every instance as the new candidate cluster during the iterations. There are many attempts to solving the first question. Also multi-objectivity gives us the opportunity to use those techniques. For the second problem, usually it is proposed to use data structures that keep data in more abstract/compressed format like k-d trees. For testing, we used two real world data sets with varying number of classes and equal/unequal number of instances per class. For both cases, we aimed at finding the desirable number of clusters by using some cluster validity indices. The results are promising and demonstrate the effectiveness and applicability of the proposed approach.

References

1. Grabmeier, J., Rudolph, A.: Techniques of cluster algorithms in data mining. Data Mining and Knowledge Discovery **6** (2003) 303–360
2. Liu, Y., Özyer, T., Alhajj, R., Barker, K.: Validity analysis of multiple clustering results on the pareto-optimal front. European Journal of Informatica (2005)

3. Liu, Y., Özyer, T., Alhajj, R., Barker, K.: Cluster validity analysis of alternative solutions from multi-objective optimization. Proceedings of SIAM International Conference on Data Mining (2005)
4. Özyer, T., Liu, Y., Alhajj, R., Barker, K.: Multi-objective genetic algorithm based clustering approach and its application to gene expression data. Proceedings of Biennial International Conference on Advances in Information Systems (2004)
5. Lu, Y., Lu, S., Fotouhi, F., Deng, Y., Brown, S.: FGKA: A fast genetic k-means clustering algorithm. ACM Symposium on Applied Computing (2004) 162–163
6. Deb, K., Agrawal, S., Pratab, A., Meyarivan, T.: A fast elitist non-dominated sorting genetic algorithm for multi-objective optimization : Nsga-ii. Number 1917, Paris, France, Springer-Verlag, LNCS (2000)
7. Dimitriadou, E., Dolnicar, S., Weingessel, A.: An examination of indexes for determining the number of clusters in binary data sets. Psychometrika **67** (2002) 137–160
8. Massachusetts Institute of Technology and Matthew Wall: GAlib Documentation. MIT, USA. (2005)
9. R Development Core Team: R: A language and environment for statistical computing. R Foundation for Statistical Computing, Vienna, Austria. (2004)

Recursive Lists of Clusters: A Dynamic Data Structure for Range Queries in Metric Spaces

Margarida Mamede*

CITI / Departamento de Informática, Faculdade de Ciências e Tecnologia da UNL, 2829–516 Caparica, Portugal
mm@di.fct.unl.pt

Abstract. We introduce a novel data structure for solving the range query problem in generic metric spaces. It can be seen as a dynamic version of the List of Clusters data structure of Chávez and Navarro. Experimental results show that, with respect to range queries, it outperforms the original data structure when the database dimension is below 12. Moreover, the building process is much more efficient, for any size and any dimension of the database.

1 Introduction

The family of algorithms and data structures for searching in metric spaces has been widely studied in recent years due to the variety of fields where they are applied. Some settings assume that the metric function is discrete (as, for example, BK-trees [4] or FQ-trees [2]), and some allow generic distance functions (c.f. AESA [11], GNAT [3], and vp-trees [13], among others). However, only a few are suitable for dealing with database updates (like dsa-trees [10, 1]). Besides, most of the approaches consider that the database fits in main memory, although some raise the issues of I/O operations [8, 9, 12]. For a complete and up-to-date survey on this subject, the reader is referred to [7].

In this work, we tackle the range query problem in generic metric spaces, considering that databases are dynamic and implemented in main memory. We propose a new data structure, called Recursive Lists of Clusters (RLC), which is built on the List of Clusters (LC) data structure, described in [5, 6]. LC is very efficient for range queries, specially in high dimensions, but is static and requires quadratic time construction in terms of the size of the database.

2 Basic Definitions

Let $(\mathcal{U}, d)$ be a *metric space*. That is, $\mathcal{U}$ is the universe of *objects*, and $d : \mathcal{U} \times \mathcal{U} \rightarrow \mathbb{R}$ is a real function, called *distance* or *metric*, that satisfies the following

* The author would like to thank Edgar Chávez and Gonzalo Navarro for some comments on this work and for kindly having sent her the source code of LC.

P. Yolum et al.(Eds.): ISCIS 2005, LNCS 3733, pp. 843–853, 2005.

properties, for all $x, y, z \in \mathcal{U}$: (strict positiveness) $d(x,y) \geq 0$ and $d(x,y) = 0 \Leftrightarrow x = y$; (symmetry) $d(x,y) = d(y,x)$; and (triangle inequality) $d(x,y) \leq d(x,z) + d(z,y)$. A *database over* $(\mathcal{U}, d)$ is a finite set $\mathbb{B} \subseteq \mathcal{U}$.

Given a database $\mathbb{B}$ over a metric space $(\mathcal{U}, d)$, and a pair (q, r_q), where $q \in \mathcal{U}$ and r_q is a non-negative real number, the *range query problem* consists in computing the set of elements of the database whose distance to q does not exceed r_q, i.e., $\{x \in \mathbb{B} \mid d(x,q) \leq r_q\}$. The object q is called *the query point* and r_q is *the query radius*.

Naturally, range queries can be answered by selecting every element of the database, one by one, and computing its distance to the query point. Nevertheless, in order to avoid this heavy linear procedure, many data structures (a.k.a. indexes) have been created and studied [7]. In spite of their many differences, all of them rely on the triangle inequality to discard elements of the database without computing the corresponding distance to the query point.

3 Lists of Clusters

We start by introducing the notions of cluster and list of clusters (which generalize the definitions presented in [5, 6]). For the sake of simplicity, from now on, let $(\mathcal{U}, d)$ denote a metric space and $\mathbb{B}$ denote a database over $(\mathcal{U}, d)$.

A *cluster* of $\mathbb{B}$ is a triple (c, r, I), where: $c \in \mathbb{B}$ is a database object, called the *center* of the cluster; r is a non-negative real number, called the *radius* of the cluster; and I is a subset of the elements of the database, excluding c, whose distance to c does not exceed r, $I \subseteq \{x \in \mathbb{B} \mid 0 < d(x,c) \leq r\}$. We call I the *interior* of the cluster. The set $I \cup \{c\}$ of objects that occur in a cluster (c, r, I) is denoted by $O_{c,r,I}$.

A *list of clusters* for $\mathbb{B}$ is a sequence of clusters of $\mathbb{B}$, $L = <(c_1, r_1, I_1), \ldots, (c_n, r_n, I_n)>$, for some $n \geq 0$, that satisfies the following properties.

1. The set of objects in L is $\mathbb{B}$: $\mathbb{B} = \bigcup_{i=1}^{n} O_{c_i,r_i,I_i}$.
2. Clusters are pairwise disjoint, that is, for every $i, j = 1, 2, \ldots, n$: $i \neq j \Rightarrow O_{c_i,r_i,I_i} \cap O_{c_j,r_j,I_j} = \emptyset$.
3. Every element occurs in the first cluster in which it fits, i.e., for every $i = 2, \ldots, n$, every $x \in O_{c_i,r_i,I_i}$, and every $j = 1, \ldots, i-1$: $d(x, c_j) > r_j$.

Figure 1, borrowed from [5, 6], illustrates the last property, depicting the "ball" associated with each cluster of a list.

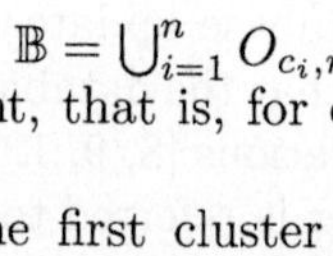

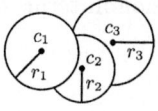

Fig. 1. Balls of the three clusters of the list $<(c_1, r_1, I_1), (c_2, r_2, I_2), (c_3, r_3, I_3)>$

The range search algorithm in a list of clusters is sketched in Fig. 2. Basically, the list is iterated and the relation between each cluster and the query is established, based on the distance from the query point to the cluster's center and on the two radii. There are six possible cases. When the center belongs to the query ball, either the query ball is completely inside the cluster, or contains the cluster, or intersects it without containment in any direction. Otherwise, the query ball may still be inside the cluster or intersect it (without containment), but the third possibility is both balls being disjoint. Notice that, whenever the query ball is inside the cluster, the iteration stops.

In order to cope with unfinished iterations, avoiding the technical details, Fig. 2 presents the recursive version of the algorithm. Function LC-search has three parameters: the list of clusters L, the query (q, r_q), and the set of objects R that belong to the answer (which should be the empty set in the initial call). It makes use of another function, C-search, which implements the range search in the interior of a cluster. Besides the cluster to be analysed (c, r, I), the query (q, r_q), and the result set R, it receives the distance from the query to the center *distQC*, to prevent repeating this computation when the triangle inequality is applied to discard the objects in I. The discussion of the algorithms on clusters is deferred until the end of this section.

```
LC-search( L, (q,r_q), R )
  if L = <> return R
  else
    let L = < (c,r,I) | L' >
    distQC ← d(q,c)
    if distQC ≤ r_q                              // Query ball contains center c.
      if distQC + r_q ≤ r                        // Query ball is inside cluster.
        return C-search((c,r,I), (q,r_q), distQC, R ∪ {c})
      else if distQC + r ≤ r_q                   // Query ball contains cluster.
        return LC-search(L', (q,r_q), R ∪ {c} ∪ I)
      else                                       // Query ball intersects cluster.
        R' ← C-search((c,r,I), (q,r_q), distQC, R ∪ {c})
        return LC-search(L', (q,r_q), R')
    else                                         // Query ball does not contain center c.
      if distQC + r_q ≤ r                        // Query ball is inside cluster.
        return C-search((c,r,I), (q,r_q), distQC, R)
      else if distQC > r_q + r                   // Query ball is outside cluster.
        return LC-search(L', (q,r_q), R)
      else                                       // Query ball intersects cluster.
        R' ← C-search((c,r,I), (q,r_q), distQC, R)
        return LC-search(L', (q,r_q), R')
```

Fig. 2. Search algorithm in a list of clusters

An important issue is the way centers and radii are chosen, when the list of clusters is built. In [5, 6], where LC is described, the construction algorithm (LC-build, outlined in Fig. 3) assumes that the database $\mathbb{B}$ is given in advance. The authors discuss five criteria for selecting centers and two for selecting radii. With regard to objects, centers can be: (1) chosen at random; (2) the objects closest to the previous center; (3) the objects farthest from the previous center; (4) the objects minimizing the sum of distances to the previous centers; (5) the objects maximizing the sum of distances to the previous centers. Radii can be all equal or such that the clusters' cardinality is constant (except, possibly, the last one). The first choice leads to *lists of clusters of fixed radius*, while the second one to *lists of clusters of fixed size.*

The main drawback of adopting global criteria, such as the last four strategies for choosing centers or clusters of fixed size, is the impossibility of performing updates efficiently. To tackle the problems raised by dynamic databases, we consider clusters of fixed radius and construct the list by means of a succession of insert operations.

The insertion algorithm in a list of clusters of fixed radius, LC-insert, is also shown in Fig. 3. Notice that an object is inserted in the first cluster where it fits. This is done by function C-insert, which returns the updated cluster. (The abuse of notation aims at emphasizing the change in the cluster's interior.) However, when an object does not belong in any existent cluster, a new cluster is created at the tail of the list. Once again, note that the distance between the object to be inserted and the cluster's center (*distOC*) is an input of function C-insert.

```
LC-build( 𝔹 )
  if 𝔹 = ∅ return <>
  else
    select c ∈ 𝔹,
    select a radius r
    I ← {x ∈ 𝔹 | 0 < d(c, x) ≤ r}
    𝔹' ← 𝔹 \ (I ∪ {c})
    return < (c, r, I) | LC-build(𝔹') >
```

```
LC-delete( L, x )
  if L = <> return L
  else
    let L = < (c, r, I) | L' >
    distOC ← d(x, c)
    if distOC ≤ r
      if distOC = 0
        return LC-insertInterior(I, L')
      else
        (c, r, I') ← C-delete((c, r, I), x, distOC)
        return < (c, r, I') | L' >
    else
      return < (c, r, I) | LC-remove(L', x) >
```

```
LC-insert( L, x )
  if L = <> return < (x, r, ∅) >
  else
    let L = < (c, r, I) | L' >
    distOC ← d(x, c)
    if distOC ≤ r
      if distOC = 0
        return L
      else
        (c, r, I') ← C-insert((c, r, I), x, distOC)
        return < (c, r, I') | L' >
    else
      return < (c, r, I) | LC-insert(L', x) >
```

```
LC-insertInterior( I, L )
  if I = <> return L
  else
    let I = < x | I' >
    L' ← LC-insert(L, x)
    return LC-insertInterior(I', L')
```

Fig. 3. Construction, insertion, and deletion algorithms in lists of clusters. Updates are performed in lists of clusters of fixed radius r.

In the same way, the deletion algorithm (c.f. LC-delete in Fig. 3) starts by searching the cluster that may contain the object. If no such cluster exists, there is nothing more to do. Otherwise, two distinct situations can hold: either the object to be removed is the cluster's center, in which case the cluster disappears, or it belongs to the cluster's interior and function C-delete performs its deletion. In the first case, all objects of the cluster's interior must be re-inserted in the remaining sub-list of clusters.

Clusters' interiors can be efficiently implemented with arrays providing there are no updates in the database. In order to reduce the number of distances computed in a range search, each array cell should store a database object and its distance to the center. Moreover, we propose that arrays are sorted in decreasing order by the distance value. The next proposition will justify these requirements.

Proposition 1. *Let $x, c, q \in \mathcal{U}$ be three objects, and r_q be a non-negative real number such that $d(x,c) < d(q,c) - r_q$. Then, $d(x,q) > r_q$.*

Proof. By triangle inequality, $d(c,q) \leq d(c,x) + d(x,q)$, which is equivalent to $d(x,q) \geq d(c,q) - d(c,x)$. But, since the distance function is symmetric, by hypothesis, $d(c,q) - d(c,x) > r_q$, which implies $d(x,q) > r_q$, as we wanted. □

Figure 4 presents the pseudo-code of the range search algorithm in a cluster whose interior is implemented with an array (Ca-search). To simplify the notation, arrays are seen as sequences of pairs of the form (d_{xc}, x), where d_{xc} represents the distance from object x to the cluster's center c.

In the first place, function Ca-search computes the minimum value d_{xc} can have that requires the evaluation of the distance from object x to query point q, and stores it in the auxiliary variable *minDist*. Then, it calls Ia-search, which is the function that examines the cluster's interior.

In Ia-search, whenever an object x such that $d_{xc} < minDist$ is found, the computation stops because neither x nor the remaining objects belong to the query ball. The justification follows directly from Proposition 1 and from the array being sorted in decreasing order by distance value.

```
Ia-search( I, (q, r_q), minDist, R )
  if I = <> return R
  else
    let I = < (d_xc, x) | I' >
    if d_xc < minDist
      return R
    else
      if d(x, q) ≤ r_q
        return Ia-search(I', (q, r_q), minDist, R ∪ {x})
      else
        return Ia-search(I', (q, r_q), minDist, R)

Ca-search( (c, r, I), (q, r_q), distQC, R )
  minDist ← distQC − r_q
  Ia-search(I, (q, r_q), minDist, R)
```

Fig. 4. Search algorithm in a cluster implemented with an array

Updates are trivially performed, unless the array is full in an insertion operation. They correspond to insertions and deletions in sorted arrays, ordered by a real number (the distance from the object to the center). That is why this value is an input of functions C-insert and C-delete.

4 Recursive Lists of Clusters

As we have already mentioned, our research focused on lists of clusters of fixed radius. As a result, we should not expect clusters to have similar sizes. In fact, experimental results show that the first clusters of the list are very densely populated, whereas the last ones often contain only the center. This means that, if the radius is small enough so as not to get half of the objects in a few initial clusters, the list becomes very large in length, having many empty or singleton clusters' interiors. Needless to say, the length of the list affects the performance of all functions introduced in the previous section, not to mention that very thinly populated clusters lead to linear running time algorithms in terms of the size of the database. On the other hand, even though large radii prevent the proliferation of clusters, they strongly increase the size of the initial clusters, whose processing may become very heavy. To overcome this difficulty, the main idea is to allow clusters to be implemented in two different ways: if the size of the cluster's interior does not exceed a certain value, its elements are stored in an array; otherwise, the interior is implemented as a list of clusters.

Let ρ be a positive real number, $\psi : \mathbb{R}^+ \to \mathbb{R}^+$ be a (positive) real function, and α be a positive integer. A *recursive list of clusters* for $\mathbb{B}$ with *radius* ρ, *radius function* ψ, and *array capacity* α is a list of clusters for $\mathbb{B}$ of fixed radius ρ, $L = < (c_1, \rho, I_1), \ldots, (c_n, \rho, I_n) >$, for some $n \geq 0$, that satisfies the following property, for every $j = 1, \ldots, n$: if the size of the interior I_j does not exceed α, I_j is implemented with an array; otherwise, I_j is a recursive list of clusters with radius $\psi(\rho)$, radius function ψ, and array capacity α. The *level* of a cluster is the number of ancestors of the cluster, excluding itself.

Figure 5 presents a graphical representation of an RLC of length three, with radius ρ, radius function $\psi(r) = kr$ (for every $r > 0$ and some $k > 0$), and array capacity 5. Apart from the center (c), the radius (r), and the interior (I), each cluster picture contains the level (l) and the interior's size (s), in order to exemplify these notions. For instance, the first cluster of the list, whose center is c_1, has 16 objects in its interior. So, the interior is an RLC of level 1: its first cluster has 6 elements (center c'_1 and 5 objects in the interior) and the second one has 10.

We assume that every object x of the database is associated with a sequence (denoted by the letter D) with the distances from x to the centers of the clusters to which x belongs. We will keep the notation of pairs used in the previous section, with (D, x) instead of (d_{xc}, x). It is worth mentioning that D is the empty sequence if, and only if, it is associated with a center of level zero. In the arrays, two orderings are preserved. On the one hand, the values $d(x, c)$ in D are ordered according to the child-parent relation on centers. On the other hand, every array is sorted in decreasing order by the first element of D.

As an example, in the recursive list of clusters of Fig. 5, the sequence associated with c''_1 is $< d(c''_1, c'_2), d(c''_1, c_1) >$. Besides, for every object x in that cluster's interior, the array contains the pair $(< d(x, c''_1), d(x, c'_2), d(x, c_1) >, x)$. The array is sorted in decreasing order by $d(x, c''_1)$.

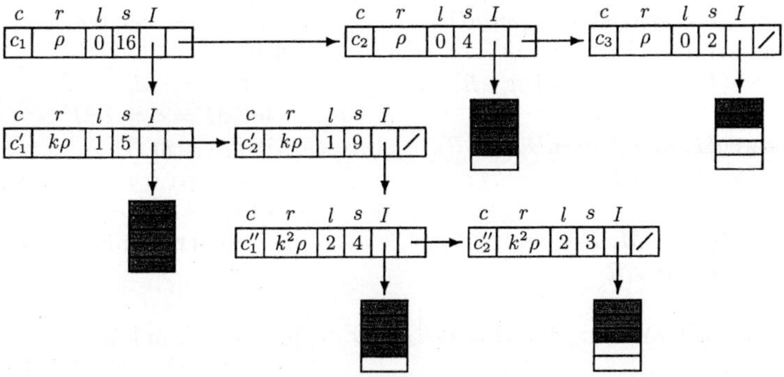

Fig. 5. An RLC with radius ρ, radius function $\psi(r) = kr$, and array capacity 5

Essentially, the algorithms on lists of clusters are still applied to recursive lists of clusters. So, our task is to show how algorithms on clusters work.

Range queries are performed by algorithm C-search, depicted in Fig. 6. First of all, remark that this function has a new parameter, called *minDists*. As we have already seen, each time we get into a cluster's interior, there is a bound for the distance between its objects and the cluster's center below which objects can be discarded without computing any other distance. Sequence *minDists* contains all these minimal bounds, from the innermost to the outermost center. In the second place, notice that, as the array is sorted by the distances to the innermost center, whenever an object that can be discarded by the first bound is found (in function A-search), all remaining objects, if any, are immediately ignored. However, this cannot be done with the other values. For this reason, the boolean function elimByAncest analyses all but the first element of the sequences. Lastly, *minDists* must be an input parameter of function LC-search (in Fig. 2). There is no need to repeat its code because this sequence should only be passed to every call of C-search and LC-search. Obviously, *minDists* has to be the empty sequence in the initial call of LC-search.

The next goal is to describe updates in a cluster. Let us start with insertions, whose pseudo-code is shown in Fig. 7. If the cluster is implemented in an array and there is space for one more element, an ordered insertion into the array is performed (A-insertOrd, by *distOC*). If the cluster is a list of clusters, function LC-insert is called. The most difficult situation arises when the array is full. In that case, if the object does not belong to the database yet, a new list of clusters is created, and the information in the array, as well as the new element, is stored in the list. The first step is done by function moveArrayToList, which calls LC-insert for every object in the array. Once more, the sequence with the distances from the object to the centers must be an input parameter of C-insert and LC-insert (Fig. 3). The expression sizeOf(I), where I is a cluster's interior of any kind, denotes the number of objects stored in I.

```
C-search((c, r, I), (q, r_q), minDists, distQC, R)
  minDists' ← < distQC − r_q | minDists >
  if I is an array
    A-search(I, (q, r_q), minDists', R)
  else
    LC-search(I, (q, r_q), minDists', R)
```

```
elimByAncest(D, M)
  if D = <> return false
  else
    let D = < d_xc | D' >
    let M = < m | M' >
    if d_xc < m
      return true
    else
      return elimByAncest(D', M')
```

```
A-search( I, (q, r_q), M, R )
  if I = <> return R
  else
    let I = < (D, x) | I' >, let D = < d_xc | D' >, let M = < m | M' >
    if d_xc < m
      return R
    else if elimByAncest(D', M')
      return A-search(I', (q, r_q), M, R)
    else
      if d(x, q) ≤ r_q
        return A-search(I', (q, r_q), M, R ∪ {x})
      else
        return A-search(I', (q, r_q), M, R)
```

Fig. 6. Search algorithm in a cluster

Deletions work the other way around (c.f. Fig. 7). Firstly, the object is deleted from the cluster interior, which is done by calling A-deleteOrd or LC-delete. Then, whenever the object is removed from a list whose size becomes equal to the array capacity, the remaining elements of the list are moved into an array.

The efficiency of updates in a recursive list of clusters can be severely affected by the changes in the clusters' interiors. The number of changes performed depends mainly on the dynamism of the database and on the distribution of the objects, but the weight of each operation depends on the array capacity. Furthermore, insertions and deletions in an array take $\Theta(n)$ both in the average and in the worst cases, if n is the number of objects in the array. For these reasons, the capacity of the arrays should be a small value.

5 Experimental Results

In this section, we present some experimental results that compare the performance of our data structure (RLC) and that of Chávez and Navarro (denoted by LC), where clusters have a fixed size and the center of the i-th cluster of the list is the element that maximizes the sum of distances to the previous centers. These choices were made by the authors in [5, 6] to compare their proposal with other structures, and are implemented in the source code they kindly sent to us.

All our metric spaces are unitary real cubes $[0,1]^k$ under the Euclidian distance, with $k = 4, 6, 8, 10, 12, 14, 16, 18, 20$. For each one of those dimensions, we

```
C-insert( (c, r, I), x, D, distOC )
  D' ← < distOC | D >
  if sizeOf(I) < α
    return (c, r, A-insertOrd(I, x, D'))
  else if sizeOf(I) = α
    if A-findOrd(I, x, D')
      return (c, r, I)
    else
      L ← moveArrayToList(I, <>)
      return (c, r, LC-insert(L, x, D'))
  else
    return (c, r, LC-insert(I, x, D'))
```

```
C-delete( (c, r, I), x, distOC )
  if sizeOf(I) ≤ α
    return (c, r, A-deleteOrd(I, x, distOC))
  else
    L ← LC-delete(I, x)
    if sizeOf(L) = α
      return (c, r, moveListToArray(L, <>))
    else
      return (c, r, L)
```

Fig. 7. Insertion and deletion algorithms in a cluster (with array capacity α)

generated six sets with uniformly random points with sizes 100, 50,000, 100,000, 150,000, 200,000, and 250,000. The smaller one was used as the set of queries, while the others were used as databases.

Both structures are parameterized. The parameters of RLC are the radius ρ, the radius function ψ, and the array capacity α. In the experiments reported here, α was set to 16, but radii varied with level, according to the following scheme: $\rho = \frac{\sqrt{k}}{\eta_1}$ and $\psi(r) = \frac{r}{\eta_2}$, for every $r > 0$, where k is the space dimension, and η_1 and η_2 are positive constants. In LC, the only parameter is the size of the cluster's interior. Table 1 presents the parameters chosen for each dimension.

Figure 8 shows the results of performing range queries (retrieving 0.01% of the database). More precisely, the charts (on the left column) present the average number of objects of the database whose distance to the query point is computed. It is easy to see that RLC outperforms LC for dimensions below 12. Above 12, LC performs better.

We have also calculated the average number of distances computed per object during the building process of the database. In the case of RLC, since the construction algorithm simply calls the insertion algorithm for each object, it corresponds to the average number of distances computed to insert an object in the database.

It turns out that, in this point, RLC is much less demanding, for any dimension (see the right column of Fig. 8). Notice that the values for RLC are, not only almost constant for each dimension, but also of a different order of magnitude from those for LC, specially with large databases. The importance of a good performance on this matter stems from the fact that these data structures

Table 1. Parameters used for each dimension

Dimension		4	6	8	10	12	14	16	18	20
RLC	η_1	2.5	3.5	4.5	4.5	4.5	4.5	4.5	4.5	4.5
	η_2	1.25	1.2	1.15	1.1	1.05	1.04	1.02	1	0.97
LC		150	100	50	35	25	15	10	7	5

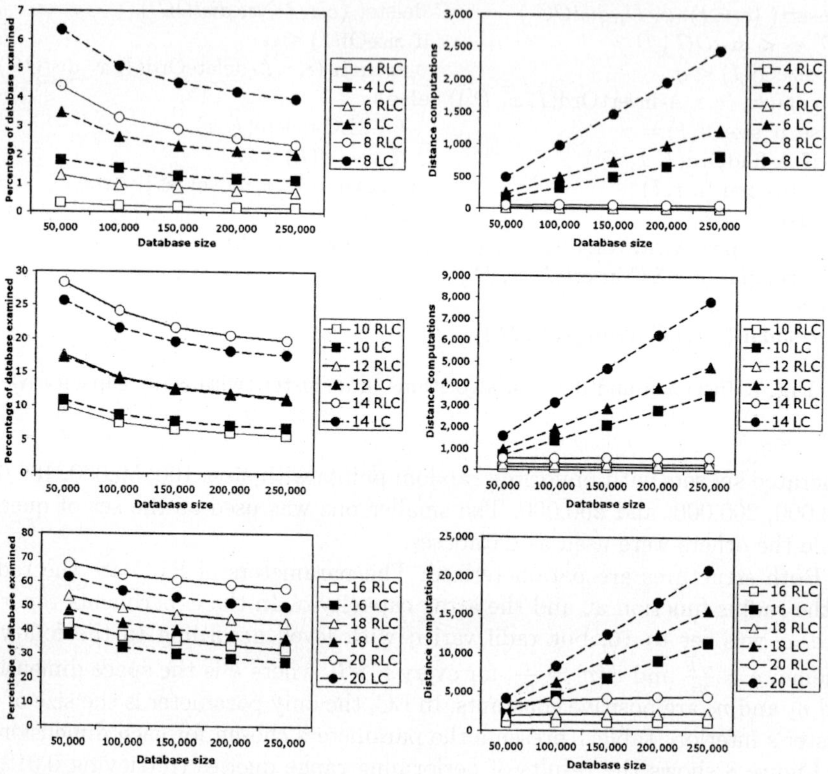

Fig. 8. (Left) Average number of distances computed to query the database, shown as a percentage of the database size. 100 queries, retrieving 0.01% of the database. **(Right)** Average number of distances computed per object to build the database. **From top to bottom:** dimensions 4, 6, and 8; 10, 12, and 14; 16, 18, and 20.

are implemented in main memory. Besides, even if LC is suitable for secondary memory implementations, its construction criterion is not compatible with updates. So, if insertions or deletions have to be performed, the data structure must be rebuilt.

6 Conclusions and Future Work

We have presented RLC, a dynamic version of the LC data structure, which outperforms significantly the original in low dimensional spaces and competes with it in medium dimensional spaces. In addition, the initial construction of RLC, insertions, and deletions are performed efficiently. It is worth mentioning that, although dynamism is crucial in many applications, only a few of the data structures for metric spaces are truly dynamic.

Concerning future work, there are two topics requiring immediate investigation: to compare RLC with other data structures (implemented in main memory) and to analyse the complexity of the algorithms, in the average case. We also want to adapt RLC to secondary memory, comparing it against the existing approaches. To this end, we plan to extend RLC with a new parameter (an integer function) that establishes the capacity of the arrays at each level. The idea is that, for the arrays to fit "exactly" into the disk pages, the arrays' capacity should decrease as the level increases, to compensate for the increment in the size of the sequences of distances associated with objects.

References

[1] Arroyuelo, D., Muñoz, F., Navarro, G., Reyes, N. : Memory-adaptative dynamic spatial approximation trees. In *Proc. of the 10th Int. Symp. on String Processing and Information Retrieval*, LNCS 2857, Springer-Verlag, (2003) 360–368

[2] Baeza-Yates, R., Cunto, W., Manber, U., Wu, S. : Proximity matching using fixed-queries trees. In *Proc. of 5th Annual Symp. on Combinatorial Pattern Matching*, LNCS 807, Springer-Verlag, (1994) 198–212

[3] Brin, S.: Near neighbor search in large metric spaces. In *Proc. of the 21st Int. Conf. on Very Large Data Bases*, Morgan Kaufmann, (1995) 574–584

[4] Burkhard, W. A., Keller, R. M: Some approaches to best-match file searching. *Communications of the ACM*, 16(4):230–236, (1973)

[5] Chávez, E., Navarro, G.: An effective clustering algorithm to index high dimensional metric spaces. In *Proc. of the 7th Symp. on String Processing and Information Retrieval*, pages 75–86. IEEE CS Press, (2000)

[6] Chávez, E., Navarro, G.: A compact space decomposition for effective metric indexing. *Pattern Recognition Letters*, 26(9):1363–1376, (2005)

[7] Chávez, E., Navarro, G., Baeza-Yates, R., Marroquín, J. L.: Searching in metric spaces. *ACM Computing Surveys*, 33(3):273–321, (2001)

[8] Ciaccia, P., Patella, M., Zezula, P.: M-tree: An efficient access method for similarity search in metric spaces. In *Proc. of the 23rd Int. Conf. on Very Large Data Bases*, pages 426–435. Morgan Kaufmann, (1997)

[9] Dohnal, V., Gennaro, C., Savino, P., Zezula, P.: D-index: Distance searching index for metric data sets. *Multimedia Tools and Applications*, 21(1):9–33, (2003)

[10] Navarro, G., Reyes, N.: Fully dynamic spatial approximation trees. In *Proc. of the 9th Int. Symp. on String Processing and Information Retrieval*, LNCS 2476, Springer-Verlag, (2002) 254–270

[11] Ruiz, E. V. An algorithm for finding nearest neighbours in (approximately) constant average time. *Pattern Recognition Letters*, 4(3):145–157, (1986)

[12] Traina Jr., C., Traina, A., Filho, R. S., Faloutsos, C.: How to improve the pruning ability of dynamic metric access methods. In *Proc. of the 11th Int. Conf. on Information and Knowledge Management*, ACM Press, (2002) 219–226

[13] Yianilos, P. N.: Data structures and algorithms for nearest neighbor search in general metric spaces. In *Proc. of the 4th Annual ACM-SIAM Symp. on Discrete Algorithms*, (1993) 311–321

Incremental Clustering Using a Core-Based Approach

Gabriela Şerban and Alina Câmpan

Department of Computer Science, “Babeş-Bolyai” University,
1, M. Kogalniceanu Street, Cluj-Napoca, Romania
tel: +40.264.405327, fax: +40.264.591.960
{gabis, alina}@cs.ubbcluj.ro

Abstract. Clustering is a division of data into groups of similar objects, with respect to a set of relevant attributes (features) of the analyzed objects. Classical partitioning clustering methods, such as *k-means* algorithm, start with a known set of objects, and all features are considered simultaneously when calculating objects' similarity. But there are numerous applications where an object set already clustered with respect to an initial set of attributes is altered by the addition of new features. Consequently, a re-clustering is required. We propose in this paper an incremental, *k-means* based clustering method, *Core Based Incremental Clustering (CBIC)*, that is capable to re-partition the objects set, when the attribute set increases. The method starts from the partitioning into clusters that was established by applying *k-means* or *CBIC* before the attribute set changed. The result is reached more efficiently than running *k-means* again from the scratch on the feature-extended object set. Experiments proving the method's efficiency are also reported.

Keywords: Data Mining, clustering, k-means.

1 Introduction

Clustering, or unsupervised classification, is a data mining activity that aims to partition a given set of objects into groups (classes or clusters) such that objects within a cluster to have high similarity with each other and low similarity with objects in other clusters. The inferring process is carried out with respect to a set of relevant characteristics or attributes of the analyzed objects. Similarity and dissimilarity between objects are calculated using metric or semi-metric functions, applied to the attribute values characterizing the objects.

A large collection of clustering algorithms is available in the literature. [4], [5] and [6] contain comprehensive overviews of the existing techniques.

A well-known class of clustering methods is the one of the partitioning methods, with representatives such as the *k-means* algorithm or the *k-medoids* algorithm. Essentially, given a set of n objects and a number $k, k \leq n$, such

P. Yolum et al.(Eds.): ISCIS 2005, LNCS 3733, pp. 854–863, 2005.

a method divides the object set into k distinct and non-empty clusters. The partitioning process is iterative and heuristic; it stops when a "good" partitioning is achieved. Finding a "good" partitioning coincides with optimizing a criterion function defined either locally (on a subset of the objects) or globally (defined over all of the objects, as in *k-means*). The criterion function used in *k-means* is the squared error criterion, which tends to work well with isolated and compact clusters ([6]).

Generally, these methods start with a known set of objects, measured against a known set of attributes. But there are numerous applications where the object set is dynamic, or the attribute set characterizing the objects evolves. Obviously, for obtaining in these conditions a partitioning of the object set, the clustering algorithm can be applied over and over again, beginning from the scratch, every time when the objects or the attributes change. But this can be inefficient. What we want is to propose an incremental, *k-means* based clustering method, named *Core Based Incremental Clustering (CBIC)*, that is capable to efficiently re-partition the object set, when the attribute set increases with one or more attributes. The method starts from the partitioning into clusters that was established by applying *k-means* or *CBIC* before the attribute set changed. The result is reached more efficiently than running *k-means* again from the scratch on the feature-extended object set.

1.1 Related Work

There are few approaches reported in the literature that take into account the problem of adapting a clustering when the object feature set is extended. Early works treat the sequential use of features in the clustering process, one by one. An example of such a monothetic approach is mentioned in [6]. A more recent paper ([11]) analyzes the same problem of adapting a clustering produced by a DBSCAN like algorithm, using some additional structures and distance approximations in an Euclidian space.

However, adapting a clustering resulted from a partitioning algorithm, using partitioning-based methods hasn't been reported by none of these works.

2 Formal Problem Study

Let $X = \{O_1, O_2, \dots, O_n\}$ be the set of objects to be classified. Each object is measured with respect to a set of m initial attributes and is therefore described by an m-dimensional vector $O_i = (O_{i1}, \dots, O_{im}), O_{ik} \in \Re, 1 \leq i \leq n, 1 \leq k \leq m$. Usually, the attributes associated to objects are standardized, in order to ensure an equal weight to all of them ([4]).

Let $\{K_1, K_2, \dots, K_p\}$ be the set of clusters discovered in data by applying the *k-means* algorithm. Each cluster is a set of objects, $K_j = \{O_1^j, O_2^j, \dots, O_{n_j}^j\}, 1 \leq j \leq p$. The centroid (cluster mean) of the cluster K_j is denoted by f_j, where

$$f_j = \left(\frac{\sum_{k=1}^{n_j} O_{k1}^j}{n_j}, \dots, \frac{\sum_{k=1}^{n_j} O_{km}^j}{n_j} \right).$$

The measure used for discriminating objects can be any *metric* function d. We used the *Euclidian distance*: $d(O_i, O_j) = d_E(O_i, O_j) = \sqrt{\sum_{l=1}^{m}(O_{il} - O_{jl})^2}$.

The measured set of attributes is afterwards extended with s ($s \geq 1$) new attributes, numbered as $(m+1), (m+2), \ldots, (m+s)$. After extension, the objects' vectors become $O'_i = (O_{i1}, \ldots, O_{im}, O_{i,m+1}, \ldots, O_{i,m+s}), 1 \leq i \leq n$.

We want to analyze the problem of recalculating the objects' grouping into clusters, after object extension and starting from the current partitioning. We aim to obtain a performance gain in respect to the partitioning from scratch process.

We start from the fact that, at the end of the initial *k-means* clustering process, all objects are closer to the centroid of their cluster than to any other centroid. So, for any cluster j and any object $O_i^j \in K_j$, inequality (1) below holds.

$$d_E(O_i^j, f_j) \leq d_E(O_i^j, f_r), \forall j, r,\ 1 \leq j, r \leq p,\ r \neq j. \tag{1}$$

We denote by $K'_j, 1 \leq j \leq p$, the set containing the same objects as K_j, after the extension. By $f'_j, 1 \leq j \leq p$, we denote the mean (center) of the set K'_j. These sets $K'_j, 1 \leq j \leq p$, will not necessarily represent clusters after the attribute set extension. The newly arrived attributes can change the objects' arrangement into clusters, formed so that the intra-cluster similarity to be high and inter-cluster similarity to be low. But there is a considerable chance, when adding one or few attributes to objects, and the attributes have equal weights and normal data distribution, that the old arrangement in clusters to be close to the actual one. The actual clusters could be obtained by applying the *k-means* classification algorithm on the set of extended objects. But we try to avoid this process and replace it with one less expensive but not less accurate. With these being said, we agree, however, to continue to refer the sets K'_j as clusters.

We therefore take as starting point the previous partitioning into clusters and study in which conditions an extended object $O_i^{j\prime}$ is still correctly placed into its cluster K'_j. For that, we express the distance of $O_i^{j\prime}$ to the center of its cluster, f'_j, compared to the distance to the center f'_r of any other cluster K'_r.

Theorem 1. When inequality (2) holds for an extended object $O_i^{j\prime}$ and its cluster K'_j

$$O_{il}^j \geq \frac{\sum_{k=1}^{n_j} O_{kl}^j}{n_j}, \forall l \in \{m+1, m+2, \ldots, m+s\} \tag{2}$$

then the object $O_i^{j\prime}$ is closer to the center f'_j than to any other center f'_r, $1 \leq j, r \leq p$, $r \neq j$.

Proof. We prove below this statement.

$$d^2(O_i^{j'}, f_j') - d^2(O_i^{j'}, f_r') = d^2(O_i^j, f_j) + \sum_{l=m+1}^{m+s} \left(\frac{\sum_{k=1}^{n_j} O_{kl}^j}{n_j} - O_{il}^j \right)^2 -$$

$$d^2(O_i^j, f_r) - \sum_{l=m+1}^{m+s} \left(\frac{\sum_{k=1}^{n_r} O_{kl}^r}{n_r} - O_{il}^j \right)^2.$$

Using the inequality (1), we have:

$$d^2(O_i^{j'}, f_j') - d^2(O_i^{j'}, f_r') \leq \sum_{l=m+1}^{m+s} \left(\frac{\sum_{k=1}^{n_j} O_{kl}^j}{n_j} - O_{il}^j \right)^2 -$$

$$\sum_{l=m+1}^{m+s} \left(\frac{\sum_{k=1}^{n_r} O_{kl}^r}{n_r} - O_{il}^j \right)^2 \Leftrightarrow d^2(O_i^{j'}, f_j') - d^2(O_i^{j'}, f_r') \leq$$

$$\sum_{l=m+1}^{m+s} \left(\frac{\sum_{k=1}^{n_j} O_{kl}^j}{n_j} - \frac{\sum_{k=1}^{n_r} O_{kl}^r}{n_r} \right) \cdot \left(\frac{\sum_{k=1}^{n_j} O_{kl}^j}{n_j} + \frac{\sum_{k=1}^{n_r} O_{kl}^r}{n_r} - 2 \cdot O_{il}^j \right).$$

If the inequality (2) holds for every new attribute of $O_i^{j'}$, then the inequality above becomes:

$$d^2(O_i^{j'}, f_j') - d^2(O_i^{j'}, f_r') \leq - \sum_{l=m+1}^{m+s} \left(\frac{\sum_{k=1}^{n_j} O_{kl}^j}{n_j} - \frac{\sum_{k=1}^{n_r} O_{kl}^r}{n_r} \right)^2 \Leftrightarrow$$

$$d^2(O_i^{j'}, f_j') - d^2(O_i^{j'}, f_r') \leq 0.$$

Because all distances are non-negative numbers, it follows that:

$d(O_i^{j'}, f_j') \leq (O_i^{j'}, f_r'), \forall r,\ 1 \leq r \leq p,\ r \neq j.$

We have to notice that the inequality in (2) imposes only intra-cluster conditions. An object is compared against its own cluster in order to decide its new affiliation to that cluster.

3 The *Core Based Incremental Clustering* Algorithm

We will use the property enounced in the previous paragraph in order to identify inside each cluster K_j', $1 \leq j \leq p$, those objects that have a considerable chance to remain stable in their cluster, and not to move into another cluster as a result of the attribute set extension. These objects form the *core* of their cluster.

Definition 1.

a) We denote by $StrongCore_j = \{O_i^{j'} | O_i^{j'} \in K_j', O_i^{j'}$ *satisfies the inequalities set (2)*$\}$ *the set of all objects in* K_j' *satisfying inequality (2) for each new attribute* l, $m+1 \leq l \leq m+s$.

b) Let $sat(O_i^{j'})$ *be the set of all new attributes* l, $m+1 \leq l \leq m+s$, *for which object* $O_i^{j'}$ *satisfies inequality (2).*

We denote by $WeakCore_j = \{O_i^{j'} | O_i^{j'} \in K_j', |sat(O_i^{j'})| \geq \frac{\sum_{k=1}^{n_j} |sat(O_k^{j'})|}{n_j}\}$ *the* *set of all objects in K'_j satisfying inequality (2) for at least so many new attributes that all objects in K'_j are satisfying (2) for, in the average.*

c) *$Core_j = StrongCore_j$ iif $StrongCore_j \neq \emptyset$; otherwise, $Core_j = WeakCore_j$. $OCore_j = K'_j \setminus Core_j$ is the set of out-of-core objects in cluster K'_j.*

d) *We denote by CORE the set $\{Core_j, 1 \leq j \leq p\}$ of all cluster cores and by OCORE the set $\{OCore_j, 1 \leq j \leq p\}$.*

For each new attribute l, $m+1 \leq l \leq m+s$, and each cluster K'_j there is at least one object that satisfies the inequality (2) in respect to the attribute l. Namely, the object that has the greatest value for attribute l between all objects in K'_j certainly satisfies the relation (the maximum value in a set is greater or equal than the mean of the values in the set). But it is not sure that there is in cluster K'_j any object that satisfies relation (2) for all new attributes $m+1, \ldots, m+s$. If there are such objects ($StrongCore_j \neq \emptyset$), we know that, according to Theorem 1, they are closer to the cluster center f'_j than to any other cluster center f'_r, $1 \leq r \leq p$, $r \neq j$. Then, $Core_j$ will be taken to be equal to $StrongCore_j$ and will be the seed for cluster j in the incremental algorithm. But if $StrongCore_j = \emptyset$, then we will choose as seed for cluster j other objects, the most stable ones between all objects in K'_j. These objects ($WeakCore_j$) can be less stable than would be the objects in $StrongCore_j$. This is not, however, a certain fact: the objects in the "weaker" set $WeakCore_j$ can be as good as those is $StrongCore_j$. This comes from the fact that Theorem 1 enounces a *sufficient* condition for the objects in K'_j to be closer to f'_j than to any other f'_r, but not a *necessary* condition too.

The *cluster cores*, chosen as we described, will serve as seed in the incremental clustering process. All objects in $Core_j$ will surely remain together in the same group if clusters do not change. This will not be the case for all core objects, but for most of them, as we will see in the results section.

We give next the *Core Based Incremental Clustering* algorithm.

We mention that the algorithm stops when the clusters from two consecutive iterations remain unchanged or the number of steps performed exceeds the maximum allowed number of iterations.

```
Algorithm Core Based Incremental Clustering is
Input: - the set X = {O_1,...,O_n} of m-dimensional objects previously
         clustered,
       - the set X' = {O'_1,...,O'_n} of (m+s)-dimensional extended objects
         to be clustered, O'_i has the same first m components as O_i,
       - the metric d_E between objects in a multi-dimensional space,
       - p, the number of desired clusters,
       - F = {F_1,...,F_p} the previous partitioning of objects in X,
       - noMaxIter the maximum number of iterations allowed.
Output: - the re-partitioning F' = {F'_1,...,F'_p} for the objects in X'.
Begin
   For all clusters F_j ∈ F
      Calculate Core_j = (StrongCore_j ≠ ∅)?StrongCore_j : WeakCore_j
```

```
        F'_j = Core_j
        Calculate f'_j as the mean of objects in F'_j
    EndFor
    While (F' changes between two consecutive steps) and
          (there were not performed noMaxIter iterations) do
        For all clusters F'_j do
            F'_j := {O'_i | d(O'_i, f'_j) ≤ d(O'_i, f'_r), ∀r, 1 ≤ r ≤ p, 1 ≤ i ≤ n}
        EndFor
        For all clusters F'_j do
            f'_j := the mean of objects in F'_j
        EndFor
    EndWhile
End.
```

The algorithm starts by calculating the old clusters' cores. The cores will be the new initial clusters from which the iterative process begins. Next, the algorithm proceeds in the same manner as the classical *k-means* method does.

Remark 1. The main characteristics of the *CBIC* algorithm are the following:

- the time complexity for calculating the cores in the clustering process does not grow the complexity of the global calculus;
- the method for calculating the core of a cluster C (using inequality (2)) depends only on the current cluster (does not depend on other clusters).

4 Experimental Evaluation

In this section we present some experimental results obtained by applying the *CBIC* algorithm described in section 3.

For this purpose, we had used a programming interface for non-hierarchical clustering described in [8]. We mention that using this interface we can simply develop non-hierarchical clustering applications for different kind of data (objects to be clusterized). As it is shown in our experiments, the objects to be clusterized are very different (patients, wine instances).

As a case study, for experimenting our theoretical results described in section 2 and for evaluating the performance of the *CBIC* algorithm, we consider some experiments that are briefly described in the following subsections.

We have to mention that most of the data were taken from the website "http://www.cormactech.com/neunet".

4.1 Quality Measures

As a quality measure for our algorithm we take the movement degree of the core objects and of the extra-core objects. In other words, we measure how the objects in either $Core_j \in CORE$, or $OCore_j \in OCORE$, remain together in clusters after the algorithm ends.

As expected, more stable the core objects are and more they remain together in respect to the initial sets $Core_j$, better was the decision to choose them as seed for the incremental clustering process. Also, as the experiments show, the movement degree was smaller for the core objects than for the extra-core objects.

We denote by $S = \{S_1, S_2, \ldots, S_p\}, S_i \subseteq K_i$, a set of clusters' subsets (as $CORE$ and $OCORE$ are). We express the *stability factor* of S as:

$$SF(S) = \frac{\sum_{j=1}^{p} \frac{|S_j|}{no\ of\ clusters\ where\ the\ objects\ in\ S_j\ ended}}{\sum_{j=1}^{p} |S_j|} \tag{3}$$

The worst case is when each object in S_j ends in a different final cluster, and this happens for every set in S. The best case is when every S_j remains compact and it is found in a single final cluster. So, the limits between which $SF(CORE)$ varies are given below, where the higher the value of $SF(CORE)$ is, better was the cores choice:

$$\frac{p}{\sum_{j=1}^{p} |Core_j|} \leq SF(CORE) \leq 1 \tag{4}$$

For comparing the informational relevance of the attributes we used the *information gain (IG)* measure ([7]).

4.2 Experiment 1. Cancer

The breast cancer database was obtained from the University of Wisconsin Hospitals, Madison, Dr. William H. Wolberg.

The objects to be clusterized in this experiment are patients: each patient is identified by 9 attributes ([10]). The attributes have been used to represent instances and each one takes integer values between 1 and 10. Each instance has one of 2 possible classes: benign or malignant. In this experiment there are 457 patients (objects).

4.3 Experiment 2. Dermatology

The objects to be clusterized in this experiment are also patients: each patient is identified by 34 attributes, 33 of which are linear valued and one of them is nominal. There are 1617 objects (patients).

The aim of the clustering process is to determine the type of Eryhemato-Squamous Disease ([3]).

The differential diagnosis of erythemato-squamous diseases is a real problem in dermatology ([3]). They all share the clinical features of erythema and scaling, with very little differences. The diseases in this group are psoriasis, seboreic dermatitis, lichen planus, pityriasis rosea, cronic dermatitis, and pityriasis rubra pilaris.

Patients were first evaluated clinically with 12 features. Afterwards, skin samples were taken for the evaluation of 22 histopathological features. The values of the histopathological features are determined by an analysis of the samples under a microscope.

In the dataset constructed for this domain, the family history feature has the value 1 if any of these diseases has been observed in the family, and 0 otherwise. The age feature simply represents the age of the patient. Every other feature (clinical and histopathological) was given a degree in the range of 0 to 3. Here, 0 indicates that the feature was not present, 3 indicates the largest amount possible, and 1, 2 indicate the relative intermediate values.

4.4 Experiment 3. Wine

These data are the results of a chemical analysis of wines grown in the same region in Italy but derived from three different cultivars. The analysis determined the quantities of 13 constituents found in each of the three types of wines ([1]).

The objects to be clusterized in this experiment are wine instances: each is identified by 13 attributes. There are 178 objects (wine instances).

We have to mention that all attributes in this experiment are continuous.

4.5 Results

In this section we present comparatively the results obtained after applying the *CBIC* algorithm for the experiments described in the above subsections. We mention that the results are calculated in average, for several executions.

From Table 1 we observe that using the *CBIC* algorithm the number of iterations for finding the solution is, usually, in the average, smaller, and also the

Table 1. The comparative results

Experiment	Cancer	Dermatology	Wine
No of objects	457	1617	178
No of attributes (m+s)	9	34	13
No of new attributes (s)	4	3	4
No of k-means iterations for (m+s) attributes	6	16	7.285
No of k-means iterations for m attributes	4.71	16.16	8
No of CBIC iterations for (m+s) attributes	7	7.16	6.571
SF(CORE)	0.9	0.930	0.524
SF(OCORE)	0.5	0.696	0.420

Table 2. The decreasing order of attributes in respect to the information gain measure

Experiment	Order of attributes	IG of new attributes / IG of old attributes (%)
Cancer	2 3 **6** **7** 5 4 **8** 1 **9**	64,7%
Dermatology	22 21 23 1 **34** 30 28 13 26 7 17 9 29 10 16 11 25 15 6 27 4 20 **32** 8 5 24 3 31 12 2 19 18 14 **33**	7,6%
Wine	7 **10** **12** **13** 6 1 2 **11** 9 4 5 3 8	57%

cores' stability factor, $SF(CORE)$, is high. We mention that for every running of each experiment, $SF(CORE) \geq SF(OCORE)$. So, every time, the stability of the objects chosen to be part or cores was greater than the stability of out-of-core objects.

In Table 2 we present, for each experiment, the attributes in decreasing order of their information gain (IG) - the new attributes are emphasized.

From Table 2 it results that the importance of the added attributes influences the number of iterations performed by the *CBIC* algorithm for finding the solution. For example, in the "cancer" experiment where the information brought by the added attributes was close to that of the initial ones, the number of iterations performed by *CBIC* is also close to the number of iterations performed by *k-means* for all the attributes.

A problem with the *k-means* algorithm is that it is sensitive to the selection of the initial partition (centroids) and may converge to a local minimum of the squared error value if the initial partition is not properly chosen. In order to properly evaluate our algorithm, we considered the same initial centroids when running *k-means* for the initial and feature-extended object set (m and $m + s$ number of attributes). It would be interesting to analyze how a good initial centroids choice affects the results.

5 Conclusions and Future Work

We proposed in this paper a new method for adapting a clustering when the attribute set describing the objects increases. The experiments on different data sets prove that, in most cases, the result is reached more efficiently using the proposed method than running *k-means* again from the scratch on the feature-extended object set. But there are some situations when it is better to resort to a full clusterization of the feature-extended object set, and not to adapt the existing clusterization using the *CBIC* algorithm. For example, such situations can be: the addition of a large number of features or the addition of new features with large information gain and contradictory information with respect to the old feature set.

Further work can be done in the following directions:

- to isolate conditions to decide when it is more effective to adapt incrementally (using *CBIC*) the clusterization of the feature-extended object set than to recalculate its clusterization (using *k-means*) from scratch;
- to apply the incremental algorithm on precise problems, from where the need of such an incremental algorithm originated;
- to study how the theoretical results described for non-hierarchical clustering could be applied/generalized for other clustering techniques.

References

1. Aeberhard, S., Coomans, D., de Vel, O.: THE CLASSIFICATION PERFORMANCE OF RDA. Tech. Rep. **92–01**, Dept. of Computer Science and Dept. of Mathematics and Statistics, James Cook University of North Queensland (1992)

2. CorMac Technologies Inc, Canada: Discover the Patterns in Your Data. http://www.cormactech.com/neunet
3. Demiroz, G., Govenir, H. A., Ilter, N.: Learning Differential Diagnosis of Eryhemato-Squamous Diseases using Voting Feature Intervals. Artificial Intelligence in Medicine
4. Han, J., Kamber, M.: Data Mining: Concepts and Techniques. Morgan Kaufmann Publishers (2001)
5. Jain, A., Dubes, R.: Algorithms for Clustering Data. Prentice Hall, Englewood Cliffs, New Jersey (1998)
6. Jain, A., Murty, M. N., Flynn, P.: Data clustering: A review. ACM Computing Surveys, **31(3)** (1999) 264-323
7. Quinlan, J. R.: C4.5: Programs for Machine Learning, Morgan Kaufmann. San Mateo, California (1993)
8. Şerban, G.: A Programming Interface for Non-Hierarchical Clustering. Studia Universitatis "Babeş-Bolyai", Informatica, **XLX(1)** (to appear)
9. Şerban, G., Câmpan, A.: Core Based Incremental Clustering. Studia Universitatis "Babeş-Bolyai", Informatica, **XLXI(2)** (to appear)
10. Wolberg, W., Mangasarian, O. L.: Multisurface method of pattern separation for medical diagnosis applied to breast cytology. Proceedings of the National Academy of Sciences, U.S.A., Volume **87**, December (1990) 9193–9196
11. Wu, F., Gardarin, G.: Gradual Clustering Algorithms. Proceedings of the 7th International Conference on Database Systems for Advanced Applications (DASFAA'01), (2001) 48–57

Indexing of Sequences of Sets for Efficient Exact and Similar Subsequence Matching

W. Andrzejewski, T. Morzy, and M. Morzy

Institute of Computing Science, Poznań University of Technology,
Berdychowo, 60-965 Poznań, Poland
{wandrzejewski, tmorzy, mmorzy}@cs.put.poznan.pl

Abstract. Object-relational database management systems allow users to define complex data types, such as objects, collections, and nested tables. Unfortunately, most commercially available database systems do not support either efficient querying or indexing of complex attributes. Different indexing schemes for complex data types have been proposed in the literature so far, most of them being application-oriented proposals. The lack of a single universal indexing technique for attributes containing sets and sequences of values significantly hinders practical usability of these data types in user applications. In this paper we present a novel indexing technique for sequence-valued attributes. Our index permits to index not only sequences of values, but sequences of sets of values as well. Experimental evaluation of the index proves the feasibility and benefit of the index in exact and similar matching of subsequences.

1 Introduction

Through unprecedented development of computer techniques witnessed in recent years, the databases are paving their way to many application areas, such as scientific, banking, industrial, retail, and financial systems. Broad applicability of database systems in diverse domains results in the development of novel data types. Traditional simple data types, such as strings, numbers, and dates, are often insufficient to describe complex structure of real-world objects. Complex data structures, such as sets and sequences, are used to reflect the complexity of the modeled reality. Sequential data are present in numerous different domains, including protein sequences, DNA chains, time series, and Web server logs. Another example of common sequence data are purchases made by customers in stores. Here, elements of a given customer sequence are not atomic, but consist of sets of products ordered by timestamps representing the date of each purchase. Contemporary object-relational database management systems support the definition and storage of complex user-defined data types as collections and nested tables. On the other hand, efficient querying and indexing of such data types is currently not supported by any commercially available database management system.

P. Yolum et al.(Eds.): ISCIS 2005, LNCS 3733, pp. 864–873, 2005.

Several indexing schemes have been proposed so far, most notably for time series and sequences of atomic values. Alas, no proposals are given for indexing of sequences of sets. The original contribution of this paper is the proposal of a new indexing structure capable of efficient retrieval of sequences of sets based on non-contiguous subsequence containment and similarity. We present the physical structure of the index and we develop algorithms for query processing based on subsequence matching and subsequence similarity. In addition, we present a novel algorithm for subsequence matching with tolerance thresholds on subsequence similarity.

The rest of the paper is organized as follows. In Section 2 we introduce basic definitions used throughout the paper. Section 3 contains an overview of the related work. We present our index in Section 4. Experimental evaluation of the index is presented in Section 5. Finally, the paper concludes in Section 6 with a summary and a future work agenda.

2 Basic Definitions

An *element of a sequence* is a pair $S_i = (v(S_i), ts(S_i))$, where $v(S_i)$ denotes the *value* of the element, and $ts(S_i)$ denotes the *timestamp* of occurrence of the element S_i. A *sequence* S is an ordered set of elements S_i arranged according to their timestamps $ts(S_i)$. We define the *length* of a sequence S as $ts(S_n) - ts(S_1)$ where S_n is the last element of the sequence S. A *subsequence* S' of the sequence S is a sequence created from the sequence S by removing arbitrary elements. A sequence $S' = \langle (v(S'_1), ts(S'_1)), \ldots, (v(S'_k), ts(S'_k)) \rangle$ is called a *continuous subsequence* of a sequence $S = \langle (v(S_1), ts(S_1)), \ldots, (v(S_n), ts(S_n)) \rangle$ (denoted $S' \subset S$) if

$$\exists w : \forall i = 1, \ldots, k \;\; v(S_{i+w}) = v(S'_i) \wedge ts(S_{i+w}) = ts(S'_i)$$

A sequence Q such that the first element of Q has the timestamp $ts(Q_1) = 0$ is called a *query sequence*. Each query sequence Q has a *tolerance sequence* T associated with it. The tolerance sequence T has the same cardinality as the query sequence Q. The elements of the tolerance sequence T are numbers, and their timestamps are consecutive integers. The elements of the tolerance sequence T form tolerance ranges for corresponding elements of the query sequence Q of the form $(ts(Q_i) - v(T_i), ts(Q_i) + v(T_i))$. In addition, tolerance ranges must not disturb the order of elements, i.e., $ts(Q_i) + v(T_i) < ts(Q_{i+1}) - v(T_{i+1})$.

An *allocation* $A(Q, S')$ is a mapping of every query sequence element to an element of S' such that $\forall i = 1, \ldots, |Q| \;\; ts(S'_i) - ts(S'_1) - ts(Q_i) \in \langle -v(T_i), +v(T_i) \rangle$.

Given a query sequence Q, the *subsequence query* retrieves all sequences S having a subsequence S', such that the following condition is fulfilled

$$l = n \wedge \forall i = 1, \ldots, n \;\; v(Q_i) \subset v(S'_i) \wedge ts(S'_i) - ts(S'_1) - ts(Q_i) \in \langle -v(T_i), +v(T_i) \rangle$$

Let ϵ denote the threshold value of minimum similarity between two sequences. Given an allocation $A(Q, S')$ of the query sequence Q to the sequence S'. The *similarity query* retrieves all sequences S such that $\exists S' \subset S : sim(Q, S') > \epsilon$, where $sim(x, y)$ is any measure of similarity between two sequences.

Given a sequence of sets S, let $sig(S_i)$ denote a binary signature of the set $v(S_i)$ and let $sig(S) = \{sig(S_i) : i = 1, \ldots, n\}$ denote the set of signatures of all the sets in the sequence S.

3 Related Work

Most research on indexing of sequence data focused on three distinct areas: indexing of time series, indexing of strings of symbols, and indexing of text. Most indexes proposed for time series support searching for similar or exact subsequences by exploiting the fact, that the elements of the indexed sequences are numbers. This is reflected both in index structure and in similarity metrics. Most popular similarity metrics include Minkowski distance [1,2], compression-based metrics [3], and dynamic time warping metrics [4]. Often, a technique for reduction of the dimensionality of the problem is employed, such as discrete Fourier transform [5,6]. String indexes usually support searching for subsequences based on identity or similarity to a given query sequence. Most common distance measure for similarity queries is the Leveshtein distance [7], and index structures are built on suffix tree [8,9,10,11] or suffix array [12].

Indexing of sequences of symbols differs significantly from indexing of strings. The main difference is the fact, that symbols in a sequence of symbols are assigned a timestamp that must be taken into consideration when processing a query. Most proposals for indexing of sequences of symbols transform the original problem into the well-researched problem of indexing of sets [13]. The transformation of a sequence into a set first maps all sequence elements into set elements, and then adds additional elements representing the precedence relation between the elements of the original sequence. The main drawback of this technique is the fact, that it ignores the timestamps associated with sequence elements. This leads to an additional verification phase, where sequences returned from the index are verified against the query sequence to prune false hits.

ISO-Depth index [14] is an indexing structure that efficiently supports searching of sequences based on subsequence containment and similarity. ISO-Depth index stores all continuous subsequences of given length in a trie structure. Additionally, trie nodes are numbered in a way permitting to quickly determine the nature of the relationship between the nodes. The order of the nodes in the trie corresponds to the order of symbols represented by those nodes in sequences pointed at in the trie leaves. Diversification of symbols in the trie (symbols differ depending on the distance from preceding symbols in a sequence) allows to answer queries containing timestamp constraints. After creating the trie structure, ISO-Depth lists and position lists are read off the trie to form the ISO-Depth index.

An interesting proposal of SEQ-join index was presented in [15]. This index uses a set of relational tables and a set of $B+$-tree indexes. Each table corresponds to a single symbol appearing in the indexed sequences and contains ordered timestamps of the symbol together with a pointer to an appropriate sequence. Preparing a subsequence query consists of creating a directed graph with nodes representing query sequence elements and edges representing order constraints between sequence elements. Answering a subsequence query consists in performing a join between symbol tables using B+-tree index joins. Detailed description of subsequence query algorithms using SEQ-join is presented in [15].

4 Generalized ISO-Depth Index

In this paper we extend the basic ISO-Depth index to support efficient indexing of sequences of sets. The new structure allows to search for similar subsequences and uses a similarity measure that is based on user-defined similarity measure for sets. We make no further assumptions on the similarity measure used to compare sets that are elements of sequences, but we require the measure to (i) increase with the increase of the size of intersection of sets, and (ii) decrease with the increase of the Hamming distance between the sets.

To the best of authors' knowledge, there are no similarity measures for sequences of sets. Therefore we introduce two new measures that can be used when formulating similarity queries on sequences of sets. Given a query sequence Q and a subsequence S' of a sequence S, such that a valid allocation $A(Q, S')$ of Q to S' exists. *Liminal similarity* is defined as the minimum similarity between any pair of sets in the allocation. Formally,

$$sim_L(Q, S') = \min_{i=1,\ldots,|Q|} \{setsim(Q_i, S'_i) : (Q_i, S'_i) \in A(Q, S')\}$$

where $setsim(Q_i, S'_i)$ is the value of user-defined similarity measure for sets that fulfills the above mentioned requirements. *Average similarity* is the average similarity between all pairs of sets in the allocation $A(Q, S')$. This similarity is given in the formula below.

$$sim_A(Q, S') = \frac{1}{|Q|} \sum_{(Q_i, S'_i) \in A(Q, S')} setsim(Q_i, S'_i)$$

It is easy to notice that for any pair of sequences (Q, S') the value of the average similarity is always greater or equal to the value of the liminal similarity between the sequences.

Below we present the algorithm for constructing the Generalized ISO-Depth index. Given a database D consisting of n sequences S^k and the width of a moving window ξ.

1. For every sequence of sets $S^k \in D$ perform the following actions
   (a) Sequence S^k is transformed into a sequence of binary signatures B^k, such that $|S^k| = |\mathcal{B}^k| \wedge \forall S_i^k : \mathcal{B}_i^k = (sig(\mathcal{S}_i^k), ts(\mathcal{S}_i^k))$. Timestamp values should be discretized prior to building binary signatures. Query sequences should be transformed analogously.
   (b) A moving window is used to read all continuous subsequences of B^k of the length lesser or equal to ξ. For each such subsequence B'^k, the sequence identifier k is stored along with the position, where B'^k starts within B^k.

(c) Subsequences B'^k are transformed into symbol sequences of the form x_i, where $x \in sig(S^k) \wedge i \in N \cup \{0\}$ using the function

$$f(B'^k) = \langle x_1, \ldots, x_n \rangle \text{ where: } x_i = \begin{cases} v(B'^k_i)_0 & \text{if } i = 1, \\ v(B'^k_i)_{ts(B'^k_i) - ts(B'^k_{i-1})} & \text{if } i > 1. \end{cases}$$

(d) Symbol sequences created in the previous step are then inserted into a modified trie structure. We modify the original trie structure in the following way: instead of defining an additional terminator symbol we add subsequence identifier to a trie node in which a given subsequence terminates. In general, there can be several subsequences terminating in a given node. Therefore, each node of the trie contains a list of subsequence identifiers.

2. The trie is traversed and all nodes are numbered using the depth-first search order. Additionally, each node is marked with the highest number of the node contained in a sub-trie starting at a given node. Those two numbers determine the range of node numbers contained in a given sub-trie. The distance of a given node from the beginning of the subsequence is simply the sum of indexes of symbols on the path to a given node.
3. The trie is used to extract ISO-Depth lists of elements of the form $(s, (a, b))$, where s is a signature of a set and the range (a, b) is the range of node numbers stored in the node pointed at by the edge representing the signature s. Each ISO-Depth list orders elements according to the value of a, and for all nodes stored in the list the distance of the node from the beginning of the subsequence is the same.
4. After creating ISO-Depth lists the trie is used to generate position lists. Each position list stores information corresponding to sequences that terminate in a given node. A position list is generated for each node where a sequence terminates.
5. ISO-Depth lists and position lists together form the Generalized ISO-Depth index. The trie structure is not used anymore and can be safely discarded.

Algorithms for processing of sequence-oriented queries using the Generalized ISO-Depth index use the following lemma.

Lemma 1. *Ranges of node numbers stored on a ISO-Depth list for a given distance from the beginning of the sequence are disjoint. Given ISO-Depth lists for distances $d_k < d_l$ from the beginning of the sequence. Let the entries on the lists be of the form $(s^k, (a^k, b^k))$ and $(s^l, (a^l, b^l))$, respectively. If $a^k < a^l \leq b^l \leq b^k$, then the database contains a sequence, such that a subsequence exists that contains sets with signatures s^k, s^l, respectively. Moreover, if the timestamp of the first element of this subsequence is subtracted from other timestamps of the subsequence elements, then the timestamps of those sets are d_k, d_l.*

The algorithm for processing of subsequence queries is given below. Let us assume that the query sequence is given as $Q = \langle (v(Q_1), 0), \ldots, (v(Q_n), ts(Q_n)) \rangle$.

1. For each timestamp $ts(Q_i)$ retrieve the ISO-Depth list for the distance equal to the timestamp.
2. Search the lists recursively. For each ISO-Depth list entry $(s^1, (a^1, b^1))$ check, if the signature $sig(Q_1)$ is contained in s^1. If true, search the ISO-Depth list corresponding to the next element of the search sequence looking for an entry $(s^2, (a^2, b^2))$, such that $a^1 < a^2 \leq b^1$ and find signatures s^2 containing $sig(Q_2)$. For each such s^2 search the list corresponding to the next element of the query sequence retrieving only the entries contained in (a^2, b^2).
3. Continue this procedure until the last element of the query sequence is reached. Signatures retrieved during each recursive call, along with the timestamps corresponding to the subsequent ISO-Depth lists, form the searched subsequence.
4. If a signature s^n is found such that s^n contains $sig(Q_n)$, use position lists to find all pointers to subsequences stored in the nodes with numbers in the range (a^n, b^n). Store those pointers for the sake of future verification. Return to the recursive traversal of ISO-Depth lists.
5. Read the subsequences accessed via stored pointers to verify the actual subsequence containment (this is required due to ambiguity introduced by binary signature generation procedure).

Algorithms for subsequence similarity matching are similar to the algorithm presented above. We design two algorithms, one capable of using tolerance sequences when searching for a similar subsequence, and one used for strict similarity subsequence searches. Both algorithms use the upper bound of approximation of similarity between compared sequences. This approximation is based on the upper bound of the intersection and the lower bound of Hamming distance between sets that are elements of the compared sequences. Using this approximation allows for significant pruning of sequences. The upper bound approximation is used during step (2) of the algorithm, instead of checking for the containment of $sig(Q_i)$ in B^i. For queries allowing tolerance sequences, the algorithm needs to retrieve in step (1) not only ISO-Depth lists for the distance equal to the timestamp $ts(Q_i)$, but all ISO-Depth lists for distances from the range $(ts(Q_i) - v(T_i), ts(Q_i) + v(T_i))$ and merge these lists into a single list.

5 Experimental Results

The efficiency of the index is experimentally evaluated and the results of the conducted experiments are presented below. For each experiment 40 different sequence databases were generated. Elements of sets contained in sequences were generated using homogeneous and Zipf distributions. Table 1 summarizes the parameters used in experiments.

After building indexes the sets of query sequences were generated. For each database 7 different sets of 10 query sequences were prepared. Each set consisted of subsequence queries and similarity queries (with and without tolerance) for similarity thresholds of 70%, 80%, and 90%.

Table 1. Synthetic data parameters

parameter	Exp.1	Exp.2	Exp.3
size of the domain	150 000	150 000	150 000
minimal distance between sets	1	1	1
maximal distance between sets	100	100	100
minimal set size	1	1	5–100
maximal set size	30	30	15–110
minimal number of sets in sequence	2	5–100	2
maximal number of sets in sequence	20	15–110	2
number of sequences	10 000–100 000	10 000	10 000
signature length	8b,16b	8b,16b	8b,16b
page/node size	4096B	4096B	4096B
window width (ξ)	250	250	250

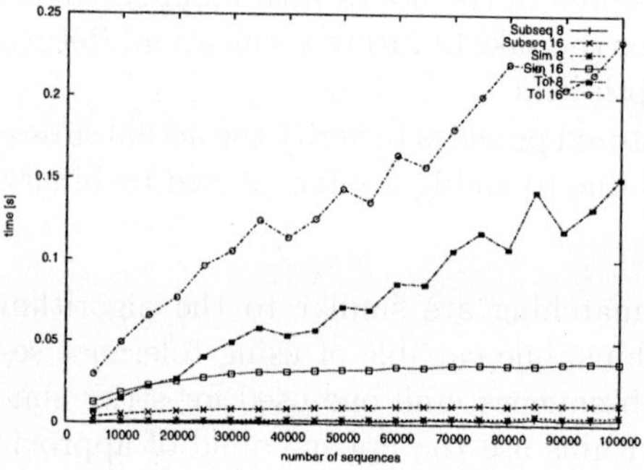

Fig. 1. Number of sequences

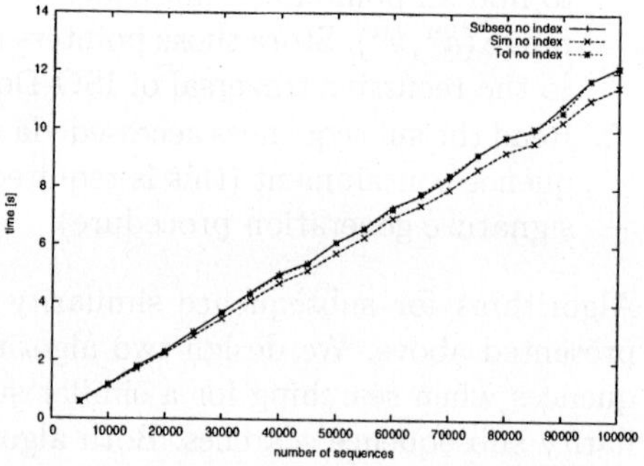

Fig. 2. Number of sequences (no index)

Experiment 1 measures the efficiency of the index with respect to increasing the size of the database. Figure 1 presents the performance of the Generalized ISO-Depth index (using 8 bit and 16 bit signatures) for subsequence queries (*Subseq*), exact similarity queries (*Sim*), and similarity queries with tolerance (*Tol*). Figure 2 presents the results for the same queries without the index. It can be easily seen that the index is 2 to 4 orders of magnitude faster than the naive approach. Query processing time grows linearly with the number of sequences stored in the database. Indexes using 8 bit signatures are faster for all classes of queries. We attribute this to the fact that shorter signatures induce smaller trie structure, less nodes in the trie, and shorter ISO-Depth lists. Of course, shorter signatures produce more ambiguity and more false hits have to be verified. Nevertheless, our experiments show that the benefit of using shorter signatures surpasses the cost of additional false hit verification.

Experiment 2 studies the impact of the average number of sets in indexed sequences on the performance of the Generalized ISO-Depth index. We vary the average number of sets from 10 to 105. Figure 3 shows the performance of our index for three classes of queries. The results for the same queries without the index are depicted in Figure 4. Both figures exhibit the results similar to the results obtained in Experiment 1. This similarity can be easily explained.

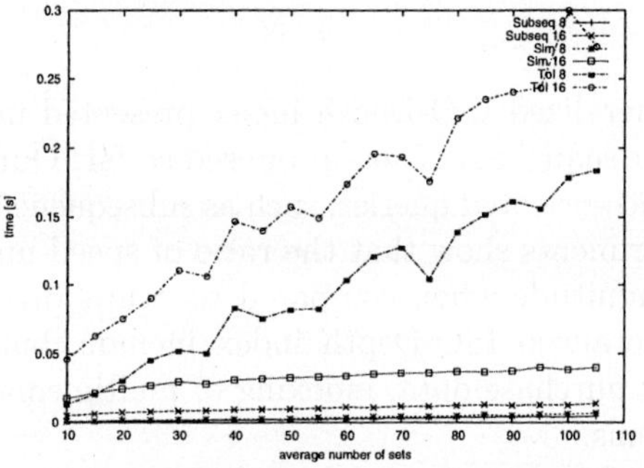

Fig. 3. Average number of sets

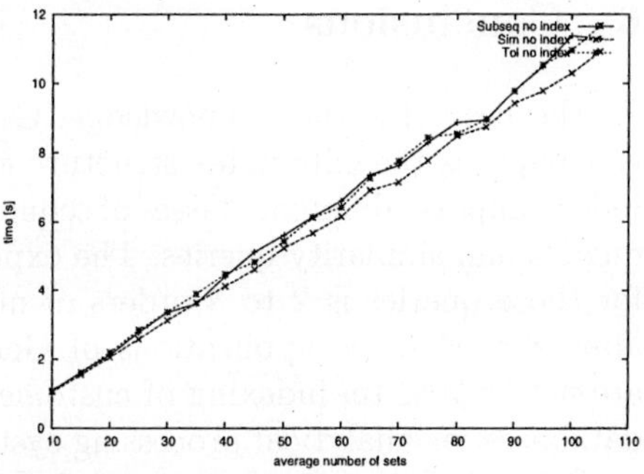

Fig. 4. Average number of sets (no index)

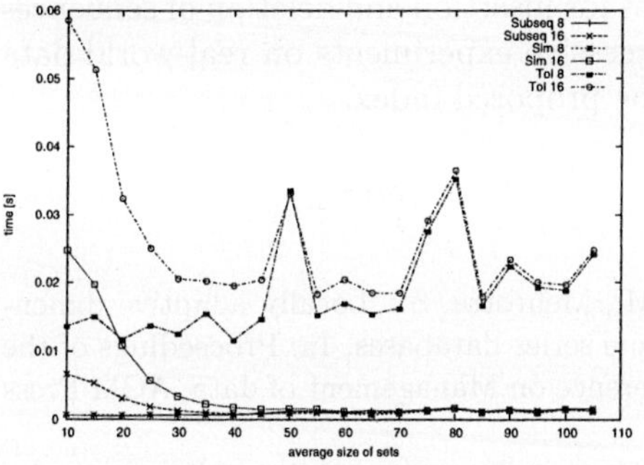

Fig. 5. Average size of sets

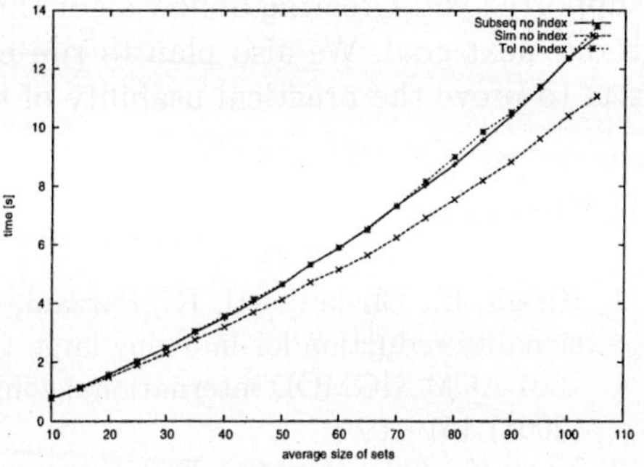

Fig. 6. Average size of sets (no index)

The number of subsequences inserted into the trie depends both on the number of sequences in the database, and the number of sets in indexed sequences. Conclusions of the Experiment 1 apply equally to the results of Experiment 2.

Experiment 3 measures the impact of the average size of sets being elements of the indexed sequences on the performance of the Generalized ISO-Depth index. We vary the average size of sets from 10 to 105. Figure 5 presents the results of three classes of queries when using the index, while Figure 6 shows the results of the same queries when not using an index. The shapes of curves presented in both figures can be easily explained. As the average size of a set grows, the probability that all positions of the signature corresponding to a given set would be set to '1' also increases. In other words, the increase of the average set size causes the saturation of signatures. Therefore, the diversity of signatures diminishes, and tho set of all signatures stored in the trie becomes more compact. As the result, the number of nodes in the trie decreases and ISO-Depth lists become shorter. This in turn results in shorter processing times, although increases the number of false hits that need to be pruned. As we have already mentioned, our experiments suggest that this additional verification phase still pays off because of the shortened access time. After reaching a certain threshold, the signatures are fully saturated with bits set to '1' and the processing time stabilizes.

6 Conclusions

To the best of authors' knowledge, Generalized ISO-Depth index presented in this paper is the only index structure for sequences of sets proposed so far. Our index supports different classes of sequence-oriented queries, such as subsequence queries and similarity queries. The experiments show that the ratio of speed-up for those queries is 2 to 4 orders of magnitude when compared to brute-force approach. Possible applications of Generalized ISO-Depth index include, but are not limited to, indexing of customer purchase data, indexing of multimedia databases, or analytical processing systems.

Still, further research is required. Our future work agenda includes optimization of the physical structure of the index and designing efficient algorithms for index maintenance. Inserting and deleting of sequences from the index is not supported yet. Creating of new algorithms for insertion and deletion of sequences is our next goal. We also plan to run excessive experiments on real-world data sets to prove the practical usability of the proposed index.

References

1. Keogh, E., Chakrabarti, K., Pazzani, M., Mehrotra, S.: Locally adaptive dimensionality reduction for indexing large time series databases. In: Proceedings of the 2001 ACM SIGMOD international conference on Management of data, ACM Press (2001) 151–162
2. Yi, B.K., Faloutsos, C.: Fast time sequence indexing for arbitrary lp norms. In: Proceedings of the 26th International Conference on Very Large Data Bases, Morgan Kaufmann Publishers Inc. (2000) 385–394
3. Keogh, E., Lonardi, S., Ratanamahatana, C.A.: Towards parameter-free data mining. In: KDD '04: Proceedings of the 2004 ACM SIGKDD international conference on Knowledge discovery and data mining, ACM Press (2004) 206–215
4. Vlachos, M., Hadjieleftheriou, M., Gunopulos, D., Keogh, E.: Indexing multidimensional time-series with support for multiple distance measures. In: ACM KDD. (2003)
5. Agrawal, R., Faloutsos, C., Swami, A.N.: Efficient similarity search in sequence databases. In: Proceedings of the 4th International Conference on Foundations of Data Organization and Algorithms, Springer-Verlag (1993) 69–84
6. Faloutsos, C., Ranganathan, M., Manolopoulos, Y.: Fast subsequence matching in time-series databases. In: Proceedings of the 1994 ACM SIGMOD international conference on Management of data, ACM Press (1994) 419–429
7. Levenshtein, V.I.: Binary codes capable of correcting deletions, insertions and reversals. Doklady Akademia Nauk SSSR **163** (1965) 845–848
8. McCreight, E.M.: A space-economical suffix tree construction algorithm. J. ACM **23** (1976) 262–272
9. Ukkonen, E.: Constructing suffix trees on-line in linear time. In J.v.Leeuwen, ed.: Information Processing 92, Proc. IFIP 12th World Computer Congress. Volume 1., Elsevier Sci. Publ. (1992) 484–492
10. Ukkonen, E.: On-line construction of suffix trees. Algorithmica **14** (1995) 249–260
11. Weiner, P.: Linear pattern matching algorithms. In: Proceedings 14th IEEE Annual Symposium on Switching and Automata Theory. (1973) 1–11

12. Manber, U., Myers, G.: Suffix arrays: a new method for on-line string searches. In: Proceedings of the first annual ACM-SIAM symposium on Discrete algorithms, Society for Industrial and Applied Mathematics (1990) 319–327
13. Nanopoulos, A., Manolopoulos, Y., Zakrzewicz, M., Morzy, T.: Indexing web access-logs for pattern queries. In: WIDM '02: Proceedings of the 4th international workshop on Web information and data management, ACM Press (2002) 63–68
14. Wang, H., Perng, C.S., Fan, W., Park, S., Yu, P.S.: Indexing weighted-sequences in large databases. In: Proceedings of International Conference on Data Engineering. (2003)
15. Mamoulis, N., Yiu, M.L.: Non-contiguous sequence pattern queries. In: Proceedings of the 9th International Conference on Extending Database Technology. (2004)

An Investigation of the Course-Section Assignment Problem

Zeki Bayram

Eastern Mediterranean University, Computer Engineering Department,
Famagusta, T.R.N. Cyprus
zeki.bayram@emu.edu.tr
http://cmpe.emu.edu.tr/bayram

Abstract. We investigate the problem of enumerating schedules, consisting of course-section assignments, in increasing order of the number of conflicts they contain. We define the problem formally, and then present an algorithm that systematically enumerates solutions for it. The algorithm uses backtracking to perform a depth-first search of the implicit search space defined by the problem, pruning the search space when possible. We derive a mathematical formula for the algorithm's average-case time complexity using a probabilistic approach, and also give a brief overview of its implementation in a WEB application.

1 Introduction

In this paper we deal with the course-section assignment problem that arises in university settings. Although the investigated problem is specific to Eastern Mediterranean University (North Cyprus), the results can easily be generalized to other university contexts.

At Eastern Mediterranean University, classes are taught Mondays through Fridays, between 8:30 a.m. and 4:30 p.m. A given course is opened in one or more sections. Each section of a course meets for 3 or 4 hours each week. The job of the student advisor during the registration period is to decide which courses the student should take, and find a set of sections for those courses such that the number of conflicts is minimized.

The problem we investigate is enumerating, in increasing order of the number of conflicts, course-section assignment schedules, given an initial list of courses that the student should take. The student advisor can then select the schedule s/he sees fit.

Course scheduling problems, when formulated as decision problems, are known to be NP-complete or even NP-hard [1], and finding the optimal solution to the problem is computationally intractable as the input sizes become large. The course-section assignment variation of the course scheduling problem is a function problem, and is at least as hard as the decision version ("Is there a course section assignment with k conflicts or less?"). However, in the real-life case we handle here, the maximum input sizes to the problem have a reasonable upper bound (i.e. a student can take only a limited number of courses which

P. Yolum et al.(Eds.): ISCIS 2005, LNCS 3733, pp. 874–883, 2005.

the advisor selects for him/her, and each course has a limited number of sections that are open at any one time) and an approach that systematically but intelligently and incrementally searches the full space of possibilities becomes feasible.

Assuming that the maximum number of courses a student takes is N and the maximum number of sections a course can have is K, then at most K^N combinations of course sections must be considered. But even then, generating all combinations of course groups at one time and then sorting them by the number of conflicts they contain can be prohibitively expensive, both in terms of time and space. Instead, the search space should be pruned when possible, and the solutions must be *incrementally* generated, in increasing order of the number of conflicts they contain. When enough solutions (defined as the best X solutions, where X is specified by the user) have been generated, the algorithm should stop.

The algorithm we describe does precisely that, and it is fast enough to be executed in a WEB browser's JavaScript engine.

The remainder of this paper is organized as follows. Section 2 formally defines the "course-section assignment problem." Section 3 contains an algorithm that systematically generates course-section assignments in increasing order of the number of conflicts. In section 4 we perform a mathematical analysis of the worst-case and average-case time complexity of this algorithm using combinatorial arguments. Section 5 gives a brief discussion of the issues concerning the JavaScript implementation of the algorithm. This is followed in section 6 by a representative survey of other approaches to course scheduling, and finally in section 7 we have the conclusion and future research directions.

2 Formal Definition of the Course-Section Assignment Problem

In this section we formally define what we mean by the "course-section assignment problem."

Definition 1. *A* `meeting-time` *is a day-period pair, such as* $< Monday, 3 >$, *meaning the third period (i.e. 10:30) on Monday.*

Definition 2. *The function* `rep(D,P)` *is defined as* $(val(D) * 8) + P$, *where* $< D, P >$ *is a meeting-time and* `val` *is a function mapping each working day to its position in the week, starting from 0, e.g.* $val(Monday) = 0$, $val(Tuesday) = 1$ *etc. Consequently, rep(D,P) is a unique integer representation of a meeting-time* $< D, P >$. *No two distinct meeting-times have the same integer representation, since there are exactly 8 periods every day.*

Definition 3. *A* `course-section assignment` *is a function that maps a course to one of its sections.*

Definition 4. *The function* `meetingTimes(C,S)` *returns the set of meeting-times of section* S *of course* C. *Formally,* $x \in meetingTimes(C, S)$ *iff* $< D, P >$ *is a meeting-time of section* S *of course* C *and* $x = rep(D, P)$.

Definition 5. *The function* `nconf(assign)` *takes a course-section assignment as an argument and returns the number of conflicts it contains. Specifically, let* $< C_1, \ldots, C_n >$ *be a list of courses and* `assign` *be a course-section assignment.* $nconf(assign)$ *is defined as*

$$|meetingTimes(C_1, assign(C_1))| + \ldots + |meetingTimes(C_n, assign(C_n))| -$$
$$|meetingTimes(C_1, assign(C_1)) \cup \ldots \cup meetingTimes(C_n, assign(C_n))|$$

Definition 6. *Given a list of courses* $< C_1, \ldots, C_n >$, *the* `course-section assignment problem` *is to generate a sequence* $< ass_1, ass_2, \ldots >$ *of course-section assignments in such a way that every assignment appears exactly once in the sequence, and if* ass_i *comes before* ass_j *in the sequence, then* $nconf(ass_i) \leq nconf(ass_j)$.

3 The Scheduling Algorithm

3.1 Data Representation

We represent the times at which a course section is taught with a bitmap consisting of 40 bits (5 days, 8 periods, one bit for each $Day - Period$ combination). A "1" in a position means that the course is taught at that time slot, and a "0" that it is not. The first 8 bits in the bitmap are used for the 8 time slots on Monday, the next 8 bits for Tuesday etc. To determine whether two course sections conflict, we just $\bigwedge$ (logical "and") the corresponding bitmaps, and if the result is other than 0, then they conflict. Using this representation, we can also determine the number of conflicts by counting the number of 1's in the result (this can be done in constant time using a lookup table t where $t[i]$ contains the number of 1's in the binary representation of i [2]). Using bitmaps with logical "or" and "and" operations, determining whether n course sections conflict has $O(n)$ time complexity.

3.2 The Algorithm in Pseudo-code

The algorithm in figure 1 finds course-section assignments in increasing order of the number of conflicts by traversing in a depth-first fashion an implicit tree whose nodes consist of a bitmap representing the day-time slots taken up by the courses considered so far. The root of this tree is always a bitmap of 40 bits that contains all "0"s.

The main identifiers in the algorithm are as follows. $current[i]$ contains the bitmap of slots taken up by $course_1$ through $course_i$. The sections of courses that are selected as we travel down the implicit tree are stored in the *result* array, i.e. $result[i]$ contains the section selected for $course_i$. $next[i]$ contains the next section to try for $course_i$ upon backtracking, or when going forward "down the tree." The function $meeting\_times(i, j)$ returns a bitmap of 40 bits which depicts the meeting-times during the week of section j of $course_i$. $nc[i]$ contains the number of conflicts in the schedule up to and including $course_i$. The function $count\_ones(bitmap)$ counts the number of "1"s in its argument.

Input:

1. C, the maximum number of conflicts that can be tolerated.
2. List of courses $course_1, course_2, \ldots, course_L$ for which we need to find schedules with at most C conflicts.
3. K, the number of sections per course.
4. The function $meeting\_times(i, j)$ that gives the bitmap for course i, section j.
5. $max\_solutions$, the maximum number of solutions that should be generated

Output: All combinations of course sections such that the number of conflicts does not exceed C and solutions are generated in increasing order of the number of conflicts they contain, up to a maximum of $max\_solutions$ solutions

```
declare current as an array[0..L] of bitmaps    // each one 40 bits long
declare nc as an array[0..L] of integer         // number of conflicts
declare next as an array[1..L + 1] of integer   // choice points for backtracking
declare result as an array[1..L] of integer     // selected sections
ns ← 0                                          // number of solutions generated
for c ← 0 to C
  i ← 1                                         // the next course to process
  next[1] ← 1                                   // process section 1 of course 1
  current[0] ← (000000...)                      // bitmap of forty zeroes
  nc[0] ← 0                                     // initial node contains no conflicts
  loop
    if ns > max_solutions then exit program end if
    if i = 0 then exit loop end if              // tree for current value of c traversed
    if next[i] > K then                         // processed all sections
      i ← i − 1; continue loop                  // backtrack to previous course
    end if
    if i = L + 1 then                           // processed all courses
      if c = nc[i − 1] then                     // check for exact number of conflicts
        print the result array
        ns ← ns + 1                             // update number of solutions found
      end if
      i ← i − 1; continue loop                  // backtrack
    end if
    new_conflicts ← count_ones(meeting_times(i, next[i]) ⋀ current[i − 1])
    if (new_conflicts + nc[i − 1]) ≤ c then     // move forward
      nc[i] ← nc[i − 1] + new_conflicts
      current[i] ← current[i − 1] ⋁ meeting_times(i, next[i])
      result[i] ← next[i]                       // store section
      next[i] ← next[i] + 1                     // prepare for backtracking
      next[i + 1] ← 1                           // start at section 1
      i ← i + 1                                 // for the next course
      continue loop
    end if
    next[i] ← next[i] + 1                       // else try next section
  end loop
end for
```

Fig. 1. Backtracking algorithm for generating course-section assignment schedules in increasing order of the number of conflicts

The algorithm assumes that each section meets the same number of times (i.e. K) during the week. This simplification does not affect the core of the algorithm and makes the ensuing mathematical analysis tractable.

4 Time-Complexity of the Algorithm

In the following discussion, let us assume that a student takes N courses, each course has K sections (for uniformity), and each section meets R times per week. Let us also ignore the maximum number of results requested by the user, as this can only improve the performance of the algorithm.

The number nodes that are "generated" in the implicit tree is an accurate measure of the time complexity of the algorithm.

4.1 Worst-Case Time-Complexity Analysis

If the root has level 0, then the level of the leaf nodes in the full implicit tree is N, the branching factor of each inner node is K and the full tree has

$$\sum_{i=0}^{N} K^i . \tag{1}$$

nodes. In the *worst case*, all these nodes are visited. Furthermore, if C is the maximum number of conflicts that are tolerated, then the algorithm makes $C+1$ passes over the tree (although each distinct solution is printed exactly once), and the number of generated (and re-generated) nodes becomes

$$\sum_{j=0}^{C} \sum_{i=0}^{N} K^i . \tag{2}$$

The above formula is an upper bound on the number of nodes that are visited. However, if a node contains more conflicts than can be tolerated, it is not visited. In a sense, the tree is pruned. We explore that case below.

4.2 Average-Case Time-Complexity Analysis

For a specific number of conflicts that we can tolerate, we can compute the probability that a node in the implicit tree will be visited by the algorithm. Let $P(Y@L_b)$ denote the probability that a node at level b with *exactly* Y number of conflicts will be visited. Let c' be the maximum number of conflicts we can tolerate in a specific iteration of the algorithm. Then, the *expected* number of visited nodes for c' *or less* number of conflicts in an iteration of the algorithm is given by:

$$\sum_{j=0}^{c'} \sum_{i=0}^{N} K^i P(j@L_i) . \tag{3}$$

However, the algorithm, in order to list solutions in increasing number of conflicts (i.e. those solutions with no conflicts, followed by those with exactly one conflict, followed by those solutions with exactly two conflicts etc.), makes multiple passes of the virtual tree. For example, the leaf node that represents a solution with 0 conflicts will be generated (visited) three times if we can tolerate 2 conflicts. The average time complexity of the algorithm in that case is:

$$\sum_{c'=0}^{C}\sum_{j=0}^{c'}\sum_{i=0}^{N} K^i P(j@L_i)\,. \tag{4}$$

Computing $P(j@L_i)$. The root of the implicit tree is always visited, so are the nodes at level 1, since there cannot be any conflicts with no courses selected, or with one course selected only. Thus,

$$\begin{aligned} P(0@L_0) &= 1\,.\\ P(0@L_1) &= 1\,.\\ P(j@L_0) &= 0 \quad for\ j \geq 1\,.\\ P(j@L_1) &= 0 \quad for\ j \geq 1\,. \end{aligned} \tag{5}$$

For nodes at level 2 we have

$$P(j@L_2) = \frac{\binom{40}{j}\binom{40-j}{R-j}\binom{40-R}{R-j}}{\binom{40}{R}^2}\,. \tag{6}$$

This formula can be justified as follows. $\binom{40}{R}^2$ is the total space of possibilities for the slots that can be taken by any two distinct courses (each course takes R slots). j slots are common to both courses, and these j slots can be taken in $\binom{40}{j}$ ways. That leaves the first course $\binom{40-j}{R-j}$ ways to choose its remaining $R-j$ slots, and the second course $\binom{40-R}{R-j}$ ways to choose *its* $R-j$ slots.

For values of i greater than 2, we need a recursive definition of $P(j@L_i)$. Let the notation $L_{i-1} \stackrel{k}{\Longrightarrow} L_i$ mean that k new conflicts are introduced by the move from a node at level $i-1$ to a node at level i, and $P(L_{i-1} \stackrel{k}{\Longrightarrow} L_i, e)$ denote the probability that k new conflicts are introduced on the move from a node at level $i-1$ to a node at level i, if at node $i-1$ we already have e conflicts. Then, for $i > 2$,

$$P(j@L_i) = \Sigma_{e=0}^{j} P(e@L_{i-1}) P(L_{i-1} \stackrel{j-e}{\Longrightarrow} L_i, e)\,. \tag{7}$$

where

$$P(L_{i-1} \stackrel{k}{\Longrightarrow} L_i, e) = \frac{\binom{(i-1)R-e}{k}\binom{40-((i-1)R-e)}{R-k}}{\binom{40}{R}}\,. \tag{8}$$

The justification for Formula (8) is as follows. At level $i-1$ we have made assignments to $i-1$ courses, and since they have e conflicts, they use $(i-1)R-e$ slots. If we introduce k new conflicts, then surely these conflicts should be caused by the slots already taken up, hence the term $\binom{(i-1)R-e}{k}$. The remaining $R-k$ slots should come from slots not already taken up, which is $40-((i-1)R-e)$, hence the term $\binom{40-((i-1)R-e)}{R-k}$. $\binom{40}{R}$ is just all possible ways of selecting R slots out of 40 slots.

5 The Implemented Solution

The implemented solution is a WEB application with a three tier architecture. The user of the application (the student advisor) fills out an HTML form concerning the courses to be taken. He has the option of specifying which sections of a course to choose from, or alternatively which sections of a course to exclude (for example, a student might insist on taking a section which is taught by his/her favorite instructor, or s/he might insist on not taking a section taught by a disliked instructor). An example form is shown in figure 2. The form is

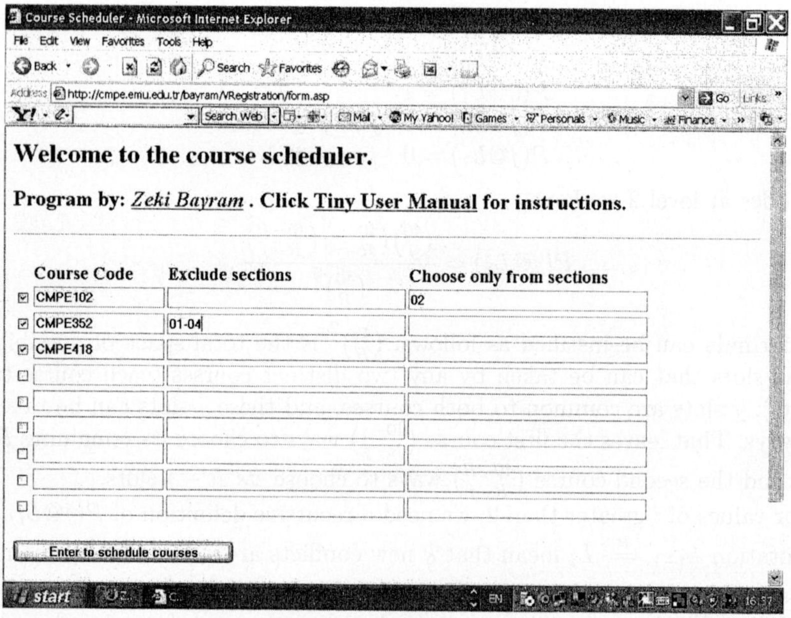

Fig. 2. The form for choosing courses

sent to an Active Server Pages (ASP) application on the server, which, after querying a *courses* database, generates and sends back an HTML page with the necessary course information and the scheduling algorithm as a JavaScript program. The course information is hard-wired into the algorithm, so that each time a user makes a request with different courses, a different JavaScript code is sent to him/her. The JavaScript code then runs on the client, generating schedules (up to a "reasonable" maximum number hard-coded in the program), in order from the least number of conflicts (ideally 0) to the most number of conflicts.

Figure 3 shows part of the result returned by the scheduler. The scheduler WEB application is available at [3].

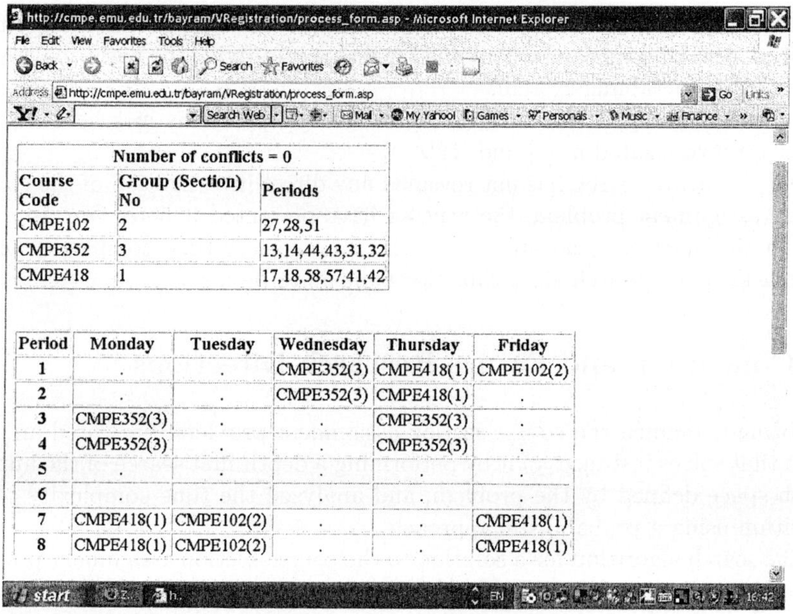

Number of conflicts = 0		
Course Code	Group (Section) No	Periods
CMPE102	2	27,28,51
CMPE352	3	13,14,44,43,31,32
CMPE418	1	17,18,58,57,41,42

Period	Monday	Tuesday	Wednesday	Thursday	Friday
1	.	.	CMPE352(3)	CMPE418(1)	CMPE102(2)
2	.	.	CMPE352(3)	CMPE418(1)	.
3	CMPE352(3)	.	.	CMPE352(3)	.
4	CMPE352(3)	.	.	CMPE352(3)	.
5	.				.
6					
7	CMPE418(1)	CMPE102(2)	.	.	CMPE418(1)
8	CMPE418(1)	CMPE102(2)	.	.	CMPE418(1)

Fig. 3. Part of the result returned by the scheduler

6 Related Work

There have been a few major venues of attack against course scheduling (sometimes called "timetabling") problems. These include constraint logic programming, genetic algorithms, simulated annealing, tabu search or some combination of these.

In [4] the authors use the Eclipse constraint logic programming system to construct optimum timetables for university courses. The application of combined deductive and object-oriented technologies to a "complex scheduling problem" which emphasizes local propagation of constraints performed with deductive rules is presented in [5].

Use of genetic algorithms for the solution of the timetabling problem is investigated in [6].

In [7] the authors investigate a variety of approaches based on simulated annealing for the course scheduling problem, including mean-field annealing, simulated annealing with three different cooling schedules, and the use of a rule-based preprocessor to provide a good initial solution for annealing.

An expert system solution to the timetabling problem is given in [8]. The expert system is written using a CLP(FD) system that extends the CHIP constraint logic system with heuristics.

In [9] the authors formulate course scheduling as a constraint satisfaction problem and apply various optimization techniques to solve it. A similar approach is taken in [10] where the potential of constraint satisfaction techniques to handle deterministic scheduling problems is investigated.

In [11], the authors present graph colouring and room allocation algorithms and show how the two can be combined together to provide the basis of a "widely applicable" timetabling system.

Tabu search algorithms for solving scheduling problems in school environments are investigated in [1] and [12].

Our literature search has not revealed any direct investigation of the course-section assignment problem, the way we have presented it here. Our approach used in the mathematical analysis of the average-case time complexity of the backtracking tree-search algorithm also appears to be novel.

7 Conclusion and Future Research Directions

We formally defined the course-section assignment problem, presented an algorithm that solves instances of it by performing a depth-first search of the implicit search space defined by the problem, and analyzed the time complexity of the algorithm using a probabilistic approach.

The search algorithm for a solution to the course-section assignment problem can be generalized to solve other kinds of scheduling problems. The mathematical approach we used here can be applied to analyze those algorithms also. Future work might include the extension of the presented framework to handle such more general scheduling problems.

References

1. Schaerf, A.: Tabu search techniques for large high-school timetabling problems. In: Proceedings of the Fourteenth National Conference on Artificial Intelligence, Portland, Oregon, USA (1996) 363–368
2. Silberchatz, Korth, S.: Database System Concepts. 4 edn. McGraw Hill (2002)
3. Bayram, Z.: Course scheduling web application, available at web site. http://cmpe.emu.edu.tr/bayram/VRegistration/form.asp (2003)
4. Frangouli, H., Harmandas, V., Stamatopoulos, P.: UTSE: Construction of optimum timetables for university courses - A CLP based approach. In: Proceedings of the 3rd International Conference on the Practical Applications of Prolog PAP'95, Paris (1995) 225–243
5. Y., C., Guillo, P., Levenez, E.: A deductive and object-oriented approach to a complex scheduling problem. In: Proceedings of Deductive and Object-Oriented Databases: Third International Conference, Phoenix, Arizona, USA (1993) 67–80
6. Colorni, A., Dorigo, M., Maniezzo, V.: Genetic algorithms - A new approach to the timetable problem. Lecture Notes in Computer Science - NATO ASI Series , Combinatorial Optimization, (Akgul et al eds) **F 82** (1990) 235–239
7. Elmohamed, M.A.S., Coddington, P., Fox, G.: A comparison of annealing techniques for academic course scheduling. Lecture Notes in Computer Science **1408** (1988) 92–114
8. Azevedo, F., Barahona, P.: Timetabling in constraint logic programming. In: Proceedings of the 2nd World Congress on Expert Systems, Lisbon, Portugal (January 1994)

9. Blanco, J., Khatib, L.: Course scheduling as a constraint satisfaction problem. In: Proceedings of the Fourth International Conference and Exhibition on The Practical Application of Constraint Technology, London, England (1998)
10. Dignum, F.W.N., Janssen, L.: Solving a time tabling problem by constraint satisfaction. Technical report, Eindhoven University of Technology (1995)
11. Burke, E.K., Elliman, D.G., Weare, R.F.: A university timetabling system based on graph colouring and constraint manipulation. Journal of Research on Computing in Education **27**(1) (1994) 1–18
12. Gaspero, L.D., Schaerf, A.: Tabu search techniques for examination timetabling. Lecture Notes in Computer Science **2079** (2001) 104–108

Crympix: Cryptographic Multiprecision Library

Ahmet Koltuksuz and Hüseyin Hışıl

Izmir Institute of Technology, College of Engineering, Dept. of Computer Engineering, Gülbahçe, Urla, 35430 Izmir, Turkey
{ahmetkoltuksuz, huseyinhisil}@iyte.edu.tr

Abstract. This paper delineates the results gained throughout the development of a cryptographic multiprecision[1] integer library, CRYMPIX. To obtain the know-how for cryptographic computation and thus being able to create the high level cryptographic protocols in an in-house-fashion are the main reasons of this development. CRYMPIX is mainly designed to supply code readability and portability plus an increased performance over other similar libraries. The whole work is achieved by detailed investigation of current algorithms and multi-precision libraries. The selected algorithms are discussed by means of efficiency and various implementation techniques. The comparative performance measurements of CRYMPIX against other multiprecision libraries show that the overall performance of CRYMPIX is not behind its predecessors if not superior.

1 Introduction

The efficiency of a cryptographic implementation considerably depends on its low-level multiprecision library. A cryptographic library is said to be competitive among its alternatives if it is engineered with not only the advanced level of coding but also with the careful selection of algorithms concerning their theoretical complexities and their inclination to the underlying hardware. However, finding the best tuning is always a tedious job because one has to switch between various algorithms with respect to some threshold values. On the other hand, once the library is developed, it is relatively easier to perform further scientific studies and go deeper inside the computational aspects of the cryptographic world. With this motivation, we strongly advise to code at least some functions if not all of a cryptographic library for every researcher who is in the field of cryptology.

Either designed for cryptographic use or not, most of the current multiprecision libraries implement arithmetic, logic and number theoretic routines. CRYMPIX also offers those capabilities. What makes CRYMPIX different from its alternatives is its design criteria as well as its performance. Our measurements showed that the overall performance is not behind the other libraries. In

[1] Arbitrary-precision, multiprecision and bignum are synonyms. In the subsequent parts of this text, the term multiprecision is preferred to address the multiple-precision.

P. Yolum et al.(Eds.): ISCIS 2005, LNCS 3733, pp. 884–893, 2005.

this paper, we explain the principles of which CRYMPIX is developed by plus will compare its performance with the others.

It is known that the asymmetrical cryptosystems require multiprecision arithmetic when they are run on fixed precision processors. For instance, if an RSA implementation uses 4096-bit key size then at least 128 computer words is needed to store and process this key on 32 bit architecture. To address this necessity, many libraries are developed up to now. The most popular ones among these libraries are GNU GMP, Shamus Software MIRACL, LibTomMath, PARI/GP, BigNum, Java BigInteger, Bouncy Castle, Magma, Maple, Mathematica, and MuPAD. All of these are implemented for related but different purposes. Therefore, it is quite likely that one needs several of them to satisfy the one's specific scientific research needs.

Excluding the scientific interpreters, the efficiency of a cryptographic library is directly proportional to the overall performance of some well known number theoretical routines such as modular powering, greatest common divisor and multiplication. Therefore, almost all of these libraries contain specialized parts for several different architectures. So, it is clear that the implementation has a tendency of multiplying very rapidly in terms of coding efforts which in turn requires handling of multiple libraries in one project thus the growing pains of code management.

In this study, we discuss how to minimize the development effort without causing any performance degradation. Finally, we compare the outcome of our design decisions with that of some other libraries.

2 Basic Design Criteria

Common design criteria of most multiprecision libraries are representation of numbers, programming language selection, memory management, portability, and functionality [1]. A well designed library is expected to satisfy optimum decisions and utilize the underlying hardware at its peak. In the following sections, we describe the design parameters of CRYMPIX and compare and contrast it with that of the corresponding parameters of other libraries.

2.1 Representation of Numbers

Almost all multiprecision libraries use positive integer vectors that are analogous to the radix representation that is given in below equation 1.

$$x = (x_{n-1}, x_{n-2}, x_{n-3}, ..., x_0)_\beta = \sum_{i=0}^{n-1} x_i \cdot \beta^i. \tag{1}$$

CRYMPIX also uses this representation. The number is partitioned into compartments and is laid along a memory space with the first variable being set to the least significant digit of the number. Radix representation is further explained in [7].

2.2 Programming Language

The preferred languages in multiprecision library development are Assembly, C, C++, FORTRAN, and Java. Excluding Assembly, the performance of any given cryptographic library depends on the coding talents of developer as well as the chosen design criteria. It is clear that performance of Assembly will always be one step ahead hence the exclusion.

ANSI C is selected as the development language of CRYMPIX. Pointer arithmetic and structural features and portability of ANSI C code play the most important role in our decision. Easy integration with Message Passing Interface (MPI) is also a distinguishing factor. In most of the other cryptographic libraries some inner-most loops are delivered to user with Assembly on the compile time as an answer to the demand of high speed computation. We are going to limit our discussion only with C and the C based versions of other libraries in this paper since CRYMPIX aims to be an educational library in which the most suitable algorithms are being implemented for cryptographic use. Nevertheless, we have included a performance table that may give the reader an idea of how Assembly affects the performance in Table 1.

On Table 1, MIRACL 4.8, GMP 4.1.4, Java BigInteger and CRYMPIX are benchmarked via their integer multiplication function. We prepared test suits of

Table 1. Integer Multiplication benchmark results. (microseconds).

Size	CRYMPIX		MIRACL		GMP		Java
	C, v1	C, v2	C	C+Asm	C	C+Asm	BigInteger
1K	21	11	17	6	23	4	32
2K	69	41	68	26	74	15	132
4K	219	133	277	104	235	47	512
8K	673	410	1097	411	731	154	2630

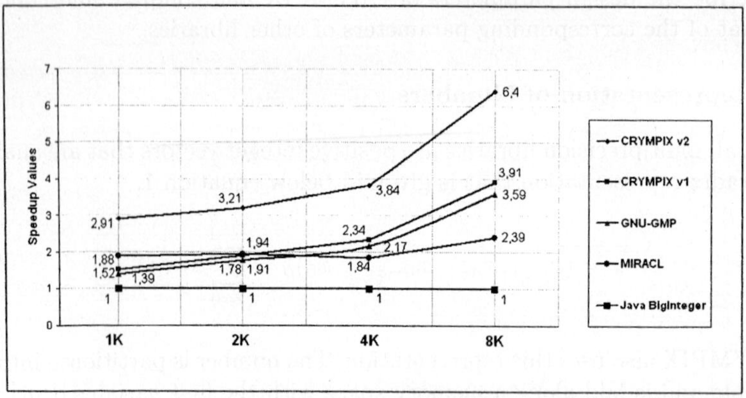

Fig. 1. Speedup values obtained by the results in Table 1

1K, 2K, 4K, and 8K each having 1000 randomly selected inputs. We decoupled the I/O time to get more accurate results. Excluding Java BigInteger, all tests are done with GNU GCC compiler at optimization levels *O*0, *O*1, and *O*2. The whole test is repeated on Intel Centrino M 1400 Mhz, Intel P4 1700 Mhz, and IBM RISC RS/6000 133 Mhz processors with no options on memory. As an operating system we used YellowDog 2.3 Linux on IBM RISC RS/6000 machine and Redhat Linux 9.0 and Microsoft Windows XP/SP2 on Intel machines. To port GNU GCC compiler to Windows we used CYGWIN platform. Java BigInteger benchmark is done on Java Virtual Machine (JVM) of Sun Microsystems, Inc., Java2 Standard Development Kit (J2SDK) v1.4.2 and applied on Intel boxes and on both Redhat Linux and Microsoft Windows XP. The whole measurements have provided us with so much data and since the speedup values are nearly constant we give results of only Intel Centrino M 1400 MHz processor with Redhat Linux operating system. The above defined test environment is used throughout this study.

ISO C'99 standard has introduced a new data type, namely `long long`, which enabled full length single-precision multiplication with C language. CRYMPIX v2 and MIRACL takes the advantage of the new double-precision data type. CRYMPIX v1 and GMP don't use this facility. What separates CRYMPIX v1 and CRYMPIX v2 is a simple compile time macro. We merely include this feature to do fair comparisons with the other libraries. Fig. 1 indicates that CRYMPIX is competitive on all test beds. MIRACL has an embedded Karatsuba/Comb routine but it is used for more costly operations such as modular exponentiation, thus it is relatively slower in this experiment. The overall performance of Java BigInteger varies with respect to the JVM but this library is slower in all circumstances and it is developed with the basecase algorithms in most cases. On the other hand, it is far easier to develop applications on such an object oriented environment. We used this library only to generate the test beds data. In Fig. 1 we have provided the performance comparison of libraries for C only built at optimization level 2 (excluding Java BigInteger).

2.3 Memory Management

Since all asymmetrical cryptosystems uses modular arithmetic, we are able to know how much the numbers grow. In this case, it is possible to prevent memory fragmentation if we fix the size of each number. Furthermore, memory allocation cost can be further decreased if a specialized kernel layer is utilized for the implementation. The kernel is responsible for fast memory allocation and subsequent release service. The whole memory needed by the application is allocated when the system initialized. This type of approach is crucial in embedded and/or real-time systems. To prevent the system run out of memory, exceeding allocations can be made by `malloc()` function. In other words, system starts dynamic memory allocations if and when necessary.

MIRACL's design is partially similar to above discussion. The space need for each number is fixed and is declared to the system as a runtime parameter. The memory allocation is done via `malloc()` function. Each number that is passed to a function is assumed to be initialized. To overcome the slowness of malloc() function, MIRACL uses an inner workspace. This approach prevents exhaustive memory allocation and release problem.

Memory allocation in GMP is done with malloc() function. The system automatically increase memory space for each number when needed. This approach is open to memory fragmentation which slows down GMP. However, GMP remedies this omission by using the stack memory. If the overall performance does not satisfy the requirements, the user is allowed to do custom memory allocation.

Java BigInteger is designed to meet object oriented programming criteria. There is no limitation or space preallocation for the numbers. JVM and its garbage collector determine the overall performance. When compared to C libraries, BigInteger is slower; on the other hand, code development is far easier.

CRYMPIX is designed to manage its own memory. Stack memory is not used for manipulating multiprecision numbers. The whole memory, needed by the application, is reserved by an initialization function. A tiny kernel supplies a fast memory allocation and release service on the preallocated space. The kernel uses a circular array data structure to speed up the allocation and release operations. Size of each number is fixed to prevent memory fragmentation. There is no built-in garbage collector mechanism in C so that programmer is responsible for the life cycle of each number. The code below introduces CRYMPIX with an integer addition example.

CRYMPIX Code Example for Integer Addition.

```
CZ a, b, c;
crympix_init(100, 20);    // Max words, max instances.
...
a = cz_init();
b = cz_init();
c = cz_init();
...
cz_add(c, a, b);    // c = a + b.
...
cz_kill(a);
cz_kill(b);
cz_kill(c);
...
crympix_finalize();
```

2.4 Code Readability and Portability

Code readability has been one of the major concerns in CRYMPIX library right from the start. Therefore, function bodies are written as plain as possible and the code organization, a standardized naming and indentation are applied throughout the development. We have observed that there are three major code portability styles in the libraries mentioned above. In the first style; which is a naive approach, the architecture-depended code is blended together with the original one. They are separated with compile time pragmas. This approach is open to *spaghetti-like* coding. The second approach is to place architecture-depended code in separate files. This approach is used in GMP library. Since GMP is developed by collection of volunteer people, no code support problem arises. A third approach is to decouple architecture-depended codes via C macros. This approach is used partially in GMP. CRYMPIX's design is solely based on this above mentioned third approach. At the lowest level, we handle single-precision arithmetic operations with C macros. A vector layer; which is on top of that, manipulates the operations between a positive integer array and a single-precision operand. The below code provides an idea about the vector layer.

```
Vector Layer Code example.

#define ccm_inc_n_mul_1(_carry, _zn, _an, _al, _b, _pad)if(1){ \
    DPUP _t; \
    POS _i; \
    _t.spu[HIGH] = _pad; \
    for(_i = 0; _i < _al; _i++){ \
        cvm_mul_2_add_2(_t, _an[_i], _b, _zn[_i], _t.spu[HIGH]); \
        _zn[_i] = _t.spu[LOW]; \
    } \
    _carry = _t.spu[HIGH]; \
}
```

At the low-level function layer which comes after vector layer, the arithmetic functions are implemented and the relevant code example is given below.

```
Low-level Function Layer Code example.

void cz_mul_basecase(POS *z, POS *a, POS al, POS *b, POS bl){
    POS i;

    ccm_mul_1(z[bl], z, b, bl, a[0], 0);
    for(i = 1; i < al; i++){
        ccm_inc_n_mul_1(z[i + bl], (z + i), b, bl, a[i], 0);
    }
}
```

The layered approach simplifies the function bodies, prevents code repetitions; hence less tedious development phase.

2.5 Selection of Algorithms

Almost all libraries use the similar algorithms in high speed multiprecision arithmetic. Therefore, we limit our decisions with algorithm selection criteria.

Table 2. Algorithms in use for multiprecision multiplication

Algorithm	Complexity	Interval
Basecase	$O(n^2)$	$0 - 1K$
Karatsuba	$O(n^{1.585})$	$1 - 6K$
Toom-Cook 3–Way	$O(n^{1.465})$	$6 - 24K$
FFT Based	$O(n^{\sim 1.4})$	$24K$–larger

Addition, Subtraction and Shift. Addition and subtraction are done as they are explained by Knuth in [5] and Menezes in [7]. The operation starts from the least significant word and carry/borrow bits are transferred to the following steps of the algorithm. For shifting multiprecision numbers the basic bitwise operators of C language are convenient to use. Generally, operations such as addition, subtraction, clone, shift, and compare are relatively cheaper therefore all of the cryptographic libraries employ the similar suites.

Multiplication. The efficiency of most cryptographic libraries depend on the cost of multiprecision multiplication operation. Table 2 summarizes the popular multiplication methods, their complexities, and of their usage intervals.

In the cryptographic applications Basecase [5,7] and Karatsuba [5,6] multiplication algorithms are frequently used. Although the above seen FFT algorithm is asymptotically faster, it is more costly as far as the cryptographic applications concerned.

Division. CRYMPIX uses basecase division algorithm explained in Knuth [5]. If numbers get slightly larger than 1500 bits, then Divide-and-conquer algorithm [2] which is a recursive variant of the basecase division, gets to be utilized often and GMP includes it too.

Greatest Common Divisor (GCD), Extended Greatest Common Divisor. The basic algorithm for GCD computation is Euclid's algorithm with $O(n^2)$ complexity. The algorithm is modified by Lehmer to fit the fixed-precision processors. Another method of GCD computation is the Binary GCD algorithm. This algorithm is faster when the numbers are few words long. For larger numbers Binary GCD algorithm is modified by many researchers. Jebelean and Weber proposed Accelerated/Generalized GCD algorithm which is faster than Lehmer GCD algorithm [4,8] by a factor of 1,45. CRYMPIX includes a slightly modified version of Lehmer GCD algorithm. It is used both for GCD and Extended GCD computations. We have provided a comparison between Lehmer GCD algorithm and its modified variant proposed by Jebelean [3] in Table 3. We have used approximative condition of GCD and double-precision techniques. The speedup values are given in Fig. 2.

We also provided the performance comparison of CRYMPIX Lehmer GCD and GMP Generalized GCD in Table 4. The expected value is a constant speedup around $0,75$ which is actually a slow down factor. This is depicted in Fig. 3. The lower performance of CRYMPIX below the expected value in smaller operands is due to the absence of binary GCD implementation.

Table 3. Standard Lehmer GCD vs. Modified Lehmer GCD (microseconds)

Length	1K	2K	4K	8K
Standard Lehmer	201	557	1746	6228
Modified Lehmer	158	351	921	3131

Table 4. CRYMPIX Lehmer GCD vs. GMP Generalized GCD. (microseconds)

Length	1K	2K	4K	8K	16K
CRYMPIX v1 GCD	186	474	1372	4449	15767
CRYMPIX v2 GCD	157	368	957	2802	9161
GNU-GMP GCD	88	266	874	3101	11592

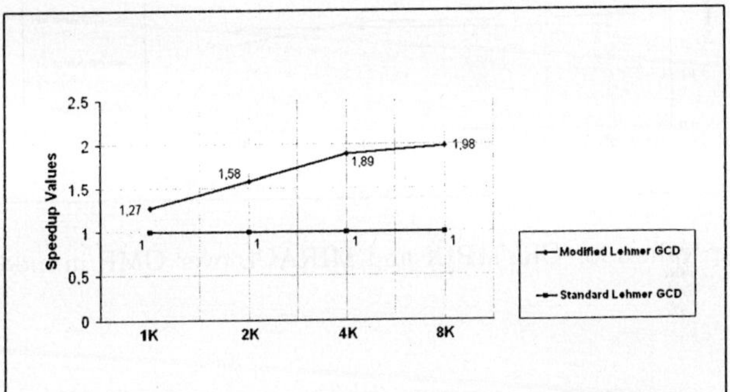

Fig. 2. Speedup values for Modified Lehmer GCD over Standard Lehmer GCD, derived from Table 3

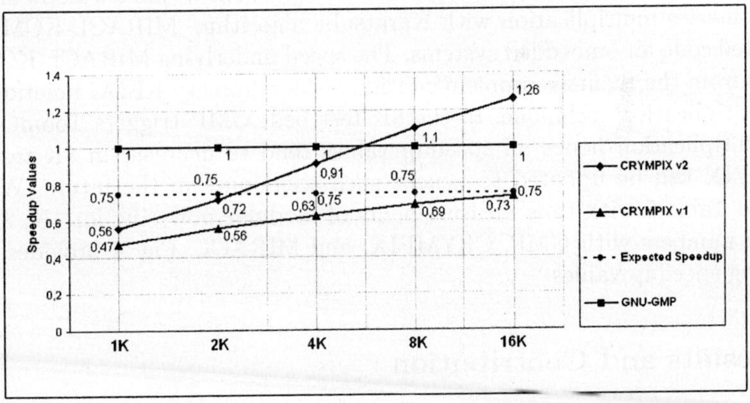

Fig. 3. Speedup values for CRYMPIX Lehmer GCD over GMP Generalized GCD, derived from Table 4

Table 5. Modular exponentiation for GMP, CRYMPIX, and MIRACL (milliseconds)

Length	**1K**	**2K**	**4K**	**8K**
GMP Mod. Exp.	54	389	2841	16734
MIRACL-KCM Mod. Exp.	31	204	1298	8132
CRYMPIX v1 Mod. Exp.	49	363	2650	19526
CRYMPIX v2 Mod. Exp.	27	195	1423	10411

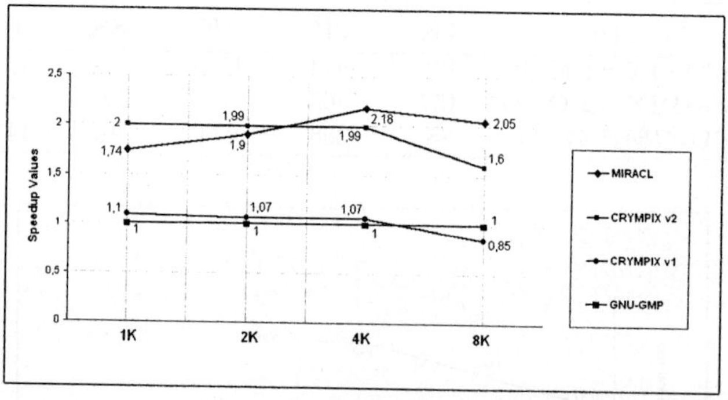

Fig. 4. Speedup values for CRYMPIX and MIRACL over GMP in modular exponentiation

Modular Exponentiation. Modular exponentiation is the most expensive operation among the other multi-precision operations. A competitive implementation takes the advantage of almost all techniques to speedup the operation. CRYMPIX uses successive squaring algorithm with left-to-right exponent scanning and variable-length-window-sliding technique with variable window size and Montgomery's multiplication with Karatsuba algorithm. MIRACL-KCM is the generated code for embedded systems. The speed underlying MIRACL-KCM references from the recursive implementation of Montgomery REDC function with half multiplication technique. In the 8K test bed, GMP triggers ToomCook-3-way multiplication hence all speedup values tend to decrease in 8K test bed. CRYMPIX will be updated to benefit such techniques in the future. We constructed Table 5 with time measurements of modular powering for 1K, 2K, 4K and 8K numbers with GMP, CRYMPIX, and MIRACL. Fig. 4 provides corresponding speedup values.

3 Results and Contribution

In this study, we have introduced a new cryptographic multiprecision library, CRYMPIX. We also provided a fair performance comparison between some libraries by providing technical comments. CRYMPIX which is developed in ANSI C, is able to take the advantage of `long long` data type of ISO C'99 whenever possible. CRYMPIX includes low level routines for multiprecision arithmetic in prime fields. The overall performance of CRYMPIX is equal to its predecessors and in some instances even superior. The first release is expected to include all functions significant for cryptography. Support for specific processors is not in the short term schedule. After the first stable release, the project is going to be extended over binary field arithmetic. Our next study will be on the layered adaptation of this library to distributed environments.

References

1. Bosselaers A., Govaerts R., Vandewalle J.: A Fast and Flexible Software Library for Large Integer Arithmetic. Proceedings 15th Symposium on Information Theory in the Benelux, Louvain-la-Neuve (B). **82-89** (1994)
2. Burnikel C.: Fast Recursive Division. Max-Planck-Institut fuer Informatik Research Report. **MPI-I-98-1-022** (1998)
3. Jebelean T.: Improving the Multiprecision Euclidean Algorithm. Proceedings of DISCO'93, Springer-Verlag LNCS 772. **45-58** (1993)
4. Jebelean T.: A Generalization of the Binary GCD Algorithm. ISSAC 93. **111-116** (1993)
5. Knuth D.E.: The Art of Computer Programming, Volume 2, Seminumerical Algorithms, 3rd edition, Addison-Wesley. (1998)
6. Koc C.K.: High Speed RSA Implementation. RSA Laboratories. **TR201** (1994)
7. Menezes A.: Handbook of Applied Cryptography. CRC Press, 608. (1993)
8. Weber K.: The Accelerated Integer GCD Algorithm. ACM Transactions on Mathematical Software, v.2. **111-122** (1995)

Optimal Control for Real-Time Feedback Rate-Monotonic Schedulers*

Tolga Ayav[1] and Giancarlo Ferrari-Trecate[2]

[1] INRIA Rhône-Alpes ZIRST 655, Avenue de l'Europe,
38334 Montbonnot, St Ismier Cedex, France. Tel: +33 4 76 61 52 17. Fax: - 54 77.
[2] INRIA, Domaine de Voluceau Rocquencourt - B.P.105
78153, Le Chesnay Cedex, France. Tel: +33 1 39 63 59 21. Fax: - 57 86.
{Tolga.Ayav, Giancarlo.Ferrari-Trecate}@inria.fr

Abstract. This paper presents an optimal control scheme for a real-time feedback control rate-monotonic scheduling (FC-RMS) system. We consider two-version tasks composed of a mandatory and an optional part to be scheduled according to the FC-RMS. In FC-RMS, the controller provides a feedback strategy for deciding about the execution or rejection of the optional sub-tasks. By modeling the task execution times as random variables, we first find the statistical model of FC-RMS and then we design a pure optimal controller and an optimal controller with feedforward integral compensation. The comparison of these two schemes with common Proportional-Integral-Derivative (PID) controller highlights the benefit of the optimal scheme with integral compensation. The results are demonstrated through the real implementation of FC-RMS on RT-Linux.

1 Introduction

Real-Time (RT) dynamic scheduling algorithms traditionally fall into two categories: static and dynamic priority-driven. One major paradigm for the static priority-driven scheduling is Rate-Monotonic (RM). The main drawback of RM is that it considers WCETs, which results in systems having spare capacity under normal operation [1]. Dynamic priority driven scheduling can be further divided into two categories: algorithms that work in *resource sufficient* environments and algorithms that work in *resource insufficient* environments. In the first category, resources are sufficient in the sense that all the tasks are schedulable at any given time despite their unknown arrival times. Earliest-Deadline-First (EDF) has been proved to be an optimal dynamic scheduling algorithm in resource sufficient environments [1]. On the other hand, it may be impossible to guarantee that the resources are sufficient in unpredictable environments.

According to [2] and [3], the next generation of real-time systems will be more complex and capable of adaptivity as well as of meeting time constraints

* This work has been partially supported by the cooperation project between İzmir Institute of Technology and Institute Aéronautique et Spatial in 2003.

P. Yolum et al.(Eds.): ISCIS 2005, LNCS 3733, pp. 894–903, 2005.

for mission and safety critical functions. A challenge of the current research is, therefore, to use more adaptive techniques such as feedback control scheduling in order to handle the transient overload, to use the spare capacity existing with traditional algorithms and to enhance the fault tolerance of real-time systems [2] [3] [4].

Although feedback control scheduling has been considered so far in different works, many questions are still open. The most important one is how to design a controller in order to guarantee the stability of the overall system. Most of the contributions in the literature focused on the use of PID controllers. In this work, we consider a FC-RMS system with optimal and feedforward compensated optimal controllers. We first construct a novel optimal controller that relies on the estimated task statistics. We show that the optimal controller is not able to track a given setpoint, while it provides better performance, during the transient, than PID. Then, in order to eliminate the steady-state error, we enhance the optimal control action with a feedforward integral action.

2 Feedback Control Rate-Monotonic Scheduling Architecture

In this section, we present the architecture we consider that integrates feedback control and rate-monotonic scheduling. The model is developed for a generic control action.

2.1 Feedback Control Rate-Monotonic Scheduling

FC-RM scheduling features a feedback control loop that is invoked at every sampling interval. It is composed of a Monitor, a Controller and a Task Level

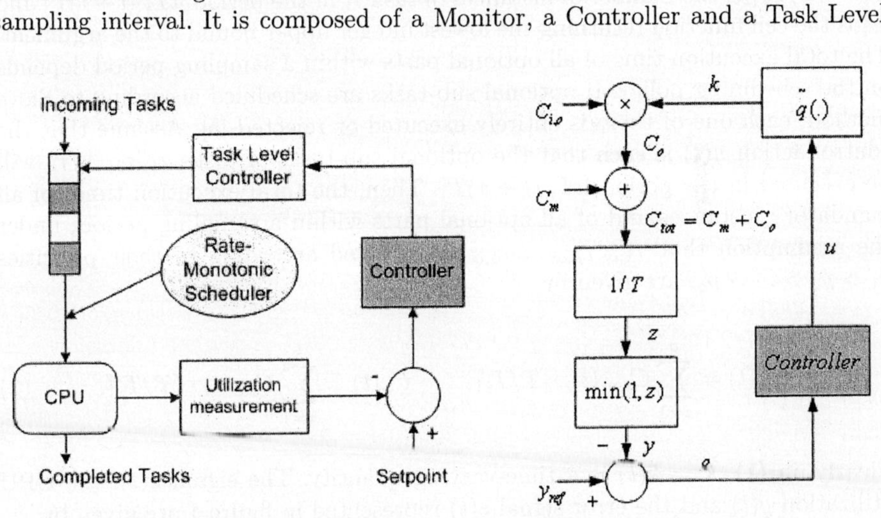

Fig. 1. Feedback Control Rate-Monotonic Scheduling. The left panel shows the schematic diagram and the right panel shows the mathematical model.

Controller (see figure 1). We choose as a controlled variable the CPU utilization (which is defined as the percentage of CPU busy time in a sampling period) since in hard real-time systems the miss ratio should be always kept zero [3]. In each sampling instance, the CPU utilization is monitored and the error is obtained by comparing it with the setpoint. The controller takes the error, produces a control value to minimize the error, i.e., to keep the utilization at a given setpoint. The task level controller takes the output of the controller and adjusts the manipulated variable (the percentage or number of the optional sub-tasks to be executed) accordingly. In order to keep the overhead at an acceptable level, the controller output is updated at a frequency $1/T$, where T denotes the sampling period (that is equal to 100 ms in our experiments, see table 1).

We use the Rate-monotonic (RM) algorithm to schedule the mandatory subtasks since, under suitable assumptions (see [1]), it can guarantee that tasks will meet their deadlines. On the other hand, making decision on which optional tasks or how many optional tasks will be executed is a much more complex problem. Feedback control scheduling is a method for solving it.

We consider a set of tasks $Tasks = \{\tau_1, \tau_2, ..., \tau_q\}$ where each task is characterized by some parameters such as deadline d_i (this is considered as period T_i if the task is periodic), processing time C_i and priority p_i. Each task consists of two sub-tasks, the mandatory part M_i and the optional part O_i. The processing times of M_i and O_i are $C_{i,m}$ and $C_{i,o}$, respectively. Thus, $C_{i,m} + C_{i,o} = C_i$, $i \in \{1, \dots, q\}$.

The evaluation of the CPU utilization in a time interval of length T can be represented by the scheme in figure 1 that we illustrate next. Let $t \in \mathbb{N}$ denote the discrete time index, i.e. the actual time $\tilde{t}$ can be computed as $\tilde{t} = Tt$. The total number N of the tasks at time t, is then given by $N = \sum_{i=1}^{q} \lceil T/T_i \rceil$. Note that $N_i = \lceil T/T_i \rceil$ is the number of instances of task τ_i in the period $[tT,\ (t+1)T]$ and $\lceil \cdot \rceil$ is the ceil function returning the lowest integer upper bound to the argument. The total execution time of all optional parts within a sampling period depends on the scheduling policy. If optional sub-tasks are scheduled according to Sieve method, each one of them is entirely executed or rejected [5]. Assume that the control action $u(t)$ is such that the optional sub-tasks of tasks $\tau_1, \tau_2, ..., \tau_k$ will be executed in the period $[tT,\ (t+1)T]$. Then, the total execution times of all mandatory instances and of all optional parts within a sampling period, under the assumption that $\tau_{1,o}, \tau_{2,o}, ..., \tau_{q,o}$ are ordered according to their priorities $p_1 > p_2 > ... > p_q$, are given by

$$C_m(t) = \sum_{i=1}^{q} C_{i,m}(t) \cdot \lceil T/T_i \rceil, \qquad C_o(t) = \sum_{i=1}^{k} C_{i,o}(t) \cdot \lceil T/T_i \rceil. \tag{1}$$

Clearly, in (1), $k = k(t)$ is a time-varying quantity. The signal $z(t)$, the CPU utilization $y(t)$ and the error signal $e(t)$ represented in figure 1 are given by

$$z(t) = \frac{C_m(t) + C_o(t)}{T}, \qquad y(t) = min\{1,\ z(t)\}, \qquad e(t) = y_{ref} - y(t). \tag{2}$$

The error signal is the difference between the requested utilization y_{ref} and the measured one, i.e. the controller takes the error, processes it and produces the value of $u(t)$ in the range of [0, 1]. Various control algorithms will be discussed in the next section. The output of the controller is then quantized by the block $\tilde{q}(.)$ seen in figure 1. The quantizer function determines the number of optional sub-tasks to be executed by mapping [0, 1] to [0, q].

2.2 Statistical Characterization of the Signals

In order to account for the unpredictability of task durations, we model them as *independent* random variables with finite average and variance over which the scheduler has no control.

If there is a sufficient number of mandatory sub-tasks and a sufficient number of optional sub-tasks to be executed within a sampling period, the Central Limit Theorem (CLT) can be used [6] in order to approximate the distributions of C_m and C_o. In our setting, the total number of mandatory sub-tasks N_m is equal to N and the total number of optional sub-tasks to be executed is $N_o = \sum_{i=1}^{k} N_i$. We point out that, despite the fact that CLT is an asymptotic theorem, it provides good approximations even if N_m and N_o are low (see [6]). In our experiments, we have $N_m = 303$ and $N_o = 181$ as can be calculated from table 1. An important fact is that CLT holds even if the task durations are not uniformly distributed. Therefore, all our results hold for general distributions (with finite average and variance) associated to $C_{i,m}$ and $C_{i,o}$.

For a generic signal ξ, we denote with $f_\xi(\xi|\kappa)$ its Probability Density Function (PDF) for the choice of executing κ optional sub-tasks at time t. Let $g(\mu, \sigma^2)$ be the Gaussian distribution with mean μ and variance σ^2. Then, for a fixed k, CLT states that C_m and C_o can be represented by

$$C_m \sim f_{C_m}(C_m|k) = g(\mu_m, \sigma_m^2),\ \mu_m = \sum_{i=1}^{q}\sum_{j=1}^{N_i} \mu_{C_{j,m}},\ \sigma_m^2 = \sum_{i=1}^{q}\sum_{j=1}^{N_i} \sigma^2_{C_{j,m}} \quad (3)$$

$$C_o \sim f_{C_o}(C_o|k) = g(\mu_o, \sigma_o^2),\ \mu_o = \sum_{i=1}^{k}\sum_{j=1}^{N_i} \mu_{C_{j,o}},\ \sigma_o^2 = \sum_{i=1}^{k}\sum_{j=1}^{N_i} \sigma^2_{C_{j,o}}. \quad (4)$$

According to the scheme reported in figure 1, C_{tot} is the sum of C_m and C_o. Thus, in view of the statistical independence of C_m and C_o, we have

$$C_{tot} \sim f_{C_{tot}}(C_{tot}|k) = g(\mu_{tot}, \sigma_{tot}^2) = g(\mu_m + \mu_o, \sigma_m^2 + \sigma_o^2). \quad (5)$$

The distribution function of z, defined in 2, is given by

$$z \sim f_z(z|k) = g(\mu_z, \sigma_z^2) = g\left(\frac{\mu_m + \mu_o}{T}, \frac{\sigma_m^2 + \sigma_o^2}{T^2}\right). \quad (6)$$

For the distribution of y, we have

$$y \sim f_y(y|k) = \begin{cases} f_z(y|k) & y < 1 \\ (1 - \int_{-\infty}^{1} f_z(z|k)dz)\delta(y-1) & y = 1 \\ 0 & y > 1 \end{cases} \quad (7)$$

Note that the block min(1, z) in figure 1 produces a Dirac delta function into the distributions of y and e (see [6]). In fact, (7) represents a truncated Gaussian distribution and the coefficient $\beta = 1 - \int_{-\infty}^{1} f_z(z|k)dz$ multiplying the δ function is significantly different from zero only if the average CPU utilization y is close to one (in fact, β represents the probability of CPU overload for a given k). On the other hand, when the setpoint is chosen sufficiently away from 1 and a stabilizing controller is used, the delta function disappears (see [7] for further details). This corresponds to remove the block $min(1, z)$ in figure 1. We highlight that this approximation is realistic since the set point should be chosen pretty far away from 1 in order to prevent undesirable saturation effects [3]. Hence, the PDFs of y and e can be approximated as

$$y \sim g\left(\frac{\mu_m + \mu_o}{T}, \frac{\sigma_m^2 + \sigma_o^2}{T^2}\right), \quad e \sim g\left(y_{ref} - \frac{\mu_m + \mu_o}{T}, \frac{\sigma_m^2 + \sigma_o^2}{T^2}\right). \tag{8}$$

The PDF of $u(t)$, $f_u(u|k)$ depends on the specific control scheme. Stankovic and Lu considered the use of PID control since it is a well-established technique in automatic control and in some cases is able to stabilize the scheduling system. For stability, it is of paramount importance to properly choose the controller parameters. Stankovic and Lu presented a method for tuning the PID parameters that relies on a deterministic scheduler model. Another approach to tune the PID parameters is given in [7], which presents the design of stabilizing PID controller based on the statistical framework presented in this paper.

On the other hand, the choice of more effective control schemes is still an important research issue. In the next section, we propose an optimal control scheme as an alternative to PID.

3 Optimal Control

Optimal control relies on the estimated task statistics. The block diagram of the optimal control rate-monotonic scheduling system is given in figure 2. The goal of the optimal control is to compute $u(t)$ that minimizes the variance of the error. For sake of clarity, it is assumed that there is no quantization in the system and the setpoint is far from 1, i.e., min(1,z) box is removed. Thus, the utilization $y(t)$ can be written as

$$y(t+1) = \frac{1}{T}(C_m(t) + C_{o,tot}(t)u(t)) \tag{9}$$

The cost function is the mean square error that, using equation 5.34 from [6], can be written as

$$J(t+1) = E[e^2(t+1)] = E^2[e(t+1)] + Var[e(t+1)]. \tag{10}$$

In (10), it holds that $E^2[e(t+1)] = (-\hat{y}(t+1|t) + y_{ref}(t+1))^2$ where $\hat{y}(t+1|t)$ is the optimal predictor of $y(t+1)$ on the basis of the information collected up to

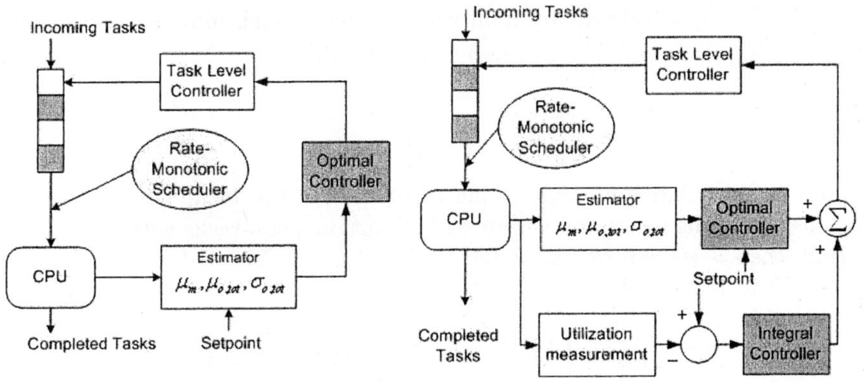

Fig. 2. Optimal Control Rate-Monotonic Scheduling. The left panel shows the system with pure optimal controller and the right panel shows the system with feedforward integral compensated optimal controller.

time t. According to certainty equivalence principle [8], the optimal prediction of $y(t)$ is given by $\hat{y}(t) = y_d(t+1)$ where $y(t) = y_d(t) + \nu(t)$. Here, $y_d(t)$ coincides with the optimal prediction of the deterministic part of $y(t)$ and $\nu(t)$ is a white noise. This principle will be applied to find $\hat{y}(t+1|t)$. First, $y(t+1)$ can be written as

$$\begin{aligned} y(t+1) &= \underbrace{\frac{1}{T}\mu_m(t) + \frac{1}{T}\mu_{o,tot}(t)u(t)}_{y_d(t)} + \underbrace{\frac{1}{T}\tilde{C}_m(t) + \frac{1}{T}\tilde{C}_{o,tot}(t)u(t)}_{\nu(t)} \end{aligned} \quad (11)$$

The uncorrelation between $\nu(t)$ and $\nu(t-\tau)$ $\forall \tau \geq 1$, can be easily proved from the following properties: 1) $u(t)$ depends only on the past history of C_m and C_o, i.e., from $C_m(t-\xi)$ and $C_o(t-\xi)$, $\xi \geq 1$; 2) $\tilde{C}_m$ and $\tilde{C}_o$ are zero mean random variables. Thus, $\nu(t)$ is a white noise with zero mean. By applying the certainty equivalence principle, the optimal predictor of $y(t+1)$ is given by

$$\hat{y}(t+1) = \frac{1}{T}(\mu_m(t) + \mu_{o,tot}(t)u(t)). \quad (12)$$

On the other hand, $Var[e(t+1)]$ takes the following form:

$$Var[e(t+1)] = E[(e(t+1) - E[e(t+1)])^2] = \frac{1}{T^2}\sigma_m^2(t) + \frac{1}{T^2}\sigma_{o,tot}^2(t)u^2(t).$$

By using equations (12) and (13) in (10), the cost function $J(t+1)$ can be written as

$$J(t+1) = \left(y_{ref}(t+1) - \frac{1}{T}\mu_m(t) - \frac{1}{T}\mu_{o,tot}(t)u(t)\right)^2 + \frac{1}{T^2}\sigma_m^2(t) + \frac{1}{T^2}\sigma_{o,tot}^2(t)u^2(t). \quad (13)$$

As a final step, $u^*(t)$ (the optimal value of $u(t)$, which minimizes $J(t+1)$) is found by imposing $\frac{dJ(t+1)}{du(t)}|_{u^*(t)} = 0$ thus obtaining

$$u^*(t) = \frac{-\mu_m(t)\mu_{o,tot}(t) + T\, y_{ref}(t+1)\mu_{o,tot}(t)}{\mu_{o,tot}^2(t) + \sigma_{o,tot}^2(t)} \tag{14}$$

Equation (14) highlights that if one can estimate the mean of all mandatory sub-tasks and the mean and variance of all optional sub-tasks within a sampling period, then $u^*(t)$ can be calculated in closed-form. When $u(t) = u^*(t)$ is used, the CPU utilization obeys to the dynamics

$$y(t+1) = \frac{1}{T}\left(\frac{\mu_m(t)\sigma_{o,tot}^2(t) + \mu_{o,tot}^2(t)T y_{ref}(t+1)}{\mu_{o,tot}^2(t) + \sigma_{o,tot}^2(t)}\right) \tag{15}$$

as $t \to \infty$. Note that even if the task statistics and the setpoint are constant in time, if $\sigma_{o,tot}^2(t) \neq 0$, one has, in general, that $y(t)$ does not converge to y_{ref} as $t \to \infty$. Moreover, incorrect estimations of the task statistics may further degrade the performance of the optimal controller.

4 Optimal Control with Feedforward Compensation

In order to avoid the bias produced by optimal control, we propose to add a feedforward integral control action. The block diagram of this scheme is given in figure 2.

In order to find a stabilizing controller, we first derive the state space form of the closed-loop system. Assume that $x \in \mathbb{R}$ is the state of the integral controller. Hence, controller equations are,

$$x(t+1) = x(t)+e(t)\,,\ u(t) = K_i x(t)+\left(\frac{-\mu_m(t)\mu_{o,tot}(t) + T\, y_{ref}(t+1)\mu_{o,tot}(t)}{\mu_{o,tot}^2(t) + \sigma_{o,tot}^2(t)}\right)$$

and the system equations are,

$$y(t) = \frac{1}{T}\left[C_m(t) + C_{o,tot}(t)\left(K_i x(t) + \frac{-\mu_m(t)\mu_{o,tot}(t) + T\, y_{ref}(t+1)\mu_{o,tot}(t)}{\mu_{o,tot}^2(t) + \sigma_{o,tot}^2(t)}\right)\right]$$

$$e(t) = -y(t) + y_{ref}(t).$$

The closed-loop system is therefore described by

$$\begin{aligned} x(t+1) &= x(t) + y_{ref}(t) - \frac{1}{T}C_m(t) \\ &- \frac{1}{T}C_{o,tot}(t)\left(K_i x(t) + \frac{-\mu_m(t)\mu_{o,tot}(t) + T\, y_{ref}(t+1)\mu_{o,tot}(t)}{\mu_{o,tot}^2(t) + \sigma_{o,tot}^2(t)}\right) \end{aligned} \tag{16}$$

By assuming that $C_{o,tot}$, C_m and y_{ref} are stationary signals, the mean state dynamics is

$$\mu_x(t+1) = \mu_x(t)+y_{ref} - \frac{1}{T}\mu_m - \frac{K_i}{T}\mu_{o,tot}\mu_x(t) - \frac{1}{T}\left(\frac{-\mu_m\mu_{o,tot}^2 + T\, y_{ref}\mu_{o,tot}^2}{\mu_{o,tot}^2 + \sigma_{o,tot}^2}\right)$$

where $\mu_x(t) = E[x(t)]$. A classical stability criterion for discrete time linear systems [9] guarantees that $\mu_x(t)$ is asymptotically stable around its equilibrium, if the following condition is fulfilled

$$\left|1 - \frac{K_i}{T}\mu_{o,tot}\right| < 1. \tag{17}$$

Then, formula (17) provides an explicit bound on the values of K_i guaranteeing the convergence of the average error to zero.

5 Implementation on RT-Linux and Experimental Results

We tested FC-RMS with PID, optimal and compensated optimal controllers using the RT-Linux system (a detailed description of FC-RMS with stabilizing PID controllers is provided in [7]).

RT-Linux has a priority-driven preemptive scheduler loaded as a kernel module [10]. In order to implement our FC-RMS method on RT-Linux 3.1, we modified the default scheduler so as to measure CPU utilization and other task statistics μ_m, $\mu_{o,tot}$ and $\sigma_{o,tot}$. A dummy application consisting of a periodic task set has also been created.

The CPU utilization y, the mean of all mandatory tasks μ_m, and the mean and variance of k optional sub-tasks within one sampling period are easy to reconstruct by resorting to the empirical estimators for the mean and variance of stationary stochastic processes [6]. However we have to estimate the mean and variance of all optional sub-tasks $\mu_{o,tot}$ and $\sigma^2_{o,tot}$ in order to use formula (14). Under the assumption that the mean and variance of each optional sub-task are constant, i.e., $\mu_{C_{j,o}} = \mu_c$ and $\sigma^2_{C_{j,o}} = \sigma_c$, $\forall j \in \{1, 2, \ldots, q\}$, one gets $\mu_{o,tot} = \mu_o \cdot \frac{q}{k}$ and $\sigma^2_{o,tot} = \sigma^2_o \cdot \frac{q}{k}$.

In the optimal controller, there is no parameter to tune. However it needs accurate estimates of the task statistics that may be difficult to obtain when the system is overloaded [3]. Another drawback is that the mean and variance of each optional sub-task are not constant in time, which results in incorrect estimations. These two pitfalls are overcome by using the feedforward integral controller.

In order to compare the performance of PID, optimal and compensated optimal controllers during transients, we used a step workload jumping from the nominal load L_{nom} to a maximum load L_{max} at a given time instant, as reported in table 1.

A comparison of figures 3.A, 3.B, and 3.C shows that pure optimal control provides the best transient characteristics in terms of settling time and overshoot. However, it cannot track the setpoint due to the bias shown in formula (15). The additional feedforward integral controller compensates this undesired phenomenon thus providing a better error tracking while preserving satisfactory performance in the transient.

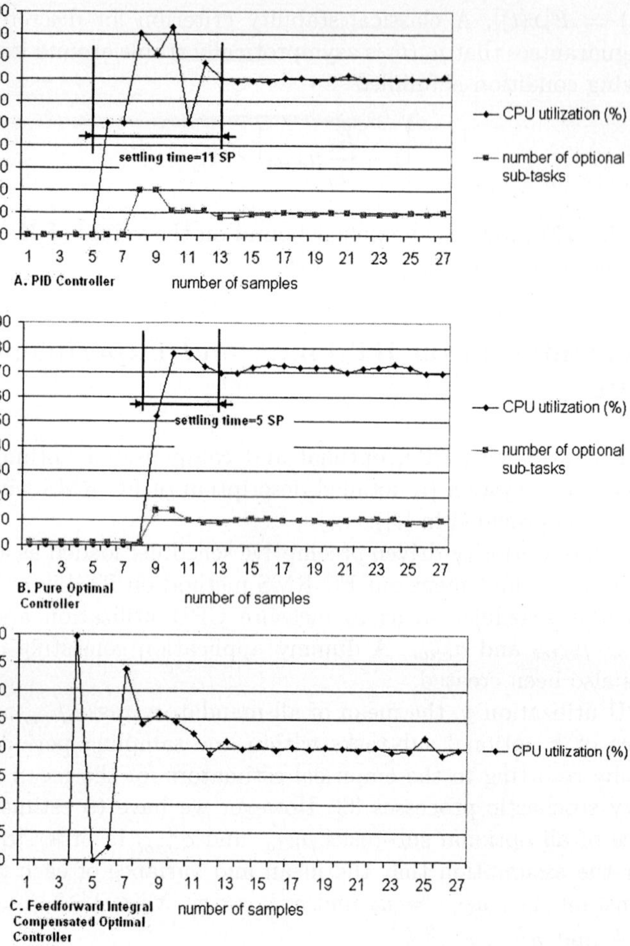

Fig. 3. Experimental results. A) CPU utilization with PID controller. $K_p = 0.1$, $K_i = 2.0$ and $K_d = 0.1$. B) CPU utilization with pure optimal controller. C) CPU utilization with feedforward integral compensated optimal controller.

Table 1. Parameters characterizing the workloads L_{nom} and L_{max}. $U[a, b]$ represents uniform distribution between a and b.

	L_{nom}	L_{max}
q	0	20
$C_{i,m}$ and $C_{i,o}$ (μs)	-	U[130, 180]
$T_{i\in\{1,\ldots,q\}}$ (ms)	-	{15,2,14,3,13,4,12,5,11,6,10,7,9,8,8,35,8,15,3,10}
T (ms)	100	100

6 Conclusions

In this paper, we presented a feedback control rate-monotonic scheduling system. By assuming that all tasks are periodic, independent and implemented with the two-version method, we first derived a statistical representation of the scheduling system. Then, we proposed a novel feedforward compensated optimal controller as an alternative to PID. The new controller achieves better performance (in terms of overshoot, settling time and error tracking) as shown in the experimental results obtained from a real implementation of FC-RMS on RT-Linux. We highlight that the developed statistical framework can be very useful for designing and analyzing feedback control scheduling systems based on other control strategies such as hybrid control. Performance comparisons of PID and optimal controllers on real applications with different types of tasks (such as aperiodic, dependent) and different implementation techniques (such as milestone and multiple-version) still require additional research, which may lead to major generalization of the proposed method.

References

1. Liu, C., Layland, J.: Scheduling algorithms for multiprogramming in a hard real-time environment. Journal of the ACM **20** (1973) 40–61
2. Lu, C., Stankovic, J., G.Tao, Son, S.: Design and evaluation of a feedback control EDF scheduling algorithm. In: Proc. 20th IEEE Real-Time Systems Symposium, Phoenix, Arizona (1999) 56–67
3. Lu, C., Stankovic, J., G.T., Son, S.: Feedback control real-time scheduling: Framework, modeling, and algorithms. Real-Time Systems Journal. Special Issue on Control Theoretical Approach to Real-Time Computing **23** (2002) 85–126
4. Lawrence, D., Guan, J., Mehta, S., Welchr, L.: Adaptive scheduling via feedback control for dynamic real-time systems. In: 20th International Performance, Computing and Communications Conference. (2001)
5. Liu, J., Shih, W.K., Lin, K.J., Bettati, R., Chung, J.Y.: Imprecise computations. Proceedings of IEEE **82** (1994) 83–94
6. Papoulis, A.: Probability, Random Variables and Stochastic Processes. McGraw-Hill International Editions (1987)
7. Ayav, T., Ferrari-Trecate, G., Yılmaz, S.: Stability properties of adaptive real-time feedback scheduling: A statistical approach. In: 12th Real-Time Embedded Systems Conference, Paris (2004) 259–277
8. Filatov, N.M., Unbehauen, H.: Adaptive Dual Control. Springer Verlag, Heidelberg (2004)
9. Franklin, G., Powell, J., Emami-Naeini, A.: Feedback Control of Dynamic Systems. Prentice-Hall International (2002)
10. Barabanov, M.: A Linux-based Real-Time Operating System. PhD thesis, New Mexico Institute of Mining and Technology (1997)

Graphical User Interface Development on the Basis of Data Flows Specification*

Tomas Danikauskas[1], Rimantas Butleris[1], and Sigitas Drąsutis[2]

[1] Department of Information Systems, Kaunas University of Technology,
Studentu str. 50, LT-51368 Kaunas, Lithuania
{tomas.danikauskas, rimantas.butleris}@ktu.lt
[2] Department of Practical Informatics, Kaunas University of Technology,
Studentu str. 50, LT-51368 Kaunas, Lithuania
sigdras@ktu.lt

Abstract. This paper introduces graphical user interface (GUI) modelling approach and it positions in information system (IS) development process. The overview of graphical user interface design methods and methodologies is presented. The main objective of the proposal is the consistency of IS development process, which includes requirements specification, system design and implementation phases. The GUI modelling process is based on the data flows specification. Detailed explanation of modelling steps is presented. Paper includes an illustrative example of the web based GUI development according to the proposed process.

1 Introduction

What gives the first impression for user about information system? Possibly we will be right, if we say that it is graphical user interface. GUI is agent between user and IS. The graphical user interface is one of the factors which determines, how fluent will be adoption of IS to business process. This article deals with GUI modelling process and development of e-commerce systems in purpose to make those IS more easily developed and maintained.

First of all a few methods and techniques for GUI design are reviewed in this work to show the variety of possible solutions for GUI modelling and design [1].

The third section of paper is dedicated to data flows specification and GUI modelling process. Data flow specification (DFS) is the result of functional requirements specification method (*FRSM*) [2,3], which is developed in Kaunas University of Technology. At this moment our research deals with IS design process, which is based on the data flows specification. The meta data source for IS design is repository of DFS.

Three phase's conception for IS design was chosen:

1. Information system workspace model composition [4];
2. Information system database model composition [5];
3. Graphical user interface model composition.

---

* The work is supported by Lithuanian State Science and Studies Foundation according to Eureka programme project "IT-Europe" (Reg. No 3473).

P. Yolum et al.(Eds.): ISCIS 2005, LNCS 3733, pp. 904–914, 2005.

Each phase already has conceptual solution based on data flows specification. The third section in detail describes GUI modelling process.

All three IS design phases are developed as autonomous modules of CASE tool prototype. Modules are implemented as MS Visio 2003 templates within the unique graphical notation stencils and encoded automated modelling processes. The final IS design models are saved as Visio2003 file (*.vst) and meta data are stored in the DFS repository. The GUI modelling template has implemented additional function: final graphical model can be transformed and saved to XML file (see fig. 4).

Section four introduces how GUI specification process and results can be used in e-commerce systems development. "User login to IS" form is as illustrative example.

2 Related Works

This section is short overview of several quite different instruments for GUI modelling and design. Our research also covered other techniques, presented in [6-10].

Oracle Designer tool along with other Oracle tools is developed on the basis of Oracle CASE method [11, 12]. Those tools gives ability to automate IS design and development process. Technology proposed by Oracle offers integrated system design and development including web based systems. Oracle tools have perfect technique for GUI requirements specification and results like forms, reports and menu generation. However Oracle CASE doesn't supply detailed process and tools for user requirements gathering and specification. The system analyst has to process and transform requirements into proper format.

Other well-known tool is UML (Unified Modelling Language) [13]. Generally it could be named as IS design, results presentation, requirements specification and documentation language [14]. UML has 12 types of diagram divided into three categories: structural diagrams (class, object, component and deployment diagrams), behaviour modelling diagrams (use case, sequence, activity, collaboration, statechart diagrams), model management diagrams (packages, subsystems and models) [13]. Statechart, sequence and collaboration diagrams enable to compose user interface architecture and behaviour. However, the IS design results like forms, reports, which meet user requirements, usually is expressed throughout the GUI elements [15]. Specification form used in UML is not adequate to user's vision of GUI specification, which traditionally consists of common graphical user interface elements.

A. Grunlund, D. Lafreniere and D. Carr proposed pattern-supported approach (PSA) to the user interface design process, which suggests a wider scope for the use of patterns by looking at the overall user-oriented interface design process. One of main goals of approach is to supply solutions to help designers to resolve GUI development problems that are common and frequently encountered. The proposed approach and the patterns need to be adapted and validated through practical usage. The descriptions, structure and level of detail must be adapted to fit actual design projects [16].

V. Balasubramanian and M. Turoff assume that GUI design being a creative process, cannot be sequential. So, they proposed design methodology containing fifteen non-sequential and highly interconnected set of design tasks. These interconnected set of tasks form a hypertext network [17]. Design process is viewed as the total set of design tasks to be carried out to transform a user's requirements into a user interface design specification. Tasks of a hypertext network are treated as design process nodes. The combination of received inputs and transformed outputs of each node produce a hypertext network. This approach provides flexibility by allowing the designer to carry out various design tasks in any order. At the same time will be ensured that the all required tasks are completed and that the rationale is captured [10].

Finally talking about the method, mentioned above, we can say:

- Oracle CASE doesn't assure the comprehensives of user requirements for IS specification, but it has perfect tool for GUI modelling and implementation.
- Both patterns and hypertext methods proposals are rational solution for GUI design, but tool support is weak.
- UML has large variety of models for IS modelling and requirements specification. But GUI specification form used in UML isn't very acceptable for users. Specification expressed through the graphical user interface elements is more understandable for users.

3 GUI Modelling on the Basis of Data Flows Specification

Functional requirements specification method is based on the analysis of data flows of the organization [18, 19]. In any organization data flows of incoming and outgoing information exist. The processing of incoming flows creates outgoing data flows. Most of those flows have a defined document or other standardized form, which is commonly used in the organization and can be analysed in the IS analysis and design process [20]. The purpose of IS is to make data flows processing and management process in organization more effective.

The result of the functional requirements specification method is data flows specification (DFS) that can be described as a system consisting from the following models:

Fh – context model of the information system;
Rds – results / data resources structure model;
Dls – model of links (data flows) between data resources, results and structure of those links;
Dp – results / data resources processing stages model;
Dst – results / data resource state transition model;
El – model of elaboration of links between data resources, results and links between data resources / results states.

The conception of FRSM CASE tool prototype is presented in figure 1. The main idea of the conception is the interaction between IS specification and IS design stages. These two stages interact with each other through the specification repository. The interaction presented in figure 1 is directed only to one side - from the specification to design; it shows the main idea of the method. In reality FRSM is an iterative process like most of methods for the requirements specification and IS design.

The main principle of FRSM is analysis of universe of discourse from results and then continuing to data resources. This principle corresponds to the natural way of activity process analysis. DFS models describe static and dynamic aspect of developing system. Fh, Rds, Dls models describe static structure of system and Dp, Dst and El models describe behaviour (dynamics) of system. All these models have graphical notation, but in order to automate IS requirements specification and design process all meta data are stored in repository. GUI models cover data input, edit, review and composition of any results (reports). The ability to use FRSM results for GUI modelling was analysed. The results have showed that FRSM meet main criteria's and it could be used for comprehensive GUI modelling [11].

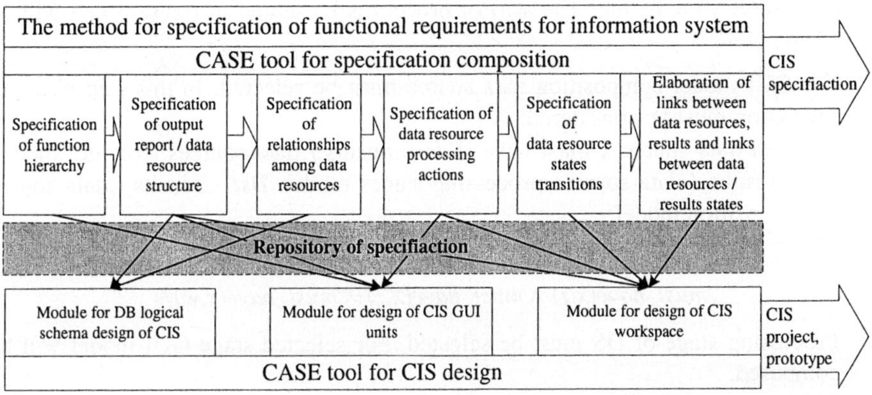

Fig. 1. Conception of FRSM CASE tool prototype

GUI model composition could be divided into two phases: abstract model composition and explicit model composition (detailed design).

GUI model design is based on three models: Rds, Dls and Dp meta data. A next section describes the GUI model template.

3.1 GUI Model Template

Abstract and detailed GUI model must be composed for every DS specified in DFS. Conceptual GUI model template is needed for abstract model composition, because this process will be computerised like all FRSM method and IS design phases. The template data will be detailed after abstract modelling phase. GUI model template is presented in figure 2. Template is divided into sections. First of all is *Title section.* It stores information, which let to identify the main purpose or function of GUI window.

In the *Data section* data input, edit, search and display is produced. Data aggregation or generalization results could be placed in *Data section* too. Functional/navigation elements are placed in *Functional/system data section.* System information such as IS state, information of IS user, system messages and etc. could be located in this section too. Another data source template could be placed into the *Data section* depending on the structure of data source. We are modelling forms and sub forms (templates and sub templates) structure using such principle. *Title* and *Functional/ system data section* isn't mandatory for sub templates.

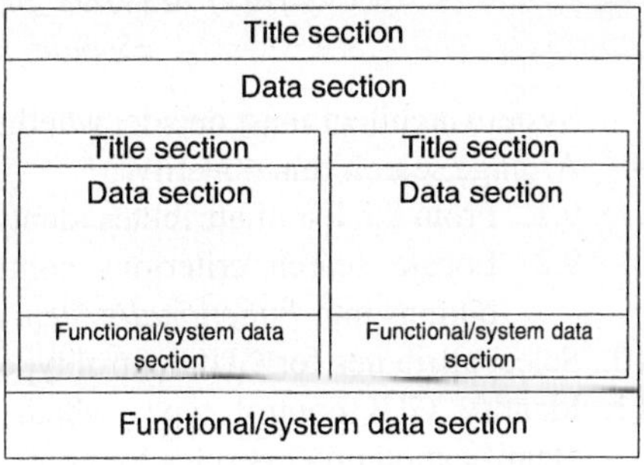

Fig. 2. Conceptual GUI model template

3.2 Process for Conceptual GUI Model Composition

Process for conceptual GUI model composition will be described in this section. This process, as it was mentioned in introduction, is implemented as CASE tool prototype module for GUI modelling. The step of process is presented in figure 3 and will be described below:

1. For GUI model composition data source must be selected. In this step also one restriction must be considered:
   Selected data source *x* must have: ***Rds*** – results / data sources structure model, ***Dp*** – results / data sources processing stages model, ***Dst*** – results / data source state transition model.

$$\forall x[DS(x) \wedge is\_selected(x,z) \Rightarrow \exists y \exists z \exists w[Rds(y) \wedge Dp(z) \wedge Dst(w) \wedge must\_have(x,z) \wedge must\_have(x,z) \wedge must\_have(x,w)]]$$

2. Processing stage of DS must be selected. For selected stage GUI model will be composed.
3. *Title section* of template must be filled using DS and Stage names and descriptions.
4. Entities of selected DS stage must be identified. All entities processed in this stage must be selected from FRSM repository.
5. Check clause: What amount of entities was identified? If one goes to step 7, if more than one, then go to step 6.
6. The primary entity must be selected. Primary entity is entity *x*, which initiates data processing in GUI form *y*.

$$\forall x[E(x) \wedge is\_primary(x) \Rightarrow \exists y[F(y) \wedge initiate\_processing(x,y)]]$$

Note: If only one entity is identified in step 4, the same entity is primary entity of form.

7. Identify attributes of primary entity. During this step all attributes from repository of selected entity must be selected. The attribute must meet following constraint:
   If *visibility* property *y* of attribute *x* is set to *true* in repository, it could be identified.

$$\forall x \forall y [A(x) \wedge P(y) \wedge is\_property\_of(y,x) \wedge value\_is\_true(y) \Rightarrow could\_be\_selected(x)]$$

8. System architect must decide, whether the form has a search functionality?
9. Arrange search functionality.
   9.1. From the list of attributes identified in step 7, select search criterions.
   9.2. Locate search criterions controls in *Data section*, and search function buttons into *Functional/system data section.*
10. Select attributes for GUI control type assignment.
11. Identify GUI control type, which will be assigned to selected attribute. In identification process rules for control type definition is used. Rules are presented below:

- If attribute don't have condition and limitary constrains, the type of attribute control will be set to *text box*;
- If attribute has limitary values stored in repository as domain of values, the type of attribute control will be set to *combo box* or *list box*;
- If attribute has Boolean data type, the type of attribute control will be *check box*.

12. In no any rule applied to attribute, than go to step 13, in other way - to step 14.
13. System architect manually must select type of control. In this case could be selected any type of traditional GUI elements.

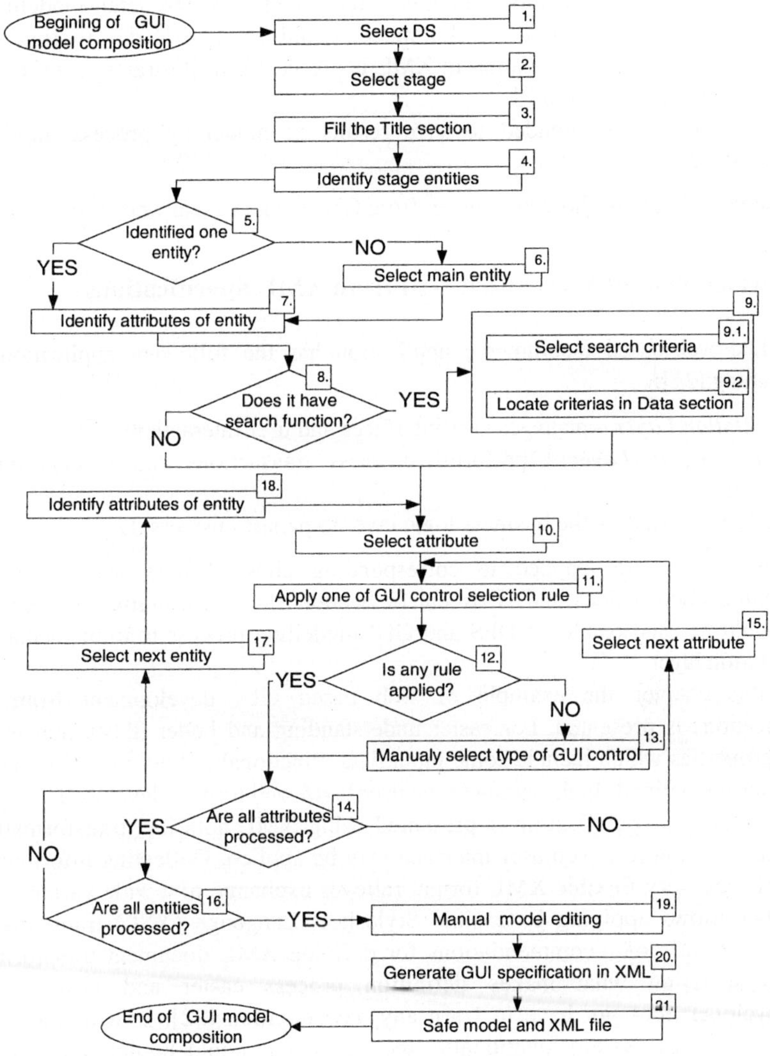

Fig. 3. Conceptual GUI model composition process

14. Are all attributes of selected entity processed? If no, then go to step 15, in other way go to step 16.
15. Select next attribute from the identified attributes list of entity.
16. Are all entities processed of selected DS? If no, then go to step 17, in other way go to step 19.
17. Next entity for the inclusion into the model has to be selected.
18. The same process, like in step 7.
19. Manual editing of GUI model could be performed after all entities of DS processed. The types, location of defined GUI controls and other non-functional requirements could be modified in this step, which performs detail-modelling.
20. The XML specification of GUI model could be generated. In figure 4 an example of GUI specification in XML is presented. It illustrates specification of form for user's login to IS.
21. The last step is intended to save results of modelling process: model and specification in XML.

Next section illustrates how we can get from GUI model to real web form.

4 Development of Web Based GUI from XML Specifications

A typical web-based e-commerce application has the following application logic partitioning [21]:

- *Presentation Layer* – manages user interfaces and user interaction;
- *Business Logic Layer* - performs business transactions and models business processes;
- *Data Layer* - used by the business logic layer to persist business data.

These layers are mapped to corresponding physical tiers where the actual application code resides and is executed. Section shows illustrative example, how easy could be used results of DFS and GUI modelling process in implementation of presentation layer.

In this chapter the example of web based GUI development from XML specifications is presented. For easier understanding and better illustration just few basic properties which include some input data, functionality buttons and visual style attributes are defined. In the example the user login web form is developed.

When system specification is presented using XML notation, transformation of this specification to a web user interface may be applied. Collecting information in a simple and very flexible XML format relieves exchange of a wide variety of data and also allows applying Extensible Stylesheet Language (XSL) transformation. XSL is a family of recommendations for defining XML document transformation and presentation what makes definition process easier and faster because the developer does not have to learn any new notation [22]. In example, for the some part of the system functionality the parameters could be defined as follows (see fig. 4):

```
<window>
<title>login</title>
<data>
 <input>
     <name>login</name>
     <dtype>varchar2</dtype>
     <length>10</length>
     <type>text</type>
 </input> <input>
     <name>password</name>
     <dtype>varchar2</dtype>
     <length>10</length>
     <type>password</type>
 </input> <input>
     <name>secure</name>
     <dtype>boolean</dtype>
     <length>1</length>
     <type>checkbox</type>
 </input>
</data>
<functionality>
  <button>
      <type>submit</type>
      <caption>Login</caption>
  </button>
  <button>
      <type>reset</type>
      <caption>Clear</caption>
  </button>
</functionality>
<style>
  <body>
      <background-
color>#669999</background-color>
      <color>#ffffcc</color>
  </body>
</style>
</window>
```

Fig. 4. GUI specification model presented in XML

Now it is time to define transformations for each specified part of the system and create code for the user web interface. Using XSL language for the transformations relieves applying them later because parameters are collected with XML. An example of the transformation for Cascading Style Sheet (CSS) file (fig. 6):

```
<?xml version='1.0'?>
<xsl:stylesheet version="1.0" xmlns:xsl="http://www.w3.org/1999/XSL/Transform">
<xsl:template match="/">
    <xsl:for-each select="window/style/*">
    <xsl:value-of select="name()"/>{
    <xsl:for-each select="./descendant::*">
        <xsl:value-of select="name()"/>:<xsl:value-of select="."/>;
    </xsl:for-each>
} <br />
</xsl:for-each> </xsl:template> </xsl:stylesheet>
```

Fig. 5. XSL transformation for CSS file

This XSL transformation generates output file (fig. 6) which will be used later:

```
body { background-color:"#669999"; color:#ffffcc; }
```

Fig. 6. Generated CSS file

An example of the transformation for a web page written in HTML language is shown in figure 7. It combines XML data of input and functionality button properties:

```
<?xml version='1.0'?>
<xsl:stylesheet version="1.0" xmlns:xsl="http://www.w3.org/1999/XSL/Transform">
<xsl:template match="/">
  <html xmlns="http://www.w3.org/1999/xhtml" lang="en" xml:lang="en">
  <head> <title><xsl:value-of select="window/title"/></title>
   <meta http-equiv="content-type" content="text/html; charset=UTF-8" />
```

```
    <link rel="stylesheet" type="text/css" href="login.css" />
  </head>
  <body>
    <form method="post" action="">
    <table>
    <xsl:for-each select="window/data/input">
    <tr><td><xsl:value-of select="name"/></td>
        <td> <xsl:element name="input">
           <xsl:attribute                           name="type"><xsl:value-of
        select="type"/></xsl:attribute>
           <xsl:attribute                      name="maxlength"><xsl:value-of
        select="length"/></xsl:attribute>
        </xsl:element> </td>
    </tr> </xsl:for-each>
    </table>
    <xsl:for-each select="window/functionality/button">
      <xsl:element name="input">
      <xsl:attribute                                name="type"><xsl:value-of
select="type"/></xsl:attribute>
      <xsl:attribute                               name="value"><xsl:value-of
select="caption"/></xsl:attribute>
      </xsl:element>
    </xsl:for-each>
    </form>
  </body> </html>
  </xsl:template>
  </xsl:stylesheet>
```

Fig. 7. XSL transformation for HMTL file

Transformations defined once could be used many times. Changes of main specification accompanied with transformation are reflected in application i.e. program code is updated automatically. This transformation is important because the proposed algorithm relieves specifying big and complex information systems and helps to avoid much iteration of system analysis and validation.

The result of system specification transformation to the program code is functional user login web form illustrated in figure 8.

Fig. 8. Generated Web form example

5 Conclusions

Several techniques for GUI design were reviewed in this paper. These techniques represent different approaches of GUI modelling.

The description of the functional requirements specification method and requirements specification process is presented. GUI modelling process is based on the results of three models:

- Results / data resources structure model;
- Links (data flows) between data resources/results and structure of those links model;
- Results / data resources processing stages model.

The proposed conceptual GUI modelling process was presented in detail. The graphical user interface modelling process is implemented as a module that includes autonomous functionality of the CASE tool. It allows a partial automation of the design process and results of a better quality can be reached faster. The tool works as a GUI design process wizard proposing solutions or suggestions for a designer.

Consistent analysis and design methods and generation of XML specification used in the GUI development process allow developing better quality systems and higher customer satisfaction. This improvement makes development of the e-commerce and other web based systems easier and more effective.

As a future work we will try to develop a process that would take into account all three layers of e-commerce systems: Presentation, Business Logic and Data Layer and extend capabilities of FRSM to specify non-functional requirements and store them in DFS.

References

1. Myers, B.A.: User-interface tools: introduction and survey. Software, IEEE Volume 6, Issue 1 (Jan.1989) 15-3
2. Butleris, R., Butkienė, R.: The Approach for the User Requirements Specification, in: A.Čaplinskas, J.Eder (Ed.), 5th East-European conference ADBIS'2001 Research Communications, Vilnius (2001) 225-240
3. Butleris, R., Butkienė, R.: Verification Rules of Computerised Information System Model with Respect to Data Resource Processing, Informatica 12(3) (2001) 347-372
4. Butleris, R., Danikauskas, T., Misevičiūtė, B.: Model based user interface design using models of requirements specifications of IS (in Lithuanian), in: Information technologies '2004, Conference papers, Technologija, Kaunas (2004) 533-538
5. Butleris, R., Danikauskas, T.: Conceptual Data model Design Using Functional Requirements Specification Method, in: Proceedings of EMMSAD'04 workshop at CaiSE'04 conference, Riga (2004) 221-232
6. Kolp, M., Giorgini, M., Mylopoulos, M.: Organizational Patterns for Early Requirements Analysis, in: CAiSE 2003, LNCS 2681, Springer-Verlag Berlin Heidelberg (2003) 617-632
7. Arisholm, E.: Incorporating Rapid User Interface Prototyping in Object-Oriented Analysis and Design with Genova, in: The Eighth Nordic Workshop on Programming Environment Research, Electronic proceedings: NWPER ' 98, Sweden (1998)
8. Molina, P.J.: A Review to Model-Based User Interface Development Technology, in: IUI/CADUI 2004 workshop, Electronic proceedings, Portugal, Madeira (2004)
9. Saiedian, H., Dale, R.: Requirements engineering: making the connection between the software developer and customer, Information and Software Technology 42, Elsevier (2000) 419-428
10. Díaz, J.S., Pastor, O., Fons, J.J.: From User Requirements to User Interfaces: A Methodological Approach, Lecture Notes In Computer Science; Vol. 2068 archive Proceedings of the 13th International Conference on Advanced Information Systems Engineering (2001) 60-75
11. Barker, R., Longman, R.: Case Method, function and process modelling, Addison-Wesley (1992)
12. Barker, R.: Case Method, Tasks and deliverables, Addison-Wesley (1989)
13. OMG. OMG Unified Modeling Language Specification ver. 1.5. Object Management Group (2003)

14. Maciaszek, L.A.: Requirements Analysis and System Design Developing Information Systems. Adison-Wesley (2001)
15. Van Harmelen, M.: Object Modeling and User Interface Design. Edison-Wesley (2001)
16. Grundlund, Å., Lafreniere, D., Carr, D.A.: A pattern-Supported Approach to the User Interface Design Process. Proceedings of HCI International 2001 9th International Conference on Human-Computer Interaction. New Orleans, USA (2001)
17. Balasubramanian, V., Turoff, M.: Supporting the User Interface Design Process with Hypertext Functionality. The International Workshop Series on Incorporating Hypertext Functionality Into Software Systems. HTF II, held in conjunction with the ACM Hypertext '96 conference, Washington USA, (1996).
18. Butkiene, R., Jasiukevicius, A., Sakys, V.: The specification of structure of information flows (in Lithuanian), Information Sciences 24 (2003) 117-124
19. Butleris, R., Butkienė, R., Danikauskas, T.: Business modeling for elicitation of information requirements, in: Business operation and its legal environment: processes, tendencies and results, Proceedings of International Conference, Turiba, Riga (2002) 67-73
20. Wangler, B.: Contributions to Functional Requirements Modelling, Ph.D. Thesis, Stockholm University, Royal Institute of Technology (1993)
21. Kounev, S.D.: Performance Prediction, Sizing and Capacity Planning for Distributed E-Commerce Applications, Information Technology Transfer Office, Germany (2001)5-6
22. W3C. XSL Transformations (XSLT) Version 2.0. W3C XSL Working Group (2005)

Generalizing Redundancy Elimination in Checking Sequences

K. Tuncay Tekle[1], Hasan Ural[2], M. Cihan Yalcin[1], and Husnu Yenigun[1]

[1] Faculty of Engineering and Natural Sciences, Sabanci University, Tuzla 34956, Istanbul, Turkey

[2] School of Information Technology and Engineering, University of Ottawa, Ottawa, Ontario, K1N 6N5, Canada

Abstract. Based on a distinguishing sequence for a Finite State Machine (FSM), an efficient checking sequence may be produced from the elements of a set $E_{\alpha'}$ of α'–sequences and a set E_T of T–sequences, that both recognize the states, and elements of E_C which represents the transitions in the FSM. An optimization algorithm may then be used to produce a reduced length checking sequence by connecting the elements of $E_{\alpha'}$, E_T, and E_C using transitions taken from an acyclic set E''. It is known that only a subset E'_C of E_C is sufficient to form a checking sequence. This paper improves this result by reducing the number of elements in E'_C that must be included in the generated checking sequence.

1 Introduction

Finite state machine (FSM) model has been widely used to specify behaviour of various types of systems [1]. An FSM M models the externally observable behaviour of a system under test (SUT) N in terms of the sequences of inputs and outputs exchanged between a "black box" representing N and its environment. When testing N to ensure its correct functionality with respect to M, a *checking sequence* (i.e., a sequence of inputs constructed from M) is applied to N to determine whether N is a correct or faulty implementation of M [2, 3]. Often, N is considered to have the same input and output alphabets of M and to have no more states than M.

A checking sequence of M is constructed in such a way that the output sequence produced by N in response to the application of the checking sequence provides sufficient information to verify that every state transition of M is implemented correctly by N. That is, in order to verify the implementation of a transition from state s to state s' under input x, firstly, N must be transferred to the state recognized as state s of M; secondly, when the input x is applied, the output produced by N in response to x must be as specified in M; i.e., there must not be an output fault; and thirdly, the state reached by N after the application of x must be recognized as state s' of M; i.e., there must not be a transfer fault. Hence, a crucial part of testing the correct implementation of each transition is recognizing the starting and terminating states of the transition which can be achieved by a distinguishing sequence [3], a characterization set [3]

P. Yolum et al.(Eds.): ISCIS 2005, LNCS 3733, pp. 915–926, 2005.

or a unique input-output (UIO) sequence [4]. It is known that a distinguishing sequence may not exist for every minimal FSM [5], and that determining the existence of a distinguishing sequence for an FSM is PSPACE-complete [6].

Nevertheless, based on distinguishing sequences, various methods have been proposed for FSM based testing (for example, [3, 7, 8]). Some of these methods aim in generating reduced length checking sequences [8, 9, 10]. A representative example of these methods is [9] which shows that an efficient checking sequence may be produced by combining the elements in some predefined set $E_{\alpha'}$ of α'–sequences that recognize subsets of states, the elements of a set E_T of T–sequences which recognize individual states, and the elements of a set E_C of subsequences that represent individual transitions, using an acyclic set E'' of transitions from M. An optimization algorithm is then used in order to produce a shortest checking sequence by connecting the elements of $E_{\alpha'}$, E_T, and E_C using transitions drawn from E''.

Recently it is shown in [10] that the length of checking sequences can be reduced even further by eliminating some elements of E_C. Those transitions in E_C, that *correspond to the last transitions traversed* when a T–sequence is applied in an α'–sequence, are taken to be the candidate transitions for which transition tests can be eliminated. A dependency relation is derived on these candidate transitions, and only an acyclic subset of them (which does not depend on each other – directly or indirectly – with respect to this dependency relation) is considered to be eliminated.

In this paper, we generalize the condition for a transition to be considered as a candidate for transition test exemption. The candidate transitions are again among the transitions traversed when a T–sequence is applied in an α'–sequence. However, they do not have to be the last transitions traversed. The condition given in this paper trivially holds for the last transitions, hence the approach of [10] is a special case of the approach given in this paper.

Besides the theoretical novelty of providing a more general condition, our approach also has the following practical implication. Since we identify more candidate transitions, the dependency relation between these candidate transitions is more relaxed. This allows us to find acyclic subsets of candidate transitions with greater cardinality, hence we can eliminate more transition tests than the approach of [10].

The rest of the paper is organized as follows. Section 2 gives an overview of the concepts used in constructing checking sequences based on distinguishing sequences, and Section 3 explains an existing approach for the construction of checking sequences. Section 4 presents the proposed method for eliminating redundant transition tests and shows the application of the method to an example. Section 5 gives the concluding remarks.

2 Preliminaries

A deterministic FSM M is defined by a tuple $(S, s_1, X, Y, \delta, \lambda)$ in which S is a finite set of *states*, $s_1 \in S$ is the *initial state*, X is the finite *input alphabet*,

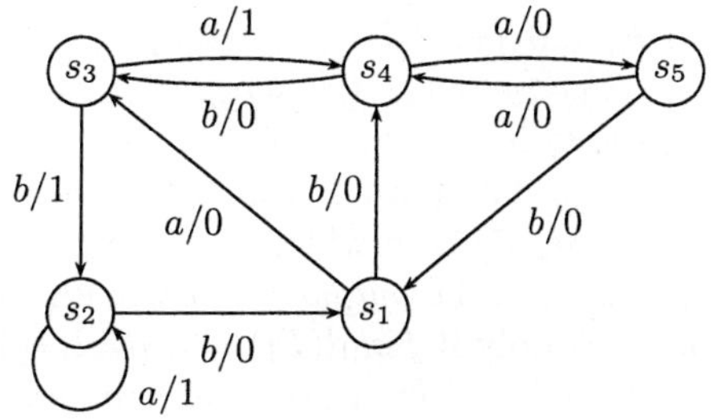

Fig. 1. The FSM M_0

Y is the finite *output alphabet*, $\delta : S \times X \rightarrow S$ is the *next state function* and $\lambda : S \times X \rightarrow Y$ is the *output function*. The functions δ and λ can be extended to input sequences in a straightforward manner. The number of states of M is denoted n and the states of M are enumerated, giving $S = \{s_1, \ldots, s_n\}$. An FSM is *completely specified* if the functions λ and δ are total.

An FSM, that will be denoted M_0 throughout this paper, is described in Figure 1. Here, $S = \{s_1, s_2, s_3, s_4, s_5\}$, $X = \{a, b\}$ and $Y = \{0, 1\}$.

Throughout the paper, we use barred symbols (e.g. $\bar{x}, \bar{P}, \ldots$) to denote sequences, and juxtaposition to denote concatenation. In an FSM M, $s_i \in S$ and $s_j \in S$, $s_i \neq s_j$, are *equivalent* if, $\forall \bar{x} \in X^*$, $\lambda(s_i, \bar{x}) = \lambda(s_j, \bar{x})$. If $\exists \bar{x} \in X^*$ such that $\lambda(s_i, \bar{x}) \neq \lambda(s_j, \bar{x})$ then $\bar{x}$ is said to *distinguish* s_i and s_j. An FSM M is said to be *minimal* if none of its states are equivalent. A *distinguishing sequence* for an FSM M is an input sequence $\bar{D}$ for which each state of M produces a distinct output. More formally, for all $s_i, s_j \in S$ if $s_i \neq s_j$ then $\lambda(s_i, \bar{D}) \neq \lambda(s_j, \bar{D})$. Thus, for example, M_0 has distinguishing sequence *abb*.

The shortest prefix of a distinguishing sequence $\bar{D}$ that distinguishes a state in M can actually be used as a special distinguishing sequence for that state [11]. Based on this observation, we use prefixes of distinguishing sequences, in order to further reduce the length of checking sequences. We will use $\bar{D}_i$ to denote the shortest prefix of a distinguishing sequence $\bar{D}$ that is sufficient to distinguish a state s_i from the other states. Formally, given a distinguishing sequence $\bar{D}$ and a state s_i, $\bar{D}_i$ is the shortest prefix of $\bar{D}$ such that for any state s_j, if $s_i \neq s_j$ then $\lambda(s_i, \bar{D}_i) \neq \lambda(s_j, \bar{D}_i)$. For example, M_0 has $\bar{D}_1 = ab$, $\bar{D}_2 = \bar{D}_3 = \bar{D}_4 = \bar{D}_5 = abb$. Below we call $\bar{D}_i$'s as *prefix distinguishing sequences*.

An FSM M can be represented by a directed graph (*digraph*) $G = (V, E)$ where a set of vertices V represents the set S of states of M, and a set of directed edges E represents all transitions of M. Each edge $e = (v_j, v_k, x/y) \in E$ represents a transition $t = (s_j, s_k, x/y)$ of M from state s_j to state s_k with input x and output y where $s_j, s_k \in S$, $x \in X$, and $y \in Y$ such that $\delta(s_j, x) = s_k$, $\lambda(s_j, x) = y$. For a vertex $v \in V$, $indegree_{E'}(v)$ denotes the number of edges from E' that enter v and $outdegree_{E'}(v)$ denotes the number of edges from E' that leave v, where $E' \subseteq E$.

A sequence $\bar{P} = (n_1, n_2, x_1/y_1)(n_2, n_3, x_2/y_2) \ldots (n_{k-1}, n_k, x_{k-1}/y_{k-1})$ of pairwise adjacent edges from G forms a *path* in which each *node* n_i represents a vertex from V and thus, ultimately, a state from S. Here $initial(\bar{P})$ denotes n_1, which is the *initial node* of $\bar{P}$, and $final(\bar{P})$ denotes n_k, which is the *final node* of $\bar{P}$. The sequence $\bar{Q} = (x_1/y_1)(x_2/y_2)\dots(x_{k-1}/y_{k-1})$ is the *label* of $\bar{P}$ and is denoted $label(\bar{P})$. In this case, $\bar{Q}$ is said to *label* the path $\bar{P}$. $\bar{Q}$ is said to be a *transfer sequence* from n_1 to n_k. The path $\bar{P}$ can be represented by the tuple $(n_1, n_k, \bar{Q})$ or by the tuple $(n_1, n_k, \bar{x}/\bar{y})$ in which $\bar{x} = x_1x_2\dots x_{k-1}$ is the *input portion* of $\bar{Q}$ and $\bar{y} = y_1y_2\dots y_{k-1}$ is the *output portion* of $\bar{Q}$. Two paths $\bar{P}_1$ and $\bar{P}_2$ can be concatenated as $\bar{P}_1\bar{P}_2$ only if $final(\bar{P}_1) = initial(\bar{P}_2)$.

A *tour* is a path whose initial and final nodes are the same. Given a tour $\bar{\Gamma} = e_1e_2\dots e_k$, $\bar{P} = e_je_{j+1}\dots e_ke_1e_2\dots e_{j-1}$ is a path formed by *starting* $\bar{\Gamma}$ with edge e_j, and hence by *ending* $\bar{\Gamma}$ with edge e_{j-1}. An *Euler Tour* is a tour that contains each edge exactly once. A set E' of edges from G is *acyclic* if no tour can be formed using the edges in E'.

A digraph is *strongly connected* if for any ordered pair of vertices (v_i, v_j) there is a path from v_i to v_j. An FSM is *strongly connected* if the digraph that represents it is strongly connected. It will be assumed that any FSM considered in this paper is deterministic, minimal, completely specified, and strongly connected.

Given an FSM M, let $\Phi(M)$ be the set of FSMs each of which has at most n states and the same input and output alphabets as M. Let N be an FSM of $\Phi(M)$. N is *isomorphic* to M if there is a one-to-one and onto function f on the state sets of M and N such that for any state transition $(s_i, s_j, x/y)$ of M, $(f(s_i), f(s_j), x/y)$ is a transition of N. A *checking sequence* of M is an input sequence starting at the initial state s_1 of M that distinguishes M from any N of $\Phi(M)$ that is not isomorphic to M. In the context of testing, this means that in response to this input sequence, any faulty implementation N from $\Phi(M)$ will produce an output sequence different from the expected output, thereby indicating the presence of a fault/faults. As stated earlier, a crucial part of testing the correct implementation of each transition of M in N from $\Phi(M)$ is recognizing the starting and terminating states of the transition which lead to the notions of state recognition and transition verification used in algorithms for constructing reduced length checking sequences (for example, [8, 9]). These notions are defined below in terms of a given distinguishing sequence $\bar{D}$ (more precisely the prefix distinguishing sequences) for FSM M.

3 An Existing Approach

3.1 Basics

Consider the digraph $G = (V, E)$ representing M and let $\bar{Q}$ be the label of a path $\bar{P}$ in G. A vertex v of $\bar{P}$ is said to be *recognized* (in $\bar{Q}$) as a state s_i of M, if the label $\bar{T}$ of a subpath $\bar{R}$ of $\bar{P}$ starting at v has a prefix $\bar{D}_i/\lambda(s_i, \bar{D}_i)$. This rule says that $initial(\bar{R})$ is recognized as state s_i if $label(\bar{R})$ has a prefix $\bar{D}_i/\lambda(s_i, \bar{D}_i)$. Alternatively, if $\bar{P}_1 = (v_i, v_j, \bar{T})$ and $\bar{P}_2 = (v_k, v, \bar{T})$ are two subpaths of $\bar{P}$ such that v_i and v_k are recognized as state s' of M and v_j is recognized as state s of M, then v is said to be recognized (in $\bar{Q}$) as state s of M. This rule says that if $\bar{P}_1$ and $\bar{P}_2$ are labeled by the same input/output sequence at their starting vertices which are recognized as the same state s' of M, then their terminating vertices correspond to the same state s of M. An edge $(v, v', x/y)$ of $\bar{P}$ is said to be *verified* (in $\bar{Q}$) as a transition $(s_i, s_j, x_i/y_i)$ of M if v is recognized as state s_i, v' is recognized as state s_j, $x = x_i$, and $y = y_i$; i.e., v is recognized as state s_i of M and there is a subpath $\bar{P}'$ of $\bar{P}$ starting at v whose label is $x\bar{D}_j/\lambda(s_i, x\bar{D}_j)$. The subpath $\bar{P}'$ is called the *transition test* for the transition $(s_i, s_j, x_i/y_i)$; i.e., $\bar{P}'$ is the transition sequence labeled by (the application of) the input sequence $x\bar{D}_j$ at state s_i. Accordingly, the following result will form the basis of the checking sequence construction method proposed in this paper.

Theorem 1. *(Theorem 1, [8]) Let $\bar{P}$ be a path of G representing an FSM M that starts at s_1 and $\bar{Q} = label(\bar{P})$. If every edge of G is verified in $\bar{Q}$, then the input portion of $\bar{Q}$ is a checking sequence of M.*

Let $\bar{Q}$ be the label of a path $\bar{P}$ in G starting at v_1 such that $\bar{Q}$ contains n subsequences of the form $\bar{D}_i/\lambda(s_i, \bar{D}_i)$, $(1 \le i \le n)$. Since $\bar{D}_i$'s are prefix distinguishing sequences for M, each of these subsequences of the form $\bar{D}_i/\lambda(s_i, \bar{D}_i)$, $(1 \le i \le n)$, is unique. If $\bar{Q}$ labels a path starting at the initial state of N from $\Phi(M)$ then, since N has at most n states, $\bar{D}_i$'s must also be prefix distinguishing sequences for N. This says that if n different expected responses to $\bar{D}_i$'s are observed in N, then $\bar{D}_i$'s define a one-to-one correspondence between the states of N and M. In this case, we say that the uniqueness of the response of each of the n states of N to $\bar{D}_i$'s are verified and hence N has n distinct states.

Let $DS(s_i)$ denote the transition sequence labeled by $\bar{D}_i/\lambda(s_i, \bar{D}_i)$ at state s_i and let $\bar{T}_i$, called henceforth T–sequence, be $label(\bar{R}_i)$ where $\bar{R}_i = DS(s_i)\bar{B}_i$ and $\bar{B}_i$ is a (possibly empty) sequence of transitions of G starting at $final(DS(s_i))$, $(1 \le i \le n)$. Since a T–sequence $\bar{T}_i$ is a sequence of input/output pairs with a prefix $label(DS(s_i)) = \bar{D}_i/\lambda(s_i, \bar{D}_i)$, it may be used to recognize the ending state of any transition terminating at state s_i [8]. $\bar{R}_i$'s can be connected to each other in a succinct manner to form the elements of an α'–set $= \{\bar{\alpha}'_1, \bar{\alpha}'_2, \ldots \bar{\alpha}'_q\}$ where each $\bar{\alpha}'_k$ $(1 \le k \le q)$ is called an α'–sequence [9]. An α'–sequence $\bar{\alpha}'_k$ is the label of an α'–path $\bar{\rho}_k = \bar{R}_{k_1}\bar{R}_{k_2}\ldots\bar{R}_{k_{r_k}}$, $1 \le k_1, k_2, \ldots, k_{r_k} \le n$, such that (a) $\exists$ an α'–path $\bar{\rho}_j = \bar{R}_{j_1}\bar{R}_{j_2}\ldots\bar{R}_{j_{r_j}}$, $1 \le j \le q$ and $1 \le j_1, j_2, \ldots, j_{r_j} \le n$, such that for some i, $1 \le i < r_j$, $k_{r_k} = j_i$; and (b) No other $\bar{R}_{k_i}$, $1 \le i < r_k$, in $\bar{\rho}_k$ satisfies (b). In other words for every α'–path $\bar{\rho}_k$, the last component and only the last component $\bar{R}_{k_{r_k}}$ in $\bar{\rho}_k$ appears in the same or in some other α'–path $\bar{\rho}_j$ before the last component in $\bar{\rho}_j$. Since $\bar{\alpha}'_k = label(\bar{\rho}_k)$, $\bar{\alpha}'_k$ will be concatenation of T–sequences. A set of α'–sequences is called an α'–set only if $\forall \bar{T}_i$, $1 \le i \le n$, $\exists\, \bar{\alpha}'_k$, $1 \le k \le q$, such that $\bar{T}_i$ is a subsequence of $\bar{\alpha}'_k$.

Let $A = \{\bar{\alpha}'_1, \bar{\alpha}'_2, \ldots, \bar{\alpha}'_q\}$ be an α'–set with the corresponding set of α'–paths $\{\bar{\rho}_1, \bar{\rho}_2, \ldots, \bar{\rho}_q\}$, and $\bar{Q}$ be the label of a path $\bar{P}$ such that each $\bar{\alpha}'_k \in A$ is a subsequence of $\bar{Q}$. Then we have the following properties:

1) Since $\bar{\alpha}'_k$ starts with a $\bar{T}_i$ that has a prefix $\bar{D}_i/\lambda(s_i, \bar{D}_i)$, $initial(\bar{\rho}_k)$ is recognized in $\bar{Q}$
2) Since every α'–sequence $\bar{\alpha}'_k$ is a subsequence of $\bar{Q}$, $final(\bar{\rho}_k)$ is recognized in $\bar{Q}$

3) Since every $\bar{T}_i$ is in some $\bar{\alpha}'_k$, $initial(\bar{R}_i)$ is recognized in $\bar{Q}$
4) Since every $\bar{T}_i$ is followed by a $\bar{T}_j$ in some $\bar{\alpha}'_k$, $final(\bar{R}_i)$ is recognized in $\bar{Q}$
5) Since $\bar{\alpha}'_k$ starts with a $\bar{T}_i$ that has a prefix $\bar{D}_i/\lambda(s_i, \bar{D}_i)$, $\bar{\alpha}'_k$ may be used to recognize the ending state of any transition terminating at state s_i [9].

3.2 Checking Sequence Construction

The checking sequence construction method given in [9] first builds a digraph $G' = (V', E')$ by augmenting the digraph $G = (V, E)$ representing an FSM where $V' = V \cup U'$, $E' = E_C \cup E_{\alpha'} \cup E_T \cup E''$ by:

- replicating each vertex v in V as a vertex v' in U' to represent the "recognized" version of v
- replacing each edge $(v_i, v_j, x/y)$ of E by an edge $(v'_i, v_j, x/y)$ in E_C so that the transition to be verified starts at the recognized vertex v'_i
- inserting an edge $(v_i, v'_j, \bar{\alpha}'_k)$ in $E_{\alpha'}$ for each $\bar{\rho}_k = (v_i, v_j, \bar{\alpha}'_k)$, $(1 \le k \le q)$ so that $\bar{\rho}_k$ ends at the recognized vertex v'_j
- inserting an edge $(v_i, v'_j, \bar{T}_m)$ in E_T for each $\bar{R}_m = (v_i, v_j, \bar{T}_m)$, $(1 \le m \le n)$ so that $\bar{R}_m$ ends at the recognized vertex v'_j
- inserting an edge $(v'_i, v'_j, x/y)$ in E'' for each edge $(v_i, v_j, x/y)$ in a subset of edges of E such that $G'' = (U', E'')$ does not have a tour and G' is strongly connected.

Note that in G' each edge in E_C is followed by an edge from $E_{\alpha'} \cup E_T$ to form a transition test for the transition corresponding to that edge of E_C. Then, the approach in [9] forms a minimal symmetric augmentation G^* of the digraph induced by $E_{\alpha'} \cup E_C$ by adding replications of edges from E' . If G^*, with its isolated vertices removed, is connected, then G^* has an Euler tour. Otherwise, a heuristic such as the one given in [8] is applied to make G^* connected and an Euler tour of this new digraph is formed. On the basis of Theorem 1, it is argued in [9] that the input portion of the label of the Euler tour of G^* starting at vertex v_1 which is followed by $\bar{D}_1$ is a checking sequence of M.

4 An Enhancement on the Existing Approach

This section explains how, given an α'–set A, we can produce a checking sequence without considering some of the edges in E_C. In the following, we first define a set of edges $L \subset E$, then show that transition tests for the edges in L are redundant, and finally explain how we can modify the algorithm to generate the checking sequence in order not to include these redundant transition tests.

4.1 Transition Test Exemption

In this section, we consistently use $\bar{P}$ to denote a path in G, and $\bar{Q}$ to denote $label(\bar{P})$. Similar to showing an edge being verified as given in Section 3.1, in order to show a sequence of edges being verified we first introduce the notion of a sequence of edges being traced.

Definition 1. *Let $\bar{P}' = e_1e_2 \ldots e_h$ be a sequence of edges in G, where $e_m = (v_{i_m}, v_{i_{m+1}}, x_m/y_m)$ for $1 \leq m \leq h$. $\bar{P}'$ is* traced *in $\bar{Q}$ if there exists a subpath $(n_1, n_{h+1}, x'_1x'_2 \ldots x'_h/y'_1y'_2 \ldots y'_h)$ in $\bar{P}$ such that n_1 is recognized as v_{i_1}, n_{h+1} is recognized as $v_{i_{h+1}}$, and $x_m/y_m = x'_m/y'_m$ for $1 \leq m \leq h$.*

Lemma 1. *Let $\bar{P}' = e_1e_2 \ldots e_h$ $(h \geq 1)$ be a sequence of edges in G traced in $\bar{Q}$, where $e_m = (v_{i_m}, v_{i_{m+1}}, x_m/y_m)$ for $1 \leq m \leq h$. Assume that $e_1, e_2, \ldots, e_l$ for some $1 \leq l < h$ are all verified in $\bar{Q}$. Then, $\bar{P}'' = e_{l+1}e_{l+2} \ldots e_h$ is also traced in $\bar{Q}$.*

Proof. The proof is by induction on l. Let's assume $l = 1$. If e_1 is verified in $\bar{Q}$, then $\bar{P}$ includes a subpath $\bar{P}_1 = (n_j, n_k, x'_1/y'_1)$ where n_j is recognized as v_{i_1}, n_k is recognized as v_{i_2} and $x_1/y_1 = x'_1/y'_1$. Since $\bar{P}'$ is traced in $\bar{Q}$, there must exist a subpath $\bar{P}_2 = (n_q, n_s, x''_1x''_2 \ldots x''_h/y''_1y''_2 \ldots y''_h)$ in $\bar{P}$ where n_q is recognized as v_{i_1}, n_s is recognized as $v_{i_{h+1}}$, and $x''_m/y''_m = x_m/y_m$ for $1 \leq m \leq h$. Let us divide the path $\bar{P}_2$ into two as $\bar{P}_{21} = (n_q, n_i, x''_1/y''_1)$ and $\bar{P}_{22} = (n_i, n_s, x''_2x''_3 \ldots x''_h/y''_2y''_3 \ldots y''_h)$. According to the definition of a recognized vertex given in Section 3.1, the paths $\bar{P}_1$ and $\bar{P}_{21}$ recognize n_i as v_{i_2}. Then, the existence of $\bar{P}_{22}$ in $\bar{P}$ implies that $\bar{P}'' = e_2e_3 \ldots e_h$ is traced in $\bar{Q}$.

For the inductive step, we can again use the arguments given above to conclude that $\bar{P}'' = e_2e_3 \ldots e_h$ is traced in $\bar{Q}$. However, we have $l - 1$ verified transitions at the beginning of $\bar{P}''$, hence the proof is completed by using the induction hypothesis. □

Definition 2. *An edge $(v, v', x_v/y_v)$ in G is said to be a* nonconverging edge *[12] if $\forall(u, u', x_u/y_u)$, $u \neq v$ and $x_u = x_v$ implies $u' \neq v'$ or $y_u \neq y_v$.*

Lemma 2. *Let $(v, v', x_v/y_v)$ be a nonconverging edge in G, and $(n_p, n_q, x/y)$ be a subpath of $\bar{P}$ such that n_q is recognized as v' and $x/y = x_v/y_v$. If all the edges $(u, u', x_u/y_u)$ in G, where $x_u = x_v$ are verified in $\bar{Q}$, then n_p is recognized as v.*

Proof. Since all the edges in G corresponding to the x_v transitions of the states in M are verified, and since the state corresponding to the node v is the only state that produces y_v and moves into the state corresponding to the node v' when x_v is applied, we can conclude that whenever x_v/y_v is seen in $\bar{Q}$ and the ending node is recognized as v', then the previous node must be the node v. □

Lemma 3. *Let $\bar{P}' = e_1e_2 \ldots e_h$ $(h \geq 1)$ be a sequence of edges in G traced in $\bar{Q}$, where $e_m = (v_{i_m}, v_{i_{m+1}}, x_m/y_m)$ for $1 \leq m \leq h$. Assume that $e_l, e_{l+1}, \ldots, e_h$ for some $1 < l \leq h$ are all verified in $\bar{Q}$. If for all $l \leq r \leq h$*
(i) $e_r = (v_{i_r}, v_{i_{r+1}}, x_r/y_r)$ is a nonconverging edge, and
(ii) For each vertex v in G, all the edges of the form $(v, v', x/y)$ (where $x = x_r$) are verified in $\bar{Q}$ then $\bar{P}'' = e_1e_2 \ldots e_{l-1}$ is also traced in $\bar{Q}$.

Proof. The proof is by induction on $h-l+1$. Let's assume $h-l+1 = 1$, i.e $l = h$. Since $\bar{P}'$ is traced in $\bar{Q}$, $\bar{P}'$ must be a subpath $(n_q, n_s, x'_1x'_2 \ldots x'_h/y'_1y'_2 \ldots y'_h)$ of $\bar{P}$ where n_q is recognized as v_{i_1}, n_s is recognized as $v_{i_{h+1}}$, and $x'_m/y'_m = x_m/y_m$ for $1 \leq m \leq h$. Let us divide $\bar{P}'$ into two as $\bar{P}_1 = (n_q, n_i, x'_1x'_2 \ldots x'_{h-1}/y'_1y'_2 \ldots y'_{h-1})$

and $\bar{P}_2 = (n_i, n_s, x'_h/y'_h)$. Note that $\bar{P}_2$ corresponds to e_h which is a nonconverging edge. Since all the edges of the form $(v, v', x_h/y)$ are verified in $\bar{Q}$, n_i is recognized as v_{i_h} by using Lemma 2. Then $\bar{P}_1 = e_1e_2\ldots e_{h-1}$ is traced in $\bar{Q}$.

For the inductive step, we can again use the arguments given above to conclude that $\bar{P}'' = e_1e_2\ldots e_{h-1}$ is traced in $\bar{Q}$. However, we have $h-l$ verified transitions at the end of $\bar{P}''$, hence the proof is completed by using the induction hypothesis. □

Lemma 4. *Let $\bar{P}' = e_1e_2\ldots e_h$ $(h \geq 1)$ be a sequence of edges in G traced in $\bar{Q}$, where $e_m = (v_{i_m}, v_{i_{m+1}}, x_m/y_m)$ for $1 \leq m \leq h$. Let e_l be an edge in $\bar{P}'$, where $1 \leq l \leq h$. If*
(i) $\forall r, 1 \leq r \leq h, r \neq l$ implies e_r is verified in $\bar{Q}$, and
(ii) $\forall r,\ l < r \leq h$
(ii.a) $e_r = (v_{i_r}, v_{i_{r+1}}, x_r/y_r)$ is a nonconverging edge; and
(ii.b) For each vertex v in G, all the edges of the form $(v, v', x/y)$ (where $x = x_r$) are verified in $\bar{Q}$ then e_l is also verified in $\bar{Q}$.

Proof. Since $\bar{P}'$ is traced in $\bar{Q}$, $\bar{P}'$ is a subpath $(n_q, n_s, x'_1x'_2\ldots x'_h/y'_1y'_2\ldots y'_h)$ of $\bar{P}$ where n_q is recognized as v_{i_1}, n_s is recognized as $v_{i_{h+1}}$, and $x'_m/y'_m = x_m/y_m$ for $1 \leq m \leq h$. Let us divide the path $\bar{P}'$ into three as follows: $\bar{P}_1 = (n_q, n_i, x'_1x'_2\ldots x'_{l-1}/y'_1y'_2\ldots y'_{l-1})$, and $\bar{P}_2 = (n_i, n_s, x'_l/y'_l)$, and finally $\bar{P}_3 = (n_s, n_t, x'_{l+1}x'_{l+2}\ldots x'_h/y'_{l+1}y'_{l+2}\ldots y'_h)$. By using Lemma 1, $\bar{P}_2\bar{P}_3$ is traced in $\bar{Q}$ and n_i is therefore recognized as v_{i_l}. By using Lemma 3, $\bar{P}_1\bar{P}_2$ is traced in $\bar{Q}$ and n_s is therefore recognized as $v_{i_{l+1}}$. Since both n_i and n_s are recognized in $\bar{P}_2 = e_l$, e_l is verified. □

Lemma 4 suggests that if there is a sequence of edges which is traced in the label $\bar{Q}$ of a path, then $\bar{Q}$ already includes what it takes to verify an edge e_l in the sequence, provided that the conditions (i), (ii.a) and (ii.b) given in the premises of Lemma 4 hold. Therefore, we can pick a transition e_l in a sequence of edges which is known to be traced, and do not include the transition test for e_l, provided that the conditions are satisfied for e_l. Note that, one can always pick e_h as e_l (the last transition in the sequence of edges) according to the conditions of Lemma 4. This is what has been proposed in [10], and therefore the approach given in [10] is a special case of our approach.

In fact, inclusion of α'–sequences in the checking sequences guarantee that there are some sequences of edges which are traced, as shown by the following lemma.

Lemma 5. *Let A be an α'–set, and $\bar{Q}$ include all the α'–sequences in A. Then $\forall i, 1 \leq i \leq n$, $\bar{R}_i = DS(s_i)\bar{B}_i$ is traced in $\bar{Q}$.*

Proof. Note that $\exists \bar{\alpha}'_k$, $1 \leq k \leq q$, with the subsequence $label(\bar{R}_i)label(\bar{R}_j)$ for some j, $1 \leq j \leq n$. Since $label(\bar{R}_i)$ starts with $\bar{D}_i/\lambda(s_i, \bar{D}_i)$, $initial(\bar{R}_i)$ is recognized. Since $label(\bar{R}_j)$ starts with $\bar{D}_j/\lambda(s_j, \bar{D}_j)$, $initial(\bar{R}_j)$, hence $final(\bar{R}_i)$ is also recognized. □

Lemma 6. *Let A be an α'-set, and $\bar{Q}$ include all the α'-sequences in A, and $\bar{R}_i = e_{j_1}e_{j_2}\dots e_{j_h}$ be the sequence of edges corresponding to the application of the T-sequence $\bar{T}_i$ at a state s_i. Let $e_{j_l} = (v_{j_l}, v_{j_{l+1}}, x_{j_l}/y_{j_l})$ be an edge in $\bar{R}_i$. If*
(i) $\forall r, 1 \le r \le h, r \ne l$ implies e_{j_r} is verified in $\bar{Q}$, and
(ii) $\forall r, l < r \le h$
(ii.a) e_{j_r} is a nonconverging edge; and
(ii.b) For each vertex v in G, all the edges of the form $(v, v', x/y)$ (where $x = x_{j_l}$) are verified in $\bar{Q}$ then e_{j_l} is also verified in $\bar{Q}$.

Proof. The result follows from Lemma 4 and Lemma 5. □

Lemma 6 suggests that one can identify an edge per state to be excluded from the transition tests. However, if we identify some edge e for a state s, exclusion of e depends on some other transitions being verified, as given in the premises of Lemma 6. We may identify another edge e' for another state s'. Nevertheless, exclusion of e may depend on e' being verified, and exclusion of e' may depend on e being verified (either directly or indirectly). The following procedure shows a possible way to calculate a set of edges that can be excluded from the transition tests without having such a cyclic dependency.

For an $\bar{R}_i = DS(s_i)\bar{B}_i = e_1e_2\dots e_h$, $1 \le i \le n$, an edge e_l $(1 \le l \le h)$ is a *candidate edge of* $\bar{R}_i$ if $\forall r, l < r \le h$, e_r is a nonconverging edge. Note that e_h is always a candidate edge of $\bar{R}_i$ according to this definition. Let $L_0 = \{e \mid e$ is a candidate edge of $\bar{R}_i, 1 \le i \le n\}$.

Note that, the generated checking sequence must start from s_1, the initial state of M. Therefore at least one incoming transition of s_1 must be tested, so that the generated tour passes over v_1. Therefore let L_1 be a maximal subset of L_0 such that, $indegree_{L_1}(v_1) < indegree_E(v_1)$.

Further note that according to Lemma 6, the test for a transition can be exempted only if some other transitions are tested. In order to avoid cyclic dependencies, the following algorithm can be used:

Construct a digraph $G_S = (V_S, E_S)$ where V_S contains one vertex for each $e \in L_1$. $(v_1, v_2) \in E_S$ if and only if $v_1 \ne v_2$, and for some $\bar{R}_i$, the edges e_1 and e_2 corresponding the vertices v_1 and v_2 appear in $\bar{R}_i$. Find a maximal subgraph $G'_S = (V'_S, E'_S)$ of G_S by removing vertices from G_S (and the edges connected to the removed vertices) such that E'_S is acyclic. Let L be the set of edges that correspond to the vertices in V'_S.

Finding G'_S is an instance of Feedback Vertex Set problem [13], which is NP–complete. However certain heuristic approaches exist for this problem [14, 15]. Note that for an $\bar{R}_i$, there will always be a cyclic dependency between the candidate edges of $\bar{R}_i$. Therefore only one of the edges in $\bar{R}_i$ will survive in G'_S. Hence, at most n transition tests can be removed from the checking sequence.

4.2 Improved Checking Sequence Construction

Now using L, we can improve on the algorithm in [9] for the checking sequence generation, by reducing the set of edges that must be included in the checking sequence. First the digraph $G' = (V', E')$ is obtained as explained in Section 3.2. E'' can be constructed similarly as discussed in [8].

Theorem 2. *Let E'_C be defined as $E'_C = \{(v'_i, v_j, x/y) : (v_i, v_j, x/y) \in E - L\}$. Let $\bar{\Gamma}$ be a tour of G' that contains all edges in $E_{\alpha'} \cup E'_C$ which is found in the same manner as in [9]. Let $e = (v'_i, v_1, x/y) \in E'_C$ be an edge in $\bar{\Gamma}$ ending at v_1 that corresponds to the initial state s_1 of M. Let $\bar{P}$ be a path of G' that is formed by ending $\bar{\Gamma}$ with edge e, and $\bar{Q} = label(\bar{P})\bar{D}_1/\lambda(s_1, \bar{D}_1)$. Then the input portion of $\bar{Q}$ is a checking sequence of M.*

Proof. All edges in $E - L$ are verified in $\bar{Q} = label(\bar{P})\bar{D}_1/\lambda(s_1, \bar{D}_1)$. According to Lemma 6 and the way L is constructed, if all edges in $E - L$ are verified in $\bar{Q}$, then all edges in L are verified in $\bar{Q}$. Thus, all edges of G are verified in $\bar{Q}$, and by Theorem 1, the input portion of $\bar{Q}$ is a checking sequence of M. □

4.3 Application

Let us consider FSM M_0 given in Figure 1. A distinguishing sequence for M_0 is $\bar{D} = abb$. The shortest prefixes of $\bar{D}$ that are sufficient to distinguish each state are: $\bar{D}_1 = ab$, $\bar{D}_2 = \bar{D}_3 = \bar{D}_4 = \bar{D}_5 = abb$. In this example, we will use $\bar{B}_i$'s in $\bar{R}_i = DS(s_i)\bar{B}_i$, as empty sequences. Hence $\bar{T}_i = \bar{D}_i/\lambda(s_i, \bar{D}_i)$, $1 \leq i \leq n$. Using these $\bar{T}_i$'s, an α'–set for M_0 is $\{\bar{\alpha}'_1 = \bar{T}_1\bar{T}_2\bar{T}_4\bar{T}_4, \bar{\alpha}'_2 = \bar{T}_3\bar{T}_2, \bar{\alpha}'_3 = \bar{T}_5\bar{T}_4\}$, with the following corresponding α'–paths: $\bar{\rho}_1 = (v_1, v_4, \bar{\alpha}'_1)$, $\bar{\rho}_2 = (v_3, v_4, \bar{\alpha}'_2)$, $\bar{\rho}_3 = (v_5, v_4, \bar{\alpha}'_3)$.

Note that in FSM M_0, all the edges except $(v_2, v_1, b/0)$ and $(v_5, v_1, b/0)$ are nonconverging edges. According to the definition of candidate edges given in Section 4.1, the set L_0 can be found as $\{(v_1, v_3, a/0), (v_1, v_4, b/0), (v_2, v_1, b/0), (v_3, v_4, a/1), (v_3, v_2, b/1), (v_4, v_3, b/0), (v_5, v_4, a/0), (v_5, v_1, b/0)\}$. Note that $\forall e \in L_0$, $\exists \bar{R}_i$, $1 \leq i \leq n$, such that e occurs in $\bar{R}_i$, and all the edges that come after e in $\bar{R}_i$ are nonconverging edges.

Since all the incoming edges of v_1 are in L_0, we need to exclude one of the incoming edges of v_1 from L_0 to get L_1. Let $L_1 = L_0 \setminus \{(v_2, v_1, b/0)\}$.

A maximal acyclic subgraph G'_S of G_S for L_1 includes the vertices corresponding to the following edges: $L = \{(v_1, v_3, a/0), (v_1, v_4, b/0), (v_2, v_1, b/0), (v_3, v_4, a/1), (v_5, v_4, a/0)\}$.

The graph $G' = (V', E')$ is given in Figure 2.

A tour $\bar{\Gamma}$ over G' that contains all the edges in $E_{\alpha'} \cup E'_C$ is

$$(v_1, v'_4, \bar{\alpha}'_1), (v'_4, v_5, a/0), (v_5, v'_4, \bar{\alpha}'_3), (v'_4, v_3, b/0), (v_3, v'_4, \bar{\alpha}'_2), (v'_4, v'_3, b/0), (v'_3, v_2, b/1), (v_2, v'_4, \bar{T}_2), (v'_4, v'_3, b/0), (v'_3, v'_2, b/1), (v'_2, v_2, a/1), (v_2, v'_4, \bar{T}_2), (v'_4, v'_5, a/0), (v'_5, v_1, b/0)$$

Note that $\bar{\Gamma}$ already starts at v_1. Hence when we consider the path $\bar{P}$ corresponding to $\bar{\Gamma}$ given above, the input portion of $\bar{Q} = label(\bar{P})\bar{D}_1/\lambda(s_1, \bar{D}_1)$ forms a checking sequence of length 40. Using the approach of [10], only the transition tests for the edges $(v_1, v_4, b/0)$ and $(v_3, v_2, b/1)$ are found to be redundant, since these are the only edges that occur as the last edges in $\bar{R}_i$'s. The

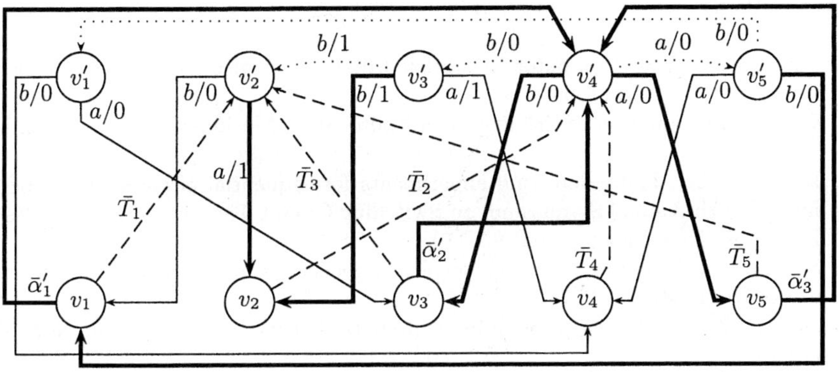

Fig. 2. $G' = (V', E')$ for M_0. The nodes in V and U' are at the bottom, and at the top respectively. The dashed lines are the edges in E_T, and the dotted lines are the edges in E''. The edges in $E_{\alpha'} \cup E_C$ are given in solid lines. The bold solid lines are the edges in $E_{\alpha'} \cup E'_C$, and the remaining solid lines are the edges in L.

checking sequence in this case is found to be of length 52, which is still shorter than the checking sequence of length 63 that would be found by applying the general method proposed in [9].

5 Conclusion

We have shown that, when α'–sequences are used in constructing a checking sequence, some transitions tests can be identified as redundant. Such tests are then eliminated by the optimization algorithm used to construct a shorter checking sequence, and hence a further reduction is obtained in the length of a resulting checking sequence. We have also shown that our approach can identify more redundant transition tests than the approach of a similar work given in [10].

The approach proposed in this paper starts with a given set of α'–sequences. We believe that selecting α'–sequences judiciously will result in further reductions in the length of a checking sequence. A recent study by Hierons and Ural [16] show how α'–sequences can be chosen so that their use minimizes the sum of the lengths of the subsequences to be combined in checking sequence generation. The related checking sequence generation algorithm then produces the set of connecting transitions *during* the optimization phase. Our proposed approach can also be incorporated to the method given in [16].

Acknowledgment

This work was supported in part by "Natural Sciences and Engineering Research Council of Canada under grant RGPIN 976".

References

1. Tanenbaum, A.S.: Computer Networks. 3rd edn. Prentice Hall International Editions, Prentice Hall (1996)
2. Gill, A.: Introduction to the Theory of Finite–State Machines. McGraw–Hill, New York (1962)
3. Hennie, F.C.: Fault–detecting experiments for sequential circuits. In: Proceedings of Fifth Annual Symposium on Switching Circuit Theory and Logical Design, Princeton, New Jersey (1964) 95–110
4. Sabnani, K., Dahbura, A.: A protocol test generation procedure. Computer Networks **15** (1988) 285–297
5. Kohavi, Z.: Switching and Finite Automata Theory. McGraw–Hill, New York (1978)
6. Lee, D., Yannakakis, M.: Testing finite state machines: state identification and verification. IEEE Trans. Computers **43** (1994) 306–320
7. Gonenc, G.: A method for the design of fault detection experiments. IEEE Transactions on Computers **19** (1970) 551–558
8. Ural, H., Wu, X., Zhang, F.: On minimizing the lengths of checking sequences. IEEE Transactions on Computers **46** (1997) 93–99
9. Hierons, R.M., Ural, H.: Reduced length checking sequences. IEEE Transactions on Computers **51** (2002) 1111–1117
10. Chen, J., Hierons, R., Ural, H., Yenigun, H.: Eliminating redundant tests in a checking sequence. In: 17th IFIP International Conference on Testing of Communicating Systems. Volume 3502 of Lecture Notes in Computer Science., Montreal, Canada (2005) 146–158
11. Lee, D., Yannakakis, M.: Principles and methods of testing finite–state machines – a survey. Proceedings of the IEEE **84** (1996) 1089–1123
12. Miller, R.E., Paul, S.: On the generation of minimal–length conformance tests for communication protocols. IEEE/ACM Transactions on Networking **1** (1993) 116–129
13. Garey, M.R., Johnson, D.S.: Computers and Intractability. W. H. Freeman and Company, New York (1979)
14. Bar-Yehuda, R., Geiger, D., Naor, J., Roth, R.: Approximation algorithms for the vertex feedback set problem with applications to constraint satisfaction and bayesian inference. In: Proceedings of Fifth ACM-SIAM Symposium on Discrete Algorithms. (1994) 344–354
15. Fujito, T.: A note on approximation of the vertex cover and feedback vertex set problems. Information Processing Letters **59** (1996) 59–63
16. Hierons, R.M., Ural, H.: Optimizing the length of checking sequences. IEEE Transactions on Computers (2004) submitted.

A Computable Version of Dini's Theorem for Topological Spaces

Tanja Grubba and Klaus Weihrauch

University of Hagen, Germany
{Tanja.Grubba, Klaus.Weihrauch}@FernUni-Hagen.de

Abstract. By Dini's theorem on a compact metric space K any increasing sequence $(g_i)_{i\in\mathbb{N}}$ of real-valued continuous functions converging pointwise to a continuous function f converges uniformly. In this article we prove a fully computable version of a generalization: a modulus of uniform convergence can be computed from a quasi-compact subset K of a computable T_0-space with computable intersection, from an increasing sequence of lower semi-continuous real-valued functions on K and from an upper semi-continuous function to which the sequence converges. For formulating and proving we apply the representation approach to Computable Analysis (TTE) [1]. In particular, for the spaces of quasi-compact subsets and of the partial semi-continuous functions we use natural multi-representations [2]. Moreover, the operator computing a modulus of convergence is multi-valued.

1 Introduction

Many problems in Computer Science, e.g. about solid modelling, about the computational complexity of fractals like the Mandelbrot set or Julia sets, about fractal dimensions or about "degenerate configurations" in Algorithmic Geometry, require a theory of real number computation. Furthermore, the increasing demand for reliable and efficient software in scientific computation and engineering requires a broad and sound foundation not only of the numerical/analytical but also of the computational aspects of real number computation. Computable Analysis is a branch of computability theory studying those functions on the real numbers and related sets which can be computed by machines such as digital computers. It combines concepts of *computability and computational complexity* from Logic and Computer Science with concepts of *approximation* from Topology, Analysis and Numerical Analysis. Although Computable Analysis has been neglected for a long time it moves more and more into focus of attention in Logic, Computabilty Theory and Computer Science, and there has been remarkable progress in recent years.

In this article we study computational aspects of *Dini's theorem* which is one of the fundamental theorems in Functional Analysis and General Topology. In [3] it is formulated as follows.

P. Yolum et al.(Eds.): ISCIS 2005, LNCS 3733, pp. 927–936, 2005.

Theorem 1 (Dini).
Let E be a compact metric space. If an increasing sequence (g_i) of real-valued continuous functions on E converges to a continuous function f, it converges uniformly to f.

Notice that (simple or pointwise) convergence means $(\forall x \in E)(\forall \varepsilon > 0)(\exists i)|f(x)-g_i(x)| < \varepsilon$ and uniform convergence means, there is a function $e : \mathbb{N} \to \mathbb{N}$, a modulus of uniform convergence, such that $(\forall n)(\forall x \in E)|f(x) - g_{e(n)}(x)| < 2^{-n}$.

The first effective version of Dini's theorem has been proved by Kamo [4]. He works in the terminology introduced by Pour-El and Richards [5] using the definitions of an "effectively compact metric space" and of "computable sequence of computable functions" introduced by Mori, Tsujii and Yasugi [6,7]. His theorem is formulated as follows.

Theorem 2 (effective Dini, Kamo' version). *Let (M, d, S) be an effectively compact metric space. Let (g_n) be a computable sequence of real-valued functions on M and f a computable real-valued function on M. If g_n converges pointwise monotonically to f as $n \to \infty$, then g_n converges effectively uniformly to f.*

Roughly speaking, on a compact metric space with natural computability assumptions on compactness and sequences of real-valued functions, **there is** a computable modulus of convergence.

The representation approach to Computable Analysis,TTE [8,9,1] allows to express more general versions of the form: **there is a computable operator** mapping any compact set, any sequence (g_i) of functions and any function f (such that the Dini-assumptions hold) to a modulus of uniform convergence. In particular, a computable operator maps computable data to computable ones. S. Chevillard [10] has proved such a uniformly computable version of Dini's theorem for the real line.

In this article we generalize both, Kamo's and Chevillard's, versions. We consider quasi-compact subsets of a computable T_0-space with countable base, lower semi-continuous real functions g_i and an upper semi-continuous real function f as inputs and prove that a modulus of uniform continuity is not only computable if the inputs are computable but that it can be computed from the input data.

2 Preliminaries

In this article we use the framework of TTE (Type 2 theory of effectivity) [1]. A partial function from X to Y is denoted by $f :\subseteq X \to Y$. We assume that Σ is a fixed finite alphabet containing the symbols 0 and 1 and consider computable functions on finite and infinite sequences of symbols Σ^* and Σ^ω, respectively. By $\iota : \Sigma^* \to \Sigma^*$ we denote the "wrapping function". The definition of the wrapping function guarantees that subwords $\iota(u)$ and $\iota(v)$ of a word w can overlap only trivially. We consider functions for finite or countable tupling on Σ^* and Σ^ω denoted by $\langle \cdot \rangle$. By "$\lhd$" we denote the subword relation. For $p \in \Sigma^\omega$ let $p^{<i} \in \Sigma^*$ be the prefix of p of length $i \in \mathbb{N}$.

Notations $\nu :\subseteq \Sigma^* \to X$ and representations $\delta :\subseteq \Sigma^\omega \to X$ are used for introducing relative continuity and computability on "abstract" sets X. For convenient formulation of our main result we apply the concept of multi-function. A *multi-valued partial function, multi-function* for short, from A to B is a triple $f = (A, B, \mathrm{R}_f)$ such that $\mathrm{R}_f \subseteq A \times B$ (the *graph* of f). Usually we will denote a multi-function f from A to B by $f :\subseteq A \rightrightarrows B$. For $X \subseteq A$ let $f[X] := \{b \in B \mid (\exists a \in X)(a,b) \in \mathrm{R}_f\}$ and for $a \in A$ define $f(a) := f[\{a\}]$. Notice that f is well-defined by the values $f(a) \subseteq B$ for all $a \in A$. We define $\mathrm{dom}(f) := \{a \in A \mid f(a) \neq \emptyset\}$

In our applications we have in mind, for a multi-function $f :\subseteq A \rightrightarrows B$, $f(a)$ is interpreted as the set of all results which are "acceptable" on input $a \in A$. Any concrete computation will produce on input $a \in \mathrm{dom}(f)$ some element $b \in f(a)$, but usually there is no method to select a specific one. In accordance with this interpretation composition is defined as follows: for $f :\subseteq A \rightrightarrows B$ and $g :\subseteq C \rightrightarrows D$ define $g \circ f :\subseteq A \rightrightarrows D$ by

$$a \in \mathrm{dom}(g \circ f) :\iff a \in \mathrm{dom}(f) \text{ and } f(a) \subseteq \mathrm{dom}(g) \quad (1)$$

$$g \circ f(a) := g[f(a)] \quad (2)$$

(Notice that (2) without (1) corresponds to ordinary relational composition of R_f and R_g.)

For a representation $\delta :\subseteq \Sigma^\omega \to M$, if $\delta(p) = x$ then the point $x \in M$ can be identified by the "name" $p \in \Sigma^\omega$. We will have applications where a sequence $p \in \Sigma^\omega$ contains information about a point x which is sufficient for some computation, although p does not identify x. We arrive at the concept of multi-representation. A *multi-representation* of a set M is a surjective multi-function $\delta :\subseteq \Sigma^\omega \rightrightarrows M$.

A "naming system" is a notation or a (multi-)representation. Occasionally we abbreviate $\nu(w)$ by ν_w and $\delta(p)$ by δ_p. A multi-representation can be considered as a naming system for the points of a set M where each name can encode many points. We generalize the concept of realization of a function or multi-function w.r.t. (single-valued) naming systems [1] to multi-representations as follows [11]:

Definition 1.
For multi-representations $\gamma_i :\subseteq Y_i \rightrightarrows M_i$ $(i = 0, \ldots, k)$, abbreviate $Y := Y_1 \times \ldots \times Y_k$, $M := M_1 \times \ldots \times M_k$, and $\gamma(y_1, \ldots, y_k) := \gamma_1(y_1) \times \ldots \times \gamma_k(y_k)$. Then a function $h :\subseteq Y \to Y_0$ is a (γ, γ_0)-realization of a multi-function $f :\subseteq M \rightrightarrows M_0$, iff for all $p \in Y$ and $x \in M$, $x \in \gamma(p) \cap \mathrm{dom}(f) \Longrightarrow f(x) \cap \gamma_0 \circ h(p) \neq \emptyset$.

The multi-function f is
- *(γ, γ_0)-continuous, if it has a continuous (γ, γ_0)-realization,*
- *(γ, γ_0)-computable, if it has a computable (γ, γ_0)-realization.*

Fig. 1 illustrates the definition.

If multi-functions on represented sets have realizations, then their composition is realized by the composition of the realizations. In particular, the computable multi-functions on represented sets are closed under composition.

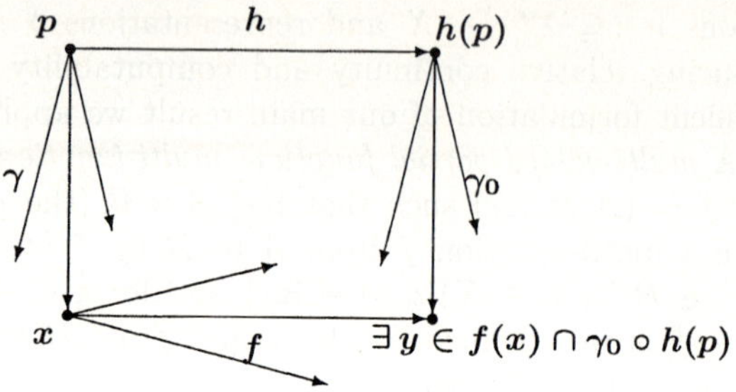

Fig. 1. $h(p)$ is a name of some $y \in f(x)$, if p is a name of $x \in \mathrm{dom}(f)$

3 The Spaces and Their Representations

Let $\nu_{\mathbb{N}} :\subseteq \Sigma^* \to \mathbb{N}$ and $\nu_{\mathbb{Q}} :\subseteq \Sigma^* \to \mathbb{Q}$ be some standard notations of the natural numbers and the rational numbers, respectively. In the following we will abbreviate $\nu_{\mathbb{Q}}(w)$ by $\overline{w}$. If $\delta :\subseteq \Sigma^\omega \to M$ is a representation, the canonical representation of the set of sequences $M^\omega := \{(x_0, x_1, x_2, \ldots) \mid x_i \in M \text{ for all } i\}$ is defined by the sequence of symbols $[\delta]^\omega\langle p_0, p_1, p_2, \ldots\rangle := (\delta(p_0), \delta(p_1), \delta(p_2), \ldots)$. Finally we need a representation of the moduli of convergence. A modulus of convergence will be a function $e : \mathbb{N} \to \mathbb{N}$, hence e is an element of Baire space $\mathbb{B}$. As a representation of $\mathbb{B}$ we choose $\delta_{\mathbb{B}}$ defined by $\delta_{\mathbb{B}}^{-1}(e) := 0^{e(0)}10^{e(1)}10^{e(2)}1\ldots$.

A topological space $\mathbf{X} = (X, \tau)$ is a T_0-space, if for all $x, y \in X$ such that $x \neq y$ there is an open set $U \in \tau$ such that $x \in U \iff y \notin U$. In a T_0-space every point can be identified by the set of its neighbourhoods $U \in \tau$. $\mathbf{X}$ is called *second-countable*, if it has a countable base [12]. We introduce *computable* T_0*-spaces* by adding a notation of a base.

Definition 2 (computable T_0-space).
A computable T_0*-space is a tuple* $\mathbf{X} = (X, \tau, \nu)$ *such that* (X, τ) *is a second countable* T_0*-space and* $\nu :\subseteq \Sigma^* \to \beta$ *is a notation of a base* β *of* τ *with recursive domain.*

The condition "dom(ν) is r.e." is not properly weaker, since for every notation with r.e. domain there is an equivalent one with recursive domain. In [1] Def. 3.2.1 a "computable topological space" is a triple $\mathbf{S} = (M, \sigma, \nu')$ such that $\nu' :\subseteq \Sigma^* \to \sigma$ is a notation of a countable subbase σ of a T_0-topology τ on M such that $\{(u, v) \mid u, v \in \mathrm{dom}(\nu') \text{ and } \nu'(u) = \nu'(v)\}$ is r.e. The set of finite intersections of elements from σ is a base of τ. With the notation ν of this base canonically derived from ν' we obtain a computable T_0-space.

Later we will need the following property of a computable T_0-space.

Definition 3 (computable intersection).
A computable T_0*-space has a computable intersection, iff there is a computable function* $h :\subseteq \Sigma^* \times \Sigma^* \to \Sigma^\omega$ *such that*

$$\nu(u) \cap \nu(v) = \bigcup \{\nu(w) \mid w \in \mathrm{dom}(\nu) \text{ and } \iota(w) \lhd h(u, v)\} \tag{3}$$

for all $u, v \in \mathrm{dom}(\nu)$.

If ν is deduced from a notation of a subbase, the computability of the intersection follows immediately.

For formulating our version of Dini's theorem we need the following computable T_0-spaces on the real numbers.

Definition 4.
Define computable T_0*-spaces* $\mathbf{R}_<$ *and* $\mathbf{R}_>$ *by*

$$\begin{aligned}
\mathbf{R} := (\mathbb{R}, \tau_\mathbb{R}, \mathrm{I}^1) \quad & \textit{with } \tau_\mathbb{R} := \{(x;y) \mid x,y \in \mathbb{R}\} \\
& \textit{and } \mathrm{I}^1(\iota(v)\iota(w)) = (\nu_\mathbb{Q}(v) - \nu_\mathbb{Q}(w); \nu_\mathbb{Q}(v) + \nu_\mathbb{Q}(w)), \\
\mathbf{R}_< := (\mathbb{R}, \tau_<, \nu_<) \; & \textit{with } \tau_< := \{(x;\infty) \mid x \in \mathbb{R}\}, \; \nu_<(w) := (\nu_\mathbb{Q}(w); \infty), \\
\mathbf{R}_> := (\mathbb{R}, \tau_>, \nu_>) \; & \textit{with } \tau_> := \{(-\infty;x) \mid x \in \mathbb{R}\}, \; \nu_>(w) := (-\infty; \nu_\mathbb{Q}(w)).
\end{aligned}$$

Obviously, $\mathbf{R}_<$ and $\mathbf{R}_>$ are computable T_0-spaces. The natural representation for $\mathbf{R}_>$ is $\rho_>$, defined by $\rho_>(p) := \inf\{\nu_\mathbb{Q}(w) \mid w \in \mathrm{dom}(\nu_\mathbb{Q}) \text{ and } \iota(w) \lhd p\}$. If τ is an arbitrary topology, the $(\tau, \tau_<)$-continuous and the $(\tau, \tau_>)$-continuous functions are called lower semi-continuous and upper semi-continuous, respectively.

For computable T_0-spaces $\mathbf{X}$ and $\mathbf{X}'$ let $\mathrm{C}_p(\mathbf{X}, \mathbf{X}')$ be the set of all continuous partial functions from X to X'. As an example consider the set $\mathrm{C}_p(\mathbf{R}_<, \mathbf{R}_<)$. Since the identity $\mathrm{id}_\mathbb{R}$ is in $\mathrm{C}_p(\mathbf{R}_<, \mathbf{R}_<)$, $f \in \mathrm{C}_p(\mathbf{R}_<, \mathbf{R}_<)$ for each restriction f of $\mathrm{id}_\mathbb{R}$. The set of these restrictions has the cardinality of the powerset of $\mathbb{R}$. Therefore, $\mathrm{C}_p(\mathbf{R}_<, \mathbf{R}_<)$ has more elements than Σ^ω and has no representation. We can, however, introduce a sufficiently meaningful multi-representation of this set.

Definition 5 (the multi-representation $\delta_{\mathbf{X},\mathbf{X}'}$ of $\mathrm{C}_p(\mathbf{X}, \mathbf{X}')$).
For all $p \in \Sigma^\omega$ *and* $f \in \mathrm{C}_p(\mathbf{X}, \mathbf{X}')$ *let*

$$f \in \delta_{\mathbf{X},\mathbf{X}'}(p) :\iff (\forall v \in \mathrm{dom}(\nu'))f^{-1}[\nu'(v)] = \bigcup_{(u,v)\in Q_p} \nu(u) \cap \mathrm{dom}(f)$$

where $Q_p := \{(u,v) \in \mathrm{dom}(\nu) \times \mathrm{dom}(\nu') \mid \iota(\iota(u)\iota(v)) \lhd p\}$ *is the set "listed" by* $p \in \Sigma^\omega$.

Notice that every continuous function $f :\subseteq X \to X'$ has at least one $\delta_{\mathbf{X},\mathbf{X}'}$-name and that every $\delta_{\mathbf{X},\mathbf{X}'}$-name p of f is also a $\delta_{\mathbf{X},\mathbf{X}'}$-name of each restriction of f. This representation has already been used for metric spaces in [13].

A subset K of a T_0-space (X, τ) is called *quasi-compact*, if every open cover of K has a finite subcover, i.e., if for any subset $\zeta \subseteq \tau$, $K \subseteq \bigcup\zeta$, then $K \subseteq \bigcup\zeta'$ for some finite subset ζ' of ζ [12]. For a computable T_0-space $\mathbf{X} = (X, \tau, \nu)$ let $\mathcal{QK}(\mathbf{X})$ be the set of all quasi compact subsets of X.

In the following we generalize the representation κ_c of the compact subsets of the Euclidean space [1] and δ_{cover} of the compact subsets of a computable metric space [14] defined by listing all finite subcovers from a countable base. For the space $\mathbf{R}_>$ the set $\mathcal{QK}(\mathbf{R}_>)$ is too big (see below) and cannot have a representation. In particular, a quasi-compact set in $\mathbf{R}_>$ cannot be identified by the set of all finite subcovers of base elements. However, we can define a meaningful multi-representation.

Definition 6 (the multi-representation $\kappa_{\mathbf{X}}$ of $\mathcal{QK}(\mathbf{X})$).
Let $\mathbf{X} = (X, \tau, \nu)$ be a computable T_0*-space. Define a multi-representation $\kappa_{\mathbf{X}} : \subseteq \Sigma^\omega \rightrightarrows \mathcal{QK}(\mathbf{X})$ as follows. For all $q \in \Sigma^\omega$ and $K \in \mathcal{QK}(\mathbf{X})$ let*

$$K \in \kappa_{\mathbf{X}}(p) :\iff \{w \in \Sigma^* \mid \iota(w) \lhd p\} = \{w \in R_\nu \mid K \subseteq \bigcup_{\iota(u) \lhd w} \nu(u)\}$$

where $R_\nu := \{w \in \Sigma^* \mid (\forall u)[\iota(u) \lhd w \Rightarrow u \in \mathrm{dom}(\nu)]\}$.

Roughly speaking, p is a name of K, if it is a list of all (!) finite subcovers of K with base elements. The example of $\mathbf{R}_>$ shows that a $\kappa_{\mathbf{X}}$-name p may denote more than one quasi-compact set.

Example 1 (multi-representation $\kappa_{\mathbf{R}_>}$ of $\mathcal{QK}(\mathbf{R}_>)$).
Consider the computable T_0-space $\mathbf{R}_> = (\mathbb{R}, \tau_>, \nu_>)$. A set $K \subseteq \mathbb{R}$ is quasi-compact iff it has a maximum.

Suppose, $K \subseteq \mathbb{R}$ has maximum m. Then for each cover of K with open intervals $(-\infty; \nu_{\mathbb{Q}}(w))$ there exists a $\nu_{\mathbb{Q}}(w_0)$ with $m < \nu_{\mathbb{Q}}(w_0)$ and $K \subseteq (-\infty; \nu_{\mathbb{Q}}(w_0))$ which is a finite subcover. If on the other hand $K \subseteq \mathbb{R}$ has no maximum and $(\nu_{\mathbb{Q}}(w_i))_{i \in \mathbb{N}}$ is an increasing sequence converging to the supremum of K then $K \subseteq \bigcup\{(-\infty; \nu_{\mathbb{Q}}(w_i) \mid i \in \mathbb{N})\}$ but there is no finite subcover of K.

Since our basis of $\mathbf{R}_>$ is closed under union, a $\kappa_{\mathbf{R}_>}$-name q of a set $K \subseteq \mathbb{R}$ with maximum $x \in \mathbb{R}$ is, roughly speaking, a list of all $a \in \mathbb{Q}$ such that $x < a$. It is a name also of every other set with the same maximum x.

While for a T_0-space the representation $\kappa_{\mathbf{X}}$ may be properly multi-valued, for a T_1-space it is single-valued. Consider quasi-compact sets $K, L \subseteq X$ such that $K \neq L$. Then w.l.o.g., $x \in L \setminus K$ for some x. By the T_1-property for each $y \in K$ there is some w_y such that $y \in \nu(w_y)$ and $x \notin \nu(w_y)$. Since $K \subseteq \bigcup_{y \in K} \nu(w_y)$, K has a finite covering of base elements not containing x. This covering cannot cover L. (A similar argument shows that every compact subset of a Hausdorff space is closed.)

4 Dini's Theorem

As the main result of this article we will prove the following computable version of Dini's theorem.

Theorem 3 (Dini's theorem, computable version).
Let $\mathbf{X} = (X, \tau, \nu)$ be a computable T_0*-space with computable intersection. Define a multi-function*

$$\mathrm{MOD} : \subseteq C_p(\mathbf{X}, \mathbf{R}_>) \times [C_p(\mathbf{X}, \mathbf{R}_<)]^\omega \times \mathcal{QK}(\mathbf{X}) \rightrightarrows \mathbb{B}$$

as follows: $e \in \mathrm{MOD}(f, (g_i), K)$, iff

1. $K \subseteq \mathrm{dom}(f)$ *and* $K \subseteq \mathrm{dom}(g_i)$ *for all* $i \in \mathbb{N}$,
2. $g_i(x) \le g_{i+1}(x)$ *for all* $x \in K$ *and* $i \in \mathbb{N}$,
3. $\lim_{i\to\infty} g_i(x) = f(x)$ *for all* $x \in K$,
4. $e : \mathbb{N} \to \mathbb{N}$ *is a modulus of uniform convergence of the sequence* $(g_i)_{i\in\mathbb{N}}$ *converging pointwise to* f.

Then MOD *is* $(\delta_{\mathbf{X},\mathbf{R}_>}, [\delta_{\mathbf{X},\mathbf{R}_<}]^\omega, \kappa_{\mathbf{X}}, \delta_{\mathbb{B}})$*-computable.*

We will proceed as follows. From (g_i) and f we compute the sequence (h_i) such that $h_i := f - g_i$. This is a decreasing sequence of real-valued $(\tau, \tau_>)$-continuous functions on K converging pointwise to 0. By Lemma 1, a slight generalization of Dini's theorem, this sequence converges uniformly on K to 0. Therefore, the sequence (m_i), $m_i := \max\{h_i(x) \mid x \in K\}$ is decreasing and converges to 0. Since $m_i = \max\{f(x) - g_i(x) \mid x \in K\}$ every modulus of convergence of (m_i) is a modulus of uniform convergence of (g_i) and vice versa. Since $m_i = \max h_i[K]$ we first compute the compact sets $h_i[K]$ in $\mathbf{R}_>$, then their maxima and finally a modulus of convergence of the sequence of maxima.

Some of the following lemmas are of interest by themselves. First we prove a non-effective generalization of Dini's theorem for quasi-compact sets and the space $\mathbf{R}_>$.

Lemma 1. *Let* (E, τ) *be a quasi-compact space and let* (h_i) *be a decreasing sequence of real-valued* $(\tau, \tau_>)$*-continuous functions converging pointwise to* 0. *Then the sequence* (h_i) *converges on* E *uniformly.*

Proof. Consider $n \in \mathbb{N}$. Then $(\forall x)(\exists i_x)(\forall i \ge i_x)\, h_i(x) < 2^{-n}$. We obtain $E \subseteq \bigcup_{x\in E} h_{i_x}^{-1}(-\infty; 2^{-n})$. Since E is quasi-compact, $E \subseteq \bigcup_{x\in F} h_{i_x}^{-1}(-\infty; 2^{-n})$ for some finite set $F \subseteq E$. Let $k := \max\{i_x \mid x \in F\}$. Then $h_k(x) < 2^{-n}$ for all $x \in E$ since $h_{i_x}^{-1}(-\infty; 2^{-n}) < h_k^{-1}(-\infty; 2^{-n})$ for all $x \in F$.

The following lemma will be used to compute differences of semi-continuous real functions.

Lemma 2 (effective difference).
Let $\mathbf{X} = (X, \nu)$ *be a computable* T_0*-space with computable intersection. The operation* DIF : $(f, g) \mapsto f - g$ *where* $f - g$ *is defined by*

$$(f - g)(x) := f(x) - g(x) \text{ and } \mathrm{dom}(f - g) := \mathrm{dom}(f) \cap \mathrm{dom}(g)$$

for $f \in \mathrm{C}_p(\mathbf{X}, \mathbf{R}_>)$, $g \in \mathrm{C}_p(\mathbf{X}, \mathbf{R}_<)$ *and* $g(x) \le f(x)$ *for all* $x \in \mathrm{dom}(f) \cap \mathrm{dom}(g)$ *is* $(\delta_{\mathbf{X},\mathbf{R}_>}, \delta_{\mathbf{X},\mathbf{R}_<}, \delta_{\mathbf{X},\mathbf{R}_>})$*-computable.*

Proof. Suppose $f \in \delta_{\mathbf{X},\mathbf{R}_>}(p)$ and $g \in \delta_{\mathbf{X},\mathbf{R}_<}(q)$, then

$$f^{-1}[(-\infty; \overline{w})] = \bigcup_{(u,w)\in Q_p} \nu(u) \cap \mathrm{dom}(f)$$

and

$$g^{-1}[(\overline{w}; \infty)] = \bigcup_{(v,w)\in Q_q} \nu(v) \cap \mathrm{dom}(g)$$

for all $w \in \mathrm{dom}(\nu_\mathbb{Q})$. For $x \in \mathrm{dom}(f-g)$ and $c \in \mathrm{dom}(\nu_\mathbb{Q})$ we have

$$\begin{aligned}
& (f-g)(x) < \overline{c} \\
\iff & f(x) - g(x) < \overline{c} \\
\iff & (\exists a, b \in \mathrm{dom}(\nu_\mathbb{Q}))\overline{a} < g(x) \wedge f(x) < \overline{b} \wedge \overline{b} - \overline{a} < \overline{c} \\
\iff & (\exists a, b \in \mathrm{dom}(\nu_\mathbb{Q}))g(x) \in (\overline{a}, \infty) \wedge f(x) \in (-\infty; \overline{b}) \wedge \overline{b} - \overline{a} < \overline{c} \\
\iff & (\exists a, b \in \mathrm{dom}(\nu_\mathbb{Q}))x \in g^{-1}(\overline{a}, \infty) \cap f^{-1}(-\infty; \overline{b}) \wedge \overline{b} - \overline{a} < \overline{c} \\
\iff & (\exists a, b \in \mathrm{dom}(\nu_\mathbb{Q}))x \in (\bigcup_{(v,a)\in Q_q} \nu(v)) \cap (\bigcup_{(u,b)\in Q_p} \nu(u)) \wedge \overline{b} - \overline{a} < \overline{c}
\end{aligned}$$

and therefore

$$\begin{aligned}
& (f-g)^{-1}[(-\infty; \overline{c})] = \{\nu(v) \cap \nu(u) \mid \\
& (\exists a, b \in \mathrm{dom}(\nu_\mathbb{Q}), \overline{b} - \overline{a} < \overline{c}).(v,a) \in Q_q, (u,b) \in Q_p\} \cap \ \mathrm{dom}(f-g)\}\,.
\end{aligned}$$

Therefore, using a computable function h realizing the intersection on the basis (Def. 3) a machine M_0 can be found which on input (p, q, c) lists a set $J_c \subseteq \mathrm{dom}(\nu)$ such that $(f-g)^{-1}(-\infty; \overline{c}) = \bigcup\{\nu(t) \mid t \in J_c\} \cap \mathrm{dom}(f-g)$. From M_0 a machine M can be determined which computes a $\delta_{X,R_>}$-name of $f-g$ from (p,q).

Classically, the continuous image of a compact set is compact. A computable version has been proved for Euclidean space in [1] and for computable metric spaces in [15]. In the following we prove a fully computable version for quasi-compact spaces.

Lemma 3 (continuous image of quasi-compact spaces). *Let $\mathbf{X} = (X, \tau, \nu)$ and $\mathbf{X}' = (X', \tau', \nu')$ be computable T_0-spaces with multi-representations $\kappa_\mathbf{X}$ and $\kappa_{\mathbf{X}'}$ of $\mathcal{QK}(\mathbf{X})$ and $\mathcal{QK}(\mathbf{X}')$, respectively. Then the operation $\mathrm{IM} : (f, K) \mapsto f[K]$ for $f \in \mathrm{C}_p(\mathbf{X}, \mathbf{X}')$ and quasi-compact $K \subseteq \mathrm{dom}(f)$ is $(\delta_{\mathbf{X},\mathbf{X}'}, \kappa_\mathbf{X}, \kappa_{\mathbf{X}'})$-computable.*

Proof. Suppose $f \in \delta_{\mathbf{X},\mathbf{X}'}(p), K \in \kappa_\mathbf{X}(q)$ and $K \subseteq \mathrm{dom}(f)$. We want to compute a list of all $w' \in R_{\nu'}$ such that $f[K] \subseteq \bigcup_{\iota(v) \lhd w'} \nu'(v)$. For any $w' \in \Sigma^*$ such that $v \in \mathrm{dom}(\nu')$ for $\iota(v) \lhd w'$,

$$\begin{aligned}
& f[K] \subseteq \bigcup\{\nu'(v) \mid \iota(v) \lhd w'\} \\
\iff & K \subseteq f^{-1} \bigcup\{\nu'(v) \mid \iota(v) \lhd w'\} \\
\iff & K \subseteq \bigcup\{\nu(u) \mid (\exists\, v)(\iota(v) \lhd w' \ \text{ and } \ (u,v) \in Q_p)\} \cap \mathrm{dom}(f)
\end{aligned}$$

(see Def. 5). Since $K \subseteq \mathrm{dom}(f)$ the "$\cap \mathrm{dom}(f)$" can be omitted. Since K is quasi-compact, finitely many u such that $(\exists\, v)(\iota(v) \lhd w' \ \text{ and } \ (u,v) \in Q_p)$ cover K. Since q is a list of all finite covers of K, there is some $w \in R_\nu$ (see Def. 6) such that $\iota(w) \lhd q$ and $(\forall\, u,\ \iota(u) \lhd w)(\exists\, v)(\iota(v) \lhd w' \ \text{ and } \ (u,v) \in Q_p))$. Therefore, the last property is equivalent to

$$(\exists\, w \in R_\nu)(\iota(w) \lhd q \ \text{ and } \ (\forall\, u,\ \iota(u) \lhd w)(\exists\, v)(\iota(v) \lhd w' \ \text{ and } \ (u,v) \in Q_p))(4)$$

There is a Type-2 machine M which on input (p,q) produces a list of all words $w' \in R_{\nu'}$ for which (4) is true. If (4) is true for w' then this follows already from finite prefixes of p and q. Let M be a machine which on input (p,q) operates in stages $i = 1,2,\ldots$ as follows. **Stage** i**:** for each word $w' \in R_{\nu'}$ of length $\leq i$ check whether (4) can be verified by reading only the first i symbols from p and from q. Whenever the answer is positive write $\iota(w')$ on the output tape. In this way the machine produces a list of all names w' of finite covers of $f[K]$. Therefore, the function $f_M :\subseteq \Sigma^\omega \times \Sigma^\omega \to \Sigma^\omega$ realizes IM.

Lemma 4 (effective maximum).
The operation $\mathrm{MAX} : K \mapsto max[K]$ *for* $K \in \mathcal{QK}(\mathbf{R}_>)\backslash\emptyset$ *is* $(\kappa_{\mathbf{R}_>}, \rho_>)$*-computable.*

Proof. For $K \in \kappa_{\mathbf{X}}(p)$ with maximum $m \in \mathbb{R}$, p is a list of all $a \in \mathbb{Q}$ such that $m < a$ and and these upper bounds approach $\max(K)$ arbitrarily closely from above. Therefore p can be interpreted as a $\rho_>$-name of m.

Lemma 5. *The multi-function* $\mathrm{MC} :\subseteq {\mathbf{R}_>}^\omega \rightrightarrows \mathbb{B}$ *mapping each decreasing sequence of real numbers which converges to* 0 *to a modulus of convergence is* $(\rho_>^\omega, \delta_\mathbb{B})$*-computable.*

Proof. There is a Type-2 machine M which on input $\langle p_0, p_1, \ldots\rangle$, $p_i \in \mathrm{dom}(\rho_<)$ operates in stages $n = 0,1,\ldots$ as follows. **Stage** n: find the smallest number k such that there are $w \in \mathrm{dom}(\nu_\mathbb{Q})$ and $i \leq k$ such that $\iota(w) \lhd p_i^{<k}$ and $\nu_\mathbb{Q}(w) < 2^{-n}$. Then print 0^i1. Since $(\rho_>(p_i))$ decreases and converges to 0, for each n there are numbers i,k and a word $w \in \mathrm{dom}(\nu_\mathbb{Q})$ such that $i \leq k$, $\iota(w) \lhd p_i^{<k}$ and $\nu_\mathbb{Q}(w) < 2^{-n}$. In this case, $\rho_>(p_j) < 2^{-n}$ for all $j \geq i$. Therefore, M prints the $\delta_\mathbb{B}$-name of a modulus of convergence of the sequence $(\rho_>(p_i))$.

Now we can proof Theorem 3:

Proof. Let $\mathbf{X} = (X, \tau, \nu)$ be a computable T_0-space with computable intersection. Notice that the function $\mathrm{T} : ((h_i), j) \mapsto h_j$ is $([\delta_{\mathbf{X},\mathbf{R}_>}]^\omega, \nu_\mathbb{N}, \delta_{\mathbf{X},\mathbf{R}_>})$-computable. For $f \in \mathrm{C}_p(\mathbf{X}, \mathbf{R}_>)$, $g_i \in \mathrm{C}_p(\mathbf{X}, \mathbf{R}_<)$, $K \in \mathcal{QK}(\mathbf{X}) \setminus \emptyset$ and $i \in \mathbb{N}$, the function

$$(f, (g_i), K, j) \mapsto \max(f - g_j)[K]$$

is $(\delta_{\mathbf{X},\mathbf{R}_>}, [\delta_{\mathbf{X},\mathbf{R}_<}]^\omega, \kappa_\mathbf{X}, \nu_\mathbb{N}, \rho_>)$-computable by Lemma 2, 3 and 4, since $\max(f - g_j)[K] = \mathrm{Max}(\mathrm{IM}(\mathrm{DIF}(f, \mathrm{T}((g_i), j), K))$. Therefore, the function

$$(f, (g_i)_{i\in\mathbb{N}}, K) \mapsto (m_i)_{i\in\mathbb{N}} \text{ where } m_i := \mathrm{MAX}(\mathrm{IM}(\mathrm{DIF}(f, g_i), K))$$

is $(\delta_{\mathbf{X},\mathbf{R}_>}, [\delta_{\mathbf{X},\mathbf{R}_<}]^\omega, \kappa_\mathbf{X}, [\rho_>]^\omega)$-computable. Finally by composition with the computable multi-function MC from Lemma 5 we obtain a $(\delta_{\mathbf{X},\mathbf{R}_>}, [\delta_{\mathbf{X},\mathbf{R}_<}]^\omega, \kappa_\mathbf{X}, \delta_\mathbb{B})$-computable function which computes a modulus of convergence whenever $K \neq \emptyset$.

Let M_0 be a machine realizing this function w.r.t. $(\delta_{\mathbf{X},\mathbf{R}_>}, [\delta_{\mathbf{X},\mathbf{R}_<}]^\omega, \kappa_\mathbf{X}, [\rho_>]^\omega)$. If $\kappa_\mathbf{X}(r) = \emptyset$ then $\iota(w) \lhd r$ for some $w \in R_\nu$ such that $\iota(u) \lhd w$ for no $u \in \Sigma^*$. Let M be a machine which works like M_0 and simultaneously by reading r checks whether $\kappa_\mathbf{X}(r) = \emptyset$. As soon as this has been detected, M continues writing $111\ldots$ forever. (Notice that any function $e : \mathbb{N} \to \mathbb{N}$ can be chosen as a modulus of convergence if $K = \emptyset$.) This machine computes a realization of our function MOD. Therefore, MOD is $(\delta_{\mathbf{X},\mathbf{R}_>}, [\delta_{\mathbf{X},\mathbf{R}_<}]^\omega, \kappa_\mathbf{X}, \delta_\mathbb{B})$-computable

We state without proof that Kamo's theorem 2 is a special case of Thm. 3.

References

1. Weihrauch, K.: Computable Analysis. Springer, Berlin (2000)
2. Schröder, M.: Effectivity in spaces with admissible multirepresentations. Mathematical Logic Quarterly **48** (2002) 78–90
3. Dieudonné, J.: Foundations of Modern Analysis. Academic Press, New York (1960)
4. Kamo, H.: Effective Dini's theorem on effectively compact metric spaces. In Brattka, V., Staiger, L., Weihrauch, K., eds.: Computability and Complexity in Analysis. Volume 320 of Informatik Berichte., FernUniversität in Hagen (2004) 69–77 Sixth International Workshop, CCA 2004, Lutherstadt Wittenberg, Germany, August 16–20, 2004.
5. Pour-El, M.B., Richards, J.I.: Computability in Analysis and Physics. Perspectives in Mathematical Logic. Springer, Berlin (1989)
6. Mori, T., Tsujii, Y., Yasugi, M.: Computability structures on metric spaces. In Bridges, D.S., Calude, C.S., Gibbons, J., Reeves, S., Witten, I.H., eds.: Combinatorics, Complexity, and Logic. Discrete Mathematics and Theoretical Computer Science, Singapore, Springer (1997) 351–362 Proceedings of DMTCS'96.
7. Yasugi, M., Mori, T., Tsujii, Y.: Effective properties of sets and functions in metric spaces with computability structure. Theoretical Computer Science **219** (1999) 467–486
8. Grzegorczyk, A.: Computable functionals. Fundamenta Mathematicae **42** (1955) 168–202
9. Kreitz, C., Weihrauch, K.: Theory of representations. Theoretical Computer Science **38** (1985) 35–53
10. Chevillard, S.: About the effectivity of Dini's Theorem. Talk at CCA04, Sixth International Workshop on Computability and Complexity in Analysis, Wittenberg (2004)
11. Weihrauch, K.: Considerations on higher level programming in Analysis. In preparation
12. Engelking, R.: General Topology. Volume 6 of Sigma series in pure mathematics. Heldermann, Berlin (1989)
13. Weihrauch, K.: Computability on computable metric spaces. Theoretical Computer Science **113** (1993) 191–210 Fundamental Study.
14. Brattka, V., Presser, G.: Computability on subsets of metric spaces. Theoretical Computer Science **305** (2003) 43–76
15. Weihrauch, K.: Computational complexity on computable metric spaces. Mathematical Logic Quarterly **49** (2003) 3–21

Improved Simulation of Quantum Random Walks

Uğur Küçük and A.C. Cem Say

Department of Computer Engineering, Boğaziçi University, 34342 İstanbul, Turkey
{ugur.kucuk, say}@boun.edu.tr

Abstract. We present an optimized version of the quantum random walk simulation algorithm. Our approach can be generalized to optimize any quantum simulation in which the linear combination rule is used to simulate a collection of constituent Hamiltonians. The method involves manipulation of the order in which the constituent Hamiltonians are simulated for small durations in the iterative step of the simulation algorithm. An analysis to illustrate the benefits of the new approach in oracle-based simulations is also given.

1 Introduction

Determining the problems which quantum computers can solve qualitatively faster than classical computers is a central issue in the field of quantum computation. Most of the quantum algorithms which exhibit exponential speedup over the best known classical algorithm for the same task, including Shor's algorithm for factorization [6], are based on the quantum Fourier transformation (QFT) method. A quantum algorithm which does *not* involve the QFT and yet is able to provide exponential speedup over its classical counterparts was demonstrated very recently, [1] and it is based on the concept of quantum simulation.

The task of simulating quantum systems is among the first classically difficult problems for which quantum computers were expected to provide means of efficient solutions [2]. In 1996, Lloyd showed that a quantum system which evolves according to local interactions could be simulated efficiently by quantum computers, and proposed a method for the quantum simulation of such systems [4]. (A conventional quantum circuit model of the quantum simulation algorithm can be found in [5].) Since then, several applications for quantum simulation have been proposed, and various ideas have been developed to improve simulation capabilities.

Several groups of researchers have proposed their models for using quantum simulation to implement quantum analogues of the classical random walk algorithms, which have a wide application area in the classical framework. It is common to state that the quantum versions of random walk algorithms have significantly different features and require qualitatively shorter time to reach the desired state, when compared to the classical random walk algorithms. The key result about quantum random walks is that for certain problems they provide exponentially faster solutions compared not only to classical random walk algorithms but also to any classical algorithm. This is a very important result since only QFT-based algorithms had previously been shown to provide this speedup.

The exponential speedup provided by quantum random walks was first demonstrated in [1]. This is done by first introducing a problem that can not be solved in sub-exponential time by classical algorithms, and then by showing how quantum

P. Yolum et al.(Eds.): ISCIS 2005, LNCS 3733, pp. 937 – 946, 2005.

random walk simulations could be used to solve it efficiently. The problem is an oracle problem defined on a graph theoretical framework and the proposed algorithm produces probabilistic results. In this paper, an improvement in the method to solve this problem will be demonstrated.

The rest of the paper is structured as follows: Section 2 presents a description of the problem. A summary of the solution proposed in [1] is given in Section 3. The details of our proposed improvement are explained in Section 4. Section 5 contains an analysis of the benefits of this technique when several additional limitations are imposed on the oracle calls that the simulator can perform. Section 6 is a conclusion.

2 The Problem

The problem is a black box graph traversal problem defined on the graphs G_n of a specific form. G_n consists of two binary trees of height n, connected by a random cycle that alternates between the leaves of the two trees. The cycle is arranged in a way that every leaf of a tree is connected to two of the leaves of the other tree. Fig. 1 contains a typical graph of the form G_4.

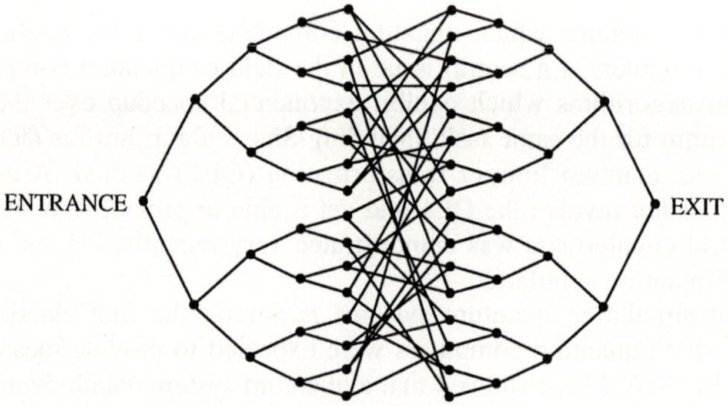

Fig. 1. Two binary trees of height four connected by a random cycle form an example of G_4

The problem assumes the existence of a black box, the functionality of which would be better understood after the following definitions. Let $G = (V(G), E(G))$ be a graph with N vertices. Let m be such that $2^m > N$. Assign each vertex $u \in V(G)$ a distinct m-bit string as its name. (Do not assign $11..1 = 1^m$ as the name of any vertex.) Let k be at least as large as the maximum vertex degree in G. For each vertex $u \in V(G)$, assign the outgoing edges of u labels from a set L of size k.

$v_c(u)$ is defined as the adjacent vertex of $u \in \{0,1\}^m$, reached by following the outgoing edge labeled by $c \in L$. If $u \notin V(G)$ or if u does not have an outgoing edge labeled by c, then $v_c(u) = 11..1$. The black box takes $u \in \{0,1\}^m$ and $c \in L$ as its inputs, and returns $v_c(u)$ as its output. Finally, a formal definition of the graph traversal problem is as follows:

Let G be a graph and ENTRANCE and EXIT be two vertices of G. The input of the traversal problem is a black box for G and the name of the ENTRANCE. The output is the name of the EXIT.

So the task is to develop an efficient mechanism which, when given the name of the *ENTRANCE* node, can manage to find out the name of the *EXIT* node by querying the black box.

3 The Quantum Walk

In [1], it is shown that the instances of the problem described above can be efficiently solved to any accuracy by a quantum algorithm, and no classical algorithm can do the same in sub-exponential time. The algorithm depends on successively using the quantum simulation algorithm presented in [5] to simulate the quantum random walk on the graph for a duration randomly chosen from a predefined interval. At the end of each simulation, a control is made to test if the measured value is the desired result or not. The overall algorithm is shown to work correctly and in an efficient manner. The quantum walk implementation of this algorithm will be of consideration here.

In order to apply the simulation algorithm to the quantum walk, first there is the need for an appropriate representation of the system, then the Hamiltonian which governs the random walk should be identified in terms of local interactions, and finally, it should be shown how to simulate each of these local interactions. Sections 3.1, 3.2 and 3.3 show how these can be done for a symmetrically labeled graph, where both vertices incident to an edge label it with the same name. (In the case of asymmetric labeling, it is possible to use a modified version of the same methods. For details, see [1].) In section 3.4, a conventional circuit model of the quantum walk simulation algorithm will be described.

3.1 The Representation

The Hilbert space for the quantum walk simulation is spanned by states of the form $|a,b,r\rangle$, where a and b are m-bit strings, and r is a bit. The states of the form $|u,0,0\rangle$ correspond to the vertices $u \in V(G)$.

The subroutines which perform the black box queries will be denoted V_c for every $c \in L$, and they will function as

$$V_c|a,b,r\rangle = |a, b \oplus v_c(a), r \oplus f_c(a)\rangle, \tag{1}$$

where $f_c(a) = \begin{cases} 0 & v_c(a) \neq 11...1 \\ 1 & v_c(a) = 11...1 \end{cases}$.

3.2 The Identification of the Local Interactions

The quantum evolution in N dimensional Hilbert space spanned by $V(G)$ can be analyzed in close analogy to a continuous Markov process [3], for which the probability of jumping to any adjacent vertex in a time ε is defined to be $\gamma\varepsilon$ in the limit case where $\varepsilon \to 0$. In the quantum case, the overall system is governed by the Schrödinger equation, which describes the time evolution of the system by relating the derivative of the state vector $|\alpha\rangle$ to the Hamiltonian H of the system.

$$i\hbar\frac{d}{dt}|\alpha\rangle = H|\alpha\rangle \tag{2}$$

If the state at time t is given by $\sum_a \alpha_a(t)|a\rangle$, then the individual entries H_{ab} of the Hamiltonian can be related to the entries in the state vector as in (3), assuming that one gets rid of the Planck constant in the usual way. Hence it would be easiest to use the derivative of the state vector to identify the Hamiltonian of the system.

$$i\frac{d}{dt}\alpha_a(t) = \sum_b H_{ab}\alpha_b(t) \tag{3}$$

The states for a random walk on a graph stand for the vertices of the graph, and the transitions between these states are ruled by the edge set of the graph, since there is a chance of jumping only between the adjacent vertices.

$$H_{ab} = \begin{cases} \gamma & \text{if } (a,b) \in E(G) \\ 0 & \text{otherwise} \end{cases} \tag{4}$$

In other words, H is the adjacency matrix of the graph times γ. Therefore, simulating the random walk on a graph for a time Δt is equivalent to simulating γ times the adjacency matrix of this graph for this duration. However, the structure of the graph is not explicitly given. It is available only through access to a black box. So it is necessary to redefine the Hamiltonian H of the system, without referring to the structure of the graph, but with the freedom to use the black box queries.

$\sum_{c\in L} V_c^\dagger T V_c$ can be shown to satisfy these conditions where T is given by (5) and $S^{(m,n)}$ is the usual swap operator between the m'th and n'th qubits [1]. ($A^\dagger$ denotes the adjoint or the complex conjugate transpose of the matrix A.)

$$T = S^{(1,m+1)} \otimes S^{(2,m+2)} \otimes \ldots \otimes S^{(m,2m)} \otimes |0\rangle\langle 0| \tag{5}$$

The equivalence of $\sum_{c\in L} V_c^\dagger T V_c$ and $1/\gamma$ times H is trivial with the fact that they both map $|a,0,0\rangle$ to $\sum_{c:v_c(a)\in V(G)} |v_c(a),0,0\rangle$. Let $\gamma = 1$ for simplicity, then H can be written as a sum of constituent Hamiltonians $H_c = V_c^\dagger T V_c$, one for each $c \in L$. The linear combination rule of quantum simulation [1] suggests that $e^{-iH\Delta t}$ can be efficiently implemented if there is an efficient way of simulating H_c for each $c \in L$.

3.3 The Simulation of Local Terms

Each of the local terms specified above yield the same unitary structure $e^{-iH_c\Delta t} = e^{-iV_c^\dagger T V_c \Delta t}$. So, in order to show that H can be simulated efficiently, it is sufficient to show that $e^{-iV_c^{\dagger}TV_c\Delta t}$ can be implemented efficiently for arbitrary $c \in L$. We can use the unitary conjugation rule of quantum simulation [1] to write $e^{-iV_c^{\dagger}TV_c\Delta t} = V_c^{\dagger} e^{-iT\Delta t} V_c$. Since V_c's for every $c \in L$ are provided as accesses to the black box, it remains only to show that T can be efficiently simulated. The circuit in Fig. 2 employs an extension of the simulation method suggested in [5] to simulate T for duration Δt. (See [1] for the description of the unitary operator W.)

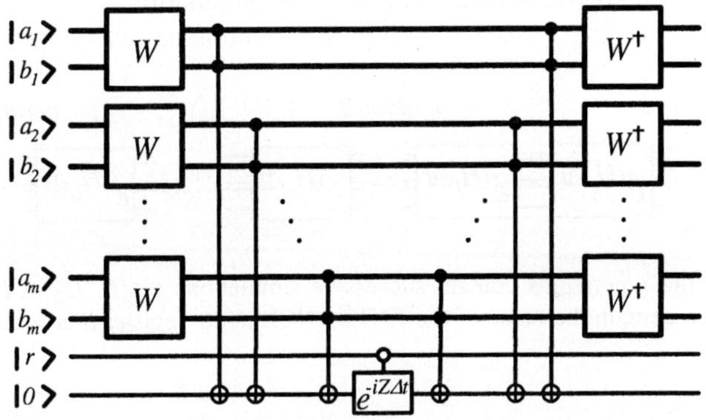

Fig. 2. The circuit for simulating T for duration Δt. The circuit contains an ancilla qubit.

3.4 The Circuit Model for Quantum Walk Simulation

Circuit models are often useful to visualize quantum algorithms. The circuit model for the quantum walk simulation algorithm is easy to construct, however, it is not so easy to display without the use of some shortcuts to abbreviate circuit segments.

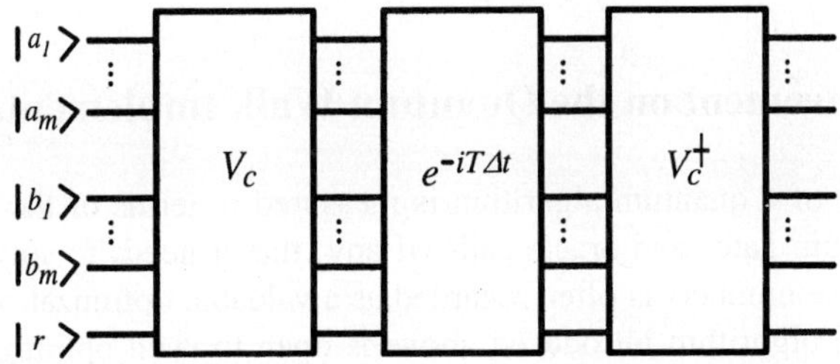

Fig. 3. A circuit simulating $H_c = V_c^{\dagger} T V_c$ for duration Δt

In the core of the model, there is the circuit shown in Fig. 2. If it is denoted as a component labeled by $e^{-iT\Delta t}$, then the circuit which simulates $H_c = V_c^{\dagger} T V_c$ can be constructed as in Fig. 3.

Let $L = \{l_1, l_2, ..., l_k\}$, in which case it is natural to name the local Hamiltonians as $H_1, H_2, ..., H_k$, so that $H = H_1 + H_2 + ... + H_k$. Then the overall circuit can be drawn as in Fig. 4, where the circuit which simulates $H_c = V_c^{\dagger} T V_c$ for a duration Δt is shown as a component labeled $e^{-iH_c\Delta t}$, for each $l_c \in L$. The circuit divides the total simulation time t into r equal slices of Δt, then in each iteration it successively simulates each of $H_1, H_2, ..., H_k$ for time Δt. The number of slices and hence the duration of each individual simulation, Δt, are dependent on the accuracy expected from the simulation. More slices would mean more accurate simulation.

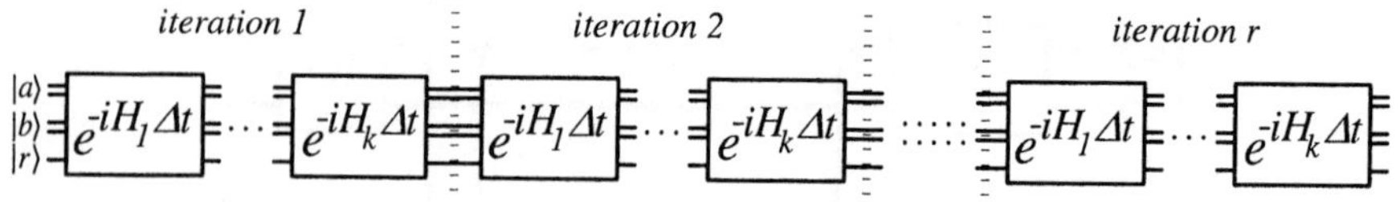

Fig. 4. Each of the r iterations contain successive simulations of $H_1, H_2, ..., H_k$. Initially the register a is set to contain the name of the ENTRANCE node, register b is set to 00..0 and the qubit r is set to 0.

In [1], it is shown that simulating the random walk for duration t with precision ε requires $O(k^2 t^2/\varepsilon)$ black box queries and $O(k^2 t^2 m/\varepsilon)$ auxiliary operations. It is also shown that for sufficiently large n, running the quantum walk for a time uniformly chosen in $[0, n^4/2\varepsilon]$ and then measuring in the computational basis yields a probability of finding the *EXIT* that is greater than $\frac{1}{2n}(1-2\varepsilon)$. When combined, these two results enable one to construct a quantum algorithm that solves the traversal problem on the graphs of type G_n with use of polynomial number of calls to the black box and polynomial number of one- and two-qubit gates.

4 An Improvement on the Quantum Walk Implementation

The complexity of a quantum algorithm is measured in terms of the number of conventional quantum gates and oracle calls (if any) that it needs to solve a problem. A reduction in these numbers is often regarded as a valuable optimization. The quantum walk simulation algorithm introduced above is open to such optimization in several ways. Here is a discussion of such an effort to improve this algorithm:

The simulation algorithm is based on the trivial fact that the Hamiltonian H, which governs the random walk, can be written as a sum of several smaller Hamiltonians H_c where $c \in L$. The iterative part of the algorithm is the successive simulation of these smaller Hamiltonians for small time slices. The order in which these simulations will take place is not specified anywhere. It is natural to ask whether this order of simulations can serve as an instrument for a possible optimization.

A simple idea is to start each iteration (with the trivial exception of the first one) with the simulation of that H_c which was the last in the previous iteration. This can be achieved by simply reversing the order at each iteration. In other words the simulation should run like H_1, H_2,..., H_k, H_k, H_{k-1},..., H_1, H_1, H_2,..., H_k,... and so on. If this method is applied, two successive simulations of the same Hamiltonian occurs r–1 times, like in the cases of H_k, H_k and H_1, H_1. Two successive simulations of a Hamiltonian, which is of the form $H_c = V_c^\dagger T V_c$, bring in a potential for optimization: $H_c H_c = V_c^\dagger T V_c V_c^\dagger T V_c = V_c^\dagger T T V_c$.

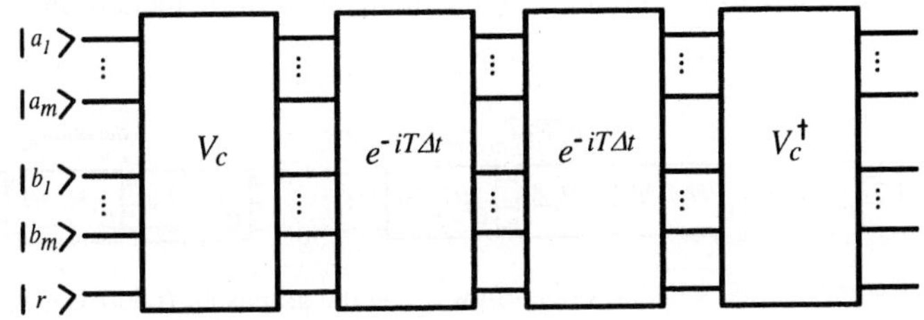

Fig. 5. Two successive simulations of H_c : $H_c H_c = V_c^\dagger T V_c V_c^\dagger T V_c = V_c^\dagger T T V_c$

With this optimization, the number of oracle calls needed for these successive simulations is reduced by half. The ratio of the improvement in the overall algorithm is dependent on k, the number of local interactions that make up the global Hamiltonian H . Each iteration of the old method requires $2k$ oracle calls, while this number is reduced to $2k-1$ for the first and last iterations, and to $2k-2$ for the others with this new method. The maximum vertex degree for the sort of graphs contained in our problem is three, so k can be taken to be 3 for this problem. In this case, the total number of oracle calls is reduced by a factor in the order of one thirds of that number for the original algorithm, which is a valuable optimization, considering how hard it is to build quantum computers. However the circuit shown in Fig. 5 is open to further improvement. A more detailed look (as in Fig. 6) at the center of this circuit would reveal the idea.

Fig. 6 offers an opportunity to improve the circuit by canceling the unitary operator $W^{\otimes m}$ and its adjoint, which, when applied one after another, act as the identity

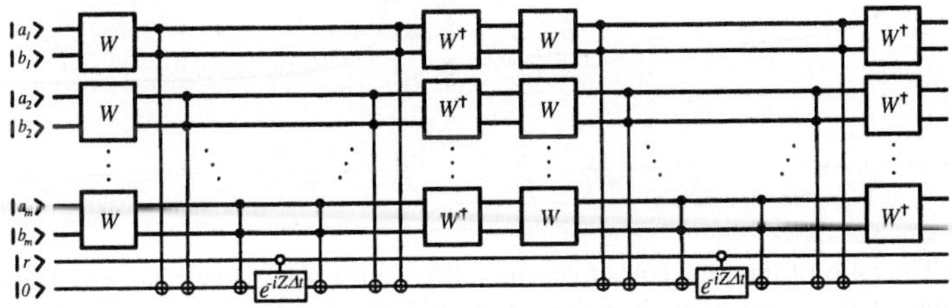

Fig. 6. The circuit for two successive simulations of T is open to improvement

operator. Then a further improvement becomes trivial by canceling the Toffoli gates to produce a circuit where two of the components for simulating the Pauli Z operator for duration Δt come together at the center. A natural choice is to replace these gates with a simulation of the Pauli Z operator for duration $2\Delta t$. Then we end up with a circuit like the one in Fig. 2, but with a controlled $e^{-iZ2\Delta t}$ gate instead of a controlled $e^{-iZ\Delta t}$ gate in the middle. Now it is also apparent that the circuit in Fig. 5 simulates H_c for time $2\Delta t$.

The new algorithm is depicted in Fig. 7. This is an improvement over the old algorithm, not only because it is computationally less expensive, but also because it eliminates more failures due to potential problems in physical implementations.

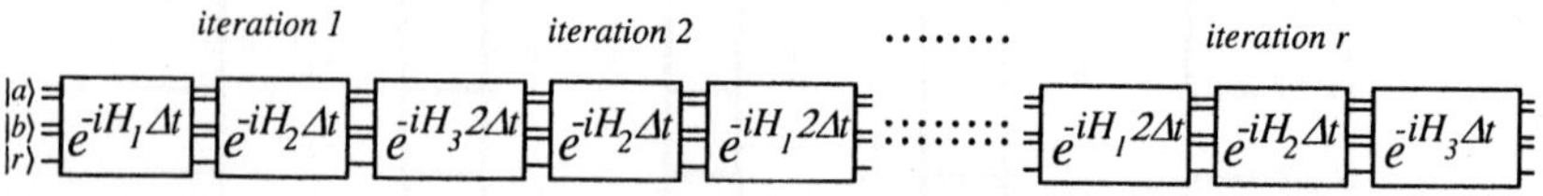

Fig. 7. The circuit that simulates random walk on the graphs G_n (odd r is assumed)

5 Performance Analyses for Various Oracle Conditions

The introduced method can be more beneficial for solving slightly modified versions of the original black box problem. This section briefly discusses several such cases.

As the first example, consider a problem that is the same as the original one, except that this time, the costs for the oracle queries are not uniform, with different costs associated with querying the oracle for different edge labels. In this case, the improved algorithm performs better if it economizes on the types of calls which are more expensive. To achieve the best performance, the simulation should start the first iteration with the second most expensive label and end with the most expensive one. Then reversing this order at each iteration would save an oracle query which is of one

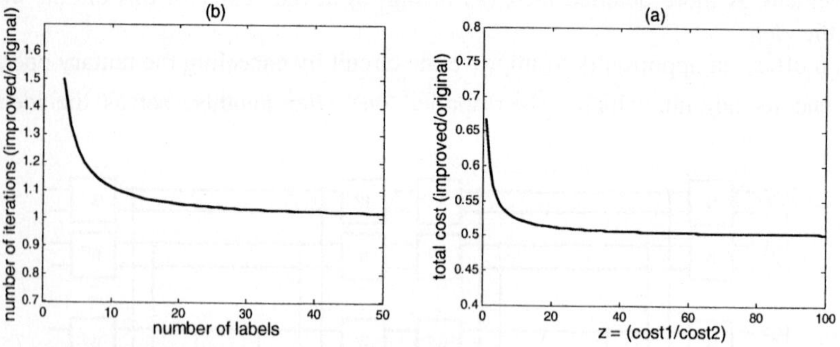

Fig. 8. (a) The ratio of the total costs over the ratio of different query costs. (b) The ratio of the total number of iterations over the number of different labels when the number of allowed oracle calls is held constant.

of the most expensive types. The ratio of improvement with respect to the original algorithm is dependent on how the costs are distributed. A simplified scenario contains three labels, two of which have the same cost (denoted as cost1 in Fig. 8), which is z times as big as the cost of the third one (denoted as cost2). Fig. 8.a contains a sketch of the ratio of improvement in total cost against the ratio of the individual label costs for this simplified scenario. For uniform label costs, the improvement over the original algorithm is in the order of one thirds of the total cost for the original algorithm, while that ratio increases to a half with the increase in the ratio of the nonuniform costs.

Another interesting case occurs when the number of oracle queries that a simulation algorithm can perform is limited. Several variations of this scenario can be considered. The most interesting alternative imposes independent limits for queries of different labels. The performance criterion in such a case is the precision of the simulation, which is a polynomial function of the number of iterations that the simulation can run. The maximum number of iterations that the original algorithm can run is half the number of the allowed queries for the label with the tightest limitation. The improved algorithm can be adjusted to run for twice as many iterations (if limitations on other labels are not so tight) and hence returns more precise results. For a better comparison of the two algorithms, the maximum number of queries allowed for each label should be taken to be the same. The number of iterations that the original algorithm can run is half that number. The performance of the improved algorithm is dependent on the number of labels k, as depicted in Fig. 8.b. For large k's, the two algorithms return similar results, while for small k's, the improved algorithm can run notably more iterations, which means better precision.

Various other scenarios can be constructed, where the improved algorithm can be shown to perform significantly better than the original one. The overall improvement in complexity, together with a flexibility that can be used in favor of more preferable types of queries can be seen to be the reasons for that improved performance.

6 Conclusion

It is evident that the optimization technique presented in this paper is not limited to the simulation of quantum random walks, but it can be generalized to optimize any quantum simulation, not necessarily involving oracle calls, in which the linear combination rule is used to simulate a collection of constituent Hamiltonians. A straightforward extension of the previous analysis shows that the performance gain that would be achieved through the use of this technique is inversely proportional to the number of constituent Hamiltonians of the simulated system, and the quantum random walk of [1], where this number is only three, is a particularly suitable example for demonstrating a significant gain.

Acknowledgements

We thank the anonymous referees for their helpful comments.

References

1. Childs, A., Cleve, R., Deotto, E., Farhi, E., Gutmann, S., Spielman D.: Exponential algorithmic speedup by a quantum walk. Proceedings of STOC'03 (2003) 59–68
2. Feynman, R.P.: Simulating physics with computers, International Journal of Theoretical Physics 21 (1982) 467–488
3. Grassmann, W. K.: Computational Probability. Kluwer Academic Publishers, Boston/Dordrecht/London (2000)
4. Lloyd S.: Universal quantum simulators, Science, Vol. 273. (1996) 1073–1078
5. Nielsen M. A., Chuang I. L.: Quantum Computation and Quantum Information. Cambridge University Press, Cambridge (2000)
6. Shor P.: Polynomial-time algorithms for prime factorization and discrete logarithms on a quantum computer. SIAM Journal on Computing, Vol. 26(5). (1997) 1484–1509

An Alternative Proof That Exact Inference Problem in Bayesian Belief Networks Is NP-Hard

Mustafa Tacettin and Tonguç Ünlüyurt

Faculty of Engineering and Natural Sciences, Sabancı University,
34956 Orhanli, Istanbul, Turkey
{tacettin@su, tonguc}@sabanciuniv.edu

Abstract. Exact inference problem in belief networks has been well studied in the literature and has various application areas. It is known that this problem and its approximation version are NP-hard. In this study, an alternative polynomial time transformation is provided from the well-known vertex cover problem. This new transformation may lead to new insights and polynomially solvable classes of the exact inference problem in Bayesian belief networks.

1 Introduction

Belief networks constitute a framework that enables us to analyze the causal relationships between the events. Belief networks have generally been applied to problems when there is uncertainty in the data or in the knowledge about the domain, and when being able to reason with uncertainty is important. This problem area overlaps with conventional knowledge based system technology, with its uncertainty handling facilities, and with fuzzy logic. Belief nets have been applied particularly to problems that require diagnosis of problems from a variety of input data (often from sensors). A few examples of fielded systems include medical diagnostic systems, real-time weapons scheduling, fault diagnosis in processors, troubleshooting and many others. They also provide a powerful tool for simulating the interactions between physical, social and economic variables [1]. Although belief networks are no substitute for high quality fieldwork, it is clear that they provide a mathematical framework that facilitates interdisciplinary data capture and analysis.

It has been shown that both exact inference problem in Bayesian belief networks (EIBBN) and its approximate version are NP-hard. In this study, an alternative transformation from the well-known vertex cover problem is provided to show that EIBBN is NP-hard.

In what follows, we will first describe EIBBN formally. In the following section a short review on the complexity of the problem is provided. After that, the proposed transformation will be described. Finally we will discuss the possible consequences of this transformation.

P. Yolum et al.(Eds.): ISCIS 2005, LNCS 3733, pp. 947–955, 2005.

2 Exact Inference Problem in Bayesian Belief Networks

A *belief network* is a directed graph whose nodes correspond to random variables. The arcs describe the existence of causal relations between the random variables. In other words, nodes are connected by causal links that point from parent nodes (causes) to child nodes (effects). Each node has a conditional probability table that quantifies the effects that the parents have on the node. A state of the node is the random variable that demonstrates the condition or the value of the node.

Exact inference problem in a belief network is the process of computing $Pr(V = v|E = e)$, or simply $Pr(v|e)$ where v is a value of a variable V and e is an assignment of values to a set of variables E in the belief network. e is also called evidence or observation. In other words, it involves the computation of the conditional probability for a certain node given the values of a subset of other nodes. In the remainder of this paper, we will use the well-known definitions of [2] for computational complexity concepts. To clarify the definition of EIBBN, a simple example will be introduced next.

$P(C=F)$	$P(C=T)$
0.5	0.5

C	$P(S=F)$	$P(S=T)$
F	0.5	0.5
T	0.9	0.1

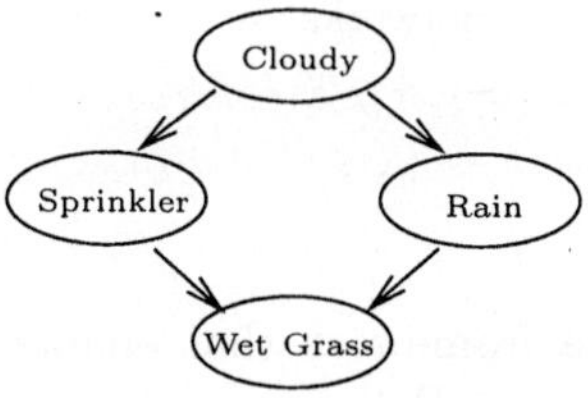

C	$P(R=F)$	$P(R=T)$
F	0.8	0.2
T	0.2	0.8

S R	$P(W=F)$	$P(W=T)$
F F	1.0	0.0
T F	0.1	0.9
F T	0.1	0.9
T T	0.01	0.99

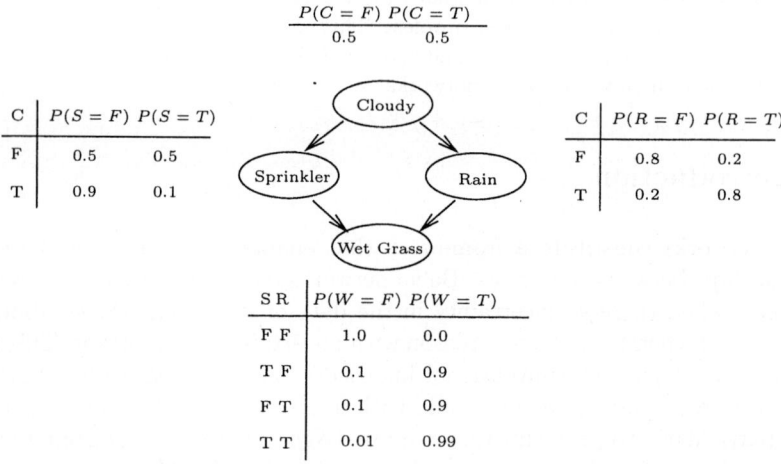

Fig. 1. An example

In this example all nodes have two possible values, denoted by T (*true*) and F (*false*). As can be sen in Fig. 1, the event "grass is wet" (*W=true*) has two possible causes: either the water sprinkler is on (*S=true*) or it is raining (*R=true*). The strength of this relationship is shown in the table. For example, we see that $Pr(W = true|S = true, R = false) = 0.9$ (second row), and hence, $Pr(W = false|S = true, R = false) = 1 - 0.9 = 0.1$, since each row must sum to one. Since node C has no parents, its probability table specifies the prior probability that it is cloudy (in this case, 0.5). An instance of the EIBBN can be computing the probability that sprinkler is on given that grass is wet and it is raining. The decision version of the EIBBN involves deciding whether or not a certain conditional probability is higher than a threshold value.

We will define Vertex Cover (VC) problem since the proposed transformation uses this problem. A *Vertex Cover* of an undirected graph $G = (V, E)$ is a subset S of V such that if (u, v) is an edge of G, then either $u \in S$ or $v \in S$ (or both). Given an undirected graph G and an integer k, the decision version of the VC problem tries to answer whether G has a vertex cover with cardinality at most k.

It is known that EIBBN can be solved in polynomial time when the belief network is a tree [3]. In [4], it is proved that exact inference problem in Bayesian belief networks is NP-hard. The proof consists of a polynomial transformation from 3-SAT problem. It is shown in [5] that approximate version of EIBBN is NP-hard. [6] showed that there is a polynomial time algorithm for approximating probabilistic inference, if conditional probabilities are arbitrarily close to zero in the case that the evidence set is empty or constant-sized. It is shown in [7] that even for surprisingly restricted cases, the problem is NP-hard. For these cases, even the approximate version of the problem remains NP-hard.

3 Transformation from Vertex Cover Problem

In this section, we will transform VC to EIBBN in polynomial time. Let's consider a graph $G = (V, E)$ for the vertex cover problem, with $V = \{V_1, \ldots, V_n\}$ and $E = \{E_1, \ldots, E_m\}$. We will define the nodes, edges and probability tables for the belief network. The idea is to construct the EIBBN in such a way that there exists a vertex cover with cardinality at most k if the marginal probability of a certain node is positive.

3.1 Nodes of Belief Network

There are six types of nodes in the belief network:

Vertex nodes: For each vertex V_i in the original graph, there is a corresponding vertex node in the belief network that will again be denoted by V_i. So there are n vertex nodes as shown in Fig. 2.

Edge nodes: For each edge E_i in the original graph, there is a corresponding node in the belief network that will be denoted by E_i. So there are m edge nodes as shown in Fig. 3.

Edge result nodes: For each edge on the graph, except the edge with the highest index number, there is a corresponding node in the belief network. So, there are $m - 1$ edge result nodes. These nodes are denoted by R_i for $i = 1, \ldots, m - 1$. These nodes are created to check whether the edge is covered in the original problem or not. Fig. 4 shows the edge result nodes.

State nodes: There are state nodes in the belief network corresponding to the number of vertices in the vertex cover for the original graph. For a vertex V_i, there are $i + 1$ state nodes in the belief network. These nodes will be denoted by S_{ij}. Fig. 5 shows a state node.

State result nodes: State result nodes are introduced in the belief network in order to see whether the number of covered vertices is less than or equal to k or not. There are $k + 1$ state result nodes that will be denoted by D_i for $i = 0, \ldots, k$. Fig. 6 shows the state result nodes.

Final Node: The node for the BN that is associated with whether the solution for VC is true or false. We will denote this node by Y. Fig. 7 shows the final node.

For each node, there are two states, true or false. Total number of nodes is $2m + k + [\frac{(n+1)\times n}{2}]$.

3.2 Edges of Belief Network

While describing the edges of the belief network, the relation of a group of nodes and their parents will be utilized.

Vertex nodes: These nodes don't have parent nodes.

Fig. 2. Vertex nodes of BN

Edge nodes: Each edge node has two parent nodes. These are the vertex nodes that form the edge in the original graph.

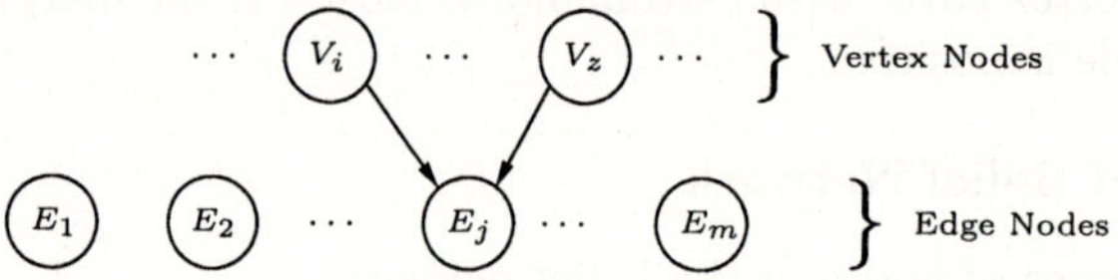

Fig. 3. The parents of node E_j where E_j is (V_i, V_z)

Edge result nodes: Each edge result node has at most two parent nodes. These are the preceding edge result node and the corresponding edge node.

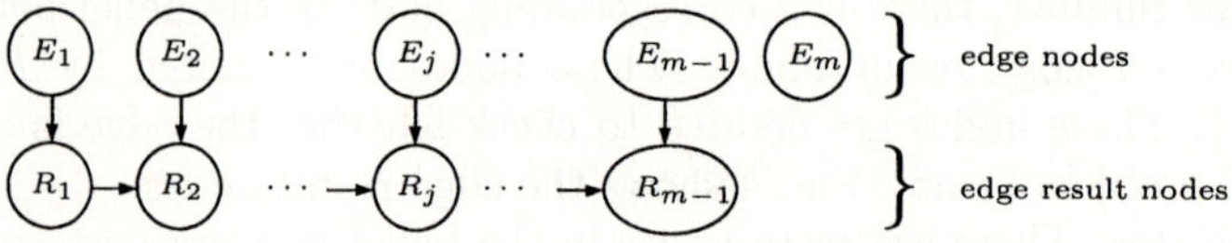

Fig. 4. The edge result nodes

State nodes: The state nodes can be classified into n groups. Each group can be matched to a vertex node. In each group there are x nodes, where x is the degree of the vertex node matched to that group. So, total number of state nodes is $\frac{n\times(n-1)}{2}$. For each state node, there are at most 3 parent nodes.

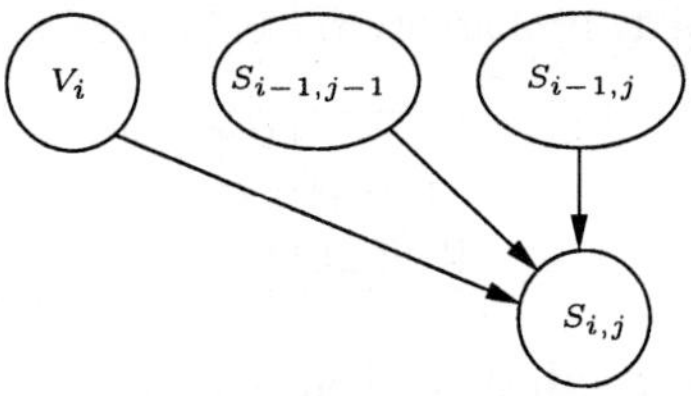

Fig. 5. The incoming arcs of the state node S_{ij}

The notation used for a state node is S_{ij}, where i is the vertex node associated with this node, and the j corresponds to the state of the first i vertices meaning; if S_{ij} is true, j of the first i vertices are covered where $j \leq i$.

There is one incoming arc for state S_{ij} emanating from V_i. In addition two other arcs are inserted emanating from $S_{i-1,j}$ and $S_{i-1,j}$, if $S_{i-1,j-1}$ and $S_{i-1,j-1}$ exist.

State result nodes: The state result nodes are constructed to check the total number of covered vertices. For each state result node there are at most 2 parent nodes. These are the predecessor node and the state node S_{nj}, where $j \leq k$.

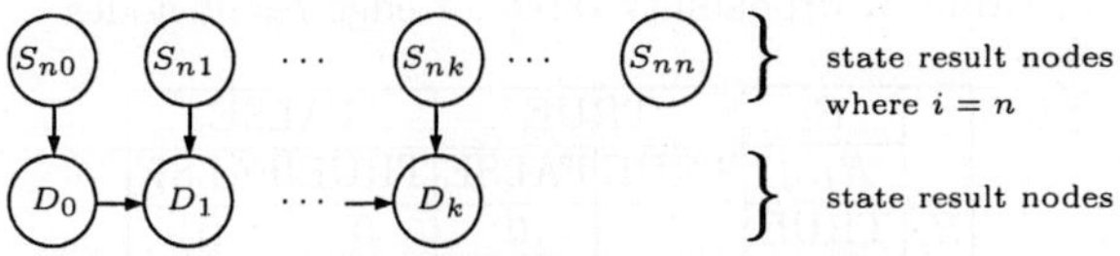

Fig. 6. The state result nodes

Final node: This is a single node that has 3 parent nodes. These are the last state result node, last edge node and last edge result node. It is only true if all parent nodes are true. We will denote the final node by Y.

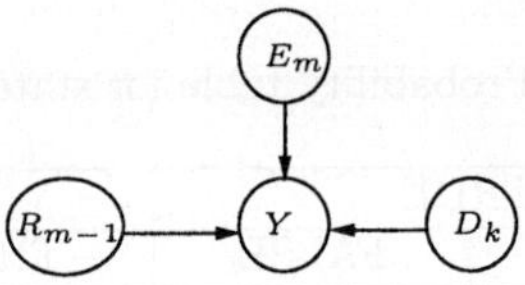

Fig. 7. Final node denoted by Y

3.3 The Probability Tables

Probability table for vertex nodes: There are 2 states for each node. And the states are probabilistic, they are not known. So, giving equal chances to each state seems reasonable. As a matter of fact, the values of the probabilities do not matter as long as they sum up to 1.

Table 1. Probability table for vertex nodes

	V_i
TRUE	0.5
FALSE	0.5

Probability table for edge nodes: There are exactly two parent nodes for each edge node. The probability table for edge E_i is as follows:

Table 2. Probability table for edge node

	V_i	TRUE		FALSE	
	V_z	TRUE	FALSE	TRUE	FALSE
E_j	TRUE	1	1	1	0
	FALSE	0	0	0	1

The table says that the node E_j with parents V_i and V_z is always true if any of the parent is true.

Probability table for Edge Result Nodes: They have two parent nodes, except the first edge result node. The probability table is as follows:

Table 3. Probability table for edge result nodes

	E_i	TRUE		FALSE	
	R_{j-1}	TRUE	FALSE	TRUE	FALSE
R_j	TRUE	1	0	0	0
	FALSE	0	1	1	1

The table says that the node R_j with parents R_{j-1} and E_j is true if both of the parents are true.

Probability table for state nodes: This type of nodes has at most three parent nodes. If the parent node does not exist, it should be removed from the table. The table is as follows:

Table 4. Probability table for state nodes

	V_i	TRUE				FALSE			
	$S_{i-1,j-1}$	TRUE		FALSE		TRUE		FALSE	
	$S_{i-1,j}$	TRUE	FALSE	TRUE	FALSE	TRUE	FALSE	TRUE	FALSE
$S_{i,j}$	TRUE	0.5	1	0	0	0.5	0	1	0
	FALSE	0.5	0	1	1	0.5	1	0	1

The state nodes are designed in order to count the number of true assignments to vertex nodes. If S_{ij} is true, then j of the first i state nodes are true. For the state nodes S_{nj}, the information gained is the total number of true vertex nodes.

Probability table for state result nodes: They have 2 parent nodes, except the first one. The probability table is as follows:

Table 5. Probability table for state result nodes

	$S_{n,j}$	TRUE		FALSE	
	D_{j-1}	TRUE	FALSE	TRUE	FALSE
D_j	TRUE	1	1	1	0
	FALSE	0	0	0	1

The table says that the result node D_j is true if any of the parents is true.

3.4 An Example Transformation

To understand the model easily, let's define a small vertex cover problem and transform it to an EIBBN as described in the previous section.

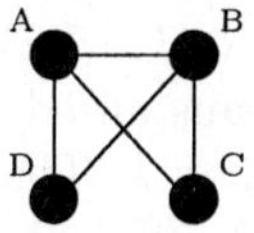

Fig. 8. A VC Problem: Is it possible to have a vertex cover V where $|V| \leq 2$?

Here, the problem is stated in Fig. 8. We are supposed to answer whether there is a vertex cover V whose size is at most 2.

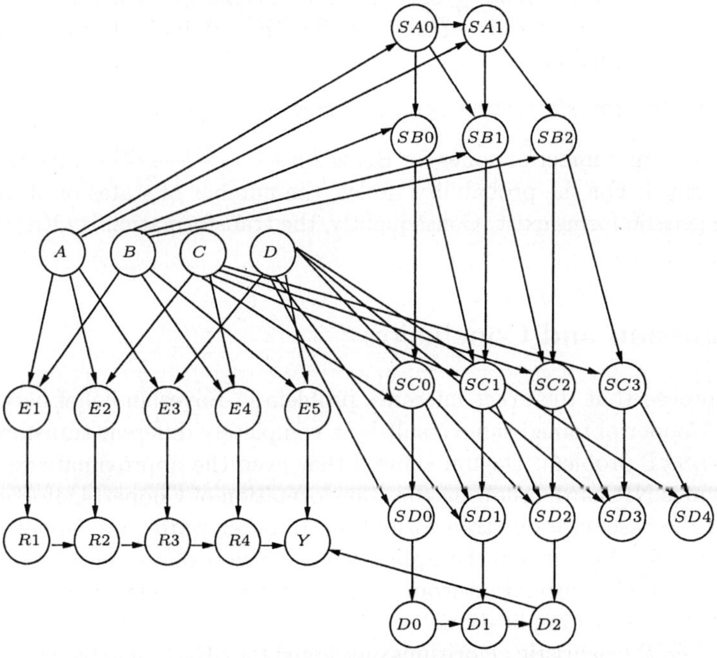

Fig. 9. The BN representation of the example problem

By using the transformation method proposed above the BN representation of this problem can be seen in Fig. 9.

If $Pr(Y = true) > 0$ then the answer to the vertex cover problem is yes, meaning that there exists a vertex cover with cardinality at most 2.

3.5 Correctness Of The Transformation

Lemma 1. *$Pr(Y = true) > 0$ in the belief network if and only if there is a vertex cover with cardinality at most k in the original graph.*

Proof: If the states of all vertex nodes are given, the probability of Y is either 0 or 1. That is the result of having deterministic relations among the nodes. The probability is 1 iff all incoming nodes for node Y is true. Then, R_{m-1}, E_m and D_k are all true. R_{m-1} and E_m are true iff all edges are covered by the vertex nodes that are true. D_k is true if the number of vertex nodes that are in state true, is smaller than or equal to k, which is the cardinality number for the original VC. So, having $Y = 1$ means all edges are covered and the number of vertex nodes in state true is less than k. There are 2^n possible assignments for vertex nodes. It means there are 2^n different evidence options for vertex nodes.

$$Pr(Y = True) = \sum_{i=1}^{2^n} Pr(Y = true|evidence\ i)\frac{1}{2^n}$$

where evidence i is an assignment of vertex nodes different than evidence j where $i \neq j$. If the probability of Y is greater than 0, then for an evidence i $Pr(Y = true|evidence\ i)$ is equal to 1. So, the original VC problem has a solution with cardinality k. □

Lemma 2. *The transformation can be carried out in polynomial time.*

Proof: The total number of nodes for BN is $2m+k+[\frac{(n+2)\times(n+1)}{2}]$. All the edges are well defined. For the probability tables, the number of states of all nodes is 2 and the generic forms exist. Consequently, the transformation is $O(n^2)$ so it is polynomial. □

4 Discussion and Conclusion

We have proved that the exact inference problem in Bayesian belief networks is NP-hard. Cooper obtained same result by a completely different transformation from the 3-SAT problem. Dagum showed that even the approximate version of the problem is NP-hard, following the transformation of Cooper. Unfortunately, this is not the case with our transformation. In other words, we cannot imitate the same transformation for the approximate version of the problem. On the other hand, the transformation from the vertex cover problem provided in this paper may have some implications.

First of all, the heuristic algorithms developed for EIBBN can be used to solve VC instances. We have tried this by off-the-shelf available software. The results were not very encouraging. Yet, the belief network obtained via the transformation has a special structure. One can exploit this special structure to develop more efficient algorithms. It is possible, for instance, to apply the node elimination method of [8].

There are certain special classes of vertex cover problem instances that can be solved in polynomial time like the case that the underlying graph is bipartite. In addition, there are polynomial time constant factor approximation algorithms for the vertex cover problem in the literature [9]. The relation between the vertex cover problem and EIBBN can be investigated further to find classes of EIBBN that can be solved in polynomial time.

References

1. Batchelor, C.: Application of belief networks to water management studies. Agricultural Water Management **40** (1999) 51–57
2. Garey, M.R., Johnson, D.S.: A Guide to the Theory of NP-Completeness. W. H. Freeman and Company, New York (1979)
3. Pearl, J.: Fusion, propagation, and structuring in belief networks. Artificial Intelligence **29** (1986) 241–288
4. Cooper, G.F.: The computational complexity of probabilistic inference using bayesian belief networks. Artificial Intelligence **42** (1990) 393–405
5. Dagum, P., Luby, M.: Approximating probabilistic inference in bayesian belief networks is np-hard. Artificial Intelligence **60** (1993) 141–153
6. Dagum, P., Luby, M.: An optimal approximation algorithm for bayesian inference. Artificial Intelligence **93** (1997) 1–27
7. Roth, D.: On the hardness of approximate reasoning. Artificial Intelligence **82** (1996) 273–302
8. Shachter, Ross, D.: Probabilistic inference and influence diagram. Operations Research **36** (1988) 586–602
9. Vazirani, V.: Approximation Algorithms. Springer, Berlin (2001)

Recovering the Lattice of Repetitive Sub-functions

Guy-Vincent Jourdan[1], Hasan Ural[1], and Hüsnü Yenigün[2]

[1] School of Information Technology and Engineering (SITE), University of Ottawa, 800 King Edward Avenue, Ottawa, Ontario, Canada, K1N 6N5
{gvj, ural}@site.uottawa.ca

[2] Faculty of Engineering and Natural Sciences, Sabancı University, Tuzla, Istanbul, Turkey 34956
yenigun@sabanciuniv.edu

Abstract. Given a set of observations of an existing concurrent system with repetitive sub-functions, we consider the construction of an MSC graph representing the functionality of the concurrent system. We first introduce a formal structure that we call "lattice of repetitive sub-functions". This lattice provides us with a global view of all the repetitive sub-functions of the system and all the compatible observations. Using the lattice, we are able to propose an algorithm that constructs the MSC graph representation of the system functionality in a more general context than in previously published work.

1 Introduction

Often, depictions of individual intended behaviors of a concurrent system are given by designers as Message Sequence Charts (MSCs) [1,2]. An MSC is a visual description of a series of message exchanges among communicating processes in a concurrent system. Figure 1, left, shows an MSC of three processes exchanging a total of five messages. The message m_1 is sent by the process P_2 and received by the process P_3, which is represented by an arrow from P_2 to P_3 and labeled m_1. Each message exchange is represented by a pair of *send* and *receive* events. The local view of the message exchanges of a process (send and receive events of a process) is a total order, but the global view is a partial order. A tuple consisting of a local view for each process of the message exchanges depicted in an MSC uniquely determines that MSC. Thus, an MSC represents a partial order execution of a concurrent system which stands for a set of linearizations (total order executions of the system) determined by considering all possible interleavings of concurrent message exchanges implied by the partial order.

To describe a functionality that is composed of several sub-functionalities, an MSC graph (a graph with a source and a sink node where edges labeled by MSCs) can be used. An MSC corresponding to the concatenation of MSCs along a path from the source node to the sink node in an MSC graph is said to be in the language of the MSC graph. In the following, M^k means that M is repeated k times, and M^* means any number of repetitions of M. Figure 1, right,

P. Yolum et al.(Eds.): ISCIS 2005, LNCS 3733, pp. 956–965, 2005.

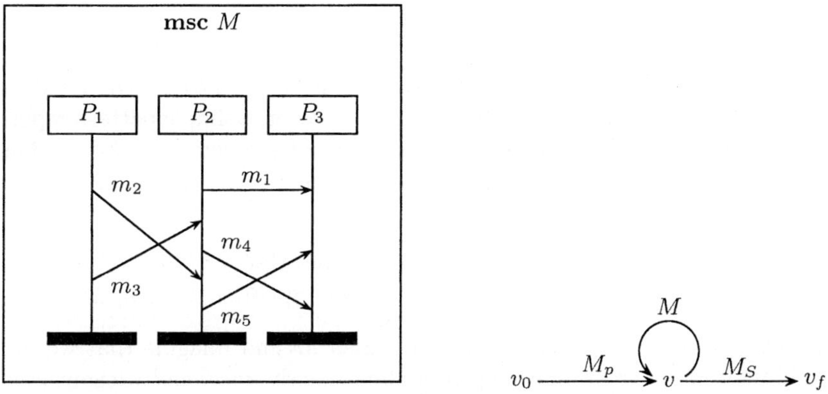

Fig. 1. An MSC of three processes (left) and an example MSC Graph (right)

shows an MSC Graph where the MSC M_p is followed by an arbitrary number of iterations of the MSC M, followed by the MSC M_s, which defines the language $M_p.M^*.M_s$. In this paper we assume that an MSC in the language of an MSC graph represents a system functionality from the initial state to the final state, without going through the initial state again during the execution.

Formal semantics associated with MSCs provides a basis for their analysis such as detecting timing conflicts and race conditions [3], non–local choices [4], model checking [5], and checking safe realizability [6,7].

One of the aims of the reverse engineering [8,9] is to recover the design of an existing system from the run time behavior of its implementation. In this paper, we consider the reverse engineering of designs of existing concurrent systems from given sets of observations of their implementations. We assume that we are given a set O of observations, each observation $o \in O$ being an arbitrary linearization of an MSC m from a set of MSCs that is not given. Some of the sub-functions of the system can be *repetitive*, in which case they can be called consecutively a different number of times in different runs of the system. We assume that a repetitive sub-function does not start (resp. end) at the initial (resp. final) state, and that every repetitive sub-function of the system (if any) is represented in the given set of observations at least twice: once with no occurrence, and once with two or more consecutive occurrences.

In [10], a method to infer repetitive sub-functions from a given set of observations is described. However, this method requires restrictive assumptions regarding the observations. In this paper, we introduce a new concept, the *lattice of the repetitive sub-functions*, to model a structure indicating all possible 2^n combinations of n repetitive sub-functions of the observed system. Using this concept, we are able to relax the following the assumptions made in [10]:

- Repetitive sub-functions do not have to be iterated the same number of times in each observation,
- Repetitive sub-functions need not be introduced in a specific order,
- The ordering of the sub-functions need not be totally unambiguous.

2 Preliminaries

A sub-function that is repeated in an observation will create a repeated pattern in the MSC corresponding to that observation. However, a simple pattern repetition is not enough. In order to deduce the existence of a repetitive sub-function, we need to have an evidence such as different number of iterations of the pattern within the same context.

Definition 1. *An MSC M is* the basic repetitive MSC *of MSC M' if $M' = M^k$ for some $k \geq 2$ and there does not exist a basic repetitive MSC of M.*

Consider the visual representation of an MSC M and imagine that we draw a line through M by crossing each process line exactly once, and without crossing any message arrows. Such a line divides M into two parts M_p (the part above the cutting line) and M_s (the part below the cutting line). M_p and M_s can be shown to be MSCs again. M_p and M_s are what we call a prefix of M and a suffix of M, respectively.

Definition 2. *Two MSCs M_1 and M_2 are said to* infer M to be repetitive within the context M_p–M_s *if all the following are satisfied:*

1. *M does not have a basic repetitive MSC,*
2. *$M_1 = M_p.M^k.M_s$ for some $k \geq 2$ and $M_2 = M_p.M_s$,*
3. *M is not a suffix of M_p and M is not a prefix of M_s.*

Definition 3. *A* common prefix (resp. suffix) *of two MSCs M_1 and M_2, is an MSC M, such that M is a prefix (resp. suffix) of both M_1 and M_2. The* maximal common prefix (resp. suffix) *of M_1 and M_2 is a common prefix (resp. suffix) M of M_1 and M_2 with the largest number of events.*

3 The Lattice of the Repetitive Sub-functions

The *lattice of the repetitive sub-functions* is a structure providing all possible selection of n repetitive sub-functions, including none of them (bottom of the lattice) and all of them (top of the lattice). We first look at the simple case, with only one level of repetitive sub-functions, and we then consider the case of nested repetitive sub-functions.

3.1 The Case Without Nested Repetitive Sub-functions

If two MSCs M_1 and M_2 infer an MSC M to be repetitive within the context M_p–M_s, we obtain a regular expression, $M_p.M^*.M_s$, which can be seen as a language whose alphabet is the set of MSCs used in the regular expression ($\{M_p, M_s, M\}$ in that case). M_1 and M_2 are two of the words of that language.

For example, lets consider the following three MSCs, corresponding to a given set of three observations: $M_1.M_3.M_5$, $M_1.M_2.M_2.M_3.M_5$ and $M_1.M_3.M_4.M_4.M_4.M_5$. The first two MSCs infer the language $M_1.M_2^*.M_3.M_5$, while the first and third MSCs infer the language $M_1.M_3.M_4^*.M_5$, using the alphabet $\{M_1, M_2, M_3, M_4, M_5\}$.

Considering the general case of n repetitive sub-functions with no nested repetitive sub-functions, the general form of the top "language" (the top of the lattice), representing the selection of all repetitive sub-function, will be of the form $M_p.M_1^*.T_1.M_2^*.T_2.M_3^* \ldots M_{n-1}^*.T_{n-1}.M_n^*.M_s$, where $\forall i \leq n$, M_i is a non empty MSC representing a repetitive sub-function, T_i is a possibly empty "transition" MSC, M_p is the non-empty prefix and M_s is the non-empty suffix. Figure 2 shows an example with $n = 3$.

Because all combinations of the repetitive sub-functions are possible, we can observe every subset of the set of n M_i's, to a total of 2^n possible different languages. All of these languages can be ordered by inclusions: $\forall L_1, \forall L_2, L_1 \subseteq L_2$ if and only if $\forall w, w \in L_1 \Rightarrow w \in L_2$. Then, we are in fact looking at an hypercube of size n, the elements being the languages, where a language L_2 includes a language L_1 if L_2 contains all the repetitive sub-functions included in L_1.

The bottom "language" (the bottom of the lattice) is actually a constant, whose only word is the MSC of the observation with no repetitive sub-function. All other observations should "introduce" a new repetitive sub-function. All in all, n languages will be directly deduced from pairs of observations, and the others will be inferred.

There are several possible sets of observations that will allow the inference of the same lattice. In Figure 2, the black dots are deduced from pairs of observations and the white dots are the languages inferred by inclusion. However, not all combination of four nodes are valid. For example, the right-most combination is invalid, since M_3 is never inferred (never given in any observation, in fact).

Note that if a "transition" T_i is empty (that is, M_i and M_{i+1} are consecutive) and if no observation is provided showing both M_i and M_{i+1}, we cannot order M_i and M_{i+1}.

3.2 The Case of the Nested Repetitive Sub-functions

Observations containing occurrences of nested repetitive sub-functions will yield the top element of a structure whose general form is the same as the one given

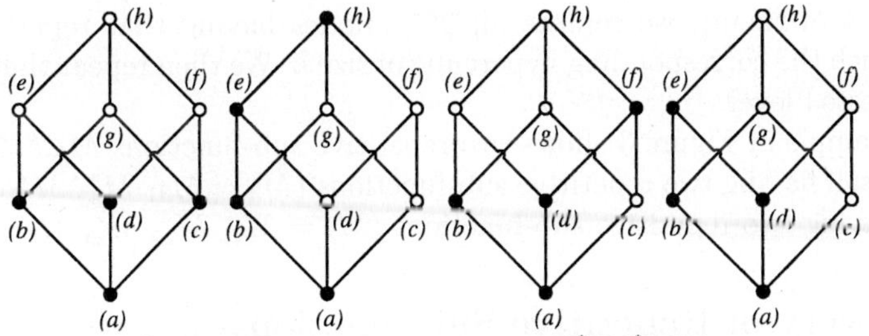

$(a) = M_pT_1T_2T_3M_s$
$(b) = M_pM_1^*T_1T_2T_3M_s$
$(c) = M_pT_1T_2M_3^*T_3M_s$
$(d) = M_pT_1M_2^*T_2T_3M_s$
$(e) = M_pM_1^*T_1M_2^*T_2T_3M_s$
$(f) = M_pT_1M_2^*T_2M_3^*T_3M_s$
$(g) = M_pM_1^*T_1T_2M_3^*T_3M_s$
$(h) = M_pM_1^*T_1M_2^*T_2M_3^*T_3M_s$

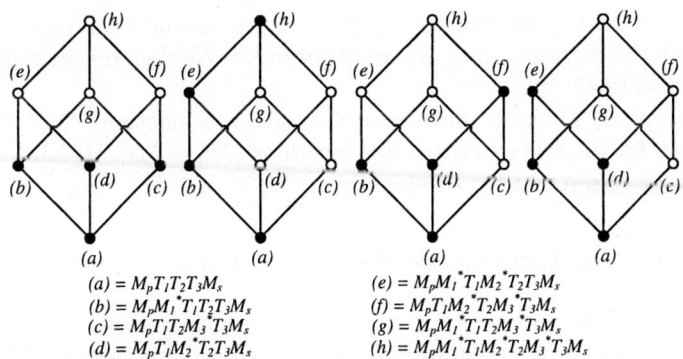

Fig. 2. Different sets of observations for the same lattice

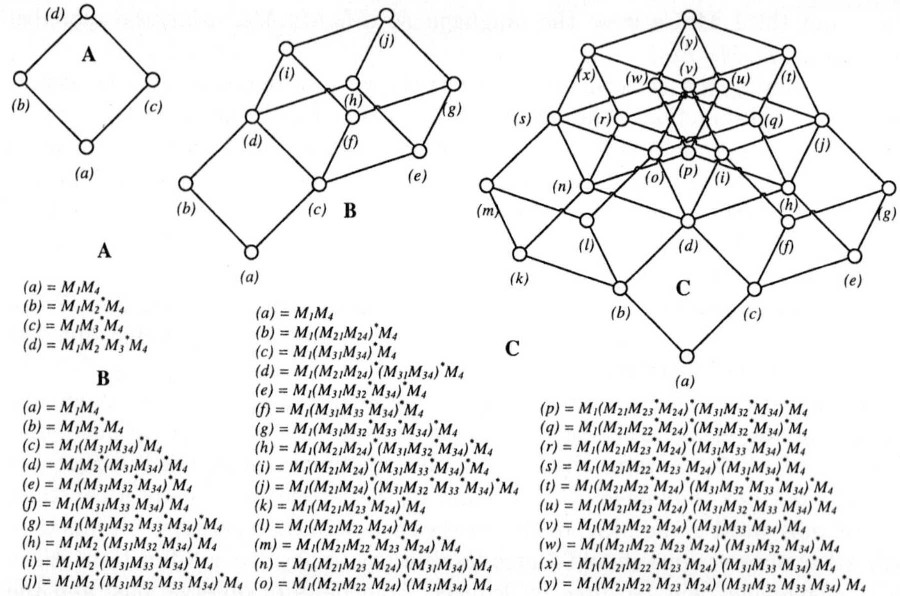

Fig. 3. Two repetitive sub-functions, each one having two nested repetitive sub-functions

in the previous section. In this general form, a sub-function containing k nested repetitive sub-functions will have a non empty prefix, a non empty suffix, and k repetitive sub-functions separated by possibly empty transition MSCs. Thus, this sub-function alone, with its k nested repetitive sub-functions, defines an hypercube of size k. Each of the nested repetitive sub-function can itself have nested repetitive sub-functions and the same idea would apply. That is, we first consider the "first level" repetitive sub-functions. With n first level repetitive sub-functions, we have an initial hypercube of size n, with each repetitive sub-function defining one "direction" or one "face" of the hypercube. Each repetitive sub-function appears in 2^{n-1} nodes of the hypercube.

For each first level repetitive sub-function having nested repetitive sub-functions (say k of them), we replace all 2^{n-1} nodes having that repetitive sub-function with the corresponding hypercube of size k. We then repeat that process for each nested level.

The example in Figure 3 shows two repetitive sub-functions $M_1.M_2^*.M_3^*.M_4$ (A), M_3 itself having two repetitive sub-functions ($M_3 = M_{31}.M_{32}^*.M_{33}^*.M_{34}$, B) and M_2 having two repetitive sub-functions ($M_2 = M_{21}.M_{22}^*.M_{23}^*.M_{24}$, C).

4 Recovery of Repetitive Sub-functions

With the help of the lattice, we can derive a repetitive sub-function recovery algorithm that has fewer assumptions than the ones assumed in [10]. We do keep the following assumptions from [10]:

1. The initial observation (without repetitive sub-function calls), and each repetitive sub-function having nested repetitive sub-functions, has a non empty, repetitive sub-function free prefix and a non empty, repetitive sub-function free suffix.
2. Repetitive sub-functions have no common prefix with the part of the MSC that starts just after them and no common suffix with the part of the MSC that leads to them.
3. Repetitive sub-functions starting at the same point do not alternate.
4. Every repetitive sub-function is introduced "individually" by at least one observation. That is, for every repetitive sub-function M, there is at least one observation o and a set of observations S such that:
   (a) M is repeated at least twice in o
   (b) M does not appear at all in any observation of S
   (c) Every other repetitive sub-function appearing at least once in at least one observation in S is also introduced individually within the set of observations of S.

   In other words, it is possible to introduce the repetitive sub-functions one at a time.

A major difference with [10] is that once a repetitive sub-function has been introduced, it can then be used (or not used), and used any number of times in the other observations. In the case of nested repetitive sub-functions, the observation that introduces the nested repetitive sub-function iterates that nested repetitive sub-function in only one occurrence of the outer repetitive sub-function.

4.1 Description of the Algorithm

We first consider the following simplified case:

- The ordering of the repetitive sub-functions is never ambiguous (there is always either a non empty transition between two consecutive repetitive sub-functions, or these repetitive sub-functions are provided incrementally).
- There are no nested repetitive sub-functions.
- There are no unnecessary observations (i.e. we are working with $n+1$ observations to uncover n repetitive sub-functions).

We are going to construct the lattice corresponding to a given set of observations step by step, starting from the bottom. Initially, we look for observations that allow us to deduce a single repetitive sub-function (assumption 4 ensures us that there is at least one). Once we have deduced all these repetitive sub-functions, we complete that portion of the lattice and infer the top of it. Then, we look for observations that allow us to deduce just one repetitive sub-function in addition to the ones that have been already deduced (again, thanks to assumption 4, there is always one at least). We complete that part of the lattice, infer the top, etc. until we are done.

We will use "topLabel" to store the current top of the lattice. Initially, topLabel is the bottom of the lattice (which is simply the MSC of the shortest observation of the whole set).

```
topLabel = the MSC of the shortest observation
S = set of all observations minus topLabel
while S ≠ ∅ do
   /* First phase: discovering the next set of repetitive sub-functions */
   for all observations o ∈ S do
      Let prefix = MaxCommonPrefix(topLabel, o)
      Let suffix = MaxCommonSuffix(topLabel, o)
      if prefix ≠ null and suffix ≠ null and prefix.suffix ∈ topLabel then
         Let M be the portion of the MSC of o between prefix and suffix
         /* MSC representation of o=prefix.M.suffix */
         if M_1 = basic_repetitive_MSC(M) then
            /* M = M_1^k for some k. We have found prefix.M_1^*.suffix */
            Add prefix.M_1^*.suffix as a successor of topLabel in the lattice
            Remove o from S
         end if
      end if
   end for
   /* second phase: reconstruction phase */
   Close the lattice by combining all the found successors of topLabel.
   Assign topLabel to the top of the lattice.
end while
```

After the first pass through the while loop, topLabel is a regular expression, using the repetition(∗). The functions MaxCommonPrefix and MaxCommonSuffix presented in [10] must be adapted as follows: trace along topLabel. Once you reach a repetition (you reach an M^*), there are two options: either follow M or skip it altogether. Thanks to assumption 2, you see immediately which way to go. If M is followed, you can loop through M any number of times. If the trace ends in the middle of M, then push back the common prefix to the beginning of that repetitive sub-function M.

Let's consider the following set of MSCs corresponding to a given set of four observations as an example:

1. $M_p.M_t.M_s$
2. $M_p.M_a.M_a.M_a.M_a.M_t.M_s$
3. $M_p.M_t.M_b.M_b.M_s$
4. $M_p.M_a.M_t.M_b.M_b.M_b.M_c.M_c.M_s$

Initially, topLabel $= M_p.M_t.M_s$ In the first pass through, topLabel and observations 2) find $M_p.M_a^*.M_t.M_s$ and topLabel and observations 3) find $M_p.M_t.M_b^*.M_s$. The lattice, a square, is closed, and $M_p.M_a^*.M_t.M_b^*.M_s$ is inferred as the top. In the second pass, topLabel $= M_p.M_a^*.M_t.M_b^*.M_s$ with observations 4) find $M_p.M_a^*.M_t.M_b^*.M_c^*.M_s$. The lattice, a cube, is closed, and $M_p.M_a^*.M_t.M_b^*.M_c^*.M_s$ is inferred as the final top.

4.2 Adding the Nested Repetitive Sub-functions

If there are nested repetitive sub-functions, the above algorithm will not find them. To handle this case, we have to waive the restriction that MaxCommonPrefix must not finish inside a repetitive sub-functions. We must trace the max-

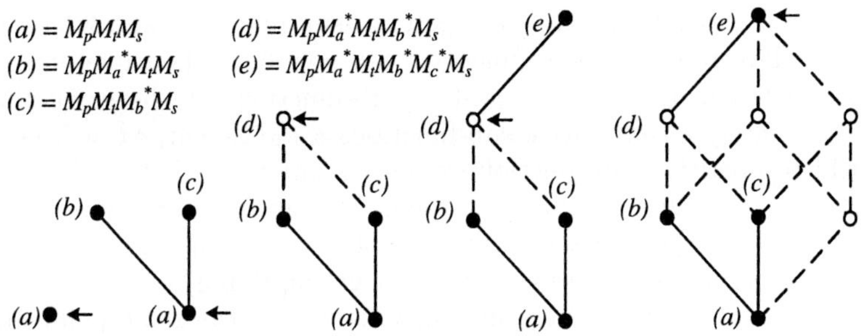

Fig. 4. The algorithm step by step

imal common prefix within the repetitive sub-function. If it finishes inside it, we trace the maximal common suffix and if it too finishes at the same point in the repetitive sub-function, then that is the candidate for the starting point of the nested sub-function.

Thus, the strategy becomes the following: we first iterate the algorithm as before, until going through the for loop (line 5) does not add new repetitive sub-functions. At that point, we have identified all the "first level" repetitive sub-functions. We then continue the algorithm, this time allowing the max common prefixes and max common suffixes to stop inside a first level repetitive sub-function. We iterate until, again, the for loop does not add new repetitive sub-functions. At that point, we have found all the second level repetitive sub-functions (repetitive sub-functions inside a repetitive sub-functions). Now, we allow suffixes and prefixes finishing inside second level repetitive sub-functions and find third level repetitive sub-functions. We go one until we have exhausted the set of observations.

4.3 Waiving the Non-ambiguity Condition

Consider the following set of MSCs corresponding to a given set of four observations:

1. $M_p.M_s$
2. $M_p.M_a.M_a.M_a.M_s$
3. $M_p.M_b.M_b.M_b.M_s$
4. $M_p.M_a.M_b.M_c.M_c.M_c.M_s$

By applying the algorithm of Section 4.1 we will first find M_a and M_b, but we don't know their respective order until later, when we find M_c.

We need to adapt the algorithm so that it records the ambiguity: during the lattice completion phase (line 19), we may end up with several repetitive sub-functions starting at the same point. We need thus to enhance our regular expression and allow alternative. In the example above, the first discovery phase finds $M_p.M_a^*.M_s$ and $M_p.M_b^*.M_s$, so the first reconstruction phase can't decide whether the top should be $M_p.M_a^*.M_b^*.M_s$ or $M_p.M_b^*.M_a^*.M_s$. So we record $M_p.(M_a^*|M_b^*).M_s$.

We thus need to modify MaxCommonPrefix and MaxCommonSuffix again: now, as we trace inside topLabel, we may reach a point where there are several choices: take any of the repetitive sub-functions starting there, or move on.

What we need to do is try all the repetitive sub-functions and follow the one that works. Two repetitive sub-functions can now have the same prefix, so we may end up following several repetitive sub-functions at the same time, but because ultimately all repetitive sub-functions are different, we will be able to decide which repetitive sub-function we must really follow before the end of the first iteration. We must record what repetitive sub-functions have been taken because we can go through several ones at that point, one after the other (the sub-functions cannot alternate according to assumption 3).

If at least two repetitive sub-functions start from the same point and have a common prefix, it is possible that MaxCommonPrefix finishes before we have reached a point allowing to decide which sub-function we are actually following. Again because all repetitive sub-functions are ultimately distinct, MaxCommonSuffix will resolve the problem: it may also end up in the middle of several repetitive sub-functions, but the set of repetitive sub-functions found by MaxCommonPrefix and the set of repetitive sub-functions found by MaxCommonSuffix will have at most one sub-function in common (the right one, if there is one).

Finally, to eventually waive the ambiguity, we have to enhance line 11: when we find a repetitive sub-function, if we have followed ambiguous branches during MaxCommonPrefix and/or during MaxCommonSuffix, then the order in which we have followed these branches is the order of the repetitive sub-functions and the ambiguity is removed.

In the example, after inferring $M_p.(M_a^*|M_b^*).M_s$ as the current top, in the next phase we trace it against $M_p.M_a.M_b.M_c.M_c.M_c.M_s$. We successfully locate M_c^*, and at that time we waive the $M_a|M_b$ ambiguity and finish with $M_p.M_a^*.M_b^*.M_c^*.M_s$.

Note that in fact, we can finish all the observations and still have ambiguity in the final top of the lattice. This means that the order of the ambiguous repetitive sub-functions was never provided. We can report that fact to the user.

4.4 Waiving the No Non-necessary Observations Conditions

So far, each observation adds something at one point. We actually don't need that. If an observation is "redundant", in that it doesn't help discovering any repetitive sub-function, at one point the current "topLabel" will be able to already generate that observation. That is, in the algorithm it simply means that MaxCommonSuffix will consume the complete observation. At that point, we just need to discard it. Note that a redundant observation can still be useful to waive ordering ambiguity. If that is the case, then we must simply record the order before discarding the observation.

5 Conclusion

We have introduced the "lattice of repetitive sub-functions", a new formal structure providing a global view of the compatible observations of a system having repetitive sub-functions. We have described an algorithm to construct an MSC graph of the functionality of a system built from a set of observations. The new algorithm introduced in this paper is an improvement over the solution presented in [10] in that some of the most restrictive assumptions on the set of observations are being waived. The last strong assumption remaining is the assumption 4 of the Section 4, stating that each repetitive sub-function must be introduced "individually". In future work, we will attempt to waive this assumption as well.

References

1. ITU Telecommunication Standardization Sector: ITU-T Recommendation Z.120. Message Sequence Charts (MSC96). (1996)
2. Rudolph, E., Graubmann, P., Gabowski, J.: Tutorial on message sequence charts. Computer Networks and ISDN Systems–SDL and MSC **28** (1996)
3. Alur, R., Holzmann, G.J., Peled, D.: An analyzer for message sequence charts. Software Concepts and Tools **17** (1996) 70–77
4. Ben-Abdallah, H., Leue, S.: Syntactic detection of progress divergence and non–local choice in message sequence charts. In: 2nd TACAS. (1997) 259–274
5. Alur, R., Yannakakis, M.: Model checking of message sequence charts. In: 10th International Conference on Concurrency Theory, Springer Verlag (1999) 114–129
6. Alur, R., Etessami, K., Yannakakis, M.: Inference of message sequence charts. In: 22nd International Conference on Software Engineering. (2000) 304–313
7. Alur, R., Etessami, K., Yannakakis, M.: Inference of message sequence charts. IEEE Transactions on Software Engineering **29** (2003) 623–633
8. Chikofsky, E., Cross, J.: Reverse engineering and design recovery. IEEE Software **7** (1990) 13–17
9. Lee, D., Sabnani, K.: Reverse engineering of communication protocols. In: IEEE ICNP'93. (1993) 208–216
10. Ural, H., Yenigun, H.: Towards design recovery from observations. In: FORTE 2004, LNCS 3235. (2004) 133–149

Erol Gelenbe's Career and Contributions

Professor Ufuk Çaglayan

Department of Computer Engineering, Bogaziçi University,
Bebek, Istanbul, Turkey
caglayan@boun.edu.tr

Abstract. We briefly summarize the career of Prof. Sami Erol Gelenbe who founded the ISCIS conference series, on the occasion of his 60th birthday, and on this 20th anniversary of the ISCIS conferences.

S. Erol Gelenbe is a native of Istanbul and a descendant of the 18th century mathematician Ismail Gelenbevî Efendi (1730-1790) who taught at the Ottoman Imperial War College. Erol's father, Yusuf Âli Gelenbe was also born in Istanbul, while his mother Maria Sacchet Gelenbe was born in the Belluno area of Northern Italy. Because his father worked at the Ankara headquarters of a Turkish bank, Erol graduated from Ankara Koleji in 1962. He entered the Middle East Technical University in Ankara and graduated with High Honours in Electrical Engineering in 1966, and was awarded the Clarke Award for Research Excellence for his Bachelor's thesis on Partial Flux Switching Memory. He completed his MS and PhD in three years as a Fulbright Scholar at Brooklyn Poly in New York, and then joined the University of Michigan in Ann Arbor. He was invited by IRIA to spend six months in 1972, and joined the University of Liège in Belgium as a chaired professor in 1974. He continued his association with IRIA (which became INRIA), and also taught at the University of Paris XIII and at Ecole Polytechnique. In 1979 he joined the University of Paris Sud where he was one of the principal architects of its program in Computer Science. After a stint as Science and Technology Adviser to the French Minister for Universities from 1984 to 1986, he joined the University of Paris V and developed its Computer Science Program. From 1991 to 2003 he was in the United States as New Jersey State Professor at NJIT, then as endowed chair professor and Department Head at Duke University, finally as University Chair Professor, School Director and Associate Dean of Engineering at the University of Central Florida in Orlando. Since the summer of 2003 he has been with Imperial College as the Dennis Gabor Chair Professor.

Erol was elected a member of the *Academia Europaea* in 2005. In 1986 he was elected a Fellow of IEEE, and subsequently a Fellow of ACM (2001) and of the IEE (2003). He was awarded the Honorary Doctorates of the University of Rome in 1996 and of Bogaziçi University in 2004, has been decorated by the French government, and has received several scientific awards.

From the early 70's to today Erol has made seminal contributions to computer systems and networks. He has published four books which have appeared

P. Yolum et al.(Eds.): ISCIS 2005, LNCS 3733, pp. 966–970, 2005.

in English, French, Japanese and Korean. In his initial work on performance modelling [1] he proved the surprising result that the FIFO paging algorithm is strictly equivalent to a random page replacement choice for the independent reference model of program behaviour, for all possible page reference frequencies. In the mid-seventies concurrently with H. Kobayashi, he derived the first diffusion approximations for queuing systems but suggested a model with holding times at the boundaries providing better accuracy at light traffic, and good accuracy at heavy traffic [2]. This work was used [3,4] in a recent IBM Patent (1999) [5] on call admission control for ATM networks. Together with G. Fayolle and J. Labetoulle, he showed that the random access ALOHA channel can only be stabilized by a control policy in which the retransmission time is proportional to the number of blocked transmissions [6,7]. In the late 70's Erol designed the "first ever" random access network on a fiber optic channel using these results. In the late seventies Erol proved [8] that in a database subject to *random* failures, the optimum checkpoint interval is a *deterministic* quantity expressed in terms of the amount of work that the database has accomplished since the most recent checkpoint. This work later gave rise to several theses by Erol's students [10,11] and further work in the USA [9]. Also during that time he published some of the first performance analyses of communication protocols. The Gelenbe-Mitrani graduate level book appeared in 1980, and was translated into Japanese in 1988. The early and mid-eighties saw him make other pioneering contributions: the classical Gelenbe-Iasnogorodski [13] result characterizing, under general arrival and service conditions, the long run waiting time at a paging disk server, the first ever work on the analytical estimation of the space and time cost of relational database operations [14], the end-to-end performance analysis of packet re-sequencing protocols [15], and the first analysis of the performance of interfering reads and writes during parallel access to shared data [16]. The Gelenbe-Pujolle book [17] appeared in French and was soon translated into English; it has gone through several editions and was published in Korean in 2000.

Over the last decade, Erol's invention of work removing "negative customers" [22] has produced a resurgence of research on "product form networks" [18,19,20,21,22,23,24,25,26,27,28] was motivated by the need to introduce control functions in queuing systems. An interesting mathematical twist is that G-networks have non-linear traffic equations, raising questions about the existence and uniqueness of solutions [20]. His work on G-networks has had a parallel development in the field of neural computation, where "negative customers" are models of the inhibitory spikes in biophysical neurons [28,29,30,31,32]. Erol has developed related learning algorithms [34,45] and his group has come up with many novel applications [33,35,36,37,38,39,40,41,42,43,44].

Erol is currently conducting innovative experimental work on computer network design [46,47,49], using performance and quality of service as the driving element and neural networks as the control units used in routers. His group has designed and built an experimental "self-routing packet" test-bed based on his Cognitive Packet Network patent. Related to this, Erol is also developing a theory of "sensible" [48] network routing.

He has attracted and mentored numerous PhD students and younger researchers. Many any of them are now technical leaders in France, Italy, Belgium, Greece, Turkey, Canada and the US. Finally, Erol has also made seminal contributions to the organization of his field by being a founding member of ACM SIGMETRICS, and of IFIP WG7.3. He has constantly served the profession through active participation in conferences and journals of the IEEE, the ACM and also of the British Computer Society. He has had significant impact on the Turkish Computer Science and Engineering community by founding and helping to organise for twenty consecutive years the International Symposia on Computer and Information Sciences series in Turkey.

References

1. E. Gelenbe "A unified approach to the evaluation of a class of replacement algorithms", Vol. C-22 (6), pp. 611-618, June 1973.
2. E. Gelenbe "On approximate computer system models", Journal ACM, Vol. 22, No. 2, 261-269, April 1975.
3. E. Gelenbe, X. Mang, R. Onvural "Diffusion based call admission control in ATM", Performance Evaluation, Vol. 27 & 28, 411-436, 1996.
4. E. Gelenbe, X. Mang, R. Onvural "Bandwidth allocation and call admission control in high speed networks", IEEE Communications Magazine, Vol. 35, No. 5, 122-129, 1997.
5. G.A. Marin, X. Mang, E. Gelenbe, R. Onvural, , U.S. Patent No. , 1999.
6. G. Fayolle, E. Gelenbe, J. Labetoulle "Stability and optimal control of the packet switching broadcast channel", Journal ACM, Vol. 24, No. 3, 375-386, 1977.
7. Banh-Tri-An, E. Gelenbe "Am?lioration d'un canal de diffusion sous contr?le", Revue d'Informatique (R.A.I.R.O), Vol. 11, No. 3, 301-321, 1977.
8. E. Gelenbe "On the optimum checkpoint interval", Journal ACM, Vol. 26, No. 2, 259-270, 1979.
9. E. Gelenbe, S. Tripathi, D. Finkel "Performance and reliability of a large distributed system", Acta Informatica, Vol. 23, 643-655, 1986.
10. E. Gelenbe, M. Hernandez "Optimum checkpoints with time dependent failures", Acta Informatica, Vol. 27, pp 519-531, 1990.
11. E. Gelenbe, M. Hernandez "Virus tests to maximize availability of software systems", Theoretical Computer Science, Vol. 125, 131-147, 1994.
12. E. Gelenbe, I. Mitrani "Analysis and Sythnesis of Computer Systems", Academic Press, New York and London, 1980.
13. E. Gelenbe, R. Iasnogorodski "A queue with server of walking type", Annales de l'Institut Henri Poincar?, S?rie B, Vol. 16, No. 1, 63-73, 1980.
14. E. Gelenbe, D. Gardy "On the size of projections I", Information Processing Letters, Vol. 14, No. 1, 1982.
15. F. Baccelli, E. Gelenbe, B. Plateau "An end-to-end approach to the resequencing problem", Journal ACM, Vol. 31, No. 3, 1984.
16. A. Chesnais, E. Gelenbe, I. Mitrani "On the modelling of parallel access to shared data", Comm. ACM, Vol. 26, No. 3, 1983.
17. E. Gelenbe, G. Pujolle "Introduction to Networks of Queues", 2nd Edition, John Wiley Ltd, New York and Chichester, 1998.

18. E. Gelenbe "Queueing networks with negative and positive customers", Journal of Applied Probability, Vol. 28, 656-663 (1991).
19. E. Gelenbe, P. Glynn, K. Sigman "Queues with negative arrivals", Journal of Applied Probability, Vol. 28, pp 245-250, 1991.
20. E. Gelenbe, M. Schassberger "Stability of product form G-Networks", Probability in the Engineering and Informational Sciences, 6, pp 271-276, 1992.
21. E. Gelenbe "G-networks with instantaneous customer movement", Journal of Applied Probability, 30 (3), 742-748, 1993.
22. E. Gelenbe "G-Networks with signals and batch removal", Probability in the Engineering and Informational Sciences, 7, pp 335-342, 1993.
23. E. Gelenbe "G-networks: An unifying model for queueing networks and neural networks," Annals of Operations Research, Vol. 48, No. 1-4, pp 433-461, 1994.
24. J.M. Fourneau, E. Gelenbe, R. Suros "G-networks with multiple classes of positive and negative customers," Theoretical Computer Science Vol. 155 (1996), pp.141-156.
25. E. Gelenbe, A. Labed "G-networks with multiple classes of signals and positive customers", European Journal of Operations Research, Vol. 108 (2), 293-305, July 1998.
26. E. Gelenbe, H. Shachnai "On G-networks and resource allocation in multimedia systems", European Journal of Operational Research, Vol. 126, No. 2, 308-318, October 2000.
27. E. Gelenbe, J.M. Fourneau "G-Networks with resets", Performance Evaluation, Vol. 49, 179-192, 2002.
28. E. Gelenbe "Reseaux stochastiques ouverts avec clients negatifs et positifs, et reseaux neuronaux", Comptes-Rendus Acad. Sci. Paris, t. 309, Serie II (1989), 979-982.
29. E. Gelenbe "Random neural networks with positive and negative signals and product form solution", Neural Computation, Vol. 1, No. 4, pp 502-510, 1989.
30. E. Gelenbe "Stable random neural networks", Neural Computation, Vol. 2, No. 2, pp 239-247, 1990.
31. E. Gelenbe "Distributed associative memory and the computation of membership functions", Information Sciences, Vol. 57-58, pp 171-180, 1991.
32. E. Gelenbe "Une generalisation probabiliste du probleme SAT", Comptes-Rendus Acad. Sci., t 313, Serie II, pp 339-342, 1992.
33. V. Atalay, E. Gelenbe "Parallel algorithm for colour texture generation using the random neural network model", International Journal of Pattern Recognition and Artificial Intelligence, Vol. 6, No. 2 & 3, pp 437-446, 1992.
34. E. Gelenbe "Learning in the recurrent random network", Neural Computation, 5, pp 154-164, 1993.
35. E. Gelenbe, V. Koubi, F. Pekergin "Dynamical random neural approach to the traveling salesman problem," ELEKTRIK, Vol. 2, No. 2, pp 1-10, 1994.
36. E. Gelenbe, C. Cramer, M. Sungur, P. Gelenbe "Traffic and video quality in adaptive neural compression", Multimedia Systems, Vol. 4, 357-369, 1996.
37. E. Gelenbe, T. Feng, K.R.R. Krishnan "Neural network methods for volumetric magnetic resonance imaging of the human brain," Proceedings of the IEEE, Vol. 84, No. 10, 1488-1496, October 1996.
38. E. Gelenbe, A. Ghanwani, V. Srinivasan "Improved neural heuristics for multicast routing", IEEE Journal of Selected Areas of Communications, Vol. 15, No. 2, 147-155, February 1997.

39. E. Gelenbe, K. Harmanci, J. Krolik "Learning neural networks for detection and classification of synchronous recurrent transient signals", Signal Processing, Vol. 64 (3), 233-247, 1998.
40. H. Bakircioglu, E. Gelenbe, T. Kocak, "Image processing with the Random Neural Network model", ELEKTRIK, Vol. 5 (1), 65-77, 1998.
41. E. Gelenbe, C. Cramer "Oscillatory corticothalamic response to somatosensory input", Biosystems, Vol. 48 (1-3), 67-75, 1998.
42. E. Gelenbe, Z.-H. Mao, Y.-D. Li "Function approximation with spiked random networks", IEEE Trans. on Neural Networks, Vol. 10, No. 1, 3-9, 1999.
43. E. Gelenbe, J.M. Fourneau "Random neural networks with multiple classes of signals", Neural Computation, Vol. 11 (4):953-963, 1999.
44. C. Cramer, E. Gelenbe "Video quality and traffic QoS in learning-based subsampled and receiver-interpolated video sequences", IEEE Journal on Selected Areas in Communications, Vol. 18 (2), 150-167, February 2000.
45. E. Gelenbe, K. Hussain "Learning in the multiple class random neural network", IEEE Trans. on Neural Networks, Vol. 13 (6), 1257-1267, 2002.
46. E. Gelenbe, R. Lent, Z. Xu, "Measurement and performance of a cognitive packet network", Computer Networks, Vol. 37, 691-791, 2001.
47. E. Gelenbe, R. Lent, Z. Xu, "Design and performance of cognitive packet networks", Performance Evaluation, Vol. 46, 155-176, 2001.
48. E. Gelenbe "Sensible decisions based on QoS", Computational Management Science, Vol. 1 (1), 1-14, 2004.
49. E. Gelenbe, R. Lent "Adhoc power aware Cognitive Packet Networks", Ad Hoc Networks Journal, Vol. 2 (3), 205-216, 2004.

Author Index

Lecture Notes in Computer Science

For information about Vols. 1–3654

please contact your bookseller or Springer

Vol. 3698: U. Furbach (Ed.), KI 2005: Advances in Artificial Intelligence. XIII, 409 pages. 2005. (Subseries LNAI).

Vol. 3697: W. Duch, J. Kacprzyk, E. Oja, S. Zadrożny (Eds.), Artificial Neural Networks: Formal Models and Their Applications – ICANN 2005, Part II. XXXII, 1045 pages. 2005.

Vol. 3696: W. Duch, J. Kacprzyk, E. Oja, S. Zadrożny (Eds.), Artificial Neural Networks: Biological Inspirations – ICANN 2005, Part I. XXXI, 703 pages. 2005.

Vol. 3695: M.R. Berthold, R. Glen, K. Diederichs, O. Kohlbacher, I. Fischer (Eds.), Computational Life Sciences. XI, 277 pages. 2005. (Subseries LNBI).

Vol. 3694: M. Malek, E. Nett, N. Suri (Eds.), Service Availability. VIII, 213 pages. 2005.

Vol. 3693: A.G. Cohn, D.M. Mark (Eds.), Spatial Information Theory. XII, 493 pages. 2005.

Vol. 3692: R. Casadio, G. Myers (Eds.), Algorithms in Bioinformatics. X, 436 pages. 2005. (Subseries LNBI).

Vol. 3691: A. Gagalowicz, W. Philips (Eds.), Computer Analysis of Images and Patterns. XIX, 865 pages. 2005.

Vol. 3690: M. Pěchouček, P. Petta, L.Z. Varga (Eds.), Multi-Agent Systems and Applications IV. XVII, 667 pages. 2005. (Subseries LNAI).

Vol. 3689: G.G. Lee, A. Yamada, H. Meng, S.H. Myaeng (Eds.), Information Retrieval Technology. XVII, 735 pages. 2005.

Vol. 3688: R. Winther, B.A. Gran, G. Dahll (Eds.), Computer Safety, Reliability, and Security. XI, 405 pages. 2005.

Vol. 3687: S. Singh, M. Singh, C. Apte, P. Perner (Eds.), Pattern Recognition and Image Analysis, Part II. XXV, 809 pages. 2005.

Vol. 3686: S. Singh, M. Singh, C. Apte, P. Perner (Eds.), Pattern Recognition and Data Mining, Part I. XXVI, 689 pages. 2005.

Vol. 3685: V. Gorodetsky, I. Kotenko, V. Skormin (Eds.), Computer Network Security. XIV, 480 pages. 2005.

Vol. 3684: R. Khosla, R.J. Howlett, L.C. Jain (Eds.), Knowledge-Based Intelligent Information and Engineering Systems, Part IV. LXXIX, 933 pages. 2005. (Subseries LNAI).

Vol. 3683: R. Khosla, R.J. Howlett, L.C. Jain (Eds.), Knowledge-Based Intelligent Information and Engineering Systems, Part III. LXXX, 1397 pages. 2005. (Subseries LNAI).

Vol. 3682: R. Khosla, R.J. Howlett, L.C. Jain (Eds.), Knowledge-Based Intelligent Information and Engineering Systems, Part II. LXXIX, 1371 pages. 2005. (Subseries LNAI).

Vol. 3681: R. Khosla, R.J. Howlett, L.C. Jain (Eds.), Knowledge-Based Intelligent Information and Engineering Systems, Part I. LXXX, 1319 pages. 2005. (Subseries LNAI).

Vol. 3679: S.d.C. di Vimercati, P. Syverson, D. Gollmann (Eds.), Computer Security – ESORICS 2005. XI, 509 pages. 2005.

Vol. 3678: A. McLysaght, D.H. Huson (Eds.), Comparative Genomics. VIII, 167 pages. 2005. (Subseries LNBI).

Vol. 3677: J. Dittmann, S. Katzenbeisser, A. Uhl (Eds.), Communications and Multimedia Security. XIII, 360 pages. 2005.

Vol. 3676: R. Glück, M. Lowry (Eds.), Generative Programming and Component Engineering. XI, 448 pages. 2005.

Vol. 3675: Y. Luo (Ed.), Cooperative Design, Visualization, and Engineering. XI, 264 pages. 2005.

Vol. 3674: W. Jonker, M. Petković (Eds.), Secure Data Management. X, 241 pages. 2005.

Vol. 3673: S. Bandini, S. Manzoni (Eds.), AI*IA 2005: Advances in Artificial Intelligence. XIV, 614 pages. 2005. (Subseries LNAI).

Vol. 3672: C. Hankin, I. Siveroni (Eds.), Static Analysis. X, 369 pages. 2005.

Vol. 3671: S. Bressan, S. Ceri, E. Hunt, Z.G. Ives, Z. Bellahsène, M. Rys, R. Unland (Eds.), Database and XML Technologies. X, 239 pages. 2005.

Vol. 3670: M. Bravetti, L. Kloul, G. Zavattaro (Eds.), Formal Techniques for Computer Systems and Business Processes. XIII, 349 pages. 2005.

Vol. 3669: G.S. Brodal, S. Leonardi (Eds.), Algorithms – ESA 2005. XVIII, 901 pages. 2005.

Vol. 3668: M. Gabbrielli, G. Gupta (Eds.), Logic Programming. XIV, 454 pages. 2005.

Vol. 3666: B.D. Martino, D. Kranzlmüller, J. Dongarra (Eds.), Recent Advances in Parallel Virtual Machine and Message Passing Interface. XVII, 546 pages. 2005.

Vol. 3665: K. S. Candan, A. Celentano (Eds.), Advances in Multimedia Information Systems. X, 221 pages. 2005.

Vol. 3664: C. Türker, M. Agosti, H.-J. Schek (Eds.), Peer-to-Peer, Grid, and Service-Orientation in Digital Library Architectures. X, 261 pages. 2005.

Vol. 3663: W.G. Kropatsch, R. Sablatnig, A. Hanbury (Eds.), Pattern Recognition. XIV, 512 pages. 2005.

Vol. 3662: C. Baral, G. Greco, N. Leone, G. Terracina (Eds.), Logic Programming and Nonmonotonic Reasoning. XIII, 454 pages. 2005. (Subseries LNAI).

Vol. 3661: T. Panayiotopoulos, J. Gratch, R. Aylett, D. Ballin, P. Olivier, T. Rist (Eds.), Intelligent Virtual Agents. XIII, 506 pages. 2005. (Subseries LNAI).

Vol. 3660: M. Beigl, S. Intille, J. Rekimoto, H. Tokuda (Eds.), UbiComp 2005: Ubiquitous Computing. XVII, 394 pages. 2005.

Vol. 3659: J.R. Rao, B. Sunar (Eds.), Cryptographic Hardware and Embedded Systems – CHES 2005. XIV, 458 pages. 2005.

Vol. 3658: V. Matoušek, P. Mautner, T. Pavelka (Eds.), Text, Speech and Dialogue. XV, 460 pages. 2005. (Subseries LNAI).

Vol. 3657: F.S. de Boer, M.M. Bonsangue, S. Graf, W.-P. de Roever (Eds.), Formal Methods for Components and Objects. VIII, 325 pages. 2005.

Vol. 3656: M. Kamel, A. Campilho (Eds.), Image Analysis and Recognition. XXIV, 1279 pages. 2005.

Vol. 3655: A. Aldini, R. Gorrieri, F. Martinelli (Eds.), Foundations of Security Analysis and Design III. VII, 273 pages. 2005.